ADVANCED
FINANCIAL
ACCOUNTING

The Dryden Press

Chicago   New York   Philadelphia
San Francisco   Montreal   Toronto
London   Sydney   Tokyo   Mexico City
Rio de Janeiro   Madrid

ADVANCED FINANCIAL ACCOUNTING

Ronald J. Huefner, Ph.D., CMA, CPA

Professor of Accounting
State University of New York at Buffalo

James A. Largay III, Ph.D., CPA

Professor of Accounting
Lehigh University

Acquisitions Editor: Feeny Lipscomb
Developmental Editor: Patricia Locke
Managing Editor: Jane Perkins
Design Director: Alan Wendt

Text and cover design by William Seabright
Copy editing by Flora Foss

Address orders to:
383 Madison Avenue
New York, New York 10017

Address editorial correspondence to:
901 North Elm Street
Hinsdale, Illinois 60521

Library of Congress Catalog Card Number: 81-67236
ISBN: 0-03-052641-8
Printed in the United States of America
234-144-987654321

CBS COLLEGE PUBLISHING
The Dryden Press
Holt, Rinehart and Winston
Saunders College Publishing

To Our Families

For, as we know, there are three things needed
by anyone who wishes to carry on business
carefully.

The most important of these is cash or any
equivalent, according to the saying *Unum
aliquid necessarium est substantia.* Without
this, business can hardly be carried on.

The second thing necessary in business
is to be a good bookkeeper and ready
mathematician. . . .

The third and last thing is to arrange all
transactions in such a systematic way that one
may understand each one of them at a glance,
i.e., by the debit (*debito*—owed to) and credit
(*credito*—owed by) method. This is very
essential to merchants, because, without
making the entries systematically, it would be
impossible to conduct their business, for they
would have no rest and their minds would be
troubled.

—Luca Pacioli, *Double Entry Bookkeeping* (1494)

The Dryden Press
Series in Accounting

Contents

Preface

This book is written with three major objectives in mind. First, we seek to reflect the changing topical emphasis and content in the advanced financial accounting course. Second, we write from the perspective of enhancing teachability. Third, we identify a unifying theme—the accounting entity—underlying many of the apparently diverse advanced accounting topics and use it as a focal point throughout the text.

In organizing the text, our goal is to provide a reasonably coherent flow of topics, beginning with relatively easy subjects and progressing to more complex ones. Our desire to focus on the accounting entity meshes with this approach. We start with simple entities—individuals and partnerships—and progress through fiduciary entities and home office and branch relationships until we reach the complex area of multiple corporations and consolidated financial statements. The different orientation inherent in governmental and nonprofit organization accounting justifies its placement toward the end of the book.

Chapter 1 deals with **the entity concept and personal financial statements,** introducing the unifying theme for the book and discussing many of the interesting accounting issues related to reporting the financial affairs of individual, family, or proprietorship entities. This material is typically not covered in depth anywhere in the accounting curriculum; it serves as a useful introduction to the diverse entities considered in advanced accounting.

Chapters 2 and 3 discuss **partnership accounting;** the partnership is seen as an entity composed of several individuals. Several of the concepts relating to individual entities are seen to also be applicable to partnerships. Income determination and allocation and various forms of capital changes—formation, admission and resignation of a partner, and liquidation—are the major topics discussed.

Chapter 4, on **fiduciary accounting,** incorporates the accounting both for estates and trusts and for corporate bankruptcies. Various aspects of fiduciary accounting are related and presented in a manner which minimizes many burdensome details and illuminates basic principles.

The chapter on **home office and branch accounting** (Chapter 5) turns to the familiar corporate entity and begins the consideration of multiple-entity accounting. Working papers and eliminating entries are introduced to prepare the student for the subsequent chapters on consolidation.

Business combinations and consolidated financial statements constitute a major topic in advanced accounting. We have streamlined the coverage and offer but six chapters in the area (Chapters 6–11). At the same time, however, we have provided expanded coverage of accounting for business combinations, accounting for income taxes in consolidated statements, and the consolidated statement of changes in financial position.

Following the material on consolidated statements, Chapter 12 succinctly stresses theoretical issues and accounting standards related to **segment and interim reporting.** Generally accepted accounting principles are critically analyzed and examples from actual annual reports are presented.

Accounting for international operations is a complex, controversial subject and can best be understood within the context of the changing economic environment which has influenced current and previous accounting standards in the area. We have developed background material which reviews elements of the international economic system and have included a section on international accounting standards. Chapters 13 and 14 present this increasingly important material.

The growing role of all types of **government and of nonprofit organizations** in our society led us to increase the coverage of fund accounting and its applications to four chapters. Chapter 15 presents a survey of governmental accounting at all levels: local, state, federal, and the national economy. Chapters 16 and 17 are then devoted to the specific accounting and reporting procedures of local government, reflecting the recently revised pronouncements of the National Council on Governmental Accounting. Finally, Chapter 18 discusses accounting and reporting for various types of nonprofit organizations.

Certain complex and perhaps optional topics are covered in the following five chapter appendices, providing the instructor with additional flexibility.

1. Tax aspects of partnerships (Appendix to Chapter 2).

2. Estate planning and taxation (Appendix to Chapter 4).

3. Determining the price in a business combination when the constituent companies are publicly traded (Appendix to Chapter 6).

4. The relationship between foreign currency translation and constant-dollar accounting (Appendix to Chapter 14).

5. Consolidated financial statements of the United States government (Chapter 15).

Citations to professional literature are cross-referenced from the original pronouncement to the related section in the Commerce Clearing House volume, *Professional Standards, Accounting, Current Text.* For example, allocation of "negative goodwill" is discussed in paragraph 91 of *APBO 16;* the cross-reference to the appropriate section of the Commerce Clearing House volume is AC § 1091.91. The pronouncements themselves are identified as follows:

APBO: Accounting Principles Board Opinion

APBS: Accounting Principles Board Statement

ARB: Accounting Research Bulletin

ASR: Accounting Series Release (SEC)

IAS: International Accounting Standard

IFAS: Interpretation of Financial Accounting Standards

NCGA: National Council on Governmental Accounting

SFAS: Statement of Financial Accounting Standards

Each chapter contains approximately thirty questions, exercises, and problems. Many of the questions can be used to review topics in the chapter, while others are more thought-provoking and challenging. Exercises and problems vary in level of difficulty and are frequently designed to reinforce and deepen the student's understanding of a topic by introducing a new element or complexity beyond the examples in the text. Numerous questions and problems have been adapted from the Uniform CPA Examination with the permission of the American Institute of Certified Public Accountants. In many cases, these materials are revised to conform with our text presentation of particular subjects.

The instructor's manual has been prepared by the authors. It includes lecture notes and examination material for each chapter as well as detailed solutions to the questions, exercises, and problems. Comments from users are invited and will be welcomed.

Acknowledg-ments

Many individuals were helpful in making this book what it is. While we gratefully acknowledge this assistance, we accept responsibility for the errors which remain. Several faculty members reviewed all or part of the manuscript, either as outside reviewers or as colleagues who used the manuscript in their classes. They are listed alphabetically below:

Raymond C. Clair State University of New York at Buffalo

Sanford C. Gunn State University of New York at Buffalo

Michelle W. Hamer University of Maryland

Susan S. Hamlen State University of New York at Buffalo

Orville R. Keister Jr. University of Akron

Frank Luh Lehigh University

Leonard E. Morrissey Jr. Dartmouth College

Richard J. Murdock Ohio State University

Jon G. Norem University of Northern Iowa

Cecily A. Raiborn Texas Women's University

Donald Tang Portland State University

Arthur L. Thomas University of Kansas

Jerry E. Trapnell Louisiana State University

Mark E. Zmijewski State University of New York at Buffalo

Special thanks are due to Phoebe W. Stevens, currently of Fox and Company, who provided editorial assistance and aided in the development of problems and solutions. Mr. William D. Szustak of Ernst & Whinney reviewed the appendix to Chapter 4. In addition, several students provided helpful comments relating to the text, problems, and solutions: Peter Gallipeau, Robert Principato, and Peter S. M. Wolcott of Dartmouth College; Bryan Bingel, Daniel D. Gasiewicz, Thomas D. Hyzy, and Jill Moosmann of the State University of New York at Buffalo; Steven Brown and John Talley of Lehigh University.

We also acknowledge the permission of the AICPA and the FASB to quote from their documents in the text. Documents issued by the AICPA are copyright © by the American Institute of Certified Public Accountants, Inc. FASB documents are copyright © by the Financial Accounting Standards Board, High Ridge Park, Stamford, Connecticut, 06905, U.S.A. Copies of the complete FASB documents are available from the FASB.

Finally, our thanks go to Audrey Hanlon, Marjorie Mahoney, and Sharon Murawski, who typed the bulk of the manuscript. Professor Largay also wishes to acknowledge the support provided him by Coopers & Lybrand and the Amos Tuck School of Business Administration, Dartmouth College. Most of his work on the manuscript was done while serving as the Coopers & Lybrand Visiting Associate Professor of Accounting at the Tuck School.

Ronald J. Huefner

James A. Largay III

About the
Authors

Ronald J. Huefner, Ph.D. (Cornell University), CMA, CPA, is Professor of Accounting in the School of Management, State University of New York at Buffalo. He is a member of the American Accounting Association, the American Institute of Certified Public Accountants, the National Association of Accountants, and other professional organizations. Articles by Professor Huefner have appeared in *The Accounting Review*, the *Journal of Accounting Research*, the *Bell Journal of Economics and Management Science*, *Management Accounting*, and other journals. He is the author of *An Introduction to New York State Income Taxation* (Horton, 1980) and is a contributor to the *Handbook of Modern Accounting*, the *Handbook of Cost Accounting*, and the *Accountant's Cost Handbook*. Professor Huefner currently teaches undergraduate and graduate courses in financial accounting and taxation. In 1977, he received the Chancellor's Award of the State University of New York for Excellence in Teaching.

James A. Largay III, Ph.D. (Cornell University), CPA, is Professor of Accounting in the College of Business and Economics, Lehigh University. He previously served on the faculties of the Amos Tuck School of Business Administration at Dartmouth College, Georgia Institute of Technology, and Rice University. Professor Largay is a member of the American Accounting Association, the American Institute of Certified Public Accountants, and other professional organizations. He has public accounting experience with Arthur Andersen & Co. Articles by Professor Largay have appeared in *The Accounting Review*, *The Journal of Finance*, the *Journal of Political Economy*, the *Financial Analysts Journal*, and other journals. He is co-author of *Accounting for Changing Prices* (Wiley, 1976) and is a contributor to the *Handbook of Modern Accounting* and the *Handbook of Cost Accounting*. Professor Largay currently teaches undergraduate and graduate courses in financial and managerial accounting.

PART ONE

SIMPLE ENTITIES

The entity concept is the theme which links the diverse topics of an advanced accounting text. This section of the text describes the entity concept and several relatively simple entities. Chapter 1 discusses individuals. It covers reporting for business activities of sole proprietorships and comprehensive reporting for individuals in the form of personal financial statements. The latter topic involves several accounting issues, including current value reporting. Chapters 2 and 3 discuss accounting for partnerships. Here the difficulty in separating the business entity from its individual partners leads to several accounting practices that differ significantly from corporate accounting. These differences affect the determination of income and accounting for capital changes. Chapter 4 covers fiduciary accounting. Fiduciaries are entities which hold and manage assets on behalf of others. Some common fiduciary entities are estates of deceased individuals, estates of bankrupt firms, and trusts of various types. Accounting and reporting are designed to show clearly how the responsibilities to the beneficiaries have been carried out. Financial statements for fiduciaries therefore differ significantly from those for other entities.

Most of the study of accounting prior to this course has been limited to the corporate business entity. Advanced accounting will introduce a variety of other entities as well as expanding the corporate entity. These first four chapters emphasize how the purposes and characteristics of each entity influence the accounting procedures and the design of financial statements.

Chapter 1

Introduction to Entity Concept and Personal Financial Statements

Advanced accounting courses cover a variety of topics in financial accounting, including accounting for individuals; partnerships; trusts, estates, and bankrupt firms; business combinations; parent-subsidiary corporate structures; multinational corporations; government units; and nonprofit organizations.

At first glance, this appears to be a list of unrelated topics. There is, however, a unifying theme which connects them—the concept of **entity**. This concept, first encountered in basic accounting courses, concerns the definition of the unit for which accounting data are accumulated and reported. Up to this point in the study of accounting, the most frequently covered entity has been the business corporation. For this entity, the affairs of the business are distinguished from the affairs of the owners by definition. The separate legal existence of the corporation facilitates this view of the reporting entity. The view may change, however, when organizations other than the simple corporation are examined. When we contemplate individuals and partnerships, we find that we cannot separate the business from the owners as easily as we can for corporations. In analyzing multiple corporations under common ownership, we will see that the fact of separate legal entities is overcome by the existence of common economic control. Thus consolidated statements are prepared for the group on the basis of a single economic entity. When we study government accounting, we will see that the reporting emphasis shifts away from an organizational unit and toward groups of resources to be expended for certain purposes. These groups of resources, known as *funds*, become the accounting and reporting entities. As a result, several reporting entities and several sets of financial statements may exist for a single government unit.

Thus, as we progress through this book, we will see how the question of defining the entity is always a basic issue. Once the entity is defined, different accounting techniques will follow from the differing entity definitions.

We begin our study of these entities and their accounting problems by considering the entity concept and its role in accounting. Later in the chapter, we will proceed to a discussion of a fundamental accounting entity—the individual —and some of the interesting reporting problems encountered in the preparation of personal financial statements.

The Entity Concept in Accounting

In its 1964 report on the business entity concept, a committee of the American Accounting Association concluded:

> In accounting, the entity with which we are concerned may be defined as *an area of economic interest to a particular individual or group*. The boundaries of such an economic entity are identifiable (1) by determining the interested individual or group, and (2) by determining the nature of that individual's or that group's interest.[1]

Several points contained in this definition of **entity concept** need to be emphasized.

1. An *accounting entity* is an area of economic activity. This is a much narrower concept than the more general notions of separate identity and distinctness applied to entity in the abstract. A faculty committee, for example, is generally considered an entity, but it can become an accounting entity only if it has a budget. An accounting entity can stand alone or be included in the accounts and reports of another entity. Thus, for managerial accounting purposes, a product line, branch, or division represents an area of economic activity. Yet, for public reporting purposes, the area of economic activity is the firm, a more inclusive entity. This latter contrast leads to the next point.

2. An accounting entity is of interest to a particular individual or group. Although there are many possible areas of economic activity, the nature of an individual's or group's interest helps delimit the accounting entity. Hence a division of a firm, which is an area of economic activity, becomes an accounting entity because of the interest of both divisional and corporate management in its performance. The corporation's stockholders, however, are more interested in the accounting entity known as the firm than in its smaller pieces. Since the focus of the stockholders' interest is on the firm, divisional data need not be reported to them. Yet, divisional or segment data are reported publicly (as will be discussed in Chapter 12), primarily because of the interests of another group—security analysts.

   The Internal Revenue Service is another interested group. Its concerns include determination of *taxable entities*, accounting entities which may have different boundaries than those of interest to other groups. For example, a partnership is generally considered to be an accounting entity, but it is not a taxable entity. An accounting entity may consist of a group of affiliated corporations; yet, each individual corpo-

---

[1] American Accounting Association, 1964 Concepts and Standards Research Study Committee —the Business Entity Concept, "The Entity Concept," *The Accounting Review*, April 1965, p. 358.

ration—an accounting entity—rather than the group may be a taxable entity because of the size of minority interests.

3. Theoretically, all the financial information gathered for an economic activity of interest to some group could be disclosed in reports to that group. The nature of the group's interest is important in deciding on the subset of information possibilities to be reported. For what purposes will the interested group—the users—use the reported information? What decisions will be made by members of the group? Corporate management may use manufacturing data prepared on a direct or variable cost basis in their decision models while full or absorption costing data may be of interest to stockholders.

  Defining the boundaries of an accounting entity is helpful in determining the totality of information relevant to that entity which is eligible for disclosure. It also assists in identifying the information needs of users. Yet the entity concept itself provides no detailed guidance for deciding which of the available information is to be disclosed, how it is to be reported, what accounting principles are to be emphasized, and so forth.[2] In the case of the Internal Revenue Service, however, identification of accounting entities of relevance to it (that is, taxable entities) also serves to define the information and disclosure requirements of those taxable entities.

4. Note the stress on the economic aspect of the accounting entity. Legal aspects play a secondary role, although they can be helpful in identifying an area of economic activity, and, in the case of corporations, legal entities and accounting entities are often one and the same. The entity concept stresses substance over form, thereby leading to the identification of partnerships and groups of related but legally separate corporations as accounting entities. Similarly, the sole proprietorship can be a legitimate accounting entity, separate from the proprietor's personal financial affairs. Of course, for other purposes, such as taxation and personal financial reporting, the individual proprietor's business and personal affairs are combined. Other entity-related considerations relevant to individuals are discussed later in the chapter.

The Relationship Between the Entity Concept and the Entity Theory in Accounting

The entity concept is central to accounting. Without it, one is hard pressed to discern any mission for accounting to perform. In contrast, the entity theory takes as given the existence of accounting entities and offers a particular view of the entity and the interests therein. In essence, the entity theory, the proprietary theory, and the fund theory are alternative approaches to understanding the nature of the relationships expressed on the right-hand side of the fundamental accounting equation: Assets = Liabilities + Owners' Equity.[3] They are briefly discussed in the following paragraphs.

---

[2] A general, though abstract, approach to the level of detail appropriate in financial reports designed to be responsive to the needs of users is given in John E. Butterworth, "The Accounting System as an Information Function," *Journal of Accounting Research*, Spring 1972, pp. 11–27.

[3] These theories and others of lesser importance are contrasted in more detail in Eldon S. Hendriksen, *Accounting Theory*, 3d. ed. (Homewood, Ill.: Irwin, 1977), pp. 487–498.

Entity Theory   The **entity theory** holds that the accounting entity has an existence separate from its owners and creditors. The entity owns or controls its assets, while various individuals and organizations have claims on those assets or equities in them. The equities of creditors (that is, liabilities) are viewed as the specific obligations of the entity subject to independent valuation, while the equities of owners consist of recorded amounts of paid-in capital and invested earnings with no particular valuation interpretation. Earnings are said to accrue to the entity rather than to the stockholders directly. Dividends represent distributions of the entity's income and at that point become income to owners.

When applied to consolidated financial statements, the entity theory implies equivalence between the majority and minority stockholders and the valuations assigned to their proportionate equities in the consolidated entity. This is discussed in Chapter 7.

Proprietary Theory   The **proprietary theory** stresses the importance of the proprietor or owner of an accounting entity and views the accounting entity itself as being coincident with the proprietor's area of economic activity. The ownership interest and income of the proprietor are of paramount importance, and accounting reports focus on the information needs of the proprietor, not the needs of other interests in the firm as is the case with the entity theory.

Thus the right-hand side of the accounting equation clearly differentiates between the liabilities of the proprietor and the proprietor's net worth. Assets are presumed to belong to the proprietor, and the earnings resulting from revenues and expenses directly affect the proprietor's net worth. In the corporate context, dividends paid to the proprietors (stockholders) represent withdrawals of capital by the owners.

A version of the proprietary theory surfaces in Chapter 7 as the parent theory of consolidated financial statements. In this setting, the parent company's shareholders emerge as the center of interest or proprietors. A clear distinction is drawn between the interests of majority and minority shareholders and the valuation of their interests. Consolidated net income accrues only to the parent company's shareholders, and only dividends paid to parent company shareholders are shown as distributions to owners.

Fund Theory   The **fund theory** offers an alternative view of the accounting entity. It forsakes the personal aspects of the proprietor's interest in the proprietary theory and the separateness of the entity and its equity holders in the entity theory. Rather, the fund theory views the accounting entity in a more operational or goal-oriented context. In short, the entity is viewed as a *fund*, a collection of resources assembled for a particular economic purpose and constrained by a set of restrictions. The right-hand side of the accounting equation specifies the types and quantities of restrictions placed on the assets of the fund. Liabilities are viewed as contractual restrictions on the assets, and "owners' equity" or "invested capital" implies legal or statutory restrictions. Financial statements describe the activities of the fund and are not oriented toward any particular interests. The focus is on sources and dispositions of cash and other resources as they relate to the activities of the fund.

Despite the effort by Vatter[4] to flesh out the fund theory and argue its applicability to accounting in general, it has not caught on in corporate accounting. Today, fund accounting is used extensively only in government and other organizations with nonprofit activities, such as colleges and universities, hospitals, and so forth. Many of these applications are studied in Chapters 15–18 of this book.

Thus the entity concept is essential to accounting, while the entity theory and its alternatives are philosophies of the nature of the entity and the interests in its assets. The entity concept cannot be employed as justification for particular accounting principles, but the nature of the accounting entity and those having interests in it do influence the type of information disclosed in financial reports. This will be especially evident in the material on individuals, estates and trusts (fiduciaries), and government organizations.

The definition of the entity can also have accounting implications. When an accounting entity includes two or more smaller entities, as in the cases of home office/branch and parent/subsidiary accounting, certain accounting procedures become necessary to correctly reflect the affairs of the smaller entities in the reports of the larger one.

Individuals and Personal Financial Statements

An individual engaged in economic activity can be viewed as the fundamental accounting entity. Yet, if the individual is also a **proprietor,** the sole owner of a business, the individual's economic activities may encompass two or more accounting entities. Categorizing the individual's financial affairs along entity lines is affected by the nature of his or her interests in those entities. A typical problem where individuals are concerned involves determining the boundaries of their proprietorship and personal activities. Such matters are discussed in the remainder of the chapter, beginning with consideration of entity and accounting issues related to proprietorships.

Proprietorships

The **proprietorship** is a common form of organization for small businesses having a sole owner. In general, proprietorship accounting is not a difficult topic. Most of the accounting procedures applicable to corporate business entities also apply to proprietorships. However, a few topics merit special discussion.

Entity   As we have seen, identification of the accounting entity in a business enterprise is a basic need. For corporations and partnerships, this identification is aided by their legal recognition as separate entities. For the proprietorship, however, legal recognition of the firm as distinct from the individual owner is lacking. While a proprietorship may have a legally recognized trade name, virtually no other legal recognition exists. Thus, identification of the business entity in accounting requires judgment in separating the affairs of the business from

---

[4] A comprehensive examination of the fund theory is given in William J. Vatter, *The Fund Theory of Accounting and Its Implications for Financial Reports* (Chicago: University of Chicago Press, 1947).

the personal affairs of the owner. In many cases, this distinction is clear; in others, it is difficult to make. To illustrate this difficulty, consider the following situations:

1.   Mr. Adams owns a building. The first floor houses a grocery store which Mr. Adams operates as a proprietorship. The second floor contains an apartment, which he rents to tenants. Should the building and the rental income be included in the financial statements of the proprietorship?

2.   Mr. Townsend is a successful attorney. He frequently receives advance fees from clients, which he invests in short-term securities. He also invests the profits of his practice in longer-term securities. Should either of the investments and the related interest income be included in the financial statements of the proprietorship?

3.   Ms. Segrist is a self-employed CPA. Each year, she contributes a percentage of her profits to a tax-qualified retirement plan for the self-employed *(Keogh plan)*. Should this expense and the value of the accumulation in the retirement plan be included in the financial statements of the proprietorship?

Generally accepted accounting principles provide little guidance in dealing with these questions. The logic of the entity concept suggests that an attempt must be made to view the business separately and to ask how the transactions would be treated if the business were a legally distinct entity. Applying this logic, we would answer the above questions as follows:

1.   Assuming the primary purpose of owning the building is to house the grocery store, the building should be reported as a proprietorship asset and the rental income as proprietorship income. Other rental properties owned by Mr. Adams, however, should not be included in proprietorship financial statements.

2.   The short-term investment of advance fees and the associated income should be reported by the proprietorship, on the basis that the earning process is not yet complete (that is, the services have not yet been rendered). It is reasonable, therefore, to view the short-term securities as an asset of the business. Once the services are complete, the profits of Mr. Townsend's practice are his to spend as he wishes. Thus the longer-term securities in which he invests the profits would be considered personal assets.

3.   The contribution to the retirement plan appears to be a business-related expense, analogous to pension expense of a corporation. In a proprietorship, however, compensation of the owner is viewed as an element of profit, not an expense. It would be appropriate, therefore, to treat indirect compensation in the same manner. Thus we would not include the expense in the proprietorship statements. The treatment of the accumulation in the retirement plan is clear. This asset belongs to Ms. Segrist, not to the business (that is, if she sold her practice, this asset would clearly not be transferred to the buyer).

Special accounting issues and the lack of a distinct legal entity create difficulty in separating, for accounting purposes, the business affairs of the proprietorship and the personal affairs of the owner. The logic of the entity concept guides the accountant in achieving this separation.

Income Reporting Net income of a proprietorship differs in definition from net income of a corporation. Corporate net income calculations include deductions for salary expense of *all* employees, including those who are also owners (stockholders). The net income of a proprietorship, however, reflects both profit and compensation for the owner's services in that compensation of the owner is not deducted as an expense. While the absence of compensation as an expense of the business is at variance with the entity concept, the lack of an arm's-length transaction hinders objective determination of compensation. Admittedly, this same situation exists in the closely-held corporation. There, the Internal Revenue Service acts as a modifying force, insisting that compensation must be "reasonable in amount" in order to be deductible. No such constraint exists for the proprietorship because no tax deduction for the owner's compensation is allowed.

No provision for federal income taxes is made in determining the net income of a proprietorship. The Internal Revenue Code does not impose a distinct tax on proprietorship income; rather, the income is included on the owner's personal income tax return. Allocation of a portion of the individual's total income tax to the business for financial reporting purposes is not attempted.

As a result of the above differences, the income statement of a proprietorship would have the following general format:

Sales and Other Revenues		$XXX
Costs and Expenses:		
Materials and Supplies	$XX	
Salaries and Wages of Employees (Excluding Any Salary to Proprietor)	XX	
Depreciation	XX	
Other Expenses	XX	XXX
Net Income		$ XX

Personal Financial Statements

In addition to the proprietorship, we may view an individual or group of individuals as an entity for which financial statements are presented. The need for personal financial statements may arise in connection with application for a bank loan; major investment in a business activity, such as formation of a partnership; estate planning; or appointment or election to public office.

Audits of Personal Financial Statements, issued by the AICPA in 1968, established generally accepted accounting principles for the preparation of personal financial statements.[5] The reporting requirements in this area are complex, involving many important accounting and reporting issues. This complexity may be increased by a lack of adequate accounting records. The accountant must often work with fragmentary data rather than with an organized set of books.

---

[5] American Institute of Certified Public Accountants, *Audits of Personal Financial Statements* (N.Y.: AICPA, 1968). As this book goes to press, revisions in these principles are being proposed.

The Entity   Normally, personal financial statements are prepared for an individual or for a husband and wife jointly. Occasionally, it may be appropriate for a larger family group to constitute the reporting entity. The purposes for which the statements will be used and the ownership status of major assets are important considerations in defining the reporting entity.

Multiple ownership of assets may complicate the definition of the reporting entity. Several forms of multiple ownership exist:

1. *Tenancy in common* means that two or more persons own undivided interests in an asset. These interests need not be equal and may be transferred to others.

2. *Joint tenancy* means that two or more persons own equal interests in an asset, with *rights of survivorship* (at death, the interest of the decedent passes to the other owners). A joint tenant may transfer the interest to a third party, in which case the joint tenancy ceases and a tenancy in common is created.

3. *Tenancy by the entireties* is a joint tenancy involving a husband and wife, in which neither party can eliminate the right of survivorship by transferring the interest to a third party.

4. *Community property laws*, which exist in some states, provide for joint ownership in any asset acquired by either spouse during a marriage, even if title is in one spouse's name, unless the asset was acquired with resources possessed by that spouse prior to the marriage.

State laws generally define the rights of multiple owners; not all of the above forms exist in all states. Where the reporting entity does not correspond to the ownership of assets or liabilities, the appropriate proportionate share should be reported in the financial statements, with full disclosure of the details of ownership in the notes. For example, if statements are being prepared for an individual who holds a one-third interest in a parcel of land as a tenant in common, one-third of the cost and value of the land would be presented with a footnote explaining the ownership.

Form and Content of Financial Statements   The major financial statement prepared for individuals, similar to the statement of financial position (balance sheet) of business firms, is called the **statement of assets and liabilities.** Often a second financial statement, the **statement of changes in net assets,** is also presented; it details the increases and decreases in an individual's net assets over a period of time, resulting both from income and expense transactions and from other transactions. Finally, a personal financial statement includes notes concerning valuation methods, details of assets and liabilities, and other disclosures. Sample personal financial statements with accompanying notes are presented in Exhibits 1.1, 1.2, and 1.3.

One important aspect of personal financial statements is that two bases of valuation are presented: the familiar *cost basis* and a *current value basis*. The principles governing the determination of cost and current value are discussed later in the chapter.

Statement of Assets and Liabilities   The title "Statement of Assets and

Exhibit 1.1   Illustrative Statement of Assets and Liabilities

Peter and Jennifer Baldwin
Statement of Assets and Liabilities
December 31, 19X7

	Cost Basis	Current Value Basis
ASSETS		
Cash	$ 11,079	$ 11,079
Marketable Securities (Note 2)	29,578	42,227
Cash Value of Life Insurance	4,647	4,647
Net Assets of ABC Proprietorship (Notes 1 and 3)	47,970	65,280
Interest in Net Assets of XYZ Corp. (Note 4)	3,000	4,730
Residence, Pledged on Mortgage Note (Note 6)	42,000	67,000
Automobiles	3,000	3,000
Jewelry (Note 6)	6,300	8,400
Paintings (Note 5)	10,000	20,000
Household Furnishings	2,000	2,000
Vested Interest in QM Corp. Pension Trust	—	17,810
Investment in Real Estate (Note 6)	30,678	41,000
Total Assets	$190,252	$287,173
LIABILITIES		
Accounts Payable and Accrued Expenses	$ 3,290	$ 3,290
6% Note Payable, Unsecured, Due January 15, 19X9	15,000	15,000
5½% Mortgage, Maturing in 19Y4 Secured by Residence (Annual Principal and Interest Payments Amount to $2,680)	19,790	19,790
Accrued Income Taxes Payable, Net of Prepayments	2,400	2,400
Accrued Income Taxes on Unrealized Asset Appreciation (Note 7)	—	24,230
Total Liabilities	$ 40,480	$ 64,710
EXCESS OF ASSETS OVER LIABILITIES	$149,772	$222,463

The notes to the financial statements are an integral part of this statement. They appear in Exhibit 1.3.

Source: The illustrative personal financial statements and notes are adapted from *Audits of Personal Financial Statements* (N.Y.: AICPA, 1968), pp. 21–25. Copyright © 1968 by the American Institute of Certified Public Accountants, Inc.

Liabilities" as opposed to the traditional "Balance Sheet" or "Statement of Financial Position" is intended to clarify to users the purpose of the statement. Consistent with this title, the major sections of the statement are subtitled "Assets," "Liabilities," and "Excess of Assets over Liabilities."

The business concepts of operating cycles and working capital do not apply to individuals. Thus, the statement of assets and liabilities is not classified into current and noncurrent categories. Assets are listed in order of liquidity, and liabilities are listed in order of maturity.

Exhibit 1.1 illustrates a typical statement of assets and liabilities. Because two bases of valuation are presented, a two-column format has been adopted. The first column presents information on the basis of historical cost, while the second column presents the assets and liabilities on a current value basis.

Exhibit 1.2 Illustrative Statement of Changes in Net Assets

Peter and Jennifer Baldwin
Statement of Changes in Net Assets
Year Ended December 31, 19X7

	Cost Basis	Current Value Basis
Net Assets, January 1, 19X7	$146,046	$215,998
Add: Income and Other Increases in Net Assets		
Dividends on Stock	$ 1,565	$ 1,565
Interest Income	845	845
Salaries and Bonuses, XYZ Corp.	4,040	4,040
Drawings from ABC Proprietorship	16,000	16,000
Gain on the Sale of Securities	3,989	1,743
Increase In Value since January 1, 19X7:		
Marketable Securities	—	2,936
Net Assets of ABC Proprietorship (Net of Drawings) . .	3,618	4,300
Interest in Net Assets of XYZ Corp.	—	613
Vested Interest in QM Corp. Pension Trust	—	547
Residence	—	1,120
Total Increases	$ 30,057	$ 33,709
Deduct: Expenses and Other Decreases in Net Assets		
Interest Expense	$ 1,870	$ 1,870
Decrease in Value of Automobiles	1,125	1,125
Income Taxes	4,000	4,000
Real Estate Taxes	1,873	1,873
Personal Expenditures	17,463	17,463
Provision for Income Taxes on Unrealized Asset Appreciation	—	913
Total Decreases	$ 26,331	$ 27,244
Net Assets, December 31, 19X7	$149,772	$222,463

Statement of Changes in Net Assets The **statement of changes in net assets** reconciles the change in net assets (excess of assets over liabilities) during the reporting period. As shown in Exhibit 1.2, the general format of this statement is:

> Net assets, beginning of period
>
> Plus: Income and other increases
>
> Minus: Expenses and other decreases
>
> Equals: Net assets, end of period

No attempt is made to separate income and expense items from other changes. The dual-column format is maintained, so that changes in both the cost basis and the current value basis are presented.

Notes to the Financial Statements Exhibit 1.3 illustrates typical notes which accompany personal financial statements. These notes provide greater detail for certain items on the statements and disclose the methods by which current values were determined.

Accounting Principles—General The broad provisions of generally accepted accounting principles apply to personal financial statements. Accrual accounting, not cash basis accounting, is the appropriate basis for preparing the financial statements. Since personal records are likely to be kept on a cash basis (if at all), conversion to an accrual basis is necessary before financial statements are prepared.

The concept of materiality applies throughout financial accounting. For example, personal effects such as jewelry and household furnishings may be immaterial to the individual's total financial condition. If so, they may be omitted or reported at a nominal amount. If the individual's personal effects are material in amount, however, costs and current values should be estimated and reported despite the difficulty of obtaining such information.

Business interests (proprietorships, partnership interests, or interests in a closely-held corporation) are presented as investments on the statement of assets and liabilities. Shown on a single line of the statement, business interests are reported as if they were unconsolidated subsidiaries. This procedure presents the individual's interest in net assets of the business as a single asset rather than combining business and personal assets and liabilities of a similar nature. For example, proprietorship cash would appear as part of the investment figure on the owner's personal financial statements rather than being combined with the individual's personal cash accounts. In Exhibit 1.3, note 1 to the personal financial statements of Peter and Jennifer Baldwin details the net assets of Peter Baldwin's business. Observe that only the net assets figure of $47,970 appears on the statement of assets and liabilities.

Accrued taxes on the statement of assets and liabilities consist of taxes currently payable and, if applicable, deferred taxes. Since individuals use the cash basis for tax reporting but must use the accrual basis for financial statements, timing differences leading to deferred tax accruals are likely.

Accounting Principles—Cost Basis The first column in the dual-column format of personal financial statements is based on historical cost. Since the cost basis is commonly used in financial reporting for all entities, relatively few special problems exist in applying the cost basis to personal financial statements. The following points are worthy of mention:

1. Acquisition cost for property acquired by gift or inheritance is the fair value at time of acquisition. Assets acquired through exchange are valued in accordance with *APBO 29* (AC § 1041).[6]

2. Depreciation is provided on income-producing assets such as rental property. Non-income-producing property (for example, a personal residence) is not depreciated; it is reported at original cost unless there is evidence of a permanent decline in value.

3. The equity method is used to value business interests presented as investments.

---

[6] Accounting Principles Board, *Opinion No. 29*, "Accounting for Nonmonetary Transactions" (N.Y.: AICPA, 1973), par. 21; AC § 1041. (Throughout the book, we cross-reference accounting publications in this short-hand method to the related section in the Commerce Clearing House volume; AC stands for *Professional Standards, Accounting, Current Text*, and, in this footnote, 1041 gives the section number in which APB *Opinion No. 29* is found.)

Exhibit 1.3   Illustrative Notes to Financial Statements

Peter and Jennifer Baldwin
Notes to the Financial Statements
December 31, 19X7

COST BASIS COLUMN

Note 1—Net Assets of ABC Proprietorship

A summary statement of the net assets of the proprietorship as of December 31, 19X7, follows:

Current Assets	$37,694
Land, Building and Equipment, Net	25,570
Other Assets	2,110
Total	$65,374
Current Liabilities	$ 5,790
Deferred Items	3,094
Long-Term Debt	8,520
Total	$17,404
Net Assets	$47,970

Income before provision for income taxes for the year ended December 31, 19X7, amounted to $19,618. Drawings by Peter Baldwin during the year were $16,000.

A certified public accounting firm has examined the financial statements of the proprietorship as of December 31, 19X7, and expressed an unqualified opinion on them.

CURRENT VALUE COLUMN

Note 2—Marketable Securities

The amounts shown as market value at December 31, 19X7, were arrived at as follows:

Stocks—Quoted closing or latest bid prices
Bonds—Quoted latest bid prices

Accounting Principles—Current Value Basis   The second column of dual-format personal financial statements represents current or fair market values, implying values determined by bona fide bargaining between well-informed buyers and sellers. Where quoted prices are available, the determination of current values is straightforward. However, estimation of current values is often required for certain securities, real estate, and other assets. While current values of marketable securities are readily determinable, individuals may own investments which are not ordinarily traded, such as shares in a closely-held corporation or interests in a partnership or proprietorship. Various approximations to current value may be considered—the capitalized value of earnings, the replacement value of net assets, or the liquidation value of net assets. In some cases, buy-out agreements may exist among partners or stockholders which specify payment in the event of withdrawal or death. These agreements could serve as a basis for approximating the current value of the firm. Notes 3 and 4 in Exhibit 1.3 illustrate current value estimations of business interests for personal financial statements.

Exhibit 1.3   Illustrative Notes to Financial Statements *continued*

Marketable securities consist of the following:

STOCKS	Shares	Cost	Market Value
American Industries, Inc.	100	$ 1,647	$ 4,003
Colleen Fabrics Corp.	1,000	9,696	15,322
Do-All Manufacturing, Ltd.	50	913	401
Thomas Lighting Company	75	1,097	4,243
Maureen Fashions, Inc.	225	7,674	8,949
United Products	500	2,312	1,676
U.S. Equipment Rentals	100	239	920
		$23,578	$35,514
BONDS			
United Products $6^{1}/_4$% due 7/1/Z4		$ 2,000	$ 2,713
U.S. Government $5^{1}/_2$% due 11/15/Y6		4,000	4,000
		$ 6,000	$ 6,713
		$29,578	$42,227

Note 3—ABC Proprietorship

Current value is based on an offer to purchase the net assets of the business, dated September 17, 19X7. Peter Baldwin has refused the offer.

Note 4—Interest in Net Assets of XYZ Corp.

Current value of the 25 percent interest in the net assets of the corporation is based on unaudited financial statements as of September 30, 19X7. Management of XYZ Corp. has reported that no material financial changes have occurred since that date.

Note 5—Paintings

Current value is based upon a bona fide offer to purchase the paintings by Modern Galleries, Inc., on December 16, 19X7.

Note 6—Appraisals

Current value is based upon independent appraisals of the following assets:

Residence	$67,000 (1)
Jewelry	8,400 (2)
Real Estate	41,000 (3)

1. Recent purchases of homes within the same general area approximate the appraised valuation. The assessed real estate value (100 percent valuation) was determined in 19X6 to be $61,000.

2. Jennifer Baldwin's jewelry has been insured in the amoutn of $8,400.

3. The assessed real estate value (100 percent valuation) was determined in 19X5 to be $38,000.

Note 7—Accrued Income Taxes on Unrealized Appreciation

Unrealized appreciation in value of assets would, if realized, require payment of taxes at capital gains rates. Therefore, the accrual has been made on that basis.

To determine the current value of real estate, the accountant may consider the following:

1. Estimates by real estate agents.
2. Data on actual sales of similar property.

3. Assessed values for property taxes, together with the general relationship between assessed values and market values.

4. Formal appraisals.

Judgment must be exercised as to which approach provides the most reliable approximation of current value. The source of current value for the residence and other real estate of the Baldwins is shown in note 6 of Exhibit 1.3. Appraisals were obtained ($67,000 for the residence and $41,000 for the other real estate) and are presented on the statement of assets and liabilities. Note 6 also comments on the reasonableness of the appraisals. Reference is made to alternative approaches to estimation of current value—recent sales and assessed values—which yielded valuations similar to the appraisals.

An individual may possess future interests such as pension rights or interests in property held in trusts. If these future interests are vested (nonforfeitable), their value should be included in the current value column. There may or may not be an amount in the cost column, depending on whether the individual has invested any resources (for example, contributed to a pension plan). It is necessary to determine the present value of these future interests based on discounted cash flows.

In presenting accrued income taxes in the current value column, the estimated tax on the unrealized appreciation of net assets must be calculated. The logic of this requirement is that when the assets are sold, the gains generally will be taxable. This calculation requires consideration of the type of asset and the anticipated tax rates (ordinary versus capital gains and the tax bracket at the time of sale). Consideration should also be given to special tax rules, such as the $100,000 exclusion on the sale of a residence when taxpayers are over fifty-five. For example, the statement of assets and liabilities for Peter and Jennifer Baldwin (see Exhibit 1.1) shows accrued income taxes on unrealized asset appreciation as $24,230. Assuming that a tax rate of 25 percent is applicable, the calculation was made as follows:

Asset	Cost	Current Value	Unrealized Appreciation
Marketable Securities	$29,578	$42,227	$12,649
ABC Proprietorship	47,970	65,280	17,310
XYZ Corporation	3,000	4,730	1,730
Residence	42,000	67,000	25,000
Jewelry	6,300	8,400	2,100
Paintings	10,000	20,000	10,000
QM Pension	—	17,810	17,810
Real Estate	30,678	41,000	10,322
Total Unrealized Appreciation			$96,921
Tax rate			× .25
Accrued Income Tax on Unrealized Appreciation			$24,230

In some circumstances, it might be appropriate to estimate estate taxes rather than income taxes, as in the case of an elderly individual who is unlikely to sell the assets.

Summary of Key Concepts

The **entity** is the organizational unit for which accounting data are accumulated and reported. Definition of the entity is an important aspect of the various areas of accounting discussed in this book.

The **entity theory, proprietary theory,** and **fund theory** are different explanations of the nature of the accounting entity and the interests in its assets. Each of these three theories will be encountered in the topics covered in this book.

A **proprietorship** is an unincorporated business entity having a single owner. While most aspects of corporate accounting apply to proprietorships, the definition of **net income** is different.

Personal financial statements consist of a **statement of assets and liabilities,** an optional **statement of changes in net assets,** and notes. Data are presented on both a **cost basis** and a **current value basis.**

Questions

Q1.1 Explain the difference between the terms *entity concept* and *entity theory* in accounting.

Q1.2 Millie Watson converted her garage to a beauty salon, which she operates as a sole proprietorship. Watson has a practice of collecting tips in a glass jar. Periodically she empties the jar and buys magazines, which she reads before setting them out for customers.
1. In preparing the financial statements for the proprietorship, how would the tips be reported?
2. In preparing the financial statements for the proprietorship, how would the cost of the magazines be reported? (Assume the cost is a material amount.)
3. Would either item be reported on Watson's personal financial statements? If so, how?

Q1.3 Kyle Johnson lives on the second floor of a three-story house which he owns. He rents the top floor to local university students. A home decorating business which Kyle owns and operates occupies the ground floor of the house. Should the house and the rental income be included in the financial statements of the proprietorship?

Q1.4 E. A. Grimes owns an insurance agency, which is operated as a sole proprietorship. Because of the substantial amount of travel connected with the business, Grimes owns two automobiles. One, a compact car, is used almost exclusively for business (about 10 percent of the use of the compact car is for personal rather than business purposes). The other, a station wagon, is used exclusively for family (personal) purposes.

In preparing a financial statement for the insurance agency only, how would you recommend that the two cars be treated?

Q1.5 In what ways do the financial statements of a proprietorship differ from the financial statements of a corporation?

Q1.6 Why are items on the statement of assets and liabilities of an individual not separated into current and noncurrent categories?

Q1.7 The statement of assets and liabilities is always prepared when reporting the personal financial position of an individual or group. The statement of changes in net assets, however, is optional. Under what circumstances might a statement of changes in net assets *not* be presented?

Q1.8 Personal financial statements are being prepared for an individual who owns and operates a grocery store as a sole proprietorship. What information concerning the grocery store would appear on the personal financial statements? What are the likely sources of that information?

Q1.9 What are future interests, and how are they presented on personal financial statements?

Q1.10 Current values of material items are presented on personal financial statements. How could the current value of the following assets be determined?

1. Postage stamp collection.
2. Vacant lot in a housing development.
3. Antique furniture.
4. Life insurance policy.
5. Household appliances.
6. Inventory of a proprietorship.
7. Jewelry.
8. Minority interest in a closely-held corporation.

Exercises **E1.1** The following is available from the books of Aston Refinishing Company:

Cash	$ 9,000
Equipment	12,000
Supplies	4,000
Prepaid Rent	3,000
Accounts Payable	(4,460)
Notes Payable	(10,000)
Capital	(6,160)
Revenues	(39,840)
Supplies Expense	9,500
Labor Expense	8,000
Salary Expense (Aston)	14,000
Interest Expense	960

Additional information:

1. Wages owed on December 31, 19X1, are $600.
2. The owner earned a salary of $15,000 in 19X1. Of this amount, $1,000 remains to be paid as of December 31.
3. Prepaid rent as of December 31 should be $1,000.
4. Semi-annual interest on the note of $720 is due on February 28. The note has been outstanding all year.
5. The corporate tax rate is 17 percent; Aston's personal tax rate is 21 percent. The accrual basis is used.

Required: Prepare income statements for Aston Refinishing Company, assuming the company is:
1. A proprietorship.
2. A corporation.

E1.2 James Cromwell, age forty-five, is employed as an engineer. He participates in his employer's pension plan, which requires that he contribute 4 percent of his annual salary to the plan. To date, he has contributed $8,947 to the plan. His benefits, which are vested, will be based on his past and future salary levels. Given reasonable assumptions about his future salary growth, he anticipates benefits of approximately $10,500 per year upon retirement at age sixty-five (at which time his life expectancy will be twelve years).

Required: Assuming that a 10 percent discount rate and 40 percent tax rate are appropriate, indicate how the pension rights would be presented on Cromwell's personal statement of assets and liabilities.

E1.3 Included on Irene Bomba's statement of assets and liabilities is an $11,350 liability for accrued income tax on unrealized appreciation of assets. A tax rate of 25 percent was used to compute the liability.
  Data relating to Bomba's assets appear below:
1. Irene Bomba bought 1,000 shares of stock in Allan Co. in 19X5 at $12 each. Since 19X5, the stock has increased in value 25 percent. Billings Co. stock, purchased at the same time, has not changed in value. Last year Bomba sold 90 of her 100 shares in Crafton Inc., at $45 each. (She had originally paid $40 a share.) The market value of Crafton stock has not changed in the past year.
2. Bomba's hobby is collecting coins. Her collection is now worth $1,850 more than the $2,000 she paid for the coins. Other personal belongings of Bomba have decreased in value by $2,000. They are now worth $38,000. These losses would not be deductible for tax purposes.
3. In addition to her house, which was recently appraised at $70,000, Irene owns a lot which has doubled in value since she bought it.

Required: If the cost of Billings Co. stock was $4,500 and the total current value of all Bomba's assets is $144,800, construct a chart showing the cost, current value, and unrealized appreciation on all her assets.

E1.4 Prepare a statement of assets and liabilities for Michael Fenway as of December 31, 19X3, given the following information:
1. Fenway's unincorporated business yielded a profit of $42,000 on the cash basis and $50,000 on the accrual basis.
2. The book value of Fenway's equity in the business is $30,000 at year-end. However, the market value of the business is estimated to be $100,000. The books are kept on the accrual basis.
3. Fenway, a cash basis taxpayer, is subject to a tax rate of 40 percent on all income. During the year, estimated tax payments of $12,000 were made.
4. Fenway's only income is derived from the business. His only other asset is cash of $15,000.

E1.5 Arthur Randolf owns 75 percent of Granitville Services Co. The book value of the firm's total assets is \$700,000; liabilities are \$300,000. The normal rate of return on total assets for similar firms in the same industry is 15 percent. Because of its long-standing reputation for quality service, Granitville Services Co. has repeatedly enjoyed excess earnings. Net income before extraordinary items for the last six years is shown below:

19X4 . . . . \$140,000		19X7 . . . . \$132,500	
19X5 . . . . \$130,000		19X8 . . . . \$120,000	
19X6 . . . . \$127,500		19X9 . . . . \$130,000	

A capitalization rate of 10 percent for excess earnings is considered appropriate.

Required: Calculate the values of the investment to be shown on Randolf's personal statement of assets and liabilities under the following assumptions:

1. Assume excess earnings will continue indefinitely.
2. Assume excess earnings will continue for fifteen years.

E1.6 Comparative statements of assets and liabilities are given below for Jonathan Flanders, along with additional information.

Jonathan Flanders
Comparative Statements of Assets and Liabilities

	12/31/X4		12/31/X5	
ASSETS	Cost	Current Value	Cost	Current Value
Cash	\$ 4,000	\$ 4,000	\$ 3,500	\$ 3,500
Marketable Securities (Note 1)	10,000	12,000	8,500	13,600
Total Assets	\$14,000	\$16,000	\$12,000	\$17,100
LIABILITIES				
Accrued Income Taxes	\$ 600	\$ 600	\$ 450	\$ 450
Accrued Income Taxes on Unrealized Asset Appreciation (Note 2)	—	300	—	765
Total Liabilities	\$ 600	\$ 900	\$ 450	\$ 1,215
EXCESS OF ASSETS OVER LIABILITIES . . .	\$13,400	\$15,100	\$11,550	\$15,885

Note 1: Marketable securities are 100 shares in Weber Co.
Note 2: Taxes on unrealized appreciation are accrued at a rate of 15 percent.

Additional information:

1. During 19X5, Flanders sold fifteen shares of Weber Company for \$195 each. He paid \$125 in taxes on the sale. No other sale or purchase regarding marketable securities occurred in 19X5.
2. Dividends of \$238 on Weber stock were received during 19X5.
3. Flanders' salary during 19X5 was \$14,000. He paid income taxes totaling \$3,700 (not including taxes on sale of stock).

Required: Prepare a statement of changes in net assets for Jonathan Flanders for 19X5.

Problems **P1.1** **Discussion and Applications of Entity Concept** The concept of the accounting entity often is considered to be the most fundamental of accounting concepts, one that pervades all of accounting.

Required:
1. a. What is an accounting entity? Explain.
   b. Explain why the accounting entity concept is so fundamental that it pervades all of accounting.
2.   For each of the following, indicate whether the accounting concept of entity is applicable. Discuss and give illustrations.
   a. A unit created by or under law.
   b. The product-line segment of an enterprise.
   c. A combination of legal units and product-line segments.
   d. All of the activities of an owner or a group of owners.
   e. An industry.
   f. The economy of the United States.

(AICPA adapted)

P1.2 **Proprietorship Accounting—Simple** Peter Becker started repairing watches in his spare time several years ago. The hobby has evolved into a business, and Becker is considering resigning from his maintenance job and opening a watch repair shop. Before taking such a drastic step, Becker wants to know how profitable the repair business will be. For tax purposes, Becker kept receipts for repair work. He did not report any expenses related to the business.

Becker's expenditures during the past year, 19X0, were recorded in his checkbook. He made no purchases for the business with cash.

Because the demand for Becker's work far exceeds the time he can currently spend, he has turned away many customers in the past year. Becker estimates he can triple 19X0 cash receipts in his first year of operation. Other clock and watch repairers in the area make $15 an hour. Becker plans to use this number in determining his salary based on a fifty-week, forty-hour-a-week, work year.

A local jewelry store has agreed to rent Becker a back room for $300 a month including utilities. Phone bills for the first year are expected to be $350.

Data from Becker's checkbook are as follows:

Groceries	$8,500
Clothing	1,000
Payment of Taxes	250
Purchases of Watch Parts	500
House Payments	3,720
Miscellaneous	2,000

Becker's tax return shows that he received $8,000 cash from repairing watches and $15,000 in salary from his maintenance job. He paid $5,700 in taxes.

Required:
1. Prepare a projected income statement for the first year of Becker's watch repair shop.
2. What other factors should Becker consider before opening the repair shop?

P1.3   **Proprietorship Statements—Cash to Accrual**   Jacob Peterson owns a warehouse, which he operates as a sole proprietorship. Jacob has applied to a lending institution for a loan to expand the facilities. Jacob maintains his accounting records on a cash basis. The lending institution has requested a balance sheet and income statement for the proprietorship prepared on the accrual basis. Below are trial balances of accounts in the general ledger as of December 31, 19X5.

General Ledger Trial Balance
December 31, 19X5

	Debit	Credit
Cash .	$ 170,000	
Investments .	425,000	
Property, Plant, and Equipment .	1,200,000	
Allowance for Depreciation .		$ 350,000
Payroll Taxes Withheld .		12,000
Capital, Jacob Peterson .		1,318,000
Rental and Service Income .		400,000
Operating Expense .	200,000	
Insurance .	30,000	
Administrative Expense .	70,000	
Investment Income .		15,000
Totals .	$2,095,000	$2,095,000

Details of unrecorded accruals and other information follow:

	December 31	
	19X4	19X5
Accounts Receivable—Rents and Services (Includes doubtful accounts totaling $700 at December 31, 19X5. All doubtful accounts were for 19X5 services.) .	$ 27,000	$ 37,000
Rental Deposits from Lessees ($7,500 of 19X5 amount was received in 19X5 and recorded in Rental and Service Income; $600 of the 19X4 amount was applied to final months' rentals in 19X5.) .	2,100	9,000
Interest Income Receivable .	1,000	2,600
Market Value of Investments (All investments are corporate bonds.) .	460,000	475,000
Accounts Payable (operating expenses) .	8,000	9,700

The amount in the Insurance account is a February 1 payment for insurance premiums: $6,000 for a one-year liability insurance policy and $24,000 for a three-year fire insurance policy. The coverage under both policies commenced on January 1.

Payroll Taxes Withheld includes employees' FICA taxes of $800. Administrative Expenses includes a payment of $300 for 19X4 employer FICA taxes.

Required: Complete a worksheet for the preparation of financial statements on the accrual basis. The worksheet should have debit and credit columns for each of the following: (a) trial balance (cash basis); (b) adjustments; (c) income statement (accrual basis); (d) balance sheet (accrual basis).   (AICPA adapted)

P1.4   **Preparation of Statement of Assets and Liabilities**   Marilyn Gray is sole owner and operator of Gray's Art Shop. The balance sheet and income statement for
the current year are presented below:

Gray's Art Shop
Balance Sheet
December 31, 19X9

ASSETS			LIABILITIES AND CAPITAL		
Cash	. . . .	$ 10,000	Accounts Payable	. . .	$ 5,000
Accounts Receivable	. .	20,000	Short-Term Loan	. . .	30,000
Inventory	. . . .	130,000	Loan on Automobile	. . .	800
Automobile (Net)	. . .	1,800			$ 35,800
Equipment, Fixtures (Net)	. .	20,000	Capital—Marilyn Gray	. . .	150,200
Prepaid Expenses	. . .	4,200			
			Total Liabilities and		
Total Assets	. . .	$186,000	Capital	. . . .	$186,000

Gray's Art Shop
Income Statement
For the Year Ended December 31, 19X9

Sales		$250,000
Cost of Goods Sold		150,000
Gross Profit		$100,000
Other Expenses:		
Rent	$24,000	
Car Expense	3,800	
Insurance and Security	10,000	
Interest	3,500	
Depreciation	5,000	
Miscellaneous	2,300	
Total Expenses		48,600
Net Income		$ 51,400

Marilyn has been renting space in a building since she began business. The
owner has offered to sell her the building if she can raise the necessary money.
As her accountant, you instructed Marilyn to assemble both personal and business financial information so that you can prepare a personal financial statement to be included with her loan application. The information received is as
follows:

1. The mortgage on her house, which she owns jointly with her husband, has
a current balance of $17,500. Marilyn and Neil, her husband, purchased
the house ten years ago for $50,000. A real estate broker estimates current
market value to be $70,000.
2. Their joint checking account shows a balance of $2,000 on the last state-
ment date. Since then, the Grays have written checks totaling $1,400 and
deposited $230.
3. A joint savings account shows a balance of $25,000 including interest to
date.

4. Outstanding charge accounts (joint) total $5,000 from the purchase of personal items.
5. Marilyn estimates that household effects purchased at various times at a cost of $30,000 now have a resale value of $10,000 (jointly owned).
6. Data on securities held in Marilyn's name are as follows:

Security	Purchase Date	Shares	Cost	Market Value
A	2/1/X6	300	$ 3.83	$ 5.60
B	4/1/X8	250	15.80	35.20
C	10/1/X8	1,500	.35	.50
D	5/1/X9	150	2.34	2.00

7. The automobile Marilyn uses only for business purposes is in her name. It cost $5,400 and has a market value of $1,000. Balance due on the loan for the car is $800. The Grays use Neil's car for personal purposes. He owes $4,000 on the principal of the car loan. Neil paid $5,900 for the car. He estimates it to be worth $3,500 now.
8. Recently a local art gallery offered to purchase Gray's Art Shop for $200,000.
9. Income taxes owed on December 31, 19X9, which are attributable to Marilyn's income are $1,200. The effective tax rate on unrealized appreciation of assets is 20 percent.

Required: Prepare a statement of assets and liabilities for Marilyn Gray with accompanying notes.

P1.5 **Statement of Assets and Liabilities—Comprehensive** James Bolan, M.D., and Louis Scott, M.D., are applying for a $115,000 loan to purchase additional equipment for their medical practice. The bank has requested a personal statement of assets and liabilities as of June 30, 19X3, from James Bolan and his wife, Frances. Pertinent facts about the Bolans follow. Unless stated otherwise, all facts are presented as of June 30, 19X3.

1. The Bolans have $8,000 in a checking account and $30,000, including interest through June 30, 19X3, in a savings account.
2. The Bolans paid $7,500 in 19X1 for a 15 percent interest in Crown Corporation, which has 100,000 shares outstanding. The stock is traded on a midwestern exchange. In recent months, the stock has traded in blocks of 100 shares or less at $1.50 per share. Dr. Bolan was offered $1.10 per share for all his shares on June 22, 19X3. The offer is still outstanding.
3. Dr. Bolan and Dr. Scott each own a 50 percent interest in the Suburban Medical Group, a partnership. The balance sheet of the Suburban Medical Group, prepared on a modified cash basis, follows at the top of page 25.
4. As of June 30, 19X3, there were unrecorded accounts receivable of $12,451 and unrecorded accounts payable of $1,327. Payments on the notes are current. The partnership prepares its tax returns on the accrual basis.
5. Dr. Scott and Dr. Bolan were offered $260,000 for their practice by Rural Medical Center. The offer is still outstanding. Counsel has advised that if

ASSETS		LIABILITIES	
Cash (in Non-Interest-Bearing Account)	$ 10,400	6% Notes Payable (Principal and Interest Payable Monthly until 19Y0)	$ 39,000
30-day Treasury Bills (Maturing July 30, 19X3) . . .	11,000	Capital	120,300
Drugs and Supplies Inventory .	6,100		
Equipment and Office Furniture (Net of $14,000 Accumulated Depreciation)	66,000		
Automobiles (Net of $1,150 Accumulated Depreciation) .	10,800		
Building (Purchased June 28, 19X3)	55,000		
Total	$159,300	Total	$159,300

the offer is accepted, any difference between the proceeds and the partners' tax bases in the partnership will be taxed as ordinary income.

6. The Bolans purchased their residence in 19X0 for $85,000. The balance of the thirty-year, 10 percent mortgage is $64,498. The current rate charged on similar mortgages is 10 percent. Payments on the mortgage are current. Similar homes in the area have increased in value approximately 30 percent since 19X0. The assessed real estate value was determined in March 19X3 to be $108,500 based on fair value.

7. Frances Bolan owns a 19X0 automobile which cost $7,100. Current newspaper advertisements indicate that her car could be sold for $4,800.

8. Fifteen years ago the Bolans bought a painting by an artist who has since become internationally famous. The Bolans paid $6,000 for the painting. In June 19X3, the painting was appraised at $16,000.

9. The Bolans have maintained cost records on their major household effects. The costs aggregate $27,500. A local business which specializes in auctioning this type of merchandise estimated in July 19X3 that the household effects have a net realizable value of $12,000. Other household effects are of nominal value.

10. Dr. Bolan has a vested interest of $14,175 in a group-participating pension plan. The present value of the vested benefits is $6,818. Dr. Bolan's contributions to the plan (tax basis) have been $5,432.

11. On July 1, 19X0, Dr. Bolan paid $9,000 for 25 percent of the capital stock of Medical Instruments, Inc., a closely-held business which designs medical instruments. A summary of financial data of the corporation follows:

	Balance Sheet at June 30, 19X2		Earnings Summary for the Years Ended June 30		Dividends Paid	
Assets	$112,800					
Liabilities	46,650		19X1	$12,050		
Equity	66,150		19X2	18,100		
	$112,800		19X3	28,050	$6,200	June 10

Similar businesses in the area have been sold recently for ten times the average of the last three years' earnings.

12. The Bolans owed $810 on charge accounts and $220 on a national credit card account at June 30, 19X3.

13. In early July 19X3, the Bolans estimated their federal income tax for their 19X3 return to be $26,000. Estimated tax payments of $8,000 had been made as of June 30, 19X3. A tax rate of 40 percent is assumed for all tax considerations, with capital gains subject to a 60 percent deduction.

Required:

1. Prepare a statement of assets and liabilities in good form as of June 30, 19X3, for James and Frances Bolan. Do not prepare accompanying notes.

2. Identify the items of the statement of assets and liabilities requiring explanatory and disclosure notes. Do not prepare the notes.

(AICPA adapted)

P1.6 **Personal Financial Statements—Current Value Basis** Z. D. Sanberry, who practices dentistry as a sole proprietor, recently filed as a candidate for mayor of his city. He has requested your assistance in preparing combined personal financial statements for himself and his wife, June. Your firm rendered an unqualified opinion on similar statements last year in connection with an examination conducted to support Dr. Sanberry's application for a bank loan, which was not made.

Dr. Sanberry's bookkeeper has provided you with a trial balance listing the Sanberry's assets and liabilities on the cost basis at April 30, 19X1. Your examination disclosed the following additional information:

1. A summary of cash receipts and disbursements for the year ended April 30, 19X1, follows:

DISBURSEMENTS		
Personal Expenditures, Including Personal Life Insurance Premium	$16,000	
Purchase of Kindred Company 6% Bonds at Par	8,000	
Income Taxes	4,100	
Interest on Mortgage	1,400	
Mortgage Principal Amortization	1,300	
Real Estate Taxes	900	$31,700
RECEIPTS		
Withdrawals from Sanberry's Dental Practice	$21,000	
Sale of Inco Stock (Purchased 6/1/W8 for $3,200; Market Value on 5/30/X0, $4,500)	6,100	
Dividends on Stock	1,540	
Interest on Bonds	240	28,880
DECREASE IN CASH		$ 2,820

2. The bonds were purchased on July 31, 19X0. Interest is payable semiannually on January 31 and July 31.

3. In 19W4, Sanberry invested $10,000 to begin his dentistry practice and

since has made additional investments. On April 2, 19X1, Sanberry was offered $31,000 for the net assets of his dental practice.
4. Sanberry owns 25 percent of the outstanding stock of the closely-held corporation, Dental Supply, Inc.
5. The April 30, 19X1, statements of net assets of Sanberry's dental practice and Dental Supply, Inc., both accompanied by unqualified opinions rendered by a CPA, were composed of the assets and liabilities shown below:

	Sanberry's Dental Practice	Dental Supply, Inc.
Current Assets	$ 6,000	$30,000
Noncurrent Assets	36,000	70,000
Current Liabilities	3,650	17,000
Long-Term Liabilities	16,350	35,000
Deferred Credits	2,500	4,000

6. Investments in marketable securities on April 30, 19X1, were composed of the following:

	April 30, 19X1, Latest Prices	
	Bid	Asked
STOCKS		
Steele, Inc.	$15,100	$15,500
Gilliam Corp.	4,000	4,200
BONDS		
Kindred Company 6% bonds	7,800	7,900
	$26,900	$27,600

7. The valuation (at 100 percent of fair market value) of other property owned by the Sanberrys on April 30, 19X1, was as follows:

Residence	$100,000
Automobile	4,300
Paintings	14,500
Household Furnishings	7,600

For records kept on a cost basis, the automobile and household furnishings were written down to reflect a permanent decline in value.
8. The accounts payable as of April 30, 19X0, and April 30, 19X1, represent liabilities for personal living costs.
9. The Sanberrys would have to pay a capital gains tax at an effective rate of 25 percent if the assets were sold. Decreases in asset values may be ignored in making this computation.
10. Accrued income taxes payable of $2,225 as of April 30, 19X1, represent the Sanberrys' total tax liability.

Required: The worksheet shown on page 28 (as Exhibit 1.4) includes items valued at cost for 19X1 and at current values for 19X0. Make the adjusting and summary entries on a worksheet and prepare, in worksheet form, a statement of changes in net assets and a statement of assets and liabilities for Z. D. and June Sanberry on the *current value basis* only.   (AICPA adapted)

Exhibit 1.4   Worksheet for P1.6

Z. D. and June Sanberry
Worksheet for Current Value Basis Financial Statements
For the Year Ended April 30, 19X1

| | Assets and Liabilities | | Summary and Adjusting Entries | | Current Value Basis—April 30, 19X1 | |
| | Cost Basis April 30, 19X1 | Current Value Basis April 30, 19X0 | | | Statement of Changes in Net Assets | Statement of Assets and Liabilities |
			Debit	Credit	Debit	Credit
ASSETS						
Cash	$ 3,300	$ 6,120				
Marketable Securities	23,000	21,400				
Cash Value of Life Insurance	4,250	3,900				
Net Assets of Sanberry's Dental Practice	19,500	27,000				
Interest in Dental Supply, Inc.	6,100	8,600				
Residence	65,000	94,000				
Automobile	4,300	5,800				
Paintings	11,000	12,700				
Household Furnishings	7,600	7,800				
	$144,050	$187,320				
LIABILITIES						
Accounts Payable	$ 3,100	$ 2,850				
Accrued Income Taxes Payable	2,225	1,900				
Accrued Income Taxes on Unrealized Asset Appreciation		10,970				
Mortgage Payable	34,000	35,300				
	$ 39,325	$ 51,020				

Chapter 2

Partnerships: Formation, Operation, and Expansion

Despite the apparent popularity of the corporate form of business organization, most businesses in the United States are organized as sole proprietorships or partnerships rather than as corporations. We discussed sole proprietorships in Chapter 1. In Chapters 2 and 3, we consider partnerships. In this chapter, we discuss the characteristics of a partnership and the accounting issues relating to its formation, operation, and expansion.

Characteristics of a Partnership

The organizational and operational rules for partnerships derive from two sources: law (the Uniform Partnership Act) and contract (the partnership agreement).

Legal Provisions

Partnerships are subject to the laws of the particular state in which they are organized. Many states have adopted the provisions of the Uniform Partnership Act. This act has sections dealing with:

1. The nature of a partnership.
2. Relations of partners to others.
3. Relations among partners.
4. Partners' property rights.
5. Termination and dissolution of the partnership.

We shall briefly discuss the major provisions of these sections.

The Nature of a Partnership The act defines a **partnership** as "an association of two or more persons to carry on as co-owners a business for profit." Thus the actions of individuals as they jointly conduct a business activity and share profits legally create a partnership even if no formal agreement among the individuals exists.

Relations of Partners to Others   Each partner is considered an agent of the partnership. That is, for most transactions, any one partner can act for the entire partnership and can legally enter into binding contracts, representing other partners as well. Only a few transactions, such as disposing of the goodwill of the business or confessing a judgment in court, require authorization of all the partners. This characteristic, known as **mutual agency,** is of great convenience to partners in transacting business. One partner may act for the entire partnership, and outsiders know that any partner with whom they deal legally represents the entire partnership.

There is another significant aspect to this section of the act. While any one partner may enter into transactions on behalf of the partnership, all partners are liable for the partnership's obligations. The partners are said to be liable *jointly and severally*. This means that as a group they are liable for the obligations of the partnership, and also that each partner has personal liability which could extend to the entire partnership obligation. In other words, creditors of the partnership could seek to collect from a single partner. Since the partners' obligations are not limited to their investments in the partnership, personal assets are also at risk. Partners are thus said to possess **unlimited liability.** We shall consider this matter more fully in the next chapter, in the discussion of partnership liquidations.

Relations among Partners   This section of the act deals with the rights and duties of partners, setting forth the following:

> The rights and duties of the partners in relation to the partnership shall be determined, subject to any agreement between them, by the following rules:
>
> a. Each partner shall be repaid his contributions, whether by way of capital or advances to the partnership property and share equally in the profits and surplus remaining after all liabilities, including those to partners, are satisfied; and must contribute toward the losses, whether of capital or otherwise, sustained by the partnership according to his share in the profits.
> b. The partnership must indemnify every partner in respect of payments made and personal liabilities reasonably incurred by him in the ordinary and proper conduct of its business, or for the preservation of its business or property.
> c. A partner, who in aid of the partnership makes any payment or advance beyond the amount of capital which he agreed to contribute, shall be paid interest from the date of payment or advance.
> d. A partner shall receive interest on the capital contributed by him only from the date when repayment should be made.
> e. All partners have equal rights in the management and conduct of the partnership business.
> f. No partner is entitled to remuneration for acting in the partnership business, except that a surviving partner is entitled to reasonable compensation for his services in winding up the partnership affairs.
> g. No person can become a member of a partnership without the consent of all the partners.
> h. Any difference arising as to ordinary matters connected with the partner-

ship business may be decided by a majority of the partners; but no act in contravention of any agreement between the partners may be done rightfully without the consent of all the partners.[1]

Note that any of the above rules are subject to modification by the partnership agreement. For example, the partners may agree to a division of profits and losses in unequal shares. However, if no specific agreement exists, then the provision of the act regarding equal sharing applies.

Partners' Property Rights　The act defines three specific property rights which a partner possesses:

1. The partner is a co-owner of all property held by the partnership and has no claim on specific assets.

2. The partner possesses a partnership interest (that is, a right to a share of the capital and profits).

3. The partner has a right to participate in the management of the partnership.

Termination and Dissolution of the Partnership　The act deals extensively with the dissolution of partnerships, covering ways in which dissolution occurs, impact of dissolution on the rights of various parties, and the rules for distribution of partnership assets. These issues are discussed in Chapter 3.

Contractual Provisions

The **partnership agreement** (sometimes referred to as the **articles of partnership**) is a contract among the partners. On certain matters, such as the distribution of income among partners, the contractual agreement takes precedence over the provisions of the Uniform Partnership Act. On other matters, such as the rights of outside parties, the contract cannot be at variance with the law. In general, the partnership agreement deals with the following matters:

1. Characteristics of the partnership—its name, nature, location of its business activity, duration, fiscal year, and so on.

2. Methods of allocating partnership income to the partners.

3. Procedures for admitting new partners and for settling a partner's interest upon withdrawal or death, including life insurance to be carried on partners, buy-sell agreements, and so on.

Thus, the partnership agreement generally addresses the various aspects of the relationship among the partners. It will have little if anything to say about the relationship of the partnership to outside parties.

Limited Partnerships

The above discussion has focused on general partnerships, in which all partners can participate in the management of the firm and all are liable for the partnership's obligations.

Another type of partnership, the **limited partnership,** has both general partners and limited partners. The *general partners* (of whom there must be at least one) manage the firm and have all the rights and obligations previously dis-

---

[1] Uniform Partnership Act, Part IV, Section 18.

Exhibit 2.1 A Comparison of General Partnership, Limited Partnership, and Corporate Forms of Business Organization

ASPECT	GENERAL PARTNERSHIP	LIMITED PARTNERSHIP	CORPORATION
Creation	By contract between two or more parties.	By contract between two or more parties, under statutory enabling legislation, with recording of certificate in prescribed office.	Under statutory enabling legislation with charter granted by a governmental entity.
Legal status and activities	Not a legal entity; may carry out any legal activity agreed upon by the partners. Each partner has authority to bind the partnership when dealing with outsiders in the usual manner.	May carry out all activities that a partnership without limited partners may undertake, except as limited by its recorded certificate.	Is a legal entity and may carry out all activities authorized by its charter.
Life of organization	Ceases at death, withdrawal, or addition of a partner, or earlier by contractual provision. Business operation may continue by contractual arrangement.	Ceases at death, withdrawal, or addition of general partner, or earlier by contractual provision. Withdrawal or addition of limited partners need not terminate the partnership. When all limited partners cease to be such, partnership is terminated.	Perpetual, unless limited by charter.
Ownership share transferability	Only with consent of all other partners.	General partners interests may be changed only with consent of all partners. Limited partner interests may be assigned;	Freely transferable.

cussed. The *limited partners* invest capital and have the right to a specified share of income or loss but have no right to participate in management. Moreover, their liability for the partnership's obligations is limited to their investment in the partnership. In other words, limited partners have *no personal liability* for partnership obligations, as general partners do.

Limited partnerships have often been used in situations where investment capital is desired. A general partner may initiate the project, such as a real estate development or an oil well, and finance it by selling limited partnership interests to a number of investors. In this way, the general partner acquires the needed capital without relinquishing management control, and investors acquire a right to share in income without bearing any personal responsibility for partnership liabilities.

Comparison of Partnership and Corporation Forms of Business Organization

Exhibit 2.1 presents a detailed comparison of general partnerships, limited partnerships, and corporations, summarizing characteristics of each form of business organization.

Exhibit 2.1   A Comparison of General Partnership, Limited Partnership, and Corporate
Forms of Business Organization *continued*

ASPECT	GENERAL PARTNERSHIP	LIMITED PARTNERSHIP	CORPORATION
		assignees may become substituted limited partners with consent of all other partners or by action of assignor if certificate gives assignor such authority.	
Management	Each partner is entitled to an equal voice unless the partnership agreement provides otherwise.	Only general partners have rights to manage.	Responsibility is vested in the board of directors.
Status of owners	Each partner is a principal and an agent of the other partners.	Each general partner is principal and agent of the other general partners. Limited partners do not serve as principal or agent for other partners.	Stockholder is neither principal nor agent, but has contractual rights only.
Liability of owners	Unlimited liability for debts of the partnership and torts of partners, unless limited by contract (subject to limitations).	Limited partners not liable to creditors unless they take part in control of the business. General partners have liability similar to that of partners in a general partnership.	Stockholder not liable for debts of corporation.
Additional owners	Creates new partnership. All current partners must consent.	Additional limited partners may be admitted upon filing amendment to original certificate, subject to rights of original partners.	Limited by charter and preemptive rights of current shareholders.

Major Accounting Issues

Because it is a business entity, a partnership uses many of the same accounting principles used by corporations. For example, general topics such as revenue and expense recognition and asset valuation are given the same treatment. There are, however, a few important areas where partnership accounting differs from corporate accounting. Most of these differences are due to the particular nature of the partnership entity.

Like a corporation, a partnership is an entity distinct from the individual partners. However, the partners typically are actively involved in the firm; they are not absentee owners. This fact influences the concept of net income for a partnership as well as the treatment of owners' equity. Corporate equity is reflected in several accounts (Common Stock, Paid-In Capital, and Retained Earnings) but no attempt is made to maintain equity accounts for each stockholder. Partnership equity, on the other hand, is recorded in a single **capital ac-**

count, which reflects both invested capital and accumulated earnings. A capital account is maintained for each partner.

Allocations versus Payments to Partners

In discussing the flow of income from the partnership to the individual partners, we must distinguish two steps. First are the *allocations* to partners, which are the credits to the partners' capital accounts reflecting the sharing of income (or debits reflecting the sharing of loss). Much of the following discussion will be devoted to these allocations. Second are the *payments* to partners (debits to capital accounts) reflecting the transfer of resources from the partnership to the partners. These payments (also called *drawings*) involve no special accounting problems, except in cases where the partnership is being liquidated. (This topic is discussed in Chapter 3.)

Income Determination

To determine net income for a partnership, we must first define *net income* as it applies to the special distinctions of the partnership form. Just as we discussed the differences between income for proprietorships and corporations, we now discuss the differences between income for partnerships and corporations. There are several similarities between income determination for proprietorships and for partnerships.

In corporate accounting, net income signifies the return to the owners (stockholders) of the corporation. In partnership accounting, we again wish to have net income signify the return to the owners (partners). A practical problem arises, however, in that in most cases partners are actually involved in the operation of the firm. In addition to being investors, partners may also render personal services in the day-to-day conduct of business and may loan money to the partnership. Stockholders of a corporation may also be employees of, or lenders to, that corporation, but no problem of income determination arises because accounting and tax requirements necessitate a careful distinction between the corporate entity and the individual, along with a distinction among the individual's possible roles as stockholder, employee, and lender. These constraints are much weaker in the case of a partnership because a partnership does not have the distinct legal status of a corporation, nor is it a taxable entity. As a result, when partners have multiple involvement in the financial affairs of the partnership—as investors, employees, and lenders—it is difficult to distinguish among: (a) compensation for services performed, (b) interest on loans, and (c) return on capital invested. While certain allocations may be called salaries, other allocations interest, and still others distribution of profit, the lack of an arm's-length transaction in establishing the amounts prompts us to disregard these distinctions and to consider *all* allocations to partners as divisions of profit. In other words, in determining the net income of a partnership, salaries to partners and interest to partners are excluded from expenses.

A second area of difference between corporation and partnership net income is the treatment of income taxes. For federal income tax purposes, a corporation is a taxable entity, but a partnership is not. A partnership is considered a conduit, whereby income flows to the individual partners. Thus, *no federal income tax is imposed directly on the partnership;* rather, the individual partners include their share of income on their personal income tax returns. The income statement of the partnership, therefore, does not provide for income tax expense.

**Allocation of
Net Income
to Partners**

After the partnership's net income is determined, the next concern is allocation of the net income among the individual partners. As discussed above, all allocations to partners are viewed as divisions of net income. It is not surprising, therefore, that in dividing net income, attention may be given to the various roles (investor, employee, lender) which each partner may hold.

The partnership agreement should specify the rules for the allocation of income. These rules may be simple or complex. Should the partnership agreement be silent as to the allocation of income, then it must be assumed that income is to be divided equally among all partners. Various approaches to allocation are discussed and illustrated in a subsequent section.

Capital Changes

The third major accounting issue is changes in the capital structure of the partnership. Such changes occur for many reasons. In this chapter and the next, we consider the formation of the partnership, the subsequent entry and exit of individual partners, and the eventual liquidation of the partnership.

**Formation
of the
Partnership**

Accounting for the formation of a partnership requires the valuation of assets contributed by the partners and determination of each partner's capital account. Following GAAP, assets contributed to a partnership in exchange for a capital interest should be valued at fair market value.[2] This often creates a difference between the accounting basis and the tax basis of particular assets. Our main concern in this chapter is the accounting basis; however, the tax basis is briefly examined in the appendix to this chapter.

**Bonus and
Goodwill
Approaches**

The determination of each partner's capital account is somewhat more complex than the valuation of assets. One straightforward approach is to set each partner's capital account equal to the fair market value of net assets invested. For example, assume that Prince and Quinn form a partnership. Prince invests $30,000 cash, and Quinn invests land and a building having a combined fair market value of $75,000, subject to a mortgage of $35,000, which the partnership assumes. Thus Quinn has invested net assets with fair market value of $40,000. If each partner's capital is to equal net assets invested at fair market value, the entry to record formation would be:

Cash	30,000	
Land and Building	75,000	
Mortgage Payable		35,000
Capital—Prince		30,000
Capital—Quinn		40,000
To record formation of partnership.		

An alternative possibility is that the partners might specify that a predetermined percentage interest in total partnership capital is to apply to each partner. This approach could generate several alternative entries for recording the partnership's formation, depending on the details of the agreement between Prince and Quinn. For example, assume that Prince and Quinn decide that

[2] Accounting Principles Board, *Opinion No. 29*, "Accounting for Nonmonetary Transactions" (N.Y.: AICPA, 1973); AC § 1041.

each is to have a 50 percent interest in partnership capital. How is this to be accomplished, given that Prince invested $30,000 and Quinn invested $40,000? Two approaches are possible: One is simply to divide the total capital of $70,000 equally, crediting each with $35,000. Thus, there is an implied transfer of $5,000 of capital from Quinn to Prince. The entry recording the formation of the partnership would then be:

Cash	30,000	
Land and Building	75,000	
Mortgage Payable		35,000
Capital—Prince		35,000
Capital—Quinn		35,000
To record formation of partnership.		

This is called the **bonus approach to partnership formation.** Quinn is assumed to be paying Prince a bonus of $5,000.

A second approach is to assume that intangible assets exist which will bring the investments (and hence the capital balances) into the desired relationship. We may argue, for example, that the reason the partners agreed on equal capital balances while making apparently unequal investments is that one partner, Prince in this case, brings certain talents, contacts, or other intangible benefits to the partnership. We may record this intangible asset, called *goodwill*, in an amount sufficient to achieve the desired relationship among the capital accounts. In our example, we would need to record $10,000 of goodwill in order to make Prince's investment equal to Quinn's. Our entry to record formation of the partnership would then be:

Cash	30,000	
Land and Building	75,000	
Goodwill	10,000	
Mortgage Payable		35,000
Capital—Prince		40,000
Capital—Quinn		40,000
To record formation of partnership.		

This approach is called the **goodwill approach to partnership formation.** In forming the partnership, the partners must specify which accounting approach is to be used.

The bonus and goodwill methods will be examined more thoroughly in connection with the admission of a new partner, which is discussed later in the chapter.

Investment of an Existing Business

Rather than investing individual assets, a partner may have an existing business entity (a proprietorship) which becomes that partner's investment in the partnership. This does not cause any substantial accounting problem.

The main question is whether the books of the existing proprietorship will be retained to serve as the books of the partnership or a new set of books will be established. If the existing books are retained, two steps are necessary:

1. Revaluations of assets may be necessary to reflect the fair market value of assets being transferred to the partnership, and intangible assets may need to be recognized.

2. Investments by partners must be recorded.

If a new set of books is to be established, each asset of the business must be recorded at its fair market value. The entry is made in the same manner as described in the preceding section. Whichever of these two approaches is followed, the asset values and capital accounts which result should be the same.

Accounting for Partnership Operations

As mentioned earlier, rules covered in introductory and intermediate accounting courses regarding corporate revenue and expense recognition and asset and liability valuation apply in general to partnerships. Thus the special accounting considerations for partnerships focus primarily on the capital accounts representing the owners' equity.

In partnership accounting, a capital account for each partner serves as the set of owners' equity accounts. This account combines invested capital and undistributed income. Three types of events affect capital account balances:

1. *Investment of capital.* An individual partner's capital account may be affected not only by the partner's own involvement (as illustrated in discussing partnership formation above) but also by the investments of new partners (as will be illustrated later in discussing the admission of partners).

2. *Distribution of net income.* When the partnership's net income is determined and allocated to the partners, the appropriate share is credited (or debited if there is a loss) to each partner's capital account.

3. *Withdrawal of capital* (including withdrawal of net income). Amounts withdrawn are debited to each partner's capital account. Often, withdrawals are made in anticipation of net income and are debited to a separate **drawing** account for each partner. This account is then closed at year-end to the capital account. For example, if partner Burns withdraws $500 per month, the following entry could be made monthly:

   Drawing—Burns   500
     Cash   500
   To record monthly withdrawal.

   At year-end, the balance in the drawing account would be closed, as follows:

   Capital—Burns   6,000
     Drawing—Burns   6,000
   To close drawing account to capital.

   Use of the drawing account is optional; withdrawals may be directly debited to capital.

Allocation of Net Income to Partners

As was discussed above, partners' salaries or interest are not considered expenses in determining the partnership's net income. Rather, all such allocations to partners are considered divisions of net income.

In allocating partnership net income to the individual partners, therefore, a multifactor allocation procedure may be used. While partners may agree to use any factors they wish, three common ones are:

1.   A salary factor, reflecting personal services which each partner provides to the operations of the partnership.

2.   An interest factor, reflecting the capital which each partner has invested.

3.   A percentage factor, reflecting an agreed ratio for the division of net income after provision has been made for any salaries and interests.

We shall discuss and illustrate each of these.

Salaries to Partners

Allocations of net income to partners in the form of salaries are typically established by formal agreement among the partners. This agreement usually specifies the amount each partner is to receive or the formula for calculating the amount (for example, a bonus formula). The amounts can be based on the time, effort, or experience that each partner contributes to the business. For example, the DEF partnership might agree that D is to receive an annual salary of $20,000, E is to receive an annual salary of $6,000, and F is to receive no salary. Any remaining income or loss is to be divided equally among the partners. If partnership net income for the year is $38,000, the allocation would first provide for the $26,000 in salaries and then divide the remaining $12,000 by the percentage formula. This yields the following allocations:

	D	E	F	Total
Salaries	$20,000	$ 6,000	$ 0	$26,000
Balance	4,000	4,000	4,000	12,000
	$24,000	$10,000	$4,000	$38,000

The salary allocation is to be fully implemented, even if it exceeds the partnership net income.[3] In the example above, assume that net income is $17,000. The salary allocation of $26,000 exceeds net income by $9,000. This $9,000 "loss" is then allocated by the percentage formula, producing the following allocations:

	D	E	F	Total
Salaries	$20,000	$ 6,000	$ 0	$26,000
Balance	(3,000)	(3,000)	(3,000)	(9,000)
	$17,000	$ 3,000	$ (3,000)	$17,000

Bonus to Partners

As mentioned above, allocation of net income to partners for services rendered might be described in terms of a bonus formula. In discussing various bonus relationships, we use the following symbols:

---

[3] The partnership agreement should specify whether salary (and interest) allocations are to be fully implemented if they exceed total net income. We assume such a provision in our discussion.

X = Net income before bonus.

B = Amount of bonus.

Y = Net income after bonus $(Y = X - B)$.

R = Percentage rate of bonus.

If the bonus is defined as a percentage of net income before bonus, its calculation is simply:

$$B = RX.$$

Sometimes the bonus is defined as a percentage of the net income which will remain after the bonus. This involves a somewhat more complex formula:

$$B = RY$$
$$B = R(X - B)$$
$$(1 + R)B = RX$$
$$B = \frac{RX}{1 + R}.$$

For example, assume net income before the bonus is $30,000, and the bonus is to be 25 percent of net income after the bonus (a figure which is presently unknown). Using the above formula, we would calculate the bonus as:

$$
\begin{aligned}
B &= \frac{RX}{1 + R} \\
&= \frac{.25(30,000)}{1.25} \\
&= \frac{7,500}{1.25} \\
&= 6,000.
\end{aligned}
$$

We can then easily verify that the $6,000 bonus is indeed 25 percent of the net income after bonus of $24,000 (= $30,000 − $6,000).

Interest to Partners

Allocations of net income may also be made on the basis of interest on partners' capital accounts. An interest rate is specified, which usually applies to weighted average capital balances.[4] We calculate the *weighted average capital balance* by multiplying each level of a partner's capital balance by the fraction of the year during which that amount existed. For example, assume that a partner's capital account has a balance of $6,000 on January 1. On March 1, additional capital of $20,000 is invested, and on September 1, $2,000 is withdrawn. The weighted average capital balance for the year would be calculated as follows:

Period	Capital Balance	Fraction of Year	Weighted Average
1/1–2/28	$ 6,000	2/12	$ 1,000
3/1–8/31	26,000	6/12	13,000
9/1–12/31	24,000	4/12	8,000
			$22,000

[4] The partnership agreement should specify the base for the calculation of interest. For example, beginning-of-year capital balance or a simple average of beginning and ending balances could be used.

If an interest rate of 8 percent were specified, net income of $1,760 (= .08 × $22,000) would be allocated to this partner.

As was the case with salaries to partners, any allocation of net income in the form of interest must be made fully, even if it exceeds total net income. Again, any remaining loss would be allocated by the percentage formula.

Percentage Allocation

A percentage allocation formula is always assumed to exist for a partnership. The entire net income of the partnership may be allocated by percentage formula. Alternatively, some income may be allocated by a salary formula, an interest formula, or both. In this case, the balance of net income after salaries and interest, whether positive or negative, is allocated by percentage formula.

The partnership agreement sets forth the percentage formula. Normally, a single set of percentages is applied to all forms of income. The partners may, however, agree that different types of income (or expense) will be divided in different ways. Should the partnership agreement be silent as to a percentage allocation formula, then it is automatically assumed that all partners share *equally*.

Illustration of Allocation of Partnership Income

Thomas, Underwood, and Vickers are partners in a printing firm. Their partnership agreement contains the following provisions regarding income allocation:

1. Thomas is to devote two days per week to partnership business and receive an annual salary of $15,000. Underwood and Vickers are to work full time and receive annual salaries of $35,000 and $30,000, respectively.

2. Vickers, who is responsible for sales, is to receive a bonus of 10 percent of any net income in excess of $100,000.

3. The partners are to receive 10 percent interest on their weighted average capital balances. Payments of salaries and bonus are ignored for purposes of this calculation.

4. After the above allocations are implemented, any remaining income or loss is to be allocated 50 percent to Thomas, 30 percent to Underwood, and 20 percent to Vickers.

Assume that net income for 19X6 was $150,000. The partners' capital balances at the beginning of the year were: Thomas, $69,000; Underwood, $40,000; and Vickers, $40,000. Underwood invested an additional $10,000 on March 31, 19X6, and Thomas withdrew $18,000 on October 31, 19X6. At the end of each quarter, the partners withdrew a total of $6,000, divided according to the percentages in item 4 above (that is, Thomas withdrew $3,000, Underwood $1,800, and Vickers $1,200).

The allocation of income for 19X6 is shown in Exhibit 2.2.

Admission of a New Partner

The admission of a new partner gives rise to another important accounting problem for partnerships. Technically, there is no such thing as "the admission of a new partner." If a new partner is admitted, the old partnership legally ends, and a new partnership is created. For practical purposes, however, business operations are likely to continue without interruption. As is often the case in ac-

Exhibit 2.2   Illustration of Income Allocation

	Thomas	Underwood	Vickers	Total
Salaries	$15,000	$35,000	$30,000	$ 80,000
Bonus[a]	—	—	5,000	5,000
Interest[b]	6,150	4,480	3,820	14,450
				$ 99,450
Balance[c]	25,275	15,165	10,110	50,550
	$46,425	$54,645	$48,930	$150,000

[a]Bonus is 10 percent of $50,000 (= $150,000 − $100,000).
[b]Weighted average capital is calculated as follows:

	Thomas		Underwood		Vickers	
1/1–3/31	$69,000 × 3/12 =	$17,250	$40,000 × 3/12 =	$10,000	$40,000 × 3/12 =	$10,000
4/1–6/30	66,000 × 3/12 =	16,500	48,200 × 3/12 =	12,050	38,800 × 3/12 =	9,700
7/1–9/30	63,000 × 3/12 =	15,750	46,400 × 3/12 =	11,600	37,600 × 3/12 =	9,400
10/1–10/31	60,000 × 1/12 =	5,000	{44,600 × 3/12 =	11,150	{36,400 × 3/12 =	9,100
11/1–12/31	42,000 × 2/12 =	7,000				
Weighted average		$61,500		$44,800		$38,200

Ten percent of the weighted average capital is the amount of interest.
[c]The balance of $50,550 is allocated 50 percent to Thomas, 30 percent to Underwood, and 20 percent to Vickers.

counting, the economic substance (of a continuing business activity) takes precedence over the legal form (the termination of the old partnership and the creation of a new one). It is in this economic sense, therefore, that we speak of the admission of a new partner.

In the illustrations which follow, assume the partnership of Arthur Associates has a balance sheet at June 30, 19X2, as follows:

Various Assets	$140,000	Liabilities		$ 50,000
		Capital:		
		Arthur	$31,000	
		Bradley	26,000	
		Crowe	33,000	90,000
	$140,000			$140,000

Assume further that the partners share income in the following ratio: Arthur 50 percent, Bradley 20 percent, and Crowe 30 percent.

Admission by Purchase of an Existing Partnership Interest

One manner in which a new partner may enter an existing partnership is by purchasing the interest of one or more existing partners. Such a transaction occurs between the old and new partners as *individuals* and usually has no direct effect on the partnership accounts. This is parallel to the case where one individual sells shares of stock in a corporation to another individual. Only those two are involved in the transaction; the corporation makes no entry other than to update its stockholder records. In a similar manner, when one individual buys an existing partnership interest, the only entry usually needed is a transfer of the capital account from the old partner to the new.

Transfer of Capital Interests The usual method of accounting for a purchase of a partnership interest is to transfer the capital balance of the selling partner to a new capital account which is established for the buyer. The amount of the entry is the existing capital balance of the selling partner, which may be different from the selling price.

Purchase from One Partner In the case of Arthur Associates, assume that on July 1, 19X2, Findley purchases Crowe's entire partnership interest for $45,000. The partnership would record the following entry to show transfer of the interest from Crowe to Findley:

```
Capital—Crowe  .    .    .    .    .    .    .    .    . 33,000
     Capital—Findley .    .    .    .    .    .    .    .                33,000
To record transfer of partnership interest
from Crowe to Findley.
```

Note that the purchase price of $45,000 has no bearing on the entry. The $45,000 was received by Crowe directly, not by the partnership. Crowe has realized a gain of $12,000 on the sale of the partnership interest, assuming Crowe's basis is the book figure of $33,000. The cost (tax basis) of Findley's partnership interest is $45,000, despite the fact that the partnership books show the capital account as $33,000. Findley's cost of $45,000 will have no effect on any capital-based distributions which the partnership may make. In contrast, the $45,000 cost will affect the subsequent recognition of gain or loss by Findley when the partnership interest is sold.

Purchase from Several Partners A new partner may purchase a portion of the interest of several partners. For example, assume that Grogan buys a 25 percent interest in Arthur Associates by purchasing 25 percent of each partner's interest for a total of $28,000. Following the procedure illustrated in the preceding section, we could simply record the transfer of capital interests. By this method, 25 percent of each partner's capital at the date of entry would be transferred to the new partner, Grogan. The entry would be:

```
Capital—Arthur   .    .    .    .    .    .    .    .    .    7,750
Capital—Bradley .    .    .    .    .    .    .    .    .    6,500
Capital—Crowe   .    .    .    .    .    .    .    .    .    8,250
     Capital—Grogan   .    .    .    .    .    .    .    .                 22,500
To record transfer of 25 percent interest to Grogan.
```

The debits to the capital accounts of the three existing partners represent 25 percent of their respective capital balances, and Grogan's capital of $22,500 is 25 percent of the total capital of $90,000. Note that, as before, the $28,000 purchase price has no bearing on the entry. The three existing partners will recognize gains or losses as individuals on the sale of part of their partnership interests.

Recognition of Implied Goodwill The admission of a new partner by purchase of an existing partnership interest is usually recorded by the transfer of capital accounts described above. Another possible method involves the recognition of implied goodwill. Under this approach, the purchase price is used to infer the value of the entire partnership. To illustrate, again assume the case where Grogan buys 25 percent of each partner's interest for a total of $28,000.

If Grogan is willing to pay $28,000 to buy a 25 percent interest in the partnership, the entire partnership capital must be worth $112,000 (= $28,000/.25). But the partnership books show only $90,000, the total capital of Arthur, Bradley, and Crowe. This implies that $22,000 (= $112,000 implied total value − $90,000 recorded capital) of unrecorded assets exist. For convenience, we call these unrecorded assets **goodwill**. We first record the goodwill, apportioning a share to each partner according to the established income-sharing ratio of 50 percent for Arthur, 20 percent for Bradley, and 30 percent for Crowe. The entry to record implied goodwill is:

Goodwill	22,000	
Capital—Arthur		11,000
Capital—Bradley		4,400
Capital—Crowe		6,600
To record implied goodwill.		

We now make an entry to transfer 25 percent of each partner's capital to Grogan.

Capital—Arthur (25% × 42,000)	10,500	
Capital—Bradley (25% × 30,400)	7,600	
Capital—Crowe (25% × 39,600)	9,900	
Capital—Grogan		28,000
To record transfer of 25 percent interest to Grogan.		

Note that when this approach is used the credit to the new partner's capital account equals the amount paid to acquire the interest.

A new income-sharing ratio must be established for the four partners. For convenience, we typically assume that the contract for the new partnership specifies that (1) the new partner's percentages of income and of the initial capital balance are equal and (2) the old partners maintain their income-sharing relationship. After Grogan joins the firm, therefore, the partners share as follows: Arthur, 37.5 percent; Bradley, 15 percent; Crowe, 22.5 percent; and Grogan, 25 percent. These percentages are based on the fact that the old partners now own 75 percent of the partnership—Arthur has 50 percent of 75 percent, or 37.5 percent; Bradley has 20 percent of 75 percent; and Crowe has 30 percent of 75 percent.

Unless the agreement covering the purchase of partners' interests specifically provides for the recognition of implied goodwill on the partnership books, the transfer of capital accounts method should be used.

Admission by Investment of New Capital

The second way in which a new partner may enter an existing partnership is by investing directly in the partnership. In this case, the new partner contributes an agreed-upon amount of assets, which may be cash, property, or services, to the partnership and receives an agreed-upon share of capital at the date of entry and a specified share of subsequent income. The share of capital percentage is used primarily to establish the new partner's initial capital balance. Thereafter, the share of income percentage is of primary importance, as this guides the division of subsequent profits and losses among the partners. In many cases, the capital percentage and income percentage are equal. If they are not equal, their use is guided by the following rule:

> *Capital percentage* (capital-sharing ratio) is used to establish the value of the firm and hence the total amount of goodwill.
> *Income percentage* (income-sharing ratio) is used to allocate goodwill or bonus to partners as well as income.

The partnership must record the investment of assets by the new partner, the capital account of the new partner, and, perhaps, some further adjustments to reconcile the two. If the investment by the new partner happens to equal the new partner's capital percentage times the new net assets (old net assets plus assets invested), then no accounting problem exists. For example, assume that on July 1, 19X2, Edwards invests $10,000 in Arthur Associates in exchange for a 10 percent interest in capital (hereafter referred to simply as a 10 percent interest). We have:

1. Investment by Edwards = $10,000.
2. Edwards' share of new net assets = 10% × ($90,000 old net assets + $10,000 invested by Edwards) = 10%($100,000) = $10,000.

Since items 1 and 2 are equal, we simply record

Assets	10,000	
Capital—Edwards		10,000
To record investment by Edwards.		

Suppose, however, that Edwards has invested $9,000 for a 10 percent interest. We would then have:

Case A
1. Investment = $9,000.
2. Share of new net assets = 10%($90,000 + $9,000) = $9,900.

Alternatively, suppose Delano invests $12,000 for a 10 percent interest, giving:

Case B
1. Investment = $12,000.
2. Share of new net assets = 10%($90,000 + $12,000) = $10,200.

In each of the two preceding cases, the investment differs from the computed share of net assets. When this situation occurs, the disparity must be reconciled before the entry recording the investment can be made. Reconciliation can be achieved in one of two ways:

1. Consider the share of assets amount (item 2 above) to be the correct entry to the new partner's capital account. The difference between this amount and the amount invested is considered to be a capital adjustment of the existing partners. This is known as the **bonus method of admission.**

2. Bring the investment (item 1) and the share of net assets (item 2) amounts into agreement by assuming the existence of intangible assets

and adding these either to the investment of the new partner or to the existing net assets of the partnership. This is known as the **goodwill method of admission.**

The agreement accepting the new partner generally specifies which of these methods is to be used. In the following sections, both are discussed and illustrated.

Bonus Method Under the bonus method, the total net assets of the new partnership after admission of the new partner equal net assets before admission plus the investment of the new partner. The new partner's capital account is credited with the appropriate share of these net assets.

Say that the new partner's investment is *less* than the computed share of net assets, as in case A above, where Edwards invests $9,000 but receives a $9,900 share in net assets. In such a case, we assume that the existing partners have some reason for admitting Edwards at this less-than-fair-share price. Perhaps Edwards brings some important talents or resources to the firm, and to obtain these, the existing partners are willing to subsidize Edwards' admission by giving a $9,900 share for only $9,000.[5] The $900 difference is charged against the existing partners' capital accounts in their income-sharing ratio. In effect, each existing partner is transferring a portion of capital to Edwards. The entry to record Edwards' admission for a 10 percent interest with an investment of $9,000 is:

Cash	9,000	
Capital—Arthur	450	
Capital—Bradley	180	
Capital—Crowe	270	
Capital—Edwards		9,900

To record Edwards' admission under the bonus method.

This situation results in a **bonus to the new partner.**

The second possibility is that the new partner's investment is *more* than the computed share of net assets, as in case B above, where Delano invests $12,000 but has a $10,200 share in net assets. In such a situation, we assume that the existing partners are able to command a premium when admitting a new partner. Perhaps the assets of the partnership are worth more than their book value. Perhaps the partnership has above-average earning potential. Or perhaps the existing partners wish to be compensated for the risk and effort they incurred in establishing the firm. In any event, to gain admittance, Delano must contribute not only a fair share of assets, $10,200, but also an additional $1,800, which will be credited to the capital accounts of the existing partners in their income-

---

[5] Another possible reason for the low price is that the partnership's assets are overvalued. However, we generally ignore this possibility. If generally accepted accounting principles have been followed, writedowns to market for current assets such as marketable securities and inventories should have been made as losses occurred. Fixed assets are generally not written down, unless there is evidence that their utility value has permanently and materially declined.

sharing ratio. The entry to record Delano's admission, reflecting an investment of $12,000 in exchange for a 10 percent interest, would be:

Cash	12,000	
Capital—Arthur		900
Capital—Bradley		360
Capital—Crowe		540
Capital—Delano		10,200

To record Delano's admission under the bonus method.

This situation results in a **bonus to the existing partners.**

We may summarize the bonus method in formula terms. We calculate the amount to be credited to the new partner's capital account *(NC)* as follows:

$$NC = S(OC + I).$$

where OC = Total capital of the old partners.

I = Amount invested by the new partner.

S = New partner's percentage share in the partnership.

For example, if two existing partners each have capital balances of $43,000, and a new partner invests $50,000 for a 25 percent interest in the partnership, the balance of the new partner's capital account would be calculated as follows:

$$\begin{aligned} NC &= S(OC + I) \\ &= 25\%(86,000 + 50,000) \\ &= 25\%(136,000) \\ &= 34,000. \end{aligned}$$

In addition, the difference between the credit to the new partner's capital account and the amount invested *(NC − I)* would be divided among the old partners in accordance with their income-sharing ratio, and debited or credited to their capital accounts, depending on whether the new investment was less than or greater than the balance in the new partner's capital account.

Goodwill Method   Under the goodwill method, the discrepancy between the amount invested by the new partner and the share of net assets initially calculated is attributed to the presence of unrecorded intangible assets. To reconcile the discrepancy, these unrecorded assets must be recorded.

For example, say that the new partner's investment of tangible assets is less than the computed share of net assets, as in case A above, where Edwards invests $9,000 cash but has a $9,900 share in net assets. To explain this imbalance, we assume that Edwards must be bringing something more to the firm than $9,000 cash—perhaps some special skills or talents—such that the existing partners are willing to admit Edwards as a 10 percent partner. Thus we conclude that, in addition to the $9,000 cash, Edwards is also investing some intangible assets or *goodwill* in the partnership. We determine this amount in such a way that the investment (cash plus goodwill) and the share of net assets will be brought into balance. Note that as we add assets in the form of goodwill, Edwards' share of net assets will increase. Our calculation proceeds as follows:

1. Determine the total value of the new firm as implied by the net assets of the existing partners. In our example, existing net assets are $90,000, and the existing partners will have a 90 percent interest in the new partnership. This implies a total value of the new partnership of $100,000 (= $90,000/.9).

2. Calculate the new partner's share of this total value. In our example, Edwards' share is $10,000 (10 percent of $100,000).

3. The goodwill invested by the new partner is the difference between the calculated share of the value of the firm and the amount of tangible assets invested. In our example, Edwards is assumed to invest $1,000 of goodwill (= $10,000 share of firm's value − $9,000 cash invested).

The entry to record Edwards' admission would be:

```
Cash   .   .   .   .   .   .   .   .   .   .   .   .     9,000
Goodwill   .   .   .   .   .   .   .   .   .   .   .     1,000
     Capital—Edwards .   .   .   .   .   .   .   .                   10,000
To record Edwards' admission under goodwill method.
```

This situation is referred to as **goodwill to the new partner.**

The second possibility is that the new partner's investment of tangible assets is more than the initially-computed share of net assets, as in case B above, where Delano invests $12,000 cash for only a $10,200 share in net assets. To explain this imbalance, we assume that the net assets of the existing partnership are understated. Perhaps some of the firm's tangible assets have market values in excess of their book values. Or perhaps the firm has unrecorded goodwill in the form of established customers, product recognition, and skillful management. The fact that a new partner is willing to pay more than book value for a partnership interest gives credence to the idea that undervalued or unrecorded assets exist. To bring the new partner's investment into balance with the share of net assets, we must acknowledge these unrecorded asset amounts. We proceed as follows:

1. Determine the total value of the new firm as implied by the investment of the new partner. In our example, Delano invests $12,000 for a 10 percent interest. This implies a total value of the new partnership of $120,000 (= $12,000/.10).

2. Calculate the amount by which assets are understated. In our example, present net assets are recorded at $90,000. Delano will invest an additional $12,000, bringing the total to $102,000. But we have calculated the value of the new firm to be $120,000. Thus assets are understated by $18,000 (= $120,000 − $102,000).

3. The understatement of assets is corrected by recognizing the existence of an intangible asset, with offsetting credits to the capital accounts of the existing partners in their income-sharing ratio. In this way, recognition is given to the fact that the unrecorded increase in net assets occurred in the past and is attributable to the old partners. Revaluation of tangible assets to remove the understatement is generally not proper unless objective evidence—for example, a quoted market value of securities—substantiates the revaluation.

The entry to record Delano's admission would be:

Cash	12,000	
Goodwill	18,000	
Capital—Arthur		9,000
Capital—Bradley		3,600
Capital—Crowe		5,400
Capital—Delano		12,000

To record Delano's admission under the goodwill method.

This situation is referred to as **goodwill to the existing partners.**

Any goodwill recorded in admitting a new partner should be amortized over its estimated life. According to *APBO 17*, this life should not exceed forty years.[6]

Comparison of Bonus and Goodwill Methods   The mechanics of the bonus and goodwill methods may be expressed in formulas, using the following notation:

I = Amount invested by new partner.

S = New partner's percentage share in the partnership.

$(1 - S)$ = Percentage share in the partnership which will be held by the existing partners.

OC = Total capital of the existing partners ("old capital").

TV = Calculated total value of the partnership.

G = Goodwill to be recorded.

B = Total amount of bonus to be recorded.

First determine whether bonus or goodwill will apply to the new partner or to the existing partners. We may identify two general cases, which correspond to the Edwards (case A) and Delano (case B) illustrations in the preceding section.

Case A: $I < S(OC + I)$ If the investment by the new partner is less than that partner's share in the firm's total capital, the difference is accounted for by recording either a bonus or goodwill to the *new* partner. Under the bonus method, the bonus to the new partner is the difference between the new partner's capital share and investment:

$$B = S(OC + I) - I.$$

Under the goodwill method, we first calculate the implied total value of the firm:

$$TV = OC/(1 - S).$$

The total amount of goodwill to be associated with the new partner is the differ-

---

[6] Accounting Principles Board, *Opinion No. 17*, "Intangible Assets" (N.Y.: AICPA, 1970), par. 29; AC § 5141.29.

ence between the calculated total value and the new capital (old capital plus investment).

$$G = TV - (OC + I).$$

The relationship between the amount of goodwill and the amount of bonus can be seen by expanding and rearranging the above goodwill formula.

$$G = TV - (OC + I)$$

$$G = \frac{OC}{(1 - S)} - (OC + I).$$

This simplifies to:

$$(1 - S)G = S(OC + I) - I.$$

Recall that the bonus formula is:

$$B = S(OC + I) - I.$$

Thus we see that:

$$B = (1 - S)G.$$

Case B: $I > S(OC + I)$ If the investment by the new partner exceeds that partner's share in the firm's total capital, we record either a bonus or goodwill to the existing partners. Under the bonus method, the total bonus to the existing partners is the difference between the new partner's investment and capital share:

$$B = I - S(OC + I).$$

Under the goodwill method, we first calculate the implied total value of the firm:

$$TV = I/S.$$

The total amount of goodwill to be allocated to the existing partners is the difference between the calculated total value and the new capital:

$$G = TV - (OC + I).$$

Again, the relationship between the amount of goodwill and the amount of bonus can be seen by expanding and rearranging the above goodwill formula:

$$G = TV - (OC + I)$$

$$G = \frac{I}{S} - (OC + I)$$

$$SG = I - S(OC + I).$$

Recall that the bonus formula is:

$$B = I - S(OC + I)$$

and thus:

$$B = SG.$$

These results may be summarized as shown in Exhibit 2.3. The formulas relating bonus and goodwill may be useful in problem solving. If the bonus has already been calculated for a given situation, the goodwill can be readily determined by use of a formula, and vice versa.

Comparison of Results   In general, the bonus and goodwill methods will *not* yield the same capital balances for the individual partners nor the same to-

Exhibit 2.3   Summary of Bonus and Goodwill Formulas

	Relation of New Partner's Investment to Capital Share	
	$I < S(OC + I)$	$I > S(OC + I)$
Bonus Method	$B = S(OC + I) - I$ (Bonus to new partner)	$B = I - S(OC + I)$ (Bonus to existing partners)
Goodwill Method	$G = \dfrac{OC}{(1 - S)} - (OC + I)$ (Goodwill to new partner)	$G = \dfrac{I}{S} - (OC + I)$ (Goodwill to existing partners)
Relationship of Bonus to Goodwill	$B = (1 - S)G$	$B = SG$

tal capital for the partnership. The total capital of the partnership after admission of a new partner is as follows:

Bonus Method	Goodwill Method
Total capital before admission + amount invested by new partner	Total capital before admission + amount invested by new partner + goodwill recorded

To illustrate, compare the results obtained in the previous illustrations for Arthur Associates. The total capital before admission was $90,000. Edwards invested $9,000 and was admitted as a partner. Under the goodwill method, $1,000 of goodwill was attributed to Edwards. The capital balances after admission are:

	Bonus Method	Goodwill Method
Arthur	$30,550	$ 31,000
Bradley	25,820	26,000
Crowe	32,730	33,000
Edwards	9,900	10,000
Total	$99,000	$100,000

In our other illustration, Delano invested $12,000 and was admitted as a partner. Under the goodwill method, $18,000 of goodwill was attributed to the existing partners. The capital balances after admission are:

	Bonus Method	Goodwill Method
Arthur	$ 31,900	$ 40,000
Bradley	26,360	29,600
Crowe	33,540	38,400
Delano	10,200	12,000
Total	$102,000	$120,000

In only one case do the bonus and goodwill approaches lead to the same initial result. This happens when the amount invested equals the new partner's capital share $[I = S(OC + I)]$. In this case, the amount of bonus is zero and the amount of goodwill is zero, and the capital balances are the same, both individually and in total, under either method.

While the bonus and goodwill methods lead to the same initial result only in the limited case where goodwill and bonus are zero, they lead to the same ultimate result in a broader set of cases. Consider the situation where goodwill is initially recorded and is subsequently written off, either all at once or by the process of amortization. After write-off, the goodwill method will yield the same capital balances as the bonus method in cases where two conditions are met:

1. The new partner's initial capital percentage and income percentage are equal, and

2. The existing partners retain their relative income-sharing ratios.

Both conditions are met in our examples above. Observe that under each method, Edwards' capital percentage and income percentage are both 10 percent. The same holds for Delano in the second example. Arthur, Bradley, and Crowe retain their 5:2:3 relationship for sharing income. Originally, their percentages were 50, 20, and 30 percent, respectively; after admitting a new partner with a 10 percent share, their percentages become 45, 18, and 27 percent.

The ultimate equivalence of the two methods may be demonstrated in the Edwards example as follows:

	Goodwill Method before Write-off	Write-off of Goodwill	Goodwill Method after Write-off	Bonus Method
Arthur	$ 31,000	$ 450 (= $1,000 × 45%)	$30,550	$30,550
Bradley	26,000	180 (= $1,000 × 18%)	25,820	25,820
Crowe	33,000	270 (= $1,000 × 27%)	32,730	32,730
Edwards . . .	10,000	100 (= $1,000 × 10%)	9,900	9,900
	$100,000	$1,000	$99,000	$99,000

Similar results would be obtained in the Delano example.

Evaluation of Bonus and Goodwill Methods   In comparing the bonus and goodwill methods, we find that the rationales for the discrepancy between investment and share of net assets are similar, but that the accounting conclusions are different. An investment which is less than the computed share of net assets (case A in our preceding illustrations) is explained in terms of the intangible benefits which the new partner brings to the firm. The goodwill method records these as an asset, while the bonus method leaves them unrecorded but shows side payments by the existing partners, in the form of a capital transfer to the new partner, in order to obtain these intangible benefits for the firm. An investment which is more than the computed share of net assets (case B in our preceding illustrations) is explained in terms of understated asset values presently existing in the partnership. The goodwill method records these increases in asset values. The bonus method leaves them unrecorded, but shows side payments by the new partner, in the form of capital transfers to the existing partners, in order to obtain an interest in these assets.

Comparison with Corporate Accounting Practices   The admission of a new partner to a partnership is conceptually similar to the acquisition of one firm by another. Thus we may compare the bonus and goodwill approaches used in partnership accounting to the purchase and pooling approaches used in corporate accounting (to be discussed in detail in Chapter 6).

The bonus approach uses methods roughly comparable to pooling-of-interests accounting. The assets of the combining entities (the acquiring and acquired corporations or the existing partnership and new partner) are simply added together. No revaluation of assets occurs in a pooling; under the bonus method, assets may be revalued to market, but no goodwill is ever recognized. The equity accounts are then adjusted in such a way that the new equity relationships are reflected. Under pooling, transfers may occur among the Capital Stock, Paid-In Capital, and Retained Earnings accounts. Under the bonus method, transfers may occur among the capital accounts of the old and new partners.

The goodwill approach shares some similarities with purchase accounting. Under both methods, assets may be revalued based on the amount of the investment. The purchase-goodwill analogy is not perfect, however. In corporate acquisitions under the purchase method, goodwill is recorded only with respect to the *acquired* firm's assets (comparable to goodwill to the new partner). This recognizes that the value of the ownership interest given exceeds the value of tangible assets acquired, and so goodwill is recorded to make up the difference. In corporate accounting, goodwill is *not* recognized with respect to the assets of the *acquiring* (existing) firm, whereas in partnership accounting, goodwill may be recognized on the existing firm's assets (goodwill to the old partners). We should, however, note an important difference in circumstances. In the corporate case, the acquiring firm continues to exist, while in the partnership case, the old partnership is terminated and a new one created. Therefore, the corporate and partnership approaches share the following results:

1.   Goodwill may be recognized with respect to an addition to the firm (an acquired corporation or a new partner).

2. A new basis of accountability may be established when a new entity is created. (The new partnership is a new entity; the acquiring corporation is not.)

Why Adjust at All?   Before evaluating the two approaches to reconciling imbalances between investment and share of net assets, we should ask why any adjustment is needed. What does it matter if the capital accounts per books do not properly reflect the actual shares in net partnership assets? Granted, the capital accounts are important for capital-based income distribution and for liquidation. However, income distribution formulas and liquidation rights could be recognized by the partners even if not recorded on the books. The only arguments for recording the adjustments are convenience (to avoid maintaining two sets of books) and better disclosure (readers of financial statements will be aware of the true capital relationship among the partners). While these arguments are compelling, we should note that partnership accounting could be carried on without either the bonus or goodwill method.

Evaluation   The bonus approach is conservative in that it avoids recording intangible assets whose presence and value are difficult to verify and which are likely to have little, if any, realizable value upon liquidation. However, the going concern principle should lead us to have little concern for liquidation situations. The bonus approach follows the accounting convention that economic substance often takes precedence over legal form. Since in substance the partnership continues upon admission of a new partner, no new accountability basis for assets is provided. On the other hand, the implied side payments that are part of the bonus method are unusual accounting procedures. In short, the bonus method is consistent with several accounting conventions, but it is difficult to defend in terms of accounting theory.

The goodwill approach, on the other hand, has a better theoretical foundation. Since the admission of a new partner creates a new legal entity, a new basis of asset accountability is appropriate. The transaction which occurs (the investment by the new partner) forms the basis for the valuation of assets. As discussed above, the goodwill method for a partnership admission is roughly analogous to the purchase method for a corporate acquisition (which is usually viewed as a superior method to pooling of interests). The goodwill approach is also consistent with the general principles set forth in *APBO 29* dealing with nonmonetary transactions. While the *Opinion* does not specifically deal with partnerships, it sets forth the general principle that "accounting for nonmonetary transactions should be based on the fair values of the assets involved."[7] It would be logical to extend this principle to the investment of the existing interests of the old partners, and any noncash assets of the new partner, into the new partnership.

---

[7] APB *Opinion No. 29*, par. 18; AC § 1041.18.

**Summary of
Key Concepts**

Partnership law provides the general conditions under which partnerships operate. Many specific details are subject to the terms established by the partners in the **partnership agreement.**

Net income of a partnership does not include deductions for salaries to partners or interest to partners. Salaries, bonus, interest, and percentage formulas all may be used to **allocate net income to partners.** Full allocation is commonly used.

In the **formation of a partnership,** assets are recorded at **fair market value.** Initial capital balances may be based on amounts actually invested or on a pre-established capital ratio. In the latter case, either the **bonus** or **goodwill** approach is applied.

Admission of a new partner may occur by **purchase** or **investment.** In the case of a purchase, **transfer of capital accounts** is the usual accounting method. In the case of investment, either the **bonus** or **goodwill** approach is applied.

The bonus and goodwill approaches are based on different conceptual views of the nature of admission. The two approaches may be related by formula. The bonus method recognizes transfers of capital among partners, while the goodwill method recognizes intangible assets.

Appendix to Chapter 2

Tax Aspects
of Partnerships

A partnership is not a taxable entity, merely a conduit through which taxable income flows to individual partners. A partnership files an information return (form 1065), but pays no tax. However, certain tax aspects of partnership activity are worthy of discussion. We shall focus primarily on differences between tax and accounting figures with respect to the basis of partnership assets and the basis of partners' capital accounts.

Tax Basis of Partnership Assets

When an individual transfers assets to a partnership in exchange for an interest in that partnership, no gain or loss is recognized on the transfer for tax purposes. Thus the tax basis of the asset carries over from the individual to the partnership. Recall, however, that for accounting purposes the asset would be recorded at its fair market value. As an example, assume that a machine having a tax basis to partner A of $6,000 has a fair market value of $15,000 when it is transferred to the AB Partnership. For accounting purposes, the machine would be recorded at $15,000, and depreciation for income statement purposes would be based on this amount. The asset would retain its tax basis of $6,000, however, and for purposes of calculating taxable income, depreciation would be based on the $6,000 amount. Similarly, if the machine were subsequently sold, the accounting gain or loss would differ from the tax gain or loss.

When differences between accounting basis and tax basis exist, dual records must be kept with respect to basis, depreciation, and income. In addition, a question arises as to how the difference between accounting income and taxable income should be allocated to the partners. Assume, for simplicity of discussion, that the machine mentioned above has a useful life of three years, that A and B share income equally, and that income before depreciation on the machine is $20,000. For accounting purposes, net income (using straight-line depreciation with zero salvage value) would be:

Income before Depreciation	$20,000
Depreciation (Book)	5,000
Net Income per Books	$15,000

and $7,500 would be allocated to each partner. For tax purposes, however, the partnership would report:

Income before Depreciation	$20,000
Depreciation (Tax)	2,000
Taxable Income	$18,000

How much income should each partner report for tax purposes? One possibility is $9,000 each, reflecting an equal division. In this case, however, partner B is being taxed on A's previously unrecognized gain. (Recall that A had an economic gain of $9,000 when the machine was transferred to the partnership, but the gain was not taxed.) Thus the partners may specify that taxable income should be allocated as follows:

	A	B	Total
Accounting Income Divided Equally	$ 7,500	$7,500	$15,000
Adjustment Resulting from Lower Tax Basis of			
Machine—Allocated to Partner A	3,000	—	3,000
Taxable Income	$10,500	$7,500	$18,000

In this way, the $9,000 gain that went untaxed when A transferred the machine to the partnership would be included in A's taxable income over three years.

Tax Basis of Partnership Interest

The tax basis of each partner's interest begins with the tax basis of property contributed to the partnership, is increased by the partner's share of taxable income, and is decreased by the partner's share of losses and by amounts withdrawn from the partnership. In addition, each partner's share of partnership liabilities is considered to constitute a part of the tax basis of that partner's interest. This latter provision is very important and is clearly different from the accounting definition of partner's capital. The tax law permits partners to deduct their share of partnership losses up to the tax basis of their partnership interest. Suppose that Keller and Lehman are equal partners whose partnership interests, excluding liabilities, have tax bases of $4,000 and $2,800, respectively. Assume that the partnership has liabilities of $6,000, and that there is a net loss for the year of $15,000. While each partner's share of the loss would be $7,500, the loss claimed on their income tax returns would be limited to $7,000 for Keller (= $4,000 capital + $3,000 liabilities) and $5,800 for Lehman (= $2,800 + $3,000).

In an illustration presented earlier in the chapter, Prince and Quinn formed a partnership. Prince contributed $30,000 in cash, while Quinn contributed land and a building having a fair market value of $75,000, subject to a mortgage of $35,000 which was assumed by the partnership. Recall that we illustrated three ways of determining the partners' initial capital for accounting purposes:

Capital Accounts Based On:	Prince	Quinn
Net Assets Invested	$30,000	$40,000
Equal Interests, Bonus Method	35,000	35,000
Equal Interests, Goodwill Method	40,000	40,000

Regardless of the method used for accounting purposes, the tax basis of their partnership interests would be calculated as follows:

> Individual's basis in assets transferred
> + Share of liabilities assumed from others
> − Share of liabilities assumed by others
> = Tax basis of partnership interest

If we assume that the tax basis of the land and building is equal to the fair market value of $75,000, we get:

	Prince	Quinn
Individual's Basis in Assets Transferred . .	$30,000	$75,000
Liabilities Assumed from (by) Others . . .	17,500	(17,500)
Tax Basis of Partnership Interest	$47,500	$57,500

These figures result from the assumption that, by having the partnership assume the $35,000 mortgage, Prince in effect assumes half of Quinn's previous obligation. We may view these same figures in another manner, which may more clearly indicate the fact that the tax basis of a partnership interest includes the partner's share of partnership liabilities:

	Prince	Quinn
Basis in *Net* Assets Transferred	$30,000	$40,000
Share of Partnership Liabilities	17,500	17,500
Tax Basis of Partnership Interest	$47,500	$57,500

If we assumed that the tax basis of the land and building was different than $75,000, then the basis of Quinn's interest (but not Prince's) would be affected accordingly. Suppose Quinn's tax basis in the land and building was $52,000. The tax basis of each partner's interest would be:

	Prince	Quinn
Individual's Basis in Assets Transferred . .	$30,000	$52,000
Liabilities Assumed from (by) Others . . .	17,500	(17,500)
Tax Basis of Partnership Interest	$47,500	$34,500

As the partnership paid off the $35,000 mortgage, the tax basis of the partners' interests would be correspondingly reduced. Similarly, as the partnership incurred new liabilities, the tax bases would be increased. In effect, incurring liabilities is treated as an investment by the partners, and repaying liabilities is treated as a distribution to partners. Partnership liabilities can logically be viewed as individual partners' liabilities, since the partners are legally liable for them.

The tax basis of the partner's interest is particularly important when there is a loss. Tax law permits a partner to deduct a loss only to the extent of the tax basis (in other words, the tax basis cannot become negative). Note, however, that even if the partner's capital account for accounting purposes is negative, the partner's **tax basis** (capital account for tax purposes plus the partner's share of partnership liabilities) may be positive.

Questions

Q2.1 Define *partnership* and identify the information that a partnership agreement contains.

Q2.2 From what two sources are the organizational and operational rules for partnerships derived? Discuss the situations in which one source takes precedence over the other.

Q2.3 What major issues does the Uniform Partnership Act address?

Q2.4 Describe briefly the power of a partner to bind fellow partners in business contracts. What is meant by saying that all partners are liable jointly and severally?

Q2.5 What are the rules of partnership law with respect to:
  1. Specific property rights which a partner possesses.
  2. Sharing of profits and losses by partners.
  3. Partners' rights to compensation for services performed for the firm.

Q2.6
  1. X and Y are forming a partnership. X invests assets worth $100,000, and Y invests assets worth $120,000. Prepare the journal entry to record the formation.
  2. If X and Y agree that each is to have a 50 percent interest in partnership capital, discuss two ways to record the investments described in item 1.

Q2.7
  1. Identify the three types of events that affect capital account balances.
  2. Identify three ways of allocating partnership net income to the individual partners.

Q2.8 Select the best answers for the following multiple choice questions.
  1. Partners Cox and Kaler share profits and losses equally after each has been credited in all circumstances with annual salary allowances of $15,000 and $12,000, respectively. Under this arrangement, Cox will benefit by $3,000 more than Kaler in which of the following circumstances?
      a. Only if the partnership has earnings of $27,000 or more for the year.
      b. Only if the partnership does not incur a loss for the year.
      c. In all earnings or loss situations.
      d. Only if the partnership has earnings of at least $3,000 for the year.

  2. Partners Hutton and Elbert share profits in a 2:1 ratio, respectively. Each partner receives an annual salary allowance of $6,000. If the salaries are recorded in the accounts of the partnership as an expense rath-

er than treated as a division of net income, the total amount allocated to each partner for salaries and net income would be:

a. Less for both Hutton and Elbert.
b. Unchanged for both Hutton and Elbert.
c. More for Hutton and less for Elbert.
d. More for Elbert and less for Hutton.

3. If A is the total capital of a partnership before the admission of a new partner, B is the total capital of the partnership after the admission of a new partner, C is the amount of the new partner's investment, and D is the amount of capital credited to the new partner, then there is

a. A bonus to the new partner if $B = A + C$ and $D < C$.
b. Goodwill to the old partners if $B > (A + C)$ and $D = C$.
c. Neither bonus nor goodwill if $B = A - C$ and $D > C$.
d. Goodwill to the new partner if $B > (A + C)$ and $D < C$.

4. If E is the total capital of a partnership before the admission of a new partner, F is the total capital of the partnership after the admission of the new partner, G is the amount of the new partner's investment, and H is the amount of capital credited to the new partner, then there is

a. Goodwill to the new partner if $F > (E + G)$ and $H < G$.
b. Goodwill to the old partners if $F = E + G$ and $H > G$.
c. A bonus to the new partner if $F = E + G$ and $H > G$.
d. Neither bonus nor goodwill if $F > (E + G)$ and $H > G$.

(AICPA adapted)

Q2.9 Identify and briefly discuss two ways a new partner can enter an existing partnership.

Q2.10 Alice, Thelma, and Dee are partners with capital balances of $50,000, $30,000, and $20,000, respectively. The partners share profits and losses equally. For an investment of $50,000 cash, Mary is to be admitted as a partner with a one-fourth interest in capital and profits. Based on this information, the amount of Mary's investment can best be justified by which of the following?

1. Mary will receive a bonus from the other partners upon her admission to the partnership.
2. Assets of the partnership were overvalued immediately prior to Mary's investment.
3. The book value of the partnership's net assets was less than their fair market value immediately prior to Mary's investment.
4. Mary is apparently bringing goodwill into the partnership, and her capital account will be credited for the appropriate amount.

If Mary invested $20,000 (rather than $50,000) for a one-fourth interest in capital and profits, how could you justify the amount of her investment using (1) the bonus method and (2) the goodwill method?

Exercises **E2.1** On March 1, 19X7, Rowen and Evans formed a partnership with each contributing assets having the following fair market values:

	Rowen	Evans
Cash	$70,000	$ 70,000
Machinery and Equipment	25,000	75,000
Building	0	225,000
Furniture and Fixtures	10,000	0

The building is subject to a mortgage loan of $180,000, which is to be assumed by the partnership. The partnership agreement provides that Rowen and Evans share profits and losses 30 percent and 70 percent, respectively.

Required:
1. Compute the balances in each partner's capital account on March 1, 19X7, if the partners do not specify any capital relationship.
2. Compute the balances in each partner's capital account if the partners agree that each is to have a 50 percent interest in partnership capital, and they specify the bonus approach to recording the formation.
3. Compute the balances as for item 2 except the partners specify the goodwill approach.

(AICPA adapted)

E2.2 Ralph Greene, a partner in the Brite Partnership, has a 30 percent participation in partnership profits and losses. Greene's capital account had a net decrease of $60,000 during the calendar year 19X4. During 19X4, Greene withdrew $130,000 (charged against his capital account) and contributed property valued at $25,000 to the partnership.

Required: Compute the net income of the Brite Partnership for 19X4.

(AICPA adapted)

E2.3 On January 1, 19X7, Melvin and Lacey formed a partnership with each contributing $75,000 cash. The partnership agreement provided that Melvin would receive a guaranteed salary of $20,000 and that partnership profits and losses (computed after deducting Melvin's salary) would be shared equally for the year ended December 31, 19X7. The partnership's operations resulted in a net income of $2,000; Melvin's entire salary was paid in cash during 19X7.

Required:
1. Compute the amount of Melvin's partnership capital as of December 31, 19X7.
2. Compute the amount of Melvin's partnership capital as of December 31, 19X7, assuming there is net income of $42,000.

(AICPA adapted)

E2.4 The January 1, 19X0, balance sheet of the partnership of Linda Kingston and Jeannette Allen is shown at the top of page 61. The partnership reported revenues of $80,000 and expenses of $55,000 for 19X0. Neither partner withdrew funds from the partnership during the year. Kingston invested $8,000 in the firm on June 28, 19X0.

ASSETS		LIABILITIES AND CAPITAL	
Cash	$ 20,000	Liabilities	$ 60,000
Other Assets	180,000	Capital—Kingston . . .	56,000
		Capital—Allen	84,000
	$200,000		$200,000

Required: Compute the December 31, 19X0, capital balance for each partner under each of the following assumptions:

1. The partnership agreement does not specify how income is to be divided.
2. The partnership agreement specifies that Kingston receives 65 percent of income and Allen 35 percent.
3. The partnership agreement specifies that income is divided equally after paying each partner 10 percent interest on her average capital balance.
4. The partnership agreement specifies that Kingston and Allen receive salaries of $12,000 and $8,000, respectively, and that each partner receives 5 percent interest on her capital balance at the beginning of the year. Salary and interest allocations are to be fully implemented if they exceed total income. Any remaining income is to be divided equally.

E2.5 The capital accounts of the partnership of Nelson, Sherman, and Johnson on June 1, 19X7, are presented below, along with their respective profit-and-loss-sharing percentages:

	Capital	Income Share
Nelson	$139,200	1/2
Sherman	208,800	1/3
Johnson	96,000	1/6

On June 1, 19X7, Berrer was admitted to the partnership when he purchased, for $132,000, a proportionate interest from each partner in the net assets and profits of the partnership. As a result of this transaction, Berrer acquired a one-fifth interest in the net assets and profits of the firm. Assume that implied goodwill is *not* to be recorded.

Required:

1. Record the journal entry for the admission of Berrer as a partner.
2. Compute the amount of combined gain realized by Nelson, Sherman, and Johnson upon the sale of a portion of their interests in the partnership to Berrer.

(AICPA adapted)

E2.6 Lancer and Day are partners with capital balances of $80,000 and $40,000, respectively. The partners share profits and losses in the ratio of 6:4, respectively. The partners agree to admit Corey, upon his investment of $30,000, as a partner with a one-third interest in capital and profits and losses.

Required: Compute the balances in the capital accounts of Lancer, Day, and Corey after Corey's admission, assuming that the parties agree that the admission is to be recorded without recognizing goodwill.

(AICPA adapted)

E2.7   The following balance sheet is for the Amos, Grant, Derrick partnership. The partners share profits and losses in the ratio of $5:3:2$, respectively.

Cash							$ 30,000	Liabilities						$ 70,000
Other Assets							270,000	Amos—Capital						140,000
								Grant—Capital						80,000
								Derrick—Capital						10,000
							$300,000							$300,000

The partnership wishes to admit Martin as a new partner with a one-fifth interest. Compute the amount of cash or other assets Martin should contribute if the partners agree that the admission is to be recorded without recognizing goodwill or bonus.

(AICPA adapted)

E2.8   Felix and Hubert are partners who share profits and losses equally in a highly successful partnership. The capital accounts of Felix and Hubert are currently $90,000 and $60,000, respectively. Taylor wishes to join the firm and offers to invest $70,000 for a one-fourth interest in the capital and profits and losses of the firm.

Required: Compute the balances in the capital accounts of Felix, Hubert, and Taylor after Taylor's admission assuming:
   1. The parties agree that the admission is to be recorded by recognizing goodwill.
   2. The parties agree that the admission is to be recorded without recognition of goodwill.

(AICPA adapted)

E2.9   Graham and Hyde are partners who share income in a $3:1$ ratio. Their respective capital balances are $50,000 and $30,000. Ingalls proposes to invest $40,000 in the firm in exchange for a 20 percent interest.

Required:
   1. How would Ingalls' admission be recorded using the goodwill method?
   2. How would Ingalls' admission be recorded using the bonus method?
   3. Suppose instead that Ingalls purchased 20 percent of Graham's interest for $30,000 and 20 percent of Hyde's interest for $10,000 (paying these amounts directly to the individuals). How would this transaction be recorded by the partnership, assuming use of the implied goodwill approach?

E2.10   Each of the following independent situations shows either a bonus or goodwill recognized upon admission of a new partner to an existing partnership. In each case, calculate the amount of bonus or goodwill that would have been recognized if the alternative accounting treatment had been followed. That is, if the bonus method was used, calculate the goodwill to be recognized under the goodwill method and vice versa.
   1. D and E admit F as an equal partner. A bonus to F of $3,000 is recorded.
   2. O, P, and Q admit R as a new partner. R is to have a one-third interest in the new partnership. Goodwill of $6,000 is attributed to R.

3. H purchases a one-fifth interest in the partnership of I, J, and K. Goodwill to the existing partners ($6,000) is recorded.
4. L and M admit N as an equal partner for $10,000. No goodwill is recognized under the goodwill method.

E2.11 **(Appendix)** Burriss, Culpepper, and Downstreet formed a partnership with each individual contributing assets as shown here:

	Cost	Fair Value
Burriss: Cash	$15,000	$15,000
Culpepper: Equipment	13,000	15,000
Accumulated Depreciation	(3,000)	
Downstreet: Land	30,000	30,000

The equipment had an original life of thirteen years, no salvage value, and has been depreciated on a straight-line basis for three years. The land has an outstanding mortgage of $15,000, which the partnership assumes.

The partners agreed to share profits and losses equally. Profit for the first year was $6,000 before depreciation.

Required:

1. Compute the tax basis of each partner's interest in the partnership at the date of formation.
2. Compute the taxable income of each partner, assuming Culpepper is to bear any tax related to the equipment appreciation.

Problems **P2.1** **Partnerships versus Corporations—Discussion Case** Twenty years ago a new partnership purchased land in Midville, erected a building, and opened a furniture and appliance merchandising store under the name of Furniture Fair. The partnership agreement specified that profits or losses would be shared equally after the allocation of partners' salary allowances and interest on average capital balances.

Midville has grown considerably, and the store is now the most prominent in a fashionable suburban area. Good management, imaginative merchandising, and the general increase in the economy have made Furniture Fair the leading and most profitable firm of its type in Midville's trade area.

Now the partners wish to admit an investor and incorporate the business, and they have obtained a charter for Furniture Fair, Inc. Each partner will purchase at par an amount of preferred stock equal to the book value of the partner's interest in the partnership and common stock equal to that portion of the fair market value which exceeds the book value. The investor will purchase at a 10 percent premium over par value common and preferred stock equal to one-third the number of shares of each purchased by the partners. The corporation will then purchase the Furniture Fair partnership at its fair market value from the partners. After the consummation of the partners' plan, the corporation will own the partnership's assets, assume its liabilities, and employ the partners as the management of the corporation.

Required:
1. List and explain the differences in items and valuations that you would expect to find between the assets to appear on the balance sheet of the proposed corporation and the assets which appear on the partnership's balance sheet.
2. List and explain the differences that would be expected in a comparison of an income statement prepared for the proposed corporation and an income statement prepared for the partnership.

(AICPA adapted)

P2.2 **Formation of Partnership** The partnership of Frank and Keller was formed on February 28, 19X3. At that date, Frank invested $25,000 cash and furniture and equipment valued at $15,000. Keller invested $35,000 cash, merchandise valued at $55,000, and a building valued at $100,000, subject to a mortgage of $30,000 (which the partnership assumes). The partnership agreement provides that Frank and Keller share profits or losses 25 percent and 75 percent, respectively.

Required:
1. Compute the amount of each partner's capital account at February 28, assuming that each partner is credited for the full amount of net assets invested.
2. Compute the amount of Frank's capital account at February 28, assuming that the partnership agreement provides that Frank and Keller should have, initially, an equal interest in partnership capital, using the bonus method.
3. Given the facts stated in requirement 2, compute the amount of Keller's capital account at February 28, using the goodwill method.

(AICPA adapted)

P2.3 **Formation of Partnership** Augustus Berrini, the sole proprietor of Berrini Company, is planning to expand the company and establish a partnership with Fiedler and Wade. The partners plan to share profits and losses as follows: Berrini, 50 percent; Fiedler, 25 percent; Wade, 25 percent. They also agree that the beginning capital balances of the partnership will reflect this same relationship.

Berrini asked Fiedler to join the partnership because his many business contacts are expected to be valuable during the expansion. Fiedler is also contributing $28,000. Wade is contributing $11,000 and a block of marketable securities which the partnership expects to liquidate as needed during the expansion. The securities, which cost Wade $42,000, are currently worth $57,500.

Berrini's investment to the partnership is Berrini Company. He plans to pay off the notes with his personal assets. The other partners have agreed that the partnership will assume the accounts payable and the mortgage. The balance sheet for Berrini Company follows. The three partners agree that the inventory is worth $85,000, the equipment is worth half its original cost, the building and land are worth $65,000 and $25,000, respectively, and the allowance established for doubtful accounts is correct.

Berrini Company
Balance Sheet
Date of Partnership Formation

ASSETS		LIABILITIES	
Cash	$ 7,000	Accounts Payable	$ 53,000
Accounts Receivable (Net) . .	48,000	Notes Payable	7,000
Inventory	72,000	Mortgage Payable	55,000
Equipment (Net of $12,000			$115,000
Accumulated Depreciation) .	18,000		
Building (Net of $20,000		OWNER'S EQUITY	
Accumulated Depreciation) .	40,000	Capital, Berrini	85,000
Land	15,000		
		Total Liabilities and	
Total Assets	$200,000	Owner's Equity . .	$200,000

Required: Prepare the balance sheet of the partnership on the date of formation under each of the following independent assumptions:
1. The partners agree to follow the bonus method to record the formation.
2. The partners agree to follow the goodwill approach to record the formation.

P2.4 Partnership Income Allocation   Grandis and Hayley formed a partnership on January 2, 19X4, and agreed to share profits 90 percent and 10 percent, respectively. Grandis contributed capital of $25,000. Hayley contributed no capital but has a specialized expertise and manages the firm full time. There were no withdrawals during the year, except for Hayley's salary. The partnership agreement provides for the following:
1. Capital accounts are to be credited annually with interest at 5 percent of beginning capital.
2. Hayley is to be paid a salary of $1,000 a month.
3. Hayley is to receive a bonus of 20 percent of income calculated before deducting his salary and interest on both capital accounts.

Income to be allocated on December 31, 19X4, after deduction of partners' interest and Hayley's salary and bonus, was $46,750.

Required:
1. Assume that the partners had initial capital interests equal to their income-sharing ratios and that no goodwill was recognized on the formation of the partnership. Determine the original capital for each partner.
2. Compute Hayley's 19X4 bonus.
3. Calculate the balances in the capital accounts at year-end.

P2.5 Partnership Income Allocation   A 19X5 balance sheet for the Silverstone Partnership appears at the top of page 66:

Silverstone Partnership
Balance Sheet
December 31, 19X5

ASSETS		LIABILITIES AND CAPITAL	
Cash	$ 10,000	Accounts Payable . . .	$ 60,000
Accounts Receivable . .	50,000	Long-Term Liabilities . .	100,000
Equipment	85,000	Capital—Lamke	55,000
Buildings	125,000	Capital—Perez	80,000
Land	30,000	Capital—Sills	5,000
		Total Liabilities and	
Total Assets	$300,000	Capital	$300,000

Additional information:
1. The partners have agreed that each will be paid 5 percent interest on the capital balance as of the beginning of the year.
2. Salaries are as follows: Lamke, $15,000; Perez, $20,000; and Sills, $10,000.
3. Sills is to receive a bonus of 10 percent of income before salaries, bonus, and interest to partners.
4. Any income remaining after salaries, bonus, and interest to partners is to be allocated equally.
5. During 19X5, Lamke withdrew $3,300 from the firm. All other allocations to Lamke for salary, interest, and profit were retained in the business.
6. Perez kept in the firm $10,000 of all 19X5 allocations.
7. In 19X5 Sills withdrew $15,000 and all salary, bonus, interest, and profit allocations.
8. Total capital investment at the beginning of the year was $120,000.
9. Income for 19X5 after deducting interest to partners but before deductions for salaries and bonus was $90,000.

Required: Prepare a schedule showing all allocations to and withdrawals by the partners in Silverstone Partnership. The schedule should begin with capital balances as of January 1, 19X5.

P2.6 **Admission by Direct Purchase** Williams wishes to purchase a one-fourth capital and profit and loss interest in the partnership of Cob, Howards, and Lee. The three partners agree to sell Williams one-fourth of their respective capital and profit and loss interests in exchange for a total payment of $40,000. The capital account and the respective percentage interests in profit and losses immediately before the sale to Williams follow:

	Capital Accounts	Percentage Interests in Profits and Losses
Cob	$80,000	60%
Howards	40,000	30
Lee	20,000	10

All other assets and liabilities are fairly valued.

Required:

1. Compute the amount of the capital balances of Cob, Howards, Lee, and Williams immediately after Williams' acquisition, assuming *no* recognition of implied goodwill.
2. Compute the amount of the capital balances of Cob, Howard, Lee, and Williams immediately after Williams' acquisition, assuming there *is* recognition of implied goodwill.

(AICPA adapted)

P2.7 **Admission—Goodwill Approach**   Wright and Koehler formed a partnership on January 1, 19X6. They have agreed to admit Robertson as a partner on January 1, 19X9. The books for the year ending December 31, 19X8, are closed. The following additional information is available:

1. Wright and Koehler shared profits equally until January 1, 19X8, when they agreed to share profits 40 percent and 60 percent, respectively. The profit-sharing ratio after Robertson is admitted will be 32 percent to Wright, 48 percent to Koehler, and 20 percent to Robertson.
2. Robertson will invest $25,000 cash for a one-fifth interest in the capital of the partnership.
3. The partnership reported earnings of $22,000 in 19X6, $35,000 in 19X7, and $32,000 in 19X8.
4. The partnership of Wright and Koehler did not use accrual accounting for some items. It was agreed that before Robertson's admission is recorded, adjustments should be made in the accounts retroactively to report properly on the accrual method of accounting.
5. Use of a modified cash basis of accounting led to net overstatements of income of $7,000 in 19X6 and $6,000 in 19X7 and a net understatement of income of $1,000 in 1978.

Required:

1. Prepare a schedule presenting computation of the adjustments necessary to report Wright's and Koehler's correct capital account balances at December 31, 19X6, 19X7, and 19X8.
2. Assume the capital balances as originally reported on December 31, 19X8, were Wright, $66,100 and Koehler, $81,900. Adjust these capital balances to reflect accrual accounting and determine (1) Robertson's capital balance if admission is recorded under the goodwill approach and (2) the amount of goodwill to be recognized.

(AICPA adapted)

P2.8 **Admission—Various Cases**   Given at the top of page 68 are account balances for the partnership of Simpson and Scott before the admission of a new partner, Lansing. Each case presents account balances of the partnership immediately after the admission of Lansing. The cases are independent of each other.

Balance Sheet Accounts	Balances before Lansing's Admission	Case 1	Case 2	Case 3	Case 4	Case 5
Cash	$ 10,000	$ 10,000	$10,000	$20,000	$ 10,000	$30,000
Other Assets . .	80,000	130,000	80,000	80,000	170,000	80,000
Goodwill . . .	10,000	10,000	10,000	10,000	30,000	20,000
Liabilities . . .	(30,000)	(30,000)	(30,000)	(30,000)	(80,000)	(30,000)
Capital—Simpson .	(35,000)	(42,500)	(35,000)	(30,000)	(35,000)	(40,000)
Capital—Scott . .	(35,000)	(42,500)	—	(30,000)	(35,000)	(40,000)
Capital—Lansing .	—	(35,000)	(35,000)	(20,000)	(60,000)	(20,000)

Required: For each independent case, answer the following questions. Show supporting computations.

1. What method of accounting was used to record the admission (bonus, goodwill, neither)?
2. How much did Lansing invest in the partnership?
3. What percentage of ownership does Lansing have in the new partnership?

P2.9 **Cash to Accrual Basis—Admission of Partner** The partnership of Kraft, Mills, and Farmer engaged you to adjust its accounting records and convert them uniformly to the accrual basis in anticipation of admitting Ward as a new partner. Some accounts are on the accrual basis and others are on the cash basis. The partnership's books were closed at December 31, 19X6, by the bookkeeper, who prepared the general ledger trial balance that appears below.

Kraft, Mills, and Farmer
General Ledger Trial Balance
December 31, 19X6

	Debit	Credit
Cash	$ 10,000	
Accounts Receivable	40,000	
Inventory	26,000	
Land	9,000	
Buildings	50,000	
Allowance for Depreciation of Buildings		$ 2,000
Equipment	56,000	
Allowance for Depreciation of Equipment		6,000
Goodwill	5,000	
Accounts Payable		55,000
Allowance for Future Inventory Losses		3,000
Kraft—Capital		40,000
Mills—Capital		60,000
Farmer—Capital		30,000
Totals	$196,000	$196,000

Your inquiries disclosed the following:
1. The partnership was organized on January 1, 19X5, with no provision in the partnership agreement for the distribution of partnership profits and

losses. During 19X5, profits were distributed equally among the partners. The partnership agreement was amended effective January 1, 19X6, to provide for the following profit-and-loss-sharing ratio: Kraft, 50 percent; Mills, 30 percent; and Farmer, 20 percent. The amended partnership agreement also stated that the accounting records were to be maintained on the accrual basis and that any adjustments necessary for 19X5 should be allocated according to the 19X5 distribution of profits.

2. The following amounts were not recorded as prepayments or accruals:

| | December 31, | |
	19X6	19X5
Prepaid Insurance	$700	$ 650
Advances from Customers	200	1,100
Accrued Interest Expense		450

The advances from customers were recorded as sales in the year the cash was received.

3. In 19X6, the partnership recorded a provision of $3,000 for anticipated declines in inventory prices. You convinced the partners that the provision was unnecessary and the provision and related allowance should be removed from the books.

4. The partnership charged equipment purchased for $4,400 on January 3, 19X6, to expense. This equipment has an estimated life of ten years and an estimated salvage value of $400. The partnership depreciates its capitalized equipment under the double-declining-balance method.

5. The partners agreed to establish an allowance for doubtful accounts at 2 percent of current accounts receivable and 5 percent of past due accounts. At December 31, 19X5, the partnership had $54,000 of accounts receivable, of which only $4,000 was past due. At December 31, 19X6, 15 percent of accounts receivable was past due, of which $4,000 represented sales made in 19X5, and was generally considered collectible. The partnership had written off uncollectible accounts in the year the accounts became worthless as follows:

| | Accounts Written Off | |
	19X6	19X5
19X6 Accounts	$ 800	—
19X5 Accounts	1,000	$250

6. Goodwill was recorded on the books in 19X6 and credited to the partners' capital accounts in the profit-and-loss-sharing ratio in recognition of an increase in the value of the business resulting from improved sales volume. No amortization of goodwill was recorded. The partners agreed to write off the goodwill before admitting the new partner.

Required:

1. Prepare the journal entries to convert the accounting records to the accrual basis and to correct the books before admitting the new partner.

2. Without prejudice to your solution to item 1 above, assume the assets were properly valued and that the adjusted total of the partners' capital account balances at December 31, 19X6, was $140,000. On that date, Ward invested $55,000 in the partnership. Record the admission of Ward using the goodwill method. Ward is to be granted a one-fourth interest in the partnership. The other partners will retain their 50:30:20 income-sharing ratio for the remaining three-fourths interest.

(AICPA adapted)

P2.10 Partnership Accounting—Comprehensive You have been engaged to prepare financial statements for the partnership of Allison, Reed, and Werner as of June 30, 19X2. You have obtained the following information from the partnership agreement as amended and from the accounting records.

1. The partnership was formed originally by Allison and Bailey on July 1, 19X1. At that date:
   a. Bailey contributed $400,000 cash.
   b. Allison contributed land, building, and equipment with fair market value of $110,000, $520,000, and $185,000, respectively. The land and building were subject to a mortgage securing an 8 percent per annum note (interest rate of similar notes at July 1, 19X1, was 8 percent). Quarterly payments of $5,000 plus interest are due on the note on January 1, April 1, July 1, and October 1 of each year. Allison made the July 1, 19X1, principal and interest payment personally. The partnership then assumed the obligation for the remaining $300,000 balance.
   c. The agreement further provided that Allison had contributed a certain intangible benefit to the partnership due to his many years of business activity in the area to be serviced by the new partnership. The assigned value of this intangible asset plus the net tangible assets he contributed gave Allison a 60 percent initial capital interest in the partnership. The intangible asset is amortized over ten years.
   d. Allison was designated the only active partner at an annual salary of $24,000 plus an annual bonus of 4 percent of net income after deducting his salary but before deducting interest on partners' capital investments.
   e. Each partner is to receive a 6 percent return on his average capital investment. The average is based on the capital balances at the beginning of each month.
   f. All remaining profits or losses are to be shared equally.
2. On October 1, 19X1, Bailey sold his partnership interest and rights as of July 1, 19X1, to Werner for $370,000. Allison agreed to accept Werner as a partner if he would contribute sufficient cash to meet the October 1, 19X1, principal and interest payment on the mortgage note. Werner made the payment from personal funds.
3. On January 1, 19X2, Allison and Werner admitted a new partner, Reed. Reed invested $150,000 cash and received a 10 percent capital interest based on the July 1, 19X1, original investments of Allison and Bailey. The January 1, 19X2, capital balances of Allison and Werner were ignored for this calculation. At January 1, 19X2, the book value of

the partnership's assets and liabilities approximated their fair market values. Reed contributed no intangible benefit to the partnership.

Similar to the other partners, Reed is to receive a 6 percent return on his average capital investment. His investment also entitles him to 20 percent of the partnership's profits or losses as defined above. However, for the year ended June 30, 19X2, Reed would receive one-half of his pro rata share of the profits or losses.

4. The accounting records show that on February 1, 19X2, Miscellaneous Expenses had been charged $3,600 in payment of hospital expenses incurred by Allison's eight-year-old daughter.

5. Allison's salary was paid in one lump sum on June 29, 19X2, and charged to his drawing account. On June 1, 19X2, Werner made a $33,000 withdrawal. These are the only transactions recorded in the partners' drawing accounts.

6. Presented below is a trial balance summarizing the partnership's general ledger balances at June 30, 19X2. The general ledger has not been closed.

	Dr.	Cr.
Current Assets	$ 307,100	
Fixed Assets, Net	1,285,800	
Current Liabilities		$157,000
8% Mortgage Note Payable		290,000
Allison, Capital		515,000
Reed, Capital		150,000
Werner, Capital		400,000
Allison, Drawing	24,000	
Reed, Drawing	0	
Werner, Drawing	33,000	
Sales		872,600
Cost of Sales	695,000	
Administrative Expenses	16,900	
Miscellaneous Expenses	11,100	
Interest Expense	11,700	

Required: Compute the ending balance of the partners' capital accounts. Show supporting calculations.

(AICPA adapted)

P2.11 **Partners' Tax Basis and Taxable Income** (Appendix) Refer to the data in P2.3 concerning the formation of a partnership by Berrini, Fiedler, and Wade.

The equipment had an original life of five years with no salvage value. The building had an original life of thirty years, also with no salvage value. The straight-line method of depreciation is used.

Accounting net income for the first year of operations is $30,000. All of the inventory transferred from the Berrini Company was charged to cost of goods sold under the FIFO method. The marketable securities contributed by Wade were sold during the year for $65,000 (the $7,500 accounting gain is included in the net income figure cited above).

The partners have agreed that accounting income will be divided according to the 50:25:25 percentage ratio. As the partnership realizes the gains or losses which were unrecognized at the time of the original transfer of assets, these will be included in the taxable income of the partner(s) who invested the assets.

Required:

1. Compute the tax basis of each partner's interest in the partnership at the date of formation.
2. Compute the taxable income to be reported by each partner.

Chapter 3

Partnerships: Contraction, Termination, and Liquidation

A partnership terminates legally whenever the composition of the partnership changes, as in the admission of a new partner or the retirement or death of an existing partner. Accounting, however, is concerned with the economic entity rather than the legal entity. This chapter addresses one legal situation—legal dissolution of a partnership—with two economic interpretations. The partnership may continue as an economic entity or may cease to exist.

When a partnership terminates legally but the business activities are maintained by a successor partnership, the economic entity is intact. This can occur when a partner leaves the business due to retirement, resignation, or death.

On the other hand, if the assets of a partnership are liquidated and distributed, the partnership ceases to exist as an economic entity. There are several possible reasons for this type of termination. Bankruptcy of the partnership will lead to termination. Or the partners may have initially specified that the partnership would exist for only a limited time or until a certain purpose was accomplished. For example, a partnership may be created to buy a tract of land and develop and sell subdivision lots. When all lots are sold and paid for, the partnership may be dissolved. In other cases, partners may mutually agree to terminate a partnership because it is unsuccessful or because they wish to pursue other activities.

Retirement of a Partner

Ownership composition of a partnership changes when a partner withdraws. Accounting for such changes varies, depending on whether the interest of the withdrawing partner is purchased by one or more remaining partners with their personal assets or by the partnership with partnership assets. Because the accounting treatment is similar regardless of the reason for withdrawal (resignation, retirement, or death), we discuss only the case of retirement.

Purchase with Individual Assets

We first consider the situation where the remaining partners, as individuals, purchase the interest of the retiring partner. Since the transaction—between the retiring partner and remaining partner(s)—occurs outside the partnership, the only entry necessary on the partnership books is a transfer of capital balances. Assume, for example, that KLM Associates shows the following information:

Partner	Capital Balance	Income Share
Keenan	$ 75,000	45%
Ludlow	60,000	30
Morris	30,000	25
Total	$165,000	100%

If Keenan and Ludlow buy Morris' interest for $60,000, Morris' $30,000 capital account must be transferred to Keenan and Ludlow. If the purchasers retain their relative shares (45:30, or 3:2), $18,000 would be credited to Keenan and $12,000 to Ludlow. The transfer of capital would be recorded as:

Capital—Morris	30,000	
Capital—Keenan		18,000
Capital—Ludlow		12,000
To record Morris' retirement.		

This treatment is similar to procedures discussed in Chapter 2 for admission of a new partner by purchase of an existing interest. In that case, however, the purchase transaction with an outside party could lead to recognition of implied goodwill on the partnership books. In this retirement case, no outside party is involved. Without the presence of an arm's-length transaction, the argument that market value has been determined and goodwill can be recognized is weak.

Purchase with Partnership Assets

The second possibility is that the retiring partner will receive assets directly from the partnership in settlement of that individual's capital interest. In effect, the partnership will buy out the retiring partner. The remainder of this section explains procedures for dealing with this situation.

Determination of Payment to Retiring Partner   The settlement with a retiring partner should be based on the *fair value* of the partner's interest. There is no reason to expect that this value is equal to the balance in the partner's capital account at time of retirement. Some equitable manner of determining the value of the retiring partner's interest, and hence the payment to the retiring partner, is needed. In general, we would expect the partnership agreement to answer the question. When forming the partnership, the partners should have considered and agreed upon a method of valuing a partner's interest in the event of resignation, retirement, or death. They might have agreed on a formula (such as "five times the partner's average share of income over the preceding three years, plus the balance in the capital account"). Or they might have agreed to base the value on an outside appraisal of the partnership's assets, both tangible and intangible. Whatever the partnership agreement specifies will be used to determine the value of the retiring partner's interest. If no provision was made in the agreement, the parties will have to agree on valuation procedures at the time of retirement.

Accounting for Retirement As stated above, payment of partnership assets to a retiring partner is not necessarily based on the balance in the retiring partner's capital account. Upon retirement, however, the capital account must be eliminated from the books, and any differences between the payment and the capital balance must be considered.

In the illustrations that follow, we assume that the retiring partner is paid with partnership cash. If part or all of the payment is made with other partnership assets, then the assets should be adjusted on the books to fair market value before their distribution to the retiring partner is recorded. Any difference between fair market value and book value should be entered in the partners' capital accounts according to their income-sharing ratio.

Accounting for the retirement of a partner via distribution of partnership assets is similar to accounting for the admission of a new partner via investment. In the simplest case, where payment to the retiring partner *does* equal that partner's capital balance, the retirement is recorded as follows:

Capital—Retiring Partner	XX	
Cash (or other assets)		XX

If, however, the payment does *not* equal the capital balance, we must account for the difference by either the bonus or goodwill method. To discuss these, we return to the data for KLM Associates:

Partner	Capital Balance	Income Share
Keenan	$ 75,000	45%
Ludlow	60,000	30
Morris	30,000	25
Total	$165,000	100%

Bonus Method To illustrate the **bonus method of recording a partner's retirement,** assume the partners determine that Morris, the retiring partner, will receive $55,000. Under the bonus method, the $25,000 difference between the payment ($55,000) and the balance in Morris' capital account ($30,000) is treated as a bonus from Keenan and Ludlow to Morris.

Capital—Keenan	15,000	
Capital—Ludlow	10,000	
Capital—Morris	30,000	
Cash		55,000

To record Morris' retirement under the bonus method.

Note that the bonus is divided between Keenan and Ludlow in relation to their respective income shares (45:30, or 3:2).

If, instead, Morris is to receive less than the $30,000 capital balance, the difference is treated as a bonus from Morris to Keenan and Ludlow. For example, if Morris receives $22,000, we record:

Capital—Morris	30,000	
Capital—Keenan		4,800
Capital—Ludlow		3,200
Cash		22,000

To record Morris' retirement under the bonus method.

Again, the bonus is divided between the remaining partners according to their income-sharing relationship.

Goodwill Method   The assumption underlying the bonus method of recording a partner's retirement is that a bonus is being paid either by or to the retiring partner. The bonus accounts for the difference between the settlement price and the retiring partner's capital balance. In contrast, the general logic of the **goodwill method of recording a partner's retirement** is that such differences, in either positive or negative directions, signify that asset revaluations are appropriate. Existing assets may be written up, intangible assets (goodwill) recorded, or both. Or, if revaluations downward are indicated, assets may be written down. In some circumstances, therefore, retirement can be recorded under the goodwill method without making an entry to an account entitled Goodwill.

Two interpretations of the goodwill method exist: the partial goodwill approach and the total goodwill approach. Either can be applied to asset revaluations upward or downward.

Under the **partial goodwill approach,** the revaluations of asset book values that are triggered by a partner's retirement are limited to the difference between the settlement price and the retiring partner's capital account. If the payment is greater than the capital balance, then undervaluations of existing assets should be corrected, with any remaining difference being attributed to goodwill. If the payment is less than the capital balance, then asset values are reduced only to the extent of the difference—even though evidence indicates that additional asset overvaluations exist. These asset revaluations are charged or credited only to the capital account of the retiring partner; the capital accounts of other partners are unaffected.

The **total goodwill approach** specifies that *all* asset revaluations apparent at the time of retirement should be recorded. These revaluations are charged or credited to the capital accounts of all partners according to their income-sharing ratio.

An illustration may help clarify the differences between these two approaches. Returning to the example of Morris' retirement from KLM Associates, assume that Morris receives $55,000, that the capital account balance is $30,000, and that the partners determine that existing assets are appropriately valued. The partial goodwill approach calls for recognition of $25,000 of goodwill—the difference between the settlement price and the capital balance. The total goodwill approach follows the logic that if $25,000 of goodwill is attributable to Morris' 25 percent interest, then total goodwill of the firm is $100,000 (= $25,000/.25), and this entire amount should be recognized.

The total goodwill approach yields total partnership capital, before Morris' retirement, of $265,000 (the original $165,000 plus $100,000 goodwill). Note that, in general, this result cannot be obtained by capitalizing the total payment

Exhibit 3.1   Comparison of the Partial and Total Goodwill Approaches: KLM Associates

Assumption	Partial Goodwill Approach			Total Goodwill Approach		

Morris' capital balance = $30,000
Payment upon retirement = $55,000
Excess payment is attributable to
    goodwill.
	Goodwill
	    Capital—Morris
	Capital—Morris
	    Cash
		25,000
		
		55,000
			25,000
			
			55,000
				Goodwill
				    Capital—Keenan
				    Capital—Ludlow
				    Capital—Morris
				Capital—Morris
				    Cash
					100,000
					
					55,000
						45,000
						30,000
						25,000
						
						55,000

Morris' capital balance = $30,000
Payment upon retirement = $55,000
Excess payment is attributable to
    undervalued existing assets
    ($15,000) and to goodwill
	Assets
	    Capital—Morris
	
	Goodwill
	    Capital—Morris
	
	Capital—Morris
	    Cash
		15,000
		
		10,000
		
		55,000
			15,000
			
			10,000
			
			55,000
				Assets
				    Capital—Keenan
				    Capital—Ludlow
				    Capital—Morris
				Goodwill
				    Capital—Keenan
				    Capital—Ludlow
				    Capital—Morris
				
				Capital—Morris
				    Cash
					15,000
					
					85,000
					
					55,000
						
						6,750
						4,500
						3,750
						
						38,250
						25,500
						21,250
						
						55,000

Morris' capital balance = $30,000
Payment upon retirement = $22,000
Difference is attributable to
    overvalued assets.
	Capital—Morris
	    Assets
	
	Capital—Morris
	    Cash
		8,000
		
		22,000
			8,000
			
			22,000
				Capital—Keenan
				Capital—Ludlow
				Capital—Morris
				    Assets
				Capital—Morris
				    Cash
					14,400
					9,600
					8,000
					
					22,000
						
						32,000
						
						22,000

to Morris ($55,000/.25, or $220,000). This latter procedure yields correct results only in the case where the dollar balances in the partners' capital accounts are exactly proportional to their percentage interests.[1] Thus, in general, total goodwill is determined from the goodwill attributable to the retiring partner rather than from the payment made to the retiring partner.

Exhibit 3.1 illustrates application of the two approaches of the goodwill method under three independent assumptions regarding Morris' retirement from KLM Associates. The usual arguments exist with respect to the choice between the two approaches. Proponents of the partial goodwill approach argue that the partnership should record goodwill only to the extent that it is purchased or paid for. Total goodwill advocates argue that the transaction provides evidence of the total value of the partnership, and that the accounts of the new entity (the successor partnership) should be based on fair market value. In essence, the argu-

---

[1] To see this, suppose that A, B, and C have capital balances of $50,000, $30,000, and $20,000, respectively, and share income in the ratio 5:3:2. C is retiring and will receive a $30,000 payment from the partnership. Partial goodwill is $10,000 (= $30,000 − $20,000), and total goodwill is $50,000 (= 5 × $10,000), giving total capital of $150,000. Capitalizing the $30,000 payment to C also gives total capital of $150,000 (= $30,000/.2).

ment comes down to an entity question. If we view the successor partnership as a continuation of the old entity, then partial goodwill is reasonable. If we view the successor partnership as a new entity, then total goodwill should be used. Following the concept of economic entity advocated in this text, we believe the partial goodwill approach is superior.

Termination and Liquidation of the Partnership

Previous discussion addressed situations in which a partnership continued as an economic entity despite legal dissolution through retirement of a partner. Now we turn to cases where a partnership terminates economically as well as legally. The business ceases operation and liquidates its assets.

Priorities for Payments

One issue central to the study of liquidations is the sequence in which the proceeds of liquidation are distributed. Outside creditors have claims against partnership assets. Partners have claims on partnership assets resulting from loans of personal assets to the partnership, investments in the partnership, and the right to share in undistributed income of the partnership. In theory, proceeds of liquidation are distributed in the following order:

1. Outside creditors.
2. Partners' loans.
3. Partners' invested capital.
4. Partners' undistributed income.

Actually, the first priority of distribution (to outside creditors) is subdivided among fully-secured, partially-secured, and unsecured creditors. Such distinctions are discussed in the section on bankruptcy accounting in Chapter 4. For purposes of illustrating partnership liquidation, we treat all outside creditors as a single category.

As a practical matter, there is little difference between partners' invested capital and undistributed income, which is closed annually to the capital accounts. Drawings by partners are typically not differentiated as to withdrawals of capital or income. Similarly, there is little practical difference between partners' loans or partners' invested capital. Liquidation often involves a loss on sale of assets, and the balance of a partner's capital account could become negative when the loss is allocated. One of the provisions of partnership law requires partners to contribute sufficient capital to cover a **capital deficiency** (debit balance in the capital account). If a partner with a capital deficiency has made loans from personal assets to the partnership, then the **right of offset** allows the loan balance to be applied to the deficiency. For example, if Partner A has a capital deficiency of $8,000 (that is, the individual owes the partnership $8,000) and has a loan account of $10,000 (that is, the partnership owes the individual $10,000), then the net effect is that Partner A is entitled to receive $2,000 of the liquidation proceeds. Examining the distribution priorities in this manner yields an effective two-step sequence for distribution of liquidation proceeds:

1. Outside creditors.
2. Partners' combined loans and capital.

As we consider partnership liquidations, therefore, our first concern is to meet obligations to outside creditors. Next we focus on determining the proper distribution to partners of any remaining proceeds from liquidation.

Rights of Creditors

Both the creditors of the partnership and the creditors of the individual partners have legal rights regarding partnership liquidation. These rights influence the accounting procedures.

Creditors of the partnership must first seek payment of their claims from partnership assets. If the partnership is insolvent, the partnership creditors may then seek payment from *any* partner. Thus, a partner can be individually liable for any and all claims against the partnership. If an individual partner pays partnership creditors, this payment is recorded as an investment of capital in the partnership.

Creditors of an individual partner must first seek payment of their claims from the individual. If the individual is insolvent, the creditors then have a claim against partnership assets remaining after satisfaction of partnership creditors. This claim is limited to the amount of that partner's equity in the partnership.

The above provisions may be restated from an asset viewpoint. In this form, they are often referred to as the **marshalling of assets rule.**

Assets of the partnership are applied in the following order:
1. Partnership creditors.
2. Creditors of individual partners, but only to the extent of that partner's capital balance.

Assets of the individual partner are applied in the following order:
1. The partner's creditors.
2. Partnership creditors.
3. Other partners (to remedy a capital deficiency).

These priorities agree with the provisions of the Uniform Partnership Act. Under common law and federal bankruptcy law, however, other partners have the same standing as the partner's creditors. In this case, liquidated assets of the individual partner would be applied in the following order:

1. The partner's creditors, including other partners.
2. Partnership creditors.

This sequence is likely to apply in states which have not adopted the Uniform Partnership Act.

Simple versus Installment Liquidations

Liquidation of a partnership may be carried out in several ways. All assets might be sold in a single transaction at a going-business price to a competitor or to others wishing to continue the business. All assets might be sold in a single transaction at distress prices (for example, at a bankruptcy auction). Some assets might be sold individually over a period of time as buyers for specific items are found, while other assets such as receivables and prepayments were liquidated by means other than sale. In this last case, the partners may request distribution of the cash as it becomes available.

The timing of cash distributions to partners influences the accounting procedures. In a **simple liquidation,** all assets are sold before any cash is distributed to partners. An **installment liquidation** occurs if cash is distributed to partners before the sale of assets is complete. Some assets are sold and cash is distributed, then additional assets are sold and more cash is distributed, and so on. The following sections consider first simple liquidations and then installment liquidations.

Simple Liquidations

Determining the distribution of cash to partners of a liquidating partnership can be a straightforward task or a complex one. Liquidation involving sales and payments by installments complicates distribution. Settlement becomes more complex, too, when any partners have capital deficiencies or develop them during the liquidation.

Successful Liquidating Partnerships   We may view a liquidating partnership as "successful" if, in the process of liquidation, all partners will receive a return of capital. In other words, the sale of all assets results in either a gain or a loss small enough that no capital deficiencies result. In this circumstance, the distribution of cash to outside creditors and partners is easy to determine.

To illustrate, assume that the JKL partnership has the following balance sheet:

Cash	$12,000	Liabilities	$17,000
All Other Assets	48,000	Capital—J	21,000
		Capital—K	6,000
		Capital—L	16,000
	$60,000		$60,000

The partners share income in a 2 : 1 : 1 ratio (that is, J has a 50 percent share; K and L, 25 percent each). If the other assets are sold for $64,000 and the resulting $16,000 gain is allocated to the partners, the accounts would show:

Cash	$76,000	Liabilities	$17,000
		Capital—J	29,000
		Capital—K	10,000
		Capital—L	20,000
	$76,000		$76,000

The distribution of the $76,000 would therefore be $17,000 to the outside creditors, $29,000 to J, $10,000 to K, and $20,000 to L.

Unsuccessful Liquidating Partnerships   We may view a liquidating partnership as "unsuccessful" if the losses from the sale of assets result in one or more capital deficiencies. If a partner still has a capital deficiency after offsetting any loans payable to that partner against the capital account, two possibilities exist. One is that the partner is able to contribute sufficient resources to remedy the deficiency. Enough assets would then be available to pay the creditors and the other partners. The other possibility is that the deficient partner is unable to contribute any resources or cannot contribute enough to eliminate the deficiency. In this case, the deficiency must be allocated to the other partners before the assets are distributed.

To illustrate, suppose that the balance sheet of the XYZ partnership appears as follows:

Cash	$ 10,000	Liabilities	$ 20,000
All Other Assets	100,000	Loan—X	6,000
		Loan—Y	4,000
		Capital—X	41,000
		Capital—Y	10,000
		Capital—Z	29,000
	$110,000		$110,000

The partners share income in a $5:3:2$ ratio, respectively. Assume now that the other assets are sold for $30,000. The loss on the sale of $70,000 must be allocated to capital balances:

	Before Loss		Capital Accounts Loss Allocation		After Loss
X	$41,000	—	$(.5 \times 70,000)$	=	$ 6,000
Y	10,000	—	$(.3 \times 70,000)$	=	(11,000)
Z	29,000	—	$(.2 \times 70,000)$	=	15,000
	$80,000				$10,000

Thus Y has a capital deficiency of $11,000.

First consider the case in which Y is able to contribute additional resources. Since the partnership owes Y $4,000, Y's net deficiency is $7,000. If Y contributes $7,000, and we offset Y's loan against the capital account, the accounts would appear as follows (the cash balance of $47,000 includes the original $10,000, the $30,000 sale proceeds, and Y's investment of $7,000):

Cash	$47,000	Liabilities	$20,000
		Loan—X	6,000
		Capital—X	6,000
		Capital—Y	0
		Capital—Z	15,000
	$47,000		$47,000

The cash should be distributed as follows:

Outside Creditors	$20,000
Partner X	12,000
Partner Y	0
Partner Z	15,000
	$47,000

In contrast, assume that Y is personally insolvent. Recall that the capital accounts after allocation of the loss are: X, $6,000; Y, ($11,000); and Z, $15,000. Y is unable to contribute any resources to remedy the deficiency. The $4,000 owed to Y by the partnership is offset against Y's capital account, reducing the deficiency to $7,000. The accounts now show:

Cash	$40,000	Liabilities	$20,000
		Loan—X	6,000
		Capital—X	6,000
		Capital—Y	(7,000)
		Capital—Z	15,000
	$40,000		$40,000

Since Y is unable to contribute, X and Z must bear this loss. We allocate Y's $7,000 deficiency to X and Z according to their income-sharing ratio (5:2). Thus, X bears $5,000 of the loss and Z bears $2,000, and the new account balances are:

Cash	$40,000	Liabilities	$20,000
		Loan—X	6,000
		Capital—X	1,000
		Capital—Y	0
		Capital—Z	13,000
	$40,000		$40,000

The $40,000 cash should be distributed as follows:

Outside Creditors	$20,000
Partner X	7,000
Partner Y	0
Partner Z	13,000
	$40,000

In summary, to account for simple partnership liquidations, we use the following sequence of accounting procedures:

1. Determine the gain or loss on the sale of assets.
2. Allocate the gain or loss to the partners' capital accounts according to the income-sharing ratio.
3. Offset loans against capital accounts in cases where a capital deficiency exists.
4. Record any investments by partners in response to capital deficiencies.
5. Allocate any remaining deficiencies to partners with positive capital account balances. (If this step produces new deficiencies, repeat steps 3 through 5.)
6. Distribute the cash.

Installment Liquidations

In the preceding sections, we discussed liquidations in which the sale of all assets is completed before any cash is distributed to the partners. In such cases, all gains and losses can be determined and allocated to the partners' capital accounts prior to determining the distribution of cash.

Suppose, however, that the partners request cash distributions before all assets are sold. Since the amount of gains and losses on future sales is unknown, it is not immediately evident how to distribute cash. Clearly, outside creditors have the first claim; they must be paid before any cash is distributed to the partners. We then require a method for determining an equitable plan for distributing cash to the partners. Two general approaches are available: determination of safe payments and preparation of a cash distribution plan.

Safe Payment Approach   The **safe payment approach** is a way of determining how a given amount of cash is to be distributed. The calculation is repeated prior to each distribution. The calculation is based on one simple assumption—that *all remaining assets will be a total loss* (that is, no more cash will be realized).

To illustrate, assume that the ABC partnership has decided to terminate business and liquidate its assets. The assets will be sold or otherwise converted into cash over a period of time, and the partners plan to distribute cash as it becomes available. Assume that the balance sheet presently appears as follows:

Cash	$ 3,000	Liabilities	$ 30,000
Receivables	30,000	Capital—A	106,000
Inventory	47,000	Capital—B	140,000
Land	25,000	Capital—C	41,000
Building (Net)	72,000		
Equipment (Net)	140,000		
	$317,000		$317,000

The partners share income in a 4:4:2 ratio.

Suppose that half of the receivables are collected and that the entire inventory is sold for $35,000. The accounts now show:

Cash	$ 53,000	Liabilities	$ 30,000
Receivables	15,000	Capital—A	101,200
Land	25,000	Capital—B	135,200
Building (Net)	72,000	Capital—C	38,600
Equipment (Net)	140,000		
	$305,000		$305,000

The decrease in the capital accounts represents the allocation of the $12,000 loss on the sale of inventory. If the partners wish to distribute the $53,000, then $30,000 will go to the outside creditors, and $23,000 will be available for the partners. How is this $23,000 to be distributed?

As stated earlier, our assumption is that all remaining assets will be a total loss, which is allocated by the income-sharing ratio. The remaining assets—receivables, land, building, and equipment—amount to $252,000. If these were a total loss, partners' capital accounts would be affected as follows:

		Capital Accounts		
	Before Loss	Loss Allocation		After Loss
Partner A	$101,200	− (.4 × 252,000)	=	$ 400
Partner B	135,200	− (.4 × 252,000)	=	34,400
Partner C	38,600	− (.2 × 252,000)	=	(11,800)
	$275,000			$23,000

Next, suppose that Partner C is unable to contribute additional capital. We allocate C's deficiency to A and B equally since they have equal income shares. We now have:

		Capital Accounts		
	Before Loss	Loss Allocation		After Loss
Partner A	$ 400	− (.5 × 11,800)	=	$ (5,500)
Partner B	34,400	− (.5 × 11,800)	=	28,500
Partner C	(11,800)			0
	$23,000			$23,000

Assuming that A is also unable to contribute additional capital, we allocate the entire deficiency to B, leading to the following capital balances:

Partner A	$ 0
Partner B	23,000
Partner C	0
	$23,000

The $23,000 will therefore be distributed entirely to Partner B. This is called a **safe payment** because it is based on the worst possible circumstances, namely that no more cash will be generated by the sale of assets and that deficient partners will be unable to contribute additional capital.

Following distribution of the $53,000 to the creditors and to Partner B, the accounts show:

Receivables	$ 15,000	Capital—A	$101,200
Land	25,000	Capital—B	112,200
Building (Net)	72,000	Capital—C	38,600
Equipment (Net)	140,000		
	$252,000		$252,000

When the next stage in the liquidation is complete and more cash becomes available for distribution, the next safe payment can be computed. Assume that receivables of $6,000 are collected, the remaining receivables are deemed uncollectible, and the equipment is sold for $90,000. Recording these transactions, including allocation to the partners of the $9,000 loss on receivables and the $50,000 loss on sale of equipment, yields:

Cash	$ 96,000	Capital—A	$ 77,600
Land	25,000	Capital—B	88,600
Building (Net)	72,000	Capital—C	26,800
	$193,000		$193,000

As before, assume no recovery of the remaining assets and allocate this potential loss to the partners as shown below:

	Capital Accounts		
	Before Loss	Loss Allocation	After Loss
Partner A	$ 77,600 −	(.4 × 97,000) =	$38,800
Partner B	88,600 −	(.4 × 97,000) =	49,800
Partner C	26,800 −	(.2 × 97,000) =	7,400
	$193,000		$96,000

Since no capital deficiencies result, the $96,000 is distributed $38,800 to A; $49,800 to B; and $7,400 to C. This process would continue until the liquidation was complete.

The safe payment approach to cash distribution is a fairly easy procedure. Its main disadvantages are (1) new calculations must be made for each distribution and (2) no information on future distributions is provided. The cash distribution plan remedies these disadvantages.

Cash Distribution Plan   Rather than recalculating payments during the liquidation process, we can develop a comprehensive **cash distribution plan.** Once this plan is prepared, we merely refer to it to determine how available cash is to be distributed.

The balances of partners' capital accounts continue to be the focus for determining cash distributions. Throughout partnership accounting, we have noted that partners' shares of net assets and profit shares are not necessarily the same. Development of a cash distribution plan is based on the concept of adjusting capital balances to the profit-sharing ratio.

We can illustrate this concept with a simple example. Suppose Black and Jones are equal partners, but Black's capital account has a balance of $45,000, while Jones' has a balance of $30,000. Despite the fact that they are equal partners, Black has more capital, due either to Black investing more or withdrawing less than Jones. Fairness suggests that when liquidating the partnership Black should receive $15,000 before Jones receives anything so as to equalize their capital positions. Once Black's capital is reduced to $30,000, they should share any remaining cash equally. Thus, we have developed a cash distribution plan for this simple situation:

1.   All liabilities are paid.

2.   Black receives the next $15,000.

3.   Any further distributions are divided equally between Black and Jones.

Where several partners with different income shares are liquidating their partnership by installments, derivation of the cash distribution plan requires a more formal approach. The logic is the same as in the simple example above: cash should be distributed so as to bring the capital accounts of the partners into proper alignment with respect to each other. This means that the partner having the largest capital balance relative to his or her ownership interest will be the first to receive cash. In the preceding example, Black, with a 60 percent capital share and a 50 percent ownership interest, received the first distribution. After all the imbalances in relative capital have been remedied, subsequent distributions are made to *all* partners in proportion to their ownership interests. The approach we will follow is:

1. Standardize the capital relationship among the partners by dividing each capital balance by that partner's income-sharing percentage. The standardized capital balance is an indicator of each partner's ability to absorb losses that may occur during liquidation. The bigger the standardized capital balance, the greater is that partner's ability to absorb losses before his or her capital balance is eliminated.

2. Equalize the standardized capital figures in steps. Begin with the largest, and determine the adjustment (subtraction) necessary to equalize it with the next largest. Continue this process until all standardized capital figures are equal. The equalization adjustments signify the *incremental* amount of loss which can be absorbed by partners with larger standardized capital balances over and above what can be absorbed by partners with smaller balances.

3. Convert the equalization adjustments back into terms of the respective partners' capital accounts by multiplying each adjustment by that partner's profit-sharing ratio. This gives the amounts and priorities of cash distributions to the partners.

4. Organize the results of step 3 into a cash distribution plan. Remember to provide first for the payment of amounts due to all outside creditors.

To illustrate preparation of a cash distribution plan, consider again the ABC partnership discussed previously. At the beginning of the liquidation process, the right-hand side of the balance sheet showed:

Liabilities	$ 30,000
Capital—A	106,000
Capital—B	140,000
Capital—C	41,000
	$317,000

The partners share income in a 4:4:2 ratio.

First, standardize the capital accounts by dividing actual capital by the income-sharing ratio:

Partner	Actual Capital	Income Ratio	Standardized Capital
A	$106,000	.4	$265,000
B	140,000	.4	350,000
C	41,000	.2	205,000

Exhibit 3.2   Work Sheet for Cash Distribution Plan

	Equalization of Standardized Capital				Actual Capital Accounts and Cash Distributions		
				Income Share	40%	40%	20%
	Partner A	Partner B	Partner C		Partner A	Partner B	Partner C
Standardized Capital	$265,000	$350,000	$205,000	Actual Capital	$106,000	$140,000	$41,000
a. Equalize A and B		(85,000)				(34,000)	
	$265,000	$265,000	$205,000		$106,000	$106,000	$41,000
b. Equalize A and B with C	(60,000)	(60,000)			(24,000)	(24,000)	
	$205,000	$205,000	$205,000		$ 82,000	$ 82,000	$41,000
				Capital Share	40%	40%	20%

This calculation tells us that when we standardize for the different income shares, partner B has the greatest amount of capital, and partner C has the least. In other words, partner B can absorb the greatest amount of loss, and partner C the least amount. It is reasonable to expect that B will receive money first, then A, then finally C.

Second, equalize the standardized capital figures, starting with the largest:

	Partner A	Partner B	Partner C
Standardized Capital	$265,000	$350,000	$205,000
a. Equalize A and B		(85,000)	
	$265,000	$265,000	$205,000
b. Equalize A and B with C	(60,000)	(60,000)	
	$205,000	$205,000	$205,000

This process is repeated in steps, noted a and b above, until all partners are equalized. The number of steps will be, at most, one less than the number of partners.

Third, convert these adjustments back into terms of the capital accounts, as follows:

Step a: Partner B $85,000 × .4 = $34,000.
Step b: Partner A $60,000 × .4 = $24,000.
            Partner B $60,000 × .4 = $24,000.

This calculation indicates that after the $30,000 of liabilities are paid, partner B should receive $34,000; then partners A and B should each receive $24,000. At this point, the relative capital of each partner would be equal, and any further distributions of cash should be made according to the partners' profit-sharing ratios (4:4:2).

A work sheet combining the second and third steps is shown in Exhibit 3.2. The left side of the work sheet shows the equalization of standardized capital. The right side shows the conversion back into terms of the partners' actual capital account balances. Figures on the left side are multiplied by the respective income percentages to get the figures on the right side. Note that the adjust-

Exhibit 3.3   ABC Partnership Cash Distribution Plan

Step	Amount	Distribution
1	First $30,000	Creditors
2	Next $34,000	Partner B
3	Next $48,000	Partners A and B in equal amounts
4	Any further amount	Partners A, B, and C, in 4:4:2 ratio

ments which equalize the standardized capital translate into cash distributions which bring the partners' capital accounts into line with the profit-sharing ratio.

Fourth, organize the results into a formal cash distribution plan, such as that shown in Exhibit 3.3. The plan shows how to distribute any amount of cash which becomes available. Remember that distributions are cumulative; that is, each distribution starts where the previous one ended.

To illustrate application of the plan, recall that we previously calculated the proper distribution of $53,000 and $96,000, proceeds from the liquidation of ABC Partnership, using the safe payment approach. We now apply the cash distribution plan to these amounts to verify the results.

First, the $53,000 is considered. The cash distribution plan states that the first $30,000 is paid to creditors and the next $34,000 is paid to partner B. A distribution of $53,000 permits us to complete the first step (to pay the creditors $30,000) and to partially complete the second step (to pay partner B $23,000 of the required $34,000). Thus the $53,000 would be distributed:

Creditors	$30,000
Partner B	23,000
	$53,000

Next, we had $96,000 to distribute. We must complete the second step of the plan (to pay partner B an additional $11,000) before moving on to the third step. Following the cash distribution plan, we get:

1. Pay $11,000 to partner B to complete the second step, leaving $85,000 (= $96,000 − $11,000) available to distribute.

2. Divide the next $48,000 equally between A and B, thus completing the third step of the plan. Left to distribute is $37,000.

3. Divide the $37,000 among A, B, and C in a 4:4:2 ratio, as specified by the fourth and final step of the plan.

The proper distribution of the $96,000 is summarized here:

Step	Amount	Distribution		
		Partner A	Partner B	Partner C
2	$11,000	$ 0	$11,000	$ 0
3	48,000	24,000	24,000	0
4	37,000	14,800	14,800	7,400
	$96,000	$38,800	$49,800	$7,400

Observe that this result is identical to that achieved by the safe payment approach.

Not all available cash need be distributed. Cash may be retained for anticipated liquidation expenses or other purposes. The approach discussed above would be applied to the amount of cash to be distributed. Occasionally, temporary deviations from the cash distribution plan may occur. For example, a specific asset may be distributed to a partner in lieu of cash, and the value of the asset may exceed the amount to which that partner is entitled. Subsequent distributions must be adjusted in favor of other partners until the excess is absorbed. For example, assume the following cash distribution plan:

Step	Amount	Distribution
1	First $10,000	Creditors
2	Next $16,000	Partner A
3	Next $30,000	Partners A and B in 2:1 ratio
4	Any further amount	Partners A, B, and C in 6:3:1 ratio

Suppose that at step 3, in lieu of $10,000 cash, B receives a truck worth $14,200. The excess distribution of $4,200 (= 3 × $1,400) to B must be remedied in step 4 by distributing $8,400 (= 6 × $1,400) to A and $1,400 (= 1 × $1,400) to C before B receives any further payment.

The derivation of the cash distribution plan has been described in terms of standardizing the capital accounts of the various partners and then distributing cash in such a way as to equalize their relative capital. The derivation may also be described in terms of ability to absorb losses. The procedures remain the same, but the numbers take on an alternative meaning. Referring to Exhibit 3.2, the result of dividing each partner's capital balance by the appropriate income share is the maximum loss that the partnership could incur without that partner's capital becoming negative. For example, partner A has capital of $140,000 and an income share of 40 percent. Dividing yields $265,000. If the partnership incurred a $265,000 loss, A's share would be 40 percent or $140,000, which would wipe out A's capital. Thus the $265,000 may be viewed as A's maximum ability to absorb losses. The partner whose ability to absorb losses is largest is in the strongest position and should receive the first distribution. We proceed to equalize the loss absorption abilities in the same manner as described earlier.

In accounting for partnership liquidations, the accountant must ensure an equitable distribution of partnership assets. Consideration must be given to actual and prospective losses on the sale of assets and to the potential inability of partners to remedy capital deficiencies. These factors are considered, either directly or indirectly, in the two procedures discussed for installment liquidations —the safe payment approach and the cash distribution plan.

Summary of Key Concepts

The interest of a **retiring partner** may be purchased with the **individual assets of one or more of the remaining partners** or with **partnership assets.** In the latter case, the **bonus, partial goodwill,** or **total goodwill** approach is used to account for any difference between the payment to the retiring partner and the amount of the retiring partner's capital account.

If the partnership is to be **liquidated,** the rights of creditors are based on the **marshalling of assets rule.** Partners' loans and capital balances are combined under the **right of offset.** If an individual partner has a **capital deficiency,** that partner is obligated to contribute additional assets to the partnership to remedy the deficiency; if this is impossible, the deficiency is remedied by the other partners.

In a **simple liquidation,** all assets are sold before any cash is distributed to the partners. In an **installment liquidation,** cash distributions occur before the sale of assets is complete. Under an installment liquidation, the equitable division of each cash distribution among the partners may be based on either the **safe payment approach** or the **cash distribution plan.**

Questions   **Q3.1**   How do the concepts of legal and economic entity relate to a partnership that continues after the retirement of one partner?

Q3.2   Identify the differences in accounting for retirement of a partner when the retiree's partnership interest is purchased (1) with personal assets of one or more existing partners and (2) with partnership assets.

Q3.3   Cite several techniques for valuing a retiring partner's interest in the partnership.

Q3.4   Upon what assumption is the goodwill method of accounting for partnership retirements based? How does this reasoning apply to the partial and total goodwill approaches?

Q3.5   What is meant by *right of offset* in accounting for partnership liquidations?

Q3.6   Assume that a partnership is being liquidated and that the obligations to creditors exceed the assets of the partnership. What, if any, rights do the creditors have in attempting to collect the full amount owed them?

Q3.7   In partnership accounting, what is the difference between a simple liquidation and an installment liquidation?

Q3.8   Discuss the procedure followed in accounting for simple partnership liquidations.

Q3.9   What advantage does the cash distribution plan have over the safe payment approach in determining cash payments to partners during liquidation? How do the results of the two approaches differ?

Q3.10 What purpose do the safe payment approach and the cash distribution plan serve during partnership liquidation? Why is this important?

Exercises **E3.1** On June 30, 19X8, the balance sheet for the partnership of Winston, Barker, and Langley, together with their respective profit-and-loss-sharing ratios, was as follows:

Assets, at Cost	$300,000
Winston—Loan	$ 15,000
Winston—Capital (20%)	70,000
Barker—Capital (20%)	65,000
Langley—Capital (60%)	150,000
	$300,000

Winston has decided to retire from the partnership, and by mutual agreement the assets are to be adjusted to their fair value of $360,000 at June 30, 19X8. It was agreed that the partnership would pay Winston $102,000 cash for his partnership interest exclusive of his loan, which is to be repaid in full. *No* goodwill is to be recorded in this transaction.

Required: After Winston's retirement, what are the capital account balances of Barker and Langley, respectively?

(AICPA adapted)

E3.2 The total of the partners' capital accounts was $105,000 before recognition of partnership goodwill in preparation for the resignation of a partner whose profit-and-loss-sharing ratio is 20 percent. He was paid $37,000 by the firm in final settlement for his interest. The remaining partners' capital accounts, excluding their share of the goodwill, totaled $80,000 after his resignation.

Required: What was the total agreed-upon goodwill of the firm?

(AICPA adapted)

E3.3 Baxter is planning to retire from the partnership of Baxter, Helman, and Caines. The partners' income-sharing ratio is 2:1:1. Helman and Caines will continue as a partnership, sharing profits and losses equally. The partners are considering various ways to pay Baxter $90,000, which is the fair market value of her interest in the business. Prior to retirement, Baxter's capital account balance is $70,000.

Required: Prepare the journal entry to record Baxter's retirement on the partnership books under each of the following assumptions:
1. Helman and Caines each pay Baxter $45,000 using personal funds.
2. Partnership cash is used to pay Baxter. The bonus method is followed.
3. Partnership cash is used to pay Baxter. The total goodwill approach is followed.
4. Partnership cash is used to pay Baxter. The partial goodwill approach is followed.

5. Helman and Caines each pay Baxter $10,000 from personal funds; the rest is paid with partnership cash.

E3.4 The following balance sheet is for the LMN partnership. The partners (L, M, and N) share profits and losses in the ratio of $5:3:2$, respectively.

Cash	$ 30,000
Other Assets	270,000
	$300,000
Liabilities	$ 70,000
L—Capital	140,000
M—Capital	80,000
N—Capital	10,000
	$300,000

Assume that L, M, and N have agreed to liquidate the partnership by selling the other assets.

Required: What should each of the partners receive if the other assets are sold for $200,000?

(AICPA adapted)

E3.5 The following balance sheet is presented for the partnership of Craven, Douglas, and Bedford, who share profits and losses in the ratio of $5:3:2$, respectively:

Cash	$ 60,000
Other Assets	540,000
	$600,000
Liabilities	$140,000
Craven—Capital	280,000
Douglas—Capital	160,000
Bedford—Capital	20,000
	$600,000

Required:
1. Assume that the assets and liabilities are fairly valued on the balance sheet and the partnership decides to admit Hank as a new partner with a one-fifth interest. *No* goodwill or bonus is to be recorded. How much should Hank contribute in cash or other assets?
2. Assume that instead of admitting a new partner, the partners decide to liquidate the partnership. If the other assets are sold for $400,000, how should the available cash be distributed to each partner?

(AICPA adapted)

E3.6 The following are data for the AB Partnership and for A and B as individuals. Assume that A and B are equal partners.

AB Partnership		Case 1	Case 2
Assets		$48,000	$31,000
Liabilities		42,000	51,000
Capital—A		3,000	(8,000)
Capital—B		3,000	(12,000)

Partner A	Case 1	Case 2
Assets	10,000	30,000
Liabilities	17,000	17,000
Partner B		
Assets	50,000	15,000
Liabilities	9,000	16,000

Required: For each case, following the marshalling of assets rule, indicate how the assets of the partnership and the assets of each partner would be applied if creditor claims were to be satisfied as fully as possible.

E3.7 Partners James, Storm, and Hadley share profits and losses in the ratio of 5:3:2, respectively. The partners vote to dissolve the partnership when its assets, liabilities, and capital are as follows:

Cash	$ 40,000
Other Assets	210,000
	$250,000
Liabilities	$ 60,000
James—Capital	48,000
Storm—Capital	72,000
Hadley—Capital	70,000
	$250,000

The partnership will be liquidated over a prolonged period of time. As cash becomes available, it will be distributed to the partners. The first sale of noncash assets having a book value of $120,000 realizes $90,000.

Required: How much cash should be distributed to each partner after this sale?

(AICPA adapted)

E3.8 Conley, Lewis, and Miller have decided to liquidate their partnership. The records show the following balances:

Cash	$ 10,000	Liabilities	$ 30,000
Receivables	50,000	Capital—Conley . . .	270,000
Inventory	130,000	Capital—Lewis	80,000
Equipment (Net)	200,000	Capital—Miller	10,000
	$390,000		$390,000

The partners share income in a 7:2:1 ratio, respectively. Assume that the entire inventory is sold for $90,000 and that the partners wish to distribute the $100,000 which is now available.

Required: Determine how the $100,000 should be divided among the three partners.

E3.9 The partnership of Jones, Brown, and Smith is to be liquidated. The partners share income and losses equally. Each partner has a capital balance of $15,000, and the balance sheet shows liabilities of the partnership as $25,000.

Required: Devise a plan for distribution of cash as it becomes available during the liquidation.

E3.10   Partners Whitehead, Ellis, and Riley had capital accounts of $72,000, $60,000, and $65,000, respectively, on the date liquidation proceedings for their partnership began. Liabilities at that date were $32,000. The partners had shared profits and losses in a 3:5:2 ratio.

Required: Prepare a plan for distribution of cash received during liquidation.

Problems   **P3.1**   **Retirement of Partner**   Horton, Fischer, and Walker are partners in a trucking firm. They share profits in a 3:4:2 ratio, respectively. On March 8, the date of Fischer's retirement from the partnership, the balances of the partners' capital accounts are Horton, $35,000; Fischer, $15,000; Walker, $21,000. Fischer has agreed to surrender his interest to Horton and Walker (who plan to continue the business) for $18,000 and a pick-up truck owned by the partnership. The cash payment is to be made from partnership funds. The truck cost $8,000 and has accumulated depreciation of $5,000. Fair value of the used truck is $3,900.

Required: Make the entries to record Fischer's retirement and compute the capital balances for Horton and Walker after the retirement (1) under the bonus approach and (2) under the partial goodwill approach.

P3.2   **Retirement of Two Partners**   Thirty years ago, five mechanics formed a partnership and established an automobile repair shop. Two of the partners, Dewitt and Galax, are now retiring. The other three partners are continuing the partnership. The original agreement called for an equal division of profits and losses. The remaining partners plan to continue this arrangement.

The following balance sheet has been prepared for the partnership as of the date of retirement:

Cash	$ 65,000	Accounts Payable	$ 90,000
Accounts Receivable	80,000	Loan Payable	40,000
Inventory of Parts	40,000	Capital—Dewitt	50,000
Equipment (Net)	90,000	Capital—Galax	40,000
Building (Net)	30,000	Capital—Farber	70,000
Land	25,000	Capital—Wayne	7,500
		Capital—Lane .	32,500
	$330,000		$330,000

All partners have agreed that Dewitt should receive $62,500 for his interest in the business and Galax should receive $50,000. Farber has proposed the bonus method for recording the retirements. Wayne objects to this method and has suggested the partial goodwill approach.

Required:

1. Prepare the journal entry to record the retirements under the bonus method.
2. Prepare the journal entry to record the retirements under the partial goodwill approach.
3. Why is Wayne objecting to the bonus method of accounting?
4. Regardless of the accounting method employed, what immediate problem for the business can you identify at the time of retirement? Propose a solution to this problem.

P3.3 **Retirement—Various Cases**   Given below are account balances for the partnership of Flint, Yancy, and Goldsmith before the retirement of Goldsmith. Each case presents account balances of the Flint and Yancy partnership immediately after Goldsmith's retirement. The cases are independent of each other. In case 4, no bonus was recorded.

Balance Sheet Accounts	Balances before Goldsmith's Retirement	Case 1	Case 2	Case 3	Case 4	Case 5
Cash	$ 50,000	$ 20,000	$ 0	$ 50,000	$ 50,000	$ 0
Other Assets	130,000	130,000	130,000	130,000	100,000	130,000
Goodwill	10,000	10,000	20,000	10,000	10,000	40,000
Liabilities	(70,000)	(70,000)	(70,000)	(70,000)	(70,000)	(70,000)
Capital—Flint	(40,000)	(45,000)	(40,000)	(80,000)	(45,000)	(50,000)
Capital—Yancy	(40,000)	(45,000)	(40,000)	(40,000)	(45,000)	(50,000)
Capital—Goldsmith	(40,000)	—	—	—	—	—

Required: For each independent case, answer the following questions. Show supporting calculations.

1. What method of accounting was used to record the retirement (bonus, goodwill, neither)?
2. How much did Goldsmith receive upon retirement?

P3.4 **Partnership Agreement—Payments to Estates of Deceased Partners**   The partnership agreement of Lee, Perng, Quinn, Robin, and Schwartz contained a buy and sell agreement, among numerous other provisions, which would become operative in case of the death of any partner. Some provisions contained in the buy and sell agreement were as follows:

ARTICLE V. Buy and Sell Agreement

1. Purposes of the Buy and Sell Agreement.
   (a) The partners mutually desire that the business shall be continued by the survivors without interruption or liquidation upon the death of one of the partners.
   (b) The partners also mutually desire that the deceased partner's estate shall receive the full value of the deceased partner's interest in the partnership and that the estate shall share in the earnings of the partnership until the deceased partner's interest shall be fully purchased by the surviving partners.

2. Purchase and Sale of Deceased Partner's Interest.

   (a) Upon the death of the partner first to die, the partnership shall continue to operate without dissolution.

   (b) Upon the decedent's death, the survivors shall purchase and the executor or administrator of the deceased partner's estate shall sell to the surviving partners the deceased partner's interest in the partnership for the price and upon the terms and conditions hereinafter set forth.

   (c) The deceased partner's estate shall retain the deceased partner's interest until the amount specified in the next paragraph shall be paid in full by the surviving partners.

   (d) The parties agree that the purchase price for the partnership interest shall be an amount equal to the deceased partner's capital account at the date of death. Said amount shall be paid to the legal representative of decedent as follows:

   (i) The first installment of 30 percent of said capital account shall be paid within sixty days from the date of death of the partner or within thirty days from the date on which the personal representative of decedent becomes qualified by law, whichever date is later, and

   (ii) The balance shall be due in four equal installments, which shall be due and payable annually on the anniversary date of said death.

3. Deceased Partner's Estate's Share of the Earnings

   (a) The partners mutually desire that the deceased partner's estate shall be guaranteed a share in the earnings of the partnership over the period said estate retains an interest in the partnership. Said estate shall not be deemed to have an interest in the partnership after the final installment for the deceased partner's capital account is paid, even though a portion of the guaranteed payments specified below may be unpaid and may be due and owing.

   (b) The deceased partner's estate's guaranteed share of the earnings of the partnership shall be determined from two items and shall be paid at different times as follows:

   (i) First, interest shall be paid on the unpaid balance of the deceased partner's capital account at the same date the installment on the purchase price is paid. The amount to be paid shall be an amount equal to accrued interest at the rate of 6 percent per annum on the unpaid balance of the purchase price for the deceased partner's capital account.

   (ii) Second, the parties agree that the balance of the guaranteed payment from the partnership earnings shall be an amount equal to 25 percent of the deceased partner's share of the aggregate gross receipts of the partnership for the full thirty-six months preceding the month of the partner's death. Said amount shall be payable in forty-eight equal monthly installments without interest, and the first payment shall be made within sixty days following the death of the partner or within thirty days from the date on which the personal representative of deceased becomes qualified, whichever date is later; provided, however, that the payments so made under this provision during any twelve-month period shall not exceed the highest annual salary on a calendar-year basis received by the partner for the three calendar years immediately preceding the date of his death. In the event that said payment would exceed said salary, then an amount per month shall be paid which does not so exceed said highest monthly salary, and the term over which payments shall be paid to the beneficiary shall be lengthened out beyond the said forty-eight months in order to complete said payment.

Lee and Schwartz were both killed simultaneously in an automobile accident on January 10, 19X6. The surviving partners notified the executors of both estates that the first payment due under the buy and sell agreement would be paid on March 10, 19X6, and that subsequent payments would be paid on the tenth day of each month as due.

The following information was determined from the partnership's records:

Partner	Income Sharing Ratio	Capital Account on January 10, 19X6	Annual Salaries to Partners by Years		
			19X3	19X4	19X5
Lee	30	$25,140	$16,500	$17,000	$17,400
Perng	25	21,970	15,000	15,750	16,500
Quinn	20	4,780	12,000	13,000	14,000
Robin	15	5,860	9,600	10,800	12,000
Schwartz	10	2,540	8,400	9,600	10,800

The partnership's gross receipts for the three prior years were:

19X3	$296,470
19X4	325,310
19X5	363,220

Required: Prepare a schedule of the amounts to be paid to the Lee Estate and to the Schwartz Estate in March 19X6, December 19X6, and January 19X7. The schedule should identify the amounts attributable to earnings and to interest in the guaranteed payments and to capital. Supporting computations should be in good form.

(AICPA adapted)

P3.5 **Partnership Admission and Liquidation** The following balance sheet is for the partnership of Alex, Stanley, and George (figures shown parenthetically reflect agreed income-sharing percentages):

Cash	$ 20,000	Liabilities	$ 50,000
Other Assets	180,000	Alex—Capital (40%) . . .	37,000
		Stanley—Capital (40%) . .	65,000
		George—Capital (20%) . .	48,000
	$200,000		$200,000

Required:

1. If the assets are fairly valued on the balance sheet and the partnership wishes to admit Day as a new partner having a one-sixth interest without recording goodwill or bonus, how much cash or other assets should Day contribute?

2. If assets on the initial balance sheet are fairly valued, Alex and Stanley consent, and Day pays George $51,000 for his interest, what would the revised capital balances of the partners be?

3. If the firm, as shown on the original balance sheet, is dissolved and liquidated by selling assets in installments, the first sale of noncash assets having a book value of $90,000 realized $50,000, and all cash avail-

able after settlement with creditors is distributed, how much cash would the respective partners receive (to the nearest dollar)?

4. If the facts are as in item 3 above, except that $3,000 cash is to be withheld for expenses of liquidation, the respective partners would then receive how much cash (to the nearest dollar)?

5. Assume that each partner properly received some cash in the distribution after the second sale, the cash to be distributed amounts to $12,000 from the third sale, and unsold assets with an $8,000 book value remain; ignoring items 3 and 4 above, which of the following would the respective partners receive?

    a. Alex, $4,800; Stanley, $4,800; George, $2,400.

    b. Alex, $4,000; Stanley, $4,000; George, $4,000.

    c. Alex, $37/150$ of $12,000; Stanley, $65/150$ of $12,000; George $48/150$ of $12,000.

    d. Alex, $0; Stanley, $8,000; George, $4,000.

(AICPA adapted)

P3.6 Partnership Liquidation—Safe Payment Several years ago, Judith Able, Leslie Bowen, Janice Cratz, and Donna Ogleby formed a partnership to operate the Abco Delicatessen. Rerouting of bus lines caused declines in patronage to the extent that the partners have agreed to dissolve the partnership and liquidate the assets.

The November 2, 19X0, balance sheet of Abco Delicatessen and other data are given below. The partnership agreement did not specify how income and losses were to be shared.

Abco Delicatessen
Balance Sheet
November 2, 19X0

Cash	$30,000	Liabilities		$40,000
Supplies	14,000	Loan—Ogleby		13,000
Equipment	35,000	Capital—Able		16,000
Fixtures	15,000	Capital—Bowen		7,000
		Capital—Cratz		3,000
		Capital—Ogleby		15,000
	$94,000			$94,000

Other information is as follows:

1. During November, half of the fixtures were sold for $4,000. Equipment with a book value of $9,000 was sold for $4,000.

2. During December, all outside creditors were paid. A neighboring restaurant bought Abco Delicatessen's supplies at 85 percent of cost. The remaining fixtures were sold for $3,100.

3. During January, equipment with a book value of $6,000 was sold for $4,500.

Required: Following the safe payment approach, specify how cash is to be distributed at the end of November, December, and January.

P3.7 **Partnership Liquidation—Cash Distribution Plan** Using the data in P3.6, develop a cash distribution plan for the liquidation of Abco Delicatessen. Show each step in the development of the plan.

P3.8 **Safe Payment Plan** After several heated disputes over management of their business, Tinsley and Shields decided to liquidate their partnership. The partnership agreement specified that the partners share profits and losses equally despite their original unequal investment of capital. Liquidation proceedings began in April, and final cash distributions to partners were made on June 30. The partners received cash as follows:

	Tinsley	Shields
April 30	$ 0	$ 0
May 31	5,000	0
June 30	47,500	22,500

The accountant followed the safe payment plan in making the distributions.
During the three-month liquidation period, the following occurred:

1. Accounts receivable collections: April, $25,000; May, $10,000; June, $10,000. At the end of June, remaining receivables of $5,000 were written off. No new receivables were added during the liquidation period.
2. Equipment was sold in June.
3. Inventory was sold for cash at three-fourths its book value; half was sold in April and half in May. Total cash received for inventory was $60,000.
4. Starting in April, liabilities were paid at the end of each month with all available cash. Total liabilities paid equaled $110,000.
5. Total assets on March 31, including $20,000 cash, had a book value of $200,000.
6. Calculation of the safe payment in May created a potential deficit in Shields' account of $12,500.

Required:

1. Prepare the balance sheets for the partnership of Tinsley and Shields on March 31, April 30, and May 31.
2. What was the gain or loss on the sale of equipment?

P3.9 **Cash Distribution Plan for Partnership Liquidation** On August 25, 19X5, Pinson, Howards, and Ropp entered into a partnership agreement to acquire a speculative second mortgage on undeveloped real estate. They invested $55,500, $32,000, and $12,500, respectively. They agreed on a profit-and-loss-sharing ratio of 4:2:1, respectively.

On September 1, 19X5, they purchased for $100,000 a mortgage note with an unpaid balance of $120,000. The amount paid included interest accrued from June 30, 19X5. The note principal matures at the rate of $2,000 each quarter. Interest at the annual rate of 8 percent computed on the unpaid balance is also due quarterly.

Regular interest and principal payments were received on September 30 and December 31, 19X5. A working capital imprest fund of $150 was established, and collection expenses of $70 were paid in December.

In addition to the regular September payment, on September 30 the mortgagor made a lump-sum principal reduction payment of $10,000 plus a penalty of 2 percent for prepayment.

Because of the speculative nature of the note, the partners agree to defer recognition of the discount until their cost has been fully recovered.

Required:

1. Assuming that no cash distributions were made to the partners, prepare a schedule computing the cash balance available for distribution to the partners on December 31, 19X5.

2. After payment of collection expenses, the partners expect to have cash in the total amount of $170,000 available for distribution to themselves for interest and return of principal. They plan to distribute the cash as soon as possible so that they can individually reinvest it. Prepare a schedule showing how the total cash of $170,000 should be distributed to the individual partners by installments as it becomes available.

(AICPA adapted)

Chapter 4

Fiduciary Accounting

Proprietorships, partnerships, and corporations are entities created to conduct business activities. Entities may be created for another purpose—the management of certain assets. Two such entities are estates and trusts. Their special purpose results in unique accounting treatment which merits attention. Estates and trusts are considered in a single chapter because the mechanics of accounting for them are similar; the differences between the two lie in the different reasons for which the assets are being managed. In both cases, the assets are managed by someone other than the owner. Estates are entities which hold and manage the assets of a deceased person until they can be properly distributed to creditors and heirs. Estates are also used to manage the assets of a "deceased" firm—one in bankruptcy or receivership—until the assets can be properly distributed to creditors, bondholders, and stockholders. Trusts may be established to manage a pool of assets on behalf of a group of people, as in the case of a pension trust or an investment trust. Trusts may also be established to manage assets for a beneficiary upon direction of the *donor* (creator of the trust), as in the case of a trust set up for a minor child by parents. In all these cases, the stewardship function of accounting dominates. Thus, the responsibility of the accountant is to report on the management of the assets to the concerned parties.

One important aspect which distinguishes an estate or trust from a corporation is the responsibility of management. The corporate manager has a considerable amount of discretion in managing the assets of the firm, and the focus is on the manager's performance as measured in terms of income or other statistics. The manager of a trust or estate has much less flexibility, being subject to legal restrictions such as wills, bankruptcy laws, and trust agreements in the management and disposition of assets. Since assets are managed on behalf of beneficiaries, the focus is on the manager's **fiduciary responsibility**—the custodial or stewardship responsibility for property belonging to others. Thus the executor of an estate, the receiver of a firm in bankruptcy, or the trustee of a trust is commonly called a **fiduciary.** Fiduciary accounting is the subject of this chapter.

Adherence to laws affecting estates and trusts is an important part of accounting for these entities. As laws exist to protect those incapable of self-protection, laws have been created to safeguard the interests of beneficiaries while their assets are managed by others. Thus the accountant must be aware of the legal framework within which estates and trusts operate. We address this issue throughout the chapter.

The assets of estates and trusts are viewed legally as belonging to two categories:

1.   **Principal** (also called **corpus**) consists of the property and rights to property (such as receivables) existing at the date the entity is created. Examples are building, marketable securities, and interest receivable.

2.   **Income** is the additional assets generated from the investment or use of principal assets. Examples are rental revenue from buildings and interest or dividends from securities which are earned after date of death.

Because laws often dictate that this division be maintained and because the beneficiaries of principal and income assets may be different, accounting for estates and trusts recognizes this distinction. Accounts for the entities are classified as to principal or income. Financial statements of estates and trusts report on the two elements separately.

Estates of Individuals

An **estate** is an entity which holds, manages, and accounts for the real and personal property of a deceased person, the **decedent,** until the property can be properly distributed to the appropriate beneficiaries. These beneficiaries and their rights to property are specified in the decedent's will or in the law if the individual died **intestate** (without a valid will). The estate is managed by a personal representative: a representative named by the will is an **executor** or **executrix;** a court-appointed representative is called an **administrator.** The personal representative of an estate has numerous duties and responsibilities and may become personally liable if lax in performance of these functions. Therefore, most states require an accounting by the fiduciary in order to enforce these duties. Interim accountings allow the court to oversee and review the fiduciary's actions, while the final accounting provides beneficiaries the opportunity to object to the representative's actions. However, once the final accounting is approved by all interested parties, the representative is released from further liability.

The estate may exist as an entity for a few months or several years. Note that the going-concern assumption underlying most business entities is absent. An estate is created with the assumption of a limited life; it ends when the assets are distributed. In this respect, it resembles a limited life partnership created to accomplish a specific purpose.

Legal Aspects of Estates

Since accounting for estates is influenced by law, understanding the legal proceedings surrounding the creation and operation of an estate is essential for the accountant. First, it must be determined if the decedent had a will. Once validated, a will governs the distribution of the decedent's property. The process of validating a will is called **probate.** Probate involves court hearings at which parties may question the validity of the will. Early in the probate proceedings, the personal representative takes possession and control of the decedent's assets to manage them until final distribution to the beneficiaries. Even if there is no will and the laws of intestacy govern the ultimate property distribution, there is a lapse of time between the death and distribution, during which the property must be managed. In either case, the time period is at least six months. A longer period is not unusual, since it may be neither practical nor desirable to distribute the assets quickly.

Once the claims are settled and the beneficiaries are determined through probate, the personal representative can distribute the assets and close the estate. Beneficiaries of real property are called **devisees;** of personal property, **legatees.** The gift of property, either a **devise** or **legacy,** can be *specific* (an identified object), *general* (an indicated quantity of something, usually an amount of cash), or *residuary* (property remaining after specific and general gifts are met). The legal classification of the beneficiaries as well as the legal classification of assets is important for the distribution of estate assets.

Following are some responsibilities of the personal representative:

1. *Notify the decedent's heirs* of the appointment as personal representative.

2. *Establish a family allowance* for the decedent's surviving spouse and dependent children. The Uniform Probate Code specifies the amount and timing of payment. The allowance is exempt from claims against the estate.

3. *Prepare an inventory of the assets.* The basis for the inventory is the fair value of property or rights owned at the date of death.

4. *List any liens* against the property.

5. *Publish a notice requesting creditors to present claims* against the estate of the decedent. The law dictates the appropriate vehicle and timing of such publication. Creditors have four months to present claims.

6. *Manage the decedent's business and investments.* If the decedent was a sole proprietor, then the personal representative has the right to manage the business for four months after the appointment.

7. *Establish an accounting system* which classifies the property as to principal or income assets. All assets existing at the date of death are principal. As income assets are generated, the personal representative must maintain records so as to retain the distinction between principal and income.

8. *Pay claims* against the estate.

9. *Distribute the assets* to the beneficiaries.

Several of these items require further discussion.

Preparing the Inventory   The fiduciary should prepare a complete inventory of the assets of the estate as soon as possible after the decedent's death. The Uniform Probate Code stipulates that within three months after appointment, the personal representative must prepare an inventory of property owned by the decedent at the time of death together with a listing of any liens against the property. If the representative anticipates a delay in appointment (for example, due to a will contest), he or she may have an objective party, such as an attorney, prepare the inventory. A prompt inventory of assets should be made in order to prevent any losses or misunderstanding which may arise regarding the existence, valuation, and location of the decedent's assets.

When preparing the inventory, the following information should be recorded:
1.   Type of asset.
2.   How the asset was held by the decedent (for example, outright or in trust).
3.   Location of the asset.
4.   Fair value of the asset at date of death.
5.   The income tax basis of the asset to the decedent.
6.   Date the asset was brought under the control of the fiduciary.
7.   Any other distinguishing features (for example, description of jewelry and antiques).

The services of a professional appraiser may be required to estimate the value of assets for which markets are not readily available.

Along with the inventory of assets, the representative should obtain any pertinent documents such as stock certificates, bankbooks, deeds, life insurance policies, and tax returns. Once the inventory is completed, it is filed with the probate court and copies may be provided to interested parties. If other assets are subsequently discovered by the representative, they should be listed on a separate schedule to be filed with the court.

Claims against the Estate   The fiduciary has the duty of satisfying all claims against the estate. However, the representative also has the authority to allow or disallow a claim. The holder of a disallowed claim can bring action to establish the validity of the claim, but the burden of proof lies with the holder of the claim. The fiduciary can also negotiate compromise settlements of claims.

As a general rule, the personal representative should publish notice to creditors in a newspaper with general circulation. The Uniform Probate Code requires that a notice be published at least once a week for three consecutive weeks. Creditors must then respond within four months from the date of first publication, or forever be barred from asserting their claims.

When the estate's assets are sufficient to cover all claims, the order of debt payment is irrelevant. However, if assets are insufficient to pay all claims in full, the following is a generally accepted order of payment, closely following that prescribed by the Uniform Probate Code:
1.   Debts secured by liens on assets (for example, mortgage on residence).
2.   Expenses of administering the estate.

3. Funeral expenses and expenses of last illness.

4. Debts given preference under federal or state law.

5. Taxes assessed on decedent's property prior to death.

6. Bonds and notes issued by the decedent.

7. All other claims.

If the will is silent as to the assets to be used for debt payment, assets should be used in the following order:

1. Personal property not bequeathed.

2. Personal property bequeathed generally.

3. Personal property bequeathed specifically.

4. Real property not devised.

5. Real property devised generally.

6. Real property devised specifically.

Distributions to Beneficiaries   Another duty of the personal representative is to distribute the estate assets to the beneficiaries named in the will. The fiduciary should, if possible and if so specified in the will, distribute the assets in kind rather than converting them into cash before distribution.

When the estate assets are insufficient to cover both creditors' claims and devises or legacies, then the devises (or legacies) are reduced (or abated) according to the sequence provided for in the will. The Uniform Probate Code provides an order of abatement (listed above) for the occasions when the will does not specify an order.

Accounting and Reporting   The personal representative must maintain proper accounting records for the estate. It is usually desirable for the representative to open a checking account in the name of the estate so that the cash transactions of the estate are kept separate from the fiduciary's personal transactions. The primary financial statement presented for estates is the **charge and discharge statement.** This statement, illustrated in Exhibit 4.1, identifies what assets were placed under the control of the personal representative and any distributions made of such property. The financial report for the estate is subject to court review in the interest of the beneficiaries. Note that the legal division of principal and income is carried into the accounting report. The accounting system for an estate must maintain this distinction to ensure legal compliance and facilitate statement preparation.

The charge and discharge statement is usually accompanied by a number of supporting schedules, which provide details of various items on the statement. For example, the assets comprising the initial inventory, the gains and losses on disposal of principal assets, and the distributions made to beneficiaries would each be detailed on supporting schedules. These schedules are illustrated in the example presented in a subsequent section.

The financial report for a small estate may be prepared only once, at the time of final distribution of estate assets. For a more complex estate, several interim reports may be made. Since an estate is a limited-life entity, reports are usually cumulative, covering the estate from date of death to the date of the report.

Exhibit 4.1   Format of Charge and Discharge Statement

Identification of Estate
Identification of Executor
Charge and Discharge Statement
For the Period _____

FIRST, AS TO PRINCIPAL

I charge myself as follows:

Inventory of Assets	$XX	
Assets Subsequently Discovered	XX	
Gain on Disposal of Principal Assets	XX	$XXX

I credit myself as follows:

Debts of Decedent Paid	$XX	
Administrative Expenses Paid	XX	
Loss on Disposal of Principal Assets	XX	
Distributions to Beneficiaries	XX	XXX
Balance, End of Period		$ XX

SECOND, AS TO INCOME

I charge myself as follows:

Revenues	$ XX

I credit myself as follows:

Expenses	$XX	
Distributions to Beneficiaries	XX	XX
Balance, End of Period		$ XX

Closing the Estate   Under the Uniform Probate Code, the fiduciary must file a petition with the probate court to close the estate. This may be done no earlier than six months after appointment and not until the time for presenting claims against the estate has expired. In the petition, the personal representative must state that he or she has:

1. Published notice to creditors at least four months prior to the date of the petition.

2. Fully administered the decedent's estate—paid all claims, administration expenses, and taxes (and perhaps distributed certain assets to beneficiaries).

3. Distributed a copy of the petition to all beneficiaries, creditors, and unpaid or barred claimants.

A charge and discharge statement must accompany the petition. Having collected all the decedent's assets, paid the debts, and carried out the appropriate tax duties and responsibilities, the personal representative is ready to prepare the final estate accounting and make the final distribution of the decedent's assets.

Accounting for Principal and Income

Since the personal representative is charged with the responsibility of managing the assets, the accounting system must be based on the concept of accountability for the assets. A significant aspect of estate accounting is the distinction between principal and income.

The Revised Uniform Principal and Income Act, drafted in 1962 and since adopted by twenty states, defines **principal** as the property which has been set aside by the owner or the person legally empowered so that it is held in trust eventually to be delivered to a beneficiary. As a general rule, principal includes any property or rights which the decedent had at date of death. For example, wages earned prior to death, interest receivable at date of death, and dividends receivable declared prior to death are all included in principal, even though payment is not received until later. The act defines **income** as "the return in money or property derived from the use of principal." Thus any earnings on principal assets which arise after the date of death are income. Each transaction of the estate must be analyzed to determine if it affects principal or income. Exhibit 4.2 shows the treatment of various common transactions. Note that certain administrative costs (such as executor's fee, attorney and accountant fees, income taxes) must be allocated between principal and income.

Principal is viewed, according to the Revised Uniform Principal and Income Act, "not as a certain amount of monetary value, but . . . as a certain group of assets which must be capable of isolation from the assets which compose the undistributed net income." Once an item is classified as a principal asset, its character is unaffected by subsequent transactions involving the item. For example, if a principal asset is sold, all proceeds are considered to be part of principal. In other words, gains and losses on sales of principal assets are recorded as principal, *not* as income.

A special aspect of estate accounting is that liabilities are generally not recorded in the accounts. Practice varies somewhat in this regard; two common practices are (1) record no liabilities at all, or (2) record only those liabilities which constitute a lien on specific property, such as a mortgage and accrued interest thereon. Our illustrations follow the second practice.

Estate accounting follows an unusual pattern with respect to the use of cash versus accrual accounting. Assets are accrued at date of death so that the principal of the estate is correctly established. Accruals are also recognized at the final settlement of the estate so that the rights of income beneficiaries are not affected by timing of receipts and payments. During the life of the estate, however, accruals are not recorded; interim charge and discharge statements are presented on a cash basis.

Other than the special accounting characteristics addressed above, estate accounting follows generally accepted accounting principles common to other entities.

Illustration of Estate Accounting   Helen Corbett, a widow with two children (Janice Nelson and William Corbett), died on June 28, 19X1. Helen was seventy-five at the time of her death. In her will, she named her daughter as executrix and specified that she receive 2 percent of the gross estate at time of death as compensation for administering the estate. This compensation was to be in addition to the following specifications in the will:

Janice is to receive the residence. The estate is to pay off the mortgage.

The Society for Prevention of Cruelty to Animals is to receive $5,000 and all income of the estate earned between the date of death and the settlement of the estate.

Exhibit 4.2   Treatment of Some Common Estate Transactions as They Affect Principal or Income

INCREASES IN PRINCIPAL

Subsequent discovery of assets existing at date of death (not included in original inventory)

Gain resulting from disposition of principal assets

CHARGES AGAINST PRINCIPAL

Cost of investing and reinvesting principal

Expenditures incurred in preparing principal property for sale or rent

Costs of administering and preserving the non-income-producing property of the estate (for example, property taxes, repairs, and maintenance)

Extraordinary repairs or permanent improvements

Income taxes on profit, gains, or other receipts allocable to principal (for example, capital gains tax)

Decedent's debts, expenses of last illness, funeral expenses

Fees of executor, estate attorney, and accountant and other administrative costs

Federal estate tax and state inheritance tax

Payment of devises and other distributions of principal

Loss resulting from any changes in the form of principal (sale, destruction, and so on)

INCREASES IN INCOME

Rent on real or personal property

Interest (but premium or discount on debt securities is generally not amortized)

Cash dividends

Business profits

Annuities

Other income earned during administration of decedent's estate

CHARGES AGAINST INCOME

Expenses of administering and preserving the income-producing property of the estate (for example, property taxes, utilities, wages, office expenses, repairs, and maintenance)

Depreciation on assets subject to depreciation under GAAP

Interest on mortgage and other indebtedness

Income taxes on profit, gains, or other receipts allocable to income

Fees of executor, estate attorney, and accountant and other administrative costs

Distributions of income

William is to receive all other assets remaining after the payment of administrative expenses, claims against the estate, mortgage, and the bequest to charity.

The will entered probate proceedings. Janice notified her brother and the Society for the Prevention of Cruelty to Animals of her appointment as executrix.

Soon after Helen Corbett's death, Janice took an inventory of her mother's assets. She valued marketable securities at their quoted prices. The residence and her mother's art collection were appraised to establish value at the date of death. Current values of other items were estimated by Janice.

The entry that follows shows the recording of the inventory. Note (1) that the only liabilities recorded are those with liens against the property and (2) that the cash account is specifically labeled "Principal Cash."

Principal Cash	25,700
Marketable Securities	22,000
Accrued Interest Receivable	250
Residence	84,000
Automobile	2,800
Furniture	3,200
Personal Effects	3,500
Art Collection	12,000
Mortgage Payable (Secured)	23,000
Accrued Interest Payable on Mortgage	140
Estate Principal Balance	130,310

To record inventory.

The Estate Principal Balance account reflects the excess of assets over liens against them. At the time of inventory, all assets are classified as principal assets.

According to the law, Janice published a notice requesting that claims against her mother's estate be filed. She received the following bills: funeral expenses, $2,000; utility bills, $91; charges at a local clothing store, $150; charges at a book store, $30. No entry was made to the accounts of the estate upon receipt of the bills.

Two months after taking the inventory, Janice discovered a cache of commemorative coins worth $6,000 at her mother's home. The discovery was recorded as follows:

Coin Collection	6,000
Assets Subsequently Discovered	6,000

To record discovered assets.

It is important to note that post-inventory discoveries of assets do not affect the Estate Principal Balance. The balance in that account remains intact until closing entries are made after court acceptance of the charge and discharge statement. This treatment enhances the accountability function of the records.

During the period of administration, $320 of dividends and $850 in interest were received by the estate and recorded as follows:

Principal Cash	250
Accrued Interest Receivable	250

To record receipt of interest.

Income Cash	920
Dividend Revenue	320
Interest Revenue	600

To record receipt of interest and dividends.

Janice then paid off the mortgage as indicated below:

Mortgage Payable	23,000
Accrued Interest Payable on Mortgage	140
Principal Cash	23,140

To record settlement of mortgage.

To generate cash needed to meet the remaining claims against the estate and to pay the general devise to the SPCA, marketable securities with a recorded value of $7,000 and the car were sold. Despite its estimated value of $2,800, the car sold for only $2,500. The marketable securities yielded $7,150.

Exhibit 4.3   Charge and Discharge Statement

Estate of Helen Corbett
Janice Nelson, Executrix
Charge and Discharge Statement
For the Period June 28 through December 28, 19X1

FIRST, AS TO PRINCIPAL

I charge myself as follows:

Inventory (Schedule 1)	$130,310	
Assets Subsequently Discovered (Schedule 2)	6,000	
Gain on Disposal of Principal Assets (Schedule 3)	150	$136,460

I credit myself as follows:

Debts of Decedent Paid (Schedule 4)	$ 2,271	
Administrative Expenses	3,189	
Loss on Disposal of Principal Assets (Schedule 5)	300	
Distributions to Beneficiaries (Schedule 6)	130,700	136,460
Balance, December 28, 19X1		$ 0

SECOND, AS TO INCOME

I charge myself as follows:

Dividend Revenue	$ 320	
Interest Revenue	600	$ 920

I credit myself as follows:

Distributions to Beneficiaries (Schedule 6)		920
Balance, December 28, 19X1		$ 0

Principal Cash	2,500	
Loss on Disposal of Principal Assets	300	
Automobile		2,800
To record sale of automobile.		
Principal Cash	7,150	
Marketable Securities		7,000
Gain on Disposal of Principal Assets		150
To record sale of securities.		

Note that any gains or losses on disposals of assets are identified as to the type of asset (principal versus income) involved.

Claims against the estate, including Janice's fee for administering the estate, were paid. Since the coin collection was part of the estate at date of death, its value was included in the calculation of the administrative fee.

Administrative Expenses	3,189	
Debts of Decedent Paid	2,271	
Principal Cash		5,460
To record payment of:		
administrative expenses (2% of $159,450)	$3,189	
funeral expenses	2,000	
various charge accounts	180	
utility bills	91	

After all claims were paid, Janice distributed the assets to the beneficiaries. The entries at the top of page 112 record those distributions.

Exhibit 4.4   Schedules for Charge and Discharge Statement

SCHEDULE 1: INVENTORY OF ASSETS

Cash	$25,700	
Marketable Securities	22,000	
Accrued Interest Receivable	250	
Residence	84,000	
Automobile	2,800	
Furniture	3,200	
Personal Effects	3,500	
Art Collection	12,000	$153,450
Less:		
Mortgage Payable	$23,000	
Accrued Interest Payable	140	23,140
Total Assets		$130,310

SCHEDULE 2: ASSETS SUBSEQUENTLY DISCOVERED

Coin Collection	$ 6,000

SCHEDULE 3: GAIN ON DISPOSAL OF PRINCIPAL ASSETS

Marketable Securities:	
Proceeds of Sale	$ 7,150
Value per Inventory	7,000
Gain on Disposal	$ 150

SCHEDULE 4: DEBTS OF DECEDENT PAID

Funeral Expenses	$ 2,000
Charge Accounts	180
Utility Bills	91
Total Debts Paid	$ 2,271

SCHEDULE 5: LOSS ON DISPOSAL OF PRINCIPAL ASSETS

Automobile:	
Proceeds of Sale	$ 2,500
Value per Inventory	2,800
Loss on Disposal	$ 300

SCHEDULE 6: DISTRIBUTIONS TO BENEFICIARIES

Principal:	
Janice Nelson	$ 84,000
William Corbett	41,700
SPCA	5,000
Total Principal Distributed	$130,700
Income:	
SPCA	$ 920

Distributions to Principal Beneficiaries   5,000
    Principal Cash   5,000
To record distribution of principal cash to the SPCA
according to the specifications of the will.

Distributions to Income Beneficiaries   920
    Income Cash   920
To record distribution of income cash to the SPCA
according to the specifications of the will.

Distributions to Principal Beneficiaries   84,000
    Residence   84,000
To record distribution of residence to Janice Nelson
according to the specifications of the will.

Distributions to Principal Beneficiaries   41,700
    Principal Cash   2,000
    Marketable Securities   15,000
    Furniture   3,200
    Personal Effects   3,500
    Art Collection   12,000
    Coin Collection   6,000
To record distribution of residuary principal assets to
William Corbett according to the specifications of the will.

The books of the estate were closed on December 28, 19X1, as follows:

Estate Principal Balance   130,310
Assets Subsequently Discovered   6,000
Gain on Disposal of Principal Assets   150
Dividend Revenue   320
Interest Revenue   600
    Loss on Disposal of Principal Assets   300
    Debts of Decedent Paid   2,271
    Administrative Expenses   3,189
    Distributions to Principal Beneficiaries   130,700
    Distributions to Income Beneficiaries   920
To close estate.

The charge and discharge statement for Janice Nelson, executrix, appears in Exhibit 4.3 with supporting schedules in Exhibit 4.4.

Estates of Bankrupt Firms	For the purposes of accounting, the bankruptcy of a firm is similar to the death of an individual. In both cases, an estate is created, and a representative is appointed via a legal process to administer the estate on behalf of the beneficiaries. In the case of a deceased individual, an executor or administrator is responsible for distributing assets to heirs in accord with the provisions of a will or intestacy law. In the case of a bankrupt firm, a trustee or receiver is responsible for distributing assets to creditors in accord with the provisions of contracts (security agreements) and bankruptcy law. In both cases, a fiduciary relationship is created, and the accounting procedures and statements are designed to show how the fiduciary responsibilities are met.
Legal Aspects of Bankruptcy	Federal bankruptcy law provides the legal process and remedies for cases of **bankruptcy,** that is, cases where individuals or business firms are unable to

meet their debts, and where either the debtor or the creditors initiate the legal process.

Three different situations are covered in the law. Chapter 7 of the Bankruptcy Reform Act of 1978, which applies to both individuals and firms, provides for liquidation of the debtor's assets in order to pay the creditors. Chapter 11, applying to business firms only, relates to reorganization. **Reorganization** permits the firm to continue to exist, without liquidation of its assets, via a fair plan to modify the rights and interests of both the creditors and the stockholders of the firm. Creditors may prefer reorganization to liquidation because their prospects of collecting what is due them may be better if the company continues to operate than if its assets are sold. Chapter 13 of the Bankruptcy Reform Act is analogous to the chapter on reorganization but applies to an individual debtor having a regular income. Rather than liquidating the debtor's assets, a repayment plan is worked out with creditors. Of these three, the liquidation process of Chapter 7 of the law is what is commonly referred to as *bankruptcy*, and will be the focus of the remainder of this section.

The Legal Process   The legal process begins with the filing of a petition with the federal bankruptcy court, stating that the debtor is unable to meet obligations and requesting that the provisions of the bankruptcy law be applied. If the petition is filed by the debtor, it is called a *voluntary petition;* if filed by creditors, it is called an *involuntary petition.* The law specifies the number of creditors and the amount of obligation to them that is required in order to file an involuntary petition.

The filing of a proper petition imposes an orderly process on the debtor's situation. Individual creditors cannot enforce liens or judgments, or repossess assets of the debtor. Rather, the claims of all creditors will be processed and satisfied, to the extent possible, according to the provisions of the law. The desire to be subject to this orderly process rather than subject to the lawsuits, repossessions, and liens of individual creditors explains why debtors may file a voluntary petition.

The court appoints an interim trustee, who may subsequently be replaced by a permanent trustee elected by the creditors. The trustee takes possession of the debtor's assets, converts them to cash, and distributes cash to creditors in accord with their legal rights and priorities. Usually, the cash is insufficient to pay all debts fully. When all available assets are distributed, the debtor is *discharged,* that is, the debtor is released from all remaining debts except those explicitly not discharged by law.

Financial Reports for a Bankruptcy

The financial reports for a bankruptcy situation fall into two categories. First is an initial report which shows the debts and available asset values of the debtor. This report, known as a **statement of affairs,** is analogous to the initial inventory in estate accounting. Both present assets at fair market value; however, the statement of affairs also includes information on liabilities. The second category is the periodic report of the fiduciary. In estate accounting, the charge and discharge statement showed how the executor had managed the estate assets on behalf of the heirs. In bankruptcy accounting, a **realization and liquidation statement** shows how the *trustee in bankruptcy,* or *receiver,* has managed the assets of the bankrupt firm on behalf of the creditors. These statements will be discussed in subsequent sections.

Statement of Affairs   The statement of affairs is a statement of financial condition of a company entering bankruptcy. Because such a company is no longer a going concern, the usual means of balance sheet valuation are not applicable. Estimated realizable values replace historical costs as the relevant measure of assets.

One purpose of the statement of affairs is to present the liabilities of the firm according to their legal preference. Liabilities are organized into four categories:

1. *Fully-secured liabilities.* For these liabilities, the creditor has a lien on specific assets, and the estimated realizable value of those assets equals or exceeds the amount of the liability. For example, a bank holds a $50,000 mortgage on a building of a bankrupt firm, and the building has an estimated realizable value of $82,000. The mortgage is, therefore, fully secured, and the bank is referred to as a fully-secured creditor.

2. *Partially-secured liabilities.* In other cases, the creditor has a lien on specific assets, but the estimated realizable value of those assets is less than the amount of the liability. For example, a finance company holds a $20,000 note secured by equipment of a bankrupt firm, but the equipment has an estimated realizable value of only $13,000. This note is partially secured, and the finance company is referred to as a partially-secured creditor.

3. *Unsecured liabilities with priority.* When the creditor has no lien on any specific assets of the bankrupt firm, but its claims rank ahead of other unsecured liabilities in order of payment, the claims are considered unsecured liabilities with priority. These liabilities, in order of priority, are:
   a. Administrative expenses of the trustee.
   b. Unpaid wages, up to $2,000 per employee, earned within 90 days prior to the bankruptcy petition.
   c. Obligations to employee benefit plans, up to $2,000 per employee, accrued within 180 days prior to the bankruptcy petition.
   d. Deposits made with the bankrupt firm by consumers for the purchase, lease, or rental of property or services, up to $900 per claimant.
   e. Taxes.

4. *Unsecured liabilities.* All other liabilities for which the creditor has no lien on any specific assets of the bankrupt firm are unsecured. This category includes the unsecured portion of the liability to partially-secured creditors. In our example above, there is a note payable to the finance company for $20,000 secured by equipment worth $13,000; the difference of $7,000 is added to the unsecured liabilities.

A second purpose of the statement of affairs is to present the assets of the firm according to any specific claims against them, and to indicate amounts expected to be available for the unsecured creditors. As mentioned earlier, all assets are valued at their estimated realizable value rather than historical cost. Assets are organized into three categories:

1. *Assets pledged to fully-secured creditors.* Certain assets may be pledged as security for a particular liability, and the estimated realizable value of the assets equals or exceeds the amount of the liability. Such assets may also yield resources to cover unsecured liabilities. The building with an estimated realizable value of $82,000, which secures a $50,000 mortgage liability, is an example of an asset pledged to a fully-secured creditor. After the mortgage is paid, $32,000 remains for unsecured creditors.

2. *Assets pledged to partially-secured creditors.* Other assets that are pledged as security for a particular liability may have estimated realizable value less than the amount of the liability. Partial satisfaction of the liability will consume the entire asset value; nothing will be left for the unsecured liabilities. The equipment with an estimated realizable value of $13,000, which secures a $20,000 note payable, is an example of an asset pledged to a partially-secured creditor.

3. *Free assets.* Assets that are not pledged as security for any particular liability, and thus are available to meet the claims of unsecured creditors, are labeled free assets. This category also includes the value of assets pledged to fully-secured creditors in excess of the related liability. In the example in item 1, $32,000 of the value of the building is included in free assets.

Format of the Statement   The statement of affairs presents assets and liabilities organized into the categories discussed in the preceding section. Secured claims and corresponding assets are offset so that the statement shows the total amount of free assets and the total amount of unsecured liabilities. These two amounts are then compared to show the **estimated deficiency to unsecured creditors**—the amount by which the unsecured liabilities exceed the assets available to pay them.

The liability section of the statement of affairs is structured as follows:

	Creditors' Claims	Unsecured Liabilities
Fully-Secured Creditors:		
(List)	$XX	
Partially-Secured Creditors:		
(List)	$XX	
Less: Value of Pledged Assets	X	$ X
Unsecured Creditors with Priority:		
(List)	$XX	
Unsecured Creditors:		
(List)		X
Total Unsecured Liabilities		$XX

Exhibit 4.5 Format of the Statement of Affairs

X Corporation
Statement of Affairs
Date

Assets

Book Value		Estimated Realizable Value	Free Assets
$ XX	Assets Pledged to Fully-Secured Creditors:		
	(List)	$XX	
	Less: Liabilities to Fully-Secured Creditors		
	(List)	XX	$ X
XX	Assets Pledged to Partially-Secured Creditors:		
	(List)	$XX	
XX	Free Assets:		
	(List)	XX	XX
	Total Free Assets		$XX
	Less: Unsecured Liabilities with Priority		X
	Net Free Assets		$XX
	Estimated Deficiency to Unsecured Creditors		X
$XXX	Total Unsecured Liabilities		$XXX

Liabilities

Book Value		Creditors' Claims	Unsecured Liabilities
$ XX	Fully-Secured Creditors:		
	(List)	$XX	
XX	Partially-Secured Creditors:		
	(List)	$XX	
	Less: Value of Pledged Assets	XX	$ X
X	Unsecured Creditors with Priority:		
	(List)	$ X	
XX	Unsecured Creditors:		
	(List)		XX
XX	Stockholders' Equity		—
$XXX	Total Unsecured Liabilities		$XX

Note that the total of the unsecured liabilities consists of the obligations to unsecured creditors plus the obligations to partially-secured creditors in excess of the value of pledged assets. Observe also that the unsecured liabilities with priority are included under Creditors' Claims but not in the total of Unsecured Liabilities.

The asset section of the statement of affairs is structured as follows:

	Estimated Realizable Value	Free Assets
Assets Pledged to Fully-Secured Creditors:		
(List)	$XX	
Less: Amount of Liability	X	$ X
Assets Pledged to Partially-Secured Creditors:		
(List)	$XX	
Free Assets:		
(List)		X
Total Free Assets		$XX
Less: Unsecured Liabilities with Priority		XX
Net Free Assets		$ X
Estimated Deficiency to Unsecured Creditors		X
Total Unsecured Liabilities		$XX

We see that the total free assets consist of the value of unpledged assets plus the value of assets pledged to fully-secured creditors in excess of the amount of the related liability. The estimated deficiency to unsecured creditors reconciles the difference between the amount of net free assets and the amount of unsecured liabilities, making the statement balance.

This simple format focuses on the key aspects of bankruptcy reporting. In practice, somewhat more complex formats may be employed. For example, book values are generally presented on the statement of affairs along with the estimated realizable values. As we have discussed, estimated realizable values are most important because the company is no longer a going concern and we wish to present information relating to the status of the various classes of creditors. However, book values are also useful, since they tie the statement of affairs to the balance sheet and, when compared to the estimated realizable values, indicate the expected gains or losses upon liquidation. Thus, the statement of affairs commonly appears in the format shown in Exhibit 4.5.

Illustration of Statement of Affairs   Bristol Corporation is entering bankruptcy proceedings on October 31, 19X4. Its balance sheet on that date shows the information at the top of page 118.

Note that, as in this example, a firm may enter into bankruptcy even though it has positive stockholders' equity. The key factor is that the firm is unable to meet its debt obligations. For example, when the Penn Central Railroad entered bankruptcy proceedings in 1970, its last annual report showed retained earnings of $495 million, and stockholders' equity of $1.8 billion. Nevertheless, the company's liquid assets were inadequate to meet its current obligations, and bankruptcy resulted.

Bristol Corp.
Balance Sheet
October 31, 19X4

ASSETS		LIABILITIES AND STOCKHOLDERS' EQUITY	
Cash	$ 4,000	Accounts Payable	$134,000
Marketable Securities	7,000	Loan Payable	100,000
Accounts Receivable	27,000	Equipment Note Payable	30,000
Inventory	63,000	Accrued Wages	41,000
Land	15,000	Taxes Payable	12,000
Building	135,000	Mortgage Payable	94,000
Equipment	163,000	Stockholders' Equity	14,000
Deferred Charges	11,000	Total Liabilities and	
		Stockholders'	
Total Assets	$425,000	Equity	$425,000

It is estimated that Bristol Corporation's assets have the following realizable values:

Cash	$ 4,000
Marketable Securities	9,000
Accounts Receivable	20,000
Inventory	44,000
Land and Building	190,000
Equipment	63,900
Deferred Charges	0
	$330,900

The receivables and inventory are pledged as security for the $100,000 loan; the land and building are pledged as security for the mortgage. The $30,000 equipment note payable is secured by a machine having an estimated realizable value of $22,000 (and a book value of $20,000).

The statement of affairs for Bristol is shown in Exhibit 4.6. The statement shows net free assets of $97,900 and unsecured liabilities of $178,000, resulting in an estimated deficiency to unsecured creditors of $80,100. This information can be converted into an **expected recovery percentage** for unsecured creditors:

$$\text{Expected recovery percentage} = \frac{\text{Net free assets}}{\text{Unsecured liabilities}}$$

$$= \frac{\$97,900}{\$178,000}$$

$$= 55\%.$$

In other words, unsecured creditors can expect to receive 55 cents per dollar owed to them by the bankrupt firm. Fully-secured creditors, of course, receive the full amount owed them, as do (typically) the unsecured creditors with priority. The partially-secured creditors receive less than 100 percent, but more than the percentage received by unsecured creditors. For the two partially-

Exhibit 4.6   Statement of Affairs for Bristol Corp.

Bristol Corp.
Statement of Affairs
October 31, 19X4

Book Value		Estimated Realizable Value	Free Assets
	Assets Pledged to Fully-Secured Creditors:		
$150,000	Land and Building	$190,000	
	Less: Mortgage Payable	94,000	$ 96,000
	Assets Pledged to Partially-Secured Creditors:		
27,000	Accounts Receivable	$ 20,000	
63,000	Inventory	44,000	
20,000	Equipment	22,000	
		$ 86,000	
	Free Assets:		
4,000	Cash	$ 4,000	
7,000	Marketable Securities	9,000	
143,000	Equipment	41,900	
11,000	Deferred Charges	0	54,900
	Total Free Assets		$150,900
	Less: Unsecured Liabilities with Priority . .		53,000
	Net Free Assets		$ 97,900
	Estimated Deficiency to Unsecured Creditors .		80,100
$425,000	Total Unsecured Liabilities		$178,000

Book Value		Creditors' Claims	Unsecured Liabilities
	Fully-Secured Creditors:		
$ 94,000	Mortgage Payable	$ 94,000	
	Partially-Secured Creditors:		
100,000	Loan Payable	$100,000	
	Less: Value of Accounts Receivable and		
	Inventory	64,000	$ 36,000
30,000	Equipment Note Payable	$ 30,000	
	Less: Value of Machine	22,000	8,000
	Unsecured Creditors with Priority:		
41,000	Accrued Wages	$ 41,000	
12,000	Taxes Payable	12,000	
		$ 53,000	
	Unsecured Creditors:		
134,000	Accounts Payable		134,000
14,000	Stockholders' Equity		
$425,000	Total Unsecured Liabilities		$178,000

secured creditors in our example, we may calculate the recovery as follows:

```
Loan Payable of $100,000:
    Secured Portion (Full Recovery)
        Value of Pledged Assets  .  .  .  .  .  .  .  .  .  .      $64,000
    Unsecured Portion (Partial Recovery)
        $36,000 × 55%   .  .  .  .  .  .  .  .  .  .  .  .         19,800
                Total Recovery .  .  .  .  .  .  .  .  .  .        $83,800

Equipment Note Payable of $30,000:
    Secured Portion (Full Recovery)
        Value of Pledged Asset   .  .  .  .  .  .  .  .  .  .      $22,000
    Unsecured Portion (Partial Recovery)
        $8,000 × 55% .  .  .  .  .  .  .  .  .  .  .  .  .          4,400
                Total Recovery .  .  .  .  .  .  .  .  .  .        $26,400
```

Thus the loan creditor will recover 83.8 percent (= $83,800/$100,000), and the equipment note creditor will recover 88 percent (= $26,400/$30,000).

Realization and Liquidation Statement   The realization and liquidation statement provides a complete record of the transactions of the receiver for a period of time. Its structure is similar to a T account, and it is composed of three elements: asset transactions, liability transactions, and income/loss transactions. First, consider the structure of T accounts for assets and liabilities. A completed and balanced T account appears as follows:

Asset Account

Beginning balance	100	70	Decreases
Increases	50	80	Ending balance
	150	150	

Liability Account

Decreases	40	60	Beginning balance
Ending balance	50	30	Increases
	90	90	

We now apply this structure to the activities of the receiver. One task of the receiver is to **realize the assets,** that is, to convert the noncash assets into cash so that creditors may be paid. The process of realization may take several forms. Certain activities of the firm may continue in operation, providing cash or other assets. Some assets may be realized via normal business operations, such as the continuing collection of receivables from customers. Other assets may be realized via sale. Since the receiver is to act in the interest of the creditors, he or she must select the means of realization which will provide the best return to the creditors. As a result, the realization process may extend over a considerable period of time. During this time, gains and losses on asset sales may occur, expenses may be incurred, and revenues may be earned. The realization activities may be described in T account format as follows:

Assets (Other Than Cash)

Beginning Balance: Assets to be realized	Decreases: Assets realized
Increases: Assets acquired	Ending Balance: Assets not realized

Income Effect of Realization

Expenses and losses	Revenues and gains

The second task of the receiver is to **liquidate the liabilities,** that is, to arrange full or partial settlement with the creditors. Again, gains or losses may occur in the process of liquidation, as may expenses or revenues. The liquidation activities may also be described in T account format as follows:

Liabilities

Decreases: Liabilities liquidated Ending Balance: Liabilities not liquidated	Beginning Balance: Liabilities to be liquidated Increases: Liabilities incurred

Income Effect of Liquidation

Expenses and losses	Revenues and gains

Accounting for Realization and Liquidation Activities   To prepare a realization and liquidation statement, the asset and liability accounts must be structured in a way that segregates the gain or loss. Consider first an asset account, which is structured as follows:

Assets (Other Than Cash)

Assets to be realized Assets acquired	Assets realized Assets not realized

Suppose that inventory having a book value of $100,000 is to be realized. Assume that a portion of the inventory, having a book value of $30,000, is sold for $12,000. Following the above format, the account would indicate that $30,000 of inventory has been realized, and $70,000 remains to be realized.

Inventory

Assets to be realized	100,000	30,000	Assets realized
Assets acquired	0	70,000	Assets not realized
	100,000	100,000	

In addition, there would be a debit to Cash of $12,000 and a debit to Loss of $18,000.

The inventory account could be restructured to show that the $30,000 of inventory that was realized resulted in $12,000 of cash and an $18,000 loss. In this case, the account would appear as:

Inventory

Assets to be realized	100,000	12,000	Assets realized (proceeds)
Assets acquired	0	18,000	Assets realized (loss)
		70,000	Assets not realized
	100,000	100,000	

If the inventory with a book value of $30,000 had been sold for $35,000, the $30,000 of assets realized would be shown as $35,000 of proceeds and a $5,000 gain as follows:

Inventory

Assets to be realized	100,000	35,000	Assets realized (proceeds)
Assets acquired	0	70,000	Assets not realized
Assets realized (gain)	5,000		
	105,000	105,000	

Note that the gain appears on the debit side, and that the balance in the account is maintained. In other words, the $30,000 retirement of inventory appears as $35,000 of proceeds less the $5,000 gain. In addition, there would be a debit to Cash of $35,000 and a credit to Gain of $5,000.

Similar considerations exist for the liability accounts. The general structure is:

Liabilities

Liabilities liquidated		Liabilities to be liquidated
Liabilities not liquidated		Liabilities incurred

Suppose that notes payable of $73,000 exist, and that the holder of a $20,000 note accepts $16,000 in full settlement. Following the above format, we have:

Notes Payable

Liabilities liquidated	20,000	73,000	Liabilities to be liquidated
Liabilities not liquidated	53,000	0	Liabilities incurred
	73,000	73,000	

We may replace the $20,000 book value of liabilities liquidated with the information that this liability was settled for an actual payment of $16,000, resulting in a $4,000 gain. We then have:

Notes Payable

Liabilities liquidated (payment)	16,000	73,000	Liabilities to be liquidated
Liabilities liquidated (gain)	4,000	0	Liabilities incurred
Liabilities not liquidated	53,000		
	73,000	73,000	

There would also be a credit to Cash of $16,000 and a credit to Gain of $4,000. It would be rare for a liability to be liquidated at a loss. Should this occur, however, the loss would appear on the credit side of the account.

Revenues and expenses (as distinct from gains and losses) usually arise from acquisition of assets or incurrence of liabilities. For example, if interest of $500 is accrued on notes receivable, we would record the following entries (the revenue and expense T accounts are presented in conventional, rather than balance, format):

Interest Receivable

Assets acquired	500	500	Assets not realized

Revenues

		500	Interest

Similarly, if administrative expenses of $1,800 were incurred by the receiver, but not paid, we record:

Accrued Administrative Expenses			
Liabilities not liquidated	1,800	1,800	Liabilities incurred

Expenses	
Administrative	1,800

The Realization and Liquidation Statement Format   The general structure of the realization and liquidation statement follows from the expanded format of the asset and liability accounts discussed in the preceding section. Various formats are found in practice; Exhibit 4.7 shows one possibility. Note that certain accounts are excluded from the statement:

1.   The Cash account.
2.   Revenues and Expenses.
3.   The income accounts for gains and losses.
4.   The Equity account.

A balance sheet and a statement of estate deficit should accompany the realization and liquidation statement. The balance sheet of the trustee has the following format:

BALANCE SHEET

Cash	Liabilities Not Liquidated
Assets Not Realized	Estate Deficit

The statement of estate deficit shows the revenues, expenses, gains and losses for a period, resulting in a net change in the estate deficit. It is analogous to a statement of income and retained earnings of a going concern. One possible format of this statement is shown below:

STATEMENT OF ESTATE DEFICIT

Revenues	$X	
Gains	X	$XX
Expenses	$X	
Losses	X	XX
Net Change in Estate Deficit		$ X
Estate Deficit—Beginning of Period		X
Estate Deficit—End of Period		$XX

One question which arises for a firm in receivership or bankruptcy is whether depreciation should be recognized. A reasonable answer is that if the firm is continuing to carry on operations, recognition of depreciation is appropriate to measure the results of operations. If little or no operating activities are being conducted—that is, the assets are being sold and liabilities settled—no depreciation charges should be made.

Exhibit 4.7 Format of Realization and Liquidation Statement

X Corporation
(Name of Receiver or Trustee)
Realization and Liquidation Statement
(Time Period Covered)

Assets to Be Realized:	Assets Realized:
(List and amounts)	(List and amounts)
Assets Acquired:	Assets Not Realized:
(List and amounts)	(List and amounts)
Liabilities Liquidated:	Liabilities to Be Liquidated:
(List and amounts)	(List and amounts)
Liabilities Not Liquidated:	Liabilities Incurred:
(List and amounts)	(List and amounts)
Gain on Realization or Liquidation	Loss on Realization or Liquidation:
Combined Total	Combined Total

Illustration Joanne Willis is appointed trustee of the Weeks Corporation, which is in bankruptcy. Her responsibilities are to administer the firm's estate, to realize the assets, and to liquidate the liabilities. At the time of her appointment, the company's balance sheet appears as follows:

Weeks Corporation
Balance Sheet
March 31, 19X3

Cash	$ 1,000	Accounts Payable	$27,000
Accounts Receivable	6,000	Accrued Wages	5,000
Inventories	11,000	Notes Payable	40,000
Equipment, Net	35,000	Stockholders' Equity	(19,000)
	$53,000		$53,000

The accounts payable and notes payable are unsecured.

Willis takes custody of the company's assets. A statement of affairs would be prepared to show the estimated realizable values of the company's assets, and the estimated recovery by each class of creditors. Willis must then establish accounting records for herself as trustee. Her initial entry records, at book value, the assets and liabilities which she is administering:

Cash	1,000	
Accounts Receivable	6,000	
Inventories	11,000	
Equipment	35,000	
Estate Deficit	19,000	
Accounts Payable		27,000
Accrued Wages		5,000
Notes Payable		40,000

To record assets and liabilities of Weeks Corporation.

Suppose that during the following three months, the following transactions occur:

1. A total of $3,300 is received in settlement of $5,000 of accounts receivable; the remaining $1,000 is expected to be collectible.
2. Inventory items having a book value of $8,000 are sold for $6,400.
3. A machine with a book value of $7,000 is sold for $12,000.
4. The accrued wages are paid.
5. Administrative expenses of $4,000 are accrued.
6. An initial payment of twenty cents per dollar of indebtedness is made to the unsecured creditors.

The trustee records these transactions as follows:

1.	Cash	3,300	
	Loss on Realization	1,700	
	Accounts Receivable		5,000
	To record collection of receivables.		
2.	Cash	6,400	
	Loss on Realization	1,600	
	Inventory		8,000
	To record sale of inventory.		
3.	Cash	12,000	
	Equipment		7,000
	Gain on Realization		5,000
	To record sale of machine.		
4.	Accrued Wages	5,000	
	Cash		5,000
	To record payment of wages.		
5.	Administrative Expenses	4,000	
	Accrued Expenses		4,000
	To accrue expenses of trustee.		
6.	Accounts Payable	5,400	
	Notes Payable	8,000	
	Cash		13,400
	To record partial payment of 20% of amount due to unsecured creditors.		

T accounts reflecting the initial entry and the six transaction entries are shown in Exhibit 4.8. The credits for assets realized are broken down between proceeds (coded P) and gain or loss (coded G or L). The T accounts enclosed in the box represent the information which will appear on the realization and liquidation statement. This statement is presented in Exhibit 4.9, on page 128.

The trustee's balance sheet and statement of estate deficit at June 30, 19X3, would appear as:

Weeks Corporation
Joanne Willis, Trustee
Balance Sheet
June 30, 19X3

Cash	$ 4,300		Accounts Payable	$21,600
Accounts Receivable	1,000		Notes Payable	32,000
Inventory	3,000		Accrued Expenses	4,000
Equipment	28,000		Estate Deficit	(21,300)
	$36,300			$36,300

Weeks Corporation
Joanne Willis, Trustee
Statement of Estate Deficit
June 30, 19X3

Gain on Realization			$ 5,000
Loss on Realization		$3,300	
Administrative Expenses		4,000	7,300
Net Change in Estate Deficit			$ (2,300)
Estate Deficit—March 31, 19X3			(19,000)
Estate Deficit—June 30, 19X3			$(21,300)

Trusts

A **trust** is an entity established by a legal process to hold and manage assets on behalf of beneficiaries. Trusts are widely used for a variety of purposes. All have certain common characteristics:

1. A *donor* or *grantor* transfers assets to the trust.

2. A *trust agreement* sets forth the purposes of the trust, the duration of the trust, the identification of the beneficiaries, the identification of (or the process for appointing) the trustee, and other relevant matters.

3. A *trustee* is appointed to take possession of the assets, to manage the assets, and to make distributions to beneficiaries.

4. One or more *beneficiaries* are identified, who are entitled to receive the income and the principal of the trust.

Types of Trusts

Despite the variety of origins and purposes for trusts, three major types of trusts can be identified. Each type has special accounting characteristics. For convenience, we label these types as personal trusts, public trusts, and group trusts.

Personal Trusts   Individuals create **personal trusts** for the benefit of other individuals. For example, an individual's will may provide for the establishment of a trust for the spouse, children, or others. Such a trust, created by will to be effective at the grantor's death, is known as a *testamentary trust*. Another example is a *living trust*, also called an *inter vivos trust*, which takes effect while the grantor is living. In both cases, the trust usually has a limited life (for example, for a spouse's lifetime or until a child reaches age twenty-one). The individual(s) who will periodically receive the trust's income is known as an *income beneficiary* or *life tenant*. The individual(s) who will receive the trust's principal, typically at the end of the trust's life, is known as a *principal beneficiary* or *remainderman*. In some cases, the income beneficiary and principal beneficiary are different individuals. For example, a man may create a testamentary trust, providing that his widow receive the income of the trust during her lifetime, and upon her death the principal be distributed to their children.

Personal trusts follow principles of fiduciary accounting similar to those discussed earlier for estates of individuals. The distinction between principal and

Exhibit 4.8   Accounts for Realization and Liquidation Activities

	Cash		
B	1,000	5,000	(4)
(1)	3,300	13,400	(6)
(2)	6,400		
(3)	12,000		

ASSETS TO BE REALIZED

Accounts Receivable				Inventory				Equipment			
B	6,000	3,300	P (1)	B	11,000	6,400	P (2)	B	35,000	12,000	P (3)
		1,700	L (1)			1,600	L (2)	G (3)	5,000	28,000	E
		1,000	E			3,000	E		40,000	40,000	
	6,000	6,000			11,000	11,000					

LIABILITIES TO BE LIQUIDATED

Accounts Payable				Accrued Wages			
(6)	5,400	27,000	B	(4)	5,000	5,000	B
E	21,600			E	0		
	27,000	27,000			5,000	5,000	

Notes Payable				Accrued Expenses			
(6)	8,000	40,000	B	E	4,000	4,000	(5)
E	32,000						
	40,000	40,000					

Administrative Expenses		Gain on Realization	
(5) 4,000		5,000	(3)

Loss on Realization		Estate Deficit	
(1) 1,700		B 19,000	
(2) 1,600			

Legend:
B = Beginning balance.
E = Ending balance.
P = Proceeds from realization.
G = Gain on realization.
L = Loss on realization.
Numbers in parentheses correspond to numbered journal entries in the text.

income is important, since different beneficiaries may exist. The financial report of the trustee may take the form of a charge and discharge statement, as was illustrated earlier. Alternatively, a **statement of trust principal** and a **statement of trust income** may be presented. The format of these two statements is shown in Exhibits 4.10 and 4.11, respectively.

Exhibit 4.9   Realization and Liquidation Statement

Weeks Corporation
Joanne Willis, Trustee
Realization and Liquidation Statement
For the Three Months Ended
June 30, 19X3

Assets to Be Realized:			Assets Realized:		
Accounts Receivable .	$ 6,000		Accounts Receivable .	$ 3,300	
Inventory	11,000		Inventory	6,400	
Equipment . . .	35,000	$ 52,000	Equipment . . .	12,000	$ 21,700
Assets Acquired:			Assets Not Realized:		
None		0	Accounts Receivable .	$ 1,000	
			Inventory	3,000	
			Equipment . . .	28,000	32,000
Liabilities Liquidated:			Liabilities to Be Liquidated:		
Accounts Payable . .	$ 5,400		Accounts Payable . .	$27,000	
Accrued Wages . .	5,000		Accrued Wages . .	5,000	
Notes Payable . .	8,000	18,400	Notes Payable . .	40,000	72,000
Liabilities Not Liquidated:			Liabilities Incurred:		
Accounts Payable . .	$21,600		Accrued Expenses . .		4,000
Notes Payable . .	32,000				
Accrued Expenses .	4,000	57,600			
Gain on Realization . .		5,000	Loss on Realization . .		3,300
Combined Total . .		$133,000	Combined Total . .		$133,000

Public Trusts   **Public trusts** are established for the benefit of a public beneficiary, that is, an institution, a group, an activity, or a cause, not one or more
specific individuals. Some examples of public trusts include:

1. A wealthy alumnus of a university establishes a trust which provides
   annual income to support athletic programs.

2. An individual establishes a trust which provides funds to be spent for
   scientific research on solar energy.

3. An individual establishes a trust which provides funds to be spent in
   support of wildlife preservation in Alaska.

These trusts are often known as *charitable trusts* or *foundations*. While typically created and endowed by individuals, these entities sometimes expand in size
and scope, generating additional resources from public contributions, government grants, and other sources.

Public trusts differ from personal trusts in several ways. A public trust usually has an indefinite life, while the life of a personal trust is limited. A public
trust is likely to be managed by a board of directors rather than a single trustee.
And, as mentioned above, a public trust benefits a group, activity, or cause,
while a personal trust has specific individual beneficiaries selected by the
grantor.

Exhibit 4.10   Format of Statement of Trust Principal

Identification of Trust
Name of Trustee
Statement of Trust Principal
For the Period January 1, 19X1, to December 31, 19X1

Trust Principal, January 1, 19X1	
(Detailed list)	$ XX
Increases	
(Detailed list)	XX
	$XXX
Decreases	
(Detailed list)	XX
Trust Principal, December 31, 19X1	$ XX

(A schedule showing the assets which make up the ending balance would be attached.)

Exhibit 4.11   Format of Statement of Trust Income

Identification of Trust
Name of Trustee
Statement of Trust Income
For the Period January 1, 19X1, to December 31, 19X1

Undistributed Trust Income, January 1, 19X1	$ X
Revenues	
(Detailed list)	X
	$XX
Expenses and Distributions	
(Detailed list)	X
Undistributed Trust Income, December 31, 19X1	$ X

(A schedule showing the assets which make up the ending balance would be attached.)

Public trusts may follow principles of fiduciary accounting. The distinction between principal and income continues to be important, but not for the reason that different beneficiaries are likely to exist. Rather, the trust agreement may provide for the principal to be maintained indefinitely and for only the income to be expended. In the case of public trusts which expand into larger, broadly supported entities, the accounting practices and reports are likely to be similar to those for nonprofit organizations (a topic discussed in Chapter 18).

Group Trusts   Group trusts are established by firms or other entities for the benefit of individuals who belong to a specified group. Some examples include:

1. A professional association establishes an insurance trust for its members. The association collects premiums from its members who desire coverage and purchases group policies from insurance companies.

2. A brokerage firm establishes an investment trust. It solicits investments and acquires a particular type of assets. Municipal bond trusts and real estate investment trusts are common examples.

3.   A firm establishes a pension trust for its employees. The firm contributes an amount (usually specified by a complex formula) to the trust each year. Contributions from the employees may also be required or permitted. The trust invests these resources and pays benefits to retired employees in accord with the provisions of the pension plan.

Group trusts typically have an unlimited life, and the trustee is often an institution (a bank, an insurance company, a brokerage house, or a professional association) rather than one or more individuals.

In accounting for group trusts, the distinction between principal and income is usually not important. All resources are combined and used for the specific purpose of the trust. A balance sheet and a statement of increases and decreases in the total capital of the trust are the common financial statements.

Summary of Key Concepts	**Fiduciary accounting** relates to entities which exist to hold and manage assets on behalf of others. **Estates of individuals, estates of bankrupt firms,** and **trusts** are the major entities to which fiduciary accounting applies.

Legal considerations, especially the distinction between **principal** and **income,** are important in fiduciary accounting.

In the case of **estates of individuals,** an **executor** or **administrator** takes charge of the decedent's assets, pays claims against the estate, and makes distributions to beneficiaries. The **charge and discharge statement** details, for both principal and income, the assets under the fiduciary's control and the disposition of those assets.

In the case of **bankrupt firms,** a **statement of affairs** is prepared to show the financial condition of the company. Assets are valued at **estimated realizable value** and are classified according to any security interests held by creditors. Liabilities are classified according to their **legal preference.** The statement shows the **estimated deficiency to unsecured creditors.**

The **statement of realization and liquidation** details the activities of the **receiver** or **trustee** in administering the estate of the bankrupt firm.

In the case of **trusts,** accounting and reporting depend upon the nature of the trust. Accounting for **personal trusts** is similar to accounting for estates of individuals. Accounting for **public trusts** and **group trusts** is usually similar to accounting for nonprofit organizations.

Appendix to Chapter 4

Estate Planning and Taxation

In addition to accounting and reporting for estates, accountants also participate in estate planning and determination of estate taxes. Both are complex topics requiring considerable study; this appendix only touches on a few major aspects of these subjects.

Estate planning may be described as a process by which an individual (1) provides for the transfer of assets to desired beneficiaries and (2) attempts to reduce taxes on the transfers. The first objective—directing assets to desired beneficiaries—can be accomplished in several ways:

1. A *will* should be prepared which specifies the disposition of the individual's property at death. If no will exists, state intestacy laws govern the distribution of property.

2. *Gifts* may be made during the individual's lifetime.

3. *Trusts* may be established, either during the individual's lifetime or at death, to hold assets on behalf of beneficiaries. There are many forms of trusts, as will be discussed later in this appendix.

By these and other means, an individual's assets are transferred, either during life or at death, to desired beneficiaries.

The second objective of estate planning is to minimize the tax cost of this transfer of assets. **Gift taxes** apply to transfers of property during the individual's lifetime, and **estate taxes** apply to transfers at death. Minimizing gift and estate taxes involves planning the timing and form of the transfer of assets.

Estate and Gift Taxation

The federal estate tax and gift tax are both taxes on the transfer of property from one individual to another. These taxes are imposed on the transferor, not on the recipient, of the property. That is, the giver is responsible for paying the gift tax, and the estate of a decedent is responsible for paying the estate tax. On the other hand, some state inheritance taxes are imposed on the recipient.

The estate and gift taxes are *unified*, that is, the same rate schedule applies to both types of transfers. The tax rates currently range from 18 to 70 percent, as shown in Exhibit 4.12. These rates are scheduled to decrease so that, by

Exhibit 4.12   Federal Estate and Gift Tax Rates

Amount Subject to Tax		Amount of Tax	
At Least	But Less Than		
$ 0	$ 10,000	18% of taxable amount	
10,000	20,000	$ 1,800 + 20% of excess over $	10,000
20,000	40,000	3,800 + 22% of excess over	20,000
40,000	60,000	8,200 + 24% of excess over	40,000
60,000	80,000	13,000 + 26% of excess over	60,000
80,000	100,000	18,200 + 28% of excess over	80,000
100,000	150,000	23,800 + 30% of excess over	100,000
150,000	250,000	38,800 + 32% of excess over	150,000
250,000	500,000	70,800 + 34% of excess over	250,000
500,000	750,000	155,800 + 37% of excess over	500,000
750,000	1,000,000	248,300 + 39% of excess over	750,000
1,000,000	1,250,000	345,800 + 41% of excess over	1,000,000
1,250,000	1,500,000	448,300 + 43% of excess over	1,250,000
1,500,000	2,000,000	555,800 + 45% of excess over	1,500,000
2,000,000	2,500,000	780,800 + 49% of excess over	2,000,000
2,500,000	3,000,000	1,025,800 + 53% of excess over	2,500,000[a]
3,000,000	3,500,000	1,290,800 + 57% of excess over	3,000,000[b]
3,500,000	4,000,000	1,575,800 + 61% of excess over	3,500,000[c]
4,000,000	4,500,000	1,880,800 + 65% of excess over	4,000,000[c]
4,500,000	5,000,000	2,205,800 + 69% of excess over	4,500,000[d]
5,000,000		2,550,800 + 70% of excess over	5,000,000[d]

NOTES
a. Rate drops to 50% in 1985.
b. Rate drops to 55% in 1984 and 50% in 1985.
c. Rate drops to 60% in 1983, 55% in 1984, and 50% in 1985.
d. Rate drops to 65% in 1982, 60% in 1983, 55% in 1984, and 50% in 1985.

Source: Internal Revenue Code, Section 2001(c).

1985, the highest rate will be 50 percent. The tax base is *cumulative*, that is, the tax is based on the aggregate amount of taxable transfers to date, including both taxable gifts during one's lifetime and the amount of the taxable estate.

Transfers Subject to Tax

Estate and gift taxes are generally based on the fair market value of the property at time of transfer. Transfers of property by gift are generally subject to the gift tax, with the following major exceptions:

1. Gifts to charity.
2. Gifts of $10,000 or less. This exclusion applies *annually* to each recipient. In other words, an individual may give up to $10,000 per year to each of an unlimited number of recipients without incurring a gift tax.
3. Gifts to a spouse are subject to an unlimited *marital deduction*.

Determining the amount of an estate subject to tax is considerably more complex. The gross estate consists of the value of all property which the decedent owned or possessed an interest in at time of death. In addition to property such as cash, securities, real estate, and automobiles, other property is also included in the decedent's gross estate, such as:

1. Life insurance, even though payable directly to a beneficiary, if the decedent possessed rights of ownership of the policy (for example, the right to cancel the policy or to change the beneficiary).

2. Value of decedent's pension and annuity benefits which will be paid to a beneficiary.

To determine the taxable amount of the estate, the gross estate is then reduced by the following deductions:

1. Funeral expenses.

2. Administrative expenses of the estate.

3. Debts of the decedent.

4. Losses of estate property due to casualty or theft during the period of administration.

5. A marital deduction for property which passes to the surviving spouse. After January 1, 1982, this deduction has no maximum.

6. Transfers or bequests to qualified charitable organizations.

7. Where no surviving spouse exists, an orphan's exclusion for each child under age twenty-one equal to $5,000 times the number of years to the child's twenty-first birthday.

Calculation of Tax

The taxable amount of gifts or taxable estate are subject to the rates shown in Exhibit 4.12. As mentioned earlier, the tax base is the cumulative amount of transfers. To determine the tax on a current transfer, the tax on all transfers to date is calculated, and the tax applicable to previous transfers is then deducted. For example, assume an individual who has previously made taxable gifts of $470,000 now makes a taxable gift of $80,000. The tax on the current gift is calculated as follows, using the rates in Exhibit 4.12:

Tax on Cumulative Gifts of $550,000 [$155,800 + (37% × $50,000)] . .	$174,300
Tax on Prior Gifts of $470,000 [$70,800 + (34% × $220,000)]	145,600
Tax on Current Gift of $80,000	$ 28,700

A lifetime tax credit of $47,000 currently exists, which is applied to gift and estate taxes until consumed. As can be verified from the rate schedule, this credit offsets the tax on the first $175,625 of taxable transfers. This credit increases to $62,800 in 1982, $79,300 in 1983, $96,300 in 1984, $121,800 in 1985, $155,800 in 1986, and $192,800 in 1987. By 1987, the credit will offset the tax on the first $600,000 of taxable transfers. Subsequent illustrations and end-of-chapter problems assume the $47,000 credit.

Illustration   George Johnson died on July 17, 19X5, leaving half his estate to his wife. The gross estate amounted to $730,000. The estate paid funeral expenses, administrative costs, and debts of the decedent in the amount of $53,000. George had made taxable gifts of $75,000 five years ago but, by applying a portion of his lifetime credit, had paid no gift tax. The calculation of the estate tax is:

Gross Estate	$730,000
Expenses	53,000
Adjusted Gross Estate	$677,000
Marital Deduction	338,500
Taxable Estate	$338,500
Previous Taxable Transfers	75,000
Cumulative Taxable Transfers	$413,500
Tax on Cumulative Transfers of $413,500 [$70,800 + (34% × $163,500)]	$126,390
Tax on Prior Transfers of $75,000 [$13,000 + (26% × $15,000)]	16,900
Estate Tax before Credit	$109,490
Less Credit ($47,000 less $16,900 applied to gift tax in prior years)	(30,100)
Estate Tax	$ 79,390

Estate Planning

Estate planning is a process whereby an individual plans for the transfer of property to beneficiaries, either during life or at death, in a way that accomplishes a number of objectives, such as:

1. Providing sufficient availability of assets to meet the individual's lifetime needs.

2. Minimizing income taxes during the individual's lifetime.

3. Minimizing estate taxes, both at the time of the individual's death and at the time of beneficiaries' deaths.

In the following sections, we briefly discuss a number of factors involved in estate planning.

Transfers During Life

The transfer of assets to beneficiaries during an individual's lifetime may be desirable for several reasons. If the individual's expected future needs are well provided for, lifetime transfers may satisfy personal objectives such as helping one's children to buy a home or begin a business. Income tax reductions will occur if the recipients are in lower tax brackets than the donor. Savings on gift and estate taxes may occur but are limited by the cumulative nature of the tax. However, the $10,000 annual exclusion does permit tax savings where transfers occur in small amounts over a period of time.

One form of transfer during life is outright gift, which permanently and irrevocably transfers ownership. Gifts are typically made to immediate family members, such as spouse or children. For example, if most of a couple's property is acquired and owned by the husband, gifts to his wife will reduce the disparity in their estates and may lead to lower total estate taxes.

Another form of transfer during life, which may be permanent or temporary, is the *inter vivos trust*. Various forms of inter vivos trusts exist. *Revocable trusts* exist at the pleasure of the grantor. There are no tax advantages to such trusts; the income is taxed to the grantor, and the trust property is included in the grantor's estate. Thus, revocable trusts are usually created for nontax reasons, some of which are relevant to estate planning. The trust assets do not go through probate, thus reducing delays and costs. Also, since wills are public documents when they are brought to probate court, while trusts are not, the use of a trust as a "will substitute" results in increased privacy. The trust assets are protected from creditors of the estate and may also be protected from control by a legal guardian should the donor become incapacitated. Finally, the trust (especially if in existence for some time) is less likely to be challenged by heirs, as a will might be. These nontax advantages, which apply to any form of inter vivos trust, are often desirable in an estate plan.

Irrevocable trusts are permanent dispositions of property. Once an irrevocable trust is established, the income is no longer taxed to the grantor, and the trust property is excluded from the grantor's estate (except that the rule covering gifts within three years of death continues to apply). Transfer of property to an irrevocable trust constitutes a gift, and thus a gift tax obligation may be incurred. The advantage of transfer to an irrevocable trust over a direct gift to the beneficiary is that control is provided over the beneficiary's access to the principal.

An intermediate type of trust, which has some characteristics of both revocable and irrevocable trusts, is a trust for a fixed period of time. Commonly referred to as *Clifford trusts*, these have become popular in estate planning in recent years. The trust must be established for a fixed term of at least ten years or for an indefinite term (for example, the lifetime of the beneficiary). A Clifford trust may be used to provide support for elderly parents or an educational fund for a child. It is like an irrevocable trust in that the grantor is not taxed on the income of the trust. The present value of the income constitutes a gift, but the principal does not. Like a revocable trust, the assets will ultimately revert to the grantor and be included in the grantor's estate.

Transfers at Death

Transfers of property at time of death are specified in the will. Before these transfers can occur, however, provision for estate taxes must be made. The marital deduction is a major factor in reducing estate taxes. Thus estate planning usually takes maximum advantage of the marital deduction by leaving much of the estate to the spouse. Note that, assuming no remarriage, the marital deduction is available only on the death of the first spouse. Consideration must be given to minimizing the estate tax upon the death of the surviving spouse. One common approach is for the first spouse to leave part of the estate to the surviving spouse, so as to qualify for the marital deduction, and to leave the other part to a trust where the surviving spouse is the income beneficiary but the children are the principal beneficiaries. In this way, the full amount of the estate will be available to provide support for the surviving spouse, but only part will be included in the surviving spouse's estate. There are some limitations on the use of trusts to minimize estate taxes. So-called *generation-skipping trusts*, in which the principal beneficiaries are grandchildren or subsequent generations but earlier generations (e.g., children) are the income beneficiaries, are subject to special estate tax rules to prevent abuse.

Joint Ownership

Property owned jointly with right of survivorship automatically passes, upon the death of one owner, to the surviving owners. While this eliminates the need to provide for disposition of the property via will, it also limits flexibility in that all owners must agree to any sale of the property. Joint ownership that seems appropriate at one point in time may later prove inappropriate, as in the case of divorce. Jointly-owned property is included in each owner's estate in a proportionate manner.

Life Insurance

Life insurance is usually a significant part of an estate. While the proceeds are paid directly to the beneficiary, the face value of the policy is included in the estate if the decedent owned the policy. Ownership is measured in terms of possession of major rights, such as the right to cancel the policy or to change the beneficiary. To remove the insurance from the estate, the policy could be transferred as a gift to another individual or to an irrevocable trust. However, this involves loss of control over a major asset.

Liquidity

An important aspect of estate planning is to ensure that sufficient cash will be available in the estate to pay expenses, living costs of surviving family members, and estate taxes. Liquidity is a particular problem for individuals whose major asset is a business or a farm. The desire may have been to leave this asset intact for heirs, but often the asset must be sold to raise necessary cash. Various techniques are available to ensure the availability of cash to the estate. For example, life insurance may be purchased with the estate named as the beneficiary.

Summary

An estate plan is not fixed or absolute. Once established, it needs regular monitoring and revision as an individual's assets, needs, and circumstances change over time. Because of the complexities involved, estate planning is usually handled by a team of professionals, including accountants, attorneys, tax experts, and perhaps others, such as investment brokers and insurance agents.

Questions   **Q4.1**   Legal terminology is important in accounting for estates, trusts, and firms in bankruptcy. Explain the meaning of the following terms:

1. executor
2. intestate
3. administrator
4. principal
5. receiver
6. probate
7. residuary devise
8. specific devise

Q4.2   Valuation of assets under fiduciary accounting often differs from historical cost valuation. Indicate the basis of asset valuation used for each of the following financial statements:

1. Charge and discharge statement (estate).
2. Statement of affairs (bankruptcy).
3. Realization and liquidation statement (bankruptcy).
4. Charge and discharge statement (trust).
5. Balance sheet (trust).

Q4.3   When principal assets are sold, are gains and losses resulting from the sale treated as income or principal items? Can you offer any explanation for such treatment?

Q4.4   Does accounting for estates follow cash basis or accrual basis accounting? Discuss your answer.

Q4.5   What is meant by fully-secured liabilities? By partially-secured liabilities?

Q4.6   In fiduciary accounting, the fiduciary manages assets on behalf of some other party. Explain the role of the fiduciary in accounting for estates, trusts, and firms in bankruptcy.

Q4.7   Briefly explain the accounting procedures appropriate to each of the following:
   1. Post-inventory discovery of assets (estates).
   2. Liabilities existing at date of death (estates).
   3. Liabilities existing at date of declaration of bankruptcy (bankruptcy).
   4. Involuntary conversion of principal assets (trusts).
   5. Permanent improvements to principal assets (trusts).
   6. Regular maintenance of principal assets (trusts).

Q4.8   Do firms entering bankruptcy always have a deficit in Retained Earnings? Explain.

Q4.9   Compare the role of the statement of realization and liquidation and the statement of affairs in bankruptcy with respect to (1) purpose of the statements, (2) timing of statement presentation, and (3) basis of asset valuation.

Q4.10   What role, if any, does depreciation play in accounting for the activities of a receiver (or trustee) in bankruptcy?

Exercises   **E4.1**   In accounting for estates and trusts, there is a problem of separating the items that should be charged against principal from the items that should be charged against income. State whether each of the following items would be charged to principal or to income, assuming the case of a testamentary trust.
   1. Taxes on vacant city lots.
   2. Interest paid on mortgage on real estate.
   3. Depreciation of real estate.
   4. Legal fees for collection of rent.
   5. Special assessment tax levied on real estate for street improvement.
   6. Amortization of premium on bonds which had been purchased by the testator.
   7. Loss on sale of trust investments.

(AICPA adapted)

E4.2   The numbered transactions below pertain to the accounts maintained by the executor of an estate. The decedent died on January 17, 19X0. The will and other documents revealed that the decedent's son had been specifically bequeathed the decedent's only rental property and bonds of the MT Corporation ($100,000 par value, 3 percent, due February 28, 19Z5); the decedent's daughter was the beneficiary of a life insurance policy (face amount $150,000), on which the decedent had paid the premiums; and his widow had been left the remainder of the estate in trust, with full powers of appointment.

For each numbered transaction below, indicate whether the amount in question should be:

      a. Allocated between principal and income.

      b. Attributed solely to principal.

      c. Attributed solely to income.

1. January 20, 19X0: $3,450 was collected in connection with the redemption of AB Corporation bonds, 3 percent, due January 15, 19X0; par value $3,000.

2. January 20, 19X0: $1,000 was collected from FG Corporation on account of dividend of $1 per share on common stock declared December 1, 19W9, payable January 15, 19X0, to stockholders of record January 2, 19X0.

3. January 20, 19X0: $3,250.50 was paid to Smith & Company, brokers, for the purchase of income bonds of A.A.R.R., 5 percent, due June 30, 19Y2; face value $3,000.

4. January 21, 19X0: thirty shares of common stock were received from the DQ Corporation, constituting receipt of an ordinary 3 percent common stock dividend declared December 14, 19W9, payable January 20, 19X0, to holders of record January 15, 19X0.

5. February 1, 19X0: $400 quarterly interest was paid on a promissory note due January 31, 19X1.

6. February 1, 19X0: Dr. Mathews, the decedent's physician, was paid $1,000 for professional services rendered during the deceased's final illness.

7. February 1, 19X0: $1,600 was collected from TC Corporation on account of a cash dividend of $.50 per share on common stock, declared January 18, 19X0, payable January 30, 19X0, to holders of record January 27, 19X0.

8. February 1, 19X0: $400 rental income for February was deposited.

9. February 10, 19X0: $500 was paid for real estate taxes covering the period February 1–July 31, 19X0.

10. March 1, 19X0: $1,572 was paid on account of the decedent's state income tax for 19W9.

(AICPA adapted)

E4.3   On August 1, 19X3, Kevin Jackson, administrator of Susan Phoenix's will, distributed the following and closed the estate:

Distributed To	Amount
George Franklin .	$3,500
Carol Phoenix .	$95,000 (gross proceeds from sale of Susan Phoenix's residence)
Darrell Phoenix .	$48,400 (cash and securities)
Linda Webster .	Personal belongings valued at $30,000

Jackson's term as administrator commenced on December 1, 19X2, immediately after the death of Susan Phoenix. During the period of administration, the following events occurred:

1. Jackson invested some estate cash in securities (Group A).
2. Real estate fees on the sale of the house ($7,500) were paid. There was no mortgage remaining on the house.
3. Dividends on Group B securities (originally purchased by Susan Phoenix) of $1,000 were declared and received. Dividends and interest on Group A securities were received, totaling $2,500.
4. Legal and administrative fees (all charged to principal) of $3,000 were paid.
5. Jackson paid $800 brokerage fees on security transactions during his administration.
6. Group B securities increased in value $1,200.

Required:

1. Reconstruct the market value of Susan Phoenix's assets on December 1, 19X2.
2. Calculate the income of the estate during the administration period. What expenses were charged to income?
3. Briefly state the terms of Susan Phoenix's will.

E4.4 During the last few years of Maynard Crowley's life, he underwent expensive surgery and medical treatments. Back taxes and other overdue bills accumulated because Maynard was too ill to manage his financial affairs properly. After Felix Crowley, Maynard's son and executor of the estate, published notice to creditors of Maynard's death, the following bills were received:

Funeral Expenses	$ 2,500
Unpaid Medical Bills, Final Illness	12,000
Taxes Due at Date of Death	10,000
Charges at Local Stores	7,000
Loan from Bank	8,000

Maynard's will contained the following provisions:

1. Bequeathed to Felix Crowley, $30,000 plus residence and automobile (both fully owned by Maynard);
2. Bequeathed to St. Angela's High School, land (fully owned by Maynard) adjoining the school;
3. Bequeathed to Katherine Hutchinson, diamond and emerald brooch;
4. Bequeathed to St. Angela's High School, all property remaining after other distributions are complete.

Executor's fee was $2,000. Felix was also beneficiary of a $40,000 life insurance policy. The net realizable values of assets at date of death were as follows:

Residence	$60,000
Certificates of Deposit	30,000
Land Adjoining St. Angela's High School	15,000
Other Land	10,000
Diamond and Emerald Brooch	4,000
Automobile	1,500

Required: State the amount and nature of the assets received by Katherine

Hutchinson, Felix Crowley, and St. Angela's High School upon settlement of Maynard Crowley's estate.

E4.5 The following information is available concerning Hopkins, Inc., on the date the company entered bankruptcy proceedings:

Account	Balance per Books
Cash	$ 2,860
Accounts Receivable	52,260
Inventory	28,000
Prepaid Expenses	430
Buildings (Net)	59,000
Equipment (Net)	5,600
Goodwill	5,650
Wages Payable	(2,500)
Taxes Payable	(1,810)
Accounts Payable	(79,000)
Notes Payable	(15,150)
Common Stock	(72,000)
Retained Earnings—Deficit	16,660

Inventory with a book value of $20,000 is security for notes of $10,100. The other notes are secured by the equipment.

Expected realizable value of the assets is:

Accounts Receivable	$44,100
Inventory	18,500
Buildings	22,000
Equipment	2,000

Required: Compute the estimated deficiency to unsecured creditors.

E4.6 Because of inability to pay its debts, the Fox Manufacturing Co. has been forced into bankruptcy as of April 30, 19X3. The balance sheet on that date shows:

ASSETS		LIABILITIES	
Cash	$ 2,700	Accounts Payable	$ 52,500
Accounts Receivable . . .	39,350	Notes Payable (First Bank) . .	15,000
Notes Receivable	18,500	Notes Payable (Suppliers) . .	51,250
Inventories	87,850	Accrued Wages	1,850
Prepaid Expenses	950	Accrued Taxes	4,650
Land and Buildings . . .	61,250	Mortgage Bonds Payable . .	90,000
Equipment	48,800	Common Stock ($100 Par) . .	75,000
		Retained Earnings	(30,850)
	$259,400		$259,400

Additional Information:
1. Accounts receivable of $16,110 and notes receivable of $12,500 are expected to be collectible. The good notes are pledged to First Bank.
2. Inventories are expected to bring in $45,100 when sold under bankruptcy conditions.

    3. Land and buildings have an appraised value of $95,000. They serve as security on the bonds.

    4. The current value of the equipment, net of disposal costs, is $9,000.

Required: Compute the following:

    1. Estimated loss on asset disposition.

    2. Estimated gain on asset disposition.

    3. Priority claims.

    4. Estimated payments to secured creditors.

    5. Expected recovery percentage.

(AICPA adapted)

E4.7   The balance sheet of Binder Company immediately prior to entering bankruptcy proceedings and a balance sheet prepared during liquidation are shown below.

Binder Company
Balance Sheet
June 30, 19X0

Cash		$ 2,000	Accounts Payable .		$ 40,000
Accounts			Accrued Wages .		7,000
Receivable . .		10,000	Taxes Payable . .		8,000
Inventories . . .		30,000	Notes Payable[a] . .		70,000
Equipment . . . $73,000			Stockholders'		
Less			Equity . . .		(15,000)
Accumulated					
Depreciation . 20,000		53,000			
Land		15,000			
		$110,000			$110,000

[a]Of the notes payable, $15,000 are secured with inventory having a book value of $15,000. The remaining notes payable and the accounts payable are unsecured.

Binder Company
Alfred Wade, Trustee
Balance Sheet
December 31, 19X0

Cash		$10,000	Liabilities Not Liquidated:	
Assets Not Realized:			Accounts	
Equipment . . $73,000			Payable . . $32,000	
Less Accumulated			Notes Payable . 48,000	
Depreciation . 20,000		53,000	Estate Deficit . . (17,000)	
		$63,000	$63,000	

    The inventory was sold at two-thirds its book value. Half of the accounts receivable were collected; the rest were written off.

Required: Reconstruct the journal entries for Binder Company from June 30 to December 31, 19X0.

E4.8 When he was sixty-six years old and his grandson Vincent had just turned eighteen, Walter Dodson established a trust for Vincent. The principal was composed of 8 percent bonds (face and market value, $80,000) and common stock (market value, $30,000) in several companies. Merchant's Bank agreed to administer the trust for an annual fee of 6 percent of gross trust income. The stocks and bonds were to come under Vincent's control when he reached age twenty-one. Until that time, yearly net income of the trust was to be paid to Vincent on his birthday. Dividends received on the stock for the three years of the trust were $1,200, $1,800, and $2,000, respectively.

Required: Record all journal entries made by Merchant's Bank for the trust of Vincent Dodson.

E4.9 At January 1, 19X4, the records of Frederick McDonald, trustee in bankruptcy for VCM Corporation, showed the following:

Cash	$ 8,200
Assets Not Realized:	
Land	10,000
Building	43,000
Equipment	28,000
Patents	4,400
Liabilities Not Liquidated:	
Accounts Payable	80,000
Loans Payable	40,000
Estate Deficit	26,400

During January, McDonald sold equipment having a book value of $15,000 for $8,800, and sold the patents for $12,000. McDonald was paid $1,300 as a trustee's fee, and $21,000 was distributed proportionately to the creditors.

Required: Prepare a statement of realization and liquidation for January and a balance sheet and statement of estate deficit as of January 31, 19X4.

E4.10 (**Appendix**) Edith Barnes died on July 17, 19X5, leaving one-half of her estate to her husband and one-half to a trust for the benefit of their children. The gross estate amounted to $430,000. The estate paid debts, funeral expenses, and administrative costs of $40,000. During her lifetime, Edith made no gifts exceeding the $10,000 exclusion. Assume a $47,000 lifetime credit.

Required:
1. Calculate the estate tax owed by the estate of Edith Barnes.
2. Calculate the estate tax assuming Edith had left her entire estate to her husband.
3. Calculate the estate tax assuming Edith had left her entire estate to the trust for the benefit of their children.

Problems **P4.1** **Estate and Trust Accounting** On May 2, 19X2, Theodosia Hale died in a boating accident. The will specified that Hale's residence was to be sold and the mortgage settled. Her personal belongings (furniture, jewelry, photographs, and so on) were bequeathed to Rosenelle Abernathy, Hale's sister and only living relative. Rosenelle Abernathy was also named beneficiary of income from the estate subject to the following limitations:

1. Maximum annual distribution is to be $18,000. Earnings of the estate in excess of that amount are to be added to principal.
2. Minimum annual distribution is to be $10,000. Any deficiency in earnings is to be met by principal.

The will also called for creation of a trust. Income from the trust was to be distributed to Rosenelle Abernathy subject to the same limitations established for income from the estate. Upon Abernathy's death, the holdings of the trust were to be given to the United Fund. Kevin Boylston was named as executor of the estate and trustee of the trust.

The following information is available:

1. Residence: estimated fair market value at date of death, $110,000; mortgage payment made on June 1, $400, of which $180 was interest; selling price, $108,000; selling and closing expenses, $9,700; payment of remaining mortgage, $25,000; selling date, June 2, 19X2.
2. Personal belongings: estimated fair market value at date of death, $27,000.
3. Estate taxes: $66,000, paid in 19X2; funeral expenses: $3,000, paid in 19X2.
4. Assets other than residence and personal belongings: cash, $20,000; securities, $200,000; undeveloped land, $40,000. Values are stated as of May 2, 19X2.
5. Accrued interest receivable on May 2, 19X2: Security A, $100, and Security B, $900.
6. Creation of the trust: April 30, 19X3.
7. Administrative expenses: May 2, 19X2 to April 30, 19X3, $5,000; May 1, 19X3 to April 30, 19X4, $4,000; divided evenly between principal and income.
8. Security transactions: Security A, interest of $600 received on July 1, 19X2 and July 1, 19X3; Security B, interest of $1,200 received on February 2, 19X3 and February 2, 19X4; dividends and interest on other securities, $16,000 in the first year of administration and $24,000 in the second year; sale of Security W in August 19X3 yielded $42,000 compared to book value of $30,000, with proceeds invested in Security G.
9. All distributions to the beneficiary were made on April 30.
10. Contents of safe deposit box discovered on July 10, 19X2: jewelry worth $9,000 and Security E worth $15,000 (values as of May 2, 19X2).

Required:

1. Prepare the journal entries made by the fiduciary for the period May 2, 19X2 to April 30, 19X3.
2. Prepare a charge and discharge statement for Kevin Boylston as of April 30, 19X3.
3. Prepare the journal entries made by the fiduciary for the period May 1, 19X3 to April 30, 19X4.
4. Prepare a charge and discharge statement for Kevin Boylston as of April 30, 19X4.

P4.2   **Estate Accounting**   The will of Albert Brown, deceased, directed that his executor, Charles Dawson, liquidate the entire estate within two years of the date of Mr. Brown's death and pay the net proceeds and income, if any, to the Sunnydale Orphanage. Mr. Brown, who was a bachelor, died on February 1, 19X4, after a brief illness.

An inventory of the decedent's property was prepared, and the fair market value of all items was determined. The preliminary inventory, before the computation of any appropriate income accruals on inventory items, follows:

	Fair Market Value
First National Bank Checking Account	$ 6,000
$60,000 City of Laguna School Bonds, Interest Rate 6% Payable January 1 and July 1, Maturity Date 7/1/X8	59,000
2,000 Shares Jones Corporation Capital Stock	220,000
Term Life Insurance (Beneficiary—Estate of Albert Brown)	20,000
Personal Residence ($45,000) and Furnishings ($5,000)	50,000

During 19X4, the following transactions occurred:

1.   The interest on the City of Laguna School Bonds was collected. The bonds were sold on July 1 for $59,000, and the proceeds and interest were paid to the orphanage.

2.   The Jones Corporation paid cash dividends of $1 per share on March 1 and December 1, as well as a 10 percent stock dividend on July 1. All dividends were declared forty-five days before each payment date and were payable to holders of record as of forty days before each payment date. On September 2, 1,000 shares were sold at $105 per share, and the proceeds were paid to the Sunnydale Orphanage.

3.   Because of a depressed real estate market, the personal residence was rented furnished at $300 per month commencing April 1. The rent is paid monthly, in advance. Real estate taxes of $900 for the calendar year of 19X4 were paid. The house and furnishings have estimated lives of forty-five years and ten years, respectively. The part-time gardener-handyman was paid four months' wages totaling $500 on April 30 for services performed, and he was released.

4.   The First National Bank checking account was closed and the balance of $6,000 was transferred to an estate bank account.

5.   The term life insurance was paid on March 1 and deposited in the estate bank account.

6.   The following disbursements were made:
    a.   Funeral expenses, $2,000.
    b.   Final illness expenses, $1,500.
    c.   April 15 income tax remittance, $700.
    d.   Attorney's and accountant's fees, $12,000.

7.   On December 31, the balance of the undistributed income, except for $1,000, was paid to the beneficiary. The balance of the cash on hand

derived from the principal of the estate was also paid to the beneficiary on December 31.

Required: As of December 31, 19X4, the executor resigned and waived all commissions. Prepare a charge and discharge statement separately stated as to principal and income, together with its supporting schedules, on behalf of the executor of the estate of Albert Brown for the period from February 1, 19X4 through December 31, 19X4.

(AICPA adapted)

P4.3 **Estate Accounting** Arthur Taine died in an accident on May 31, 19X2. His will, dated February 28, 19X1, provided that all just debts and expenses be paid and that his property be disposed of as follows:

United States Treasury bonds and Puritan Company stock—to be placed in trust. All income to go to Bertha Taine during her lifetime, with right of appointment upon her death.

Seneca Company mortgage notes—bequeathed to Wanda Taine Langer, daughter.

Cash—a bequest of $10,000 to David Taine, son.

Remainder of estate—to be divided equally between the two children, Wanda Taine Langer and David Taine.

The will further provided that during the administration period Bertha Taine was to be paid $300 a month out of estate income, and estate and inheritance taxes were to be paid out of principal. David Taine was named as executor and trustee.

Bertha and Arthur owned their personal residence jointly with rights of survivorship.

An inventory of the decedent's property was prepared. The fair market value of all items as of the date of death was determined. The preliminary inventory, before the computation of any appropriate income accruals on inventory items, follows:

Personal Residence Property	$ 95,000
Jewelry—Diamond Ring	9,600
York Life Insurance Co.—Term Life Insurance Policy on Life of Arthur Taine. Beneficiary—Bertha Taine, Widow	120,000
Granite Trust Co.—3% Savings Bank Account, Arthur Taine, in Trust for Philip Langer (Grandchild), Interest Credited January and July 1; Balance May 31, 19X2	400
Fidelity National Bank—Checking Account; Balance May 31, 19X2	143,000
$100,000 United States Treasury Bonds, 3%, (Maturing in 30 Years), Interest Payable Mar. 1 and Sept. 1	100,000
$9,700 Seneca Co. First Mortgage Notes, 6%, 19X6, Interest Payable May 31 and November 30	9,900
800 Shares Puritan Co. Common Stock	64,000
700 Shares Meta Mfg. Co. Common Stock	70,000

The executor opened an estate bank account to which he transferred the decedent's checking account balance. Other deposits, through July 1, 19X3, were as follows:

Interest Collected on Bonds:
  $100,000 United States Treasury
      September 1, 19X2 . . . . $ 1,500
      March 1, 19X3 1,500
Dividends Received on Stock:
  800 Shares Puritan Co.
      June 15, 19X2, Declared May 7, 19X2, Payable to Holders of Record
        May 27, 19X2 800
      September 15, 19X2 800
      December 15, 19X2 1,200
      March 15, 19X3 800
      June 15, 19X3 800
  Net Proceeds of June 19, 19X2, Sale of 700 Shares Meta Mfg. Co. . . . 68,810

Payments were made from the estate's checking account through July 1, 19X3, for the following:

Funeral Expenses . . . . $ 2,000
Assessments for Additional 19X0 Federal and State Income Tax ($1,700)
  Plus Interest ($110) to May 31, 19X2 1,810
19X2 Income Taxes of Arthur Taine for the Period January 1, 19X2 through
  May 31, 19X2, in Excess of Amounts Paid by the Decedent on
  Declarations of Estimated Tax 9,100
Federal and State Fiduciary Income Taxes, Fiscal Years Ending June 31,
  19X2 ($75) and June 30, 19X3 ($1,400) 1,475
Federal and State Estate Taxes 58,000
Monthly Payments to Bertha Taine—13 payments of $300 3,900
Attorney's and Accountant's Fees 25,000

The executor waived his commission. However, he desired to receive his father's diamond ring in lieu of the $10,000 specific legacy. All parties agreed to this in writing, and the court's approval was secured. All other specific legacies were delivered by July 15, 19X2.

Required: Prepare a charge and discharge statement as to principal and income, together with its supporting schedules, on behalf of the executor of the estate of Arthur Taine for the period from May 31, 19X2 through July 1, 19X3.

(AICPA adapted)

P4.4 **Statement of Affairs** The Statton Corporation is facing bankruptcy proceedings. The balance sheet of Statton Corporation at June 30, 19X6, and supplementary data are presented here:

ASSETS

Cash	$ 2,000
Accounts Receivable, Less Allowance for Doubtful Accounts	70,000
Inventory, Raw Material	40,000
Inventory, Finished Goods	60,000
Marketable Securities	20,000
Land	13,000
Buildings, Less Accumulated Depreciation	90,000
Machinery, Less Accumulated Depreciation	120,000
Goodwill	20,000
Prepaid Expenses	5,000
Total Assets	$440,000

LIABILITIES AND CAPITAL

Accounts Payable	$ 80,000
Notes Payable	135,000
Accrued Wages	15,000
Mortgages Payable	130,000
Common Stock	100,000
Retained Earnings (Deficit)	(20,000)
Total Liabilities and Capital	$440,000

Supplementary data:

1. Cash should be reduced by $500 for a travel advance which has been expended.
2. Accounts Receivable of $40,000 have been pledged in support of Notes Payable of $30,000. Credit balances of $5,000 are netted in the Accounts Receivable total.
3. Marketable Securities consists of government bonds costing $10,000 and 500 shares of Bartlett Company stock. The market value of the bonds is $10,000 and the stock is $18 per share. The bonds have accrued interest due of $200. The securities are collateral for a $20,000 bank loan.
4. Appraised value of raw materials is $30,000 and of finished goods is $50,000. For an additional cost of $10,000, the raw materials would realize $70,000 as finished goods.
5. The appraised values of fixed assets are: Land, $25,000; Buildings, $110,000; Machinery, $75,000.
6. Prepaid Expenses will be exhausted during the liquidation period.
7. Accounts Payable include $15,000 of withheld payroll taxes and $6,000 owed to creditors who had been reassured by the president they would be paid. There are unrecorded employer's payroll taxes in the amount of $500.
8. Accrued Wages are not subject to any limitations under bankruptcy laws.
9. Mortgages Payable consist of $100,000 on land and buildings and a $30,000 mortgage on machinery. Total unrecorded accrued interest for these mortgages amounts to $2,400.
10. Estimated legal fees and expenses in connection with the liquidation are $10,000.
11. Probable judgment on a pending damage suit is $50,000. This meets the accrual criteria of FASB No. 5.
12. There is an unrecorded invoice for $5,000 for last year's audit, and it is estimated that the fee for liquidation work will be $1,000.

Required:

1. Prepare a statement of affairs.
2. Compute the estimated settlement per dollar of unsecured liabilities.

(AICPA adapted)

P4.5 **Statement of Affairs** The Bellow Company, Inc., has been finding it more and more difficult to meet its obligations. Although its sales volume appeared to be satisfactory and it was showing a profit, the requirements for capital for inventory and payments on current liabilities were greater than the company could provide. Finally, after pledging all of its installment accounts, it found itself unable to meet the bills falling due on October 10, 19X4. Management feels that if the company could obtain an extension of time in which to pay its obligations it could meet its liabilities in full. The corporation has arranged for a meeting of creditors to determine if the company should be granted an extension or be forced into bankruptcy.

The trial balance for the current calendar year of the company on September 30, 19X4, is as follows:

	Debit	Credit
Cash on Hand	$ 500	
Cash in Bank	1,620	
Installment Contracts—Pledged	215,000	
Allowance for Bad Contracts		$ 13,440
Accounts Receivable—30 day	20,830	
Allowance for Doubtful Accounts		1,050
Inventories—January 1, 19X4	151,150	
Prepaid Insurance	1,490	
Autos and Trucks	22,380	
Accumulated Depreciation (Autos and Trucks)		14,960
Furniture and Equipment	12,500	
Accumulated Depreciation (Furniture and Equipment)		2,140
Buildings	89,760	
Accumulated Depreciation (Building)		7,530
Land	10,240	
Organization Expense	880	
Trade Accounts Payable		132,100
Contract Payable (Furniture and Equipment)		5,800
Installment Note on Auto and Trucks		10,000
Bank Loan—Secured by Installment Contracts		161,250
Taxes Payable (Prior Years)		14,220
Accrued Salaries and Wages		4,680
Accrued Interest		10,990
Notes Payable—Stockholder		100,000
First Mortgage		49,000
Capital Stock		100,000
Retained Earnings	65,290	
Sales		708,900
Purchases	527,630	
Expenses and Miscellaneous Income (Net)	216,790	
	$1,336,060	$1,336,060

From further investigation, the following additional data are obtained:

1. Depreciation, doubtful accounts, and prepaid and accrued items had all been adjusted as of September 30, 19X4.
2. All installment contracts had been pledged with the bank on September 30, 19X4; the bank had deducted its interest to date and had increased the company loan to equal 75 percent of face amount of the contracts, in accordance with a loan agreement. It was estimated that a forced liquidation

would result in a loss of $40,000 from the face amount of the contracts.

3. Thirty-day accounts receivable were not pledged, and it was estimated that they would provide $16,500 on a liquidation basis.

4. It was estimated that since January 1, 19X4, the company had made a gross profit of 33⅓ percent but that the inventory on hand would provide only $100,000 in a forced liquidation.

5. Cancellation of the insurance would provide $990.

6. All the autos and trucks were covered by an installment note, and their total market value was $8,000.

7. The store had been remodeled in 19X3, and the furniture and equipment had been acquired on contract. Because of its specialized nature, it was estimated that in a forced sale no more than $5,000 could be realized.

8. The land and buildings were subject to a 6 percent first mortgage, on which interest had been paid to July 30, 19X4. It was estimated the property could be sold for $75,000.

9. The notes payable to stockholders had not been subordinated to general creditors. The notes carried a 6 percent rate of interest, but no interest had been paid since December 31, 19X2.

10. Since prior income tax returns disclosed a large available net operating loss carryover, no current income tax need be considered.

11. The cost of liquidation proceedings was estimated to be $5,000.

12. There appeared to be no other values on liquidation and no unrecorded liabilities.

Required:

1. Prepare a statement of affairs for Bellow Company, Inc., as of September 30, 19X4.

2. Compute the percentage of recovery by the unsecured creditors if Bellow Company, Inc., is forced into bankruptcy.

(AICPA adapted).

P4.6 Statement of Realization and Liquidation Barnwell Corporation, which has had a history of profitable operations, has recently encountered serious difficulty in paying its bills. Attempts to acquire bank financing have been unsuccessful, due to the advanced age and ill health of the firm's sole owner and manager, Amos Barnwell. Attempts to sell the company have also proven unsuccessful. Faced with the prospect of the firm's bankruptcy, Barnwell's creditors met and proposed the following terms to Mr. Barnwell:

1. Operations would be continued until the present raw materials and work-in-process inventories were used or completed and sold.

2. The creditors would advance $9,000 to finance the necessary operating costs.

3. A trustee would be appointed by the creditors to manage the remaining operations and subsequent liquidation.

Amos Barnwell agreed to these terms and on August 1, 19X1, Frank Carrington was appointed trustee. The company's balance sheet on that date showed the following:

Cash	$ 397	Accounts Payable . . .	$ 37,933
Accounts Receivable . .	6,093	Common Stock ($10 Par) .	30,000
Raw Materials Inventory .	24,000	Additional Paid-In Capital .	60,000
Work-in-Process Inventory .	51,600	Retained Earnings . . .	12,783
Finished Goods . . .	8,550		
Equipment (Net) . . .	50,075		
	$140,716		$140,716

During the first six months of Carrington's term as trustee, the following occurred:

1. The creditors advanced the company $9,000.
2. Additional raw materials were purchased on account for $9,450.
3. Expenses incurred on account were $22,500. Expenses paid with cash were $31,732, of which $24,937 was for labor. All expenses were charged to work in process.
4. Cash in the amount of $1,125 was expended for new equipment.
5. Of the accounts receivable outstanding on August 1, $570 were deemed uncollectible. The balance was collected.
6. Depreciation of $1,500 was recorded and charged to work in process.
7. Sales on account of $108,450 were collected during the six-month period.
8. No equipment was sold.

On January 31, 19X2, account balances were as follows: Accounts Receivable (new), $5,073; Accounts Payable (new), $133; Raw Materials, $3,000; and Finished Goods, $45,000.

Required:

1. Prepare a schedule showing transactions affecting the cash account of Barnwell Corporation.
2. Prepare a statement of realization and liquidation for Barnwell Corporation for the six-month period ending January 31, 19X2.

P4.7 **Statement of Affairs—Partnership** The Adams-Story Partnership has had difficulty in meeting its obligations as the debts matured. If the business is dissolved, the process will take six months. Burke, the part-time bookkeeper, prepared the following trial balance:

Adams-Story Partnership
Trial Balance
April 15, 19X8

Cash in Banks	$ 20,000	
Accounts Receivable	100,000	
Allowance for Doubtful Accounts		$ 4,000
Notes Receivable	58,000	
Notes Receivable Discounted		12,000
Raw Materials	9,000	
Work in Process	20,000	
Finished Goods	15,000	
Prepaid Insurance	1,200	
Property Held in Trust	18,000	
Machinery and Equipment, Cost	9,000	
Building	33,000	

Land	12,000	
Accumulated Depreciation		6,000
Interest Receivable	700	
Payroll Taxes Payable		200
Real Estate Taxes Payable		1,200
Wages Payable		3,450
Notes Payable		60,000
Accounts Payable		125,700
Mortgage Payable—4%		40,000
Equipment Contract Payable (Purchased on a Conditional Sales		
Contract)		6,400
Interest Payable		1,000
Adams, Capital		15,975
Story, Capital		1,975
Trust Principal		18,000
	$295,900	$295,900

An analysis of the accounts revealed the following:

1. Cash in First Bank, $8,000; in Second Bank, $12,000.
2. Of the accounts receivable, 60 percent are good and fully collectible, 30 percent are doubtful and considered to be only 80 percent collectible, the remaining 10 percent are worthless.
3. All notes are good and are pledged as security on notes payable to the Factor House of $50,000 with accrued interest of $500.
4. Of the notes which were discounted at the Manning Bank, it is estimated that one, amounting to $2,000, will not be paid at maturity or thereafter.
5. All finished goods will be sold for 20 percent less than their cost. Work in process cannot be sold until finished and can be completed by incurring labor and material costs of $9,000, of which $3,000 will be from raw material inventory. The balance of the raw material inventory will realize $5,000.
6. The prepaid insurance, which expires October 15, has a short-term cancellation value on April 15 of $900.
7. Property held in trust is in the form of stocks and bonds with realizable value of $24,000. The partnership is entitled to a fee of $600 per year, payable April 15, for its services. Cash was not available in the trust for the payment, therefore the fee was not recorded.
8. The machinery and equipment with a book value of $8,000 will realize $5,000.
9. The land and building may be sold for $38,000; however, the mortgage holder has indicated a willingness to cancel the debt and assume all encumbrances for the surrender of title to the real estate. Interest on the mortgage was paid on January 15.
10. The wages and commissions were last paid in full on January 31. Commission salesmen were dismissed on February 15. Accrued wages in the trial balance are:

Burke, Bookkeeper (to April 15)	$1,400
Maxwell, Commission Salesman (to February 15)	300
Josephs, Manager (to April 15)	1,750
	$3,450

11. The partnership owes the Second Bank a note of $10,000. The note is secured by the balance in the Adams-Story account in Second Bank.
12. The estimated administrative expenses are $3,000.
13. While Adams has personal liabilities which are approximately equal to his personal assets, Story's personal assets exceed his personal liabilities by $2,800.

Required:

1. Prepare a statement of affairs for the Adams-Story Partnership as of April 15, 19X8.
2. What percentage of liabilities is expected to be recovered by each class of creditors?

(AICPA adapted)

P4.8   **Personal Trust**   Shortly before her death, Theresa Letterman established a $120,000 trust for the daughters of a friend. Emily and Janet Wallace, the beneficiaries of the trust, were each to receive half the income from the trust until their twenty-first birthdays. Upon reaching her majority, Emily was to receive $20,000. Janet (the younger sister) would continue to receive one-half of trust income with the remainder being added to the principal. On Janet's twenty-first birthday, the remaining trust principal was to be divided equally and distributed to both women. Emily and Janet were sixteen and eleven years old at the time Theresa Letterman made the arrangements.

Data concerning earnings and expenses of the trust are as follows:

	Total for First Five Years	Total for Second Five Years
Gross Earnings	$36,000	$43,000
Administrative Expenses (Allocated 60% to Principal and 40% to Income)	2,000	2,500
Gains (Losses) on Sales of Securities . .	(500)	3,000

Required:

1. Calculate the distribution of principal on Janet's twenty-first birthday.
2. Calculate the total dollar amount received by Janet from the trust. Calculate the total dollar amount received by Emily from the trust.
3. Calculate the distribution in the third year of the trust, assuming trust investment revenue was $7,000, administrative expenses were $400, and gains on sales of securities were $800 that year.

P4.9   **Profit-Sharing Trust**   The Habler Company established a non-contributing profit-sharing trust for its employees, effective January 1, 1981. Contributions to the trust have been determined to be allowable as a deduction on the company tax return. The records of the trust have been kept by the company bookkeeper who has computed prior years' distributions accurately. The following trial balance of the trust at December 31, 1983, is available:

Habler Employee Profit-Sharing Trust
Trial Balance
December 31, 1983

Cash in Bank	$1,505	
Savings and Loan Shares	1,000	
Government Securities	2,000	
Stocks	1,095	
Loans to Members	500	
Accrued Interest Receivable	85	
Liability to Members		$6,000
Interest Earned		260
Dividends		50
Payment on Account to Separated Employee	115	
Brokers' Fees	10	
	$6,310	$6,310

Employee records and records of the trust show the following:

Name	Date Employed	1983 Salaries	Trust Account Balances December 31, 1982
John Jones	2/1/63	$ 40,000	$2,500
Mary Smith	12/10/78	10,000	500
Oscar Johnson	1/20/68	30,000	1,500
Wendell Davis (Quit 8/31/83)	8/10/77	11,800	500
James Saunders	6/2/75	20,000	1,000
Susan Jacobs	8/10/81	10,000	0
Sam Dodd	10/20/82	10,000	0
		$131,800	$6,000

The profit-sharing trust agreement provides:
1. The annual company contribution to the trust is to be computed on the basis of income as determined for tax purposes, but before deduction of the profit-sharing contribution. The contribution is to be made at the rate of 10 percent of the first $50,000 of such income and 15 percent of the excess over $50,000.
2. Company contributions and relinquishments (forfeitures) are to be distributed to members in the employ of the company at the close of each year on the basis of service and salary points—one point for each full year of company service and one point for each $200 of earnings for the year.
3. Annual earnings of the trust are to be distributed to members having balances in their membership accounts at the beginning of the year in the ratio that each such beginning balance bears to the total beginning balances.
4. An employee must have two full years of service to be eligible for participation in the trust. Eligibility for new members is to be determined as of the end of each fiscal year.

5. A member leaving the employment of the company for any reason other than at the instigation of the employer for cause is entitled to receive a percentage of his trust balance based on the number of full years of service with the company, as set forth in the following table:

Years of Service	Percentage Received	Years of Service	Percentage Received
1	10%	6	60%
2	20	7	70
3	30	8	80
4	40	9	90
5	50	10	100

Employees do not participate in the company contribution for the year of separation. Income of the company for the year ended December 31, 1983, amounted to $60,666.67 before income taxes and deduction for its contribution to the plan.

Required:

1. Compute the profit-sharing contribution by the company for 1983.
2. Compute:
   a. The distribution of company contributions to members' accounts.
   b. The allocation of the trust income to members' accounts.
   c. The severance settlement and forfeiture of Wendell Davis.
3. Complete the chart illustrated below and compute the ending balance of liabilities of the trust to members and to the separated employee.

Employee Profit-Sharing Trust
Statement of Changes in Member Accounts
For Year Ending December 31, 1983

Members	Beginning Balance	Company Contributions	Trust Income	Relinquishments (Forfeitures)	Total	Payments During Year	Ending Balance
John Jones	$2,500						
Mary Smith	500						
Oscar Johnson	1,500						
James Saunders	1,000						
Susan Jacobs							
Separated Employee—Wendell Davis	500						
	$6,000						

4. Record the 1983 adjusting entries for the profit-sharing trust and prepare the balance sheet of the trust as of December 31, 1983.

(AICPA adapted)

P4.10 **Estate Taxation** **(Appendix)** Refer to P4.3, relating to the death of Arthur Taine. The following additional data are available:

1. Both Arthur and Bertha were employed, and both contributed equally to the acquisition of their jointly-owned residence.
2. Arthur made two gifts during his lifetime that exceeded his $10,000 annual exclusion:

    a. A $20,000 wedding gift to his daughter, Wanda, for a down payment on a house, given five years ago.

    b. A $15,000 sports car to his son David upon his graduation from college four years ago.

Required: Calculate the estate tax owed by the estate of Arthur Taine (ignore the $58,000 figure for federal and state estate taxes given in P4.3). Assume that the lifetime credit is $47,000.

PART TWO

MULTIPLE CORPORATE ENTITIES

Corporate financial accounting and reporting have long been the focus of much of accounting theory, standards, and practice. In this part of the book, we address accounting problems arising when multiple corporate entities are viewed as a single accounting entity or area of economic interest to shareholders. We look beyond legal and organizational distinctions to identify the inclusive accounting entity, which often consists of several subentities, to serve as the basis for reports on financial position, operations, and changes in financial position.

Chapters 5 through 11 deal with the aggregation of accounting information. Many business units are, in themselves, legitimate accounting entities. Yet such units are often parts of a larger collection of economic resources in which common ownership interests exist. Bringing together the accounts of these business units involves more than a simple summation.

Chapter 5 offers an introduction to this aggregation problem within the relatively simple framework of a single corporation organized around subfirm entities, called branches, which have separate financial accounting systems. In Chapter 6, the accounting problems arising when separate corporations are brought under common control are studied. When corporations under common control remain as separate legal entities, their accounts are normally consolidated for financial reports reflecting the status and performance of the commonly-controlled economic resources. Chapters 7 through 11 provide comprehensive analyses of typical problems arising when consolidated statements are prepared and the aggregation problem is more complex.

Consolidated financial statements offer many advantages to the controlling shareholders. However, they tend to average the accounts of the constituent corporations, some of which may have different risk, return, and growth characteristics. In such situations, shareholders may require financial information broken down along industry and geographic lines in addition to the primary consolidated statements. Such matters are studied in Chapter 12, along with consideration of interim reporting problems which arise when financial information is presented for short periods within a year.

Chapter 5

Home Office and Branch Accounting

Within a firm, there are various accounting or reporting entities. These entities range from production, service, and marketing *departments* to *branches*, *divisions*, and separately controlled corporations known as *subsidiaries*. The concept of *responsibility accounting* provides the basis for identifying departments as cost or profit centers; accordingly, expense and revenue data are accumulated for these units of activity in the firm's management accounting system. On a larger scale, divisions and subsidiaries of a firm often have considerable autonomy and may include many departments.

The degree of financial accounting responsibility varies among these business units. While individual departments normally do not have their own financial accounting systems, they are viewed as accounting entities because their activities are separately identified in the firm's management or cost accounting system. In contrast, the subsidiaries under common corporate control have complete financial accounting systems. Between departments on the one hand and subsidiaries on the other lie sales agencies, branches, and divisions. These subfirm entities have varying degrees of financial accounting responsibility. This chapter addresses the financial accounting procedures employed by such subfirm entities.

Sales Agencies

We begin with a discussion of accounting for sales agencies. A **sales agency** is a business unit physically removed from the firm's main or home office. Its limited functions include serving as a base for sales personnel in the field, processing customer orders, and maintaining limited inventories of the company's products. From an accounting standpoint, the sales agency's accounts are carried on the books of the home office. Transactions are recorded in accounts which identify the particular sales agency. An imprest fund is established to

Exhibit 5.1   Accounting for the Operation of a Sales Agency by the Home Office

Oceanside Company decides to open a sales agency to promote its leisure-time products in Longport, a popular resort town. A $10,000 imprest fund is established for the Longport Agency:

Imprest Fund: Longport Agency	10,000	
Cash		10,000
To establish a $10,000 imprest fund for use of the Longport Agency.		

The following transactions related to the Longport agency are recorded by the Oceanside Company during the month of July:

Merchandise Samples: Longport Agency	25,000	
Inventory		25,000
To record the cost of samples shipped to the Longport Agency. Oceanside uses a perpetual inventory system. Under a periodic inventory system, an account such as Merchandise Shipments: Longport Agency rather than Inventory would be credited.		

Accounts Receivable	50,000	
Sales: Longport Agency		50,000
To record sales generated by the Longport Agency.		

Operating Expenses: Longport Agency (details omitted) . .	7,000	
Cash		7,000
To reimburse the Longport Agency's imprest fund for various cash expenses.		

Operating Expenses: Longport Agency	9,000	
Depreciation Expense—Furniture and Fixtures: Longport Agency	1,500	
Accounts Payable		9,000
Accumulated Depreciation—Furniture and Fixtures . . .		1,500
To charge the Longport Agency for expenses incurred by Oceanside on behalf of the agency.		

Cost of Goods Sold: Longport Agency	22,000	
Inventory		22,000
To charge the Longport Agency for the cost of merchandise sold by its personnel.		

Selling Expenses: Longport Agency	5,000	
Merchandise Samples: Longport Agency		5,000
To record use of sample merchandise by the Longport Agency; samples costing $20,000 are still on hand.		

provide the agency with cash used for various small expenses. Since rent, payroll, utilities, and asset accounting are all handled by the home office, the agency's primary accounting responsibility relates to the imprest fund. Entries made by the home office to account for typical transactions of a sales agency are illustrated in Exhibit 5.1. Note that the sales agency itself makes no entries because it has no financial accounting system.

From Exhibit 5.1, we see that accounting for a sales agency creates no special problems. Except for the imprest fund, the accounting identifies transac-

Exhibit 5.1   Accounting for the Operation of a Sales Agency by the Home Office *continued*

At the end of July, Oceanside prepares an income statement for the Longport Agency and closes the revenue and expense accounts to Oceanside's income summary. The income statement is given below:

Longport Sales Agency
Income Statement for the Month of July

Sales	$50,000
Cost of Goods Sold	$22,000
Operating Expenses	16,000
Depreciation Expense	1,500
Selling Expenses	5,000
Total Expenses	$44,500
Net Income	$ 5,500

tions made *by* or *for* the sales agency rather than *between* the sales agency and the home office. The transfer of merchandise samples indicates their new physical location. As an alternative to maintaining home office accounts identified by sales agency, as in Exhibit 5.1, entries could be made in control accounts at the home office with simultaneous updating of subsidiary records for the various sales agencies.

We now turn to consideration of accounting for home office/branch (or divisional) relationships. The major factors distinguishing these business units from sales agencies for accounting purposes are (1) separate accounting systems and (2) greater variety of transactions *between* the home office and its branches.

Branches and Divisions

We have seen that a sales agency is a business unit with limited functions and, aside from the imprest fund, with no accounting functions. In contrast, branches and divisions are typically larger business units which perform many functions. Accounting for such business units requires special consideration when a more complete chart of accounts is maintained by the unit and numerous transactions with the home office are recorded in the accounts of *both* the branch or division *and* the home office. The equivalent of sales agency accounting could be used for a division if the division has no financial accounting responsibility. Profitability of such a division would be measured by the internal accounting system, and the home office/branch accounting procedures which we describe below would not be needed. To simplify the terminology, the term **branch** will be used to identify a business unit (branch office or division) which has more than a minimal financial accounting responsibility. Transactions between the home office and branch are recorded by *both* units in their separate accounts.

Reciprocal Accounts

A key element both in identifying home office/branch situations and in providing the needed accounting is the presence of *reciprocal accounts.*

> **Reciprocal accounts** have equal and offsetting balances on both the home office and branch books. They are used by both business units to record those transactions *between* the units or made *on behalf of* one unit by the other.

Note that when a company's financial statements are prepared, all internal transactions among the units of the company are netted out so that the statements reflect only transactions with outside parties. The procedures for netting out the reciprocal accounts—which represent internal transactions—when combined financial statements for the home office and branches are prepared are discussed later in the chapter.

Investment in Branch and Home Office Accounts   From the home office point of view, all resources transferred to the branch and earnings generated by the branch are included in the home office's investment in the branch. To keep track of its claim on branch assets, the home office uses an **Investment in Branch** account (sometimes called *Branch Office* or *Branch Current*). After periodic results of branch operations are recorded, Investment in Branch reflects the equity of the home office in the branch. Similarly, the branch uses an account called **Home Office** (or *Home Office Current*) to record transactions with the home office from the branch perspective. The balance in the Home Office account represents the dollar amount of the branch's obligations to the home office or, alternatively, may be viewed as an owners' equity account where the home office is the owner. In normal circumstances, the Investment in Branch account on the home office books has a debit balance, while the Home Office account on the branch books has a credit balance.

As an example, suppose the home office transfers the following items to a newly established branch:

Item	Amount per Home Office Books
Cash	$20,000
Unexpired Insurance	1,400
Office Supplies	800
Furniture and Fixtures	35,000
Accumulated Depreciation—Furniture and Fixtures	(10,000)
Net Book Value of Items Transferred	$47,200

These transfers would be recorded by the home office and branch as shown on page 163.

Note that after the transfer has been recorded there is no difference in the firm's total assets or liabilities. Rather, the fact that assets have changed their location within the organization is recorded in the reciprocal accounts. In order to avoid overstatement of assets and liabilities when combined financial statements are prepared, the offsetting balances in both the Investment in Branch and Home Office accounts will be netted out. This procedure is discussed later in the chapter.

RECORDING THE TRANSFER OF ASSETS
BETWEEN HOME OFFICE AND BRANCH

Account	Home Office Books		Branch Books	
	Dr.	Cr.	Dr.	Cr.
Investment in Branch	47,200	—	—	—
Cash		20,000	20,000	
Unexpired Insurance		1,400	1,400	
Office Supplies		800	800	
Furniture and Fixtures		35,000	35,000	
Accumulated Depreciation—Furniture and Fixtures	10,000			10,000
Home Office	—	—		47,200

Treatment of Start-Up Costs of New Branches Establishing a new branch often requires that considerable start-up costs be incurred before revenues are generated. The matching principle might be invoked by some to justify deferring or capitalizing those costs pending the realization of revenue. *SFAS 7* (AC § 2062) offers some guidance in this area.[1] Technically, *SFAS 7* applies to development stage enterprises (as defined therein) which will issue separate financial statements; its thrust is given in the following excerpt:

> Generally accepted accounting principles that apply to established operating enterprises shall govern the recognition of revenue by a development stage enterprise and shall determine whether a cost incurred by a development stage enterprise is to be charged to expense when incurred or is to be capitalized or deferred. Accordingly, capitalization or deferral of costs shall be subject to the same assessment of recoverability that would be applicable in an established operating enterprise.[2]

Although separate financial statements are not issued externally for a branch, whether in a "development stage" or not, it seems clear that *future benefit* is the main criterion when capitalization is being considered. No special accounting principles apply. This means that conventional organization costs could be capitalized and amortized but that training costs or early operating losses must be expensed as incurred and not deferred.

Merchandise Shipments to Branches

Branches are often established to serve as retail outlets for a company's products. Merchandise inventories carried at the branch locations are periodically replenished with shipments of merchandise from the home office. The internal transfer price used to bill shipments to branches affects the accounting for shipments and the procedures employed to combine the accounts of the home office and its branches when financial statements are prepared. Transfer prices may be based on any of the following:

    1.   Cost to the home office.

---

[1] Financial Accounting Standards Board, *Statement of Financial Accounting Standards No. 7*, "Accounting and Reporting by Development Stage Enterprises" (Stamford, Conn.: FASB, 1975).

[2] Ibid., par. 10; AC § 2062.10.

2.   An amount in excess of cost:
   a. Cost plus an internal markup percentage.
   b. Retail or market value.

Merchandise Shipments Billed at Cost   The simplest practice is to bill shipments of merchandise to the branch at cost; it creates no special accounting problems and results in a branch income statement that provides management with a straightforward view of the results of branch operations. On the other hand, it has the effect of attributing the entire gross profit on merchandise sales to the branch, even though the home office may have played a substantial role in the manufacture or procurement of merchandise from outside sources. Evaluation of the performance of the branch relative to the home office may therefore be clouded—some of the ultimate gross profit attributed to the branch may legitimately have been attributable to operation of the home office. Further discussion of such transfer pricing issues appears in Chapter 12. A comprehensive treatment, however, is beyond the scope of this book.

Periodic Inventory System   When the home office and branch use periodic inventory accounting, shipments are recorded in two additional offsetting reciprocal accounts, as follows:

HOME OFFICE BOOKS

Investment in Branch   XXX
   Shipments to Branch   XXX
To record the shipment of inventory to the branch.

BRANCH BOOKS

Shipments from Home Office   XXX
   Home Office   XXX
To record the receipt of inventory shipped from the home office.

If the branch pays the freight cost, it will charge Freight In and credit Cash. No entry need be made by the home office. In contrast, payment of the freight by the home office means that additional entries are required to assign the freight cost to the branch.

HOME OFFICE BOOKS

Investment in Branch   XXX
   Cash   XXX
To record payment of shipping costs on behalf of the branch.

BRANCH BOOKS

Freight In   XXX
   Home Office   XXX
To record freight expense on inventory paid by home office.

Perpetual Inventory System   When both the home office and branch employ perpetual inventory systems, the additional reciprocal accounts—Shipments to Branch and Shipments from Home Office—are unnecessary. Instead, the home office credits Inventory when shipments are made and the branch debits Inventory when the shipments are received. Cost of freight for the shipments is handled the same as under the periodic system.

Merchandise Shipments Billed above Cost   The billing of shipments at an amount above cost is often appropriate for performance evaluation and optimal decision making within the firm. It has the effect of attributing some, or all, of the gross profit on sales to the home office. The practice has also been motivated by the desire to conceal the true profitability of the branch operation from the branch manager. An added advantage arises when shipments are billed at *retail prices*. Even if a periodic inventory system is used, billing at retail has the effect of creating a perpetual system at the branch. If shipments are billed at retail, the branch inventory account will reflect retail prices. Sales made by the branch are, of course, made at retail. Therefore, the home office record of shipments to the branch at retail less sales reported by the branch tells the home office the branch inventory which should be on hand, at retail. Periodic physical inventory counts by home office personnel will reveal any shortages in the branch inventory with a high degree of accuracy. In this way, a system of billing shipments to the branch at retail prices enhances internal control over branch inventories.

These internal control benefits associated with billing intrafirm shipments at retail must be weighed against the possible distortion of branch operating results. When shipments are billed at retail, branch sales revenue will approximate its cost of goods sold. Consequently, the branch will consistently report an operating loss equal to its operating expenses. This is not an accurate picture of branch operations. It might impede proper managerial analysis of the branch and have a demoralizing effect on branch personnel.

Periodic Inventory System   Once a firm begins pricing merchandise shipments to branches at amounts in excess of cost, a new accounting problem arises. When the home office computes its own cost of goods sold for a reporting period, it reduces its own merchandise purchases from outside sources by the amount shown in the Shipments to Branch account. Similarly, if the home office manufactures the goods itself, the shipments to the branch go to reduce cost of goods manufactured.

For financial reporting purposes, the home office carries its inventory accounts at cost (or lower of cost or market). This cost basis will be disturbed if merchandise purchases are reduced by branch shipments measured at more than cost. To accommodate this problem, the home office employs an account entitled **Overvaluation of Branch Inventory,** sometimes called *Unrealized Profit in Branch Inventory*. Such an account cannot be viewed as deferred profit (as in installment sales) because no external sale has occurred. Although this overvaluation account relates to the branch inventory, it is normally carried on the home office books as a contra to Inventory. It will have the desired effect on the branch inventory when combined statements are prepared. The markup on each shipment to the branch will be entered and accumulated in this account, which becomes another reciprocal account. The Shipments to Branch balance at cost plus the Overvaluation account balance on the home office books will offset the Shipments from Home Office balance at billed prices on the branch books.

As an example, suppose the home office bills the branch $25,000 for a shipment of merchandise which cost the home office $15,000. The branch pays freight costs of $800. Journal entries made by the home office and branch are as follows:

HOME OFFICE BOOKS

Investment in Branch	25,000	
Shipments to Branch		15,000
Overvaluation of Branch Inventory		10,000
To record the shipment of inventory costing $15,000 to the branch at a billed price of $25,000.		

BRANCH BOOKS

Shipments from Home Office	25,000	
Freight In	800	
Home Office		25,000
Cash		800
To record the receipt of inventory shipped from the home office, $25,000, and payment of the freight, $800.		

Perpetual Inventory System   Again, when the home office and branch both have perpetual systems, the shipments accounts are no longer needed—the Inventory accounts are debited and credited directly. The home office continues to account for the markup in the overvaluation account in order to avoid disturbing the cost basis of its inventory. The entries needed in a perpetual inventory system to record the $25,000 shipment just mentioned follow:

HOME OFFICE BOOKS

Investment in Branch	25,000	
Inventory		15,000
Overvaluation of Branch Inventory		10,000
To record the shipment of inventory costing $15,000 to the branch at a billed price of $25,000.		

BRANCH BOOKS

Inventory	25,000	
Freight In	800	
Home Office		25,000
Cash		800
To record the receipt of inventory shipped from the home office, $25,000, and payment of the freight, $800.		

Transfer of merchandise to branches at prices above cost generates the need for certain end-of-period adjustments when the home office and branch accounts are combined. Branch inventory must be reduced to cost and the Overvaluation account balance must be eliminated. We defer discussion of these adjustments to the section which describes all the end-of-period procedures.

Treatment of Freight In   Freight costs on merchandise purchases or shipments from the home office attach to the merchandise and are inventoriable costs. When recording the ending inventory, the accountant must include either the actual freight costs on those goods or a pro rata share of total freight in. We assume throughout that the cost of merchandise to the home office includes the appropriate freight. Branch inventories at prices billed by the home office, with or without markup, must be increased by the applicable freight amount.

Charging the Branch with Expenses Incurred by the Home Office

Since the branch is not autonomous, the home office will incur various expenses on its behalf. This situation occurs for two major reasons:

1.   Certain accounting records, such as those for plant assets and payroll, may be retained in the home office. As a result, depreciation expense, salaries and wages, and payroll taxes pertaining to the branch are initially recorded by the home office.

2.   Various general and administrative overhead expenses as well as certain marketing expenses (such as advertising) are normally incurred at the home office. Such expenses are generally not separable, although some portion obviously relates to the branch operations.

How these expenses are accounted for varies across firms. Some companies may not charge expenses to their branches in formal accounting entries. Rather, they may simply make memorandum allocations for internal reporting purposes. In other situations, expenses incurred on behalf of branches are credited in the home office accounts and entered in the accounts of the branch. We briefly illustrate the latter case:

HOME OFFICE BOOKS

Investment in Branch   XXX
     Various Credits (details omitted)   XXX
To charge the branch for expenses incurred on its behalf by the
home office. Credits are to expenses such as advertising, assets
such as prepayments, and accumulated depreciation.

BRANCH BOOKS

Various Expenses (details omitted)   XXX
     Home Office   XXX
To record expenses attributable to the branch which were
originally incurred by the home office.

Observe that these entries affect the reciprocal Home Office and Investment in Branch accounts. Incurrence of these expenses by the home office clearly increases the resources committed to the branch and, concurrently, increases the obligation of the branch to the home office.

Transactions among Branches

Although it is possible for a branch to have reciprocal accounts with other branches, there is little need to do so. As part of its control system, the home office coordinates and controls any transactions between branches through its investment in branch accounts. Branch offices record any transactions with other branches in their respective home office accounts.

Merchandise shipments between branches are probably the most common type of interbranch transaction. Excess inventory at one branch location is frequently moved to cover a shortage at another location. In considering such interbranch transactions, one must also address the treatment of freight costs. The freight cost associated with direct shipment of the merchandise from the home office to the branch where it is sold is properly inventoriable. Shipments between branches, however, may cause the total freight cost incurred in getting the merchandise to its ultimate destination to exceed the cost of direct shipment from the home office. This excess is not inventoriable and is an expense of the current period generally attributable to the home office, which usually makes decisions on shipments.

To illustrate, suppose that the Hanover branch had received $10,000 of merchandise at cost from its home office and had paid freight of $500. Subsequently, Hanover is instructed to ship these items to the Concord branch at an additional shipping cost of $200, paid by Hanover. Had the items been shipped direct to Concord from the home office, the freight cost would have been $600. This shipment is recorded on the three sets of books in the following way:

HANOVER BRANCH BOOKS

Home Office	10,700	
Shipments from Home Office		10,000
Freight In		500
Cash		200

To record shipment of merchandise to the Concord branch as directed by the home office and charge the home office for all freight costs incurred by Hanover in connection with this merchandise.

CONCORD BRANCH BOOKS

Shipments from Home Office	10,000	
Freight In	600	
Home Office		10,600

To record receipt of inventory shipped from the home office via the Hanover branch and inventoriable freight costs of $600.

HOME OFFICE BOOKS

Investment in Concord Branch	10,600	
Shipments to Hanover Branch	10,000	
Excess Freight Expense	100	
Investment in Hanover Branch		10,700
Shipments to Concord Branch		10,000

To record the movement of inventory from Hanover to Concord, credit Hanover for the shipment and freight cost of $700 it paid, charge Concord for the shipment and freight cost of $600, and record the excess freight cost of $100 as a home office expense.

After these entries have been made, all reciprocal accounts have the proper offsetting balances. The home office, of course, must carefully monitor both the movement of goods and the related accounting entries in order to keep things straight.

End-of-Period Procedures

At the end of an accounting period, three types of procedures are required in home office/branch accounting. First, the accountant must determine that the offsetting balances in the reciprocal accounts are equal, as intended. If discrepancies exist, the reciprocal accounts must be reconciled and their balances adjusted accordingly. Second, to account for the operations of the period, conventional closing entries must be made on the home office and branch books. Third, the accountant must prepare combined financial statements for the home office, often using a working paper to facilitate their preparation. We discuss each procedure in turn.

Reconciliation of Reciprocal Accounts   Reciprocal accounts must be reconciled, and any necessary adjustments must be made to bring these accounts into balance before end-of-period procedures can be continued. Differences in reciprocal account balances can result from errors but usually arise when intrafirm transactions occur near the end of an accounting period. Such transactions are normally recorded by *either* the home office *or* the branch, but not by both. Delays in shipping, mailing, or the processing of information can mean the second half of the transaction goes unrecorded until the next accounting period. Some common examples of these transactions include:

1. Shipments in transit at the end of a period, which are recorded by the home office but not by the branch.
2. Remittances from the branch mailed on the last day of an accounting period and therefore not yet received and recorded by the home office.
3. Collections of home office receivables by the branch close to the end of a period, which are not recorded in the home office records.
4. If all fixed asset records are maintained at the home office, a last-minute fixed asset purchase by the branch does not yet appear on the home office books at the end of the period.

All such transactions are recorded in only one reciprocal account by the end of the period. A reconciliation of reciprocal accounts and appropriate adjusting entries are needed so that the offsetting account balances are brought into agreement.

Closing Entries   After the reciprocal accounts have been reconciled, closing entries are made on both the branch and home office books. When a periodic inventory system is used, these closing entries include the recognition of home office and branch ending inventories. The branch revenue and expense accounts are closed to the branch's income summary. If the branch had net income (loss), closing the branch's income summary generates a credit (debit) to the Home Office account. The home office records the income (loss) of the branch and increases (decreases) its Investment in Branch account accordingly. Similarly, home office revenue and expense accounts are closed to the home of-

Exhibit 5.2   Typical Closing Entries Made on Branch and Home Office Books

BRANCH BOOKS

Sales	XXX	
Inventory, December 31	XXX	
Shipments from Home Office		XXX
Expenses (details omitted)		XXX
Inventory, January 1		XXX
Income Summary		XXX

To close the branch revenue and expense accounts to Income Summary and record the net income for the period. Cost of goods sold for the branch equals Inventory, January 1 + Shipments from Home + Freight In − Inventory, December 31.

Income Summary	XXX	
Home Office		XXX

To close the net income for the period to the Home Office account.

HOME OFFICE BOOKS

Investment in Branch	XXX	
Income from Branch		XXX

To record the net income reported by the branch, thereby increasing the investment in the branch.

Overvaluation of Branch Inventory	XXX	
Realized Intrafirm Profit		XXX

To credit the home office for the markup on the intrafirm shipments realized on sales to external customers during the period.

Sales	XXX	
Shipments to Branch	XXX	
Inventory, December 31	XXX	
Realized Intrafirm Profit	XXX	
Purchases		XXX
Freight In		XXX
Expenses (details omitted)		XXX
Inventory, January 1		XXX
Income Summary		XXX

To close the home office revenue and expense accounts to Income Summary and record the net income from home office operations. Cost of goods sold for the home office equals Inventory, January 1 + Purchases − Shipments to Branch + Freight In − Inventory, December 31.

Income from Branch	XXX	
Income Summary		XXX

To close the branch's net income to Income Summary.

Income Summary	XXX	
Retained Earnings		XXX

To close combined net income for the period to Retained Earnings.

fice income summary account. When shipments to the branch are billed at prices above cost, the overvaluation account must be reduced by the amount of intrafirm markup realized during the period through branch sales to external customers. Whether the realized intrafirm markup should be attributed to branch operations or home office operations is related to the previously discussed reasons for setting the transfer price above cost. The typical closing entries presented in Exhibit 5.2 reflect the realized intrafirm markup in home office operations by assigning it to an account entitled Realized Intrafirm Profit.

Working Papers for Combined Statements   Financial statements issued to external users report the financial position and operations of the home office and its branches as a *single business unit,* the firm. Preparation of these combined financial statements is facilitated by use of a **working paper** designed to organize the preclosing account balances and ending inventories of the home office and branch along income statement and balance sheet lines. As mentioned earlier, transactions between the home office and branch must be netted out (or **eliminated**) in combining the accounts to avoid overstating combined assets, liabilities, revenues, and expenses. These internal transactions are reflected in the offsetting reciprocal account balances on the home office and branch books. The Investment in Branch and Home Office reciprocal account balances are eliminated on the working paper as part of this netting-out or **elimination process.** If they are not eliminated, combined assets and equities will both be overstated by the balance in these accounts. This part of the elimination process is depicted graphically in Figure 5.1. Be aware, however, that the elimination process is a working paper technique only. Because the reciprocal accounts reflect bonafide transactions between the home office and branch, their balances are not eliminated on the books.

The shipments and overvaluation accounts also are reciprocal accounts and are eliminated on the working paper to avoid overstatement of revenues and cost of goods sold and to reduce the branch inventories to cost. Although the shipments accounts are closed and the overvaluation account adjusted as part of the normal closing procedures, their elimination on the working paper is not entered in the books of the home office and branch. They, too, reflect bonafide transactions between the home office and branch. In sum, *working paper eliminations are not posted to the books.*

Branch Inventories Priced above Cost   Recall that when the home office prices merchandise shipments to the branch above cost, it accounts for the excess in an account such as Overvaluation of Branch Inventory. This practice creates two problems when combined statements are prepared:

1.   Since the branch ending inventory includes an intrafirm markup, the markup must be removed before home office and branch inventories can be combined in the firm's balance sheet.

2.   Markup in both the beginning and ending inventories of the branch distorts the firm's cost of goods sold and, accordingly, must be eliminated.

Since preclosing account balances are used in the combined financial statement working paper, the above problems necessitate working paper elimina-

Figure 5.1   Diagramatic Approach to Eliminating Reciprocal Account Balances When Preparing Combined
Statements for a Home Office and Branch

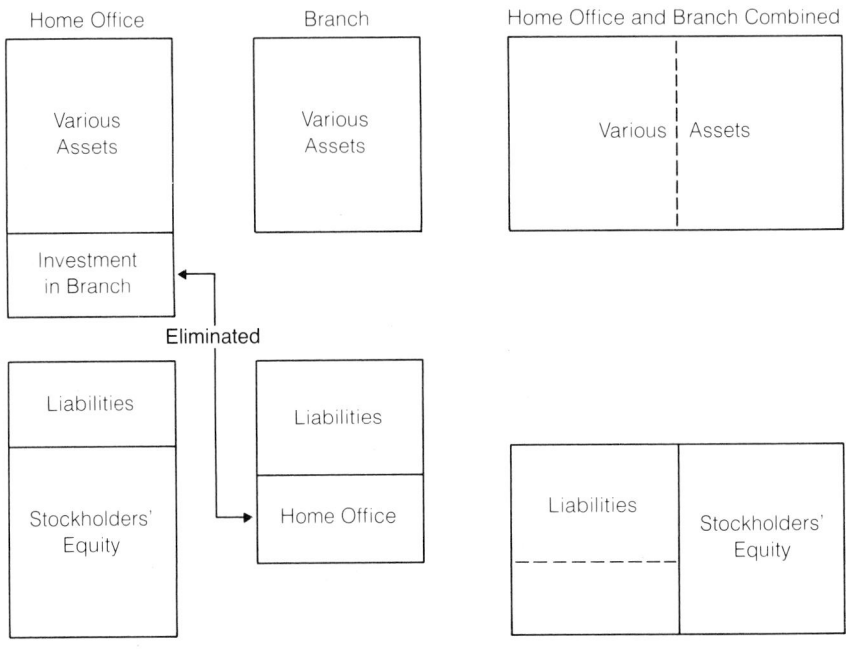

tions even though the formal closing entries achieve the same result on the
books. To see how these complications are treated on the working paper, suppose we have the following set of account balances (a periodic inventory system
is used):

HOME OFFICE BOOKS: (CR.)

Shipments to Branch	$(100,000)
Overvaluation of Branch Inventory	(58,000)

BRANCH BOOKS: DR.

Inventory, January 1	$ 24,000
Shipments from Home Office	150,000
Inventory, December 31	30,000

Merchandise shipments to the branch are marked up 50 percent above cost
by the home office. The balance of $58,000 in Overvaluation of Branch Invento-
ry includes the $50,000 markup on current period shipments and the $8,000
markup reflected in the branch's January 1 inventory balance of $24,000. To
eliminate the reciprocal account balances and adjust the inventories to cost, the
eliminating entries shown in Exhibit 5.3 would be made on the combined financial statement working paper.

The exact form of the third entry in Exhibit 5.3 depends upon the working
paper format being used. Our objective is to remove the markup and reduce
ending inventory to cost. Since ending inventory appears on the balance sheet

Exhibit 5.3 Illustration of End-of-Period Eliminating Entries Relating to Merchandise Shipments Priced Above Cost

COMBINED FINANCIAL STATEMENT WORKING PAPER

Shipments to Branch	100,000	
Overvaluation of Branch Inventory	50,000	
Shipments from Home Office		150,000
To eliminate the offsetting reciprocal account balances relating to intrafirm merchandise shipments.		
Overvaluation of Branch Inventory	8,000	
Inventory, January 1, Income Statement (or Cost of Goods Sold) .		8,000
To reduce the branch beginning inventory to cost, thereby reducing cost of goods sold.		
Inventory, December 31, Income Statement (or Cost of Goods Sold) .	10,000	
Inventory (Balance Sheet)		10,000
To reduce the branch ending inventory to cost, thereby increasing cost of goods sold.		

and also enters into the computation of cost of goods sold, removing the markup from the ending inventory affects both the balance sheet and income statement. Our working paper (illustrated later, in Exhibit 5.7) is arranged in financial statement format. It includes the income statement, statement of retained earnings, and balance sheet. Furthermore, within the income statement separate lines are provided for beginning and ending inventories and merchandise purchases. Therefore, since removing the markup from ending inventory affects that ending inventory on both the balance sheet and income statement, our working paper elimination must debit and credit inventory by the same amount but in two different financial statements. An alternative format would replace these three lines with a single cost-of-goods-sold line.

Accounting for Shipments to Branch as Sales The preferred treatment for merchandise shipments to branches is to use a *shipments* account, which reduces home office purchases, and a separate overvaluation account to keep track of any markup. Some firms, however, may treat all shipments to branches as *sales* at billed prices. This practice requires that the interoffice sales be eliminated on the working paper against the branch's shipments account. As before, branch inventories are maintained at billed prices, and any markup must be removed on the combined financial statement working paper.

Markup in ending inventory is eliminated from the ending inventory on both the income statement and balance sheet in the way illustrated in Exhibit 5.3. If there is markup in *beginning inventory*, however, it is eliminated against beginning inventory on the income statement and against *beginning retained earnings*. In the normal closing procedures, home office "sales" to the branch are closed to the home office income summary. Thus the home office net income includes the markup on the sales to the branch, even though some of it is reflected in the branch's inventory and is not realized. Since the markup reflected in last period's net income is in this period's beginning retained earnings, the elimination is against beginning retained earnings.

Exhibit 5.4   Comparison of Gross Profits Reported under the Shipments and Sales Alternatives

SHIPMENTS AND OVERVALUATION ACCOUNTS	Year One	Year Two
Branch Sales	$130,000	$240,000
Branch Cost of Goods Sold	(75,000)	(175,000)[a]
Branch Gross Profit on Sales	$ 55,000	$ 65,000
Intrafirm Markup Realized on External Sales	15,000	35,000[b]
Total Gross Profit on Branch Sales	$ 70,000	$100,000

[a]$175,000 = $25,000 + $150,000.
[b]$35,000 = $5,000 + ($150,000 − $120,000).

RECORDING INTRAFIRM SHIPMENTS AS SALES	Year One	Year Two
Branch Gross Profit (as Above)	$ 55,000	$ 65,000
Home Office Sales to Branch	$100,000	$150,000
Cost of Goods Sold to Branch	(80,000)	(120,000)
Home Office Gross Profit on Sales to Branch	$ 20,000	$ 30,000
Total Reported Gross Profit on Branch Sales	$ 75,000	$ 95,000
Working Paper Elimination Needed	(5,000)	5,000
Corrected Total Gross Profit on Branch Sales (as Above)	$ 70,000	$100,000

To contrast this sales treatment with the use of the shipments and overvaluation accounts, consider the following example. During year one, the home office bills a newly-established branch $100,000 for merchandise shipped to it. The merchandise cost the home office $80,000. At year-end, $25,000 of this merchandise remains in the branch inventory, reflecting unrealized intrafirm markup of $5,000. The branch records sales of $130,000 in year one. In year two, $150,000 is billed to the branch for merchandise costing the home office $120,000. Branch sales during year two amounted to $240,000, and there is no ending inventory. Total gross profit on branch sales over the two-year period is $170,000 [= ($130,000 + $240,000) − ($80,000 + $120,000)]. Comparative gross profit data under the two methods are presented in Exhibit 5.4.

The correct gross profits for the two years are computed in the top half of Exhibit 5.4, where the shipments and overvaluation accounts are used. After the normal closing procedures in year one, the unrealized intrafirm markup of $5,000 remains in the overvaluation account. It is counted as realized at the end of year two, when the overvaluation account is adjusted to reflect the external sale of all the inventory.

In contrast, when shipments to the branch are treated as sales, the results in the bottom half of Exhibit 5.4 occur. Although the $5,000 unrealized intrafirm markup is eliminated on the working paper in both cases, it remains in the home office reported net income for year one and is closed to retained earnings. The $5,000 actually belongs in year two's net income, and the working paper entry that follows achieves the result. Note that the debit is to beginning retained earnings rather than the overvaluation account, as was illustrated in Exhibit 5.3.

COMBINED FINANCIAL STATEMENT WORKING PAPER

Retained Earnings, Jan. 1 (year two) 5,000
   Inventory, Jan. 1 (year two)   5,000
To reduce the beginning inventory to cost and remove the
markup from beginning retained earnings. Recording
intrafirm shipments as sales led to inclusion of the unrealized
markup in year one income and in retained earnings at the
end of year one.

Comprehensive Illustration of Home Office and Branch Accounting

The Hardy Corporation established a branch office in Blockville on January 2, 19X1. Hardy bills all shipments of merchandise to Blockville at 25 percent over cost. At January 1, 19X4, the beginning of the current year, the condensed trial balance of the Blockville branch is as follows:

Blockville Branch
Trial Balance at January 1, 19X4

Account	Amount Dr. (Cr.)
Cash	$ 14,000
Accounts Receivable	65,000
Inventory	77,000
Furniture and Fixtures	100,000
Accumulated Depreciation	(49,090)
Accounts Payable	(8,000)
Salaries Payable	(5,000)
Home Office	(193,910)
	$ 0

The furniture and fixtures were acquired on January 2, 19X1. They are being depreciated by Blockville over ten years by the sum-of-the-years'-digits (SYD) method and have no salvage value. All other property accounts and prepayments are maintained at the home office. The beginning inventory includes $2,000 of freight costs. Home office and branch books are closed annually, and combined financial statements are prepared. A summary of transactions involving the branch during 19X4 follows:

1. Merchandise costing $300,000 was shipped to the branch; $8,000 was in transit at December 31, 19X4. Freight on the in-transit shipment to be paid by the branch is $100.

2. Freight costs on shipments received from the home office amounted to $9,000; $7,000 of this was paid in cash by the home office, $2,000 by the branch.

3. Sales of $500,000 were made by Blockville, including $125,000 of cash sales.

Exhibit 5.5   Accounting Entries Made by Hardy Corporation and Its Blockville Branch to Record
Transactions Involving the Branch in 19X4

HOME OFFICE BOOKS				BLOCKVILLE BRANCH BOOKS		
	Dr.	Cr.	Transaction		Dr.	Cr.
Investment in Branch .	375,000		1	Shipments from Home		
Shipments to Branch .		300,000		Office	365,000	
Overvaluation of				Home Office . . .		365,000
Branch Inventory. .		75,000		To record merchandise		
To record merchandise				received from the home		
shipped to the branch at				office, at billed prices.		
125 percent of cost.						
Investment in Branch . .	7,000		2	Freight In	9,000	
Cash		7,000		Cash		2,000
To record freight cost paid				Home Office . . .		7,000
on merchandise shipments				To record freight cost on		
to the branch.				merchandise shipments		
				received, including that		
				paid by the home office.		
			3	Cash	125,000	
				Accounts Receivable . .	375,000	
				Sales		500,000
				To record cash and credit		
				sales made during the year.		
			4	Cash	390,000	
				Accounts Receivable .		390,000
				To record collection of		
				receivables.		

4. Collections on accounts receivable in the amount of $390,000 were received in the Blockville branch.

5. Operating expenses incurred by the branch amounted to $35,000; salaries were $50,000. Payments of $31,000 were made for operating expenses, and $53,000 was paid to employees (disregard payroll taxes).

6. Cash remittances to the home office were $410,000, of which $20,000 was in transit on December 31, 19X4.

7. On December 29, 19X4, a $7,800 payment from a home office customer was received in the branch. Branch personnel deposited the check but had not informed the home office by December 31, 19X4.

8. The home office allocated $27,000 of its operating expenses to the branch.

9. Depreciation expense of $12,727 [= (7/55) × $100,000] on furniture and fixtures was recorded by the branch on December 31, 19X4.

10. Ending inventory at the branch was $60,000 at billed prices and the applicable freight was $1,500; home office ending inventory, at cost, was $275,000.

Exhibit 5.5   Accounting Entries Made by Hardy Corporation and Its Blockville Branch to Record Transactions Involving the Branch in 19X4 *continued*

HOME OFFICE BOOKS				BLOCKVILLE BRANCH BOOKS		
	Dr.	Cr.	Transaction		Dr.	Cr.
			5	Operating Expenses . .	35,000	
				Salaries Expense . . .	50,000	
				Salaries Payable . . .	3,000	
				Accounts Payable . .		4,000
				Cash		84,000
				To record operating expenses, salaries expense, and payments to employees and suppliers.		
Cash	390,000		6	Home Office	410,000	
Investment in Branch .		390,000		Cash		410,000
To record cash received from the branch during 19X4.				To record cash remitted to the home office during 19X4.		
			7	Cash	7,800	
				Home Office . . .		7,800
				To record payment received from a home office customer and deposited.		
Investment in Branch . .	27,000		8	Operating Expenses . .	27,000	
Operating Expenses .		27,000		Home Office . . .		27,000
To record allocation of home office expenses to the branch.				To record expenses allocated by the home office.		
			9	Depreciation Expense . .	12,727	
				Accumulated Depreciation . . .		12,727
				To record depreciation expense on furniture and fixtures in 19X4.		

Accounting entries made by the home office and branch during 19X4 are given in Exhibit 5.5. After the entries in Exhibit 5.5 are posted, preclosing trial balances for the home office and branch are prepared (Exhibit 5.6).

Reconciliation of Reciprocal Accounts

Exhibit 5.6 shows a discrepancy between the Investment in Branch and Home Office reciprocal accounts. The Investment in Branch account has a debit balance of $212,910, while the Home Office account has a credit balance of $190,710. Before we can proceed with our end-of-period procedures, these reciprocal accounts must be reconciled and brought into balance.

To accomplish this, we refer back to our summation of the year's transactions. *First*, we note from 1 that a merchandise shipment costing $8,000 with

Exhibit 5.6   Hardy Corporation and Blockville Branch: Preclosing Trial Balances

Hardy Corporation and Its Blockville Branch
Preclosing Trial Balances at December 31, 19X4

| | Amount: Dr. (Cr.) | |
Account	Home Office	Branch
Cash	$ 110,000	$ 40,800
Accounts Receivable	260,000	50,000
Inventory, January 1, 19X4	280,000	77,000
Overvaluation of Branch Inventory	(90,000)	—
Prepayments	40,000	—
Property, Plant, and Equipment	750,000	100,000
Accumulated Depreciation	(200,000)	(61,817)
Investment in Branch	212,910	—
Accounts Payable	(162,000)	(12,000)
Salaries Payable	(18,000)	(2,000)
Other Liabilities	(300,000)	—
Capital Stock	(200,000)	—
Retained Earnings, January 1, 19X4	(352,910)	—
Home Office	—	(190,710)
Sales	(1,700,000)	(500,000)
Shipments to Branch	(300,000)	—
Purchases	1,150,000	—
Shipments from Home Office	—	365,000
Freight In	25,000	9,000
Salaries Expense	250,000	50,000
Operating Expenses	195,000	62,000
Depreciation Expense	50,000	12,727
	$ 0	$ 0

freight of $100 was in transit to the branch at December 31. At the 25 percent markup being used by the home office, this shipment has a billed value of $10,000. To record this shipment, the branch makes the following entry:

BLOCKVILLE BRANCH BOOKS
1(a)

Shipments from Home Office (in transit)	10,000	
Home Office		10,000

To record the merchandise shipment in transit from the home office. *Note: this transaction increases the branch's ending physical inventory by $10,000 to $71,500,* the amount to be recorded in the closing entries given in the next section.

Freight In (in transit)	100	
Accounts Payable		100

To accrue the freight cost on the merchandise shipment in transit. *Note: this transaction increases the branch's ending inventory by another $100, to $71,600.*

Second, transaction 6 indicated that cash remittances to the home office of

$20,000 were in transit at December 31. The home office will record this as shown:

HOME OFFICE BOOKS

6(a)

Cash (in transit)	20,000	
Investment in Branch		20,000
To record the cash remittance in transit to the home office at December 31.		

Third, we see that in transaction 7 the branch recorded the collection of a home office receivable but had not informed the home office. Since the receivable was not on the branch books, the credit was made to Home Office. Now, of course, the home office must recognize that this receivable has been collected.

HOME OFFICE BOOKS

6(a)

Investment in Branch	7,800	
Accounts Receivable		7,800
To record the collection of a home office receivable made by the branch.		

These adjustments are posted to the reciprocal accounts as shown next:

Investment in Branch					Home Office		
Bal., 12/31/X4	212,910	6(a)	20,000			Bal., 12/31/X4	190,710
7(a)	7,800					1(a)	10.000
Adj. bal.	200,710					Adj. bal.	200,710

Closing Entries

Both the home office and branch must record the typical closing entries at the end of the accounting period. These entries are posted to the accounts of the home office and branch. Be aware of the distinction, however, between the closing entries made here and the subsequent preparation of combined financial statements. In preparing the combined balance sheet and statements of income and retained earnings, we start with *preclosing trial balances* and make working paper eliminations that are *not* posted to the accounts of the home office or branch.

Branch Closing Entries   Branch personnel record the ending inventory and close all revenue and expense accounts, including Shipments from Home Office, first to an income summary account and then to the Home Office account. Any net income (loss) recorded by the branch increases (decreases) its obligation to the home office. After adjusting for the merchandise shipment in transit, the branch's ending inventory is $71,600, and Shipments from Home Office is $375,000.

BLOCKVILLE BRANCH BOOKS

Sales	500,000	
Inventory, December 31	71,600	
Income Summary	14,227	
Shipments from Home Office		375,000
Freight In		9,100
Salaries Expense		50,000
Operating Expenses		62,000
Depreciation Expense		12,727
Inventory, January 1		77,000

To close the revenue and expense accounts for 19X4 to
Income Summary and record the net loss of $14,227.

Home Office	14,227	
Income Summary		14,227

To close the net loss for 19X4 to the Home Office
account.

Home Office Closing Entries   In addition to recording its own ending inventory and closing its own revenue and expense accounts to Income Summary and then to Retained Earnings, the home office must accrue the net income (loss) of the branch and adjust the Overvaluation of Branch Inventory account. Ending inventory of the Blockville branch *at billed prices* is $70,000, which is 25 percent or $14,000 [= $70,000 − ($70,000/1.25)] above cost. The overvaluation account must be reduced to $14,000; the other $76,000 (= $90,000 − $14,000) has been realized through sales by the branch to outsiders. Should the realization of this $76,000, which is now profit, be attributed to the branch or the home office? This question can only be answered by recalling the reasons for billing merchandise shipments at a markup.

If the markup in fact represents a profit element attributable to the home office, the home office could include it in income from its own operations. In contrast, when the markup is actually a portion of branch profit, the home office will increase the profit reported by the branch accordingly. As before, *assume that the home office attributes the markup to home office operations* and records it as Realized Intrafirm Profit. The home office closing entries appear on page 181.

Note that neither the Investment in Branch nor the Home Office account has been closed out. The shipments accounts are closed because they are purchases to the branch and a reduction in purchases to the home office. As the next section makes evident, however, all reciprocal account balances are eliminated when combined financial statements are prepared.

Working Paper Preparation of Combined Financial Statements

Because the balances of certain of the reciprocal accounts are carried forward on the home office and branch books, combined financial statements are often prepared using a working paper. The working paper includes the preclosing trial balance data and ending inventory balances for the home office and branch as well as columns for adjustments and eliminations. The *columns for adjustments and eliminations* have two purposes:

    1.   To record any adjusting entries not reflected in the preclosing trial bal-

HOME OFFICE BOOKS

Income from Branch	14,227	
Investment in Branch		14,227
To record the operating loss reported for 19X4 by		
the Blockville branch, thereby reducing the		
investment in the branch.		
Overvaluation of Branch Inventory	76,000	
Realized Intrafirm Profit		76,000
To credit the home office for the markup on		
merchandise shipments realized on sales to		
external customers during 19X4.		
Sales	1,700,000	
Shipments to Branch	300,000	
Inventory, December 31	275,000	
Realized Intrafirm Profit	76,000	
Purchases		1,150,000
Freight In		25,000
Salaries Expense		250,000
Operating Expenses		195,000
Depreciation Expense		50,000
Inventory, January 1		280,000
Income Summary		401,000
To close the revenue and expense accounts for		
19X4 to Income Summary and record net income		
from home office operations of		
$325,000(= $401,000 − $76,000).		
Income Summary	14,227	
Income from Branch		14,227
To close the branch's net loss to Income Summary,		
thereby decreasing net income for 19X4 to		
$386,773(= $401,000 − $14,227).		
Income Summary	386,773	
Retained Earnings		386,773
To close net income for 19X4 to Retained Earnings.		

ances. In our example, the preclosing trial balances used in the working paper do reflect the adjustments made earlier to reconcile the reciprocal accounts.

2.   To record eliminating entries whose purpose is to remove the offsetting balances in the intrafirm reciprocal accounts. *Eliminations are made on working papers only and are not posted to the accounts.*

Combined Financial Statement Working Paper   We have chosen a working paper format organized around three principal financial statements— the income statement, statement of retained earnings, and balance sheet. The trial balance data from Exhibit 5.6 have been adjusted to reconcile the reciprocal accounts and have been organized to fit under one of these three financial statements. This is a **combined financial statement working paper.** An alternative approach, illustrated later, is to use the trial balances themselves, gen-

Exhibit 5.7 Combined Financial Statement Working Paper

Hardy Corporation and Blockville Branch
Combined Financial Statement Working Paper
For the Year Ended December 31, 19X4

	Home Office	Blockville Branch	Adjustments and Eliminations		Combined
			Dr.	Cr.	
INCOME STATEMENT					
Sales	1,700,000	500,000			2,200,000
Inventory, Dec. 31, 19X4 . .	275,000	71,600 [a]	(3) 14,000		332,600
Shipments to Branch . . .	300,000	—	(1) 300,000		—
Total Credits	2,275,000	571,600	314,000		2,532,600
Inventory, Jan 1, 19X4 . . .	280,000	77,000		(2) 15,000	342,000
Purchases	1,150,000	—			1,150,000
Shipments from Home Office .	—	375,000 [a]		(1) 375,000	—
Freight In	25,000	9,100 [a]			34,100
Salaries Expense	250,000	50,000			300,000
Operating Expenses . . .	195,000	62,000			257,000
Depreciation Expense . . .	50,000	12,727			62,727
Total Debits	1,950,000	585,827		390,000	2,145,827
Net Income—to Ret. Earn. Stmt.	325,000	(14,227)	314,000	390,000	386,773
RETAINED EARNINGS STATEMENT					
Retained Earnings, Jan. 1, 19X4	352,910	—			352,910
Net Income—from Inc. Stmt. .	325,000	(14,227)	314,000	390,000	386,773
Dividends	—	—			—
Retained Earnings, Dec. 31, 19X4—to Balance Sheet . .	677,910	(14,227)	314,000	390,000	739,683
BALANCE SHEET					
Cash	130,000 [a]	40,800			170,800
Accounts Receivable . . .	252,200 [a]	50,000			302,200
Inventory	275,000	71,600 [a]		(3) 14,000	332,600
Overval. of Branch Inventory .	(90,000)	—	(1) 75,000 (2) 15,000		—
Prepayments	40,000	—			40,000
Investment in Branch . . .	200,710 [a]	—		(4) 200,710	—
Property, Plant, & Equipment .	750,000	100,000			850,000
Accumulated Depreciation . .	(200,000)	(61,817)			(261,817)
Total	1,357,910	200,583	90,000	214,710	1,433,783
Accounts Payable	162,000	12,100			174,100
Salaries Payable	18,000	2,000			20,000
Other Liabilities	300,000	—			300,000
Home Office	—	200,710 [a]	(4) 200,710		—
Capital Stock	200,000	—			200,000
Ret. Earnings—from Ret. Earn. Stmt.	677,910	(14,227)	314,000	390,000	739,683
Total	1,357,910	200,583	514,710	390,000	1,433,783
			604,710	604,710	

[a]These balances reflect adjustments 1(a), 6(a), and 7(a) made to reconcile the reciprocal accounts.

Explanations of Working Paper Entries

(1) To eliminate the balance in Shipments from Home Office against the reciprocal Shipments to Branch and the related portion of the overvaluation account.
(2) To eliminate the remaining portion of the overvaluation account and remove the markup in the beginning inventory of the branch.
(3) To remove the markup included in the ending inventory of the branch on both the income statement and balance sheet.
(4) To eliminate the Investment in Branch against the reciprocal Home Office account.

---

erate a combined trial balance, and reorganize the combined accounts into the appropriate financial statement format.

We believe that the financial statement working paper format has some procedural advantages, including several total and subtotal points which help ensure accuracy. Furthermore, this format is used extensively in the chapters involving consolidated financial statements.

The completed working paper from which formal combined statements may be prepared appears in Exhibit 5.7. Note that the combined net income of $386,773 equals the total net income recorded by the home office in its closing entries, as it should.

Compare the closing entry which adjusted the overvaluation account down to $14,000 with the working paper eliminations that remove it entirely. In making our closing entries, we did not reduce the branch inventory to cost. The overvaluation account is actually a contra-asset account and, when subtracted from the marked-up inventory, provides us with inventory at cost. On the working paper, $75,000 of the overvaluation account balance is eliminated in conjunction with eliminating the shipments accounts. The remaining $15,000 is eliminated against the branch's *beginning* inventory, thereby reducing it to cost. Branch ending inventory appears on the working paper in both the income statement and balance sheet. In both places, it must be written down to cost by removing $14,000 from the ending inventory. Entry 3 accomplishes this and provides the same result as the book balance of $14,000 in the overvaluation account.

Combined Trial Balance Working Paper   Another approach to the preparation of combined financial statements for the home office and branch calls for a **combined trial balance working paper.** The combined accounts are then rearranged in financial statement format. Such a combined trial balance working paper is given in Exhibit 5.8 for the Hardy Corporation and its Blockville branch. In comparing it with the combined financial statement working paper in Exhibit 5.7, we make the following observations:

1.   Adjusting entries 1(a), 6(a), and 7(a) made to reconcile the Investment in Branch and Home Office reciprocal accounts are entered on the combined trial balance working paper. Alternatively, adjusted trial balances could have been used.

2.   Note the treatment of the ending inventory. The preclosing trial balance given in Exhibit 5.6 reflects only the beginning January 1 inventory. Ending inventory at December 31 is entered in the trial balance as *both* a debit and credit, thereby maintaining the integrity of the

Exhibit 5.8   Combined Trial Balance Working Paper

Hardy Corporation and the Blockville Branch
Combined Trial Balance Working Paper
For the Year Ended December 31, 19X4

Account	Home Office Dr. (Cr.)	Branch Dr. (Cr.)	Adjustments and Eliminations Dr.		Adjustments and Eliminations Cr.		Combined Dr. (Cr.)
Cash	110,000	40,800	6(a)	20,000			170,800
Accounts Receivable . .	260,000	50,000			7(a)	7,800	302,200
Inventory, January 1, 19X4 .	280,000	77,000			(2)	15,000	342,000
Inventory, December 31, 19X4 (Balance Sheet) .	275,000ª	71,600ª			(3)	14,000	332,600
Prepayments	40,000	—					40,000
Property, Plant, and Equipment	750,000	100,000					850,000
Accumulated Depreciation . . .	(200,000)	(61,817)					(261,817)
Investment in Branch .	212,910		7(a)	7,800	6(a)	20,000	—
					(4)	200,710	
Accounts Payable . . .	(162,000)	(12,000)			1(a)	100	(174,100)
Salaries Payable . . .	(18,000)	(2,000)					(20,000)
Other Liabilities . . .	(300,000)	—					(300,000)
Capital Stock	(200,000)	—					(200,000)
Retained Earnings . . .	(352,910)	—					(352,910)
Home Office	—	(190,710)	(4)	200,710	1(a)	10,000	—
Sales	(1,700,000)	(500,000)					(2,200,000)
Shipments to Branch . .	(300,000)	—	(1)	300,000			—
Inventory, December 31, 19X4 (Income Statement)	(275,000)ª	(71,600)ª	(3)	14,000			(332,600)
Overvaluation of Branch Inventory	(90,000)	—	(1)	75,000			—
			(2)	15,000			
Purchases	1,150,000	—					1,150,000
Shipments from Home Office	—	365,000	1(a)	10,000	(1)	375,000	—
Freight In	25,000	9,000	1(a)	100			34,100
Salaries Expense . . .	250,000	50,000					300,000
Operating Expenses . .	195,000	62,000					257,000
Depreciation Expense . .	50,000	12,727					62,727
	0	0		642,610		642,610	0

ªThe ending inventory of the home office and branch [reflecting adjustment 1(a)] is entered twice. The debit entry will be carried to the balance sheet and the credit is carried to the income statement as a component of cost of goods sold.

Explanations of Working Paper Entries

1(a) To record the merchandise shipment in transit from the home office and the related freight.

6(a) To record the cash remittance in transit to the home office.

7(a) To record the collection of a home office receivable made by the branch.

(1)   To eliminate the balance in Shipments from Home Office against the reciprocal Shipments to Branch and the related portion of the overvaluation account.

(2)   To eliminate the remaining portion of the overvaluation account and remove the markup in the beginning inventory of the branch.

(3)   To remove the markup included in the ending inventory of the branch on both the income statement and the balance sheet.

(4)   To eliminate the Investment in Branch against the reciprocal Home Office account.

trial balance. The debit entry will be carried to the balance sheet while the credit entry and the January 1 inventory (a debit) will be carried to the income statement as the ending and beginning inventories used in computing cost of goods sold.

3. The eliminating entries made on the combined trial balance working paper are the same as those made on the combined financial statement working paper.

Formal Combined Statements   Using the data in the Combined column of Exhibit 5.7 or 5.8, we prepare formal financial statements for the Hardy Corporation, which include the accounts of the Blockville branch. These statements are presented in Exhibits 5.9 and 5.10.

Disposal of a Branch

As mentioned earlier, home office/branch accounting is used in a variety of intrafirm entity situations. Indeed, branch accounting can be used for business units significant enough for their activities to represent a *separate major line of business or class of customer*. When such business units are closed down or sold, the provisions of *APBO 30* (AC § 2012) relating to **discontinued operations** must be followed.[3] Closing down or selling a branch activity that is one of several similar branch activities does not constitute disposal of a separate identifiable business segment. On the other hand, discontinuing operation of a particular manufacturing division, accounted for as a branch, may be subject to the rules in *APBO 30*. The relevant sections of *APBO 30* have two principal objectives in connection with discontinued operations:

1. Separate disclosure of income or loss from discontinued operations, net of applicable income taxes, between income from continuing operations and extraordinary items.

2. Disclosure of gain or loss on disposal of the business segment, net of applicable income taxes, along with the income or loss from discontinued operations.

This information should first appear in the financial statements covering the **measurement date,** the date at which management formally adopts a plan leading to the termination of operations. Descriptive information regarding the disposal should be disclosed in the notes to the financial statements encompassing the measurement date and in subsequent reporting periods until disposal is complete.

Item 1 above will reflect income or loss generated by the discontinued operation during the current period up to the measurement date. Prior period financial statements should be revised to disclose the results of operating the discontinued segment in those periods, net of applicable income taxes, as a separate component of income before extraordinary items. Item 2 above will also be disclosed in the period covering the measurement date. If the actual disposal has

---

[3] Accounting Principles Board, *Opinion No. 30*, "Reporting the Results of Operations" (N.Y.: AICPA, 1973).

Exhibit 5.9 Statement of Income and Retained Earnings of Hardy Corporation

Hardy Corporation
Statement of Income and Retained Earnings
For the Year Ended December 31, 19X4

Sales .	$2,200,000
Cost of Goods Sold	$1,193,500[a]
Salaries Expense	300,000
Operating Expenses .	257,000
Depreciation Expense	62,727
Total Expenses	$1,813,227
Net Income	$ 386,773
Retained Earnings, January 1, 19X4 .	352,910
Retained Earnings, December 31, 19X4 .	$ 739,683

[a]$1,193,500 = $342,000 + $1,150,000 + $34,100 − $332,600.

Exhibit 5.10 Balance Sheet of Hardy Corporation

Hardy Corporation
Balance Sheet at December 31, 19X4

ASSETS

Cash .	$ 170,800
Accounts Receivable	302,200
Inventory .	332,600
Prepayments .	40,000
Total Current Assets .	$ 845,600
Property, Plant, and Equipment .	$ 850,000
Less Accumulated Depreciation .	(261,817)
Total Noncurrent Assets .	$ 588,183
Total Assets .	$1,433,783

LIABILITIES AND STOCKHOLDERS' EQUITY

Accounts Payable	$ 174,100
Salaries Payable .	20,000
Other Liabilities .	300,000
Total Liabilities	$ 494,100
Capital Stock	$ 200,000
Retained Earnings	739,683
Total Stockholders' Equity	$ 939,683
Total Liabilities and Stockholders' Equity	$1,433,783

not taken place during that period, any estimated loss from disposal, net of applicable taxes, must be provided as of the measurement date. This provision includes the anticipated loss from disposal itself and from operations of the discontinued unit between the measurement date and the **disposal date**—the date when the segment is actually disposed of. The treatment differs if the disposal itself and the remaining period of operations are expected to result in an overall gain. In this case, the gain is not recognized at the measurement date and is deferred until actually realized at the disposal date.

As an example, suppose management of Amalgam Corporation decides to dispose of an unprofitable manufacturing operation, the Toy Branch. The branch is shut down shortly after the decision is made. It had incurred pretax losses of $300,000 in the current year and is sold at a pretax loss of $800,000. Toy's property and liability accounts are maintained at the branch and, after closing the books immediately prior to disposal, the Home Office account has a credit balance of $1,500,000, reflecting various branch assets of $3,000,000, accumulated depreciation of $1,000,000, and liabilities of $500,000. Entries made by the branch and home office to record the disposal follow:

TOY BRANCH BOOKS

Accumulated Depreciation	1,000,000	
Liabilities	500,000	
Home Office	1,500,000	
Assets		3,000,000

To record termination of operations as a unit of
Amalgam Corporation.

AMALGAM CORPORATION BOOKS

Cash	700,000	
Loss on Disposal of Toy Branch	800,000	
Investment in Branch		1,500,000

To record the sale of Toy Branch for $700,000 and to
recognize the pretax loss of $800,000.

Assuming Amalgam's marginal income tax rate is 40 percent, Amalgam would disclose the following information in its income statement for the period in which the disposal occurred.

Income from Continuing Operations after Taxes		XXX
Discontinued Operations:		
Loss from Operation of Discontinued Toy Division (after		
Taxes of $120,000)	$180,000	
Loss on Disposal of Toy Division (after Taxes of $320,000) .	480,000	$660,000
Income before Extraordinary Items		XXX

Concluding Remarks

Branches are integral units of a business firm, which have varying degrees of autonomy and accounting responsibility, perform various functions, and are normally physically removed from the home office. The term *branch accounting* is used in this chapter to identify a type of internal accounting system characterized by the presence of offsetting *reciprocal accounts* at both the branch and home office. These reciprocal accounts enable the home office and branch to easily account for transactions between them or made on behalf of one unit by the other. Since reciprocal accounts reflect internal and not external transactions, their balances must be eliminated when financial statements including the combined home office and branch accounts are prepared. Mastery of this elimination concept is critical, for it will be encountered repeatedly in the chapters describing the preparation of consolidated financial statements.

The chapter has stressed the accounting procedures for a branch which is a going concern. To round out the subject area, we have related generally accepted accounting principles for development stage enterprises and discontinued operations to the start-up and termination phases of branch operations.

Summary of Key Concepts	Accounting for a **sales agency** generally entails only an imprest fund and subsidiary accounting records maintained at the home office.

Home office/branch accounting refers to the type of accounting system used when a business unit of a larger firm has substantial financial accounting responsibilities and engages in various kinds of transactions with the home office.

Criteria for assessing whether **capitalization of start-up costs** of new branches is appropriate are no different than those employed for any going concern.

Reciprocal accounts are accounts with equal and offsetting balances maintained by the home office and branch, which are used to record transactions between home office and branch or made by one business unit on behalf of the other.

Merchandise shipments by the home office to the branch may be billed at cost to the home office or at cost plus a markup (which may equal retail price). Such shipments are normally accounted for in reciprocal accounts established for that purpose. Any difference between home office cost and amount billed should be separately accounted for as **overvaluation of branch inventory.**

Adjusting and closing entries are made at the end of an accounting period to reconcile reciprocal accounts, record the branch closing entries, accrue the branch's reported net income on the home office books, and adjust the overvaluation account.

Preparation of **combined financial statements** for the home office and branch is facilitated by the use of a working paper designed for that purpose. A key working paper procedure involves eliminating the offsetting reciprocal accounts to avoid double counting and to remove intrafirm markup from branch inventories. **Working paper eliminations are not posted to the books.**

Closing down or selling a branch that represents a separate major line of business or class of customer may call for special disclosures on the combined income statement. Under *APBO 30*, both **income or loss from discontinued operations** and **gain or loss on disposal** must be separately disclosed.

Questions

Q5.1 The term *branch* is broad enough to include business organizations of varying complexity. In advising a client on the installation of an accounting system, what factors would have to be present for you to recommend the use of home office/branch accounting procedures?

Q5.2 Briefly discuss the major differences between accounting for a sales agency and accounting for a branch from the home office point of view.

Q5.3 Reciprocal accounts are a key characteristic of home office/branch accounting. Briefly explain why they are important and the ways in which they are used.

Q5.4 You have been engaged to audit the Clifford Company. When you arrive at the client's office to begin the preliminary audit work, you learn that several new branches have been opened by Clifford during the year. What principles should you use to decide the appropriateness of capitalizing the start-up costs of those branches? The costs are material to Clifford's overall operations.

Q5.5 Under what conditions will the reciprocal accounts Shipments to Branch and Shipments from Home Office not have equal and offsetting balances?

Q5.6 The controller of Barret, Inc., decides that merchandise shipments to its branch are to be priced at an amount greater than cost. What advantage could be cited for setting the transfer price equal to Barret's external selling price?

Q5.7 In discussing the end-of-period accounting procedures employed in home office/branch accounting, a student makes the following objection: "This is just so much hocus-pocus and duplication. I see no need for both closing entries and a combined financial statement working paper." Do you agree with the student's objection? Explain.

Q5.8 In preparing a combined financial statement working paper, we find it necessary to make eliminating entries. What is the purpose of such entries, and why are they made only on the working paper?

Q5.9 Reciprocal accounts must be reconciled and brought into balance, before combined financial statement working papers can be prepared. List four common reasons reciprocal accounts may be out of balance.

Q5.10 Disposal of a branch may fall under the provisions of *APBO 30* for public reporting purposes. Under what condition is *APBO 30* relevant to disposal of a branch? Briefly describe and evaluate the principal disclosure requirements of the *Opinion*.

Exercises

E5.1 The TOTO Company operates a branch in a small town in West Texas. During June of the current year, a tornado swept through the town and destroyed the warehouse in which the branch's inventory was stored. TOTO is self-insuring but needs to compute the amount of the loss for tax purposes. You have gathered the following information:

1. Goods are acquired from the home office and from outside suppliers. Historically, about 60 percent of the merchandise purchases, at billed prices, is acquired from the home office at prices 20 percent over home office cost; the balance is purchased from external sources. Freight charges are 5 percent of all merchandise purchases at billed prices. The branch's selling prices reflect a markup of 20 percent on purchases from the home office and 30 percent on other purchases, excluding the freight costs.
2. Inventory at January 1 was $105,000 on the branch books.
3. Shipments from the home office received at the branch prior to the tornado amounted to $150,000.
4. Payments to outside suppliers made during the year and before the tornado were $125,000. No unpaid invoices existed at the time of the tornado, but accounts payable to suppliers at the previous year-end showed a balance of $25,000.
5. Sales made prior to the tornado amounted to $320,000, net of sales returns of $20,000.

Required:

1. Calculate the amount of the loss suffered by TOTO in connection with the destruction of its branch's inventory by the tornado. Show all computations in good form.
2. Prepare the journal entry made by the branch to record the loss.

E5.2   The Morrissey Company established a branch office early this year. Merchandise is shipped to the branch from the home office at prices 25 percent over cost. Freight costs are inventoriable and are paid by the branch in cash and amount to 4 percent of billed prices. Transactions for the year are summarized here:

1. Merchandise was shipped to the branch at billed prices amounting to $200,000.
2. The branch recorded sales of $320,000, all in cash.
3. Operating expenses of the branch amounted to $75,000, paid in cash.
4. A physical inventory at year-end showed merchandise on hand of $50,000 at billed prices.

Required:

1. Prepare journal entries made by the home office and branch during the year for the above transactions. Periodic inventory systems are used, and the home office accounts for the markup in an overvaluation account.
2. Prepare closing entries made by the branch and by the home office related to branch operations. The home office attributes the realized markup to home office operations.

E5.3   The Winery, seller of fine imported and domestic table wines, opened a branch office on December 20 of the current year. Not being familiar with the accounting procedures used in home office and branch operations, the firm's owner has asked your assistance in updating his accounting records and preparing combined statements at December 31. No entries have been made to record transactions involving the home and branch offices, but the following information is available:

1. Set-up costs of the branch: $30,000.
2. Shipments to branch (at 25 percent over cost): $10,000.
3. Sales by branch (at price billed from home office): $4,000.
4. Branch salaries paid by home office: $1,500.
5. Cash remitted by branch: $2,000.

Required:

1. Determine the balances in the Home Office and Investment in Branch reciprocal accounts at December 31.
2. What amount of inventory overvaluation must be recognized as income on December 31? Give the journal entry necessary to do this on the home office books.
3. Explain *how* the reciprocal accounts should be treated for combined statement purposes and *why* this treatment is necessary.

E5.4 The controller of the Paran Company recently resigned. You are engaged on July 1 to assist the new controller after it is discovered that several transactions relating to its branch have not been posted since the beginning of the year. After considerable work, the following data are assembled:

1. The Investment in Branch and Home Office accounts at January 1 are not in agreement. The Investment in Branch account shows a debit balance of $385,000 while the Home Office account has a credit balance of $340,000. The shipments accounts have zero balances.
2. Merchandise costing $160,000 has been shipped to the branch during the year. Such shipments are billed at cost.
3. Year-to-date depreciation expense is $40,000. One-fifth of all depreciable assets are located at the branch office. The home office had charged the branch for its share but had failed to notify the branch of the charge.
4. Cash remitted by the branch during the year totals $200,000.
5. A review of last year's working paper for combined statements revealed adjustments of $40,000 for inventory in transit to the branch and $5,000 for cash in transit from the branch to the home office at December 31.
6. Paran uses a periodic system to account for all inventories.
7. At July 1, the books show:

	Dr. (Cr.)
Investment in Branch	$493,000
Home Office .	(300,000)
Shipments from Home Office	160,000
Shipments to Branch	(100,000)

Required: Prepare a schedule to reconcile all reciprocal accounts.

E5.5 Ajax, Inc., accounts for all its inventories under a perpetual system and bills all shipments to the branch at cost. The branch obtains all its merchandise from the home office. At year-end, a discrepancy appears to exist in the merchandise accounts. Aside from the transactions causing the discrepancy, all other transactions between the home office and branch have been recorded correctly. Merchandise purchased by the home office during the year amounted to $800,000. Relevant account balances at December 31 are shown here:

	Amount Dr. (Cr.)	
	Home Office	Branch
Investment in Branch	$430,000	
Home Office .		($430,000)
Inventory, January 1 .	100,000	70,000
Inventory, December 31 .	120,000	40,000
Cost of Goods Sold .	600,000	280,000

Required: Compute the amount of the discrepancy. Assuming that the home office records are correct and that all inventories have been verified by physical count, explain what must have happened.

E5.6 The Wicket Company bills merchandise to its branch at retail selling prices which represent a 100 percent markup over cost. Transportation costs on shipments amount to 5 percent of billed prices. The following data relate to Wicket's intrafirm merchandise transactions during the year:

Inventory, January 1, Branch Office .	$210,000
Home Office Shipments to the Branch	500,000
Freight Cost on Shipments	25,000
Branch Sales .	546,000

Required:
1. Compute the cost of goods sold on the branch books.
2. Compute the amount of ending inventory on the branch books.
3. Give the closing entry made by the home office to adjust the overvaluation account.
4. If the ending inventory of the home office is $400,000 at cost, compute the ending inventory to be reported on a combined balance sheet.
5. Give the eliminating entries relative to inventories that must be made on the combined financial statement working paper.

E5.7 The Marble Company operates several branches and records all merchandise shipments to those branches as sales. Freight costs are trivial. The branches acquire all of their merchandise from the home office at markups approximating 30 percent of home office cost. Intrafirm merchandise transactions are summarized here:

Inventory, January 1 (All Branches at Billed Prices) .	$ 390,000
Inventory, December 31 (All Branches at Billed Prices) .	520,000
Sales (from Home Office to Branches) .	1,950,000

Required: Give the necessary eliminating entries to be made on the combined financial statement working paper.

E5.8 On May 15, 19X1, Marine, Inc., shipped outboard motors costing $12,000 to its Seaport branch. Seaport was billed $18,000 plus freight (prepaid by Marine) of

$760. On June 22, 19X1, Marine directed Seaport to ship 25 percent of this merchandise to the Bayview branch, which was temporarily out of stock for certain models. Additional freight cost, paid by Bayview, was $200. Periodic inventory systems are used.

Required:
1. Prepare the journal entries made by Marine, Inc., and the Seaport branch relative to the shipment made on May 15, 19X1.
2. Prepare the journal entries made by all three business units relative to the June 22 shipment, assuming that transportation direct from Marine to Bayview cost $300.

E5.9   On September 30, 19X1, the board of directors of Mills Corporation decided to close down the Low Cost Branch, an unprofitable retailing unit of the firm. Shortly thereafter, Low Cost was sold to an optimistic buyer for $160,000, which is $20,000 over the postclosing balance in the Investment in Low Cost Branch account. Low Cost reported a pretax operating loss of $70,000 during the portion of the current year prior to the sale. Mills' marginal income tax rate is .45.

Required: Assuming that Mills reported pretax income of $600,000 from home office continuing operations and that *APBO 30* applies, prepare the section of Mills' 19X1 income statement in which the information required by *APBO 30* relative to the disposal of Low Cost is disclosed.

Problems   **P5.1**   **Propriety of Capitalizing Start-Up Operating Losses**   You are engaged in the audit of the Willis Corporation, which opened its first branch office in 19X0. During the audit, Willis' president raises the question of the accounting treatment of the branch office operating loss for its first year—a material amount.

The president proposes to capitalize the operating loss as a starting-up expense to be amortized over a five-year period. He states that branch offices of other firms engaged in the same field generally suffer a first-year operating loss which is invariably capitalized, and you are aware of this practice. He argues, therefore, that the loss should be capitalized so that the accounting will be conservative; further, he argues that the accounting must be consistent with established industry practice.

Required: Discuss the president's use of the words "conservative" and "consistent" from the standpoint of accounting terminology. Discuss the accounting treatment you would recommend.

(AICPA adapted)

P5.2   **Reconciliation of Reciprocal Accounts—Combined Trial Balance**   The preclosing general ledger trial balances at December 31, 19X5, for the Baltimore Wholesale Company and its Atlanta branch are shown:

Baltimore Wholesale Co.
General Ledger Trial Balance
December 31, 19X5

Account	Home Office Dr. (Cr.)	Branch Office Dr. (Cr.)
Cash	$ 36,000	$ 8,000
Accounts Receivable	35,000	12,000
Inventory, January 1	70,000	15,000
Fixed Assets, Net	90,000	
Investment in Branch	20,000	
Accounts Payable	(36,000)	(13,500)
Accrued Expenses	(14,000)	(2,500)
Home Office		(9,000)
Capital Stock	(50,000)	
Retained Earnings, January 1	(45,000)	
Sales	(440,000)	(95,000)
Purchases	290,000	24,000
Purchases from Home Office		45,000
Expenses	44,000	16,000
	$ 0	$ 0

Additional information:

1. On December 23, the branch manager purchased $4,000 of furniture and fixtures but failed to notify the home office. The bookkeeper, knowing that all fixed assets are carried on the home office books, recorded the proper entry on the branch records. It is the company's policy not to take any depreciation on assets acquired in the last half of the year.

2. On December 27, a branch customer erroneously paid his account of $2,000 to the home office. The bookkeeper made the correct entry on the home office books but did not notify the branch.

3. On December 30, the branch office remitted cash of $5,000 which was received by the home office in January 19X6.

4. On December 31, the branch erroneously recorded the December allocated expenses from the home office as $500 instead of $1,500.

5. On December 31, the home office shipped merchandise billed at $3,000 to the branch. It was received in January 19X6.

6. The entire opening inventory of the branch had been purchased from the home office at billed prices. Home office 19X5 shipments to the branch were purchased by the home office in 19X5. The physical inventories at December 31, 19X5, excluding the shipment in transit, were: home office, $55,000 (at cost); branch, $20,000 (comprised of $18,000 from home office and $2,000 from outside vendors).

7. The home office consistently bills shipments to the branch at 20 percent above cost. The Sales account is credited for the invoice price. Since the home office does not use an overvaluation account for shipments to the branch, the markup included in the branch's beginning inventory is reflected in beginning Retained Earnings.

Required:
1. Prepare a schedule to reconcile the Investment in Branch and Home Office reciprocal accounts.
2. Using a trial balance worksheet with columns for adjustments and eliminations, prepare a combined trial balance. Formal combined statements are not required. Supporting computations must be in good form.
3. Prepare formal adjusting and eliminating entries and indicate which are adjustments (A) and which are eliminations (E).

(AICPA adapted)

P5.3   **Combined Financial Statement Working Paper**   You are engaged to audit the records of the Pacific Import Company, which have not previously been audited. The trial balance at December 31, 19X6, follows:

DEBITS	Home Office	Branch
Cash	$ 15,000	$ 2,000
Accounts Receivable	20,000	17,000
Inventory, December 31, 19X6	30,000	8,000
Fixed Assets, Net	150,000	
Investment in Branch	44,000	
Cost of Sales	220,000	93,000
Expenses	70,000	41,000
Total	$549,000	$161,000
CREDITS		
Accounts Payable	$ 23,000	
Mortgage Payable	50,000	
Capital Stock	100,000	
Retained Earnings, January 1, 19X6	26,000	
Sales	350,000	$150,000
Accrued Expenses		2,000
Home Office		9,000
Total	$549,000	$161,000

Additional information:
1. The branch receives all of its merchandise from the home office. The home office bills goods to the branch at 125 percent of cost. During 19X6, the branch was billed for $105,000 on shipments from the home office.
2. The home office credits Sales for the invoice price of goods shipped to the branch.
3. On January 1, 19X6, the inventory of the home office was $25,000. The branch books showed a $6,000 inventory.
4. On December 31, 19X6, the home office billed the branch for $12,000—the branch's share of expenses paid by the home office. The branch has not recorded this billing.
5. All cash collections made by the branch are deposited in a local bank to the account of the home office. Deposits of this nature included the following:

Amount	Date Deposited by Branch	Date Recorded by Home Office
$5,000	December 28, 19X6	December 31, 19X6
3,000	December 30, 19X6	January 2, 19X7
7,000	December 31, 19X6	January 3, 19X7
2,000	January 2, 19X7	January 5, 19X7

6. Expenses incurred locally by the branch are paid from an imprest bank account, which is reimbursed periodically by the home office. Just prior to the end of the year, the home office forwarded a reimbursement check in the amount of $3,000, which was not received by the branch office until January 19X7.

Required:

1. Prepare a reconciliation of the Investment in Branch and Home Office accounts showing the corrected book balances. (Hint: recompute the branch's cost of sales).
2. Prepare a combined financial statement working paper for the Pacific Import Company. Rearrange the trial balance data given in the problem into financial statement format. Use the Adjustments and Eliminations columns to post the entries reconciling the reciprocal accounts as well as to make the eliminations. Formal journal entries and formal financial statements are not required.

(AICPA adapted)

P5.4   **Adjusting and Eliminating Entries—Formal Combined Statements**   Trial balance data for The Azure Company and its branch at December 31, 19X3, prior to the annual audit, are as follows:

The Azure Company
Trial Balances
December 31, 19X3

DEBITS	Home	Branch
Cash	$ 17,000	$ 200
Inventory, January 1 (at Billed Prices)	23,000	11,550
Other Assets	200,000	48,700
Investment in Branch	60,000	—
Purchases	190,000	—
Shipments from Home	—	105,000
Freight In from Home	—	5,250
Various Expenses	42,000	24,300
Totals	$532,000	$195,000

CREDITS		
Various Liabilities	$ 35,000	$ 3,500
Home Office	—	51,500
Sales	155,000	140,000
Shipments to Branch	110,000	—
Overvaluation of Branch Inventory, January 1	1,000	—
Capital Stock	200,000	—
Retained Earnings, January 1	31,000	—
Totals	$532,000	$195,000

The audit at December 31, 19X3, disclosed the following:

1. The branch deposits all cash receipts in a local bank for the account of the home office. The audit worksheet for the cash cut-off revealed:

Amount	Deposited by Branch	Recorded by Home Office
$1,050.	December 27, 19X3	December 31, 19X3
1,100.	December 30, 19X3	January 2, 19X4
600.	December 31, 19X3	January 3, 19X4
300.	January 2, 19X4	January 6, 19X4

2. The branch pays expenses incurred locally from an imprest bank account that is maintained with a balance of $2,000. Checks are drawn once a week on this imprest account, and the home office is notified of the amount needed to replenish the account. At December 31, an $1,800 reimbursement check was mailed to the branch.

3. The branch receives all of its goods from the home office. The home office bills the goods at cost plus a markup of 10 percent of cost. At December 31, a shipment with a billing value of $5,000 was in transit to the branch. Freight costs are typically 5 percent of billed values, are considered to be inventoriable costs, and are paid by the branch.

4. The trial balance opening inventories are shown at their respective costs to the home office and the branch. The inventories at December 31, excluding the shipment in transit, are:

Home Office (at Cost)	$30,000
Branch Office (at Billing Value)	10,400

Required:

1. Prepare a reconciliation of the Investment in Branch and Home Office reciprocal accounts.

2. Prepare the formal adjusting and eliminating entries needed on working papers for the preparation of combined financial statements. Entries should be identified as adjusting (A) or eliminating (E), and supporting computations should be in good form. Do not prepare closing entries.

3. Prepare a statement of income and retained earnings and a balance sheet for the Azure Company as of December 31, 19X3.

(AICPA adapted)

P5.5 **Combined Financial Statement Working Paper** Saffron Company has a branch located in Loadsville, 200 miles away. The branch purchases about 40 percent of its inventory for resale from local suppliers; the rest is acquired from Saffron at billed prices representing a markup equal to 20 percent of selling price. Freight on merchandise purchases and shipments to the branch is 2 percent of billed prices. Trial balances for both business units at December 31, 19X6, follow:

Saffron Company and Branch
Preclosing Trial Balances at December 31, 19X6

	Amount Dr. (Cr.)	
Account	Home Office	Branch
Cash	$ 263,200	$ 50,000
Accounts Receivable	300,000	158,000
Inventory, January 1	90,000	81,600
Prepayments	60,000	10,400
Plant Assets	800,000	—
Accumulated Depreciation	(100,000)	—
Investment in Branch	182,000	—
Current Liabilities	(330,000)	(150,000)
Capital Stock	(400,000)	—
Retained Earnings, January 1	(268,600)	—
Home Office	—	(138,000)
Sales	(2,100,000)	(800,000)
Shipments to Branch	(240,000)	—
Overvaluation of Branch Inventory	(69,600)	—
Purchases	1,300,000	200,000
Shipments from Home Office	—	290,000
Freight In	42,000	9,800
Operating Expenses	471,000	288,200
	$ 0	$ 0

The following information has been gathered by Saffron's controller:

1. On Friday, December 31, 19X6, the branch mailed a check for $27,000 to the home office.
2. Expenses incurred by Saffron on behalf of the branch and allocated to the branch amounted to $7,000. The branch was never notified.
3. The final merchandise shipment to the branch left Saffron on December 28; invoice amount was $10,000. Freight will be paid by the branch.
4. Ending inventories of the home office and branch amounted to $98,000 and $76,500, respectively, at invoice prices plus applicable freight. Sixty percent of the branch beginning and ending inventory (excluding the shipment in transit) was acquired from the home office.

Required: Prepare a combined financial statement working paper for Saffron Company and its branch at December 31, 19X6. Formal adjusting and eliminating entries and combined statements are not required.

P5.6   Two Branches—Reconcile Reciprocal Accounts and Make Adjusting and Closing Entries   Following are the preclosing trial balances of Wash Company and its two branches at June 30, 19X8, the end of Wash Company's fiscal year.

Account	Amount: Dr. (Cr.)		
	Home Office	Branch A	Branch B
Cash and Receivables	$ 281,000	$214,000	$105,000
Inventory, July 1, 19X7	560,000	180,000	80,000
Plant Assets	940,000	155,000	100,000
Accumulated Depreciation	(250,000)	(25,000)	(10,000)
Investment in Branch A	470,000	—	—
Investment in Branch B	300,000	—	—
Current Liabilities	(580,000)	(130,600)	(60,000)
Capital Stock	(500,000)	—	—
Retained Earnings, July 1, 19X7	(750,000)	—	—
Home Office	—	(376,000)	(230,000)
Sales	(2,800,000)	(790,000)	(430,000)
Shipments to Branch A	(280,000)	—	—
Shipments to Branch B	(190,000)	—	—
Overvaluation of Branch A Inventory . . .	(180,000)	—	—
Overvaluation of Branch B Inventory . . .	(115,000)	—	—
Purchases	2,400,000	180,000	70,000
Shipments from Home Office	—	380,000	255,000
Freight In on Merchandise	24,000	—	—
Operating Expenses	670,000	212,600	120,000
	$ 0	$ 0	$ 0

Additional information regarding Wash Company and its branches is as follows:

1. Home office ships merchandise to the branches at cost plus 50 percent. Of the beginning inventory of Branch A, $120,000 had been acquired from home office; of Branch B, $60,000.

2. The following shipments of merchandise originally acquired by the home office were in transit at June 30, 19X8:

From	To	Amount
Home	Branch A	$10,000
Home	Branch B	9,000
Branch B	Branch A	21,000 [a]
Branch A	Home	30,000

[a]Not recorded by home office.

3. Cash payments in transit among the three business units at June 30, 19X8, are:

From	To	Amount
Branch B	Branch A	$40,000 [a]
Branch A	Home	54,000

[a]Not recorded by home office.

4. Ending inventories of Branch A and Branch B amounted to $150,000 and $110,000, respectively; about 60 percent of each had been acquired from the home office. Home office ending inventory was $600,000.

Required:
1. Prepare a schedule to reconcile all reciprocal accounts, including the shipments and overvaluation accounts.
2. Prepare formal adjusting and closing entries, assuming the realized intra-

firm markup on merchandise sales is attributed to home office operations. A separate set of entries should be made for each of the three entities.

P5.7   **Combined Trial Balance Working Paper**   Refer to the data in P5.6 for the Wash Company.

Required: Prepare a combined trial balance working paper for the Wash Company and its branches.

P5.8   **Worksheet—Branch Treated as Sales Agency**   You are examining the financial statements of Conrad Sales Company for the year ended December 31, 19X7. Conrad has not had an audit before. Sales are made from Conrad's home office and a newly opened branch office.

A general ledger trial balance as of December 31, 19X7, appears on page 201. The following information was also available:

1. An inventory taken at the home office on December 31, 19X7, showed merchandise costing $345,200 with a fair market value of $347,300. A perpetual inventory system is maintained.
2. The Investments account balance at December 31, 19X7, in the general ledger was composed of the following:

Cost of 40,000 Shares of Conrad Treasury Stock Purchased in 19X5 . .	$ 68,000
Marketable Securities at Cost (Market Value December 31, 19X7,	
$82,000)	80,000
Cost of Exclusive Distribution Franchises with Unlimited Lives	17,000
Total	$165,000

3. Conrad paid $20,000 for an incentive bonus on December 22, 19X7, before the bonus was due on December 31, 19X7. The entire bonus of $35,000 was accrued at December 31, 19X7, and the balance of $15,000 was paid on January 15, 19X8.
4. Other assets included $10,000 of market survey costs for a sales project undertaken and abandoned in 19X7, $1,000 of deposits held by utility companies, and $153,000 of net fixed assets. Examination of fixed asset records revealed that Conrad deducted the correct amount of depreciation each year from the recorded cost of fixed assets. The $153,000 was comprised of original costs of $53,000 for land, $100,000 for a building, and $28,000 for furniture and equipment less accumulated depreciation of $22,000 on the building and $6,000 on the furniture and equipment.
5. On September 15, 19X7, Conrad established a branch and shipped it merchandise having a retail value of $140,000 (140 percent of Conrad's cost). At December 31, 19X7, the branch inventory was $56,000, priced at retail value. The branch reported 19X7 sales of $84,000, of which $50,400 had been collected by the branch and represented cash in transit to Conrad at December 31, and $33,600 was receivable from branch customers. This information on branch sales has not been recorded by the home office. The branch considered all its accounts collectible at December 31, 19X7. Branch administrative expenses totaling $4,100 were paid by Conrad in 19X7 and charged to the General and Administrative Expenses—Branch

account. Prepaid expenses of $1,200 related to the branch were also charged to this account.

6. Formal home office/branch accounting procedures have not yet been adopted by Conrad. In effect, the branch is being accounted for as if it were a sales agency. All branch accounts are to be identified as such and maintained on the home office books.

7. The home office Accounts Receivable consist of the following:

Various small 19X6 balances in dispute (not likely to be collected) .	$	2,000
Account balances of bankrupt customers (uncollectible) . . .		9,500
Remaining accounts (estimated 3 percent uncollectible) . . .		300,000
Total		$311,500

Bad debts expense of $4,000 was included in the General and Administrative Expenses—Home Office account at December 31, 19X7.

Conrad Sales Company
General Ledger Trial Balance
December 31, 19X7

Account	Debit	Credit
Cash	$ 65,400	
Accounts Receivable—Home Office	311,500	
Allowance for Bad Debts		$ 9,000
Merchandise Inventory—Home Office	349,600	
Merchandise Inventory—Branch	100,000	
Investments	165,000	
Prepaid Incentive Bonus	20,000	
Prepaid Expenses	32,100	
Other Assets	164,000	
Accounts Payable		205,600
Accrued Incentive Bonus		35,000
Capital Stock, $1 Par Value		500,000
Retained Earnings, January 1, 19X7		366,600
Sales—Home Office		1,043,800
Cost of Sales—Home Office	746,800	
Selling Expenses—Home Office	98,000	
Selling Expenses—Branch	9,600	
General and Administrative Expenses—Home Office . .	92,700	
General and Administrative Expenses—Branch	5,300	
Totals	$2,160,000	$2,160,000

Required: Prepare a work sheet to adjust the accounts of Conrad Sales Company at December 31, 19X7, and to provide the basis for preparation of combined financial statements. The work sheet should have columns labeled Trial Balance (Dr., Cr.), Adjustments (Dr., Cr.), Income Statement (Dr., Cr.), and Balance Sheet (Dr., Cr.). Formal adjusting and closing entries are not required.

(AICPA adapted)

Chapter 6

Business Combinations

Business combinations occur when two or more companies are brought under common control. They have long been present in the American economy and have occurred for many reasons. In the short run, a business combination leads to a larger single entity than previously existed; more transactions are controlled and more decisions are made by the combined firm than by either previous single entity. Outside an individual firm, price movements direct production through an exchange mechanism called the *market*. After a business combination, the combined firm has substituted its own decision-making apparatus for that of the market's in respect to the factors of production acquired in the combination. The acquiring firm initiates the combination because it believes that it can accomplish its objectives more efficiently and at lower cost than it could in dealing directly with the input and output markets. It follows that a primary motivating principle behind business combinations can be identified as follows.

> In general, a business combination will occur when management believes that the cost of achieving a set of objectives (for example, contracting for sources of supply, increasing sales volume, diversification) through the market exceeds the cost of acquiring existing firms and bypassing the market altogether.

This principle is reflected in the practical reasons typically cited to explain the business combination phenomenon. We now turn to these as we review the history of business combinations in the United States.

Business Combinations: Incentives, Incidence, and Insights

Growth is a major objective of most corporate enterprises and may take many forms. *Growth in sales* is needed to increase the firm's share of the market and solidify its position. *Growth in earnings and earnings per share* is seen as essential if the firm's securities are to become more attractive in the capital markets. *Growth in diversity* is pursued in order to reduce or spread business risk, insulate earnings from downturns in business and decrease the cost of capital. Although growth in these areas can be achieved internally as well as externally, there are several reasons why combination with other existing firms may be preferred to expansion from within.

1. A going concern has its own historical records, experienced personnel, network of suppliers, customers, and creditors. Combination with such a firm eliminates the need to start from scratch. Although managerial and other changes may be necessary, the inescapable fact is that growth from within, whether for reasons of market share or diversification, would usually require duplication of many of the efforts already made by an existing firm. The cost of duplicating these efforts could exceed the cost of acquiring the firm outright.

2. Combination with an existing firm often leads to lower levels of actual or potential competition. If two competing firms combine, competition is actually reduced. Similarly, if a firm enters an industry by acquiring one of the firms currently competing, the number of competing firms remains unchanged. Entry via investment in a new firm, however, increases the number of competitors, thereby making it more difficult for the entering firm to succeed.

3. Desired expansion or entry into a new market may be achieved more quickly through combination with an existing firm.

4. The cost of growth may be cut substantially by combining with a firm possessing large tax loss carryforwards. A profitable firm may be able to combine with one that has generated losses and provide the taxable income needed to realize tax benefits from the losses.

Business Combinations in the American Economy

A large number of business combinations, or mergers, have taken place in the last hundred years, contributing significantly to the development of the American economy. Economic historians often identify three time periods coincidental with large "merger movements."

The first of these occurred around the turn of the century. During the period 1898–1902, there were some 360 business combinations per year. At this time, American companies were acquiring their competitors and expanding their geographic markets. This type of business combination is generally referred to as **horizontal integration.**

A second period of high merger activity took place during the 1920s. For the years 1920–1929, an average of 680 mergers per year took place, with an average of over 900 per year in 1925–1929. The characteristics of most mergers during this period differed from those of the earlier period. Whereas the earlier horizontal combinations meant that firms were expanding the scale of their activities by entering new markets and increasing productive capacity, **vertical integration** was far more common during the 1920s. Vertical combinations involved firms having a supplier/customer relationship. For example, a manufacturing firm would merge with a mining company to insure the continued supply of raw materials. Or a manufacturing company might combine with a retailing firm in order to secure ready outlets for its products.

The third merger movement began during the late 1950s and reached its peak during the period 1965–1969. From 1955 to 1969, an average of 1,062 business combinations occurred each year, and an average of 1,642 occurred during each of the years from 1965 to 1969. The combining companies of this period often had fundamentally different characteristics, giving rise to a new type of merger—the **conglomerate merger.** Unlike traditional horizontal and vertical integration, in which the combining companies were engaged in similar or related activities, conglomerates were formed by groups of unrelated companies. Food companies and tobacco companies combined. Motion picture, mining, and manufacturing firms were brought under common management, and so on.

The motivation for conglomerate enterprises can be attributed to the desire to diversify business risks. As previously mentioned, such diversification may provide stability in earnings by insulating the combined firm against economic forces which affect different industries at different times. Furthermore, it was found during the "go-go" years of the 1960s that cleverly executed business combinations could provide instant growth in earnings per share.

Antitrust Law and Business Combinations   Business combinations often result in improved economic efficiency, particularly through achieving economies of scale. Nevertheless, the concentrations of economic power represented by large firms occasionally lead to abuses, such as anticompetitive behavior and monopolistic pricing. The antitrust statutes were enacted primarily to promote competition, restrict monopoly, and to serve as countervailing forces against the misuse of economic power often concentrated in large firms resulting from business combinations.

First among these statutes was the *Sherman Act*, passed by Congress in 1890. In Section 1, the act declared every contract, business combination, or conspiracy in restraint of trade or commerce to be illegal. This section prohibited "unreasonable" behavior such as predatory pricing and other practices aimed at coercing competitors and unfairly limiting their ability to compete effectively. Section 2 declared that those who monopolize, or attempt to monopolize, or combine or conspire to monopolize any part of trade or commerce are outside the law. Whereas Section 1 tended to emphasize market conduct and behavior, Section 2 became a vehicle for attacking market structure. That is, a dominant firm (or firms) may be found guilty under Section 2 even though it engaged in no unscrupulous practices and did not conspire to restrain trade.

Although in 1911 the Sherman Act was responsible for breaking up two giant trusts—Standard Oil and American Tobacco—it did not represent a wholly satisfactory solution to the abuses of the time. To complement and strengthen the Sherman Act, Congress enacted additional legislation in 1914.

One of these new laws, the *Clayton Act*, attacks specific business policies which would substantially reduce competition or promote monopoly. Price discrimination, arrangements whereby sellers would force their customers not to buy from competitors, and mergers which would substantially lessen competition are among the activities forbidden by the Clayton Act. The *Celler-Kefauver*

Act of 1950 further strengthened the prohibition against those mergers which would lead to reduced competition by broadening the scope of the relevant section in the Clayton Act.

A second statute, the *Federal Trade Commission Act,* was also passed in 1914. It created the Federal Trade Commission (FTC) and provided it with the potentially wide-ranging mandate to declare unfair methods of competition in commerce as unlawful, a role not substantively different from that of Section 1 of the Sherman Act. The *Wheeler-Lea Act* of 1938 authorized the FTC to prohibit unfair or deceptive acts or practices in commerce, thus establishing the basis for its action against unfounded or misleading advertising claims.[1]

Accounting for Business Combinations

At the outset of this section, it is important to recognize that *accounting for business combinations* and *preparation of consolidated financial statements* are two separate and distinct topics in accounting theory and practice. The rules governing accounting for business combinations are employed to determine how the combination should be recorded. Not all business combinations lead to the subsequent preparation of consolidated statements. When consolidated statements are prepared, however, the method used in accounting for the business combination will affect certain details in their preparation. These matters are discussed in Chapters 7 and 8.

In a business combination, two or more companies are joined as one under common control. The combination may occur in various ways, but to simplify and standardize the discussion, we define and use the following terms.

> An **acquiring company** is one whose shareholders as a group control the ownership interests in the combined enterprise. These ownership interests will also be referred to as the **controlling interest.**

Other companies involved in a business combination are considered to be acquired companies. Although some might argue that neither company in a particular business combination is being acquired, a distinction must be made between the relative status of the various ownership interests before and after a business combination.

> Therefore, an **acquired company** is one whose ownership interests are substantially eliminated in the combined enterprise or whose ownership interests become part of the controlling interest in the combined enterprise.

A completed combination is typically the outcome of negotiations between the acquiring and acquired companies. An analytical approach to these negotiations when the constituent companies are publicly traded is discussed in the appendix to this chapter.

---

[1] For more on the subject of antitrust law, see Richard Caves, *American Industry: Structure, Conduct, Performance,* 4th ed. (Englewood Cliffs, N.J.: Prentice-Hall, 1977), especially Chapter 6; and Richard A. Posner, *Economic Analysis of Law* (Boston: Little, Brown, 1973), especially Chapter 7.

Four types of business combinations can be identified from a legal and organizational point of view.

1. A **statutory merger** results when Company B is absorbed into Company A. Company B ceases to exist as a legal entity and its shares are retired. Only the surviving firm, Company A, remains as a legal entity.

2. A **statutory consolidation** takes place when a new corporation, Company C, is organized to absorb the activities of two or more existing corporations. Thus, if Company C is formed out of Companies A and B, the shares of A and B are retired and only Company C continues to exist as a legal entity.

    The above two types of combinations are *statutory* in the sense that the reorganization, issue and retirement of shares, and so forth are governed by the laws of a state. Even though the absorbed firms cease to exist as legal entities, their operations may continue undisturbed as divisions of the combined firm.

3. An **asset acquisition** reflects the acquisition by one firm of all or part of the assets (and liabilities) and business operations of another firm. The selling firm may continue to survive as a legal entity, perhaps with an equity interest in the buying firm, or it may liquidate entirely.

4. A **stock acquisition** occurs when the acquiring firm obtains all or most of the voting shares of another firm. Both firms continue as separate legal entities, and the investment in the acquired firm is treated as an intercorporate investment. Furthermore, a **parent/subsidiary relationship** is created between the two firms by virtue of the acquiring (parent) firm's controlling equity interest in the acquired (subsidiary) firm.

Note that in items 1–3 above the surviving or acquiring firm records the assets and liabilities acquired on its books. A single legal entity with a single set of financial accounting records remains, and consolidated statements are not necessary. In contrast, a stock acquisition (item 4) results in an intercorporate investment whereby the shares acquired are recorded in an *Investment in Subsidiary* account. Since both of the combining firms remain as separate legal entities, with their own financial accounting records, preparation of consolidated statements normally follows.

APBO 16 (AC § 1091) contains authoritative guidance relative to accounting for business combinations.[2] During the three years subsequent to the issue of *APBO 16* in August 1970, thirty-nine unofficial interpretations were published by the AICPA (AC § U1091).[3] Together, *APBO 16* and the unofficial interpretations represent the bulk of generally accepted accounting principles in the business combinations area. *SFAS 38* clarifies and amends *APBO 16* with respect to the accounting treatment of contingent assets, contingent liabilities, and contingent impairments of assets at date of business combination.[4]

---

[2] Accounting Principles Board, *Opinion No. 16*, "Business Combinations" (N.Y.: AICPA, 1970).

[3] American Institute of Certified Public Accountants, *Unofficial Interpretations of* APB Opinion No. 16 (N.Y.: AICPA, 1970–1973).

[4] Financial Accounting Standards Board, *Statement of Financial Accounting Standards No. 38*, "Accounting for Preacquisition Contingencies of Purchased Enterprises" (Stamford, Conn.: FASB, 1980).

Additional technical issues are discussed in the following pronouncements:

1. *SFAS 10* (AC § 1092). *APBO 16* had provided an exemption from some of the pooling conditions in certain situations for business combinations completed within five years of October 31, 1970. *SFAS 10* extends this exemption indefinitely by removing the five-year limitation.[5]

2. *IFAS 4* (AC § 4211–1). The general requirement of *SFAS 2* that research and development costs be expensed as incurred is not waived in a purchase combination. That is, the cost assigned to identifiable assets used in research and development is expensed unless the test of alternative future use is met.[6]

3. *IFAS 9* (AC § 1091–1). The portion of this *Interpretation* relating to *APBO 16* indicates that the *individual* assets and liabilities of savings and loan associations or similar institutions are to be accounted for at their fair values. An aggregate or institution-wide valuation approach is not permitted.[7]

Further changes in accounting for business combinations are likely to occur. On August 19, 1976, the FASB published a massive Discussion Memorandum entitled "Accounting for Business Combinations and Purchased Intangibles." To date, however, this Discussion Memorandum has not generated any specific proposals.

The two generally accepted methods of accounting for a business combination are the purchase and pooling of interest methods. Technically, the method of accounting depends upon the characteristics of the combination—only one of the two methods is acceptable for a particular combination. As we shall see, however, sufficient flexibility often exists to enable the parties to choose the accounting by tailoring the combination to conform with the requirements of the desired accounting method.

Purchase Method of Accounting for Business Combinations

The first generally accepted method of accounting for business combinations is the purchase method.

> Under the **purchase method** of accounting for business combinations, the business combination is accounted for as an *acquisition of assets or equity shares*, the outcome of a completed exchange transaction in the open market. The consideration surrendered by the acquiring firm provides the basis for valuing the assets or equities acquired.

---

[5] Financial Accounting Standards Board, *Statement of Financial Accounting Standards No. 10*, "Extension of 'Grandfather' Provisions for Business Combinations" (Stamford, Conn.: FASB, 1975).

[6] Financial Accounting Standards Board, *Interpretation of Financial Accounting Standards No. 4*, "Applicability of *FASB Statement No. 2* to Business Combinations Accounted for by the Purchase Method" (Stamford, Conn.: FASB, 1975).

[7] Financial Accounting Standards Board, *Interpretation of Financial Accounting Standards No. 9*, "Applying *APB Opinions No. 16 and 17* When a Savings and Loan Association or a Similar Institution Is Acquired in a Business Combination Accounted for by the Purchase Method" (Stamford, Conn.: FASB, 1976).

Use of the purchase method normally assumes the presence of a dominant firm in the business combination. The acquiring firm engages in an arm's-length market transaction to obtain its interest in the assets or equity of the acquired firm. An exchange transaction has therefore occurred in the market, and, consistent with the principles of historical cost accounting, the assets and liabilities (or equities) acquired are recorded at their cost to the acquiring firm. Cost is measured by either the fair market value of the consideration surrendered or the fair market value of the property acquired, whichever is the more readily determinable.

The purchase method has several postcombination accounting implications. First, *a new basis of accountability for the property acquired is established when the purchase transaction is completed.* Subsequent depreciation and amortization is computed on this new basis. Second, property has been acquired; it only begins generating earnings for the new owners (the controlling interest) *after* the date of business combination. Third, any retained earnings of the acquired firm at the date of business combination relate to the previous stockholders; these prior earnings are not included in postcombination retained earnings. In sum, the purchase method of accounting for business combinations provides the shareholders of the acquiring firm with a new firm. Since the new firm can have neither earnings nor retained earnings until after it begins operations, the controlling shareholders' interest in the earnings of the new (acquired) firm begins at the date of acquisition.

Pooling of Interests Method of Accounting for Business Combinations

The second generally accepted method of accounting for business combinations is the pooling of interests method.

> Under the **pooling of interests method** of accounting for business combinations, the business combination is accounted for as a *union of previously separate ownership interests* achieved through the exchange of equity securities. Since these equity securities are neither purchased nor sold, no new basis of accountability arises out of this exchange.

This method also has some postcombination accounting implications. First, the assets and liabilities of the constituent firms are carried forward to the combined firm at their existing book values. If the separate companies used different accounting methods for similar assets and liabilities, the amounts may be adjusted to the same accounting basis so long as the change is appropriate for the separate company. Any such changes in accounting method should be applied retroactively, and prior period statements presented for comparative purposes should be restated to reflect the changes.[8] Second, all of the current period's earnings of the constituent firms attributable to the controlling interest are added together, regardless of when the pooling occurred. This follows from the fact that, in a pooling of interests, the previous ownership interests remain intact but are simply combined. Aggregate income remains the same because the

---

[8] See Accounting Principles Board, *Opinion No. 20*, "Accounting Changes" (N.Y.: AICPA, 1971), pars. 34 and 35; AC § 1051.34–35. Such accounting changes are viewed as resulting in financial statements for a different reporting entity—the pooled companies.

Exhibit 6.1   Postcombination Accounting Implications of the Purchase and Pooling of Interests Methods

Accounting Implication	Purchase	Pooling of Interests
1. Value of Property Acquired	Fair market value at date of combination, generally measured by the fair market value of the consideration given in the combination. Subsequent depreciation and amortization charges based on fair market value.	Book value as recorded in the accounts of the acquired company. Subsequent depreciation and amortization charges continue to be based on book value.
2. Combined Net Income in the Period of Acquisition	Includes the acquiring company's net income plus the controlling interest's share of the acquired company's earnings *after* date of combination.	Includes the acquiring company's net income plus the controlling interest's share of the acquired company's earnings for the *entire period*.
3. Combined Retained Earnings	Includes the acquiring company's retained earnings plus the controlling interest's share of the acquired company's earnings *after* date of combination.	Includes the acquiring company's retained earnings plus the controlling interest's share of the acquired company's retained earnings both *before* and *after* date of combination.

total resources of the combined firm have not changed. Similarly, since the ownership interests in the combined firm are the same interests which existed in the constituent firms prior to combination, earnings of the current period prior to the date of combination are reflected in the net income attributable to the controlling interest. Third, retained earnings of the combined firm includes the controlling shareholders' interest in all retained earnings of the constituent firms.

A short example will serve to illustrate how the post-combination accounting implications differ between the two methods. Suppose Park Corporation wishes to acquire all of the outstanding voting stock of Street Corporation and is evaluating the two accounting methods. The combination is scheduled for December 31. Street Corporation's books show net assets of $1,000,000, retained earnings of $250,000, and current net income of $30,000 at December 31.

1. *Purchase.* Park issues shares of its own stock for $1,500,000 cash and uses the proceeds to purchase Street's outstanding stock in the market. Combined or consolidated statements at December 31 include the assets and liabilities of Street valued at a net of $1,500,000. None of Street's retained earnings or current period income is included.

2. *Pooling of Interests.* Park exchanges additional shares of its own stock for the shares of Street owned by Street's shareholders. No cash changes hands. Combined or consolidated statements at December 31 now reflect Street's assets and liabilities valued at a net of $1,000,000 *and* Street's retained earnings of $250,000 and current period net income of $30,000.

These accounting implications of the purchase and pooling of interests methods are summarized in Exhibit 6.1.

Exhibit 6.2   Business Combinations Recorded as Purchases or Poolings of Interest by the 600 Companies Surveyed in *Accounting Trends and Techniques* 1967–1978

| Year | Business Combinations | | | | |
| | Purchase | | Pooling of Interests | | |
	Number	Percent	Number	Percent	Total
1978	149	73%	56	27%	205
1977	118	71	48	29	166
1976	103	71	43	29	146
1975	75	71	31	29	106
1974	143	74	50	26	193
1973	163	65	89	35	252
1972	160	61	102	39	262
1971	133	57	100	43	233
1970 *APBO 16, APBO 17* . . .	155	53	139	47	294
1969	195	51	185	49	380
1968	190	51	184	49	374
1967	116	45	144	55	260

Source: American Institute of Certified Public Accountants, *Accounting Trends and Techniques,* various issues. Copyright © by the American Institute of Certified Public Accountants, Inc.

Prior period financial statements and financial information of the constituent companies are to be restated to the combined basis to furnish information comparable to the current period which reflects the pooling. In contrast, prior period information presented after a purchase combination is disclosed on a pro forma combined basis only in the notes to the statements and only for the immediately preceding fiscal period.

These accounting implications suggest that, over the years, combined net income in a pooling is likely to exceed combined net income in a purchase. This phenomenon begins in the period of the combination. Companies which complete a pooling of interests combination at any time during a reporting period can include the acquired company's net income for the entire period in combined net income. Another factor contributes to this phenomenon in periods subsequent to the combination. Recall that a purchase combination produces a new basis of accountability for depreciable and amortizable assets. If the new basis is higher than the original book value, the purchase method will result in larger charges for depreciation and amortization made against combined net income after the date of business combination.

Prior to the issuance of *APBO 16*, the search for companies capable of providing these kinds of benefits in a pooling of interest combination had almost become a national pastime. Abuses of pooling were common. While the rules enabled a company disappointed with its own profit prospects to improve net income by consummating a pooling of interests combination late in the reporting period, some companies went even further. For example, poolings completed between the end of the reporting period and the date that period's financial statements were issued were sometimes included in those statements.

In Exhibit 6.2, we tabulate purchase and pooling combinations reported by the 600 companies surveyed by *Accounting Trends and Techniques* from 1967 to 1978. The relative significance of poolings declined sharply after *APBO 16* was issued in 1970.

The Fall from Favor of Pooling of Interests Accounting   The pooling of interests concept in a business combination is not new;[9] it was incorporated as part of the authoritative literature in *ARB 40* published in September 1950 and was included in 1953 as Chapter 7–C of *ARB 43*.[10] Additional elaboration of the concept and discussion of the criteria governing its application were presented in *ARB 48*, issued in January 1957. The thrust of *ARB 48* with respect to the definition and propriety of pooling of interests accounting provided the basis for *APBO 16*. Unfortunately, *ARB 48* can now be seen as an inadequate guide to practice because it permitted too much interpretation. Paragraph 7 (reproduced below) best sums up how *ARB 48* became virtually irrelevant as a guide to accounting for business combinations in the years following its publication. Its ambiguities are, we believe, obvious.

> 7. No one of the factors discussed in paragraphs 5 and 6 would necessarily be determinative and any one factor might have varying degrees of significance in different cases. However, their presence or absence would be cumulative in effect. Since the conclusions to be drawn from consideration of these different relevant circumstances may be in conflict or partially so, determination as to whether a particular combination is a purchase or a pooling of interests should be made in light of all such attendant circumstances.[11]

To fully appreciate how the thrust of *ARB 48* was twisted and distorted, one must examine some of the business combinations which were accounted for as poolings. Most combinations now viewed as abuses of the pooling concept took place during the 1960s. This was the decade when the conglomerate merger came of age. It was also a period known in investment circles as the "go-go" years on Wall Street.[12] Reported earnings per share were considered of paramount importance to investors and, correspondingly, to corporate managements. The achievement of robust, systematic growth in earnings per share (or, as we shall see, the *appearance* of such growth) became the overriding objective of many business firms. Business combinations, and the pooling of interests method to account for them, were employed almost ruthlessly to promote growth in earnings per share by many companies during the 1960s.

As stated earlier, a major reason for the popularity of the pooling concept is its ability to create instant growth in earnings and earnings per share. This growth in earnings may arise in two ways. First, in the year of the pooling, the

---

[9]   See Arthur R. Wyatt, *Accounting Research Study No. 5*, "A Critical Study of Accounting for Business Combinations" (N.Y.: AICPA, 1963).

[10]   Committee on Accounting Procedure, *Accounting Research Bulletin No. 43*, "Restatement and Revision of Accounting Research Bulletins" (N.Y.: AICPA, 1953).

[11]   Committee on Accounting Procedure, *Accounting Research Bulletin No. 48*, "Business Combinations" (N.Y.: AICPA, 1957), par. 7.

[12]   For a colorful and entertaining view of this period, see Adam Smith [pseud.], *The Money Game* (N.Y.: Random House, 1968).

net incomes of the constituent companies for the whole year are combined, regardless of when the combination was completed. Second, by combining assets at their book values rather than at their generally higher fair values any unrealized gains become a reservoir of potential income which may be recognized almost at will by the combined company. To accomplish this, the unrealized gains are gradually realized and recognized as income as the undervalued assets are sold or used. We now consider how some actual companies bent, twisted, or stretched the pooling concept to achieve these ends.

Retrospective Poolings—Western Equities, Inc. (Westec)   The Westec case is a prominent example of the creative accounting practices which came to light during the 1960s. In September 1964, Westec's stock was selling for about $3.50 on the American Stock Exchange. Over the next nineteen months, the price of Westec stock climbed to over $67 a share, while the financial statements were presenting a picture of incredible growth. On August 25, 1966, trading in Westec stock was halted by the exchange as certain manipulative securities transactions by Westec executives were revealed and the bubble burst. The questionable pooling transactions which contributed to that growth are now discussed briefly. A complete account of the case can be found in *Accounting Series Release (ASR) 248*, issued by the SEC on May 31, 1975, following a lengthy investigation.

In order to bolster earnings for calendar year 1964, Westec acquired three companies at the end of March 1965 and retrospectively included the pooled income statements in 1964 earnings. These acquisitions contributed about 23 percent of Westec's total earnings for 1964. Westec's auditors approved of this accounting treatment.

In April 1966, a similar situation occurred. To maintain the growth pattern for calendar year 1965, Westec again retrospectively pooled two acquisitions, which contributed 32 percent of the 1965 earnings.

These and other transactions contributed to the increase in Westec's reported earnings per share from $.12 in 1963 to $.43 in 1964 (23 percent from poolings) to $1.10 in 1965 (32 percent from poolings).

Retrospective Poolings—National Student Marketing Corporation (NSMC)   Although this case is famous primarily because of its improper revenue recognition practices (see *ASR 173*), it too had a number of retrospective poolings. Subsequent to NSMC's year ended August 31, 1969, eight major acquisitions were completed and their profits pooled with those of NSMC for fiscal 1969. These acquisitions contributed some $3,750,000 in earnings, thereby turning a loss into a substantial profit.[13]

Pooling via the Issue of Treasury Stock—American Tobacco and Sunshine Biscuits, Inc.   *APBO 16* prohibits the use of pooling when substantial transactions in treasury stock are made in contemplation of a business combination. When American Tobacco Company acquired Sunshine Biscuits,

---

[13] See Abraham J. Briloff, *Unaccountable Accounting* (N.Y.: Harper & Row, 1972), Chapter 3, "Dirty Pooling and Polluted Purchase," especially pp. 86–87.

Inc., in May 1966 (prior to *APBO 16*), almost 40 percent of the shares issued to effect the pooling were treasury shares acquired for about $30,000,000. [14] Not only did the acquisition of the treasury shares eliminate a component of American's ownership interest, it involved a cash payment which, although indirect, seems to violate the pooling concept. Furthermore, this $30,000,000 cash cost never entered subsequent income statements because, consistent with accounting for treasury stock, the excess of cost over par value of the shares was charged to stockholders' equity accounts.

Implications of Pooling of Interests—A Final Note

As mentioned earlier, pooling of interests accounting preserves the book values of the pooled firms' assets and liabilities. If the book values of assets acquired are far below their fair values, the unrealized gains are not recorded since zero cost is assigned to the appreciation in the assets' values. As the gains are realized in subsequent periods, they are attributed to the post-combination entity and flow through the income statement unreduced by the (suppressed) costs which were incurred to obtain them. Two examples follow.

1. The pooling of Paramount Pictures and Desilu into Gulf & Western (G & W) in 1967 enabled G & W to acquire many motion picture films having substantially amortized costs. By negotiating television distribution contracts which reflected the fair value of the films, G & W was able to recognize income on the unrealized gains attributable to the films. [15] Because of the pooling, G & W's statements never reflected the true cost of the films; the concurrent overstatement of income was hidden.

2. When International Telephone and Telegraph Corporation (ITT) acquired The Hartford Fire Insurance Company in 1969–1970, it also acquired a stock portfolio with total unrealized gains approximating $282 million. Starting with 1970, profits on the investment portfolio exceeding $260 million were realized over five years. As a comparison, total investment portfolio profits were a mere $2.5 million in the five years including 1964–1968, suggesting that the unrealized gains were systematically realized as income once ITT took over. [16]

   Overall, a number of ITT's poolings in the 1964–1970 period involved some $2.4 billion in consideration. Yet, the properties acquired were booked at $1.02 billion, indicating that, for these poolings, the cost of properties acquired was understated in ITT's financial statements by approximately $1.4 billion.

APBO 16 and the Conditions for Pooling of Interest

In order to curtail these abuses while continuing to allow pooling to be used under appropriate circumstances, the Accounting Principles Board issued *APBO 16* in August

---

[14] Ibid., p. 94.

[15] Ibid., pp. 65–67.

[16] See Abraham J. Briloff, *More Debits than Credits* (N.Y.: Harper & Row, 1976), Chapter 8, "Of Pools and Fools," especially pp. 219–226.

Exhibit 6.3   Necessary and Sufficient Conditions for the Use of the Pooling of Interests Method

Attributes of the Combining Companies

a. Each of the combining companies is autonomous and has not been a subsidiary or division of another corporation within two years before the plan of combination is initiated.

b. Each of the combining companies is independent of the other combining companies.

Manner of Combining Interests

a. The combination is effected in a single transaction or is completed in accordance with a specific plan within one year after the plan is initiated.

b. A corporation offers and issues only common stock with rights identical to those of the majority of its outstanding voting common stock in exchange for substantially all of the voting common stock interest of another company at the date the plan of combination is consummated.

c. None of the combining companies changes the equity interest of the voting common stock in contemplation of effecting the combination either within two years before the plan of combination is initiated or between the dates the combination is initiated and consummated; changes in contemplation of effecting the combination may include distributions to stockholders and additional issuances, exchanges, and retirements of securities.

d. Each of the combining companies reacquires shares of voting common stock only for purposes other than business combinations, and no company reacquires more than a normal number of shares between the dates the plan of combination is initiated and consummated.

e. The ratio of the interest of an individual common stockholder to those of other common stockholders in a combining company remains the same as a result of the exchange of stock to effect the combination.

f. The voting rights to which the common stock ownership interests in the resulting combined corporation are entitled are exercisable by the stockholders; the stockholders are neither deprived of nor restricted in exercising those rights for a period.

g. The combination is resolved at the date the plan is consummated and no provisions of the plan relating to the issue of securities or other consideration are pending.

Absence of Planned Transactions

a. The combined corporation does not agree directly or indirectly to retire or reacquire all or part of the common stock issued to effect the combination.

b. The combined corporation does not enter into other financial arrangements for the benefit of the former stockholders of a combining company, such as a guaranty of loans secured by stock issued in the combination, which in effect negates the exchange of equity securities.

c. The combined corporation does not intend or plan to dispose of a significant part of the assets of the combining companies within two years after the combination other than disposals in the ordinary course of business of the formerly separate companies and to eliminate duplicate facilities or excess capacity.

Source: Accounting Principles Board, *Opinion No. 16,* "Business Combinations" (N.Y.: AICPA, 1970), pars. 46–48; AC § 1091.46–48. Copyright © 1970 by the American Institute of Certified Public Accountants, Inc.

1970. The *Opinion* includes twelve conditions, *all* of which must be satisfied if a business combination is to be accounted for as a pooling of interests. These conditions are reproduced verbatim in Exhibit 6.3. We summarize them in the following paragraphs.

Attributes of the Combining Companies   These conditions were designed to ensure that a pooling will reflect only a legitimate union of previously independent ownership interests undertaken to share the risks and rights of ownership in the combined enterprise. Precluded are piecemeal combinations (unless completed within one year of the initiation of a formal plan for the combination) and combinations between companies already holding more than a 10 percent interest in the outstanding voting shares of any combining company (the *"10 percent rule"*).

Manner of Combining Interests   The conditions in this section have a bearing on the consummation of the combination. Fundamental to the concept of pooling is the notion that substantially all of the ownership interests in the combining companies continue as ownership interests in the combined companies. This can be achieved only through the exchange of voting common shares. The issue of cash, debt, or other nonvoting equity consideration in the combination would eliminate or alter some of the previously existing ownership interests. Therefore, the exchange of voting stock for "substantially all" of the voting stock of an acquired company means that at least 90 percent of the acquired company's voting stock is exchanged (the *"90 percent rule"*). Note, however, that the issue of cash or debt for related expenses such as consultants' and attorneys' fees does not violate these conditions.

Conditions (c) and (d) (in Exhibit 6.3) prohibit the rearrangement of capital structures and the retirement or reacquisition of shares in contemplation of a business combination. Such changes in capital structure and shares outstanding could represent a buy-out of certain ownership interests, which would defeat the pooling concept. Condition (d) is known as the *"treasury stock rule."* It specifically precludes the application of pooling of interests accounting when combining companies acquire treasury stock in connection with a business combination. This condition does not apply to treasury stock acquired more than two years prior to the combination. Any such shares should first be retired and then treated as previously unissued shares.

Condition (g) indicates that future consideration contingent upon the occurrence of the specified events has no place in a pooling of interests because of its incompatibility with the mutual exchange of ownership interests fundamental to pooling.

Absence of Planned Transactions   These conditions emphasize the importance of substance over form in pooling of interests accounting. For example, a combination satisfying the "90 percent rule" in form would not satisfy it in substance if (1) former stockholders of a combining company also received contracts employing them as "consultants" at excessive "wages" or (2) the stock issued in a business combination was repurchased by the combined firm shortly after the combination occurred.

Packaging a Pooling as a Purchase   Before we turn to the process of recording a business combination, one further observation on the twelve conditions for a pooling is appropriate. In their entirety, these conditions are restrictive and effectively limit the use of pooling of interests accounting to those combinations which faithfully reflect the pooling concept. Although it may be difficult to package a purchase transaction to meet the pooling criteria, the reverse is clearly not true. For example, management of the acquiring company may favor a purchase in order to bolster the resulting combined balance sheet. Yet the Internal Revenue Code provisions governing nontaxable corporate reorganizations often motivate the shareholders of the acquired firm to insist on a complete exchange of equity shares. To achieve the tax-free corporate reorganization *and* the purchase accounting treatment, the negotiating companies might agree to some contingent consideration in the plan of combination, thereby failing to conform to the pooling of interest rules in their entirety.

Recording the Business Combination

How a business combination is to be recorded depends primarily on two factors:
1. The nature of the business combination—whether it is a statutory merger, a statutory consolidation, an asset acquisition, or a stock acquisition.
2. The accounting method appropriate in the circumstances—purchase or pooling of interests.

The Nature of the Business Combination In a statutory merger, the acquired company is absorbed into the acquiring company, its stock is retired, and it ceases to exist as a legal entity. A statutory consolidation differs in degree only because two or more acquired firms cease to exist as legal entities. They are absorbed into a new firm, which is the legal entity that survives the combination. Thus *the acquiring firm records the assets and liabilities obtained in the statutory merger or consolidation on its books.* Furthermore, an asset acquisition is recorded in the same way, even though the firm from which the assets are acquired continues in business or liquidates in an unrelated transaction.

The method of recording a business combination which is a stock acquisition differs from the above. A parent/subsidiary relationship is created between the acquiring and the acquired companies. The acquired company remains as a separate legal entity and is treated as an intercorporate investment by the acquiring firm. Consequently, *the acquiring firm does not record the assets and liabilities of the acquired firm on its books.* Rather, the acquiring firm uses an **Investment in Subsidiary account** to record the shares of stock acquired. The Investment in Subsidiary account gives a one-line summation of the acquiring company's interest in the underlying assets and liabilities of the acquired company. As we shall see in subsequent chapters, this parent/subsidiary relationship normally calls for the preparation of consolidated financial statements. In a consolidated balance sheet, the Investment in Subsidiary account is replaced by the underlying assets and liabilities of the subsidiary.

The Method of Accounting We have already indicated that a major difference between purchase and pooling of interests accounting involves the basis for recording the property acquired. Under purchase accounting, the fair value of the consideration given typically provides the total dollar amount used to record the assets or stock acquired. In contrast, the acquiring firm uses book values for recording the acquired company's assets or stock obtained in a pooling of interests. Other rules applicable to the recording of business combinations are discussed below in the context of the two allowable accounting methods.

Application of the Purchase Method

The cost of the stock or assets acquired in a purchase combination is normally based on the fair value of the consideration surrendered. This amount is increased by certain direct costs associated with the combination, such as fees paid to consultants and finders and the cost of legal services related to the combination. Costs of registering and issuing equity securities are also part of the investment cost. Care must be taken, however, not to count these costs twice. In an unofficial interpretation (number 35) of paragraph 76 of *APBO 16* (AC § U1091.138–140), the AICPA indicated that while such costs effectively reduce the otherwise determinable fair value of securities issued, the costs themselves are part of the total investment cost. That is, the investment cost includes the total fair value of the securities issued. The registration and issue costs reduce the amount otherwise recorded as additional paid-in capital. If the registration costs have not been incurred when the securities are issued, an estimate must be accrued as a liability and charged to the investment account (or to Additional Paid-In Capital if the costs were not considered in recording the fair value of the securities issued). In the final analysis, it is the total fair value of securities issued that enters the investment account.

Indirect expenses and the recurring costs of mergers and acquisitions departments within the acquiring company are not capitalized but are treated as normal operating expenses of the period. Once the total cost of the property acquired is determined, it must be allocated among the assets and liabilities acquired.

The fair value of consideration given in a purchase combination is rarely equal to the book values of the assets acquired less liabilities assumed. To simplify dealing with this difference, we use the following terminology.[17]

> A **purchase premium** is said to exist when the cost of the acquisition is *greater than* the book values of the underlying assets acquired less liabilities assumed. Similarly, a **purchase discount** arises when the cost of the acquisition is *less than* the book values of the underlying assets acquired less liabilities assumed.

Purchase premiums and discounts must be allocated among the assets acquired and liabilities assumed as part of the following process whereby the total cost of the acquisition is allocated:

> A portion of the total cost is then assigned to each individual asset acquired [and liability assumed] on the basis of its fair value. A difference between the sum of the assigned costs of the tangible and identifiable intangible assets less liabilities assumed and the cost of the group is evidence of unspecified intangible values [goodwill].[18]

---

[17] Our thanks to Mr. Peter S. M. Wolcott, MBA, 1979, the Amos Tuck School of Business Administration, Dartmouth College, for suggesting this terminology to us.

[18] Accounting Principles Board, *Opinion No. 16*, par. 68; AC § 1091.68; parenthetical phrases added by the authors.

Exhibit 6.4   Schedule for Determining and Allocating a Purchase Premium or Discount

P Company and S Company
Schedule for Determining and Allocating the Purchase Premium (Discount)
Arising in the 100 Percent Purchase Acquisition on December 31, 19X1

Total Cost of the Acquisition	$1,000,000
Book Value of the Net Assets or Stockholders' Equity Acquired	800,000
Purchase Premium (Discount)	$ 200,000

Assets and Liabilities of S Company	Fair Value	Book Value	Fair Value Less Book Value	Allocation Based On P's Interest (100%)
Current Assets . . .	$1,150,000	$1,125,000	$ 25,000	$ 25,000
Noncurrent Assets . .	1,080,000	1,030,000	50,000	50,000
Current Liabilities . .	(600,000)	(600,000)	—	—
Noncurrent Liabilities .	(700,000)	(755,000)	55,000	55,000
	$ 930,000	$ 800,000	$130,000	$ 130,000
Goodwill				70,000
Total Purchase Premium (Discount)				$ 200,000

Since application of the purchase method results in a new basis of accountability for the property acquired, depreciation, amortization, and other asset expirations (costs) in subsequent years are to be based on the amounts assigned at date of combination. *APBO 16* requires, however, that any *goodwill previously recorded* by the acquired company is to be ignored in allocating the investment cost among the assets and liabilities acquired. Such goodwill is not an "identifiable intangible asset."[19] Exhibit 6.4 provides us with a systematic approach to this process of allocating the cost of an acquisition in a purchase combination.

In the great majority of cases, a purchase combination involves consideration with fair value greater than the book values of the property acquired. Moreover, the cost of the acquisition often exceeds the fair value of the tangible assets and identifiable intangible assets acquired less liabilities assumed, thereby generating a residual intangible called **goodwill.** A problem arises, however, if the fair value of the property acquired less liabilities assumed exceeds the cost of the investment. Or, in other words, the problem occurs if the fair value of the consideration given up is less than the fair value of the net assets acquired. When this occurs, we have what might be considered a *bargain purchase.* Yet the bargain purchase interpretation arises essentially because of a disagreement between estimates of the fair value of the consideration surrendered and the fair value of the property acquired. The fair value of the property acquired dominates the transaction only if it is more clearly evident than the fair value of the consideration given.

For example, cash or the market value of securities traded on the New York or American Stock Exchange would be more reliable evidence of the cost of an

---

[19]   Accounting Principles Board, *Opinion No. 16*, par. 89; AC § 1091.89.

acquired company than appraisals of the acquired company's assets and liabilities. On the other hand, competent appraisals may have more validity in establishing cost than prices of thinly-traded, over-the-counter securities. If the fair value of the consideration given more clearly represents the actual combination cost, then the amounts assigned to assets acquired less liabilities assumed cannot exceed that cost. Furthermore, when the investment cost is less than the fair values of the net assets acquired, a *two-stage allocation process* is called for.

1. The first stage simply involves stating the assets and liabilities acquired at their fair values. The difference between fair and book values is then compared with the purchase premium or discount, which is the difference between investment cost and book value. If fair value exceeds investment cost, **negative goodwill** arises. This general procedure has been illustrated in Exhibit 6.4 and is applied to an example involving negative goodwill in Exhibit 6.8.

2. *APBO 16* provides that any excess of fair value of assets over investment cost (negative goodwill) must be allocated proportionately among noncurrent assets except long-term investments in marketable securities.[20] This is the second stage of the allocation process. If there is sufficient negative goodwill to reduce the book values of eligible noncurrent assets to zero, any remaining (unallocated) amount is classified as a *deferred credit*. Under the provisions of *APBO 17* (AC § 5141), both positive goodwill arising in a business combination and deferred credits arising from unallocated negative goodwill must be *systematically amortized to income over a period not to exceed forty years. Straight-line amortization is required.*[21]

Observe that the existence of a purchase discount does not in itself guarantee that negative goodwill will arise. Nor will a purchase premium always mean that positive goodwill is present. In short, the purchase premium or discount determination is based on a comparison between the investment cost and the *book value* of the net assets acquired. Whether positive or negative goodwill exists follows from the relationship between investment cost and the *fair value* of the net assets acquired. For example, if investment cost exceeds book value, a purchase premium was paid. Yet negative goodwill will be present if investment cost is less than fair value. Similarly, if book value exceeds investment cost, a purchase discount exists, but positive goodwill will result if investment cost is more than fair value.

The following examples illustrate how purchase accounting is applied in a business combination.

Purchase Accounting—Statutory Merger   S Company is to be merged into P Company on December 31, 19X1, pursuant to the laws of the state in which P is incorporated. The condensed balance sheet of S Company at the date of combination appears in Exhibit 6.5, along with estimated fair values.

As consideration, P Company is issuing 10 percent bonds with par value and current market value of $900,000 to the shareholders of S in exchange for their

---

[20] Accounting Principles Board, *Opinion No. 16*, par. 91; AC § 1091.91.

[21] Accounting Principles Board, *Opinion No. 17*, "Intangible Assets" (N.Y.: AICPA, 1970).

Exhibit 6.5   Balance Sheet of S Company at December 31, 19X1

S Company
Balance Sheet at December 31, 19X1

ASSETS		Book Value	Fair Value
Cash and Receivables		$ 100,000	$100,000
Inventory		250,000	375,000
Plant and Equipment	$1,000,000		
Less Accumulated Depreciation . .	(200,000)	800,000	960,000 (net)
Total Assets		$1,150,000	
LIABILITIES AND STOCKHOLDERS' EQUITY			
Current Liabilities		$ 200,000	200,000
Bonds Payable, 6%, Par Value			
$500,000		500,000	400,000 [a]
Common Stock, Par Value $1 . . .		100,000	
Additional Paid-In Capital		125,000	
Retained Earnings		225,000	
Total Liabilities and Stockholders'			
Equity		$1,150,000	

[a]With current interest rates approximating 10 percent, the market value of the debt has fallen since the bonds were initially issued.

---

entire equity interest in the net assets (that is, assets less liabilities) of S Company. Direct costs associated with the merger (consultants' and attorneys' fees) amount to $25,000. Since the stockholders' equity of S Company amounts to only $450,000, P Company has paid a *purchase premium*. In Exhibit 6.6, we compute this purchase premium and determine how it is to be allocated among the assets and liabilities of S Company.

To record the merger, P Company makes the following journal entry on its books:

Cash and Receivables	100,000	
Inventory	375,000	
Plant and Equipment (Net)	960,000	
Discount on 6% Bonds Payable	100,000 [a]	
Goodwill	90,000 [b]	
Current Liabilities		200,000
Cash		25,000 [c]
Bonds Payable, 6%		500,000 [a]
Bonds Payable, 10%		900,000

To record the statutory merger of P Company and S Company, accounted for as a purchase.

[a]The 6 percent bonds payable assumed by Company P are recorded at their current market value of $400,000 by entering the liability at par value, $500,000, and recording a discount on bonds payable of $100,000.

[b]Goodwill of $90,000 arises because the consideration given exceeded the fair values of the identifiable assets acquired reduced by liabilities assumed (see Exhibit 6.6).

[c]The $25,000 credit to Cash reflects payment of the direct costs of the merger.

Exhibit 6.6   Determination and Allocation of the Purchase Premium Paid by P in Its Acquisition of S on December 31, 19X1

P Company and S Company
Schedule for Determining and Allocating the Purchase Premium
Arising in the Statutory Merger on December 31, 19X1

Cost of the Acquisition:

Market Value of Long-Term Debt Issued	$900,000
Consultants' and Attorneys' Fees	25,000
Total Cost of the Acquisition	$925,000

Book Value of the Net Assets or Stockholders' Equity Acquired:

Common Stock	$100,000
Additional Paid-In Capital	125,000
Retained Earnings	225,000
Total Book Value of S Company	$450,000
Purchase Premium	$475,000

Assets and Liabilities of S Company	Fair Value	Book Value	Fair Value Less Book Value	Allocation Based on P's Interest (100%)
Cash and Receivables	$100,000	$100,000	—	—
Inventory	375,000	250,000	$125,000	$125,000
Plant and Equipment (Net)	960,000	800,000	160,000	160,000
Current Liabilities	(200,000)	(200,000)	—	—
Bonds Payable, 6%	(400,000)	(500,000)	100,000	100,000
	$835,000	$450,000	$385,000	$385,000
Goodwill				90,000
Total Purchase Premium				$475,000

Accounting for Accumulated Depreciation of the Acquired Company   In a purchase combination, the acquiring company has purchased the assets and liabilities of the acquired company either directly or indirectly through the purchase of shares. Allocation of the purchase price is dependent upon the fair values of the properties acquired, and any accumulated depreciation recorded by the acquired company becomes irrelevant after the combination. The fair values established for assets, whether new or used, become their carrying values after the combination. These new carrying values (net of any estimated salvage proceeds) are then depreciated over their remaining useful lives. In the statutory merger just recorded, only the net fair value of S's plant and equipment, $960,000, is entered on P's books.

Purchase Accounting—Statutory Consolidations and Asset Acquisitions   The principles involved in recording statutory consolidations and asset acquisitions under the purchase method are no different from the statutory merger case and will not be repeated here. Nevertheless, we shall illustrate how the problem associated with negative goodwill is treated within the context of a statutory consolidation. In this case, companies S and T will be absorbed into P

Exhibit 6.7   Balance Sheet of T Company at December 31, 19X1

T Company
Balance Sheet at December 31, 19X1

ASSETS		Book Value	Fair Value
Cash and Receivables		$ 150,000	$ 150,000
Marketable Equity Securities—			
Current		100,000	120,000
Inventory		300,000	350,000
Marketable Equity Securities—Long-			
Term		500,000	600,000
Plant and Equipment	$2,000,000		
Less Accumulated Depreciation . .	(600,000)	1,400,000	1,600,000 (net)
Total Assets		$2,450,000	
LIABILITIES AND STOCKHOLDERS' EQUITY			
Current Liabilities		$ 500,000	500,000
Other Liabilities		800,000	1,200,000 [a]
Common Stock, Par Value $5 . .		250,000	
Additional Paid-In Capital . . .		400,000	
Retained Earnings		500,000	
Total Liabilities and Stockholders' Equity		$2,450,000	

[a]The fair value of Other Liabilities exceeded their book value due to the recognition of certain pension obligations which, consistent with generally accepted accounting principles, had not been booked by T Company. See footnote 13 to par. 88 (h) of *APBO 16* [AC § 1091.88(h)].

Company, a new corporation organized for carrying on the combined business operations of S and T. The assets and liabilities of S Company were given in Exhibit 6.5 in conjunction with estimates of their fair values. Similar data are provided for T Company in Exhibit 6.7.

The statutory consolidation of companies S and T into P Company is to be accomplished by an exchange of stock and cash by P for the stock of S and T. The shares of S and T will be retired, and only P Company will survive as a legal entity. Since P Company is a new corporation, no market exists for its common stock. We assume that we have reliable market prices for the stock of S Company and T Company. It is these prices which will be used to establish the cost of the acquired companies in the statutory consolidation. The terms of these acquisitions follow.

Relative to S Company   S Company's stockholders agreed to exchange all of their stock for 70,000 shares of P Company's $7.50 par value stock and $200,000 cash. The total market value of S Company's outstanding stock is assumed to be $900,000. Therefore, the implicit market value of these 70,000 shares of P Company stock is $700,000 (= $900,000 − $200,000). In addition, P Company incurred registration and issue costs of $15,000 and other direct costs of $25,000.

Relative to T Company   T Company's stockholders agreed to exchange all of their stock for 88,000 shares of P Company's $7.50 par value stock and $120,000 cash. The total market value of T Company's stock is assumed to be $1,000,000, and the implicit market value of the 88,000 P Company shares is $880,000 (= $1,000,000 − $120,000). P Company also incurred registration and issue costs in the amount of $20,000 and other direct costs of $40,000.

To record the statutory consolidation on P's books, the accountant must allocate the purchase premium or discount among the assets acquired and liabilities assumed. This procedure was applied to S Company in Exhibit 6.6. Exhibit 6.8 gives a similar schedule for T Company and also summarizes the details of the S Company acquisition.

The T Company acquisition, however, requires additional work. Specifically, it appears that the acquisition of T Company was a *bargain purchase*. Following paragraph 91 of *APBO 16*, we illustrate how the "excess of fair value over cost" or *negative goodwill* of $80,000 is to be treated in allocating the overall purchase discount of $110,000 to the assets and liabilities of T Company. This is the second stage of the two-stage allocation process. Negative goodwill must be used to reduce the cost assigned to noncurrent assets, exclusive of long-term investments in marketable securities. Current assets and all liabilities are to be recorded at their fair values. We have indicated that T's plant and equipment had a net fair value of $1,600,000. The entire $80,000 of negative goodwill would go to reduce the cost assigned to plant and equipment to $1,520,000. Suppose the Plant and Equipment account consisted of the following:

	Book Value	Fair Value Amount	Fair Value Percent
Buildings and Equipment	$1,200,000	$1,300,000	81%
Land	200,000	300,000	19
Total	$1,400,000	$1,600,000	100%

Allocation of the negative goodwill of $80,000 between Buildings and Equipment and Land is based on their relative proportions of total fair value, as shown below:

	(1) Percent of Fair Value	(2) Allocation of Negative Goodwill [(1) × $80,000]	(3) Fair Value	(4) Cost Assigned [(3)−(2)]
Buildings and Equipment	81%	$64,800	$1,300,000	$1,235,200
Land	19	15,200	300,000	284,800
Total	100%	$80,000	$1,600,000	$1,520,000

Exhibit 6.8   Determination and Allocation of the Purchase Premium and Discount in the P, S, and T Statutory Consolidation on December 31, 19X1

P Company, S Company, and T Company
Schedule for Determining and Allocating the Purchase Premium (Discount)
Arising in the Statutory Consolidation on December 31, 19X1

	S Company	T Company
Cost of the Acquisition:		
Fair Value of Stock Given, Net of Registration and Issue Costs	$685,000	$ 860,000
Plus Registration and Issue Costs	15,000	20,000
Cash Given	200,000	120,000
Direct Costs Incurred	25,000	40,000
Total Cost of the Acquisition	$925,000	$1,040,000
Book Value of the Net Assets or Stockholders' Equity Acquired:		
Common Stock	$100,000	$ 250,000
Additional Paid-In Capital	125,000	400,000
Retained Earnings	225,000	500,000
Total Book Values of Acquired Companies	$450,000	$1,150,000
Purchase Premium (Discount)	$475,000	$ (110,000)

Assets and Liabilities of T Company	Fair Value	Book Value	Fair Value Less Book Value	Allocation Based on P's Interest (100%)
Cash and Receivables	$ 150,000	$ 150,000	—	—
Marketable Equity Securities —Current	120,000	100,000	$ 20,000	$ 20,000
Inventory	350,000	300,000	50,000	50,000
Marketable Equity Securities —Long-Term	600,000	500,000	100,000	100,000
Plant and Equipment (Net)	1,600,000	1,400,000	200,000	200,000
Current Liabilities	(500,000)	(500,000)	—	—
Other Liabilities	(1,200,000)	(800,000)	(400,000)	(400,000)
	$1,120,000	$1,150,000	$ (30,000)	$ (30,000)
Negative Goodwill				(80,000)
Total Purchase Discount				$(110,000)

The entry to record the statutory consolidation on the books of P is given in Exhibit 6.9. It incorporates the data previously used to reflect fair values of S Company's assets and liabilities as well as the data just developed relative to T Company.

Purchase Accounting—Stock Acquisitions   Recall that from a legal and organizational point of view, a business combination may occur even though the combining companies remain as separate entities. A parent/subsidiary relationship may be established, in which the acquiring company accounts for its interest in the acquired company by means of an Investment in Subsidiary account ("Subsidiary" is generally referred to as "S"). The parent/subsidiary relationship is established when the acquiring company secures control of more than 50 percent of the voting shares of the acquired company. This controlling interest may be secured through a purchase of shares in the market, an exchange of equity shares, or some similar means.

When a stock acquisition is accounted for as a purchase, the cost of the investment is measured by the fair value of the consideration given if this amount is clearly more obvious than the fair value of the property underlying the equity shares. *If a purchase premium or discount exists, it is allocated subsequently when consolidated statements are prepared.* To illustrate the accounting for stock acquisitions, we use companies S and T as previously introduced.

Consider first the acquisition of S Company. If S Company is to remain as a separate legal entity, the acquisition of its shares would be recorded on the books of P Company by the following journal entry:

Investment in S	925,000	
Cash		240,000
Common Stock (70,000 × $7.50)		525,000
Additional Paid-In Capital		160,000

To record the acquisition of all the outstanding common stock of S Company. Consideration to the former shareholders of S included cash of $200,000 and 70,000 shares of P Company $7.50 par value stock. The P Company stock had an implicit market value of $700,000, derived from the market value of S Company's stock. Net market value of the P stock issued was $685,000 *after* deducting registration and issue costs of $15,000, which were paid in cash and are part of the total investment cost of $925,000. Additional direct costs associated with this acquisition were consultants' and attorneys' fees of $25,000.

With respect to the acquisition of T Company, if a parent/subsidiary relationship is to be maintained, P Company makes a similar journal entry:

Investment in T	1,040,000	
Cash		180,000
Common Stock		660,000
Additional Paid-In Capital		200,000

To record the acquisition of all the outstanding common stock of T Company. Consideration to the former shareholders of T included cash of $120,000 and 88,000 shares of P Company $7.50 par value stock. The P Company stock had an implicit market value of $880,000 derived from the market value of T Company's stock. Net market value of the P stock issued was $860,000 *after* deducting registration and issue costs of $20,000, which were paid in cash and are part of the total investment cost of $1,040,000. Additional direct costs associated with this acquisition were consultants' and attorneys' fees of $40,000.

In Chapters 7 and 8, we discuss how the Investment in Subsidiary account is to be accounted for after the business combination. Whether the proper accounting requires consolidated statements or not, we still need to know both book values *and* fair values of the assets and liabilities of companies S and T.

Exhibit 6.9   Recording the Statutory Consolidation of S Company and T Company into P Company on the Books of P Company as a Purchase

	Relative to S Company		Relative to T Company		Total Statutory Consolidation	
	Dr.	Cr.	Dr.	Cr.	Dr.	Cr.
Cash and Receivables .	100,000		150,000		250,000	
Marketable Equity Securities—Current .	—		120,000		120,000	
Inventory	375,000		350,000		725,000	
Marketable Equity Securities—Long-Term	—		600,000		600,000	
Plant and Equipment (Net) . .	960,000		1,520,000 [c]		2,480,000	
Discount on 6% Bonds Payable.	100,000		—		100,000	
Goodwill	90,000		—		90,000	
Current Liabilities . .		200,000		500,000		700,000
Other Liabilities . .		—		1,200,000		1,200,000
Cash		240,000 [a]		180,000 [a]		420,000
Bonds Payable, 6% .		500,000		—		500,000
Common Stock . .		525,000		660,000		1,185,000
Additional Paid-In Capital		160,000 [b]		200,000 [b]		360,000

[a]The credits to Cash include the cash given to the former shareholders of S and T companies plus the direct costs paid and the issue and registration costs.

[b]The credits to Additional Paid-In Capital are net of the registration and issue costs. For example, stock having an implicit market value of $880,000 was issued to the shareholders of Company T. This stock had a par value of $660,000 (= 88,000 shares × $7.50). The registration and issue costs of $20,000 effectively reduce the implicit market value of the 88,000 shares to $860,000 and additional paid-in capital of $200,000 (= $860,000 − $660,000) results.

[c]This is the total of the amounts previously assigned to buildings and equipment ($1,235,200) and land ($284,800).

A stock acquisition often involves less than 100 percent of the subsidiary's outstanding voting stock. Regardless of the percentage of ownership, the cost of the shares acquired is accounted for as an investment in subsidiary. Partially owned subsidiaries, however, generate additional problems for the accountant who must prepare consolidated financial statements. These problems will be studied in subsequent chapters.

Contingent Consideration in Purchase Accounting   Paragraphs 77–86 of *APBO 16* provide guidance for accounting for various types of **contingent consideration agreements** which often arise in a business combination. Such agreements call for the payment of additional cash or the issuance of additional securities in the future if specified events occur. The existence of a contingent consideration arrangement violates pooling condition (g) (see Exhibit 6.3) and will therefore only be dealt with in the context of a purchase combination. These arrangements generally benefit the shareholders of the acquired company and are of two general types:

1.   Contingencies based on earnings.

2.   Contingencies based on security prices.

A **contingency based on earnings** typically derives from the beliefs of the former shareholders of the acquired company that they are entitled to more consideration for their shares because their company will substantially bolster post-combination earnings. Although there may be no evidence on this point, the acquiring company may agree that if earnings equal or exceed a given amount in a specified period of time, additional consideration will be paid to the former shareholders of the acquired company. Such payments, when they materialize, represent *an addition to the cost of the acquired company*. The parties are, in effect, agreeing that *the total cost will not be known until the contingency period elapses*. Accordingly, payments resulting from the resolution of an earnings contingency will increase a previously existing purchase premium or decrease a previously existing purchase discount. Any change in the purchase premium or discount is viewed as a change in accounting estimate. Allocation of the new amount to depreciable or amortizable assets simply increases the costs which must now be depreciated or amortized over the assets' remaining lives.

As an example, suppose P Company agrees that if average post-combination earnings over the next two years exceed $250,000, payments of $100,000 in cash or stock will be made to former S Company shareholders. Footnote disclosure of the contingency is required in P's financial statements. If, at the close of the second year, average earnings for the two year period are $275,000, P Company may settle the contingency by issuing additional shares. P's shares have a par value of $7.50 and, assuming a per share market value of $20 at the end of the contingency period, the accountant will record the issuance of 5,000 (= $100,000/$20) shares. According to our initial allocation of the cost of the S Company acquisition in Exhibit 6.6, the additional market value of $100,000 (= 5,000 × $20) would be allocated in its entirety to goodwill.

Goodwill	100,000	
Common Stock		37,500
Additional Paid-In Capital		62,500

To record the issue of 5,000 shares of P Company's
$7.50 par value stock at their per share market value of
$20 in settlement of the earnings contingency arranged
as part of the combination with S Company.

In contrast, a **contingency based on security prices** does not affect the cost of the acquired company. Such a contingency guarantees the former shareholders of the acquired company that the market value of securities (stock or debt) issued to them in exchange for their stock will be at least a specified amount at a specified time. It is this *guaranteed amount* that *measures the cost of the acquired company*. Although additional consideration may be required in the future to restore the economic position of the acquired company's former shareholders, the cost of the acquired company has not changed.

To illustrate, suppose that, in acquiring T Company, P Company agreed to guarantee that the 88,000 P Company shares issued would be worth at least $10 per share in one year. If the closing market price was $8 per share at the end of one year, P must issue additional consideration worth $176,000 (= 88,000 shares issued × $2 per share). Whether more shares are now issued or cash is paid, the debit is to Additional Paid-In Capital. We assume that P Company satisfies the contingent consideration agreement by issuing more shares of its stock. At $8 per share, 22,000 (= $176,000/$8) new shares must be issued.

Additional Paid-In Capital	165,000	
Common Stock		165,000

To record the additional shares issued at their total par
value of $165,000 (= 22,000 × $7.50) in settlement of
the contingent consideration agreement made with the
former shareholders of S Company.

This entry has the effect of properly stating both the total par value of stock issued in the combination and the additional paid-in capital which, in the final analysis, resulted. We demonstrate this point by observing:

Agreed-Upon Value of Stock Given (88,000 × $10)	$880,000
Total Par Value of 110,000 (= 88,000 + 22,000) Shares at $7.50	
per Share	$825,000
Registration and Issue Costs	20,000
Net Additional Paid-In Capital	35,000 ←
	$880,000
Amount Originally Credited to Additional Paid-In Capital . . .	$200,000
Amount Debited to Additional Paid-In Capital When 22,000	
Additional Shares Are Issued	(165,000)
Net Additional Paid-In Capital	$ 35,000 ←

Accounting for Preacquisition Contingencies　　In September 1980, the FASB issued *SFAS 38*.[22] This statement clarifies the application of *SFAS 5* (AC § 4311)[23] and *SFAS 16* (AC § 2014)[24] to *APBO 16* as to the valuation of preacquisition contingencies of purchased enterprises and subsequent adjustments generated by the resolution of those contingencies. More specifically, the issues are: What criteria should govern the allocation of investment cost to unrecorded (and perhaps unknown) contingent assets, contingent impairments of assets, or contingent liabilities existing at date of business combination? Should subsequent adjustments to or resolutions of such contingencies enter the income statement or be used to revise the original purchase price allocation?

SFAS 38 addresses these issues by identifying an **allocation period,** normally not to extend beyond one year after a business combination, during which the initial purchase price allocations may be revised as new information regarding preacquisition contingencies arises. After this allocation period expires, subsequent adjustments to recorded preacquisition contingencies enter the income statement.

For example, suppose that a lawsuit was filed against an acquired company alleging defective products and claiming damages of $100,000. If the lawsuit was filed during the allocation period and meets three criteria, allocation of the purchase price would include recognizing an estimated liability of $100,000. The criteria are:

1.　　The alleged defects related to goods manufactured *before* the business combination.

2.　　The loss outcome is probable.

[22] Financial Accounting Standards Board, *Statement No. 38.*

[23] Financial Accounting Standards Board, *Statement of Financial Accounting Standards No. 5,* "Accounting for Contingencies" (Stamford, Conn.: FASB, 1975).

[24] Financial Accounting Standards Board, *Statement of Financial Accounting Standards No. 16,* "Prior Period Adjustments" (Stamford, Conn.: FASB, 1977).

3.   The amount of the loss can be reasonably estimated.

If the contingency is resolved (settled or withdrawn) during the allocation period, the original (or revised) purchase price allocation would be adjusted, if necessary, to reflect the resolution. In cases where the contingency remains unresolved at the end of the allocation period, all information then available should be analyzed to determine whether the allocation for the contingency should be increased or decreased. Once the allocation period has expired, however, any further increases or decreases in the contingent item are accounted for as gains or losses.

Preacquisition contingencies can also relate to assets. Suppose that a patent was applied for prior to the combination and subsequently approved after the combination but during the allocation period. The original purchase price allocation would be adjusted to reflect the estimated fair value of the approved patent.

Application of the Pooling of Interests Method

In a pooling of interests, the assets and liabilities of the acquired company are carried forward in the business combination at their *book values*. No new basis of accountability arises, and, accordingly, information regarding the fair value of consideration given, assets acquired, or liabilities assumed is not considered in recording the combination. Furthermore, any *direct or indirect costs of the combination are treated as expenses of the period*. The primary problem encountered in recording a pooling of interests lies in combining the stockholders' equity accounts. Under the pooling concept, the total contributed capital (that is, capital stock plus additional paid-in capital) of the combined firm should not be less than the sum of the contributed capital accounts of the combining firms. The exchange of shares in a pooling implies that simply adding the contributed capital accounts together is not sufficient. Rather, the par or stated value of the acquiring company's shares which are issued in the combination must be properly accounted for. Any difference between the par value of new shares issued and the total contributed capital of the acquired company is credited or debited to the acquiring company's Additional Paid-In Capital (APIC) account. Retained earnings of the constituent companies are added together without adjustment unless the acquiring company's APIC would be driven below zero in recording the combination.

To systematically analyze how a pooling of interests combination is recorded, consider the following format for the journal entry to be made on the books of the acquiring company, as it pools with an acquired company.

Net Assets (= Assets − Liabilities) . . Book Value[a]	
Common Stock	Par Value[b]
Additional Paid-In Capital	Contributed Capital of S Less Par Value of Stock Issued[c]
Retained Earnings	Book Value[a]

[a] *Book Value* refers to the appropriate account balances on the books of the acquired company.
[c] *Par Value* is the total par or stated value of the shares issued by the acquiring company in the combination.
[c] If the par value of the stock issued by the acquiring company *exceeds* the total contributed capital of the acquired company, the excess is *debited* to APIC. If the excess is greater than the acquiring company's credit balance in APIC, it is necessary to debit retained earnings for any amount remaining after the credit balance in APIC is exhausted.

To see how this journal entry would be used to record a particular pooling of interests combination, consider the following stockholders' equity data for P Company and S Company:

	P Company	S Company
Common Stock, Par Value $7.50, Authorized 300,000 Shares;		
Issued and Outstanding 135,000 Shares	$1,012,500	—
Common Stock, Par Value $1, Authorized, Issued, and		
Outstanding 100,000 Shares	—	$100,000
Additional Paid-In Capital	50,000	125,000
Retained Earnings	2,000,000	225,000
Total Precombination Stockholders' Equity (= Net Assets) .	$3,062,500	$450,000

In Exhibit 6.10, we record the pooling of interests of P and S under four different possible exchanges of equity shares.

Pooling of Interests—Statutory Mergers and Consolidations   Earlier in the chapter, we recorded the statutory merger of P and S under purchase accounting. We now assume that the combination will be accomplished as a pooling of interests solely through the exchange of equity shares. P Company is issuing 20,000 of its $7.50 par value shares for the 100,000 shares of S Company (case 2 in Exhibit 6.10). Out-of-pocket costs for related expenses—consultants' and attorneys' fees, registration and issue costs—amount to $40,000. Using the balance sheet data (book values) for S Company from Exhibit 6.5, we record the statutory merger as a pooling with the following journal entry made on the books of P Company. Note that, in contrast with purchase accounting, the Accumulated Depreciation balance of the "acquired" company is carried over in the combination. Moreover, had goodwill been recorded on the books of S Company, it would be carried over in the pooling.

Cash and Receivables	100,000	
Inventory	250,000	
Plant and Equipment	1,000,000	
Expenses of Business Combination	40,000	
Cash		40,000
Accumulated Depreciation		200,000
Current Liabilities		200,000
Bonds Payable, 6%		500,000
Common Stock		150,000
Additional Paid-In Capital		75,000
Retained Earnings		225,000

To record the statutory merger of P Company and S Company, accounted for as a pooling of interests.

If S Company and T Company were to pool their interests with P Company in a statutory consolidation, the pooling would be recorded as in Exhibit 6.11. Say that P Company issues 50,000 shares of its $7.50 par value common stock for all 50,000 shares of T Company stock issued and outstanding. Out-of-pocket costs amount to $60,000 and the balance sheet data for T Company (book values) are from Exhibit 6.7. The entry given above to record the pooling with S Company is also included as part of the statutory consolidation in Exhibit 6.11.

Exhibit 6.10 Recording a Pooling of Interests under Alternative Exchanges of Equity Shares

Recording the Pooling of Interests of P Company and S Company under Alternative Exchanges of Equity Shares

	Case 1		Case 2		Case 3		Case 4	
	Dr.	Cr.	Dr.	Cr.	Dr.	Cr.	Dr.	Cr.
Net Assets	450,000		450,000		450,000		450,000	
Common Stock		75,000		150,000		240,000		375,000
Additional Paid-In Capital . .		150,000		75,000	15,000		50,000	
Retained Earnings		225,000		225,000		225,000		125,000

Case 1: P exchanges 10,000 of its $7.50 par value shares for the 100,000 shares of S's outstanding stock.

Case 2: P exchanges 20,000 of its $7.50 par value shares for the 100,000 shares of S's outstanding stock.

Case 3: P exchanges 32,000 of its $7.50 par value shares for the 100,000 shares of S's outstanding stock.

Case 4: P exchanges 50,000 of its $7.50 par value shares for the 100,000 shares of S's outstanding stock.

Exhibit 6.11   Recording a Statutory Consolidation as a Pooling of Interests

Recording the Statutory Consolidation of S Company and T Company
into P Company on the Books of P Company as a Pooling of Interests

	Relative to S Company		Relative to T Company		Total Statutory Consolidation	
	Dr.	Cr.	Dr.	Cr.	Dr.	Cr.
Cash and Receivables . .	100,000		150,000		250,000	
Marketable Equity Securities—Current . .	—		100,000		100,000	
Inventory	250,000		300,000		550,000	
Marketable Equity Securities—Long-Term .	—		500,000		500,000	
Plant and Equipment . .	1,000,000		2,000,000		3,000,000	
Expenses of Business Combination	40,000 [a]		60,000 [a]		100,000	
Cash		40,000 [a]		60,000 [a]		100,000
Accumulated Depreciation . . .		200,000		600,000		800,000
Current Liabilities . . .		200,000		500,000		700,000
Other Liabilities . . .		—		800,000		800,000
Bonds Payable, 6% . .		500,000		—		500,000
Common Stock . . .		150,000 [b]		375,000 [b]		525,000
Additional Paid-In Capital		75,000 [b]		275,000 [b]		350,000
Retained Earnings . .		225,000 [c]		500,000 [c]		725,000

[a]Following paragraph 58 of *APBO 16,* expenses incurred in connection with a pooling of interests are not capitalized but are charged directly against income.
[b]Common Stock is credited for the par value of P Company stock issued; the total credits to Common Stock and Additional Paid-In Capital equal the total contributed capital of companies S and T.
[c]In a pooling of interests, unlike the purchase case, the retained earnings of the acquired companies become part of the post-combination retained earnings.

Pooling of Interests—Stock Acquisition   Pooling of interests accounting may also be used to account for a stock acquisition, provided that the pooling conditions are satisfied. Since the acquired company survives as a separate legal entity, P Company records the acquisition on its books by debiting the Investment in Subsidiary account for its interest in the net assets (at book value) of S Company. The entries to the stockholders' equity accounts are identical to those just presented in connection with statutory mergers and consolidations. Therefore, to record the pooling of P Company and S Company as a stock acquisition, we give P Company's entry for the case in which P issues 20,000 shares of its $7.50 par value stock for all 100,000 outstanding shares of S Company. The out-of-pocket costs were $40,000.

Investment in S	450,000	
Expenses of Business Combination	40,000	
Cash		40,000
Common Stock		150,000
Additional Paid-In Capital		75,000
Retained Earnings		225,000
To record the pooling of P Company and S Company as a stock acquisition.		

Recording a Less Than 100 Percent Pooling

Stock acquisitions often involve the acquisition of less than 100 percent of the subsidiary's outstanding common shares. In a pooling of interests, at least 90 percent of these shares must be acquired. To facilitate this discussion, we define α as the percent of voting shares acquired by P.

> In a business combination, $\boldsymbol{\alpha}$ refers to the percent of a subsidiary's outstanding voting shares acquired by the parent or controlling interest; α = number of shares of S acquired by P/total number of shares of S outstanding.

Our journal entry format for recording a stock acquisition may now be modified as follows:

Investment in S (= Assets − Liabilities) . . . . . . α(Book Value)[a]	
Common Stock	Par Value[b]
Additional Paid-In Capital . .	α(Contributed Capital of S) Less Par Value of Stock Issued[c]
Retained Earnings	α(Book Value)[a]

To record a stock acquisition as a pooling of interests, where $.9 \leq \alpha < 1$.

[a]Book Value refers to the appropriate account balances on the books of S, the acquired company.
[b]*Par Value* is the total par or stated value of the shares issued by P in the combination.
[c]If the par value of stock issued by P exceeds P's share (α) of the total contributed capital of S, the excess is *debited* to APIC. If the excess is greater than P's credit balance in APIC, it is necessary to debit retained earnings for any amount remaining after the credit balance in APIC is exhausted.

As an example, consider the pooling with S Company. Suppose P Company exchanges 19,000 shares of its $7.50 par value stock for 95 percent of S Company's 100,000 shares. Ignoring any out-of-pocket costs, P Company records the stock acquisition as follows:

Investment in S (.95 × $450,000)	427,500	
Common Stock (19,000 × $7.50)		142,500
Additional Paid-In Capital [.95($100,000 + $125,000) − $142,500]		71,250
Retained Earnings (.95 × $225,000)		213,750

To record the pooling of P Company and S Company, in which 19,000 shares of P Company's Stock were exchanged for 95 percent of S Company's outstanding shares.

Issue of Treasury Stock in a Pooling of Interests

Although the acquisition of treasury stock in contemplation of a business combination defeats the pooling concept (see condition d, Exhibit 6.3), it does not follow that treasury stock may never be used in a pooling. Specifically, there is no prohibition against the use of *treasury stock acquired more than two years prior* to initiating the business combination. Paragraph 54 of *APBO 16* instructs us to first account for these shares as retired, and then reissue them. Since the shares issued in a pooling are to be accounted for at the book value of the shares (or net assets) acquired, the basis of previously acquired treasury stock is not relevant.

If P Company were issuing 20,000 shares of treasury stock previously acquired several years ago at a cost of $220,000 in a pooling, the stock, par value $7.50, would be retired.

Common Stock	150,000	
Additional Paid-In Capital	70,000	
Treasury Stock		220,000

To record the retirement of 20,000 shares of $7.50 par value common stock in contemplation of their reissue in a pooling of interests combination. Total par value of the retired stock is $150,000 (= 20,000 shares × $7.50).

The issue of such stock in a pooling would now be treated as if the shares had been previously unissued, consistent with our other illustrations.

Accounting for Business Combinations: The Future

Despite the publication of *APBO 16* and the interpretations that followed, considerable dissatisfaction with generally accepted accounting principles still exists. Prior to *APBO 16*, two *Accounting Research Studies* (*ARS*s) recommended elimination of the pooling of interests method. In *ARS 5*, Wyatt concluded that

> no basis exists in principle for a continuation of what is presently known as "pooling of interests" accounting *if* the business combination involves an exchange of assets and/or equities between independent parties.[25]

Five years later, in their conclusion to *ARS 10*, Catlett and Olson stated:

> Except in a few business combinations in which the combination is not a purchase transaction but creates a new enterprise, the proper accounting for business combinations is found in the general concepts underlying purchase accounting. Pooling of interests is not a valid method of accounting for business combinations.[26]

With respect to *APBO 16* itself, six of the eighteen board members dissented. In particular, the *Opinion* states that "Messrs. Davidson, Horngren and Seidman dissent to the Opinion because it seeks to patch up some of the abuses of pooling. The real abuse is pooling itself. On that, the only answer is to eliminate pooling."[27] Nevertheless, it appears that *APBO 16* had an impact on the incidence of business combinations recorded as poolings of interest (see Exhibit 6.2).

The obvious questions are: why has pooling survived for so long, and can we forecast its demise? We will attempt an answer. First, the pooling concept has some intuitive appeal. The notion of companies pooling their resources and adopting a new form of business organization in which the previous ownership interests remain to share in the risks and rewards flowing from the combined enterprise cannot be condemned outright. Yet the pooling takes place not in a vacuum, but in a world in which securities having determinable economic value are exchanged. Can this exchange of value be safely ignored when financial

---

[25] Wyatt, *ARS No. 5*, p. 105.

[26] George R. Catlett and Norman O. Olson, "Accounting for Goodwill," *Accounting Research Study No. 10* (N.Y.: American Institute of Certified Public Accountants, 1968), p. 110.

[27] Accounting Principles Board, *Opinion No. 16*, par. 99; AC § 1091.99.

statements are prepared? We think not. Formation of a partnership could be viewed as a sort of pooling of interests. Does it then follow that the fair value of property invested in a partnership is irrelevant, and that the partners' capital interests should be based on previous book values which may bear no relationship to the fair values of assets invested? Again, we think not.

Second, pooling of interests accounting does possess distinct potential for improving the *appearance* of the income statement. Many continue to value this potential. We question whether accounting principles should be based on this type of argument.

In sum, we acknowledge the intuitive and economic appeal of the pooling method but question the legitimacy of the pooling concept in a business combination. We believe that pooling will ultimately disappear from the scene. Its demise will be hastened if some form of current value accounting becomes more widely used.

Summary of Key Concepts

A business combination occurs when two or more companies are brought under common control. From a legal and organizational perspective, business combinations may be classified as **statutory mergers, statutory consolidations, asset acquisitions,** and **stock acquisitions.** In a stock acquisition, the combining companies remain as separate legal entities.

For simplicity, we define the surviving or controlling company in a business combination as the **acquiring company.** Similarly, the **acquired company** is one whose ownership interests are substantially eliminated in the combined enterprise or whose ownership interests become part of the controlling interest in the combined enterprise.

A given business combination is accounted for under either the purchase or pooling of interests method. In a **purchase** combination, an arm's-length exchange transaction has occurred, and the assets and liabilities of the acquired company are stated at their **fair market values** at the date of combination. A **pooling of interests** is viewed as a union of previously separate ownership interests, not as an arm's-length exchange transaction. Assets and liabilities of the "acquired" company in a pooling are stated at the **book values** to the acquired company.

If the investment cost in a purchase combination is greater than (less than) the book value of the net assets acquired, a **purchase premium (discount)** results. This premium or discount is allocated among the identifiable assets and liabilities acquired in order that they be stated at their fair values. Any **unallocated debit balance** is reclassified as **goodwill.** If the process of stating the assets and liabilities of the acquired company at their fair values produces an unallocated **credit balance,** it is viewed as **negative goodwill.** Negative goodwill must in turn be allocated among the noncurrent assets of the acquired company (except long-term investments in marketable securities) in proportion to their fair market values.

In a **pooling of interests,** the total contributed capital of the combined entity should not be less than the sum of the contributed capital accounts of the combining firms. To achieve this, capital stock is increased by the par value of the additional shares issued by the "acquiring" company. Combined additional paid-in capital is increased if the acquired company's contributed capital exceeds the par value of stock issued; otherwise it is decreased. The acquired company's retained earnings becomes part of combined retained earnings.

Contingent consideration is frequently part of a purchase combination. If the contingency is based on **future earnings,** any additional payments made at the end of the contingency period go to increase the cost of the acquired company. In contrast, a contingency based on **future security prices** does not result in a change to the cost of the acquired company when the contingency period ends, even if additional payments are required to satisfy the contingency clause.

Contingent liabilities, contingent assets, and contingent impairments of assets are often present when a business combination is consummated. Establishing valuations for these items in a purchase combination is often made difficult by uncertainty. *SFAS 38* allows adjustments to be made to these valuations during an **allocation period,** which generally expires one year after the combination. Subsequent adjustments enter the postcombination income statement and cannot be used to make retroactive changes in the purchase price allocation.

Appendix to Chapter 6

Determining the Price in a Business Combination When the Constituent Companies Are Publicly Traded

As we have seen, merger and acquisition activities have been widespread in the American economy. The terms under which business combinations have taken place are varied. Whether publicly-traded or privately-held companies are involved, however, the parties must decide upon the amount of economic value to be exchanged and its composition. The *composition of the economic value transferred* in a business combination refers to that mix of cash, common stock, preferred stock, debt, and warrants which make up the agreed-upon economic value. Since the possible arrays of cash and securities are almost limitless, we cannot begin to explore them here. Indeed, such a comprehensive treatment of price and payment negotiations in business combinations is beyond the scope of this book.

To give an idea of the nature of merger negotiations and the role played by accounting data in these negotiations, we will focus on companies whose shares are publicly traded. To further simplify the analysis, we will assume that a single class of stock—voting common—will be exchanged. In this way, we can concentrate on determining the amount of economic value to be exchanged.[28]

A company analyzing a potential acquisition has, in effect, a capital budgeting problem. When the target company is privately held, its economic value must be estimated. A schedule of estimated future cash flows to be generated by the target company must be prepared, adjusted for applicable taxes, and discounted to its present value at the combination date. Because any such estimate of economic value will be sensitive to (1) the amounts and timing of the estimated cash flows and (2) the choice of discount rate, qualitative and subjective factors are likely to play large roles in the decision-making process.

The situation differs, however, when the target company is publicly held and its shares are traded on a major stock exchange. In this case, the market provides us with independently-determined information regarding the economic value and risk of the target company. These data are:

1.   The *per-share* value or *price* (P) of the target company's stock.
2.   The target company's *price/earnings* (P/E) *ratio*.

---

[28]   For a more detailed and formal treatment of this approach, see Kermit D. Larson and Nicholas J. Gonedes, "Business Combinations: An Exchange Ratio Determination Model," *The Accounting Review*, October 1969, pp. 720–728.

Similar data relative to the acquiring company are also available, assuming that it too is publicly held and its shares are traded on a major stock exchange.

Just as the risk associated with the privately-held company will usually be an important factor in the choice of discount rate, the P/E ratio gives us the market's estimate of the risk associated with the publicly-held company. Literally, the P/E ratio is interpreted as the number of dollars investors are willing to pay for $1 of earnings. A low P/E ratio often means that investors view the company as risky and are not willing to pay much for its earnings. Alternatively, a low P/E ratio could indicate slow projected earnings growth.

Stock Exchange Ratios

When a business combination is to be achieved solely through the exchange of common stock, a mutually acceptable price is set when a mutually acceptable *stock exchange ratio* (ER) is negotiated.

> A **stock exchange ratio** is defined as the number of shares of the acquiring company's stock to be exchanged for one share of the target company's stock.

Consider a business combination involving S Company and T Company. Since the value of ER will determine the total number of shares outstanding after the combination, it will also determine the postcombination earnings per share, E_{ST}. Given that the price of a share of stock, $P = E(P/E)$, and that we can compute postcombination E_{ST} for any exchange ratio, ER, the value of the stock after the combination will depend on the postcombination P/E ratio assigned by the market. We call this the *ex post* P/E ratio and emphasize that it is *unknown prior to completion of the combination*. Because of this, the best we can do is identify the boundaries of the range within which the final, mutually acceptable ER must be negotiated. Subjective factors continue to have importance. For example, the target company may have a large tax loss carryforward. If its eventual realization is uncertain, its potential value may only be partially reflected in the target company's stock price, if at all. Such a loss carryforward may have significant value to the acquiring company if consolidated tax returns are envisioned. It will surely have an impact on the acceptability of alternative exchange ratios to the acquiring company.

Thus we emphasize that the agreed-upon ER will typically not be the outcome of a mathematical model. Rather, it will fall within a range, but its precise determination will be based on managerial judgment, accounting and tax advice, and the relative bargaining positions of the constituent companies. We now illustrate the application of these concepts with a numerical example.

Stock Exchange Ratio Negotiating Range: An Example   S Company and T Company are planning to merge through an exchange of common stock if terms acceptable to the shareholders of both companies can be negotiated. Relevant data for S and T are given here:

	S Company	T Company
Net Income	$9,000,000	$2,000,000
Shares Outstanding	3,000,000	1,000,000
Earnings per Share	$ 3	$ 2
Market Price per Share	$ 30	$ 16
P/E Ratio	10	8

To introduce the method of analysis, a reasonable exchange ratio might simply be based on the inverse of the companies' share prices. That is, ER = $1/(P_S/P_T) = P_T/P_S = \$16/\$30 = .5333$. S Company will exchange .5333 share for each share of T Company. Total shares of S Company outstanding increase to 3,533,300 [= 3,000,000 + .5333(1,000,000)]. Earnings per share for the combined firm, E_{ST}, will equal \$3.1132 [= (\$9,000,000 + \$2,000,000)/3,533,300]. The value of S Company's shares will now reflect T Company and will depend on the ex post price/earnings ratio, P/E_{ST}. One might expect P/E_{ST} to accurately reflect the relative significance of companies S and T. If so, it would be a *weighted average* of the separate price earnings ratios, which we will denote $\overline{P/E_{ST}}$.

$$\overline{P/E_{ST}} = \left(\frac{\text{Net income of S}}{\text{Combined net income}} \right) P/E_S + \left(\frac{\text{Net income of T}}{\text{Combined net income}} \right) P/E_T.$$

For our example, then,

$$\overline{P/E_{ST}} = \left(\frac{\$9,000,000}{\$11,000,000} \right) 10 + \left(\frac{\$2,000,000}{\$11,000,000} \right) 8$$

$$\overline{P/E_{ST}} = 8.1818 + 1.4545$$

$$\overline{P/E_{ST}} = 9.6363.$$

Therefore, the per share price for the combined firm, $P_{ST} = \$30$ [= $E_{ST}(P/E_{ST})$ = \$3.1132(9.6363)]. This is exactly what should be expected. Each shareholder is in precisely the same economic position as before. The original shareholders of S Company still own 3,000,000 shares worth \$30 each for a total of \$90,000,000. The former shareholders of T now own 533,300 shares of S stock worth \$16,000,000, the same as the value of their 1,000,000 T shares surrendered. Under some combinations of ER and P/E_{ST}, however, the total market value of the 3,000,000 shares held by the original shareholders of S *would be less than* \$90,000,000. Presumably, these original shareholders would not accept any ER which, at some P/E_{ST}, would reduce their wealth. We can therefore identify the upper boundary of the negotiating range by finding the *maximum* ER, denoted ER_S, which would be acceptable to S shareholders at any given P/E_{ST}. By allowing P/E_{ST} to vary, we can solve for the ER_S which maintains the market value of the 3,000,000 original S shares at \$90,000,000.

Similarly, T Company's former shareholders would reject an exchange ratio which, at some potential P/E_{ST}, reduced the market value of the S shares they receive below \$16,000,000. Thus, the lower boundary of the negotiating range will consist of a set of *minimum* ER, denoted ER_T, which the T shareholders would find acceptable at any given P/E_{ST}.

To demonstrate how these exchange ratios are calculated, we use alternative postcombination price/earnings ratios of 9, 10, 12, and 15 and compute the max-

Exhibit 6.12   Determination of Minimum and Maximum Acceptable Stock Exchange Ratios

Determination of Maximum (Minimum) Stock Exchange Ratios, ER_S (ER_T),
Acceptable to Shareholders of S(T) at Alternative Postcombination Price/Earnings Ratios

	P/E_{ST}				
	9	9.6363	10	12	15
ER_S	.3000[1]	.5333	.6667	1.4000	2.5000
ER_T	.5873	.5333	.5106	.4138[2]	.3221

EXAMPLES OF THE CALCULATIONS

(1) $\$90,000,000 = 3,000,000 \left[\dfrac{\$11,000,000}{3,000,000 + ER_S(1,000,000)} \right] 9.$

Dropping 000,000, we have

$$\$90 = \frac{\$297}{3 + ER_S}$$

$$\$270 + \$90 ER_S = \$297$$
$$90 ER_S = 27$$
$$ER_S = 27/90$$
$$\boxed{ER_S = .3000.}$$

Note: If $P/E_{ST} = 9$, any $ER > .3$ will, by reducing E_{ST}, cause the market value of 3,000,000 shares of S Company to fall below $90,000,000.

(2) $\$16,000,000 = ER_T(1,000,000) \left[\dfrac{\$11,000,000}{3,000,000 + ER_T(1,000,000)} \right] 12.$

Dropping 000,000, we have

$$\$16 = ER_T \left[\frac{\$132}{3 + ER_T} \right]$$

$$\$48 + \$16\, ER_T = \$132\, ER_T$$
$$116\, ER_T = 48$$
$$ER_T = 48/116$$
$$\boxed{ER_T = .4138.}$$

Note: If $P/E_{ST} = 12$, any $ER < .4138$ will, by reducing the number of shares going to the former shareholders of T, result in a total market value of the S shares received of less than $16,000,000.

imum (minimum) ER acceptable to the shareholders of S(T) for each of these P/E_{ST}. First, we note that

$$3,000,000 + ER(1,000,000) = \text{Number of shares of S Company stock}$$
$$\text{outstanding after the combination.}$$

Second, with knowledge of the shares outstanding, E_{ST} may be written as

$$\frac{\$11,000,000}{3,000,000 + ER(1,000,000)} = \text{Earnings per share of the combined firm, ST.}$$

Third, the price of a share of postcombination S Company stock is

$$P_{ST} = E_{ST} \times P/E_{ST}$$

$$P_{ST} = \left[\frac{\$11,000,000}{3,000,000 + ER(1,000,000)} \right] P/E_{ST}.$$

Fourth, the total market value of the original 3,000,000 shares of S Company stock after the combination is given by

$$3,000,000 \times P_{ST} = 3,000,000 \left[\frac{\$11,000,000}{3,000,000 + ER(1,000,000)} \right] P/E_{ST}.$$

Fifth, the total postcombination market value of the S Company shares now held by the former T Company shareholders is the following:

$$ER(1,000,000) \times P_{ST} = ER(1,000,000) \left[\frac{\$11,000,000}{3,000,000 + ER(1,000,000)} \right] P/E_{ST}.$$

We have already determined that at the weighted average price/earnings ratio, $\overline{P/E_{ST}} = 9.6363$, an ER = .5333 is acceptable to all shareholders. Indeed, we shall see that if $P/E_{ST} = 9.6363$, then ER = .5333 is the *only* acceptable stock exchange ratio. The calculations pertaining to the alternative values of P/E_{ST} of 9, 10, 12, and 15 are summarized in Exhibit 6.12.

The stock exchange ratio negotiating range is graphed in Figure 6.1. In the first panel, ER_S is graphed. The curve for ER_T appears in the second panel. Finally, the ER_S and ER_T curves are combined, thereby identifying the area between them as the negotiating range in the third panel.

Conclusion

Accounting information can be of significant help in establishing the terms of a business combination. As we see in Figure 6.1, however, the final exchange ratio must be negotiated, for there are many that would injure neither group of stockholders. If one draws a horizontal line through ER = .5333, one has identified the only exchange ratio that will have an equivalent effect on both groups of stockholders at any P/E_{ST}. To the right of $P/E_{ST} = 9.6363$, exchange ratios between the curves will be such that all stockholders will be better off. Unless ER = .5333, however, either the original S shareholders or the former T shareholders will benefit disproportionately.

Questions

Q6.1 Describe the various motivating factors behind business combinations.

Q6.2 In discussing the history of authoritative pronouncements on accounting for business combinations, the text quotes a passage from *ARB 48*. Read *ARB 48*. Has the pooling concept changed substantially from *ARB 48* to *ARBO 16*? Why or why not?

Q6.3 See Q6.2 above. Why has *APBO 16* apparently succeeded in preventing abuses of pooling, while *ARB 48* failed? The two pronouncements seem to suggest a fundamentally different approach to accounting principles. What is the nature of this difference? Are you troubled by it?

Q6.4 A publishing company owns the copyrights to many books. The original cost of these copyrights has been substantially amortized, yet, due to the reissue of many books as paperbacks, the copyrights have high market values. The publishing company is about to be acquired by a conglomerate whose management insists on structuring the combination as a pooling. Why might management be so adamant about the choice of accounting method?

Figure 6.1   Graphing ER_S, ER_T, and the Negotiating Range

Panel 1   Graph of Maximum Stock Exchange Ratio (ER$_S$) Acceptable to the Original Shareholders of S Company

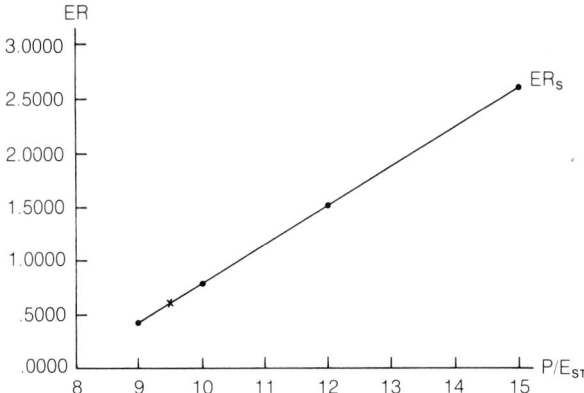

Panel 2   Graph of Minimum Stock Exchange Ratio (ER$_T$) Acceptable to the Original Shareholders of T Company

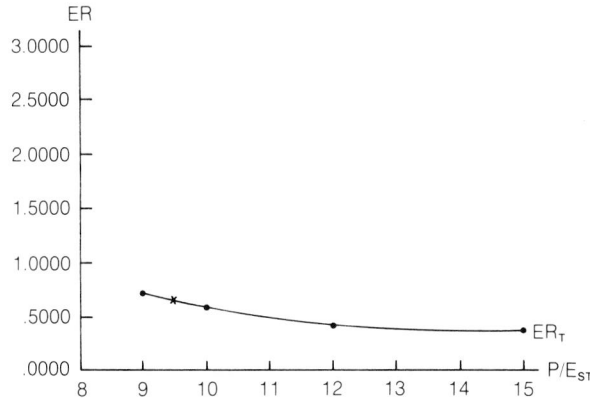

Panel 3   Graph of Stock Exchange Ratio Negotiating Range within Which All Shareholders Will Be at Least as Well Off as They Were before the Combination

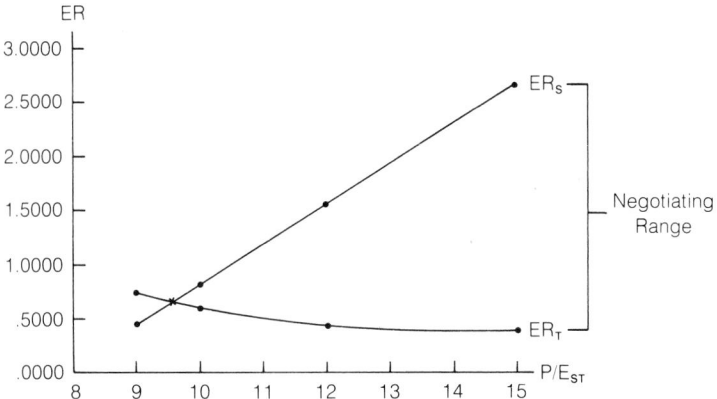

Q6.5   In a purchase combination, a purchase premium is to be allocated to the acquired company's identifiable assets and to goodwill. There is potential for some abuse here. Describe how it can occur.

Q6.6   Any negative goodwill arising in a purchase combination must be allocated among noncurrent assets, excluding long-term investments in marketable securities. Also, no negative goodwill is allocated among current assets and liabilities. Briefly discuss the apparent reasons for these rules.

Q6.7   Describe the accounting rules governing the composition of combined stockholders' equity following a pooling. Briefly indicate the reasoning which led to these rules.

Q6.8   Suppose bonds are issued by the acquiring company as the consideration in a purchase combination. Former stockholders of the acquired company are guaranteed that the bonds they receive will be worth at least some minimum amount in two years. At the end of the two years, a substantial number of new bonds are issued under the terms of the guarantee. Explain what must have happened during the two years, the accounting treatment by the acquiring company when the new bonds are issued, and whether the accounting is sound.

Q6.9   The general prohibition against the use of treasury stock in a pooling of interests is waived when the treasury stock was acquired more than two years prior to initiating the business combination. What message is implied by this two-year rule?

Q6.10   Suppose current value accounting were adopted. Would this defeat the pooling concept? How would the traditional advantages attributed to pooling be affected?

Exercises   **E6.1**   Pen Company has agreed to acquire all of the outstanding common stock of Simpson Company through an exchange of 55,000 shares of Pen Company stock. The stock has an aggregate fair market value of $2,500,000. Since the method of accounting for this combination is not yet certain, you have been asked to reflect the contemplated combination both as a purchase and as a pooling of interests. Prior to the combination, the stockholders' equity accounts of both companies are as follows:

	Pen Company	Simpson Company
Common Stock Outstanding:		
530,000 Shares, Par Value $1	$ 530,000	—
40,000 Shares, Par Value $5	—	$ 200,000
Additional Paid-In Capital	5,665,000	1,350,000
Retained Earnings	12,373,000	378,000
Total Stockholders' Equity	$18,568,000	$1,928,000

Required: Give the postcombination components of Pen Company's stockholders' equity under both purchase and pooling. Show all calculations.

E6.2   The Nugget Company's balance sheet on December 31, 19X1, is as follows:

ASSETS

Cash	$ 100,000
Accounts Receivable	200,000
Inventories	500,000
Property, Plant, and Equipment, Net	900,000
	$1,700,000

LIABILITIES AND STOCKHOLDERS' EQUITY

Current Liabilities	$ 300,000
Long-Term Debt	500,000
Common Stock (Par Value $1)	100,000
Additional Paid-In Capital	200,000
Retained Earnings	600,000
	$1,700,000

On December 31, 19X1, the Bronc Company purchases all of the outstanding common stock of Nugget for $1,500,000 cash. On that date, the fair (market) value of Nugget's inventories is $450,000 and the fair value of Nugget's property, plant, and equipment (net) is $1,000,000. The fair values of all other assets and liabilities of Nugget are equal to their book values.

Required:
1. As a result of the acquisition of Nugget by Bronc, the consolidated balance sheet of Bronc and Nugget should show goodwill in the amount of:
    a. $500,000.
    b. $550,000.
    c. $600,000.
    d. $650,000.
2. Assuming that the balance sheet of Bronc (unconsolidated) at December 31, 19X1, shows retained earnings of $2,000,000, what amount of retained earnings should be shown in the December 31, 19X1, consolidated balance sheet of Bronc and its new subsidiary, Nugget?
    a. $2,000,000.
    b. $2,600,000.
    c. $2,800,000.
    d. $3,150,000.

(AICPA adapted)

E6.3   Following are balance sheet data for Samuel, Inc., as of January 31, 19X0:

	Book Value	Fair Value
Current Assets	$150,000	$140,000
Property and Equipment, Net	300,000	380,000
Liabilities	130,000	130,000
Common Stock (Par Value $1)	50,000	—
Retained Earnings	270,000	—

On January 31, 19X0, Patrick, Inc., merges with Samuel by exchanging 3,000 shares of its $10 par value common stock for all of the outstanding shares of Samuel, Inc. The Patrick stock has a fair market value of $120 per share.

Required:
1. Give the journal entry made by Patrick to record the merger as a pooling of interests.
2. Give the journal entry made by Patrick to record the merger as a purchase.

E6.4   Pack Company has paid $2,000,000 cash to the shareholders of Sack Company for all of Sack's outstanding shares. Attorneys' fees related to the combination were $50,000. A comparison of the book and fair values of Sack's assets and liabilities appears here:

	Book Value	Fair Value
Cash and Receivables	$ 120,000	$ 120,000
Marketable Equity Securities	175,000	150,000
Inventory	610,000	800,000
Plant Assets, Net	1,600,000	2,000,000
Current Liabilities	(340,000)	(340,000)
Long-Term Debt	(1,000,000)	(850,000)
Accrued Pension Liability[a]	(90,000)	(130,000)
Net Assets	$1,075,000	$1,750,000

[a]Sack's pension accrual is in conformity with generally accepted accounting principles. The amount in the fair value column is the amount by which the present value of vested benefits exceeds the amount in the pension fund.

Required:
1. Give the journal entry made by Pack to record the business combination as a merger.
2. Give the journal entry made by Pack to record the business combination as a stock acquisition.

E6.5   Scott Corporation's noncurrent assets have book and fair values as described below. The book values of other assets and all liabilities of Scott approximate their fair values.

	Book Value	Fair Value
Land	$240,000	$720,000
Buildings, Net	570,000	660,000
Equipment, Net	200,000	180,000
Investment in Ace Corporation (2%)	70,000	60,000

Paper Company pays $2,500,000 for the net assets of Scott, which have a book value of $2,260,000, implying a purchase premium of $240,000. The shares of Ace Corporation are traded in the over-the-counter market.

Required: Prepare a schedule to allocate the purchase premium among the noncurrent assets of Scott.

E6.6   Plank Company surrenders $5,000,000 plus 250,000 shares of its own $1 par value stock worth $10,000,000 for all of the outstanding shares of Stud Company in a stock acquisition. Management of Plank also makes the following guarantees to the former shareholders of Stud. Each should be viewed independently.

1. If total earnings from continuing operations of the combined entity exceed $2,000,000 over the next two years, additional shares of Plank will be issued to the former shareholders of Stud. Sufficient shares will be issued so that the market value of the additional shares equals the amount by which total earnings exceed $2,000,000. In no case, however, will additional shares having a market value in excess of $500,000 be issued to satisfy this provision.

2. If the total market value of the original shares issued to Stud is less than $10,000,000 at the end of two years, Plank will issue sufficient additional shares to the former owners of Stud in order to restore the market value of all Plank shares issued in the acquisition to $10,000,000.

Two years later, total earnings from continuing operations amount to $2,076,000, and Plank's stock is selling for $38 a share.

Required: In view of the above events, prepare any journal entries which must be made by Plank at the end of the two-year period. Give explanations and show all calculations.

E6.7   The book value of Simon Company's stockholders' equity is $750,000 including $350,000 in retained earnings. Peterson Corporation plans a merger and is to acquire all the outstanding stock of Simon Company in a pooling of interests. At the date of the business combination, Peterson's stockholders' equity accounts have the following book balances:

Common Stock, Par Value $5, Authorized 1,000,000 Shares,	
Issued and Outstanding 100,000 Shares	$ 500,000
Additional Paid-In Capital	200,000
Retained Earnings	1,300,000
Total Precombination Stockholders' Equity	$2,000,000

Required:

1. Record the pooling assuming Peterson issues 50,000 shares.
2. Record the pooling assuming Peterson issues 100,000 shares.
3. Record the pooling assuming Peterson issues 150,000 shares.
4. Record the pooling assuming Peterson issues 200,000 shares.

E6.8   **(Appendix)** Alpha Company and Beta Company are contemplating a merger in which shares of Alpha will be exchanged for shares of Beta. Alpha earned $6,000,000 last year ($2.50 per share); its stock currently sells at $25. Beta earned $2,000,000 ($2.00 per share), and its stock currently sells at $8.

In negotiating the terms of the merger, managements of the two companies estimate that the ex post combined price/earnings ratio will be 9.

Required: Compute the upper and lower boundaries of the stock exchange ratio negotiating range for Alpha and Beta at the given ex post combined price/earnings ratio of 9.

E6.9 On January 1, 19X2, Peters, Inc., issued 200,000 additional shares of voting common stock in exchange for 100,000 shares of Clarkin Company's outstanding voting common stock in a business combination appropriately accounted for by the pooling of interests method. The market value of Peters' voting common stock was $40 per share on the date of the business combination. The balance sheets of Peters and Clarkin immediately before the business combination contained the following information:

PETERS, INC.

Common Stock, Par Value $5 per Share; Authorized 1,000,000 Shares; Issued and Outstanding 600,000 Shares	$ 3,000,000
Additional Paid-In Capital	6,000,000
Retained Earnings	11,000,000
Total Stockholders' Equity	$20,000,000

CLARKIN COMPANY

Common Stock, Par Value $10 per Share; Authorized 250,000 Shares; Issued and Outstanding 100,000 Shares	$1,000,000
Additional Paid-In Capital	2,000,000
Retained Earnings	4,000,000
Total Stockholders' Equity	$7,000,000

Additional information:

1. Net income for the year ended December 31, 19X2, was $1,150,000 for Peters and $350,000 for Clarkin.
2. During 19X2, Peters paid $900,000 in dividends to its stockholders, and Clarkin paid $210,000 in dividends to Peters.

Required: Prepare the postcombination stockholders' equity section of the balance sheet of Peters, Inc., and its subsidiary, Clarkin Company, at December 31, 19X2. Provide a supporting schedule for retained earnings. Ignore income tax and deferred tax considerations.

(AICPA adapted)

Problems **P6.1** **Propriety of Purchase and Pooling under Various Conditions** The boards of directors of Kessler Corporation, Bar Company, Cohen, Inc., and Mason Corporation are meeting jointly to discuss plans for a business combination. Each of the corporations has one class of common stock outstanding; Bar also has one class of preferred stock outstanding. Although terms have not as yet been settled, Kessler will be the acquiring or issuing corporation. Because the directors want to conform to generally accepted accounting principles, they have asked you to attend the meeting as an advisor.

Required: Consider each of the following questions independently of the others and answer each in accordance with generally accepted accounting principles. Explain your answers.

1.   Assume that the combination will be consummated August 31, 19X3.

Explain the philosophy underlying the accounting and how the balance sheet accounts of each of the four corporations will appear on Kessler's consolidated balance sheet on September 1, 19X3, if the combination is accounted for as a

    a. Pooling of interests.

    b. Purchase.

2.   Assume that the combination will be consummated August 31, 19X3. Explain how the income statement accounts of each of the four corporations will be accounted for in preparing Kessler's consolidated income statement for the year ended December 31, 19X3, if the combination is accounted for as a

    a. Pooling of interests.

    b. Purchase.

3.   Some of the directors believe that the terms of the combination should be agreed upon immediately and that the method of accounting to be used (whether pooling of interests, purchase, or a mixture) may be chosen at some later date. Others believe that the terms of the combination and the method to be used are very closely related. Which position is correct?

4.   Kessler and Mason are comparable in size; Cohen and Bar are much smaller. How do these facts affect the choice of accounting method?

5.   Bar was formerly a subsidiary of Tucker Corporation, which has no other relationship to any of the four companies discussing combination. Eighteen months ago Tucker voluntarily spun off Bar. What effect, if any, do these facts have on the choice of accounting method?

6.   Kessler holds 2,000 of Bar's 10,000 outstanding shares of preferred stock and 15,000 of Cohen's 100,000 outstanding shares of common stock. All of Kessler's holdings were acquired during the first three months of 19X3. What effect, if any, do these facts have on the choice of accounting method?

7.   It is almost certain that Mrs. Victor Mason, Sr., who holds 5 percent of Mason's common stock, will object to the combination. Assume that Kessler is able to acquire only 95 percent (rather than 100 percent) of Mason's stock, issuing Kessler common stock in exchange.

    a. Which accounting method is applicable?

    b. If Kessler is able to acquire the remaining 5 percent at some future time—say in five years—in exchange for its own common stock, which accounting method will be applicable to this second acquisition?

8.   Since the directors feel that one of Mason's major divisions will not be compatible with the operations of the combined company, they anticipate that it will be sold as soon as possible after the combination is consummated. They expect to have no trouble in finding a buyer. What effect, if any, do these facts have on the choice of accounting method?

(AICPA adapted)

P6.2 **Combining a Partnership and a Corporation: Pooling and Purchase** The B & Q Company was organized on July 1, 19X1. Under the partnership agreement, $900,000 was provided by Beke and $600,000 by Quinn as initial capital;

income and losses were to be shared in the same ratio as the initial capital contributions. No additional capital contributions have been made. The June 30, 19X6, balance sheet of the B & Q Company follows:

B & Q Company
Balance Sheet at June 30, 19X6

ASSETS

Cash	$ 500,500
Accounts Receivable, Net	950,000
Inventory (LIFO Basis)	1,500,000
Prepaid Insurance	18,000
Land	58,000
Machinery and Equipment, Net	1,473,500
Total Assets	$4,500,000

LIABILITIES AND CAPITAL

Current Liabilities	$1,475,000
Beke, Capital	1,815,000
Quinn, Capital	1,210,000
Total Liabilities and Capital	$4,500,000

Assume that Beke and Quinn have engaged in lengthy discussions with the executives and directors of Preston Corporation during the past few months. With the permission of Beke and Quinn, the auditors of Preston Corporation conducted an examination and expressed an unqualified opinion on the historical cost financial statements of B & Q Company as of June 30, 19X6. The allowance for doubtful accounts and accumulated depreciation on June 30, 19X6, amounted to $300,000 and $536,500, respectively.

Beke agrees to accept 8,700 shares, and Quinn agrees to accept 5,800 shares of Preston Corporation common stock in exchange for all partnership interests. During the month of June 19X6, the market value of a share of Preston Corporation was $265. The stockholders' equity account balances of Preston Corporation as of June 30, 19X6, follow:

Common Stock, Par Value $100	$2,000,000
Additional Paid-In Capital	580,000
Retained Earnings	2,496,000
	$5,076,400

Required:
1. Prepare the necessary journal entry (or entries) to record the business combination as a pooling of interests on July 1, 19X6, on the books of Preston Corporation.
2. Assume that the combination is to be recorded as a purchase. The assets and liabilities of Beke and Quinn are stated at their fair values except for inventory and land, with fair values of $1,800,000 and $100,000, respectively. Prepare the necessary journal entry (or entries) to record the combination as a purchase on July 1, 19X6, on the books of Preston Corporation.

(AICPA adapted)

P6.3   **Calculating Pooled Retained Earnings and Recording the Pooling**   On December 31, 19X2, Cole Company and Bond Company entered into a business combination appropriately accounted for as a pooling of interests. As a result of this combination, a new company, Gold Corporation, was formed with 500,000 authorized shares of no par, $1 stated-value common stock. The management of Gold did not intend to retain either Cole or Bond as subsidiaries.

On December 31, 19X2, Gold issued its common stock in exchange for all of the outstanding common stock of Cole and Bond as follows:

>   Cole: 300,000 shares of Gold common stock for all 10,000 outstanding shares of Cole's $5 par value common stock.
>
>   Bond: 200,000 shares of Gold common stock for all 4,000 outstanding shares of Bond's $10 par value common stock.

Presented below are condensed financial statements of Cole and Bond for the year ended December 31, 19X2, prior to the pooling of interests.

Balance Sheets
December 31, 19X2
(Precombination)

	Cole Company	Bond Company
ASSETS		
Current Assets	$260,000	$235,000
Property, Plant, and Equipment (Net)	410,000	320,000
Other Assets	90,000	65,000
Total Assets	$760,000	$620,000
LIABILITIES AND STOCKHOLDERS' EQUITY		
Current Liabilities	$167,000	$124,000
Long-Term Debt	300,000	—
Common Stock	50,000	40,000
Capital in Excess of Par Value	10,000	160,000
Retained Earnings	233,000	296,000
Total Liabilities and Stockholders' Equity	$760,000	$620,000

Statements of Income and Retained Earnings
For the Year Ended December 31, 19X2

	Cole Company	Bond Company
Net Sales	$1,600,000	$2,200,000
Costs and Expenses:		
Cost of Sales	$1,120,000	$1,560,000
Operating and Other Expenses	330,000	480,000
	$1,450,000	$2,040,000
Net Income	$ 150,000	$ 160,000
Retained Earnings, January 1, 19X2	83,000	136,000
Retained Earnings, December 31, 19X2	$ 233,000	$ 296,000

Cole values its inventory using the FIFO method; Bond uses the LIFO method for its inventory. Bond agreed to change its method of inventory valuation from LIFO to FIFO prior to the business combination.

Bond began operations on January 1, 19X1, and data relevant to Bond's inventory are as follows:

	LIFO Method	FIFO Method
Inventory, December 31, 19X1	$42,000	$62,000
Inventory, December 31, 19X2	55,000	85,000

Required:
1. Prepare the adjusting journal entry with the appropriate explanation and supporting calculations to be made by Bond Company on December 31, 19X2, to change its inventory from LIFO cost to FIFO cost. Income taxes should not be considered in your solution.
2. Prepare a schedule computing pooled retained earnings of Gold Corporation as of December 31, 19X2.
3. Prepare the December 31, 19X2, journal entry on the books of Gold Corporation to record the business combination as a pooling of interests.

(AICPA adapted)

P6.4 Recording a Purchase Combination: Purchase Premium and Discount Plastic Corporation is contemplating a business combination with Steel Corporation at December 31, 19X3. Steel's post-closing trial balance on that date appears below:

	Book Value	Fair Value (If Different)
Cash and Receivables	$ 35,000	
Inventory	35,000	$45,000
Long-Term Investments in Marketable Securities	18,000	20,000
Land	8,000	11,000
Buildings and Equipment, Net	7,000	14,000
Patents	5,000	10,000
	$108,000	
Liabilities	$ 22,000	
Common Stock	50,000	
Retained Earnings	36,000	
	$108,000	

Required: Give the journal entry to record the business combination of Plastic and Steel as a purchase for each of the following purchase prices and combination methods:
1. Plastic merges with Steel by acquiring all of Steel's stock for $100,000 cash. Other direct cash costs are $25,000.
2. Plastic merges with Steel by acquiring all of Steel's stock for $90,000 cash. Other direct cash costs are $10,000.
3. Plastic merges with Steel by acquiring all of Steel's stock for $50,000 cash. Other direct cash costs are $10,000.

4. Plastic acquires 80 percent of Steel's stock for $90,000 cash in a stock acquisition. Other direct cash costs are $15,000.

P6.5 **Combining a Partnership and a Proprietorship to Form a Corporation**
Howard & Sanders Electrical Contracting Company, a partnership, and Grover Wholesale Electricians' Hardware Company, a proprietorship, have agreed to transfer the assets and liabilities of their companies on November 1, 19X9, to a newly chartered corporation, Major Electrical, Inc., in exchange for Major's stock. The agreement provides that the combination is to be accounted for as a purchase and:

1. Preferred stock shall be issued at par value of $100 per share to each of the parties in exchange for his share of the net assets (assets minus liabilities) transferred to Major Electrical, Inc. John Grover shall receive at least 900 shares of preferred stock and Bill Howard and Joe Sanders shall receive together a total of not more than 480 shares of preferred stock. Cash shall be contributed to the companies by the respective parties or distributed by the companies to the parties to accomplish the proper net asset transfers.

2. Common stock shall be issued in a total amount equal to the earnings expected to be contributed by the companies to Major Electrical, Inc., for the next five years to the extent that the earnings of each company, based on the past three calendar years, exceed the average earnings of its respective industry. The common stock shall be issued at par value of $10 per share to the owners of the companies in the ratio of the amount that each company's average earnings are expected to exceed the average industry earnings of the company with the lesser earnings. The par value of the common stock issued shall represent goodwill.

Trial balances for the ten months ended October 31, 19X9, for both companies are shown in Exhibit 6.13.

Additional information follows:

1. Howard & Sanders maintain the partnership books on the cash basis of accounting. Grover maintains his proprietorship books on the accrual basis. Major's books are to be maintained on the accrual basis. Items not recorded on Howard & Sanders' books at October 31, 19X9, follow:

Accounts Receivable	$20,300
Allowance for Bad Debts	400
Unbilled Contract in Progress	8,000
Prepaid Expenses	1,200
Accounts Payable	6,200
Accrued Expenses Payable	2,400

All accounts receivable are for jobs completed and billed. The unbilled contract in progress is for a $10,000 contract, which was 80 percent complete (to be recorded as revenue) and upon which a $2,500 deposit was paid to Howard & Sanders when the contract was signed. Cash payments by Howard & Sanders for work on the contract to October 31, 19X9, total $3,500 and were recorded on the partnership books as inventory. Accounts payable includes $2,800 owed to Grover Wholesale Electricians' Hardware Company.

Exhibit 6.13   Trial Balances for Grover Hardware Company and Howard & Sanders Company (P6.5)

Grover Wholesale Electricians' Hardware Company and
Howard & Sanders Electrical Contracting Company
Trial Balances
November 1, 19X9

Account	Grover Hardware Debit	Grover Hardware Credit	Howard & Sanders Debit	Howard & Sanders Credit
Cash	$ 17,000		$ 20,700	
Accounts Receivable	43,000			
Allowance for Bad Debts . . .		$ 3,000		
Inventory	63,000		3,500	
Prepaid Expenses	2,000		1,300	
Land, Building, and Equipment .	44,000		26,000	
Allowance for Depreciation . .		27,000		$ 12,000
Accounts Payable		54,000		
Accrued Expenses Payable . .		4,000		
Deposit on Contract				2,500
Grover, Capital		75,000		
Grover, Drawing	5,000			
Howard, Capital				11,300
Sanders, Capital				7,700
Revenues		200,000		70,000
Cost of Producing Revenues . .	160,000		31,000	
Partners' Salaries (Drawings) . .			7,000	
Operating Expenses	29,000		14,000	
Totals	$363,000	$363,000	$103,500	$103,500

2. The partnership agreement specified Bill Howard would receive a salary of $12,000 per year and share 60 percent of any profit or loss, and Joe Sanders would receive a salary of $9,000 per year and share 40 percent of any profit or loss. Each partner will receive the same annual salary from the corporation. In 19X9, each partner drew one-third of the annual salary.

3. John Grover withdraws an amount each month from his proprietorship equal to a normal salary. Grover's annual salary from the corporation will be $15,000.

4. Based on the past three years, John Grover could expect his proprietorship to earn an average of $39,000 per year for the next five years before any salary allowance, with average expected sales of $600,000 per year. The industry average net income (after deducting all salaries and income taxes) for electrical hardware wholesalers for the next five years is expected to be 1.35 percent of sales.

5. Based on the past three years, Bill Howard and Joe Sanders could expect their partnership to earn an average of $55,500 per year for the next five years before deducting partners' salaries, with average expected revenues of $240,000 per year. The industry average net income (after deducting all salaries and income tax) for electrical contractors for the next five years is expected to be 7.5 percent of sales.

6. The parties expect the corporation to pay income tax at an average rate of 40 percent during the next five years.
7. The final distribution of partnership income to Howard and Sanders is to reflect all accrual basis adjustments.
8. Net book values of assets approximate their current fair values.

Required: Prepare a worksheet to determine the pro forma opening account balances of Major Electrical, Inc., giving effect to the agreement to transfer the assets and liabilities and issue stock. The worksheet should have columns for Grover Hardware Trial Balance (Dr., Cr.), Howard & Sanders Trial Balance (Dr., Cr.), Grover Hardware Adjusting and Eliminating Entries (Dr., Cr.), Howard & Sanders Adjusting and Eliminating Entries (Dr., Cr.), and Major Electrical, Inc., Opening Account Balances (Dr., Cr.). Prepare supporting schedules computing (1) any cash contributions or distributions necessary and preferred stock to be issued to each party and (2) the number of shares of common stock to be issued to each party. Formal adjusting and closing entries and formal financial statements are not required.

(AICPA adapted)

P6.6 **Multiple Choice Questions on Business Combinations**

1.   Pluto Corporation issued 100,000 shares of its $1 par (current fair value, $10) capital stock for all 1,000 shares of the issued and outstanding capital stock of Saturn Company. At the date of the business combination, the stockholders' equity of Saturn was as follows:

Capital Stock, Par Value $10 .	$ 10,000
Additional Paid-In Capital	82,300
Retained Earnings	60,900
Total Stockholders' Equity	$153,200

If the business combination is recorded as a pooling, the effect on Pluto's Additional Paid-In Capital account (precombination balance of $136,000) would be:

a. A credit of $900,000.
b. A credit of $82,300.
c. A debit of $10,000.

d. A debit of $7,700.
e. None of the above.

2.   On May 17, 19X8, Port Corporation paid $600,000 cash for all of the outstanding common stock of Short Company in a purchase combination. Short's assets and liabilities at May 17, 19X8, had the following book values:

Cash .	$ 80,000
Inventories	320,000
Plant and Equipment, Net	260,000
Liabilities	(190,000)
	$470,000

Appraisals as of May 17, 19X8, indicated that Short's inventory had a fair value of $295,000 and that the fair value of Short's plant and equipment (net) was $300,000. If Port is to recognize goodwill in the combination, the amount is:

a. $0.
b. ($25,000).

c. $115,000.
d. $130,000.
e. None of the above.

3. P acquired all of the outstanding shares of S for a cost below the book value of S Company's identifiable net assets at the date of the business combination. The difference is related to the technological obsolescence of some of S Company's equipment. In a combined or consolidated balance sheet, this difference is accounted for by
a. Decreasing the equipment account.
b. Increasing consolidated additional paid-in capital.
c. Recognizing an extraordinary loss.
d. Recording negative goodwill.
e. None of the above.

4. Which of the following is *not* a postcombination financial statement difference between the pooling and purchase methods?
a. Par value of postcombination capital stock.
b. The financial statements which are combined or consolidated in the year of the combination.
c. Composition of postcombination retained earnings.
d. Valuation of the acquired company's assets and liabilities.
e. None of the above.

Items 5, 6, and 7 are based on information presented in the following balance sheets of two companies prior to their combination.

		January 1, 19X0	
		P Company	S Company
Cash	. . . .	$ 3,000	$ 100
Inventory (at FIFO Cost, which Approximates Fair Value)	. . . .	2,000	200
Fixed Assets (Net) .	. . . .	5,000	700 [a]
Total Assets .	. . . . . .	$10,000	$1,000
Current Liabilities	. . . .	$ 600	$ 100
Common Stock ($1 Par Value) .	. . . . .	1,000	100
Additional Paid-In Capital .	. . . . . .	3,000	200
Retained Earnings .	. . . .	5,400	600
Total Equities	. . . .	$10,000	$1,000

[a]Fair value at January 1, 19X0, is $1,500.

5. On January 1, 19X0, P Company acquires 100 percent of the common stock of S Company by issuing, in a tax-free exchange, 200 shares of its (P's) common stock, which has a fair value of $10 per share on that date. The requirements for use of pooling of interests accounting are met and will be followed. A balance sheet of the two companies combined as of January 1, 19X0, is to be prepared. The amount of addition-

al paid-in capital that would be shown on this combined balance sheet is:

   a. $3,000.   c. $3,200.
   b. $3,100.   d. $3,900.

6.   On January 1, 19X0, P Company acquires 100 percent of the common stock of S Company in a taxable purchase by payment of $2,000 cash. The amount that would be shown as "goodwill" on the combined balance sheet as of January 1, 19X0, is:

   a. $200.   c. $1,100.
   b. $900.   d. $300.

7.   On January 1, 19X0, P Company acquires 100 percent of the common stock of S Company in a taxable purchase by payment of $1,500 cash. The amount that would be shown as fixed assets in the combined balance sheet is:

   a. $5,700.   c. $6,300.
   b. $6,500.   d. $6,700.

8.   During 19X8, the Henderson Company purchased the net assets of John Corporation for $800,000. On the date of the transaction, John had no long-term investments in marketable securities and had $100,000 of liabilities. The fair value of John's assets when acquired were as follows:

Current Assets	$ 400,000
Noncurrent Assets	600,000
	$1,000,000

How should Henderson account for the $100,000 difference between the fair value of the net assets acquired ($900,000) and the cost ($800,000)?

   a. The $100,000 difference should be credited to retained earnings.
   b. The noncurrent assets should be recorded at $500,000.
   c. The current assets should be recorded at $360,000, and the noncurrent assets should be recorded at $540,000.
   d. A deferred credit of $100,000 should be set up and then amortized to income over a period not to exceed forty years.

(Items 5–8, AICPA adapted.)

P6.7 Postcombination Balance Sheets: Pooling and Purchase   The Cooper family owns all of the outstanding stock of Cooper Corporation. Reynolds Corporation is planning to merge with Cooper by exchanging its common stock for all of the outstanding common stock of Cooper. In addition, Reynolds will issue $100,000 par value, 6 percent, cumulative, non-participating preferred stock to the holders of Cooper's long-term bonds. The Cooper family intends to sell 80 percent of its Reynolds shares through a pre-arranged secondary offering to the public shortly after the combination takes place. So as to keep the family name associated with the company, the Cooper family will continue to hold its remaining 20 percent of its interest in Reynolds Corporation.

The number of $10 par value Reynolds Corporation common shares given will be based on the relationship between the market value of the recorded net assets of Cooper Corporation and the market price of Reynolds' stock, which is currently $30 per share.

The following balance sheet data are obtained:

	Reynolds Corp.	Cooper Corp.	Cooper Corp. (Market Value)
Current Assets	$400,000	$100,000	$115,000
Plant Assets (Net)	500,000	350,000	427,000
Total	$900,000	$450,000	
Current Liabilities	$200,000	$ 50,000	50,000
Long-Term Liabilities	300,000	100,000	90,000
Common Stock ($10 Par Value) . .	60,000	100,000	
Additional Paid-In Capital . . .	40,000	—	
Retained Earnings	300,000	200,000	
Total	$900,000	$450,000	

Required:

1. Should this combination be accounted for as a purchase or a pooling of interests? Support your response with reference to applicable provisions of *APBO 16* (AC § 1091) and the related AICPA Accounting Interpretations (AC § U1091), especially Interpretations Nos. 21 and 37.
2. Prepare postcombination balance sheets for the merged companies under the method selected in part 1 and the alternative method.

(Adapted from a problem prepared by Clyde P. Stickney.)

P6.8 **Computation of Stock Exchange Ratios (Appendix)** Bate Company and Tate Company are planning a merger to be accounted for as a pooling of interests. Representatives of each company's board of directors are trying to work out a set of mutually acceptable stock exchange ratios. These stock exchange ratios are expressed in terms of the number of new shares of Bate's stock to be exchanged for one share of Tate's stock. Financial data for the two companies are given here:

	Bate Company	Tate Company
Net Income	$8,000,000	$4,000,000
Shares Outstanding	4,000,000	1,000,000
Earnings per Share	$ 2	$ 4
Market Price per Share	$ 30	$ 40
P/E Ratio	15	10

Required:

1. Compute the stock exchange ratio and ex post combined price/earnings ratio which leave all shareholders in exactly the same economic position they had prior to the merger.
2. Assume the ex post combined price/earnings ratio is 15. Compute the *maximum* stock exchange ratio likely to be acceptable to the stockholders of Bate and the *minimum* stock exchange ratio likely to be acceptable to the stockholders of Tate.

Chapter 7

Introduction to Consolidated Financial Statements: The Balance Sheet

The Nature of Consolidated Statements

The preceding chapter discussed four types of business combinations: statutory mergers, statutory consolidations, asset acquisitions, and stock acquisitions. For the first three types of combinations, a single set of accounting records remained—those of the acquiring company. Moreover, only the acquiring company survived as a separate and distinct legal entity. In a *stock acquisition*, however, the combining companies remain as separate and distinct legal entities under common ownership control. That is, the shareholders of P Company control S Company by virtue of their ownership of more than 50 percent of S's outstanding voting shares. Furthermore, if P's control over S were 100 percent, financial statements for P and S together should not differ from those prepared if P and S had merged, with P Company the only surviving legal entity. With some refinements, of course, this is precisely the motivating force behind the preparation of consolidated financial statements.

Corporations which maintain a parent/subsidiary relationship are often referred to as **affiliated corporations.** Accordingly, we can state the following:

> The purpose of **consolidated financial statements** is to report the financial affairs of two or more affiliated corporations as if they were a single *unified economic entity*.

Consolidated statements stress substance over form. The mere fact that affiliated corporations remain as separate legal entities does not detract from the fact that they are under common ownership control. In *APBS 4* (AC § 1027.22), the Accounting Principles Board pointed out:

> Consolidated financial statements present the financial position and results of operations of a parent company and its subsidiaries essentially as if the group

258

were a single enterprise comprised of branches or divisions. The resulting accounting entity is an economic rather than a legal unit, and its financial statements are considered to reflect the substance of the combined economic relationships to an extent not possible by merely providing the separate financial statements of the corporate entities comprising the group.[1]

In this chapter, we begin consideration of the preparation of consolidated financial statements. Experience has shown that approaching this subject one step at a time is wise. Accordingly, our major emphasis in this chapter is on preparation of a consolidated balance sheet. To further simplify the presentation, we make the assumption that the balance sheet is being prepared *at the date of the business combination*. This assumption is made for pedagogical reasons only—in the business world, a balance sheet is prepared at the end of the reporting period, not during the period to coincide with a merger or acquisition. Consolidation at date of business combination offers the important advantage of focusing on the problems of consolidating balance sheets without the added complexities associated with consolidating income statements.

Criteria for Consolidation

When one company has a controlling interest in another, a presumption exists "that consolidated statements are more meaningful than separate statements and that they are usually necessary for a fair presentation."[2] A controlling interest generally exists when P Company owns, either directly or indirectly, a majority of the outstanding voting shares of S Company. Ownership of more than 50 percent of S Company's voting shares means that management of P Company can control 100 percent of S Company's assets and operations. The dividend and investment policies of S Company, as well as other tactical and strategic business decisions, are controlled by P Company. Although P Company may effectively control S Company with an ownership interest of less than 50 percent, consolidated statements are not prepared in such instances. Ownership of a unified block (say, 40 percent) of S Company's voting shares might enable P Company to dominate S's management. Yet, the shares not held by P —the "minority" interest—would be larger than the "controlling" interest. Moreover, maintaining control under such circumstances is more uncertain than it would be if P actually owned (directly or indirectly) a majority of S Company's outstanding voting shares. It is hard to see how consolidated financial statements could provide a fair presentation to P's shareholders in these situations, where their equity in the subsidiary is smaller than that of the outside shareholders, the majority.

ARB 51 notes, however, that ownership of a majority of S's shares is *not a sufficient condition* for *consolidation* for the following reasons:

1. Control may be temporary, or a long-term investment position may not be contemplated. That is, a majority interest may be acquired for the purpose of facilitating other business deals and not with a managerial commitment to the acquired company.

---

[1] Accounting Principles Board, *Statement No. 4*, "Basic Concepts and Accounting Principles Underlying Financial Statements of Business Enterprises" (N.Y.: AICPA, 1970), par. 194.

[2] Committee on Accounting Procedure, *Accounting Research Bulletin No. 51*, "Consolidated Financial Statements" (N.Y.: AICPA, 1959), par. 1; AC § 2051.02.

2.   For companies in financial difficulty, effective control may rest not with the majority shareholders but with fiduciaries. Similarly, effective control of foreign subsidiaries may rest with foreign governments and not with the majority shareholders.

3.   A subsidiary in a line of business unrelated to the parent's business may be excluded from consolidation. This frequently occurs when finance companies are owned by manufacturing companies. Even though control exists, consolidation of companies with significantly different asset and liability structures can result in a misleading presentation. The component companies are far different from the "average" portrayed in consolidation.

After evaluating its subsidiaries in terms of these criteria, a parent company must decide which of its subsidiaries are to be included in consolidated statements. This decision involves an **accounting policy** and is subject to *APBO 22*, (AC § 2045).[3] When investments in subsidiaries become a significant factor in the parent's overall financial picture, the **consolidation policy** followed by the parent must be disclosed in a note to the financial statements. Pursuant to this requirement, a recent annual report of the General Electric Company stated, in part,

> The financial statements consolidate the accounts of the parent General Electric Company and those of all majority-owned and controlled companies ("affiliated companies"), except finance companies whose operations are not similar to those of the consolidated group.

A summary of consolidation policies followed by the 600 companies surveyed in *Accounting Trends and Techniques* over the period 1976–1978 is shown in Exhibit 7.1. The types of subsidiaries which are not consolidated follow from reasons 1 and 3 above.

Overview of Consolidation Procedures

When approaching the preparation of consolidated statements, the accountant must keep in mind the basic objective: to report the financial affairs of affiliated corporations as if they were those of a single unified economic entity. Thus the consolidated statements must reflect only the outcomes of transactions between firms within the affiliated group and *external* parties—individuals, corporations, and government agencies, for example. Achieving this state of affairs necessitates the use of eliminating entries.

> An **eliminating entry,** as made in the preparation of consolidated statements, *neutralizes, reverses, or removes* an existing intercompany financial relationship or transaction between two or more affiliated corporations.

Before proceeding to a discussion of the kinds of eliminating entries that are used, we must recognize that such entries are *not booked* or journalized by any

---

[3]   Accounting Principles Board, *Opinion No. 22*, "Disclosure of Accounting Policies" (N.Y.: AICPA, 1972).

Exhibit 7.1   Consolidation Policies

NATURE OF SUBSIDIARIES NOT CONSOLIDATED	1978	1977	1976
Finance Related:			
Credit	94	97	93
Insurance	31	35	36
Leasing	18	17	20
Banks	6	10	10
Real Estate	25	30	33
Foreign	33	37	38
NUMBER OF COMPANIES			
Consolidating All Significant Subsidiaries	428	423	411
Consolidating Certain Significant Subsidiaries	163	167	178
Not Presenting Consolidated Financial Statements	9	10	11
Total Companies	600	600	600

Source: American Institute of Certified Public Accountants, *Accounting Trends and Techniques* (N.Y.: AICPA, 1979), p. 49.
Copyright © 1979 by the American Institute of Certified Public Accountants, Inc.

of the affiliated companies and appear on consolidated statement working papers only.

> Because eliminating entries are used to prepare consolidated statements, they have *no substantive effect* on the economic or legal relationships between the *separate legal entities* comprising an affiliated group. Accordingly, they do not affect the internal accounting records of any of the affiliated companies and are *not booked*.

The preparation of consolidated financial statements consists of *combining* the trial balances or financial statements of the affiliates after any adjusting entries and the appropriate eliminating entries have been made. Adjusting entries involve no new concepts, so we shall focus on a description of the kinds of eliminating entries used and the rationale behind them. Subsequent examples in this and later chapters will thoroughly illustrate how these entries are developed in the consolidation process.

Types of Eliminating Entries

As was mentioned, the objective of consolidated statements is to provide financial statements for a group of affiliated companies as if they were a single company. Our use of eliminating entries accomplishes this objective in two fundamental ways:

1. Double counting of assets, liabilities, revenues, and expenses is avoided.

2. Gains and losses arising from transactions among the companies are removed when no transactions with external parties substantiate the realization of these gains and losses.

The various types of eliminating entries will be discussed. As part of this discussion, we mention several principles central to consolidated statements from which the reasoning behind the eliminations follows.

Eliminating the Investment in S and the Stockholders' Equity of S

In a stock acquisition, the *Investment in S account* reflects the cost of the net assets (= assets less liabilities) or stockholders' equity of S Company owned by the parent, P Company. Since it is carried as an asset on the books of P Company, *the Investment in S must be eliminated against the stockholders' equity of S Company* in consolidation to avoid double counting. The need for this elimination can be viewed from two perspectives.

First, note that the investment account reflects the cost of S Company's net assets to P Company. If we simply combined the balance sheets of P and S, without eliminating the investment account, S's net assets would be counted twice, once in the investment account and again in the asset and liability accounts themselves. This elimination accomplishes what we refer to as the **substitution principle,** in which the underlying assets and liabilities of S Company are substituted in consolidated statements for the Investment in S account in the parent's unconsolidated statements.

Second, observe that the stockholders' equity of S Company is embodied in the stockholders' equity of P Company. Because P Company owns S's stock, the stockholders of P become the stockholders of S. With respect to P and S consolidated, the shares of S are held *internally* in the Investment in S account. Failure to eliminate the Investment in S and the stockholders' equity of S would also overstate consolidated stockholders' equity. Thus the stockholders' equity of S would be duplicated—first by the stockholders' equity accounts of S and second by the stockholders' equity of P, which, by definition, includes the ownership interest in S.

To illustrate, suppose that P Company purchases 100 percent of S Company's outstanding voting shares for $1,000,000 cash, and that this amount equals the stockholders' equity of S Company. P uses the following journal entry to record the stock acquisition:

BOOKS OF P COMPANY

Investment in S	1,000,000	
Cash		1,000,000

To record the acquisition of all of S Company's outstanding voting shares at a cost of $1,000,000.

If a consolidated balance sheet is prepared at the date of acquisition, the working paper would include an eliminating entry:

CONSOLIDATED FINANCIAL STATEMENT WORKING PAPER

Stockholders' Equity—S Company	1,000,000	
Investment in S		1,000,000

To eliminate the Investment in S against the stockholders' equity (details omitted) of S Company.

This eliminating entry is posted to the condensed consolidated balance sheet working paper appearing in Exhibit 7.2.

Therefore, using the *substitution principle*, we substitute the underlying assets ($3,500,000) and liabilities ($2,500,000) of S Company for the Investment in S account ($1,000,000 = $3,500,000 − $2,500,000) when the consolidated balance sheet is prepared. Moreover, consolidated stockholders' equity now

Exhibit 7.2   Condensed Consolidated Balance Sheet Working Paper

P Company and S Company
Condensed Consolidated Balance Sheet Working Paper

	P Company	S Company	Adjustments and Eliminations Dr.	Adjustments and Eliminations Cr.	Consolidated
Investment in S	1,000,000	—		(1) 1,000,000	—
Other Assets . . .	5,000,000	3,500,000			8,500,000
	6,000,000	3,500,000		1,000,000	8,500,000
Liabilities	3,000,000	2,500,000			5,500,000
Stockholders' Equity .	3,000,000	1,000,000	(1) 1,000,000		3,000,000
	6,000,000	3,500,000	1,000,000		8,500,000

Explanation of Working Paper Entry
(1) To eliminate the Investment in S against the Stockholders' Equity of S.

equals the stockholders' equity of the controlling interest, the stockholders of P Company.

Eliminating Intercompany Receivables and Payables   Keeping in mind that consolidated statements report the affairs of affiliated companies as those of one company, *amounts due to or from affiliated companies must be eliminated* in order to avoid overstatement of consolidated assets and liabilities. Intercompany obligations do not represent amounts due to or from external parties and thus are excluded from consolidated statements.

For example, if P Company loans $20,000 to S Company, have total consolidated assets and liabilities increased? Of course not. Yet P Company's books show a receivable of $20,000 due from S, and a payable of $20,000 to P is recorded on S Company's books. From a legal entity perspective, this is a valid $20,000 debt; from a consolidated statement point of view, the $20,000 debt does not exist. The cash has moved from P to S, but we eliminate the intercompany debt on the working paper.

CONSOLIDATED FINANCIAL STATEMENT WORKING PAPER
Loan Payable to P 20,000
     Loan Receivable from S 20,000
To eliminate the intercompany loan of $20,000 by P to S.

Although our introduction to consolidated statements begins with the balance sheet, we briefly mention two other types of eliminating entries, which will be used often in the preparation of a consolidated income statement.

Eliminating Intercompany Revenues and Expenses   Affiliated companies often sell merchandise to one another or perform services for each other, thereby generating revenue and expense entries on the books of the participating firms. Consolidated statements, however, show revenues and expenses that arise through transactions with parties outside the affiliation. Furthermore, there is a double counting problem. Suppose P Company purchases goods in the open market and sells them to S. S Company subsequently sells the goods outside. In this case, purchases and sales have each been recorded twice within the P and S affiliation. Elimination of the intercompany purchase and sale means the consolidated revenue and expense accounts reflect only the transactions with outside parties.

Eliminating Unconfirmed Intercompany Gains and Losses   We have just discussed why the amounts recorded as revenues and expenses generated by intercompany transactions must be eliminated in consolidated statements. Unfortunately, intercompany revenue and expense transactions often lead to a second problem requiring treatment in consolidated statements. Suppose S Company purchases merchandise from P Company for $9,000—150 percent of the cost to P. At year-end, S Company's inventory includes $3,000 of this merchandise. The original cost to P was $2,000. Realization of the gain of $1,000 is not confirmed—there has been no sale outside the P and S affiliation—and it must be eliminated. The elimination will reduce both consolidated net income and consolidated inventory. In this way, we recognize the important **confirmation principle**: gains and losses arising out of intercompany transactions are not recognized in consolidated net income until they are confirmed by transactions outside the affiliated group. These matters will be discussed in detail in Chapters 9 and 10.

A Note on Our "Principles" of Consolidation   The overriding objective in the preparation of consolidated statements is to report the affairs of a group of affiliated corporations as if it were a single economic entity. Hence, the eliminations are designed to remove the effects of reported transactions and relationships between components of the entity. In this way, the financial statements for the consolidated entity are guided by the same accounting principles that guide any financial statement—namely, that information (revenues, expenses, gains, assets, liabilities, and so on) is reported based on transactions with outside parties. Our principles—substitution, confirmation, and removal of intercompany assets, liabilities, and revenues and expenses—are simply specific applications of the single entity approach underlying consolidated statements. We use them to provide some structure to the various eliminations and, accordingly, view them as a learning device to complement, but not substitute for, an understanding of this single entity concept.

Consolidated Balance Sheet at Date of Business Combination	In this section, we discuss the preparation of a consolidated balance sheet on the date that the business combination occurs. There are several cases to be considered.

1. Investment cost *equals* book value of the amount of S Company's stockholders' equity acquired. Although the book values of individual assets and liabilities could differ from their fair values, in presenting

this case we assume there are no such differences. This assumption provides a convenient starting point for discussing the preparation of a consolidated balance sheet following a purchase combination or a pooling of interests. In a pooling, fair values are irrelevant and investment cost equals the book value of S Company's stockholders' equity by definition.

2.   Investment cost is *greater than* the book value of S Company's stockholders' equity. This case arises only in business combinations accounted for as purchases and is referred to as a **purchase premium.**

3.   Investment cost is *less than* the book value of S Company's stockholders' equity. This case also arises only in business combinations accounted for as purchases and is referred to as a **purchase discount.**

Many business combinations include subsidiaries that are not wholly owned by their parents. Consolidated statements including such subsidiaries will reflect the separate interests of shareholders outside of the controlling interest in the subsidiaries' net assets. An account entitled **Minority Interest in Subsidiary** will be used to reflect the equity interest of these outside shareholders. Because of certain theoretical issues related to the valuation of the minority interest, we defer considering the consolidation of partially-owned subsidiaries until later in the chapter and address consolidation of wholly-owned subsidiaries first.

We assume that the date of business combination is January 1, 19X2, the beginning of year 1, so that income statement issues can be safely postponed. The balance sheet of P Company at January 1, 19X2, *prior to the combination* with S Company, appears in Exhibit 7.3. The balance sheet of S Company at the same date is given in Exhibit 7.4. The data in these two exhibits provide the basis for our balance sheet consolidations until we reach the purchase discount case.

Consolidated Balance Sheet at Date of Business Combination: P's Investment Cost Equals S's Book Value

This case assumes that P's investment cost equals the book value of the S Company stock acquired. Given our additional assumption that the book values of S's individual assets and liabilities equal their fair values, we may encounter this case in either a purchase or pooling combination. In a purchase combination, the amount recorded by P in the Investment in S account depends on the fair value of the consideration given by P in the combination. We assume here that this fair value equals the book value of the acquired portion of S's stockholders' equity. In practice, such an equality is strictly coincidental. Under the pooling of interest rules, however, the amount recorded in the Investment in S account is *based* on the book value of the stockholders' equity of S acquired and will *always* be equal to it at date of combination.

Assuming no intercompany receivables and payables exist, consolidation requires a single eliminating entry. This entry applies the substitution principle and substitutes the underlying assets and liabilities of S for the Investment in S account. A diagram which visually portrays this process appears in Figure 7.1.

Purchase Combination: S Wholly Owned   On January 1, 19X2, P Company acquires all the outstanding voting shares of S Company in an exchange of

Exhibit 7.3   Precombination Balance Sheet of P Company at January 1, 19X2

P Company
Balance Sheet at January 1, 19X2
(Precombination)

ASSETS

Cash and Receivables		$ 800,000
Inventory		600,000
Plant and Equipment	$4,000,000	
Less Accumulated Depreciation	(1,700,000)	2,300,000
Total Assets		$3,700,000

LIABILITIES AND STOCKHOLDERS' EQUITY

Current Liabilities		$ 400,000
Other Liabilities		300,000
Common Stock, Par Value $7.50, Authorized 1,000,000		
Shares, Issued and Outstanding 200,000 Shares . . .		1,500,000
Additional Paid-In Capital		900,000
Retained Earnings		600,000
Total Liabilities and Stockholders' Equity		$3,700,000

Exhibit 7.4   Balance Sheet of S Company at January 1, 19X2

S Company
Balance Sheet at January 1, 19X2

ASSETS

Cash and Receivables		$ 100,000
Inventory		250,000
Plant and Equipment	$1,000,000	
Less Accumulated Depreciation	(200,000)	800,000
Total Assets		$1,150,000

LIABILITIES AND STOCKHOLDERS' EQUITY

Current Liabilities		$ 200,000
Bonds Payable, 6%, Par Value $500,000		500,000
Common Stock, Par Value $1		100,000
Additional Paid-In Capital		125,000
Retained Earnings		225,000
Total Liabilities and Stockholders' Equity		$1,150,000

equity shares plus some contingent consideration based on postcombination earnings. The use of contingent consideration will cause this transaction to be accounted for as a purchase, *not* a pooling. P Company will issue 20,000 shares

Figure 7.1 Diagrammatic Approach to Consolidating the Balance Sheets of P and S When Investment Cost Equals Book Value (Purchase and Pooling of Interests Combinations)

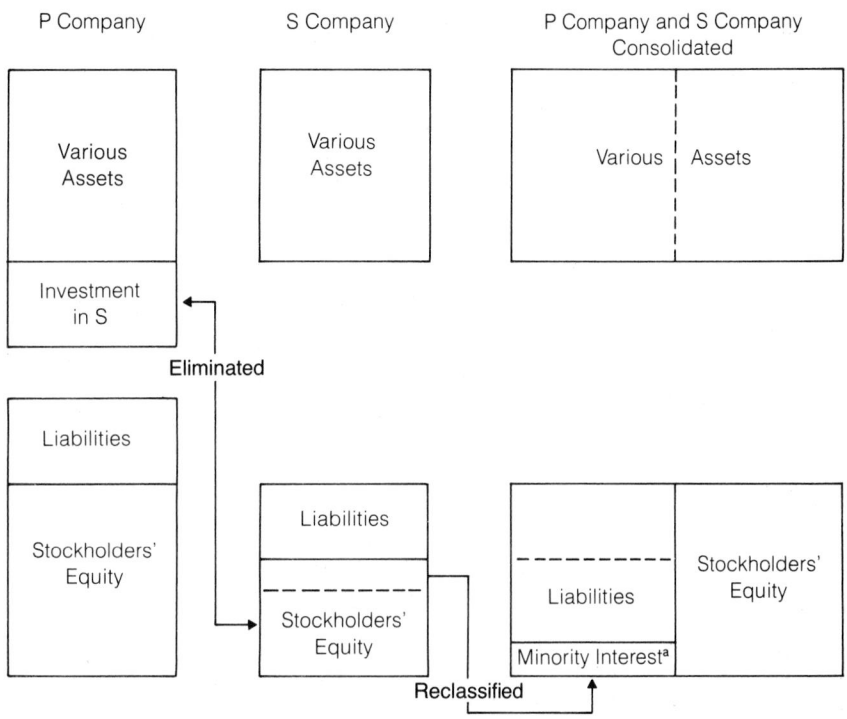

^aIf P owns 100 percent of the outstanding voting shares of S, the entire stockholders' equity of S is eliminated, and there is no minority interest.

of its $7.50 par value stock to the shareholders of S in exchange for their 100,000 shares of S Company's outstanding stock. Market value of the 20,000 P Company shares is assumed to be $450,000. The stockholders' equity of S equals $450,000; we assume that the book values of S's assets and liabilities equal their fair values. It is important to recognize that the acquisition generates no entries on the books of S Company. The shares are acquired directly from S Company's shareholders and no resources flow in or out of S Company itself. P records the acquisition on its books with the following journal entry:

BOOKS OF P COMPANY

Investment in S	450,000	
Common Stock (20,000 × $7.50)		150,000
Additional Paid-In Capital		300,000

To record the acquisition of all 100,000 outstanding shares of S Company for 20,000 shares of P Company stock worth $450,000.

If a consolidated balance sheet is prepared immediately after the combination occurs, an eliminating entry is made on the consolidated financial statement working paper:

Exhibit 7.5   Consolidated Balance Sheet at January 1, 19X2 (Purchase)

P Company and S Company
Consolidated Balance Sheet at January 1, 19X2
(Purchase Combination)

ASSETS

Cash and Receivables		$ 900,000
Inventory		850,000
Plant and Equipment	$4,800,000	
Less Accumulated Depreciation	(1,700,000)	3,100,000
Total Assets		$4,850,000

LIABILITIES AND STOCKHOLDERS' EQUITY

Current Liabilities	$ 600,000
Other Liabilities	300,000
Bonds Payable, 6%	500,000
Total Liabilities	$1,400,000
Common Stock, Par Value $7.50, Authorized 1,000,000	
Shares, Issued and Outstanding 220,000 Shares . . .	$1,650,000
Additional Paid-in Capital	1,200,000
Retained Earnings	600,000
Total Stockholders' Equity	$3,450,000
Total Liabilities and Stockholders' Equity	$4,850,000

CONSOLIDATED FINANCIAL STATEMENT WORKING PAPER

Common Stock	100,000	
Additional Paid-In Capital	125,000	
Retained Earnings	225,000	
Investment in S		450,000

To eliminate the Investment in S account against the
stockholders' equity accounts of S Company.

The resulting consolidated balance sheet is presented in Exhibit 7.5.

Pooling of Interests Combination: S Wholly Owned   Alternatively, P Company and S Company may decide against the contingent consideration and pool their interests through the exchange of equity shares just described. P Company will issue 20,000 shares of its $7.50 par value stock to the shareholders of S. In recording this pooling combination, three items must be remembered:

1.   The amount assigned to the Investment in S reflects the book value of the stockholders' equity or net assets of S, $450,000 (the market value of the 20,000 shares of P Company stock is irrelevant).

2.   The entries to paid-in capital (par value of common stock plus additional paid-in capital) should equal the total paid-in capital as recorded on the books of S Company, $225,000.

3. The retained earnings of S Company at date of combination ($225,000) become part of consolidated retained earnings and must be included when P Company records the combination.

Therefore, the journal entry we make on P Company's books to record the pooling is:

BOOKS OF P COMPANY

Investment in S	450,000	
Common Stock (20,000 × $7.50)		150,000
Additional Paid-In Capital ($225,000 − $150,000) .		75,000
Retained Earnings		225,000

To record the acquisition of all the outstanding shares of S
Company through the exchange of 20,000 P Company
shares in a pooling of interest.

A consolidated balance sheet prepared for P Company and its new subsidiary, S Company, on January 1, 19X2, would require that the following eliminating entry be made on the consolidated financial statement working paper:

CONSOLIDATED FINANCIAL STATEMENT WORKING PAPER

Common Stock	100,000	
Additional Paid-In Capital	125,000	
Retained Earnings	225,000	
Investment in S		450,000

To eliminate the Investment in S account against the
stockholders' equity accounts of S Company.

In recording the pooling, the retained earnings of S are brought onto P's books. This procedure is consistent with the notion that a pooling unites previously separate stockholder interests. Since S's retained earnings are recorded by P, the working paper entry eliminates the retained earnings of S on S's separate statements. An alternative procedure is to record only the amount of S's paid-in capital accounts on P's books and sum the retained earnings of the two companies on the working paper. We do not use the alternative procedure in this book.

Observe that the investment elimination entries in the pooling and purchase cases are *identical*. While this is coincidental in general, it is not coincidental here. In both cases being examined, the balance in the investment account equals the book value of S Company's stockholders' equity.

Consolidated Stockholders' Equity Accounts under Purchase and Pooling When S Is Wholly Owned   Even though the investment elimination entries made at date of business combination under purchase and pooling are the same, not all of the individual consolidated stockholders' equity accounts are. This is because the acquisition is recorded differently in the purchase and pooling cases. To see this, consider the comparison of the stockholders' equity accounts in Exhibit 7.6. We can make several observations:

1. Consolidated paid-in capital (par value of common stock plus additional paid-in capital) includes the market value of the shares issued in the purchase ($450,000) versus the book value of S's paid-in capital in the pooling ($225,000).

2. Consolidated retained earnings includes none of S Company's retained

Exhibit 7.6   Comparison of Consolidated Stockholders' Equity Accounts in the Purchase and Pooling of Interests Cases

PURCHASE: EXCHANGE OF SHARES

Stockholders' Equity Accounts	P before Acquisition	Acquisition Entry	P after Acquisition	S Company	Eliminations	Consolidated
Common Stock at Par . . .	$1,500,000	$150,000	$1,650,000	$100,000	$(100,000)	$1,650,000
Additional Paid-In Capital . .	900,000	300,000	1,200,000	125,000	(125,000)	1,200,000
Retained Earnings	600,000	—	600,000	225,000	(225,000)	600,000
Total	$3,000,000	$450,000	$3,450,000	$450,000	$(450,000)	$3,450,000

POOLING: EXCHANGE OF SHARES

Stockholders' Equity Accounts	P before Acquisition	Acquisition Entry	P after Acquisition	S Company	Eliminations	Consolidated
Common Stock at Par . . .	$1,500,000	$150,000	$1,650,000	$100,000	$(100,000)	$1,650,000
Additional Paid-In Capital . .	900,000	75,000	975,000	125,000	(125,000)	975,000
Retained Earnings	600,000	225,000	825,000	225,000	(225,000)	825,000
Total	$3,000,000	$450,000	$3,450,000	$450,000	$(450,000)	$3,450,000

earnings in the purchase but all of S Company's retained earnings in the pooling.

3. Total consolidated stockholders' equity is the same in both the purchase and pooling cases because of our assumption that the investment cost equals the book value of the shares acquired. In general, total consolidated stockholders' equity differs under the two methods.

4. S Company's stockholders' equity accounts are unaffected by the acquisition in both cases.

5. Because S Company's stockholders' equity accounts are eliminated in consolidation, the consolidated stockholders' equity accounts are equal to P Company's stockholders' equity accounts after the acquisition.

Purchase Combination: S Partially Owned   As previously mentioned, failure to acquire all of S Company's outstanding shares means that a group of *minority shareholders,* separate from the controlling shareholders of P, continues to have an equity interest in S Company. In making the investment elimination entry, then, the entire stockholders' equity of S Company is not eliminated against the Investment in S account. Rather, the portion which pertains to the shares owned by the minority shareholders is reclassified and reported as *Minority Interest in Subsidiary* in the consolidated balance sheet. This latter point can be seen by referring back to Figure 7.1; the portion of S Company's stockholders' equity *above* the dashed line represents the equity attributable to those shares not held by P Company and is appropriately reclassified as minority interest.

Suppose P Company acquires 90 percent ($\alpha = .9$) of S Company's outstanding shares by issuing 18,000 shares of its own stock (having a market value of $405,000) and agreeing to an earnings contingency. The journal entry made by P to record the acquisition is:

BOOKS OF P COMPANY

Investment in S	405,000	
Common Stock (18,000 × $7.50)		135,000
Additional Paid-In Capital		270,000

To record the acquisition of 90,000 shares of S Company
for 18,000 shares of P Company stock worth $405,000.

We begin by illustrating the investment elimination in this case with *two working paper entries*. The first entry *eliminates* the Investment in S account against P's share (90 percent) of S Company's stockholders' equity. The second entry *reclassifies* the remaining 10 percent of S's stockholders' equity as Minority Interest in S.

CONSOLIDATED FINANCIAL STATEMENT WORKING PAPER

Common Stock (.9 × $100,000)	90,000	
Additional Paid-In Capital (.9 × $125,000) . . .	112,500	
Retained Earnings (.9 × $225,000)	202,500	
Investment in S		405,000

To eliminate the Investment in S against 90 percent of the
stockholders' equity accounts of S Company.

Common Stock (.1 × $100,000)	10,000	
Additional Paid-In Capital (.1 × $125,000) . . .	12,500	
Retained Earnings (.1 × $225,000)	22,500	
Minority Interest in S		45,000

To reclassify as minority interest the remaining balances
in S Company's stockholders' equity accounts which
pertain to outstanding shares not owned by P.

Throughout the subsequent consolidation material, however, we use a single entry to eliminate the investment account and establish the minority interest. Thus, the above two entries are combined into the following single eliminating entry:

CONSOLIDATED FINANCIAL STATEMENT WORKING PAPER

Common Stock	100,000	
Additional Paid-In Capital	125,000	
Retained Earnings	225,000	
Investment in S		405,000
Minority Interest in S		45,000

To eliminate the Investment in S against 90 percent of
the stockholders' equity accounts of S Company and to
reclassify the remaining 10 percent as minority interest.

Pooling of Interests Combination: S Partially Owned   For the combination to qualify as a pooling, at least 90 percent of S Company's shares must be exchanged for shares of P Company. If we now assume that the earnings contingency is removed from the combination plan, we may proceed with a pooling in which 18,000 shares of P's stock are exchanged for 90,000 shares of S's stock.

BOOKS OF P COMPANY

Investment in S [.9($100,000 + $125,000 +
$225,000)] 405,000
    Common Stock (18,000 × $7.50) 135,000
    Additional Paid-In Capital [.9($100,000 +
    $125,000) − $135,000] 67,500
    Retained Earnings (.9 × $225,000) 202,500
To record the acquisition of 90,000 shares of S Company
stock through the exchange of 18,000 shares of P
Company stock in a pooling of interests.

Moving to the consolidated financial statement working paper, we use a single entry to accomplish investment elimination and minority interest reclassification:

CONSOLIDATED FINANCIAL STATEMENT WORKING PAPER

Common Stock 100,000
Additional Paid-In Capital 125,000
Retained Earnings 225,000
    Investment in S 405,000
    Minority Interest in S 45,000
To eliminate the Investment in S against 90 percent of the
stockholders' equity accounts of S Company and to
reclassify the remaining 10 percent as minority interest.

Balance Sheet Classification of Minority Interest   Recall that *minority interest* refers to the equity of shareholders outside the controlling interest in partially-owned subsidiaries. Having said this, however, it may not be obvious where the minority interest may be found in published consolidated balance sheets. Both theoretical issues and methods adopted in practice affect placement of the minority interest among the liabilities and stockholders' equity accounts. There seem to be three possibilities:

1.   Report the minority interest as a noncurrent liability, perhaps of indeterminate term. According to *Accounting Trends and Techniques,* of 591 firms issuing consolidated statements in 1978, 150 included minority interest among the noncurrent liabilities; of 590 in 1977, 156 did so.[4]

2.   Report the minority interest in a separate caption between noncurrent liabilities and stockholders' equity.

3.   Report the minority interest as part of consolidated stockholders' equity.

Accounting Trends and Techniques does not indicate the proportions of its survey companies which treat minority interest in the manner suggested in 2 or 3 above. Nevertheless, approximately 75 percent of the companies surveyed did not report the minority interest as a noncurrent liability.

Noncurrent Liability   Reporting minority interest as a noncurrent liability is consistent with the **parent theory of consolidated statements,** which consid-

---

[4] American Institute of Certified Public Accountants, *Accounting Trends and Techniques* (N.Y.: AICPA, 1979), pp. 49, 191.

ers consolidated statements to be nothing more than an extension of parent company statements. The statements are prepared solely for the stockholders of the parent company, and, from their point of view, the outside minority interest represents a liability. Although we acknowledge that consolidated statements are prepared primarily for the controlling interest, we are skeptical when that position is invoked as support for a liability concept of minority interest. This emphasis on the controlling interest certainly suggests that the equity of minority shareholders differs from the equity of the controlling interest. Liability treatment does not follow, however, because we see no obligation on the part of the controlling interest to pay a reasonably determinable amount at a reasonably determinable time to minority shareholders.

Between Noncurrent Liabilities and Stockholders' Equity This treatment is also an outgrowth of the so-called parent theory. It recognizes that minority interest is neither a liability nor a part of the equity of the majority or controlling interest. It is felt that minority interest is not part of consolidated stockholders' equity and thus a new balance sheet caption must be devised for it. We are sympathetic with this view but are uncomfortable with the notion of a special nonliability, non–stockholders' equity balance sheet caption.

Stockholders' Equity The problem with minority interest arises, it seems to us, for two reasons. First, minority shareholders do not have a proportional interest in specific assets but rather in the subsidiary as a whole. In other words, the interests of the majority and minority shareholders in the subsidiary's net assets are *inseparable*. One cannot be factored out from the other, and the total net assets must equal all stockholders' equity. Second, the parent company controls 100 percent of the net assets of the subsidiary by virtue of its ownership of more than 50 percent of S's shares. Thus there exists an arithmetic gap between the net assets *controlled* and the net assets *owned*. This gap is filled by the minority interest, and its disclosure is important because it defines the extent of the stockholders' equity of the controlling interest.

Elements of this view of inseparability are embodied in the **entity theory of consolidated statements,** which holds that consolidated statements reflect the viewpoint of the total business entity.[5] The resources controlled by the consolidated entity relate to both the majority and minority shareholders and, in consolidation, both sets of interests must be treated consistently. From this perspective, minority shareholders may be viewed as shareholders in the consolidated entity even though their interest is limited to *part* of the consolidated entity. Therefore, the amount assigned to the minority interest should be separately disclosed and included within consolidated stockholders' equity.

---

[5] A comprehensive development of this view of consolidated statements can be found in Maurice Moonitz, *The Entity Theory of Consolidated Statements*, American Accounting Association Monograph No. 4 (Evanston: American Accounting Association, 1944).

Authors' Conclusion We believe that the minority interest problem is one of *disclosure*—disclosure of the fact that not all of S's shares are held internally. No basis exists for treating such ownership interests as liabilities. In our view, adequate disclosure is achieved either by reporting the minority interest in a separate caption between noncurrent liabilities and stockholders' equity or by clearly identifying it within consolidated stockholders' equity.

Consolidated Balance Sheet at Date of Business Combination: Purchase Premium

In a purchase combination, the surrender of consideration which has a fair value in excess of the acquired stockholders' equity of S indicates that a *purchase premium* has been paid by P Company. We addressed the accounting treatment of this premium in the previous chapter as part of our discussion of statutory mergers and consolidations accounted for as purchases. Our objective was to allocate the cost of the investment to the identifiable assets and liabilities of the acquired company. Any premium unallocated in this way is recorded as an unspecified intangible asset, goodwill.

Accounting for a stock acquisition differs from a statutory merger in that the acquired company does not lose its legal identity. Further, the cost of the investment is not directly allocated among the assets and liabilities of S Company by a journal entry on P Company's books. Rather, in a *stock acquisition, the allocation of investment cost* among the assets and liabilities of S Company takes place *only on the consolidated statement working paper.* In this way, the new basis of accountability established by the fair value of the consideration given in the acquisition of S Company is reported on the consolidated balance sheet.

If a consolidated balance sheet is prepared immediately following the stock acquisition and a purchase premium exists, three working paper entries are required.

1. Remove the excess of investment cost over book value of S's shares from the Investment in S account and reclassify it as Purchase Premium.

2. Allocate the purchase premium among the identifiable assets and liabilities of S Company in accordance with their fair values, assigning any amount unallocated in this way to goodwill. If negative goodwill exists, it must be allocated using the two-stage allocation process discussed later.

3. Eliminate the Investment in S account, now adjusted to the book value of the S Company shares owned, against the stockholders' equity accounts of S Company and, if appropriate, recognize the existence of a minority interest by reclassifying the remaining stockholders' equity of S as Minority Interest in S. These procedures are diagrammed in Figure 7.2.

Purchase Premium: S Wholly Owned When we dealt with recording the business combination of P and S in the last chapter, we compared the estimated

Figure 7.2   Diagrammatic Approach to Consolidating the Balance Sheets of P and S When a Purchase Premium Exists (Purchase Combinations Only)

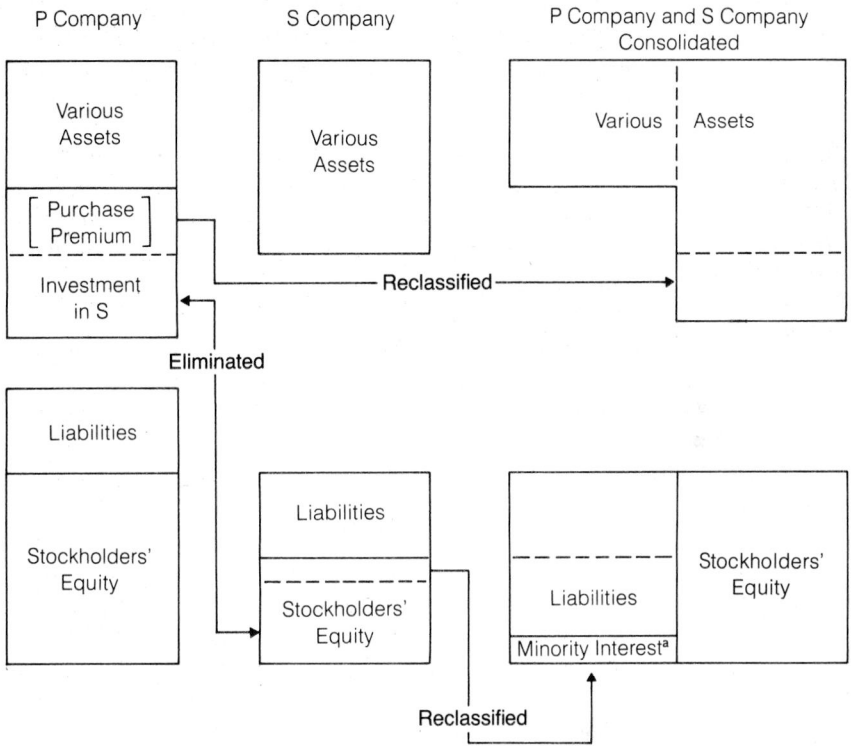

^aIf P owns 100 percent of the outstanding voting shares of S, the entire stockholders' equity of S is eliminated, and there is no minority interest.

fair values of S Company's assets and liabilities with their book values, as shown in Exhibit 7.7.

P Company acquires all the outstanding shares of S Company through an exchange of equity shares and a cash payment. S Company shareholders receive $200,000 cash and 70,000 shares of P Company stock worth $700,000. Direct out-of-pocket costs incurred by P in connection with the stock acquisition amount to $40,000, as follows:

Registration and Issue Costs	$15,000
Consultants' and Attorneys' Fees	25,000
Total Direct Costs of Stock Acquisition	$40,000

Conforming to the rules stated in *APBO 16*, the registration and issue costs have no net effect on the cost of the acquisition. Although they are part of the investment cost, their incurrence decreases the fair value of the P Company stock

Exhibit 7.7   Book Values and Fair Values of S Company's Assets and Liabilities

S Company
Assets and Liabilities at January 1, 19X2

ASSETS		Book Value	Fair Value
Cash and Receivables		$ 100,000	$ 100,000
Inventory		250,000	375,000
Plant and Equipment	$1,000,000		
Less Accumulated Depreciation . .	(200,000)	800,000	960,000 (net)
Total Assets		$1,150,000	$1,435,000
LIABILITIES			
Current Liabilities		$ 200,000	$ 200,000
Bonds Payable, 6%, Par Value			
$500,000		500,000	400,000
Total Liabilities		$ 700,000	$ 600,000
Net Assets		$ 450,000	$ 835,000

issued. In contrast, the consultants' and attorneys' fees are added to the cost of the investment. The journal entry made on P's books to record this stock acquisition is as follows:

BOOKS OF P COMPANY

Investment in S	925,000	
Cash		240,000
Common Stock (70,000 × $7.50)		525,000
Additional Paid-In Capital		160,000

To record the acquisition of all the outstanding common stock of S Company. Consideration to the former shareholders of S included cash of $200,000 and 70,000 shares of P Company $7.50 par value stock. The P Company stock had a market value of $10 per share; net market value of the P stock issued was $685,000 *after* deducting registration and issue costs of $15,000, which were paid in cash and are part of the total investment cost of $925,000. Additional direct costs associated with this acquisition were consultants' and attorneys' fees of $25,000.

Since $925,000 of cost was incurred to acquire stock having a $450,000 book value in the accounts of S Company, a purchase premium of $475,000 results. Preparation of our consolidated balance sheet requires that this purchase premium be allocated among the assets and liabilities of S on the working papers. The basis for this allocation was made in a schedule originally prepared in Chapter 6. We reproduce this information in Exhibit 7.8.

Three working paper entries are required to consolidate P and S on January 1, 19X2. These are given in Exhibit 7.9. No minority interest is present because 100 percent of S's shares are owned by P. Note that when a purchase premium

Exhibit 7.8   Determination and Allocation of the Purchase Premium Paid by P in the January 1, 19X2, Acquisition of S (100%)

P Company and S Company
Schedule for Determining and Allocating Purchase Premium
Arising in the Stock Acquisition on January 1, 19X2 ($\alpha = 1$)

Cost of the Acquisition:

Fair Value of Stock Given, Net of Registration and Issue Costs	$685,000
Plus Registration and Issue Costs	15,000
Cash Given	200,000
Direct Costs Incurred (Consultants' and Attorneys' Fees)	25,000
Total Cost of the Acquisition	$925,000

Book Value of the Net Assets or Stockholders' Equity Acquired:

Common Stock	$100,000
Additional Paid-In Capital	125,000
Retained Earnings	225,000
Total Book Value of S Company	$450,000
Purchase Premium	$475,000

Assets and Liabilities of S Company	Fair Value	Book Value	Fair Value Less Book Value	Allocation Based on P's Interest (100%)
Cash and Receivables	$100,000	$100,000	—	—
Inventory	375,000	250,000	$125,000	$125,000
Plant and Equipment (Net)	960,000	800,000	160,000	160,000
Current Liabilities	(200,000)	(200,000)	—	—
Bonds Payable, 6%	(400,000)	(500,000)	100,000	100,000
	$835,000	$450,000	$385,000	$385,000
Goodwill				90,000
Total Purchase Premium				$475,000

exists, it is not eliminated. Instead, it finds its way to the consolidated balance sheet through its inclusion in S's identifiable assets or liabilities, or goodwill. Only the portion of the Investment in S account which equals the book value of the shares of S owned is eliminated.

Purchase Premium: S Partially Owned   An interesting issue in the theory of consolidated statements arises when a subsidiary is partially acquired at a purchase premium or purchase discount. The issue concerns measurement of the minority interest: should it be based on the book values of S's assets and liabilities, or should it be based on the fair values of S's assets and liabilities established by the price paid by P? Current generally accepted accounting principles do not provide a definitive answer. Instead, room for interpretation remains, and alternatives for measuring the minority interest exist. We shall examine these alternatives following our presentation of the treatment most

Exhibit 7.9   Working Paper Entries to Consolidate P and S ($\alpha = 1$; Purchase Premium = \$475,000)

CONSOLIDATED FINANCIAL STATEMENT WORKING PAPER

Purchase Premium	475,000	
Investment in S		475,000

To reclassify amount paid by P in excess of book value of S Company's
shares as a purchase premium.

Inventory	125,000	
Plant and Equipment (Net)	160,000	
Discount on Bonds Payable	100,000	
Goodwill	90,000	
Purchase Premium		475,000

To allocate the purchase premium paid for S's shares among the
assets and liabilities of S Company and goodwill according to
Exhibit 7.8.

Common Stock	100,000	
Additional Paid-In Capital	125,000	
Retained Earnings	225,000	
Investment in S		450,000

To eliminate the Investment in S against the stockholders' equity
accounts of S Company.

widely used in practice.[6] This treatment can be summarized in the following
way.

> Payment of a purchase premium in a less-than-100-percent stock acquisi-
> tion results in reporting the *parent's share (α)* of S's assets and liabilities at
> their *fair values* in a consolidated balance sheet and the minority's share at
> book value. The amount of *minority interest* reported is derived from the
> *book value* of S's net assets and is not imputed from the purchase premium
> paid by P. Any unspecified intangibles *(goodwill)* established by the pur-
> chase premium relate solely to the *controlling interest*.

Before proceeding, we use a short numerical example to clarify this treatment. Suppose A pays \$800,000 for 80 percent of B's outstanding voting shares
($\alpha = .8$). The net assets of B Company have a book value of \$700,000 and a fair
value of \$900,000. Therefore,

Purchase premium = Investment Cost $-$ α (Book value of B's net assets)

Purchase premium = \$800,000 $-$ .8(\$700,000)

Purchase premium = \$240,000.

Of this \$240,000, \$160,000 [= .8(\$900,000 $-$ \$700,000)] is allocated to the identifiable assets of B, and \$80,000 (= \$240,000 $-$ \$160,000) to goodwill on the con-

---

[6] See the FASB Discussion Memorandum, "Accounting for Business Combinations and Purchased Intangibles" (1976), pars. 367–371, 866, and 867.

solidated balance sheet. The minority interest is reported as $140,000 (= .2 × $700,000). *Only the controlling interest's portion* of the assets and liabilities of B included in consolidated totals *is recorded at fair value;* the minority interest's portion is recorded at book value.

Returning to the acquisition of S Company, we now assume that P Company acquired 80 percent of the outstanding voting shares at a total cost of $740,000. Stock worth $560,000 and $160,000 cash were given to the shareholders of S Company. Registration and issue costs amounted to $12,000; consultants' and attorneys' fees were $20,000.

BOOKS OF P COMPANY

Investment in S	740,000	
Cash		192,000
Common Stock (56,000 × $7.50)		420,000
Additional Paid-In Capital		128,000

To record the acquisition of 80 percent of the outstanding common stock of S Company. Consideration to the former shareholders of S included cash of $160,000 and 56,000 shares of P Company $7.50 par value stock. The P Company stock had a market value of $10 per share; net market value of the P stock issued was $548,000 *after* deducting registration and issue costs of $12,000, which were paid in cash and are part of the total investment cost of $740,000. Additional direct costs associated with this acquisition were consultants' and attorneys' fees of $20,000.

Determination and allocation of the purchase premium is given in Exhibit 7.10. The working paper eliminations are presented in Exhibit 7.11.

Alternative Approaches to Measuring the Minority Interest   We believe that the measurement of minority interest by reference to the book values of S Company's assets and liabilities is consistent with the principles of historical cost accounting. The price paid by the parent in an acquisition establishes the value of the *parent's* share of properties acquired but not the minority's share. Since *APBO 6* (AC § 4072) prohibits S Company from recording any write-ups on its own books,[7] an approach designed to achieve an equivalent result on the working paper is inappropriate. This position is consistent with *the parent theory of consolidated statements.* Nevertheless, this position is not without flaws, and the alternatives found in practice deserve some attention here.

The Entity Theory of Consolidated Statements   The most important alternative approach to measuring minority interest follows from the *entity theory of consolidated statements,* which we discussed in connection with the balance sheet classification of minority interest. Observe that the approach we use in this book does have a flaw—the assets and liabilities of S Company are reported on two different bases in the same consolidated balance sheet. The parent's portion is reported at fair value, while the minority's portion is reflected at book value. Under the entity theory, this would not be the case. The entity the-

---

[7] Accounting Principles Board, *Opinion No. 6,* "Status of Accounting Research Bulletins" (N.Y.: AICPA, 1965), par. 17.

Exhibit 7.10   Determination and Allocation of the Purchase Premium Paid by P in the January 1, 19X2, Acquisition of S (80%)

P Company and S Company
Schedule for Determining and Allocating Purchase Premium
Arising in the Stock Acquisition on January 1, 19X2 ($\alpha = .8$)

Cost of the Acquisition:

Fair Value of Stock Given, Net of Registration and Issue Costs	$548,000
Plus Registration and Issue Costs	12,000
Cash Given	160,000
Direct Costs Incurred (Consultants' and Attorneys' Fees)	20,000
Total Cost of the Acquisition	$740,000

Book Value of the Net Assets or Stockholders' Equity Acquired (80%):

Common Stock	$ 80,000
Additional Paid-In Capital	100,000
Retained Earnings	180,000
Total Book Value of S Company (80%)	$360,000
Purchase Premium	$380,000

Assets and Liabilities of S Company	Fair Value	Book Value	Fair Value Less Book Value	Allocation Based on P's Interest (80%)
Cash and Receivables	$100,000	$100,000	—	—
Inventory	375,000	250,000	$125,000	$100,000
Plant and Equipment (Net)	960,000	800,000	160,000	128,000
Current Liabilities	(200,000)	(200,000)	—	—
Bonds Payable, 6%	(400,000)	(500,000)	100,000	80,000
	$835,000	$450,000	$385,000	$308,000
Goodwill				72,000
Total Purchase Premium				$380,000

ory infers the *total* fair value of S's identifiable assets, liabilities, and goodwill from the price paid by P for its fractional interest. Thus, the assets and liabilities of S Company and goodwill reported in a consolidated balance sheet prepared according to the entity theory would be shown at their *total fair value*, and the minority interest would be recorded at its proportional interest in the fair value of assets, liabilities, and goodwill for the entity as a whole.

The total fair value of S is computed by "grossing up" the price paid by P for its partial interest, α.

$$\text{Fair Value of S Company} = \text{Price Paid by P Company}/\alpha$$

In our last example, P acquired 80 percent of S's shares at a cost of $740,000. From that we infer that the fair value of S Company as a whole is $925,000 (= $740,000/.8). Using the approach just described, the net assets of S would be re-

Exhibit 7.11   Working Paper Entries to Consolidate P and S ($\alpha = .8$; Purchase Premium = $380,000)

CONSOLIDATED FINANCIAL STATEMENT WORKING PAPER

Purchase Premium	380,000	
Investment in S		380,000

To reclassify amount paid by P in excess of book value of the 80 percent of S Company's shares acquired as a purchase premium.

Inventory	100,000	
Plant and Equipment (Net)	128,000	
Discount on Bonds Payable	80,000	
Goodwill	72,000	
Purchase Premium		380,000

To allocate the purchase premium paid for S's shares among the assets and liabilities of S Company and goodwill according to Exhibit 7.10.

Common Stock	100,000	
Additional Paid-In Capital	125,000	
Retained Earnings	225,000	
Investment in S		360,000
Minority Interest in S		90,000

To eliminate the Investment in S against 80 percent of the stockholders' equity accounts of S Company and to reclassify the remaining 20 percent of the stockholders' equity accounts of S Company as minority interest.

ported at their total fair value of $835,000 (see Exhibit 7.10) in the consolidated balance sheet, and goodwill would amount to $90,000 (= $925,000 − $835,000 = $72,000/.8). The minority interest, reflecting a 20 percent share of net assets at fair value *and* goodwill, would be measured at $185,000 [= .2($835,000 + $90,000)], an increase of $95,000 [= .2($385,000 + $90,000)] over its book value.

This application of the entity theory is rarely encountered in practice today. If accounting reports depart from historical cost and become more reliant on current values, however, the entity theory could provide a more appropriate valuation basis for consolidated statements when subsidiaries are partially owned.

The Entity Theory Modified   A third approach to the measurement of subsidiaries' assets and liabilities and of the minority interest in a consolidated balance sheet focuses on the nature of goodwill. Under this approach, the identifiable assets and liabilities of S are recorded at their total fair values in the consolidated balance sheet, and the appropriate portion is reflected in the minority interest. The existence of goodwill, however, is believed to be evidence of value which will accrue only to the parent by virtue of its control over the subsidiary. Thus the goodwill does not relate to the subsidiary standing alone and hence does not relate to the minority interest.

Taking up the example in Exhibit 7.10 where P owns 80 percent of S, the modified entity theory would report (1) total fair value of S's net assets, $835,000, (2) the minority interest at $167,000 (= .2 × $835,000), and (3) goodwill of $72,000, pertaining only to the controlling interest.

Authors' Conclusion   Although these alternative approaches to measuring minority interest do occasionally appear in practice, we shall not use them in the text. Text examples and problem solutions reflect the method previously developed, unless a particular problem calls for alternatives. Our method may be summarized as follows:

1. The minority interest is based on the book value of S Company's stockholders' equity. It does not include a pro rata share of asset and liability restatements to fair value or of goodwill.

2. The consolidated balance sheet includes the identifiable assets and liabilities of P and S at book value *plus P's share* of the difference between the fair values and book values of S's identifiable assets and liabilities. Goodwill is a residual, attributable to P Company, and is the excess of investment cost over P's share of the fair value of S Company's assets and liabilities.

Consolidated Balance Sheet at Date of Business Combination: Purchase Discount

A *purchase discount* exists when the cost of P's investment in S is less than the book value of the shares acquired. As in the case of a purchase premium, the discount must be allocated among the assets and liabilities of the subsidiary. While the discount allocation could imply the existence of positive goodwill (an unallocated debit balance), the more likely result is an unallocated credit balance, commonly referred to as *negative goodwill*. This negative goodwill must then be allocated among the subsidiary's noncurrent assets—except long-term investments in marketable securities—in accordance with their relative fair values. Thus the procedure for allocating a purchase discount with negative goodwill is somewhat more complex than the typical purchase premium allocation involving positive goodwill (negative goodwill could exist along with a purchase premium, but it is not likely). In the premium case with positive goodwill, the goodwill remains and is amortized in subsequent periods. In contrast, none of the negative goodwill arising in a purchase discount (or occasionally in a purchase premium) remains unless the subsidiary has no noncurrent assets to which it can be allocated. Unallocated negative goodwill appears in the consolidated balance sheet as a deferred credit and is amortized into income by the straight-line method over a period not to exceed forty years.

We first encountered the purchase discount case with negative goodwill in Chapter 6, when the statutory consolidation of P, S, and T took place. The purchase discount and negative goodwill related to T Company; we followed their allocation among T's assets and liabilities in Exhibit 6.8 and related schedules. In the stock acquisition case which we are now addressing, however, the purchase discount is allocated only on the consolidated financial statement working paper. A diagram of this process appears in Figure 7.3.

Purchase Discount: T Wholly Owned   We now consider the acquisition of T Company at a purchase discount. The book value of T Company's stockholders' equity is $1,150,000. To acquire the shares of T, P Company issues both stock and cash and makes the following journal entry on its books:

Figure 7.3 Diagrammatic Approach to Consolidating the Balance Sheets of P and S When a Purchase Discount Exists (Purchase Combinations Only)

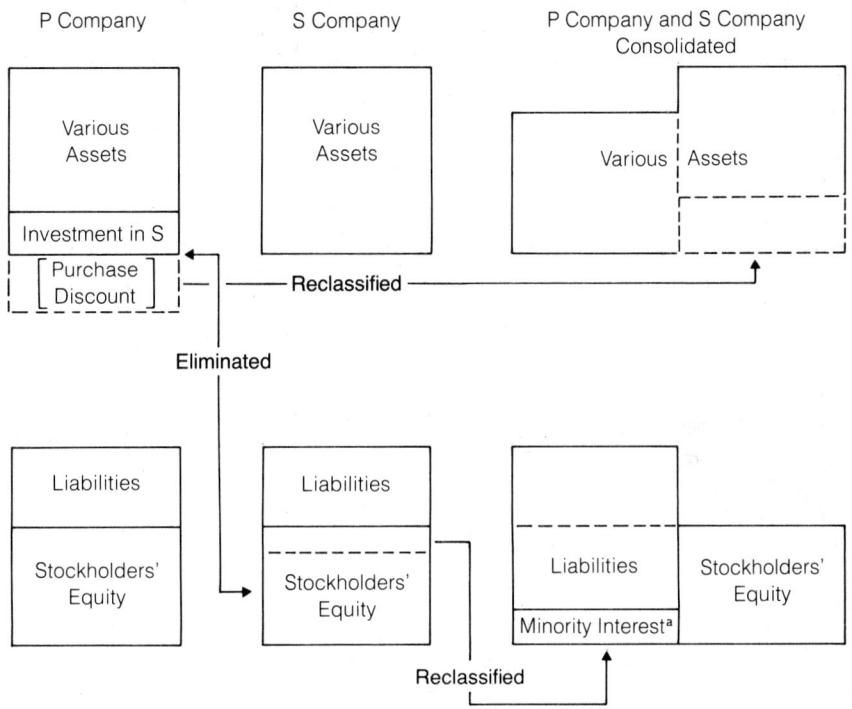

[a]If P owns 100 percent of the outstanding voting shares of S, the entire stockholders' equity of S is eliminated, and there is no minority interest.

BOOKS OF P COMPANY

Investment in T	1,040,000	
Cash		180,000
Common Stock (88,000 × $7.50)		660,000
Additional Paid-In Capital		200,000

To record the acquisition of all the outstanding common stock of T Company. Consideration to the former shareholders of T included cash of $120,000 and 88,000 shares of P Company $7.50 par value stock. The P Company stock had a market value of $10 per share; net market value of the P stock issued was $860,000 *after* deducting registration and issue costs of $20,000, which were paid in cash and are part of the total investment cost of $1,040,000. Additional direct costs associated with this acquisition were consultants' and attorneys' fees of $40,000.

Thus, the shares of T are acquired at a purchase discount of $110,000 (= $1,150,000 − $1,040,000). The initial allocation of the purchase discount is illus-

Exhibit 7.12   Determination and Allocation of the Purchase Discount Realized by P in the January 1, 19X2, Acquisition of T (100%)

P Company and T Company
Schedule for Determining and Allocating Purchase Discount
Arising in the Stock Acquisition on January 1, 19X2 ($\alpha = 1$)

Cost of the Acquisition:

Fair Value of Stock Given, Net of Registration and Issue Costs	$ 860,000
Plus Registration and Issue Costs	20,000
Cash Given	120,000
Direct Costs Incurred	40,000
Total Cost of the Acquisition	$1,040,000

Book Value of the Net Assets or Stockholders' Equity Acquired:

Common Stock	$ 250,000
Additional Paid-In Capital	400,000
Retained Earnings	500,000
Total Book Value of T Company	$1,150,000
Purchase Discount	$ (110,000)

Assets and Liabilities of T Company	Fair Value	Book Value	Fair Value Less Book Value	Allocation Based on P's Interest (100%)
Cash and Receivables	$ 150,000	$ 150,000	—	—
Marketable Equity Securities—Current	120,000	100,000	$ 20,000	$ 20,000
Inventory	350,000	300,000	50,000	50,000
Marketable Equity Securities—Long-Term	600,000	500,000	100,000	100,000
Plant and Equipment (Net)	1,600,000	1,400,000	200,000	200,000
Current Liabilities	(500,000)	(500,000)	—	—
Other Liabilities	(1,200,000)	(800,000)	(400,000)	(400,000)
	$1,120,000	$1,150,000	$ (30,000)	$ (30,000)
Negative Goodwill				(80,000)
Total Purchase Discount				$(110,000)

trated in Exhibit 7.12. Following *APBO 16*,[8] we now allocate the negative good-will to T Company's Plant and Equipment. This is the second stage of the two-stage allocation process developed in Chapter 6. Exhibit 7.12 indicates that the total book value of T's Plant and Equipment (Net) is $1,400,000; total fair value is $1,600,000. An analysis of the Plant and Equipment account and related appraisal information reveals the following plant asset accounts in terms of book and fair values.

---

[8] Accounting Principles Board, *Opinion No. 16*, "Business Combinations" (N.Y.: AICPA, 1970), par. 91; AC § 1091.91.

		Fair Value	
	Book Value	Amount	Percent
Buildings and Equipment	$1,200,000	$1,300,000	81%
Land	200,000	300,000	19
Total	$1,400,000	$1,600,000	100%

Allocating the negative goodwill of $80,000 to the components of Plant and Equipment reduces their tentative fair value adjustment from $200,000 to $120,000. Since preparation of consolidated statements starts with the book values of T's plant and equipment items, only the final purchase premium or discount allocation is entered on the working paper. The next schedule is used to compute this final allocation. This is somewhat different from the approach developed in Chapter 6, where we computed the total cost assigned to these items, which was recorded in a journal entry on P's books and did not separately identify the increment or decrement to book value. In the present case, we calculate this increment or decrement which is to be entered on the working paper.

	(1)	(2)	(3)		(4)
		Allocation of Negative	Fair Value − Book Value		Final
	Percent of	Goodwill		P's Interest	Allocation
	Fair Value	[(1) × $80,000]	Total	(100%)	[(3) − (2)]
Buildings and Equipment	81%	$64,800	$100,000	$100,000	$ 35,200
Land	19	15,200	100,000	100,000	84,800
Total	100%	$80,000	$200,000	$200,000	$120,000

Consolidating P and T requires three working paper entries, given in Exhibit 7.13. The first entry, which reclassifies the purchase discount, deserves some explanation. Since the purchase discount has a credit balance, recording it on the working paper requires that some account be debited. The account to be debited is Investment in T. By so doing, the balance in the Investment in T is increased up to the book value of T Company's stockholders' equity so that it can be cleanly eliminated. In contrast, reclassification of a purchase premium decreases the balance in the Investment account so that it equals the book value of the subsidiary's stockholders' equity.

Purchase Discount: T Partially Owned   The final case of consolidation at date of acquisition involves P and T, with a minority interest present. The entries are familiar by now, so we shall illustrate this case using a consolidated balance sheet working paper. We assume that P has acquired 80 percent ($\alpha =$ .8) of the outstanding voting shares of T Company for stock and cash at a total cost of $832,000. The book value of 80 percent of T's stockholders' equity is $920,000 (= .8 × $1,150,000), implying a purchase discount of $88,000. P records the acquisition as follows:

Exhibit 7.13   Working Paper Entries to Consolidate P and T ($\alpha = 1$; Purchase Discount = $110,000)

CONSOLIDATED FINANCIAL STATEMENT WORKING PAPER

Investment in T	110,000	
Purchase Discount		110,000

To recognize the purchase discount implicit in the Investment in T by
increasing the Investment in T to the book value of T Company's
stockholders' equity.

Marketable Equity Securities—Current	20,000	
Inventory	50,000	
Marketable Equity Securities—Long-Term	100,000	
Buildings and Equipment	35,200	
Land	84,800	
Purchase Discount	110,000	
Other Liabilities		400,000

To allocate the purchase discount related to the acquisition of T
Company among the assets and liabilities of T, in accordance with
Exhibit 7.12 and the second stage of the allocation process applied
to Buildings and Equipment and Land.

Common Stock	250,000	
Additional Paid-In Capital	400,000	
Retained Earnings	500,000	
Investment in T		1,150,000

To eliminate the Investment in T against the stockholders' equity
accounts of T Company.

BOOKS OF P COMPANY

Investment in T	832,000	
Cash		144,000
Common Stock (70,400 × $7.50)		528,000
Additional Paid-In Capital		160,000

To record the acquisition of 80 percent of the
outstanding common stock of T Company. The former
shareholders of T received cash of $96,000 and 70,400
shares of P Company $7.50 par value stock. Net market
value of the P stock issued was $688,000 *after*
deducting registration and issue costs of $16,000,
which were paid in cash and are part of the total
investment cost of $832,000. Additional direct costs
associated with this acquisition were consultants' and
attorneys' fees of $32,000.

The $88,000 purchase discount includes some negative goodwill. Accordingly, the allocation is handled in the two-stage process. Stage one, the analysis of book and fair values of T's assets and liabilities, appears on page 287.

The negative goodwill of $64,000 is now allocated among Buildings and Equipment and Land, the components of T's Plant and Equipment account, in proportion to their relative fair values. This is stage two of the purchase discount allocation process; it also appears on page 287.

Assets and Liabilities of T Company	Fair Value	Book Value	Fair Value Less Book Value	Allocation Based on P's Interest (80%)
Cash and Receivables	$ 150,000	$ 150,000	—	—
Marketable Equity Securities—Current	120,000	100,000	$ 20,000	$ 16,000
Inventory	350,000	300,000	50,000	40,000
Marketable Equity Securities—Long-Term	600,000	500,000	100,000	80,000
Plant and Equipment (Net)	1,600,000	1,400,000	200,000	160,000
Current Liabilities	(500,000)	(500,000)	—	—
Other Liabilities	(1,200,000)	(800,000)	(400,000)	(320,000)
	$1,120,000	$1,150,000	$ (30,000)	$ (24,000)
Negative Goodwill				(64,000)
Total Purchase Discount				$ (88,000)

	(1) Percent of Fair Value	(2) Allocation of Negative Goodwill [(1) × $64,000]	(3) Fair Value − Book Value		(4) Final Allocation [(3) − (2)]
			Total	P's Interest (80%)	
Buildings and Equipment	81%	$51,840	$100,000	$ 80,000	$28,160
Land	19	12,160	100,000	80,000	67,840
Total	100%	$64,000	$200,000	$160,000	$96,000

The consolidation of P and T appears in Exhibit 7.14. P Company's balance sheet data, drawn from those given in Exhibit 7.3, are updated in this exhibit for the acquisition entry just recorded. A formal consolidated balance sheet is shown in Exhibit 7.15.

Consolidated Balance Sheet at Date of Business Combination: Other Issues

Preparation of a consolidated balance sheet at date of business combination is often complicated by some other matters not yet addressed. We briefly discuss several of these in this section.

Dividends of Subsidiary Unpaid at Combination Date   When the parent company acquires the subsidiary's stock *after* a dividend declaration by the subsidiary but *before* the record date for payment, consolidated statements are affected in two ways:

1.   The declared dividends which are attached to ownership of S Company's shares reduce the amount otherwise recorded as Investment in S. The Investment in S account is credited and Dividends Receivable is debited for the amount of the subsidiary's dividends to be received by P. Since the subsidiary's retained earnings has already been decreased by the dividend declaration, the credit to the Investment in S effectively recognizes the reduction in the subsidiary's stockholders' equity by the parent.

Exhibit 7.14   Consolidated Balance Sheet Working Paper

P Company and T Company
Consolidated Balance Sheet Working Paper, January 1, 19X2
($\alpha = .8$; Purchase Discount $= \$88,000$)

			Adjustments and Eliminations			
ASSETS	P Company	T Company		Dr.	Cr.	P and T Consolidated
Cash and Receivables	656,000	150,000				806,000
Marketable Equity Securities—Current . .	—	100,000	(2)	16,000		116,000
Inventory	600,000	300,000	(2)	40,000		940,000
Marketable Equity Securities—Long-Term	—	500,000	(2)	80,000		580,000
Buildings and Equipment	4,000,000	1,200,000	(2)	28,160		5,228,160
Accumulated Depreciation	(1,700,000)	—				(1,700,000)
Land	—	200,000	(2)	67,840		267,840
Investment in T	832,000	—	(1)	88,000	(3) 920,000	—
Purchase Discount . . .	—	—	(2)	88,000	(1) 88,000	—
Total Assets	4,388,000	2,450,000		408,000	1,008,000	6,238,000
LIABILITIES AND STOCKHOLDERS' EQUITY						
Current Liabilities	400,000	500,000				900,000
Other Liabilities	300,000	800,000			(2) 320,000	1,420,000
Common Stock—P . . .	2,028,000	—				2,028,000
Common Stock—T . . .	—	250,000	(3)	250,000		—
APIC—P	1,060,000	—				1,060,000
APIC—T	—	400,000	(3)	400,000		—
Retained Earnings—P	600,000	—				600,000
Retained Earnings—T	—	500,000	(3)	500,000		—
Minority Interest in T . . .	—	—			(3) 230,000	230,000
Total Liabilities and Stockholders' Equity	4,388,000	2,450,000		1,150,000	550,000	6,238,000

Explanations of Working Paper Entries

(1) To recognize the purchase discount implicit in the Investment in T by increasing the Investment in T to 80 percent of the book value of T Company's stockholders' equity.

(2) To allocate the purchase discount related to the acquisition of T Company among the assets and liabilities of T. The amounts allocated to Buildings and Equipment and Land are from the second stage of the allocation process.

(3) To eliminate the Investment in T against 80 percent of the stockholders' equity accounts of T Company and to reclassify the remaining 20 percent of the stockholders' equity of T Company as minority interest.

Exhibit 7.15   Formal Consolidated Balance Sheet for P Company and T Company

P Company and T Company
Consolidated Balance Sheet at January 1, 19X2 ($\alpha = .8$)

ASSETS

Cash and Receivables		$ 806,000
Marketable Equity Securities—Current		116,000
Inventory		940,000
Total Current Assets		$1,862,000
Marketable Equity Securities—Long-Term		$ 580,000
Land		267,840
Buildings and Equipment	$5,228,160	
Less Accumulated Depreciation	(1,700,000)	3,528,160
Total Noncurrent Assets		$4,376,000
Total Assets		$6,238,000

LIABILITIES AND STOCKHOLDERS' EQUITY

Current Liabilities	$ 900,000
Other Liabilities	1,420,000
Total Liabilities	$2,320,000
Minority Interest in T	$ 230,000
Common Stock	2,028,000
Additional Paid-In Capital	1,060,000
Retained Earnings	600,000
Total Stockholders' Equity	$3,918,000
Total Liabilities and Stockholders' Equity	$6,238,000

2.   Establishment of a Dividends Receivable account generates an inter-company relationship with the Dividends Payable account recorded by S. Dividends Receivable is therefore eliminated against the portion of Dividends Payable relating to the shares owned by P on the consolidated balance sheet working paper.

Treasury Stock Held by Subsidiary   We have stressed the point that P's ownership interest in S is determined by the percentage of S's outstanding voting shares owned. Should S Company hold some of its own stock as treasury stock, this amount must be eliminated. This is done in recognition of the fact that treasury stock held by S is of no consequence in a consolidated balance sheet reporting the stockholders' equity of P Company.

The elimination would reflect the "retirement" of these treasury shares. How the shares were accounted for when reacquired affects the specifics of the elimination and readers are referred to any standard text in intermediate accounting for an explanation of the proper treatment.

Goodwill Previously Recorded by Subsidiary   In allocating purchase premiums and discounts among the identifiable assets and liabilities of a subsidiary, any goodwill previously recorded by a subsidiary is to be disregarded. *APBO 16* also states that "an acquiring corporation should not record as a separate asset the goodwill previously recorded by an acquired company."[9] Such goodwill is treated as having a book value and fair value equal to zero. This does not affect the minority interest, which is based on the book value of the subsidiary's stockholders' equity. Rather, the effect is to increase the otherwise determinable purchase premium (or decrease the purchase discount). Only one goodwill caption appears in a consolidated balance sheet, and it relates to the existence of *unspecified* intangible value established by the price paid in the business combination. In a pooling of interests, however, any goodwill recorded by the subsidiary is carried directly to the consolidated balance sheet at its book value.

Investment in Subsidiary Improperly Recorded   A minor technical problem arises if the Investment in S account is erroneously recorded. In a purchase combination, the accountant must ascertain that the investment account correctly measures the fair value of stock and other consideration given in exchange for the shares of S. If the investment account reflects only the book value of S's shares, fair values will not be properly reflected in the consolidated balance sheet.

In contrast, a pooling requires that the book value of S's shares provides the basis for the investment account balance. If the issue of P's shares is recorded at fair value, it is generally impossible to make a clean elimination of the investment account against the stockholders' equity of S. These problems are readily solved simply by recording the appropriate adjusting entry on P Company's books prior to consolidation.

Parent and Subsidiary with Different Fiscal Years   Financial statements of companies to be consolidated need not cover identical fiscal years. *ARB 51* indicates that if the fiscal years end on different dates, the separate statements may be consolidated if the difference is not much greater than three months.[10] If such is the case, the resulting consolidated statements, or the notes thereto, should reflect any intervening events which materially affect the financial position or results of operations of the constituent companies. Should the difference between the closing dates of the separate companies' fiscal years be much more than three months, separate statements conforming to a common fiscal year should be prepared and used in the consolidation.

Summary of Key Concepts	When a business combination takes place as a **stock acquisition,** the acquired company remains as a separate legal entity. A parent/subsidiary relationship is established between these **affiliated corporations.** For reporting purposes, consolidated statements are prepared in order that the financial affairs of two

---

[9]   Accounting Principles Board, *Opinion No. 16*, par. 88; AC § 1091.88.

[10]   Committee on Accounting Procedure, *ARB No. 51*, par. 4; AC § 2051.05.

or more affiliated corporations will be reported as if they were a single **unified economic entity.**

Preparation of consolidated statements requires that the separate statements of the affiliated corporations be brought together for reporting purposes and that the books of the individual affiliates not be disturbed by the consolidation process. The consolidation process entails removing all financial relationships between the affiliates in order that combined assets, liabilities, and revenues and expenses not be overstated. **Eliminating entries** recorded on a working paper specifically designed to facilitate the preparation of consolidated statements remove the various intercompany financial relationships. After the eliminations, the separate statements are combined.

Consolidated statements incorporating wholly-owned subsidiaries should be the same as if the subsidiaries had been merged and their assets and liabilities recorded by the acquiring company as explained in Chapter 6. In parent/subsidiary relationships, the "combining" of the asset and liability balances occurs on the working paper instead of on the books.

Any **purchase premium** or **discount** arising in a purchase stock acquisition is allocated among the identifiable assets and liabilities of the subsidiary. This has the effect of reporting the parent's portion of the subsidiary's assets and liabilities at their fair values. If the investment cost exceeds net fair value of the property acquired, the excess is reported as **goodwill** in the consolidated balance sheet. In contrast, **negative goodwill** is created if net fair value of the property acquired exceeds the investment cost. Negative goodwill is then allocated among the noncurrent assets of the subsidiary, except long-term investments in marketable securities, in accordance with their relative fair values.

If the parent company does not acquire all of the subsidiary's shares in a stock acquisition, the shares not held by the parent represent **minority interest** in the subsidiary's net assets or stockholders' equity. Under the **parent theory of consolidated statements,** minority interest is classified as a noncurrent liability on the balance sheet and is based on a proportional amount of the subsidiary's net assets at **book value.** The **entity theory of consolidated statements,** an alternative view, classifies minority interest as part of consolidated stockholders' equity and assigns it a value based on the price paid by the parent for the stock it acquired. Current practice contains features of both theories, but minority interest is almost always based on the **book value** of the subsidiary's stockholders' equity.

Consolidating a stock acquisition accounted for as a **pooling of interests** is procedurally much simpler. No determination and subsequent allocation of fair values is necessary. The investment account reflects book value of the subsidiary's shares owned and is eliminated directly and cleanly against the subsidiary's stockholders' equity. Book values of the subsidiary's assets and liabilities are then added to the parent's balance sheet in consolidation.

Questions **Q7.1** Consolidated statements are prepared so that the financial affairs of affiliated corporations are reported as a single, unified economic entity under common control. Given this, explain why, in certain situations, the financial affairs of affiliated corporations should *not* be consolidated.

Q7.2   Working paper eliminations are central to the consolidation process and are used in many situations to eliminate double counting. What is meant by double counting, and why must it be eliminated in consolidation?

Q7.3   To simplify the introduction to consolidated statements, we began with a situation in which no differences existed between (1) investment cost and book value of S Company's stockholders' equity and (2) fair values and book values of S Company's identifiable assets and liabilities. Suppose (1) were true and (2) were not. Explain the procedure needed to state S's identifiable assets and liabilities at their fair values in consolidation following a purchase combination.

Q7.4   Explain how a purchase premium *and* negative goodwill could both be present in a business combination.

Q7.5   In Chapter 6, a purchase premium or discount was allocated immediately among the assets and liabilities of S for all purchase combinations except stock acquisitions. Why is the allocation made only on a consolidated statement working paper in the stock acquisition case? Would the results be different if the combination were accounted for as a statutory merger?

Q7.6   Suppose P acquires 90 percent of S Company's stock for $600,000. The book value of S Company's stockholders' equity is $500,000, and all assets and liabilities are fairly valued except land, which is understated by $60,000. Compute the three alternative amounts for valuing minority interest. Which is preferred in practice?

Q7.7   On January 1, 19X8, the net assets of P Company and S Company were $350,000 and $150,000, respectively. On that date, P acquired an 80 percent interest in S for $140,000 cash. One accountant believes that, at date of acquisition, consolidated net assets should be reported as $380,000. Another accountant argues that $385,000 is the correct amount. Explain the basis for the difference of opinion.

Q7.8   P Company acquired 80 percent of S Company's 100,000 outstanding common shares on March 18, 19X2, for $1,700,000. S's board of directors had declared a per share dividend of $1 on February 22, 19X2, payable to holders of record on April 4, 19X2. S Company reported stockholders' equity of $2,000,000 on March 18, 19X2. Compute the amount of the purchase premium. If the investment account is not properly stated at $1,700,000 for purposes of consolidation, give the necessary correcting entry.

Q7.9   S Company reports net assets of $790,000, including goodwill of $70,000, on January 31, 19X5. How much of the $790,000 is reported in consolidated assets if P acquires all of S's outstanding stock in (1) a pooling of interests and (2) a purchase for $720,000.

Q7.10 At a time when P's $5 par value shares were selling for $21 per share, 100,000 shares were exchanged for 80 percent of S Company's outstanding stock. S's stockholders' equity amounted to $2,000,000 on that date. P recorded the stock acquisition as follows:

Investment in S .	1,600,000	
Common Stock .		500,000
Additional Paid-In Capital .		1,100,000

Comment on the above entry and make a correcting entry if needed.

Exercises **E7.1** Below are the condensed balance sheets of P and S at December 31, 19X1. On January 1, 19X2, P acquired 90 percent of the voting shares of S by issuing 15,000 shares of its $1 par value common stock. P's stock is currently selling at $10 in an active over-the-counter market.

	P	S
Various Assets	$1,000,000	$200,000
Liabilities .	$ 200,000	$ 60,000
Common Stock	100,000	30,000
Additional Paid-In Capital	400,000	70,000
Retained Earnings	300,000	40,000
	$1,000,000	$200,000

Required:

1. Give the journal entry to record the business combination as a *purchase* and give the eliminating entry that would be made if a consolidated balance sheet were prepared on January 1. Compute consolidated assets and consolidated retained earnings. Assume that the book values of S's assets and liabilities approximate their fair values.
2. Give the journal entry to record the business combination as a *pooling of interests* and give the eliminating entry that would be made if a consolidated balance sheet were prepared on January 1. Compute consolidated assets and consolidated retained earnings. Assume that S's net assets are undervalued by $10,000.

E7.2 Pluto Company is acquiring shares of Saturn Company's stock. At December 31, 19X3, selected account balances of Saturn are as follows:

Common Stock, Par Value $10	$1,000,000
Additional Paid-In Capital .	300,000
Donated Capital	100,000
Appropriation of Retained Earnings for Contingencies	150,000
Retained Earnings .	350,000
Long-Term Debt	800,000

Required: Give the working paper entry which eliminates the investment account, establishes any purchase premium (discount), and records the minority interest, if appropriate, under each of the following sets of conditions.

1. Pluto acquires all 100,000 shares of Saturn in the open market for $20 a share.
2. Pluto acquires all 100,000 shares of Saturn in the open market for $19 a share.
3. Pluto acquires all 100,000 shares of Saturn in the open market for $16 a share.
4. Pluto acquires 80,000 shares of Saturn in the open market for $20 a share.
5. Pluto acquires 80,000 shares of Saturn in the open market for $19 a share.
6. Pluto acquires 80,000 shares of Saturn in the open market for $16 a share.
7. Pluto acquires 400,000 previously unissued shares directly from Saturn for $20 a share.

E7.3   Refer to the data in E7.2. Pluto and Saturn are now planning a pooling of interests. Pluto's stockholders' equity accounts are given next:

Common Stock, Par Value $5; 2,000,000 Shares Authorized,	
600,000 Issued and Outstanding	$3,000,000
Additional Paid-In Capital	200,000
Retained Earnings	2,200,000
Total Stockholders' Equity	$5,400,000

Required: In each of the following situations, prepare the consolidated stockholders' equity section and include the minority interest where appropriate.

1. Pluto exchanges 200,000 of its shares for all 100,000 shares of Saturn.
2. Pluto exchanges 300,000 of its shares for all 100,000 shares of Saturn.
3. Pluto exchanges 400,000 of its shares for all 100,000 shares of Saturn.
4. Pluto exchanges 200,000 of its shares for 90,000 shares of Saturn.
5. Pluto exchanges 300,000 of its shares for 90,000 shares of Saturn.
6. Pluto exchanges 400,000 of its shares for 90,000 shares of Saturn.

E7.4   Describe the nature of the Minority Interest in Subsidiary account which often appears in consolidated balance sheets. Disagreement exists with respect to (1) the classification of minority interest in the consolidated balance sheet and (2) the measurement or valuation assigned to the minority interest. Discuss the alternative approaches to (1) and (2) and, where possible, match the classification alternatives with their logically consistent measurement alternatives.

E7.5   On January 31, 19X0, Bates, Inc., acquired 90 percent of the outstanding common stock of Wilkens Corporation for $300,000 cash plus 20,000 shares of Bates' $10 par value common stock having a market value of $80 per share. Immediately prior to the acquisition, the trial balances of the two companies were as follows:

Account	Bates	Wilkens
Current Assets	$1,000,000	$200,000
Plant and Equipment, Net	3,500,000	700,000
Current Liabilities	(500,000)	(150,000)
Long-Term Liabilities	(2,000,000)	(300,000)
Common Stock	(300,000)	(100,000)
Additional Paid-In Capital	(600,000)	(50,000)
Retained Earnings	(1,100,000)	(300,000)

The acquisition is to be treated as a purchase. A review of the fair values of Wilkens' assets indicates that current assets are undervalued by $50,000 and plant and equipment is undervalued by $600,000.

Required: Prepare a consolidated balance sheet immediately following the acquisition.

E7.6 Below are condensed balance sheet data for Pitman Company and Stone Company prior to their proposed business combination. Book values of Stone's assets and liabilities approximate their fair values.

ASSETS	Pitman	Stone
Current Assets	$2,000,000	$ 800,000
Noncurrent Assets	4,500,000	1,200,000
Total Assets	$6,500,000	$2,000,000
LIABILITIES AND STOCKHOLDERS' EQUITY		
Liabilities	$2,700,000	$1,200,000
Common Stock (Par Value $1)	500,000	100,000
Additional Paid-In Capital	1,500,000	300,000
Retained Earnings	1,800,000	400,000
Total Liabilities and Stockholders' Equity	$6,500,000	$2,000,000

Required: Assume that Pitman acquires 80,000 shares of Stone for cash of $240,000 and short-term notes payable of $400,000. Prepare a consolidated balance sheet working paper as of the date of the acquisition.

E7.7 Pond Company recently acquired 70 percent of the shares of Stream Corporation for $2,000,000 cash. After the acquisition, the net assets (assets − liabilities) of Pond and Stream had book values of $10,000,000 and $2,500,000, respectively. Fair value of Stream's net assets is $2,600,000.

Required: Compute consolidated net assets, goodwill, and minority interest under each of the following alternatives:
1. The approach used in this book.
2. The entity theory of consolidated statements.
3. The entity theory modified.

E7.8   Stiles Corporation just acquired 80 percent of the outstanding stock of Thom Company by issuing 200,000 shares of its $10 par common stock valued at $10,000,000. Immediately prior to the acquisition, condensed balance sheet data for the two companies appeared as follows:

ASSETS	Stiles	Thom
Current Assets	$45,000,000	$12,000,000
Plant and Equipment, Net	19,000,000	11,000,000
Total Assets	$64,000,000	$23,000,000
LIABILITIES AND STOCKHOLDERS' EQUITY		
Liabilities	$24,000,000	$ 8,000,000
Common Stock (Par Value $10)	5,000,000	1,000,000
Additional Paid-In Capital	20,000,000	4,000,000
Retained Earnings	15,000,000	10,000,000
Total Liabilities and Stockholders' Equity	$64,000,000	$23,000,000

Although Thom's plant and equipment was fairly stated, Thom's current assets and liabilities had fair values of $13,000,000 and $12,000,000, respectively.

Required: Prepare a consolidated balance sheet for Stiles and Thom immediately after the acquisition.

E7.9   Refer to the data in P6.4 in Chapter 6. Assume that Plastic acquired 80 percent of Steel's outstanding stock for $90,000. Other direct cash costs incurred in the acquisition amounted to $15,000.

Required: Prepare a schedule allocating the purchase premium or discount, and compute the minority interest in Steel at December 31, 19X3.

Problems   P7.1   **Consolidated Balance Sheet Working Paper—Purchase Premium**   Pearson Corporation and Saunders Corporation have entered negotiations leading to a possible business combination. At December 31, 19X4, Saunders' condensed balance sheet was as follows:

Saunders Corporation
Balance Sheet at December 31, 19X4

ASSETS	
Cash	$ 50,000
Receivables, Net	300,000
Inventories	1,600,000
Prepayments	47,000
Noncurrent Assets, Net	2,003,000
Total Assets	$4,000,000

LIABILITIES AND STOCKHOLDERS' EQUITY

Current Liabilities	$2,200,000
Common Stock, Par Value $100	1,000,000
Retained Earnings	800,000
Total Liabilities and Stockholders' Equity	$4,000,000

During the negotiations, it was determined that the fair value of Saunders' noncurrent assets, net of accumulated depreciation, approximated $3,203,000. Initially, Pearson offered to acquire all of Saunders' stock for $3,000,000. Forty percent of Saunders' stockholders objected, however, because they felt that the purchase price should reflect about $500,000 in goodwill. Ultimately, Pearson acquired 60 percent of Saunders' outstanding stock for $300 per share.

After the acquisition was completed on December 31, 19X4, a balance sheet was prepared for Pearson.

Pearson Corporation
Balance Sheet at December 31, 19X4

ASSETS

Cash	$ 5,200,000
Receivables, Net	2,400,000
Inventories	11,200,000
Prepayments	422,000
Investment in Saunders	1,800,000
Noncurrent Assets, Net	18,978,000
Total Assets	$40,000,000

LIABILITIES AND STOCKHOLDERS' EQUITY

Current Liabilities	$ 9,487,000
Common Stock, Par Value $100	10,000,000
Retained Earnings	20,513,000
Total Liabilities and Stockholders' Equity	$40,000,000

Required:

1. Prepare a consolidated balance sheet working paper at December 31, 19X4.
2. Prepare a formal consolidated balance sheet at December 31, 19X4.

(AICPA adapted)

P7.2   **Preparation of Consolidated Balance Sheet—Purchase Premium**   On June 30, 19X3, Paul Corporation acquired for cash of $19 per share all of the outstanding voting common stock of Sand Corporation. Both companies continued to operate as separate entities. After closing the nominal accounts, Sand's condensed balance sheet on June 30, 19X3, was as follows:

Sand Corporation
Balance Sheet at June 30, 19X3

ASSETS

Cash	$ 700,000
Accounts Receivable, Net	600,000
Inventories	1,400,000
Property, Plant, and Equipment, Net	3,300,000
Other Assets	500,000
Total Assets	$6,500,000

LIABILITIES AND STOCKHOLDERS' EQUITY

Current Liabilities	$ 700,000
Long-Term Debt	2,600,000
Other Liabilities	200,000
Common Stock, Par Value $1	1,000,000
Additional Paid-In Capital	400,000
Retained Earnings	1,600,000
Total Liabilities and Stockholders' Equity	$6,500,000

On June 30, 19X3, Sand's assets and liabilities having fair values different than the book values were as follows:

	Fair Value
Property, Plant, and Equipment, Net	$16,400,000
Other Assets	200,000
Long-Term Debt	2,200,000

The amount paid by Paul in excess of the fair value of the net assets of Sand is attributable to expected future earnings of Sand.

Paul's balance sheet immediately *after* the acquisition appears next:

Paul Corporation
Balance Sheet at June 30, 19X3

ASSETS

Cash	$ 3,500,000
Accounts Receivable, Net	1,400,000
Inventories	1,000,000
Property, Plant, and Equipment, Net	2,000,000
Investment in Sand	19,000,000
Other Assets	100,000
Total Assets	$27,000,000

LIABILITIES AND STOCKHOLDERS' EQUITY

Current Liabilities	$ 1,500,000
Long-Term Debt	4,000,000
Other Liabilities	750,000
Common Stock, Par Value $1	10,000,000
Additional Paid-In Capital	5,000,000
Retained Earnings	5,750,000
Total Liabilities and Stockholders' Equity	$27,000,000

Required:
1. Prepare a schedule to determine and allocate the purchase premium.
2. Give the eliminating entries that would appear on a consolidated balance sheet working paper.
3. Prepare a formal consolidated balance sheet for Paul Corporation and Sand Corporation at June 30, 19X3.

(AICPA adapted)

P7.3 **Consolidated Balance Sheet—Partially-Owned Subsidiary and Negative Goodwill**   On December 31, 19X2, Paxon Corporation acquired 100 percent of the outstanding common stock of Saxon Company for $1,800,000 cash. The balance sheets of Paxon and Saxon, immediately *prior* to the combination, are now shown:

Balance Sheets at December 31, 19X2
(Precombination)

ASSETS		Paxon	Saxon
Cash and Receivables		$2,860,000	$ 720,000
Inventory		1,700,000	900,000
Marketable Equity Securities—Long-Term		—	300,000
Land		650,000	175,000
Buildings and Equipment . . .	$3,400,000		
Less Accumulated Depreciation . .	(1,000,000)	2,400,000	600,000 (net)
Total Assets		$7,610,000	$2,695,000
LIABILITIES AND STOCKHOLDERS' EQUITY			
Current Liabilities		$1,500,000	$1,000,000
Long-Term Debt		2,000,000	400,000
Common Stock, Par Value $1 . .		500,000	100,000
Additional Paid-In Capital . . .		1,200,000	350,000
Retained Earnings		2,410,000	845,000
Total Liabilities and Stockholders' Equity . .		$7,610,000	$2,695,000

Several of Saxon's assets and liabilities had fair values different from their book values. Estimates of the fair values of these items follow:

Account	Estimated Fair Value
Inventory	$1,000,000
Marketable Equity Securities—Long-Term	250,000
Land	420,000
Buildings and Equipment, Net	900,000
Long-Term Debt	(290,000)

Required:
1. Prepare a consolidated balance sheet at December 31, 19X2.
2. Prepare a consolidated balance sheet assuming that Paxon paid $1,620,000 for a 90 percent interest in Saxon.

P7.4 **Allocation of Purchase Discount and Negative Goodwill** Refer to the data in P7.3. Assume that Paxon paid $1,000,000 for an 80 percent interest in Saxon. Give the final allocation of the purchase premium or discount. Show all calculations.

P7.5 **Consolidated Balance Sheet Working Paper—Purchase Discount** Following a period of protracted negotiations, Penn Company and Stark Company have agreed on terms for a business combination, scheduled to occur on January 2, 19X6. On that date, the following condensed precombination balance sheet data are prepared:

		Stark Company	
ASSETS	Penn Co.	Book Value	Fair Value
Cash and Receivables	$ 8,000,000	$1,000,000	$ 900,000
Inventories	10,000,000	3,000,000	3,200,000
Plant Assets, Net	12,000,000	5,000,000	4,500,000
Investment in Bonds	1,000,000	500,000	300,000
Total Assets	$31,000,000	$9,500,000	
LIABILITIES AND STOCKHOLDERS' EQUITY			
Current Liabilities	$ 6,000,000	$2,500,000	2,500,000
Noncurrent Liabilities	8,000,000	3,000,000	(Note)
Common Stock, Par Value $10 . . .	4,000,000	1,000,000	—
Retained Earnings	13,000,000	3,000,000	—
Total Liabilities and Stockholders' Equity . . .	$31,000,000	$9,500,000	

Note: Noncurrent liabilities of Stark include $2,000,000 of bonds payable and $1,000,000 accrued pension liability. At January 2, 19X6, Stark's pension fund had assets of $500,000; the present value of vested benefits was $2,500,000.

Required: Assuming that Penn acquired all the outstanding stock of Stark for a cash payment of $3,500,000, prepare a consolidated balance sheet working paper as of January 2, 19X6.

P7.6 **Consolidated Balance Sheet Working Paper; Purchase Discount, Minority Interest** Refer to the data in P7.5. Assume that Penn acquired 80 percent of Stark's outstanding stock for a cash payment of $3,000,000 and that the fair value of Stark's Plant Assets is $6,500,000.

Required: Prepare a consolidated balance sheet working paper as of January 2, 19X6.

P7.7 **Consolidated Balance Sheet Working Paper; Purchase Premium, Minority Interest** Placid Corporation acquired 70 percent of the outstanding stock of Stagnant Company on June 30, 19X0, by issuing 100,000 shares of its $1 par value common stock valued at $41.80 per share. Direct cash costs associated with the acquisition were $35,000, and the cost of registering and issuing the stock was $20,000. On June 15, 19X0, Stagnant's board of directors had declared $80,000 of cash dividends on its common stock to holders of record on July 15, 19X0, and recorded a liability for that amount. Condensed balance sheet data for the two companies immediately *prior* to the combination are given:

		Stagnant Company	
ASSETS	Placid Corp.	Book Value	Fair Value
Cash and Receivables	$ 8,000,000	$2,000,000	$1,800,000
Marketable Equity Securities, Current . .	—	600,000	1,000,000
Inventory	7,000,000	2,400,000	2,600,000
Plant Assets, Net	10,000,000	3,600,000	3,600,000
Copyrights	1,000,000	200,000	2,000,000
Goodwill	—	500,000	100,000
Total Assets	$26,000,000	$9,300,000	
LIABILITIES AND STOCKHOLDERS' EQUITY			
Current Liabilities	$ 6,000,000	$2,000,000	2,000,000
Noncurrent Liabilities	4,000,000	3,300,000	3,000,000
Common Stock, Par Value $1	100,000	100,000	—
Additional Paid-In Capital	900,000	400,000	—
Retained Earnings	15,000,000	3,500,000	—
Total Liabilities and Stockholders' Equity	$26,000,000	$9,300,000	

Required: Prepare a consolidated balance sheet working paper as of June 30, 19X0, for Placid and Stagnant.

P7.8 **Consolidated Balance Sheet; Pooling of Interests**   Refer to the data in P7.7. Assume that Placid exchanged 100,000 shares of its $1 par value common stock for 90 percent of Stagnant's outstanding capital stock in a business combination qualifying as a pooling of interests. Other data in P7.7 are unchanged.

Required: Prepare a consolidated balance sheet for the two companies as of June 30, 19X0.

Chapter 8

Consolidated Financial Statements after Date of Business Combination

We indicated in the last chapter that once a company acquires a controlling interest in a subsidiary, the preparation of consolidated financial statements generally follows. Consolidated statements were introduced in Chapter 7 under the assumption that a consolidated balance sheet is prepared on the effective date of a business combination. After that date, however, the full range of financial statements must be prepared at the regular reporting intervals. Thus the passage of time requires that consolidated statements of income, retained earnings, and changes in financial position be generated. Furthermore, subsequent consolidated balance sheets must reflect the financial activities of the affiliated companies since the combination occurred.

The presentation of consolidated financial statements is a *reporting requirement* and not an *accounting requirement* (recall that eliminations are made on working papers only). For accounting purposes, however, the Investment in Subsidiary is an intercorporate investment. Preparation of postcombination consolidated financial statements is influenced not only by transactions among the affiliates but also by the method the parent company uses to account for the Investment in Subsidiary on its books. We begin the chapter with a brief review of accounting for intercorporate investments and marketable equity securities before concentrating on the equity method used in most parent/subsidiary relationships. We then introduce the preparation of consolidated statements of income, retained earnings, and changes in financial position and end the chapter with a discussion of certain issues in accounting for income taxes which are germane to these subjects.

Accounting for Intercorporate Investments

Accounting for marketable equity securities carried as current assets is subject to the provisions of *SFAS 12* (AC § 5132).[1] The *Statement* also covers the accounting for marketable equity securities carried as noncurrent assets when the investor company owns a small portion—generally less than 20 percent—of the voting shares of the investee. The accounting for other nonconsolidated intercorporate investments follows the rules set down in *APBO 18* (AC § 5131).[2] According to *APBO 18*, ownership of 20 percent or more of the voting shares of an investee leads to the presumption that the investor may exercise significant influence over the affairs of the investee. Absent evidence refuting the ability of an investor to significantly influence or control an investee, the *Opinion* requires that the *equity method* be used to account for such intercorporate investments. *IFAS 35* lists five examples of factors which, if present, may overcome the presumption that ownership of 20 percent or more of an investee's stock is sufficient for the investor to exercise significant influence.[3]

1. Opposition by the investee, in the form of litigation or complaints to regulatory agencies, which challenge the investor's influence.

2. Agreements between investor and investee in which the investor relinquishes significant stockholder rights.

3. Majority ownership of the investee concentrated among a few stockholders who control the investee and severely limit the investor's influence.

4. The investor thwarted in its attempts to obtain information, not generally available to stockholders, which is needed to apply the equity method.

5. The investor unable to obtain representation on the investee's board of directors.

As previously indicated, ownership of more than 50 percent of the investee's shares generally invokes the reporting requirement for presentation of consolidated statements. Because of this, the parent company has the option of accounting for its subsidiary investment with either the *equity method* or an alternative known as the *cost method*. Strictly speaking, however, neither method is an accounting requirement when consolidated statements are presented. A flowchart summarizing these matters appears in Figure 8.1.

As we shall see, the method used by an investor company to account for intercorporate investments has no effect on consolidated financial statements, although it does affect the *procedures* required to prepare these statements. For this reason, parent companies which consolidate their subsidiaries sometimes use the cost method to account for intercorporate investments which are to be consolidated, even though the equity method is otherwise required by *APBO 18*.

---

[1] Financial Accounting Standards Board, *Statement of Financial Accounting Standards No. 12,* "Accounting for Certain Marketable Securities" (Stamford, Conn.: FASB, 1975).

[2] Accounting Principles Board, *Opinion No. 18,* "The Equity Method of Accounting for Investments in Common Stock" (N.Y.: AICPA, 1971).

[3] Financial Accounting Standards Board, *Interpretation of Financial Accounting Standards No. 35,* "Criteria for Applying the Equity Method of Accounting for Investments in Common Stock" (Stamford, Conn.: FASB, 1981), par. 4.

Figure 8.1   Accounting for Intercorporate Investments

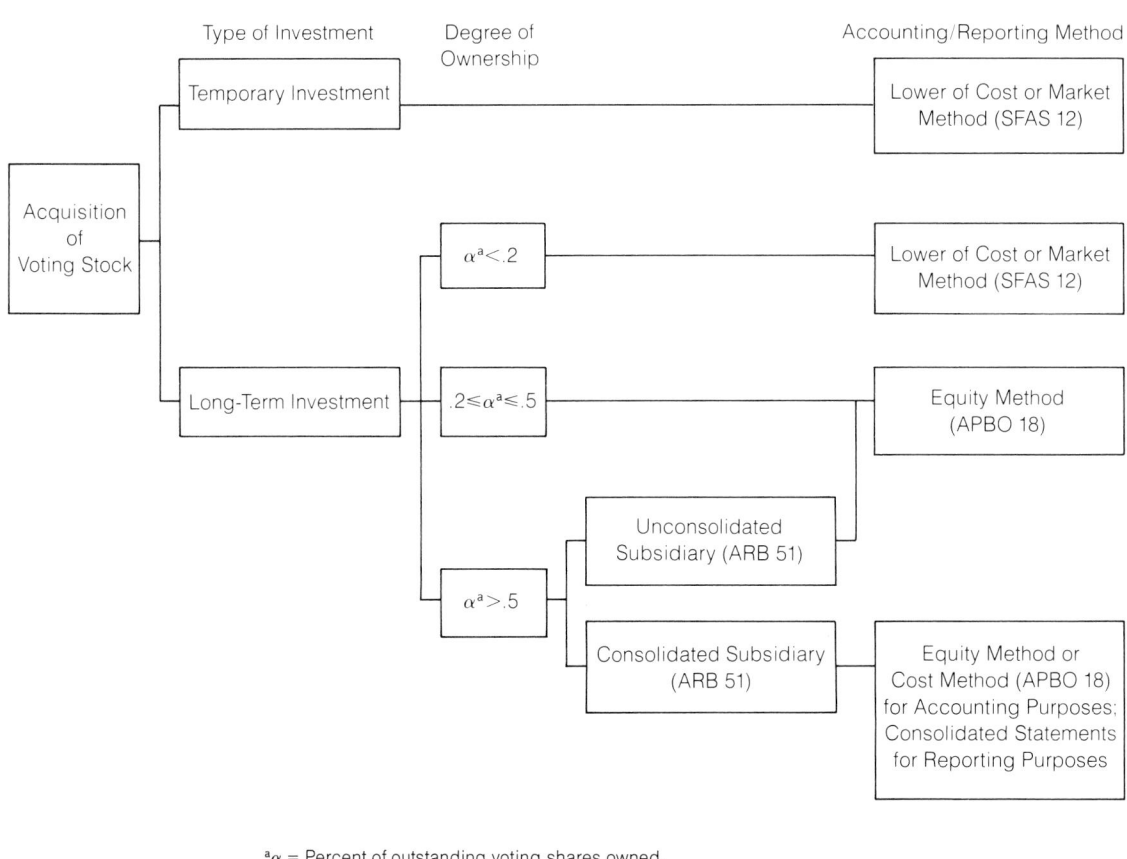

ᵃα = Percent of outstanding voting shares owned.

Since most parent companies which consolidate their subsidiaries use the equity method, it is emphasized throughout this book. Moreover, the parent company *must* use the equity method to account for its subsidiaries if it issues separate (unconsolidated) parent company statements. We do not, however, completely ignore the cost method. As we review the equity method in the next section, we contrast it with the cost method and, later in this chapter, we provide a comprehensive illustration of consolidation when the cost method is being used by the parent company.

The Equity Method

Under the **equity method of accounting for intercorporate investments,** the parent increases (decreases) the Investment in S account for its share of the subsidiary's earnings (loss), and decreases the account by its share of the subsidiary's dividends. If there is no purchase premium or discount and there are no intercompany gains or losses, application of the equity method simply means that the Investment in S account changes as the retained earnings of the subsidiary changes. Assuming no capital changes in the subsidiary's stockholders' equity, the balance in the investment account moves in tandem with the book value of the subsidiary's shares owned.

Unfortunately, such a simple, straightforward situation seldom prevails because application of the equity method is viewed as a **one-line consolidation.** Those events—amortization of purchase premium or discount and intercompany gains and losses—which must be dealt with in consolidation must also be reflected in the parent's application of the equity method. *APBO 18* makes this quite clear:

> The difference between consolidation and the equity method lies in the details reported in the financial statements. Thus an investor's net income for the period and its stockholders' equity at the end of the period are the same whether an investment in a subsidiary is accounted for under the equity method or the subsidiary is consolidated. [4]

Some of the complicating factors will not appear until later chapters. Nevertheless, proper application of the equity method actually *facilitates* the consolidation procedure because the parent must deal with many consolidation issues when it records its share of the subsidiary's periodic income or loss.

The Cost Method

The equity method need not be used by a parent company to account for subsidiaries which are to be consolidated. It becomes a factor in financial statements *only* when intercorporate investments of 20 percent or more are *not* consolidated. Because of this, some parent companies use the **cost method of accounting for intercorporate investments** which are to be consolidated. Under the cost method, the balance in the Investment in S account generally remains constant unless additional shares are bought or sold. Income is recorded by the parent only when dividends are declared by the subsidiary and only to the extent of the parent's share of those dividends. Accordingly, there is no relationship between the balance in P's investment account and changes in the book value of P's share of S Company's stockholders' equity. An exception arises when the subsidiary distributes dividends in excess of its earnings since the parent's acquisition by purchase (not pooling). Such dividends represent a return of capital and are credited to the investment account rather than being accounted for as income.

When consolidation occurs, however, it becomes necessary to make working paper entries which update P's investment account to reflect changes in S Company's stockholders' equity since date of combination in order that clean eliminations can be made. A **clean elimination** can be made when the balance in the investment account is equal to the dollar amount of S Company's stockholders' equity owned by P plus (minus) any unamortized purchase premium (discount).

Comparing the Cost and Equity Methods

The essence of the cost and equity methods can be grasped by working through a simple example. On January 1, 19X1, P acquires 90 percent of S Company's outstanding voting stock for $900,000 cash. The total book value of S Company's stockholders' equity is $1,000,000—P's share is $900,000—and the book values of S's assets and liabilities equal their fair values. The condensed stockholders' equity section of S Company follows:

---

[4] Accounting Principles Board, *Opinion No. 18*, par. 19; AC § 5131.19.

S Company
Stockholders' Equity at January 1, 19X1

Common Stock	$ 100,000
Additional Paid-In Capital	400,000
Retained Earnings	500,000
Total Stockholders' Equity	$1,000,000

During the year, S Company reports net income of $80,000 and pays dividends of $30,000 on June 30, 19X1. Rather than debiting Retained Earnings for the dividends, S Company debits a Dividends account which effectively reduces retained earnings. Thus at December 31, 19X1, S Company's retained earnings of $550,000 consist of:

Retained Earnings, January 1, 19X1	$500,000
Dividends	(30,000)
Net Income	80,000
Retained Earnings, December 31, 19X1	$550,000

The journal entries made on P Company's books, and the eliminating entries made on the working paper under the two methods appear in Exhibit 8.1. Note that when S Company's dividends are eliminated, the credit is to *Dividends — S*, rather than to Retained Earnings—S, January 1, 19X1. Furthermore, S Company's revenues and expenses are not eliminated; they flow into consolidated net income.

Before proceeding, we wish to clarify the elimination of intercompany dividends and P's share of S's net income illustrated in Exhibit 8.1. This is done in order to avoid *double counting*. When we consolidate the income statements of P and S, we add them together. Under the cost method, P's separate income statement includes dividend income from S, while under the equity method, P's separate income statement reflects P's share of S's net income. If we summed the income statements without eliminating these intercompany income components, they would be counted twice, once through inclusion in P's net income and again in S's net income. This process can be visualized by studying the diagram in Figure 8.2.

When the equity method is used, elimination of the entries recorded by P during the year adjusts the investment account to its balance at the *beginning* of the year. Assuming that retained earnings is the only component of S's stockholders' equity to have changed during the year, we can eliminate the investment account against S Company's beginning-of-year stockholders' equity. The change in S Company's retained earnings during the current year will be reflected in consolidated retained earnings and in the minority interest. The last working paper entry in Exhibit 8.1 records the minority's share of the current year change in S Company's retained earnings. It establishes the *Minority Interest in Net Income*, eliminates the minority's share of S Company's dividends, and shows the difference as the change in the minority interest during the current year. At consolidation points more than one year after date of business combination, an additional working paper entry will be necessary under

Exhibit 8.1   Cost and Equity Methods Compared

	Cost Method		Equity Method	
BOOKS OF P COMPANY	Dr.	Cr.	Dr.	Cr.
1/1/X1				
Investment in S	900,000		900,000	
Cash		900,000		900,000
To record the acquisition of 90 percent of S Company's stock for $900,000.				
6/30/X1				
Cash	27,000		—	
Dividend Income		27,000		—
Cash	—		27,000	
Investment in S		—		27,000
To record the receipt of $27,000 (= .9 × $30,000) of dividends from S Company.				
12/31/X1				
Investment in S	No entry		72,000	
Income from S				72,000
To record P's share of S's net income; $72,000 (= .9 × $80,000).				

	Dr.	Cr.	Dr.	Cr.
CONSOLIDATED FINANCIAL STATEMENT WORKING PAPER				
Dividend Income	27,000		—	
Dividends—S		27,000		—
To eliminate intercompany dividends received from S Company.				
Income from S			72,000	
Dividends—S		—		27,000
Investment in S		—		45,000
To eliminate P's share of S's net income and intercompany dividends thereby adjusting the Investment in S account to its beginning-of-year balance.				
Common Stock—S	100,000		100,000	
Additional Paid-In Capital—S	400,000		400,000	
Retained Earnings—S, January 1, 19X1	500,000		500,000	
Investment in S		900,000		900,000
Minority Interest in S		100,000		100,000
To eliminate the Investment in S against 90 percent of S Company's stockholders' equity at the beginning of the year and reclassify the remaining 10 percent as minority interest.				
Minority Interest in Net Income	8,000		8,000	
Dividends—S		3,000		3,000
Minority Interest in S		5,000		5,000
To establish the change in minority interest during the current year —the minority's share of S's net income less dividends paid by S Company to the minority; $8,000 (= .1 × $80,000).				

Figure 8.2   Diagrammatic Approach to Consolidating the Income Statements of P and S When P Uses the Equity Method

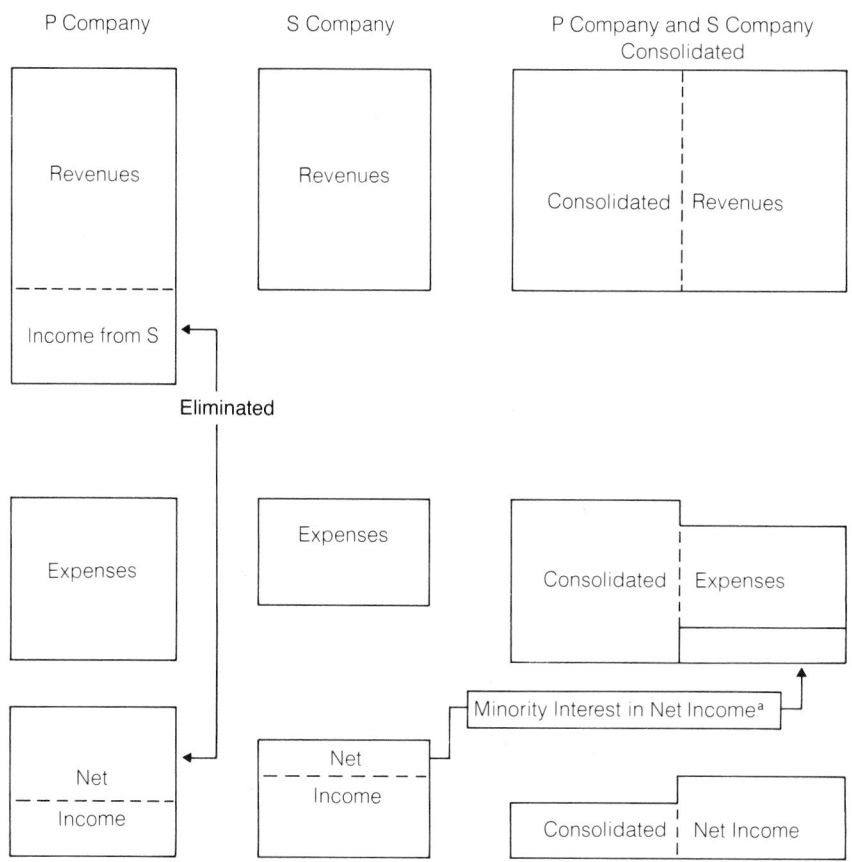

[a]If P owns 100 percent of the outstanding voting shares of S, then P's income from S and S's net income are the same, and there is no minority interest in net income.

the cost method to permit a clean elimination. The purpose of this entry is to adjust the investment account to the equity basis. Without such an entry, a discrepancy will exist between S's stockholders' equity, which has changed since acquisition, and the investment account, which has not changed.

Amortization of Purchase Premium (Discount)

In a purchase combination, the fair value of the consideration given for S Company's shares establishes the postcombination accounting basis of the underlying net assets and liabilities of S Company. The allocation of a purchase premium or discount to depreciable or amortizable assets or liabilities determines the amounts to be depreciated or amortized in subsequent consolidated financial statements. We now discuss this problem within the context of a purchase premium.

Suppose that the acquisition of S by P resulted in a purchase premium attributed entirely to goodwill. *APBO 17* (AC § 5141.29) requires that goodwill be amortized by the straight-line method over a period of forty years or less.[5] Furthermore, *APBO 18* provides "a difference between the cost of an investment and the amount of underlying equity in net assets of an investee should be accounted for as if the investee were a consolidated subsidiary."[6] Therefore, the amortization of goodwill arising in a business combination must be reflected by P Company when it records its share of S Company's net income under the equity method. This is done by reducing the amount of S's income which otherwise would be accrued under the equity method by the amount of the goodwill amortization. Note, however, that no separate account for the goodwill appears on P's balance sheet and no separate expense account for goodwill amortization appears on P's income statement. Rather, the unamortized goodwill is shown separately as an asset only on the consolidated balance sheet, and the periodic amortization expense is reported only on the consolidated income statement. The working paper entry we make to allocate a purchase premium places the goodwill on the consolidated balance sheet. Another working paper entry is required to record the periodic amortization.

These principles are easily extended to cases in which the purchase premium allocation is more complex. Assume that P acquires a 90 percent interest in S on January 1, 19X1, for $1,200,000 cash. The stockholders' equity of S amounts to $1,000,000. Determination of the amount and allocation of the purchase premium is given in Exhibit 8.2, which shows that the purchase premium is allocated to inventory, buildings and equipment, and goodwill. Assume that these costs expire as follows:

1. The inventory is sold during 19X1.
2. Depreciation of buildings and equipment is straight-line, based on an average remaining life of fifteen years.
3. Goodwill is amortized on the straight-line basis over forty years.

Consolidation at End of First Year: Equity Method Used by Parent

During 19X1, S Company realizes net income of $350,000 and pays dividends of $100,000. As in the earlier illustration, S Company's dividends are debited to a Dividends account rather than to retained earnings. To simplify the mechanics of applying the equity method, we use a schedule to determine the net amount of equity method income to be recorded by P. In this way, we keep the number of entries to a minimum.

Schedule to Determine the Equity Method Accrual for the Year Ended December 31, 19X1	
P's Share of S's Net Income (.9 × $350,000)	$315,000
Less Amortization of Purchase Premium:	
Sale of Revalued Inventory	$ 45,000
Additional Depreciation ($180,000/15)	12,000
Amortization of Goodwill ($75,000/40)	1,875
Total Amortization	$ 58,875
Net Equity Method Accrual for 19X1	$256,125

---

[5] Accounting Principles Board, *Opinion No. 17*, "Intangible Assets" (N.Y.: AICPA, 1970), par. 29.

[6] Accounting Principles Board, *Opinion No. 18*, par. 196; AC § 5131.196.

Exhibit 8.2   Determination and Allocation of the Purchase Premium Paid by P in its 90 Percent Acquisition of S

P Company and S Company
Schedule for Determining and Allocating Purchase Premium
Arising in the Stock Acquisition on January 1, 19X1 ($\alpha = .9$)

Cost of the Acquisition	$1,200,000
Book Value of the Net Assets or Stockholders' Equity Acquired (90%) . . .	900,000
Purchase Premium	$ 300,000

Assets and Liabilities of S Company	Fair Value	Book Value	Fair Value Less Book Value	Allocation Based on P's Interest (90%)
Cash and Receivables . .	$ 300,000	$ 300,000	—	—
Inventory	450,000	400,000	$ 50,000	$ 45,000
Buildings and Equipment				
(Net)	1,000,000	800,000	200,000	180,000
Land	200,000	200,000	—	—
Liabilities	(700,000)	(700,000)	—	—
	$1,250,000	$1,000,000	$250,000	$225,000
Goodwill				75,000
Total Purchase Premium				$300,000

Exhibit 8.3 on pages 312–313 presents the entries made by P Company during 19X1 under the equity method and the related working paper eliminations. The working paper eliminations are numbered to tie-in with the completed working paper appearing in Exhibit 8.4 on pages 314–315.

Consolidated Statements of Income and Retained Earnings

The objectives of consolidated statements of income and retained earnings are to report consolidated net income and the changes in consolidated retained earnings. Both statements focus on those amounts relevant to the *controlling interest*, the shareholders of P Company. Indeed, when the equity method is used, consolidated net income equals the net income of P Company, and consolidated retained earnings equals P Company's retained earnings.

These interpretations of consolidated net income and retained earnings follow from the *parent theory of consolidated statements* by reason of their emphasis on the controlling interest. Under the *entity theory*, consolidated net income and retained earnings include the minority interest and relate to all shareholders of P and S, not just the majority. We support the emphasis on the controlling interest derived from the parent theory because it is consistent with current accounting practices and with the historical rationale for consolidated statements. Therefore, we offer the following definitions.

> **Consolidated net income** is the net income of P and S attributable to the stockholders of P and, as such, includes the net income of P Company from its own operations plus P's share of S Company's net income, after adjustments for unconfirmed gains and losses on intercompany transactions and for amortization of any purchase premium or discount.
>
> **Consolidated retained earnings** consist of P Company's retained earnings at date of business combination, increased (decreased) by consolidated net income (loss) in subsequent periods and decreased by dividends paid by P Company to its shareholders. In a pooling of interests, consolidated retained earnings also include any retained earnings of the subsidiary recorded by P when the pooling took place.

Consolidated Financial Statement Working Paper

All but the simplest consolidation situations require a systematic approach to the preparation of consolidated statements; otherwise the mechanics become unmanageable. An appropriately designed working paper provides such a systematic approach. A working paper incorporating the format of the consolidated financial statements to be prepared offers some clear advantages. One alternative is to use a trial balance working paper. (An example of this format appears later in the chapter, where consolidation under the cost method is illustrated.) Regardless of the working paper format selected, however, the working paper entries are basically the same.

The consolidated financial statement working paper is organized to accommodate the income statement, statement of retained earnings, and balance sheet data. It is not used for preparation of the consolidated statement of changes in financial position, which is derived from comparative consolidated balance sheets and the consolidated statements of income and retained earnings. An example of our consolidated financial statement working paper is given in Exhibit 8.4. It has been completely filled out and incorporates the information from our last example. Since this working paper format will be used again and again, spend the time necessary to become thoroughly familiar with it now. The last line of the working paper—total debits and credits—summarizes the adjustments and eliminations related to balance sheet accounts. Entries affecting the income statement and retained earnings statement accounts are reflected on the balance sheet in the Retained Earnings line.

There are four aspects of the consolidated financial statement working paper which we mention in order to link it to the working paper entries presented in Exhibits 8.1 and 8.3:

1. Consistent with our earlier discussion, since the statement of retained earnings discloses dividends declared or paid, we have *separate captions for the dividends of both companies,* which decrease (are debited to) retained earnings. Therefore, when P's share of S's dividends—the intercompany dividends—is eliminated and when the minority's share of S's dividends is charged to the minority interest, the credits are to Dividends—S rather than to Retained Earnings—S.

2. The income statement portion of the working paper has no Cost of Goods Sold caption. Rather, it includes captions for the components of cost of goods sold—*Beginning Inventory* plus *Purchases* less *Ending*

Exhibit 8.3 P Company's Equity Method Journal Entries and Related Working Paper Entries
For the Year Ended December 31, 19X1 ($\alpha = .9$)

BOOKS OF P COMPANY

Investment in S	1,200,000	
Cash		1,200,000

To record the acquisition of 90 percent of S Company's
outstanding voting shares for $1,200,000 cash.

Cash	90,000	
Investment in S		90,000

To record receipt of dividends from S Company.

Investment in S	256,125	
Income from S		256,125

To record P's share of S's net income for 19X1, $315,000, less
amortization of purchase premium amounting to $58,875.

CONSOLIDATED FINANCIAL STATEMENT WORKING PAPER

(1)

Income from S	256,125	
Dividends—S.		90,000
Investment in S		166,125

To eliminate the equity method entries recorded by P, thereby
adjusting the investment account to its balance on January 1,
19X1.

(2)

Common Stock—S	100,000	
Additional Paid-In Capital—S	400,000	
Retained Earnings—S, January 1, 19X1	500,000	
Purchase Premium	300,000	
Investment in S		1,200,000
Minority Interest in S		100,000

To reclassify the purchase premium, eliminate the Investment in S
against 90 percent of the stockholders' equity of S, and reclassify
the remaining stockholders' equity as minority interest, all as of
January 1, 19X1.

Inventory. Allocation of a purchase premium to Inventory at January 1,
19X1—for inventory assumed sold during the year—has the desired
effect of increasing the cost of goods sold. The advantage of this breakdown will become clear in the next chapter as we address intercompany transactions involving merchandise.

3. Our *Operating Expenses caption* includes depreciation and amortization expense. Thus we debit operating expenses for the amount of extra
depreciation and amortization expense resulting from the purchase
premium.

4. The Capital Stock captions reflect *total* paid-in capital—par value of
common stock plus additional paid-in capital. When the investment account is eliminated against the stockholders' equity of S and the minor-

Exhibit 8.3 *continued*

(3)

Inventory, Balance Sheet .	45,000	
Buildings and Equipment (Net)	180,000	
Goodwill .	75,000	
Purchase Premium		300,000

To allocate the purchase premium to the assets of S Company and goodwill as of January 1, 19X1.

(4)

Inventory, December 31, Income Statement (or Cost of Goods Sold) .	45,000	
Depreciation Expense	12,000	
Amortization Expense	1,875	
Inventory, Balance Sheet .		45,000
Accumulated Depreciation		12,000
Goodwill .		1,875

To recognize current year amortization of the purchase premium in the consolidated income statement for 19X1.

(5)

Minority Interest in Net Income	35,000	
Dividends—S .		10,000
Minority Interest in S .		25,000

To record the change in the minority interest during 19X1, consisting of the minority's interest in net income decreased by S Company's dividends paid to minority shareholders.

ity interest is established, the debit to Capital Stock—S on the working paper serves to remove both components of paid-in capital.

Consolidating a Pooling of Interests   Recall that in a pooling of interests, the Investment in S account reflects the *book value* of S Company's net assets. Furthermore, the assets and liabilities of S Company are brought into the consolidated balance sheet at their book values. Application of the equity method by P Company is therefore not complicated by the need to amortize a purchase premium or discount, as there is none.

Consolidation procedures in a pooling differ from those we have described only in that the working paper entries made to reclassify, allocate, and amortize a purchase discount or premium are not used. The working paper entries to eliminate the equity method accrual, intercompany dividends, and the investment account and to establish the minority interest continue to be central to the consolidation process.

Consolidation in Subsequent Years: Equity Method Used by Parent

Use of the equity method simplifies the consolidation process in later years because the Investment in S account continues to reflect (1) the book value of P's equity interest in S and (2) any unamortized purchase premium or discount. At each consolidation point we accomplish the following:

Exhibit 8.4   P Company and S Company: Consolidated Financial Statement Working Paper

Consolidated Financial Statement Working Paper
for the Year Ended December 31, 19X1
(Equity Method)

	P Company	S Company (90%)	Adjustments and Eliminations Dr.		Adjustments and Eliminations Cr.		Consolidated
INCOME STATEMENT							
Sales and Other Revenue . .	1,960,000	1,300,000					3,260,000
Income from S	256,125	—	(1)	256,125			—
Inventory, December 31, 19X1 .	75,000	390,000					465,000
Total Credits	2,291,125	1,690,000		256,125			3,725,000
Inventory, January 1, 19X1 . .	100,000	400,000	(3)	45,000			545,000
Purchases	900,000	600,000					1,500,000
Operating Expenses . . .	480,000	340,000	(4)	13,875			833,875
Total Debits	1,480,000	1,340,000		58,875			2,878,875
Minority Interest in Net Income .	—	—	(5)	35,000			(35,000)
Net Income—to Ret. Earn. Stmt.	811,125	350,000		350,000			811,125
RETAINED EARNINGS STATEMENT							
Retained Earnings, 1/1/X1—P .	900,000	—					900,000
Retained Earnings, 1/1/X1—S .	—	500,000	(2)	500,000			—
Net Income—from Inc. Stmt. .	811,125	350,000		350,000			811,125
Dividends—P	(200,000)	—					(200,000)
Dividends—S	—	(100,000)			(1)	90,000	—
					(5)	10,000	
Ret. Earn., 12/31/X1—to Bal. Sht.	1,511,125	750,000		850,000		100,000	1,511,125
BALANCE SHEET							
Cash and Receivables . . .	275,000	360,000					635,000
Inventory	75,000	390,000					465,000
Investment in S	1,366,125	—			(1)	166,125	—
					(2)	1,200,000	
Other Investments . . .	100,000	—					100,000
Purchase Premium	—	—	(2)	300,000	(3)	300,000	—
Land	200,000	200,000					400,000
Buildings and Equipment . .	2,000,000	1,000,000	(3)	180,000			3,180,000
Accumulated Depreciation .	(800,000)	—			(4)	12,000	(812,000)
Goodwill	—	—	(3)	75,000	(4)	1,875	73,125
Total	3,216,125	1,950,000		555,000		1,680,000	4,041,125
Current Liabilities	175,000	200,000					375,000
Other Liabilities	730,000	500,000					1,230,000
Capital Stock—P	800,000						800,000
Capital Stock—S	—	500,000	(2)	500,000			—
Ret. Earn.—from Ret. Earn. Stmt.	1,511,125	750,000		850,000		100,000	1,511,125
Minority Interest in S . . .	—	—			(2)	100,000	125,000
					(5)	25,000	
Total	3,216,125	1,950,000		1,350,000		225,000	4,041,125
				1,905,000		1,905,000	

Explanations of Working Paper Entries
(1) To eliminate the equity method entries made by P during 19X1.
(2) To eliminate the investment account and reclassify the purchase premium and minority interest as of January 1, 19X1.
(3) To allocate the purchase premium as of January 1, 19X1.
(4) To recognize current year amortization of the purchase premium.
(5) To record the change in the minority interest during 19X1.

1. Eliminate the equity method entries, thereby restoring the investment account to its balance at the beginning of the current year.

2. Eliminate the investment account and reclassify the unamortized purchase premium or discount and the minority interest, all as of the beginning of the current year.

3. Allocate the unamortized purchase premium or discount.

4. Record the additional expenses associated with current year amortization of the purchase premium or discount.

5. Recognize the change in minority interest during the year by recording the minority's share of S's net income and charging any remaining subsidiary dividends against the minority interest.

We now work through consolidation at the end of 19X2 using the equity method. This will provide us with a good basis for subsequent comparison to the cost method as well as giving us the opportunity to add a few complications to the procedure.

During 19X2, S Company reported net income of $400,000. On November 30, 19X2, S Company declared dividends of $110,000, payable on January 5, 19X3. Finally, S Company made a short-term loan of $50,000 to P Company on October 1, 19X2. The loan bears interest at the rate of 10 percent; principal and interest are to be repaid on March 31, 19X3. S Company has properly accounted for the loan on its books. P Company determines its equity method accrual as shown in the following schedule:

**Schedule to Determine the Equity Method Accrual
for the Year Ended December 31, 19X2**

P's Share of S's Net Income (.9 × $400,000)	$360,000
Less Amortization of Purchase Premium:	
Additional Depreciation ($180,000/15)	$ 12,000
Amortization of Goodwill ($75,000/40)	1,875
Total Amortization	$ 13,875 [a]
Net Equity Method Accrual for 19X2	$346,125

[a]Recall that $45,000 of the purchase premium was allocated to inventory of S Company that was sold during 19X1.

The entries made by P Company in connection with these developments are shown next:

BOOKS OF P COMPANY

<u>10/1/X2</u>

Cash	50,000	
Current Liabilities		50,000

To record receipt of cash borrowed from S Company.
This amount, plus 10 percent interest, is to be repaid on
March 31, 19X3.

<u>11/30/X2</u>

Dividends Receivable	99,000	
Investment in S		99,000

To record P's share of dividends declared by S
Company; (.9 × $110,000).

<u>12/31/X2</u>

Investment in S	346,125	
Income from S		346,125

To record P's share of S's net income for 19X2, reduced
by purchase premium amortization for 19X2.

Recall that our consolidated financial statement working paper includes columns for adjustments *and* eliminations. We are now in a position to illustrate a typical adjusting entry which would be made on the working papers and which also would be entered in P Company's accounting records. An adjustment is necessary because P failed to accrue the interest due on its loan from S Company for the period October 1–December 31; S has recorded the accrual. This adjusting entry, which will be posted to P's books, is given below and is denoted on the working papers by an asterisk.

ADJUSTING ENTRY—BOOKS OF P COMPANY

Operating Expenses	1,250	
Current Liabilities		1,250

To record interest accrued on the loan from S Company for the
three-month period, October 1–December 31; $1,250 (= $3/_{12}$
× .1 × $50,000).

The working paper entries needed to consolidate P and S at December 31, 19X2, are given in Exhibit 8.5. In Exhibit 8.6, the complete balance sheet, income statement, and statement of retained earnings data for P and S at December 31, 19X2, are given in our working paper format. The adjusting entry above and the numbered entries in Exhibit 8.5 are posted to the working paper and the consolidated financial statement balances are computed.

The balance in the Investment in S account at December 31, 19X2, reflects the equity method transactions which occurred during 19X1 and 19X2. These are summarized in the following T account:

Investment in S

1/1/X1	Acquisition of Stock	1,200,000				
12/31/X1	Equity Method		19X1	Share of S		
	Accrual	256,125		Company's Dividends	90,000
12/31/X1	Balance	1,366,125				
12/31/X2	Equity Method		19X2	Share of S		
	Accrual	346,125		Company's Dividends	99,000
12/31/X2	Balance	1,613,250				

Exhibit 8.5   Consolidated Financial Statement Working Paper Entries
For the Year Ended December 31, 19X2 (α = .9)

CONSOLIDATED FINANCIAL STATEMENT WORKING PAPER

(1)

Income from S	346,125	
Dividends—S		99,000
Investment in S		247,125

To eliminate the equity method entries recorded by P, thereby adjusting the investment account to its balance on January 1, 19X2.

(2)

Retained Earnings—S, January 1, 19X2	750,000	
Capital Stock—S	500,000	
Purchase Premium ($300,000 − $45,000 − $12,000 − $1,875)	241,125	
Investment in S		1,366,125
Minority Interest in S		125,000

To reclassify the purchase premium, now reduced by the amortization recorded at December 31, 19X1, eliminate the Investment in S against 90 percent of the stockholders' equity of S, and reclassify the remaining stockholders' equity as minority interest, all as of January 1, 19X2.

(3)

Buildings and Equipment	180,000	
Goodwill ($75,000 − $1,875)	73,125	
Accumulated Depreciation		12,000
Purchase Premium ($300,000 − $58,875)		241,125

To allocate the unamortized purchase premium at January 1, 19X2, to the assets of S Company and goodwill. The original purchase premium allocations made at January 1, 19X1, and the 19X1 amortization amounts are shown in parentheses.

(4)

Operating Expenses	13,875	
Accumulated Depreciation		12,000
Goodwill		1,875

To recognize current year amortization of the purchase premium in the consolidated income statement for 19X2.

(5)

Minority Interest in Net Income	40,000	
Dividends—S		11,000
Minority Interest in S		29,000

To record the change in the minority interest during 19X2, consisting of the minority's interest in net income decreased by S Company's dividends paid to minority shareholders.

(6)

Current Liabilities	150,250	
Cash and Receivables		150,250

To eliminate intercompany receivables and payables consisting of interest ($1,250), dividends ($99,000), and loans ($50,000).

(7)

Sales and Other Revenue	1,250	
Operating Expenses		1,250

To eliminate intercompany interest revenue and expense.

P Company and S Company
Consolidated Financial Statement Working Paper For the Year
Ended December 31, 19X2 (Equity Method)

	P Company	S Company (90%)	Adjustments and Eliminations Dr.	Adjustments and Eliminations Cr.	Consolidated
INCOME STATEMENT					
Sales and Other Revenue . .	2,210,000	1,560,000	(7) 1,250		3,768,750
Income from S	346,125	—	(1) 346,125		—
Inventory, December 31, 19X2 .	80,000	410,000			490,000
Total Credits	2,636,125	1,970,000	347,375		4,258,750
Inventory, January 1, 19X2 . .	75,000	390,000			465,000
Purchases	1,120,000	740,000			1,860,000
Operating Expenses . . .	520,000	440,000	*1,250 (4) 13,875	(7) 1,250	973,875
Total Debits	1,715,000	1,570,000	15,125	1,250	3,298,875
Minority Interest in Net Income .	—	—	(5) 40,000		(40,000)
Net Income—to Ret. Earn. Stmt.	921,125	400,000	402,500	1,250	919,875
RETAINED EARNINGS STATEMENT					
Retained Earnings, 1/1/X2—P .	1,511,125	—			1,511,125
Retained Earnings, 1/1/X2—S .	—	750,000	(2) 750,000		—
Net Income—from Inc. Stmt. .	921,125	400,000	402,500	1,250	919,875
Dividends—P	(230,000)	—			(230,000)
Dividends—S	—	(110,000)		(1) 99,000 (5) 11,000	—
Ret. Earn., 12/31/X2—to Bal. Sht.	2,202,250	1,040,000	1,152,500	111,250	2,201,000
BALANCE SHEET					
Cash and Receivables . . .	399,000	436,250		(6) 150,250	685,000
Inventory	80,000	410,000			490,000
Investment in S	1,613,250	—		(1) 247,125 (2) 1,366,125	—
Other Investments	109,000				109,000
Purchase Premium	—	—	(2) 241,125	(3) 241,125	—
Land	341,000	300,000			641,000
Buildings and Equipment . .	2,400,000	1,250,000	(3) 180,000		3,830,000
Accumulated Depreciation .	(920,000)	(100,000)		(3) 12,000 (4) 12,000	(1,044,000)
Goodwill	—	—	(3) 73,125	(4) 1,875	71,250
Total	4,022,250	2,296,250	494,250	2,030,500	4,782,250
Current Liabilities	320,000	256,250	(6) 150,250	*1,250	427,250
Other Liabilities	700,000	500,000			1,200,000
Capital Stock—P	800,000	—			800,000
Capital Stock—S	—	500,000	(2) 500,000		—
Ret. Earn.—from Ret. Earn. Stmt.	2,202,250	1,040,000	1,152,500	111,250	2,201,000
Minority Interest in S . . .	—	—		(2) 125,000 (5) 29,000	154,000
Total	4,022,250	2,296,250	1,802,750	266,500	4,782,250
			2,297,000	2,297,000	

Explanations of Working Paper Entries

*   Adjusting entry to accrue interest on P Company's loan from S Company.

(1) To eliminate the equity method entries made by P Company during 19X2.

(2) To eliminate the investment account and reclassify the purchase premium and minority interest as of 1/1/X2.

(3) To allocate the purchase premium as of 1/1/X2.

(4) To recognize current year amortization of the purchase premium.

(5) To record the change in the minority interest during 19X2.

(6) To eliminate intercompany receivables and payables.

(7) To eliminate intercompany interest expense and revenue.

Consolidation Under the Cost Method in a Trial Balance Format

When P uses the cost method to account for an intercorporate investment, the Investment in S will not reflect changes in the book value of S's stockholders' equity. Similarly, P Company's retained earnings will include only the cumulative dividend income received from S but not P's equity in S's undistributed earnings since acquisition.

For these reasons, the investment account cannot be cleanly eliminated against S Company's stockholders' equity. If S Company's retained earnings have grown since acquisition, the growth would remain after the investment account, as recorded at date of acquisition, was eliminated. There are two ways to deal with this problem.

1.   Prepare a working paper entry which would restate the Investment in S account and P's retained earnings to the equity basis at the beginning of the current year. After eliminating the dividend income recorded by P under the cost method against Dividends—S, we would proceed with the consolidation as before; *or*

2.   Eliminate the Investment in S, as recorded at date of acquisition, against S Company's stockholders' equity at date of acquisition. Then, after eliminating the intercompany dividends as in item 1 above, we allocate the growth in S Company's retained earnings between the retained earnings of P and the minority interest. This can be done with a working paper entry or by adding a column entitled "Minority Interest" and extending the appropriate amounts to the "Minority" and "Consolidated" columns.

Of these two options, we prefer the first. We believe that this approach is more systematic in that it places all working paper manipulations in journal entry form.

To illustrate consolidation under the cost method, we use the data developed in our previous example for the year ended December 31, 19X2. The first step is to determine the amount needed to restate the investment account and P's retained earnings to the equity basis at January 1, 19X2. This is done in the schedule given in Exhibit 8.7.

In our example, an adjustment of $166,125 is required to bring both the investment account and the parent's retained earnings up to their balances at January 1, 19X2, under the equity method. An additional working paper entry must be made to reflect this restatement; it will be given shortly.

After this has been accomplished, the only remaining difference between the cost and equity methods involves intercompany dividends. Under the equity method, dividends received by P from S were credited to the investment account. In contrast, intercompany dividends are recorded by P as *Dividend In-*

Exhibit 8.7   Determining the Needed Restatement of the Investment Account and the Retained Earnings of P (Cost Method Used by P)

Schedule to Determine the Amount of Restatement Necessary to
Place the Investment in S and Retained Earnings—P on the Equity
Basis at January 1, 19X2, When P Employs the Cost Method

	Investment in S	Retained Earnings—P
Balance at Acquisition, January 1, 19X1 . .	$1,200,000	$ 900,000
90 Percent of S's Net Income—Year 1 . . .	315,000	315,000
90 Percent of S's Dividends—Year 1 . . .	(90,000)	—
Amortization of Purchase Premium—Year 1 .	(58,875)	(58,875)
P's Income from Its Own Operations—Year 1 .	—	555,000 [a]
P's Dividends Declared—Year 1	—	(200,000)
Equity Method Balances, December 31, 19X1 .	$1,366,125	$1,511,125
Balances per Books, December 31, 19X1, Cost Method	1,200,000	1,345,000 [b]
Required Restatement	$ 166,125	$ 166,125

[a]P's income from its own operations ($555,000) is simply its net income as recorded in Exhibit 8.4 ($811,125) less the equity method accrual of $256,125. Alternatively, $555,000 = $811,125 − ($315,000 − $58,875).
[b]This amount consists of P's retained earnings at January 1, 19X1 ($900,000), plus P's net income from its own operations ($555,000) plus dividend income from S ($90,000) less dividends declared by P ($200,000).

come when the cost method is used. Therefore, the debit part of the eliminating entry which removes the intercompany dividends is to the Dividend Income account. Both of these entries appear below. All other working paper entries, including the adjustment for accrued interest, are the same as under the equity method.

CONSOLIDATED TRIAL BALANCE WORKING PAPER

Investment in S	166,125	
Retained Earnings—P		166,125

To restate the Investment in S and Retained Earnings—P, as carried under the cost method, to the equity method as of January 1, 19X2.

Dividend Income	99,000	
Dividends—S		99,000

To eliminate the intercompany dividends under the cost method.

Consolidated Trial Balance Working Paper   Consolidation procedures can readily be executed by using a working paper including the adjusted trial balances of P and S. The trial balance working paper is generally fashioned in one of two ways.

1.   The final column (following the Adjustments and Eliminations columns) contains the consolidated trial balance. Once the consolidated trial balance is prepared, the resulting consolidated account balances are used in the formal consolidated financial statements.

2.   Additional columns labeled "Balance Sheet," "Income Statement," and "Statement of Retained Earnings" may be included. Then, after

the consolidation entries are recorded on the working paper, the consolidated account balances can be extended directly into the appropriate financial statement columns.

Our illustration incorporates both of the above. We provide a column for the consolidated trial balance and additional columns for the three financial statements. Having studied the consolidated financial statement working paper, the reader may wish to compare it with the trial balance working paper approach. The completed trial balance working paper for 19X2 appears in Exhibit 8.8.

Note that the trial balance working paper includes the same accounts as our financial statement working paper, although the format differs. As a result, under our system *working paper entries are the same, whether the trial balance or financial statement format is being used.* Refer back to Exhibits 8.5 and 8.6 to convince yourself of this. In doing so, remember that P's use of the cost method is being illustrated on this trial balance working paper, while the equity method was used previously. Had the financial statement working paper format been used to illustrate the cost method, it would include those working paper entries —(1) and (2) in Exhibit 8.8—which are specific to the cost method.

Business Combinations during an Accounting Period

To this point, our examples always involved business combinations at the beginning or end of an accounting period in order to avoid the minor technical problems caused by combination during an accounting period. When a purchase combination occurs *during* an accounting period, one must decide how to report the subsidiary's current period earnings *prior* to the combination when the consolidated statements are prepared at year-end. In a pooling, the consolidated income statement always includes the affiliate's revenues and expenses for the entire year. There are, however, two alternative treatments for the purchase case:

1. Include only the subsidiary's revenues and expenses arising *after* the date of acquisition in the consolidated income statement. This follows from the fact that in purchase combinations the subsidiary's retained earnings at date of combination are eliminated. In effect, this treatment eliminates the subsidiary's revenues, expenses, and earnings prior to the business combination date.

2. Report the subsidiary's sales and expenses for the entire year but show a deduction for **preacquisition earnings**—the subsidiary's net income prior to date of combination—in the consolidated income statement. *ARB 51* (AC § 2051.10) expresses a preference for this approach:

   One method, which usually is preferable . . . is to include the subsidiary in the consolidation as though it had been acquired at the beginning of the year, and to deduct at the bottom of the consolidated income statement the preacquisition earnings. . . . This method presents results which are more indicative of the current status of the group, and facilitates future comparison with subsequent years.[7]

---

[7] Committee on Accounting Procedure, *Accounting Research Bulletin No. 51*, "Consolidated Financial Statements" (N.Y.: AICPA, 1959), par. 11.

Exhibit 8.8   Consolidated Trial Balance Working Paper For the Year Ended December 31, 19X2 (Cost Method)

P Company and S Company
Consolidated Trial Balance Working Paper For the Year Ended December 31, 19X2
(Cost Method)

ACCOUNT	P Company Dr. (Cr.)	S Company (90%) Dr. (Cr.)	Adjustments and Eliminations Dr.	Adjustments and Eliminations Cr.	Consolidated Trial Balance	Consolidated Income Statement	Consolidated Retained Earnings Statement	Consolidated Balance Sheet
Cash and Receivables	399,000	436,250		(7) 150,250	685,000			685,000
Inventory, January 1, 19X2	75,000	390,000			465,000	465,000		
Inventory, December 31, 19X2	80,000	410,000			490,000			490,000
Investment in S	1,200,000	—	(1) 166,125 (3) 241,125	(3) 1,366,125 (4) 241,125	—			
Purchase Premium	—	—						
Other Investments	109,000				109,000			109,000
Land	341,000	300,000			641,000			641,000
Buildings and Equipment	2,400,000	1,250,000	(4) 180,000		3,830,000			3,830,000
Accumulated Depreciation	(920,000)	(100,000)		(4) 12,000 (5) 12,000	(1,044,000)			(1,044,000)
Goodwill	—	—	(4) 73,125	(5) 1,875	71,250			71,250
Current Liabilities	(320,000)	(256,250)	(7) 150,250	(5) *1,250	(427,250)			(427,250)
Other Liabilities	(700,000)	(500,000)			(1,200,000)			(1,200,000)
Capital Stock—P	(800,000)	—			(800,000)			(800,000)
Capital Stock—S	—	(500,000)	(3) 500,000		—			
Retained Earnings—P, January 1, 19X2	(1,345,000)	—		(1) 166,125	(1,511,125)		(1,511,125)	
Retained Earnings—S, January 1, 19X2	—	(750,000)	(3) 750,000		—			
Dividends—P	230,000	—			230,000		230,000	
Dividends—S	—	110,000		(2) 99,000 (6) 11,000	—			
Minority Interest in S	—	—		(3) 125,000 (6) 29,000	(154,000)			(154,000)
Sales and Other Revenue	(2,210,000)	(1,560,000)	(8) 1,250		(3,768,750)	(3,768,750)		
Dividend Income from S	(99,000)	—	(2) 99,000		—			
Purchases	1,120,000	740,000		(8) 1,250	1,860,000	1,860,000		
Operating Expenses	520,000	440,000	(5) *1,250 13,875		973,875	973,875		
Inventory, December 31, 19X2	(80,000)	(410,000)			(490,000)	(490,000)		
Minority Interest in Net Income	—	—	(6) 40,000		40,000	40,000		
Totals	0	0	2,216,000	2,216,000	0			
Consolidated Net Income						(919,875)	(919,875)	
Consolidated Retained Earnings, December 31, 19X2							(2,201,000)	(2,201,000)
						(919,875)	(919,875)	0
							(2,201,000)	(2,201,000)

Explanations of Working Paper Entries

*   To accrue interest on P Company's loan from S Company.

(1) To adjust the Investment in S and Retained Earnings of P to the equity basis as of January 1, 19X2.

(2) To eliminate the intercompany dividends.

(3) To eliminate the investment account and reclassify the purchase premium and minority interest as of January 1, 19X2.

(4) To allocate the purchase premium as of January 1, 19X2.

(5) To recognize current year amortization of the purchase premium.

(6) To record the change in the minority interest during 19X2.

(7) To eliminate intercompany receivables and payables.

(8) To eliminate intercompany interest expense and revenue.

In our view, each method has advantages and disadvantages. Including only revenues and expenses generated by the subsidiary after date of acquisition (method 1) seems more conceptually sound as long as some indication of the magnitude of the effect on consolidated net income is disclosed. Adopting the position favored by *ARB 51* (method 2) does provide investors with a pro forma view of the entire year. Yet, when acquisition occurs late in the year, almost all of the subsidiary's net income would be deducted as preacquisition earnings, a somewhat odd treatment. We have a slight preference for including only the revenues and expenses generated by the subsidiary after acquisition—method 1—but will illustrate both alternatives.

Suppose Praxon Corporation acquires 80 percent of the outstanding stock of Sonnet Company on April 1, 19X2, at a cost of $40,000,000. Sonnet's contributed capital was recorded at $25,000,000 on January 1, 19X2, and has not changed. An analysis of Sonnet's retained earnings and 19X2 operations appears in Exhibit 8.9.

Praxon is paying a purchase premium of $9,600,000 [= $40,000,000 − .8($25,000,000 + $13,000,000)], which we assume is attributed entirely to goodwill. Given that Praxon had revenue of $150,000,000 and operating expenses of $110,000,000 from its own operations, we prepare consolidated income statements under the two methods in Exhibit 8.10.

Assuming that Praxon uses the equity method, it would record 80 percent of Sonnet's postacquisition income, $11,200,000 [= .8($48,000,000 − $34,000,000)], less goodwill amortization for three-fourths of the year, $180,000 [= ($9,600,000/40) (3/4)], for a total of $11,020,000. Similarly, Praxon would reduce the investment account by 80 percent of Sonnet's postacquisition dividends, $800,000 (= .8 × $1,000,000). These entries are identical under methods 1 and 2, and they will be reversed on the working paper in consolidation at December 31, 19X2.

If method 1 is used, Sonnet's books should be closed as of April 1 so that in consolidation, beginning retained earnings—now dated April 1—reflect net income and dividends for the first three months of the year. The usual eliminating entries are then made. Under method 2, however, Sonnet's books are not closed as of April 1, and beginning retained earnings is dated January 1, not reflecting net income and dividends through March 31. Therefore, both Sonnet's retained earnings at January 1 and the change (net income less dividends) during the preacquisition period must be eliminated. This is accomplished in two working paper entries.

1.   The investment account balance at April 1 is eliminated against

Exhibit 8.9   Analysis of Sonnet's Retained Earnings Account during 19X2

Sonnet Company
Analysis of Changes in Retained Earnings during 19X2

Retained Earnings, January 1, 19X2	$10,400,000
Less Dividends Declared and Paid, February 15, 19X2	(1,400,000)
Plus Revenue Realized, January 1, 19X2–March 31, 19X2	15,000,000
Less Operating Expenses, January 1, 19X2–March 31, 19X2	(11,000,000)
Retained Earnings if Books Closed on March 31, 19X2	$13,000,000
Less Dividends Declared and Paid, August 15, 19X2	(1,000,000)
Plus Revenue Realized, April 1, 19X2–December 31, 19X2	48,000,000
Less Operating Expenses, April 1, 19X2–December 31, 19X2	(34,000,000)
Retained Earnings after Closing on December 31, 19X2	$26,000,000

Exhibit 8.10   Alternative Consolidated Income Statements in the Praxon and Sonnet Intraperiod Business Combination

Condensed Consolidated Income Statements for Praxon and Sonnet
Reflecting the Two Alternative Treatments of Sonnet's Preacquisition Earnings

	Praxon and Sonnet Consolidated	
	Method 1	Method 2
Sales	$198,000,000	$213,000,000
Operating Expenses	(144,000,000)	(155,000,000)
Goodwill Amortization	(180,000) [a]	(180,000) [a]
Minority Interest in Net Income	(2,800,000) [b]	(3,600,000) [c]
Preacquisition Earnings	—	(3,200,000) [d]
Consolidated Net Income	$ 51,020,000	$ 51,020,000

[a]$180,000 = .75($9,600,000/40).
[b]$2,800,000 = .2($48,000,000 − $34,000,000); based on Sonnet's net income during the postacquisition period only.
[c]$3,600,000 = .2[($15,000,000 + $48,000,000) − ($11,000,000 + $34,000,000)]; based on Sonnet's net income for the entire year.
[d]$3,200,000 = .8($15,000,000 − $11,000,000).

(a) Sonnet's stockholders' equity at January 1 and (b) 80 percent of Sonnet's earnings and dividends during the preacquisition period. The minority interest in Sonnet as of January 1 is also established in this entry.

2.   The *change in the minority interest* is computed on a pro forma basis for the *entire year*. The working paper entry establishes 20 percent of Sonnet's net income for the entire year as minority interest in net income and eliminates the remaining 20 percent of Sonnet's dividends for the entire year.

We now present the working paper entries made at December 31, 19X2, under *method 2*, assuming that the investment account is carried at equity.

CONSOLIDATED FINANCIAL STATEMENT WORKING PAPER

(Method 2)

Income from Sonnet	11,020,000	
Dividends—Sonnet		800,000
Investment in Sonnet		10,220,000

To eliminate the investment income and intercompany dividends recorded under the equity method; $11,020,000 = .8($48,000,000 − $34,000,000) − $180,000.

Preacquisition Earnings	3,200,000	
Contributed Capital—Sonnet	25,000,000	
Retained Earnings—Sonnet	10,400,000	
Goodwill	9,600,000	
Dividends—Sonnet		1,120,000
Investment in Sonnet		40,000,000
Minority Interest in Sonnet		7,080,000

To eliminate the investment account against the stockholders' equity of Sonnet Company, establish the minority interest, eliminate Praxon's share of the preacquisition dividends, and record the preacquisition earnings. The minority interest is calculated as of January 1, 19X2; $7,080,000 [= 2($25,000,000 + $10,400,000)].

Amortization Expense	180,000	
Goodwill		180,000

To record amortization of goodwill for 3/4 of the year.

Minority Interest in Net Income	3,600,000	
Dividends—Sonnet		480,000
Minority Interest in Sonnet		3,120,000

To record the change in the minority interest during 19X2, consisting of the minority's interest in net income decreased by the minority's share of Sonnet Company's dividends; [$480,000 = .2($1,400,000 + $1,000,000)]. Minority interest in Sonnet at December 31, 19X2, is $10,200,000 [= .2($25,000,000 + $26,000,000) = $7,080,000 + $3,120,000].

Two observations should be made about the above working paper entries. First, the amount of Sonnet's net income for the year not included in consolidated net income is $6,800,000 [= ($15,000,000 − $11,000,000) + .2($48,000,000 − $34,000,000)]. The entries break this into two components: preacquisition earnings of $3,200,000 and minority interest in net income of $3,600,000. Second, $1,600,000 [= $1,400,000 + (.2 × $1,000,000)] of Sonnet's dividends were not paid to the controlling stockholders during the year. This amount also has two components: preacquisition dividends of $1,120,000 and 20 percent of Sonnet's total dividends, $480,000.

Consolidated Statement of Changes in Financial Position

Although the statement of changes in financial position (SCFP), or "funds" statement, is not a new disclosure device, it was not required as part of a firm's basic financial statements until 1971, when *APBO 19* (AC § 2021) was issued; it set forth the following requirement:

> When financial statements purporting to present both financial position (balance sheet) and results of operations (statement of income and retained earnings) are issued, a statement summarizing changes in financial position should also be presented as a basic financial statement for each period for which an income statement is presented.[8]

Nature of the Statement of Changes in Financial Position

The SCFP filled a significant gap in corporate reporting. It provided a much more complete link between successive balance sheets than statements of income and retained earnings alone. This linkage was established by the objectives of the SCFP, given in *APBO 19:*

> The objectives of a funds statement are (1) to summarize the financing and investing activities of the entity, including the extent to which the enterprise has generated funds from operations during the period, and (2) to complete the disclosure of changes in financial position during the period.[9]

The term *funds* refers to a short-term concept of net assets, typically working capital (current assets less current liabilities) or cash. In either case, the SCFP usually reports a computation of funds provided by operations and the other significant investing and financing activities which took place, even if they did not directly affect funds (for example, the issuance of common stock to retire bonds). If funds are defined as working capital, the SCFP may be viewed as an analysis of the change in working capital through reference to the changes in the non–working capital accounts. An algebraic approach to understanding the SCFP is given in Exhibit 8.11.

We will not duplicate the more complete discussions of the statement of changes in financial position found in intermediate accounting textbooks. Rather, we shall highlight the particular items that tend to show up on a consolidated SCFP and work through an example using the **T account solution method.**

Preparation of the Consolidated Statement of Changes in Financial Position

A consolidated statement of changes in financial position is prepared from comparative consolidated balance sheets, consolidated statements of income and retained earnings, and any necessary supplementary information. Attempts to prepare a consolidated SCFP from the unconsolidated SCFPs of P and S are relatively inefficient. Eliminations would have to be made both here and again when the other financial statements are consolidated. We now consider some items that are often encountered in a consolidated SCFP.

1.   In determining funds provided by operations, *amortization of goodwill* arising in consolidation must be *added back to consolidated net in-*

---

[8] Accounting Principles Board, *Opinion No. 19*, "Reporting Changes in Financial Position" (N.Y.: AICPA, 1971), par. 7; AC § 2021.07.

[9] Ibid., par. 4; AC § 2021.04.

Exhibit 8.11   An Algebraic Approach to Understanding the Statement of Changes in Financial Position

CA = Current assets.   NCL = Noncurrent liabilities.

CL = Current liabilities.   SE = Stockholders' equity.

NCA = Noncurrent assets. Δ = Greek letter *delta*, indicating *change in*.

The fundamental accounting equation provides that

$$\text{Assets} = \text{Liabilities} + \text{Stockholders' Equity}$$
$$CA + NCA = CL + NCL + SE,$$

which is the definition of a balance sheet. Since this equation holds for successive balance sheets, we can add the Δ to indicate change in the various balance sheet categories:

$$\Delta CA + \Delta NCA = \Delta CL + \Delta NCL + \Delta SE.$$

Using working capital as our definition of funds, we rearrange terms and have

$$\Delta CA - \Delta CL = \Delta NCL + \Delta SE - \Delta NCA.$$

Thus our solution technique and the formal SCFP itself are based upon the concept of using changes in the *non-working capital accounts* to explain the change in *working capital*. If funds are defined as *cash*, then the change in cash is explained through reference to changes in the *noncash accounts*.

come. It is a deduction from net income which does not use working capital—it decreases a noncurrent asset, goodwill.

2.   *Minority interest in net income* is deducted in computing consolidated net income. Since it does not use working capital—it increases a stockholders' equity account—it must be *added back* in computing working capital provided by operations. Similarly, the *minority interest in a net loss* is added in computing consolidated net income. Since this does not provide working capital—it decreases a stockholders' equity account —it must be *deducted* in computing working capital provided by operations.

3.   *Dividends paid to minority shareholders* are shown as a *nonoperating use of working capital*. Payment of such dividends reduces Minority Interest in S, a stockholders' equity account.

4.   *Purchase of additional subsidiary shares* in the open market constitutes a *nonoperating use of working capital*. In contrast, if the shares are purchased directly from the subsidiary, there is no effect on consolidated working capital or on the parent's capital stock account. Hence, no disclosure is needed on the funds statement.

5.   *Undistributed equity method income (loss)* from unconsolidated subsidiaries or other equity method investments must be *subtracted (added)* in computing working capital provided by operations. The accrual of such equity method income increases other noncurrent assets—long-term (unconsolidated) equity investments—and does not itself provide working capital; it must be subtracted from consolidated net income. Dividends received from such investments, however, represent a realization of the equity method income and *do* increase working capital.

Exhibit 8.12   Consolidated Financial Statements for P and S to be Used in Consolidated Funds Statement Illustration

P Company and S Company
Comparative Consolidated Balance Sheets
at December 31, 19X2 and 19X1

		12/31/X2	12/31/X1
ASSETS			
Cash and Receivables		$ 685,000	$ 635,000
Inventory		490,000	465,000
Total Current Assets		$1,175,000	$1,100,000
Other Investments		$ 109,000	$ 100,000
Land		641,000	400,000
Buildings and Equipment	$3,830,000		
	$3,180,000		
Less Accumulated Depreciation	(1,044,000)		
	(812,000)	2,786,000	2,368,000
Goodwill		71,250	73,125
Total Noncurrent Assets		$3,607,250	$2,941,125
Total Assets		$4,782,250	$4,041,125
LIABILITIES AND STOCKHOLDERS' EQUITY			
Current Liabilities		$ 427,250	$ 375,000
Other Liabilities		1,200,000	1,230,000
Total Liabilities		$1,627,250	$1,605,000
Capital Stock		$ 800,000	$ 800,000
Retained Earnings		2,201,000	1,511,125
Minority Interest in S		154,000	125,000
Total Stockholders' Equity		$3,155,000	$2,436,125
Total Liabilities and Stockholders' Equity		$4,782,250	$4,041,125

P Company and S Company
Consolidated Statement of Income and Retained
Earnings For the Year Ended December 31, 19X2

Sales and Other Revenue		$3,768,750
Cost of Goods Sold:		
Inventory, January 1, 19X2	$ 465,000	
Purchases	1,860,000	
Inventory, December 31, 19X2	(490,000)	$1,835,000
Operating Expenses		973,875
Minority Interest in Net Income		40,000
Total Expenses		$2,848,875
Net Income		$ 919,875
Retained Earnings, January 1, 19X2		1,511,125
Dividends Declared		(230,000)
Retained Earnings, December 31, 19X2		$2,201,000

Other Information:

1. Consolidated depreciation expense was $232,000.
2. Sales and Other Revenue includes $15,000 income from equity method investments; $6,000 in dividends was received.

These dividends must be included in funds provided by operations. Therefore, the net effect is to subtract the undistributed equity method income (not received in dividends) in arriving at funds provided by operations.

Consolidated Funds Statement: An Illustration   Our illustration is based on the data previously developed for P and S. We now have comparative consolidated balance sheets for P and S at December 31, 19X1 and 19X2, and a consolidated statement of income and retained earnings for 19X2. These statements are presented in Exhibit 8.12. The formal consolidated statement of changes in financial position for 19X2 appears in Exhibit 8.13 and the T account worksheet used in its preparation appears in Exhibit 8.14.

Accounting for Income Taxes and Consolidated Statements	Intercorporate investments create some interesting complications in accounting for income taxes. We introduce certain of these issues now but defer considering the tax effects of unconfirmed intercompany gains and losses until Chapter 9.

Recall that *APBO 11* (AC § 4091) requires comprehensive interperiod income tax allocation.[10] Under this concept, a distinction is drawn between *income tax expense*—which accrues as income subject to tax is recognized in the accounting records—and *income tax liability*—which reflects taxes actually due to the government. The amount of income tax expense is based on pretax book income, while the amount of income tax liability is based on the income tax return. Most income tax accounting problems are traceable to differences between the firm's pretax book income and tax return income for a given reporting period. These differences are of two general types:

1.   **Timing differences:** Some items affect book income and tax return income in different reporting periods, thereby creating temporary dissimilarities between book income and tax return income. In time, these dissimilarities *reverse*. When straight-line depreciation is used for book purposes and accelerated depreciation for tax purposes, tax depreciation will first exceed and then fall short of book depreciation over the asset's life. It is the existence of such timing differences that generated the perceived need for comprehensive interperiod tax allocation and the accrual of deferred income taxes.

2.   **Permanent differences:** Some items affect *only* book income or tax return income, thereby creating lasting dissimilarities between book income and tax return income. The tax effect of such items does not reverse over time. For example, interest on municipal bonds is properly includable as book income but is permanently exempt from taxation under current law. Permanent differences do not give rise to deferred income taxes.

With these definitions in mind, we turn to their significance when intercorporate investments are concerned. Many groups of affiliated corporations issue

---

[10]   Accounting Principles Board, *Opinion No. 11,* "Accounting for Income Taxes" (N.Y.: AICPA, 1967).

Exhibit 8.13 Consolidated Statement of Changes in Financial Position

P Company and S Company
Consolidated Statement of Changes in Financial Position
For the Year Ended December 31, 19X2

Working Capital Provided by Operations:
Net Income	$ 919,875
Add (Subtract) Items Not Using (Providing) Working Capital	
Depreciation Expense	232,000
Goodwill Amortization	1,875
Minority Interest in Net Income	40,000
Undistributed Equity Method Income	(9,000)
Working Capital Provided by Operations	$1,184,750
Working Capital Used For:	
Payment of Dividends to P Company Shareholders	$ 230,000
Payment of Dividends to Minority Shareholders	11,000
Purchase of Land	241,000
Purchase of Buildings and Equipment	650,000
Reduction in Other Liabilities	30,000
Total Uses of Working Capital	$1,162,000
Increase in Working Capital	$ 22,750

Schedule of Changes in Working Capital Accounts

	12/31/X2	12/31/X1	Increase (Decrease) in Working Capital
Cash and Receivables	$685,000	$635,000	$50,000
Inventory	490,000	465,000	25,000
Current Liabilities	(427,250)	(375,000)	(52,250)
Total	$747,750	$725,000	$22,750

consolidated income statements but do not file consolidated income tax returns. We defer discussion of consolidated tax returns to a later section and now examine how use of the equity method affects accounting for income taxes when consolidated returns are not filed.

Undistributed Equity Method Income

The rules governing provision of deferred taxes on undistributed equity method income depend on whether the investee is considered a *subsidiary* ($\alpha > .5$) or a *nonsubsidiary investment* ($.2 \leq \alpha \leq .5$). We discuss each in turn.

Subsidiary Equity Method Investments Unless a consolidated income tax return is filed, an investor corporation is taxed only for dividends received from investees. Furthermore, these dividends are generally eligible for the 85 percent corporate deduction for dividends received. Therefore, if P carries its investment in S on the equity basis and separate income tax returns are filed, a difference arises. Recall that, under the equity method, the net income of P

Exhibit 8.14 T Account Worksheet Used to Prepare Consolidated Statement of Changes in Financial Position

P Company and S Company
T Account Worksheet for Consolidated Statement of Changes in Financial Position

WORKING CAPITAL

Balance, 1/1/X2	725,000	

From Operations

(Net Income and Additions)			(Subtractions)		
Net Income	(1)	919,875	Equity Method Income from Other		
Depreciation Expense	(2)	232,000	Investments	(3)	15,000
Dividends from Other Investments	(4)	6,000			
Goodwill Amortization	(5)	1,875			
Minority Interest in Net Income	(6)	40,000			
		(15,000)			
W/C Provided by Operations		1,184,750			

Nonoperating

(Sources)			(Uses)		
			Purchase of Land	(7)	241,000
			Purchase of Buildings and Equipment	(8)	650,000
			Decrease in Other Liabilities	(9)	30,000
			Parent Company Dividends	(10)	230,000
			Dividends Paid to Minority Interest	(11)	11,000
			Total Nonoperating Uses of W/C		1,162,000

Balance, 12/31/X2	747,750	

Other Investments					Land					Buildings and Equipment		
1/1	100,000				1/1	400,000				1/1	3,180,000	
(3)	15,000	(4)	6,000		(7)	241,000				(8)	650,000	
12/31	109,000				12/31	641,000				12/31	3,830,000	

Accumulated Depreciation					Goodwill					Other Liabilities		
		1/1	812,000	1/1	73,125						1/1	1,230,000
		(2)	232,000			(5)	1,875	(9)	30,000			
		12/31	1,044,000	12/31	71,250						12/31	1,200,000

Capital Stock					Retained Earnings					Minority Interest in S		
		1/1	800,000			1/1	1,511,125				1/1	125,000
				(10)	230,000	(1)	919,875	(11)	11,000	(6)		40,000
		12/31	800,000			12/31	2,201,000				12/31	154,000

equals consolidated net income—the amount of the equity method accrual is reflected in each. In contrast, P's tax return includes the dividends received from S, net of the 85 percent dividends received deduction; it does not include the equity method accrual.[11]

Accounting treatment of this difference was clarified in *APBO 23* (AC § 4095), superseding the conflicting positions which had appeared in *ARB 51*, *APBO 11*, and *APBO 18*. The general rule regarding undistributed earnings of subsidiaries is that they represent *timing differences* to the parent and are subject to interperiod tax allocation. Nevertheless, under certain conditions—known as the **indefinite reversal criteria**—a *permanent difference* results, and deferred taxes need not be provided. From *APBO 23*, we have:

> **Timing difference.** The Board believes it should be presumed that all undistributed earnings of a subsidiary will be transferred to the parent company. Accordingly, the undistributed earnings of a subsidiary included in consolidated income (or in income of the parent company) should be accounted for as a timing difference, except. . . .[12]
>
> **Permanent difference: indefinite reversal criteria.** The presumption that all undistributed earnings will be transferred to the parent company may be overcome, and no income taxes should be accrued by the parent company, if sufficient evidence shows that the subsidiary has invested or will invest the undistributed earnings indefinitely or that the earnings will be remitted in a tax-free liquidation.[13]

Since parent company management can effectively control the investment and dividend policies of its subsidiaries, it is often able to argue successfully that undistributed equity method income will be permanently invested by its subsidiaries. In such cases, the indefinite reversal criteria apply, and no deferred income taxes on the undistributed equity method income are accrued by the parent.

Nonsubsidiary Equity Method Investments   When $.2 \leq \alpha \leq .5$, the percentage of ownership is sufficient to require use of the equity method but not sufficient to justify preparation of consolidated statements. Use of the equity method in nonsubsidiary investments, then, will likely result in a difference between the equity method income reported in P Company's income statement and the dividend income included in the tax return. *APBO 24* (AC § 4096.07) concludes that the *undistributed equity method income of nonsubsidiary investments constitutes a timing difference* to the investor. The indefinite reversal criteria do not apply here.

---

[11] While the 85 percent dividends received deduction is generally available to any domestic corporation, affiliated corporations (as defined in the Internal Revenue Code) are often able to elect to deduct 100 percent of any intercompany dividends from tax return income. A consolidated income tax return need not be filed. In such situations, equity method income—whether distributed or not—represents a permanent difference between pretax book income and tax return income; no deferred taxes need be provided.

[12] Accounting Principles Board, *Opinion No. 23*, "Accounting for Income Taxes—Special Areas" (N.Y.: AICPA, 1972), par. 10; AC § 4095.10.

[13] Ibid., par. 12; AC § 4095.12.

The Board concludes that the *tax effects of differences between taxable income and pretax accounting income* attributable to an investor's share of earnings of investee companies (other than subsidiaries and corporate joint ventures) . . . are related either to probable future distributions of dividends or to anticipated realization on disposal of the investment and therefore have the essential characteristics of *timing differences.* The Board believes that the ability of an investor to exercise significant influence over an investee differs significantly from the ability of a parent company to control investment policies of a subsidiary and that *only control can justify the conclusion that undistributed earnings may be invested for indefinite periods.* [14] [Emphasis added.]

Thus when $\alpha > .5$, the parent may be able to justify the indefinite reversal concept by virtue of its control over the subsidiary's dividend and investment policies. If $\alpha \leq .5$, however, this control is presumed not to exist and deferred taxes must be provided on undistributed equity method earnings.

Illustration of Interperiod Tax Allocation on Undistributed Equity Method Income   We continue to assume that a consolidated income tax return is not filed. Therefore, the investor corporation is taxed only on the dividends received from the investee. Unless indefinite reversal can be substantiated (in the case of subsidiary investments only), the investor must accrue deferred taxes on undistributed equity method income. In determining the income tax provision, the following two items are important:

1.   The investor must decide the form in which the undistributed income will ultimately be realized. If dividends are expected, the tax is accrued on the undistributed income as if it were dividends subject to the 85 percent dividends received deduction. In contrast, if the undistributed income is expected to be realized as a capital gain by virtue of the sale of the investment, the tax provision must be based on applicable capital gain tax rates.

2.   Any adjustments to the investor's share of the investee's net income made under the one-line consolidation requirement of *APBO 18* are irrelevant in determining the tax provision. Such amounts are not allowable tax deductions against dividend income. Thus, the equity method accrual must be cleansed of any purchase premium amortization. In addition, any intercompany gains or losses which normally would be eliminated in computing the equity method accrual must be reinstated for purposes of the tax provision. These issues will be discussed in Chapter 9.

Suppose that Paul Corporation owns 70 percent of the voting shares of Sam Corporation. Sam earned $90,000 after taxes during the current year and paid dividends of $20,000. A purchase premium of $100,000 was allocated as follows: $75,000 to depreciable equipment and $25,000 to goodwill. Paul faces a combined federal and state income tax rate of 60 percent. At year-end, Paul makes the following entry to provide for income taxes on its investment income from

---

[14] Accounting Principles Board, *Opinion No. 24*, "Accounting for Income Taxes—Investments in Common Stock Accounted for by the Equity Method" (N.Y.: AICPA, 1972), par. 7.

Exhibit 8.15   Paul Corporation's Computation of Income Taxes on Investment Income from Sam Corporation

Paul's 70% Share of Sam's Aftertax Income of $90,000 (Expected to Be Realized as Dividends)	$63,000
Less 85% Dividend Received Deduction (Expected to Be Available When Dividends Are Distributed)	(53,550)
Income Subject to Tax When Distributed	$ 9,450
Income Tax Expense (.6 × $9,450)	$ 5,670
Dividends Received during Current Year Subject to Income Tax [1 − .85)(.7)($20,000)]	$ 2,100
Income Tax Currently Payable at 60% (.6 × $2,100)	1,260
Undistributed Income Subject to Tax in Future Years ($9,450 − $2,100)	7,350
Deferred Income Taxes at 60% (.6 × $7,350)	4,410
Income Tax Expense	$ 5,670

Notes

1. The purchase premium allocation (and amortization) has been disregarded in the income tax computations.
2. Even if consolidated financial statements are prepared and reflect the purchase premium amortization, the income tax provision remains as computed.

Sam; computation of tax amounts are shown in Exhibit 8.15. Management of Paul expects that the undistributed income will eventually be realized as dividends received from Sam.

BOOKS OF PAUL CORPORATION

Income Tax Expense	5,670	
Income Taxes Payable		1,260
Deferred Income Taxes		4,410
To provide for income taxes on income from Sam.		

Consolidated Income Tax Returns

The set of corporate affiliations eligible to file consolidated income tax returns is substantially smaller than the set eligible to issue consolidated financial statements. Section 1501 of the Internal Revenue Code indicates that an *affiliated group of corporations* shall have the privilege of filing a consolidated return, subject to the Treasury regulations prescribed in Section 1502.

Section 1504 goes on to define an *affiliated group* as one or more chains of corporations connected through stock ownership with a common parent. The common parent must directly own stock possessing at least 80 percent of the voting power of all classes of stock and at least 80 percent of each class of the nonvoting stock of at least one of the other corporations. Furthermore, at least 80 percent of each class of nonvoting stock of each corporation, except the parent, must be owned directly by one or more of the corporations in the group. Certain corporations, such as tax exempt corporations, foreign companies, and Domestic International Sales Corporations, are specifically excluded from filing consolidated returns. Criteria for issuing consolidated financial statements are far less restrictive than these.

Advantages of Filing a Consolidated Income Tax Return An affiliated group of corporations benefits from the filing of a consolidated income tax return in the following ways:

1. Offsetting operating losses of one company against the operating profits of another provides immediate tax benefits, whereas the net operating loss provisions of the code would defer those benefits to future periods if the tax return were not consolidated.

2. Offsetting capital losses of one company against the capital gains of another accelerates the deductibility of capital losses.

3. Taxes on intercompany dividends are completely eliminated.

4. The tax on unconfirmed gains resulting from intercompany sales or exchanges of property is deferred until the gains are ultimately realized.

5. A company's investment credit or foreign tax credit may be available for use in a consolidated return although it exceeds the limitation applying to a separate return.

Disadvantages of Filing a Consolidated Return On the other hand, the decision by an affiliated group to file a consolidated income tax return carries with it certain disadvantages:

1. The election to file a consolidated income tax return must be made with the consent of each affiliated corporation and is binding for future years. Permission must be obtained to revert to the filing of separate returns.

2. Deferral of unconfirmed losses resulting from intercompany sales or exchanges of property also defers their tax benefits.

3. Risk of increased minimum tax on preference items is greater.

Amortization of Purchase Premium or Discount in a Consolidated Income Tax Return Many business combinations are treated as tax-free corporate reorganizations under Section 368 of the Internal Revenue Code. While these rules tend to result in the nonrecognition of gains and losses for tax purposes in eligible corporate reorganizations, they also provide for the carryover of existing tax bases of depreciable property. Thus, if purchase accounting is used for a business combination qualifying as a tax-free corporate reorganization, the existence and amortization of a purchase premium or discount is not considered for tax purposes and creates a *permanent difference* between the consolidated income statement and consolidated income tax return. Deferred taxes are not provided.

In contrast, if a purchase business combination is treated as a taxable exchange, with recognition of gain or loss for tax purposes, any purchase premium or discount must be allocated in conformity with Treasury regulations. Accordingly, consolidated tax depreciation may approximate consolidated book depreciation. *In no case, however, is amortization of goodwill an allowable tax deduction; it always creates a permanent difference.*

Concluding Comments

The major remaining problem of accounting for income taxes in consolidated financial statements arises when unconfirmed intercompany gains and losses exist and a consolidated income tax return is not filed. We deal with this situation in Chapter 9.

In order to concentrate on the major consolidation issues in subsequent chapters, we shall leave behind the interperiod tax allocation generally required under the equity method. To do so, we make the simplifying assumption that, unless otherwise stated, *undistributed equity method income is permanently reinvested and no tax allocation is necessary.*

Summary of Key Concepts

When a business combination is recorded as a **stock acquisition,** it is carried on the parent's books as an **intercorporate investment.** The parent accounts for such intercorporate investments using the equity or cost method. If the subsidiary is not consolidated, the equity method must be used for both accounting and reporting purposes. The **equity method** is stressed in this book.

Consolidated statements are prepared for reporting purposes only and do not represent accounting requirements. **Whether the equity or cost method is used** by the parent to account for its investments in subsidiaries, the **resulting consolidated statements are the same.** Only the procedures used to prepare them are affected by the choice of accounting method.

Under the **equity method,** the parent increases the investment account for its share of the subsidiary's net income and decreases the investment account for its share of the subsidiary's dividends. According to *APBO 18,* the equity method accrual is viewed as a **one-line consolidation** and must reflect all consolidation adjustments to net income. The only adjustment to the equity method accrual considered in this chapter is periodic purchase premium (discount) amortization. Other adjustments are considered in Chapters 9 and 10.

Consolidation under the equity method requires that the equity method entries made by the parent during the current year be eliminated on the working paper. By so doing, the parent's share of the subsidiary's net income is not counted twice—once in the equity method accrual and again when the revenue and expense accounts of the affiliates are combined.

Use of the **cost method** requires that the parent's share of the subsidiary's dividends be recognized as income when declared and the investment account balance **not** be periodically updated to reflect the subsidiary's net income. On the working paper, the investment account must be adjusted to the equity basis at the beginning of the year so it can be cleanly eliminated against the subsidiary's beginning stockholders' equity. Since the intercompany dividends were recorded by the parent as income, they must be eliminated in consolidation to avoid double counting of the parent's share of the subsidiary's net income.

A **consolidated financial statement working paper** is used to facilitate preparation of the consolidated balance sheet and statements of income and retained earnings. Preclosing trial balance data of the affiliates are rearranged in financial statement format on the working paper. Alternatively, a **consolidated trial balance working paper** may be used.

Preparation of the consolidated income statement for the year in which a **purchase combination** takes place can be complicated if the combination occurs **during** the year. The two alternatives are (1) to include only those revenues and expenses of the subsidiary arising **after** the date of combination and (2) to include the subsidiary's revenues and expenses for the **entire** year while deducting **preacquisition earnings.**

Consolidated net income covering the acquisition year should not include more than P's share of the subsidiary's earnings **after** date of acquisition. This result is achieved for the second alternative above in two steps. The first involves the deduction of the **minority interest in net income** for the **entire year.** The second concerns the deduction of **preacquisition earnings,** the parent's share of the subsidiary's earnings in the months prior to the intrayear combination. Observe that the deductions for preacquisition earnings and the portion of the minority interest in net income pertaining to the months prior to the intrayear combination add up to the subsidiary's total earnings in those prior months.

The **consolidated statement of changes in financial position (SCFP)** is prepared from comparative consolidated balance sheets, consolidated statements of income and retained earnings, and any necessary supplementary information. If this approach is followed, no further eliminations need be made when preparing the consolidated SCFP. Amortization of consolidated goodwill and the minority interest in net income must be added back to consolidated net income in determining funds provided by operations. Dividends paid to minority shareholders are shown as a nonoperating use of funds.

When the affiliates do not file a consolidated income tax return, undistributed equity method income normally represents a timing difference, and deferred taxes are provided. Under the **indefinite reversal criteria,** the parent may provide evidence that undistributed equity method income is permanently invested by the subsidiary and constitutes a **permanent difference.** In such situations, accrual of deferred taxes is not called for.

Questions   **Q8.1**   Proper application of the equity method by the parent results in the parent's net income and retained earnings being equal to consolidated net income and retained earnings, respectively. Explain why this happens.

Q8.2   "The parent's share of the subsidiary's dividends is recorded by the parent as dividend income under the cost method." Is this always true? Explain.

Q8.3   P Company owns 80 percent of S Company, acquired for $400,000 over book value. S's assets and liabilities are fairly stated at their book values. If S reports net income of $200,000 from its own operations in the current year, what is the maximum amount that P can accrue as income from S?

Q8.4   Minority Interest in Subsidiary appears on the consolidated balance sheet, and Minority Interest in Net Income appears on the consolidated income statement. Are they the same? What is the relationship between them?

Q8.5 How does the Minority Interest in Subsidiary change during the year? What working paper entries are made to record the change? Why are the entries necessary?

Q8.6 The consolidated financial statement working paper and the consolidated trial balance working paper presented in the chapter are set up so that the same working paper eliminations can be used in either format. Give the reason underlying this equivalence.

Q8.7 A pooling of interests combination recorded as a stock acquisition will normally lead to preparation of consolidated financial statements. In what significant way are the consolidation procedures different from those used in the purchase case?

Q8.8 When a purchase combination occurs *during* an accounting period, only that portion of S's net income earned *after* date of acquisition is eligible for inclusion in consolidated net income, and only to the extent of P's ownership of it. How do the consolidation procedures of method 2 (including S's revenues and expenses for the entire year) described in the text achieve this result?

Q8.9 In reviewing a consolidated financial statement working paper, you notice the following entry:

Preacquisition Earnings	390,000	
Dividends—S		160,000
Investment in S		230,000

Interpret the entry and indicate what it accomplishes on the working paper.

Q8.10 How are the components of the change in minority interest during the current year treated on the consolidated statement of changes in financial position?

Q8.11 When affiliated companies *do not* file a consolidated income tax return, only intercompany dividends (after the 85 percent deduction) are included in tax return income. Yet pretax consolidated book income includes P's entire share of S's net income, whether distributed in dividends or not. How does this affect the computation of book consolidated income tax expense?

Q8.12 Explain why the indefinite reversal criteria are irrelevant to many equity method investments.

Exercises **E8.1** During 19X2, P's 70-percent-owned subsidiary reported net income of $1,600,000 and declared dividends of $600,000. P had acquired its interest in the subsidiary on January 2, 19X2, at a cost of $5,200,000, which was $1,000,000 in excess of the net assets acquired. Of this $1,000,000, $500,000 was allocated to equipment with a five-year life and $200,000 related to inventory—of which 40 percent was sold during 19X2. The remaining $300,000 could not be allocated to identifiable assets and liabilities. P Company amortizes its intangibles over the longest possible period.

Required: Give the journal entries recorded by P under the equity method in 19X2 and the working paper eliminations. Show all calculations.

E8.2   Refer to the data in E8.1. Assume that the remaining revalued inventory was sold during 19X3, and give all working paper entries made at December 31, 19X3, relative to the purchase premium.

E8.3   On December 31, 19X2, P acquired 80 percent of S's outstanding shares for $200,000, $40,000 more than their book value. S's assets and liabilities were fairly stated except for certain motor vehicles, which were appraised at $30,000 more than their book value. The vehicles' remaining life at December 31, 19X2, was five years. Any goodwill arising in consolidation is to be amortized over twenty years. P accounts for its investment in S using the cost method.

As of January 1, 19X5, the beginning of the current year, S had total earnings of $90,000 since the acquisition by P and had paid out dividends of $70,000. In 19X5, S reported net income of $32,000 and paid dividends of $20,000.

Required: Prepare the entries made by P during 19X5 relative to its investment in S and give the working paper eliminations. Compute the minority interest in S at December 31, 19X5.

E8.4   The separate income statements of Parson and Soaper Companies for the year ended June 30, 19X7, are given below. When Parson acquired 80 percent of Soaper on July 1, 19X6, it was found that Soaper's inventory was undervalued by $160,000, plant assets with a ten-year life were overvalued by $200,000, and long-term debt which matures in five years was overvalued by $100,000. No goodwill arose in the combination. All Parson's depreciation and amortization charges are based on the straight-line method. The undervalued inventory was sold during the year ended June 30, 19X7.

	Parson	Soaper
Sales .	$5,000,000	$2,000,000
Income from Soaper .	112,000	—
Cost of Goods Sold .	(3,000,000)	(800,000)
Depreciation Expense	(500,000)	(140,000)
Interest Expense .	(100,000)	(60,000)
Other Expenses .	(600,000)	(700,000)
Net Income .	$ 912,000	$ 300,000

Required: Prepare a consolidated income statement for Parson and Soaper for the year ended June 30, 19X7.

E8.5   P Company, a calendar year corporation, acquired 90 percent of S Company's shares on September 30, 19X0, in a stock acquisition qualifying as a pooling of interests. S Company also reports on a calendar year basis. Its business is non-seasonal. P accounts for the investment in S using the cost method. Separate income statements of the two companies for the year ended December 31, 19X0, follow:

	P Company	S Company
Sales	$10,000,000	$3,000,000
Dividend Income from S	90,000	—
Cost of Goods Sold	(6,000,000)	(2,000,000)
Selling and Administrative Expenses	(1,500,000)	(400,000)
Net Income	$ 2,590,000	$ 600,000

Required:

1. Prepare a consolidated income statement for the year ended December 31, 19X0.
2. Suppose P used the equity method. Compute the equity method accrual and consolidated net income.

E8.6 On June 30, 19X5, Portly Company purchased 70 percent of the outstanding stock of Stout Corporation for $15,000,000 cash. Both companies report on a calendar year basis. Portly earned $5,000,000 in 19X5 from its own operations and accounts for its investment in Stout by the equity method. Stout's business is seasonal, and its controller determined that 30 percent of its net income of $2,000,000 was earned in the first six months of 19X5. Stout's dividend rate was increased late in 19X5, and, accordingly, 60 percent of its annual dividends of $1,200,000 were declared after June 30.

Assume that Stout's capital stock and retained earnings on June 30, 19X5, amounted to $7,000,000 and $13,000,000, respectively, and that its assets and liabilities are fairly stated. Portly amortizes intangibles over the maximum period allowed by *APBO 17*.

Required:

1. Compute consolidated net income for 19X5.
2. Prepare the working paper eliminations made in consolidation at December 31, 19X5, under the preacquisition earnings approach.

E8.7 Following are the condensed income statements of P Company and its 80-percent-owned subsidiary, S Company, for the year ended December 31, 19X8. P acquired its interest in S on September 30, 19X8. The purchase discount of $1,900,000 on the acquisition was allocated entirely to assets of S being depreciated on the straight-line method over a remaining life of ten years. Because of the nature of S's business, 50 percent of its revenues and expenses arose in the last quarter of 19X8.

	P Company	S Company
Sales	$10,000,000	$4,000,000
Cost of Goods Sold	(6,000,000)	(3,000,000)
Other Operating Expenses	(3,200,000)	(900,000)
Net Income	$ 800,000	$ 100,000

Required: Prepare condensed consolidated income statements for P and S for 19X8 under *both* of the alternative presentations mentioned in the chapter.

E8.8 Using the following data, prepare the "Working Capital Provided by Operations" section of a consolidated statement of changes in financial position.

Consolidated Net Income	$1,000,000
Purchase Premium Amortization: Goodwill ($30,000), Trademarks ($25,000), Inventory ($45,000)	100,000
Consolidated Depreciation Expense	180,000
Net Income Reported by 80-Percent-Owned Consolidated Subsidiary	200,000
Dividends Declared by 80-Percent-Owned Consolidated Subsidiary	60,000
Net Income Reported by 30-Percent-Owned Equity Investment	150,000
Dividends Declared by 30-Percent-Owned Equity Investment	90,000

E8.9 Prep Corporation has owned 80 percent of Strep Company since Strep's inception. The condensed consolidated balance sheets of Prep and Strep at the beginning and end of the current year and other relevant pieces of information are presented next:

Prep Corporation and Subsidiary
Condensed Consolidated Balance Sheets

ASSETS	End of Year	Beginning of Year
Current Assets	$2,000,000	$1,700,000
Plant Assets	4,000,000	4,200,000
Accumulated Depreciation	(1,500,000)	(1,600,000)
Goodwill	300,000	330,000
Total Assets	$4,800,000	$4,630,000

LIABILITIES AND STOCKHOLDERS' EQUITY	End of Year	Beginning of Year
Current Liabilities	$1,282,000	$1,550,000
Noncurrent Liabilities	1,800,000	1,700,000
Minority Interest in Strep	288,000	280,000
Stockholders' Equity	1,430,000	1,100,000
Total Liabilities and Stockholders' Equity	$4,800,000	$4,630,000

Additional information:
1. Consolidated net income for the year is $400,000.
2. Strep Company reported net income from its own operations of $120,000 and declared $80,000 in dividends.
3. Consolidated depreciation expense was $350,000.
4. Plant assets with an original cost of $500,000 and a net book value of $50,000 were retired from service and scrapped.
5. Prep declared $70,000 in dividends during the year.

Required: Prepare, in good form, a consolidated statement of changes in financial position for the current year.

E8.10 Press Company acquired 70 percent of the outstanding stock of Stalwart Company several years ago and uses the equity method to account for its investment. Stalwart has paid no dividends (85 percent of which would be excluded from taxation under current law) and has net earnings of $840,000 since acquisition, including $120,000 in the current year. Press reported pretax book income of $500,000 from its own operations in the current year and has had no timing differences related to its own operations. Press expects that all of Stalwart's earnings will ultimately be distributed as dividends. Both companies face a combined federal and state income tax rate of 40 percent.

Required:

1. Prepare the journal entry made by Press to record its income tax expense for the year.
2. Compute the balance in Press' Deferred Income Taxes account at the end of the current year.

E8.11 Plant Company owns 80 percent of the outstanding stock of Seed Company. Seed reported net income of $200,000 after taxes during the current year and made dividend distributions of $80,000. In computing its equity method accrual, Plant recognized consolidated goodwill amortization of $20,000. Plant and Seed file separate federal income tax returns, and both companies face a marginal income tax rate of 40 percent. Current law provides for deduction of 85 percent of intercorporate dividends.

Required:

1. Give the journal entry made by Plant to provide for income taxes on its investment income in Seed. Show all supporting computations. Assume that Plant expects that Seed's undistributed income will eventually be received as dividends.
2. Same as requirement 1, except that the indefinite reversal criteria apply.

Problems **P8.1** **Investor Accounting and Consolidation—Cost and Equity Methods Compared** On January 1, 19X1, Todd Corporation made the following investments:

1. Acquired 80 percent of the outstanding common stock of Meadow Corporation for cash at $70 per share. The stockholders' equity of Meadow on January 1, 19X1, consisted of the following:

Common Stock, Par Value $50 . . . . $50,000
Retained Earnings 20,000

2. Acquired 70 percent of the outstanding common stock of Van Corporation for cash at $40 per share. The stockholders' equity of Van on January 1, 19X1, consisted of the following:

Common Stock, Par Value $20		$60,000
Capital in Excess of Par Value		20,000
Retained Earnings		40,000

An analysis of the retained earnings of each company for 19X1 is as follows:

	Todd	Meadow	Van
Balance, January 1, 19X1	$240,000	$20,000	$40,000
Net Income (Loss) from Own Operations . .	104,600	36,000	(12,000)
Cash Dividends Paid	(40,000)	(16,000)	(9,000)
Balance, December 31, 19X1	$304,600	$40,000	$19,000

Required:

1. Assume Todd accounts for its investments in subsidiaries using the cost method. Give the entries made by Todd to record these investments and to account for them during 19X1. (Hint: Consider the nature of the "dividends" paid by Van.)
2. Again, assuming Todd uses the cost method, give the necessary working paper entries to consolidate Todd and its subsidiaries at December 31, 19X1.
3. Repeat requirement 1, assuming that Todd uses the equity method.
4. Repeat requirement 2, assuming that Todd uses the equity method.
5. Compute the amount of minority interest in each subsidiary's stockholders' equity at December 31, 19X1.
6. Compute consolidated net income for the year ended December 31, 19X1.
7. Compute consolidated retained earnings at December 31, 19X1. Show all calculations. (AICPA adapted)

P8.2 **Consolidated Financial Statement Working Paper and Purchase Premium Amortization** Padre Company, a wholesaler, purchased 80 percent of the issued and outstanding stock of Sun, Inc., a retailer, on December 31, 19X2, for $120,000. At that date, Sun, Inc., had one class of common stock outstanding at a stated value of $100,000 and retained earnings of $25,000. Padre Company had a $50,000 deficit balance in retained earnings.

Padre Company purchased the Sun, Inc., stock from Sun's major stockholder, primarily to acquire control of signboard leases owned by Sun. The leases will expire on December 31, 19X7, and Padre Company executives estimate the leases, which cannot be renewed, were worth at least $25,000 more than their book value when the stock was purchased.

The financial statements for both companies for the year ended December 31, 19X6, appear at the top of page 344.

Additional information:

1. Sun declared a $9,000 cash dividend on December 20, 19X6, payable on January 16, 19X7, to stockholders of record on January 2, 19X7. Padre carries its investment at equity but had not recorded this dividend on December 31, 19X6. No dividend payments occurred during 19X6.

Padre Company and Subsidiary
Financial Statements
For the Year Ended December 31, 19X6

BALANCE SHEET

ASSETS	Padre Company	Sun, Inc.
Other Current Assets	$117,200	$113,500
Inventories	54,800	85,600
Investment in Sun, Inc.	151,200	—
Signboard Leases (Net)	—	12,000
Land	25,000	10,500
Plant and Equipment	200,000	40,000
Accumulated Depreciation	(102,000)	(10,600)[a]
Total Assets	$446,200	$251,000

LIABILITIES AND STOCKHOLDERS' EQUITY		
Other Current Liabilities	$ 60,000	$ 67,000
Dividends Payable	—	9,000
Capital Stock	300,000	100,000
Retained Earnings	86,200	75,000
Total Liabilities and Stockholders' Equity . . .	$446,200	$251,000

[a]Balance allocated since acquisition on December 31, 19X2.

INCOME STATEMENT

	Padre Company	Sun, Inc.
Sales	$420,000	$300,000
Income from Sun	16,000	—
Cost of Goods Sold	(315,000)	(240,000)
Expenses	(65,000)	(35,000)
Net Income	$ 56,000	$ 25,000

2. Inventories at January 1, 19X6, amounted to $52,300 and $89,000 for Padre and Sun, respectively.

Required:
1. Prepare a consolidated financial statement working paper for the Padre Company and its subsidiary, Sun, Inc., as of December 31, 19X6. Formal statements and journal entries are not required. You may assume that both companies made all the adjusting entries required for separate financial statements unless an obvious discrepancy exists.
2. Prepare a schedule explaining how the investment account balance changed between December 31, 19X2, and December 31, 19X6.

(AICPA adapted)

P8.3   Consolidated Balance Sheet—Purchase Premium Amortization   Paul Corporation acquired all of the outstanding stock of Sand Corporation on June 30,

19X3, for $19,000,000. The Sand stock had a book value of $3,000,000, giving a purchase premium of $16,000,000, which was allocated as follows:

Account	Amount Dr. (Cr.)	Amortization Period (Straight-Line)
Property, Plant, and Equipment, Net	$13,100,000	13.1 years
Other Assets	(300,000)	15
Long-Term Debt	400,000	40
Goodwill	2,800,000	40
	$16,000,000	

During the six-month period from July 1 to December 31, 19X3, Sand earned $1,250,000 and paid no dividends. Paul carries its Investment in Sand at equity but has *not* reflected the purchase premium amortization in its equity method accrual.

The balance sheets of Paul and Sand prior to consolidation at December 31, 19X3, are as follows:

	Paul Corporation	Sand Corporation
ASSETS		
Cash	$ 3,500,000	$ 600,000
Accounts Receivable, Net	1,400,000	1,500,000
Inventories	1,000,000	2,500,000
Property, Plant, and Equipment, Net	2,000,000	3,100,000
Investment in Subsidiary, at Equity	20,250,000	—
Other Assets	100,000	500,000
Total Assets	$28,250,000	$8,200,000
LIABILITIES AND STOCKHOLDERS' EQUITY		
Current Liabilities	$ 1,500,000	$1,100,000
Long-Term Debt	4,000,000	2,600,000
Other Liabilities	750,000	250,000
Common Stock, Par Value $1 per Share	10,000,000	1,000,000
Additional Paid-In Capital	5,000,000	400,000
Retained Earnings	7,000,000	2,850,000
Total Liabilities and Stockholders' Equity	$28,250,000	$8,200,000

Required: Prepare a consolidated balance sheet of Paul Corporation and its wholly-owned subsidiary, Sand Corporation, as of December 31, 19X3. Show supporting computations in good form.

(AICPA adapted)

P8.4 **Equity Method Entries, Eliminations, and Consolidation Computations**
On December 31, 19X0, P acquired 60 percent of S's outstanding voting shares for $150,000—$30,000 more than their book value. S's assets and liabilities were all fairly stated at date of acquisition except for manufacturing equipment, which was appraised for $30,000 more than its book value. The equipment's re-

maining useful life at December 31, 19X0, was ten years. Any goodwill arising in consolidation is to be amortized over forty years.

As of January 1, 19X3, the beginning of the current year, S had total net income of $70,000 since the acquisition by P and had paid out dividends of $40,000. Aside from retained earnings, S's only other owners' equity account is capital stock of $100,000, unchanged since S was organized.

During 19X3, S had net income of $20,000 and paid dividends of $8,000. P accounts for its investment in S using the equity method. P's net income from its own operations was $36,000.

Required:

1. Give the journal entries made by P during 19X3 relative to its investment in S.
2. Give the eliminating entries which would appear on the consolidated working paper at December 31, 19X3.
3. Compute consolidated retained earnings and the minority interest in S at December 31, 19X3. P's retained earnings from its own operations are $220,000 at that date.
4. What is consolidated net income for 19X3?

P8.5   **Investor Accounting—Cost and Equity Methods, Purchase Premium**   On December 31, 19X3, Paint Corporation acquired 90 percent of the stock of Soil Company. During 19X4, Soil reported net income of $200,000 and paid dividends of $90,000. The market value of the consideration given by Paint was $3,200,000, which exceeded the book value of Paint's 90 percent interest by $500,000. Allocation of the purchase premium produced the following:

Account	Amount	Amortization Period
Inventory	$ 75,000	Sold during 19X4
Depreciable Assets	225,000	Ten years
Goodwill	200,000	Maximum allowable
	$500,000	

Required:

1. Give the journal entries made by Paint Corporation during 19X4, assuming the equity method is used. Supporting computations must be in good form.
2. Same as requirement 1, except the cost method is used by Paint.
3. Give the working paper entries necessary to consolidate Paint and Soil at December 31, 19X4, under the equity method.
4. Same as requirement 3, except the cost method is used by Paint.
5. If Paint reports net income from its own operations in 19X4 of $500,000, compute consolidated net income.

P8.6   **Consolidated Statement of Changes in Financial Position**   Comparative consolidated balance sheets and the intervening consolidated income statement for P Company and S Company follow.

P Company and S Company
Comparative Consolidated Balance Sheets
at December 31, 19X7 and 19X6

ASSETS	12/31/X7	12/31/X6
Current Assets	$1,400,000	$1,000,000
Property, Plant, and Equipment	3,100,000	2,500,000
Accumulated Depreciation	(1,000,000)	(800,000)
Goodwill	275,000	300,000
Total Assets	$3,775,000	$3,000,000

LIABILITIES AND STOCKHOLDERS' EQUITY		
Current Liabilities	$ 900,000	$ 650,000
Other Liabilities	950,000	800,000
Capital Stock	700,000	500,000
Retained Earnings	1,065,000	900,000
Minority Interest in S	160,000	150,000
Total Liabilities and Stockholders' Equity	$3,775,000	$3,000,000

P Company and S Company
Consolidated Statement of Income and Retained Earnings
For the Year Ended December 31, 19X7

Sales and Other Revenue	$3,555,000
Cost of Goods Sold	$1,700,000
Operating Expenses	1,243,000
Minority Interest in Net Income	12,000
Total Expenses	$2,955,000
Net Income	$ 600,000
Retained Earnings, January 1, 19X7	900,000
Dividends Declared	(435,000)
Retained Earnings, December 31, 19X7	$1,065,000

Additional information:
   1. Consolidated depreciation expense was $250,000.
   2. During the year, plant assets with an original cost of $75,000 and accumulated depreciation of $50,000 were sold for $25,000.

Required: Prepare, in good form, a consolidated statement of changes in financial position (working capital basis) for the year ended December 31, 19X7.

P8.7 **Consolidated Financial Statement Working Paper—Purchase Premium**
Paltry Corporation purchased all of the outstanding stock of Slim Company on January 2, 19X7, for $2,000,000 cash. On that date, Slim's inventory was undervalued by $100,000, plant assets with a twenty-year life remaining were undervalued by $200,000, and, due to rising interest rates, the market value of its

long-term debt stood at $400,000. The debt matures in five years. Paltry always uses straight-line amortization over the maximum period allowable. Inventories are accounted for using the FIFO cost-flow assumption.

Following are the preclosing trial balances for the two companies at December 31, 19X7:

Account	Paltry	Slim
Cash and Receivables	$2,800,000	$ 880,000
Inventory, January 2, 19X7	3,000,000	1,400,000
Investment in Slim	1,920,000	—
Plant Assets	5,000,000	2,300,000 (net)
Accumulated Depreciation	(1,200,000)	—
Current Liabilities	(2,600,000)	(2,300,000)
Long-Term Debt	(1,700,000)	(500,000)
Capital Stock	(800,000)	(200,000)
Retained Earnings	(4,200,000)	(1,000,000)
Dividends	300,000	80,000
Sales	(12,780,000)	(5,400,000)
Purchases	8,000,000	3,000,000
Operating Expenses	2,100,000	1,700,000
Interest Expense	160,000	40,000
	$ 0	$ 0
Inventory, December 31, 19X7	$3,200,000	$1,350,000

Required:

1. Compute the equity method accrual to be made by Paltry at December 31, 19X7, and record it.
2. Prepare a consolidated financial statement working paper for Paltry and Slim at December 31, 19X7, after the equity method accrual has been recorded.

P8.8   **Consolidated Financial Statement Working Paper: Purchase Discount**   P Company acquired 80 percent of the outstanding shares of S Company on January 2, 19X1, for $1,470,000 cash. Direct cash costs associated with the acquisition amounted to $50,000. S Company's stockholders' equity had a book value of $2,000,000 on that date; some of its assets and liabilities had fair values different from their book values, as shown below:

Accounts of S Company	Book Value	Fair Value
Inventory (LIFO Cost-Flow Assumption)	440,000	500,000
Notes Receivable, Noncurrent	110,000	130,000
Buildings and Equipment, Net (Twenty-Year Life Remaining)	500,000	400,000
Long-Term Debt (Face Value $200,000)	(220,000)	(300,000)

All depreciation and amortization are allocated by the straight-line method. Preclosing trial balances for the two companies at December 31, 19X1, follow:

Account	P Company	S Company
Cash and Receivables	$1,000,000	$1,580,000
Inventory, January 2, 19X1	1,700,000	440,000
Notes Receivable, Noncurrent (Face Value $100,000) . .	—	108,000
Investment in S	1,480,000	—
Land	600,000	330,000
Buildings and Equipment	2,200,000	600,000
Accumulated Depreciation	(700,000)	(50,000)[a]
Current Liabilities	(1,400,000)	(500,000)
Long-Term Debt (10 Percent Coupon Rate)	(600,000)	(218,000)
Capital Stock	(200,000)	(100,000)
Retained Earnings	(2,810,000)	(1,900,000)
Dividends	120,000	50,000
Sales	(7,000,000)	(3,200,000)
Interest Income	—	(8,000)
Purchases	4,800,000	2,440,000
Operating Expenses	750,000	410,000
Interest Expense	60,000	18,000
	$ 0	$ 0
Inventory, December 31, 19X1	$1,800,000	$ 500,000

[a]Amount allocated in 19X1.

Required:
1. Compute the equity method accrual to be made by P at December 31, 19X1.
2. Prepare a consolidated financial statement working paper for P and S at December 31, 19X1.

P8.9 **Consolidated Statement of Changes in Financial Position: Cost Method**
On page 350, in Exhibit 8.16, are the trial balances of P Company and its subsidiary, S Company, subsequent to closing the nominal accounts. P accounts for its investment in S using the cost method.

Additional information:
1. P Company acquired 90 percent of the outstanding stock of S Company on January 2, 19X1, in exchange for:

500 Shares P Company Capital Stock; Par Value $50, Market Value $200	$100,000
Note Payable, due December 20, 19X2	78,400
Total	$178,400

The above note payable due December 20, 19X2, was paid on December 1, 19X2. On January 2, 19X1, the stockholders' equity of S Company had a book value of $151,900. The entire excess of cost over book value is attributed to undervalued land on the books of S Company. P carries its investment in S at cost.

2. In January 19X2, P Company sold for $101,300 some "other investments" that cost $85,400. In March 19X2, P Company sold a parcel of land that cost $10,500 for $18,800.

Exhibit 8.16 Comparative Trial Balances of P Company and S Company to Be Used in P8.9

	December 31, 19X2		December 31, 19X1	
	P Company	S Company	P Company	S Company
Cash	$ 21,100	$ 34,700	$ 56,700	$ 9,800
Accounts Receivable	49,700	64,200	54,200	31,500
Inventories	46,600	64,400	49,800	48,400
Other Receivables—Current	41,300	22,400	32,300	24,500
Investment in S Company	178,400	—	178,400	—
Other Investments	10,800	33,400	92,800	33,400
Land	18,200	15,000	28,700	15,000
Buildings	135,800	87,000	106,700	65,000
Equipment	61,000	45,000	48,000	45,000
Total Debits	$562,900	$366,100	$647,600	$272,600
Allowance for Bad Debts	$ 4,500	$ 3,900	$ 4,100	$ 3,700
Allowance for Depreciation	69,500	50,600	41,300	31,200
Accounts Payable	22,900	45,900	31,200	36,800
Notes Payable, Current	41,000	25,000	88,400	—
Dividends Payable	—	14,000	—	—
Other Accruals	5,900	20,800	12,700	12,600
Income Taxes Payable	19,600	19,400	36,500	12,300
Bonds Payable	—	—	30,000	—
Capital Stock	175,000	75,000	175,000	75,000
Capital Contributed in Excess of Par Value . . .	117,000	38,200	117,000	38,200
Retained Earnings, Beginning of Year	87,400	48,800	62,300	38,700
Net Income for Year	20,100	24,500	49,100	24,100
Total Credits	$562,900	$366,100	$647,600	$272,600

3. On June 30, 19X2, P Company demolished an unneeded warehouse building that cost $18,900 and had a net book value of $5,400 on that date.

4. During 19X2, P Company declared and paid cash dividends totaling $24,000. S Company declared a cash dividend totaling $14,000 on December 1, 19X2, payable on January 10, 19X3, to holders of record on December 15, 19X2. The dividend receivable was recorded in P Company's Other Receivables account.

5. The P Company bonds, which had a maturity date of December 1, 19X4, were retired in 19X2 at a total consideration of $32,500, including $600 for accrued interest and $1,900 penalty for early retirement.

6. At December 31, 19X2, P Company's Other Receivables account included a $25,000 non-interest bearing note receivable from S Company. S Company's Accounts Receivable included $18,500 due from P Company for merchandise purchases; the amount is equal to the original cost of the merchandise to S.

7. The amounts for the net income for the year are after all deductions; no expenses or income were recorded in the retained earnings accounts.

Required: Prepare a formal consolidated statement of changes in financial position (working capital basis) for P Company and its subsidiary for the year ended December 31, 19X2. All supporting computations, including the computation of consolidated net income, should be in good form. [Hint: Combine the beginning and ending trial balances, and use the T account solution procedure (not required); eliminate all intercompany receivables and payables when computing working capital at December 31, 19X2.]

(AICPA adapted)

Chapter 9

Consolidated Financial Statements: Intercompany Transactions I

This is the first of two chapters in which we study how **intercompany transactions**—transactions among affiliated corporations—affect the preparation of consolidated financial statements. Many of the intricacies common to the consolidation process are encountered in these two chapters.

Intercompany transactions are of two general types. The first type occurs when goods or services are sold between affiliated corporations. In consolidation, intercompany revenues and expenses are eliminated. Neither arose out of transactions with outside parties; both must be eliminated to avoid overstatement of consolidated revenues and expenses. Any related intercompany receivables and payables must also be eliminated. The second type of intercompany transaction requiring working paper eliminations arises when assets transferred among affiliates at a gain or loss to the selling company are still on hand at the end of an accounting period. Since such gains and losses have not yet been confirmed by transactions with outside parties, they too must be eliminated and the assets' balances adjusted in consolidation.

This chapter looks at intercompany revenues and expenses and the problems created by unconfirmed profits and losses arising out of intercompany transfers of land, merchandise inventory, and depreciable assets. These unconfirmed profits and losses are also related to the parent's equity method accrual and, where appropriate, to the minority interest in net income. Income tax effects of intercompany transactions and the computation of consolidated income tax expense are discussed at the end of the chapter.

In Chapter 10, the study of intercompany transactions is continued with emphasis on intercompany bondholdings and a comprehensive numerical example involving a variety of intercompany transactions. Chapter 10 concludes with a discussion of situations in which the subsidiary has preferred stock *and* common stock outstanding.

As the problems created by intercompany transactions are addressed, the accountant is guided by the overriding objective in the preparation of consolidated statements: to report the affairs of a group of affiliated corporations as if it were a single economic entity. The **principles of confirmation** and **removal of intercompany assets, liabilities, and revenues and expenses,** which follow from this overriding objective, are used over and over again in this chapter and the next.

Intercompany Revenues and Expenses

When affiliated corporations perform services or transfer merchandise to one another, the intercompany transaction causes one company to record revenues and the other to record expenses (or merchandise purchases). Because the companies have recorded (or will record) purchase and sales transactions with outside parties which incorporate these internally transferred goods or services, such intercompany revenue and expense items are always eliminated in their entirety in consolidated statements. The eliminating entry is:

CONSOLIDATED FINANCIAL STATEMENT WORKING PAPER

Revenues (Intercompany)	XXX	
Expenses (Intercompany)		XXX

To eliminate the revenue and expense amounts recorded by the affiliates on an intercompany sale of merchandise or services.

This removes the double counting of revenue and expense items which otherwise would exist without affecting the amount of consolidated net income. The effect of such an elimination can be seen in Figure 9.1. Notice that consolidated revenues and expenses are reduced by equal amounts and that the area labeled "Consolidated Net Income" is identical to the total area within the separate net incomes of P and S.

To illustrate, suppose that Park Company performs some management services for South Company. Personnel compensation, supplies, travel, and overhead result in out-of-pocket costs of $25,000 to Park, which have been recorded in Park's accounting records. The management services are billed to South Company at $40,000, thereby generating the following bookkeeping entries by Park and South:

BOOKS OF PARK COMPANY

Cash	40,000	
Service Revenue		40,000

To record the performance of services for South Company at a price of $40,000.

BOOKS OF SOUTH COMPANY

General and Administrative Expenses	40,000	
Cash		40,000

To record the procurement of management services from Park Company at a cost of $40,000.

We assume that the cost of these management services is, like all costs of being in business, reflected in the prices of goods and services sold to outside parties. When Park and South are consolidated, we view them as a single economic entity. Therefore, from a consolidated point of view, we are interested

Figure 9.1   Effect of Eliminating Intercompany Revenues and Expenses

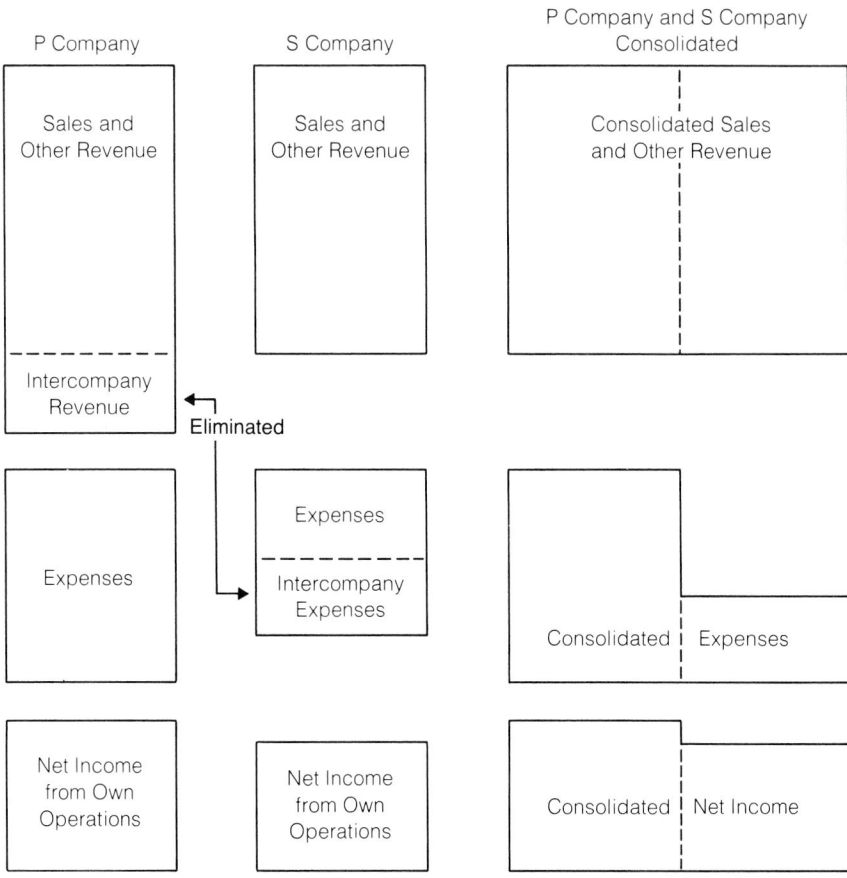

only in (1) the costs originally incurred by Park Company and (2) the sales to external parties by South Company. The intercompany revenues and expenses are of no concern to the controlling interest, and consolidated revenue and expenses will be overstated by $40,000 if these entries are not eliminated. At the next consolidation point, then, the following eliminating entry is made on the working paper:

CONSOLIDATED FINANCIAL STATEMENT WORKING PAPER

Service Revenue 40,000
    General and Administrative Expenses   40,000
To eliminate the intercompany revenue and expense
resulting from the management services provided by
Park to South in the amount of $40,000.

Note that since this elimination reduces consolidated revenues and expenses by equal amounts, it has no effect on consolidated net income. Moreover, neither P's equity method accrual nor the minority interest in net income is affected. As we shall see in the section on intercompany merchandise transactions, however, income of the affiliates is affected *only* if there are unconfirmed intercompany profits or losses. Eliminating intercompany sales and purchases is done to avoid double counting; removal of unconfirmed intercompany profits is a separate issue.

Intercompany Profits: Some Preliminaries	To simplify the discussion, we distinguish between intercompany sales or transfers *from* parent *to* subsidiary and *to* parent *from* subsidiary, as follows.

> A **downstream sale** or **transfer** occurs when the *parent sells to a subsidiary*. An **upstream sale** or **transfer** indicates that a *subsidiary is selling to the parent*.

Determination of the Intercompany Profit

The intercompany profits which require elimination relate only to transfer of assets which remain inside the affiliated group at the end of the reporting period. These are the profits (or losses) which have not yet been confirmed by further sale to outside parties; confirmed profits require no elimination. Calculation of the intercompany profit is straightforward, although a minor complication arises when shipping or installation costs are incurred on an intercompany transfer.

$$\text{Intercompany profit} = \text{Intercompany transfer price} - \text{Cost (net book value)}$$
$$\text{to selling affiliate.}$$

Shipping and Installation Costs   Frequently, intercompany transfers of merchandise and equipment result in shipping or installation costs. If these costs are paid by the purchasing affiliate, they represent valid costs to the affiliated group and do not affect the intercompany profit. In contrast, payment of such costs by the selling affiliate indicates a concession in the intercompany transfer price, and the intercompany profit is reduced accordingly. Observe that in both cases the resulting consolidated asset reflects original acquisition cost plus any shipping and installation costs incurred in the transaction, regardless of which company actually pays for the costs. To convince yourself of this point, consider the following data:

Intercompany Merchandise Transfer Price	$100
Cost to Selling Affiliate	80
Shipping Cost	5

If the *purchasing affiliate pays the shipping cost*, it records the inventory at $105. Assuming the inventory is unsold at consolidation, unconfirmed intercompany profit of $20 (= $100 − $80) would be eliminated, reducing consolidated inventory to $85 (= $105 − $20).

In contrast, *payment of the shipping cost by the selling affiliate* indicates that the transfer price is actually $95 (= $100 − $5), and the intercompany profit is $15 (= $95 − $80). The purchasing affiliate records the inventory at $100. Assuming it is unsold at consolidation, unconfirmed intercompany profit of $15 is eliminated, reducing consolidated inventory to $85 (= $100 − $15), as in the previous case.

How Much Intercompany Profit Should Be Eliminated?

Elimination of intercompany profits on asset transfers within an affiliated group derives from the fundamental argument that, since P and S are under common control, transactions between them are *not* the outcome of arm's-length bargaining. Therefore, any profits (or losses) recorded in such transactions are *tentative*, subject to confirmation via arm's-length transactions with external parties.

Total Elimination in Downstream Sales   There is general agreement that intercompany profits arising in downstream sales should be entirely eliminated against the controlling interest. This simply follows from the notion that no part of the unconfirmed intercompany profit benefits the controlling interest (P Company) until the assets are sold outside the affiliated group. Furthermore, the existence of a minority interest is irrelevant in downstream sales. Since elimination of the unconfirmed intercompany profit is entirely against the controlling interest, there is no effect on the minority interest in net income.

Total versus Partial Elimination in Upstream Sales   In cases where the subsidiary is selling to the parent, recorded unconfirmed intercompany profits show up first in the net income of S and then—by the equity method—in the net income of P. Clearly, if S is a wholly-owned subsidiary, P has in effect made a sale to itself, and the distinction between downstream and upstream sales vanishes. P's net income should include none of these unconfirmed intercompany profits. The presence of a minority interest, however, complicates the issue.

Remember that P and S are separate legal entities. One could argue, with some merit, that the minority's share of intercompany profits on upstream sales needs no further confirmation. Indeed, once the upstream sale to P has occurred, the minority's share of the profit is fixed. Yet P may arbitrarily decide to void the sale and transfer the unsold items back to S, in which case the intercompany profit, along with the minority share thereof, vanishes. This is the problem when non-arm's-length transactions occur between companies under common control. Nevertheless, some accountants believe that unconfirmed intercompany profits on upstream sales ought to be eliminated only to the extent of P's interest in S—the partial or fractional elimination position. The *parent theory of consolidated statements* supports partial elimination on upstream sales.

We believe that total elimination of all unconfirmed intercompany profits or losses is appropriate for consolidated statements. Whether upstream or downstream, intercompany sales are not likely to be arm's-length transactions, and realization of any intercompany profits prior to sale outside the firm is premature. Furthermore, failure to remove the entire unconfirmed intercompany profit is inconsistent with reporting consolidated assets at cost to the consolidated entity. This position is consistent with the *entity theory of consolidated statements* and with *ARB 51*, which states, in part:

> Accordingly, any intercompany profit or loss on assets remaining within the group should be eliminated; the concept usually applied for this purpose is gross profit or loss. . . .[1]
>
> The amount of intercompany profit to be eliminated . . . is not affected by the existence of a minority interest. The complete elimination of the intercompany profit or loss . . . *may* be allocated proportionately between the majority and minority interests.[2] [Emphasis added.]

The quotation indicates that elimination of the intercompany profit *may* be allocated proportionately between the controlling and minority interest. *ARB 51* seems to be suggesting that, when the subsidiary is partially owned, total elimination of the intercompany profit against the controlling interest is an acceptable alternative treatment. Such a procedure would have the unfortunate effect of reducing consolidated net income below what it would have been had the intercompany transaction not occurred at all!

To illustrate, suppose Post Corporation owns 80 percent of Staff Corporation. Net income of Post was $200,000. Staff earned $100,000 during the year, including $40,000 on sales to Post, as yet unconfirmed by external transactions. If Staff's upstream sales had not occurred at all, consolidated net income would be $248,000 [= $200,000 + (.8 × $60,000)]; minority interest in net income is $12,000 (= .2 × $60,000). The same result is obtained if the intercompany profit is eliminated proportionately against the controlling and minority interests. Elimination of the $40,000 intercompany profit against only the majority, however, leads to consolidated net income of $240,000 [= $200,000 + (.8 × $100,000) − $40,000] and minority interest in net income of $20,000 (= .2 × $100,000). In effect, the minority's share is recognized by charging the majority for $8,000 and shifting the $8,000 to the minority. We find no basis in principle for such a shift. Consistent application of this approach calls for crediting the majority for the same $40,000 when the intercompany profit is ultimately confirmed. Hence, consolidated net income is misstated by $8,000 in each of two accounting periods. Even though the misstatements cancel out, we see no justification for the first misstatement, let alone the second.

The treatment of unconfirmed intercompany gains and losses adopted throughout this book can be summarized as follows. We believe this treatment is theoretically sound and consistent with current practice.

> Preparation of consolidated statements requires *total elimination* of unconfirmed intercompany gains and losses. Unconfirmed gains or losses on upstream sales are *allocated proportionately* against the controlling and minority interests.

---

[1] Note that the *gross profit* on intercompany merchandise transfers is eliminated if unconfirmed. An alternative is to eliminate the *net profit*, gross profit reduced by selling and administrative expenses. Elimination of net profit only, however, would overstate consolidated inventories. The overstatement arises because the inventory account would include some period costs— selling and administrative expenses—which are not considered to be inventoriable costs. Therefore, we believe that elimination of net profit is *not* an acceptable alternative.

[2] Committee on Accounting Procedure, *Accounting Research Bulletin No. 51*, "Consolidated Financial Statements" (N.Y.: AICPA, 1959), pars. 6, 14; AC § 2051.07, 13.

Impact on the Equity Method Accrual

As we have mentioned, *APBO 18* indicates that the equity method accrual is a *one-line consolidation*. Under this one-line consolidation concept, P's share of any unconfirmed intercompany gains (losses) are deducted from (added to) P's share of S's reported net income in computing the equity method accrual. Thus the equity method accrual is affected by unconfirmed intercompany gains and losses on upstream *and* downstream sales. Intuitively, P's unconfirmed intercompany profit on downstream sales would seem to have nothing to do with the income P accrues from S. Nevertheless, since these unconfirmed profits are eliminated in consolidation, they are also removed in determining the equity method accrual. This leads to the result called for in *APBO 18*—namely, that the reported net income of P equals consolidated net income and that P's retained earnings equal consolidated retained earnings.[3]

Intercompany Transfers of Land

Transfers of land between affiliated companies represent the most straightforward application of the concepts inherent in accounting for unconfirmed intercompany profits. Land is not depreciable and is not integrated into a cost of goods sold computation.

The intercompany sale of land generates a gain or loss to the selling affiliate, which is recorded in its accounting records. The purchasing affiliate records the purchase of land at the price paid. In addition, the parent company will reduce its equity method accrual by the amount of unconfirmed intercompany profit— proportionately, if the sale is upstream. At each consolidation point, we prepare working paper entries to eliminate the effects of the intercompany land transfer until the land is sold externally. In the year of sale, the recorded intercompany gain is eliminated against the land account, and, in the case of an upstream sale, the minority interest in net income is reduced by its share of the eliminated gain. This working paper entry is as shown:

CONSOLIDATED FINANCIAL STATEMENT WORKING PAPER

Gain on Sale of Land   XXX
    Land   XXX
To eliminate the unconfirmed gain on intercompany sale of
land during the current year and reduce the land account to
original acquisition cost.

Eliminations in Subsequent Years— Upstream Sales

If the land was sold *upstream* in a prior period, the unconfirmed gain must be eliminated from the *beginning retained earnings of S*. Although it was eliminated on the working paper, the gain remained intact on S's books and was closed to S's retained earnings in the year of sale.

CONSOLIDATED FINANCIAL STATEMENT WORKING PAPER

Retained Earnings—S, January 1   XXX
    Land   XXX
To eliminate the unconfirmed gain on an *upstream*
intercompany sale of land made in a prior year and to reduce
the land account to original acquisition cost.

---

[3] Accounting Principles Board, *Opinion No. 18*, "The Equity Method of Accounting for Investments in Common Stock" (N.Y.: AICPA, 1971), par. 19; AC § 5131.19.

Treatment If Land Is Sold to Outside Party   Sale of the land to an outside party in a subsequent year requires a working paper entry to transfer the original intercompany gain out of S's beginning retained earnings and into current year income.

CONSOLIDATED FINANCIAL STATEMENT WORKING PAPER

Retained Earnings—S, January 1 XXX
    Gain on Sale of Land   XXX
To include in current income the previously recorded
intercompany gain on an *upstream* sale of land, which is now
confirmed through external sale.

The minority interest in net income is now increased by the minority's share of the original intercompany gain confirmed by the external sale. Often, the external sale results in a gain or loss *in addition* to the original intercompany gain or loss. This additional gain or loss is attributed entirely to the company selling the land externally (that is, the company which purchased the land internally). To illustrate these concepts, consider the following transactions for Port Corporation and its 80-percent-owned subsidiary, Side Corporation:

1.   On July 29, 19X1, Side Corporation sold a parcel of land to Port Corporation for $80,000. The land had originally cost Side $65,000.

2.   Port continues to hold the land at December 31, 19X2.

3.   Port sells the land outside for $78,000 at September 30, 19X3.

Exhibit 9.1 shows the entries made by Port and Side to record these transactions and the related working paper eliminations.

Eliminations in Subsequent Years— Downstream Sales

With *downstream* sales, in subsequent years the unconfirmed gain must be added to the *Investment in S* account. In this case, the intercompany gain was originally charged against the accrual of equity method income from S, thereby reducing the investment account, but there was no corresponding effect on S Company's net income at time of consolidation. Hence, a discrepancy exists between the investment account and S Company's stockholders' equity. Removal of this discrepancy is necessary for a clean elimination. This simply means that, where unconfirmed downstream sales are concerned, we debit or credit the investment account at subsequent consolidation points instead of the beginning retained earnings of S Company. P's retained earnings were previously reduced when the unconfirmed intercompany gain was subtracted from the equity method accrual. P's retained earnings (and consolidated retained earnings) are therefore properly stated. This reduction in P's retained earnings is also reflected in the investment account. Elimination of the investment account against the stockholders' equity of S *without* adding back the unconfirmed gain would result in an incomplete elimination. A portion of S's stockholders' equity equal to the unconfirmed downstream gain would remain. The addback to the investment account is needed to remedy this situation. No further working paper adjustments to P's retained earnings are necessary. In all other respects, the eliminations for downstream sales are the same as for upstream sales.

Exhibit 9.1 Intercompany Sale of Land Made Upstream: Journal Entries and Working Paper Eliminations

BOOKS OF SELLING OR PURCHASING AFFILIATE

July 29, 19X1

(Side Corporation)

Cash	80,000	
Land		65,000
Gain on Sale of Land . . .		15,000

To record sale of land to Port Corporation.

(Port Corporation)

Land	80,000	
Cash		80,000

To record purchase of land from Side Corporation.

December 31, 19X1

Port's equity method accrual is reduced by $12,000 (= .8 × $15,000).

December 31, 19X2

No entries

September 30, 19X3

(Port Corporation)

Cash	78,000	
Loss on Sale of Land . . .	2,000	
Land		80,000

To record sale of land to outside party.

December 31, 19X3

Port's equity method accrual is increased by $12,000 (= .8 × $15,000) now that the intercompany gain is confirmed.

CONSOLIDATED FINANCIAL STATEMENT WORKING PAPER

December 31, 19X1

Gain on Sale of Land . . .	15,000	
Land		15,000

To eliminate the unconfirmed gain on intercompany sale of land and reduce the land account to original acquisition cost.

Note:

The minority interest in S Company's net income for 19X1 is reduced by $3,000 (= .2 × $15,000).

December 31, 19X2

Retained Earnings—S, January 1, 19X2 . . .	15,000	
Land		15,000

To eliminate the unconfirmed intercompany gain arising in 19X1 and reduce the land account to original acquisition cost.

December 31, 19X3

Retained Earnings—S, January 1, 19X3 . . .	15,000	
Gain on Sale of Land . . .		15,000

To credit 19X3 income for the $15,000 intercompany gain, which is now confirmed.

Note:

The minority interest in S Company's net income for 19X3 is increased by $3,000 (= .2 × $15,000).

We return to the Port and Side example and use the following transactions to illustrate the entries for downstream sales. Recall that Port owns 80 percent of Side.

1. On March 15, 19X1, Port sold land to Side Corporation for $125,000. Port had purchased the land several years before for $100,000.

2. Side continued to hold the land at December 31, 19X2.

3. The land was sold outside for $165,000. Settlement took place on January 8, 19X3.

The entries made to record these transactions and the related working paper eliminations are given in Exhibit 9.2.

| **Intercompany Transfers of Merchandise** | Transfers of merchandise inventory items between affiliated corporations are quite common. Component parts are often manufactured by one affiliate and assembled by another. Or finished goods may be produced by one affiliate and marketed by another. In all such cases, the preparation of consolidated statements requires elimination of intercompany revenues and expenses. If the intercompany transfer price differs from cost, unconfirmed gains or losses must also be eliminated when merchandise remains unsold to outside parties. Similarly, P's equity method accrual is reduced by the total amount of unconfirmed intercompany inventory profit on downstream sales and by a proportional amount of the profit on upstream sales. The minority interest in S's net income will be decreased by the minority's share of unconfirmed upstream gains. |

The principles involved in intercompany inventory profit eliminations parallel those encountered in eliminations arising from land transfers among affiliates. Nevertheless, the procedures may seem more complex because merchandise inventory is reflected in the income statement through its inclusion in cost of goods sold. There is no gain on sale of merchandise indicated separately on the income statement. Rather, the unconfirmed gain is part of the ending (or beginning) inventory balance. Elimination of the unconfirmed gain in ending inventory results in an increase in consolidated cost of goods sold. Our consolidated financial statement working paper is set up to show the *components* of cost of goods sold in the income statement—beginning inventory + purchases − ending inventory—rather than cost of goods sold itself. Ending inventory *also appears* in the balance sheet section of the working paper. Since the amount of ending inventory reduces cost of goods sold, it is shown as a credit in the income statement. Removal of the gain, therefore, means debiting ending inventory (or cost of goods sold) on the income statement, while crediting the inventory account on the balance sheet. At the same time, *total* intercompany merchandise sales (purchases) must also be eliminated so that consolidated revenues and expenses are not overstated. This entry *does not* affect consolidated net income, while the entry made to remove the unconfirmed profit on intercompany merchandise sales *does*. Both entries are now illustrated:

Exhibit 9.2   Intercompany Sale of Land Made Downstream: Journal Entries and Working Paper Eliminations

BOOKS OF SELLING OR PURCHASING AFFILIATE

(Port Corporation)

March 15, 19X1

Cash	125,000	
Land		100,000
Gain on Sale of Land . .		25,000

To record sale of land to Side Corporation.

(Side Corporation)

Land	125,000	
Cash		125,000

To record the purchase of land from Port Corporation.

December 31, 19X1   Port's equity method accrual is reduced by $25,000.

December 31, 19X2   No entries

January 8, 19X3

(Side Corporation)

Cash	165,000	
Land		125,000
Gain on Sale of Land . .		40,000

To record sale of land to outside party.

December 31, 19X3   Port's equity method accrual is increased by $25,000, now that the gain is confirmed.

CONSOLIDATED FINANCIAL STATEMENT WORKING PAPER

December 31, 19X1

Gain on Sale of Land . . .	25,000	
Land		25,000

To eliminate the intercompany sale of land and reduce the land account to original acquisition cost.

Note:

The minority interest in S's net income for 19X1 is *not* affected.

December 31, 19X2

Investment in S	25,000	
Land		25,000

To add the unconfirmed intercompany gain to the investment account to maintain equivalence with retained earnings of S and reduce land account to original acquisition cost.

December 31, 19X3

Investment in S	25,000	
Gain on Sale of Land . .		25,000

To credit 19X3 income for the $25,000 intercompany gain now confirmed and add to the investment account.

Note:

The minority interest in S's net income for 19X3 will reflect the minority's share of the external gain, $8,000 (= .2 × $40,000).

CONSOLIDATED FINANCIAL STATEMENT WORKING PAPER

Sales　.　.　.　.　.　.　.　.　.　.　.　.　.　.　.　.　.　XXX
　　　Purchases (or Cost of Goods Sold)　.　.　.　.　.　.　.　　　　　XXX
To eliminate intercompany merchandise sales by reducing
consolidated sales and purchases (or cost of goods sold).

Inventory, December 31, Income Statement (or Cost of Goods
　　Sold)　.　.　.　.　.　.　.　.　.　.　.　.　.　.　.　XXX
　　　Inventory (Balance Sheet)　.　.　.　.　.　.　.　.　.　　　　　XXX
To eliminate unconfirmed intercompany profit in ending
inventory by increasing cost of goods sold and decreasing the
asset account to original acquisition cost.

The existence of unconfirmed gains in the *ending* inventory of one period
means that those gains are also reflected in next period's *beginning* inventory.
Working paper eliminations do not affect the companies' books, so at the next
consolidation point the beginning inventory (or cost of goods sold) on the income
statement is overstated by the unconfirmed gain. Another working paper elimination is needed so that these gains are transferred into current year income by
reducing (crediting) beginning inventory (or cost of goods sold) on the income
statement. (Of course, any such gains not actually confirmed during the current
year will be included in unconfirmed gains removed from the ending inventory.)
The offsetting *debit* is to Beginning Retained Earnings of S for *upstream sales*
and to Investment in S for *downstream sales*. Since the unconfirmed gains on
downstream sales were removed from P's equity method accrual made at the
end of the last period, P's retained earnings are properly stated, while S's retained earnings are not affected. As in the land case, the increase to the Investment in S is necessary to restore equivalence with S's stockholders' equity.

The need to transfer unconfirmed intercompany gains in beginning inventory
into current year income also extends to P's equity method accrual. Whereas
unconfirmed intercompany gains in *ending* inventory were *deducted* from
the equity accrual, unconfirmed intercompany gains in *beginning* inventory are *added* to the equity accrual. As before, such adjustments are total
(for downstream sales) or proportional (for upstream sales). The needed entries
follow:

CONSOLIDATED FINANCIAL STATEMENT WORKING PAPER

Retained Earnings—S, January 1　.　.　.　.　.　.　.　.　XXX
　　　Inventory, January 1 (Income Statement)　.　.　.　.　.　　　　　XXX
To eliminate intercompany profit on *upstream* sales in the
beginning inventory, assumed confirmed in the current year,
by decreasing beginning retained earnings and cost of goods
sold.

Investment in S　.　.　.　.　.　.　.　.　.　.　.　.　.　.　XXX
　　　Inventory, January 1 (Income Statement)　.　.　.　.　.　　　　　XXX
To eliminate intercompany profit on *downstream* sales in the
beginning inventory, assumed confirmed in the current year,
by increasing the investment account and decreasing cost of
goods sold.

Note that the elimination of both beginning and ending unconfirmed intercompany profits on upstream sales of merchandise affects the minority interest
in net income. Under proportional allocation of eliminated intercompany profits, the eliminated amount affects consolidated net income and minority inter-

est in net income in proportion to the interests of majority and minority share-holders.

Intercompany Profits and Inventory Cost-Flow Assumptions

Most companies do not use specific identification when accounting for invento-ries and cost of goods sold. Rather, they employ a cost-flow assumption such as LIFO or FIFO. The reader should note that the intercompany profit elimination techniques discussed here are compatible with any cost-flow assumption. Our eliminations seem to imply a FIFO cost flow because any intercompany profit in beginning inventory is assumed confirmed and is added to current income. Then the intercompany profit in the ending inventory is eliminated.

Suppose, however, that LIFO was being used and, to simplify matters, that the ending LIFO inventory was unchanged from the beginning LIFO inventory. Following our procedure, the beginning intercompany profit is added to current income, and the ending intercompany profit is deducted from current income. What is the effect on current income? Absolutely zero! Since the LIFO invento-ry is assumed constant, so is the unconfirmed intercompany profit, and its elim-ination from beginning and ending inventories on the income statement has no net effect on current period income. Moreover, in making the elimination from ending inventory on the income statement, we also remove the unconfirmed gain from the overstated inventory on the balance sheet.

Under FIFO, of course, our procedure shows as confirmed the old (begin-ning) intercompany profit and eliminates as unconfirmed the new (ending) inter-company profit—precisely what is needed.

Numerical Illustration

Our numerical example involves Presento and Solento Corporations. Presento acquired 80 percent of Solento's voting stock several years ago. A summary of the intercompany inventory transactions between these affiliates for 19X2 is shown next:

Presento Corporation and Solento Corporation
Intercompany Transactions in Merchandise Inventory, 19X2

	Presento Corporation	Solento Corporation	Total
Intercompany Profits in Inventory, January 1, 19X2	$ 10,000	$40,000	$ 50,000
Intercompany Sales of Merchandise during 19X2	300,000	80,000	380,000
Intercompany Profits in Inventory, December 31, 19X2	8,000	50,000	58,000

During 19X2, the affiliates recorded the intercompany sales as follows:

BOOKS OF PRESENTO CORPORATION

| Cash | 300,000 | |
| Sales | | 300,000 |

To record sale of merchandise to Solento Corporation.

| Purchases | 80,000 | |
| Cash | | 80,000 |

To record purchase of merchandise from Solento Corporation.

BOOKS OF SOLENTO CORPORATION

Cash	80,000	
Sales		80,000

To record sale of merchandise to Presento
Corporation.

Purchases	300,000	
Cash		300,000

To record purchase of merchandise from Presento
Corporation.

P's equity method accrual will be increased by P's share of the unconfirmed intercompany profits in beginning inventory, $48,000 [= $40,000 + .8($10,000)], and decreased by P's share of the unconfirmed intercompany profits in ending inventory, $56,400 [= $50,000 + .8($8,000)], a net decrease of $8,400.

We now show the working paper eliminations to be made when consolidated statements are prepared at the end of 19X2. Our eliminations deal with intercompany sales and intercompany profits in beginning and ending inventories, in that order.

CONSOLIDATED FINANCIAL STATEMENT WORKING PAPER

Sales	380,000	
Purchases		380,000

To eliminate intercompany sales and purchases made
in 19X2.

Retained Earnings—S, January 1	10,000	
Inventory, January 1 (Income Statement) . . .		10,000

To eliminate unconfirmed intercompany profits on
upstream sales from beginning inventory, assuming
confirmation in 19X2, and include in 19X2 operations.

Investment in S	40,000	
Inventory, January 1 (Income Statement) . . .		40,000

To eliminate unconfirmed intercompany profits on
downstream sales from beginning inventory, assuming
confirmation in 19X2, and include in 19X2 operations.

Inventory, December 31 (Income Statement) . . .	58,000	
Inventory (Balance Sheet)		58,000

To eliminate unconfirmed intercompany profits in
ending inventory by increasing cost of goods sold and
reducing inventory to original acquisition cost.

The net effect of these eliminations of intercompany profits on *upstream* merchandise sales is to increase the minority interest in net income by $400, calculated as follows:

Minority interest in net income *increased* by 20 percent of intercompany profit in Presento's beginning inventory, assumed confirmed in current year [.2($10,000)]	$2,000
Minority interest in net income *decreased* by 20 percent of intercompany profit in Presento's ending inventory [.2($8,000)] .	(1,600)
Net increase in minority interest in net income	$ 400

**Effect of
Lower of Cost
or Market
Adjustments**

Chapter 4 of *ARB 43* calls for inventories to be valued at *lower of cost or market (LCM)*. The "market value" to be compared with acquisition cost is presumed to be current replacement cost except that *market* cannot exceed net realizable value (NRV, the "ceiling") or be less than NRV minus a normal profit margin (the "floor"). These considerations are reflected in the following expression which, when correctly evaluated, identifies the appropriate LCM inventory amount:

$$LCM = Min \: [OC, \: NRV, \: max(RC, \: NRV - \pi)],$$

where

OC = Original acquisition cost.

NRV = Net realizable value; selling price less estimated cost to complete and sell.

RC = Current replacement cost.

π = Normal profit margin.

At year-end, a member of an affiliated group may find it necessary to reduce inventory acquired from another member of the group to market to conform with the LCM rule. How should this adjustment, which generates a loss to the purchasing affiliate, affect our intercompany profit eliminations? We see two possibilities.

1. Attribute the loss to the *purchasing* affiliate and use it to reduce the amount of intercompany profit to be eliminated. This treatment follows from the notion that the LCM adjustment is recognition of another economic event. Its effect is to confirm this portion of the intercompany profit to the selling affiliate.

2. Attribute the loss to the *selling* affiliate on the grounds that the write-down was necessitated by an artificially high transfer price determined in a non-arm's-length transaction. Under this interpretation, the LCM adjustment is considered as an exogenously determined reversal of the tentative intercompany profit, and none of the intercompany profit is confirmed to the selling affiliate.

Some individuals support the first treatment. We believe that it is flawed because it allows affiliates to shift gains and losses among the members and to misstate consolidated net income. For example, suppose P owns 60 percent of S and sells inventory marked up $10,000 to S. Assume that S still owns the goods at year-end and, under the LCM rule, recognizes a loss of $10,000 by reducing the inventory to market. Under the first treatment above, the intercompany transaction increases consolidated net income by $4,000! The $10,000 intercompany profit assumed confirmed to P is not eliminated but is reduced only by $6,000, P's share of the LCM loss booked by S. In contrast, the second treatment effectively eliminates the entire $10,000 of intercompany profit, leaving consolidated net income unchanged.

For these reasons, the second treatment should be used but probably only in the year of sale. This practice would neutralize any short-term manipulative practices. After some passage of time, then, the LCM rule would operate as it was intended to do.

Intercompany Transfers of Depreciable Assets

Though less common than intercompany merchandise sales, transfers of depreciable assets between members of an affiliated group also require special treatment when consolidated statements are prepared. The complication arises because of the way in which intercompany gains on depreciable assets are assumed confirmed. Recall that gains arising on intercompany transfers of land and merchandise are confirmed when the items are sold to outsiders. In contrast, *the confirmation or realization of intercompany gains on depreciable assets normally is linked to their depreciation.* As the book values of depreciable assets are written down, their services are assumed to be embodied in the goods and services sold externally by the purchasing affiliate. Hence recorded depreciation, which represents the expiration of assets' services, also represents their "sale" to outsiders. For reasons of simplicity and materiality, we typically assume that *all* of the annual depreciation is "sold" outside and an identical portion of the gain confirmed. This is, of course, not strictly true. If the purchasing affiliate is a manufacturing concern, a part of its annual depreciation is included in manufactured inventories under full or absorption costing. We may further complicate the issue by suggesting that some of the manufactured goods are sold to other affiliates and not to outsiders at all. Generally, however, the cost flows are not traced to their ultimate external disposition because the amounts involved are not material. For this reason, we assume that recorded depreciation adequately measures the expiration of assets' services and their "sale" to outsiders, and attempt no further investigation of actual cost flows.

Objectives of the Eliminations

When a depreciable asset is transferred from one affiliate to another, the amount recorded by the purchasing affiliate typically differs from the asset's net book value (original acquisition cost less accumulated depreciation) to the selling affiliate. Since the selling affiliate normally records a gain on the transfer, the resulting asset balance on the books of the purchaser exceeds the net book value of the asset. From this, we derive three specific objectives for our working paper eliminations.

1. Eliminate the unconfirmed intercompany gain and reduce the asset account to its net book value at date of intercompany sale.

2. Reduce the annual depreciation expense to the amount based on original acquisition cost. The excess, which is eliminated, represents confirmation of the gain in the current period and is allocated to the selling affiliate.

3. Restate the balances in the asset and accumulated depreciation accounts so they are based on original acquisition cost.

The format of the necessary working paper entries follows.

Eliminations in the Year of Intercompany Sale   First, we consider the eliminations required in the *year of sale* when an intercompany gain has arisen on the transfer of a depreciable asset. Each working paper entry achieves one of the objectives just mentioned.

CONSOLIDATED FINANCIAL STATEMENT WORKING PAPER

Gain on Sale of Depreciable Assets   XXX
    Depreciable Assets   XXX
To eliminate the recorded intercompany gain. The amount
remaining in the asset account is the net book value at date of
intercompany sale.

Accumulated Depreciation XXX
    Depreciation Expense   XXX
To eliminate the excess annual depreciation expense
recorded by the purchasing affiliate on the increased
depreciable basis generated in the intercompany transaction.
The remaining accumulated depreciation is based on original
acquisition cost.

Depreciable Assets XXX
    Accumulated Depreciation   XXX
To restate the asset and accumulated depreciation accounts
to their original acquisition cost basis. *The amount of
adjustment is equal to the accumulated depreciation at date
of intercompany sale.* The *net book value* of the depreciable
asset is not affected.

Taken together, the above entries restate the asset, accumulated depreciation, and depreciation expense accounts so that they reflect *original acquisition cost*. The reduction in depreciation expense is allocated to the selling affiliate; it represents the amount of intercompany gain confirmed in the current year. If the subsidiary was the selling affiliate, *minority interest in net income* is decreased by the minority's share of the total intercompany gain and increased by the minority's share of the portion confirmed during the year (that is, the excess depreciation expense).

Both the total intercompany gain and the portion assumed confirmed during the year through depreciation affect P's *equity method accrual*, proportionately if the sale was upstream. The accrual is decreased by the total gain and increased by the portion assumed confirmed.

Eliminations in Subsequent Years   At consolidation points subsequent to the year of sale, eliminations must be made to achieve the three consolidation objectives previously discussed. Fortunately, only the entry made to eliminate the unconfirmed intercompany gain will differ. The same entries which were made in the year of sale to eliminate the excess annual depreciation expense and to restate the assets and accumulated depreciation accounts to their original cost basis are also made at each subsequent consolidation point. Of course, the excess depreciation expense eliminated each year will be different if straight-line depreciation is not used. Recall that in the year of sale we first eliminated the entire gain and then recognized the amount confirmed through a reduction in depreciation expense. In subsequent years, however, we face a new set of conditions.

1.   The original intercompany gain has been:
    a. Eliminated from the investment account under the one-line consolidation approach of the equity method if the transfer was *downstream*, thereby creating a discrepancy between the investment account and P's interest in S Company's retained earnings; or

b. Buried in S Company's retained earnings if the transfer was *upstream*. P's share of the gain was removed from the investment account under the one-line consolidation approach of the equity method.

2. Some portion of the gain has been confirmed through prior years' depreciation recorded on the purchasing company's books.

3. Accumulated depreciation is overstated by the total excess depreciation expense (= portion of gain confirmed) recorded since date of intercompany sale.

Taking these conditions into account, we now show the general form of the working paper entry needed to eliminate the unconfirmed portion of the intercompany gain when straight-line depreciation is used. Define:

Y = Total intercompany gain recorded by the selling affiliate.

T = Remaining depreciable life of the asset at the date of the intercompany sale.

t = Year subsequent to the date of sale; $t = 1, ..., T$.

Y/T = Annual excess depreciation; amount of gain confirmed annually.

The entry recorded at consolidation point t follows:

CONSOLIDATED FINANCIAL STATEMENT WORKING PAPER

Investment in S (*downstream* sale)
    or   . $(T - t + 1)(Y/T)$
Retained Earnings—S, January 1 (*upstream* sale)
Accumulated Depreciation . . . . $(t - 1)(Y/T)$
 Depreciable Assets . . . . Y
To eliminate the amount of intercompany gain
unconfirmed in prior years $[(T - t + 1)(Y/T)]$,
remove the excess depreciation recorded in prior
years (the amount of gain *confirmed*) $[(t - 1)(Y/T)]$,
and reduce the asset account to its net book value at
date of intercompany sale.

[Note: $(T - t + 1)(Y/T) + (t - 1)(Y/T) = T(Y/T) = Y$].

For $T = 4$ and $t = 2$, the eliminating entry is:

Investment in S (*downstream* sale)
    or   . . . . $3(Y/4)$
Retained Earnings—S, January 1 (*upstream* sale)
Accumulated Depreciation . . . . $(Y/4)$
 Depreciable Assets . . . . Y

Strictly speaking, the above working paper eliminations hold only when straight-line depreciation is used. For other depreciation methods, one must compute the amount of intercompany gain confirmed in prior years. This amount is charged to Accumulated Depreciation. The total gain less the amount confirmed in prior years is the amount still unconfirmed. It is charged to Investment in S (downstream sale) or to Retained Earnings—S (upstream sale).

The portion of the gain assumed confirmed each year through depreciation increases P's *equity method accrual*, proportionately in upstream sales. Moreover, if the original sale was upstream, the *minority interest in net income* is also increased by the minority's share of the annual excess depreciation expense.

A Numerical Example   To illustrate these concepts, consider the case of Pump Company and Slide Company. Pump owns 80 percent of Slide. On January 1, 19X1, Slide sells Pump a piece of machinery for $150,000. Slide had acquired the machinery two years before for $140,000 (useful life of seven years) and had recorded accumulated depreciation of $40,000 (net book value = $100,000). The asset has a remaining useful life of five years, and use of straight-line depreciation will continue. No salvage value has been or is anticipated. We begin by showing the entries made by Slide and Pump on their own books during 19X1:

BOOKS OF SLIDE COMPANY

1/1/X1

Cash	150,000	
Accumulated Depreciation	40,000	
Machinery		140,000
Gain on Sale of Machinery		50,000

To record the sale of machinery to Pump Company.

BOOKS OF PUMP COMPANY

1/1/X1

Machinery	150,000	
Cash		150,000

To record the purchase of machinery from Slide Company.

12/31/X1

Depreciation Expense	30,000	
Accumulated Depreciation		30,000

To record depreciation expense for 19X1; $30,000 = $150,000/5.

We now turn to the eliminations made at December 31, 19X1.

CONSOLIDATED FINANCIAL STATEMENT WORKING PAPER

12/31/X1

Gain on Sale of Machinery	50,000	
Machinery		50,000

To eliminate the recorded intercompany gain and to reduce the machinery account to net book value at date of intercompany sale.

Accumulated Depreciation	10,000	
Depreciation Expense		10,000

To eliminate the annual excess depreciation recorded by Pump Company. On the original acquisition cost basis, annual depreciation expense is $20,000 (= $140,000/7). The excess of $10,000 is simply the difference between the $30,000 recorded by Pump and the $20,000 based on original acquisition cost. Equivalently, $10,000 = $50,000/5.

Machinery	40,000
Accumulated Depreciation	40,000

To restate the machinery and accumulated depreciation
accounts to their original acquisition cost basis. This is
the accumulated depreciation recorded by Slide prior to
the intercompany sale.

These eliminations effectively reduce the *minority interest in net income* by
$8,000. In consolidation, Slide's net income is first decreased by $50,000 (the
total intercompany gain) and then increased by $10,000 (the portion of the gain
realized through depreciation). The net effect on Slide's net income is a decrease of $40,000 (= $50,000 − $10,000), of which the minority's share is $8,000
(= .2 × $40,000). Similarly, Pump's 19X1 *equity method accrual* is decreased
by the controlling interest's share of the unconfirmed gain, $32,000 [=
.8($50,000 − $10,000)].

If the intercompany transaction had not occurred, the machinery would be
reported at $140,000 and accumulated depreciation (after three years) at
$60,000. From the T accounts below, we see that our entries accomplish this.

Machinery				Accumulated Depreciation			
1/1/X1 (P)	150,000					12/31/X1 (P)	30,000
12/31/X1 (E)	40,000	12/31/X1 (E)	50,000	12/31/X1 (E)	10,000	12/31/X1 (E)	40,000
12/31/X1 (C)	140,000					12/31/X1 (C)	60,000

(P): Entry made by Pump Company.
(E): Working paper elimination.
(C): Consolidated balance.

During year 2, the only bookkeeping entry made is when Pump records the
annual $30,000 depreciation expense. At December 31, 19X2 ($t = 2$), when the
consolidated statements are prepared, the following eliminating entries are
made.

CONSOLIDATED FINANCIAL STATEMENT WORKING PAPER

12/31/X2

Retained Earnings—Slide, January 1, 19X2	40,000
Accumulated Depreciation	10,000
Machinery	50,000

To eliminate the intercompany gain unconfirmed in prior
years ($40,000 = $50,000 − $10,000), remove the
excess depreciation recorded in prior years ($10,000),
and reduce the machinery account to its net book value
at date of intercompany sale ($100,000 = $150,000 −
$50,000). Note that $Y/T = \$50,000/5 = \$10,000$;
$(T - t + 1)(Y/T) = (5 - 2 + 1)\$10,000 = \$40,000$, and
$(t - 1)(Y/T) = (2 - 1)\$10,000 = \$10,000$.

Accumulated Depreciation	10,000
Depreciation Expense	10,000

To eliminate the annual excess depreciation expense
recorded by Pump Company.

Machinery	40,000
Accumulated Depreciation	40,000

To restate the machinery and accumulated depreciation
accounts to their acquisition cost basis.

The $10,000 gain confirmed in 19X2 through depreciation is allocated proportionately between the controlling and minority interests. The *equity method accrual* is increased by Pump's share, $8,000, and the *minority interest in net income* is increased by $2,000, the minority's share.

If the machine is sold outside the affiliated group before it is fully depreciated, the previously recorded intercompany gain is assumed fully confirmed and is allocated to the income of the original selling affiliate at the next consolidation point. Should Pump subsequently sell the machine externally, consolidated net income in that period would include (1) Pump's gain or loss on the external sale and Pump's share of (2) the remaining intercompany gain not previously confirmed through depreciation. Item 2 would be reflected proportionately in Pump's equity method accrual and in the minority interest in net income in the period of external sale.

Computing the Equity Method Accrual and the Minority Interest in Net Income: An Example

We have now examined the procedures for dealing with several common types of intercompany transactions. In Chapter 10, additional intercompany transactions are analyzed, and a comprehensive numerical example complete with working paper is presented. Before moving to Chapter 10, however, it will be useful to summarize the effects of the transactions studied so far on the equity method accrual made by P, on the minority interest in net income, and on the consolidated financial statement working paper. Although the equity method accrual is eliminated in consolidation, it does become a component of the Investment in S and Retained Earnings accounts on P's books. Furthermore, we have seen that elimination of the unconfirmed intercompany gains and losses in the equity method accrual—under the one-line consolidation concept of *APBO 18*—influences the working paper entries needed to eliminate them at subsequent consolidation points.

This example is based on information which was discussed earlier in the chapter and is summarized below. Other financial statement data included on the working paper are assumed.

1. P owns 80 percent of S. S reported $200,000 of net income from its own operations and paid dividends of $50,000 in the current year, 19X2.

2. During the current year, S sold a parcel of land to P for $80,000. The land had originally cost S $65,000. P owns the land at year-end.

3. S's ending inventory includes $50,000 of unconfirmed intercompany profits on $300,000 of merchandise purchased from P.

4. On January 1 of the current year, S sold P a piece of machinery for $150,000. S had acquired the machinery two years ago for $140,000 (useful life of seven years) and had recorded accumulated depreciation of $40,000 (net book value = $100,000). The equipment has a remaining life of five years, and straight-line depreciation will continue.

5. Current period amortization of P's purchase premium (goodwill) is assumed to be $18,000. The unamortized goodwill at the beginning of the year is $108,000.

Schedules to compute P's equity method accrual and the minority interest in

Exhibit 9.3   Computation of P's Equity Method Accrual and the Minority Interest in Net Income, 19X2

Schedule to Compute the Equity Method Accrual

P's Share of S's Reported Net Income (.8 × $200,000)	$160,000
Less Amortization of Purchase Premium	(18,000)
Less P's Unconfirmed Intercompany Profit of $50,000 on Sale of Merchandise to S	(50,000)
Less 80% of S's Unconfirmed Intercompany Profit of $15,000 on Sale of Land to P	(12,000)
Less 80% of S's Unconfirmed Intercompany Gain of $40,000 on the Sale of Equipment to P[a]	(32,000)
Net Equity Method Accrual	$ 48,000

Schedule to Compute the Minority Interest in Net Income

Minority's Share of S's Reported Net Income (.2 × $200,000)	$ 40,000
Less 20% of S's Unconfirmed Intercompany Profit of $15,000 on Sale of Land to P	(3,000)
Less 20% of S's Unconfirmed Intercompany Gain of $40,000 on the Sale of Equipment to P[a]	(8,000)
Minority Interest in Net Income	$ 29,000

[a]The unconfirmed $40,000 gain consists of the gain on sale of $50,000 (= $150,000 − $100,000) recorded by S reduced by the excess depreciation of $10,000 [= ($150,000/5) − ($140,000/7)] recorded by P during the year.

net income for 19X2 are given in Exhibit 9.3. The completed consolidated financial statement working paper appears in Exhibit 9.4.

Income Tax Effects of Unconfirmed Intercompany Profits

When members of an affiliated group file separate income tax returns, unconfirmed intercompany gains and losses give rise to timing differences in consolidation. This happens because the eliminated items are removed only on the consolidated financial statement working paper; pretax book incomes of the affiliates are not affected. Therefore, elimination of unconfirmed intercompany gains in consolidation means that pretax consolidated book income is often smaller than the total unconsolidated pretax book income of all companies in the consolidated group. Similarly, consolidated income tax expense is often smaller than the sum of the unconsolidated separate companies' income tax expenses. In these cases, total income tax expense must be reduced in the working paper so that it bears the appropriate statutory relationship to pretax consolidated book income. This is achieved by reclassifying the income taxes pertaining to the unconfirmed intercompany gains on the working paper with the following entry:

CONSOLIDATED FINANCIAL STATEMENT WORKING PAPER

Prepaid Income Taxes	XXX	
Income Tax Expense		XXX

To show as *prepaid* those taxes accrued or paid on current period, unconfirmed intercompany gains eliminated in consolidation.

In each subsequent year that these gains (or some portion of them) remain unconfirmed, a working paper entry must be made to reflect the appropriate amount of prepaid income taxes. The credit is made to the Investment in S (for downstream sales) or beginning Retained Earnings—S (for upstream sales),

Exhibit 9.4   Consolidated Financial Statement Working Paper

P Company and S Company
Consolidated Financial Statement Working Paper
For the Year Ended December 31, 19X2

	P Company	S Company (80%)	Adjustments and Eliminations Dr.		Adjustments and Eliminations Cr.		Consolidated
INCOME STATEMENT							
Sales	3,000,000	1,000,000	(3)	300,000			3,700,000
Income from S	48,000	—	(1)	48,000			—
Gain on Sale of Land	—	15,000	(2)	15,000			—
Gain on Sale of Machinery	—	50,000	(5)	50,000			—
Inventory, Dec. 31, 19X2	420,000	200,000	(4)	50,000			570,000
Total Credits	3,468,000	1,265,000		463,000			4,270,000
Inventory, January 1, 19X2	400,000	210,000					610,000
Purchases	2,000,000	600,000			(3)	300,000	2,300,000
Operating Expenses	510,000	255,000	(9)	18,000	(6)	10,000	773,000
Total Debits	2,910,000	1,065,000		18,000		310,000	3,683,000
Minority Interest in Net Income			(10)	29,000			(29,000)
Net Inc.—to Retained Earn. Stmt.	558,000	200,000		510,000		310,000	558,000
RETAINED EARNINGS STATEMENT							
Retained Earnings, 1/1/X2—P	1,500,000	—					1,500,000
Retained Earnings, 1/1/X2—S	—	750,000	(8)	750,000			—
Net Income—from Income Stmt.	558,000	200,000		510,000		310,000	558,000
Dividends—P	(250,000)	—					(250,000)
Dividends—S	—	(50,000)			(1)	40,000	—
					(10)	10,000	
Ret. Earn., 12/31/X2—to Balance Sheet	1,808,000	900,000		1,260,000		360,000	1,808,000
BALANCE SHEET							
Cash and Receivables	547,000	300,000					847,000
Inventory	420,000	200,000			(4)	50,000	570,000
Investment in S	1,116,000	—			(1)	8,000	—
					(8)	1,108,000	
Land	400,000	140,000			(2)	15,000	525,000
Buildings and Machinery	2,600,000	1,600,000	(7)	40,000	(5)	50,000	4,190,000
Accumulated Depreciation	(800,000)	(300,000)	(6)	10,000	(7)	40,000	(1,130,000)
Goodwill			(8)	108,000	(9)	18,000	90,000
Total	4,283,000	1,940,000		158,000		1,289,000	5,092,000
Current Liabilities	475,000	340,000					815,000
Other Liabilities	1,000,000	200,000					1,200,000
Capital Stock—P	1,000,000	—					1,000,000
Capital Stock—S	—	500,000	(8)	500,000			—
Ret. Earn.—from Ret. Earn. Stmt.	1,808,000	900,000		1,260,000		360,000	1,808,000
Minority Interest in S		—			(8)	250,000	269,000
					(10)	19,000	
Total	4,283,000	1,940,000		1,760,000		629,000	5,092,000
				1,918,000		1,918,000	

Explanations of Working Paper Entries

 (1) To eliminate the equity method entries recorded by P during the year.
 (2) To eliminate the unconfirmed intercompany gain on the sale of land during the year and reduce the land account to original acquisition cost.
 (3) To eliminate intercompany merchandise sales.
 (4) To eliminate the unconfirmed intercompany profit in ending inventory.
 (5) To eliminate the gain on intercompany sale of machinery and reduce the machinery to its net book value at date of intercompany sale.
 (6) To eliminate the excess depreciation recorded by P during the current year.
 (7) To restate the machinery and accumulated depreciation accounts to their original acquisition cost basis.
 (8) To eliminate the Investment in S amount against the stockholders' equity of S and establish the unamortized purchase premium (goodwill) and the minority interest in S, all as of the beginning of the year.
 (9) To record current year amortization of the goodwill.
(10) To record the change in the minority interest during the year.

and it signifies that the original timing difference occurred in a prior year. When the gains are confirmed, the timing difference reverses and the related income tax expense must be reflected in the consolidated income statement. A working paper entry debiting Income Tax Expense and crediting the investment account or beginning retained earnings of S achieves this. Substantial reversals of these timing differences in a given period could lead to consolidated income tax expense greater than the sum of the separate companies' income tax expenses.

Impact of Taxes on the Equity Method Accrual

As mentioned previously, *APBO 18* indicates that the equity method accrual is a one-line consolidation, requiring that any unconfirmed intercompany gains (losses) be deducted from (added to) P's share of S's reported net income in computing the equity method accrual. With the introduction of income taxes, the equity method accrual is based on S Company's net income *after taxes*. Therefore, the removal of any unconfirmed intercompany gains must also be on an aftertax basis; the related taxes will be reclassified as *prepaid* in consolidation. We illustrate these procedures using the familiar schedular format for computing the equity method accrual.

Assume Pant Corporation owns 80 percent of Slack Corporation ($\alpha = .8$). Slack's reported net income, after income tax expense of $300,000, was $200,000. Slack had recorded $40,000 of unconfirmed profits on upstream merchandise sales, while Pant's net income of $350,000 (after income tax expense of $525,000) included $10,000 of unconfirmed gain on a downstream sale of land. Both companies face combined state and federal income tax rates of 60 percent and file separate income tax returns. Purchase premium amortization of $15,000 is assumed. Computation of the equity method accrual follows:

Pant Corporation and Slack Corporation
Schedule to Compute the Equity Method Accrual

Pant's Share of Slack's Net Income, after Taxes of 60 Percent (.8 × $200,000)	$160,000
Less Amortization of Purchase Premium[a]	(15,000)
Less Pant's Unconfirmed Intercompany Profits of $10,000, Net of Applicable Income Taxes of $6,000 (= .6 × $10,000) . . .	(4,000)
Less 80% of Slack's Unconfirmed Intercompany Profits of $40,000, Net of Applicable Income Taxes of $24,000 (=.6 × $40,000); [.8($40,000 − $24,000) = $12,800]	(12,800)
Net Equity Method Accrual	$128,200

[a]Since purchase premium amortization is a permanent difference, there is no tax effect.

If we also assume that Slack declared $55,000 in dividends during the year, the equity method requires the following entries:

BOOKS OF PANT CORPORATION

| Cash | 44,000 | |
| Investment in Slack | | 44,000 |

To record dividends received from Slack Company, $44,000 = (.8 × $55,000).

| Investment in Slack | 128,200 | |
| Income from Slack | | 128,200 |

To record Pant's share of Slack's net income, net of purchase premium amortization, intercompany gains, and applicable taxes.

Computation of Consolidated Income Tax Expense

Consolidated income tax expense for the P and S group has five basic components:

1. Income tax expense accrued by P on book income from its own operations.

2. Income tax expense accrued by S on book income from its own operations.

3. Adjustments for the taxes of both companies which relate to unconfirmed intercompany gains eliminated in consolidation.

4. Income tax expense related to P's income from S. This component consists of the taxes to be paid by P on dividends received from S.

5. Income tax expense accrued on undistributed equity method income not assumed to be permanently reinvested.

Item 5 was introduced at the end of Chapter 8. We bring it up again only for this example, to show how it would affect consolidated income tax expense.

We now return to the Pant and Slack example. Consolidated income tax expense for Pant and Slack is computed in Exhibit 9.5. We assume that the undistributed equity method income will *not* be permanently reinvested, will ultimately be received by Pant as dividends, and that there are no other permanent or timing differences.

The following working paper entries are needed to reflect the tax effects computed in Exhibit 9.5 and the related intercompany profit eliminations.

CONSOLIDATED FINANCIAL STATEMENT WORKING PAPER

| Gain on Sale of Land | 10,000 | |
| Land | | 10,000 |

To eliminate the unconfirmed intercompany gain on the *downstream* sale of land.

| Prepaid Income Taxes | 6,000 | |
| Income Tax Expense | | 6,000 |

To classify as prepaid the income taxes accrued or paid on the unconfirmed intercompany gain on sale of land eliminated in consolidation.

| Inventory, December 31 (Income Statement) | 40,000 | |
| Inventory (Balance Sheet) | | 40,000 |

To eliminate the unconfirmed intercompany inventory profit on *upstream* sales.

Exhibit 9.5   Computation of Consolidated Income Tax Expense

Pant Corporation and Slack Corporation
Computation of Consolidated Income Tax Expense
(α = .8; Tax Rate = .6; No Permanent Reinvestment of Slack's Earnings)

Income Tax Expense Recorded by Pant on Book Income from Its Own Operations	$525,000
Income Tax Expense Recorded by Slack on Book Income from Its Own Operations	300,000
Total Income Tax Expense Recorded per Books	$825,000
Less Income Tax Expense on Pant's Unconfirmed Intercompany Profit on Sale of Land (.6 × $10,000)	$ (6,000)
Less Income Tax Expense on Slack's Unconfirmed Intercompany Inventory Profits (.6 × $40,000)[a] .	(24,000)
Total Reduction for Income Tax Expense on Unconfirmed Intercompany Profits to Be Eliminated . .	$ (30,000)
Income Tax Currently Payable by Pant on Dividends Received from Slack [.8 × .6 × (1 − .85) × $55,000]	$ 3,960
Deferred Income Taxes on Pant's Undistributed Equity Method Income from Slack [.8 × .6 × (1 − .85) × ($200,000 − $55,000)][b]	10,440
Total Income Tax Expense on Pant's Equity Method Income Received or to Be Received from Slack .	$ 14,400
Consolidated Income Tax Expense	$809,400

[a]Recall that we eliminate 100 percent of the unconfirmed intercompany profit on upstream sales; 20 percent will be allocated to the minority interest. Similarly, by removing 100 percent of the tax expense attributable to intercompany profit, 20 percent of the tax reduction will be allocated to the minority interest.
[b]When computing the tax on Pant's income from Slack that is or will be received as dividends, Pant's share of Slack's *reported income* is the critical amount. The adjustments which were made in determining the equity method accrual are not allowable tax deductions against dividend income. In particular, *purchase premium amortization* represents a *permanent* rather than a timing difference. It is ignored in the computation of consolidated income tax expense.

Prepaid Income Taxes	24,000	
Income Tax Expense		24,000

To classify as prepaid the income taxes accrued or paid
on the unconfirmed intercompany inventory profit
eliminated in consolidation.

Income Tax Expense	14,400	
Income Tax Payable		3,960
Deferred Income Taxes		10,440

To record income taxes currently payable and deferred
on P's share of S's net income received or to be received
in dividends.

Note that once the above entries are made, consolidated income tax expense—
on the working paper—equals $809,400 (= $825,000 − $30,000 + $14,400).

Income Tax Effects in the Following Year

To complete the discussion of tax effects, consider the working paper entries made at the end of the following year. The gain on the land remains unconfirmed and Pant's ending inventory included $25,000 of intercompany profits recorded by Slack during the year. Intercompany profits of $40,000 in the beginning inventory are assumed confirmed this year. The entries relate only to the intercompany profits and related taxes.

CONSOLIDATED FINANCIAL STATEMENT WORKING PAPER

Investment in Slack	10,000	
Land		10,000
To add the unconfirmed intercompany gain to the investment account and reduce the land account to original acquisition cost.		
Prepaid Income Taxes	6,000	
Investment in Slack		6,000
To classify as prepaid the income taxes paid on the intercompany gain which arose last year and to reduce the investment account accordingly.		
Income Tax Expense	24,000	
Retained Earnings—S, January 1	16,000	
Inventory, January 1 (Income Statement)		40,000
To eliminate unconfirmed intercompany inventory profits on *upstream* sales from the beginning inventory, charge the related income taxes against current income, and remove the net-of-tax profit from S's beginning retained earnings.		
Prepaid Income Taxes	15,000	
Inventory, December 31 (Income Statement)	25,000	
Income Tax Expense		15,000
Inventory (Balance Sheet)		25,000
To eliminate unconfirmed intercompany inventory profits on upstream sales from the ending inventory and classify the related income taxes as prepaid.		

The first two entries add the $4,000 aftertax gain on sale of land to the investment account; $4,000 (= $10,000 − $6,000) was removed in computing the prior year's equity method accrual. The third entry removes the aftertax intercompany inventory profit of $16,000 from S's retained earnings, transfers it to current operations, and reduces the beginning inventory to original acquisition cost. Minority interest in net income is then *increased* by $3,200 (= .2 × $16,000). The fourth entry eliminates the unconfirmed intercompany profit in ending inventory and reclassifies the related taxes. This results in a *decrease* in the minority interest in net income of $2,000 [= .2($25,000 − $15,000)].

Summary of Key Concepts

Transactions between affiliated companies often must be eliminated by working paper entries in consolidation. **Intercompany revenues and expenses** (for example, intercompany merchandise sales and purchases) and **intercompany assets and liabilities** (such as intercompany receivables and payables) are **eliminated to avoid double counting** in consolidation. In addition, any profits or losses recognized by the affiliates on intercompany transactions and **not confirmed** by transactions with external parties **are eliminated** in consolidation.

Intercompany profit refers to the difference between the **intercompany trans-**

fer price and the **net book value** (acquisition cost plus capital improvements minus accumulated depreciation, if applicable) to the selling affiliate. In consolidation, the entire amount of the unconfirmed intercompany profit is eliminated on the working paper. Elimination of unconfirmed intercompany profits on **upstream sales**—from subsidiary to parent—is **proportionate** between the controlling and minority interests. The minority interest in net income is affected by such elimination. Elimination of unconfirmed intercompany profit on **downstream sales**—from parent to subsidiary—is entirely against P's net income.

Following the one-line consolidation concept of *APBO 18,* the **equity method accrual reflects the same eliminations of unconfirmed intercompany profits as those made in computing consolidated net income.** P's share of S's reported net income is reduced by the total unconfirmed intercompany profits on downstream sales and by P's share (α) of the unconfirmed intercompany profits on upstream sales.

When the affiliates **do not** file a consolidated tax return, elimination of unconfirmed intercompany profit on the working paper creates a timing difference between consolidated pretax book income and the combined tax return income of the affiliates. Thus the income taxes accrued separately by the affiliates are, to the extent that they relate to unconfirmed intercompany profits, reclassified as **prepaid** on the working paper. Similarly, the **aftertax** unconfirmed intercompany profits are removed in determining P's equity method accrual.

Intercompany profits often remain wholly or partially unconfirmed in years subsequent to the year in which the intercompany transfer occurred. When P uses the equity method, unconfirmed intercompany profits originating in prior years are eliminated against the Investment in S (for downstream sales) or the Retained Earnings—S (for upstream sales) account. Reclassification of the related income taxes as **prepaid** reduces the net amount of the elimination against Investment in S or Retained Earnings—S.

Intercompany profits or losses on transfers of inventory, land, and other **nondepreciable assets** are confirmed upon subsequent **sale to external parties.** In contrast, intercompany profits or losses on transfers of **depreciable or amortizable assets** are assumed confirmed as the assets's book values are written down by recording **depreciation or amortization expense.** This represents expiration of the assets' services which, in turn, are generally assumed reflected in the prices of goods and services sold to outsiders.

Elimination of unconfirmed intercompany profits in **beginning inventory** has the effect of **decreasing** current period **cost of goods sold.** On the other hand, elimination of unconfirmed intercompany profit in **ending inventory increases** consolidated cost of goods sold.

Intercompany transfers of depreciable or amortizable assets generally result in (1) confirmation of the gain over several accounting periods and (2) asset balances that differ from the original cost to the consolidated entity. Working paper entries deal with these facts by eliminating the amount of gain unconfirmed at the beginning of the year, recognizing the current period gain confirmation by eliminating "excess" depreciation expense, and restating the asset and related accumulated depreciation or amortization accounts to balances based on original cost to the consolidated entity.

Proper application of the **one-line consolidation concept** to the equity method will assure that **P's net income equals consolidated net income** and **P's retained earnings equal consolidated retained earnings.**

Questions   **Q9.1**   The term *intercompany profit* generally refers to *gross profit* on intercompany transfers. An alternative view mentioned in the chapter suggests that *net profit* is the relevant intercompany profit concept. Discuss the difference between the two concepts and indicate the differential effects of applying them in consolidation.

Q9.2   Unconfirmed intercompany profits on *upstream* sales could be eliminated in three different ways: (1) elimination of the controlling interest's share only; (2) proportional elimination of the total amount against the majority and minority; and (3) elimination of the total amount against the majority. Evaluate these three possibilities.

Q9.3   The income tax effects of unconfirmed intercompany gains may seem unnecessarily complex, yet they represent a straightforward extension of the fact that taxable gains are reduced by income taxes. Explain how the working paper eliminations achieve this extension in consolidation.

Q9.4   The basis for charging P's equity method accrual with P's share of S's unconfirmed intercompany profits on upstream sales seems clear—in consolidation, S's income will be reduced as these gains are eliminated. What is the basis for charging the equity method accrual with *P's* unconfirmed intercompany gains on downstream sales?

Q9.5   Intercompany merchandise sales and purchases generate working paper entries in consolidation. Either one or two different types of eliminations might be needed. What are the purposes of the two types of eliminations? Identify the situations which call for either or both types of eliminations to be made. Ignore income taxes.

Q9.6   When P applies the equity method as prescribed in *APBO 18*, intercompany gains on downstream sales which remain unconfirmed in subsequent years are eliminated against the Investment in S account. Why is this necessary?

Q9.7   The following eliminating entry appears on a consolidated financial statement working paper:

Investment in S	60,000	
Prepaid Income Taxes	40,000	
Land		100,000

Carefully explain the circumstances lying behind such an entry.

Q9.8   Explain the following eliminating entry which appears on a consolidated financial statement working paper:

Retained Earnings—S	20,000	
Accumulated Depreciation	30,000	
Buildings		50,000

Q9.9   The text recommends that lower of cost or market write-downs following intercompany merchandise sales be charged to the selling affiliate in consolidation, effectively reducing any intercompany profit. It has been suggested that this treatment might not be consistent with the general approach to recognizing gains and losses on intercompany transactions. Briefly discuss the basis for this objection.

Q9.10   In dealing with unconfirmed intercompany profits in inventories, we decrease the cost of goods sold by the amount in the beginning inventory and increase the cost of goods sold by the amount in ending inventory. Will this approach work for all of the cost-flow assumptions? Why or why not?

Exercises   **E9.1**   P acquired 90 percent of S Company's stock in a pooling of interests during 19X4. On June 15, 19X5, S transferred a parcel of land to P for $150,000 and recorded a gain of $25,000. P Company continues to hold the land. During the current year, 19X7, P sold $300,000 of merchandise to S, reflecting a markup of $60,000 over P's cost. S Company's inventory at December 31, 19X7, includes $50,000 of this merchandise. S Company reports net income of $225,000 in 19X7. P accounts for its investment in S under the equity method.

Required:
1. Give the working paper eliminations required when consolidated statements are prepared on December 31, 19X7. Ignore income taxes and effects on the minority interest.
2. Give the additional working paper entries required if P and S file separate tax returns and face income tax rates of 60 percent.
3. How is the minority interest in S affected by the eliminations made in requirement 1? requirement 2?

E9.2   P owns 80 percent of S Company's capital stock, acquired at par value at the date of organization in year 1. At the beginning of year 2, P purchased from S for $60,000 equipment which S had manufactured at a cost of $40,000. P Company has depreciated this equipment on a straight-line basis at the rate of 20 percent per year. (S Company had claimed no depreciation on this equipment.)

During year 2, P sold to S merchandise for $40,000, reflecting a markup of $10,000; 30 percent of this merchandise remained in the ending inventory of S that year. P and S file separate income tax returns and both face marginal tax rates of 40 percent.

Required:

1. Give the eliminating entries to be made on the consolidated financial statement working papers at the end of year 2 in respect to the intercompany sale of equipment. Disregard the reversal of the equity method entries made by P.

2. Give the eliminating entries to be made on the consolidated financial statement working papers at the end of year 2 in respect to the intercompany sale of merchandise. Disregard the reversal of the equity method entries made by P.

3. Compute consolidated net income for year 2, assuming P and S reported net income from their own operations of $50,000 and $40,000, respectively.

4. Using the data from requirement 3, compute the minority interest in net income for year 2.

E9.3 Partridge Corporation owns 80 percent of Seagull's outstanding common stock. During the current year, Partridge sold merchandise to Seagull for $6,000,000. At year-end, half of this merchandise is still on hand and makes up 60 percent of Seagull's ending inventory. In discussing preparation of consolidated statements, controllers of both companies disagree on the amount of intercompany profit to be eliminated. Partridge's controller believes that Partridge's earnings/sales ratio of 10 percent should be used, while Seagull's controller feels that Partridge's gross margin/sales ratio of 30 percent is the critical number.

Required: Compute the appropriate intercompany profit elimination according to generally accepted accounting principles. Criticize the other position and show the net difference between the two approaches on consolidated net income and inventories. Ignore income taxes.

E9.4 Portland Corporation owns 80 percent of the outstanding stock of Salem Company and carries the investment at equity. Portland sells merchandise to Salem at a 30 percent markup over cost and Salem sells to Portland at a markup of 25 percent over cost. Merchandise transactions between the affiliates during the year ended December 31, 19X4, are given next:

	Portland	Salem
Inventories at January 1, 19X4, Acquired from Affiliate . . .	$ 50,000	$ 78,000
Sales Made to Affiliate during 19X4	460,000	380,000
Inventories at December 31, 19X4, Acquired from Affiliate . .	40,000	91,000

Required:

1. Prepare the working paper eliminations to be made at December 31, 19X4. Ignore income taxes.

2. Assuming that Portland and Salem file separate income tax returns and face income tax rates of 40 percent, prepare the additional working paper eliminations necessary at December 31, 19X4.

E9.5 Parker Company sold equipment (carried at equity) to its wholly-owned subsidiary, Spencer Company, on January 2, 19X1. At time of sale, Parker's books showed the equipment at a cost of $60,000 and accumulated depreciation of $15,000. Spencer bought the equipment for $50,000 and depreciated it over its remaining five-year life (straight-line method, no salvage value).

Required:
1. Prepare the necessary consolidation elimination entries at December 31, 19X1.
2. Prepare the necessary consolidation elimination entries at December 31, 19X2.

E9.6 P Company and its 60-percent-owned subsidiary, S Company, both face income tax rates of 40 percent. Income tax expense of $800,000 and $200,000 has been accrued on the separate books of P and S, respectively. At the end of the current year, P's ending inventory reflects intercompany profit of $100,000 on goods purchased from S, while S's ending inventory includes goods purchased from P which reflect P's gross margin of $40,000. S Company declared no dividends during the year.

Required: Compute consolidated income tax expense and prepare the necessary working paper eliminations. Assume that the indefinite reversal criteria apply.

E9.7 Pin Company owns all of the outstanding stock of Stick Corporation. At the beginning of the current year, unconfirmed intercompany profits included in the inventories of Pin and Stick amounted to $42,000 and $17,000, respectively. During the year, Pin sold merchandise to Stick for $200,000 at an average markup equal to 20 percent of selling price. Stick's physical inventory of goods purchased from Pin did not change during the year. In contrast, Pin's ending inventory of goods purchased from Stick was twice that of the beginning inventory. Pin purchased $600,000 worth of goods from Stick at an average markup equal to 20 percent over Stick's cost.

Required: Assume that the physical units in Pin's and Stick's beginning inventories equaled 40 percent of each company's intercompany purchases (in physical units) during the current year. Compute the net effect on consolidated net income of eliminating unconfirmed intercompany profit under LIFO and FIFO.

E9.8 P owns 70 percent of S. P's ending inventory includes $100,000 of unconfirmed intercompany profit on merchandise purchased from S. After applying the lower-of-cost-or-market test, P's auditors insist that the inventory acquired from S be written down by $20,000.

Required: Compute the effect on consolidated net income assuming that (1) the LCM loss is charged to the purchasing affiliate in consolidation and (2) the LCM loss is charged to the selling affiliate in consolidation.

Problems **P9.1** **Eliminating Entries—Various Intercompany Transactions** On October 1, 19X0, the Arba Company acquired a 90 percent interest in the common stock of Braginetz Company on the open market for $750,000; the book value was

$712,500 at that date. Since the excess could not be attributed to the undervaluation of any specific assets, Arba reported $37,500 of consolidated goodwill on its consolidated balance sheet at September 30, 19X1. During fiscal 19X2, it was decided that the consolidated goodwill should be amortized in equal amounts over ten years beginning with fiscal 19X2. Arba uses the equity method.

On October 1, 19X1, Arba purchased new equipment for $14,500 from Braginetz. The equipment cost Braginetz $9,000 and had an estimated life of ten years as of October 1, 19X1. Arba uses the sum-of-the-years'-digits depreciation method for both financial and income tax reporting.

During fiscal 19X3, Arba made merchandise sales to Braginetz of $100,000; the merchandise was priced at 25 percent above Arba's cost. Braginetz still owed Arba $17,500 on open account and had 20 percent of this merchandise in inventory at September 30, 19X3.

On August 1, 19X3, Braginetz borrowed $30,000 from Arba by issuing twelve, $2,500, 9 percent, ninety-day notes. Arba discounted four of the notes at its bank with recourse on August 31 at 6 percent. Braginetz reported net income from its own operations of $200,000 in fiscal 19X3.

Required:

1. What criteria could influence Arba in its decision to include or exclude Braginetz as a subsidiary in consolidated financial statements? Explain.
2. Prepare a schedule to compute Arba's equity method accrual for fiscal 19X3. Ignore income taxes.
3. For each of the following items, give the elimination entry (including explanation) that should be made on the working paper for the preparation of the indicated consolidated statement(s) at September 30, 19X3. Ignore income taxes throughout.
    a. For the consolidated goodwill—to prepare all consolidated statements. Goodwill amortization did not appear on consolidated statements in fiscal 19X1.
    b. For the equipment: (1) To prepare only a consolidated balance sheet; (2) To prepare all consolidated statements.
    c. For the intercompany merchandise transactions—to prepare all consolidated statements.
    d. For the note transactions—to prepare only a consolidated balance sheet.

(AICPA adapted)

P9.2 **Computation of Consolidated Income Tax Expense** Percy Corporation owns 80 percent of Stetson Company. Both firms file separate income tax returns and face a marginal tax rate of .6. The following information relates to their operations during 19X5.

1. Percy reported pretax book income of $1,200,000 from its own operations. Unconfirmed intercompany profits in Percy's beginning and ending inventories amounted to $70,000 and $80,000, respectively.
2. Percy's beginning retained earnings includes a $40,000 pretax gain recognized on a prior period transfer of land to Stetson Company.

3. Stetson reported pretax book income of $400,000 from its own operations and declared dividends of $100,000 during 19X5. The indefinite reversal criteria do not apply.

4. Stetson began buying merchandise from Percy during 19X5. Its ending inventory included goods marked up $25,000 by Percy. During 19X5, Stetson recognized a loss of $50,000 on land sold to Percy.

5. Stetson leased equipment from Percy during 19X5. Total intercompany billings were $200,000.

Required: Prepare a schedule to compute consolidated income tax expense for Percy and Stetson in 19X5.

P9.3 **Consolidated Financial Statement Working Paper—Intercompany Transactions** Preclosing trial balances of Power Company and its 60-percent-owned subsidiary, Sour Company, at December 31, 19X0, are as shown here:

Account	Power Co.	Sour Co.
Cash and Receivables	$ 960,000	$ 700,000
Inventory	1,000,000	500,000
Investment in Sour	1,192,000	—
Plant Assets	7,200,000	4,270,000
Accumulated Depreciation	(2,100,000)	(1,600,000)
Current Liabilities	(820,000)	(420,000)
Noncurrent Liabilities	(2,600,000)	(1,600,000)
Capital Stock	(500,000)	(200,000)
Retained Earnings	(3,200,000)	(1,300,000)
Sales	(8,000,000)	(3,200,000)
Income from Sour	(92,000)	—
Gain on Sale of Land	(100,000)	—
Purchases	5,000,000	2,100,000
Operating Expenses	1,300,000	550,000
Income Tax Expense	760,000	200,000
	$ 0	$ 0
Ending Inventory	$1,100,000	$ 450,000

Additional information:

1. The Investment in Sour account reflects a purchase premium of $200,000, entirely attributable to goodwill amortizable over a remaining life of twenty years.

2. Power recognized a gain of $100,000 on land sold to Sour Company.

3. Power's ending inventory includes $50,000 of unconfirmed intercompany profits on goods acquired from Sour. Total intercompany sales were $600,000 during 19X0.

4. Sour declared no dividends during the year; the indefinite reversal criteria apply.

5. Both companies' Income Tax Expense accounts relate to their own operations; the marginal income tax rate is .4.

Required: Prepare a consolidated financial statement working paper for Power and Sour.

P9.4 **Equity Method Accrual—Various Intercompany Transactions** Silver Company, an 80-percent-owned subsidiary of Platinum, Inc., reported net income from its own operations of $600,000. Both firms face a 40 percent marginal tax rate and use straight-line depreciation and amortization. As the new assistant controller at Platinum, you have been asked to compute Platinum's equity method accrual and are given the following information.

1. A summary of unconfirmed intercompany inventory profits is as follows:

	Platinum	Silver
Intercompany Profits in Ending Inventory	$200,000	$80,000
Intercompany Profits in Beginning Inventory	150,000	90,000

2. On January 2, the beginning of the accounting period, Silver sold a piece of equipment to Platinum for $320,000. The net book value to Silver had been $240,000; the equipment had a remaining useful life of five years at January 2.

3. When Platinum purchased Silver three years ago, it paid a purchase premium of $100,000. Allocation of the $100,000 consisted of a $150,000 decrease to Silver's Long-Term Debt account and a $50,000 decrease to Silver's Patents account. At date of acquisition, the debt had a maturity date six years in the future, and the revalued patent had a remaining economic life of ten years.

4. During the year in which the acquisition took place, Platinum recognized a gain of $180,000 on a sale of land to Silver. Silver still owns the land.

5. Silver declared dividends of $400,000 during the year. Its undistributed earnings are assumed to be permanently reinvested.

Required: Prepare a schedule to compute the equity method accrual to be made by Platinum at the end of the current year.

P9.5 **Consolidated Trial Balance Working Paper—No Income Taxes** Following are the preclosing trial balances of P Company and its 80-percent-owned subsidiary, S Company, at December 31, 19X4.

Account	P Company	S Company
Cash and Receivables	$ 2,000,000	$1,100,000
Inventory	1,500,000	800,000
Investment in S	2,930,000	—
Plant Assets	9,600,000	5,200,000
Accumulated Depreciation	(2,800,000)	(1,400,000)
Current Liabilities	(1,900,000)	(700,000)
Noncurrent Liabilities	(3,000,000)	(1,000,000)
Capital Stock	(1,000,000)	(500,000)
Retained Earnings	(6,226,000)	(3,000,000)
Dividends	800,000	200,000
Sales	(15,000,000)	(7,000,000)
Income from S	(704,000)	—
Purchases	10,000,000	5,000,000
Operating Expenses	3,800,000	1,300,000
	$ 0	$ 0
Ending Inventory	$ 1,200,000	$1,000,000

Additional information:

1. P uses the equity method to account for the investment in S Company.
2. P recorded a gain of $150,000 on land sold to S during 19X3. S continues to hold the land.
3. A summary of intercompany merchandise transactions is as follows:

	P Company	S Company	Total
Intercompany Profits in Inventory, January 1, 19X4	$ 80,000	$ 200,000	$ 280,000
Intercompany Sales of Merchandise during 19X4	2,000,000	1,000,000	3,000,000
Intercompany Profits in Inventory, December 31, 19X4	50,000	240,000	290,000

4. Unpaid invoices on intercompany sales amounted to $375,000 at December 31, 19X4.

Required: Prepare a consolidated trial balance working paper. Ignore income taxes.

P9.6 **Consolidated Income Statement—Pooling of Interests** Pow Company and Sow Company united in a pooling of interests several years ago as Pow exchanged its own shares for 95 percent of the outstanding stock of Sow. Pow recorded its share of Sow's retained earnings at that time. Condensed income statements for the two companies are given below. Although Pow uses the equity method, the current year's equity method accrual has not been made and can be ignored in your solution.

	Pow Company	Sow Company
Sales	$25,000,000	$10,000,000
Other Income	1,200,000	500,000
Total Revenue	$26,200,000	$10,500,000
Cost of Goods Sold	$19,000,000	$ 7,600,000
Operating Expenses	4,100,000	1,800,000
Other Expenses	800,000	300,000
Total Expenses	$23,900,000	$ 9,700,000
Net Income	$ 2,300,000	$ 800,000
Retained Earnings, January 1	15,700,000	6,200,000
Dividends	(1,000,000)	(400,000)
Retained Earnings, December 31	$17,000,000	$ 6,600,000

Additional information:

1. Pow's *beginning* inventory included $400,000 of intercompany profit on goods purchased from Sow and Sow's *ending* inventory included $200,000 of intercompany profit on purchases of $3,000,000 from Pow.
2. Sow's Other Expenses balance includes a loss of $100,000 on an intercompany sale of land to Pow.
3. Pow's Other Income balance reflects a $250,000 gain on sale of machinery to Sow at the beginning of the year. At date of sale, the machinery had a remaining life of five years; it is being depreciated by the straight-line method.

4. Several years ago, Pow had recorded a gain of $60,000 on land sold to Sow for $280,000. Sow sold the land externally during the year for $390,000. The current gain is reflected in Sow's Other Income account.

Required: Prepare a consolidated statement of income and retained earnings for Pow and Sow. Ignore income taxes.

P9.7 **Intercompany Transfers of Depreciable Assets** Pert Corporation acquired 80 percent of Smart Company ten years ago. In the intervening years, Pert and Smart have engaged in several intercompany transfers of depreciable assets. Pert's controller is beginning the process of preparing consolidated statements for the current year ended December 31, 19X8. As the new assistant controller, you have been asked to develop the working paper eliminations for the following group of intercompany transactions. Pert uses the equity method to account for its investment in Smart. All depreciation is allocated according to the straight-line method.

Transaction No.	Date	Original Cost	Accumulated Depreciation	Transfer Price	Remaining Life	Upstream (U) Downstream (D)
1	6/30/X2	$100,000	$ 20,000	$160,000	8 years	D
2	1/2/X4	450,000	300,000	200,000	10	U
3	1/1/X7	600,000	360,000	200,000	5	D

Required:

1. Prepare the needed working paper eliminations for consolidation at December 31, 19X8. All computations must be in good form.
2. Assume that the item in transaction 2 was sold outside on January 1, 19X8, for $400,000. Prepare the working paper eliminations needed for transaction 2 at December 31, 19X8, reflecting the sale to an external party during 19X8.

P9.8 **Consolidated Financial Statement Working Paper—No Income Taxes** Plato Company owns 90 percent of Socrates Company. Socrates was acquired for a price $500,000 greater than its book value on January 2, 19X3. The entire $500,000 was allocated to goodwill and is being amortized over twenty years according to the straight-line method. On January 2, 19X7, Plato sold a depreciable asset to Socrates for $200,000. The asset originally cost $300,000 and had been fully depreciated by Plato, yet, due to a shift in consumption patterns, the asset was believed to have an economic life of four more years as of January 2, 19X7. Socrates uses sum-of-the-years'-digits depreciation.

Socrates regularly sells merchandise to Plato for further processing and external sale. In 19X9, Plato's beginning and ending inventories reflected intercompany profits on purchases from Socrates of $30,000 and $45,000, respectively. Intercompany sales during 19X9 were $1,400,000. Trial balances of the two companies at December 31, 19X9, follow.

Account	Plato Company	Socrates Company
Cash and Receivables	$ 1,700,000	$ 490,000
Inventory	2,100,000	510,000
Investment in Socrates	1,596,500	—
Plant Assets	8,000,000	2,100,000
Accumulated Depreciation	(2,000,000)	(500,000)
Current Liabilities	(1,900,000)	(340,000)
Noncurrent Liabilities	(4,000,000)	(800,000)
Capital Stock	(1,000,000)	(100,000)
Retained Earnings	(4,043,000)	(1,200,000)
Dividends	400,000	100,000
Sales	(10,000,000)	(4,000,000)
Income from Socrates	(253,500)	—
Purchases	7,800,000	3,100,000
Operating Expenses	1,600,000	640,000
	$ 0	$ 0
Ending Inventory	$ 2,000,000	$ 530,000

Required: Prepare a consolidated financial statement working paper for Plato and Socrates at December 31, 19X9. Ignore income taxes.

Chapter 10

Consolidated Financial Statements: Intercompany Transactions II

In this chapter, we complete our study of intercompany transactions in consolidated statements. After considering the consolidation problems created when one affiliate holds bonds issued by another affiliate, we present a comprehensive example incorporating various intercompany transactions and a consolidated financial statement working paper. The chapter ends with a discussion of consolidation issues relating to subsidiary companies that have preferred stock as well as common stock outstanding.

Intercompany Bondholdings

Study of the consolidation techniques called for when intercompany bondholdings are present can become very involved. Following the single entity concept, when the bonds of one affiliate are held by another affiliate, no external relationship exists insofar as the consolidated entity is concerned (that is, transactions regarding the bondholding are internal). If the bonds are acquired directly from the issuing affiliate, the purchaser's *investment in bonds* will equal the issuer's *bond liability*. Each year the intercompany debt and related interest expense can be cleanly and simply eliminated. The only requirement is that both companies use the same method to amortize any offsetting discount or premium on the bonds. As the following illustration shows, such a simple situation presents no accounting complications.

Suppose P Company owns 80 percent of S Company. On January 1, 19X3, P issues $1,000,000 par value bonds for $950,000. The bonds pay 10 percent interest annually and mature in twenty years. S Company acquires 40 percent of the bond issue directly from P Company. Therefore, $400,000 par value bonds are held by an affiliate and are viewed as being **constructively retired** from a consolidated point of view. The accounts relative to this intercompany bondholding at January 1, 19X3, are as follows:

	P Company			S Company	
Bonds Payable (Par) . . .	$400,000		Investment in Bonds (Par) .	$400,000	
Discount on Bonds Payable .	(20,000)		Discount on Investment in Bonds	(20,000)	
Net Bond Liability . . .	$380,000		Net Bond Investment . .	$380,000	

Both companies amortize their discounts by the straight-line method. In consolidation at December 31, 19X3, the intercompany bondholding and the intercompany interest revenue and expense must be eliminated. The three working paper entries that follow accomplish this:

CONSOLIDATED FINANCIAL STATEMENT WORKING PAPER

Bonds Payable	400,000	
Investment in Bonds		400,000
To eliminate the par value of the intercompany bonds.		

| Discount on Investment in Bonds . . . . . . | 19,000 | |
| Discount on Bonds Payable . . . . . | | 19,000 |

To eliminate the unamortized discounts on the intercompany bondholding; $19,000 = $20,000 − $20,000/20.

| Interest Revenue . . . . | 41,000 | |
| Interest Expense . . . . | | 41,000 |

To eliminate the interest revenue and expense on the intercompany bonds; $41,000 = (.1 × $400,000) + $20,000/20.

These eliminations are repeated at each subsequent consolidation point as long as the bonds are held internally. While the annual interest and par value of the intercompany bondholding are unchanged in future years, the unamortized discounts decline by $1,000 (= $20,000/20) each year. At December 31, 19X4, for example, the first and third working paper entries above would be made in the same amounts. In the second entry, however, the unamortized discounts would have decreased to $18,000 [= $20,000 − 2($20,000/20)]. We now turn to a more intricate set of circumstances.

Intercompany Bonds Acquired in the Open Market

When bonds are acquired directly from the issuing company, their price equals the proceeds received by the issuer. Thus if the bonds are issued at a discount from par, they will be purchased at an equal discount; the intercompany bond accounts will be equal and offsetting. Unfortunately, this is not normally the case if the bonds are acquired in the open market after they were originally issued. Changes in interest rates affect the present value of the cash payments promised by the bonds and thus also affect bond prices. Therefore, a dramatic increase in interest rates can cause bonds originally issued at a premium to subsequently sell at a discount. Similarly, a decline in interest rates can cause bonds originally issued at a discount to sell at a premium.

If interest rates have changed since the bonds were issued, problems will arise when consolidated statements are prepared following the purchase of intercompany bonds in the open market. The two major problems are:

1. Because of interest rate changes since date of issue, the *investment in bonds* will not equal the carrying value of the *bond liability*.

2. As a consequence of this first problem, the *interest expense* recorded by the *issuing affiliate* will *differ* from the *interest revenue* recorded by the *purchasing affiliate*. Even though the amount of coupon interest paid equals the amount received, *different amounts of premium or discount amortization* cause the intercompany interest expense and revenue amounts to be unequal.

Several controversial issues are involved in dealing with these problems; they are discussed later in the chapter. However, our resolution of these issues is reflected in the following summary regarding treatment of these problems in consolidated statements.

> Because they are held inside the affiliated group, intercompany bonds are considered to be *constructively retired* and are eliminated. In the year of acquisition, a consolidated gain (loss) arises if the net bond liability is greater than (less than) the net investment in bonds. This gain or loss is attributed to the affiliates according to their recorded premium or discount and is confirmed over time through discount or premium amortization on the affiliates' books. At each subsequent consolidation point, P's portion of the consolidated gain or loss not yet confirmed must be removed from the Investment in S account (it was originally entered via the equity method). S's unconfirmed portion must be entered in its beginning retained earnings. Finally, the unamortized premium and discount and current interest expense and revenue on intercompany bonds must be eliminated.

Before proceeding, we note one very important difference between intercompany bondholdings and other transactions generating intercompany gains and losses. In the other intercompany transactions, the gains or losses have been recorded by the affiliates as part of their own operations; *at consolidation the unconfirmed portion is eliminated.* An intercompany bondholding, however, gives rise to a gain or loss which will not be recorded by the affiliates, except through P's equity method accrual. Since the equity accrual is eliminated in consolidation, the gain or loss related to the intercompany bondholding *must be recorded at the first consolidation point after the bonds are acquired internally.*

Eliminations When the Bonds Are Acquired   To introduce the eliminations, assume that the bonds are acquired on December 31, 19X1, and consolidated statements are prepared immediately. (This assumption allows us to sidestep, for now, the complications created by premium/discount amortization after acquisition.) Our presentation incorporates the following facts:

1. The bonds were originally issued at a premium over par. When acquired in the open market, however, they were selling at a discount under par.

2. The issuing affiliate has its bond liability recorded in two accounts: Bonds Payable for the par value and an adjunct account having a credit balance, Premium on Bonds Payable, for the unamortized balance of the proceeds in excess of par.

3.   The purchasing affiliate has its bond investment recorded in two accounts: Investment in Bonds for the par value and a contra account having a credit balance, Discount on Investment in Bonds, for the discount from par.

In a situation such as this, we eliminate the par value of the intercompany bonds and eliminate the unamortized premium and discount separately, thereby simplifying the elimination process.

We now present the eliminations to be made when the bonds are first acquired within the affiliated group at December 31, 19X1.

CONSOLIDATED FINANCIAL STATEMENT WORKING PAPER

Bonds Payable XXX
    Investment in Bonds   XXX
To eliminate the *par value* of the intercompany bonds.

Premium on Bonds Payable XXX
Discount on Investment in Bonds XXX
    Gain on Retirement of Consolidated Debt   XXX
To eliminate the premium and discount on intercompany
bonds and to recognize a gain attributable to the constructive
retirement of the debt. The gain equals the excess of bond
liability over bond investment; in effect, less money was spent
to acquire (and retire) the bonds than was owed by the
issuing affiliate.

Nature of the Gain or Loss on Retirement of Consolidated Debt

When one affiliate acquires the bonds of another, the acquisition has the same effect as retirement of the bonds by the selling firm from the point of view of the consolidated firms (or, we say that the bonds have been *constructively retired*). If the cost of the bonds is less than the issuing affiliate's bond liability, a consolidated gain arises. In contrast, if the investment in bonds exceeds the bond liability, a consolidated loss is incurred. Once the amount of gain or loss is determined, the accountant must decide to what extent it should accrue to the issuing and purchasing affiliates. Four alternative treatments have been proposed to answer this question.

1.   ***Allocate entirely to issuing affiliate***   This position rests on the notion that when companies are under common control, the affiliate purchasing the bonds is acting as an *agent* for the issuing affiliate. Hence the entire gain or loss should be attributed to the issuing affiliate. We see no basis, however, for allocating to the issuing affiliate the portion of the gain or loss to be realized by the purchasing affiliate over time.

2.   ***Allocate entirely to purchasing affiliate***   Under this interpretation, it is the purchasing affiliate's investment which led to the constructive retirement of the bonds. In our opinion, this is adequate justification for attributing the difference between par and the cost of the bonds to the purchasing affiliate; however, we see no basis for allocating to the purchaser the issuer's unamortized discount or premium.

3.   ***Allocate entirely to controlling interest***   Parent company management controls its subsidiaries and therefore is responsible for decisions involving material investments, debt issues, and debt retire-

ments. Hence it could be argued that the entire gain or loss accrues to the parent. This certainly does follow if the parent is the issuing company, and the bonds actually are retired or if the purchasing affiliate is a wholly-owned subsidiary. Otherwise, the minority interest shares in the gain or loss as it is realized over time. If a minority interest is present, allocation of the entire gain or loss to the controlling interest seems to be at odds with the facts.

4. ***Allocate between the issuing and purchasing affiliates***   We believe this to be the most consistent treatment of gain or loss on constructive retirement of consolidated debt. It recognizes the *fact that both affiliates will typically record a discount or premium and will realize a gain or loss as the bonds are held to maturity.* If a partially-owned subsidiary is involved, the minority interest will clearly absorb some portion of the gain or loss due to discount or premium amortization over time.

In our view, the first three treatments described are not consistent with the fact acknowledged in the fourth treatment. Therefore, in the illustrations that follow, *both affiliates share in the gain or loss to the extent of their respective discounts or premiums.* Moreover, if a partially-owned subsidiary is involved, Minority Interest in Net Income is affected. When there are *offsetting* premiums or discounts such that there is no *net* gain or loss, the minority interest nevertheless absorbs its share of the gain or loss attributable to the subsidiary.

Impact of Intercompany Bondholdings on the Equity Method Accrual   In order to understand the working paper entries required to eliminate intercompany bondholdings, it is necessary to grasp the dual role played here by the equity method. To simplify the discussion, we assume that the intercompany bondholding resulted in *gains* being attributed to both P and S.

1. P's equity method accrual made during the year the bonds are acquired includes the gain attributable to itself *plus* its share (α) of the gain attributable to S. Therefore, in that year of acquisition, both the Investment in S and the net income of P include P's share of the total consolidated gain. At the same time, S Company's net income does not include its portion of the gain, nor does it include P's portion of the gain.

2. At consolidation points *following* the date the bonds are acquired, the books of P and S both reflect their current year amortization of premium and discount on the intercompany bondholding. This amortization of premium and discount represents partial recognition of the consolidated gain previously recorded by P under the equity method (in item 1). Consequently, these annual amounts of premium and discount amortization are charged *against* the equity method accrual in postacquisition years *so that the total gain is counted only once.*

Put another way, the total consolidated gain arising out of the intercompany bondholding consists of the affiliates' unamortized discount and premium on the intercompany bonds when the bonds are acquired. P's share of the gain is recorded as part of the equity method accrual in the year the bonds are acquired. On the working paper in that year, the total gain is recognized and allocated to consolidated net income (P's share) and the minority interest in net income (the minority's share of S's portion of the gain). After the bonds are acquired, both P and S recognize a portion of the gain on their books each year as P's discount and S's premium on the bonds are amortized. If the periodic discount and premium amortization are not eliminated from the equity method accruals (and on the working papers) in subsequent years, the total gain will be counted in income twice—once in the year the bonds are acquired internally and a second time through periodic discount and premium amortization by P and S.

In sum, at any consolidation point following the year in which the bonds are acquired, the Investment in S account will include P's share of the total consolidated gain not yet recorded by the affiliates through discount and premium amortization. Working paper entries are necessary to adjust the investment account and the retained earnings of S to permit clean eliminations and to avoid recognizing the consolidated gain twice.

Eliminations in Subsequent Years   As indicated above, the affiliates involved in the intercompany bondholding recognize their portions of the total gain over time through amortization of the discount and premium on their own books. Consistent application of the equity method leads to differences between the investment account and the retained earnings of S. For these reasons, the following must be accomplished at each subsequent consolidation point:

1.   *Par value* of the intercompany bondholding must be eliminated.

2.   The *unamortized premium and discount* as of the end of the current year must be eliminated; items 3 and 4 below achieve this.

3.   *Intercompany interest expense and revenue* must be eliminated. Since the recorded amounts represent the coupon payment plus or minus the current discount and premium amortization, the elimination reverses the current year's amortization and adjusts the discount and premium to their beginning-of-year balances.

4.   One of these beginning-of-year balances is *S's unconfirmed portion of the gain;* it is eliminated and allocated to the beginning retained earnings of S. The other balance is *P's unconfirmed portion of the gain;* its elimination goes to reduce the investment account.

The entry used at acquisition to eliminate the par value of the intercompany bondholding is also used at each subsequent consolidation point. We do not repeat that entry here. Rather, we will provide a general form of the entry needed to eliminate intercompany interest and the premium and discount, and to deal with the portion of the gain not recorded by the individual companies. Assume that S Company originally issued the bonds, P subsequently acquired them, and both companies use straight-line amortization. We first establish the following definitions:

D = Discount on investment in bonds when acquired by P Company.

B = Unamortized premium on bonds payable at date bonds are acquired by P Company.

T = Number of years to maturity when bonds are acquired by P Company.

t = Year subsequent to date bonds are acquired by P Company, $t = 1, ..., T$.

D/T = Annual straight-line amortization of discount on bond investment by P Company.

B/T = Annual straight-line amortization of premium on bonds payable by S Company.

I = Annual intercompany coupon interest.

Using this notation, we can express symbolically the amounts in the eliminating entry, as follows:

$I + D/T$ = Annual interest revenue recorded by P Company.

$I - B/T$ = Annual interest expense recorded by S Company.

$D - t(D/T)$ = Unamortized discount on investment in bonds at *end* of year t.

$B - t(B/T)$ = Unamortized premium on bonds payable at *end* of year t.

$D - (t - 1)(D/T)$ = Unamortized discount on investment in bonds at *beginning* of year t.[a]

$B - (t - 1)(B/T)$ = Unamortized premium on bonds payable at *beginning* of year t.[b]

Amortization of bond premium and discount via the effective interest amortization method would change none of the principles involved here. Of course, it would make the computation more complex because we would not have constant annual amortization. Regardless of whether straight-line or effective interest amortization is used, however, the principles embodied in the eliminating entry are as follows:

1. Each affiliate's unamortized premium or discount on the intercompany bonds at the *end* of the current year is part of the total intercompany bondholding and must be eliminated.

2. The periodic intercompany interest revenue and expense as recorded by the affiliates is eliminated. The difference between the coupon amount and the interest revenue or expense is the amount of total gain or loss realized or confirmed by each affiliate during the year.

3. The portion of the total gain or loss which has *not* been recorded on the affiliates' books via periodic discount or premium amortization in prior years is also dealt with in consolidation. This is the amount of unamortized discount or premium at the *beginning* of the current year (the amortized portion *has* been recorded in the affiliates' books by inclusion in prior years' interest revenue and expense). The Investment in S account is adjusted by the portion pertaining to P and Retained Earnings—S is adjusted by the portion pertaining to S.

[a] This is the portion of P Company's gain *not* recorded through discount amortization as of the *beginning* of year t but recorded via the equity method when the bonds were acquired.

[b] This is the portion of S Company's gain *not* recorded through premium amortization as of the *beginning* of year t.

Now, the entry itself:

CONSOLIDATED FINANCIAL STATEMENT WORKING PAPER

Interest Revenue	$I + D/T$	
Discount on Investment in Bonds	$D - t(D/T)$	
Premium on Bonds Payable	$B - t(B/T)$	
Retained Earnings—S, January 1		$B - (t - 1)(B/T)$
Investment in S		$D - (t - 1)(D/T)$
Interest Expense		$I - B/T$

To eliminate the unamortized premium and discount on intercompany bonds and the intercompany interest expense and revenue. P had acquired the bonds of S in the open market on December 31 of a previous year.

After the preceding entry and the entry eliminating the par value of the intercompany bonds have been made, the following consolidated results are obtained:

1. The intercompany bondholdings, including premium and discount, have vanished.

2. Intercompany interest revenue and expense are gone.

3. The portion of the gain directly attributable to P and previously recorded under the equity method has been removed from the Investment in S account. Furthermore, the unrecorded portion of the gain attributable to S is now part of S's retained earnings. The Investment in S account still includes P's share of S's portion of the gain and can be eliminated cleanly.

Illustration of Intercompany Bondholdings

On December 31, 19X1, Pinto Corporation purchases $100,000 par value bonds issued by its 80-percent-owned subsidiary, Stallion Corporation. The bonds pay 8 percent interest annually on December 31 and were acquired in the open market for $95,000, reflecting a current market yield of approximately 9.3 percent. They mature in five years, on December 31, 19X6. Stallion had an unamortized premium of $10,000 related to the bonds recorded on its books. Both companies use the straight-line method of amortizing bond discounts and premiums. These data are summarized as follows.

Pinto Corporation		Stallion Corporation	
Investment in Bonds (Par)	$100,000	Bonds Payable (Par)	$100,000
Discount on Investment in		Premium on Bonds Payable	10,000
Bonds	(5,000)		
Net Bond Investment	$ 95,000	Net Bond Liability	$110,000

From the foregoing, we can make two observations:

1. P's bond investment ($95,000) does not equal S's bond liability ($110,000).

2. P's annual interest revenue will not equal S's annual interest expense; $9,000 (= $8,000 + $5,000/5) does not equal $6,000 (= $8,000 − $10,000/5).

At the end of 19X1, when Pinto records its equity method accrual, it must reflect its share of the intercompany gain on constructive retirement of consolidated debt. The total gain is $15,000 (= $110,000 − $95,000), of which $5,000 (the discount) is allocated directly to Pinto and $10,000 (the premium) to Stallion. If Stallion earns $50,000 in 19X1, Pinto makes the following accrual under the equity method:

BOOKS OF PINTO CORPORATION

Investment in S	53,000	
Income from S		53,000

To record Pinto's 80 percent share of Stallion's net income $40,000 (= .8 × $50,000) plus Pinto's portion of the gain on intercompany bonds ($5,000) plus 80 percent of Stallion's portion of the gain on intercompany bonds $8,000 (= .8 × $10,000).

Preparation of consolidated financial statements then occurs; the working paper entries made to prepare the statements are as follows:

CONSOLIDATED FINANCIAL STATEMENT WORKING PAPER

Income from S	53,000	
Investment in S		53,000

To eliminate the equity method accrual and restate the investment account to its balance at January 1, 19X1.

Bonds Payable	100,000	
Investment in Bonds		100,000

To eliminate the intercompany bonds at par value.

Premium on Bonds Payable	10,000	
Discount on Investment in Bonds	5,000	
Gain on Retirement of Consolidated Debt		15,000

To eliminate the discount and premium on intercompany bonds and establish the gain on constructive retirement of the intercompany bonds.

In the following year, 19X2, three very important matters must be kept in mind:

1. Both the Investment in S and Retained Earnings accounts of Pinto now reflect Pinto's portion of the gain ($5,000) plus 80 percent of Stallion's portion of the gain ($8,000), a total of $13,000. These amounts were recorded on P's books as part of the 19X1 equity method accrual and are not affected by working paper eliminations.

2. Stallion's Retained Earnings account does *not* reflect any part of its portion of the gain on intercompany bonds.

3. During 19X2, $3,000 of the total gain of $15,000 will be recorded by the affiliates as they amortize the discount ($1,000) and premium ($2,000). This amortization causes the inequality between P's annual interest revenue of $9,000 and S's annual interest expense of $6,000.

Impact on Equity Method Accrual in 19X2   To illustrate how amortization of the discount and premium on intercompany bonds affects the equity method accrual, let us take a typical subsequent year, 19X2. In 19X2, $3,000 of gain will be recorded by the affiliates as they amortize the bond discount ($1,000) and premium ($2,000), thereby increasing interest revenue and decreasing interest expense, respectively. As we have previously stated, this amortization must be eliminated in consolidation of financial statements to avoid counting the $3,000 twice—once in beginning consolidated retained earnings and again in current period consolidated net income.

Under the one-line consolidation concept, Pinto Corporation must incorporate those eliminations affecting consolidated net income in the equity method accrual. Assume that Stallion earned $30,000 in 19X2. Pinto's share is $24,000 (= .8 × $30,000). Stallion's income, however, includes $2,000 of premium amortization which will be eliminated. Pinto's share of this is $1,600 (= .8 × $2,000); the other $400 will be charged against the minority interest in net income in consolidation. In addition, Pinto's bond discount amortization of $1,000 will also be eliminated (the entire amount relates to Pinto).

If these were the only intercompany items affecting the equity method accrual, Pinto would record $21,400 (= $24,000 − $1,600 − $1,000) of income from Stallion in 19X2. After five years of reducing the equity method accrual by $2,600, Pinto's $13,000 share of the total gain on retirement of intercompany debt, $15,000, will have been removed from the investment account. Pinto will have recorded $5,000 of interest revenue on its books through the periodic discount amortization. Stallion will have recorded $10,000 of reductions to interest expense on its books through the periodic premium amortization, $2,000 of which relates to the minority interest. The total $15,000 gain will have been counted only once.

Starting with 19X2, then, the first year after the intercompany bonds are acquired, bookkeeping entries made by Pinto and Stallion affect the working paper eliminations as follows:

1. The discount and premium are reduced each year by $1,000 and $2,000, respectively, as they are amortized.

2. Retained earnings of Stallion begin to reflect Stallion's portion of the gain as $2,000 of bond premium is amortized each year.

3. The Investment in S account is reduced by $1,000 each year, as elimination of the $1,000 bond discount amortization is reflected in the equity method accrual.

Bond Eliminations Made in the Years Remaining until Maturity   The eliminating entries made at the end of the five remaining years to maturity incorporate the developments just discussed; they are presented in Exhibit 10.1 and are related to the general form of the elimination given earlier.

| **Intercompany Transactions: A Comprehensive Example** | In this section of the chapter, we bring together the various intercompany transactions and consider them as parts of a complex consolidation problem using a consolidated financial statement working paper. P Company acquired 80 percent of S Company's outstanding common stock several years ago on December 31, 19X1, for $2,400,000. When the stock was acquired, S's stockholders' equity was $2,500,000, and the book values of S's assets and liabilities ap- |

Exhibit 10.1 Working Paper Eliminations for Intercompany Bondholdings in Years Subsequent to Acquisition by Pinto Corporation

	General Form		12/31/X2; $t = 1$		12/31/X3; $t = 2$	
	Dr.	Cr.	Dr.	Cr.	Dr.	Cr.
1. Bonds Payable	Par Value		100,000		100,000	
Investment in Bonds . . .		Par Value		100,000		100,000
2. Interest Revenue	$I + D/T$		9,000		9,000	
Discount on Investment in Bonds .	$D - t(D/T)$		4,000		3,000	
Premium on Bonds Payable . .	$B - t(B/T)$		8,000		6,000	
Retained Earnings—S,						
January 1		$B - (t-1)(B/T)$		10,000		8,000
Investment in S		$D - (t-1)(D/T)$		5,000		4,000
Interest Expense		$I - B/T$		6,000		6,000

1. To eliminate the intercompany bonds at par.
2. To eliminate the unamortized premium and discount on intercompany bonds and the intercompany interest expense and revenue.

Notation:
D = Discount on investment in bonds when acquired by Pinto Corporation; $5,000.
B = Unamortized premium on bonds payable to date bonds acquired by Pinto; $10,000.
T = Number of years to maturity when bonds acquired by Pinto; 5.
t = Year subsequent to date bonds acquired by Pinto; $t = 1, ..., 5$.
D/T = Annual straight-line amortization of discount on bond investment by Pinto; $1,000 = \$5,000/5$.
B/T = Annual straight-line amortization of premium on bonds payable by Stallion Corporation; $2,000 = \$10,000/5$.
I = Annual intercompany coupon interest; $8,000 = .08 \times \$100,000$.

proximated their fair values with one exception. A factory owned by S had an estimated fair value of $500,000; it was recorded on S's books at a net book value of $300,000. The factory had an estimated remaining life of ten years when the acquisition was made by P. Determination and allocation of the purchase premium implicit in the acquisition price are given in Exhibit 10.2.

We are now beginning the preparation of consolidated financial statements at December 31, 19X4, three years after the stock acquisition on December 31, 19X1. P accounts for its investment in S by the equity method and amortizes the goodwill on the straight-line basis over forty years. The following information regarding intercompany transactions is provided:

1. P sold merchandise to S for $125,000 during 19X4; the cost to P was $100,000. Of this $125,000 of merchandise purchased from P, $30,000 remained in the ending inventory of S Company. Furthermore, S Company's beginning inventory included $1,000 of intercompany profits on purchases from P during 19X3, which were not confirmed at December 31, 19X3.

2. During 19X4, S Company transferred a parcel of land to P Company for $60,000. The original cost was $35,000; S Company recorded a gain of $25,000.

12/31/X4; $t = 3$		12/31/X5; $t = 4$		12/31/X6; $t = 5$	
Dr.	Cr.	Dr.	Cr.	Dr.	Cr.
100,000		100,000		100,000	
	100,000		100,000		100,000
9,000		9,000		9,000	
2,000		1,000		—	
4,000		2,000		—	
	6,000		4,000		2,000
	3,000		2,000		1,000
	6,000		6,000		6,000

3.   On December 31, 19X2, P Company sold some equipment to S Company for $112,000. Immediately prior to the sale, the equipment and related accumulated depreciation accounts showed $200,000 and $120,000, respectively. Thus the net book value was $80,000 at time of sale, and P recorded a gain of $32,000. Previous depreciation expense had been $10,000 annually; the equipment had a remaining useful life of eight years at December 31, 19X2. Annual excess depreciation will therefore be $4,000 (= $32,000/8).

4.   On January 1, 19X4, P Company acquired all of the outstanding bonds of S Company for $924,180. The bonds have a par value of $1,000,000, pay 8 percent interest annually on December 31, and mature on December 31, 19X8. The yield to maturity on the bonds at January 1, 19X4, was 10 percent as indicated in the following calculation:

Present Value of $1,000,000, to Be Received in Five Years (December
31, 19X8), Discounted at 10%; .62092 × $1,000,000 . . . . . . $620,920
Present Value of Five Annual Interest Payments of $80,000 (= .08 ×
$1,000,000), Discounted at 10%; 3.79079 × $80,000 303,260
    Price Paid by P Company $924,180

When the bonds were acquired on January 1, 19X4, S Company's books showed an unamortized premium on bonds payable of $20,000. P Company recorded a discount on investment in bonds of $75,820 (= $1,000,000 − $924,180). Thus at January 1, 19X4, the total gain on constructive retirement of consolidated debt was $95,820, of which $75,820 pertained to P and $20,000 to S. The gain will be realized by both companies over the five years remaining to maturity as the discount and premium are amortized at the straight-line annual rates of $15,164 (= $75,820/5) and $4,000 (= $20,000/5), respectively.

Exhibit 10.2   Determination and Allocation of the Purchase Premium

P Company and S Company
Schedule for Determining and Allocating Purchase Premium
Arising in the Stock Acquisition on December 31, 19X1

Cost of the Acquisition	$2,400,000
Book Value of the Net Assets or Stockholders' Equity Acquired (80%):	
Capital Stock	$1,200,000
Retained Earnings	800,000
Total Book Value of S Company (80%)	$2,000,000
Purchase Premium	$ 400,000

Assets and Liabilities of S Company	Fair Value	Book Value	Fair Value Less Book Value	Allocation Based on P's Interest (80%)
Cash and Receivables . .	$ 550,000	$ 550,000	—	—
Inventory . . .	750,000	750,000	—	—
Land	600,000	600,000	—	—
Buildings and Equipment (Net) .	2,400,000	2,200,000	$200,000	$160,000
Current Liabilities .	(672,000)	(672,000)	—	—
Bonds Payable, 8% .	(1,000,000)	(1,000,000)	—	—
Premium on Bonds Payable . . .	(28,000)	(28,000)	—	—
	$2,600,000	$2,400,000	$200,000	$160,000
Goodwill				240,000
Total Purchase Premium				$400,000

S Company paid dividends of $200,000 and reported net income of $500,000 in 19X4. Upon receipt of this information, P Company determines the accrual required under the equity method and records it. Exhibit 10.3 explains how the accrual is computed, and the equity method entries made by P are given below:

BOOKS OF P COMPANY

Investment in S	430,456	
Income from S		430,456
To record income from S accrued under the equity method.		
Cash	160,000	
Investment in S		160,000
To record the receipt of dividends from S according to the equity method.		

After the equity method entries are made at December 31, 19X4, the Investment in S account has a balance of $2,917,456. Exhibit 10.4 shows how this amount is determined. The calculation reflects consistent application of the

Exhibit 10.3   Schedule to Compute the Equity Method Accrual

P Company and S Company
Schedule to Compute the Equity Method Accrual
For the Year Ended December 31, 19X4

	100%	80%	
P's Share of S's Reported Net Income (.8 × $500,000)			$400,000
Less Amortization of Purchase Premium:			
Additional Depreciation Expense on P's Share of Factory ($160,000/10)	$(16,000)		
Amortization of Goodwill ($240,000/40)	(6,000)		(22,000)
Less P's Unconfirmed Intercompany Inventory Profits of $6,000 (= .2 × $30,000; Markup Is 20% of Selling Price) at December 31, 19X4 . .			(6,000)
Plus P's Intercompany Inventory Profits of $1,000 in Beginning (January 1, 19X4) Inventory Assumed Confirmed in 19X4			1,000
Less 80% of S's Unconfirmed Profit on Intercompany Sale of Land to P (.8 × $25,000)			(20,000)
Plus Excess Depreciation Expense of $4,000 on Intercompany Sale of Equipment to S at December 31, 19X2			4,000 [a]
Plus Gain on Constructive Retirement of Intercompany Bonds:			
	100%	80%	
Amount Attributable to P ($1,000,000 − $924,180)	$75,820	—	
Less P's Amortization of Discount in 19X4 ($75,820/5) Included in P's 19X4 Interest Income	(15,164)	—	
Amount Attributable to S ($1,020,000 − $1,000,000)	—	$16,000	
Less S's Amortization of Premium in 19X4 ($20,000/5) Reflected in S's 19X4 Interest Expense	—	(3,200)	
	$60,656	$12,800	73,456
Net Equity Method Accrual			$430,456

[a]This is the portion of P's gain realized in 19X4 [$4,000 = ($112,000/8) − $10,000].

equity method since acquisition on December 31, 19X1, and assumes that S Company's retained earnings increased by $400,000 between December 31, 19X1 and December 31, 19X3 (January 1, 19X4).

Working Paper Eliminations

Complete financial statement data for P Company and S Company appear a little later in the chapter on the consolidated financial statement working paper in Exhibit 10.7. We first explain these entries in the narrative, then show their impact on the completed working paper and prepare formal consolidated financial statements. Numbers assigned to the working paper entries in the narrative also appear on the working paper in Exhibit 10.7 for ease in cross-reference.

Elimination of the Equity Method Entries   Under the equity method, P increases its Investment in S by its share of S's reported net income adjusted for intercompany items arising in consolidation. Dividends received from S during the year reduce the Investment in S balance. Since the effects of these entries are duplicated in consolidation, we eliminate them, thereby adjusting the Investment in S to its balance at the beginning of the year.

Exhibit 10.4   Analysis of the Investment in S Account at December 31, 19X4

P Company and S Company
Determining the Balance in the Investment in S
Account at December 31, 19X4

Acquisition Cost at December 31, 19X1	$2,400,000
P's Share of Growth in S Company's Retained Earnings from December 31, 19X1 to January 1, 19X4 [.8($1,400,000 − $1,000,000)]	320,000
Less Amortization of Purchase Premium in 19X2 and 19X3 [2 × $16,000 (factory) + 2 × $6,000 (goodwill)]	(44,000)
Less P Company's Unconfirmed Inventory Profits in Beginning (January 1, 19X4) Inventory	(1,000)
Less Gain on Intercompany Sale of Equipment Removed from Equity Method Accrual at December 31, 19X2	(32,000)
Plus Excess Depreciation Expense of $4,000 on Intercompany Sale of Equipment to S at December 31, 19X2	4,000 [a]
Balance in Investment in S at January 1, 19X4	$2,647,000
Plus Equity Method Accrual for 19X4 (Exhibit 10.3)	430,456
Less Dividends Received from S Company in 19X4 (.8 × $200,000) . . .	(160,000)
Balance in Investment in S at December 31, 19X4	$2,917,456

[a]This is the portion of P's gain realized in 19X3.

CONSOLIDATED FINANCIAL STATEMENT WORKING PAPER

(1)

Income from S	430,456	
Dividends—S		160,000
Investment in S		270,456

To eliminate the equity method entries recorded by P,
thereby adjusting the investment account to its
January 1, 19X4, balance.

Elimination of the Intercompany Transactions   As we have seen, proper use of the equity method treats P's equity in the earnings of S as a one-line consolidation. Thus the equity method accrual is not based simply on a fraction of S's reported net income; it must be adjusted for those items which affect consolidated statements. In this process, differences develop over time between the balance in the Investment in S account and the book value of S Company's underlying stockholders' equity. Therefore, before we are able to eliminate the beginning-of-year Investment in S balance, we must adjust it for those items reflected there but not in S Company's beginning retained earnings. Only in this way can a clean elimination of the investment account be made. At the same time, however, note that P Company's retained earnings equal consolidated retained earnings—each period's equity method accrual reflects all the items which affect the computation of consolidated net income.

Intercompany Inventory Transactions   Three eliminating entries are necessary to remove all intercompany inventory transactions. The first eliminates total intercompany sales of merchandise. The second removes unconfirmed intercompany profit from the ending inventory. The third transfers the intercompany profit in the beginning inventory to current income and increases the Investment in S account, thus replacing an item never removed from S Company's beginning retained earnings.

CONSOLIDATED FINANCIAL STATEMENT WORKING PAPER

(2)

Sales	125,000	
Purchases		125,000

To eliminate intercompany sales and purchases.

(3)

Inventory, December 31 (Income Statement) . . .	6,000	
Inventory (Balance Sheet)		6,000

To eliminate unconfirmed intercompany profit in ending inventory, consistent with the confirmation principle. Consolidated inventories are reduced and cost of goods sold increased.

(4)

Investment in S	1,000	
Inventory, January 1 (Income Statement) . . .		1,000

To remove the unconfirmed intercompany profit from the beginning inventory and decrease cost of goods sold. This amount was eliminated in computing last year's equity method accrual and must now be added to the investment account.

Intercompany Sale of Land   Another elimination must be made to remove the gain recorded by S Company in 19X4 and reduce the land account to its original acquisition cost.

CONSOLIDATED FINANCIAL STATEMENT WORKING PAPER

(5)

Gain on Sale of Land	25,000	
Land		25,000

To eliminate the unconfirmed gain on intercompany sale of land, in accordance with the confirmation principle.

Intercompany Sale of Equipment   This transaction took place two years ago, on December 31, 19X2. The gain originally recorded by P Company and eliminated in the equity method accrual was $32,000. Each year, $1/8$ of that gain, or $4,000, is realized by P as the equipment depreciates; $4,000 is the excess depreciation generated by the intercompany transaction. The $4,000 is included each year in the equity method accrual. At each consolidation point, then, the portion of the gain *not yet realized* by P via the annual depreciation represents a difference between the investment account and S's retained earnings and must be added to the investment account. Also, on the working paper we eliminate the excess depreciation and restate the asset and related accumulated depreciation accounts to their original acquisition cost balances.

CONSOLIDATED FINANCIAL STATEMENT WORKING PAPER

(6)

Investment in S	28,000	
Accumulated Depreciation	4,000	
Equipment		32,000

To eliminate the excess depreciation recorded in
19X3, reduce the equipment account to its net book
value at date of intercompany sale, and add the
intercompany gain unconfirmed in prior years to the
investment account.

(7)

Accumulated Depreciation	4,000	
Depreciation Expense		4,000

To eliminate the annual excess depreciation expense
recorded by S Company in 19X4.

(8)

Equipment	120,000	
Accumulated Depreciation		120,000

To restate the equipment and accumulated
depreciation accounts to their original acquisition cost
basis ($120,000 was the amount of accumulated
depreciation at date of sale).

Intercompany Bondholding   Here we eliminate the intercompany bondholding and establish the gain on constructive retirement of consolidated debt.
We also eliminate the intercompany interest revenue and expense.

CONSOLIDATED FINANCIAL STATEMENT WORKING PAPER

(9)

Bonds Payable	1,000,000	
Investment in Bonds		1,000,000

To eliminate the par value of the intercompany bonds.

Premium on Bonds Payable	16,000	
Discount on Investment in Bonds	60,656	
Interest Income	95,164	
Interest Expense		76,000
Gain on Retirement of Consolidated Debt . . .		95,820

To eliminate the unamortized premium and discount
on intercompany bonds acquired on January 1, 19X4,
the intercompany interest (net of premium and
discount amortization), and to establish the gain on
constructive retirement of consolidated debt.

Elimination of the Investment in S Account   Since 80 percent of S Company's outstanding shares are now held internally by P, we eliminate the Investment in S against the stockholders' equity of S to avoid counting these items
twice. The investment account balance at the beginning of 19X4, after the preceding eliminations, is $2,676,000, including the unamortized purchase premi-
um of $356,000 [= $400,000 − 2($22,000)]. Exhibit 10.5 presents an analysis of

how those eliminations affect the investment account and why a balance of $2,676,000 is needed for a clean elimination. We now make the elimination and establish both the unamortized purchase premium and the minority interest at January 1, 19X4:

CONSOLIDATED FINANCIAL STATEMENT WORKING PAPER

(11)

Capital Stock—S	1,500,000	
Retained Earnings, January 1, 19X4—S . . .	1,400,000	
Purchase Premium (Differential)	356,000	
Investment in S		2,676,000
Minority Interest in S		580,000

To eliminate the Investment in S against the stockholders' equity of S Company and establish the unamortized purchase premium and minority interest in S, all as of January 1, 19X4.

Allocation and Amortization of Purchase Premium   Once the unamortized purchase premium has been established in the working paper, it must be allocated to the assets of S Company, and the current year depreciation and amortization must be recorded. As of January 1, 19X4, two years have expired since the stock acquisition. Hence our allocation of the purchase premium must reflect two years' amortization applied to the original values given in Exhibit 10.2. The net book value of the portion attributable to the factory is down by $32,000—two years' annual depreciation of $16,000—while the original goodwill of $240,000 has an unamortized balance of $228,000 at January 1, 19X4. We now record the allocation and current amortization of the purchase premium:

CONSOLIDATED FINANCIAL STATEMENT WORKING PAPER

(12)

Buildings and Equipment	160,000	
Goodwill	228,000	
Accumulated Depreciation		32,000
Purchase Premium (Differential) . . .		356,000

To allocate the unamortized purchase premium at January 1, 19X4.

(13)

Operating Expenses	22,000	
Accumulated Depreciation		16,000
Goodwill		6,000

To record current year amortization of the purchase premium. Depreciation on the portion allocated to the factory equals $16,000 (= $160,000/10) and amortization of goodwill is $6,000 (= $240,000/40).

Recording the Minority Interest in Net Income   Two of the intercompany transactions affect the minority interest in net income. First, the $25,000 gain recorded by S on the upstream sale of land to P has been eliminated in consolidation. The minority should be charged for 20 percent of this amount, or

Exhibit 10.5   Analysis of the Effect of Intercompany Profit Eliminations on the Investment in S and Equivalence between the Adjusted Balance of $2,676,000 and P's Share of S Company's Stockholders' Equity

Investment in S

Balance, December 31, 19X4	2,917,456	(1) Equity method entries	270,456
(4) Profit in January 1, 19X4, inventory	1,000		
(6) Unrealized gain on equipment sale	28,000		
Adjusted balance, January 1, 19X4	2,676,000		

Stockholders Equity of S Company, January 1, 19X4:

Capital Stock	$1,500,000
Retained Earnings	1,400,000
	$2,900,000
P's Share (.8 × $2,900,000)	$2,320,000
Unamortized Purchase Premium at January 1, 19X4	356,000
Investment Account Balance Needed for Clean Elimination	$2,676,000

Exhibit 10.6   Determination of the Minority Interest in Net Income

P Company and S Company
Computation of Minority Interest in Net Income, 19X4

Reported Net Income of S Company	$500,000
Elimination of Unconfirmed Intercompany Gain on Upstream Sale of Land	(25,000)
Unamortized Premium on Intercompany Bonds When Constructively Retired at January 1, 19X4 (S Company's Portion of the Gain on Retirement of Consolidated Debt)	20,000
Partial Realization of the Gain through Premium Amortization in 19X4	(4,000)
Adjusted Net Income of S Company	$491,000
Minority Interest (.2 × $491,000)	$ 98,200

$5,000, under the principle of proportional allocation of intercompany profit eliminations. Second, the unamortized premium on the bonds of S Company now held by P represents S's portion of the gain on retirement of consolidated debt. This amount was $20,000 at January 1, 19X4, but $4,000 of the premium was amortized during 19X4 and is reflected in S's net income. The minority is entitled to 20 percent of the remaining $16,000, or $3,200. The computation of minority interest in net income appears in Exhibit 10.6; the eliminating entry is as follows:

CONSOLIDATED FINANCIAL STATEMENT WORKING PAPER

(14)

Minority Interest in Net Income	98,000	
Dividends—S		40,000
Minority Interest in S		58,200

To record the minority's interest in S Company's
adjusted net income and eliminate the minority's
share of S Company's dividends.

The completed consolidated financial statement working paper is presented in
Exhibit 10.7.

Formal Consolidated Financial Statements

To complete this example, we have prepared formal consolidated financial
statements from the consolidated account balances on the working paper in Exhibit 10.7. The consolidated statement of income and retained earnings appears
in Exhibit 10.8. Cost of goods sold consists of the beginning inventory of
$1,659,000, plus purchases of $4,025,000, less ending inventory of $1,664,000.
Finally, the consolidated balance sheet is presented in Exhibit 10.9.

Subsidiaries with Preferred Stock

Preferred stock may be issued by companies which are already controlled by
another company as well as by those that might become subsidiaries in the future. The two major issues that arise when consolidating a subsidiary that has
outstanding preferred stock are indicated below.

1.   How is the stockholders' equity of the subsidiary to be apportioned
     among the preferred and common stockholders? This apportionment
     affects the elimination of the common stockholders' interest, the mi-
     nority interest in common stock, *and*, when preferred shares are held
     externally, the minority interest in preferred stock.

2.   If the parent company acquires some or all of the subsidiary's preferred
     stock, how is any difference between cost and book value of the pre-
     ferred to be treated in consolidation? How is the Investment in Pre-
     ferred to be accounted for?

Note that the parent's equity method accrual relating to its investment in the
subsidiary's common stock is based on the subsidiary's income available to
common shareholders (*after* preferred dividends are deducted).

Establishing the Correct Book Value of the Preferred Stockholders' Interest

Preferred stock has priority over common stock in regard to dividends and to
proceeds in liquidation. Regardless of the market value of the preferred stock,
the preferred stockholders' interest in the subsidiary is often not adequately
measured by the amount shown for Preferred Stock on the subsidiary's balance
sheet. The preferred stock may be recorded at par value, yet its call price or
liquidation value may exceed par value. In the event the stock is purchased by
call or retired in a liquidation of the corporation, the par value does not measure
the claim of the preferred shareholders.

Exhibit 10.7   Consolidated Financial Statement Working Paper

P Company and S Company
Consolidated Financial Statement Working Paper
For the Year Ended December 31, 19X4

	P Company	S Company (80%)	Adjustments and Eliminations Dr.	Adjustments and Eliminations Cr.	Consolidated
INCOME STATEMENT					
Sales	6,000,000	2,800,000	(2) 125,000		8,675,000
Income from S	430,456	—	(1) 430,456		—
Interest Income	95,164	—	(10) 95,164		—
Gain on Sale of Land	—	25,000	(5) 25,000		—
Gain on Ret. of Cons. Debt	—	—		(10) 95,820	95,820
Inventory, 12/31/X4	1,000,000	670,000	(3) 6,000		1,664,000
Total Credits	7,525,620	3,495,000	681,620	95,820	10,434,820
Inventory, 1/1/X4	1,040,000	620,000		(4) 1,000	1,659,000
Purchases	2,800,000	1,350,000		(2) 125,000	4,025,000
Operating Expenses	1,860,000	949,000	(13) 22,000	(7) 4,000	2,827,000
Interest Expense	300,000	76,000		(10) 76,000	300,000
Total Debits	6,000,000	2,995,000	22,000	206,000	8,811,000
Minority Interest in Net Income	—	—	(14) 98,200		(98,200)
Net Inc.—to Ret. Earn. Stmt.	1,525,620	500,000	801,820	301,820	1,525,620
RETAINED EARNINGS STATEMENT					
Retained Earnings, 1/1/X4—P	2,500,000	—			2,500,000
Retained Earnings, 1/1/X4—S	—	1,400,000	(11) 1,400,000		—
Net Income—from Inc. Stmt.	1,525,620	500,000	801,820	301,820	1,525,620
Dividends—P	(400,000)	—			(400,000)
Dividends—S	—	(200,000)		(1) 160,000	—
				(14) 40,000	
Retained Earnings, Dec. 31, 19X4—to Balance Sheet	3,625,620	1,700,000	2,201,820	501,820	3,625,620
BALANCE SHEET					
Cash and Receivables	950,000	700,000			1,650,000
Inventory	1,000,000	670,000		(3) 6,000	1,664,000
Investment in S	2,917,456	—	(4) 1,000	(1) 270,456	—
			(6) 28,000	(11) 2,676,000	
Investment in Bonds	1,000,000	—		(9) 1,000,000	—
Discount on Inv. in Bonds	(60,656)	—	(10) 60,656		—
Land	1,000,000	800,000		(5) 25,000	1,775,000
Buildings and Equipment	6,000,000	3,600,000	(8) 120,000	(6) 32,000	9,848,000
			(12) 160,000		
Accumulated Depreciation	(3,221,180)	(832,000)	(6) 4,000	(12) 32,000	(4,213,180)
			(7) 4,000	(8) 120,000	
				(13) 16,000	
Purchase Premium	—	—	(11) 356,000	(12) 356,000	—
Goodwill	—	—	(12) 228,000	(13) 6,000	222,000
Total	9,585,620	4,938,000	961,656	4,539,456	10,945,820
Current Liabilities	960,000	722,000			1,682,000
Bonds Payable	3,000,000	1,000,000	(9) 1,000,000		3,000,000
Premium on Bonds Payable	—	16,000	(10) 16,000		—
Capital Stock—P	2,000,000	—			2,000,000
Capital Stock—S	—	1,500,000	(11) 1,500,000		—
Ret. Earn.—from Ret. Earn. Stmt.	3,625,620	1,700,000	2,201,820	501,820	3,625,620
Minority Interest in S	—	—		(11) 580,000	638,200
				(14) 58,200	
Total	9,585,620	4,938,000	4,717,820	1,140,020	10,945,820
			5,679,476	5.679,476	

Explanations of Working Paper Entries

(1) To eliminate the equity method entries made by P in 19X4.
(2) To eliminate intercompany merchandise sales.
(3) To eliminate unconfirmed intercompany profit in ending inventory.
(4) To remove unconfirmed intercompany profit from the beginning inventory and increase the Investment in S accordingly.
(5) To eliminate the unconfirmed gain on intercompany sale of land in 19X4 and reduce land account to original acquisition cost.
(6) To eliminate excess depreciation recorded in prior years, reduce the equipment account to its net book value on date of intercompany sale, and add the unrealized portion of the gain to the investment account.
(7) To eliminate the annual excess depreciation expense recorded by S in 19X4.
(8) To restate the equipment and accumulated depreciation accounts to their original acquisition cost basis.
(9) To eliminate the par value of the intercompany bonds.
(10) To eliminate the unamortized premium and discount on the intercompany bonds and the intercompany interest and to establish the gain on retirement of consolidated debt.
(11) To eliminate the Investment in S against the stockholders' equity of S and establish the unamortized purchase premium and the minority interest in S, all as of January 1, 19X4.
(12) To allocate the unamortized purchase premium at January 1, 19X4.
(13) To record amortization of the purchase premium for 19X4.
(14) To record the minority's interest in S's adjusted net income and eliminate the minority's share of S's dividends.

Exhibit 10.8   Consolidated Statement of Income and Retained Earnings

P Company and S Company
Consolidated Statement of Income and Retained Earnings
For the Year Ended December 31, 19X4

Sales .	$8,675,000
Gain on Retirement of Consolidated Debt	95,820
Total Revenues	$8,770,820
Cost of Goods Sold	$4,020,000
Operating Expenses .	2,827,000
Interest Expense .	300,000
Total Expenses	$7,147,000
Minority Interest in Net Income of S .	$ 98,200
Consolidated Net Income	$1,525,620
Retained Earnings, January 1, 19X4 .	2,500,000
Dividends	(400,000)
Retained Earnings, December 31, 19X4 .	$3,625,620

Preferred stock issues may be cumulative, participating, or both. **Cumulative** preferred stock requires that payment of preferred dividends which had not been paid in prior years and those for the current year be made before any profits can be distributed to common stockholders. Preferred stock that is **participating** shares any profit distributions in excess of preferred dividends with the common stockholders in an agreed-upon ratio. Since participating preferred stock is rarely encountered today, we will assume that preferred stock in our examples is cumulative but not participating.

If the preferred stock is *cumulative*, the preferred stockholders' interest is

Exhibit 10.9   Consolidated Balance Sheet

P Company and S Company
Consolidated Balance Sheet
December 31, 19X4

ASSETS

Cash and Receivables	$ 1,650,000
Inventory	1,664,000
Total Current Assets	$ 3,314,000
Land	$ 1,775,000
Buildings and Equipment	9,848,000
Less Accumulated Depreciation	(4,213,180)
Goodwill	222,000
Total Noncurrent Assets	$ 7,631,820
Total Assets	$10,945,820

LIABILITIES AND STOCKHOLDERS' EQUITY

Current Liabilities	$ 1,682,000
Bonds Payable	3,000,000
Total Liabilities	$ 4,682,000
Minority Interest in S Company	$ 638,200
Capital Stock	2,000,000
Retained Earnings	3,625,620
Total Stockholders' Equity	$ 6,263,820
Total Liabilities and Stockholders' Equity	$10,945,820

increased by the amount of any preferred dividends in arrears. This arrearage is not normally recorded in the accounts of the issuing company.

By properly stating the equity of preferred stockholders, the minority interest in preferred, if any, can be correctly measured. This is necessary because preferred stockholders' equity is *not a residual*. Similarly, the minority interest in preferred reflects the preferences inherent in preferred stock. In this sense, it differs from the true residual nature of minority interest in common stock.

Before turning to a numerical example, consider whether call price or liquidation value should be used to measure the claims of preferred stockholders, aside from any dividend arrearage. The **call price** or **redemption price** gives the amount to which preferred stockholders are entitled if the issuing corporation as a going concern purchases or calls the preferred stock. The use of call price to measure the claims of preferred stockholders could therefore be justified by the *going concern assumption* which underlies financial accounting.

In contrast, preferred stock's **liquidation value** indicates the claim of preferred stockholders when the corporation is in liquidation. It has practical meaning only in the event of a liquidation and has no relevance to a going concern. Its use to measure the claims of preferred stockholders is derived from the notion that *only* in the event of liquidation do preferred stockholders have a *claim* on the corporation's net assets as opposed to the *right* to receive a given sum of money if their stock is redeemed by the corporation.

> In our judgment, a going concern should use *call* or *redemption price* when establishing the preferred shareholders' interest in consolidation. When a preferred stock issue does not specify a call price but does indicate a liquidation value in excess of par, the liquidation value should be used.

To illustrate, suppose Parsons Company owns 80 percent of Stone's outstanding common stock. Stone's stockholders' equity at January 1, 19X4, is given here:

Stone Company: Components of Stockholders' Equity

10 Percent Cumulative, Nonparticipating Preferred Stock, $100 Par Value, Redemption Price $103, Liquidation Value $105	$1,000,000
Additional Paid-In Capital: Preferred	150,000
Common Stock, Par Value $1	1,000,000
Additional Paid-In Capital: Common	2,700,000
Retained Earnings	5,000,000
Total Stockholders' Equity	$9,850,000

Note: Preferred dividends for the prior two years are in arrears.

We now compute the proper book value of the preferred stockholders' equity and indicate the needed working paper adjustment. Since all preferred shares are held externally, this amount will appear as "Minority Interest in Stone: Preferred" on the consolidated balance sheet.

Total Redemption Price of Preferred Stock (10,000 × $103)	$1,030,000
Dividends in Arrears (10% of Par Value for Two Years; .1 × $1,000,000 × 2)	200,000
Corrected Book Value of Preferred Shareholders' Interest	$1,230,000
Less Amount Recorded by Stone ($1,000,000 + $150,000)	1,150,000
Working Paper Adjustment Required	$ 80,000

This required adjustment has the effect of earmarking $80,000 of Stone Company's retained earnings for the preferred stockholders. The adjustment is made only on the consolidated financial statement working paper, does not affect the accounts of Stone Company, and is part of the working paper entry which reclassifies the corrected book value of the preferred stock as Minority Interest in Preferred.

CONSOLIDATED FINANCIAL STATEMENT WORKING PAPER

Retained Earnings—Stone	80,000
Preferred Stock	1,000,000
Additional Paid-In Capital: Preferred	150,000
Minority Interest in Stone: Preferred . . .	1,230,000

To establish the book value of the preferred stockholders' equity in Stone Company by earmarking $80,000 of Stone's retained earnings and to reclassify Stone's preferred stock held outside the affiliation as Minority Interest in Stone: Preferred. *Note:* A single account could be used to identify the total minority interest in Stone, including both common and preferred.

In this case, the Additional Paid-In Capital: Preferred (APIC:P) is part of the preferred stockholders' interest because it, plus the par value, is less than the call price. It is not always true that the APIC:P "belongs" to the preferred stockholders. If par plus APIC:P is more than the call or redemption value, some of that APIC:P is actually part of the common stockholders' interest.

Suppose that, in addition to the prior two years' preferred dividends being in arrears, the *current* year's preferred dividends are also in arrears. On the working paper, the amount of the current year's preferred dividends would be included in the Minority Interest in Net Income; it would not be charged to Stone's beginning retained earnings.

Treatment at Date of Business Combination   In determining the book value of the common stockholders' equity acquired at the date of a business combination, the parent must consider the proper amount of the preferred stockholders' interest. If the common stockholders' equity is decreased when the correct book value of the preferred stock is established, the purchase premium (discount) is increased (decreased). Assuming a purchase premium was paid to acquire the common stock in the example just given, the purchase premium is increased by $80,000.

Parent's Investment in the Subsidiary's Preferred Stock

When the parent company acquires some or all of the subsidiary's preferred stock, the following two issues arise:

1. If the cost of the preferred shares differs from their book value, properly computed, how is the difference treated in consolidation?

2. How should the parent account for the investment in preferred on its books?

Difference between Cost and Book Value of Investment in Preferred
To simplify the discussion, consider only the case of an *excess* of cost over book value. This implies a *purchase premium* on the investment in preferred. An analysis of the debt/equity characteristics of preferred stock and an understanding of why the market prices of preferred stocks change will help show how this purchase premium should be treated in consolidation.

Preferred stock is neither pure debt nor pure equity. It does carry a specified dividend rate, but there is no contractual agreement specifying that the firm *must* pay the stated dividend or *must* redeem the shares at a specified time. In terms of debt instruments, preferred stock is not like a conventional bond, but it is close to a *consol* or *perpetual bond*. Consols have occasionally been issued by the British and Canadian governments. A consol's price equals the present value of the stated interest payments in perpetuity. As the market rate of interest (the rate used to discount the interest payments) changes, the price of the consol moves inversely to the change.

Moreover, most preferred stocks, especially the cumulative and nonparticipating issues, are quite different from common equity. There is a stated dividend rate, similar to a stated interest rate. Passing the preferred dividend does not remove the preferred dividend obligation. Finally, preferred stock is not a residual. Its priority is lower than bonds but higher than common stock.

We believe that the fixed dividend characteristic of preferred stock suggests that changes in its price are due primarily to changes in the market rate of interest. Whether the firm's net assets are undervalued or overvalued has little relevance, except insofar as firm-specific risk influences the discount rate.

Suppose Parsons Company acquired 2,000 of Stone's preferred shares at a cost of $300,000 on January 1, 19X4. In the last section, we found the book value per preferred share to be $123 (= $1,230,000/10,000). The book value of the 2,000 shares is $246,000, and a purchase premium of $54,000 (= $300,000 − $246,000) arises. From a consolidated point of view, these 2,000 preferred shares are retired. Since the purchase premium is the result of a change in market yields and not of undervalued assets, it should not be allocated to the assets and liabilities of Stone.[1]

The purchase premium on preferred has all the characteristics of a *loss*. One approach is to assign the loss to the consolidated income statement, as in the case of intercompany debt. Another is to view the internally held preferred stock as retired treasury stock and to charge the loss against the parent's additional paid-in capital. We support the latter position.

> In our judgment, *retirement of preferred stock held internally* for the purposes of consolidation is more like the *retirement of treasury stock*. Any purchase premium (discount) on the preferred should be charged (credited) to additional paid-in capital.

This leads to the following working paper entries. The first entry establishes the correct value of the preferred stock, and the second eliminates the investment in preferred.

---

[1] In the case of *convertible* preferred stock or preferred stock that *participates* in the earnings available to common shareholders, it may be that the preferred stock price behaves more like equity than like debt. If so, the purchase premium or discount on an investment in preferred should be treated in the same way as a purchase premium or discount on an investment in common.

CONSOLIDATED FINANCIAL STATEMENT WORKING PAPER

Retained Earnings: Stone	80,000	
Additional Paid-In Capital: Preferred		80,000

To establish the correct book value of the preferred stockholders' equity in Stone Company by reducing Stone's retained earnings. APIC:P now has a balance of $230,000.

Preferred Stock	1,000,000	
Additional Paid-In Capital: Preferred	230,000	
Additional Paid-In Capital: Common (Parsons) . .	54,000	
Investment in Stone: Preferred		300,000
Minority Interest in Stone: Preferred		984,000

To eliminate the investment in preferred against the preferred stock of Stone, charging the purchase premium against consolidated additional paid-in capital and reclassifying the remaining 8,000 preferred shares as minority interest; $984,000 (= 8,000 × $123).

Cumulative Preferred Stock and the Consolidated Income Statement

Current dividends on preferred stock of a subsidiary which is held outside the affiliated group become a component of the Minority Interest in Net Income and therefore represent a deduction in computing consolidated net income. In the Stone Company example, 80 percent of Stone's preferred stock is owned by outsiders. Each year, the dividends of $80,000 (= .8 × .1 × $1,000,000) on those shares are charged against consolidated net income and credited to Preferred Stock whether or not they were actually declared. The cumulative feature reduces the amount of earnings available for distribution to common stockholders; declaration is not required to achieve this reduction.

This is a departure from conventional treatment of preferred dividends. In the single firm case, preferred dividends are not accrued and charged against income available to the common stockholders unless they have been declared. The consolidation case is different because all dividends on S's cumulative preferred stock not held by P Company, whether declared or not, reduce the amount of S's retained earnings available for distribution to the controlling common stockholders. The charge in the consolidated income statement signifies this reduction.

If the parent accounts for its investment in the subsidiary's preferred using the *equity method*—which follows from P's control over S's preferred dividend policy—P's equity method accrual will include the preferred dividends attributable to the shares owned by P. The Investment in Preferred will be increased by the amount of the preferred dividends and will be decreased when the preferred dividends are actually declared. Thus the Investment in Preferred will move in tandem with the book value of the preferred stockholders' equity after the previously discussed working paper entry establishing the correct book value is made.

Use of the *cost method* to account for the investment in preferred will require that the investment account be restated to the equity basis as of the beginning of the current year. At each consolidation point, another working paper entry will be needed to reflect P's share of any dividend arrearage in the Investment in Preferred account. This is similar to the working paper entry required when the investment in common is carried at cost (as was discussed in Chapter 8).

Preferred Stock: A Numerical Example

To illustrate these preferred stock matters on a consolidated financial statement working paper, consider the Parsons and Stone data just discussed. Parsons' investment in Stone's common was at book value at a time when no dividend arrearages existed on the preferred stock but the redemption price was $103 per share. This excess of $30,000 [= ($103 − $100)10,000] was allocated to the preferred stock in determining the book value of the common equity acquired.

On January 1, 19X4, Parsons acquired the 2,000 shares (20 percent interest) of Stone's preferred stock for $300,000; the investment is carried at equity. Stone earned $600,000 from its own operations in 19X4, of which $100,000, representing the current year's preferred dividend, is allocated to the preferred stockholders. Parsons' equity method accrual is therefore $420,000, consisting of $400,000 [= .8($600,000 − $100,000)] for the common and $20,000 (= .2 × $100,000) for the preferred.

At consolidation on December 31, 19X4, we assume that three years of preferred dividends are in arrears—the current year *and* the two prior years. There were no intercompany transactions in 19X4, and Stone declared no common dividends. The completed consolidated financial statement working paper is presented in Exhibit 10.10. All detailed financial statement data are assumed.

Summary of Key Concepts

When the bonds of one affiliate are acquired by another affiliate, the resulting **intercompany asset and liability** must be **eliminated** when consolidated statements are prepared. If the bonds are acquired on the **open market,** the carrying value of the purchaser's **bond investment** will normally differ from the carrying value of the issuer's **bond liability.** Thus the **constructive retirement** of the intercompany bondholding in consolidation produces a **consolidated gain or loss** on retirement of intercompany debt.

The **total consolidated gain or loss** consists of the sum of the **premium** or **discount** related to the intercompany bondholding which is recorded on each company's books. Since each company systematically amortizes its premium or discount, the gain or loss is recognized by the companies through interest expense and revenue over the time remaining to maturity.

At the **first consolidation point** following the acquisition of intercompany bonds, **the total consolidated gain or loss** on retirement of the intercompany bondholding is recognized in the consolidated income statement. Any premium or discount amortization by the respective companies after acquisition of the bonds is part of the total gain or loss and must not be counted twice. In this book, we allocate the consolidated gain or loss between the affiliates according to the unamortized premium or discount at the date the bonds were acquired internally.

Exhibit 10.10   Parsons Company and Subsidiary Stone Company Consolidated Financial Statement Working Paper For the Year Ended December 31, 19X4

	P Company	S Company (80%)	Adjustments and Eliminations Dr.	Adjustments and Eliminations Cr.	Consolidated
INCOME STATEMENT					
Sales	50,000,000	20,000,000			70,000,000
Income from Stone	420,000	—	(1) 420,000		—
Inventory, Dec 31, 19X4	8,000,000	5,000,000			13,000,000
Total Credits	58,420,000	25,000,000	420,000		83,000,000
Inventory, January 1, 19X4	7,500,000	4,800,000			12,300,000
Purchases	35,000,000	15,000,000			50,000,000
Operating Expenses	13,920,000	4,600,000			18,520,000
Total Debits	56,420,000	24,400,000			80,820,000
Minority Interest in Net Income	—	—	(5) 180,000		(180,000)
Net Income—to Ret. Earn. Stmt.	2,000,000	600,000	600,000		2,000,000
RETAINED EARNINGS STATEMENT					
Ret. Earn., Jan. 1, 19X4—P	10,000,000	—			10,000,000
Ret. Earn., Jan. 1, 19X4—S	—	5,000,000	(2) 80,000 (4) 4,920,000		—
Net Income—from Inc. Stmt.	2,000,000	600,000	600,000		2,000,000
Dividends—P	(1,000,000)	—			(1,000,000)
Dividends—S	—	—			
Ret. Earn., Dec. 31, 19X4—to Balance Sheet	11,000,000	5,600,000	5,600,000		11,000,000
BALANCE SHEET					
Cash and Receivables	5,884,000	3,000,000			8,884,000
Inventory	8,000,000	5,000,000			13,000,000
Invest. in Stone—Common	7,296,000	—		(1) 400,000 (4) 6,896,000	—
Invest. in Stone—Preferred	320,000	—		(1) 20,000 (3) 300,000	—
Land	4,000,000	2,000,000			6,000,000
Buildings and Equipment	13,000,000	9,000,000			22,000,000
Accumulated Depreciation	(2,500,000)	(1,550,000)			(4,050,000)
Total	36,000,000	17,450,000		7,616,000	45,834,000
Current Liabilities	8,000,000	4,000,000			12,000,000
Other Liabilities	12,000,000	3,000,000			15,000,000
Preferred Stock—Stone	—	1,150,000	(3) 1,230,000	(2) 80,000	—
Common Stock—Parsons	5,000,000	—	(3) 54,000		4,946,000
Common Stock—Stone	—	3,700,000	(4) 3,700,000		—
Ret. Earn.—from Ret. Earn. Stmt.	11,000,000	5,600,000	5,600,000		11,000,000
Minority Interest in Stone	—	—		(3) 984,000 (4) 1,724,000 (5) 180,000	2,888,000
Total	36,000,000	17,450,000	10,584,000	2,968,000	45,834,000
			10,584,000	10,584,000	

Explanations of Working Paper Entries
(1) To eliminate the equity method entries made by Parsons during 19X4.
(2) To establish the correct book value of Stone's preferred stock as of January 1, 19X4.
(3) To eliminate the investment in preferred against Stone's preferred stock, charge the purchase premium of $54,000 against Parsons' common stock (APIC), and establish the minority interest in preferred, all as of January 1, 19X4; $984,000 (= .8 × $1,230,000).
(4) To eliminate the investment in common against the common stockholders' equity of Stone and establish the minority interest in common, all as of January 1, 19X4; $1,724,000 [= .2($4,920,000 + $3,700,000)].
(5) To record the minority interest in net income for 19X4; $80,000 (= .8 × $100,000), preferred; $100,000 [= .2($600,000 − $100,000)], common.

Under the **one-line consolidation concept** of *APBO 18*, the parent company will record its share of the total gain or loss in the equity method accrual made in the year the bonds are acquired. In subsequent years, P's share of the periodic premium or discount amortization recorded by the companies is charged **against** the equity method accrual in order that the total gain not be counted twice.

The effects of intercompany bondholdings on the equity method accrual create a discrepancy between the balance in the Investment in S and P's share of S Company's stockholders' equity. At each subsequent consolidation point, this discrepancy must be removed by (1) eliminating P's unconfirmed portion of the gain or loss (P's unamortized discount or premium at the beginning of the year) from the investment account and (2) allocating S's unconfirmed portion of the gain or loss (S's unamortized premium or discount at the beginning of the year) to Retained Earnings—S.

When a subsidiary has **preferred stock outstanding,** the correct book value of the preferred stock must be established on the working paper. If the preferred stock is cumulative and dividends are in arrears, common shareholders' equity must be reduced. A similar approach is required when the call or redemption price of the preferred exceeds the par value plus additional paid-in capital attributable to the preferred shareholders. Each year, on the **consolidated income statement,** consolidated net income must be **charged for the dividends** on cumulative preferred stock held externally.

The parent company may own some (or all) of the subsidiary's preferred stock. If so, the **Investment in Preferred** would normally be carried at **equity,** being increased by the periodic preferred dividend amount and decreased as preferred dividends are actually declared. A purchase premium or discount will exist if the amount paid for the preferred shares differs from their book value. While this **purchase premium or discount** ultimately represents a gain or loss to the consolidated entity, we believe that it should be **credited or debited to Additional Paid-In Capital in consolidation.** This treatment follows from the treatment accorded to the retirement of treasury stock, which we feel is analogous to the retirement of internally held preferred stock in consolidation.

Questions   Q10.1   When the bonds in an intercompany bondholding are acquired directly from the issuing company, consolidation problems are minimized. Explain why.

Q10.2   Briefly describe the two major problem areas which typically arise when the bonds of one affiliate are acquired in the open market by another affiliate.

Q10.3   Most unconfirmed intercompany gains or losses are recorded on the selling affiliate's books; in consolidation they must be *eliminated*. The gain or loss on an intercompany bondholding, however, is somewhat different. Explain the nature of the difference and how the consolidation procedures deal with it.

Q10.4   The one-line consolidation concept of *APBO 18* requires some working paper entries which may seem unusual. Specifically, a gain on constructive retirement of an intercompany bondholding generally means that the Investment in S is *credited* at subsequent consolidation points. Carefully explain what is happening here.

Q10.5   In most intercompany bondholding situations, intercompany interest expense differs from intercompany interest revenue. How should this difference be interpreted? To what is the sum of these periodic differences equal?

Q10.6   Describe the ways in which the minority interest in net income can be affected in an intercompany bondholding.

Q10.7   In a consolidated balance sheet, the Stockholders' Equity caption normally refers to the equity of the controlling shareholders in consolidated net assets. The presence of externally held preferred stock often requires that action be taken on the working paper so that consolidated stockholders' equity is properly stated. What action is taken? Does it make sense?

Q10.8   While reviewing a consolidated financial statement working paper, you notice the following working paper entry:

Minority Interest in Net Income XXX
    Preferred Stock—S (or Dividends—S)   XXX

Indicate the purpose of such an entry.

Q10.9   Criticize the position taken by the authors regarding the treatment of purchase premium or discount arising on an investment in a subsidiary's preferred stock.

Q10.10   Suppose P carries its investment in S Company's preferred stock at cost rather than at equity. How would consolidation procedures differ under the cost method?

Exercises   E10.1   On January 1, 19X7, Solid Corporation purchased $2,000,000 par value of bonds issued several years ago by its parent company, PBR, Inc., for $2,200,000. The bonds pay 11 percent annually and mature ten years after January 1, 19X7. PBR's books show the carrying value of this bond liability to be $2,080,000. Both companies amortize bond premiums and discounts by the straight-line method.

Required: Prepare the working paper entries relative to the intercompany bondholding when consolidated statements are prepared at December 31, 19X7 and December 31, 19X8. Assuming that PBR owns 70 percent of Solid's stock, also give the effect on the Minority Interest in Net Income during the two years.

E10.2 On December 31, 19X3, Sampson Company acquired $1,000,000 face value of Petersen Company's 12 percent annual bonds for $1,122,888. The bonds mature in ten years, and the price reflects a 10 percent yield to maturity. At date of issue, the bonds were sold to yield 15 percent. Sampson is wholly owned by Petersen, and the book value of Petersen's bond liability is $849,432.

Required:
1. Give the working paper eliminations required at December 31, 19X3 and December 31, 19X4, assuming that the straight-line method of premium and discount amortization is used by both companies.
2. Same as requirement 1, except that both companies use the effective interest method of premium and discount amortization.

E10.3 P Company owns 80 percent of S Company's stock (carried at equity) and 60 percent of S Company's outstanding 10 percent bonds. Data relative to the intercompany bondholding are as follows:

P COMPANY

Investment in Bonds (Par) Made on December 31, 19X1	$ 6,000,000
Discount on Investment in Bonds at December 31, 19X1	(639,390)
Net Investment in Bonds	$ 5,360,610

S COMPANY

Bonds Payable (Par), 10% Interest Paid Annually on December 31 and Maturing in 9 years on December 31, 19Y0	$10,000,000
Premium on Bonds Payable at December 31, 19X1	1,249,388
Total Bond Liability	$11,249,388

When originally issued by S Company, the bonds yielded 8 percent. At the time they were acquired by P, however, their price had fallen, reflecting a yield to maturity on December 31, 19X1, of 12 percent.

Required:
1. Give the working paper entries required to eliminate the effects of the intercompany bondholding at consolidation on December 31, 19X1 and December 31, 19X2. Both companies use the straight-line method to amortize the discount and premium.
2. Same as requirement 1, except that both companies use the effective interest method of discount and premium amortization.
3. Explain how the minority interest in S is affected at December 31, 19X1, (a) when the straight-line method is used and (b) when the effective interest method is used.

E10.4 On December 31, 19X3, Scythe Company took out a twenty-year, $100,000 mortgage from the Second National Bank of Odon. The equal annual mortgage payments are based on a 10 percent interest rate and are made at the end of each year. One year later, when Scythe is acquired by Pond Corporation, Pond purchases the mortgage from the bank at an amount which provides Pond with a 12 percent internal rate of return on the mortgage. Both companies amortize premiums and discounts on long-term notes by the effective interest method. Pond accounts for its investment in Scythe using the equity method.

Required: Assuming Scythe is wholly owned by Pond, give the working paper eliminations relative to the above intercompany loan which would be made at December 31, 19X4, 19X5, and 19X6. Show all computations.

E10.5 P owns 80 percent of S's outstanding common stock. Included in S's capital structure are 1,000,000 outstanding shares of 8 percent, $100 par value cumulative preferred stock. The preferred shares have a call price of $102 and have a two-year dividend arrearage (including the current year).

Required: Prepare the needed working paper eliminations relative to the preferred stock when consolidated statements are prepared at the end of the current year.

E10.6 Punch Corporation acquired 70 percent of Stun Company's outstanding common stock for $1,000,000. The book value of Stun's common stockholders' equity at date of acquisition was $1,000,000. In addition, Stun had 5,000 shares of preferred stock with par value of $500,000 outstanding. The preferred has a stated dividend rate of 12 percent, has a call price of $101, and is three years in arrears on dividends.

Required: Compute the purchase premium paid by Punch on its investment in Stun's common stock. Show all calculations.

E10.7 The Stockholders' Equity section of Steedle Corporation's balance sheet is shown here:

10 Percent Cumulative, Nonparticipating Preferred Stock, $200	
Par Value, Liquidation Value $208	$ 2,000,000
Additional Paid-In Capital: Preferred	270,000
Common Stock, Par Value $10	500,000
Additional Paid-In Capital: Common	4,800,000
Retained Earnings	7,900,000
Total Stockholders' Equity	$15,470,000

Pundit owns 90 percent of Steedle's common stock and 10 percent of Steedle's preferred stock. Steedle's board of directors has just voted to omit the current year's preferred dividend for the first time in twenty years.

Required: Show how Steedle's preferred stock will appear on the consolidated balance sheet. All computations must be in good form.

E10.8 Selected account balances from the books of P Company and its subsidiary, S Company, appear as follows:

P COMPANY

Investment in S (Common; 80%)	$5,800,000
Investment in S (Preferred; 40%)	300,000

S COMPANY

Common Stock, $1 Par Value	$ 100,000
10 Percent Cumulative Preferred Stock, $100 Par Value, Call	
Price $105, Liquidation Price $102	800,000
Additional Paid-In Capital	2,400,000
Retained Earnings	4,000,000

Assume that the above account balances existed at the *beginning* of the current year, the day that P purchased the common and preferred shares. This year's preferred dividend has not yet been declared, and there is no prior arrearage. The fair values of S's net assets, both individually and collectively, approximate their book values. No intercompany transactions occurred during the year. Both investment accounts are carried at equity.

Required: Prepare the working paper eliminations needed to consolidate P and S at the *end* of the current year. Show all computations.

Problems P10.1   **Consolidated Financial Statement Working Paper—Incomplete Equity Method**   Following are the trial balances of Pierce Corporation and Stanley Corporation as of March 31, 19X6, the close of the fiscal year. Assume that each company's individual books are correct and include all necessary adjustments unless it is otherwise apparent. Assume that any depreciation and amortization are allocated on a straight-line basis.

Account	Pierce	Stanley
Cash	$ 50,000	$ 30,000
Accounts Receivable	120,000	35,000
Interest and Dividends Receivable	24,000	—
Inventories	95,000	40,000
Investment in Stanley	309,600	—
Investment in Bonds	94,000	—
Plant Assets	406,000	488,000
Accumulated Depreciation	(240,000)	(78,000)
Current Liabilities	(40,000)	(18,000)
Interest and Dividends Payable	—	(32,000)
Bonds Payable	—	(200,000)
Capital Stock	(550,000)	(150,000)
Retained Earnings	(133,400)	(80,000)
Sales	(750,000)	(350,000)
Purchases	585,000	255,000
Operating Expenses	104,000	82,000
Other Revenue	(70,000)	(42,000)
Dividends	30,000	20,000
Income from Stanley	(34,200)	—
	$ 0	$ 0
Ending Inventory	$ 80,000	$ 45,000

Additional information:

1. Pierce acquired 90 percent of Stanley's common stock on April 1, 19X3, for a cash price of $270,000. At that time, Stanley's stockholders' equity accounts were:

Capital Stock $150,000
Retained Earnings 50,000

It was further estimated that certain equipment having a ten-year remaining life was undervalued by $20,000 and that land was undervalued by $80,000 on Stanley's books.

2. An analysis of Pierce's Investment in Subsidiary account shows the following:

4/1/X3	Original Investment	$270,000
3/31/X4	Share of Stanley's $10,000 Income, Less Adjustment for	
	Depreciation on Revaluation of Equipment	7,200
3/31/X5	Share of Stanley's $20,000 Income, Less Adjustment for	
	Depreciation on Revaluation of Equipment	16,200
3/31/X6	Share of Stanley's $40,000 Income, Less Adjustment for	
	Depreciation on Revaluation of Equipment	34,200
3/31/X6	Share of $20,000 Dividend Declared by Stanley on 3/31 . .	(18,000)
	Balance	$309,600

3. Pierce sold merchandise to Stanley during the year in the amount of $125,000. This price reflects a 25 percent markup over cost. Stanley had $25,000 of intercompany merchandise in its inventory at both the beginning and end of the year.

4. Pierce charges Stanley $3,000 per month for administrative services. Pierce credits the Other Revenue account, and Stanley charges Operating Expenses. Two months' charges are unpaid at year-end.

5. On April 1, 19X5, Stanley sold Pierce a building for $190,000. The building originally cost $200,000 and had a net book value of $168,000 when it was sold. On April 1, 19X5, the building had a remaining useful life of eleven years.

6. On April 2, 19X5, Pierce acquired one-half of Stanley's outstanding twenty-year bonds at a price of $94,000. The bonds had been issued fourteen years before at their par value. They pay 6 percent interest annually on April 1; current year discount amortization has not been recorded.

Required: Prepare a consolidated financial statement working paper for Pierce and Stanley for the year ended March 31, 19X6. Formal eliminating entries and financial statements are not required, but each working paper entry should be numbered and a brief explanation provided. Supporting computations should be in good form. Ignore income taxes.

P10.2   Consolidated Trial Balance: Complex Purchase Premium and Intercompany Transactions   On June 30, 19X9, Linskey, Inc., purchased 100 percent of the outstanding common stock of Cresswell Corporation, paying $3,605,000 cash and Linskey's common stock valued at $4,100,000. At the date of purchase, the book and fair values of Cresswell's assets and liabilities were as follows:

	Book Value	Fair Value
Cash	$ 160,000	$ 160,000
Accounts Receivable, Net	910,000	910,000
Inventory	860,000	1,025,186
Furniture, Fixtures, and Machinery (Net)	3,000,000	2,550,000
Building	9,000,000	7,250,000 (net)
Accumulated Depreciation—Building	(5,450,000)	—
Intangible Assets, Net	150,000	220,000
	$8,630,000	
Accounts Payable	$ 580,000	580,000
Note Payable	500,000	500,000
5% Mortgage Note Payable	4,000,000	3,710,186
Common Stock	2,900,000	—
Retained Earnings	650,000	—
	$8,630,000	

By the year-end, December 31, 19X9, the net balance of Cresswell's accounts receivable at June 30, 19X9, had been collected; the inventory on hand at June 30, 19X9, had been charged to cost of goods sold; the accounts payable at June 30, 19X9, had been paid; and the $500,000 note had been paid.

As of June 30, 19X9, Cresswell's furniture, fixtures and machinery, and building had estimated remaining lives of eight and ten years, respectively. All intangible assets had estimated remaining lives of twenty years. All depreciation and amortization is to be computed using the straight-line method.

As of June 30, 19X9, the 5 percent mortgage note payable had eight equal annual payments remaining with the next payment due in one year. The fair value of the note was based on a 7 percent rate. The discount of $289,814 (= $4,000,000 − $3,710,186) will be amortized using the effective interest method.

Prior to June 30, 19X9, there were no intercompany transactions between Linskey and Cresswell; however, during the last six months of 19X9, the following intercompany transactions occurred:

1. Linskey sold $400,000 of merchandise to Cresswell. The cost of the merchandise to Linskey was $360,000. Of this merchandise, $75,000 (at billed prices) remained on hand at December 31, 19X9.

2. On December 31, 19X9, Cresswell purchased $300,000 of Linskey's 7½ percent bonds payable in the market for $312,500, including $22,500 of accrued interest. Linskey had issued $1,000,000 of these twenty-year 7½ percent bonds payable on January 1, 19X2, for $960,000.

3. Many of the management functions of the two companies have been consolidated since the merger. Linskey charges Cresswell a $30,000 per month management fee.

4. At December 31, 19X9, Cresswell owes Linskey two months' management fees and $18,000 for merchandise purchases.

Trial balances of Linskey and Cresswell at December 31, 19X9, appear in

Exhibit 10.11. Linskey has not recorded the equity method accrual for the last six months of 19X9. It may be ignored in your solution.

Linskey's profit and loss figures are for the twelve-month period, while Cresswell's are for the last six months. You may assume that both companies made all the adjusting entries required for separate financial statements unless an obvious discrepancy exists. Income taxes should not be considered in your solution. Round all computations to the nearest dollar.

Required:
1. Prepare formal eliminating entries with explanations and supporting calculations.
2. Prepare a worksheet for the preparation of a consolidated trial balance for Linskey, Inc., and its subsidiary, Cresswell Corporation, for the year ended December 31, 19X9. Provide computations in good form where appropriate to support entries.

(AICPA adapted)

P10.3   **Consolidated Financial Statement Working Paper: Purchase Premium and Intercompany Transactions**   On April 1, 19X3, Jared, Inc., purchased 100 percent of the common stock of Munson Manufacturing Company for $5,850,000. At the date of purchase, the book and fair values of Munson's assets and liabilities were as follows:

	Book Value	Fair Value
Cash and Receivables	$1,093,000	$ 1,093,000
Inventories	1,000,000	872,000
Land	1,560,000	2,100,000
Machinery and Equipment	7,850,000	6,600,000 (net)
Accumulated Depreciation	(3,250,000)	—
Other Assets	140,000	50,000
	$8,393,000	
Current Liabilities	$ 515,000	515,000
Other Liabilities	750,000	750,000
Subordinated Debentures—7%	5,000,000	5,000,000
Capital Stock	1,122,000	—
Retained Earnings	1,006,000	—
	$8,393,000	

Additional information:
1.   By December 31, 19X3, the following transactions had occurred:
   a. The balance of Munson's net accounts receivable at April 1, 19X3, had been collected.
   b. The inventory on hand at April 1, 19X3, had been charged to cost of sales. Munson used a perpetual inventory system in accounting for inventories.
   c. Prior to 19X3, Jared had purchased at face value $1,500,000 of Munson's 7 percent subordinated debentures. These debentures mature on October 31, 19X9, with interest payable annually on October 31.
   d. As of April 1, 19X3, the machinery and equipment had an estimated

Exhibit 10.11 Trial Balances of Linskey and Cresswell at December 31, 19X9, to Be Used in P10.2

Account	Linskey, Inc.	Cresswell Corporation
Cash	$ 507,000	$ 200,750
Accounts Receivable, Net	1,890,000	817,125
Inventory	2,031,000	1,009,500
Furniture, Fixtures, and Machinery	4,200,000	3,000,000
Buildings	17,000,000	9,000,000
Accumulated Depreciation—Buildings	(8,000,000)	(6,050,000)
Intangible Assets, Net	—	146,250
Investment in Subsidiary	7,705,000	—
Investment in Linskey 7¹/₂% Bonds Payable	—	300,000
Interest Receivable	—	22,500
Discount on 7¹/₂% Bonds	24,000	(10,000)
Accounts Payable	(1,843,000)	(575,875)
Interest Payable	(200,500)	(100,000)
Mortgage Notes Payable	(6,786,500)	(4,000,000)
7¹/₂% Bonds Payable	(1,000,000)	—
8¹/₄% Bonds Payable	(3,900,000)	—
Common Stock	(8,772,500)	(2,900,000)
Retained Earnings	(2,167,500)	(650,000)
Sales	(26,000,000)	(6,000,000)
Cost of Goods Sold	18,000,000	3,950,000
Selling, General, and Administrative Expenses . . .	3,130,000	956,000
Management Service Income	(180,000)	—
Management Service Expense	—	180,000
Interest Expense	662,000	100,000
Depreciation Expense	3,701,000	600,000
Amortization Expense	—	3,750
	$ 0	$ 0

remaining life of six years. Munson uses the straight-line method of depreciation. Munson's depreciation expense calculation of $588,750 (included in Operating Expenses) for the nine months ended December 31, 19X3, was based upon the old depreciation rates.

e. The other assets consist entirely of long-term investments made by Munson and do *not* include any investment in Jared.

f. During the last nine months of 19X3, the following intercompany inventory transactions occurred between Jared and Munson:

	Jared to Munson	Munson to Jared
Net Sales	$158,000	$230,000
Included in Purchaser's Inventory at December 31, 19X3 . .	36,000	12,000
Balance Unpaid at December 31, 19X3	16,800	22,000

Jared sells merchandise to Munson at cost. Munson sells merchandise to Jared at regular selling price, including a normal gross profit margin of 35 percent of selling price. There were *no* intercompany sales between the two companies prior to April 1, 19X3.

2. Accrued interest on intercompany debt is recorded by both companies in their respective Accounts Receivable and Accounts Payable accounts.

3. Jared's policy is to amortize intangible assets over a twenty-year period.

4. Trial balances for Jared and Munson at December 31, 19X3, are as shown in Exhibit 10.12.

5. Jared's revenue and expense figures are for the twelve-month period, while Munson's are for the last nine months of 19X3. You may assume that both companies made all the adjusting entries required for separate financial statements unless stated to the contrary. Round all computations to the nearest dollar. Ignore income taxes.

Required:

1. Prepare a schedule to determine and allocate the purchase premium arising in the acquisition of Munson's stock.

2. Prepare a schedule to show how the equity method accrual was computed.

3. Prepare formal eliminating entries with explanations and supporting calculations in good form.

4. Complete a consolidated financial statement working paper for Jared and Munson at December 31, 19X3. Show any supporting computations in good form.

(AICPA adapted)

P10.4   Consolidated Financial Statement Working Paper—Intercompany Transactions   The trial balances of Preston Corporation and Stanton Corporation as of March 31, 19X6, the close of their current fiscal year, appear in Exhibit 10.13. Assume that each company's individual books are correct and reflect all necessary adjustments unless it is otherwise apparent.

Additional information:

1. Preston acquired 80 percent of the outstanding common stock of Stanton on April 1, 19X4, for a cash price of $240,000. At that time, it was estimated that a certain parcel of land was undervalued by $56,000. Stanton's Capital Stock and Retained Earnings accounts on the trial balance are unchanged since April 1, 19X4. The investment in Stanton is carried at equity.

2. Stanton declared and paid dividends of $5,000 in January 19X6. During the year ended March 31, 19X5, Stanton had zero profit and paid no dividends.

3. Intercompany sales of merchandise during the year were as follows. Preston sold Stanton merchandise at a price of $96,000, while Stanton sold Preston merchandise at a price of $65,000 (of which $10,000 had not yet been paid at March 31, 19X6). At the beginning and end of the current year, Preston's inventories of intercompany merchandise (bought from Stanton) were $26,000 and $13,000, respectively. Stanton's inventories

Exhibit 10.12   Jared, Inc., and Munson Manufacturing Company Trial Balances at December 31, 19X3, to Be Used in P10.3

Account	Jared, Inc.	Munson Manufacturing Company
Cash and Receivables	$ 3,580,000	$1,983,400
Inventories, December 31, 19X3	3,204,000	1,182,000
Land	4,000,000	1,560,000
Machinery and Equipment	15,875,000	7,850,000
Accumulated Depreciation—Machinery and Equipment	(6,301,000)	(3,838,750)
Buildings	1,286,000	—
Accumulated Depreciation—Buildings	(372,000)	—
Investment in Munson Manufacturing Company	6,364,700	—
Investment in Debentures	1,500,000	—
Other Assets	413,000	140,000
Current Liabilities	(1,364,000)	(319,000)
Other Liabilities	(10,000,000)	(750,000)
Subordinated Debentures—7%	—	(5,000,000)
Capital Stock	(2,640,000)	(1,122,000)
Retained Earnings	(12,683,500)	(1,006,000)
Sales	(18,200,000)	(5,760,000)
Purchases	10,804,000	3,342,000
Operating Expenses	4,551,500	1,652,650
Inventories, January 1, 19X3 (April 1, 19X3, for Munson)	3,000,000	1,000,000
Inventories, December 31, 19X3	(3,204,000)	(1,182,000)
Income from Munson	(514,700)	—
Interest Revenue	(105,000)	(1,700)
Interest Expense	806,000	269,400
	$ 0	$ 0

(bought from Preston) were $12,000 and $18,000. Preston's selling price reflects a 20 percent markup over cost, while Stanton's sales reflect a 30 percent markup over cost.

4. On August 8, 19X4, Preston sold land having a book value of $30,000 to Stanton at a price of $50,000.

5. On October 1, 19X5, Stanton sold equipment to Preston for $60,000. The equipment had a net book value of $48,000 and a remaining life of six years on that date. The gain was recorded in Other Revenue.

6. On April 1, 19X5, Preston acquired 25 percent of Stanton's outstanding bonds for $48,000, debiting this amount to its Investment in Subsidiary account. The total bond issue had a par value of $200,000 and was issued by Stanton ten years prior to April 1, 19X5. The bonds pay 7 percent interest annually on March 31 and mature twenty years from the issue date. Preston used the straight-line method to amortize the discount during the current year.

Required: Prepare a consolidated financial statement working paper for Preston and Stanton for the year ended March 31, 19X6. Formal eliminating entries

Exhibit 10.13   Preston Corporation and Stanton Corporation Trial Balances at March 31, 19X6, to Be Used in P10.4

Account	Preston	Stanton
Cash .	$ 75,000	$ 80,000
Accounts Receivable	120,000	65,000
Inventories	70,000	90,000
Investment in Stanton	274,040	—
Advance to Stanton	25,000	—
Plant Assets .	500,000	315,000
Accumulated Depreciation .	(180,000)	(55,000)
Current Liabilities	(90,000)	(30,000)
Advance from Preston	—	(25,000)
Bonds Payable	(400,000)	(200,000)
Capital Stock	(250,000)	(150,000)
Retained Earnings	(106,520)	(50,000)
Sales	(720,000)	(377,000)
Purchases	610,000	275,000
Operating Expenses	55,000	42,000
Other Revenue	(20,000)	(15,000)
Other Expense	35,000	30,000
Dividends	20,000	5,000
Income from Stanton	(17,520)	—
	$ 0	$ 0
Ending Inventory	$ 80,000	$ 75,000

and financial statements are not required, but each working paper entry should be numbered and a brief explanation provided. Supporting computations should be in good form. Ignore income taxes and assume that all depreciation and amortization (forty years for goodwill) is allocated on the straight-line basis.

P10.5   Consolidated Trial Balance—Preferred Stock; Cost Method   Parent, Inc., purchased for $151,000 cash 100 percent of the common stock and 20 percent of the 5 percent noncumulative, nonparticipating preferred stock of Subsidiary Manufacturing Corporation on June 30, 19X1. At that date, Subsidiary's stockholders' equity was as follows: 5,000 shares of $10 par value preferred stock, $50,000; 100,000 shares of $1 par value common stock, $100,000; and retained earnings, $41,000. The fair values of the assets, liabilities, and preferred stock did not differ materially from their book values. Subsidiary has made no adjustments to its books to reflect the purchase by Parent. At December 31, 19X1, Parent and Subsidiary prepared consolidated financial statements.

Transactions between Parent and Subsidiary during the year ended December 31, 19X2, follow:

1. On January 3, 19X2, Parent sold land with an $11,000 book value to Subsidiary for $15,000. Subsidiary made a $3,000 down payment and signed an 8 percent mortgage note payable in twelve equal quarterly payments of $1,135, including interest, beginning March 31, 19X2.
2. Subsidiary produced equipment for Parent under two separate contracts. The first contract, which was for office equipment, was begun and com-

Exhibit 10.14 Parent, Inc., and Subsidiary Manufacturing Corporation Trial Balances at December 31, 19X2, to Be Used in P10.5

Account	Parent, Inc.	Subsidiary Corp.
Cash	$ 43,000	$ 31,211
Accounts Receivable	119,000	53,000
Costs and Estimated Earnings in Excess of Billings on		
Uncompleted Contracts	—	87,100
Dividends Receivable	500	—
Mortgage Receivable	8,311	—
Unsecured Notes Receivable	18,000	—
Inventories	217,000	117,500
Land	34,000	42,000
Plant and Equipment, Net	717,000	408,000
Investment in Subsidiary Corporation	151,000	—
Accounts Payable	(203,000)	(97,000)
Dividends Payable	—	(2,500)
Mortgages Payable	(592,000)	(397,311)
Preferred Stock	—	(50,000)
Common Stock	(250,000)	(100,000)
Retained Earnings	(139,311)	(47,000)
Sales	(1,800,000)	—
Earned Revenues on Contracts	—	(1,289,000)
Cost of Sales	1,155,000	—
Cost of Earned Revenues on Contracts	—	852,000
Selling, General, and Administrative Expenses	497,000	360,000
Interest Revenue	(20,000)	—
Interest Expense	49,000	32,000
Dividend Revenue	(500)	—
Gain on Sale of Land	(4,000)	—
	$ 0	$ 0

pleted during the year at a cost to Subsidiary of $17,500. Parent paid $22,000 cash for the equipment on April 17, 19X2. The second contract was begun on February 15, 19X2, but will not be completed until May 19X3. Subsidiary has incurred $45,000 costs as of December 31, 19X2, and anticipates an additional $30,000 cost to complete the $95,000 contract. Subsidiary accounts for all contracts under the percentage-of-completion method of accounting. Parent has made no entry on its books for this uncompleted contract as of December 31, 19X2.

3. On December 1, 19X2, Subsidiary declared a 5 percent cash dividend on its preferred stock, payable on January 15, 19X3, to stockholders of record as of December 14, 19X2.

4. Parent sells merchandise to Subsidiary at an average markup of 12 percent of cost. During the year, Parent charged Subsidiary $238,000 for merchandise purchased, of which Subsidiary paid $211,000. Subsidiary has $11,200 of this merchandise on hand at December 31, 19X2.

Parent depreciates all its equipment over a ten-year estimated economic life with no salvage value. Parent takes a half-year's depreciation in year of purchase.

Both companies have made all of the adjusting entries required for separate financial statements unless an obvious discrepancy exists. Their trial balances for the year ended December 31, 19X2, appear in Exhibit 10.14.

Required: Prepare a consolidated trial balance working paper for Parent and Subsidiary for the year ended December 31, 19X2. Formal statements and journal entries are not required. Round all computations to the nearest dollar. Ignore income tax considerations.

(AICPA adapted)

P10.6 **Consolidated Stockholders' Equity Calculations—Preferred Stock** Nickles, Inc., a manufacturer of restaurant and kitchen equipment, was incorporated thirty years ago. Its stock is closely held. You have been assigned to analyze certain transactions affecting a portion of the income statement and the stockholders' equity section of Nickles, Inc., and its subsidiaries. In accomplishing this assignment, income taxes and earnings per share calculations are to be ignored.

The stockholders' equity section of the balance sheet at September 30, 19X1, and the income statement for the year then ended follow. At that time, Nickles held no investments in other corporations.

STOCKHOLDERS' EQUITY

$1 Cumulative Preferred Stock, Par Value $15 per Share, Shares Authorized 500,000; Issued and Outstanding 4,000	$ 60,000
Common Stock, $10 Par Value per Share, Shares Authorized 1,000,000; Issued and Outstanding 110,000	1,100,000
Retained Earnings	622,000
Total Stockholders' Equity	$1,782,000

INCOME STATEMENT

Sales	$1,050,000
Cost of Goods Sold	725,000
Gross Operating Income	$ 325,000
Selling, General, and Administrative Expenses	135,000
Net Income	$ 190,000

Additional information:

1. On May 1, 19X1, an empty warehouse with a book and fair market value of $145,000 was completely destroyed by fire. Though the building was insured, the insurance company refused to pay for the loss. Nickles, Inc., immediately instigated litigation, and management was confident of winning; hence, no provision was made for a possible loss in fiscal 19X1. The trial was completed October 5, 19X2, finding for the insurance company.

2. The 4,000 shares of preferred stock were issued for cash at incorporation, and no other preferred shares have been issued prior to fiscal 19X2. No dividends have been declared on the common stock prior to fiscal 19X2.

3.   Nickles' capital stock transactions during fiscal 19X2 were:

  a. Preferred stock: On September 30, 19X2, 8,000 shares were issued to the stockholders of Wixon, Inc., to acquire 100 percent of the outstanding common stock of the corporation, whose fiscal year ends September 30. The fair value of Wixon at acquisition was $140,000.

  b. Common stock:

January 17, 19X2—Sold 4,500 shares for cash to Horace Edwards at $25 per share.

May 5, 19X2—Sold 5,500 shares for cash to James Morgan at $25 per share.

September 14, 19X2—Purchased dissident stockholder Edwards' 4,500 shares at $27 per share. The shares are to be held as treasury shares and accounted for at cost. (Edwards violently opposed Nickles' expansion program. It was necessary to pay a $2 premium to eliminate his interest.)

September 28, 19X2—Contracted with Charles Trenton for the sale of 10,000 previously unissued shares at $25 per share to be issued when purchase price is fully paid. At September 30, only $195,000 had been paid. Trenton agreed to pay the balance on or before November 3, 19X2.

September 30, 19X2—Issued 51,000 previously unissued shares to the stockholders of Acme, Inc., in exchange for 100 percent of the outstanding common stock of the corporation, whose fiscal year ends September 30.

4.   Dividends declared by Nickles during fiscal 19X2 were:

  a. Preferred stock—A cash dividend of $1 per share was declared on May 15, 19X2, for shares of record on May 27, 19X2, and paid on June 12, 19X2. There were no dividends in arrears on preferred stock at September 30, 19X2.

  b. Common stock—A cash dividend of $1.25 per share and a 2 percent common stock dividend were declared on September 15, 19X2, for shares of record on September 27, 19X2, payable October 10, 19X2.

5.   Data on Acme and Wixon:

  a. Both corporations are authorized to issue only no-par-value common stock. Data applicable at September 30, 19X0 and 19X2, (no change) follow:

	Acme	Wixon
Shares Authorized	50,000	25,000
Shares Issued and Outstanding	34,000	2,500
Dollar Balance in the Common Stock Account . .	$631,000	$105,000

  b. An analysis of retained earnings (deficit) for the two years ended September 30, 19X2, follows:

	Acme	Wixon
Balance September 30, 19X0	$(147,000)	$ 32,000
Net Income [Loss] for the Year Ended:		
September 30, 19X1[a]	112,000	(15,000)
September 30, 19X2	125,000	(6,000)
Balance September 30, 19X2	$ 90,000	$ 11,000

[a]Also net operating income [loss].

    c. Prior to September 30, 19X2, Acme and Wixon have never had any intercompany transactions with Nickles or between each other.

6. Nickles' unconsolidated net income (also net operating income) was $215,000 for the year ended September 30, 19X2.

7. You have previously determined that the acquisitions of Acme and Wixon must be accounted for as a pooling of interests and a purchase, respectively.

Required:

1. Prepare a comparative consolidated statement of income beginning with net operating income and arriving at net income for the years ended September 30, 19X2 and 19X1. This statement should be supported by a schedule calculating consolidated net operating income.

2. Assuming consolidated net income of $405,000 and $240,000 for the years ended September 30, 19X2 and 19X1, respectively, prepare a comparative stockholders' equity section of the consolidated balance sheet for the years ended September 30, 19X2 and 19X1. This statement should be supported by the following schedules presented in the order given:

    a. Changes in preferred stock account.

    b. Changes in common stock account.

    c. Calculation of number of shares to be issued for common stock dividend.

    d. Calculation of paid-in capital in excess of par.

    e. Changes in retained earnings.

(AICPA adapted)

P10.7 Consolidated Financial Statement Working Paper—Intercompany Bonds and Preferred Stock The trial balances of Pawn Corporation and its 80-percent-owned subsidiary, Standish Company, at December 31, 19X3, are given in Exhibit 10.15. Pawn acquired these common shares and 20 percent of Standish's outstanding cumulative preferred shares on January 1, 19X1, for $1,990,400 and $200,000, respectively. On January 1, 19X1, Pawn's common shareholders' equity accounts amounted to $2,000,000; the preferred stock was $600,000. No dividends have been declared on the preferred stock since 19X0. Also on January 1, 19X1, Pawn purchased one-half of Standish's $4,000,000 par value outstanding bonds for $1,800,000. The bonds mature ten years after the date they were acquired; straight-line amortization has been used by both companies. No other intercompany transactions occurred between the two com-

Exhibit 10.5 Pawn Corporation and Standish Company Trial Balances at December 31, 19X3, to Be Used in P10.7

Account	Pawn Corp.	Standish Co.
Cash and Receivables	$ 2,601,600	$1,805,000
Inventory	3,250,000	2,400,000
Investment in Standish—Common (Equity)	3,598,400	—
Investment in Standish—Preferred (Cost)	200,000	—
Investment in Bonds	1,860,000	—
Plant Assets, Net	7,300,000	5,300,000
Current Liabilities	(3,514,000)	(1,000,000)
Bonds Payable, 8% Annual Coupons	—	(4,105,000)
Preferred Stock, 10%, Par Value, $100; Call Price, $102 .	—	(600,000)
Capital Stock	(2,000,000)	(500,000)
Retained Earnings	(10,000,000)	(3,000,000)
Dividends	400,000	—
Sales	(11,000,000)	(6,005,000)
Income from Standish	(316,000)	—
Interest Revenue	(180,000)	—
Purchases	5,800,000	4,200,000
Operating Expenses	2,000,000	1,200,000
Interest Expense	—	305,000
	$ 0	$ 0
Ending Inventory	$ 3,100,000	$2,600,000

panies during 19X3. Any purchase premium attributable to the investment in common is goodwill amortized over forty years.

Required: Prepare a consolidated financial statement working paper for Pawn and Standish for the year ended December 31, 19X3.

P10.8 **Compute Consolidated Retained Earnings—Intercompany Transactions and Preferred Stock** P owns 80 percent of S's common stock and 10 percent of S's preferred stock. Both investments were acquired on January 1, 19X4, for $5,000,000 and $200,000, respectively. Because certain accounting records on the computer have been "lost," you must reconstruct the correct balance in consolidated retained earnings as of December 31, 19X5. The following data are available.

Additional information:
1. On January 1, 19X4, S's common shareholders' equity amounted to $5,000,000, and its assets and liabilities were recorded at amounts which approximated their fair values.
2. S's preferred stock consists of 20,000 shares of $100 par value 10 percent cumulative preferred stock. The stock has a call price of $105. Dividends have always been declared on a timely basis except for the 19X4 and 19X5 dividends which were omitted.
3. P's policy is to amortize intangibles over forty years.
4. On January 1, 19X5, P sold a machine to S for $200,000. The machine had

a remaining life of five years and a net book value of $120,000 on that date.

5. P's January 1, 19X5, and December 31, 19X5, inventories include intercompany profits of $25,000 and $15,000, respectively, on goods purchased from S.

6. On December 31, 19X5, P acquired all of S's outstanding 10 percent bonds for $860,000. The bonds have par value of $800,000, mature in ten years, and were recorded by S at $780,000. Both companies amortize their premiums and discounts by the straight-line method.

7. During 19X4–19X5, P reported income from its own operations of $2,000,000 (excluding intercompany dividends) and declared dividends of $900,000.

8. During 19X4–19X5, S reported income from its own operations of $800,000. The only dividend declared was the preferred dividend for 19X4.

9. On January 1, 19X4, the retained earnings of P and S were $10,000,000 and $3,000,000, respectively.

Required: Compute consolidated retained earnings at December 31, 19X5. Show all computations.

Chapter 11

Consolidated Financial Statements: Special Topics

In this chapter, we examine some additional topics in consolidated financial statements which may be encountered in practice. The two principal areas developed are (1) changes in the parent's ownership interest in the subsidiary and (2) complex ownership relationships among the affiliated companies. Although other consolidation issues—such as intercompany transactions and preferred stock—may be present in an actual situation, for the most part we assume such complications away in this chapter.

Changes in the Parent's Ownership Interest

To this point, our discussions and examples of business combinations and consolidated financial statements involved one-time acquisitions of controlling interest. This was done in order to avoid additional complexities when control is achieved after a series of purchases or when the parent's ownership interest changes. In practice, of course, the world is not so neatly ordered. Our objective in this section is to deal with some of these problems. Some theoretical issues as well as technical issues will arise. We begin with a discussion of consolidation issues when control is achieved after a series of purchases.

Control Achieved in a Series of Purchases

When an acquiring company achieves a controlling interest in a subsidiary after two or more acquisitions of stock, the mechanics of allocating purchase premiums and discounts become more complex. The original guidance provided in *ARB 51* is presented on page 438.

> If two or more purchases are made over a period of time, the earned surplus of the subsidiary at acquisition should generally be determined on a step-by-step basis; *however, if small purchases are made over a period of time and then a purchase is made which results in control, the date of the latest purchase, as a matter of convenience, may be considered the date of acquisition.*[1] (Emphasis added.)

Times have changed since *ARB 51* was published in 1959. The guidance quoted above was expressive of a concern over eliminating the correct amount of the subsidiary's retained earnings in consolidation. This is not a burning issue today. Rather concern has turned to determination of the appropriate time(s) for estimating the fair values of the subsidiary's assets and liabilities. When *ARB 51* was published, most unconsolidated intercorporate investments were carried at *cost*. Today, substantial intercorporate investments are carried at *equity*, reflecting the one-line consolidation concept of *APBO 18*. Under *APBO 18*, once an investor company's position in the investee's voting stock passes 20 percent (or less, if substantial influence over the investee's affairs can be demonstrated), the equity method is to be used, estimates of fair values made, and goodwill established and amortized. It seems that if small purchases are made over a period of time, the acquiring company must enter the equity method range and fair values will be established before control is actually achieved. The issue was specifically addressed in an unofficial 1973 AICPA accounting interpretation of *APBO 17* (AC § U5141.004):

> When a company in a series of purchases on a step-by-step basis acquires either a subsidiary which is consolidated or an investment which is accounted for under the equity method, the company should identify the cost of each investment, the fair value of the underlying assets acquired and the goodwill for each step purchase.[2]

For these reasons, we believe that the old "convenience" provision of *ARB 51* governing the date of acquisition when control is achieved after a series of small purchases is no longer relevant. Note that a step acquisition can occur only in a purchase combination. In a pooling, control must be achieved in a single "acquisition" of at least 90 percent of the stock. If any further acquisitions are made to buy out the minority interest, however, these subsequent acquisitions are treated as purchases. We now illustrate the mechanics of a step acquisition in which the acquiring company uses the equity method.

To illustrate, consider the following data. Puck Company acquires an 80 percent interest in Stick Company after three purchases spanning two years. Stick Company has 100,000 outstanding shares. Details concerning the acquisitions follow.

---

[1] Committee on Accounting Procedure, *Accounting Research Bulletin No. 51*, "Consolidated Financial Statements" (N.Y.: AICPA, 1959), par. 10; AC § 2051.09.

[2] American Institute of Certified Public Accountants, *Unofficial Interpretation No. 2 of APB Opinion No. 17*, "Goodwill in a Step Acquisition" (N.Y.: AICPA, 1973).

Acquisition Date	Percent Acquired	Cost of Shares	Net Assets of Stick Company Fair Value	Book Value	Stick Company Net Income Year	Amount
5/1/X1	25%	$180,000	$500,000	$400,000	19X1	$ 60,000
4/1/X2	20	190,000	600,000	470,000	19X2	120,000
10/1/X2	35	400,000	700,000	530,000		

Note: No dividends were paid by Stick during 19X1 and 19X2.

In analyzing the purchase premium paid at each step, we assume that any which is allocated to Stick's net assets will be depreciated on the straight-line basis over 10 years. Any remaining purchase premium is evidence of goodwill, which is to be amortized over forty years. Determination and allocation of the purchase premium at each step are summarized in the following schedule:

Acquisition Date	(1) Cost of Shares	(2) Book Value of Net Assets Acquired	(3) [(1) − (2)] Purchase Premium	Net Assets of Stick Company (4) Fair Value	(5) Book Value	(6) [(4) − (5)] (FV − BV)	(7) Puck's Interest	(8) [(3) − (7)] Goodwill
5/1/X1	$180,000	$100,000 (25%)	$ 80,000	$500,000	$400,000	$100,000	$ 25,000 (25%)	$ 55,000
4/1/X2	190,000	94,000 (20%)	96,000	600,000	470,000	130,000	26,000 (20%)	70,000
10/1/X2	400,000	185,500 (35%)	214,500	700,000	530,000	170,000	59,500 (35%)	155,000
	$770,000	$379,500	$390,500				$110,500	$280,000

Our next concern involves computing the equity method accrual made by Puck in each year. This is given in Exhibit 11.1. Then we calculate the un-amortized purchase premium to be included in consolidated assets on the first consolidated balance sheet prepared at December 31, 19X2.

To keep track of the unamortized purchase premium which will be included in consolidated assets, it is helpful to prepare a schedule which separates the portions attributable to identifiable assets and to goodwill. Such a schedule giving information for the Puck and Stick case is summarized next:

Schedule of Unamortized Purchase Premium

Date Acquired	Identifiable Assets 5/1/X1	4/1/X2	10/1/X2	Total	Goodwill 5/1/X1	4/1/X2	10/1/X2	Total
Acquired: 19X1	$25,000	—	—	$ 25,000	$55,000	—	—	$ 55,000
Amort.: 19X1	(1,650)	—	—	(1,650)	(921)	—	—	(921)
Bal., 12/31/X1	$23,350	—	—	$ 23,350	$54,079	—	—	$ 54,079
Acquired: 19X2	—	$26,000	$59,500	85,500	—	$70,000	$155,000	225,000
Amort.: 19X2	(2,500)	(1,950)	(1,488)	(5,938)	(1,375)	(1,313)	(969)	(3,657)
Bal., 12/31/X2	$20,850	$24,050	$58,012	$102,912	$52,704	$68,687	$154,031	$275,422

This schedule will be updated annually.

Whenever the parent's investment in a particular subsidiary reflects two or more blocks of stock acquired at different times, a record is needed to keep their book values separate. If some of the shares are ultimately sold, the correct

Exhibit 11.1   Computation of Equity Method Accruals

Puck Company and Stick Company
Computation of the Equity Method Accruals
For the Years Ended December 31, 19X1 and 19X2

19X1

Puck's Share of Stick's Net Income [.25 × $60,000 × ($^8/_{12}$)]	$10,000
Less Amortization of Purchase Premium:	
Additional Depreciation ($25,000/10) × ($^8/_{12}$)	$ 1,650
Amortization of Goodwill ($55,000/40) × ($^8/_{12}$)	921
Total Purchase Premium Amortization	$ 2,571
Net Equity Method Accrual for 19X1	$ 7,429

19X2

Puck's Share of Stick's Net Income:	
May 1, 19X1, Acquisition (.25 × $120,000)	$30,000
April 1, 19X2, Acquisition [.20 × $120,000 × ($^9/_{12}$)]	18,000
October 1, 19X2, Acquisition [.35 × $120,000 × ($^3/_{12}$)]	10,500
Total Share of Stick's 19X2 Net Income	$58,500
Less Amortization of Purchase Premium:	
Additional Depreciation:	
May 1, 19X1, Acquisition ($25,000/10)	$ 2,500
April 1, 19X2, Acquisition [$26,000/10 × ($^9/_{12}$)]	1,950
October 1, 19X2, Acquisition [($59,500/10) × ($^3/_{12}$)]	1,488
Amortization of Goodwill:	
May 1, 19X1, Acquisition ($55,000/40)	1,375
April 1, 19X2, Acquisition [($70,000/40) × ($^9/_{12}$)]	1,313
October 1, 19X2, Acquisition [($155,000/40) × ($^3/_{12}$)]	969
Total Purchase Premium Amortization	$ 9,595
Net Equity Method Accrual for 19X2	$48,905

book value is needed to determine gain or loss. A schedule like the following enables the accountant to identify the book values of the various blocks of stock. It too will be updated annually.

Schedule of Carrying Values of Stock Purchases in a Step Acquisition

Date of Acquisition	Block A (25%) 5/1/X1	Block B (20%) 4/1/X2	Block C (35%) 10/1/X2	Total
Cost of Acquisition . .	$180,000	$190,000	$400,000	$770,000
Equity Accrual: 19X1 . .	7,429	—	—	7,429
Dividends: 19X1 . . .	—	—	—	—
Equity Accrual: 19X2 . .	26,125	14,737	8,043	48,905
Dividends: 19X2 . . .	—	—	—	—
Balance: December 31,				
19X2	$213,554	$204,737	$408,043	$826,334

Transactions Involving the Subsidiary's Shares

Although accounting theory tends to stress substance, or the actual outcome of transactions, over form (the way in which the result was achieved), the form of a transaction involving the subsidiary's shares may influence its accounting treatment. From the standpoint of the affiliated group, different transactions involving the subsidiary's shares which have the same economic end result can be accounted for differently. Consider the following three ways in which the subsidiary's shares could be sold outside the affiliated group:

1. The parent could reduce its ownership interest by selling some of the subsidiary's shares which it owns to outsiders.

2. The parent could reduce its ownership interest by instructing the subsidiary to sell previously unissued shares to outsiders.

3. The parent could reduce its ownership interest by instructing the subsidiary to sell its own treasury shares to outsiders.

All of these transactions involve a reduction in the parent's ownership interest. If the shares are sold for more than their book value, consolidated stockholders' equity will increase even though the controlling interest's ownership percentage has decreased. Is the increase in consolidated stockholders' equity an income item or a capital item? Does it depend on whether the parent or the subsidiary sold the shares? In our judgment, current accounting practice in this area is inconsistent, as the following numerical example illustrates.

P Company owns 8,000 of S Company's 10,000 outstanding common shares, for an ownership interest of 80 percent. P Company carries the shares at equity, $80,000. No purchase premium or discount exists. The stock currently sells in the market for $30 a share.

Case 1: P Company sells 1,000 of the shares it owns for $30,000. Since the book value of those shares was $10,000, P's shareholders have realized an increase in their equity of $20,000 (= $30,000 − $10,000), and they now own 70 percent of S Company's outstanding shares.

Case 2: S Company issues 1,429 shares for $42,870 (= $30 × 1,429), increasing S Company's stockholders' equity to $142,870 (= $100,000 + $42,870).[3] The portion of S Company's stockholders' equity now owned by P is 70 percent (= 8,000/11,429), and it has a book value of $100,000 (= .7 × $142,870). P's shareholders have realized an increase in their equity of $20,000 (= $100,000 − $80,000).

In our judgment, cases 1 and 2 are fundamentally identical. Yet, current accounting practice would treat the case 1 "gain" as *income* and, although some might object, would treat the case 2 "gain" as a capital transaction and record it as *additional paid-in capital*. It would be argued that in case 1 P has realized income on the sale of an investment and in case 2 S has sold its own stock—a capital transaction—and P has realized no income.

---

[3] Given that the 8,000 shares presently owned by P are to represent a 70 percent ownership interest after the new issue, the additional number of shares is determined as follows: Define X as the total number of shares of S outstanding after the new issue. Then,

$$.7 = 8,000/X$$
$$.7X = 8,000$$
$$X = 11,429.$$

This represents an increase of 1,429 shares over the 10,000 originally outstanding.

We believe that these accounting treatments are inconsistent. From the viewpoint of the parent company, *both* transactions provide income to its shareholders. On the other hand, from the standpoint of the total entity, *neither* transaction provides income—the parent's sale of the subsidiary's shares is, in effect, a sale of treasury stock.

A major contributing factor to the treatment of subsidiary stock issues (case 2) as capital transactions is the position taken by the SEC: "No profits on the person's own equity securities, or profits of its affiliates on their own equity securities, shall be included under this caption [*profits on securities*]."[4]

It is widely acknowledged that sound accounting theory relies on substance, not form. Unfortunately, these inconsistent accounting treatments arise in practice because form is being stressed over substance. We favor treating the gains arising in both case 1 and case 2 as income in consolidated statements because the economic position of the controlling interest has been improved by a completed market transaction. Our position is consistent with the *parent theory* of consolidated statements, while the capital transaction approach follows from the *entity theory*. Either approach consistently followed is preferable to the inconsistency that currently exists in practice.

We now illustrate the accounting for (1) a sale of part of the parent's ownership interest in the subsidiary and (2) a sale of additional shares by the subsidiary, which also reduces the parent's ownership interest. Transactions in which the subsidiary purchases or sells treasury stock are, in substance, quite similar to the transactions in cases 1 and 2 above. We will briefly illustrate and comment on them later in the section.

Parent Sells Shares of the Subsidiary to Outsiders   The two major issues of interest when the parent sells a portion of its holdings of the subsidiary's stock are:

1.   Establishing the book value of the interest sold.
2.   Adjusting the purchase premium or discount.

Book Value of Shares Sold   Use of the equity method by the parent enables it to account for the current book value of its interests in the subsidiary. If the shares are sold *during* an accounting period, the change in book value since the beginning of the accounting period must be estimated. An adjustment may be necessary at year-end if subsequent information calls for a revision in that estimate. When the parent's investment in the subsidiary consists of two or more separate blocks of shares, management must decide which shares have been sold. Since one share of a company's stock is indistinguishable from another, identifying the particular shares sold becomes difficult. *Specific identification* of shares sold is not really possible unless an entire block is disposed. The use of *first-in, first-out* (FIFO) is a reasonable though arbitrary policy for identifying shares sold. Another approach involves computing the *average book*

---

[4]   Louis H. Rappaport, *SEC Accounting Practice and Procedure*, 3d ed. (N.Y.: Ronald Press, 1972), p. 18.28.

value of all shares owned and assumes that shares chosen at random are sold. In our judgment, the last approach has the most conceptual appeal because of the identical nature of the shares. If it is used, there is no need to keep track of the separate book value of each block of shares.

Purchase Premium (Discount) Adjustment   If the carrying value of the shares sold includes a purchase premium, the amount of unamortized purchase premium remaining in the investment account is reduced. Subsequent allocation and amortization of the purchase premium on consolidated financial statement working papers are affected because some portion of the purchase premium has been "sold." The adjustment process is most vividly illustrated when a *particular*, rather than *average*, block of stock is sold. Therefore, we shall use the data developed in the Puck and Stick example here, employing FIFO rather than specific identification, to identify the particular block of stock assumed sold.

Suppose that on December 31, 19X2, Puck sells 10,000 shares of Stick Company stock for $105,420. This is 10 percent of Stick's outstanding stock and is assumed to be taken from Puck's first acquisition made on May 1, 19X1 (that is, block A). After the sale, the shares remaining in that initial acquisition represent 15 percent of Stick's outstanding shares. Each share in block A has a book value of $8.542 (= $213,554/25,000). Included in this book value is $73,554 (= $20,850 of identifiable assets + $52,704 of goodwill) of unamortized purchase premium, or $2.942 (= $73,554/25,000) per share. Thus the shares sold had a book value of $85,420 (= 10,000 × $8.542), and a gain of $20,000 (= $105,420 − $85,420) resulted. Puck records the sale as follows, and the gain shows up on the consolidated income statement for the year ended December 31, 19X2.

BOOKS OF PUCK COMPANY

Cash	105,420	
Investment in Stick		85,420
Gain on Sale of Investment		20,000

To record the sale of 10,000 shares of Stick
Company stock for $105,420, thereby reducing
our ownership interest to 70 percent.

Allocation of the remaining unamortized purchase premium on the consolidated balance sheet at December 31, 19X2, yields the following results:

	Amount Allocated to		Total Unamortized
	Identifiable Assets	Goodwill	Purchase Premium
Balance, 80% Interest . .	$102,912	$275,422	$378,334
Portion Sold, 10% Interest			
(from Block A Acquired			
May 1, 19X1)	(8,340)[a]	(21,082)[b]	(29,422)
Balance, 70% Interest . .	$ 94,572	$254,340	$348,912

[a]$8,340 = $20,850(10,000/25,000).
[b]$21,082 = $52,704(10,000/25,000).

Subsidiary Issues Additional Shares to Outsiders   Sale of its own stock by a subsidiary is handled in the usual way on the subsidiary's books. In consolidation, however, two additional matters must be considered:

1. Establishing the book value of the parent's new ownership interest.
2. Adjusting the purchase premium or discount.

Book Value of Ownership Interest   If the additional stock issued by the subsidiary is at a price *other than book value* of the shares issued, the monetary value of the ownership interest in the investment account must be adjusted. The amount of the adjustment is the controversial "gain or loss" discussed earlier. No entry is made by P when the new shares are issued at book value. In this case, the decline in the percentage of shares owned by the parent is exactly offset by the percentage of increase in the stockholders' equity of the subsidiary.

Purchase Premium (Discount) Adjustment   The decline in the fraction of subsidiary shares owned by the parent following an issue of subsidiary shares to outsiders is equivalent to the sale of a portion of the parent's ownership interest. As was the case with the sale by the parent, any purchase premium or discount must be reduced in proportion to the decrease in ownership interest. This will be necessary even if there is no gain or loss; the portion of the purchase premium "sold" will have been replaced by an increase in the subsidiary's stockholders' equity.

To illustrate this type of transaction and contrast it directly with the sale of shares by the parent, we assume that Stick Company issues an additional 14,286 shares of stock in the market on December 31, 19X2. This increases the number of shares outstanding to 114,286 (= 100,000 + 14,286), of which the 80,000 shares owned by Puck represent a 70 percent (= 80,000/114,286) interest. All shares are purchased by outside interests at an average price of $10.542, for a total of $150,603 (= 14,286 × $10.542). The book value of Stick's stockholders' equity now stands at $710,603. Recall that as of October 1, 19X2, the date the third block of Stick's stock was acquired, the net assets of Stick amounted to $530,000. If we assume that 25 percent of the 19X2 net income of $120,000 was earned in the last three months of 19X2, the book value of Stick's stockholders' equity prior to the issue of securities was $560,000. Adding the proceeds from the issue brings the book value up to $710,603.

Puck now owns 70 percent (= 80,000/114,286) of Stick's outstanding shares, and 70 percent of Stick's stockholders' equity is now $497,422 (= .7 × $710,603). The net effect of this new security issue will be to increase the Investment in Stick account balance by $20,000. An entry will be made recording the $20,000 either as a *gain* to Puck—to be consistent with the outright sale of shares by Puck—or as *additional paid-in capital* to Puck, following the SEC rule. As can be seen from the following analysis, the $20,000 is the difference between two partially offsetting effects on the investment account. First, the monetary amount of Puck's interest in Stick, now 70 percent, has risen by $49,422 [= $497,422 − .8($560,000)]. Second, a portion of the purchase premium associated with block A, $29,422 [= ($20,850 + $52,704)(10,000/25,000)], is assumed sold.

Composition of the Investment in Stick Company

	Equity in Stick's Net Assets	Purchase Premium	Total
Combined Acquisitions	$379,500	$390,500	$770,000
19X1 Equity Accrual	10,000	(2,571)	7,429
19X2 Equity Accrual	58,500	(9,595)	48,905
Balance, December 31, 19X2, before			
Stock Issue	$448,000	$378,334	$826,334
Stick's Issue of New Stock.	49,422	(29,422)	20,000
Balance, December 31, 19X2, after			
Stock Issue	$497,422	$348,912	$846,334

At December 31, 19X2, Puck Company makes the following entry on its books to record the net increase in the monetary value of the investment account:

BOOKS OF PUCK COMPANY

Investment in S 20,000	
Gain (or Additional Paid-In Capital)	20,000

To record the net increase in the investment in Stick generated by the issue of additional shares by Stick Company in the open market at more than their book value (to Stick).

When the consolidated balance sheet is prepared at December 31, 19X2, the unamortized purchase premium will be allocated as follows. The reductions are the same as those previously indicated when the shares owned by Puck were actually sold outside.

	Amount Allocated to		Total Unamortized
	Identifiable Assets	Goodwill	Purchase Premium
Balance, 80% Interest . .	$102,912	$275,422	$378,334
Portion "Sold," 10% Interest			
(from Block A) . . .	(8,340)[a]	(21,082)[b]	(29,422)
Balance, 70% Interest . .	$ 94,572	$254,340	$348,912

[a]$8,340 = $20,850(10,000/25,000).
[b]$21,082 = $52,704(10,000/25,000).

The case we have illustrated involves the issue of stock by the subsidiary to outsiders only. It is reasonable to expect that the parent company will often acquire some of those shares. If so, the transaction becomes a combination of (1) an additional acquisition of stock by the parent and (2) an issue of subsidiary stock to outsiders. It must be analyzed accordingly and is not discussed further or illustrated here.

Subsidiary Transactions in Treasury Stock   Sales of treasury stock by a subsidiary create no new problems. The effects of such transactions on the investment account are analyzed and treated as if they arose from sales of unissued stock by the subsidiary.

Purchases of treasury stock from outsiders by the subsidiary decrease the number of shares outstanding and increase the parent's ownership interest. There are three possibilities:

1. Treasury shares acquired at book value have no effect on the investment account. The decrease in the subsidiary's stockholders' equity is exactly offset by the increase in the parent's ownership percentage.

2. Treasury shares acquired at *more* than book value reduce the subsidiary's stockholders' equity by more than the increase in the parent's ownership percentage. Although the balance in the investment account will fall, it is difficult to justify recognizing a loss on what is, in effect, a purchase. Hence the debit will be to Additional Paid-In Capital. An alternative procedure, which has some merit, calls for leaving the investment account balance undisturbed and increasing the unamortized purchase premium by the amount of the decrease in equity. Our preference is to charge Additional Paid-In Capital for the difference, on the grounds that the acquisition of treasury stock should not increase an amortizable asset.

3. Treasury shares acquired at *less* than book value have the opposite effect, reducing the subsidiary's stockholders' equity by less than the increase in the parent's ownership percentage. In this case, the balance in the investment account rises. To avoid recognizing a gain on a purchase, we suggest crediting Additional Paid-In Capital. As before, we believe that this treatment is preferable to a reduction in the unamortized purchase premium which offsets the increase in equity and leaves the investment account balance unchanged.

To illustrate these three possibilities, we return to our Puck and Stick example. At December 31, 19X2, Puck owns 80 percent of Stick's 100,000 outstanding common shares. The book value of Stick's stockholders' equity per share is $5.60 (= $560,000/100,000). The effects of purchases of 11,111 shares of treasury stock at prices of $5.60, $5.00, and $6.20 are illustrated in Exhibit 11.2.

Complex Affiliation Relationships

Our last set of special topics deals with the preparation of consolidated statements when affiliation relationships are more intricate than those **direct holdings** (parent's direct ownership of controlling interest in a subsidiary) studied to this point. The basic types of affiliation relationships are diagrammed in Figure 11.1.

Indirect holdings arise when the parent company's controlling interest in a subsidiary enables the parent to control a second subsidiary even though it owns few or none of the second subsidiary's shares directly. The main problems generated by indirect holdings relate to the interpretation of a purchase premium or discount and the order in which the procedures for preparing consolidated financial statements are carried out. **Mutual holdings** occur when one or more subsidiaries own stock in the parent or in each other. Such shares are

Exhibit 11.2   Effects of Stick's Acquisition of 11,111 Treasury Shares at Alternative Prices of $5.60, $5.00, and $6.20 per Share

	Stockholders' Equity of Stick Company			
	Without Purchase of Treasury Stock	With Purchase of 11,111 Shares of Treasury Stock		
		At $5.60	At $5.00	At $6.20
Stockholders' Equity, before .	$560,000	$560,000	$560,000	$560,000
Less Treasury Stock	—	(62,222)	(55,555)	(68,888)
Stockholders' Equity, after . .	$560,000	$497,778	$504,445	$491,112
Puck's Percentage Interest . . .	.8	.9 [a]	.9 [a]	.9 [a]
Puck's Share . .	$448,000	$448,000	$454,000	$442,000
Increase (Decrease) .	—	—	$ 6,000 [b]	$ (6,000)[c]

[a] .9 = 80,000/88,889.
[b] $6,000 = $454,000 − $448,000.
[c] $(6,000) = $442,000 − $448,000.

not shown as outstanding in a consolidated balance sheet.[5] The principal conceptual problem arises when there is a minority interest in a parent-subsidiary mutual holding. In this case, there are two acceptable alternative treatments which result in different consolidated statements.

Indirect Holdings

The first issue to be addressed is the interpretation of the purchase premium or discount in an indirect holding. Note that the **father-son-grandson (FSG)** and **connecting affiliate (CA)** configurations have one thing in common—one subsidiary's interest in the second subsidiary enables the parent to control the second subsidiary. In the FSG case, P controls T because P controls S and S controls T. In the CA case, P controls T because P controls S *and* P and S *together* have a controlling interest in T.

Suppose we have an FSG affiliation in which P controlled S *before* S acquires its controlling interest in T. Any purchase premium arising when S acquires T is allocated in the usual way across T's assets and liabilities, with any residual being assigned to goodwill. Modify this to the situation where P acquires S *after* S acquired its controlling interest in T. Assuming that P pays a purchase premium for its interest in S (and through S its interest in T), the accountant's allocation problem has a new dimension. There are now three possible explanations for this purchase premium:

1.   The fair value of S Company's net assets, *excluding the Investment in T*, may exceed their book value.

---

[5] The subsidiaries' shares are, as usual, eliminated in consolidation. Similarly, *ARB 51* states that "shares of the parent held by a subsidiary should not be treated as outstanding stock in the consolidated balance sheet." Committee on Accounting Procedure, *ARB 51*, par. 13; AC § 2051.12.

Figure 11.1   Basic Types of Affiliation Relationships

Direct Holdings

One Subsidiary

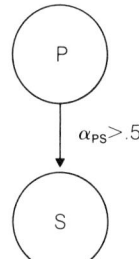

Several Subsidiaries

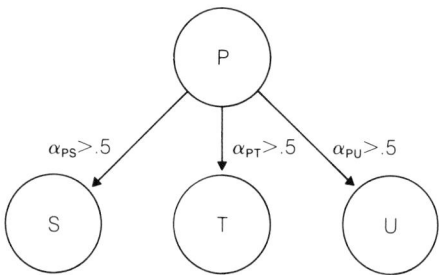

Indirect Holdings

Father-Son-Grandson

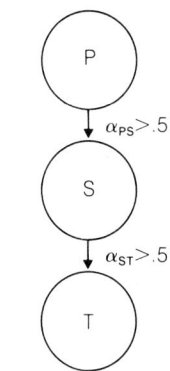

Connecting Affiliates

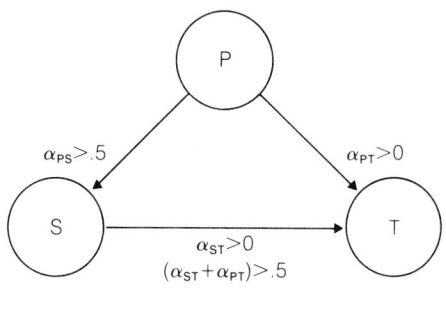

Mutual Holdings

Parent and Subsidiary

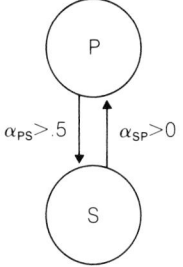

Connecting Affiliates

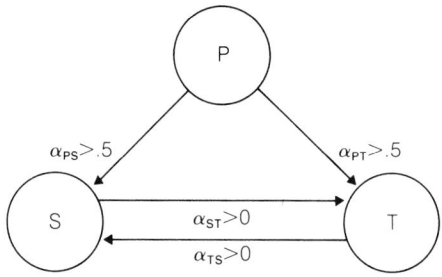

2. The fair value of T's net assets may exceed the amount reflected in the Investment in T on S Company's books.

3. Net assets of both S and T may be fairly stated and the premium be evidence of purchased goodwill.

Of course, any given purchase premium may easily represent a combination of these three factors. When consolidating P, S, and T, the net assets of S may require revaluation, the net assets of T may require revaluation beyond that implied by S's investment in T, and goodwill may be present as well. Before we illustrate these points with a numerical example, observe that the same situation may hold in the CA case. If P acquires S *after* S acquired its minority interest in T, a portion of P's purchase premium in S may be attributable to an excess of fair value over book value of T's assets. This can be complicated further if P acquires its interest in T at a time different from when the interest in S is acquired.

To illustrate some of these possibilities, assume that two companies, S and T, have the following condensed balance sheet data at December 31, 19X3:

Balance Sheet Data as of December 31, 19X3

	S Company		T Company	
	Book Value	Fair Value	Book Value	Fair Value
Various Assets . .	$8,000,000	$10,000,000	$3,000,000	$4,000,000
Liabilities . . .	$4,000,000	3,000,000	$2,000,000	2,000,000
Stockholders' Equity . . .	4,000,000	—	1,000,000	—
Totals . .	$8,000,000		$3,000,000	

S Acquires T   On December 31, 19X3, S Company acquires a 70 percent interest in T ($\alpha_{ST} = .7$) for $1,800,000 in cash. The book value of 70 percent of T's stockholders' equity is $700,000 (= .7 × $1,000,000), and a purchase premium of $1,100,000 (= $1,800,000 − $700,000) results. Allocation of this purchase premium is as follows:

Allocation of Purchase Premium Paid When S
Acquires 70 Percent of T at December 31, 19X3

Assets and Liabilities of T Company	Fair Value	Book Value	Fair Value Less Book Value	Allocation Based on S's Interest (70%)
Various Assets	$4,000,000	$3,000,000	$1,000,000	$ 700,000
Liabilities	(2,000,000)	(2,000,000)	—	—
	$2,000,000	$1,000,000	$1,000,000	$ 700,000
Goodwill				400,000
Total Purchase Premium				$1,100,000

The straight-line method will be used to depreciate the write-up of the various assets over ten years and the goodwill over forty years. Consolidating the balance sheets of S and T at December 31, 19X3, requires the following combined working paper entry:

CONSOLIDATED FINANCIAL STATEMENT WORKING PAPER

Various Assets—T	700,000	
Goodwill	400,000	
Stockholders' Equity—T	1,000,000	
Investment in T		1,800,000
Minority Interest in T		300,000

To allocate the purchase premium, eliminate the Investment in T against the stockholders' equity of T, and establish the minority interest in T as of December 31, 19X3.

During 19X4, S and T report income from their own operations and make dividend payments as follows:

	Year Ended December 31, 19X4	
	S Company	T Company
Net Income from Own Operations	$1,200,000	$500,000
Dividends Declared and Paid	400,000	200,000

S Company's equity method accrual is computed in the following schedule:

S Company and T Company
Schedule to Determine the Equity Method Accrual
For the Year Ended December 31, 19X4

S's Share of T's Net Income (.7 × $500,000)	$350,000
Less Amortization of Purchase Premium:	
Additional Depreciation ($700,000/10)	$ 70,000
Amortization of Goodwill ($400,000/40)	10,000
Total Amortization	$ 80,000
Net Equity Method Accrual for 19X4	$270,000

Therefore, at December 31, 19X4, S's Investment in T account has a balance of $1,930,000 (= $1,800,000 + $270,000 − $140,000), reflecting the $140,000 (= .7 × $200,000) of T's dividends received by S. Condensed balance sheet data at December 31, 19X4, for companies S and T are given here:

Balance Sheet Data as of December 31, 19X4

	S Company		T Company	
	Book Value	Fair Value	Book Value	Fair Value
Various Assets .	$ 9,200,000	$10,000,000	$3,600,000	$5,000,000
Investment in T .	1,930,000	—	—	—
Total . .	$11,130,000		$3,600,000	

	S Company		T Company	
	Book Value	Fair Value	Book Value	Fair Value
Liabilities . . .	$ 6,060,000	4,500,000	$2,300,000	2,300,000
Stockholders' Equity . . .	5,070,000	—	1,300,000	—
Total . .	$11,130,000		$3,600,000	

S Company's stockholders' equity of $5,070,000 consists of the $4,000,000 balance at December 31, 19X3, plus S's 19X4 net income from its own operations of $1,200,000 plus the 19X4 equity method accrual of $270,000 minus dividends paid during 19X4 of $400,000.

P Acquires S   On December 31, 19X4, P Company acquires an 80 percent interest in S Company for $7,200,000 cash. Since the book value of S Company's stockholders' equity is $5,070,000, a purchase premium of $3,144,000 [= $7,200,000 − .8($5,070,000)] was paid for the 80 percent interest. In analyzing the acquisition of S, P's management may also have considered the differences between fair and book values of the assets and liabilities of T Company. Therefore, we have two alternative approaches to analyzing and allocating the purchase premium paid to acquire the 80 percent interest in S.

Allocate Only to S   Allocation of the purchase premium among the assets (except the Investment in T) and liabilities of S and goodwill yields the following results:

Allocation of Purchase Premium Paid
When P Acquires 80 Percent of S at December 31, 19X4 (Fair Value of T Ignored)

Assets and Liabilities of S Company	Fair Value	Book Value	Fair Value Less Book Value	Allocation Based on P's Interest (80%)
Various Assets	$10,000,000	$9,200,000	$ 800,000	$ 640,000
Liabilities	(4,500,000)	(6,060,000)	1,560,000	1,248,000
	$ 5,500,000	$3,140,000	$2,360,000	$1,888,000
Goodwill				1,256,000
Total Purchase Premium				$3,144,000

This procedure leaves the Investment in T undisturbed and, if a consolidated balance sheet were prepared immediately, the various assets of S would be increased by $640,000, the liabilities decreased by $1,248,000, and goodwill increased by $1,256,000. Allocation of S's purchase premium in T will, as before, result in an increase of $700,000 in T's assets and $400,000 in goodwill before deduction of the $80,000 amortization expense for the current year.

Allocate to S and T   Using the alternative approach, we would first allocate the purchase premium to the assets and liabilities of S, in accordance with the 80 percent interest owned by P. Any remaining purchase premium would then be allocated among the assets and liabilities of T and goodwill. The portion of P's purchase premium attributable to the increase in fair value of S's 70 percent interest in T is transferred from the Investment in S account to the Investment in T account on the working paper. The previous allocation left us with $1,256,000 in goodwill. After the allocation shown next, in which an additional $350,000 is allocated to the identifiable assets of T Company, only $906,000 remains as goodwill.

Allocation of Purchase Premium Paid
When P Acquires 80 Percent of S at December 31, 19X4 (Fair Value of T Recognized)

Assets and Liabilities of T Company	Fair Value	Book Value	Fair Value Less Book Value	Allocation Based on S's Interest (70%)
Various Assets . .	$5,000,000	$3,600,000	$1,400,000	$ 980,000
Liabilities	(2,300,000)	(2,300,000)	—	—
	$2,700,000	$1,300,000	$1,400,000	$ 980,000

Amount Already Included in Investment in T ($700,000 − $70,000 Depreciation)	(630,000)
Write-Up of Investment in T	$ 350,000
Amount Attributed to Undervaluation of S Company's Assets and Liabilities .	1,888,000
Goodwill Included in Price Paid by P	906,000
Total Purchase Premium	$3,144,000

If in fact the price paid for the interest in S reflected a premium attributable to the undervalued net assets of T, then allocating the total premium to S and T would best reflect the facts. Nevertheless, some accountants would prefer to allocate the entire amount to S on the grounds that there is only *indirect evidence* in support of the needed revaluations of T's assets and liabilities. In other words, it may be very difficult to determine whether the excess premium represents purchased goodwill or recognition of undervalued net assets held by T. We do not share this view; careful estimates of the fair values of T's assets and liabilities should be as reliable as those made for the assets and liabilities of S.

We illustrate the preparation of consolidated balance sheets of P, S, and T on a working paper prepared for this purpose in Exhibit 11.3. Balance sheet data for P Company are assumed and are independent of other examples. Note that S's purchase premium in T is dependent upon the allocation of P's purchase premium in S. To facilitate consolidation, the purchase premiums should be dealt with early in the consolidation process, and the allocation of P's purchase premium in S should precede allocation of S's purchase premium in T.

Consolidating the Income Statements in an Indirect Holding   Consolidation of income statements in the case of an indirect holding is not complicated by special problems, but the order in which working paper adjustments affecting income statement items are made is important. At year-end, S Company will determine and book its equity method accrual from T. S's share of T's reported net income will be adjusted by any purchase premium amortization and unconfirmed intercompany profits. Once this is accomplished, P's equity method accrual from S—which will reflect P's share of S's equity accrual from T—can be computed and booked by P Company.

Moving to the consolidated financial statement working papers, note that the effects of any working paper entries to remove unconfirmed intercompany profits from the income of T affect the minority interest in T's net income. Similarly, since S Company's stockholders own a portion of T's income, working paper adjustments to T's income also affect the minority interest in S Company's net income. Hence working paper entries affecting the income statement items of S and T normally precede entries affecting the income statement items of P and S.

Consolidation of S and T on the working paper is outlined in the following steps. Subsequent consolidation of P and S is handled in the usual way on the same working paper.

1. Reverse the equity method entries, thereby adjusting the Investment in T to its beginning-of-year balance.

2. Eliminate any intercompany revenues, expenses, and unconfirmed profits from the appropriate income statement and balance sheet accounts.

3. If P's acquisition of S called for further revaluation of T Company's assets and liabilities, adjust the Investment in T by removing the amount of P's purchase premium attributable to T from the Investment in S [see entry (1) in Exhibit 11.3].

4. Reclassify and allocate the purchase premium—as adjusted in item 3 —among the assets and liabilities of T Company.

5. Record the purchase premium amortization for the year.

6. Eliminate the Investment in T against the stockholders' equity of T Company and establish the minority interest in T, all as of the beginning of the year.

7. Record the minority's share of T Company's adjusted net income and eliminate the minority's share of T Company's dividends.

Mutual Holdings

Mutual holdings arise when one or more subsidiaries own stock in the parent or in each other. Those ownership relationships are also known as **bilateral** or **reciprocal holdings.** None of the affiliates' shares held by other members of the group are treated as outstanding in the consolidated balance sheet. Although this consolidated result is achieved in all mutual holding situations, acceptable alternative treatments can lead to different consolidated statements when a partially-owned subsidiary owns some of the parent's stock.

We now analyze consolidation of the four basic mutual holding configurations, beginning with those situations in which no minority interest is present.

Exhibit 11.3   Consolidated Balance Sheet Working Paper

P Company, S Company, and T Company
Consolidated Balance Sheet Working Paper, December 31, 19X4

	P Company	S Company	T Company	Adjustments and Eliminations Dr.	Adjustments and Eliminations Cr.	P, S, and T Consolidated
ASSETS						
Various Assets	30,000,000	9,200,000	3,600,000	(3) 980,000 (6) 640,000		44,420,000
Investment in S (80%) . . .	7,200,000	—	—		(1) 350,000 (5) 2,794,000 (7) 4,056,000	—
Investment in T (70%) . . .		1,930,000	—	(1) 350,000	(2) 1,370,000 (4) 910,000	—
Purchase Premium—T . . .				(2) 1,370,000	(3) 1,370,000	—
Purchase Premium—S . . .				(5) 2,794,000	(6) 2,794,000	—
Goodwill				(3) 390,000 (6) 906,000		1,296,000
Total Assets	37,200,000	11,130,000	3,600,000			45,716,000
LIABILITIES AND STOCKHOLDERS' EQUITY						
Liabilities	12,000,000	6,060,000	2,300,000	(6) 1,248,000		19,112,000
Stockholders' Equity—P . .	25,200,000					25,200,000
Stockholders' Equity—S . .		5,070,000		(7) 5,070,000		—
Stockholders' Equity—T . .			1,300,000	(4) 1,300,000		—
Minority Interest in S . .		—			(7) 1,014,000	1,014,000
Minority Interest in T . .		—	—		(4) 390,000	390,000
Total Liabilities and Stockholders' Equity . .	37,200,000	11,130,000	3,600,000	15,048,000	15,048,000	45,716,000

Explanations of Working Paper Entries

(1) To increase Investment in T by amount of P's purchase premium in S attributable to T.

(2) To reclassify purchase premium related to T; $1,020,000 (= $1,100,000 − $80,000) of the $1,370,000 is the unamortized portion of the purchase premium paid by S; $350,000 is S's share (70 percent) of the further increase in the fair value of T's assets imputed from P's investment in S.

(3) To allocate the total purchase premium related to T; the $980,000 allocated to various assets consists of the original $700,000 less one year's depreciation of $70,000 plus the $350,000 imputed from P's investment in S; the balance is unamortized goodwill.

(4) To eliminate the Investment in T against the stockholders' equity of T and establish the Minority Interest in T; $390,000 = .3($1,300,000).

(5) To reclassify the purchase premium attributable to P's investment in S; $2,794,000 = $3,144,000 − $350,000.

(6) To allocate the portion of P's purchase premium related to the investment in S to the assets and liabilities of S Company and to goodwill.

(7) To eliminate the Investment in S against the stockholders' equity of S and establish the Minority Interest in S; $1,014,000 = .2($5,070,000).

Parent and Subsidiary: No Minority Interest   In the first mutual holding case we consider, the subsidiary is wholly owned. This case is diagrammed below; it is the simplest because there is no minority interest.

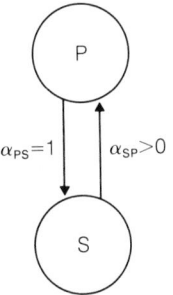

The treatment in consolidation is straightforward and follows from the facts of the case. *First*, the shares of P owned by S are, in consolidation, held internally. Hence they are treated as *treasury shares* by reclassifying the Investment in P as Treasury Stock on the consolidated financial statement working paper. Note that, had the parent reacquired the shares instead of the subsidiary, the same result would be achieved.

Second, P owns all of the shares of S, and thus all of S Company's earnings accrue to the controlling interest, the shareholders of P. Therefore, even though S Company owns some of P's shares, and conceptually S's net income should include a pro rata share of P's net income under the equity method, any attempt at allocation would be unnecessary and superfluous. For these reasons, the Investment in P should be carried at *cost*, not equity, on S Company's books. Intercompany dividends received by S would be recorded as dividend income and would be eliminated against P's Dividends account on the working papers. To illustrate this case, consider the following situation.

On January 1, 19X1, P acquired all of S Company's outstanding shares for $340,000. One day later, S Company acquired 20 percent of P's outstanding shares at a cost of $150,000. There were purchase premiums involved in both cases, as shown at the top of page 456.

	P Company	S Company
Cost of Investment in	$150,000	$340,000
Retained Earnings, January 1, 19X1	$400,000	$200,000
Capital Stock, January 1, 19X1	200,000	100,000
Total Stockholders' Equity, January 1, 19X1 . . .	$600,000	$300,000
α_{SP}	.20	—
α_{PS}	—	1.00
Purchase Premium	$ 30,000 [a]	$ 40,000 [b]

[a]$30,000 = $150,000 − .2($600,000).
[b]$40,000 = $340,000 − 1($300,000).

Since the shares of P held by S are considered to be treasury stock in consolidation, the purchase premium of $30,000 paid by S remains as part of the cost of the treasury stock and is not allocated and amortized. We assume that the purchase premium of $40,000 paid by P is entirely attributable to goodwill, which will be amortized over forty years.

For the year ended December 31, 19X1, P and S reported the following summary data:

	P Company	S Company
Income from Own Operations	$131,000	$75,000
Dividends Paid	80,000	20,000
Intercompany Merchandise Sales	40,000	—
Unconfirmed Profit in Ending Inventory . . .	—	5,000

The equity method accrual made at December 31, 19X1, by P Company was $69,000, as shown in the following schedule:

P Company and S Company
Schedule to Compute the Equity Method Accrual
For the Year Ended December 31, 19X1

P's Share of S's Net Income from Its Own Operations (1 × $75,000) .	$75,000
Less Amortization of Purchase Premium (Goodwill, $40,000/40) . .	(1,000)
Less P's Unconfirmed Intercompany Inventory Profit	(5,000)
Net Equity Method Accrual	$69,000

Consolidation of P and S at December 31, 19X1, is given in the working paper displayed in Exhibit 11.4. Detailed balance sheet and income statement data are assumed. Note that the balance of $389,000 in the Investment in S account reflects original cost of $340,000 plus the equity method accrual of $69,000 less S Company's dividends of $20,000.

Connecting Affiliates: No Minority Interest   In a situation involving **connecting affiliates** with no minority interest, there are two subsidiaries controlled by the same parent company, and each owns some of the other subsidiary's shares. None of the parent's shares are held by the subsidiaries.

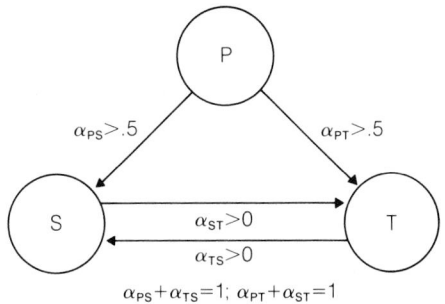

$$\alpha_{PS}+\alpha_{TS}=1; \; \alpha_{PT}+\alpha_{ST}=1$$

The *treasury stock* interpretation is not relevant here, since none of the parent's shares are held by the subsidiaries and, in consolidation, all of the subsidiaries' paid-in capital is eliminated. Hence only the parent's outstanding common stock appears on the consolidated balance sheet. Since there is no minority interest (that is, $\alpha_{PS} + \alpha_{TS} = 1$; $\alpha_{PT} + \alpha_{ST} = 1$), all of the subsidiaries' earnings accrue to P, the controlling interest, and no allocation of these earnings is required. The subsidiaries' investments in each other are carried at *cost*, and intercompany dividends are eliminated in consolidation by debiting Dividend Revenue and crediting Dividends—S and Dividends—T on the working paper.

It would not be unusual if the amount paid by one subsidiary to acquire the shares of another reflected a purchase premium or discount. Any such purchase premium or discount must be reclassified, allocated, and amortized in consolidation, *just as if the parent company had acquired the shares directly.* Again, we argue that substance should govern rather than form; it makes no difference whether the parent or a subsidiary acquires the shares. A numerical example follows.

Suppose that P Company acquired 80 percent of the shares of S and 70 percent of the shares of T on January 2, 19X2. Two years later, on January 2, 19X4, S acquired the remaining 30 percent of T's shares, and T acquired the remaining 20 percent of S's shares. Details of the acquisitions are as follows:

	S Company	T Company
Price Paid by P on January 2, 19X2, to Acquire		
Shares of	$530,000	$400,000
Book Value of P's Share of Net Assets . . .	400,000 (80%)	350,000 (70%)
Purchase Premium Paid by P to Acquire . .	$130,000	$ 50,000
Price Paid by S on January 2, 19X4, for		
Remaining Shares of	—	$200,000
Price Paid by T on January 2, 19X4, for		
Remaining Shares of	$300,000	—
Book Value of Remaining Share of Net Assets at		
January 2, 19X4	220,000 (20%)	192,000 (30%)
Purchase Premium Paid on January 2, 19X4 .	$ 80,000	$ 8,000

Exhibit 11.4   Consolidated Financial Statement Working Paper

P Company and S Company
Consolidated Financial Statement Working Paper
For the Year Ended December 31, 19X1

	P Company (20%)	S Company (100%)	Adjustments and Eliminations Dr.	Adjustments and Eliminations Cr.	Consolidated
INCOME STATEMENT					
Sales	800,000	300,000	(3) 40,000		1,060,000
Income from S	69,000	—	(1) 69,000		—
Dividend Revenue	—	16,000	(2) 16,000		—
Inventory, December 31,19X1	120,000	40,000	(4) 5,000		155,000
Total Credits	989,000	356,000	130,000		1,215,000
Inventory, January 1, 19X1	100,000	35,000			135,000
Purchases	400,000	140,000		(3) 40,000	500,000
Operating Expenses	289,000	90,000	(8) 1,000		380,000
Total Debits	789,000	265,000	1,000	40,000	1,015,000
Net Income—to Ret. Earn. Stmt.	200,000	91,000	131,000	40,000	200,000
RETAINED EARNINGS STATEMENT					
Ret. Earnings, Jan. 1, 19X1—P	400,000	—			400,000
Ret. Earnings, Jan. 1, 19X1—S	—	200,000	(6) 200,000		—
Net Income—from Income Stmt.	200,000	91,000	131,000	40,000	200,000
Dividends—P	(80,000)	—		(2) 16,000	(64,000)
Dividends—S	—	(20,000)		(1) 20,000	—
Ret. Earnings, Dec. 31, 19X1— to Balance Sheet	520,000	271,000	331,000	76,000	536,000
BALANCE SHEET					
Cash and Receivables	241,000	116,000			357,000
Inventory	120,000	40,000		(4) 5,000	155,000
Investment in S (100%)	389,000	—		(1) 49,000	—
				(6) 340,000	
Investment in P (20%)	—	150,000		(5) 150,000	—
Land	100,000	75,000			175,000
Buildings and Equipment	380,000	180,000			560,000
Accumulated Depreciation	(100,000)	(20,000)			(120,000)
Purchase Premium	—	—	(6) 40,000	(7) 40,000	—
Goodwill	—	—	(7) 40,000	(8) 1,000	39,000
Total	1,130,000	541,000	80,000	585,000	1,166,000
Current Liabilities	200,000	75,000			275,000
Other Liabilities	210,000	95,000			305,000
Treasury Stock	—	—	(5) 150,000		(150,000)
Capital Stock—P	200,000	—			200,000
Capital Stock—S	—	100,000	(6) 100,000		—
Ret. Earn.—from Ret. Earn. Stmt.	520,000	271,000	331,000	76,000	536,000
Minority Interest in S	—	—			—
Total	1,130,000	541,000	581,000	76,000	1,166,000
			661,000	661,000	

Explanations of Working Paper Entries
(1) To eliminate the equity method entries made by P in 19X1.
(2) To eliminate intercompany dividends received by S.
(3) To eliminate intercompany merchandise sales.
(4) To eliminate unconfirmed intercompany profit in ending inventory.
(5) To reclassify the Investment in P as Treasury Stock.
(6) To eliminate the Investment in S and establish the unamortized purchase premium.
(7) To allocate the unamortized purchase premium at January 1, 19X1.
(8) To record amortization of the purchase premium for 19X1.

All purchase premiums are assumed attributable to land and are not amortized. During 19X4, the only intercompany transactions involved the payment of dividends; net income and dividend activity for 19X4 are summarized below.

	P Company	S Company	T Company
Income from Own Operations	$300,000	$180,000	$140,000
Dividends Paid	200,000	100,000	40,000

The consolidated financial statement working paper for the year ended December 31, 19X4, is given in Exhibit 11.5. The detailed financial statement data are assumed. Note an unusual feature of this working paper. The net income and ending retained earnings of P are *not equal* to the consolidated amounts. This happens for two reasons. First, the subsidiaries' investments in each other are carried on the cost basis, meaning that their respective incomes do not include equity accruals. Second, P's equity accruals are based only on its share of the subsidiaries' incomes from their own operations. Since P owns all of the subsidiaries' shares, directly or indirectly, consolidated net income includes the total income of all three affiliates from their separate operations. The working paper properly reflects this fact. Alternative approaches to consolidating P, S, and T given this affiliate relationship do exist but have not been utilized in our example. In the following paragraphs, we briefly explain each of these alternative approaches.

Alternative 1   Allocate the subsidiaries' income among them in order to provide them with equity method accruals, and base P's equity method accrual on the reported net incomes of the subsidiaries, which now include their shares of each other's income. This is the so-called **traditional allocation method** and is equivalent to accounting for the subsidiaries' investments in each other on the *equity* rather than the *cost* basis. This allocation method is used in later examples where mutual holdings have minority interests present. Using this alternative, the net income and ending retained earnings of P will equal the consolidated amounts.

Alternative 2   Continue to account for the subsidiaries' investments in each other on the cost method, but base P's equity accruals on the *total* subsidiaries' incomes from their own operations, excluding intercompany dividend revenue. This approach also makes P's income and ending retained earnings equal to the corresponding consolidated amounts.

Exhibit 11.5   Consolidated Financial Statement Working Paper

P Company and Subsidiaries S Company and T Company
Consolidated Financial Statement Working Paper
For the Year Ended December 31, 19X4

	P Company	S Company (80%, 20%)	T Company (70%, 30%)	Adjustments and Eliminations Dr.		Adjustments and Eliminations Cr.		Consolidated
INCOME STATEMENT								
Sales	1,000,000	600,000	400,000					2,000,000
Income from S (= .8 × 180,000)	144,000	—	—	(1)	144,000			—
Income from T (= .7 × 140,000)	98,000	—	—	(2)	98,000			—
Dividend Revenue . .	—	12,000	20,000	(3)	12,000			—
				(4)	20,000			
Inventory, Dec. 31, 19X4 .	150,000	110,000	80,000					340,000
Total Credits . . .	1,392,000	722,000	500,000		274,000			2,340,000
Inventory, Jan. 1, 19X4 .	160,000	105,000	83,000					348,000
Purchases	500,000	300,000	200,000					1,000,000
Operating Expenses . .	190,000	125,000	57,000					372,000
Total Debits . . .	850,000	530,000	340,000					1,720,000
Net Inc.—to Ret. Earn. Stmt.	542,000	192,000	160,000		274,000			620,000
RETAINED EARNINGS STATEMENT								
Ret. Earn., Jan. 1, 19X4—P	2,600,000	—	—					2,600,000
Ret. Earn., Jan. 1, 19X4—S	—	800,000	—	(7)	640,000			—
				(8)	160,000			
Ret. Earn., Jan. 1, 19X4—T	—	—	390,000	(9)	273,000			—
				(10)	117,000			
Net Inc.—from Inc. Stmt. .	542,000	192,000	160,000		274,000			620,000
Dividends—P . . .	(200,000)	—	—					(200,000)
Dividends—S . . .	—	(100,000)	—	(1)		80,000		—
				(4)		20,000		
Dividends—T . . .	—	—	(40,000)	(2)		28,000		—
				(3)		12,000		
Ret. Earn., Dec. 31, 19X4— to Balance Sheet . .	2,942,000	892,000	510,000		1,464,000		140,000	3,020,000
BALANCE SHEET								
Inventory	150,000	110,000	80,000					340,000
Other Assets	2,368,000	952,000	490,000					3,810,000
P's Investment in S (80%)	1,074,000	—	—			(1)	64,000	—
						(5)	130,000	
						(7)	880,000	
T's Investment in S (20%)	—	—	300,000			(5)	80,000	—
						(8)	220,000	
P's Investment in T (70%)	568,000	—	—			(2)	70,000	—
						(5)	50,000	
						(9)	448,000	
S's Investment in T (30%)	—	200,000	—			(5)	8,000	—
						(10)	192,000	
Land	450,000	330,000	180,000	(6)	268,000			1,228,000
Purchase Premium . .	—	—	—	(5)	268,000	(6)	268,000	—
Total	4,610,000	1,592,000	1,050,000		536,000		2,410,000	5,378,000
Liabilities	1,168,000	400,000	290,000					1,858,000
Capital Stock—P . .	500,000	—	—					500,000
Capital Stock—S . .	—	300,000	—	(7)	240,000			—
				(8)	60,000			
Capital Stock—T . . .	—	—	250,000	(9)	175,000			—
Ret. Earn.—from Ret. Earn. Stmt. . . .	2,942,000	892,000	510,000	(10)	75,000			
					1,464,000		140,000	3,020,000
Total	4,610,000	1,592,000	1,050,000		2,014,000		140,000	5,378,000
					2,550,000		2,550,000	

Explanations of Working Paper Entries
 (1) To eliminate the equity method entries made by P in connection with its investment in S during 19X4.
 (2) To eliminate the equity method entries made by P in connection with its investment in T during 19X4.
 (3) To eliminate intercompany dividends received by S from T.
 (4) To eliminate intercompany dividends received by T from S.
 (5) To reclassify the purchase premiums reflected in the intercompany investments.
 (6) To allocate the purchase premium entirely to land.
 (7) To eliminate P's investment in S.
 (8) To eliminate T's investment in S.
 (9) To eliminate P's investment in T.
(10) To eliminate S's investment in T.

Alternative 3 Continue to account for the subsidiaries' investments in each other on the cost method, but base P's equity accruals on the reported net incomes of the subsidiaries, including intercompany dividend income. P's net income and ending retained earnings will not equal the consolidated amounts *unless* the subsidiaries distribute all the income from their own operations in the form of dividends.

We believe that our approach conforms with proper use of the equity and cost methods and is the simplest to apply. Under our approach, the subsidiaries' investments in each other are carried at cost, and P's equity accruals are based only on P's share of the subsidiaries' income from their own operations. Nevertheless, any of these alternatives is acceptable when there is no minority interest. In consolidation, all three approaches yield identical results *and* P's shareholders will receive only the consolidated reports, not P's separate statements.

Parent and Subsidiary: Minority Interest Is Present The following diagram of the affiliation relationship indicates that, although the parent controls the subsidiary, the subsidiary is not wholly owned.

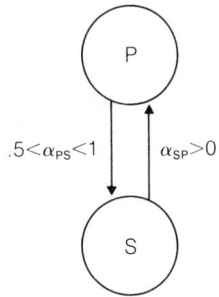

As previously indicated, shares of the parent held by a subsidiary are not to be treated as outstanding in the consolidated balance sheet. The cost of such shares is eliminated or reclassified as treasury stock on the working paper, depending on the context. We have seen that when no minority interest is present, it is convenient to carry the subsidiary's investment in the parent at *cost* and simply eliminate the subsidiary's intercompany dividend revenue and any other intercompany transactions on the working paper.

In the present case, however, existence of a minority interest in the subsidiary can complicate the consolidation process when income statement data are consolidated. Two alternative acceptable approaches are found in practice; each normally leads to different consolidated results.

Treasury Stock Method   The **treasury stock method** is simply an extension of the treasury stock approach encountered when there is no minority interest present. It is supported by an early position taken by the American Accounting Association:

> Shares of the controlling company's capital stock owned by a subsidiary should be treated in consolidation as treasury stock. Any subsequent acquisition or sale by a subsidiary should likewise be treated in the consolidated statements as though it had been the act of the controlling company.[6]

Under this approach, the minority interest in the subsidiary's net income includes a pro rata share of any dividend revenue from the parent. The intercompany dividends are, of course, eliminated on the working paper, but the minority interest in net income is based on the subsidiary's reported net income, which reflects the intercompany dividend revenue. In applying the equity method, the parent company accrues its share of the subsidiary's net income from its own operations excluding the minority share of intercompany dividend revenue. An identical result is achieved by determining the parent's share of the subsidiary's reported net income and then subtracting all the intercompany dividend revenue.

To illustrate, suppose P owns 90 percent of S ($\alpha_{PS} = .9$), and S owns 10 percent of P ($\alpha_{SP} = .1$). P and S had net incomes from their own operations of $131,000 and $75,000, respectively. During the year, P paid $80,000 in dividends and S paid $20,000. The following schedule shows how the equity method accrual is determined:

P Company and S Company
Schedule to Compute the Equity Method Accrual

P's Share of S's Net Income from Its Own Operations (.9 × $75,000) .	$67,500
Less Minority's Share of P's Dividends Received by S (.1 × $8,000) .	(800)
Net Equity Method Accrual	$66,700

OR

P's Share of S's Reported Net Income [.9($75,000 + $8,000)] . .	$74,700
Less Intercompany Dividends Received by S (.1 × $80,000) . .	(8,000)
Net Equity Method Accrual	$66,700

Under this approach, consolidated net income is $197,700 (= $131,000 + $66,700), and the minority interest in S Company's net income is $8,300 [= .1 × ($75,000 + $8,000)] for a total of $206,000 (= $131,000 + $75,000).

---

[6] Committee on Accounting Concepts and Standards, *Accounting and Reporting Standards for Corporate Financial Statements* (Columbus: AAA, 1957), p. 44.

Traditional Allocation Method The **traditional allocation method** involves application of the equity method to *both* P and S. Hence the combined earnings of P and S from their own operations must be allocated between the two companies and, subsequently, between the controlling and minority interests. P's total earnings under the equity method depend in part on S's earnings. But because S owns some of P's shares, S's earnings (and the minority interest in S's earnings) also depend on P's earnings. Thus the earnings of P and S are interdependent (and the relationship is circular in nature) because each is influenced by the other.

Proper allocation of combined earnings between the controlling and minority interests calls for computation of the net incomes of P and S on an equity basis. Determination of these equity basis incomes is facilitated by the use of simultaneous equations which take into account the interdependence between P and S. The following general relationships are used:

$P^* = $ P Company's net income on an equity basis.

$S^* = $ S Company's net income on an equity basis.

$Y_P = $ Net income of P from its own operations.

$Y_S = $ Net income of S from its own operations.

$\alpha_{PS} = $ Percentage of S's shares owned by P.

$\alpha_{SP} = $ Percentage of P's shares owned by S.

We can express P* and S* as follows.

$$P^* = Y_P + \alpha_{PS}S^* \text{ and } S^* = Y_S + \alpha_{SP}P^*.$$

Note that $(P^* + S^*) > (Y_P + Y_S)$ because some income is double counted. The solutions, denoted P^* and S^*, are *tentative* and will be reduced to reflect the controlling and minority interest in these equity basis incomes. By substitution, we have

$$P^* = Y_P + \alpha_{PS}(Y_S + \alpha_{SP}P^*)$$

$$(1 - \alpha_{PS}\alpha_{SP})P^* = Y_P + \alpha_{PS}Y_S$$

$$\boxed{P^* = \frac{Y_P + \alpha_{PS}Y_S}{(1 - \alpha_{PS}\alpha_{SP})}}, \text{ and}$$

$$S^* = Y_S + \alpha_{SP}(Y_P + \alpha_{PS}S^*)$$

$$(1 - \alpha_{SP}\alpha_{PS})S^* = Y_S + \alpha_{SP}Y_P$$

$$\boxed{S^* = \frac{Y_S + \alpha_{SP}Y_P}{(1 - \alpha_{SP}\alpha_{PS})}}$$

Since α_{SP} of P's shares are owned by S, only $(1 - \alpha_{SP})$ of P^*, P Company's net income on an equity basis, pertains to the controlling interest. Similarly, since α_{PS} of S's shares are owned by the controlling interest, only $(1 - \alpha_{PS})$ of S^*, S Company's net income on an equity basis, pertains to the minority interest.

Using the facts from our last example, suppose P owns 90 percent of S ($\alpha_{PS} = .9$) and S owns 10 percent of P ($\alpha_{SP} = .1$). The net incomes of P and S from their own operations, Y_P and Y_S, respectively, are \$131,000 and \$75,000.

P^* = P Company's net income on an equity basis.
S^* = S Company's net income on an equity basis.

$$P^* = \frac{\$131,000 + .9(\$75,000)}{[1 - (.9)(.1)]} = \frac{\$198,500}{.91} = \boxed{\$218,132.}$$

$$S^* = \frac{\$75,000 + .1(\$131,000)}{[1 - (.1)(.9)]} = \frac{\$88,100}{.91} = \boxed{\$96,813.}$$

Note that $(P^* + S^*) = \$314,945$, while the net incomes of P and S from their own operations total \$206,000 (= \$131,000 + \$75,000). Since the total of the income shares attributable to the controlling and minority interests *must equal* \$206,000, we adjust P^* and S^* as follows:

P Company's Net Income on an Equity Basis (P*)	\$218,132
Less Amount Attributable to S (.1 × \$218,132)	21,813
Controlling Interest's Share of Combined Income	\$196,319 [a]
S Company's Net Income on an Equity Basis (S*)	\$ 96,813
Less Amount Attributable to P (.9 × \$96,813)	87,132
Minority Interest's Share of Combined Income	\$ 9,681 [b]
Combined Net Incomes of P and S from Their Own Operations	\$206,000

[a]$(1 - \alpha_{SP}) = (1 - .1) = .9$; $\$196,319 = .9(\$218,132)$.
[b]$(1 - \alpha_{PS}) = (1 - .9) = .1$; $\$9,681 = .1(\$96,813)$.

Consider the equity method accruals which now will be recorded by both companies. First we consider P's equity method accrual.

P Company and S Company
Schedule to Compute P Company's Equity Method Accrual
$(\alpha_{PS} = .9; \alpha_{SP} = .1)$

P's Share of S Company's Equity Basis Net Income	
(.9 × \$96,813)	\$ 87,132
Less S Company's Share of P's Equity Basis Net Income	
(.1 × \$218,132)	(21,813)
Net Equity Method Accrual Made by P	\$ 65,319

OR

Controlling Interest's Share of Combined Income	\$196,319
Less P Company's Income from Its Own Operations	131,000
Net Equity Method Accrual Made by P	\$ 65,319

We now give the entries made by P to record the dividends received from S during the year and the equity method accrual:

BOOKS OF P COMPANY

Cash 18,000
    Investment in S 18,000
To record intercompany dividends received from S;
$18,000 (= .9 × $20,000).

Investment in S 65,319
    Income from S 65,319
To record income from S accrued under the equity
method.

The equity method accrual for S Company equals $21,813 as shown in the following schedule.

P Company and S Company
Schedule to Compute S's Equity Method Accrual
$(\alpha_{PS} = .9; \alpha_{SP} = .1)$

S's Share of P's Equity Basis Net Income (.1 × $218,132) . . . $21,813

OR

S's Equity Basis Net Income $96,813
Less S Company's Income from Its Own Operations 75,000
Net Equity Method Accrual Made by S $21,813

Entries made during the year by S Company to record the dividends received from P and the equity method accrual are given below:

BOOKS OF S COMPANY

Cash 8,000
    Investment in P 8,000
To record intercompany dividends received from P;
$8,000 (= .1 × $80,000).

Investment in P 21,813
    Income from P 21,813
To record income from P accrued under the equity
method.

A Numerical Comparison   We now prepare working papers to contrast the *treasury stock* and *traditional allocation* methods to consolidate mutual holdings. On January 1, 19X1, P acquired 90 percent of S Company's stock for $306,000, while S acquired 10 percent of P Company's stock for $80,000. The book value of the S Company shares acquired was $270,000 (90 percent of the total book value of $300,000), while the 10 percent interest in P had a book value of $60,000. The purchase premium of $36,000 (= $306,000 − $270,000) paid by P is attributable to land. S Company also paid a purchase premium of $20,000 (= $80,000 − $60,000). Treatment of S Company's purchase premium in consolidation depends on the method being used.

    1.   Under the *treasury stock method*, the purchase premium is included in the Investment in P account, which is reclassified as Treasury Stock. The working paper reflecting this method appears in Exhibit 11.6.

Exhibit 11.6 Consolidated Financial Statement Working Paper (Treasury Stock Method)

P Company and S Company
Consolidated Financial Statement Working Paper For the Year Ended December 31, 19X1
(Treasury Stock Method)

	P Company (10%)	S Company (90%)	Adjustments and Eliminations Dr.	Adjustments and Eliminations Cr.	Consolidated
INCOME STATEMENT					
Sales	800,000	300,000			1,100,000
Income from S	66,700	—	(1) 66,700		—
Dividend Revenue	—	8,000	(2) 8,000		—
Inventory, December 31, 19X1	120,000	40,000			160,000
Total Credits	986,700	348,000	74,700		1,260,000
Inventory, January 1, 19X1	100,000	35,000			135,000
Purchases	400,000	140,000			540,000
Operating Expenses	289,000	90,000			379,000
Total Debits	789,000	265,000			1,054,000
Minority Interest in Net Income	—	—	(6) 8,300		8,300
Net Income—to Ret. Earn. Stmt.	197,700	83,000	83,000		197,700
RETAINED EARNINGS STATEMENT					
Ret. Earn., Jan. 1, 19X1—P	400,000	—			400,000
Ret. Earn., Jan. 1, 19X1—S	—	200,000	(4) 200,000		—
Net Inc.—from Inc. Stmt.	197,700	83,000	83,000		197,700
Dividends—P	(80,000)	—		(2) 8,000	(72,000)
Dividends—S	—	(20,000)		(1) 18,000	—
				(6) 2,000	
Ret. Earn., Dec. 31, 19X1—to					
Balance Sheet	517,700	263,000	283,000	28,000	525,700
BALANCE SHEET					
Cash and Receivables	273,000	178,000			451,000
Inventory	120,000	40,000			160,000
Investment in S (90%)	354,700			(1) 48,700	—
				(4) 306,000	
Investment in P (10%)		80,000		(3) 80,000	—
Land	100,000	75,000	(5) 36,000		211,000
Buildings and Equipment	380,000	180,000			560,000
Accumulated Depreciation	(100,000)	(20,000)			(120,000)
Purchase Premium			(4) 36,000	(5) 36,000	—
Total	1,127,700	533,000	72,000	470,700	1,262,000
Current Liabilities	200,000	75,000			275,000
Other Liabilities	210,000	95,000			305,000
Treasury Stock	—	—	(3) 80,000		(80,000)
Capital Stock—P	200,000	—			200,000
Capital Stock—S	—	100,000	(4) 100,000		—
Ret. Earn.—from Ret. Earn Stmt.	517,700	263,000	283,000	28,000	525,700
Minority Interest in S	—	—		(4) 30,000	36,300
				(6) 6,300	
Total	1,127,700	533,000	463,000	64,300	1,262,000
			535,000	535,000	

Explanations of Working Paper Entries
(1) To eliminate the equity method entries made by P in 19X1.
(2) To eliminate intercompany dividends received by S.
(3) To reclassify the Investment in P as Treasury Stock.
(4) To eliminate the Investment in S, establish the purchase premium and minority interest, all as of the beginning of the year.
(5) To allocate the unamortized purchase premium at 1/1/X1.
(6) To record the change in the minority interest in S during 19X1.

2. Under the *traditional allocation method,* the stock of P held by S is assumed to be *constructively retired.* Hence the Investment in P will be eliminated on the working paper against the stockholders' equity of P. Since the retirement of stock cannot generate gain or loss, the purchase premium is debited to P's Additional Paid-In Capital account. In our example, the caption "Capital Stock" includes the additional paid-in capital. This method is illustrated in a working paper presented in Exhibit 11.7.

We previously pointed out that the two methods lead to different amounts of consolidated net income. This can be seen clearly from the working papers. Note also that consolidated retained earnings differ under the two methods. This difference in consolidated retained earnings arises because (1) consolidated net income under each method differs and (2) the portion of P's retained earnings owned by S is eliminated in the traditional allocation method. Of somewhat lesser importance is the fact that consolidated paid-in capital is also affected by the method being used.

Authors' Conclusion We have observed that in a parent/subsidiary mutual holding situation, two acceptable alternative accounting treatments can lead to materially different results. In our example, consolidated retained earnings under the treasury stock method amounted to $525,700, or about $8^{1}/_{2}$ percent more than the $484,319 reported by the traditional allocation method. We conclude that the *treasury stock method* is more appropriate, for the following reasons:

1. From the standpoint of the controlling interest, any shares of P held by S have all of the characteristics of treasury stock.

2. Use of the equity method for S's investment in P seems improper in most situations. The entire equity method concept is based on the notion that the *investor* can exercise significant influence over the *investee.*[7] This will hardly be true in the present case, for P (the investee) *controls* S (the investor). Of course, one can conceive of circumstances in which the minority shareholders in S are also large holders of P's stock. In such a situation, the equity method—and the traditional allocation method—may well be appropriate.

---

[7] See Accounting Principles Board, *Opinion No. 18,* "The Equity Method of Accounting for Investments in Common Stock" (N.Y.: AICPA, 1971), par. 12; AC § 5131.12.

Exhibit 11.7 Consolidated Financial Statement Working Paper (Traditional Allocation Method)

P Company and S Company
Consolidated Financial Statement Working Paper For the Year Ended December 31. 19X1
(Traditional Allocation Method)

	P Company (10%)	S Company (90%)	Adjustments and Eliminations Dr.	Adjustments and Eliminations Cr.	Consolidated
INCOME STATEMENT					
Sales	800,000	300,000			1,100,000
Income from S	65,319	—	(1) 65,319		—
Income from P	—	21,813	(2) 21,813		—
Inventory, December 31, 19X1	120,000	40,000			160,000
Total Credits	985,319	361,813	87,132		1,260,000
Inventory, January 1, 19X1	100,000	35,000			135,000
Purchases	400,000	140,000			540,000
Operating Expenses	289,000	90,000			379,000
Total Debits	789,000	265,000			1,054,000
Minority Interest in Net Income	—	—	(6) 9,681		(9,681)
Net Inc.—to Ret. Earn. Stmt.	196,319	96,813	96,813		196,319
RETAINED EARNINGS STATEMENT					
Ret. Earn., Jan. 1, 19X1—P	400,000	—	(3) 40,000		360,000
Ret. Earn., Jan. 1, 19X1—S	—	200,000	(4) 200,000		—
Net Inc.—from Inc. Stmt.	196,319	96,813	96,813		196,319
Dividends—P	(80,000)	—		(2) 8,000	(72,000)
Dividends—S	—	(20,000)		(1) 18,000	—
				(6) 2,000	
Ret. Earn., Dec. 31, 19X1—to Balance Sheet	516,319	276,813	336,813	28,000	484,319
BALANCE SHEET					
Cash and Receivables	273,000	178,000			451,000
Inventory	120,000	40,000			160,000
Investment in S (90%)	353,319	—		(1) 47,319	—
				(4) 306,000	
Investment in P (10%)	—	93,813		(2) 13,813	—
				(3) 80,000	
Land	100,000	75,000	(5) 36,000		211,000
Buildings and Equipment	380,000	180,000			560,000
		(20,000)			(120,000)
Accumulated Depreciation	(100,000)				
Purchase Premium			(4) 36,000	(5) 36,000	—
Total	1,126,319	546,813	72,000	483,132	1,262,000
Current Liabilities	200,000	75,000			275,000
Other Liabilities	210,000	95,000			305,000
Capital Stock—P	200,000	—	(3) 40,000		160,000
Capital Stock—S	—	100,000	(4) 100,000		—
Ret. Earn.—from Ret. Earn. Stmt.	516,319	276,813	336,813	28,000	484,319
Minority Interest in S				(4) 30,000	37,681
				(6) 7,681	
Total	1,126,319	546,813	476,813	65,681	1,262,000
			548,813	548,813	

Explanations for Working Paper Entries

(1) To eliminate the equity method entries made by P in 19X1.
(2) To eliminate the equity method entries made by S in 19X1.
(3) To eliminate the Investment in P against the stockholders' equity of P. The implicit purchase premium of $20,000 is charged against the APIC of P which is included in Capital Stock—P.
(4) To eliminate the Investment in S, establish the purchase premium and minority interest, all as of the beginning of the year.
(5) To allocate the unamortized purchase premium to Land.
(6) To record the change in the minority interest in S during 19X1.

Connecting Affiliates: Minority Interest Is Present In the case diagrammed below (involving connecting affiliates and minority interest), we observe that, while the subsidiaries own some shares in each other, they do not hold any of the parent's shares. As a result, the treasury stock approach is not applicable, and the traditional allocation method must be used for S and T.

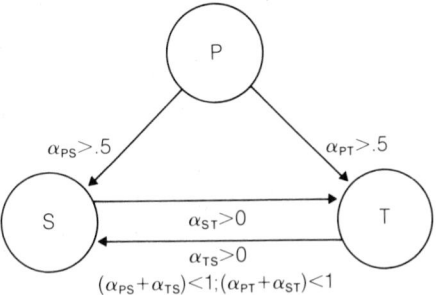

Notice that one could argue against use of the equity method by S and T on the grounds that their investments in each other are minimal compared to P Company's clear control over both subsidiaries. P's control over S and T, however, is reflected both by its *direct* interest in S and T and by its *indirect* interest in the subsidiaries' mutual holdings. Hence P's equity accrual and the controlling interest's share of total earnings are influenced by the circularity between S and T. Consider a numerical example.

All acquisitions of stock are assumed to have occurred at January 1, 19X1. We recognize that purchase premiums or discounts paid by S or T are treated as if the parent had made the acquisition, but, to simplify the analysis, we ignore these items in our example. Data for the example are summarized here:

	P Company	S Company	T Company
Interest in S Company	$\alpha_{PS} = .8$	—	$\alpha_{TS} = .1$
Interest in T Company	$\alpha_{PT} = .7$	$\alpha_{ST} = .2$	—
Net Income from Own Operations	$300,000	$180,000	$150,000
Dividends Paid	200,000	100,000	40,000
Intercompany Merchandise Sales	90,000	60,000	50,000
Unconfirmed Intercompany Inventory Profit in Net Income	8,000	10,000	5,000

Exhibit 11.8   Computation of Equity Method Accruals

P Company, S Company, and T Company
Schedule to Compute the Equity Method Accruals Made by P, S, and T
$(\alpha_{PS} = .8, \alpha_{PT} = .7, \alpha_{ST} = .2, \alpha_{TS} = .1)$

P COMPANY

P's Share of S Company's Equity Basis Net Income (.8 × $203,061)	$162,449
P's Share of T Company's Equity Basis Net Income (.7 × $165,306)	115,714
Less Unconfirmed Intercompany Profit Recorded by P	(8,000)
Net Equity Method Accrual Made by P Company	$270,163

S COMPANY

S's Share of T Company's Equity Basis Net Income (.2 × $165,306)	$ 33,061
Less Unconfirmed Intercompany Profit Recorded by S	(10,000)
Net Equity Method Accrual Made by S Company	$ 23,061

T COMPANY

T's Share of S Company's Equity Basis Net Income (.1 × $203,061)	$ 20,306
Less Unconfirmed Intercompany Profit Recorded by T	(5,000)
Net Equity Method Accrual Made by T Company	$ 15,306

Note: For P, $570,163 = $300,000 + $270,163; for S, $203,061 = $180,000 + $23,061; for T, $165,306 = $150,000 + $15,306.

We have included unconfirmed intercompany profits to show how they are handled under the traditional allocation method. As long as the treatment of intercompany profits set forth in this text is used (100 percent elimination, proportionately against the controlling and minority interests), these profits can be deducted directly from income from own operations before solving the simultaneous equations. We first solve for the equity basis incomes of S and T and then use these tentative solutions to compute P's equity method accrual and the minority interest in net income. Note the reductions made for unconfirmed intercompany profits.

$$S^* = (\$180,000 - \$10,000) + .2T^*.$$
$$T^* = (\$150,000 - \$5,000) + .1S^*.$$

$$S^* = \frac{\$170,000 + .2(\$145,000)}{[1 - (.2)(.1)]} = \frac{\$199,000}{.98} = \boxed{\$203,061.}$$

$$T^* = \frac{\$145,000 + .1(\$170,000)}{[1 - (.1)(.2)]} = \frac{\$162,000}{.98} = \boxed{\$165,306.}$$

Since P's net income from its own operations is $292,000 (= $300,000 − $8,000), total income to be allocated among the controlling and minority interests is $607,000 (= $292,000 + $170,000 + $145,000). This allocation is as follows:

P's Net Income on an Equity Basis (Consolidated Net Income); $292,000 + .8S*
    + .7T* = $292,000 + .8($203,061) + .7($165,306) . . . .
Minority Interest in Net Income of S; .1S* = .1($203,061)   20,306
Minority Interest in Net Income of T; .1T* = .1($165,306)   16,531
    Combined Net Income Less Unconfirmed Intercompany Profits $607,000

    Computation of the equity method accruals for the three companies is shown in Exhibit 11.8. A working paper to consolidate P, S, and T is presented in Exhibit 11.9. Detailed financial statement data are assumed.

Conclusion

This completes our study of consolidated financial statements. In Chapters 7–11, we have stressed substance over form and have been guided by the single entity concept. Although a group of affiliated corporations consists of several legal entities, the fact that the group is under common control creates a new accounting entity, an area of economic activity of interest to the controlling shareholders. Thus all transactions and other intercompany relationships between members of the affiliated group are eliminated in consolidation.

Summary of Key Concepts

When the parent achieves its controlling interest by a series of smaller purchases, the purchase premium or discount related to **each block of stock** must be determined and allocated among the assets and liabilities of S and to goodwill. To do so, the fair values of S's identifiable assets and liabilities at the dates the several blocks are acquired must be estimated.

Care must be taken to insure that **consistent accounting treatment** is afforded those various transactions in the **subsidiary's shares** that have **identical effects** on the economic position of the **controlling interest.** We believe that if the controlling interest's position is improved following the issue of additional shares by the subsidiary, a consolidated gain should be recognized just as if P had sold at a gain shares of S which P owned.

A new dimension of the problem of allocating a purchase premium arises when P acquires a company that **already** has its own subsidiary, T. In this type of **indirect holding,** the accountant is faced with the dilemma of whether to attribute some of P's purchase premium or discount in the acquisition of S to the assets and liabilities of T. If the fair values of T's assets and liabilities are to be considered in the purchase premium allocation, the premium is *first* allocated among the assets and liabilities of S. Any **remaining** unallocated premium, which otherwise would be classified as goodwill, is *then* allocated among the assets and liabilities of T.

A **mutual holding** arises when one or more subsidiaries own stock in the parent or in each other. Any shares of the parent held by a subsidiary are treated as **treasury stock** in consolidation. We believe that subsidiary investments in

Exhibit 11.9   Consolidated Financial Statement Working Paper

P Company, S Company, and T Company
Consolidated Financial Statement Working Paper for the Year
Ended December 31, 19X1

	P Company	S Company (80%, 10%)	T Company (70%, 20%)	Adjustments and Eliminations Dr.		Adjustments and Eliminations Cr.		Consolidated
INCOME STATEMENT								
Sales	1,000,000	600,000	400,000	(5)	200,000			1,800,000
P's Income from S . . .	154,449	—	—	(1)	154,449			—
P's Income from T . . .	115,714	—	—	(2)	115,714			—
S's Income from T . . .	—	23,061	—	(3)	23,061			—
T's Income from S . . .	—	—	15,306	(4)	15,306			—
Inventory, Dec. 31, 19X1 .	150,000	110,000	80,000	(6)	23,000			317,000
Total Credits . . .	1,420,163	733,061	495,306		531,530			2,117,000
Inventory, Jan. 1, 19X1 . .	160,000	105,000	83,000					348,000
Purchases	500,000	300,000	200,000			(5)	200,000	800,000
Operating Expenses . .	190,000	125,000	47,000					362,000
Total Debits	850,000	530,000	330,000				200,000	1,510,000
Minority Int. in Net Inc. of S .	—	—	—	(13)	20,306			(20,306)
Minority Int. in Net Inc. of T .	—	—	—	(14)	16,531			(16,531)
Net Inc.—to Ret. Earn. Stmt.	570,163	203,061	165,306		568,367		200,000	570,163
RETAINED EARNINGS STATEMENT								
Ret. Earn., Jan. 1, 19X1—P .	2,600,000	—	—					2,600,000
Ret. Earn., Jan. 1, 19X1—S .	—	800,000	—	(7)	640,000			—
				(8)	80,000			
				(11)	80,000			
Ret. Earn., Jan. 1, 19X1—T .	—	—	400,000	(9)	280,000			—
				(10)	80,000			
				(12)	40,000			
Net Inc.—from Inc. Stmt.	570,163	203,061	165,306		568,367		200,000	570,163
Dividends—P	(200,000)	—	—					(200,000)
Dividends—S	—	(100,000)	—			(1)	80,000	—
						(4)	10,000	
						(13)	10,000	
Dividends—T	—	—	(40,000)			(2)	28,000	—
						(3)	8,000	
						(14)	4,000	
Ret. Earn., Dec. 31, 19X1— to Balance Sheet . . .	2,970,163	903,061	525,306		1,768,367		340,000	2,970,163
BALANCE SHEET								
Inventory	150,000	110,000	80,000			(6)	23,000	317,000
Other Assets	3,023,000	1,348,000	880,000					5,251,000
P's Investment in S (80%) .	954,449	—	—			(1)	74,449	—
						(7)	880,000	
T's Investment in S (10%) .	—	—	115,306			(4)	5,306	—
						(8)	110,000	
P's Investment in T (70%) .	542,714	—	—			(2)	87,714	—
						(9)	455,000	
S's Investment in T (20%) .	—	145,061	—			(3)	15,061	—
						(10)	130,000	
Total	4,670,163	1,603,061	1,075,306				1,780,530	5,568,000
Liabilities	1,200,000	400,000	300,000					1,900,000
Capital Stock—P . . .	500,000	—	—					500,000
Capital Stock—S . . .	—	300,000	—	(7)	240,000			—
				(8)	30,000			
				(11)	30,000			
Capital Stock—T . . .	—	—	250,000	(9)	175,000			—
				(10)	50,000			
				(12)	25,000			
Ret. Earn.—from Ret. Earn. Stmt.	2,970,163	903,061	525,306		1,768,367		340,000	2,970,163
Minority Interest in S . .	—	—	—			(11)	110,000	120,306
						(13)	10,306	
Minority Interest in T . .	—	—	—			(12)	65,000	77,531
						(14)	12,531	
Total	4,670,163	1,603,061	1,075,306		2,318,367		537,837	5,568,000
					2,318,367		2,318,367	

Explanations of Working Paper Entries
(1) To eliminate the equity method entries made by P in connection with its investment in S during 19X1.
(2) To eliminate the equity method entries made by P in connection with its investment in T during 19X1.
(3) To eliminate the equity method entries made by S in connection with its investment in T during 19X1.
(4) To eliminate the equity method entries made by T in connection with its investment in S during 19X1.
(5) To eliminate intercompany sales and purchases.
(6) To eliminate unconfirmed intercompany profit in ending inventory.
(7) To eliminate P's investment in S.
(8) To eliminate T's investment in S.
(9) To eliminate P's investment in T.
(10) To eliminate S's investment in T.
(11) To establish the minority interest in S at January 1, 19X1.
(12) To establish the minority interest in T at January 1, 19X1.
(13) To record the change in the minority interest in S during 19X1.
(14) To record the change in the minority interest in T during 19X1.

---

shares of the parent should be carried at *cost*, although a case could be made for use of the equity method when a minority interest exists.

The **treasury stock method** is the preferred consolidation method in a parent/subsidiary mutual holding for two principal reasons. First, from the viewpoint of the controlling interest, any shares of P held by S have all of the characteristics of treasury stock. Second, use of the equity method for S's investment in P seems inappropriate in most situations.

The **traditional allocation method** *may* be used in a parent/subsidiary mutual holding with minority interest present and *must* be used in a connecting affiliate mutual holding when a minority interest is present. A computational problem arises in allocating the affiliates' total income to the controlling and minority interests in these cases. The mutual holding creates a situation in which one company's equity accrual from another company is also dependent on the second company's equity accrual from the first. This interdependence or circularity is best dealt with by the use of simultaneous equations.

The existence of **unconfirmed intercompany profits** is easily handled under the traditional allocation method as long as consolidation policy calls for elimination of 100 percent of the intercompany profit proportionately against the controlling and minority interests. Such unconfirmed intercompany profits are simply deducted from the selling companies' incomes from their own operations before solving the simultaneous equations.

Questions Q11.1 P may obtain control over S after several blocks of S's stock are purchased over time. Generally accepted accounting principles seem to suggest that, in such situations, "the date of the latest purchase, as a matter of convenience, may be considered the date of acquisition." Comment.

Q11.2 Briefly explain the nature of the accounting problems which arise when P sells a portion of its holdings of S's stock.

Q11.3   We believe that if the economic position of the controlling interest is improved by the sale of some of S's shares—either by P or by S—the resulting gain should flow through the consolidated income statement. How might you criticize this approach?

Q11.4   Suppose S reacquired its own stock for a total of $30,000, $10,000 less than its book value. As a result, P's ownership interest increased from 70 percent to 80 percent. What entry would be made by P using the treatment recommended in the text?

Q11.5   The father-son-grandson (FSG) type of indirect holding is a common ownership configuration. Suppose P paid $5,000,000 for an 80 percent interest in S. The estimated fair value of S's identifiable assets less liabilities was $4,000,000 at date of acquisition. Discuss the conceptual difference in accounting for this combination under two alternatives: (1) S controls no subsidiaries, and (2) S controls two subsidiaries, T Company and U Company.

Q11.6   Why is the order of consolidation important in an indirect holding?

Q11.7   In the connecting affiliation involving P, S, and T with no minority interest, alternative accounting treatments can cause P's net income and retained earnings to differ from their respective consolidated amounts, even if P uses the equity method. Explain how this situation can arise.

Q11.8   Explain the basic consolidation problem often encountered in a mutual holding situation with minority interest present.

Q11.9   "In a mutual holding involving a partially-owned subsidiary, application of either the treasury stock method or the traditional allocation method will yield identical amounts of minority interest in net income." Comment.

Q11.10   The chapter presents formulas for the computation of P^* and S^*, *tentative* measurements of the net incomes of P and S on an equity basis. Why are these solutions tentative, and how must they be adjusted so that they are no longer tentative?

Exercises **E11.1**   P acquired control of S Company by purchasing two large blocks of S's stock. The details are as follows:

Acquisition Date	Percent Acquired	Cost of Shares	Net Assets of S Company		Net Income (Dividends) of S Company for the Year	
			Fair Value	Book Value		
1/2/X8	25%	$ 300,000	$1,100,000	$1,000,000	$100,000	$(40,000)
1/2/X9	60	1,000,000	1,400,000	1,060,000	150,000	(60,000)

S Company's undervalued assets are being depreciated by the straight-line method over a remaining life of ten years at date(s) of acquisition. P's policy is to amortize intangibles over twenty years.

Required:
  1. Prepare a schedule to determine and allocate the purchase premiums reflected in the acquisition prices paid by P.
  2. Prepare a schedule to compute the equity method accruals recorded by P in 19X8 and 19X9.

E11.2 Petri Corporation owns 60,000 of Storrs Company's 100,000 shares of outstanding common stock. The balance in the Investment in S, carried at equity, is $1,400,400, including an unamortized purchase premium of $200,000. S Company's stock currently sells for $35 per share.

Required: Given the current price at which S's shares are selling, the controlling interest believes that now might be a good time to realize $60,000 of the unrealized holding gains attributable to its investment in S's shares. Determine how many shares must be (1) sold by P or (2) issued by S, to achieve this desired result.

E11.3 Pidgeon Corporation owns 90 percent of Starling's 100,000 outstanding common shares. The investment account is carried at equity, has a balance at December 31, 19X4, of $1,700,000, and reflects an unamortized purchase *discount* of $100,000. Starling is contemplating the purchase of 5,263 shares of treasury stock.

Required: Determine the effects on the dollar amount of Pidgeon's investment in Starling if the treasury shares are purchased at (1) $22 per share, (2) $20 per share, and (3) $18 per share.

E11.4 At December 31, 19X1, condensed balance sheet data for S Company and T Company are as follows:

Balance Sheet Data as of December 31, 19X1

	S Company		T Company	
	Book Value	Fair Value	Book Value	Fair Value
Various Assets . .	$2,000,000	$2,400,000	$1,100,000	$1,300,000
Investment				
in T (80%) . . .	480,000	—	—	—
	$2,480,000		$1,100,000	
Liabilities . . .	$ 800,000	710,000	$ 500,000	540,000
Stockholders' Equity .	1,680,000	—	600,000	—
	$2,480,000		$1,100,000	

S had acquired its interest in T several years before, when the book values of T's assets and liabilities equalled their fair values. On December 31, 19X1, P

Company acquired 90 percent of S's outstanding shares for a total cash price of $2,200,000. This price was based, in part, on a careful analysis of the fair values of T's assets and liabilities as well as those of S.

Required: Prepare a schedule to determine and allocate P's purchase premium in S among the assets and liabilities of S and T.

E11.5   P Company, S Company, and T Company are related in a connecting affiliation, diagrammed here:

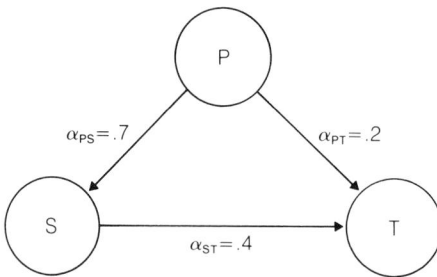

The three companies' condensed statements of income and retained earnings from their own operations for the year ended December 31, 19X6, appear as follows. Although P carries its investments in S and T at equity, the current year's equity accruals have not been made.

	P Company	S Company	T Company
Sales	$10,000,000	$5,000,000	$4,000,000
Cost of Goods Sold	5,500,000	3,000,000	2,000,000
Operating Expenses	3,000,000	1,400,000	1,600,000
Net Income	$ 1,500,000	$ 600,000	$ 400,000
Retained Earnings, January 1, 19X6 . .	8,000,000	2,000,000	1,900,000
Dividends Declared	500,000	300,000	200,000
Retained Earnings, December 31, 19X6 .	$ 9,000,000	$2,300,000	$2,100,000

Required: Prepare a condensed consolidated statement of income and retained earnings for 19X6. There were no purchase premiums or discounts and no intercompany transactions.

E11.6   P owns 100 percent of S's stock. S recently purchased 20 percent of P's stock in the open market on July 1 for $2,000,000. The book value of those shares was $1,800,000 at time of purchase. Following the acquisition by S, P declared $100,000 in dividends. During the current year, P Company reported net income of $340,000 from its own operations, earned evenly throughout the year.

Required: Prepare the working paper entries relative to S's investment in P's stock necessary for consolidation at December 31.

E11.7   Companies P, S, and T are related in a connecting affiliation.

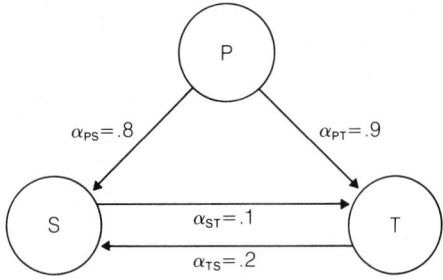

Information relative to these investments is summarized next:

	S Company	T Company
Price Paid by P on December 31, 19X7, to Acquire Shares of	$4,000,000	$2,000,000
Book Value of P's Share of Net Assets at Acquisition . . .	3,500,000	1,800,000
Price Paid by S on December 31, 19X8, for Remaining Shares of	—	200,000
Price Paid by T on December 31, 19X8, for Remaining Shares of	1,000,000	—
Book Value of Remaining Share of Net Assets at December 31, 19X8	950,000	240,000

Any purchase premiums are attributed to goodwill amortizable over twenty years. Purchase discounts are allocated to depreciable assets with a remaining life of ten years at acquisition. Neither S nor T engaged in any capital transactions after 19X7. P carries its investments in S and T at equity.

Required: From the information given, prepare the working paper eliminations necessary to consolidate the financial statements of P, S, and T at December 31, 19X9.

E11.8 P owns 90 percent of S and S owns 20 percent of P. During the current year, P earned $500,000 from its own operations and paid dividends of $200,000. S earned $300,000 from its own operations and paid dividends of $100,000.

Required: Compute consolidated net income and the minority interest in net income under (1) the treasury stock method and (2) the traditional allocation method.

E11.9 Akron, Inc., owns 80 percent of the capital stock of Benson Company and 70 percent of the capital stock of Cashin, Inc. Benson Company owns 15 percent of the capital stock of Cashin, Inc. Cashin, Inc., in turn, owns 25 percent of the capital stock of Akron, Inc. These ownership relationships are illustrated in the diagram at the top of page 478.

Net income of each corporation from its own operations follows:

Akron, Inc.	$190,000
Benson Company	170,000
Cashin, Inc.	230,000

Required: For each multiple choice item that follows, select the correct answer.

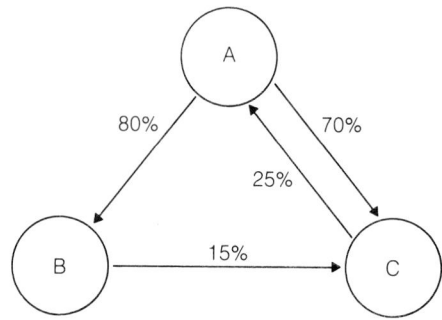

Ignore all income tax considerations. The following notations relate to items 1 through 4:

A_e = Akron's net income on an equity basis.

B_e = Benson's net income on an equity basis.

C_e = Cashin's net income on an equity basis.

1.   The equation, in a set of simultaneous equations, which computes A_e is:
   a. $A_e = .75(190,000 + .8B_e + .7C_e)$.
   b. $A_e = 190,000 + .8B_e + .7C_e$.
   c. $A_e = .75(190,000) + .8(170,000) + .7(230,000)$.
   d. $A_e = .75(190,000) + .8B_e + .7C_e$.

2.   The equation, in a set of simultaneous equations, which computes B_e is:
   a. $B_e = 170,000 + .15C_e - .75A_e$.
   b. $B_e = 170,000 + .15C_e$.
   c. $B_e = .2(170,000) + .15(230,000)$.
   d. $B_e = .2(170,000) + .15C_e$.

3.   Cashin's minority interest in net income is:
   a. $.15(230,000)$.
   b. $230,000 + .25A_e$.
   c. $.15(230,000) + .25A_e$.
   d. $.15C_e$.

4.   Benson's minority interest in net income is:
   a.   34,316.
   b.   25,500.
   c.   45,755.
   d.   30,675.

(AICPA adapted)

E11.10   The following information relates to the P, S, and T affiliation:

	P Company	S Company	T Company
Ownership Interest of P Company in . . .	—	.7	.8
Ownership Interest of S Company in . . .	—	—	.1
Ownership Interest of T Company in . . .	—	.2	—
Net Income from Own Operations of . . .	$100,000	$70,000	$40,000

Required: Compute consolidated net income and the minority interest in net income for the P, S, and T affiliation, using the traditional allocation method as appropriate.

Problems **P11.1** **Consolidated Financial Statement Working Paper after Sale of Partial Interest**   Prune Corporation owns 60 percent of the outstanding common stock of Squash Company, having held an 80 percent interest through June 30, 19X7, the current year. A gain of $50,000 was recognized on the sale, based on January 1, 19X7, book value, and was recorded as Other Income. The original acquisition of the 80 percent interest occurred on January 2, 19X2, at a transaction price of $400,000, $160,000 more than the portion of Squash's stockholders' equity acquired. The $160,000 was allocated to depreciable assets with a ten-year life ($120,000) and to goodwill amortized over 40 years ($40,000).

On April 20, 19X7, Squash sold a parcel of land to Prune and recorded a gain of $20,000. Later in the year, Squash sold merchandise costing $50,000 to Prune for $75,000. This sale occurred on October 15 and, as of December 31, 19X7, one-half of the merchandise was still on hand and it had not been paid for. Squash makes semi-annual dividend payments of $10,000 on February 15 and August 15 of each year. Its net income is earned evenly throughout the year.

The preclosing trial balances of the two companies at December 31, 19X7, are given below. Prune's controller has not yet made the 19X7 equity method accrual as there is confusion over how it is affected by the mid-year sale.

Prune Corporation and Squash Company
Preclosing Trial Balances at December 31, 19X7

Account	Prune Corp.	Squash Company
Cash and Receivables	$ 477,750	$ 180,000
Inventory, January 1, 19X7	200,000	120,000
Inventory, December 31, 19X7	230,000	100,000
Plant Assets	1,300,000	720,000
Accumulated Depreciation	(270,000)	(130,000)
Investment in Squash	345,250	—
Current Liabilities	(275,000)	(160,000)
Noncurrent Liabilities	(400,000)	—
Capital Stock	(100,000)	(100,000)
Retained Earnings	(828,000)	(380,000)
Dividends	100,000	20,000
Sales	(2,100,000)	(1,400,000)
Other Income	(50,000)	(20,000)
Inventory, December 31, 19X7	(230,000)	(100,000)
Purchases	1,100,000	700,000
Operating Expenses	500,000	450,000
	$ 0	$ 0

Required: Prepare a consolidated financial statement working paper for Prune and Squash at December 31, 19X7.

P11.2 **Consolidated Balance Sheet Working Paper—Step Acquisition; Incomplete Equity Method**   The December 31, 19X8, postclosing trial balances of the Major Corporation and its two subsidiaries are as shown in Exhibit 11.10.

Exhibit 11.10   Postclosing Trial Balances of the Major Corporation and Subsidiaries to Be Used in P11.2

Major Corporation and Subsidiaries
Postclosing Trial Balances
December 31, 19X8

ASSETS	Major Corporation	Minor Corporation	Mode Corporation
Cash	$ 100,000	$ 75,000	$ 95,000
Accounts Receivable	158,200	210,000	105,000
Inventories	290,000	90,000	115,000
Advance to Minor Corporation	17,000		
Dividends Receivable	24,000		
Property, Plant, and Equipment	777,600	325,000	470,000
Allowance for Depreciation	(180,000)	(55,000)	(160,000)
Investment in Minor Corporation:			
6% Bonds	23,800		
Common Stock	308,600		
Investment in Mode Corporation:			
Preferred Stock	7,000		
Common Stock	196,000		
Totals	$1,722,200	$645,000	$625,000
LIABILITIES AND STOCKHOLDERS' EQUITY			
Accounts Payable	$ 170,000	$ 96,000	$ 86,000
Notes Payable	45,000	14,000	44,000
Bonds Payable	285,000	150,000	125,000
Discount on Bonds Payable	(8,000)	(12,000)	
Dividends Payable	22,000	30,000	
Preferred Stock, $20 Par	400,000		
Mode Corporation			50,000
Common Stock, $10 Par	600,000		
Minor Corporation		250,000	
Mode Corporation			200,000
Retained Earnings	208,200		
Minor Corporation		117,000	
Mode Corporation			120,000
Totals	$1,722,200	$645,000	$625,000

Additional information available includes the following:

1. The investment in Minor Corporation stock by the Major Corporation is composed of the following items:

Date	Description	Amount
4/1/X7	Cost of 5,000 Shares of Minor Corporation Stock	$ 71,400
12/31/X7	20% of the Dividends Declared in December 19X7 by Minor Corporation	(9,000)
12/31/X7	20% of the 19X7 Net Income of Minor Corporation	12,000
7/1/X8	Cost of 15,000 Shares of Minor Corporation Stock	226,200
12/31/X8	80% of the Dividends Declared in December 19X8 by Minor Corporation	(24,000)

Date	Description	Amount
12/31/X8	80% of the 19X8 Net Income of Minor Corporation	32,000
12/31/X8	Total	$308,600

2. Major Corporation acquired 250 shares of noncumulative fully participating preferred stock for $7,000 and 14,000 shares of common stock for $196,000 (their book value) of the Mode Corporation on January 2, 19X8. Mode Corporation had a net income of $20,000 in 19X8 and did not declare any dividends. Under the fully participating provision, Mode's common and preferred shareholders have interests in current and retained earnings equal to the ratios of common stock ($200,000) and preferred stock ($50,000) to total contributed capital ($250,000), respectively.

3. Mode Corporation's inventory includes $22,400 of merchandise acquired from Minor Corporation for which no payment has been made. Minor charged Mode an amount 40 percent above its own cost for the merchandise.

4. Major Corporation acquired in the open market twenty-five $1,000 face-value, 6 percent bonds of Minor Corporation for $21,400 on January 5, 19X5. The Minor Corporation bonds mature in two years, on December 31, 19Y0. Interest is paid each June 30 and December 31.

5. The three corporations are all in the same industry, and their operations are similar. Major Corporation exercises control over the boards of directors of both Minor Corporation and Mode Corporation and has installed new principal officers in both.

Required: Prepare a consolidated balance sheet working paper as of December 31, 19X8, for Major Corporation and its subsidiaries. The consolidation is to be accounted for as a purchase. Formal financial statements and journal entries are not required. Supporting computations should be in good form.

(AICPA adapted)

P11.3 **Intrayear Step Acquisition—Eliminations and Consolidated Calculations**
Phydeaux Corporation now owns a controlling interest in Styx Company and uses the equity method of accounting. Three blocks of stock were acquired over a period of eighteen months; the related data are as follows:

Acquisition Date	Percent Acquired	Cost of Shares	Net Assets of Styx		Net Income and Dividends of Styx		
			Fair Value	Book Value	Year	Net Income	Dividends
1/3/X4	25%	$500,000	$1,800,000	$1,600,000	19X4	$450,000	$50,000
1/5/X5	20	600,000	2,400,000	2,000,000	19X5	830,000	230,000
7/2/X5	30	900.000	2,500,000	2,300,000			

Styx Company's undervalued assets are being depreciated by the straight-line method at an annual rate of 20 percent. Phydeaux amortizes intangibles over the maximum period allowable by *APBO 17*. Phydeaux's retained earnings from its own operations at December 31, 19X4, amounted to $7,200,000. During 19X5, Phydeaux earned $1,500,000 from its own operations and declared dividends of $800,000. All earnings and dividends occur evenly during each year.

Required:

    1. Compute the balance in the investment account at December 31, 19X5.

    2. Compute consolidated net income for 19X5 and consolidated retained earnings at December 31, 19X5.

    3. Give the working paper eliminations made in consolidation at December 31, 19X5. Use the preacquisition earnings approach where appropriate.

P11.4 **Mutual Holdings—Connecting Affiliates with Minority Interest Present** P, S, and T are affiliated according to the relationship diagrammed here:

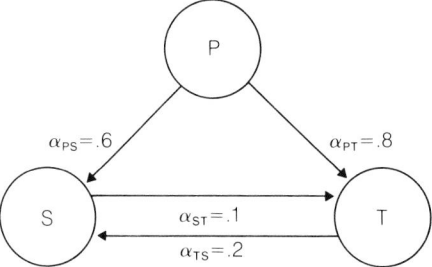

Companies P, S, and T reported income from their own operations of $900,000, $200,000, and $500,000, respectively. No dividends were declared during the year. P Company's beginning and ending inventories included unconfirmed intercompany profits on goods purchased from S of $30,000 and $40,000, respectively. T's net income included a gain of $50,000 on a sale of land to S Company. S Company still owned the land at year-end.

Required:

    1. Compute consolidated net income and the minority interest in net income.

    2. Prepare a schedule to determine the equity method accruals of P, S, and T.

P11.5 **Derive Expressions for P*, S*, and T* in a Complex Mutual Holding** Consider the following ownership configuration:

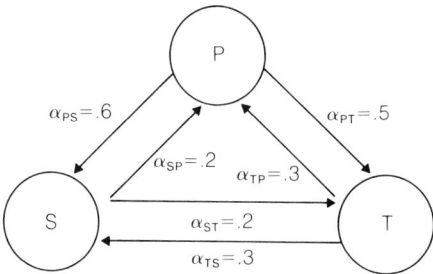

Required: Derive formulas to compute P*, S*, and T*. Explain how P*, S*, and T* must be adjusted in order that the total net income of the group be allocated between the controlling and minority interests on the equity basis.

Chapter 12	Segment and Interim Reporting

Chapters 5 through 11 have focused on the preparation of financial statements for business firms with several components. Certain procedures are required to combine or consolidate the firm with its branches or subsidiaries on the grounds that the appropriate reporting entity is the *total enterprise*. Furthermore, "the basic time period for which financial statements are presented is one year," according to *APBS 4* (AC § 1027).[1] Traditionally, the most prevalent financial reporting model called for the issuance of total enterprise statements at annual intervals. However, increases in the complexity of firms, improvements in communications technology, and the growing sophistication of investors and analysts have led to modifications in the traditional financial reporting model. For many firms, annual consolidated statements are no longer sufficient to meet the information needs of users and regulatory agencies. This chapter addresses two major dimensions of accounting's response to this problem: *segment reporting* and *interim reporting*.

The Entity Question

The total enterprise continues to be the principal reporting entity, yet the increased diversity of operations within a business firm often means that total enterprise statements provide insufficient information about this diversity. Recall that the third merger movement discussed in Chapter 6 was characterized by large numbers of *conglomerate* mergers. Such business combinations often brought totally unrelated business operations under common control in an effort to diversify business risks. As a consequence, however, traditional financial

---

[1] Accounting Principles Board, *Statement No. 4*, "Basic Concepts and Accounting Principles Underlying Financial Statements of Business Enterprises" (N.Y.: AICPA, 1970), par. 194.

statements portrayed the *total* financial position and results of operations of the business units in the firm but revealed nothing about the *components* of the total. Similarly, enterprise-wide financial ratios are weighted averages of the underlying individual ratios and may bear no resemblance to the individual ratios —some may be much higher and others much lower.

To assist statement users in understanding these complex business enterprises, the notion of reporting information about the components of the enterprise became popular. These components, labeled **business segments,** have become quasi-entities in their own right. As a result, generally accepted accounting principles have come to require **segment reporting,** the disclosure of extensive supplementary information on these business segments in the firm's financial statements or notes thereto. The major source of these requirements is *SFAS 14* (AC § 2081), which we examine in a subsequent section.[2]

A related issue concerns the time frame covered by financial reports. The demand for more timely financial statement information, which could be processed and acted on quickly by investors and others, has been accompanied by growth in the incidence of **interim reporting.** Even though interim reports cover the total enterprise, they are typically released at quarterly intervals as the year between annual reports unfolds. Interim reports are less complete than annual reports and are generally unaudited. As we shall see, generally accepted accounting principles do not require interim reporting but *APBO 28* (AC § 2071) governs the preparation and disclosure of interim information if the firm releases it.[3]

Figure 12.1 shows the relationship between annual total enterprise financial statements, the supplementary business segment data that accompany them, and the interim data released quarterly during the year.

Segment Reporting: A Disclosure Issue	Demand for segment reports by investors and analysts is motivated by two separate yet related factors. In considering these factors, the reader should note that **segment reporting** provides information relating to lines of business, areas of geographical activity, export sales, and major customers.

1. Better forecasts of total enterprise earnings are possible when the various components of earnings are known. Different product lines and industry activities have different growth rates and varying degrees of susceptibility to general economic conditions. Relating forecasts of these factors to specific segments of a firm's operations can produce more meaningful earnings forecasts for the firm as a whole.

2. Modern investment theory is heavily concerned with both the risk and return of alternative investments. The earnings forecast mentioned above is one key element in the analysis of returns. At the same time, however, adequate segment data can also assist the analyst in evaluating the riskiness of investing in a particular company. This is accom-

---

[2] Financial Accounting Standards Board, *Statement of Financial Accounting Standards No. 14,* "Financial Reporting for Segments of a Business Enterprise" (Stamford, Conn.: 1976).

[3] Accounting Principles Board, *Opinion No. 28,* "Interim Reporting" (N.Y.: AICPA, 1973).

Figure 12.1   Enterprise, Segment, and Interim Financial Reports

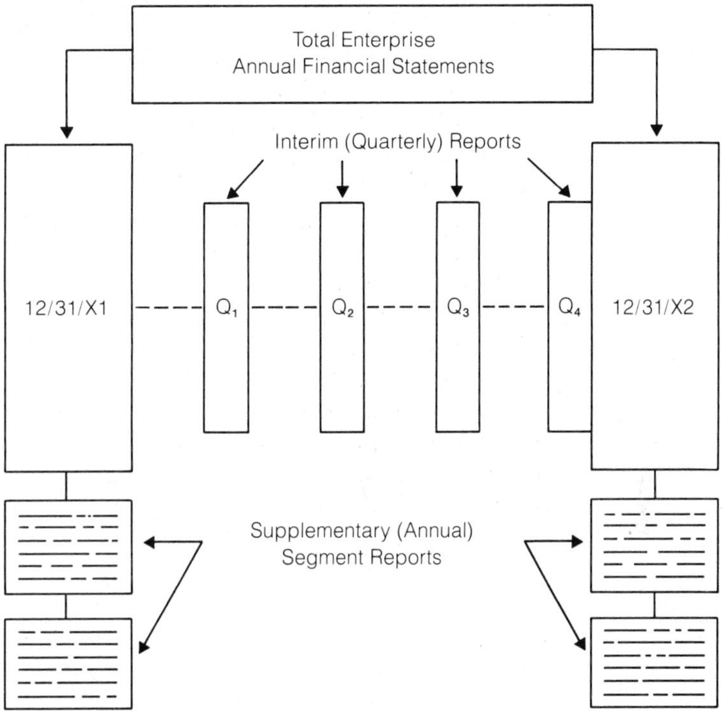

plished through an understanding of the firm's capital commitments to various industry activities and foreign operations.

The FASB alluded to these factors in its statement of the purpose of segment information in *SFAS 14:*

> The purpose of the information . . . about an enterprise's operations in different industries and different areas of the world and about the extent of its reliance on export sales or major customers is to assist financial statement users in analyzing and understanding the enterprise's financial statements by permitting better assessment of the enterprise's past performance and future prospects.[4]

Segment information as presently disclosed is supplementary in nature and is intended not to replace total enterprise financial statements but rather to enhance the interpretability of those statements.

Problem Areas in Segment Reporting

Accounting information generally lacks the precision attributed to it by the assignment of specific numbers of dollars to specific items, transactions, and events. Estimates, allocations, and other subjective judgments lie behind those

---

[4] Financial Accounting Standards Board, *Statement No. 14,* par. 75; AC § 2081.075.

perfectly clear, perfectly articulated columns of numbers. Total enterprise reporting tends to be less subjective in this respect than segment reporting. Despite their limitations, however, financial statements of the total enterprise reflect the relationship and performance of that enterprise relative to external parties and markets. The transactions entered into by the firm and recorded and reflected in the accounts are, for the most part, the result of arm's-length negotiations with outsiders. Furthermore, allocation decisions tend to relate to *time periods* only, as in the case of depreciation and amortization. In contrast, segment reporting in any detail tends to require disclosure of some *internal* transactions *among* the firm's segments as well as the segments' transactions with outsiders. Of equal concern is the need to allocate many costs incurred on behalf of two or more segments of the business among those segments in order to generate certain segment information. This is the familiar joint cost or common cost allocation problem which inevitably entails arbitrary judgments by those performing the allocations.

For these reasons, segment reports are of doubtful value when used for comparison with (1) similar segments in other firms and (2) free-standing firms in the same line of business. We now proceed to discuss problems arising from internal transactions and common cost allocations. Later we shall see how the existing segment reporting requirements have tried to cope with these difficulties.

Pricing Internal Transfers   We know that when combined or consolidated statements are prepared, transactions among the components of the firm are eliminated. Thus the pricing of internal transfers may affect internal performance measurements but not the firm's external financial statements. In developing income statement information for the segments of a business enterprise, however, internal pricing issues assume importance when the segment data are reported externally. Internal prices, known as **transfer prices,** affect the reported revenues of the selling segments and reported costs of the purchasing segments.

The **transfer pricing problem** is a major stumbling block to optimal management and control within a decentralized corporation. In its purest form, a decentralized firm is one with several autonomous divisions under the common control of corporate headquarters. Most decision-making authority is concentrated at the divisional level. The divisions may do business with each other as well as in the open market, and divisional managers are supposed to react to internal prices no differently than they react to external market prices. In practice, one finds the following bases for transfer prices:

1.   Variable cost of production.
2.   Full cost of production, including allocated fixed overhead.
3.   Full cost plus a percentage markup.
4.   "Market" prices.

A transfer pricing system which uses external competitive market prices to price internal transfers is probably the best. Unfortunately, competitive prices do not always exist, due to market imperfections. And there may be no external market prices at all for certain manufactured products, especially subassemblies or specialized parts. Finally, determination of "market" prices is complicated by the facts that list prices are not necessarily transaction prices and that prices are often dependent upon order size and freight cost absorption. The reasons for placing quotation marks around "market," then, are that several comparable but different market prices may exist or no truly comparable external price may be available. When no external market price exists, transfer prices based on variable or marginal cost of production generally lead to the correct internal decisions.

Complete analysis of the transfer pricing problem is beyond the scope of this text.[5] We will, however, use a simple example to illustrate how transfer prices based on full cost, with or without markup, can lead to suboptimal decisions in a decentralized firm.

Suppose Division X manufactures a component part used by Division Y in its manufacturing operations. Variable manufacturing costs per unit produced by Division X amount to $5, while allocated fixed cost is $2 per unit, for a full cost of $7. Division Y's variable cost of manufacturing is $4 per unit. Suppose further that both divisions have excess capacity and there is no intermediate market for the component produced by X. Division Y has the opportunity to expand its output and realize $10.50 per unit sold. If Y has to pay $7 for each component part purchased from X, it will incur a loss [$10.50 < ($7.00 + $4.00)] and will not produce the added units. This is suboptimal from the corporate point of view because Y's revenue of $10.50 exceeds total variable costs of $9 (= $5 + $4); $1.50 (= $10.50 − $9.00) per unit of corporate profit contribution will be lost.

Although the transfer pricing problem is most crucial in internal decision-making, it also has implications for externally-reported segment information. Under *SFAS 14*, business segments report revenue and profitability information which reflects sales to outside customers and to other segments within the firm. Hence such information is influenced by the sales and purchases among business units within the firm which are not completed market transactions. Methods for pricing internal transfers may vary from company to company, making comparisons among segments difficult. Even disclosure of the method used may not be of much help, as can be seen from the following excerpt from page 51 of the 1977 annual report of Norton Simon Inc.: "Intersegment sales are recorded at fair value adjusted for quantity and production efficiencies." Readers are left to their own imaginations to determine precisely what that statement means.

Common Cost Allocations   Common costs incurred on behalf of two or more segments in a diversified firm can be a significant problem if (1) the common costs are material and (2) the segment reports reflect a common cost allocation. All common costs, however, are not the same, and several categories can be listed: (1) corporate services, (2) corporate administration, and (3) corporate taxes.

---

[5] For further discussion of transfer pricing issues see, for example, David Solomons, "Divisional Reports," in Sidney Davidson and Roman L. Weil, eds., *Handbook of Modern Accounting*, 2d ed. (N.Y.: McGraw-Hill, 1977), Chap. 44, and the sources cited by Solomons in his bibliography.

Corporate Services The **corporate services** category includes common costs incurred by corporate departments which provide services to the several operating divisions. Examples include personnel, accounting, data processing, and printing and reproduction departments. These kinds of costs are related to divisional activities and requests for services. Hence they often can be allocated in a sensible way at year-end or be charged to the divisions on an ongoing basis.

Corporate Administration Expenses of operating corporate headquarters; compensation of corporate managers, staff, and support personnel; and directors' fees fall into the category of **corporate administration.** Other costs which would be included in this category for purposes of allocation are interest expense and institutional advertising. These costs are farther removed from divisional activities and, indeed, the divisions have little control over how much of such "services" they "use." Allocations of corporate administrative costs are coarser than those related to corporate services. Such gross measurements as assets, sales, investment, employment, and gross profits by segment are employed to allocate corporate administrative costs. One single allocation base, such as assets, is often not sufficient, so various combinations of these bases may be used. Alternatively, some costs may be allocated on one basis and other costs on other bases.

Corporate Taxes If segment income statements are to reflect a share of corporate taxes, care must be taken not to determine that share by a general allocation scheme. External financial statement users are concerned about the segments affected by special tax treatments. Therefore, the best approach is to estimate the tax expense for each segment as if it were standing alone.

Users' Evaluation of Common Cost Allocation Bases Mautz's 1967 survey of financial analysts revealed substantial diversity with respect to analysts' *preferences* for allocation bases and the *acceptability* of those bases to the analysts, as shown:[6]

Basis of Common Cost Allocation	Percent of Financial Analysts Indicating	
	a Preference for the Basis	the Basis Would Be Acceptable
Sales or Gross Revenue	18.4%	25.8%
Assets Employed	29.5	28.1
Benefits Received	24.9	19.2
Net Income before Common Costs	21.8	23.8
Other	5.4	3.1
	100.0%	100.0%

These data lead one to wonder whether analysts perceived little difference among the major bases or whether the allocations were likely to be disregarded no matter what basis was used. On this point, these analysts did feel that when

---

[6] Robert K. Mautz, *Financial Reporting by Diversified Companies* (N.Y.: Financial Executives Research Foundation, 1968), p. 120.

common costs amount to 10 percent or more of segment revenue, profit figures reflecting common cost allocations tend to lose their significance.

Allocations Based on Sales: A Special Danger   We believe it is worth illustrating a particular danger that can arise when material amounts of common cost are allocated to segments based on their sales or total revenue. As the ratio of total common costs to total traceable segment costs increases, the use of sales as a basis for allocating common costs tends to *equalize* segment profit margin ratios. Consider a company with three identifiable segments. Segments X, Y, and Z have sales revenues of $140,000, $270,000, and $160,000, respectively. Total costs are $400,000, and we will vary the common portion of those costs from zero up to $400,000; the portion of traceable costs will therefore be decreasing from $400,000 to zero. After determining segment costs and profits for several intermediate traceable cost/common cost combinations, we will compute segment profit margins (profit/sales) and plot them on a graph. This analysis is given in Exhibit 12.1.

The main point of Exhibit 12.1 is that, as allocated common costs become a large portion of total costs, use of sales revenue to allocate these costs across products or business segments drives profit margin ratios toward equality. This is best seen in the last panel of Exhibit 12.1, where all costs are charged to the segments in proportion to their sales revenue, leading to equal profit/sales ratios. The effect of such an allocation scheme applied when common costs are significant is to destroy the usefulness of segment profitability data. Note that the initial diverse profit/sales ratios (case 1, Exhibit 12.1) were chosen to vividly illustrate how common cost allocations based on sales lead to identical segment profit ratios. In practice, profit/sales ratios reflecting no common costs (as in case 1) may not be so different from each other.

Segment Reporting under SFAS 14

SFAS 14 was published in December 1976. To conform to generally accepted accounting principles, companies must disclose the information required by this *Statement*. Other segment reporting requirements affect certain reports submitted to the SEC and the Federal Trade Commission (FTC). To bring SEC requirements into line with *SFAS 14, ASR 236* was issued in December 1977.[7] Shortly thereafter, in March 1978, the SEC released *ASR 244* to indicate its intention to review the industry segments reported by registrants "to determine whether their segmentation is consistent with *SFAS 14* and thus achieves the goals of industry segment reporting."[8] The FTC program is somewhat outside the mainstream of financial reporting. Indeed, one of its major purposes is to assess the degree of competition in American industries. For an analysis of this program see the study by Benston.[9]

---

[7] Securities and Exchange Commission, *Accounting Series Release No. 236*, "Industry Segment Reporting: Adoption of Disclosure Regulation and Amendments of Disclosure Forms and Rules" (Washington, D.C.: SEC, 1977).

[8] Securities and Exchange Commission, *Accounting Series Release No. 244*, "Industry Segment Determination" (Washington, D.C.: SEC, 1978).

[9] George J. Benston, "FTC's Line of Business Program: A Benefit-Cost Analysis," in H. J. Goldschmid, ed., *Government Information Needs and Business Disclosure* (N.Y.: McGraw-Hill, 1978).

Exhibit 12.1   Effect on Segment Profit Margins of Using Sales as the Basis for Allocating Common Costs to Segments

	Segment			
DATA FOR ILLUSTRATION	X	Y	Z	Total
Sales Revenue	$140,000	$270,000	$160,000	$570,000
Sales/Total Sales[a]	.245	.474	.281	1.000
CASE 1: $0 COMMON COSTS (0%)				
Sales	$140,000	$270,000	$160,000	$570,000
Traceable Costs	140,000	180,000	80,000	400,000
Common Costs	0	0	0	0
Profit	$ 0	$ 90,000	$ 80,000	$170,000
Profit/Sales	0	.333	.500	.298
CASE 2: $100,000 COMMON COSTS (25%)				
Sales	$140,000	$270,000	$160,000	$570,000
Traceable Costs	105,000	135,000	60,000	300,000
Common Costs	24,500	47,400	28,100	100,000
Profit	$ 10,500	$ 87,600	$ 71,900	$170,000
Profit/Sales	.075	.324	.450	.298
CASE 3: $200,000 COMMON COSTS (50%)				
Sales	$140,000	$270,000	$160,000	$570,000
Traceable Costs	70,000	90,000	40,000	200,000
Common Costs	49,000	94,800	56,200	200,000
Profit	$ 21,000	$ 85,200	$ 63,800	$170,000
Profit/Sales	.150	.316	.399	.298
CASE 4: $300,000 COMMON COSTS (75%)				
Sales	$140,000	$270,000	$160,000	$570,000
Traceable Costs	35,000	45,000	20,000	100,000
Common Costs	73,500	142,200	84,300	300,000
Profit	$ 31,500	$ 82,800	$ 55,700	$170,000
Profit/Sales	.224	.307	.349	.298
CASE 5: $400,000 COMMON COSTS (100%)				
Sales	$140,000	$270,000	$160,000	$570,000
Traceable Costs	0	0	0	0
Common Costs	98,000	189,600	112,400	400,000
Profit	$ 42,000	$ 80,400	$ 47,600	$170,000
Profit/Sales	.300	.298	.298	.298

[a]These percentages are used to allocate the firm-wide common costs among the three segments.

Exhibit 12.1   *continued*

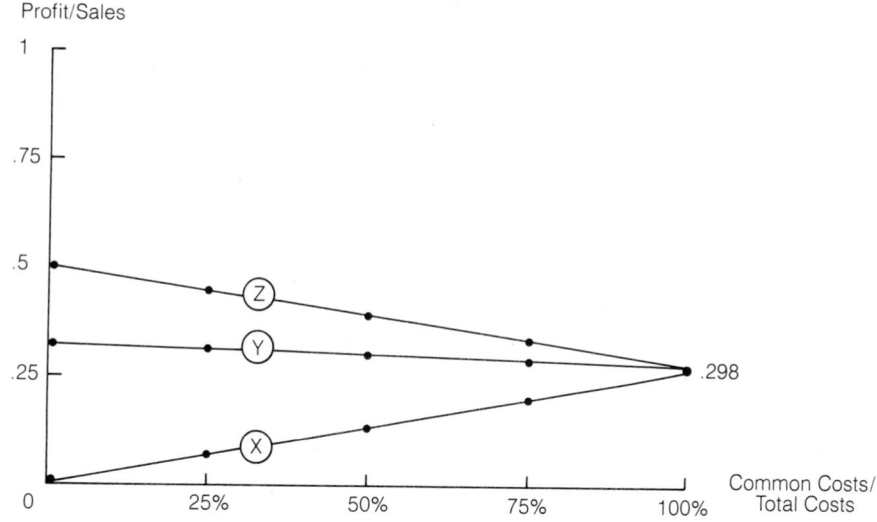

Graph of the Relationship between Common Costs as a Percentage
of Total Costs and Segment Profit Margins

SFAS 14 calls for disaggregated information to be prepared and reported for each reportable segment in accordance with the same accounting principles underlying the aggregate information. Requirements for information and rules for determining reportable segments in the following three categories will be discussed in turn.

1.   Operations in different industries.
2.   Foreign operations and export sales.
3.   Major customers.

Operations in Different Industries   The principal industry-related information to be disclosed for the firm's reportable industry segments is:

1.   *Sales* to unaffiliated customers, total sales to other segments of the firm, and the basis for pricing the sales to other segments.

2.   *Operating profit or loss* net of traceable expenses and the *corporate service* type of expenses mentioned earlier in the chapter. Corporate administrative expenses, domestic and foreign income taxes, extraordinary items, minority interest in net income, and other items listed in paragraphs 10(d) and 24 of *SFAS 14* are not to be allocated in computing segment operating profit.

3.   *Identifiable assets*, including both assets used exclusively in particular segments and those used jointly by two or more segments where a reasonable allocation of the jointly-used assets can be made. Intersegment advances shall *not* be counted as identifiable assets unless they are

made by a *finance segment*. Income from intersegment advances made by a finance segment will be included in the finance segment's operating profit.

4. *Depreciation, depletion, and amortization expense* (in total).

5. *Capital expenditures*—additions to property, plant, and equipment.

6. *Equity method investment in and income of vertically integrated investees* and the geographic areas in which these investees operate.

7. *Effects of changes in accounting principles on segment operating profits*, following *APBO 20*, "Accounting Changes," (AC § 1051).

Determining Reportable Industry Segments   *SFAS 14* provides both guidance to assist management in identifying industry segments and significance tests to assure that management identifies neither too few nor too many segments. Approaches adopted by the federal government to classify business activities, such as the Standard Industrial Classification (SIC) and Enterprise Standard Industrial Classification (ESIC) systems, are mentioned in paragraph 12 of *SFAS 14*. These systems, however, often bear little relationship to the organization of business operations. As a result, the selection of industry segments is generally based on the judgment of the company's management.

The basic approach is to start with a firm's *profit centers*, generally the smallest units of business activity selling to customers outside the firm, and to group the products and services of these profit centers along industry lines. For example, a company's profit centers for production and sales of spark plugs, instrument panels, and windshield wiper blades may be designated as a segment in the automobile parts industry. When possible, industry segmentation should incorporate the worldwide operations of the enterprise. If some or all of an enterprise's foreign operations cannot be broken down by industry segments, those foreign operations will constitute an industry segment themselves.

Only *significant* industry segments need be reported. Unless the firm has a single dominant segment, however, *sufficient industry segments* must be identified so that *combined sales* to unaffiliated customers of reportable segments is at least *75 percent* of the firm's total sales to unaffiliated customers (the "75 percent test"). Generally, the number of reportable segments should not exceed ten.

A single *dominant segment* exists when that segment accounts for at least 90 percent of the revenue, operating profit or loss, and identifiable assets of all the firm's industry segments. Also, no other industry segment within that firm can meet any of the significance tests indicated below. Whatever industry such a firm's operations are concentrated in must be identified.

Satisfaction of *any one* of the following **significance tests** (paragraph 15 of *SFAS 14*) by an industry segment indicates that it is sufficiently significant to be reported separately. In applying these significance tests, we have assumed away any unconfirmed intersegment profits in inventory, land, and so on. If there were unconfirmed intercompany profits, they would not be removed from the segments' operating profit and identifiable asset amounts. In reconciling to the consolidated totals, however, the unconfirmed intercompany profits would be eliminated in 2 and 3 below, just as intersegment revenue is eliminated in 1 below.

1. The segment's *total revenue*—intersegment sales plus external sales—is at least 10 percent of the combined total revenue of all the company's industry segments. Note that *combined total revenue* includes intersegment sales and hence differs from *consolidated revenue*. *Example:*

	Segment W	Segment X	Segment Y	Segment Z	Combined	Elimination	Consolidated
External Sales	$6,000	$80,000	$10,000	$ 5,000	$101,000	—	$101,000
Intersegment Sales	3,000	—	2,000	20,000	25,000	$(25,000)	—
Total Revenue	$9,000	$80,000	$12,000	$25,000	$126,000	$(25,000)	$101,000

> *Result:* Segments X and Z are reportable because their total revenues of $80,000 and $25,000 are at least 10 percent of combined total revenue of $126,000, as shown in the third row of the example. Segments W and Y are not reportable under the revenue test.

2. The segment's *operating profit or loss*, in absolute value, is at least 10 percent of the *greater* of the absolute value of (a) the combined operating profit of profitable segments or (b) the combined operating loss of loss segments. *Example:*

	Segment W	Segment X	Segment Y	Segment Z	Corporate Revenue (Expense)	Consolidated
Operating Profit (Loss)	$ 3,000	$30,000	$(4,000)	$(1,000)	—	$28,000
Other Rvenue (Expense)	7,000	(6,000)	—	—	$(8,500)	(7,500)
Total Income before Taxes	$10,000	$24,000	$(4,000)	$(1,000)	$(8,500)	$20,500

> *Result:* As indicated in the first row of the example, segments X and Y are reportable because the absolute values of their operating profit or loss of $30,000 and $4,000 are at least 10 percent of the combined operating profit of $33,000 (= $3,000 + $30,000). The combined operating profit of $33,000 exceeds the absolute value of combined operating losses of $5,000. Segments W and Z are not reportable under the operating profit or loss test.

3. The segment's *identifiable assets* are at least 10 percent of the combined identifiable assets of all the company's industry segments.

Example:

	Segment W	Segment X	Segment Y	Segment Z	Combined	Corporate Assets	Elimination	Consolidated
Indentifiable Assets	$120,000	$280,000	$80,000	$ 50,000	$530,000	$75,000	—	$605,000
Intersegment Advances	8,000	—	5,000	25,000	38,000	10,000	$(48,000)	—
Total Assets	$128,000	$280,000	$85,000	$75,000	$568,000	$85,000	$(48,000)	$605,000

> *Result:* Segments W, X, and Y are reportable because the first row of the example shows that their identifiable assets of $120,000, $280,000, and $80,000 are at least 10 percent of combined identifiable assets of $530,000. Segment Z is not reportable under the identifiable assets test.

Since each industry segment is significant in at least one test, all must be reported separately. Note that in these examples, the *75 percent test* is of no concern because the $80,000 external sales of Segment X alone make up more than 75 percent of combined external sales of $101,000.

Financial information is to be presented in dollar terms (percentages are optional) and revenue, operating profit or loss, and identifiable assets are to be reconciled to the consolidated totals. We illustrate these disclosures and reconciliations in Exhibit 12.2 with an excerpt from a recent annual report of Caterpillar Tractor Company.

Comments on the Industry Disclosure Requirements   *SFAS 14* has compromised in the troubling area of common costs (see definition of operating profit or loss above). Major categories of corporate-wide expenses are not to be allocated to segments, although other common costs more closely related to segments' activities must be allocated.

The transfer pricing issue has been only partially accommodated. Each segment must disclose its total sales to other segments as well as the basis for pricing those sales. This is an inadequate approach to the problems created by intersegment transfers large enough to be considered material. Such transfers are both sales *and* purchases, yet there are no requirements to (1) disclose each segment's internal purchases and (2) disclose the amounts of intersegment sales and purchases between *each pair* of industry segments. As a result, the financial statement reader cannot determine the total impact of internal transactions on each segment when three or more segments are reported. Although one can ascertain the extent to which each segment makes *sales* to internal and external customers, one cannot determine the amount of *purchases* made by each segment from internal and external suppliers. This is important because, in our judgment, when either substantial intersegment sales or purchases are present it becomes difficult to evaluate true segment profitability.

Foreign Operations and Export Sales   Foreign operations generally face different risks than domestic operations. To appreciate the extent of foreign op-

Exhibit 12.2   Example of Industry Segment Disclosures under *SFAS 14:* The Caterpillar Tractor Company

13. SEGMENT INFORMATION

The following information on the company's business and geographic segments is prepared and presented in accordance with the requirements of Statement of Financial Accounting Standards No. 14—*Financial Reporting for Segments of a Business Enterprise.*

BUSINESS SEGMENTS

The company is engaged in the manufacture and sale of earthmoving, construction and materials handling machinery and equipment (Machinery and Equipment),

such as track-type tractors, bulldozers, rippers, track and wheel loaders, lift trucks, pipelayers, motor graders, wheel dozers, compactors, wheel tractor-scrapers, hydraulic excavators, skidders, off-highway trucks and related parts and equipment. The company also manufactures diesel engines for incorporation in its machines, and diesel and natural gas engines for sale as on-highway truck engines, marine and industrial engines, electric power generation systems, and related equipment (Engines). Data on these business segments is as follows:

Caterpillar Tractor Co.
and Consolidated Subsidiary Companies
Notes to Financial Statements (Continued)
(Millions of Dollars)

	Machinery and Equipment	Engines	Eliminations	Consolidated
For the Year Ended December 31, 1977:				
Sales	$5,077.7	$ 771.2	$ —	$5,848.9
Transfers between Business Segments	—	487.7	(487.7)	—
Total	$5,077.7	$1,258.9	$ (487.7)	$5,848.9
Operating Profit	$ 804.3	$ 155.6	$ 3.9	$ 963.8
General Corporate Expenses				(131.6)
Interest on Borrowed Funds				(95.4)
Miscellaneous Income				40.3
Taxes Based on Income				(334.1)
Equity in Profit of Affiliated Companies				.3
Profit of Subsidiary Credit Companies				1.8
Profit for Year—Consolidated				$ 445.1
Capitalized Expenditures for Land, Buildings, Machinery and Equipment	$ 329.3	$ 168.4		
Depreciation	$ 151.4	$ 57.4		
At December 31, 1977:				
Identifiable Assets	$2,911.1	$1,012.1	$ (23.3)	$3,899.9
General Corporate Assets				373.2
Investments in Affiliated Companies				54.9
Investments in and Advances to Subsidiary Credit Companies				17.6
Total Assets				$4,345.6

The major portion of transfers between business segments occurs within the parent company. Transfer values reflect cost and a proportionate share of total operating profit. The high degree of integration of the Company's manufacturing operations necessitates the use of a substantial number of allocations in the preparation of the business segment information.

erations, the following information is to be disclosed for domestic operations in total[10] and for the various significant foreign geographic areas (segments).

1. *Sales* to unaffiliated customers, total sales to other geographic segments, and the basis for pricing the sales to other geographic segments.

2. *Operating profit or loss* as previously defined *or* net income *or* another measure of profitability *between* operating profit or loss and net income.

3. *Identifiable assets* as previously defined.

Export Sales   When sales to unaffiliated customers in foreign countries *(export sales)* amount to 10 percent or more of consolidated sales to unaffiliated customers, the firm's *domestic operations* must report export sales separately. They must be reported in total and by geographic areas deemed appropriate by management.

Determining Foreign Geographic Segments   There are two stages involved in determining whether information about foreign operations must be disclosed and, if disclosure is necessary, how many geographic segments must be identified.

1. Information about foreign operations must be disclosed if *either* sales by foreign operations to unaffiliated customers are at least 10 percent of consolidated revenue *or* assets identified with the foreign operations are at least 10 percent of consolidated assets.

2. If foreign operations are conducted in two or more geographical areas (countries or groups of countries), more than one geographical segment must be reported if a segment's sales to unaffiliated customers or identifiable assets are at least 10 percent of the consolidated amounts. That is, the segment(s) meeting the 10 percent test must be reported separately from the others; the others may be combined for reporting purposes.

The financial information must be presented in dollars; percentages are optional. Foreign geographic segments are to be identified and the sales, profitability, and identifiable assets of each segment shall be reconciled to the consolidated totals. These disclosures and reconciliations are illustrated in Exhibit 12.3, again using Caterpillar Tractor Company.

Major Customers   To alert investors to the possible dependence of a firm on one or more large customers, the following information about major customers must be disclosed, even if the firm need not disclose industry or foreign segment information.

1. If at least 10 percent of consolidated revenue is derived from a single customer (or group of customers under common control), the firm must disclose that fact and the revenue from each such major customer.

---

[10] The firm need not report separate information about domestic operations if domestic sales to unaffiliated customers and domestic identifiable assets are less than 10 percent of the consolidated amounts.

Exhibit 12.3   Example of Foreign Operations and Export Sales Disclosures under *SFAS 14:* The Caterpillar
Tractor Co.

GEOGRAPHIC SEGMENTS

Manufacturing activities are carried on in fourteen plants in the United States, three in the United Kingdom, two each
in Brazil and France, and one each in Australia, Belgium, Canada and Mexico. Four major parts warehousing and
distributing facilities are located in the United States and eight are located abroad.

The product of manufacturing operations located outside the United States in most instances consists of components
manufactured or purchased abroad which are assembled with components manufactured in the United States and
transferred at intercompany prices. As a result, the profits of these operations do not bear any definite relationship to
their assets. The Company's intercompany pricing philosophy is that prices between Caterpillar companies are
established at levels deemed equivalent to those which would prevail in arm's-length transactions.

Caterpillar Tractor Co.
and Consolidated Subsidiary Companies
Notes to Financial Statements (Concluded)
(Millions of Dollars)

Data on the Company's geographic segments, based on the location of the manufacturing operation, is as follows:

	United States	Outside United States Europe	Outside United States All Other	Eliminations	Consolidated
For the Year Ended December 31, 1977:					
Sales	$4,740.0	$773.8	$335.1	$ —	$5,848.9
Transfers between Geographic Areas	161.8	5.9	—	(167.7)	—
Total	$4,901.8	$779.7	$335.1	$(167.7)	$5,848.9
Operating Profit	$ 872.5	$ 77.4	$ 15.0	$ (1.1)	$ 963.8
General Corporate Expenses					(131.6)
Interest on Borrowed Funds					(95.4)
Miscellaneous Income					40.3
Taxes Based on Income					(334.1)
Equity in Profit of Affiliated Companies					.3
Profit of Subsidiary Credit Companies					1.8
Profit for Year—Consolidated					$ 445.1
At December 31, 1977:					
Identifiable Assets	$3,150.1	$486.4	$284.3	$ (20.9)	$3,899.9
General Corporate Assets					373.2
Investments in Affiliated Companies					54.9
Investments in and Advances to Subsidiary Credit Companies					17.6
Total Assets					$4,345.6

Data on the Company's 1977 sales outside the United States, based on dealer location, are as follows:

	Europe	Africa, Middle East	Canada	Latin America	Australasia	Sales Outside United States
Export Sales of U.S. Manufactured Product	$340.5	$508.9	$279.1	$438.2	$290.9	$1,857.6
Sales of Non-U.S. Manufactured Product	398.3	375.9	53.5	161.8	119.4	1,108.9
Total	$738.8	$884.8	$332.6	$600.0	$410.3	$2,966.5

The sales outside the United States of $2,966.5 million were 50.7% of consolidated sales in 1977.

2.   If at least 10 percent of consolidated revenue is derived from domestic government agencies or foreign government agencies, the firm must so indicate and disclose the revenue from each group of government agencies.

In both cases, the industry segments making the sales to major commercial and governmental customers must be identified. Names of specific customers, however, need not be revealed. Examples of such disclosures appear in Exhibit 12.4.

Pronouncements Amending *SFAS 14*   Following its publication in 1976, *SFAS 14* has been amended by the following pronouncements of the FASB:

1.   *SFAS 18* (AC § 2082) eliminated the requirement for disclosure of segment information in interim reports.[11] Voluntary disclosure, however, must conform with *SFAS 14*.

2.   *SFAS 21* (AC § 2083) removed nonpublic enterprises from the provisions of *SFAS 14*, pending further action by the FASB.[12] A *nonpublic enterprise* is an enterprise (1) whose debt or equity securities are not publicly traded or (2) which is not required to file financial statements with the SEC.

3.   *SFAS 24* (AC § 2084) deals with the *separate* financial statements of enterprises which are presented along with consolidated or combined statements that *include* the enterprise.[13] Such enterprises include the parent company, subsidiaries, and corporate joint ventures. The combined or consolidated statements including such enterprises must comply with *SFAS 14*, but separate compliance is generally not required for their separate statements presented as notes or exhibits to the combined or consolidated statements.

Authors' Comments on *SFAS 14*   Disclosure of segment information in external reports is necessary if complex, diversified firms are to satisfy any reasonable standard of full disclosure. We have seen that some inherent conceptual problems—transfer pricing and common cost allocations—can limit the usefulness of segment data when intersegment transactions and common costs are material. *SFAS 14* presents a reasonable compromise on these conceptual

---

[11] Financial Accounting Standards Board, *Statement of Financial Accounting Standards No. 18,* "Financial Reporting for Segments of a Business Enterprise—Interim Financial Statements" (Stamford, Conn.: FASB, 1977).

[12] Financial Accounting Standards Board, *Statement of Financial Accounting Standards No. 21,* "Suspension of the Reporting of Earnings per Share and Segment Information by Nonpublic Enterprises" (Stamford, Conn.: FASB, 1978).

[13] Financial Accounting Standards Board, *Statement of Financial Accounting Standards No. 24,* "Reporting Segment Information in Financial Statements That Are Presented in Another Enterprise's Financial Report" (Stamford, Conn.: FASB, 1978).

Exhibit 12.4   Examples of *SFAS 14* Major Customer Disclosures

LOCKHEED CORPORATION, which reported sales of $3,485 million in 1978 and $3,348 million in 1977, disclosed the following:

By customer category, sales to the U.S. government totaled $1,968 million in 1978 and $2,076 million in 1977, and to foreign governments $998 million in 1978 and $749 million in 1977 excluding sales to foreign airlines that are owned by their respective governments of $174 million in 1978 and $162 million in 1977. Sales to one foreign government including sales to its national airline totaled $515 million in 1978 and $418 million in 1977.

WESTINGHOUSE ELECTRIC CORPORATION disclosed the following:

The largest single customer of the Corporation is the United States Government and its agencies, whose purchases accounted for 10.8 per cent of total consolidated sales in 1977 and 10.2 per cent in 1976. Of these purchases, 22 per cent in 1977 and 18 per cent in 1976 were made from Power Systems, 4 per cent in 1977 and 4 per cent in 1976 from Industry Products, and 71 per cent in 1977 and 74 percent in 1976 from Public Systems. In addition, Other Income includes fees generated through United States Government–owned Westinghouse-operated facilities.

issues, requiring disclosures that enable the careful reader to estimate the limitations in a given segment report. Unfortunately, we believe that the *Statement* suffers from two additional flaws as it relates to firms with significant intersegment transactions.

1. Disclosure of the volume of intersegment sales *and* purchases between each pair of selling and buying segments is not required but should be, so the reader can ascertain the degree of interdependence among the various segments. Remember that intersegment transactions are *not* market transactions, even though transfer prices may be based on market prices. Furthermore, it would be useful to know which of the segments are most heavily influenced by the behavior of other segments.

2. Meaningful selection of reportable segments is made more difficult by the failure to include the volume of intersegment transactions as a significance criterion. In this case, however, the significance test would be in the opposite direction. For example, if the volume of intersegment transactions is at least 10 percent, the segment should *not* be separately reported. Recall our earlier reference to the 1977 annual report of Norton Simon Inc. On page 56 of that report, we are told that "operating results of the packaging segment are affected by the volume of intersegment transactions." Of the six segments reported in 1977, packaging ranked second in operating profit and third in terms of the ratio of operating profit to sales. Fully *40 percent* of packaging's sales were to other segments in the firm. Our proposed significance test would require that packaging be combined with another segment and not be reported separately.

Interim Reporting: Accounting Theory and Disclosure Issues

Whereas segment reporting involved disaggregating information of the reporting *entity* into relevant areas of economic activity, interim reporting concerns a breakdown of information for the annual reporting *period* into shorter periods. Allocations were a problem in segment reporting because some costs benefited more than one business segment. In **interim reporting,** we seek to divide the annual reporting period into several reporting periods of shorter duration. But many costs incurred benefit more than one interim period and allocations may also be a problem here. This part of the chapter addresses these and other problems associated with interim reporting as they relate to conceptual issues, generally accepted accounting principles, and actual practice.

The Problem

Although not *required* by generally accepted accounting principles, interim reports have been issued by major companies for years. The New York Stock Exchange requires listed companies to release interim information, and the SEC calls for registrants to file Form 10–Q, a quarterly report to the SEC. There are, however, accounting rules regarding the form, content, and principles underlying interim reports released to investors. The rules simply specify that *if* interim information is reported, *then* these principles and practices are to be followed. Official pronouncements setting forth these guidelines include *APBO 28,*[14] *SFAS 3* (AC § 2072),[15] and *IFAS 18* (AC § 2071–1).[16] Interim reporting, however, continues to be a controversial subject because of the difficulties created by the fundamental problem in interim reporting, that is, defining *the nature of the interim reporting period.*

> When contemplating the measurement of earnings for an interim period, one must decide whether the interim period is to be viewed as an *integral* but subordinate portion of a longer period—the year—or as a *discrete* reporting period, standing on its own and unaffected by the other interim periods within the year.

These are the polar positions regarding the nature of the interim reporting period. Adoption of one or the other provides an overall orientation for more detailed interim reporting rules. Accommodating the characteristics of some items, however, may require that an intermediate position be accepted.

The Integral Position   The **integral position** views the interim reporting period as an integral part of the annual reporting period and avoids many strange results that would otherwise occur. For example, major maintenance costs undertaken early in the year but benefiting the entire year are charged against each of the four quarterly periods on a pro rata basis. Bonuses deter-

---

[14] Accounting Principles Board, *Opinion No. 28;* AC § 2071.

[15] Financial Accounting Standards Board, *Statement of Financial Accounting Standards No. 3,* "Reporting Accounting Changes in Interim Financial Statements" (Stamford, Conn.: FASB, 1974).

[16] Financial Accounting Standards Board, *Interpretation of Financial Accounting Standards No. 18,* "Accounting for Income Taxes in Interim Periods" (Stamford, Conn.: FASB, 1977).

mined in the last quarter of the year are estimated and charged proportionately against the four quarterly periods. However, other problems arise in connection with intrayear impairment of LIFO layers and income taxes. They will be discussed later.

The FASB Discussion Memorandum on interim reporting identifies the following characteristics of the *integral position:*

1. Interim period profit margins are reasonably constant throughout the year.

2. Expenses are allocated to interim periods on the basis of annual estimates of revenues and costs.

3. Inaccuracies in those estimates require adjustments in subsequent interim periods.

4. Earnings fluctuate less than under other approaches if those estimates are reasonably accurate.

5. Components of financial statements, such as assets, liabilities, revenues, expenses, and earnings are defined differently for interim periods than for annual periods.

6. Unforeseen events, such as catastrophic losses, gains or losses from discontinued segments of a business, and settlements of major litigations are not allocated to all periods but are recognized when they occur.[17]

The major thrust of the integral view is to estimate "annual" operating expenses —not those costs traceable to specific production and sales in particular interim periods—and allocate them to the quarterly periods on some basis of activity. The result is to smooth earnings over the four quarterly periods; the principal reporting period is the entire year.

The *integral position* seems consistent with the view that the *primary function of interim reports is prediction.* Quarterly reports are progress reports between annual closing dates and, as such, should be helpful in predicting future quarterly and annual results. The smoothing of interim income achieved by allocating annual items to quarterly periods on some activity basis aids in the prediction effort. On the other hand, there is some cost in terms of reduced objectivity because the estimates, allocations, and accruals called for under the integral view involve subjective judgments.

The Discrete Position   The **discrete position** sees each interim period standing on its own, reporting what occurred in that period, unaffected by accountants' subjective judgments regarding estimates and allocations of "annual" expenses. In principle, the quarterly interim report becomes a mini–annual report, covering three months rather than twelve.

Characteristics of the *discrete position* identified in the FASB Discussion Memorandum (pp. iv–v) are:

1. Expense recognition standards do not change with the length of the reporting period.

---

[17] Financial Accounting Standards Board, Discussion Memorandum, "Interim Financial Accounting and Reporting" (Stamford, Conn.: FASB, 1978), p. iv.

2.   Interim reporting requires no estimates or allocations different from those required for annual reporting.

3.   Components of financial statements such as assets, liabilities, expenses, and earnings are defined in the same way as they are for annual statements.

4.   The shorter the reporting period, the more likely it is that seasonal influences and discretionary costs will cause fluctuations in period-to-period earnings.[18]

Those who favor the discrete position believe that quarterly reporting periods are principal reporting periods, fundamentally different than annual periods only in the amount of time spanned. They make no special claims for the discrete period view except to observe that it requires no resources devoted to making the estimates, accruals, deferrals, and adjustments prescribed by the integral position and needs fewer subjective judgments.

In contrast to the predictive role envisioned by the integral position, the *discrete position* sees the *major function of interim reports as historical.* Under the discrete view, whatever usefulness is possessed by annual reports is also possessed by interim reports. Such reports may be helpful in prediction only insofar as any objectively determined historical record is helpful. No special effort should be made to improve the predictive ability of interim reports at the expense of objectivity.

Comparing the Two Positions with a Numerical Example   To illustrate the differences in interim earnings that can arise under these two polar approaches, we concentrate on two items that would be handled differently in interim reports prepared under the integral and discrete views:

1.   Maintenance costs are incurred in the first quarter but benefit the entire year.

2.   Quantity purchase discounts are realized in the fourth quarter but depend on the purchases made in all four quarters.

Suppose the Johnson Company projects the following activity and cost levels during the year's four quarterly periods:

	Quarter 1	Quarter 2	Quarter 3	Quarter 4
Units Produced and Sold . . .	40,000	60,000	30,000	80,000
Unit Selling Price	$2.00	$2.25	$2.30	$2.30
Traceable Costs per Unit . . .	$1.00	$1.10	$1.20	$1.20
Major Maintenance	$50,000	—	—	—
Credit for Quantity Purchase Discounts	—	—	—	$(20,000)

Exhibit 12.5 gives condensed quarterly income statements under the integral and discrete views, assuming that all projected amounts come to be realized. Allocation of the major maintenance and quantity purchase discounts across

---

[18]   Ibid., pp. iv–v.

Exhibit 12.5   Comparison of the Integral and Discrete Approaches to Interim Reporting

The Johnson Corporation
Condensed Quarterly Income Statements

INTEGRAL APPROACH	Quarter 1	Quarter 2	Quarter 3	Quarter 4	Total
Sales	$ 80,000	$135,000	$ 69,000	$184,000	$468,000
Traceable Costs	$ 40,000	$ 66,000	$ 36,000	$ 96,000	$238,000
Maintenance Costs[a]	9,500	14,500	7,000	19,000	50,000
Quantity Purchase Discount Credit[a]	(3,800)	(5,800)	(2,800)	(7,600)	(20,000)
Total Expenses	$ 45,700	$ 74,700	$ 40,200	$107,400	$268,000
Income before Taxes	$ 34,300	$ 60,300	$ 28,800	$ 76,600	$200,000
Deferred Costs at End of Period	$ 40,500	$ 26,000	$ 19,000	—	—
Accrued Income at End of Period	(3,800)	(9,600)	(12,400)	$ (20,000)	—

DISCRETE APPROACH	Quarter 1	Quarter 2	Quarter 3	Quarter 4	Total
Sales	$ 80,000	$135,000	$ 69,000	$184,000	$468,000
Traceable Costs	$ 40,000	$ 66,000	$ 36,000	$ 96,000	$238,000
Maintenance Costs	50,000	—	—	—	50,000
Quantity Purchase Discount Credit	—	—	—	(20,000)	(20,000)
Total Expenses	$ 90,000	$ 66,000	$ 36,000	$ 76,000	$268,000
Income (Loss) before Taxes	$(10,000)	$ 69,000	$ 33,000	$108,000	$200,000
Deferred Costs at End of Period	—	—	—	—	—
Accrued Income at End of Period	—	—	—	—	—

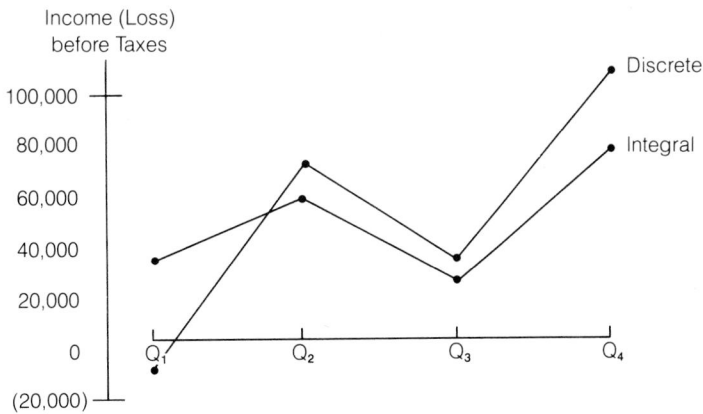

Graph of Quarterly Income (Loss)
before Taxes under the
Integral and Discrete Approaches

[a]Allocation of these items based on the following percentages: $Q_1 = 19\%$; $Q_2 = 29\%$; $Q_3 = 14\%$; $Q_4 = 38\%$.

the four quarters under the integral position is based on the percentage of total units produced and sold in each quarter.

We can see how one's view of the nature of the interim period affects the accounting information produced. Note that the pattern of quarterly income portrayed in the graph under the integral approach is smoother or less variable than under the discrete approach. In this case, the differences are due to large annual items, the maintenance costs and purchase discounts. Supporters of the integral view might also allocate fixed overhead costs which occur uniformly during the year to the four quarters based on some measure of quarterly activity. If this is done, differences appear even if there are no annual items.

Evaluation of the Integral and Discrete Positions   We believe that by reporting on the past, financial statements provide information helpful in judging the future. Interim reports should also serve this purpose, although the future may be interpreted more narrowly as the time when annual financial statements are prepared. Similarly, the timeliness of interim reports has particular value if the reports are capable of revealing any changes or turning points in the firm's performance. The *integral position* as it relates to the interim reporting period seems most consistent with these objectives. Our objection to the *discrete position* is that in reporting each interim period's information just as it occurs, without making adjustments and allocations, the discrete view may distort the quarterly results. The seasonal nature of a firm's business ought to be made clear in the interim reports, but the lumpiness of many annual expenses can conceal such seasonality. Charging such expenses entirely against the quarterly period when they are incurred may cause quarterly earnings to behave randomly or in some other pattern unrelated to underlying seasonal influences.

We hasten to add, however, that in favoring the integral approach we would allocate only *annual items*. Fixed costs incurred uniformly throughout the year should be reported as incurred and not be shifted to other quarterly periods by an allocation scheme related to quarterly sales or some other measure of activity. Such allocations could lead to a different picture of seasonality than actually exists.

Therefore, the integral position seems to us to provide the most useful frame of reference within which detailed interim reporting principles can be developed. On specific items, however, intermediate or compromise positions may be appropriate.

Income Taxes in Interim Reports

Reporting income taxes in interim reports is a particularly thorny problem for two reasons:

1. The corporate tax rate schedule is progressive, and the marginal tax rate can change from quarter to quarter.

2. The effective tax rate may differ from the statutory rate and, furthermore, may change from period to period as investment tax credits are earned, timing differences between pretax accounting income and taxable income arise and reverse, and permanent differences arise.

If the interim reporting period is viewed as an *integral* portion of a longer period, the year, the firm estimates its effective tax rate for the entire year and applies that rate to income before taxes in each quarter. This practice smooths income tax expense for the year over the four quarters and removes fluctuations in net income due to tax items which arise in individual interim periods but are meaningful only within the context of a full year.

In contrast, viewing the interim period as a *discrete* reporting period normally gives different results. Quarterly income tax expense is based on developments in each quarter rather than over the entire year. For example, suppose a firm's quarterly pretax income is fairly constant, and large investment tax credits are earned in the third quarter. Income tax expense in the third quarter could fall, even though pretax income is constant, and net income would appear to jump.

These two approaches to accounting for income taxes in interim periods are illustrated in Exhibit 12.6. The smoothing of quarterly income tax expense under the integral approach permits the quarterly results to accurately reflect the firm's stable, nonseasonal operations.

Using LIFO in Interim Periods

Accounting for inventories under the LIFO cost-flow assumption gives rise to another issue in the context of interim reporting. When physical inventories at interim reporting dates change, and LIFO is being used, should the changes be accounted for within the context of the (estimated) year-end LIFO inventory or be based on the actual change occurring at the end of the interim period? In short, how should LIFO layers added or deleted at interim dates be valued? The question is important because its answer affects both cost of goods sold and net income for the interim period.

The question assumes even greater practical importance when LIFO layers include very old low costs. Suppose inventory at the end of a quarterly period *falls*, but the firm plans to replace it by year-end. Should cost of goods sold for the interim period reflect the old costs of the temporarily impaired LIFO layer(s)? Is it misleading to do so when the impairment will be restored later in the year?

The Integral Position on LIFO   As one might expect, the integral position supports the notion that it is not the change in *interim* inventory that is important; it is the change in the *annual* inventory that counts. Under this concept, the estimated annual change in inventory is allocated to the interim periods on a systematic and rational basis, perhaps on the basis of interim sales.

The Discrete Position on LIFO   If each interim period is considered to be a discrete reporting period, standing alone, the principles and procedures used to determine LIFO inventory at year-end are also used at the end of each interim period. While no estimates or allocations are called for here, the total income reported for the four quarters may not equal annual net income, a troubling result. To see this, suppose a LIFO layer in the beginning inventory is used up at June 30 but is fully replenished by the end of the year, December 31. Impairment of the layer at June 30 would be reflected in quarter two's reported net income yet, because the layer was not impaired at December 31, annual net income would be unaffected. This leads to a discrepancy between annual net income and the sum of the quarterly net incomes.

Exhibit 12.6   Accounting for Income Taxes in Interim Periods

DATA FOR ILLUSTRATION

The West Corporation predicts income before taxes of $50,000 in each of the four quarterly periods during the next calendar year. Furthermore, it expects to earn $20,000 in investment credits on property placed in service in June. Under current law, the West Corporation faces the following United States corporate income tax schedule:

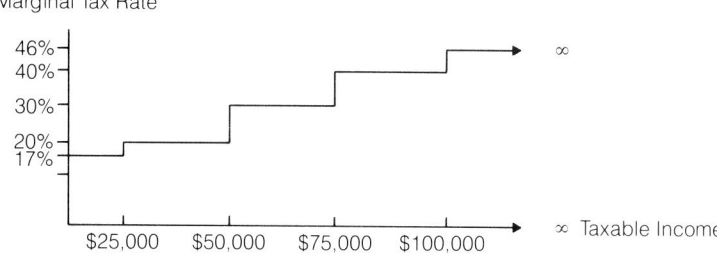

NOTE: Under the Economic Recovery Act of 1981, the marginal tax rates on the two lowest brackets of corporate taxable income decline to 16 percent and 19 percent in 1982 and to 15 percent and 18 percent in 1983 and thereafter.

Condensed quarterly income statements for the integral and discrete approaches are as follows:

INTEGRAL APPROACH	Quarter 1	Quarter 2	Quarter 3	Quarter 4	Total
Income before Taxes	$50,000	$50,000	$50,000	$50,000	$200,000
Income Tax Expense[a]	13,187	13,187	13,188	13,188	52,750
Net Income	$36,813	$36,813	$36,812	$36,812	$147,250

DISCRETE APPROACH	Quarter 1	Quarter 2	Quarter 3	Quarter 4	Total
Income before Taxes	$50,000	$50,000	$50,000	$50,000	$200,000
Income Tax Expense	9,250 [b]	(2,500)[c]	23,000 [d]	23,000 [d]	52,750
Net Income	$40,750	$52,500	$27,000	$27,000	$147,250

[a]Effective tax rate for the year is $26.375\% = [.17(\$25,000) + .20(\$25,000) + .30(\$25,000) + .40(\$25,000) + .46(\$100,000) - \$20,000]/\$200,000$.
[b]$\$9,250 = .17(\$25,000) + .2(\$25,000)$.
[c]$(\$2,500) = .3(\$25,000) + .4(\$25,000) - \$20,000$.
[d]$\$23,000 = .46(\$50,000)$.

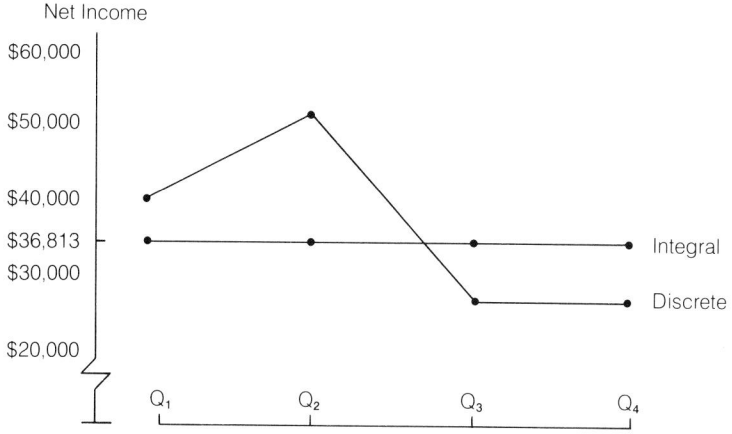

Graph of Quarterly Net Income
under the
Integral and Discrete Approaches

An Intermediate Position on LIFO   One way to avoid the discrepancy that might result under the discrete approach to LIFO also limits the smoothing effect of inventory changes when the integral position is applied. This intermediate position calls for charging cost of goods sold for the current replacement cost of any LIFO layers used during the year but expected to be replenished by the end of the year. An expected annual change in the LIFO inventory, however, is not estimated and allocated to the quarterly periods.

To illustrate how this discrepancy arises, we have prepared a numerical example in Exhibit 12.7. Since the example focuses on the temporary impairment of a LIFO layer, and not on a change in the annual LIFO inventory, the integral and intermediate positions provide the same results. Note the $20,000 difference between the total quarterly gross profit reported under the discrete approach and the annual gross profit. On the annual basis, the LIFO inventory is unchanged. The ending inventory implied by the discrete approach, however, includes a new layer of 10,000 units valued at current cost of $6. Thus the year-end inventory under the discrete approach is $20,000 higher and cost of goods sold $20,000 lower than either would be if LIFO was simply applied on an annual basis.

Alternative approaches are available to account for the excess of current cost over LIFO cost of temporarily impaired LIFO layers. In the third quarter, the 10,000 units sold from inventory were charged to cost of goods sold at their current cost of $60,000 rather than their LIFO inventory cost of $40,000. The $20,000 difference is accounted for in interim periods as a reduction to inventory or as a deferred credit such as Interim Inventory Allowance. In the fourth quarter, when the sold LIFO layer is replenished, the LIFO cost of $40,000 is restored to the inventory, not the current replacement cost of $60,000. The following adjusting journal entries made at the end of quarters 3 and 4 would accomplish this:

QUARTER 3

Cost of Goods Sold	60,000	
Inventory		40,000
Interim Inventory Allowance (or Inventory)		20,000

To charge Cost of Goods Sold for the current cost of the goods sold from inventory and record the excess over LIFO cost in an allowance until the LIFO layer is replenished. Cost of Goods Sold of $300,000 = $90,000 + $240,000 − [$90,000 − ($40,000 + $20,000)].

QUARTER 4

Inventory	40,000	
Interim Inventory Allowance (or Inventory)	20,000	
Cost of Goods Sold		60,000

To restore the replenished LIFO layer to Inventory at its LIFO cost, remove the allowance, and adjust the Cost of Goods Sold accordingly. Cost of Goods Sold of $240,000 = [$90,000 − ($40,000 + $20,000)] + $300,000 − $90,000.

This interim inventory allowance can fluctuate during the interim periods in order to provide the needed amounts of cost of goods sold. At year-end, when the firm knows exactly what LIFO layers have been replenished and what the

Exhibit 12.7   Alternative Treatments of Temporary Impairment of LIFO Layer in Interim Reports

DATA FOR ILLUSTRATION

The Webster Corporation uses LIFO and begins the year with an inventory of $90,000, consisting of the following LIFO layers: (1) 10,000 units @ $4, (2) 10,000 units @ $3, and (3) 10,000 units @ $2. Quarterly sales and purchases occur according to the following schedule:

	Quarter 1	Quarter 2	Quarter 3	Quarter 4
Sales	40,000 @ $10	40,000 @ $10	50,000 @ $10	40,000 @ $10
Purchases	40,000 @ $6	40,000 @ $6	40,000 @ $6	50,000 @ $6

Notice that sales exceed purchases by 10,000 units in quarter 3, while purchases exceed sales by 10,000 units in quarter 4. Units in inventory are used in quarter 3, but they are replenished in quarter 4. From an annual point of view, the beginning and ending inventories valued at LIFO are identical. Condensed quarterly income statements under the integral and discrete approaches and a condensed annual income statement are as follows:

INTEGRAL APPROACH	Quarter 1	Quarter 2	Quarter 3	Quarter 4	Total
Sales	$400,000	$400,000	$500,000	$400,000	$1,700,000
Cost of Goods Sold	(240,000)	(240,000)	(300,000)[a]	(240,000)	(1,020,000)
Gross Profit	$160,000	$160,000	$200,000	$160,000	$ 680,000

DISCRETE APPROACH	Quarter 1	Quarter 2	Quarter 3	Quarter 4	Total
Sales	$400,000	$400,000	$500,000	$400,000	$1,700,000
Cost of Goods Sold	(240,000)	(240,000)	(280,000)[b]	(240,000)	(1,000,000)
Gross Profit	$160,000	$160,000	$220,000	$160,000	$ 700,000

[a]Valued at current replacement cost; the LIFO layer temporarily "used" is ignored.
[b]Consists of 40,000 units at current replacement cost of $6 ($240,000) plus the most recent LIFO layer of 10,000 units with a LIFO cost of $4($40,000).

ANNUAL STATEMENT

Sales (170,000 @ $10)	$1,700,000
Cost of Goods Sold (170,000 @ $6)	(1,020,000)
Gross Profit	$ 680,000

annual cost of goods sold is, the allowance is closed out and fourth quarter cost of goods sold adjusted accordingly. If the actual cost of replacing the LIFO layers differs from the estimated cost at date of impairment, the difference is reflected in cost of goods sold in the period in which replacement occurs.

Interim Reporting under *APBO* 28, as Amended

APBO 28 provides most of the authoritative guidance governing the principles and practices to be used in developing interim financial information.[19] Specific provisions involving income taxes and accounting changes have been amended and are discussed following this overview of *APBO 28*.

APBO 28   This *Opinion* was issued in response to the great diversity existing in interim reporting practices. Its objective was to clarify the application of

---

[19]   Accounting Principles Board, *Opinion No. 28*; AC § 2071.

generally accepted accounting principles to interim reports and to prescribe minimum disclosures for publicly traded companies choosing to issue interim reports. Early in the *Opinion*, the board "concluded that each interim period should be viewed primarily as an *integral part of an annual period*."[20] Much of the *Opinion* is devoted to describing how annual reporting principles and practices must be modified in order to conform to the integral position. As previously indicated, *APBO 28* does *not* impose a requirement for the disclosure of interim information as *SFAS 14* did for segment information. Rather, if the decision is made to issue interim information, it should conform with the provisions of *APBO 28*, even though the information is not audited. The principal requirements of *APBO 28* are summarized in Exhibit 12.8.

Note that these requirements relate almost entirely to income statement information; no mention is made of information normally included in balance sheets and statements of changes in financial position. Indeed, the *Opinion* provides no guidance as to the form and content of interim financial *statements*. It deals with interim financial *information* disclosed in an unspecified format. The minimum disclosure requirements for publicly traded companies are listed in item 7 of Exhibit 12.8. Again, this is not a requirement that publicly traded companies issue interim reports; rather it provides guidelines for minimum disclosures by those publicly traded companies that do report on an interim basis.

Consider some ways in which *APBO 28*'s provisions are consistent with the integral position:

1. Temporary impairment of LIFO layers expected to be replenished by year-end should not be reflected in interim cost of sales or inventories (paragraph 14.b). Permanent impairment of LIFO layers in interim periods and inventory increases should be recognized in those interim periods. Interim income is not to be smoothed by an allocation of expected inventory change to the interim periods. This is the *intermediate position* on LIFO previously discussed rather than the pure integral position.

2. Inventory losses resulting from application of the lower-of-cost-or-market principle should not be recognized in the interim period if they are viewed as being restored by year-end (paragraph 14.c).

3. Costs and expenses not associated with revenue *may* be expensed as incurred, or, if more than one interim period is benefited, the cost or expense *may* be allocated among the periods benefited (paragraph 15). This provision undercuts an important feature of the integral view— namely, that costs benefiting more than one interim period *must* be allocated. *APBO 28* does not preclude allocation but does not require it either. Paragraph 16 offers some examples of costs that might or might not be allocated, such as quantity discounts based on annual sales volume, property taxes, and advertising costs clearly benefiting more than one interim period.

4. Income tax expense in interim periods will be based on the firm's best estimate of its annual effective tax rate (paragraph 19). If the estimate

---

[20] Ibid., par. 9; AC § 2071.9; emphasis added.

Exhibit 12.8   Principal Requirements of APB *Opinion No. 28*, "Interim Financial Reporting"

1. Revenue from products sold or services rendered should be recognized as earned during an interim period on the same basis as that followed for the full year.

2. Those costs and expenses that are associated directly with or allocated to the products sold or to the services rendered for annual reporting purposes (including, for example, material costs, wages and salaries and related fringe benefits, manufacturing overhead, and warranties) should be similarly treated for interim reporting purposes. The following exceptions relate to interim inventory valuation.

   a. Companies often use methods to estimate interim inventories which differ from the methods used at annual inventory dates. These companies should disclose the method used at the interim date and any significant adjustments which result from reconciliations with the annual physical inventory.

   b. Companies using LIFO may encounter temporary impairment of base period inventories which are expected to be replaced by the end of the annual period. In such cases, neither interim inventories nor cost of sales should reflect this temporary impairment; cost of sales should include the expected cost of replacing the liquidated LIFO base.

   c. Inventory losses from market declines should not be deferred beyond the interim period in which the decline occurs unless they are temporary and can reasonably be expected to be restored by the end of the annual period.

   d. For companies using standard cost systems, variances that are planned and expected to be absorbed by the end of the annual period should ordinarily be deferred at interim reporting dates.

3. Costs and expenses other than product costs should be charged to income in interim periods as incurred or be allocated among interim periods on the basis of an estimate of time expired, benefit received, or activity associated with the periods.

4. To avoid the possibility that interim results with material seasonal variations may be taken as fairly indicative of the estimated results for a full fiscal year, businesses should disclose the seasonal nature of their activities and consider supplementing their interim reports with information for twelve-month periods ended at the interim date for the current and preceding years.

5. At the end of each interim period, the company should make its best estimate of the effective tax rate expected to be applicable for the full fiscal year. The rate so determined should be used in providing for income taxes on a current year-to-date basis.

6. Extraordinary items should be disclosed separately and included in the determination of net income for the interim period in which they occur.

7. When publicly traded companies report summarized financial information to their security holders at interim dates (including reports on fourth quarters), the following data should be reported, as a minimum:

   a. Sales or gross revenues, provision for income taxes, extraordinary items (including related income tax effects), cumulative effect of a change in accounting principles or practices, and net income.

   b. Primary and fully diluted earnings per share data for each period presented.

   c. Seasonal revenue, cost, or expenses.

   d. Significant changes in estimates or provisions for income taxes.

   e. Disposal of a segment of a business and extraordinary, unusual, or infrequently occurring items.

   f. Contingent items.

   g. Changes in accounting principles or estimates.

   h. Significant changes in financial position.

Source: Accounting Principles Board, *Opinion No. 28*, "Interim Financial Reporting" (N.Y.: AICPA, 1973); AC § 2071; Copyright © 1973 by the American Institute of Certified Public Accountants, Inc.

of the effective tax rate is revised in a period, that period's income tax expense equals the year-to-date income tax expense (the new rate times the year-to-date pretax income) minus total income tax expense reported in prior interim periods. The following table illustrates computation of income tax expense in interim periods:

Period	Pretax Income Period	Pretax Income Year-to-Date	Estimated Annual Effective Tax Rate[a]	Income Tax Expense Year-to-Date	Income Tax Expense Total Prior Periods	Income Tax Expense Current Period
Q$_1$	$150,000	$150,000	42%	$ 63,000	—	$ 63,000
Q$_2$	120,000	270,000	44	118,800	$ 63,000	55,800
Q$_3$	130,000	400,000	38	152,000	118,800	33,200
Q$_4$	160,000	560,000	41	229,600	152,000	77,600
	$560,000					$229,600

[a]Based on the corporation income tax schedule given in Exhibit 12.6.

IFAS 18 was issued in March 1977 to clarify and elaborate on the original provisions in paragraphs 19 and 20 of *APBO 28*.[21] Specific problem areas addressed by the *Interpretation* include intraperiod tax allocation, loss carryforwards, multiple tax jurisdictions, and changes in tax legislation. We will not discuss these areas.

5. Attempts should be made to estimate certain year-end adjustments in order that each interim period bear a reasonable portion of the expected annual amount (paragraph 17). Some examples are bad debt expense, inventory shrinkage, and year-end bonuses.

Accounting Changes in Interim Reports The original provisions in *APBO 28* called for reporting any accounting changes made during the year in the appropriate interim periods and required that the accounting treatment of those changes conform to *APBO 20*. Unfortunately, a problem arose with respect to the treatment of *cumulative effect* accounting changes adopted in other than the first interim period. The problem concerned a potential discrepancy between interim income statements and balance sheets issued *prior* to a cumulative effect accounting change which were restated in interim periods *after* the change. In order to remedy this, *SFAS 3*[22] provides that the cumulative effect of a change in accounting principles be recognized only in the first quarter. If the change occurs in another quarter, the cumulative effect of the change on retained earnings at the beginning of the first quarter shall be included in (restated) first quarter net income. Other interim reports issued prior to the occurrence of the change are to be restated to reflect the new accounting principle.

Examples of Interim Reports Substantial diversity in interim reporting continues to exist. Some companies mail small pamphlets to stockholders containing selected data and no financial statements. Other companies develop elaborate brochures, complete with a full set of financial statements and notes. We reproduce portions of three of the latter type of interim report in Exhibits 12.9, 12.10, and 12.11 and comment briefly on each.

---

21 Financial Accounting Standards Board, *Interpretation No. 18*; AC § 2071–1.
22 Financial Accounting Standards Board, *Statement No. 3*; AC § 2072.

Exhibit 12.9   Extract from TRW Interim Report

TRW
First Quarter Report
1979

Consolidated Condensed Statement
of Change in Financial Position
(Dollars in Thousands)

	First Quarter Ended March 31	
	1979	1978
SOURCES OF WORKING CAPITAL		
Working Capital from Operations	$ 70,076	$62,556
Increases in Long-Term Obligations	$ 27,810	$23,119
Less Portion Representing Refinancing	(10,598)	(9,557)
	$ 17,212	$13,562
Other	$ 5,292	$ 3,333
Total Sources of Working Capital	$ 92,580	$79,451
APPLICATIONS OF WORKING CAPITAL		
Dividends Declared	—	$17,057
Additions to Property, Plant and Equipment	$ 34,564	25,172
Purchases of Businesses (Exclusive of Working Capital Acquired)	27,180	6,199
Payments and Maturities of Long-Term Obligations . . .	38,792	5,354
Other	2,799	8,922
Total Applications of Working Capital	$103,335	$62,704
Increase (Decrease) in Working Capital	$ (10,755)	$16,747

NOTES TO FINANCIAL STATEMENTS

PRINCIPLES OF CONSOLIDATION. The consolidated financial statements include the accounts of the Company and all significant subsidiaries. Investments in unconsolidated subsidiaries, which include a subsidiary engaged in insuring certain risks of the Company, and associated companies are accounted for by the equity method.

During the first quarter the Company acquired 100% ownership of C. E. Niehoff & Co. and Optron, Inc., for $29.0 million and $16.8 million in cash, respectively.

In addition, the Company purchased an additional 25% of Tokai TRW & Co., Ltd. for $11.4 million. Prior to this purchase TRW had a 49% ownership and its earnings were recorded on the equity method.

The above acquisitions have been accounted for as purchases. The results of operations of these companies, which were not significant in relation to the consolidated results, have been recorded since the dates of acquisition.

RESEARCH AND DEVELOPMENT. Research and development expenses included in pretax earnings amounted to approximately $14.0 million and $11.9 million for the first quarters in 1979 and 1978 respectively.

Exhibit 12.9 *continued*

CONTINGENT LIABILITIES. Renegotiation of government contracts has been completed for all years prior to 1970. Sales for 1970 and subsequent years include amounts subject to renegotiation for the limitation of profit, but the Company believes that no adjustments of reported net earnings will be required.

The Company is involved in litigation incidental to its business. In the opinion of management, the expected outcome of such litigation will not materially affect the Company's financial position.

EARNINGS PER SHARE. Fully diluted earnings per share have been computed based on the weighted average number of shares of Common Stock outstanding during each period including common stock equivalents and assuming the conversion of the 5% Guaranteed Debentures, the Serial Preference Stock—Series B, the Serial Preference Stock II—Series 1 and 3. Primary earnings per share have been computed based on the weighted average number of shares of Common Stock outstanding during each period including common stock equivalents of the Serial Preference Stock—Series A, and outstanding stock options.

INTERIM STATEMENTS. The financial statements included in this report are based in part on approximations and are subject to adjustments that may develop, such as unsettled contract and renegotiation matters and matters that arise in connection with the annual audit of the accounts; however, in the opinion of management all adjustments (which consist only of normal recurring accruals) necessary for a fair presentation of the results of operations for the periods presented have been included.

AUTHORS' COMMENTS: *There is no mention in the TRW report that the interim statements are not audited. Yet TRW does provide a note (Interim Statements) which attempts to convey the approximate nature of interim statements.*

Authors' Comments on *APBO 28*   Any evaluation of *APBO 28* must take into account the controversy over the nature of the interim reporting period. Insofar as accounting principles are concerned, the *Opinion* reflects a reasonable intermediate position embodying elements of both the integral and discrete views. These issues are not settled, however, and interim reporting continues to be an active item on the FASB's agenda. The Discussion Memorandum mentioned previously uses 126 pages to analyze all sides of the various issues.

Our major concerns with *APBO 28* relate primarily to disclosure rather than accounting principles. In the area of accounting principles, we believe that annual items of expense or revenue *must* be allocated to the quarterly periods benefited. *APBO 28* says such items *may* be allocated. While we see no need to require firms to issue interim reports, we do believe that the format of interim reports, when issued, ought to be comparable across firms. Such an objective probably implies a complete set of interim financial statements, condensed in a standard way. Unaudited statements should be clearly labeled as *unaudited*. Explanatory notes to the statements are needed. Specifically, one of these notes should describe accounting policies followed in preparing the interim financial information. Such a note would include a reference to *APBO 28* and give some indication of the nature and extent of the accruals, estimates, deferrals, and adjustments reflected in the interim information. We believe that these modifications to present interim reporting practices would improve the overall quality of interim reporting.

Exhibit 12.10   Extract from United States Steel Corporation Interim Report

Consolidated Balance Sheet
(Unaudited)
United States Steel Corporation and Subsidiary Companies
(Dollars in Millions)

	June 30	
ASSETS	1979	1978
Current Assets:		
Cash	$ 449.7	$ 336.1
Marketable Securities, at Cost (Approximates Market)	$ 143.0	$ 564.7
Receivables, Less Allowance for Doubtful Accounts of		
$16.5 and $14.4	$ 1,712.4	$ 1,303.4
Inventories, at Lower of Cost (Primarily LIFO) or Market:		
Raw Materials	$ 169.6	$ 191.4
Semifinished Products	408.9	416.4
Finished Products	376.0	311.5
Other	294.2	225.7
Total Inventories	$ 1,248.7	$ 1,145.0
Total Current Assets	$ 3,553.8	$ 3,349.2
Long-Term Receivables and Other Investments, Less		
Estimated Losses of $36.9 and $40.2	790.8	692.1
Property, Plant and Equipment, Less Accumulated		
Depreciation of $7,443.5 and $7,000.8	6,229.4	5,854.0
Operating Parts and Supplies	121.0	115.8
Costs Applicable to Future Periods	343.0	341.7
Total Assets	$11,038.0	$10,352.8
LIABILITIES		
Current Liabilities:		
Notes Payable	$ 187.7	$ 155.8
Accounts Payable	884.6	765.4
Payroll and Benefits Payable	705.1	587.0 [a]
Accrued Taxes	421.1	367.4
Long-Term Debt Due within One Year	56.0	123.0
Total Current Liabilities	$ 2,254.5	$ 1,998.6 [a]
Long-Term Debt, Less Unamortized Discount	2,310.8	2,171.9
Deferred Income Taxes	448.0	432.6
Deferred Credits and Other Liabilities	116.4	92.8 [a]
Preferred Stock of Consolidated Subsidiary	500.0	500.0
Total Liabilities	$ 5,629.7	$ 5,195.9
OWNERSHIP EVIDENCED BY		
Common Stock (Par Value $1 per Share, Authorized		
150,000,000 Shares) Outstanding—86,087,001 Shares and		
85,105,211 Shares, Stated at $20 per Share	$ 1,721.7	$ 1,702.1
Other Stockholders' Equity	3,686.6	3,454.8
Total Ownership	$ 5,408.3	$ 5,156.9
Total Liabilities and Ownership	$11,038.0	$10,352.8

[a] Reflects reclassification of long-term occupational injury and disease liabilities.

Exhibit 12.10 *continued*

NOTES TO FINANCIAL STATEMENTS

(Unaudited)

United States Steel Corporation and Subsidiary Companies

1. The information furnished in these financial statements is unaudited but, in the opinion of management, reflects all adjustments necessary to a fair statement of results for the periods covered.

2. Income per share calculations are based on the following:

					(Dollars in Millions)				
		Quarter Ended June 30				Six Months Ended June 30			
		1979		1978		1979		1978	
Income . . .	$	145.4	$	117.3	$	187.4	$	58.6	
Interest Expense and Other Costs on Convertible Debentures . . .		3.0		3.0		5.9		—	a
Adjusted Income for Calculation of Fully Diluted Income per Share . . .	$	148.4	$	120.3	$	193.3	$	58.6	
Weighted Average Number of Common Shares:									
Shares Outstanding Used in Calculation of Primary Income per Share . .		85,881,232		84,926,773		85,752,520		84,657,593	
Shares Issuable Assuming Conversion of 5³/₄% Convertible Subordinated Debentures . .		5,997,609		6,374,502		5,997,609		—	a
Shares Used in Calculation of Fully Diluted Income per Share		91,878,841		91,301,275		91,750,129		84,657,593	

ªConversion of convertible debentures excluded from computation of fully diluted earnings because of anti-dilutive effects.

3. Interest, dividends and other income includes gains of $13.0 million in 1979 ($1.6 million occurred in the second quarter) resulting from the repurchase of debt securities to satisfy sinking fund requirements. Similar gains for 1978 were $14.7 million ($2.9 million occurred in the second quarter).

4. Included in cost of sales and income before taxes are estimated benefits of $86.2 million in 1979 ($30.7 million occurred in the second quarter) from LIFO inventory liquidations which, in the opinion of management, are expected to exist at year-end. In 1978, the benefits from these liquidations amounted to $74.7 million ($42.5 million occurred in the second quarter).

Exhibit 12.10 *continued*

5. The provision for income taxes is based on an effective tax rate which recognizes for the periods reported management's best estimate of annual financial and taxable income. The six months of 1978 also included an $(18.5) million credit adjustment for estimated taxes on income related to prior years.

AUTHORS' COMMENTS: The United States Steel interim statements are clearly labeled as unaudited. Some explanation is provided for some of the information reported. Note item 4, which indicates impairment of LIFO layers is expected to exist at year-end and gives the effect on quarterly income.

Exhibit 12.11 Extract from American Motors Corporation Interim Report

Nine Months
Report to Stockholders
American Motors Corporation

Consolidated Statement of Net Earnings
American Motors Corporation and Consolidated Subsidiaries
(Dollars in Thousands)

	Three Months Ended June 30		Nine Months Ended June 30	
REVENUES	1979	1978	1979	1978
Net Sales	$797,621	$702,854	$2,285,724	$1,902,710
Other Income	5,275	5,274	20,138	12,922
	$802,896	$708,128	$2,305,862	$1,915,632
COSTS AND EXPENSES				
Cost of Products Sold, Other Than Items Below	$681,243	$606,763	$1,928,110	$1,632,805
Selling, Advertising, and Administrative Expenses . .	70,877	61,689	203,924	175,052
Amortization of Tools and Dies .	10,795	11,796	31,727	31,106
Depreciation and Amortization of Plant and Equipment . . .	4,540	4,727	13,594	14,320
Cost of Pensions	10,479	10,595	31,566	33,070
Interest	4,512	5,436	15,599	16,167
	$782,446	$701,006	$2,224,520	$1,902,520
Earnings before Taxes on Income and Extraordinary Credits . .	$ 20,450	$ 7,122	$ 81,342	$ 13,122
Taxes on Income	5,305	4,010	22,285	7,010
Earnings before Extraordinary Credits	$ 15,145	$ 3,112	$ 59,057	$ 6,102
Extraordinary Credits . . .	—	3,010	14,258	4,610
Net Earnings	$ 15,145	$ 6,122	$ 73,315	$ 10,712
Per Share:				
Primary:				
Earnings before Extraordinary Credits .	$ .49	$ .10	$ 1.94	$ .20
Net Earnings	.49	.20	2.41	.35

Exhibit 12.11   *continued*

Fully Diluted:				
Earnings before				
Extraordinary Credits .	.47	.10	1.79	.20
Net Earnings . . .	.47	.20	2.21	.35
Average Number of Shares and				
Equivalents Outstanding . .			30,397,184	30,186,651

Taxes on income are provided based on an estimated annual effective tax rate for the year. The three and nine months ended June 30, 1979, include United States income taxes of $3,265,000 and $13,835,000, respectively, and foreign and other income taxes of $2,040,000 and $8,450,000, respectively. The extraordinary credits in the nine months ended June 30, 1979, represent deferred income tax benefits of $6,682,000 which can now be reflected in the financial statements because the corporation has fully utilized its tax loss carryforward and $7,576,000 attributable to the effect of tax loss and foreign tax credit carryforwards.

The three and nine months ended June 30, 1978, include a charge of $3,010,000 and $4,610,000, respectively, representing United States income taxes, and a provision of $1,000,000 and $2,400,000, respectively, for foreign and other income taxes. The extraordinary credit in the three and nine months ended June 30, 1978, represents the reduction of income taxes attributable to a tax loss carryforward.

AUTHORS' COMMENTS: American Motors does not indicate that its interim statements are unaudited, nor does it provide extensive notes. Some explanation of taxes and extraordinary items, however, is given.

Summary of Key Concepts

Segment reporting refers to the disclosure of financial information along **lines of business** and **geographical areas.** To provide such information, companies must break down information along those lines in their combined or consolidated financial statements. The principal pronouncement in this area is *SFAS 14,* which also requires that **information about major customers** be reported.

Any attempt at segment reporting must consider the **pricing of internal transfers** and the **allocation of common costs** among segments. If segments must report revenue from sales to internal and external customers, the revenue from internal customers is based on prices that are not the result of completed market transactions. Allocations of the costs of shared facilities or other jointly-used resources inject a degree of **arbitrariness** into financial data which reflect them.

Management is responsible for **identifying reportable segments** according to several criteria which make it difficult to report either too many segments or too few. These criteria employ data on segment revenue, operating profit or loss, and identifiable assets to establish the significance of a potentially reportable segment. Generally, a potentially reportable segment having at least 10 percent of the sum of any of the criteria items for all such segments is significant enough to be reported separately.

Interim reporting is concerned with the regular issuance of financial statements covering **time periods of less than one year.** A fundamental issue in interim reporting is whether to treat the interim period as part of a larger period —the **integral position**—or as a **separate,** identifiable and complete reporting period—the **discrete position.**

The **integral approach** reflects the position that items such as income taxes, year-end bonuses, quantity discounts, and investment tax credits are meaningful only within the context of a full year and should be **allocated among the interim periods.** In contrast, proponents of the **discrete position** reject any additional allocations beyond those normally made for annual periods.

Accounting for **income taxes** and **LIFO inventories** is particularly **troublesome** under the **discrete approach** to interim reporting. The progressive nature of the corporation income tax, losses in interim periods, and the uneven flow of tax credits during the year all lead one to question the usefulness of interim income tax expense based **only** on the events of that interim period. The seasonal aspects of many businesses might result in **temporary impairment of LIFO layers** which will be replenished by the end of the annual period. Interim cost of goods sold amounts reflecting the impairment of old LIFO layers which are not impaired at year-end seem questionable.

APBO 28 provides guidance for the preparation and disclosure of interim financial information but **does not require** that companies issue interim reports. It reflects the APB's conclusion that an **interim period** does not stand alone and is properly viewed as **an integral part of an annual period.** The treatment of annual items, particularly income taxes and LIFO cost of goods sold, in interim reports is based on the best estimates of them for the entire annual period.

Questions **Q12.1** What is segment reporting, and why are many financial statement users interested in it?

Q12.2 Describe the major conceptual problems inherent in any segment reporting scheme. Evaluate the ways in which *SFAS 14* deals with these problems.

Q12.3 In its 1979 annual report, Ford Motor Company stated that "the company and its consolidated subsidiaries comprise a vertically integrated business operating primarily in a single industry segment consisting of the manufacture, assembly and sale of cars and trucks and related parts and accessories." In effect, Ford reported no supplementary information for *industry* segments. Later in the report, Ford noted that it sold 2,322,902 cars and 1,301,172 trucks in North America during 1979. Does Ford really have a single dominant segment? Comment.

Q12.4 One of the significance tests employed in identifying reportable industry segments relates to segments' identifiable assets. *SFAS 14* does not count inter-segment advances as identifiable assets unless made by a finance segment. What is the purpose of this rule? Does it seem consistent with the inclusion of intersegment revenue in applying the total revenue significance test?

Q12.5 We have taken the position that *SFAS 14* is seriously flawed because it pays too little attention to the volume of intersegment transactions in determining reportable segments and in selecting information to be disclosed. Do you agree? Explain.

Q12.6 A well-known accountant once observed that "accountants know the limitations of quarterly or other very short-term financial statements, but persons to whom the reports are addressed cannot be depended upon to treat them with adequate caution." To what limitations is the accountant referring? Why do you think that concern is expressed about users' ability to properly interpret interim statements?

Q12.7 Interim reporting continues to be a controversial subject because of the alternative ways in which accountants view the nature of the interim reporting period. Describe these alternative views, and indicate why each of them is likely to require modification before being accepted by the profession.

Q12.8 Suppose a corporation expected to earn taxable income of $1,000,000 evenly over the calendar year and to receive investment tax credits of $50,000 for property placed in service during the month of May. The flow-through method of accounting for investment tax credits is used. Calculate the effective tax rate reported by the corporation in its second quarter interim report under the integral and discrete views of the interim reporting period using the tax rate schedule given in Exhibit 12.6 in the chapter.

Q12.9 The use of LIFO requires special consideration in discussions of interim reporting, yet no particular concern is expressed over the use of FIFO. Why?

Q12.10 *APBO 28* provides that costs and expenses (other than product costs) incurred in one interim period but benefiting more than one interim period *may* (not *must*) be allocated among the interim periods benefited. Do you agree with this position? Explain.

Exercises **E12.1** The following summary data have been gathered for the Carson Company's industry segments:

	Industry Segment (Amounts in Millions)				
	A	B	C	D	E
Sales to Unaffiliated Customers	$400	$700	$200	$1,400	$1,000
Intersegment Sales	100	300	200	400	—
Operating Profit (Loss)	(50)	60	(30)	500	200
Identifiable Assets	300	800	200	1,500	900

Required: Identify the reportable industry segments for Carson Company, and indicate all significance tests which were satisfied by each reportable segment.

E12.2   Management of Manchester Corporation is trying to decide how many of the company's industry segments must be separately reported under *SFAS 14*. Revenue data for the various segments are as follows; divisional operating profit or loss and identifiable assets show the same pattern.

	Industry Segment					
	A	B	C	D	E	F
Sales to Unaffiliated Customers	$4,000	$3,000	$1,000	$1,200	$ 800	$1,100
Intersegment Sales	1,000	500	100	—	500	—
Total Sales	$5,000	$3,500	$1,100	$1,200	$1,300	$1,100

Required: Indicate how these industry segments are to be reported in accordance with *SFAS 14* and explain why.

E12.3   During the course of your audit of the Abbott Corporation, you ask the client's personnel to develop the necessary supplementary disclosures under *SFAS 14*. After several days' hard work, the assistant controller returns with the following list of data. Confused by some of the provisions of the *Statement*, the assistant asks you which of the items indicated below are to be disclosed under *SFAS 14*.

1. Abbott does business in several industries, and none of its industry segments transact with other segments in the firm. Total sales and identifiable assets are $580,000,000 and $400,000,000, respectively. Amounts for the three largest segments appear next:

	Segment A	Segment B	Segment C
Sales	$264,000,000	$200,000,000	$50,000,000
Identifiable Assets	180,000,000	120,000,000	65,000,000

2. Abbott operates in the United States and in foreign countries. Its domestic operations recorded sales of $65,000,000 to customers in Europe and South America. The foreign operations themselves generated $175,000,000 in sales on $130,000,000 in assets. Breaking the foreign operations down by geographical area yields the following:

Geographical Area	Sales	Identifiable Assets
Europe	$60,000,000	$38,000,000
Asia	20,000,000	10,000,000
South America	50,000,000	37,000,000
Australia	45,000,000	45,000,000

3. Sales to Abbott's major customers appear as follows:

Customer	Sales
U.S. Department of Defense	$61,000,000
U.S. Auto Companies (Equally Divided among GM, Ford, and	
Chrysler)	65,000,000
Qantas Airlines (Privately Owned)	20,000,000
Ministry of Defense, U.K.	40,000,000
Office of the Admiralty, U.K.	20,000,000
Air Brazil (Privately Owned)	24,000,000

Required: Identify which of the above information is to be reported separately under the various provisions of *SFAS 14*. Give reasons for your answers.

E12.4   Russell, Inc., is a diversified company. All of its industry segments are profitable. A condensed version of Russell's consolidated income statement for 19X3 follows:

Sales	$100,000,000
Equity in Income of Unconsolidated Subsidiaries	17,700,000
Interest Income	4,000,000
Total Revenue	$121,700,000
Cost of Goods Sold	$ 60,000,000
Selling Expenses	15,000,000 [a]
General and Administrative Expenses	8,000,000 [b]
Interest Expense	2,000,000
Income Tax Expense	15,000,000
Minority Interest in Net Income	2,800,000
Total Expenses	$102,800,000
Income from Continuing Operations	$ 18,900,000
Gain on Sale of ASAP Division, Net of Taxes of $1,000,000	1,500,000
Income before Extraordinary Loss	$20,400,000
Extraordinary Loss, Net of Taxes of $450,000	1,250,000
Net Income	$ 19,150,000

[a]Includes $1,900,000 of corporate advertising.
[b]Includes $2,200,000 of corporate administrative expenses.

Required: Using the concept of operating profit employed in *SFAS 14*, prepare a schedule to determine the combined operating profit of all of Russell's reportable industry segments. Total intersegment sales during the year amounted to $8,000,000. There are no unconfirmed intercompany inventory profits.

E12.5   Mill Company is a diversified firm with four reportable industry segments. Mill's controller has identified $10,000,000 of costs not directly traceable to the individual segments. The historical behavior of these cost categories shows fairly high correlation between the levels of these costs and the operating activity of the segments.

Cost Categories	Amounts
Computer Center	$5,000,000
Industrial Relations and Personnel Department	2,000,000
Central Purchasing Department	3,000,000

Data for the four segments follow:

Segment	Sales	Traceable Costs	Employees	Identifiable Assets
A	$60,000,000	$38,000,000	600	$34,000,000
B	15,000,000	10,000,000	100	15,000,000
C	30,000,000	22,000,000	1,000	20,000,000
D	45,000,000	30,000,000	300	40,000,000

Required: Prepare a schedule to allocate the common costs among the four segments for purposes of complying with *SFAS 14*. Give reasons to support the allocation bases you choose.

E12.6 The unaudited quarterly statements of income issued by many corporations to their stockholders are usually prepared on the same basis as annual statements, the statement for each quarter reflecting the transactions of that quarter.

Required:
1. Why do problems arise in using such quarterly statements to predict the income (before extraordinary items) for the year? Explain.
2. Discuss the ways in which quarterly income can be affected by the behavior of the costs recorded in a Repairs and Maintenance of Factory Machinery account.
3. Do such quarterly statements give management opportunities to manipulate the results of operations for a quarter? If so, explain or give an example.   (AICPA adapted)

E12.7 Interim financial reporting has become an important topic in accounting. There has been considerable discussion as to the proper method of reporting results of operations at interim dates. Accordingly, the Accounting Principles Board issued *APBO 28* clarifying some aspects of interim financial reporting.

Required:
1. Discuss generally how revenue should be recognized at interim dates and specifically how revenue should be recognized for industries subject to large seasonal fluctuations in revenue and for long-term contracts using the percentage-of-completion method at annual reporting dates.
2. Discuss generally how product and period costs should be recognized at interim dates. Also discuss how inventory and cost of goods sold may be afforded special accounting treatment at interim dates.
3. Discuss how the provision for income taxes is computed and reflected in interim financial statements.

(AICPA adapted)

E12.8 Many corporations issue quarterly financial statements. In general, the accounting concepts underlying these interim statements are the same as those underlying annual statements. However, certain concepts are modified in the development of interim statements because to treat the fiscal quarter as an independent accounting period might limit the usefulness of the interim statements to management, investors, and the public.

Required:
  1. On what matters does the knowledgeable reader attempt to draw conclusions from interim financial statements? (Assume the statements are reliable, even though they are unaudited.)
  2. An objective of income presentation should be the avoidance of any practice that is adopted for the purpose of equalization of reported income. Discuss the modifications, if any, of this generally accepted principle that would be made in developing interim income statements with regard to
    a. Sales.
    b. Manufacturing costs, including over- or underabsorbed overhead.
    c. Selling expenses, including advertising.   (AICPA adapted)

E12.9 The Greer Company issues quarterly reports to stockholders. Below, we present annual estimates of income and related tax items and actual quarterly results for 19X2. The initial estimate prepared at the end of the first quarter is revised in each subsequent quarter. At the end of the fourth quarter, the actual annual results are used as the basis for the fourth quarter's results.

	Quarter 1	Quarter 2	Quarter 3	Quarter 4
Estimated Annual Taxable				
Income	$600,000	$650,000	$610,000	$620,000 [a]
Estimated Annual Tax Credits.	10,000	11,000	16,000	15,000 [a]
Actual Quarterly Taxable				
Income	160,000	160,000	150,000	150,000

[a]Actual for the year.

Required: Compute the amount of income tax expense reported by Greer Company in each of its four quarterly reports according to the provisions of *APBO 28*, using the rate schedule given in Exhibit 12.6 in the chapter. Carry calculation of effective tax rates to tenths of one percent.

E12.10 Inventory quantities at the Mascoma Company change considerably during the year, due to the seasonal nature of Mascoma's business. Mascoma uses LIFO, and, because it is growing rapidly, management fully expects that ending inventory quantities will exceed those in the beginning inventory. Selected interim and annual financial data for the Mascoma Company are given at the top of page 524.

Required: Compute quarterly cost of goods sold according to (1) *APBO 28* and (2) the discrete approach to interim reporting, and compare the quarterly totals

	12/31/X0	3/31/X1	6/30/X1	9/30/X1	12/31/X1
LIFO Layers at Reporting Dates	(1) $400,000 (2) 600,000 (3) 500,000	(1) $ 400,000 (2) 600,000 (3) 200,000	(1) $ 400,000 (2) 300,000	(1) $ 400,000 (2) 600,000 (3) 300,000	(1) $ 400,000 (2) 600,000 (3) 500,000 (4) 200,000
Merchandise purchases during the quarter	—	3,000,000	2,400,000	3,200,000	3,600,000
Current cost of replacing impaired part of LIFO layer(s) at time of original impairment	—	(3) 400,000	(3) 700,000 (2) 500,000	(3) 300,000	

with annual cost of goods sold. Comment on any troubling aspects of the results in the discrete case.

Problems **P12.1**   **Discuss Various Issues in Segment Reporting**   Many accountants and financial analysts contend that companies should report financial data for segments of the enterprise.

Required:

1. What does financial reporting for segments of a business enterprise involve?
2. Identify the reasons for requiring financial data to be reported by segments.
3. Identify the possible disadvantages of requiring financial data to be reported by segments.
4. Identify the accounting difficulties inherent in segment reporting.

(AICPA adapted)

P12.2   **Explain Provisions of *SFAS 14***

1.   In order to properly understand current generally accepted accounting principles with respect to accounting for and reporting upon segments of a business enterprise, as stated by the Financial Accounting Standards Board in *SFAS 14*, it is necessary to be familiar with certain unique terminology. With respect to segments of a business enterprise, explain the following terms:
   a. Industry segment.
   b. Revenue.
   c. Operating profit and loss.
   d. Identifiable assets.

2.   A central issue in reporting on industry segments of a business enterprise is the determination of which segments are reportable.
   a. What are the tests to determine whether or not an industry segment is reportable?
   b. What is the test to determine if enough industry segments have been separately reported upon and what is the guideline on the maximum number of industry segments to be shown?   (AICPA adapted)

P12.3   **Criticize Segment Report**   The Airguide Company is having an independent audit by CPAs for the first time this year. It must comply with *SFAS 14*, and, in connection therewith, the assistant controller provides you with the following draft of an industry segment report for Airguide.

	Division A	Division B	Division C	Total
Sales	$110,000	$220,000	$550,000	$880,000
Cost of Goods Sold . . .	(80,000)	(125,000)	(300,000)	(505,000)
Gross Profit	$ 30,000	$ 95,000	$250,000	$375,000
Variable Selling and				
Administrative Expenses .	(20,000)	(20,000)	(100,000)	(140,000)
Fixed Selling and				
Administrative Expenses .	(5,000)	(40,000)	(50,000)	(95,000)
Corporate Administrative				
Expenses	(5,000)	(10,000)	(25,000)	(40,000)
Operating Profit before				
Taxes	$ 0	$ 25,000	$ 75,000	$100,000
Income Tax Expense . .	0	(10,000)	(30,000)	(40,000)
Operating Profit . . .	$ 0	$ 15,000	$ 45,000	$ 60,000

In speaking with the assistant controller, you determine the following additional information:

1. Division A sells only to Division B, while Divisions B and C sell to customers outside the firm.
2. Corporate administrative expenses were allocated to the divisions based on sales.
3. Divisional income tax expense is based on Airguide's firm-wide effective corporate income tax rate.

Required: Using the information given, explain whether the proposed segment report conforms with the requirements of *SFAS 14*. If necessary, recast the report in a format which would be acceptable under *SFAS 14*.

(Adapted from a problem prepared by Clyde P. Stickney.)

P12.4   **Presentation of Industry Segment Information**   MacDonald Company has four reportable industry segments. The following data have been gathered for these segments:

	Industry W	Industry X	Industry Y	Industry Z
External Sales	$40,000	$20,000	$15,000	$30,000
Internal Sales	1,500	—	2,000	1,000
Traceable Costs	30,000	15,000	10,000	20,000
Allocated Joint Costs . .	3,000	2,000	1,000	4,000
Identifiable Assets . . .	38,000	19,000	12,000	27,000
Depreciation Expense[a] . .	4,000	2,000	1,300	2,200
Capital Expenditures . .	5,000	3,000	2,000	4,000
Allocated Income Taxes . .	1,200	400	1,000	1,100
Share of Corporate Interest				
Expense	400	200	150	300

[a]Included in Traceable Costs above.

Additional information:

1. General corporate administrative expenses were $12,000.
2. Dividend income from nonequity investments was $5,000.
3. Corporate assets not identified with any segment amounted to $18,000.

Required: Prepare a report of supplementary financial information for the Mac-Donald Company's industry segments as required by *SFAS 14.*

P12.5 **Presentation of Geographic Segment Information**   Webster, Inc., has extensive business operations in the United States and in two distinct foreign geographical areas. Financial information for these three geographical segments is summarized here:

	United States	Foreign Area A	Foreign Area B
External Sales	$120,000	$40,000	$20,000
Transfers between Geographic			
Areas	10,000	—	6,000
Traceable Costs	75,000	30,000	12,000
Allocated Joint Costs	15,000	5,000	2,000
Share of Corporate Administrative			
Expenses	12,000	3,000	1,500
Share of Equity Method Income . .	6,000	2,000	1,000
Depreciation Expense[a]	9,000	4,000	3,000
Identifiable Assets	100,000	35,000	15,000
Capital Expenditures	30,000	10,000	5,000
Allocated Income Taxes	20,000	2,000	4,800
Allocated Interest Income . . .	5,000	2,700	1,200

[a]Included in Traceable Costs above.

Additional information:

1. U.S. operations made sales of $25,000 to unaffiliated customers in Europe.
2. General corporate assets, not identified with any segment, amounted to $27,000.

Required: Prepare a report of supplementary financial information for the geographic segments identified by Webster, Inc., as required by *SFAS 14.*

P12.6 **Using Quarterly Data to Predict Annual Income**   The controller of Navar Corporation wants to issue to stockholders quarterly income statements that will be predictive of expected annual results. He proposes to allocate all fixed costs for the year among quarters in proportion to the number of units expected to be sold in each quarter, stating that the annual income can then be predicted through use of the following equation:

$$\text{Annual income} = \text{Quarterly income} \times \frac{100\%}{\substack{\text{Percent of unit sales} \\ \text{applicable to quarter}}}.$$

Navar expects the following activity for the year:

	Units	Average Per Unit	(Amount in Thousands)
Sales Revenue			
First Quarter	500,000	$2.00	$1,000
Second Quarter	100,000	1.50	150
Third Quarter	200,000	2.00	400
Fourth Quarter	200,000	2.00	400
	1,000,000		$1,950
Costs to Be Incurred			
Variable:			
Manufacturing		$ .70	$ 700
Selling and Administrative . . .		.25	250
		$ .95	$ 950
Fixed:			
Manufacturing			$ 380
Selling and Administrative . . .			220
			$ 600
Income before Income Taxes			$ 400

Required: Ignoring income taxes, complete the following:

1. Assuming that Navar's activities do not vary from expectations, will the controller's plan achieve his objective? If not, how can it be modified to do so? Explain and give illustrative computations. Be sure to prepare quarterly income statements under the controller's plan *and*, if you suggest a modification, under the modified plan.
2. How should the effect of variations of actual activity from expected activity be treated in Navar's quarterly income statements?
3. What assumption has the controller made in regard to inventories? Discuss.

(AICPA adapted)

P12.7 **Multiple Choice Questions on Interim Reporting**

1.   Which of the following is an inherent difficulty in the determination of the results of operations on an interim basis?
   a. Cost of sales reflects only the amount of product expense allocable to revenue recognized as of the interim date.
   b. Depreciation on an interim basis is a partial estimate of the actual annual amount.
   c. Costs expensed in one interim period may benefit other periods.
   d. Revenues from long-term construction contracts accounted for by the percentage-of-completion method are based on annual completion and interim estimates may be incorrect.

2.   In considering interim financial reporting, how did the Accounting Principles Board conclude that such reporting should be viewed?
   a. As a "special" type of reporting that need *not* follow generally accepted accounting principles.
   b. As useful only if activity is evenly spread throughout the year so that estimates are unnecessary.
   c. As reporting for a basic accounting period.

   d. As reporting for an integral part of an annual period.
 3.   For annual reporting purposes, Storrar Company appropriately ac-
        counts for revenues from long-term construction contracts under the
        percentage-of-completion method. In December 19X5, for budgeting
        purposes, Storrar estimated that these revenues would be $1,600,000
        for 19X6. Favorable business conditions occurred in October 19X6,
        and, as a result, Storrar recognized revenues of $2,000,000 for the year
        ended December 31, 19X6. If the percentage-of-completion method
        had been used for the quarterly income statements on the same basis
        followed for the year-end income statement, revenues would have
        been as follows:

Three months ended March 31, 19X6	$ 300,000
Three months ended June 30, 19X6	400,000
Three months ended September 30, 19X6	200,000
Three months ended December 31, 19X6	1,100,000
Total	$2,000,000

        What amount of revenues from long-term construction contracts
        should be reflected in Storrar's quarterly income statement for the
        three months ended December 31, 19X6?
   a. $500,000.
   b. $800,000.
   c. $1,100,000.
   d. $2,000,000.
 4.   In January 19X7, Hunter, Inc., estimated that its year-end bonus to
        executives would be $240,000 for 19X7. The actual amount paid for the
        year-end bonus for 19X6 was $224,000. The estimate for 19X7 is sub-
        ject to year-end adjustment. What amount, if any, of expense should
        be reflected in Hunter's quarterly income statement for the three
        months ended March 31, 19X7?
   a. $0.
   b. $56,000.
   c. $60,000.
   d. $240,000.
 5.   On January 1, 19X6, Perry, Inc., paid property taxes of $40,000 on its
        plant for the calendar year 19X6. In March 19X6, Perry made its an-
        nual major repairs to its machinery, which cost $120,000. These re-
        pairs will benefit the entire calendar year's operations. How should
        these expenses be reflected in Perry's quarterly income state-
        ments?

	Three Months Ended			
	March 31, 19X6	June 30, 19X6	September 30, 19X6	December 31, 19X6
a.	$ 22,000	$46,000	$46,000	$46,000
b.	$ 40,000	$40,000	$40,000	$40,000
c.	$ 70,000	$30,000	$30,000	$30,000
d.	$160,000	$ 0	$ 0	$ 0

6. A $420,000 inventory loss from market decline occurred in April 19X6. The Manny Company recorded this loss in April 19X6 after its March 31, 19X6, quarterly report was issued. None of this loss was recovered by the end of the year; how should it be reflected in Manny's quarterly income statements?

| | | Three Months Ended | | |
	March 31, 19X6	June 30, 19X6	September 30, 19X6	December 31, 19X6
a.	$ 0	$ 0	$ 0	$420,000
b.	$ 0	$140,000	$140,000	$140,000
c.	$ 0	$420,000	$ 0	$ 0
d.	$105,000	$105,000	$105,000	$105,000

7. A company that uses the last-in, first-out (LIFO) method of inventory pricing finds at an interim reporting date that there has been a partial liquidation of the base period inventory level. The decline is considered temporary, and the partial liquidation will be replaced prior to year-end. The amount shown as inventory at the interim reporting date should:

a. *Not* give effect to the LIFO liquidation, and cost of sales for the interim reporting period should include the expected cost of replacement of the liquidated LIFO base.

b. Be shown at the actual level, and cost of sales for the interim reporting period should reflect the decrease in LIFO base period inventory level.

c. *Not* give effect to the LIFO liquidation, and cost of sales for the interim reporting period should reflect the decrease in the LIFO base period inventory level.

d. Be shown at the actual level, and the decrease in inventory level should *not* be reflected in the cost of sales for the interim reporting period.

8. The Doll Company estimates the cost of its physical inventory at March 31, 19X2, for use in an interim financial statement. The rate of markup on cost is 25 percent. The following account balances are available:

Inventory, March 1, 19X2	$160,000
Purchases during March	86,000
Purchase Returns	4,000
Sales during March	140,000

The estimate of the cost of inventory at March 31 would be:

a. $137,000.

b. $130,000.

c. $112,000.

d. $102,000.

e. None of the above.

9. Q Company prepares monthly income statements. A physical inventory is taken only at year-end; hence, month-end inventories must be estimated. All sales are made on account. The rate of markup on cost

is 50 percent. The following information relates to the month of June 19X3:

Accounts Receivable, June 1, 19X3	$10,000
Accounts Receivable, June 30, 19X3	15,000
Collection of Accounts Receivable during June 19X3	25,000
Inventory, June 1, 19X3	18,000
Purchases of Inventory during June 19X3	16,000

The estimated cost of the June 30, 19X3, inventory would be:

a. $12,000.
b. $14,000.
c. $19,000.
d. $22,000.

(AICPA adapted)

P12.8   Disclosure and Treatment of Items in Interim Reports   The Anderson Manufacturing Company, a California corporation listed on the Pacific Coast Stock Exchange, budgeted activities for 19X5 as follows:

	Amount	Units
Net Sales	$6,000,000	1,000,000
Cost of Goods Sold	3,600,000	1,000,000
Gross Margin	$2,400,000	
Selling, General, and Administrative Expenses	1,400,000	
Operating Earnings	$1,000,000	
Nonoperating Revenues and Expenses	0	
Earnings before Income Taxes	$1,000,000	
Estimated Income Taxes (Current and Deferred)	550,000	
Net Earnings	$ 450,000	
Earnings per Share of Common Stock	$4.50	

Anderson has operated profitably for many years and has experienced a seasonal pattern of sales volume and production similar to the following ones forecasted for 19X5. Sales volume is expected to follow a quarterly pattern of 10, 20, 35, and 35 percent, respectively, because of the seasonality of the industry. Also, due to production and storage capacity limitations, it is expected that production will follow a pattern of 20, 25, 30, and 25 percent per quarter, respectively.

At the conclusion of the first quarter of 19X5, the controller of Anderson has prepared and issued the interim report for public release as shown at the top of page 531.

The following additional information is available for the first quarter just completed but was not included in the public information released:

1. The company uses a standard cost system in which standards are set at currently attainable levels on an annual basis. At the end of the first quarter, there was underapplied fixed factory overhead (volume variance) of $50,000 that was treated as an asset at the end of the quarter. Produc-

	Amount	Units
Net Sales	$ 600,000	100,000
Cost of Goods Sold	360,000	100,000
Gross Margin	$ 240,000	
Selling, General, and Administrative Expenses	275,000	
Operating Loss	$ (35,000)	
Loss from Warehouse Fire	(175,000)	
Loss before Income Taxes	$(210,000)	
Estimated Income Taxes	0	
Net Loss	$(210,000)	
Loss Per Share of Common Stock	$ (2.10)	

tion during the quarter was 200,000 units, of which 100,000 were sold.

2. The selling, general, and administrative expenses were budgeted on a basis of $900,000 fixed expenses for the year plus $0.50 variable expenses per unit of sales.

3. The warehouse fire loss met the conditions of an extraordinary loss. The warehouse had an undepreciated cost of $320,000; $145,000 was recovered from insurance on the warehouse. No other gains or losses are anticipated this year from similar events or transactions, nor has Anderson had any similar losses in preceding years; thus, the full loss will be deductible as an ordinary loss for income tax purposes.

4. The effective income tax rate, for federal and state taxes combined, is expected to average 55 percent of earnings before income taxes during 19X5. There are no permanent differences between pretax accounting earnings and taxable income.

5. Earnings per share were computed on the basis of 100,000 shares of capital stock outstanding. Anderson has only one class of stock issued, no long-term debt outstanding, and no stock option plan.

Required:
1. Without referring to the specific situation described above, list and explain the standards of disclosure for interim financial data (published interim financial reports) for publicly traded companies.
2. Identify the weaknesses in form and content of Anderson's interim report without reference to the additional information.
3. For each of the five items of additional information, indicate the preferable treatment for each item for interim reporting purposes, and explain why that treatment is preferable.

(AICPA adapted)

P12.9 **Prepare Quarterly Income Statements** After carefully planning its operations for the coming year, West Corporation prepared the forecast of results for the four quarters in the year as shown at the top of page 532.

	Quarter 1	Quarter 2	Quarter 3	Quarter 4
Sales	$10,000,000	$8,000,000	$12,000,000	$15,000,000
Interest Received on Investments	—	80,000	—	80,000
Cost of Goods Sold (at Standard)	6,000,000	4,800,000	7,200,000	9,000,000
Fixed Overhead Volume Variance	—	120,000 (U)	—	120,000 (F)
Labor Efficiency Variance . .	—	100,000 (F)	—	—
Material Price Variance . . .	100,000 (F)	—	50,000 (U)	—
Other Selling Expenses . . .	1,000,000	800,000	1,200,000	1,500,000
Annual Advertising Campaign .	900,000	—	—	—
Annual Sales Quantity Discounts	—	—	—	500,000
Executive Bonuses	—	—	—	900,000
Annual Maintenance Program .	600,000	—	—	—
Provision for Bad Debts (1% of Sales)	—	—	—	450,000
Investment Tax Credits . . .	140,000	—	160,000	—
Other General and Administrative Expenses	1,100,000	1,000,000	1,000,000	1,200,000

Additional information:

1. West Corporation uses a standard cost system in its manufacturing operations. Its standards represent currently attainable expectations and are reviewed and adjusted if necessary shortly after the end of each year. The favorable labor efficiency variance is expected to result from the temporary shutdown of less efficient equipment during the second quarter. Market forecasts of prices of several raw materials used in production are expected to generate the material price variances shown. All standard cost variances are charged or credited to cost of goods sold.

2. The Adco Advertising Agency has been retained to develop radio and television commercials which will be broadcast throughout the year. Adco will be paid in full on March 15.

3. Sales quantity discounts and executive bonuses are both tied to gross sales.

4. The annual maintenance work on the office building is performed during the first quarter of each year.

5. Other general and administrative expenses are incurred uniformly throughout the year except for payment of the annual insurance premium ($100,000) in the first quarter and recognition of other prepayment amortization of $200,000 for the year in the fourth quarter.

6. Market value of the company's inventory is expected to fall below cost by $160,000 during the second quarter. Management anticipates that $90,000 of this will be recouped by the end of the year.

7. Semiannual payments of interest on bonds held for investment occur on June 30 and December 31.

8. West faces a combined federal, state, and city statutory income tax rate of 60 percent.

9. The company had 1,000,000 shares of common stock outstanding during the year.

10. The flow-through method of accounting is used for investment tax credits.

Required: Assuming that actual results do not deviate from the estimates given above, prepare a schedule of quarterly income statements in accordance with *APBO 28* for West Corporation. Show all supporting calculations.

P12.10   **Interim Reporting under Discrete Approach and *APBO 28***   The Hanlon Corporation projects the following results for the four quarters of 19X1:

	Quarter 1	Quarter 2	Quarter 3	Quarter 4
Units Sold	50,000	40,000	60,000	100,000
Selling Price	$5.00	$5.25	$5.50	$5.75
Units Produced	40,000	70,000	40,000	120,000
Variable Costs of Production . .	$2.00	$2.10	$2.20	$2.30
Fixed Manufacturing Overhead .	$50,000	$50,000	$50,000	$50,000
Rental of Delivery Equipment . .	$25,000	$25,000	$25,000	$25,000

Additional information:
1. Hanlon uses the LIFO cost-flow assumption to account for inventories. At the beginning of the year, inventory consisted of two batches of 10,000 units each. The oldest batch has a unit cost of $2.40, and the newest, $2.60.
2. Usage of the rented delivery equipment is related to sales.
3. Hanlon uses full absorption costing for manufacturing operations based on actual costs of the quarterly period.
4. Property taxes for the year, $60,000, are recognized in the second quarter when the tax assessment is made.
5. General and administrative expenses are $40,000 per quarter.
6. During November, cumulative sales to one of the company's best customers passed 20,000 units and grew to 25,000 units at year-end. The customer buys an equal amount each quarter. On December 31, the company rebates $.10 per unit to customers who have purchased more than 20,000 units during the year.
7. The company is taxed according to the federal corporation income tax rate schedule given in Exhibit 12.6 in the chapter. Investment tax credits of $20,000 were earned in both the third and fourth quarters.

Required: Assuming that all events occur as anticipated, prepare quarterly income statements for the Hanlon Corporation in 19X1 under (1) the discrete approach to interim reporting, and (2) *APBO 28*.

PART THREE

ACCOUNTING FOR INTERNATIONAL OPERATIONS

The continuing growth in world trade and the increasing significance of foreign operations to U.S. corporations lead us to devote two chapters to the area of international operations. Our primary objective in these chapters is to present the United States' generally accepted accounting principles as they relate to foreign currency transactions and the translation of foreign currency financial statements. A related objective of considerable importance is to present these matters not in isolation but within the context of business practices in import/export transactions and recent changes in the international monetary system. In addition, we offer an overview of accounting principles around the world and summarize pronouncements of the International Accounting Standards Committee.

We begin Chapter 13 with a discussion of foreign exchange rates and the economic environment which produces them. The spot and forward markets are explained, and their use is related to the widespread business practice of hedging foreign currency transactions. A frame of reference is therefore provided within which the accounting rules germane to forward contracts can be considered. The chapter then proceeds to explain the accounting for import and export transactions, foreign borrowing and lending, and related operations in the forward market for foreign currencies.

Chapter 14 discusses the extent of U.S. firms' business operations abroad and deals specifically with the accounting standards governing the translation of foreign currency financial statements. Financial statements of branches and subsidiaries located in foreign lands must be translated or converted into dollar equivalents before they can be included in U.S. firms' combined or consolidated financial statements. Several translation methods are compared, but current generally accepted accounting principles are emphasized. Exchange gains and losses which are produced by the translation process are carefully explained and related to similar items arising out of the foreign currency transactions discussed in Chapter 13.

To show the diversity of accounting principles and practices around the world, we compare different societal orientations toward accounting and illustrate the wide variety of accounting practices in selected areas. Finally, we conclude Chapter 14 with a discussion of international accounting organizations, giving special emphasis to the work of the International Accounting Standards Committee.

Chapter 13

Accounting for Foreign Currency Transactions

This is the first of two chapters dealing with the subject of accounting for international operations. In it we discuss the accounting for various kinds of foreign currency transactions made by U.S. firms, focusing on the treatments prescribed by *SFAS 8*. The FASB is currently considering proposals in an *Exposure Draft* which, if adopted, would replace *SFAS 8* (AC § 1083).[1] These proposals, however, would have relatively little impact on the subject matter of this chapter, and few references are made to them in Chapter 13. Since their principal concern is with the material in Chapter 14, they will be discussed in more detail in that chapter. As background information, a description of the operation of foreign exchange markets and the interrelation between the spot and forward markets is presented, along with some important history of the international monetary system.

Foreign Exchange Rates and Markets

Accounting for, reporting, and analyzing the financial affairs of multinational corporations are complicated by the fact that, worldwide, the accounts are denominated in various currencies. Just as Ford's subsidiary in the United Kingdom keeps its accounts in pounds sterling, the U.K. currency, Volkswagen's automobile assembly plant in New Stanton, Pennsylvania, records its transactions in dollars. Yet both Ford and Volkswagen must express their financial statements in a single currency, in order that the amounts reported will be

---

[1] Financial Accounting Standards Board, *Statement of Financial Accounting Standards No. 8*, "Accounting for the Translation of Foreign Currency Transactions and Foreign Currency Financial Statements" (Stamford, Conn.: FASB, 1975). The *Exposure Draft*, "Foreign Currency Translation," was issued by the FASB in June 1981, and, if adopted, would become effective at the end of 1982. It revised an earlier exposure draft on the same subject issued by the FASB in August 1980.

based on a common monetary measuring unit. The process of converting or translating foreign currency amounts into units of domestic currency employs *foreign exchange rates*. Foreign exchange rates are themselves the results of various sets of forces operating within the *international monetary system*. To set the stage for our discussion of accounting for foreign currency transactions by U.S. firms, we now define foreign exchange rates, describe the operation of foreign exchange markets, and review the international monetary system.

Foreign Exchange Rates

Foreign exchange rates are *prices*. They are not, however, prices for automobiles, television sets, or bananas. Rather,

> **a foreign exchange rate** is the price of a unit of foreign currency expressed in terms of the domestic currency.

Foreign currencies, like commodities, are traded in markets. Business transactions made in the United States by foreigners are often *denominated* in dollars. Foreign individuals and companies must sell their own currencies and purchase dollars in order to execute these transactions. Similarly, U.S. companies wishing to do business abroad must often sell dollars to purchase the needed foreign currencies. Moreover, when any firm obtains foreign currency through an international transaction, it generally sells the foreign currency and purchases the domestic currency for use in its home country. Buyers and sellers of foreign currencies use the foreign exchange markets for these purposes.

Foreign currencies are traded on both **spot markets** and **forward** (or **futures**) **markets**. Transactions involving *immediate delivery* of the foreign currency are executed at **spot rates**. In contrast, many business dealings require that foreign currency be bought or sold at some future date. To satisfy these demands, prices for futures—**forward rates**—in many foreign currencies are also quoted. A typical quotation of both spot and future foreign exchange rates is shown next. Readers should consult the financial pages of the *Wall Street Journal* or the *New York Times* for current rate quotations.

Foreign Exchange

Britain (Pound Sterling)	U.S. $ Price	Foreign Currency Price per U.S. $
Spot Rate	$2.1950	£.4555
30-day Futures	2.2005	.4544
90-day Futures	2.2105	.4523
180-day Futures	2.2262	.4491

The preceding foreign exchange rates are expressed in both the direct and indirect forms. The *direct form* gives the dollar price of one unit of foreign currency (the left-hand column), while the *indirect form* shows the foreign currency price of one dollar (the right-hand column). Consider first the spot rate for the British pound sterling (£). At the time of this quote, $2.1950/£ was the dollar price for immediate delivery of pounds (the direct form). Similarly, £.4555/$ was the pound price for immediate delivery of dollars (the indirect form). Forward (or futures) rates are also listed for the British pound. In this case, the dollar *(direct)* price for delivery of pounds in 180 days was $2.2262/£. Reasons for the differences which typically exist between spot and forward rates follow the discussion of hedging.

Hedging   The forward (futures) markets in foreign currencies serve many of the same purposes as the commodities futures markets. In both sets of markets, the intent of nonspeculative traders is to guarantee the prices at which transactions will be consummated in the future by entering into contracts establishing such prices today. This process is known as **hedging.** The foreign exchange risk inherent in commitments to accept or deliver foreign currency in the future can be removed by contracting today, at a known price, to sell or purchase foreign currency at the future time.

As an example, consider an American firm importing worsted wool fabrics from the United Kingdom. In order to set selling prices to permit sufficient profit, the firm's management must know costs. Suppose the fabric is to be delivered and payment made in ninety days. The agreed price of the fabric is £100,000. Relevant foreign exchange quotations are as follows:

	U.S. $ Price ($/£)	Foreign Currency Price (£/$)
Spot Price	$1.90	£.526
30-day Futures	1.89	.529
90-day Futures	1.88	.532
180-day Futures	1.85	.541

The pattern of forward rates indicates that the market expects the dollar to appreciate relative to the pound or that, as we shall shortly see, differences in U.S. and U.K. interest rates exist. At the spot rate, the fabric costs $190,000 (= 100,000 × $1.90); a ninety-day futures contract changes the cost to $188,000 (= 100,000 × $1.88). By purchasing pounds forward (that is, for delivery in) ninety days, the actual dollar price of the fabric is fixed. In this way, the commitment to deliver £100,000 is *hedged*. Should the firm elect not to hedge this foreign currency commitment, it must purchase pounds on the spot market in ninety days. If the forward contract is purchased at $1.88/£, the U.S. firm will gain, so long as the spot rate in ninety days is greater than $1.88. On the other hand, if the spot rate actually *declines* to $1.80 in ninety days, the firm incurs an opportunity loss of $8,000 [= ($1.88 − $1.80) × 100,000]. By fixing the price for future delivery, the hedging process removes the chance of gain as well as loss.

Why Forward Rates Differ from Spot Rates   Forward rates differ from spot rates for two reasons:

1. Market-makers expect the spot rate to change in the future, perhaps because of economic forecasts or upcoming political developments. If, for example, the U.S. demand for Japanese automobiles is expected to decrease and the value of the dollar relative to the Japanese yen is expected to increase, the forward rate for yen will be lower than the spot rate.

2.   Investors observe that interest rates differ between countries and, through the practice of covered interest arbitrage, explained next, cause the observed difference between spot and forward foreign exchange rates.

Covered Interest Arbitrage   The practice of **covered interest arbitrage** takes place when investors (1) react to higher interest rates abroad by purchasing foreign investments and (2) protect themselves against adverse exchange rate movements by *covering* their foreign investments with forward contracts to sell the foreign currency when the investments mature. It is the major reason why some currencies sell at a premium and others at a discount in the forward market. Suppose that interest rates on 180-day certificates of deposit are 4 percent per 180-day period in the United States and 5 percent in West Germany. In a free market, American investors in search of a higher yield will move their funds from dollars into deutsche marks (DM). To hedge against the foreign exchange risk associated with converting DM back into dollars, investors will *cover* their investment in DM by *selling* DM forward for dollars with delivery in 180 days. These forward sales of DM produce a downward pressure on the 180-day forward rate for DM until the discount on DM sold forward 180 days approximately equals the interest rate differential of 1 percent. At this point, U.S. investors stop moving their funds from dollars into DM because the West German interest rate advantage has been offset by a decline in the dollar value of DM when the investments mature in 180 days. Therefore, in New York, 180-day futures in DM would sell at a discount of approximately 1 percent, while in Frankfurt 180-day futures in dollars would sell at a premium of approximately 1 percent.

> In general, if the *foreign interest rate exceeds the U.S. interest rate*, the spot rate is higher than the forward rate, and forward contracts sell at a *discount* from the spot rate. Similarly, if the *U.S. interest rate exceeds the foreign interest rate*, the forward rate is higher than the spot rate, and forward contracts sell for a *premium* over the spot rate.

To illustrate the interplay between spot and forward exchange rates and interest rate differentials, we consider an investment of $10,000 in Exhibit 13.1. The interest rate differential of 1 percent is acted upon by covered interest arbitragers to create the necessary equilibrating discount in the forward rate for deutsche marks in New York and premium in the forward rate for dollars in Frankfurt. Investing the $10,000 in a U.S. certificate of deposit generates $10,400 ($= 1.04 \times \$10,000$) in six months. Converting dollars to deutsche marks at the spot rate of $.5/DM permits an investment of DM20,000 ($= \$10,000/\$.5$) in West Germany. This investment provides DM21,000 ($= 1.05 \times$ DM20,000) in six months. If deutsche marks had been sold forward to hedge the foreign currency conversion, the DM21,000 provided by the investment would also be worth $10,400 ($\approx$ DM21,000/DM2.0182).

Exhibit 13.1   The Effects of Covered Interest Arbitrage

FOREIGN EXCHANGE RATES   INTEREST RATES

	Spot	6-Month Futures	6-Month Certificates of Deposit (CD)	
New York . .	$.5/DM	$.4955/DM	4%	
Frankfurt . .	DM2/$	DM2.0182/$	5%	Differential = 1%

CASE 1: DOMESTIC INVESTMENT

Time 0

Investor in New York invests $10,000 in a six-month CD.

Six Months Later

CD matures, producing $10,400 (= 1.04 × $10,000).

CASE 2: FOREIGN INVESTMENT COVERED WITH A FORWARD CONTRACT

Time 0

a. Investor in New York converts $10,000 into DM20,000 (= $10,000/.5) and invests in a six-month CD.
b. Investor in New York enters a six-month forward contract to convert DM into dollars (at $.4955/DM) when the West German CD matures.

Six Months Later

CD matures, producing DM21,000 (= 1.05 × DM20,000).

Forward contract matures and the DM21,000 from the CD are converted into $10,400 (≈ 21,000 × $.4955).

CONCLUSION:

In both cases, the investor ends up with $10,400. The fact that the six-month forward rate of $.4955 is approximately one percent lower than the spot rate offsets the fact that six-month CD rates in Frankfurt are one percent higher than in New York.

Maintaining Consistency among Foreign Exchange Rates   The structure of foreign exchange rates is kept consistent by a group of traders known as **arbitragers.** When inconsistencies in the structure of exchange rates appear, the prospect of immediate and risk-free gains will motivate arbitragers to buy and sell the appropriate currencies until the inconsistencies are removed. For example, **two-point arbitrage** removes any difference between the exchange rates for the same currency on two different markets. Suppose that in New York the rate $/£ = 2.000 and in London $/£ = 2.001. Arbitragers would quickly purchase pounds with dollars in New York and sell the pounds for dollars in London until both rates equalize and the arbitrage gains disappear.

A more intricate scheme involves **three-point arbitrage.** This technique exploits inconsistencies existing among the exchange rates of three currencies and, by so doing, removes them.

To see this, consider the following set of foreign exchange quotations:

In New York	In Tokyo
$/£ = 2.00	Yen/£ = 410
$/Yen = .005	

Alert traders would observe that a pound could be bought for $2 in New York and exchanged for 410 yen in Tokyo. The 410 yen could each be sold for $.005 in New York for a total of $2.05, a gain of $.05 per pound purchased. Holding the rate in Tokyo constant, arbitragers in New York might purchase pounds for dollars and cause the price of pounds to gradually rise, perhaps to $2.0295. At the same time, the arbitragers would sell yen for dollars in New York until the price of yen fell to $.00495, thereby eliminating any further gains from arbitraging. Alternatively, the same result would be achieved by bidding up the dollar price of pounds to $2.05, holding the other rates constant. Whatever new exchange rates result, however, they too will be kept consistent with the rates in other markets and for other currencies by arbitragers.

In the contemporary world economy, foreign exchange rates are generally the result of free market forces. Some of the underlying factors affecting exchange rates are relative rates of inflation, relative interest rates, and the terms of trade (or international commodity exchange ratios) between countries. As these conditions change, the foreign exchange rates change. Economists refer to this as a system of **floating** or **flexible exchange rates.** It was not always so. During most of the post–World War II period, exchange rates were generally *fixed* under the terms of an international agreement. The established set of exchange rates was maintained (or *pegged*) by central banks as they purchased and sold foreign currencies in the foreign exchange markets.

We believe that the study of accounting for international operations is enriched by an understanding of the international monetary system, an important part of the international environment. Accordingly, the next section is devoted to a discussion of developments in the international monetary system.

| **The International Monetary System** | The growth in the world economy and the relative international economic stability experienced since World War II followed, in large measure, from negotiations undertaken near the end of the war. Determined to create an orderly international economic environment after the war, representatives of the Western allied powers met at Bretton Woods, New Hampshire, in the summer of 1944 to fashion the elements of a sound international monetary system. The USSR did not participate. Renowned British economist John Maynard Keynes played an important role at the conference. |

The exchange rate instability experienced between the First and Second World Wars had been attributed, rightly or wrongly, to freely floating exchange rates and the abuses perpetrated by international speculators. The desire for stability in the short run and flexibility in the long run led the Bretton Woods conferees to adopt what has been termed an **adjustable peg system.** Currency exchange rates were set, by agreement, in terms of the United States dollar. The value of the dollar, in turn, was tied to gold; the official price of gold was set at $35 per ounce. The discipline in the system was that the dollar was freely convertible into gold. In other words, if the dollar became overvalued, making an ounce of gold worth more than $35, foreigners would convert their dollars into gold at the U.S. Treasury. This would deplete the finite U.S. gold reserves; shortly we will see that this is exactly what eventually happened.

The other countries which subscribed to the Bretton Woods agreements were to attempt to maintain the values of their currencies within one percent of the par or pegged exchange rate. Therefore, if the exchange rate for a particular currency began to move above or below the allowable one percent deviation from par, that country's central bank was obliged to intervene in the foreign exchange market. The home currency was purchased with dollars or another acceptable international reserve (such as gold) to raise the exchange rate; to lower the exchange rate, the home currency was sold.

To assist countries facing temporary shortages of international reserves, the International Monetary Fund (IMF) was established as an integral part of the Bretton Woods agreements. Member countries can borrow specified quantities of international reserves from the IMF to tide them over transitory deficits in international payments. The resources of the IMF consist of mandatory contributions made by member countries.

Flexibility in the system was to be achieved by permitting countries to change the official rate by as much as 10 percent without approval of the International Monetary Fund. IMF approval was required for larger changes in the official exchange rate. An increase in the official peg was termed a **devaluation,** while a reduction in the official peg implied **revaluation.** To see this, observe that by raising the price of a foreign currency in terms of the home currency, the home currency *loses value.* That is, after the increase in the exchange rate, the home currency has been devalued because more units of it are needed to acquire the foreign currency. In the United States, the dollar would be devalued by raising the dollar price of gold. Concurrently, a devaluation of one currency means that at least one other currency experiences a revaluation. In November 1967, the British pound sterling was devalued by the United Kingdom from $2.80 to $2.40. The effects of this action on the exchange rate between dollars and pounds were:

	In New York ($/£)	In London (£/$)
Before the Sterling Devaluation	2.80	.357
After the Sterling Devaluation	2.40	.417

Note that, under the Bretton Woods agreements, the ability of a country to defend its currency in the face of a declining exchange rate was directly influenced by that country's supply of international reserves, including borrowing rights from the IMF. In contrast, keeping the exchange rate from rising usually generated an expanding domestic money supply which created inflationary pressures.

The Fatal Flaw

The problem with an adjustable peg system is that when the rate becomes more difficult to maintain through intervention, the direction of the forthcoming change in the official exchange rate is clear and "bear speculators are then presented with that rare, and greatly desired phenomenon, a 'sure thing.'."[2] Under

---

[2] Frank Graham, "Achilles' Heels in Monetary Standards," *American Economic Review* (March 1940), p. 19.

the Bretton Woods system, a large adjustment in the exchange rate occurred in a single discrete step. As the underlying economic conditions gradually changed, the exchange rate was not allowed to change accordingly. Eventually, as the central bank intervened more and more in the foreign exchange market, a forthcoming change in the official peg, usually a devaluation, was signaled. Speculators would sell large amounts of the suspect currency and short sales would increase. The central bank became the buyer of last resort and often engaged in extremely costly counterspeculative policies. In connection with the devaluation of the British pound mentioned earlier, on November 17, 1967, the Bank of England lost $250 million. This amount was expended to support the pound in the face of a massive speculative outflow of that currency. Deliberations regarding a devaluation were shrouded in secrecy, and announcements were made when markets were closed, typically on weekends or holidays.

Unfortunately, this fundamental problem was aggravated by the general unwillingness of governments to adjust the peg frequently. Devaluations were seen as assaults on national pride. Hence the crises, when they came, were massive and abrupt.

The requirement that central banks intervene in foreign exchange markets to support their currencies often created problems in domestic economic policy. Government intervention in the economy has grown in significance since World War II, so that the conflicting use of policy tools to achieve policy objectives had not been forecast by the Bretton Woods conferees. As an example, suppose a particular country were confronted with both excessive domestic unemployment and an international deficit. Domestic monetary policy would likely be expansionary, leading to a larger money supply and lower interest rates to combat unemployment. Yet just the opposite would be called for to cope with the international deficit. High interest rates attract the international investment funds which would help alleviate the international deficit. Such conflicts in economic policy were often caused by the need to support the official exchange rate.

The Evolution of Flexible Exchange Rates

As time passed, changes in international economic relations simply outgrew the capability of the pegged exchange rate system to accommodate them.

> It is not possible to date precisely the end of the international monetary system established at Bretton Woods in 1944. Different aspects of the system died at different times. And the basic principles of international financial cooperation on which the Bretton Woods system was based never died at all.
>
> There is general agreement that the final end of the adjustably pegged par value exchange rate system established at Bretton Woods was marked by the initiation of generalized floating of exchange rates by the major industrial countries following the second devaluation of the dollar in early 1973. But many who viewed the gold convertibility of the dollar as the linchpin of the system would point to the formal termination of the convertibility of official dollar holdings into gold in August 1971 as the symbolic death date of the system. Still others would point out that, de facto, the unfettered gold convertibility of the dollar as envisioned at Bretton Woods had already ended years before.[3]

---

[3]   Thomas D. Willett, *Floating Exchange Rates and International Monetary Reform* (Washington D.C.: American Enterprise Institute for Public Policy Research, 1977), p. 1.

Essentially untouched by the devastation of World War II, the United States emerged as the major economic power in the free world. It had most of the free world's supply of gold and its currency, the dollar, was in great demand throughout the world as an international medium of payment. As the countries of the world were rebuilt, with significant aid from the United States through such programs as the Marshall Plan, American economic dominance began to decline. The flow of dollars abroad became a flood in the late 1960s as the persistent balance of payments[4] deficits which began in the late 1950s grew substantially larger. The dollar shortage had become a glut; conversion of dollars into gold had reduced the United States gold reserve to a low of $10.2 billion in 1971 from a high of $24.6 billion in 1949.

In August 1971, President Nixon reacted to the growing crisis of confidence in the dollar. Anticipating the record balance of payments deficit in 1971 (which amounted to $29.7 billion on the official reserve transactions balance), the president unilaterally suspended convertibility of the dollar into gold as one of several economic policy initiatives announced on August 15, 1971. Subsequent appreciation of major foreign currencies led to an increase in the official price of gold to $38 per ounce in December 1971. A second devaluation of the dollar in February 1973 raised the official price of gold to $42 per ounce.

Serious negotiations for the reform of the international monetary system began in earnest in 1972 and reached their culmination in Kingston, Jamaica, on January 7 and 8, 1976. At the Jamaica meetings, representatives of the 128 member nations of the International Monetary Fund ratified amendments to the IMF's Articles of Agreement, officially sanctioning flexible or floating exchange rates as the basis for our international monetary system. As Nobel laureate economist Milton Friedman had suggested many years before,

> Our problem is not to solve *a* balance of payments problem. It is to solve *the* balance of payments problem by adapting a mechanism that will enable free market forces to provide a prompt, effective, and automatic response to changes in conditions affecting international trade.[5]

This movement away from pegged exchange rates has led to a new international economic environment, one in which foreign exchange rates constantly fluctuate in response to market forces. Not only has this environment affected the international operations of corporations, it has also made the accounting for international operations more complex. We begin our study of these accounting matters with a thorough examination of accounting for foreign currency transactions.

Accounting for Foreign Currency Transactions

Accounting problems resulting from various transactions involving foreign currencies are examined in the remainder of this chapter. *Import/export* transactions are considered first, then those which involve *borrowing and lending abroad*. We discuss the accounting for *forward contracts* as used to hedge such transactions and as used in speculation.

---

[4] The *balance of payments* refers to the net flow of funds in or out of a particular country. A deficit occurs when the quantity of funds flowing out exceeds the quantity flowing in.

[5] Milton Friedman, *Capitalism and Freedom* (Chicago: University of Chicago Press, 1962), p. 67.

One major class of accounting problems for U.S. firms doing business in foreign countries occurs because the firms must deal in foreign currencies while maintaining books of account in dollars. A purchase of goods from a foreign manufacturer by a U.S. firm often typifies this class of problem. The U.S. company may have to agree that the invoice be stated (or *denominated*) in units of the foreign currency and that the foreign manufacturer be paid in the foreign currency. Yet only transactions *measured* in dollars can meaningfully be entered into the U.S. firm's accounting records.

Import/Export Transactions

Import/export transactions would present no particular accounting problem *if* all sales, purchases, payments, and receipts were made in dollars. Such an unlikely situation would mean that our international customers and suppliers did business in terms of the dollar, a currency foreign to *them*.

The basic problem caused by the need to transact in a foreign currency may be summarized as follows:

> When a transaction is denominated in a foreign currency, its value in dollars is determined by the appropriate foreign exchange rate. The *passage of time* between the inception of the transaction and its ultimate settlement with cash *allows the dollar value of the transaction to change as the appropriate foreign exchange rate changes.*

Therefore, if a U.S. company makes a credit sale abroad and the transaction price is stated in units of foreign currency, the dollar value of the account receivable may change before payment is received in the foreign currency and converted into dollars. Similarly, when a U.S. company purchases goods from abroad on account at a price denominated in foreign currency units, the dollar amount owed may change before dollars are converted into the foreign currency and payment is made. These changes in the dollar value of receivables and payables generate gains and losses to the U.S. firm which must be recognized at settlement and at intervening balance sheet dates. Since the ultimate settlement of these transactions involves the conversion of dollars into foreign currency or foreign currency into dollars, we label them **exchange conversion gains or losses.**

Separate identification and reporting of exchange conversion gains and losses as accounting events *apart* from the related sale (revenue) or purchase (expense) transactions has been referred to as the **dual transaction approach.** The alternative **single transaction approach** views a transaction denominated in a foreign currency as incomplete until settled. Any intervening exchange gain or loss is used to adjust the dollar basis of the revenue or expense transaction and is not reported separately. The FASB specifically rejected this single transaction view in *SFAS 8* by observing that "the exchange exposure in a purchase or sale transaction whose price is denominated in a foreign currency stems not from the purchase or sale itself but from a delay in payment or receipt of the equivalent dollars."[6] No exchange gain or loss can occur if the transaction is

---

[6] Financial Accounting Standards Board, *Statement No. 8*, par. 114; AC § 1083.114.

settled immediately. To accommodate the dual transaction approach, we identify the following three accounting rules:

1. Record the transaction in dollars, determined by translating the foreign currency invoice price into dollars using the appropriate foreign exchange spot rate.

2. Record an exchange conversion gain or loss when the transaction is settled if the number of dollars received or paid differs from that originally recorded at date of transaction in item 1.

3. If the transaction has not been settled at a balance sheet date, record an exchange conversion gain or loss on the existing receivable or payable by adjusting it to the dollar equivalent implied by the spot rate at the balance sheet date.

Observe the dual objectives of these rules. First, recognition is given to changes in value of receivables and payables attributable to movements in the exchange rate. Second, this recognition is based on accrual accounting and is not deferred until eventual settlement if a balance sheet date occurs prior to settlement.

We now illustrate the accounting for import and export transactions with the following series of transactions.

1. On October 16, 19X1, Acme International purchased lamb's wool at an invoice price of 17,000 New Zealand dollars ($NZ17,000) from a New Zealand rancher. The exchange rate was $.92/$NZ. Payment was to be made on December 16, 19X1.

10/16/X1

Purchases	15,640	
Accounts Payable		15,640

To record the purchase of wool from New Zealand;
$15,640 = $.92 × 17,000.

2. On December 16, 19X1, Acme purchased 17,000 New Zealand dollars at an exchange rate of $.93/$NZ and transmitted them to the rancher's bank in New Zealand.

12/16/X1

Exchange Conversion Loss	170	
Accounts Payable		170

To recognize the exchange conversion loss on the
account payable; $170 = ($.93 − $.92)17,000.

Foreign Currency	15,810	
Cash		15,810

To purchase sufficient foreign currency to pay off the
New Zealand rancher; $15,810 = $.93 × 17,000.

Accounts Payable	15,810	
Foreign Currency		15,810

To record payment of the liability to the New Zealand
rancher; $15,810 = $15,640 + $170.

Consider the exchange conversion loss recorded in transaction 2. Acme had a liability to the New Zealand rancher denominated in New Zealand dollars. Since the exchange rate had risen (so that it took more U.S. dollars to purchase

New Zealand dollars), the dollar value of the liability had increased, and Acme had incurred a loss. The loss was accounted for separately from the cost of the merchandise under the *dual transaction approach*.

3. On December 20, 19X1, Acme purchased worsted wool fabrics from a British mill for 40,000 pounds sterling (£40,000), when the exchange rate was $2/£. Payment was due on January 20, 19X2.

12/20/X1

Purchases	80,000	
Accounts Payable		80,000

To record the purchase of wool fabric from Great Britain; $80,000 = $2 × 40,000.

4. On December 22, 19X1, Acme sold a quantity of deluxe wool blankets to a Canadian concern for 9,800 Canadian dollars ($CN9,800). The exchange rate was $.97/$CN. Acme's terms are sixty days, net.

12/22/X1

Accounts Receivable	9,506	
Sales		9,506

To record the sale of blankets to Canada; $9,506 = $.97 × 9,800.

5. On December 29, 19X1, Acme purchased buttons valued at 10,000 pesos (P10,000) from a Mexican manufacturer. The exchange rate was $.05/P; a check was mailed immediately.

12/29/X1

Purchases	500	
Cash		500

To record the cash purchase of buttons from Mexico; $500 = $.05 × 10,000.

6. Financial statements were prepared at December 31, 19X1, and the following adjusting entries were made. Relevant exchange rates were $1.96/£ and $.985/$CN.

12/31/X1

Accounts Payable	1,600	
Exchange Conversion Gain		1,600

To record the exchange conversion gain accrued on the liability to the British mill; $1,600 = ($2.00 − $1.96)40,000. The dollar value of this liability has decreased to $78,400 (= $1.96 × 40,000).

Accounts Receivable	147	
Exchange Conversion Gain		147

To record the exchange conversion gain accrued on the receivable from Canada; $147 = ($.985 − $.97)9,800. The dollar value of this asset has increased to $9,653 (= $.985 × 9,800).

Contrast the two exchange conversion gains accrued at December 31, 19X1, in transaction 6. Since the exchange rate for pounds sterling had declined, the dollar value of Acme's liability had declined accordingly, and an exchange conversion gain resulted. Although the exchange rate of Canadian dollars had risen at year-end, it also generated an exchange conversion gain. This is because Acme had a receivable denominated in Canadian dollars. As the value of Canadian dollars rose, so did the U.S. dollar value of Acme's receivable from the Canadian firm.

7.   Acme paid its obligation to the British mill on January 20, 19X2. The exchange rate was $1.93/£.

1/20/X2

Accounts Payable.	1,200	
Exchange Conversion Gain		1,200

To recognize the exchange conversion gain on the account payable; $1,200 = ($1.96 − $1.93)40,000.

Foreign Currency	77,200	
Cash		77,200

To record the purchase of foreign currency to pay off the British mill; $77,200 = $1.93 × 40,000.

Accounts Payable.	77,200	
Foreign Currency		77,200

To record payment of the liability to Great Britain; $77,200 = $80,000 − $1,600 − $1,200.

8.   On February 20, 19X2, payment was received from the Canadian customer on the sale of the blankets; $8,918 = $.91 × 9,800.

2/20/X2

Exchange Conversion Loss	735	
Accounts Receivable		735

To recognize the exchange conversion loss on the receivable; $735 = ($.985 − $.91)9,800.

Foreign Currency	8,918	
Accounts Receivable		8,918

To record receipt of foreign currency from Canada in payment of the receivable; $8,918 = $9,506 + $147 − $735.

Cash	8,918	
Foreign Currency		8,918

To record sale of the Canadian currency for U.S. dollars.

To summarize, accounts receivable and accounts payable arising in international transactions are often denominated in a foreign currency and are recorded at the dollar equivalent of a fixed quantity of foreign currency. As the exchange rate changes, the dollar equivalent also changes. The effects of changing exchange rates on these dollar equivalents and the resulting exchange conversion gains and losses are as follows:

Effects of Changing Exchange Rates on Receivables and Payables
with Dollar Values Based on Foreign Currency Quantities
and Resulting Exchange Conversion Gains and Losses

Account	Change in Exchange Rate ($ Price of Foreign Currency)	
	Increase	Decrease
Accounts Receivable (A/R)	A/R Increases; Gain	A/R Decreases; Loss
Accounts Payable (A/P)	A/P Increases; Loss	A/P Decreases; Gain

Using Forward Contracts to Hedge Import and Export Transactions

We indicated earlier in the chapter how foreign exchange rates have fluctuated in recent years. One result of these fluctuations has been a growing recognition by managers that their foreign currency transactions have to be *hedged*. Hedging, as previously defined, involves contracting in the forward market to purchase or to sell foreign currency at a specified time in the future for a fixed price. In this way, managers neutralize the impact of changing exchange rates on their foreign currency commitments.

Publication of *SFAS 8* provided detailed accounting rules for forward contracts and probably promoted their use by calling attention to the gains and losses resulting from exposure to changing exchange rates. We begin our discussion by examining a forward purchase contract.

Forward Purchase Contracts   A **forward purchase contract** would be used by an *importer*. Such a contract gives the importer the right to purchase foreign currency at a specified time in the future for a known price. When the importer's obligations to foreign suppliers come due, the needed amount of foreign currency will be available for a price agreed upon in advance. For accounting purposes, three components of a forward purchase transaction are important:

1. The *liability* to the foreign exchange broker, denoted *Due to Exchange Broker*, which is stated at the agreed-upon dollar value of the foreign currency to be purchased, that is, the quantity of foreign currency translated at the applicable *forward rate*. Since the rate is fixed by the contract, the liability is unaffected by changes in the exchange rate and generates no exchange conversion gain or loss.

2. The *forward purchase contract* itself, consisting of the right to the foreign currency, which is stated at the current value of the foreign currency to be purchased, that is, the quantity of foreign currency translated at the *spot rate*. This asset is based upon the current translated value of foreign currency; its dollar value will change with the *spot rate*.

3. The *premium or discount on the forward purchase contract*, the difference between the current and future values of the foreign currency to be purchased. As mentioned previously, it generally is attributable to interest rate differentials and represents a revenue or expense to the firm. Amortization of this premium or discount is accounted for separately from any exchange conversion gain or loss.

For example, suppose £1,000 were purchased for delivery in thirty days at the thirty-day forward rate of $2.20/£. The spot rate is $2.10/£. The *liability to the exchange broker* is fixed at $2,200 (= $2.20 × 1,000) and will not be affected by subsequent movements in the exchange rate. Translating the £1,000 at the spot rate gives us the current value of the foreign currency, $2,100 (= $2.10 × 1,000), which we call the *forward purchase contract*. Since the foreign currency was purchased in the forward market for *more* than the current spot rate, a *premium on the forward purchase contract* of $100 [= ($2.20 − $2.10)1,000] results.

Many transactions are preceded by the issuance of purchase orders or other contractual agreements. Accordingly, forward contracts may be entered before the transaction occurs and is recorded. There may be a further period of time after the transaction is recorded until settlement, and the forward contract often remains in effect during this period to hedge the liability exposed to exchange rate risk. If the contract was entered into *before* a transaction denominated in the foreign currency is recorded and meets the conditions described below, it is considered a **hedge of an identifiable foreign currency commitment.** Should the contract remain in effect (or be entered into) *after* a payable or receivable transaction denominated in the foreign currency is recorded, it is treated as a **hedge of an exposed asset or liability position.** These situations are depicted as follows for a forward purchase contract:

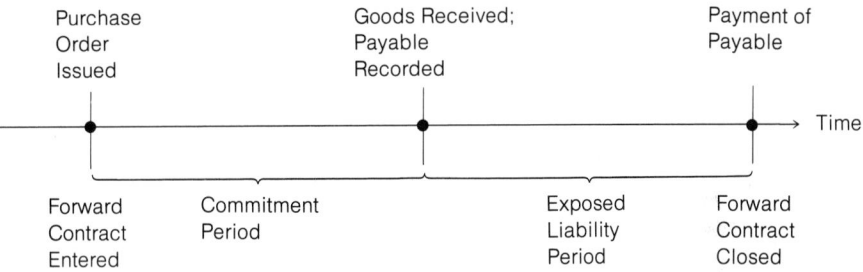

Hedging an Identifiable Foreign Currency Commitment   *SFAS 8* specifies the accounting for the exchange conversion gains and losses and premium or discount on the forward contract. The forward contract is a *hedge of an identifiable currency commitment* if all of the following conditions are met:

1. The life of the contract extends from the date of the commitment to the anticipated transaction date or later.

2. The contract is for the same currency being committed and does not exceed the amount of the foreign currency commitment.[7]

3. The foreign currency commitment is firm and noncancelable.

Under proposals currently being considered in the FASB *Exposure Draft,* the conditions for a hedge of an identifiable foreign currency commitment would become less restrictive. Management's *intent* that the forward contract be a hedge of an identifiable foreign currency commitment would replace condition 1 above. Condition 2 would be broadened to include forward contracts in currencies *economically linked* to (that is, moving in tandem with) the currency being committed. Finally, the foreign currency commitment need only be *firm,* not noncancelable. The accounting, however, remains the same in the *Exposure Draft.*

Note that for the importer an identifiable foreign currency commitment is based on a purchase order issued prior to the actual receipt of the goods. Any exchange conversion gain or loss on the forward contract is deferred until the

[7] *SFAS 20* (AC § 1084) permits the contract to exceed the amount of the foreign currency commitment if necessary to hedge the commitment on an aftertax basis; Financial Accounting Standards Board, *Statement of Financial Accounting Standards No. 20,* "Accounting for Forward Exchange Contracts" (Stamford, Conn.: FASB, 1977).

payable to the foreign supplier is booked. In effect, the forward contract is viewed as an integral part of the purchase transaction. At the time the purchase is recorded, the deferred gain or loss is included in the dollar basis of the purchase transaction. After this, exchange conversion gains and losses on both the forward contract and the payable are recorded but are offsetting. The premium or discount may either be deferred until the transaction is recorded or be amortized proportionately over the life of the contract. If it is deferred until the transaction is recorded, the portion pertaining to the commitment period is used to adjust the dollar basis of the transaction, as entered in the Purchases (or Inventory) account.

Say, for example, that on August 10, 19X2, Acme signs a contract with Queens, Ltd., a U.K. exporter, to purchase fabric valued at £100,000; the spot rate is $1.80/£. Delivery of the fabric in the United States is expected on November 30, 19X2, and payment is due on January 10, 19X3. This future payment of £100,000 is an identifiable foreign currency commitment, and Acme elects to hedge it by purchasing £100,000 for delivery on January 10, 19X3. The *commitment period*, however, runs from August 10, 19X2, to November 30, 19X2, a period of $3^2/_3$ months. With a five-month forward rate of $1.83/£, the forward contract results in a premium of $3,000, which Acme elects to defer. The spot rate on November 30, 19X2, is $1.82/£. Entries made during the commitment period are:

8/10/X2

Forward Purchase Contract ($1.80 × 100,000) . . . 180,000		
Premium on Forward Contract [($1.83 −		
$1.80)100,000] 3,000		
Due to Exchange Broker ($1.83 × 100,000) . .		183,000
To record the forward purchase contract engaged in to		
hedge the identifiable foreign currency commitment to		
Queens, Ltd.		

11/30/X2

Forward Purchase Contract 2,000		
Deferred Exchange Conversion Gain		2,000
To record as deferred the exchange conversion gain		
accrued on the forward purchase contract during the		
commitment period; $2,000 = ($1.82 −		
$1.80)100,000.		

Hedging an Exposed Liability Position   The commitment period expires once the fabric is received. After the purchase and related payable are recorded, the forward contract acts as a hedge of an exposed liability position— the account payable. Because the payable is denominated in pounds, its dollar value changes as the $/£ exchange rate changes. Thus the payable is *exposed* to foreign exchange rate risk.

At the time the purchase and related payable are recorded, the accountant must adjust Purchases by (1) the deferred exchange gain or loss accrued on the forward purchase contract during the commitment period and (2) the portion of the premium on the forward purchase contract pertaining to the commitment period. The spot rate at November 30, 19X2, is $1.82/£. The entries are:

11/30/X2

Purchases	182,000	
Accounts Payable		182,000

To record the purchase of fabric from Queens, Ltd., in
the United Kingdom; $182,000 = $1.82 × 100,000.

Deferred Exchange Conversion Gain	2,000	
Purchases		2,000

To adjust the dollar basis of purchases recorded by
the accrued exchange conversion gain on the forward
exchange contract during the commitment period.

Purchases	2,200	
Premium on Forward Contract		2,200

To adjust the dollar basis of purchases recorded by
the portion of the premium on the forward contract
pertaining to the commitment period.

The second and third entries record the adjustments to the Purchases account. Purchases are decreased by the deferred exchange conversion gain of $2,000 which accrued on the forward purchase contract during the commitment period. The commitment period covered $3^{2}/_{3}$ months of the five-month forward purchase contract. Since the premium represents an implied interest cost, $2,200 $\{= [(3^{2}/_{3})/5] \times \$3,000\}$ is recorded as an increase in Purchases. In sum, Purchases is increased by $200 (= $2,200 − $2,000).

At December 31, 19X2, a financial reporting date, both the payable to Queens, Ltd., and the forward purchase contract are still outstanding. The spot rate has risen to $1.84/£ at December 31 from $1.82/£ on November 30. In the next two entries, we accrue the exchange conversion loss and gain on these items:

12/31/X2

Exchange Conversion Loss	2,000	
Accounts Payable		2,000

To record the exchange conversion loss accrued on the
liability to Queens, Ltd., $2,000 = ($1.84 − $1.82)100,000.

Forward Purchase Contract	2,000	
Exchange Conversion Gain		2,000

To record the exchange conversion gain accrued on the
forward purchase contract for £100,000; $2,000 = ($1.84 −
$1.82)100,000.

Note that the exchange conversion loss on the account payable is offset by the exchange conversion gain on the forward purchase contract. Amortization of the premium for December 19X2 is as follows:

12/31/X2

Expense—Premium Amortization	600	
Premium on Forward Contract		600

To amortize $^{1}/_{5}$ of the premium related to December 19X2;
$600 = .2 × $3,000.

On January 10, 19X3, the forward purchase contract matures, and the payable to Queens, Ltd., becomes due. The spot rate is $1.835/£. The next six entries record the closing out of the forward purchase contract, amortization of the remaining premium, disbursement of the foreign currency to Queens, Ltd., and accrual of the offsetting exchange conversion loss and gain on the forward purchase contract and the account payable.

1/10/X3

Exchange Conversion Loss	500	
Forward Purchase Contract		500
To recognize the exchange conversion loss accrued on the forward purchase contract since December 31, 19X2; $500 = ($1.84 − $1.835)100,000.		
Due to Exchange Broker	183,000	
Cash		183,000
To record payment to foreign exchange broker.		
Foreign Currency	183,500	
Forward Purchase Contract		183,500
To record receipt of the foreign currency from the broker; $183,500 = $1.835 × 100,000.		
Expense—Premium Amortization	200	
Premium on Forward Contract		200
To expense the remaining premium on the forward contract; $200 = $3,000 − ($2,200 + $600).		
Accounts Payable	500	
Exchange Conversion Gain		500
To recognize the exchange conversion gain accrued on the account payable since December 31, 19X2; $500 = ($1.84 − $1.835)100,000.		
Accounts Payable	183,500	
Foreign Currency		183,500
To record payment of the liability to Queens, Ltd.; $183,500 = $180,000 + $2,000 + $2,000 − $500.		

In sum, the importer uses the hedging process to fix the dollar amount of the liability to the foreign supplier at $183,000. Of the $3,000 premium, $2,200 went to increase Purchases and the other $800 was expensed. Had the hedging not taken place in the above example, Acme would have lost $3,500 [= ($1.835 − $1.80)100,000] due to the adverse exchange rate movement from the time the purchase was negotiated to final payment. Hence the hedging saved Acme $500 (= $3,500 − $3,000). The decrease in Purchases from the contemplated amount of $183,000 to the recorded amount of $182,200 (= $182,000 − $2,000 + $2,200) was offset by the remaining premium amortization of $800 (= $600 + $200).

Forward Sale Contracts   *Exporters* use **forward sale contracts** to permit the sale of foreign currency at a specified time in the future for a known price. As foreign customers remit payments in foreign currency to the exporter, the foreign currency can be converted to pre-arranged quantities of dollars by using forward sale contracts. These contracts also have three components of importance for accounting.

1. The *receivable* from the foreign exchange broker, designated *Due From Exchange Broker*, consists of the agreed-upon dollar value of the foreign currency to be sold. This is the quantity of foreign currency translated at the applicable *forward rate*. The receivable is denominated in dollars, is unaffected by any change in the exchange rate and generates no exchange conversion gain or loss.

2.   *The forward sale contract* itself represents the obligation to deliver the foreign currency. It is stated at the current dollar equivalent of the currency to be sold, and its dollar value changes with the *spot rate*.

3.   *The premium or discount on the forward contract* equals the difference between the current and future values of the currency to be sold. As before, this is generally attributable to interest rate differentials and is accounted for separately from any exchange conversion gain or loss.

Hedging an Identifiable Foreign Currency Commitment   The accounting for a forward sale contract follows from that used for a forward purchase contract. In the sale case, the exporter will be receiving foreign currency and contracts to sell it for dollars to a broker at a specified time in the future for a given price. When the contract is entered before the exporter records the foreign sale and the conditions specified in *SFAS 8* are met, any exchange conversion gain or loss which accrues during the commitment period is deferred and generates an adjustment to the dollar basis of the sale transaction. The premium or discount may be amortized proportionately over the life of the forward contract or be deferred. If the premium or discount is deferred, that portion relating to the commitment period is used to adjust the dollar basis of the sale transaction. When the contract remains in force after the sale is recorded until the receivable is subsequently collected, it becomes a *hedge of an exposed asset position*—in this case, the receivable. During this time, the remaining premium or discount is amortized. Any exchange conversion gain or loss accruing on the forward sale contract is now recognized at a financial reporting date and is not deferred. The commitment period and the exposed asset period for a forward sale contract are depicted below.

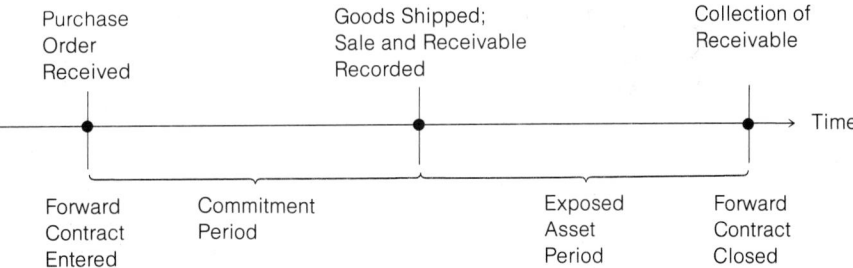

We illustrate the accounting for a forward sale contract with an example in which the sale and collection take place simultaneously. Therefore, the forward sale contract will be hedging only the foreign currency commitment; there will be no exposed asset to be hedged following the sale.

Acme International negotiated a sale of wool coats to Corsin, a Canadian retailer, on October 21, 19X2. Corsin is to pay on January 19, 19X3, when the coats are delivered (and the sale is recorded). The sale price was stated in Canadian dollars ($CN) and amounted to $CN50,000. On October 21, 19X2, the spot rate was $.96/$CN. Simultaneously, Acme sold $CN50,000 for future delivery on January 19, 19X3, at a forward rate of $.94/$CN. The discount of $1,000 will be amortized over the life of the contract. Since the discount is not deferred, no portion of it will be used to adjust the dollar value of the sale transaction. Subsequent spot rates were $.965/$CN on December 31, 19X2, and $.93/$CN on January 19, 19X3. Note that the balance sheet date of December 31, 19X2, falls during the commitment period, after seventy-one days of the ninety-day commitment period have expired. The entries recording these events follow:

10/21/X2

Due from Exchange Broker ($.94 × 50,000)	47,000	
Discount on Forward Contract [($.96 − $.94)50,000] .	1,000	
Forward Sale Contract ($.96 × 50,000)		48,000

To record the forward sale contract engaged in to hedge the identifiable foreign currency commitment with Corsin.

12/31/X2

Deferred Exchange Conversion Loss	250	
Forward Sale Contract		250

To record the exchange conversion loss accrued on the forward sale contract for $CN50,000; $250 = ($.965 − $.96)50,000.

Expense—Discount Amortization	789	
Discount on Forward Contract		789

To amortize the portion of the discount relating to 19X2; $789 = (71/90)$1,000.

1/19/X3

Accounts Receivable	46,500	
Sales		46,500

To record the sale of wool coats to Corsin of Canada; $46,500 = $.93 × $CN50,000.

Foreign Currency	46,500	
Accounts Receivable		46,500

To record receipt of the foreign currency ($46,500 = $.93 × 50,000) from Corsin.

Forward Sale Contract	1,750	
Deferred Exchange Conversion Gain		1,750

To recognize the deferred exchange conversion gain which accrued on the forward sale contract since December 31, 19X2; $1,750 = ($.965 − $.93)50,000.

Forward Sale Contract	46,500	
Foreign Currency		46,500

To record disbursement of the foreign currency to the broker; $46,500 = $48,000 + $250 − $1,750.

Cash	47,000	
Due from Exchange Broker		47,000

To record payment received from the foreign exchange broker.

Deferred Exchange Conversion Gain	1,750	
Deferred Exchange Conversion Loss		250
Sales		1,500

To adjust the dollar basis of recorded sales by the net deferred exchange gain ($1,500 = $1,750 − $250) accrued on the forward contract during the commitment period. In the example, the entire three-month life of the contract is the commitment period.

Expense—Discount Amortization 211
    Discount on Forward Contract 211
To expense the remaining discount on the forward
contract in 19X3; $211 = (19/90)$1,000.

Here the exporter used the hedging process to fix the dollar amount to be received from the foreign customer at $47,000. The $1,000 discount was expensed, $789 in 19X2 and $211 in 19X3. If hedging had not been undertaken, Acme would have lost $1,500 [= ($.96 − $.93)50,000]. Therefore, as in the previous example, Acme saved $500 (= $1,500 − $1,000) by using the forward market. The increase in Sales from the contemplated amount of $47,000 to the recorded amount of $48,000 (= $46,500 + $1,500) was offset by the discount amortization of $1,000.

In this example, the forward contract expired when the transaction was recorded at the end of the commitment period. The account receivable was collected immediately, so there was no exposed asset position to be hedged. If the receivable was not collected immediately and the forward sale contract extended beyond the transaction date, offsetting exchange conversion gains and losses would continue to accrue. Finally, the remaining period of the forward sale contract would absorb a portion of the discount amortization.

Determining Whether a Discount or Premium Exists on a Forward Contract

We have developed the following rules to assist in identifying a premium or discount on a forward contract.

Case	Type of Contract	Forward Rate (FR) ⪌ Spot Rate (SR)	Discount/Premium	Income Statement Effect
1	Forward Sale	FR < SR	Discount	Expense
2	Forward Purchase	FR < SR	Discount	Revenue
3	Forward Sale	FR > SR	Premium	Revenue
4	Forward Purchase	FR > SR	Premium	Expense

For example, if the foreign currency is sold forward and the forward rate is *less than* the current spot rate (case 1), the currency is sold at a *discount* from the current spot rate. Alternatively, if the foreign currency is purchased forward and the forward rate is *greater than* the current spot rate (case 4), the currency is purchased at a *premium* over the current spot rate.

Foreign Lending and Borrowing Transactions

The growth in the volume of international capital flows indicates that substantial investment funds move across national boundaries. U.S. companies may engage in the following investment transactions requiring foreign currency conversions:

1. Investment in securities of foreign companies, banks, and governments.
2. Borrowing from foreign lenders.
3. Direct investment in branches and subsidiaries abroad.

Of these three, direct investment in branches and subsidiaries abroad is the most complex. These investment funds provide a basis for setting up a business operation, acquiring assets, and incurring debts in the foreign country. The problems associated with the translation of these items for inclusion in U.S. company financial statements are addressed in Chapter 14.

Loans and investments in securities of foreign entities often require the U.S. firm to convert dollars into the foreign currency to acquire the security and then convert the foreign currency into dollars when the security matures or is sold. Similarly, borrowing from abroad may mean that the U.S. firm borrows a quantity of foreign currency, converts it into dollars for use domestically and later purchases sufficient foreign currency to repay the amount borrowed.

When an interest-bearing investment or note payable is denominated in a foreign currency, what exchange rate should the U.S. firm use to record the interest income or expense? Theoretically, the average exchange rate in effect while the interest is being earned should be used. In contrast, the receivable, payable, or collection or disbursement of cash when the interest is accrued is recorded at the current exchange rate. Taken together, these practices will result in a discrepancy between the revenue or expense and the asset or liability when exchange rates are fluctuating. We avoid this by *recording interest income and expense at the current exchange rate when the interest is accrued.* If interest receivable or interest payable is recorded, it will be subject to exchange conversion gains or losses due to subsequent movements in the exchange rate.

Since all such transactions expose the U.S. firm to the risk of loss from adverse changes in the foreign exchange rate, forward contracts may be used to neutralize the risk. As we illustrate these transactions, we shall introduce another way in which forward contracts can be used for hedging purposes and the related accounting rules. In the preceding section, we discussed accounting for forward contracts used to hedge an *identifiable foreign currency commitment.* We also saw how the commitment period expired once the transaction was recorded. If payment takes place at a date subsequent to recording the transaction (as it did in our forward purchase contract example), treatment of the related forward exchange contract changes. The contract is now being used to hedge an exposed asset or liability. Any accrued exchange conversion gains or losses are recognized currently and any premium or discount on the forward contract is amortized and not deferred.

This new treatment applies to *all hedges* which are *not* hedges of identifiable foreign currency commitments. Forward contracts used to hedge any exposed net asset or net liability position fall into this category. Thus the items being hedged need not be specific assets or liabilities. We illustrate this with a foreign lending transaction, although it applies equally to trade receivables and payables, as in the preceding section.

Hedging an Exposed Net Asset or Exposed Net Liability Position

Foreign lending and borrowing transactions will, on an individual basis or in the aggregate, result in an **exposed net asset position** or an **exposed net liability position.** Furthermore, a U.S. company's business operations abroad may involve exposure to exchange rate risk because its monetary assets denominated in the foreign currency exceed its monetary liabilities, or vice versa. **Monetary assets and liabilities** in this context refer to cash, claims to cash, and obligations to disburse cash which are denominated in the foreign currency. These items must represent fixed quantities of foreign currency and are not susceptible to price changes; only movements in the exchange rate cause their dollar equivalents to change.

SFAS 8 identifies the accounting rules for those forward contracts undertaken to hedge an exposed net asset (liability) position as follows. They are retained in the FASB *Exposure Draft.*

1.   Accrued exchange conversion gains or losses are to be recognized currently in income and not deferred.

2.   The premium or discount on the forward contract *must* be amortized to operations over the life of the contract.

As an example, we consider a U.S. investment in a foreign bank certificate of deposit and a forward sale contract to hedge an exposed net asset position. Although investment in the bank certificate of deposit contributes to the exposed net asset position, there need be no particular link between the investment and the forward contract. All we assume is that the company has sufficient asset exposure abroad to justify the forward contract.

On August 15, 19X2, Acme International purchases a ninety-day certificate of deposit from a Swiss bank. The certificate has a face value of 1,000,000 Swiss Francs (SF1,000,000), costs $600,000, and pays interest at the annual rate of 10 percent. At maturity on November 13, 19X2, Acme will receive SF1,025,000 [= SF1,000,000 + .1(SF1,000,000)/4]. Also on August 15, 19X2, Acme needed to hedge an exposed net asset position and sold SF2,000,000 forward for delivery on February 11, 19X3; the forward rate was $.63/SF. On November 13, 19X2, December 31, 19X2, and February 11, 19X3, the spot rates were $.59/SF, $.62/SF and $.635/SF, respectively. Acme's journal entries appear below; the books are closed on December 31.

8/15/X2

Temporary Investments	600,000	
Cash		600,000
To record the purchase of a Swiss certificate of deposit with face value of SF1,000,000 (the spot rate is $.60/SF).		

Due from Exchange Broker ($.63 × 2,000,000) .	1,260,000	
Premium on Forward Contract [($.63 − $.60)		
2,000,000]		60,000
Forward Sale Contract ($.60 × 2,000,000) . .		1,200,000
To record the forward sale contract engaged in to hedge an exposed net asset position.		

11/13/X2

Exchange Conversion Loss	10,000	
Temporary Investments		10,000
To recognize the exchange conversion loss accrued on the certificate of deposit; $10,000 = ($.60 − $.59)1,000,000.		

Foreign Currency ($.59 × 1,025,000)	604,750	
Temporary Investments ($600,000 − $10,000) .		590,000
Interest Income ($.59 × 25,000)		14,750
To record the foreign currency (SF1,025,000) received at maturity of the certificate of deposit and record the interest income based on the exchange rate when the interest is accrued.		

| Cash   .   .   .   . | 604,750 | |
| Foreign Currency   .   .   .   . | | 604,750 |

To record the exchange of SF1,025,000 for
$604,750.

12/31/X2

| Exchange Conversion Loss   .   .   .   .   . | 40,000 | |
| Forward Sale Contract .   .   .   .   .   . | | 40,000 |

To record the exchange conversion loss accrued
on the forward sale contract in 19X2; $40,000 =
($.62 − $.60)2,000,000.

| Premium on Forward Contract .   .   .   .   . | 46,000 | |
| Revenue—Premium Amortization   .   .   .   . | | 46,000 |

To amortize the portion of the premium relating to
19X2; $46,000 = (138/180)$60,000.

2/11/X3

| Exchange Conversion Loss   .   .   .   .   . | 30,000 | |
| Forward Sale Contract .   .   .   .   .   . | | 30,000 |

To recognize the exchange conversion loss
accrued on the forward sale contract since
December 31, 19X2; $30,000 = ($.635 −
$.62)2,000,000.

| Forward Sale Contract .   .   .   . | 1,270,000 | |
| Foreign Currency   .   .   .   . | | 1,270,000 |

To record disbursement of foreign currency
assumed to be on hand $1,270,000 (= $.635 ×
2,000,000) to the broker.

| Cash   .   .   .   . | 1,260,000 | |
| Due from Exchange Broker .   .   .   .   . | | 1,260,000 |

To record payment from the foreign exchange
broker.

| Premium on Forward Contract .   .   .   .   . | 14,000 | |
| Revenue—Premium Amortization   .   .   .   . | | 14,000 |

To amortize the portion of the premium relating to
19X3; $14,000 = (42/180)$60,000.

Use of Forward Contracts for Speculation

Forward contracts engaged in for hedging purposes represent defensive measures to protect against exchange rate movements adversely affecting the firms' foreign currency exposure. In contrast, firms may often sell or purchase foreign currency forward for **speculative purposes**—to gain from anticipated changes in the exchange rate. Suppose Acme's management believed that, despite the 180-day forward rate of $.63/SF, the spot rate for Swiss francs would be $.57/SF in 180 days. To speculate, Acme might sell 5,000,000 Swiss francs forward for delivery in 180 days. Such a contract would be for $3,150,000 (= $.63 × 5,000,000). If Acme is right, in 180 days it will be able to purchase SF5,000,000 for $2,850,000 (= $.57 × 5,000,000) to cover the forward sale and realize a gain of $300,000. Should the spot rate in 180 days be above $.63/SF, of course, Acme will incur a loss. *SFAS 8* and the FASB *Exposure Draft* provide the following accounting rules for such speculative forward contracts:

1.   Both the amount due to or from the exchange broker and the forward

exchange contract are recorded at the *forward* rate. As a result, neither discount nor premium is separately measured.

2. Exchange conversion gains or losses are to be based on the difference between the forward rate specified in the contract and the forward rate for the period remaining until settlement and are to be recorded currently.

Note the contrast with the accounting rules governing hedges. Forward exchange contracts used for hedging are measured using the current spot rate; speculative contracts are measured using the forward rate for the remaining period in the contract. Exchange conversion gains and losses for hedges derive from movements in the spot rate; for speculations, they derive from movements in the forward rates. Finally, any discount or premium is explicitly accounted for in the hedge and implicitly in the speculative contract.

To illustrate, suppose Acme decides to speculate in the Dutch guilder (G) by purchasing, on November 1, 19X2, G8,000,000 for delivery in ninety days. Acme will cover the contract by selling guilders in the spot market on January 29, 19X3. Relevant exchange rates ($/G) are as follows:

Date	Spot Rate	Forward Rate
November 1, 19X2	$.50	$.47 (90-day)
December 31, 19X2	.495	.465 (30-day)
January 29, 19X3	.462	—

Acme records the events relating to this speculative forward contract as follows:

11/1/X2

Forward Purchase Contract	3,760,000	
Due to Exchange Broker		3,760,000

To record a forward purchase contract calling for delivery of G8,000,000 in ninety days at the forward rate of $.47/G; $3,760,000 = $.47 × 8,000,000.

12/31/X2

Exchange Conversion Loss	40,000	
Forward Purchase Contract		40,000

To recognize the exchange conversion loss accrued on the forward contract, $40,000 = [$.47 − $.465)8,000,000], and to revalue it based on the thirty-day forward rate; $3,720,000 = $.465 × 8,000,000.

1/29/X3

Exchange Conversion Loss	24,000	
Forward Purchase Contract		24,000

To recognize the exchange conversion loss accrued on the forward purchase contract since December 31, 19X2; $24,000 = ($.465 − $.462)8,000,000.

Foreign Currency	3,696,000	
Forward Purchase Contract		3,696,000

To record receipt of the foreign currency from the
broker; $3,696,000 = $.462 × 8,000,000 =
$3,760,000 − $40,000 − $24,000.

Due to Exchange Broker	3,760,000	
Cash		3,760,000

To record payment of the foreign exchange broker.

Cash	3,696,000	
Foreign Currency		3,696,000

To record sale of the G8,000,000 in the spot
market at $.462/G.

We can see clearly that the total exchange conversion loss recognized in the accounts, $64,000 (= $40,000 + $24,000), equals the net cash loss of $64,000 (= $3,760,000 − $3,696,000) from the speculative activity. Note that had a discount been recorded at November 1, 19X2, when the forward contract was entered, the total loss would still be $64,000. The discount would have a credit balance of $240,000 [= ($.50 − $.47)8,000,000], but the forward purchase contract would have produced an exchange conversion loss of $304,000 [= ($.50 − $.462)8,000,000], exactly $64,000 more than the revenue effect of the discount amortization.

Summary of Accounting for Forward Exchange Contracts

In all forward contracts, the account *Due to (from) Exchange Broker* is denominated in dollars. It fixes the number of dollars to be paid to (or received from) the exchange broker based on the appropriate forward rate when the contract is signed. Consequently, it does not move with the exchange rate and does not generate exchange conversion gains and losses. It is the account *Forward Exchange Contract* which is denominated in the foreign currency. Its dollar value does change with the exchange rate and exchange conversion gains and losses accrue to it.

The accounting treatments prescribed for forward exchange contracts by *SFAS 8* are summarized in Exhibit 13.2. These rules may seem unnecessarily complex. Nevertheless, the underlying rationale appears reasonable. Since the hedge of an identifiable foreign currency commitment is an integral part of the entire transaction, it is appropriate to defer exchange conversion gains and losses until the transaction is recorded. Other hedges may not be related to specific transactions and may contain an element of speculation. Hence the exchange conversion gains and losses on other hedges are recognized currently, but a portion of the premium or discount is deferred when the contract's life spans more than one accounting period. Finally, speculative contracts have as their main product the generation of gains or losses from movements in exchange rates. These exchange conversion gains and losses are recognized currently as they occur with no deferral at all, and there is no separate measurement of the premium or discount on a speculative forward contract.

This completes our discussion of accounting for foreign currency transactions. In the next chapter, we turn to the problems associated with the need to translate foreign currency financial statements into dollars for inclusion in U.S. accounting reports and to consideration of international accounting standards.

Exhibit 13.2   Summary of Accounting for Forward Exchange Contracts

Purpose of Contract	Balance Sheet Valuation		Treatment of Exchange Conversion Gain or Loss	Treatment of Discount or Premium
	Amount Due to (from) Broker	Forward Exchange Contract		
To hedge an identifiable foreign currency commitment.	Fixed at the dollar equivalent of the foreign currency translated at the forward rate.	Varies with the dollar equivalent of the foreign currency translated at the spot rate.	Deferred during the commitment period until the transaction is recorded;[a] used to adjust the dollar basis of the recorded transaction.	Deferred during the commitment period or amortized over the life of the contract. If deferred, the portion pertaining to the commitment period is used to adjust the dollar basis of the recorded transaction. Any remaining amount is amortized over the contract's remaining life.
To hedge an exposed net asset or net liability position.	Fixed at the dollar equivalent of the foreign currency translated at the forward rate.	Varies with the dollar equivalent of the foreign currency translated at the spot rate.	Recognized currently as it accrues; not deferred.	Amortized over the life of the contract.
Speculation.	Fixed at the dollar equivalent of the foreign currency translated at the forward rate.	Varies with the dollar equivalent of the foreign currency translated at the forward rate for the remaining life of the contract.	Recognized currently as it accrues; not deferred.	Included as part of gain or loss but not recognized separately.

[a]Paragraph 24 of *SFAS 8* states that deferral of exchange conversion losses on forward contracts is not appropriate if deferral could lead to recognition of losses in subsequent periods. For example, if the loss exceeds the expected gross profit (less costs of sale or disposal) on a sale transaction that has been hedged, it should *not* be deferred until that sale transaction is complete.

Source: Financial Accounting Standards Board, *Statement of Financial Accounting Standards No. 8,* "Accounting for the Translation of Foreign Currency Transactions and Foreign Currency Financial Statements" (Stamford, Conn.: FASB, 1975), pars. 22–28; AC § 1083.022–028.

Summary of Key Concepts

The price of one currency in terms of another is called a **foreign exchange rate.** The **spot rate** is the price for immediate delivery of the foreign currency. Delivery at a specified time in the future can be contracted at the appropriate **forward** or **futures rate** with a foreign exchange broker or dealer.

Import/export transactions and borrowing and lending abroad by domestic companies often generate **receivables and payables denominated in a foreign currency.** As the exchange rate rises (falls), the number of dollars ultimately to be received or paid increases (decreases). These changes in the dollar equivalents of these receivables and payables generate **exchange conversion gains and losses** which are recognized by the domestic company as they occur.

Forward exchange contracts are often used to **hedge** the risk of gain or loss from movements in the exchange rate as explained above. When the contract covers some time after a transaction has been negotiated but before it is recorded, it hedges an **identifiable foreign currency commitment.** If the contract remains in effect after the transaction is recorded, it hedges an **exposed asset (liability) position.** Many forward contracts cover both the commitment and exposed periods.

When the forward rate is greater than (less than) the current spot rate, there will be a premium (discount) on the forward contract. The **premium or discount** may be deferred during **the commitment period** or **amortized over the entire life of the contract.** The amount deferred during the commitment period should be proportional to the total life of the contract and is used to adjust the dollar basis of the transaction. The balance is amortized over the remaining life of the contract.

Exchange conversion gains and losses accrue to the forward purchase (sale) contract, **not** to the amount due to (from) the exchange broker. The net exchange conversion gain or loss accruing during the **commitment period** is **deferred** and is used to adjust the dollar basis of the transaction. **Once the transaction is recorded,** an exposed liability or asset position results. **Further** exchange conversion gains or losses accruing to the forward contract **are recognized as they occur.**

A forward purchase (sale) contract may be entered solely in anticipation of an increase (decrease) in the spot rate, that is, for **speculative reasons.** In such cases, there is **no hedging,** no separate measurement of premium or discount, and all exchange conversion gains and losses are recognized currently as they accrue.

Questions   Q13.1   What is the major change that took place in the international monetary system during the 1970s? Briefly explain why this change took place.

Q13.2   Those U.S. firms engaged in transactions denominated in currencies other than the dollar generally have additional decisions to make. Describe the basic cause of these extra decisions. What can management do to deal with this problem?

Q13.3   The Barber Corporation is considering developing some overseas markets for its products. Credit and payment policies for overseas customers are two of several matters being considered. You have been engaged by Barber to explain the accounting implications of export transactions as well as to give general advice on the subject to Barber's controller. What special risks would be faced by Barber in overseas markets? What kinds of general information should be considered in formulating credit and payment policies for foreign customers?

Q13.4   Describe the *hedging* process and identify its costs and benefits.

Q13.5   Suppose that interest rates on six-month certificates of deposit are 12 percent in the United States and 10 percent in the United Kingdom. Based on this information alone, would you expect pounds sterling to be delivered in six months to sell at a premium over or discount from the spot rate? Explain.

Q13.6   A manager once remarked that "all of these accounting problems related to import/export transactions and forward contracts represent unnecessary complications. Denominating all foreign transactions of domestic firms in units of domestic currency would render these problems irrelevant." Is the manager's analysis correct? Explain.

Q13.7   If a forward contract is entered to hedge an identifiable foreign currency commitment, exchange conversion gains and losses accruing during the commitment period are deferred and used to adjust the dollar basis of the transaction. What is the logic behind this rule?

Q13.8   The Camel Company purchases 1,000,000 deutsche marks (DM) for delivery in six months at the forward rate of $.57/DM, recognizing a liability to the exchange broker of $570,000. As the weeks and months pass, both the spot and forward rates for deutsche marks fluctuate. How is Camel's liability to the exchange broker affected as the exchange rates move up and down?

Q13.9   *SFAS 8* requires that the premium or discount on a forward contract entered to hedge an exposed asset or liability position be amortized to operations over the life of the contract. Comment on the propriety of this treatment.

Q13.10 Accounting for a forward contract entered for speculative purposes calls for valuation of the forward exchange contract at the forward rate for the remaining life of the contract. No premium or discount is separately measured, even though one will typically exist. Explain why you feel this rule is consistent or inconsistent with accounting for forward contracts entered for nonspeculative reasons.

Exercises E13.1   Eastern Merchandise Company imports a variety of items for resale to U.S. retailers. During one month it made the following purchases (on credit) and payments:

Country				Amount	Currency	Spot Rate at Purchase	Spot Rate at Payment
Australia	.	.	.	15,000	Australian Dollar	$1.100	$1.130
Finland .	.	.	.	42,000	Markka	.260	.250
Indonesia	.	.	.	730,000	Rupiah	.002	.003
Turkey .	.	.	.	80,000	Lira	.060	.060

Required: Give the journal entries made by Eastern to record the above purchase and payment transactions.

E13.2 Western Exports sells many different items abroad. During one month it made the following sales (on credit) and collections:

Country	Amount	Currency	Spot Rate at Sale	Spot Rate at Collection
Austria	25,000	Schilling	$ .074	$ .082
Greece	400,000	Drachma	.028	.025
Iraq	300,000	Dinar	.014	.017
South Africa	10,000	Rand	1.150	1.140

Required: Give the journal entries made by Western to record the above sale and collection transactions.

E13.3 On September 15, 19X3, Haskell Company agreed to purchase 5,000 radios from a South Korean company for a total invoice price of 12,000,000 won (W). The radios are received on October 15 and payment made on November 14. Concurrently, on September 15, 19X3, Haskell purchased W12,000,000 for delivery on November 14, 19X3. Haskell's accounting practice is to defer a premium or discount on a forward contract during the commitment period. Relevant exchange rates ($/W) are as follows:

	9/15/X3	10/15/X3	11/14/X3
Spot Rate	$.002	$.0021	$.0022
Sixty-day Forward Rate	.00185	—	—

Required: Prepare the journal entries made by Haskell on September 15, 19X3, October 15, 19X3, and November 14, 19X3.

E13.4 On December 1, 19X1, Diversified Industries purchased merchandise from a Belgian firm, at a price of 32,000 francs, payable in sixty days. Diversified also sold merchandise to a firm in Uruguay, at a price of 40,000 pesos, to be collected in sixty days. No forward exchange contracts were used. The following exchange rates existed:

Date	$/Franc	$/Peso
December 1, 19X1	$.029	$.220
December 31, 19X1	.032	.225
January 29, 19X2	.033	.207

Required: Determine the amount of exchange conversion gain or loss to be reported by Diversified Industries in its 19X1 and 19X2 income statements. Show all calculations.

E13.5 On August 18, 19X9, Cup-of-Kava Company imports 6,000 bags of coffee from a Brazilian grower. The invoice price is for 20,000,000 cruzeiros, payable in cruzeiros on October 31, 19X9. Cup-of-Kava Company immediately enters into a forward exchange contract for delivery of 20,000,000 cruzeiros on October 31, 19X9. The forward rate specified in the contract is $.072. The spot rate on August 18, 19X9, is $.07. On October 31, 19X9, the spot rate is $.069.

Required:
1. Calculate the discount or premium on the forward exchange contract.
2. Calculate the exchange gain or loss incurred by Cup-of-Kava Company.
3. Calculate the exchange gain or loss that would have been incurred if Cup-of-Kava Company had not hedged by entering into the forward exchange contract.

E13.6 Livingstone Company, a calendar-year corporation, manufactures various kinds of filter materials. On April 15, 19X4, Livingstone received an order from a diamond mining company in South Africa for a large quantity of reusable filters to be used in the dust masks of diamond miners. The total price in rands (R) was R12,000. Livingstone planned on shipping the filters on April 30, 19X4, and payment is to be received in rands on May 15, 19X4. Upon receipt of the purchase order, Livingstone immediately sells R12,000 for delivery in thirty days. The firm's practice is to amortize any premium or discount on a forward contract over the life of the contract. Relevant exchange rates ($/R) are shown:

	4/15/X4	4/30/X4	5/15/X4
Spot Rate	$1.15	$1.16	$1.19
Thirty-day Forward Rate	1.18	—	—

Required: Prepare the journal entries made by Livingstone on April 15, 19X4, April 30, 19X4, and May 15, 19X4.

E13.7 To take advantage of high short-term interest rates, Carlton Enterprises purchased a 1,000,000 deutsche mark (DM) six-month certificate of deposit from a West German bank for $500,000 on October 1, 19X8. The annual interest rate is 15 percent. Exchange rates ($/DM) at December 31, 19X8, and March 31, 19X9, are $.52 and $.465, respectively.

Required:
1. Prepare the journal entries recorded by Carlton on October 1, 19X8, December 31, 19X8, and March 31, 19X9.
2. Was this a good investment? Explain with calculations.

E13.8 Fallon Associates is a firm making markets in certain foreign currencies. On December 15, 19X6, Fallon's net speculative position in the forward market consisted of (1) an agreement to purchase 2,000,000 Hong Kong dollars ($H) in sixty days and (2) an agreement to sell 5,000,000 Singapore dollars ($S) in thirty days. Relevant exchange rates are given next:

	12/15/X6	12/31/X6	1/14/X7	2/13/X7
Forward Rate for Remaining Life of Contract ($/$H)	$.2108	$.2101	—	$.2112 [a]
Forward Rate for Remaining Life of Contract ($/$S)	.4619	.4620	.4610 [a]	—

[a] Spot rate.

Required: Prepare the journal entries made by Fallon on December 15, 19X6, December 31, 19X6, January 14, 19X7, and February 13, 19X7.

Problems **P13.1**   **Accounting for Forward Contracts: Hedging and Speculation** The Futura Corporation, a calendar-year corporation, is an active trader in foreign exchange, both for purposes of hedging its international activities and for outright speculation. In particular, it had several transactions in the futures market for rands (R), the currency of South Africa, during 19X7. Relevant exchange rates ($/R) are shown:

	11/1/X7	12/31/X7	1/29/X8
Spot Rate	$1.15	$1.17	$1.19
Thirty-day Futures	1.13	1.16	1.20
Sixty-day Futures	1.11	1.15	1.21
Ninety-day Futures	1.09	1.14	1.22

On November 1, 19X7, Futura entered into the following forward contracts. The contracts were settled on January 29, 19X8.
1. Sold R100,000 forward to hedge a forthcoming sale to a South African firm; the sale price of R100,000 has been negotiated although delivery and collection will not take place until January 29, 19X8.
2. Purchased R200,000 forward to hedge the exposed net liability position of its South African branch.
3. Sold R100,000 forward in anticipation of a fall in the spot rate.

Required:
1. Prepare the journal entries made by Futura on November 1, 19X7, December 31, 19X7, and January 29, 19X8. Assume that Futura defers the premium or discount on a forward contract when permitted to do so under *SFAS 8*.
2. Comment on the specific use of the forward market by Futura in the problem.

P13.2   **Computation of Exchange Conversion Gain or Loss** Wheelstick Corporation, incorporated in the state of Delaware, is active in the import/export business. An analysis of Wheelstick's receivables, payables, and other assets (liabilities) prior to adjustment at December 31, 19X2, disclosed the following:

RECEIVABLES

U.S. Customers	$100,000
Belgian Customers (300,000 Francs)	9,000
Indian Customers (120,000 Rupees)	14,400
Saudi Arabian Customers (90,000 Riyal)	27,000
Exchange Broker (Forward Sale Contract for 300,000 Francs)	9,300
Total Receivables	$ 159,700

PAYABLES

U.S. Suppliers	$ (47,000)
Ecuadorian Suppliers (600,000 Sucre)	(24,000)
Mexican Suppliers (500,000 Pesos)	(19,000)
Exchange Broker (Forward Purchase Contract for 500,000 Pesos)	(20,000)
Total Payables	$(110,000)

OTHER ASSETS (LIABILITIES)

Trademarks	$ 75,000
Forward Purchase Contract (500,000 Pesos)	19,000
Forward Sale Contract (300,000 Francs)	(9,000)
Total Other Assets (Liabilities)	$ 85,000

Spot rates for the above currencies at December 31, 19X2, are:

Currency	Exchange Rate
Belgian Francs	$.036
Rupees	.125
Riyal	.287
Sucre	.042
Mexican Pesos	.035

Required: Prepare a schedule to compute the exchange conversion gain or loss recognized by Wheelstick in 19X2.

P13.3 **Recording International Transactions** The following international transactions were entered into during 19X3 by CONNCO, an American corporation:

1. April 1, 19X3: Purchased a six-month (182-day) certificate of deposit from the Bank of England—face value, £1,000,000; interest rate is 12 percent per annum; cost, $2,000,000.
2. June 15, 19X3: Entered into a firm commitment to purchase goods from Italy which will be resold in the United States. The invoice price was 40,000,000 lira, delivery and payment were to be made in sixty days, and the spot rate is $.0014. Concurrently, 40,000,000 lira were purchased in the forward market for delivery in sixty days at the forward rate of $.0012.
3. August 14, 19X3: The transactions in 2 were settled; the spot rate was $.0015.
4. September 1, 19X3: Agricultural products priced at 30,000 rial were sold to a concern in Iraq when the spot rate was $3.44. Payment was to be received in ninety days.
5. September 28, 19X3: The certificate of deposit purchased in transaction 1 matured, and the pounds were converted into dollars at an exchange rate of $2.02.
6. October 15, 19X3: After considering the worsening political situation in Thailand, CONNCO's management decided to sell 50,000,000 baht forward ninety days in order to hedge the exposed net asset position of the

Bangkok branch. The spot and ninety-day futures rates were $.05 and $.044, respectively.

7. November 30, 19X3: The receivable in transaction 4 was collected and the rial were converted to dollars at a spot rate of $3.47.

8. December 31, 19X3: The books were closed and made ready for the preparation of financial statements. The spot rate for baht was $.046, and the fifteen-day futures rate is $.045.

Required:

1. Prepare the journal entries made by CONNCO to record its international transactions during 19X3. Amortize any discount or premium arising on a forward contract.

2. Compare the exchange conversion gain or loss recognized on transaction 6 with the amounts to be recognized had the forward contract been entered into for the other reasons identified in *SFAS 8*.

P13.4   **Recording Hedged Import and Export Transactions**   International Molding Machinery, Inc., produces plastic molding machinery. During November 19X1, it purchased raw materials and sold finished goods abroad as explained below:

1. On November 7, 19X1, a special steel alloy was purchased from a Japanese company, invoice price 6,000,000 yen, payable in sixty days. The spot rate was $.0041. International immediately entered into a forward contract to purchase 6,000,000 yen on January 6, 19X2; the forward rate was $.004. When International's books were closed on December 31, 19X1, the spot rate was $.0045; it is $.005 on January 6, 19X2.

2. On November 28, 19X1, some machinery was sold to a Venezuelan firm, invoice price 180,000 bolivar, payment to be received on January 27, 19X2. The spot rate was $.233. To hedge this transaction, International signed a forward contract to sell 180,000 bolivar on January 27, 19X2, at a forward rate of $.236. The spot rate was $.227 on December 31, 19X1, when International's books were closed and is $.236 on January 27, 19X2.

Required: Prepare the journal entries made by International on November 7, 19X1, November 28, 19X1, December 31, 19X1, January 6, 19X2, and January 27, 19X2.

P13.5   **Recording a Hedged Foreign Loan**   Roderick Company borrowed 50,000 pounds (£) from a London bank on December 16, 19X1. The £50,000 were immediately converted to dollars for use in the United States and are scheduled to be repaid with interest of £500 on January 15, 19X2. To hedge the risk of an unfavorable change in the exchange rate, Roderick purchased £50,500 for delivery on January 15, 19X2. Roderick's accounting period ends on December 31, 19X1. Exchange rates ($/£) on the various dates are as follows:

	12/16/X1	12/31/X1	1/15/X2
Spot Rate	$2.10	$2.08	$2.05
Thirty-day Forward Rate	2.13	—	—

Exhibit 13.3   Bush Specialty Products: Summary of Import/Export Department Activities to Be Used in P13.6

IMPORT TRANSACTIONS

Quantity—Part No.	Unit Cost (FC)	Spot Rate When Purchased	Spot Rate When Paid	Unit Net Realizable Value
2,000—K14	6.4	$ .83	$ .80	$ 7.75
17,000—KR08	10.0	.49	.58	6.00
5,000—L16	8.2	1.13	1.22	10.00
10,000—M290	25.2	.37	.32	9.20

EXPORT TRANSACTIONS

Quantity—Part No.	Unit Selling Price (FC)	Spot Rate When Sold	Spot Rate When Collected	Unit Cost
14,000—A24	8.4	$ .27	.29	$ 1.98
6,000—DD2	12.5	2.00	1.92	24.00
20,000—A27	10.0	1.10	1.16	8.90
1,000—B23	14.6	.63	.58	8.50

FORWARD CONTRACTS

Quantity of FC Purchased (Sold)	Average Spot Rate at Inception	Average Forward Rate at Inception	Average Spot Rate at Maturity	Purpose of Contract
210,000	$.57	$.62	$.59	Hedge
(300,000)	.88	.90	.87	Hedge
1,000,000	.28	.25	.22	Speculation
(1,000,000)	.75	.74	.85	Speculation

Required: Prepare the journal entries made by Roderick on December 16, 19X1, December 31, 19X1, and January 15, 19X2.

P13.6   **Analyzing the Performance of an Import/Export Department**   William Johnston manages the import/export department of Bush Specialty Products. Because of the complexities of foreign currency transactions and the continual changes in exchange rates, Bush's management is having difficulty determining exactly how Johnston's operation is performing. You have been called in as a consultant to give advice on this performance evaluation task.

After you discuss the problem with Mr. Johnston, he produces the summary of his department's activities shown in Exhibit 13.3. The letters FC identify foreign currency units, and exchange rates are defined as $/FC. Premiums and discounts on forward contracts are always amortized over the contracts' lives, never deferred.

Required:
1. Prepare, in good form, schedules to calculate the profit contribution or loss realized by the import/export department.
2. Write a short memorandum to top management regarding your findings. Should Mr. Johnston be fired? Explain.

Exhibit 13.4 Schedule of Warner Corporation's Assets and Liabilities to Be Used in P13.7

ACCOUNTS RECEIVABLE

Domestic Customers	$ 25,000,000
Australian Customers (2,000,000 Australian Dollars)	2,280,000
Norwegian Customers (5,000,000 Krone)	1,000,000
Peruvian Customers	1,900,000
Spanish Customers (10,000,000 Pesetas)	200,000
ABC Foreign Exchange Specialists (10,000,000 Drachma)	300,000
Union Bank Foreign Exchange Department (10,000,000 Pesetas)	210,000
Total Accounts Receivable	$ 30,890,000

ACCOUNTS PAYABLE

Domestic Suppliers	$(15,000,000)
Brazilian Suppliers (4,000,000 Cruzeiros)	(200,000)
Colombian Suppliers (6,000,000 Pesos)	(180,000)
Dutch Suppliers (10,000,000 Guilders)	(5,000,000)
Swedish Suppliers	(800,000)
BR Foreign Exchange Service (5,000,000 Rupees)	(500,000)
Union Bank Foreign Exchange Department (10,000,000 Guilders)	(5,500,000)
Total Accounts Payable	$(27,180,000)

OTHER ASSETS (LIABILITIES)

Note Payable, Nippon Bank, Japan (200,000,000 Yen)	$ (1,000,000)
Forward Purchase Contract (5,000,000 Rupees)	500,000
Forward Purchase Contract (10,000,000 Guilders)	4,800,000
Forward Sale Contract (10,000,000 Drachma)	(300,000)
Forward Sale Contract (10,000,000 Pesetas)	(190,000)
Total Other Assets (Liabilities)	$ 3,810,000

P13.7 **Adjusting Entries at Balance Sheet Date** You have been engaged to audit the books of Warner Corporation as of December 31, 19X7. Assets and liabilities recorded by Warner but denominated in foreign currencies have required extensive audit adjustments in the past so you look sharply at the schedule prepared by Warner's controller. It appears in Exhibit 13.4.

Spot rates at December 31, 19X7, are given as follows:

Currency	Rate		Currency	Rate
Australian Dollar	$1.20		Pesetas	.02
Cruzeiro	.06		Pesos	.032
Drachma	.028 [a]		Rupees	.102 [a]
Guilder	.49		Yen	.006
Krone	.19			

[a]Forward rates for remaining terms of speculative contracts are $.025 and $.11 for drachma and rupees, respectively.

Required: Prepare the necessary adjusting entries for Warner Corporation as of December 31, 19X7. Support with calculations in good form.

P13.8 **Evaluation of Domestic and Foreign Investments**   The treasurer of Enormo Corporation is always on the lookout for short-term, high-yielding investments. Six-month low-risk domestic investments currently yield 12 percent per annum. Two foreign investments of comparable risk are presented:

1. A six-month certificate of deposit issued by the Bank of England has a coupon rate of 14 percent per annum. Spot and six-month forward exchange rates are $2.00 and $2.03, respectively.
2. A six-month certificate of deposit issued by the Bundesbank in West Germany carries a coupon rate of 8 percent per annum. Spot and six-month forward rates are $.50 and $.55, respectively.

Required:

1. Assuming that Enormo has $1,000,000 to invest, cannot tolerate exchange rate risk, and wants to maximize the number of dollars at the end of six months, analyze the three alternative investments and make a recommendation. Support your analysis with calculations.
2. Do you expect the results in requirement 1 to be maintained over time? Holding everything constant except the forward rates for pounds and deutsche marks, calculate the forward exchange rates which should prevail under the theory of covered interest arbitrage.

<table>
<tr><td>Chapter 14</td><td># Translating Foreign Currency Financial Statements and International Accounting Standards</td></tr>
</table>

Chapter 14

Translating Foreign Currency Financial Statements and International Accounting Standards

Our discussion in Chapter 13 focused on the structure of foreign exchange markets and how those markets are used by U.S. firms to facilitate various transactions involving foreign currency. Generally accepted accounting principles governing foreign currency transactions were explained in detail.

Another major accounting problem arises when U.S. firms have branches, divisions, or subsidiaries operating in foreign countries. When a U.S. company prepares its financial statements, the foreign currency financial statements of these overseas business units must be translated into dollars for inclusion in the U.S. statements. This is necessary so that all amounts are expressed in a common unit of measurement, the dollar. The various methods of translating these data are studied first in this chapter. In the latter part of the chapter, the diversity of accounting principles and practices around the world and the development of international accounting standards are discussed.

Growth in International Operations of U.S. Corporations

An important economic characteristic of the post–World War II period is the expanded scope of domestic corporations' activities in foreign markets. Many corporations domiciled in the United States, Japan, West Germany, and the United Kingdom, for example, all now have extensive foreign operations.

A recent study reported that the number of foreign subsidiaries owned by 180 manufacturing corporations domiciled in the United States increased from 2,196 at the end of 1950 to 11,198 at the end of 1975.[1] During this twenty-five-

---

[1] Joan P. Curhan, William H. Davidson, and Rajan Suri, *Tracing the Multinationals* (Cambridge, Mass.: Ballinger Publishing Company, 1977), pp. 19–20.

year period, 13,795 foreign subsidiaries were established, and 4,793 subsidiary relationships were terminated. The U.S. parent corporations held a majority ownership interest in 78 percent of these subsidiaries. Exhibit 14.1 presents some profitability and net asset data for U.S.-based multinational corporations to further demonstrate the significance of the foreign operations to U.S. business. The upper panel in Exhibit 14.1 shows that in 1979 many of the industries surveyed generated substantial portions of their earnings abroad (the FE/TE column) and had much of their total assets invested in foreign operations (the FNA/TNA column). The lower left panel plots the profitability of U.S. versus foreign operations for the period from 1973 to 1979, while the lower right panel expresses the changing importance of foreign earnings and assets to the respective total amounts. These data provide some indication of the relative scope of U.S. corporations' activities abroad as well as the dynamic character of these activities.

Import/export business, foreign manufacturing facilities, investments in foreign corporations, and obligations to foreign suppliers of capital are all indicative of the growing reliance of business on foreign markets. Although the expansion of world trade, coinciding with the reconstruction of areas devastated by World War II, has obviously contributed to the current importance of international business activities, the *structure* of international funds flows has also been a significant factor. Whereas international operations were once characterized primarily by the import and export of goods among countries, international flows of *capital* now heavily influence relations among countries. Exhibit 14.2 shows the changing pattern of international economic relations experienced by the United States during the postwar period. Note the substantial increases in the volume of U.S. and foreign capital flows during the 1970s. Even though merchandise imports and exports continued to expand during this period, capital flows assumed a greater relative importance—see the (UCF)/(ME) and (FCF)/(MI) rows.

This changing character of the world economy has meant new challenges for corporate managements, professional accountants, and financial analysts. These challenges have developed as the multinational operations of domestic corporations have grown and as the international monetary system has evolved from a fixed exchange rate regime to one in which exchange rates fluctuate as conditions in foreign exchange markets change.

The Multinational Corporate Entity

Consider a diversified conglomerate corporation domiciled in the United States, such as LTV or Gulf & Western. Two major problems faced by the managements of such firms are (1) controlling wide-ranging, geographically diverse operations and (2) measuring the performance of the various divisions or subsidiaries included in the conglomerates. The fundamental managerial issue of centralization versus decentralization and accounting concerns such as transfer pricing schemes and cost allocation techniques are familiar. Indeed, the discussion of segment reporting presented in Chapter 12 emphasized the importance of these accounting matters on subfirm performance measurement. In addition

Exhibit 14.1   Domestic and Foreign Net Earnings and Net Assets of U.S.-Based Multinational Corporations

1979 Profitability: Industry-by-Industry Rundown
(Amounts in Thousands)

INDUSTRY CATEGORY	Companies	Foreign			Net Earnings after Taxes (USE)	U.S.		FE/ TE (%)	FNA/ TNA (%)
		Net Earnings after Taxes (FE)	Net Assets (FNA)	FE/ FNA (%)		Net Assets (USNA)	USE/ USNA (%)		
Building and Industrial Products	6	$ 169,421	$ 1,378,142	12.3	$ 958,179	$ 7,254,373	13.2	15.0	16.0
Business and Office Equipment	6	1,978,428	10,411,762	19.0	2,399,040	13,407,246	17.9	45.2	43.7
Capital Goods	14	486,010	3,200,246	15.2	854,663	6,688,285	12.8	36.3	32.4
Chemicals	10	647,505	4,516,411	14.3	1,288,800	9,711,326	13.3	33.4	31.7
Consumer Goods	19	873,994	6,270,899	13.9	3,138,758	21,920,749	14.3	21.8	22.2
Electrical and Electronics	7	523,179	4,290,902	12.2	2,187,326	12,245,532	17.9	19.3	25.9
Food	10	196,700	1,754,867	11.2	861,681	5,961,460	14.5	18.6	22.7
Health Care	6	614,454	3,129,194	19.6	914,822	4,675,605	19.6	40.2	40.1
Metals and Mineral Products	5	292,497	1,758,366	16.6	484,559	4,715,884	10.3	37.6	27.2
Miscellaneous	4	174,291	1,146,794	15.2	372,680	3,132,550	11.9	31.9	26.8
Transportation Equipment	11	948,510	7,509,878	12.6	1,912,946	23,337,224	8.2	33.1	24.3
Total	98	6,904,989	45,367,461	15.2	15,373,454	113,050,234	13.6	31.0	28.6
Petroleum[a]	9	4,330,972	40,139,064	10.8	5,536,077	66,104,841	8.4	43.9	37.8

[a]Assets are total assets.

Abbreviations: TE: total net earnings after taxes; TNA: total net assets.

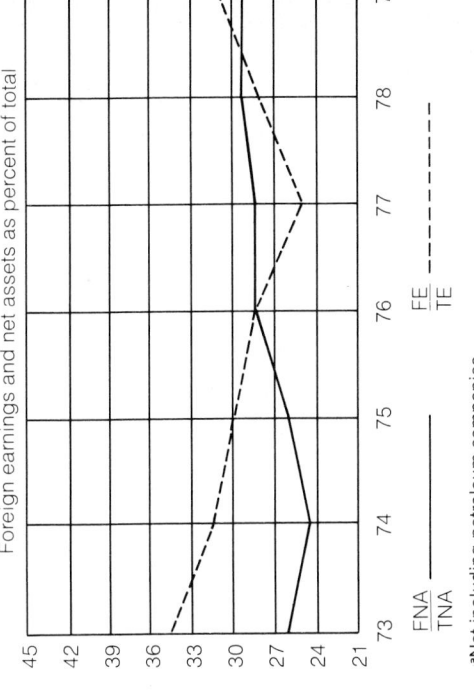

I. All Companies Surveyed[a]

Earnings as percent of net assets

US ────── Foreign ─ ─ ─ ─ ─ ─ ─

[a]Not including petroleum companies.

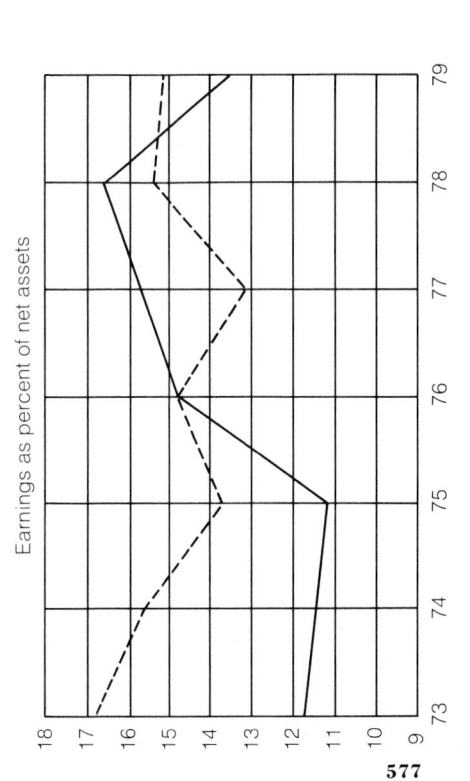

II. All Companies Surveyed[a]

Foreign earnings and net assets as percent of total

$\frac{FNA}{TNA}$ ────── $\frac{FE}{TE}$ ─ ─ ─ ─ ─ ─ ─

[a]Not including petroleum companies.

Source: Reprinted from the August 1, 1980, issue of *Business International*, page 243, with the permission of the publisher, Business International Corp. (New York).

Exhibit 14.2 Comparative Merchandise Exports and Imports, Domestic Capital Outflows, and Foreign Capital Inflows for the United States

	1946	1950	1955	1960	1965	1970	1975	1977	1978	1979
						(Amounts in Millions of Dollars)				
Merchandise Exports (ME)[a]	$11,764	$10,203	$14,424	$19,650	$26,447	$42,469	$107,088	$120,585	$142,054	$182,074
Merchandise Imports (MI)	5,067	9,081	11,527	14,744	21,496	39,866	98,041	151,644	175,813	211,524
U.S. Capital Outflows (UCF)[a]	4,055	(337)	1,383	2,883	4,176	6,164	31,548	35,793	60,957	63,423
Foreign Capital Inflows (FCF)[a]	(985)	1,912	1,357	2,120	383	5,923	14,336	50,823	63,713	33,902
(UCF)/(ME)[b]	34.5%	—	9.6%	14.7%	15.8%	14.5%	29.5%	29.7%	42.9%	34.8%
(FCF)/(MI)[b]	—	21.1%	11.8%	14.4%	1.8%	14.9%	14.6%	32.5%	36.2%	16.0%

[a]Excludes undistributed profits of subsidiaries.
[b]These ratios indicate the growing importance of capital flows relative to merchandise transactions.

Source: U.S. Department of Commerce, Bureau of Economic Analysis, *Survey of Current Business*, various issues.

to these, the following difficulties are common to multinational operations:

1. Corporate headquarters frequently separated from foreign operations by large geographical distances.

2. Books of account maintained in units of various currencies.

3. Interest rates, inflation rates, and growth rates which vary widely across countries.

4. Political conditions and economic institutions which differ among nations.

5. Language and other cultural barriers to effective communication.

6. Alternative sets of accounting principles and reporting standards around the globe.

Considering such obstacles to smooth operation, we can begin to grasp the dimensions of the planning, organizing, and control problems which confront top managements of multinational enterprises. Such problems must also be considered by the accountant who will define the boundaries of the reporting entity appropriate in a multinational enterprise.

The Entity Concept in Multinational Corporations

We have already indicated that many public reporting and disclosure issues in accounting are tied to questions concerning the entity appropriate in the circumstances. For accounting purposes, the corporation is separate from its shareholders. In consolidated statements, treatment of minority interest often differs from that of the controlling interest. *SFAS 14* requires the entity known as the *firm* to identify those *segments* which also appear to have the characteristics of a proper accounting entity. Finally, government and nonprofit units will later be seen to consist of several entities. What, then, is the appropriate entity or group of entities for accounting and reporting purposes of the multinational corporation?

The multinational corporation having foreign subsidiaries is a case in point. Ford Motor Company manufactures and sells automobiles at several locations outside the United States. Currently, Ford issues worldwide consolidated financial statements. An alternative reporting posture would be for Ford not to consolidate its foreign subsidiaries and divisions but to report them as long-term investments and include their separate financial statements in the notes. Such a posture has an advantage. Ford's owners and creditors would have a better understanding of the financial status of the various pieces included in their ownership interest. At the same time, however, their view of the big picture with respect to Ford would be clouded. Ford stockholders have an interest in the *totality* of Ford's operations. Their interests are not divisible among the pieces of Ford spread around the world.

Therefore, the entity concept appropriate for reporting the status of the stockholders' and creditors' interests in multinational enterprises is generally one which includes the foreign operations. As we shall see later in the chapter, however, there are circumstances which create exceptions to this general rule. When effective control over the assets of domestically-owned foreign subsidiaries is in jeopardy, a less inclusive entity definition may be warranted.

Translating Foreign Currency Financial Statements

We now turn to the accounting problems associated with the translation of foreign currency financial statements into dollars. Many U.S. companies have branches and subsidiaries located in foreign countries and doing business in those countries. Such companies may not engage in foreign currency transactions of the type described in Chapter 13 at all. Nevertheless, they too must be concerned with foreign exchange rates when they include these foreign operations in their U.S. financial statements.

The discussion in Chapter 13 indicated that recent changes in the international monetary system have resulted in the replacement of pegged or fixed foreign exchange rates with a flexible, or floating, structure of rates. Foreign exchange rates now change as the underlying relationships between the supply and demand of the various currencies change. The implications of this new environment for the translation of foreign currency financial statements are described in the next section.

Flexible Exchange Rates and Translating Foreign Currency Financial Statements

The present system of flexible exchange rates has removed the element of short-run stability provided by pegged rates. In addition, many foreign exchange rates have changed dramatically during the last decade. Taken together, these factors have produced new and sometimes alarming information in translated financial statements.

Many foreign exchange rates *have* changed substantially since the early 1970s, with the dollar losing ground against some of the major currencies. To show this, we reproduce in Figure 14.1 a plot of movements in several foreign exchange rates from 1977 to 1980. The exchange rates are expressed in the *indirect* form (foreign currency/$) as ratios of the rates existing in May 1970.

First, notice that all of the exchange rates are volatile. Second, observe that the dollar has lost ground against several of the major currencies. These currencies—such as the Japanese yen and the German mark—have *revalued* against the dollar because the price of dollars in those currencies has declined. For example, at the end of 1980, the West German deutsche mark price of dollars was about half that prevailing in May 1970 (the index had fallen from 100 to about 50). Because of this, the dollar equivalents of debts denominated in these strong currencies are growing, leading some foreign currency translation methods to report large losses. New concerns over whether these accounting methods are reflecting economic reality have arisen.

The constant and unpredictable fluctuations in exchange rates can cause translated account balances to become obsolete quickly. The fact that exchange rates do move up *and* down differentiates this problem from a similar one caused by domestic inflation. As a result, the inclusion of exchange gains and losses arising in the translation process in current income may be responsible for excessive and unwarranted instability in reported earnings.

In Chapter 13, we described the *exchange conversion gains and losses* produced by transactions involving the actual conversion to and from foreign currencies. In such exchange conversion cases, we saw how increases in the dollar equivalents of foreign currencies directly affect the economic position of the firm. Today, there is little controversy over including exchange conversion gains and losses in the U.S. income statement. Controversy does exist, how-

Figure 14.1   Indexes of Foreign Currency Price of the U.S. Dollar (May 1970 = 100)

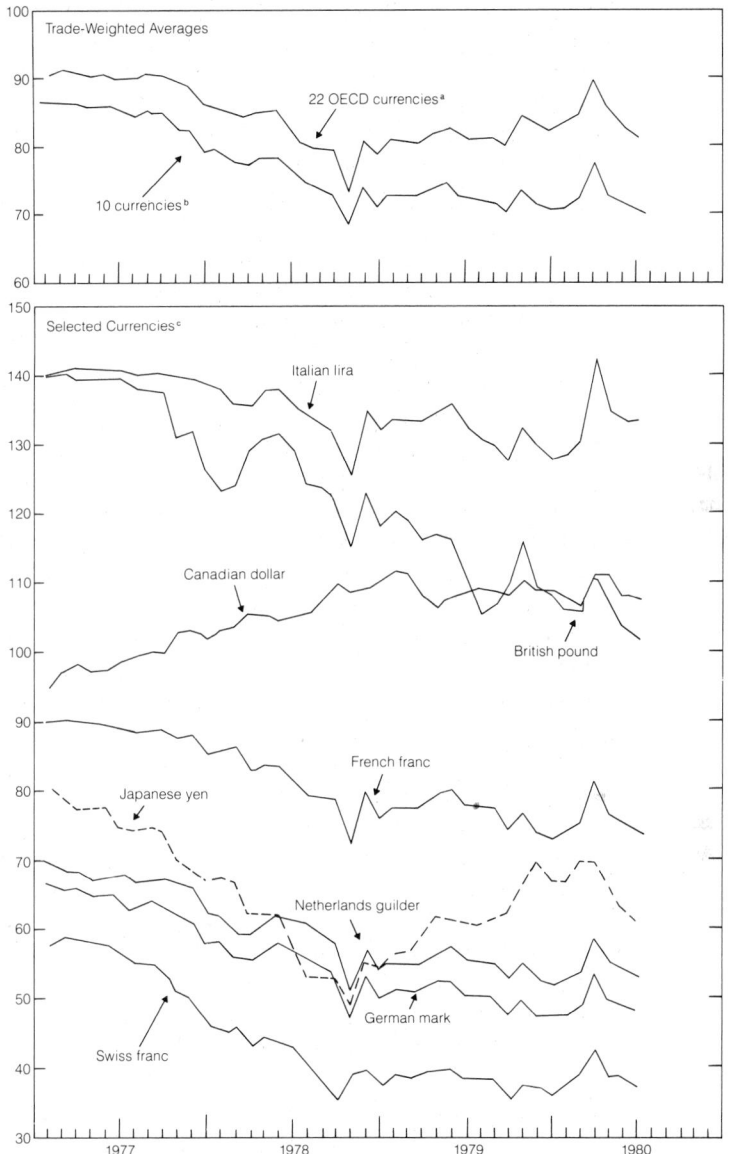

[a]Australia, Austria, Belgium, Luxembourg, Canada, Denmark, Finland, France, Germany, Greece, Iceland, Ireland, Italy, Japan, the Netherlands, New Zealand, Norway, Portugal, Spain, Sweden, Switzerland, Turkey, United Kingdom. Data: U.S. Department of the Treasury.
[b]Belgium, Canada, France, Germany, Italy, Japan, the Netherlands, Sweden, Switzerland, United Kingdom. Data: Federal Reserve Board. The Index has been revised as a result of a change in the method of computation. For details see the August 1978 Federal Reserve Bulletin. The new FRB index was rebased by BEA.
[c]Data: International Monetary Fund.
NOTE—Data are for end of month.

Source: U.S. Department of Commerce, Bureau of Economic Analysis, *Survey of Current Business*, September 1980, p. 33.

ever, over the inclusion of exchange gains and losses resulting from the translation process in income. To sharpen the distinction between exchange gains and losses arising from transactions and those arising in the translation process, we label the latter *exchange translation gains and losses*.

Exchange Translation Gains and Losses

As foreign exchange rates change, **exchange translation gains and losses** arise when some accounts are translated at the *current rate* and others at *historical rates*. Those accounts translated at the current rate change in dollar equivalents, while those translated at historical rates remain fixed in dollar equivalents.

> The **current exchange rate** is the spot rate at the end of a reporting period. It is the rate in existence on the balance sheet date. A **historical exchange rate** is a past spot rate, in existence when a particular transaction occurred.

Unlike exchange *conversion* gains and losses, exchange *translation* gains and losses may have little economic significance. For example, suppose the London branch of a U.S. company purchases merchandise from a U.K. supplier on credit. The resulting payable will be liquidated with pounds sterling generated from business in the United Kingdom. If the exchange rate ($/£) *increases*, the dollar equivalent of the payable rises, but the quantity of pounds required to discharge it does not change. Has the U.S. firm incurred a loss when this happens? Probably not, yet current accounting practice would record an exchange translation loss at year-end when the statements of the London branch are translated into dollars.

A similar situation occurs when plant assets are acquired in the foreign country with debt denominated in that foreign currency. The debt is to be retired with foreign currency generated in normal business operations. If the exchange rate ($/£) *falls*, fewer dollars would be required to retire the debt. Has the U.S. firm now realized a gain? Current accounting practice would record one at translation time, although management does not intend to use dollars to retire the debt. In cases such as these, there are neither actual nor intended conversions of foreign currency, and the U.S. firm is only affected indirectly, if at all. Thus it seems to us that *translation* gains and losses may not have the same economic significance as *conversion* gains and losses.

Exchange translation gains and losses arise because all approaches to translating foreign currency financial statements translate some accounts at the current rate and other accounts at historical rates. Determining those accounts to be translated at the current rate and those to be translated at historical rates is the most controversial issue in accounting for international operations. The position taken by *SFAS 8* in this area has been the subject of severe and ongoing criticism. Proposals contained in the FASB *Exposure Draft* (mentioned in Chapter 13) would, if adopted, replace *SFAS 8* with a translation approach which overcomes this criticism. We now discuss and compare the major approaches to translating foreign currency financial statements before providing a detailed explanation of the relevant provisions in *SFAS 8* and an overview of the related proposals in the *Exposure Draft*.

**Approaches
to Translating
Foreign
Currency
Financial
Statements**

The various approaches differ in their choices of accounts to be translated at current and historical rates. Four major approaches may be identified—current/noncurrent, monetary/nonmonetary, temporal, and current rate. We discuss each in turn.

Current/Noncurrent Method   The **current/noncurrent method** is prescribed in Chapter 12 of *ARB 43* (AC § 1083.060)[2] and incorporates the following dichotomy. *Current assets* and *current liabilities* are to be translated at the *current rate* in effect at the balance sheet date. Other assets and liabilities, as well as the stockholders' equity accounts, are all *noncurrent* and are translated at the *historical rates* in existence when those items originated. There seems to be no stated theoretical basis for the current/noncurrent dichotomy, although the method itself suggests a rationale. Current assets and liabilities are, by definition, either cash or items that are relatively close to being converted to cash or to being liquidated with cash. Being denominated in units of foreign currency, like cash, they are exposed to the effects of movements in the exchange rate. Hence it could be argued that translation at the current rate best expresses the dollar equivalents of these "near cash" items.

Revenues and expenses which occur evenly over the year are translated at average spot rates. Uneven revenue and expense flows should be translated at the rates in effect when they occur. Alternatively, a weighted average rate could be used for all revenue and expense items, except those representing amortization of balance sheet accounts which are translated at historical rates. For example, depreciation expense is translated at the historical rate used to translate the related asset.

The current/noncurrent method predominated in practice until the 1960s. In that decade, the monetary/nonmonetary method increased in favor because it remedied some logical inconsistencies in the current/noncurrent method.

Monetary/Nonmonetary Method   Hepworth's classic work, *Reporting Foreign Operations*, points out some flaws in the current/noncurrent method.[3] He first questions translation of inventory (a current asset) at the current rate on the grounds that it is not a clearly-defined foreign currency value—as are cash and receivables—but a *potential* foreign currency value. That is, since inventory is not a claim to a fixed quantity of foreign currency, it is more like plant assets (translated at historical rates) than cash (translated at the current rate).

Hepworth's second concern is with translation of long-term debt at historical rates under the current/noncurrent method. He argues that long-term debt, like accounts payable, is a contractual obligation to disburse a fixed number of foreign currency units. Although the disbursement will take place in the future, the current rate better reflects the dollar equivalent of the foreign currency obligation than a past rate.

---

[2] Committee on Accounting Procedure, *Accounting Research Bulletin No. 43*, "Restatement and Revision of Accounting Research Bulletins" (N.Y.: AICPA, 1953).

[3] Samuel R. Hepworth, *Reporting Foreign Operations* (Ann Arbor: University of Michigan, Bureau of Business Research, 1956).

Observe that both of Hepworth's objections cited above derive from a common theme: current exchange rates should be used to translate those items which represent cash or contractual claims to receive or disburse cash. Other items, which do not represent fixed quantities of foreign currency, should be translated at historical rates. This approach to the translation problem is known as the **monetary/nonmonetary method.** *Monetary assets and liabilities* are measured in fixed quantities of foreign currency; their dollar value changes only if the exchange rate changes. These are to be translated at the *current rate. Nonmonetary assets and liabilities* (all others) are therefore properly translated at the appropriate *historical rates.* Translation of revenues and expenses under the monetary/nonmonetary method is the same as under the current/noncurrent method.

The monetary/nonmonetary approach was widely used in practice during the late 1960s and early 1970s, prior to the adoption of *SFAS 8. APBO 6* (1965) amended *ARB 43* to allow translation of long-term receivables and payables at the current exchange rate, thereby effectively granting permission to use the monetary/nonmonetary approach. Publication of *SFAS 8* in 1975 required firms to translate according to the *temporal method,* a method which closely approximates the monetary/nonmonetary method when applied to the historical cost accounting model.

Temporal Method   The **temporal method** of translation was comprehensively developed by Leonard Lorensen in *Accounting Research Study No. 12.*[4] It is based on two fundamental principles:

1.   Translation changes the unit of measurement.
2.   Translation changes no other accounting principle.

Thus foreign currency translation is, like general price-level accounting, viewed as an arithmetic technique designed to convert disparate measurement units to a common one. Valuation or other attributes of the items being translated are not (and should not be) affected by the translation process. The appendix to this chapter provides a formal explanation of the relationship between the foreign currency translation process and general price-level or constant-dollar restatements.

Lorensen proceeds to establish that the major attribute of assets and liabilities which accountants measure is the **money price.** *APB Statement No. 4* refers to money prices as "ratios at which money and other resources are or may be exchanged."[5] It follows that the *date* at which an item's money price is measured should govern the date of the foreign exchange rate used to translate the item. This notion of dating the money price measured and using the foreign exchange rate on the same date to translate the money price is known as the **temporal principle of translation.** Lorensen summarizes its meaning as follows:

Thus assets and liabilities valued at current prices are translated at the cur-

---

[4]   Leonard Lorensen, *Accounting Research Study No. 12,* "Reporting Foreign Operations of U.S. Companies in U.S. Dollars" (N.Y.: AICPA, 1972).

[5]   Accounting Principles Board, *Statement No. 4,* "Basic Concepts and Principles Underlying Financial Statements of Business Enterprises" (N.Y.: AICPA, 1970), par. 70; AC § 1023.31.

> Money and receivables and payables measured at the amounts promised should be translated at the foreign exchange rate in effect at the balance sheet date. Assets and liabilities measured at money prices should be translated at the foreign exchange rate in effect at the dates to which the money prices pertain.[6]

rent rate and those valued at past prices are translated at historical rates. The temporal method is the translation method required by *SFAS 8*. At the present time, the temporal method is very similar to the monetary/nonmonetary method. Note that if current value accounting were to become accepted, assets such as buildings and equipment, which are both noncurrent and nonmonetary, would be translated at the current rate under the temporal method because they would be valued at current money prices. Translation of revenues and expenses denominated in a foreign currency involves using the foreign exchange rates in effect when the money prices measuring revenues and expenses occurred. This is really no different from the approach used in both the current/noncurrent and monetary/nonmonetary methods to translate most revenues and expenses. Revenues and expenses occurring evenly over the year are translated at average exchange rates for the year under all three methods. Depreciation and amortization are translated at whatever rates are used to translate the related assets or liabilities.

Current Rate Method   Professional societies of chartered accountants in England, Wales, and Scotland propose the **current rate method**—translating all assets, liabilities, and contributed capital accounts in foreign currency financial statements at the current exchange rate as of the balance sheet date. Foreign currency revenues and expenses are also translated at the current rate under this method.

The current rate method represents a substantial departure from U.S. accounting principles and practice. It would seem to be entirely inappropriate so long as the underlying accounting is based on historical cost. A move to current value accounting would, according to the temporal principle, provide justification for the current rate method. Nevertheless, the FASB *Exposure Draft* proposes a version of the current rate method which, if adopted, would replace the temporal method required by *SFAS 8*.

At first glance, it seems as though the current rate method eliminates exchange translation gains and losses. Unfortunately, such is not the case. A translation gain or loss arises when we attempt to reconcile retained earnings; translation of beginning-of-period retained earnings at the end-of-period exchange rate produces a translation gain or loss.

Comparing the Four Translation Approaches   In order to better explain the differences between these methods, and the diverse accounting results portraying the same underlying facts, we have prepared three exhibits. The first, Exhibit 14.3, contrasts the use of current versus historical rates to trans-

---

[6] Lorensen, *ARS No. 12*, p. 19.

Exhibit 14.3   Exchange Rates Used by Four Translation Methods to Translate Selected Financial Statement Items

BALANCE SHEET	Current/ Noncurrent	Monetary/ Nonmonetary	Temporal Principle	Current Rate
Cash and Receivables . . .	C	C	C	C
Inventory at Cost	C	H	H	C
Inventory at Market	C	H	C	C
Investments at Cost . . .	H	H	H	C
Investments at Market . . .	H	H	C	C
Plant Assets	H	H	H	C
Accounts Payable	C	C	C	C
Deferred Taxes	H	H	H, C [a]	C
Long-Term Debt	H	C	C	C
Obligations under Warranties, Current	C	H	C	C
Capital Stock	H	H	H	C
Retained Earnings	[b]	[b]	[b]	[b]
INCOME STATEMENT				
Sales Revenue	A	A	A	C
Variable Expenses	A	A	A	C
Fixed Expenses	H, A [c]	H, A [c]	H, A[c]	C

Legend and Notes

C = Current rate; H = Historical rate; A = Average rate during the year.

[a]The rate(s) applied to translate deferred taxes are those used to translate the items giving rise to the timing differences; both historical and current rates may be included. See Lorensen, *ARS No. 12,* p. 28; and Financial Accounting Standards Board, *Statement No. 8,* pars. 50–52; AC § 1083.50–52.

[b]"Translated" retained earnings is a residual, consisting of current rates of previous periods.

[c]Fixed expenses such as depreciation and amortization are translated at the same historical rates as the related assets. Other fixed expenses which involve current outlays, such as rent and property taxes, are translated at the average rate during the year.

late specific financial statement items. Although the monetary/nonmonetary method often approximates the temporal method, Exhibit 14.3 points out major differences. For example, nonmonetary items carried at current market (inventory, investments and warranty obligations) are translated at the current rate under the temporal method but at historical rates under the monetary/nonmonetary method.

The underlying data for a numerical example which contrasts the four foreign currency translation methods are presented in Exhibit 14.4. Our objective in this illustration is to clearly differentiate among the accounting results of the four methods. This can be done using an uncomplicated situation with few transactions. The four methods are applied to these data in Exhibit 14.5.

Note the dramatically different results reported under the four methods. Translated assets (equities) range from $331.2 to $394.4, which is 19 percent higher. The translated net *loss* is $75.20 under the current/noncurrent method, more than five times the net income reported by the current rate method.

Understanding the Exchange Translation Loss   At one level, the exchange translation loss is simply a *plug*. It is the amount required in the trans-

Exhibit 14.4   Data for Foreign Currency Translation Illustration

Balance Sheet as of January 1, 19X1

Cash: £200   Contributed Capital: £200

	January 1, 19X1	July 31, 19X1	December 31, 19X1
Exchange Rate	$2.00/£	$1.60/£	$1.44/£
Transactions	1. Buy 2 widgets at £50 each.	1. Sell 1 widget for £120.	1. Record straight-line depreciation on furniture, £10.
	2. Purchase furniture (5-year life) for £50.	2. Replace widget for £80.	2. Close books and prepare financial statements.
		3. Pay other expenses of £30.	
		4. Accrue current warranty liability of £20 (current price of estimated warranty service).[a]	

[a]The warranty liability pertains to services expected to be rendered during 19X2. As such, it is a current liability, and, although it reflects the current cost of providing warranty service, it is not a commitment for a fixed amount of foreign currency.

lated income statement which, through its inclusion in retained earnings, brings the balance sheet into balance. It is at another level, however, that one is able to grasp what actually is happening in the translation process. A central concept is the *exposed position*.

> For accounting purposes, a firm's **exposed position** is the difference between its assets and liabilities denominated in the foreign currency which are to be translated at the *current rate*.

The exposed position under each of the four translation methods discussed in this book is defined as follows:

Translation Method	Definition of Exposed Position
Current/Noncurrent	Current assets − Current liabilities
Monetary/Nonmonetary	Monetary assets − Monetary liabilities
Temporal	Assets measured at current money prices − Liabilities measured at current money prices
Current Rate	Retained earnings (= Assets − Liabilities − Contributed capital)

Exhibit 14.5 Illustration of Four Methods for Translating Foreign Currency Financial Statements (Year Ended December 31, 19X1)

BALANCE SHEET	£	Historical (H) Exchange Rate	Current (C) Exchange Rate	Current/Noncurrent Method		Monetary/Nonmonetary Method		Temporal Method		Current Rate Method	
Cash	60	—	$1.44/£	C	$ 86.4	C	$ 86.4	C	$ 86.4	C	$ 86.4
Inventory: Unit 2	50	$2.00/£	$1.44/£	C	72.0	H	100.0	H	100.0	C	72.0
Inventory: Unit 3	80	$1.60/£	$1.44/£	C	115.2	H	128.0	H	128.0	C	115.2
Furniture, Net	40	$2.00/£	$1.44/£	H	80.0	H	80.0	H	80.0	C	57.6
Total Assets	230				$353.6		$394.4		$394.4		$331.2
Warranty Liability, Current	20	$1.60/£	$1.44/£	C	$ 28.8	H	$ 32.0	C	$ 28.8	C	$ 28.8
Contributed Capital	200	$2.00/£	$1.44/£	H	400.0	H	400.0	H	400.0	C	288.0
Retained Earnings	10	—	—	—	(75.2)	—	(37.6)	—	(34.4)	—	14.4
Total Equities	230				$353.6		$394.4		$394.4		$331.2

INCOME STATEMENT	£	Historical (H) Exchange Rate	Current (C) Exchange Rate	Current/Noncurrent Method		Monetary/Nonmonetary Method		Temporal Method		Current Rate Method	
Sales	120	$1.60/£	$1.44/£	H	$192.0	H	$192.0	H	$192.0	C	$172.8
Cost of Goods Sold	(50)	$2.00/£	$1.44/£	H	(100.0)	H	(100.0)	H	(100.0)	C	(72.0)
Warranty Expense	(20)	$1.60/£	$1.44/£	H	(32.0)	H	(32.0)	H	(32.0)	C	(28.8)
Other Expenses	(30)	$1.60/£	$1.44/£	H	(48.0)	H	(48.0)	H	(48.0)	C	(43.2)
Depreciation Expense	(10)	$2.00/£	$1.44/£	H	(20.0)	H	(20.0)	H	(20.0)	C	(14.4)
Exchange Translation Loss					(67.2)		(29.6)		(26.4)		—
Net Income (Loss)	10				$(75.2)		$(37.6)		$(34.4)		$ 14.4

COMPUTATION OF EXCHANGE TRANSLATION LOSS

	Current/Noncurrent			Monetary/Nonmonetary			Temporal			Current Rate		
	£	E.R.	$	£	E.R.	$	£	E.R.	$	£	E.R.	$
Exposed Position, January 1, 19X1	150 [a]	2.0	$300.0	50 [c]	2.0	$100.0	50 [e]	2.0	$100.0	0 [g]	—	$ 0
Plus Sale of Inventory	120	1.6	192.0	120	1.6	192.0	120	1.6	192.0	120	1.44	172.8
Less: Purchase of Inventory	—			(80)	1.6	(128.0)	(80)	1.6	(128.0)			
Payment of Expenses	(30)	1.6	(48.0)	(30)	1.6	(48.0)	(30)	1.6	(48.0)	(30)	1.44	(43.2)
Recognition of Cost of Goods Sold	(50)	2.0	(100.0)	—			—			(50)	1.44	(72.0)
Recognition of Depreciation Expense	—			—			—			(10)	1.44	(14.4)
Recognition of Warranty Liability (Expense)	(20)	1.6	(32.0)	—			(20)	1.6	(32.0)	(20)	1.44	(28.8)
Exposed Position, December 31, 19X1	170 [b]	1.44→	$312.0 / 244.8	60 [d]	1.44→	$116.0 / 86.4	40 [f]	1.44→	$ 84.0 / 57.6	10 [h]	1.44→	$ 14.4 / 14.4
Exchange Translation Loss			$ 67.2			$ 29.6			$ 26.4			$ 0

588

Exhibit 14.5   *continued*

NOTES

a150 = Cash(50) + Inventory(100).
b170 = Cash(60) + Inventory(130) − Warranty Liability, Current(20).
cCash(50).
dCash(60).
eCash(50).
f40 = Cash(60) − Warranty Liability, Current(20).
g0 = Assets(200) − Contributed Capital(200).
h10 = Assets(230) − Warranty Liability, Current(20) − Contributed Capital(200).

The exposed position generates the translation gain or loss caused by movements in the exchange rate. The exposed position at any balance sheet date, the *ending* exposed position, is translated at the current rate. Increases and decreases which occurred in the exposed position during the year just ended are, under double entry accounting, also reflected in accounts which are translated at historical rates. The beginning exposed position is implicitly translated at the beginning-of-period current rate, which now is a historical rate. These concepts are illustrated in the lower part of Exhibit 14.5. Note that in the *current rate method* any translation gain or loss accrues only to the beginning retained earnings. All other balance sheet and income statement items are translated at the current rate under this method. The translated balance of beginning retained earnings reflects *previous* current rates; hence the discrepancy when included in ending retained earnings.

To further analyze a portion of the translation gain or loss, consider the inventory sale and purchase transactions in our example. Since these items are all translated at the current rate under the current rate method, they produce no translation gains and losses when the current rate method is used. Therefore, the following analysis is confined to a comparison of the other three translation methods.

In the *current/noncurrent method*, the *purchase* of inventory with cash has no net effect on the exposed position because total current assets have not changed. Both the increase in inventory and the £80 decrease in cash are translated at the current rate of $1.44/£, and no *translation gain or loss* results. Under the *monetary/nonmonetary and temporal methods*, however, the purchase of inventory for £80 reduces the amount of net monetary assets which will be translated at the current rate of $1.44/£, while creating a nonmonetary asset (inventory) which will be translated at the historical rate of $1.60/£. This generates an *exchange translation gain* of $12.8 [= ($1.60 − $1.44)80] because the exchange rate moved against pounds sterling during the year and £80 fewer were affected by the declining exchange rate (£/$). These effects are summarized in journal entry format at the top of page 590.

The effect of the inventory sale for £120 is opposite to that of the purchase, yet the same result is produced in the current/noncurrent, monetary/nonmonetary, and temporal translation methods. In each case, the exposed position—

| | Current/Noncurrent Method | | | | Monetary/Nonmonetary and Temporal Methods | | | |
| | £ | | $ | | £ | | $ | |
	Dr.	Cr.	Dr.	Cr.	Dr.	Cr.	Dr.	Cr.
Inventory	80		115.2		80		128	
Cash		80		115.2		80		115.2
Translation Gain		—		—		—		12.8

Notes: $115.2 = \$1.44 \times 80$; $128 = \$1.60 \times 80$; $12.8 = (\$1.60 - \$1.44)80$.

net current assets or net monetary assets,[7] depending on the context—is increased. The £120 cash will be translated at the current rate of $1.44/£. At the same time, £120 of sales revenue to be translated at the historical rate of $1.60/£ is recognized. This produces an *exchange translation loss* of $19.2 [= ($1.60 − $1.44)120] because the £120 were held during a year in which their dollar equivalent declined. These effects are also shown in journal entry format:

| | Current/Noncurrent Method | | | | Monetary/Nonmonetary and Temporal Methods | | | |
| | £ | | $ | | £ | | $ | |
	Dr.	Cr.	Dr.	Cr.	Dr.	Cr.	Dr.	Cr.
Cash	120		172.8		120		172.8	
Translation Loss	—		19.2		—		19.2	
Sales		120		192		120		192

Notes: $172.8 = \$1.44 \times 120$; $192 = \$1.60 \times 120$; $19.2 = (\$1.60 - \$1.44)120$.

We can now sum up the explanation for these translation gains and losses as follows:

> Translation gains and losses arise because the *current rate* is used to translate the *ending exposed position,* net of the *beginning exposed position* and all *changes* during the current year which are translated at *historical rates.*

The Temporal Method and SFAS 8

The FASB concluded that the translation of foreign currency financial statements should (1) be applied to statements prepared in conformity with U.S. generally accepted accounting principles and (2) change the unit of measurement and not the accounting principles used to measure items in the statements. To achieve these objectives, the board found the temporal method to be the most useful, yet it was not adopted intact.[8] Although the monetary/nonmonetary method will often generate results similar to the temporal method, the board believed it was deficient as a comprehensive basis for translation. The mone-

---

[7] Net monetary assets *is* the exposed position under the monetary/nonmonetary method; it is a large part of the exposed position according to the temporal method.

[8] Financial Accounting Standards Board, *Statement of Financial Accounting Standards No. 8,* "Accounting for the Translation of Foreign Currency Transactions and Foreign Currency Financial Statements" (Stamford, Conn.: FASB, 1975), par. 122; AC § 1083.122.

Exhibit 14.6   Exchange Rates Used to Translate Assets and Liabilities under *SFAS 8*

	Translation Rates	
ASSETS	Current	Historical
Cash on Hand and Demand and Time Deposits	X	
Marketable Equity Securities:		
Carried at Cost		X
Carried at Current Market Price	X	
Accounts and Notes Receivable and Related Unearned Discount	X	
Allowance for Doubtful Accounts and Notes Receivable	X	
Inventories:		
Carried at Cost		X
Carried at Current Replacement Price or Current Selling Price	X	
Carried at Net Realizable Value	X	
Carried at Contract Price (Produced under Fixed Price Contracts)	X	
Prepaid Insurance, Advertising, and Rent		X
Refundable Deposits	X	
Advances to Unconsolidated Subsidiaries	X	
Property, Plant, and Equipment		X
Accumulated Depreciation of Property, Plant, and Equipment		X
Cash Surrender Value of Life Insurance	X	
Patents, Trademarks, Licenses, and Formulas		X
Goodwill		X
Other Intangible Assets		X
LIABILITIES		
Accounts and Notes Payable and Overdrafts	X	
Accrued Expenses Payable	X	
Accrued Losses on Firm Purchase Commitments	X	
Refundable Deposits	X	
Deferred Income		X
Bonds Payable or Other Long-Term Debt	X	
Unamortized Premium or Discount on Bonds or Notes Payable	X	
Convertible Bonds Payable	X	
Accrued Pension Obligations	X	
Obligations under Warranties	X	

Source: Financial Accounting Standards Board, *Statement of Financial Accounting Standards No. 8*, "Accounting for the Translation of Foreign Currency Transactions and Foreign Currency Financial Statements," Appendix A (Stamford, Conn.: FASB, 1975); AC § 1083.038.

tary/nonmonetary method is a classification scheme; it does not stress the underlying measurement of items to be translated. It closely parallels the temporal method within the historical cost framework but cannot accommodate translation of nonmonetary items at the current rate if current value accounting is implemented.

Appendix A of *SFAS 8* provides guidance regarding the exchange rates to be used in translating principal assets and liabilities. Most of this guidance is tabulated in Exhibit 14.6.

Applying the Lower-of-Cost-or-Market Rule in Translated Statements
Under the conservatism principle, items such as inventories and marketable equity securities are shown on the balance sheet at lower of cost or market. Application of the *lower-of-cost-or-market rule* in translated statements involves

comparing *translated historical cost* with *translated market* (that is, market as determined in the foreign country). Cost is translated at historical rates, while market is translated at the current rate. A write-down to market in the translated statements may therefore be required, even though none occurred in the foreign currency statements. Furthermore, if translated market exceeds translated historical cost, any write-down in the foreign statements must be reversed. As examples, consider the following:

1. A unit of inventory owned by a U.K. subsidiary was purchased when the price was £10 and the exchange rate $2.00/£. At year-end, market in the United Kingdom is £12, and the exchange rate is $1.50/£. No write-down in the foreign statements is required (£12 > £10). In the translated statements, however, translated historical cost of $20 (= 10 × $2) exceeds translated market of $18 (= 12 × $1.5) and a loss of $2 (= $20 − $18) is recognized.

2. Use the facts in item 1, except that at year-end market in the United Kingdom is £9 and the exchange rate is $2.5/£. This results in a loss of £1 (= £10 − £9) recognized in the foreign currency statements. Translated market is $22.50 (= 9 × $2.5), which exceeds translated historical cost of $20 by $2.50. Hence the loss recognized in the foreign currency statements is reversed, and the appropriate translated inventory value is translated historical cost of $20.

Treatment of Exchange Gains and Losses   Fluctuating foreign exchange rates are responsible for the exchange gains and losses which arise in accounting for foreign operations. *SFAS 8* requires that such *"exchange gains and losses shall be included in determining net income for the period in which the rate changes."* [Emphasis added.][9] No distinction is made between *conversion* and *translation* gains and losses. Prior to *SFAS 8*, generally accepted accounting principles (Chapter 12 of *ARB 43*) called for including realized exchange gains and losses in income.[10] Realization occurred when the actual conversion to or from the foreign currency took place. Other exchange gains or losses were said to be *unrealized* and generally were credited or debited to a "reserve" or "suspense" account which kept track of the net unrealized exchange gain or loss. If this suspense account had a debit balance at year-end (net unrealized loss), it would be closed against income. In contrast, a credit balance (net unrealized gain) would be carried over to the next accounting period. Under *SFAS 8*, however, the following disclosures related to exchange gains and losses are required:

1. The aggregate exchange gain or loss included in net income shall be disclosed either in the financial statements or in a note.

2. Effects of exchange rate fluctuations on reported operations shall, if practicable, be described and quantified.

3. A significant change in exchange rates *after* the balance sheet date may require an explanatory disclosure, even though the financial statements need not be adjusted.

---

[9] Financial Accounting Standards Board, *Statement No. 8*, par. 17; AC § 1083.17.

[10] Committee on Accounting Procedure, *ARB 43*, pars. 10, 11; AC § 1083.060.

Interpretation of the foreign exchange gain or loss is complicated by these accounting and reporting requirements. In particular, use of the reported exchange gain or loss to determine how well a firm is coping with foreign exchange risk can lead to erroneous conclusions. The two major reasons for this are discussed next.

Components of the Aggregate Exchange Gain or Loss   We have differentiated between exchange *conversion* and *translation* gains and losses because they have different economic significance. Gains and losses on import/export transactions caused by fluctuating exchange rates directly affect the economic position of the firm. In contrast, exchange gains and losses arising in the process of translating foreign statements may be mere bookkeeping entries. Their economic significance depends heavily on the intentions of management. If foreign currency rather than dollars is to be used to liquidate debts denominated in that currency, a translation loss on those debts has little economic significance.

Most firms do not divide their reported exchange gain or loss into conversion and translation components. Hence the economic significance of the information is difficult to ascertain. As an exception, American Brands Corporation provided the following disaggregation of its 1976 exchange loss:

Foreign Currency Transactions	$ (1,855,000)
Translation of Foreign Financial Statements	(42,768,000)
Total Exchange Loss	$(44,623,000)

We believe that such disaggregated disclosure should be the rule rather than the exception.

Income Tax Effects   Exchange gains and losses enter into taxable income when receivables or payables are *settled* and conversion from or to foreign currency takes place. If reported exchange gains or losses exceed the amount currently taxable, deferred taxes must be provided on timing differences. Many translation gains or losses, however, are actually permanent differences. To the extent that the timing differences are large, the *aftertax* exchange gain or loss may be significantly different from the *pretax* amount. Yet these tax effects need not be specifically disclosed. This is another reason why attempting to evaluate the economic significance of reported exchange gains or losses may be a hazardous undertaking.

We return again to American Brands. A disclosure of their foreign exchange losses and related tax effects for 1976 is given in Exhibit 14.7. This is an extremely informative disclosure, and we recommend the format strongly.

Overview of the FASB *Exposure Draft*   In its 1981 *Exposure Draft* on foreign currency translation, the FASB made proposals designed to defuse some of the criticisms leveled at *SFAS 8*. The two principal complaints are discussed next.

First, it is contended that the inclusion of exchange translation gains and losses in income under *SFAS 8* produces unwarranted large and frequent fluctuations in reported earnings. For example, the exchange rate exposure on foreign currency debt may be effectively hedged by the foreign currency revenue potential of a foreign entity's operating assets. Because *SFAS 8* does not recog-

Exhibit 14.7 Disaggregation of Exchange Loss for 1976 for American Brands Corporation

FOREIGN CURRENCY TRANSACTIONS

Losses (Net of Gains)	$ (2,391,000)

Tax Effect:

Taxes Saved Currently	18,906,000 [a]	
Taxes Deferred	(18,370,000)[b]	
Net after Taxes		$ (1,855,000)

TRANSLATION OF FOREIGN FINANCIAL STATEMENTS

Gallaher Limited and Its Subsidiaries	$(42,922,000)	
Other	154,000	
Total		(42,768,000)[c]
Net Exchange Loss		$(44,623,000)

[a]Results from net loss recognized currently for book and tax purposes, probably from closed foreign currency transactions.
[b]Results from net gain recognized currently for book but deferred for tax, accrued net exchange gains on transactions to be closed in future periods (timing differences).
[c]Because this net loss is not deductible for tax purposes in the current year or in a future year, it represents a permanent difference. Additional taxes paid amount to $21,198,000, as shown in the tax reconciliation schedule in the American Brands 1976 notes to financial statements.

nize this "hedge," exchange translation gains or losses on foreign currency debt may have little economic significance and reporting them in income may be misleading. In drawing the distinction between exchange *conversion* and *translation* gains and losses, we have indicated our agreement with this view.

Second, it is contended that the temporal method of translation, as used in *SFAS 8*, produces distortions in the financial results and relationships reported by a foreign entity. As an example, consider a foreign subsidiary's *current ratio*, the ratio of its current assets to its current liabilities. Translation by the temporal method distorts the current ratio measured in units of foreign currency. This happens because some of the current assets, such as cash and receivables, and all current liabilities are translated at the current rate while other current assets, such as inventory carried at cost, are translated at historical rates. If exchange rates ($/FC) are rising, the current ratio translated according to *SFAS 8* might be substantially lower than the same ratio measured in the foreign currency. While we sympathize with this concern, we suspect that the fundamental problem lies in the historical cost accounting model, not in the temporal method of translation.

To address these concerns, the *Exposure Draft* sets forth the views that a U.S. company's interest in a foreign entity is a *net investment*, rather than an interest in *individual assets and liabilities*, and that the U.S. dollar is not the only relevant unit of measure. It proposes that the translation process preserve the financial results and relationships of the foreign entity as measured in its functional currency. The **functional currency** is the currency most clearly related to the entity's operations. It normally is the currency of the country in which the entity is located. In cases where the foreign entity is an integral component of the U.S. company's domestic operations, the functional currency might be the U.S. dollar. In cases where the foreign entity conducts most of its business in a country other than the country in which it is located, the currency of the *other* country might be the entity's functional currency.

The *Exposure Draft's* Proposed Translation Process   Under the *Exposure Draft*, a version of the **current rate method** is used to translate the foreign entity's financial statements measured in its *functional currency*. If the functional currency is *not* the entity's *local currency*, the local currency statements are first translated into the functional currency by a method essentially the same as that used in *SFAS 8*. The functional currency statements are then translated into U.S. dollars. Note that if the foreign entity's functional currency *is* the U.S. dollar, translation into the functional currency (the dollar) completes the process, thereby yielding essentially the same results as currently prevail under *SFAS 8*. The version of the current rate method proposed in the *Exposure Draft* incorporates the following:

1.   Translation of all assets and liabilities at the *current rate*, the exchange rate in effect on the balance sheet date.

2.   Translation of contributed capital accounts—Common Stock and Additional Paid-In Capital—at the *historical rates* in effect when the items originated. Retained Earnings is a residual.

3.   Translation of revenues and expenses at an appropriate *weighted average exchange rate* for the period.

The version of the current rate method presented earlier in the chapter called for translation of the accounts in items 2 and 3 above (except Retained Earnings) at the current rate, a difference from the *Exposure Draft* proposal.

If a foreign entity's functional currency has experienced cumulative inflation of at least 100 percent over the past three years, the *Exposure Draft* requires a *general price level restatement* of the functional currency statements *before* they are translated into dollars.

Reporting of Exchange Gains and Losses Proposed in the *Exposure Draft*   The proposed reporting requirements reflect our distinction between exchange conversion and translation gains and losses. First, exchange gains and losses from settled and unsettled foreign currency transactions—exchange *conversion* gains and losses—are generally included in net income. Exceptions relate to forward contracts entered in to hedge identifiable foreign currency commitments and foreign currency transactions intended as an economic hedge of a net investment in a foreign entity. Second, exchange gains and losses produced by translation of the functional currency statements into U.S. dollars —exchange *translation* gains and losses—are *not* included in net income. Rather, they are to be accumulated and disclosed in a separate component of stockholders' equity. This component will also include exchange gains and losses from foreign currency transactions intended as an economic hedge of a net investment in a foreign entity.

Authors' Views on the FASB *Exposure Draft*   Our principal concern with the *Exposure Draft* relates to its proposal that the *current rate* be used to translate *all* foreign assets and liabilities. We believe that this approach conflicts with the historical cost accounting model. The serious problems with the historical cost accounting model in periods of changing prices are well known; we do not address them here. Rather, we conclude that as long as accounting embraces historical costs, a translation method consistent with that model should be used. In short, we support the temporal principle as employed in *SFAS 8.* Using the current rate to translate foreign currency accounts reflecting historical costs does *not* produce current values in U.S. dollars. Note that preservation of the financial results and relationships reflected in the foreign currency financial statements, such as the current ratio mentioned earlier, could be achieved by multiplying the accounts by *any* constant. While the current exchange rate may be the most appropriate constant to use, it can lead to hybrid translated amounts having no clear interpretation.

On the other hand, we do support the distinction between exchange *conversion* and *translation* gains and losses adopted by the *Exposure Draft.* The accumulation of translation adjustments in stockholders' equity, and not in periodic net income, appears to adequately reflect their different economic significance.

As this book goes to press, it is unclear whether all or parts of the *Exposure Draft* will be adopted. If it is adopted, it is scheduled to become effective for fiscal years beginning after December 14, 1982. For this reason, we remind the reader that the discussion and examples in this book, as well as the end-of-chapter assignment material, reflect the provisions of *SFAS 8.*

Foreign Branches and Subsidiaries

Translation of foreign currency financial statements is required when the operations of foreign branches and subsidiaries are to be included in the U.S. financial statements of the parent company. The foreign accounts are generally translated according to the rules presented in the previous section. We will illustrate this process in a later section by translating the complex trial balance of a domestically owned foreign business activity. Issues peculiar to translating and reporting these foreign operations are discussed below.

Reporting on Foreign Operations   *ARB 43* expresses concern over the inclusion of translated foreign operations in U.S. company statements.[11] Given the inherent riskiness of foreign operations—distant geographical locations subject to foreign sovereign states—extreme care should be taken in reporting earnings in excess of amounts received in cash or available in cash for unrestricted transmission to the United States. Similarly, uncertainty with respect to the ultimate realization of other foreign assets is an issue to be resolved in determining the propriety of combined or consolidated statements which include translated foreign assets and liabilities.

ARB 43 also identifies four possible ways of reporting information related to foreign subsidiaries or branches:

---

[11] Committee on Accounting Procedure, *ARB 43*, Chap. 12; AC § 1081.

(a) To exclude foreign subsidiaries from consolidation and to furnish (1) statements in which only domestic subsidiaries are consolidated and (2) as to foreign subsidiaries, a summary in suitable form of their assets and liabilities, their income and losses for the year, and the parent company's equity therein. The total amount of investments in foreign subsidiaries should be shown separately, and the basis on which the amount was arrived at should be stated. If these investments include any surplus of foreign subsidiaries and such surplus had previously been included in consolidated surplus, the amount should be separately shown or earmarked in stating the consolidated surplus in the statements here suggested. The exclusion of foreign subsidiaries from consolidation does not make it acceptable practice to include intercompany profits which would be eliminated if such subsidiaries were consolidated.

(b) To consolidate domestic and foreign subsidiaries and to furnish in addition the summary described in (a) (2) above.

(c) To furnish (1) complete consolidated statements and also (2) consolidated statements for domestic companies only.

(d) To consolidate domestic and foreign subsidiaries and to furnish in addition parent company statements showing the investment in and income from foreign subsidiaries separately from those of domestic subsidiaries.[12]

Translation Differences under the Pooling and Purchase Methods

After a business combination accounted for as a *pooling of interests,* the foreign assets and liabilities retain their book values. They are generally translated at the historical exchange rates in effect when they were originally recorded by the foreign enterprise, except that those carried at current money prices (cash, receivables, etc.) are translated at the current rate. If a *minority interest* exists, its translated amount is a pro rata share of the subsidiary's net assets translated in the above manner.

In contrast, the current rate at date of business combination is used to translate *all* of the foreign assets and liabilities in a *purchase* combination. Following the procedure adopted earlier in this book, the translated amounts will reflect the parent's share of the foreign assets and liabilities adjusted to their fair values at date of business combination. Therefore, the translated amount of a *minority interest* at date of business combination is a pro rata share of the book value of the foreign enterprise's net assets translated at the current rate on that date. This rate then becomes the historical rate used in subsequent year translations.

Translation of Reciprocal Accounts

Both home office/branch accounting and parent/subsidiary accounting involve the use of **reciprocal accounts.** Reciprocal accounts are those that have equal and offsetting balances on the home/branch books or the parent/subsidiary books. Such accounts are *eliminated* when combined or consolidated financial statements are prepared. The simplest approach to translating reciprocal accounts in the foreign statements is to use the dollar balances from the reciprocal accounts on the home office or parent company's books as the translated balances.

---

[12] Ibid., AC § 1081.09. Copyright © 1953 by the American Institute of Certified Public Accountants, Inc.

In the *home office/branch* situation, the following reciprocal accounts are affected:

1.   Investment in Branch (Dr.)/Home Office (Cr.).
2.   Shipments from Home Office (Dr.)/Shipments to Branch (Cr.), Overvaluation of Branch Inventory (Cr.).
3.   Remittances to Home Office (Dr.)/Remittances from Branch (Cr.).

Observe that translating in this way removes the built-in check possessed by the reciprocal accounts in domestic home office/branch settings. The home office must now obtain a complete list of transactions recorded in the branch's reciprocal accounts and reconcile the reciprocal accounts. Since the translated foreign balance will by definition equal the U.S. dollar balance, there is no automatic way of determining whether all intrafirm transactions have been recorded properly on both sets of books.

Similarly, the preparation of consolidated financial statements in the *parent/subsidiary* setting requires that reciprocal intercompany accounts be eliminated. As in the home office/branch case, intercompany accounts in the foreign statements are given translated balances equal to the dollar balances of the offsetting accounts on the parent's books. Where intercompany sales, purchases, receivables, and payables are concerned, the foreign subsidiary must inform the parent of the transactions it recorded. Only in this way can the parent reconcile the offsetting accounts without separate translation of each entry made by the foreign subsidiary.

The investment account must be eliminated against the stockholders' equity of the subsidiary. Just as the amount recorded in the investment account becomes a function of the pooling or purchase choice, so do the exchange rates used to translate the subsidiary's stockholders' equity. In a pooling, the investment account reflects the translated book value of the subsidiary's stockholders' equity, using the original historical exchange rates (retained earnings is a residual). In the future, the subsidiary's contributed capital accounts should continue to be translated at the original historical rates. Beginning retained earnings has a translated value equal to the dollar amount of the last period's ending retained earnings.

Under purchase accounting, however, the fair value of the subsidiary's stockholders' equity is included in the investment account (that is, the fair value of the subsidiary's net assets in foreign currency translated at the spot rate at date of acquisition). Once the purchase premium or discount is determined, the amount remaining in the investment account is equal to the translated portion of the stockholders' equity owned by the parent. This provides the basis for the translated stockholders' equity of the subsidiary at date of acquisition, just as if the individual stockholders' equity accounts were translated at the spot rate on that date. At subsequent consolidation points, translated beginning retained earnings is simply the dollar amount of the prior period's ending retained earnings. This fits nicely with use of the equity method and elimination of beginning-of-period balances.

With respect to other intercompany transactions involving land, unsold inventories, and depreciable assets, records must be kept to ensure that the proper translated amounts are eliminated. Intercompany bondholdings can present a different type of problem. Consider the case in which the foreign subsidiary's bonds are held by the U.S. parent. Under *SFAS 8*, such bonds would be translated at the current rate, generating exchange gains and losses on internally held debt, an absurdity. To neutralize these exchange gains and losses and to ensure clean eliminations, the foreign bonds payable should be translated at the spot rate in effect when they were acquired by the parent. Translation of the bonds payable and any unamortized premium or discount at this rate would maintain the necessary relationship with the investment in bonds on the parent's books.

Illustrating the Translation of a Complex Foreign Trial Balance

We have prepared a complex foreign currency trial balance to serve as an example of the translation process. Since many translation issues are common to both foreign branches and foreign subsidiaries, we have not identified Paris Company, Ltd., our example firm, as either a branch or a subsidiary. The intercompany accounts could easily be branch reciprocal accounts and Owners' Equity could be interpreted as the Home Office account on the branch books or a subsidiary's stockholders' equity.

Paris Company, Ltd., a unit of American Corporation, was organized several years ago in France when the exchange rate was $.35/F. No additional investments have been made since then. The balance in the Investment in Paris account on American's books, $750,000, represents the dollar equivalent of Paris' owners' equity accounts. Exhibit 14.8 contains Paris' end-of-year trial balance in francs and illustrates the translation process. Supporting schedules with detailed calculations are provided as needed. Once the trial balance of the foreign unit is translated into dollars, combined or consolidated statements can be prepared. The trial balance data are simply rearranged to fit into the financial statement working paper format.

International Accounting Standards

Reporting international operations is complicated by the fact that accounting principles and practices vary widely across countries. Not only is the accounting function in the multinational firm affected, the task faced by investors attempting to compare and evaluate alternative investment opportunities around the world is extremely difficult. In this section, we discuss the dimensions of the problem and review the development of international accounting standards.

Diversity in Accounting Principles and Practices Throughout the World

We begin by providing some evidence regarding the lack of uniformity in accounting around the globe.[13] Certain accounting matters and the extent to which they are generally accepted in various countries are tabulated in Exhibit 14.9. Note that there are relatively few countries in which a given accounting matter is *required*. Furthermore, the extent of acceptability of any individual item tends to range all the way from *required* to *not permitted*.

---

[13] In addition to the reference provided in Exhibit 14.9, a detailed and comprehensive analysis of comparative accounting principles and practice can be found in: American Institute of Certified Public Accountants, *Professional Accounting in 30 Countries* (N.Y.: AICPA, 1975).

Exhibit 14.8   Translation of Foreign Trial Balance and Supporting Computations

Translation of Trial Balance of Paris Company, Ltd., a French
Business Unit of American Corporation

	Foreign Currency (Francs; F) Dr. (Cr.)	Applicable Exchange Rate[a] $/F		Translated Balances, Dollars Dr. (Cr.)
Cash	F1,000,000	(C)	.25	$ 250,000
Marketable Equity Securities, at Cost	250,000	(H)	.29	72,500
Marketable Equity Securities, at Market	120,000	(C)	.25	30,000
Accounts Receivable, Net	1,400,000	(C)	.25	350,000
Inventory, at Cost, January 1	300,000	(H)	(1)	94,300
Inventory, at Cost, December 31	320,000	(H)	(1)	99,900
Prepayments	280,000	(H)	(2)	80,800
Intercompany Receivables	100,000	(R)	(3)	26,000
Land	800,000	(H)	(4)	259,000
Buildings and Equipment	4,000,000	(H)	(5)	1,296,000
Accumulated Depreciation	(1,200,000)	(H)	(5)	(400,600)
Accounts Payable	(1,300,000)	(C)	.25	(325,000)
Customer Advances (Deferred Income)	(260,000)	(H)	(6)	(71,300)
Accrued Pension Obligations	(150,000)	(C)	.25	(37,500)
Estimated Warranty Liability	(90,000)	(C)	.25	(22,500)
Long-Term Debt	(2,000,000)	(C)	.25	(500,000)
Intercompany Payables	(200,000)	(R)	(3)	(51,000)
Owners' Equity	(2,500,000)	(R)	(3)	(750,000)
Sales to Outside Customers	(3,400,000)	(A)	.27	(918,000)
Intercompany Sales (Shipments)	(400,000)	(R)	(3)	(110,000)
Purchases from Outside Suppliers	1,700,000	(A)	.27	459,000
Intercompany Purchases (Shipments)	310,000	(R)	(3)	83,700
Salaries and Wages	420,000	(A)	.27	113,400
Pension Expense	150,000	(A)	.27	40,500
Warranty Expense	90,000	(A)	.27	24,300
Depreciation Expense	200,000	(H)	(5)	64,600
Other Operating Expenses	380,000	(H)	(2)	107,400
Inventory, at Cost, December 31	(320,000)	(H)	(1)	(99,900)
Translation Gain (plug)	—			(165,600)
	F 0			$ 0

LEGEND:
(C) = Current exchange rate; assumed to be $.25/F.
(H) = Historical exchange rate in effect when the item originated.
(A) = Average exchange rate for the year, assumed to be $.27/F.
(R) = Dollar balance in the reciprocal account on American Company's books.
[a]Items (1) through (6) in this column refer the reader to the numbered supporting schedules for details on the calculations.

Paris Company, Ltd.
Supporting Schedules for Translation of Trial Balance

(1) Inventory, January 1 (LIFO) consists of the following batches:

Amount(F)	Exchange Rate ($/F)	Amount($)
F 50,000	.35	$ 17,500
180,000	.31	55,800
70,000	.30	21,000
F300,000		$ 94,300

Exhibit 14.8   *continued*

Inventory, December 31 (LIFO) includes an additional layer of F20,000, acquired when the exchange rate was $.28/F. Total translated December 31 inventory is $99,900 [= $94,300 + ($.28 × 20,000)].

(2) Prepayments reflect expenditures of F80,000, made when the exchange rate was $.31/F and F200,000, made when the exchange rate was $.28/F; $80,800 = ($.31 × 80,000) + ($.28 × 200,000).
Other Operating Expenses include prepayment amortization and other expenses as follows:

Type	Amount(F)	Exchange Rate ($/F)	Amount($)
Prepayment Amortization	F 40,000	.32	$ 12,800
Prepayment Amortization	70,000	.31	21,700
Other Expenses	270,000	.27	72,900
	F380,000		$107,400

(3) Offsetting dollar balances of intercompany accounts on American's books are given below. All accounts have been reconciled and all transactions accounted for.

Account Title on Books of Paris Company, Ltd.	Dollar Balance of Offsetting Account on American's Books
Intercompany Receivables	$ 26,000
Intercompany Payables	51,000
Owners' Equity	750,000
Intercompany Sales	110,000
Intercompany Purchases	83,700

(4) Land was purchased with francs as follows:

	Amount(F)	Exchange Rate ($/F)	Amount($)
	F250,000	.35	$ 87,500
	400,000	.32	128,000
	150,000	.29	43,500
	F800,000		$259,000

(5) An analysis of the Buildings and Equipment, Accumulated Depreciation, and Depreciation Expense accounts is as follows:

Exchange Rate ($/F)	Buildings and Equipment (Original Cost) Francs	Dollars	Accumulated Depreciation, January 1 Francs	Dollars	Depreciation Expense Francs	Dollars	Accumulated Depreciation, December 31 Francs	Dollars
.35	F2,000,000	$ 700,000	F 720,000	$252,000	F100,000	$35,000	F 820,000	$287,000
.30	1,800,000	540,000	280,000	84,000	80,000	24,000	360,000	108,000
.28	200,000	56,000	—	—	20,000	5,600	20,000	5,600
	F4,000,000	$1,296,000	F1,000,000	$336,000	F200,000	$64,600	F1,200,000	$400,600

(6) Customer Advances (deferred income) arose during the year as follows:

	Amount(F)	Exchange Rate ($/F)	Amount($)
	F200,000	.28	$ 56,000
	60,000	.255	15,300
	F260,000		$ 71,300

Exhibit 14.9 Some Examples of the Variability in Accounting Worldwide

19. ACCOUNTING POLICIES
A change in accounting principles or methods without a change in circumstances is accounted for by restatement of financial informaiton currently presented in respect of prior periods.

FIXED ASSETS—LEASES 52.
The amount and period of commitments under long-term leases for future years are disclosed.

Accounting Policies (19)

Required	Insisted upon	Predominant practice	Minority practice	Rarely or not found	Not accepted	Not permitted	SOURCE	Country
						■	LEG	Argentina
			■					Australia
						■	LEG	Austria
		■						Bahamas
						■	LEG	Belgium
		■						Bermuda
				■				Bolivia
		■						Botswana
■							LEG	Brazil
		■						Canada
			■					Chile
						■	LEG	Colombia
			■					Costa Rica
			■					Denmark
					■			Dominican Rep.
			■					Ecuador
			■					El Salvador
			■					Fiji
			■					France
						■	LEG	Germany
			■					Greece
			■					Guatemala
			■					Honduras
■							HKSA	Hong Kong
			■					India
		■						Iran
■							SSAP 6	Ireland, Rep. of
		■						Italy
			■					Ivory Coast
■							SSAP 3	Jamaica
					■			Japan
		■						Jersey, Channel Is.
		■						Kenya
						■	ASR	Korea
		■						Malawi
		■						Malaysia
			■					Morocco
						■	CPC A7	Mexico
			■					Netherlands
■							SSAP 7	New Zealand
						■	CN 6	Nicaragua
		■						Nigeria
			■					Norway
			■					Pakistan
		■						Panama
			■					Paraguay
			■					Peru
			■					Philippines
			■					Portugal
			■					Senegal
		■						Singapore
						■	GAAP 3	South Africa
			■					Spain
					■			Sweden
						■	LEG	Switzerland
■							GAAP	Taiwan
			■					Trinidad and Tobago
■							SSAP 6	United Kingdom
						■	APB 20	United States
			■					Uruguay
						■	AC	Venezuela
						■	LEG	Zaire
		■						Zambia
■							RM 4	Zimbabwe Rhodesia

Fixed Assets—Leases (52)

Required	Insisted upon	Predominant practice	Minority practice	Rarely or not found	Not accepted	Not permitted	SOURCE	Country
				■				Argentina
			■					Australia
				■				Austria
			■					Bahamas
				■				Belgium
■							3065	Bermuda
				■				Bolivia
				■				Botswana
■							LEG	Brazil
■							3065	Canada
				■				Chile
			■					Colombia
			■					Costa Rica
				■				Denmark
		■						Dominican Rep.
			■					Ecuador
			■					El Salvador
		■						Fiji
				■				France
				■				Germany
				■				Greece
		■						Guatemala
				■				Honduras
				■				Hong Kong
				■				India
		■						Iran
		■						Ireland, Rep. of
				■				Italy
				■				Ivory Coast
				■				Jamaica
				■				Japan
				■				Jersey, Channel Is.
				■				Kenya
■							ASR	Korea
				■				Malawi
				■				Malaysia
				■				Morocco
■							CPC C6	Mexico
■							LEG	Netherlands
		■						New Zealand
			■					Nicaragua
			■					Nigeria
■							LEG	Norway
			■					Pakistan
			■					Panama
				■				Paraguay
■							CNSEV	Peru
■							LEG	Philippines
				■				Portugal
				■				Senegal
				■				Singapore
				■				South Africa
				■				Spain
				■				Sweden
				■				Switzerland
		■						Taiwan
			■					Trinidad and Tobago
			■					United Kingdom
■							FAS 13	United States
				■				Uruguay
■							AC	Venezuela
				■				Zaire
				■				Zambia
			■					Zimbabwe Rhodesia

Exhibit 14.9   *continued*

BUSINESS COMBINATIONS 246.

When, in a business combination accounted for as a purchase, the consideration is an issue of shares, their fair value is determined by reference either to the value of the underlying net assets acquired or to the market value of the shares issued, whichever is more clearly evident.

	Required	Insisted upon	Predominant practice	Minority practice	Rarely or not found	Not accepted	Not permitted	SOURCE
Argentina			■					
Australia		■						
Austria							■	LEG
Bahamas			■					
Belgium			■					
Bermuda	■							1580
Bolivia				■				
Botswana			■					
Brazil			■					
Canada	■							1580
Chile		■						
Colombia				■				
Costa Rica			■					
Denmark			■					
Dominican Rep.		■						
Ecuador				■				
El Salvador		■						
Fiji				■				
France	■							LEG
Germany							■	LEG
Greece			■					
Guatemala			■					
Honduras			■					
Hong Kong		■						
India	NOT APPLICABLE							
Iran				■				
Ireland, Rep. of		■						
Italy			■					
Ivory Coast				■				
Jamaica				■				
Japan			■					
Jersey, Channel Is.				■				
Kenya			■					
Korea			■					
Malawi			■					
Malaysia			■					
Morocco			■					
Mexico				■				
Netherlands			■					
New Zealand			■					
Nicaragua			■					
Nigeria				■				
Norway		■						
Pakistan				■				
Panama				■				
Paraguay				■				
Peru			■					
Philippines			■					
Portugal				■				
Senegal				■				
Singapore			■					
South Africa	■							LEG
Spain							■	LEG
Sweden				■				
Switzerland				■				
Taiwan			■					
Trinidad and Tobago			■					
United Kingdom		■						
United States	■							APB 16
Uruguay				■				
Venezuela				■				
Zaire				■				
Zambia			■					
Zimbabwe Rhodesia			■					

FOREIGN CURRENCIES 252.

In translating foreign currency financial statements, the closing exchange rate is applied to all assets and liabilities.

	Required	Insisted upon	Predominant practice	Minority practice	Rarely or not found	Not accepted	Not permitted	SOURCE
Argentina					■			
Australia			■					
Austria							■	LEG
Bahamas				■				
Belgium					■			
Bermuda							■	1650
Bolivia					■			
Botswana			■					
Brazil					■			
Canada							■	1650
Chile				■				
Colombia			■					
Costa Rica					■			
Denmark			■					
Dominican Rep.					■			
Ecuador					■			
El Salvador					■			
Fiji			■					
France			■					
Germany				■				
Greece			■					
Guatemala			■					
Honduras					■			
Hong Kong			■					
India			■					
Iran					■			
Ireland, Rep. of			■					
Italy				■				
Ivory Coast			■					
Jamaica							■	SSAP 7
Japan			■					
Jersey, Channel Is.			■					
Kenya			■					
Korea						■		
Malawi				■				
Malaysia			■					
Morocco					■			
Mexico					■			
Netherlands			■					
New Zealand				■				
Nicaragua				■				
Nigeria					■			
Norway			■					
Pakistan					■			
Panama						■		
Paraguay			■					
Peru						■		
Philippines				■				
Portugal					■			
Senegal			■					
Singapore			■					
South Africa				■				
Spain					■			
Sweden				■				
Switzerland			■					
Taiwan						■		
Trinidad and Tobago			■					
United Kingdom			■					
United States							■	FAS 8
Uruguay	■							BCCU 1
Venezuela				■				
Zaire						■		
Zimbabwe Rhodesia			■					

Source: Price Waterhouse, *International Survey of Accounting Principles and Reporting Practices*, Butterworths (Canada) Scarborough, Ontario, 1979.

At first glance, it might appear that the diversity illustrated in Exhibit 14.9 is the outcome of some unspecified random process. Upon reflection, however, it becomes apparent that the existence of alternative patterns of development in accounting leads both to diversity and to similarities in accounting across countries. Choi and Mueller identify four approaches or orientations to accounting development which provide starting points for analyzing the differences and similarities in accounting around the world.[14]

1.   A **macroeconomic orientation** results in accounting systems of individual units in the economy designed to interface closely with national programs, goals, and information requirements. One implication of a macroeconomic orientation involves accounting principles. For example, income smoothing might be encouraged in order that fluctuations in the national income and product accounts and, hence, in reported business cycles, be dampened. Moreover, a macroeconomic orientation could lead to the design of accounting systems and reports along the lines dictated by governmental central planning activities.

2.   In contrast, a **microeconomic orientation** has as its focal points individual firms and other economic entities. Under such an orientation, accounting and reporting tend to have a distinct managerial flavor. Information is structured to facilitate good (if not optimal) decisions relating to the prosperity of the firm. Replacement cost accounting and line-of-business reporting are examples of what might flow from a microeconomic orientation to accounting.

3.   Another approach views accounting as an **independent discipline,** for which conventions, principles, and procedures are derived primarily from experience in the world of business affairs. Development of a theoretical structure grounded in scientific disciplines from which logical rules of behavior can be deduced is difficult for accounting to achieve. The evolution of generally accepted accounting principles in the United States is representative of the independent discipline approach. The realization convention and historical cost valuation illustrate the pragmatic—perhaps expedient—process from which rules in the independent discipline of accounting emerge.

4.   Choi and Mueller also identify a stress on **uniform rules** as an approach to accounting development. This orientation emphasizes the importance of administrative fiat; detailed regulations prescribing uniform systems, reports, and accounting treatments; and the resulting comparability of reported information. The uniformity might be limited to particular industries or might encompass all entities in an economy. We tend to see uniform accounting in regulated industries and, from the relatively uniform perspective of the tax code, in all industries. A specific example of the influence of uniformity on accounting in the United States appears in *SFAS 2*, which prescribes a single accounting treatment for research and development costs.

---

[14]   Frederick D. S. Choi and Gerhard G. Mueller, *An Introduction to Multinational Accounting* (Englewood Cliffs, N.J.: Prentice-Hall, 1978), Chapter 2.

Note that the development of accounting in the United States is not exclusively the result of any of the four approaches mentioned above. Rather, it has elements of all. The microeconomic and independent discipline approaches are probably dominant, although increasing emphasis is being placed on uniform rules.

Efforts to Achieve Standardization Attempts aimed at standardizing accounting principles and practices are underway both nationally and internationally. Groups like the FASB and AICPA in the United States and the Canadian Institute of Chartered Accountants (CICA) in Canada are examples of private organizations which have national standardization as one of their objectives. In France, however, the government and the tax laws are most influential in shaping accounting principles and promoting standardization. Through its *Plan Comptable Général*, French accounting principles and practice are highly standardized. The *Plan* includes a detailed uniform chart of accounts adaptable to all industries, complete with definitions and regulations comparable to those of prescribed accounting systems for regulated industries in the United States.

Regional groups working toward standardization across national boundaries include the Confederation of Asian and Pacific Accountants (CAPA), the Inter-American Accounting Association (IAA; composed primarily of Spanish-speaking Western Hemisphere nations) and the Union Européenne des Experts Comptables Economiques (UEC). Membership in the UEC includes most of the member countries of the European Economic Community or "Common Market" as well as other European nations.

Member nations of the European Economic Community (EEC)[15] are also active in developing accounting principles. The EEC Commission periodically issues **directives** relating to companies in the common market. Some of these deal with accounting matters and are briefly summarized below. They are currently in various stages of implementation.

The *Fourth Directive* (1978) specifies in detail the form and content of financial statements and the requirements for disclosure. Consistency, the going-concern concept, and accrual accounting are among the basic concepts provided for in the *Fourth Directive*. Various valuation methods are also prescribed.

Consolidated financial statements are called for in the *Seventh Directive* (1981) as being appropriate when one company is under the *dominant influence* of another, even though a controlling degree of ownership does not exist. Furthermore, the directive states that independent companies within the EEC which are controlled by an enterprise *outside* the EEC should be consolidated. It also specifies consolidation principles, mechanics, and disclosure requirements.

In addition to the above organizations, the Accountants International Study Group (AISG), consisting of representatives of professional accounting organizations in Canada, the United Kingdom, and the United States, was active from the late 1960s through the late 1970s. Its mission was not to promulgate interna-

---

15 The member nations of the EEC are Belgium, Denmark, France, Greece, Republic of Ireland, Italy, Luxembourg, the Netherlands, United Kingdom and West Germany.

Exhibit 14.10   *Accountants International Studies* by the Accountants International Study Group

Study No.	Title	Date
1	Accounting and Auditing Approaches to Inventories	1968
2	The Independent Auditor's Reporting Standards	1969
3	Using the Work and Report of Another Auditor	1969
4	Accounting for Corporate Income Taxes	1971
5	Reporting by Diversified Companies	1972
6	Consolidated Financial Statements	1973
7	The Funds Statement	1973
8	Materiality in Accounting	1974
9	Extraordinary Items, Prior Period Adjustments, and Changes in Accounting Principles	1974
10	Published Profit Forecasts	1975
11	International Financial Reporting	1975
12	Glossary of Accounting Terms	1975
13	Accounting for Goodwill	1975
14	Interim Financial Reporting	1975
15	Going Concern Problems	1976
16	Independence of Auditors	1977
17	Audit Committees	1977
18	Accounting for Pension Costs	1977
19	Revenue Recognition	1978
20	Related Party Transactions	1978

tional accounting standards; rather, it produced a series of studies dealing with various accounting topics of concern to the three countries. To bring them to the reader's attention, a complete list is provided in Exhibit 14.10. They are available from the American Institute of CPAs.

International Accounting Standards Committee

We have seen that there are many accounting organizations which have an interest in studying international accounting issues and promoting communication and cooperation among accountants in many countries. Among these groups, the **International Accounting Standards Committee (IASC)** stands out for its breadth of membership and its promulgation of quasi-authoritative worldwide accounting standards. The IASC was founded on June 29, 1973, by the leading professional accounting associations of Australia, Canada, France, Germany, Japan, Mexico, the Netherlands, the United Kingdom and Ireland, and the United States. Today, about forty-five countries are members. The IASC has been and continues to be active in issuing official pronouncements known as **International Accounting Standards.** Before a brief overview of the standards currently in force and the outstanding exposure drafts is presented, two matters must be made clear:

1. The IASC *cannot require* the accounting profession in any country to adhere to its standards. Rather, the focus is on voluntary cooperation and on the good faith efforts pledged by member countries to promote the worldwide acceptance and observance of the standards.

2. The intention of the IASC is to concentrate on essentials and not to make the *International Accounting Standards* so complex and detailed that they cannot be effectively applied throughout the world.

Pronouncements of the IASC   The following is an annotated list of final *International Accounting Standards (IAS)* and *Exposure Drafts (ED)*. Effective dates of *Standards* and issue dates of *Exposure Drafts* are in parentheses. Where a particular item differs from generally accepted accounting principles in the United States, we indicate the difference in the annotation.

IAS 1: **"Disclosure of Accounting Policies" (January 1, 1975).**   This *Standard* identifies *going concern, consistency,* and *accrual accounting* as fundamental accounting assumptions. It states that major accounting policies are to be disclosed, as is the failure to follow any of the above fundamental assumptions. Material effects of changes in accounting policies must be explained and quantified. Financial statements should show corresponding figures for the preceding period.

Note: Although the issuance of comparative financial statements is a common practice in the United States, GAAP do not require it.

IAS 2: **"Valuation and Presentation of Inventories in the Context of the Historical Cost System" (January 1, 1976).**   Inventories are to be valued at the lower of acquisition cost or net realizable value. When LIFO is used, a disclosure of the difference between the LIFO inventory and either (1) the lower of FIFO (or weighted average) cost and net realizable value or (2) the lower of current cost and net realizable value is required. If direct (or variable) costing is used to value manufactured inventories, that fact should be disclosed.

Note: Under GAAP, certain inventories, such as precious metals, may be valued at market, and the lower-of-cost-or-market rule differs from that specified in *IAS* 2. Finally, direct or variable costing is not an acceptable method for valuing inventories in the United States.

IAS 3: **"Consolidated Financial Statements" (January 1, 1977).**   This *Standard* provides for consolidation of controlled subsidiaries' with the parent's financial statements unless a subsidiary's activities are substantially dissimilar from those of the other companies in the group. Investments in companies influenced but not controlled (that is, *associated companies*) are to be accounted for by the equity method. Investments in nonconsolidated companies are to be written down to market value when such value is determined to have permanently declined below its carrying value (either cost or equity) on the parent's books. Where accounting policies are not uniform within the consolidated group, the proportions of assets and liabilities to which the different accounting policies apply are to be disclosed.

Note: Disclosure of the proportions of consolidated assets and liabilities subject to different accounting policies is not required by GAAP in the United States.

IAS 4: **"Depreciation Accounting" (January 1, 1977).**   This *Standard* requires consistent and systematic depreciation of long-lived assets over their useful lives. The effect of a change in rates or methods should be disclosed in the accounting period in which it occurs. For each major class of depreciable assets, the *Standard* requires disclosure of depreciation methods and rates, depreciation expense, gross book value, and accumulated depreciation.

Note: Disclosures required by GAAP generally include only depreciation expense, gross book value, and accumulated depreciation in total. Disclosure of rates, methods, and breakdowns by asset class are not mandatory but are often presented in the notes to the financial statements.

IAS 5: "Information to be Disclosed in Financial Statements" (January 1, 1977).

This pronouncement provides general and specific disclosure principles for a company's balance sheet, income statement, notes, and supplementary statements. The components of assets, liabilities, owners' equity, revenue, and expense are listed. No particular format for presenting the information is given. Material intercompany transactions are to be disclosed. No statement of changes in financial position is required here, but see *IAS 7*.

Note: In the United States, use of either the equity method or consolidation requires elimination of intercompany profits and losses, and intercompany transactions are not disclosed. However, material *related-party transactions* are disclosed.

IAS 6: "Accounting Responses to Changing Prices" (January 1, 1978).

The *Standard* requires companies to disclose the procedures used to reflect the effects of specific price changes, changes in the general price level, or both in their financial statements. Similarly, failure to reflect the effects of changing prices in the financial statements must also be disclosed.

Note: Under current U.S. GAAP, the presumption is that financial statements are presented in historical dollars; any departure for the purpose of reflecting the effects of changing prices must be disclosed and explained. Disclosure of supplementary data regarding the effects of changing prices is required by *SFAS 33*. [16]

IAS 7: "Statement of Changes in Financial Position" (January 1, 1979).

This *Standard* establishes the requirement for a statement of changes in financial position to be an integral part of the financial statements. Flexibility in the definition of funds is permitted, but funds generated by operations should be shown separately from other sources and uses of funds.

IAS 8: "Unusual and Prior-Period Items and Changes in Accounting Policies" (January 1, 1979).

Unusual items should be separately disclosed as part of current net income. Effects of changes in estimates are not treated as unusual items and are reflected in the income of current and future periods if both are affected. The cumulative effect of a change in accounting policy should be either (1) separately disclosed in current income or (2) treated as a prior-period adjustment with restatement of comparative information for prior years. Corrections of errors are the only other permissible prior-period adjustment.

---

[16] Financial Accounting Standards Board, *Statement of Financial Accounting Standards No. 33,* "Financial Reporting and Changing Prices" (Stamford, Conn.: FASB, 1979).

Note: APBO 20 (AC § 1051.18) specifies that, in most cases, the cumulative effect of a change in accounting policy should be recognized in current period income and *not* as a prior-period adjustment.[17]

IAS 9: "Accounting for Research and Development Costs" (January 1, 1980).

Although R and D costs are generally expensed when incurred, this proposal permits deferral of costs incurred on behalf of a technically and commercially feasible product or process if the company has the resources to produce and market it. Separate disclosure is required for (1) R and D costs charged against income and (2) deferred costs, a description of the projects to which they relate, and the basis for amortization.

Note: SFAS 2 (AC § 4211.12) requires immediate expensing of research and development costs; there is no provision for deferral as described above.[18]

IAS 10: "Contingencies and Events Occurring after the Balance Sheet Date" (January 1, 1980).

This pronouncement provides for the accrual of those contingent losses which are expected to be confirmed and can be measured with reasonable accuracy. Other likely contingent gains and losses are to be disclosed but not booked. Subsequent events which have a material impact on the reported statements make it necessary to adjust the statements.

IAS 11: "Accounting for Construction Contracts" (January 1, 1980).

The percentage-of-completion method of revenue recognition can be used if the outcome of the contract can be reliably estimated. Specific conditions must be satisfied for both fixed-price and cost-plus contracts before the required degree of reliability can be met. The completed contract method is to be used in all other situations; various disclosure requirements are prescribed.

Note: ARB 45 (AC § 4031) requires neither reliable estimates of the contract's outcome nor specific conditions relating to this "reliability."[19]

IAS 12: "Accounting for Taxes on Income" (January 1, 1981).

Deferred income taxes are to be provided on timing differences using either the liability or deferral method. However, deferred taxes need *not* be provided *if* there is reasonable assurance that reversal of timing differences will not affect taxable income at least three years in the future.

Note: APBO 11 (AC § 4091.34) requires that only the deferral method be used. No exception is given for those timing differences whose reversal may or may not affect taxable income at particular times.[20]

---

[17] Accounting Principles Board, *Opinion No. 20*, "Accounting Changes" (N.Y.: AICPA, 1971), par. 18.

[18] Financial Accounting Standards Board, *Statement of Financial Accounting Standards No. 2*, "Accounting for Research and Development Costs" (Stamford, Conn.: FASB, 1974).

[19] Committee on Accounting Procedure, *Accounting Research Bulletin No. 45*, "Long-Term Construction-Type Contracts" (N.Y.: AICPA, 1955).

[20] Accounting Principles Board, *Opinion No. 11*, "Accounting for Income Taxes" (N.Y.: AICPA, 1967).

IAS 13: "Presentation of Current Assets and Current Liabilities (January 1, 1981).

This *Standard* provides broad guidance for determination of current and noncurrent assets and liabilities for companies wishing to so classify assets and liabilities on the balance sheet. The major criterion for making this determination is that the asset or liability be payable or receivable within *one year*. There is no requirement that companies adopt a current/noncurrent distinction. When the distinction is not made, subtotals on the balance sheet should not imply that items are current or noncurrent.

Note: In the United States, companies usually classify their assets and liabilities into current and noncurrent categories, unless industry characteristics render that distinction meaningless. Chapter 30 of *ARB 43* relates current assets and liabilities to the duration of a business' operating cycle, not strictly to one year.[21]

ED 14: "Accounting for Foreign Transactions and Translation of Foreign Financial Statements" (December 1977).

Under this proposal, financial statements denominated in foreign currencies could be translated by either the temporal or current rate methods. Companies could elect to defer translation gains and losses or recognize them currently.

Note: SFAS 8 requires (a) that the temporal method be used in translation and (b) that translation gains and losses, unless related to hedges of identifiable foreign currency commitments, not be deferred.[22]

ED 15: "Reporting Financial Information by Segment" (March 1980).

This document proposes that companies disclose certain financial information by industry and geographical segments. Sales, profitability, and identifiable assets are the major items to be disclosed. Segments significant enough to be reportable are to be selected by management based on a number of judgmental factors.

Note: SFAS 14 ties identification of reportable segments to a series of percentage significance tests and requires more extensive disclosures than *ED 15* —capital expenditures, depreciation expense, export sales, and major customers.[23]

ED 16: "Accounting for Retirement Benefits in the Financial Statements of Employers" (April 1980).

This proposal specifies accounting and disclosure requirements for pension plans in the financial statements of employers. Accrual accounting is to be used, with current service costs being charged to income consistently over employees' working lives. Past service costs or "experience adjustments" for present employees could be recognized when they arise or be allocated over the remaining working lives of the employees. Disclosure of accounting policies, unfunded vested benefits, amount of

---

[21]   Committee on Accounting Procedure, *ARB 43;* AC § 2031.05.

[22]   Financial Accounting Standards Board, *Statement No. 8;* AC § 1083.

[23]   Financial Accounting Standards Board, *Statement of Financial Accounting Standards No. 14,* "Financial Reporting for Segments of a Business Enterprise" (Stamford, Conn.: FASB, 1976); AC § 2081.

pension accruals or prepayments, funding policy, and date of most recent actuarial valuation are required.

Note: Provisions of GAAP for pension plan accounting and reporting are more extensive than those proposed in *ED 16*. Also, GAAP do not permit immediate recognition of past service costs or "sweeteners" when they arise; allocation under one of a variety of alternatives is required.

ED 17: "Information Reflecting the Effects of Changing Prices" (August 1980).

This proposal calls for large publicly-traded enterprises and other economically significant entities to disclose the effects of changing prices on: depreciation of property, plant, and equipment; cost of goods sold; financial instruments, if such instruments would be affected by the adjustment method used (for example, purchasing power gain or loss on monetary items under constant dollar accounting, unrealized holding gains on debt under current value accounting); and the status and performance of the enterprise, reflecting the preceding adjustments. The information may be presented in the primary financial statements or as supplementary information. Enterprises not presenting such information, even if not required to do so, should disclose that fact.

Note: SFAS 33 calls for more extensive disclosures than *ED 17* by requiring the dual constant-dollar, current-cost presentation and the five-year summary.[24] These data, however, are *not* part of the primary financial statements.

ED 18: "Accounting for Property, Plant, and Equipment in the Context of the Historical Cost System" (August 1980).

This proposed *Standard* sets forth accounting principles and disclosure requirements related to plant assets. It does not consider natural resources, expenditures on real estate development, assets acquired in a business combination, and capitalization of interest cost on self-constructed assets. Assets acquired in exchange for other assets are usually recorded at fair value but may be recorded at the book value of the asset given, increased (decreased) by any boot given (received). If some or all of an enterprise's plant assets are carried at current value, appropriate disclosures must be provided.

Note: Following APBO 29 (AC § 1041), assets acquired for other assets must be recorded at fair value unless they are similar assets.[25] Moreover, U.S. GAAP do not permit substitution of current value for historical cost of plant assets in the financial statements, only as supplementary information as provided in *SFAS 33*.

ED 19: "Accounting for Leases" (November 1980).

Compatible with *SFAS 13* (AC § 4053), this proposed standard defines a *finance lease* as one in which substantially all the risks and rewards of ownership are transferred to the lessee, whether or not title actually passes.[26] All other leases are *operating*

---

[24] Financial Accounting Standards Board, *Statement No. 33*.

[25] Accounting Principles Board, *Opinion No. 29*, "Accounting for Nonmonetary Transactions" (N.Y.: AICPA, 1973).

[26] Financial Accounting Standards Board, *Statement of Financial Accounting Standards No. 13*, "Accounting for Leases" (Stamford, Conn.: FASB, 1976).

leases. Lessees are to capitalize finance leases, and lessors are to account for them as sale and financing transactions. With an operating lease, the lessee (lessor) is to recognize the periodic rental payments as expense (revenue) over the term of the lease.

***ED 20:* "Revenue Recognition" (April 1981).** This proposal prescribes basic revenue recognition principles such as completion of the earnings process (transfer of title to goods or performance of services) and receipt of consideration with reasonable expectation of ultimate collection. When collection is sufficiently uncertain, revenue should be recognized only as cash is received. In these cases, either the installment sale method or the cost recovery method (revenue is not recognized until sufficient cash has been received to recover the cost of the item sold) may be used. Revenue may be recognized on the basis of production (that is, prior to sale) for certain agricultural crops or minerals which have guaranteed or homogeneous markets such that sale is virtually assured.

Summary of Key Concepts

Corporations now do business abroad within the context of an international monetary system characterized by **flexible** or **floating exchange rates.** These constantly changing exchange rates make the tasks of accounting and reporting foreign operations more difficult.

Domestic corporations with branches, divisions, and subsidiaries abroad must translate the accounts of those business units into dollars for inclusion in the U.S. financial statements. Most of the translation methods devised to accomplish this use the **current exchange rate** at the balance sheet date to translate some accounts and **historical exchange rates** to translate other accounts.

The four major approaches to this translation process are the **current/noncurrent, monetary/nonmonetary, temporal,** and **current rate** methods. Translation rules in *SFAS 8* are based on the **temporal method.** Each method defines an **exposed position** consisting of accounts to be translated at the current rate; other accounts are translated at historical rates.

Fluctuating exchange rates produce an **exchange translation gain or loss** which normally differs across methods. This translation gain or loss arises because the **exposed position** is translated at the **current rate,** while many **changes in the exposed position** are translated at **historical rates.** Under *SFAS 8*, the exchange translation gain or loss is recognized currently as a component of net income.

The **dollar balances** of **home office reciprocal accounts** are generally used as the translated balances of the **offsetting reciprocal accounts at foreign branches.** In parent/subsidiary accounting, foreign intercompany accounts should be translated at the dollar balances of the parent's offsetting accounts.

Translation of a foreign subsidiary's assets and liabilities differs under the **purchase** and **pooling of interests** methods. If **purchase accounting** is used, the **spot rate at date of business combination** is used to translate the subsidiary's assets and liabilities in existence at date of business combination. Under **pool-**

ing, the book values of the subsidiary's accounts at date of business combination are carried forward, and whatever **historical rates** existed when those account balances arose are to be used.

Significant differences exist among accounting principles and practices around the world. Factors contributing to these differences include the social, economic, and political conditions and institutions in various countries as well as the different ways that accounting has developed in those countries. Organizations such as the **International Accounting Standards Committee (IASC)** seek to promote uniformity in accounting principles and practices internationally. The **standards issued by the IASC,** however, are **not mandatory** and rely on good faith and cooperation for their implementation.

The Relationship between Foreign Currency Translation and Constant-Dollar Accounting

A study of the process of translating foreign currency financial statements into units of domestic currency reveals its similarity to constant-dollar, or general price-level restatements. Some elements common to both techniques are:

1. A change in the measuring unit, either from one currency to another or from historical dollars to current dollars.

2. A distinction between current and historical items.

3. A special gain or loss arising out of the translation or restatement process.

Use of the monetary/nonmonetary approach to foreign currency translation provides the most direct comparison with constant-dollar restatements. Both methods distinguish between monetary and nonmonetary items and treat each category differently. The simplest case is one in which a firm is organized at the beginning of the year and engages in no transactions during the year. At year-end, we prepare either translated or restated financial statements, depending on the method being analyzed. We begin with the fundamental accounting equation.

$$\text{Assets } (A) = \text{Liabilities } (L) + \text{Stockholders' Equity } (SE).$$

Recognizing that both assets and liabilities have monetary (M) and nonmonetary (N) components, we have

$$MA + NA = ML + NL + SE, \text{ or} \tag{1}$$
$$MA - ML = NL - NA + SE$$

Foreign Currency Translation

Define R as the percentage change between the ending (e) and beginning (b) foreign exchange rates; $R = (R_e/R_b) - 1$ and $R_e = R_b (1 + R) = R_b + R_b R$. Thus R_b is the *historical rate*, and R_e is the *current rate*. The following manipulations of equation 1 provide the translated foreign currency accounts. We first multiply the ending exchange rate by each of the account categories in equation 1:

$$R_e MA - R_e ML = R_e NL - R_e NA + R_e SE. \tag{2}$$

In foreign currency translation, the monetary items are translated at the current rate by multiplying them by R_e. The nonmonetary items are translated at the historical beginning-of-period rate, in this case R_b.

We now expand the right-hand side of equation 2, after replacing R_e with $R_b + R_bR$,

$$R_eMA - R_eML = R_bNL + R_bRNL - R_bNA - R_bRNA + R_bSE + R_bRSE,$$

and group the *potential change* in the translated nonmonetary items $[R_bR(NL - NA + SE)]$ on the right:

$$R_eMA - R_eML = R_bNL - R_bNA + R_bSE + R_bR(NL - NA + SE) \quad (3)$$

Since the historical exchange rate R_b is used to translate the nonmonetary items, their translated amounts do not change. Therefore, this potential change in the translated nonmonetary items must equal the effect of a change in the exchange rate on the translated monetary items.

The quantity $\boldsymbol{R_bR(NL - NA + SE)}$ is the **exchange translation gain or loss.** It is the exact amount by which the translated monetary items change as the exchange rate moved from R_b to R_e. If $R_bR(NL - NA + SE)$ is positive, we have a *gain*. In contrast, if $R_bR(NL - NA + SE)$ is negative, we have a *loss*.

Constant-Dollar Restatement

Define P as the percentage change between the ending *(e)* and beginning *(b)* general price levels as measured by the Consumer Price Index, Gross National Product Implicit Price Deflator, or some other broad-based index; $P = (P_e/P_b) - 1$ and $P_e = P_b(1 + P) = P_b + P_bP$. Thus P_b is the *historical price level* and P_e is the *current price level*. Again using our fundamental accounting equation (as arranged in 1), the year-end constant dollar restatement is based on the following:

$$(P_e/P_b)MA - (P_e/P_b)ML = (P_e/P_b)NL - (P_e/P_b)NA + (P_e/P_b)SE \quad (4)$$

Since monetary items are *not* restated in constant-dollar accounting, we expand the left-hand side of equation 4, after replacing P_e with $P_b + P_bP$,

$$(P_b/P_b)MA + (P_bP/P_b)MA - (P_b/P_b)ML - (P_bP/P_b)ML = (P_e/P_b)NL - (P_e/P_b)NA + (P_e/P_b)SE,$$

or

$$MA + PMA - ML - PML = (P_e/P_b)NL - (P_e/P_b)NA + (P_e/P_b)SE,$$

and transfer the *potential restatement* of the monetary items $[P(ML - MA)]$ to the right-hand side:

$$MA - ML = (P_e/P_b)NL - (P_e/P_b)NA + (P_e/P_b)SE + P(ML - MA).$$

Since there is no restatement of monetary items under constant dollar accounting, their restated amounts do not change. Therefore, the potential restatement in the monetary items must equal the effect of a change in the general price level on the restated nonmonetary items.

The quantity $\boldsymbol{P(ML - MA)}$ is the familiar **purchasing power gain or loss** on monetary items. It represents the amount by which monetary items should have changed in the face of a changing price level, but didn't. In a period of rising prices, if $(ML - MA) > 0$, then $P(ML - MA)$ is positive, a *gain*. If $(ML - MA) < 0$, then $P(ML - MA)$ is negative, a *loss*.

Compare the *exchange translation gain or loss*, $R_bR(NL - NA + SE)$, with the *purchasing power gain or loss*, $P(ML - MA)$. These are the *special gains or losses* mentioned in the introduction to this appendix. First, note that the items inside the brackets are those not affected by a changing exchange rate (general price level) in the translation (restatement) process. Second, the terms outside the brackets represent percentage changes (with foreign currency translation, R is the percentage change, while R_b is needed to translate the foreign currency amounts of NL, NA, and SE into dollars). In both the foreign currency and constant dollar cases, these special gains and losses refer to the *potential* effect of a change in the measuring unit (exchange rate or price level) on items not affected by that change in the translation or restatement process. Under double entry accounting, these special gains and losses are needed to balance the fundamental accounting equation when some items are affected by a change in the measuring unit and others are not.

Moving to a multiperiod, multitransaction setting complicates but does not change the above relationships. It simply requires the replacement of P or R with a set of P_t and R_t, where t identifies the time that a transaction occurred and hence the change in price level or exchange rate since that time. In the foreign currency translation case, use of one of the other three translation methods merely affects the way balance sheet items are grouped in equation 1 and the components of the exposed position on the left-hand side.

A Numerical Example

At the beginning of the year, a firm is formed with account balances as shown in the following table. No transactions take place during the year, and beginning and ending exchange rates and price levels are also given in the table. The account balances are measured in either units of foreign currency or beginning-of-year dollars, depending on the context.

MA = 1,000	R_b = 1.00
NA = 2,000	R_e = 1.10
ML = 800	R = .10
NL = 400	P_b = 100
SE = 1,800	P_e = 110
	P = .10

The end-of-period translated/restated balance sheets are given in Exhibit 14.11.

A careful look at these balance sheets reveals both a fundamental similarity and a fundamental difference between the two methods when they are applied to identical data. As expected, the similarity is that the exchange translation gain and the purchasing power loss are equal in absolute value but have opposite signs. In this example, net monetary items $(ML - MA)$ equals net monetary assets (debit balance) of $200. Concurrently, net nonmonetary items $(NL - NA + SE)$ indicates net nonmonetary equities (credit balance) of $200, which grows by 10 percent in the restatement process, producing a loss of $20. The exchange translation gain of 20 represents the amount by which the net monetary

Exhibit 14.11   Translated/Restated Balance Sheets

Translated Foreign Currency Balance Sheet		Restated Constant-Dollar Balance Sheet	
Monetary Assets (1,000 × 1.10)	1,100	Monetary Assets (1,000 × 1.00)	1,000
Nonmonetary Assets (2,000 × 1.00) . . .	2,000	Nonmonetary Assets (2,000 × 1.10) . . .	2,200
Total Assets	3,100	Total Assets	3,200
Monetary Liabilities (800 × 1.10)	880	Monetary Liabilities (800 × 1.00)	800
Nonmonetary Liabilities (400 × 1.00) . . .	400	Nonmonetary Liabilities (400 × 1.10) . . .	440
Stockholders' Equity (1,800 × 1.00) . . .	1,800	Stockholders' Equity (1,800 × 1.10) . . .	1,980
Exchange Translation Gain	20 [a]	Purchasing Power Loss	(20) [b]
Total Liabilities and Stockholders' Equity .	3,100	Total Liabilities and Stockholders' Equity .	3,200

[a] 20 = .1(400 − 2,000 + 1,800)
[b] 20 = .1(1,000 − 800)

assets in foreign currency *increased* in translated value. In contrast, the purchasing power loss of 20 in constant-dollar accounting arose because the net monetary assets *did not change* in the face of inflation, which sapped their value.

The difference in the translated (restated) balances occurs because the nonmonetary items are translated at the lower historical rate but are restated at the higher current general price level. Moreover, since the nonmonetary items are larger than the monetary items, total *restated* assets and equities exceed total *translated* assets and equities.

Questions **Q14.1**   Briefly discuss the nature of the financial accounting problems peculiar to multinational corporations.

Q14.2   Why is it necessary for domestic companies to translate the accounts of their overseas branches, divisions, and subsidiaries?

Q14.3   How has the historical-cost accounting model influenced the methods most frequently used to translate foreign currency financial statements?

Q14.4   Compare the effect on the translation gain or loss associated with translation of inventory at the current rate (under the current/noncurrent method) and at the historical rate (under the temporal method) when exchange rates are (1) rising and (2) falling.

Q14.5   Compare the effect on the translation gain or loss associated with translation of long-term debt at the historical rate (under the current/noncurrent method) and at the current rate (under the temporal method) when exchange rates are (1) rising and (2) falling.

Q14.6   This text has drawn a distinction between exchange *conversion* gains and losses and exchange *translation* gains and losses. What is the basis for the distinction? As a financial statement user, would you prefer separate disclosure of both types of exchange gains and losses? Explain.

Q14.7   It is recommended that translation of the reciprocal accounts of foreign branches be accomplished by using the dollar balances in the related reciprocal accounts at the domestic home office. What are the advantages and disadvantages of this procedure?

Q14.8   Explain how the minority interest in a partially-owned foreign subsidiary should be translated by its U.S.-based parent for purposes of preparing consolidated financial statements.

Q14.9   Explain the approach and rationale for the translation of the assets and liabilities of foreign subsidiaries for inclusion in consolidated financial statements when the business combination was accounted for (1) as a purchase and (2) as a pooling of interests.

Q14.10   Describe the role of the International Accounting Standards Committee (IASC). What obstacles does it face?

Exercises   E14.1   In each of the following independent situations, give the appropriate translated amount under (a) the current/noncurrent method and (b) the method prescribed by *SFAS 8*.

1. On January 1, 19X8, the Ben Company formed a foreign subsidiary. On February 15, 19X8, Ben's subsidiary purchased 100,000 local currency units (LCU) of inventory. 25,000 LCU of the original inventory purchased on February 15, 19X8, made up the entire inventory on December 31, 19X8. The exchange rates were 2.2 LCU to $1 from January 1, 19X8 to June 30, 19X8, and 2 LCU to $1 from July 1, 19X8 to December 31, 19X8. What is the translated inventory balance of Ben's foreign subsidiary at December 31, 19X8?

2. The France Company owns a foreign subsidiary with 2,400,000 local currency units (LCU) of property, plant, and equipment before accumulated depreciation at December 31, 19X8. Of this amount, 1,500,000 LCU were acquired on January 1, 19X6, when the rate of exchange was 1.5 LCU to $1, and 900,000 LCU were acquired on January 1, 19X7, when the rate of exchange was 1.6 LCU to $1. The rate of exchange in effect at December 31, 19X8, was 1.9 LCU to $1. The weighted average of exchange rates which were in effect during 19X8 was 1.8 LCU to $1. Assuming that the property, plant, and equipment are depreciated using the straight-line method over a ten-year period with no salvage value, how much depreciation expense relating to the foreign subsidiary's property, plant, and equipment should be charged in France's income statement for 19X8?

Calculate the translated balances of property, plant, and equipment and accumulated depreciation at December 31, 19X8.

(AICPA adapted)

E14.2 	 On September 10, 19X6, Globe Trading Company advanced $30,000 to its representative in Bogota, Colombia, to establish a small sales office. The representative, Mr. Moreno, converted the $30,000 into 1,000,000 pesos (P) and opened a bank account in Bogota. No formal accounting system is established in Bogota. At December 31, 19X6, Mr. Moreno submitted the following report to Globe Trading:

	Pesos
Funds Received on September 10, 19X6	1,000,000
Payments:	
Purchase of Equipment on September 10	270,000
Office Rent	70,000
Secretary's Salary	120,000
Telephone and Other Expenses	100,000
Total Payments	560,000
Cash (Pesos) on Hand, December 31, 19X6	440,000

The exchange rate was $.033/P on December 31, 19X6, and averaged $.031/P during the period from September 10 to December 31, 19X6.

Required:
1. Prepare a schedule to compute the exchange translation gain or loss related to the Bogota sales office in 19X6.
2. Assume that Globe treats the $30,000 as an advance. Give the journal entries which would be made by Globe on September 10 and on December 31, when Globe's books are closed.

E14.3 	 The following two questions relate to *SFAS 8*.
1. The Financial Accounting Standards Board discusses certain terminology essential to both the translation of foreign currency transactions and foreign currency financial statements in *SFAS 8*. Included in the discussion is a definition of and distinction between the terms *measure* and *denominate*.

Required: Define the terms *measure* and *denominate* as discussed by the Financial Accounting Standards Board and give a brief example that demonstrates the distinction between accounts measured in a particular currency and accounts denominated in a particular currency.

2. There are several methods of translating foreign currency transactions or accounts reflected in foreign currency financial statements. These are the current/noncurrent, monetary/nonmonetary, current rate, and temporal methods (the method adopted by the Financial Accounting Standards Board).

Required: Define the temporal method of translating foreign currency financial statements. Specifically include in your answer the treatment of the following four accounts:

1. Long-term accounts receivable.
2. Deferred income.
3. Inventory valued at cost.
4. Long-term debt.

(AICPA adapted)

E14.4   U.S. Industries has a subsidiary in Switzerland. The subsidiary's financial statements are maintained in Swiss francs. Exchange rates for selected dates are as follows:

January 1, 19X4 . . . $.75	January 1, 19X6 . . . $.68
January 1, 19X5 70	December 31,19X6 . . .65

Required: Following *SFAS 8*, calculate the correct dollar amount for each of the following items appearing in the subsidiary's trial balance at December 31, 19X6:

1. Cash in Bank, 400,000 Swiss francs.
2. Inventory on LIFO basis, 300,000 Swiss francs. The inventory cost consists of 100,000 Swiss francs acquired in January 19X4 and 200,000 Swiss francs acquired in January 19X6.
3. Machinery and Equipment, 1,100,000 Swiss francs. A review of the records indicates that the company bought equipment costing 500,000 Swiss francs in January 19X4 (20% of this was sold in January 19X6) and additional equipment costing 700,000 Swiss francs in January 19X5. Ignore accumulated depreciation.
4. Depreciation Expense on machinery and equipment, 110,000 Swiss francs (depreciated over ten years, straight-line basis).

E14.5   The following data relate to Sterling, Limited, located in the city of Liverpool, England. Sterling is controlled by a U.S. company.

Net Monetary Assets (Liabilities), January 1, 19X1	£ 70,000
Acquisition of Plant Assets for Debt, February 15, 19X1	100,000
Purchase of Inventory Made Evenly during 19X1	350,000
Collection of Receivables Outstanding at January 1, 19X1	270,000
Sales Made Evenly during 19X1	600,000
Depreciation of Assets Acquired When the Exchange Rate Was $1.80/£ . . .	40,000
Operating Expenses (Excluding Depreciation and Amortization), Incurred Evenly during 19X1	120,000
Refinancing or "Rollover" of Commercial Paper	80,000

Exchange rates ($/£) during 19X1 were as follows:

January 1, 19X1 . . . $1.90	Average for 19X1 . . $1.97
February 15, 19X1 . . 1.95	December 31, 19X1 . . 2.01

Required: Prepare a schedule to compute the exchange translation gain or loss for Sterling during 19X1 in conformity with *SFAS 8*.

E14.6   Following is the condensed balance sheet of the Cheung Company on September 15, 19X8. On that date, Wint Corporation, headquartered in Chicago, acquired 90 percent of Cheung's outstanding stock in exchange for its own stock valued at $2,000,000. Both book value and fair value data are given in units of foreign currency (FC).

Cheung Company
Condensed Balance Sheet at September 15, 19X8

	Book Value (FC)	Fair Value (FC)
Current Assets	3,000,000	3,400,000
Noncurrent Assets	5,000,000	6,000,000
Total Assets	8,000,000	
Current Liabilities	2,000,000	2,000,000
Noncurrent Liabilities	2,000,000	2,600,000
Stockholders' Equity	4,000,000	—
Total Liabilities and Stockholders' Equity . .	8,000,000	

The exchange rate at September 15, 19X8, is $.40/FC. The noncurrent assets and noncurrent liabilities (mostly long-term debt) were acquired (incurred) at average exchange rates of $.45 and $.50, respectively. Cheung's current assets and liabilities are monetary items except for inventory of FC1,000,000, acquired when the exchange rate was $.42. Capital stock of FC2,000,000 was issued when the exchange rate was $.45. Wint Corporation follows *SFAS 8*.

Required:
  1. Assuming the purchase method of accounting, give the eliminating entries made on a consolidated balance sheet prepared at September 15, 19X8. Show all calculations.
  2. Repeat requirement 1, assuming the pooling of interests method of accounting.

E14.7 The following transactions were recorded by Larson Company's subsidiary in Finland during 19X3. The Finnish currency is the markka (M).

	Amount (M)	Exchange Rate ($/M)
Purchase of Inventory	4,000,000	$.30
Proceeds from Sale of Equipment	500,000	.32
Book Value of Equipment Sold	350,000	.40 [a]
Sales	5,000,000	.33
Cost of Goods Sold	3,000,000	.29 [a]
Issue of Long-Term Debt for Cash	1,000,000	.35
Amortization of Prepayments	100,000	.34 [a]

[a] Exchange rates when assets sold or amortized were acquired by the Finnish subsidiary.

Required: The exchange rate ($/M) at December 31, 19X3, is $.36. Calculate the effect of each of the above transactions on the exchange translation gain or loss reported by Larson in 19X3 under (1) *SFAS 8* and (2) the current/noncurrent method of translation.

E14.8   Kasha, Limited, is located in India and is owned by Caldwell, Inc., a U.S. corporation. The lower-of-cost-or-market rule is being applied to Kasha's inventory for inclusion in Caldwell's consolidated financial statements. The inventory consists of four different categories of merchandise. Items within each category are similar. Data on cost, market, and average exchange rates when the goods were acquired by Kasha are given below. The current exchange rate is $.12.

Category	Cost (Rupees)	Average Exchange Rate When Acquired	Current Market (Rupees)
A	5,000,000	$.14	6,500,000
B	10,000,000	.11	9,900,000
C	8,000,000	.18	12,000,000
D	2,000,000	.10	1,600,000

Required: Compute the dollar value of each category of inventory that will be reflected in Caldwell's consolidated balance sheet and the dollar amount of the write-down to market included in the consolidated income statement for each category of inventory as provided for in *SFAS 8*.

Problems   P14.1   **Translating a Condensed Trial Balance—Equity Method Accrual**   The trial balance of Valiant Corporation, a small Swedish company involved in merchandising is given below. The account balances are for the year ended December 31, 19X4, and are measured in krone (K), the Swedish currency.

Account	Amount (K) Dr. (Cr.)
Cash	240,000
Accounts Receivable	400,000
Allowance for Uncollectible Accounts	(40,000)
Plant and Equipment, Net	2,000,000
Accounts Payable	(200,000)
Notes Payable	(600,000)
Capital Stock	(400,000)
Retained Earnings, January 1, 19X4	(1,160,000)
Sales	(1,200,000)
Depreciation Expense	320,000
Other Expenses	640,000
	0

Valiant Corporation was formed, and its stock issued, when the exchange rate was $.20/K. The plant assets were acquired and the notes payable executed when the exchange rate was $.25/K. Sales and Other Expenses occurred evenly during 19X4. The translated (dollar) balance of Valiant's January 1 retained earnings was $150,000. Exchange rates in 19X4 were as follows:

Time	Rate ($/K)
January 1, 19X4	$.30
Average for 19X4	.33
December 31, 19X4	.35

Required:
1. Translate the Valiant Corporation's trial balance into dollars.
2. Prepare a translated income statement and balance sheet for Valiant Corporation.
3. If Domestic Corporation, a U.S. firm, owned 70 percent of Valiant's outstanding stock, prepare the journal entry made by Domestic to record the equity method accrual at December 31, 19X4. There were no intercompany transactions and no purchase premium or discount. Your solutions should conform with *SFAS 8*.

P14.2 **Translation of Selected Accounts** On January 1, 19X1, the Franklin Company formed a foreign subsidiary which issued all of its currently outstanding common stock on that date. Selected captions from the balance sheets, all of which are shown in local currency units (LCU), are as follows:

	December 31	
ACCOUNTS RECEIVABLE	19X2	19X1
(Net of Allowance for Uncollectible Accounts of 2,200 LCU at December 31, 19X2, and 2,000 LCU at December 31, 19X1)	40,000 LCU	35,000 LCU
INVENTORIES, at Cost	80,000	75,000
PROPERTY, PLANT, AND EQUIPMENT		
(Net of Accumulated Depreciation of 31,000 LCU at December 31, 19X2, and 14,000 LCU at December 31, 19X1)	163,000	150,000
LONG-TERM DEBT	100,000	120,000
COMMON STOCK		
Authorized 10,000 Shares, Par Value 10 LCU per Share, Issued and Outstanding 5,000 Shares at December 31, 19X2 and December 31, 19X1	50,000	50,000

Additional information:
1. Exchange rates are as follows:

January 1, 19X1–July 31, 19X1	2 LCU to $1
August 1, 19X1–October 31, 19X1	1.8 LCU to $1
November 1, 19X1–June 30, 19X2	1.7 LCU to $1
July 1, 19X2–December 31, 19X2	1.5 LCU to $1
Average monthly rate for 19X1	1.9 LUC to $1
Average monthly rate for 19X2	1.6 LCU to $1

2. An analysis of the accounts receivable balance is as follows:

ACCOUNTS RECEIVABLE	19X2	19X1
Balance at Beginning of Year	37,000 LCU	— LCU
Sales (36,000 LCU per Month in 19X2 and 31,000 LCU		
per Month in 19X1)	432,000	372,000
Collections	(423,600)	(334,000)
Write-offs (May 19X2 and December 19X1)	(3,200)	(1,000)
Balance at Year-end	42,200 LCU	37,000 LCU

ALLOWANCE FOR UNCOLLECTIBLE ACCOUNTS		
Balance at Beginning of Year	2,000 LCU	— LCU
Provision for Uncollectible Accounts	3,400	3,000
Write-offs (May 19X2 and December 19X1)	(3,200)	(1,000)
Balance at Year-end	2,200 LCU	2,000 LCU

3. An analysis of inventories, for which the first-in, first-out (FIFO) inventory method is used, is as follows:

	19X2	19X1
Inventory at Beginning of Year	75,000 LCU	— LCU
Purchases (June 19X2 and June 19X1)	335,000	375,000
Goods Available for Sale	410,000	375,000
Inventory at Year-end	80,000	75,000
Cost of Goods Sold	330,000 LCU	300,000 LCU

4. On January 1, 19X1, Franklin's foreign subsidiary purchased land for 24,000 LCU and plant and equipment for 140,000 LCU. On July 4, 19X2, additional equipment was purchased for 30,000 LCU. Plant and equipment is being depreciated on a straight-line basis over a ten-year period with no salvage value. A full year's depreciation is taken in the year of purchase.

5. On January 15, 19X1, 7 percent bonds with a face value of 120,000 LCU were sold. These bonds mature on January 15, 19X7, and interest is paid semiannually on July 15 and January 15. Bonds with a face value of 20,000 LCU were retired on January 14, 19X2.

Required: Prepare a schedule translating the selected captions above into U.S. dollars at December 31, 19X2 and December 31, 19X1, respectively, following *SFAS 8.* Show supporting computations in good form.

(AICPA adapted)

P14.3 Translating a Foreign Subsidiary's Trial Balance The Wiend Corporation acquired the Dieck Corporation on January 1, 19X5, by the purchase at book value of all outstanding capital stock. The Dieck Corporation is located in a Central American country whose monetary unit is the peso (P). The Dieck Corporation's accounting records were continued without change; a trial balance, in pesos, of the balance sheet accounts at the purchase date follows at the *bottom* of page 625.

Exhibit 14.12   Trial Balance Data to Be Used in P14.3

The Dieck Corporation
Trial Balance (in Pesos)
December 31, 19X6

	Debit	Credit
Cash	P 25,000	
Accounts Receivable	20,000	
Allowance for Uncollectible Accounts		P 500
Due from the Wiend Corporation	30,000	
Inventory, December 31, 19X6	110,000	
Prepayments	3,000	
Machinery and Equipment	210,000	
Accumulated Depreciation		79,900
Accounts Payable		22,000
Income Taxes Payable		40,000
Notes Payable		60,000
Capital Stock		50,000
Retained Earnings		100,600
Sales—Domestic		170,000
Sales—Foreign		200,000
Cost of Sales	207,600	
Depreciation Expense	22,400	
Selling and Administrative Expenses	60,000	
Gain on Sale of Assets		5,000
Income Tax Expense	40,000	
Total	P728,000	P728,000

The Dieck Corporation
Trial Balance (in Pesos)
January 1, 19X5

	Debit	Credit
Cash	P 3,000	
Accounts Receivable	5,000	
Inventory	32,000	
Machinery and Equipment	204,000	
Accumulated Depreciation		P 42,000
Accounts Payable		81,400
Capital Stock		50,000
Retained Earnings		70,600
Total	P244,000	P244,000

The Dieck Corporation's trial balance, in pesos, at December 31, 19X6, appears in Exhibit 14.12.

The following additional information is available:

1. All the Dieck Corporation's export sales are made to its parent company

and are accumulated in the account, Sales—Foreign. The balance in the account, Due from the Wiend Corporation, is the total of unpaid invoices. All foreign sales are billed in United States dollars. The reciprocal accounts on the parent company's books show total 19X6 purchases as $471,000 and the total of unpaid invoices as $70,500.

2. Depreciation is computed by the straight-line method over a ten-year life for all depreciable assets. Machinery costing 20,000 pesos was purchased on December 31, 19X5, and no depreciation was recorded for this machinery in 19X5. No other depreciable assets have been acquired since January 1, 19X5, and no assets are fully depreciated.

3. Certain assets that were included in fixed assets at January 1, 19X5, were sold on December 31, 19X6. For 19X6, a full year's depreciation was recorded before the assets were removed from the books. Information regarding the sale follows:

	Pesos
Cost of Assets	14,000
Accumulated Depreciation	4,900
Net Book Value	9,100
Proceeds of Sale	14,100
Gain on Sale	5,000

4. Cost of sales consists mostly of goods purchased evenly throughout 19X6. Inventory (LIFO cost) was acquired late in 19X5.

5. Prepayments were acquired evenly during 19X6.

6. Notes payable are long-term obligations that were incurred on December 31, 19X5.

7. No entries have been made in the Retained Earnings account of the subsidiary since its acquisition, other than the net income for 19X5. The Retained Earnings account at December 31, 19X5, was translated to $212,000.

8. The prevailing rates of exchange follow:

Date	Exchange Rate ($/P)
January 1, 19X5	$2.00
19X5 Average	2.10
December 31, 19X5	2.20
19X6 Average	2.30
December 31, 19X6	2.40

Required: Prepare a worksheet to translate the December 31, 19X6, trial balance of the Dieck Corporation from pesos to dollars, in accordance with *SFAS 8.* The worksheet should show the trial balance in pesos, the appropriate translation rates, and the translated trial balance. All supporting computations should be in good form.

(AICPA adapted)

P14.4 Multiple Choice Questions on Foreign Currency Translation

1. The Marvin Company has a receivable from a foreign customer which is payable in the local currency of the foreign customer. The amount receivable for 900,000 local currency units (LCU), has been translated into $315,000 on Marvin's December 31, 19X5, balance sheet. On January 15, 19X6, the receivable is collected in full when the exchange rate is 3 LCU to $1. What journal entry should Marvin make to record the collection of this receivable?

	Debit	Credit
a. Cash	300,000	
Accounts Receivable		300,000
b. Cash	300,000	
Exchange Loss	15,000	
Accounts Receivable		315,000
c. Cash	300,000	
Deferred Exchange Loss	15,000	
Accounts Receivable		315,000
d. Cash	315,000	
Accounts Receivable		315,000

2. The Clark Company owns a foreign subsidiary which had net income for the year ended December 31, 19X5, of 4,800,000 local currency units (LCU), which was appropriately translated into $800,000. On October 15, 19X5, when the rate of exchange was 5.7 LCU to $1, the foreign subsidiary paid a dividend to Clark of 2,400,000 LCU. The dividend represented the net income of the foreign subsidiary for the six months ended June 30, 19X5, during which time the weighted average of exchange rates was 5.8 LCU to $1. The rate of exchange in effect at December 31, 19X5, was 5.9 LCU to $1. What rate of exchange should be used to translate the dividend for the December 31, 19X5, financial statements?
   a. 5.7 LCU to $1.
   b. 5.8 LCU to $1.
   c. 5.9 LCU to $1.
   d. 6.0 LCU to $1.

3. Certain balance sheet accounts in a foreign subsidiary of the Brogan Company at December 31, 19X7, have been translated into U.S. dollars as follows:

	Translated at	
	Current Rates	Historical Rates
Marketable Equity Securities Carried at Cost . . .	$100,000	$110,000
Marketable Equity Securities Carried at Current Market Price	120,000	125,000
Inventories Carried at Cost	130,000	132,000
Inventories Carried at Net Realizable Value . . .	80,000	84,000
	$430,000	$451,000

What amount should be shown in Brogan's balance sheet at December 31, 19X7, as a result of the above information?

a. $430,000.
b. $436,000.
c. $442,000.
d. $451,000.

4.   On January 1, 19X6, the Ace Company formed a foreign subsidiary. On February 15, 19X6, Ace's subsidiary purchased 175,000 local currency units (LCU) of inventory. 50,000 LCU of the original inventory purchased on February 15, 19X6, made up the entire inventory on December 31, 19X6. The exchange rates were 2.2 LCU to $1 from January 1, 19X6 to June 30, 19X6, and 2 LCU to $1 from July 1, 19X6 to December 31, 19X6. The December 31, 19X6, inventory balance for Ace's foreign subsidiary should be translated into U.S. dollars of:

a. $23,077.
b. $22,727.
c. $23,810.
d. $25,000.

5.   The Dease Company owns a foreign subsidiary with 3,600,000 local currency units (LCU) of property, plant, and equipment before accumulated depreciation at December 31, 19X5. Of this amount, 2,400,000 LCU were acquired in 19X3, when the rate of exchange was 1.6 LCU to $1, and 1,200,000 LCU were acquired in 19X4, when the rate of exchange was 1.8 LCU to $1. The rate of exchange in effect at December 31, 19X5, was 2 LCU to $1. The weighted average of exchange rates which were in effect during 19X5 was 1.92 LCU to $1. Assuming that the property, plant, and equipment are depreciated using the straight-line method over a ten-year period with no salvage value, how much depreciation expense relating to the foreign subsidiary's property, plant, and equipment should be charged in Dease's income statement for 19X5?

a. $180,000.
b. $187,500.
c. $200,000.
d. $216,667.

6.   The Witter Company owns a foreign subsidiary with 4,800,000 local currency units (LCU) of property, plant, and equipment before accumulated depreciation at December 31, 19X4. Of this amount, 3,000,000 LCU were acquired in 19X2, when the rate of exchange was 1.5 LCU to $1, and 1,800,000 LCU were acquired in 19X3, when the rate of exchange was 1.6 LCU to $1. The rate of exchange in effect at December 31, 19X4, was 1.9 LCU to $1. The weighted average of exchange rates which were in effect during 19X4 was 1.8 LCU to $1. Assuming that the property, plant, and equipment are depreciated using the straight-line method over a ten-year period with no salvage value, how much depreciation expense relating to the foreign subsidiary's property, plant, and equipment should be charged in Witter's income statement for 19X4?

    a. $252,632.

    b. $266,667.

    c. $300,000.

    d. $312,500.

7.   Lochlann Company purchased with U.S. dollars all the outstanding common stock of Dey Company, a Canadian corporation. At the date of purchase, a portion of the investment account was appropriately allocated to goodwill. One year later, after an exchange rate decrease (U.S. dollars have become less valuable), the goodwill should be shown in the consolidated balance sheet at what amount?

    a. An increased amount, less amortization.

    b. The same amount, less amortization.

    c. A lesser amount, less amortization.

    d. An increased or lesser amount depending on management policy, less amortization.

8.   If a parent company bills all sales to a foreign subsidiary in terms of dollars and is to be repaid in the same number of dollars, the purchases account on the subsidiary's trial balance will be converted to U.S. dollars by using:

    a. The average exchange rate for the period.

    b. The exchange rate at the beginning of the period.

    c. The exchange rate at the end of the period.

    d. The amount shown in the parent's accounts for sales to the subsidiary.

    (AICPA adapted)

P14.5 **Multiple Choice Questions on Foreign Currency Translation**

1.   How should exchange gains and losses resulting from translating foreign currency financial statements into U.S. dollars be accounted for?

    a. Included as an ordinary item in net earnings for the period in which the rate changes.

    b. Included as an extraordinary item in net earnings for the period in which the rate changes.

    c. Included in the statement of financial position as a deferred item.

    d. Included as an ordinary item in net earnings for gains, but deferred for losses.

2.   A material loss arising from the devaluation of the currency of a country in which a corporation was conducting foreign operations through a branch would be reflected in the company's year-end financial statements as:

    a. An asset to be subsequently offset against gains from foreign currency revaluations.

    b. A factor in determining earnings before extraordinary items in the year during which the loss occurred.

    c. An extraordinary item on the earnings statement of the year during which the loss occurred.

    d. A prior-period adjustment, unless the operations of the foreign branch had begun during the year in which the loss occurred.

3.   A change in the foreign currency exchange rate between the date a

transaction occurred and the date of the current financial statements gives rise to an exchange gain or loss if:

a. The asset or liability being translated is carried at a current money price.

b. The asset or liability being translated is carried at a price from a past purchase or sale exchange.

c. The revenue or expense item relates to an asset or liability that is translated at historical rates.

d. The revenue or expense item relates to a deferred asset or liability shown on a previous statement of financial position.

4.   Seed Company had a receivable from a foreign customer which is payable in the customer's local currency. On December 31, 19X6, this receivable was appropriately included in the accounts receivable section of Seed's balance sheet at $450,000. When the receivable was collected on January 4, 19X7, Seed converted the local currency of the foreign customer into $440,000. Seed also owns a foreign subsidiary in which exchange gains of $45,000 resulted as a consequence of translation in 19X7. What amount, if any, should be included as an exchange gain or loss in Seed's 19X7 consolidated income statement?

a. $0.

b. $10,000 exchange loss.

c. $35,000 exchange gain.

d. $45,000 exchange gain.

5.   Fore Company had a $30,000 exchange loss resulting from the translation of the accounts of its wholly-owned foreign subsidiary for the year ended December 31, 19X8. Fore also had a receivable from a foreign customer which was payable in the customer's local currency. On December 31, 19X7, this receivable for 500,000 local currency units (LCU) was appropriately included in the accounts receivable section of Fore's balance sheet at $245,000. When the receivable was collected on February 5, 19X8, the exchange rate was 2 LCU to $1. What amount should be included as the total exchange gain or loss in the 19X8 consolidated income statement of Fore Company and its wholly-owned foreign subsidiary as a result of the above?

a. $5,000 exchange gain.

b. $20,000 exchange loss.

c. $25,000 exchange loss.

d. $30,000 exchange loss.

6.   When preparing combined or consolidated financial statements for a domestic and a foreign company, account balances expressed in the foreign currency must be translated into the domestic currency. The objective of the translation process is to obtain currency valuations that:

a. Are conservative.

b. Reflect current monetary equivalents.

c. Are expressed in domestic units of measure and are in conformity with domestic generally accepted accounting principles.

d. Reflect the translated account at its unexpired historical cost.

7. The year-end balance of accounts receivable on the books of a foreign subsidiary should be translated by the parent company for consolidation purposes at the:
   a. Historical rate.
   b. Current rate.
   c. Negotiated rate.
   d. Forward rate.

8. When translating an amount for fixed assets shown on the statement of financial position of a foreign subsidiary, the appropriate rate of translation is the:
   a. Current exchange rate.
   b. Average exchange rate for the current year.
   c. Historical exchange rate.
   d. Average exchange rate over the life of each fixed asset.

(AICPA adapted)

P14.6 **Principles of Consolidating and Translating Foreign Accounts** Dhia Products Company was incorporated in the state of Florida to do business as a manufacturer of medical supplies and equipment. Since incorporating, Dhia doubled in size about every three years and is now considered one of the leading medical supply companies in the country.

During January 19X1, Dhia established a subsidiary, Ban, Ltd., in the emerging nation of Shatha. Dhia owns 90 percent of the outstanding capital stock of Ban; the remaining 10 percent of Ban's outstanding capital stock is held by Shatha citizens, as required by Shatha constitutional law. The investment in Ban, accounted for by Dhia by the equity method, represents about 18 percent of the total assets of Dhia at December 31, 19X4, the close of the accounting period for both companies.

Required:

1. What criteria should Dhia Products Company use in determining whether it would be appropriate to prepare consolidated financial statements with Ban, Ltd., for the year ended December 31, 19X4? Explain.

2. Independent of your answer to requirement 1, assume it has been appropriate for Dhia and Ban to prepare consolidated financial statements for each year 19X1 through 19X4. But before consolidated financial statements can be prepared, the individual account balances in Ban's December 31, 19X4, adjusted trial balance must be translated into the appropriate number of U.S. dollars. For each of the ten accounts listed, taken from Ban's adjusted trial balance, specify what exchange rate (for example, average exchange rate for 19X4 or current exchange rate at December 31, 19X4) should be used to translate the account balances into dollars, according to *SFAS 8*, and explain why that rate is appropriate. Assign letters *a* through *j* to your answers, to correspond with each account in the following list:
   a. Cash in Shatha National Bank.
   b. Trade Accounts Receivable (all from 19X4 revenues).

Exhibit 14.13   Phillips Company and Standard, Limited, Condensed Financial Statements to Be Used in P14.7

	Balance Sheets	
	Phillips ($)	Standard (£)
Cash and Receivables	$ 7,680,000	£ 3,000,000
Inventory	4,000,000	3,000,000
Property, Plant, and Equipment, Net	12,000,000	5,000,000
Investment in Standard	8,320,000	—
Total Assets	$32,000,000	£11,000,000
Current Liabilities	$ 8,000,000	£ 4,000,000
Long-Term Debt	4,000,000	1,000,000
Capital Stock	10,000,000	2,000,000
Retained Earnings	10,000,000	4,000,000
Total Liabilities and Stockholders' Equity	$32,000,000	£11,000,000

	Statements of Income and Retained Earnings	
	Phillips ($)	Standard (£)
Sales	$30,000,000	£10,000,000
Cost of Goods Sold	$20,000,000	£ 6,000,000
Depreciation Expense	1,000,000	500,000
Other Operating Expenses	5,000,000	2,000,000
	$26,000,000	£ 8,500,000
Net Income	$ 4,000,000	£ 1,500,000
Dividends Declared and Paid	(2,000,000)	(1,000,000)
Increase in Retained Earnings	$ 2,000,000	£ 500,000

c. Supplies Inventory (all purchased during the last quarter of 19X4).
d. Land (purchased in 19X1).
e. Short-Term Note Payable to Shatha National Bank.
f. Capital Stock (no par or stated value and all issued in January 19X1).
g. Retained Earnings, January 1, 19X4.
h. Sales Revenue.
i. Depreciation Expense (on buildings).
j. Salaries Expense.

(AICPA adapted)

P14.7   **Prepare Consolidated Financial Statements with Purchased Foreign Subsidiary**   On January 1, 19X4, Phillips Company acquired 80 percent of the outstanding shares of Standard, Limited, a U.K. firm, for $10,000,000 cash. At the end of 19X4, the two companies presented the condensed financial statements appearing in Exhibit 14.13.

At date of acquisition, the exchange rate was $2/£. Standard's inventory and buildings were undervalued by £100,000 and £500,000, respectively. All of the undervalued inventory was sold during the year, and the buildings are being depreciated over a twenty-year life. Other relevant information is as follows:

1. The exchange rate at December 31, 19X4, was $2.30/£.

2. Standard's sales and other operating expenses occurred evenly during the year. The average exchange rate was $2.15/£.

3. Standard's inventory and goods sold were acquired when the exchange rate was $2.10/£.

4. Standard's plant assets were acquired when the exchange rate was $1.80/£.

5. Phillips' policy is to amortize intangibles over forty years.

6. Phillips carries its Investment in Standard at equity. However, the equity method accrual for 19X4 has not been booked and can be disregarded in this problem. Intercompany dividends, paid when the exchange rate was $2.10, were credited to the investment account.

Required: Prepare a consolidated balance sheet and a consolidated statement of income and retained earnings for Phillips and Standard. Neither a working paper nor formal working paper entries are required. All supporting computations should be in good form. Follow the provisions of *SFAS 8.*

P14.8   **Translated Financial Statements under Four Alternative Translation Methods**   The SA Company was organized in Mexico on January 5, 19X2, with a capital stock issue that yielded 1,000,000 pesos (P). Transactions engaged in during 19X2 and the relevant exchange rates follow:

Date	January 5, 19X2	June 30, 19X2	December 21, 19X2
Exchange rate	$.10/P	$.12/P	$.15/P
Transactions:	1. Buy 2,000 wood carvings at P200 each.	1. Sell 1,000 carvings for P300,000.	1. Record straight-line depreciation on office equipment.
	2. Purchase office equipment (10-year life) for P200,000.	2. Buy 1,500 carvings for P360,000.	2. Write-down the carvings bought on June 30 to market of P320,000.
		3. Pay rent of P30,000.	3. Close books and prepare financial statements.

Required: Using a schedule like the one presented in Exhibit 14.5 in the chapter, prepare translated balance sheets and income statements under the current/noncurrent, monetary/nonmonetary, temporal, and current rate translation methods. Show the calculation of the exchange translation gain or loss in each of the four methods.

P14.9   **Translation of Branch Accounts and Combined Trial Balance Working Paper**   Copra Trading Company established a foreign branch office in Arpoc Cay in 19X0 to purchase local products for resale by the home office and to sell company products.

Exhibit 14.14   Trial Balance Data to Be Used in P14.9

Copra Trading Company and Branch Office
Trial Balances
At December 31, 19X7

DEBITS	Branch Office (in Pesos)	Home Office (in Dollars)
Cash	P 110,000	$ 90,000
Trade Accounts Receivable	140,000	160,000
Branch Current Account	—	10,000
Inventory, January 1	80,000	510,000
Prepaid Expenses	10,000	18,000
Fixed Assets	1,000,000	750,000
Deferred Marketing Research	—	12,000
Purchases	488,889	3,010,000
Purchases from Home	711,111	—
Purchases from Branch	—	140,000
Operating and General Expenses	190,000	680,000
Depreciation Expense	100,000	50,000
Total Debits	P2,830,000	$5,430,000
CREDITS		
Allowance for Depreciation	P 650,000	$ 350,000
Current Liabilities	220,000	240,000
Home Office Current Account	50,000	—
Long-Term Debt	230,000	200,000
Capital Stock	—	300,000
Retained Earnings, January 1	—	142,500
Sales	1,057,778	4,035,000
Sales to Branch	—	120,000
Sales to Home	622,222	—
Overvaluation of Branch Inventory	—	42,500
Total Credits	P2,830,000	$5,430,000

You were engaged to examine the company's financial statements for the year ended December 31, 19X7, and engaged a chartered professional accountant in Arpoc to examine the branch office accounts. He reported that the branch accounts were fairly stated in pesos, the local currency, except a franchise fee, and any possible adjustments required by home office accounting procedures were not recorded. Trial balances for both the branch office and home office appear in Exhibit 14.14.

Your examination disclosed the following information:

1. The peso was devalued July 1, 19X7, from 4 pesos per $1 to 5 pesos per $1. The former rate of exchange had been in effect for ten years. Branch ending inventory and prepaid expenses were acquired after the devaluation.

2. Sales to the branch are marked up 33⅓ percent and shipped F.O.B. home office. Branch sales to home office are made at branch cost.

3. The branch had a beginning and ending inventory on hand valued at 80,000 pesos, of which one-half at each date had been purchased from the home office. The home office had an inventory at December 31, 19X7, valued at $520,000.

4. The Deferred Marketing Research is the unamortized portion of a $15,000 fee paid in January 19X6 to a U.S. firm for continuing marketing research for the branch. Currency restrictions prevented the branch from paying the fee, which was paid by the home office. The home office charges the branch $3,000 annually during the five-year amortization period and the branch records the expense.

5. The branch incurred its long-term indebtedness in 19X2 to finance its most recent purchase of fixed assets.

6. The government of Arpoc imposes a franchise fee of 10 pesos per 100 pesos of net income of the branch in exchange for certain exclusive trading rights granted. The fee is payable each May 1 for the preceding calendar year's trading rights and had not been recorded by the branch at December 31, 19X7.

Required: Prepare a combined trial balance working paper for Copra Trading Company and its foreign branch office with all amounts stated in U.S. dollars. Your working paper should have headings for: Branch Trial Balance (pesos); Translation Rate; Branch Trial Balance (dollars); Home Office Trial Balance; Adjustments and Eliminations; Combined Trial Balance. Ending inventories must be included and supporting computations must be in good form. Number the working paper adjusting and eliminating entries.

(AICPA adapted)

PART FOUR

GOVERNMENT
AND NONPROFIT
ENTITIES

The growth of the government and nonprofit sectors and their increasing importance in our economy lead us to devote four chapters to accounting for these entities. Our primary objective is to highlight the areas in which accounting and reporting for government and nonprofit entities differ from accounting and reporting for corporate business entities.

Chapter 15 provides an overview of the field of governmental accounting. In this introductory chapter, local, state, and federal levels of government are discussed as well as the overall economy. Because a good deal of practice centers around local government accounting, Chapters 16 and 17 are devoted to a detailed coverage of this subject. Recently, local government accounting has experienced changes in accounting and reporting standards; these new standards are discussed and illustrated. Each of the numerous accounting entities that exist in local government are considered. In Chapter 18, attention is given to the nongovernment, nonprofit entity. Although many types of nonprofit organizations exist, voluntary health and welfare organizations, colleges, and hospitals are given primary attention. Many of the accounting and reporting practices for these three types apply equally to other types of nonprofit organizations. Again, recent developments in this area of accounting are considered.

Chapter 15

Introduction to Governmental Accounting

Government, at all levels, is an increasingly important segment of the economy. As the scope and diversity of government services and programs expand, so too does the importance of governmental accounting and reporting. Governmental accounting and reporting practices differ from those of commercial enterprises. Legal considerations, organization objectives, and decentralization of control over resources create special reporting needs of government units. In this chapter, we examine how the entity concept applies to governmental accounting. We also discuss accounting and reporting principles for local, state, and federal levels of government, as well as for the national economy.

Accounting by Local Government

Since the level of government most frequently served by accountants is the local government, the first section of this chapter presents an overview of accounting principles for local government. Detailed accounting and reporting procedures will be discussed in Chapters 16 and 17.

The term **government unit** used in this section and in subsequent chapters refers to a local government unit. The accounting concepts and procedures discussed apply equally to towns, cities, counties, school districts, water districts, fire protection districts, and other local government units.

The Entity

A government unit constitutes one legal entity. We may, however, find additional legal entities within a government unit or overlapping it. For example, a school district may be a legally separate entity from a city or town, and the two may or may not geographically coincide. A municipality may contain "special districts"—legally separate entities which provide a particular service such as sewers, sidewalks, street lighting, or fire protection to a particular area. Each of these units—the city, the town, the school district, the fire district—constitutes a separate legal entity. Each is likely to have its own taxing authority, ability to issue debt, and other powers.

Initially, we focus on the legal entity as the one whose activities must be accounted for and reported to the taxpayers or other constituencies. *Within each legal entity, however, the concept of economic entity dominates.* In corporate accounting, the entity concept led to presentation of consolidated financial statements (one economic entity) for several corporations (separate legal entities). Conversely, following the economic entity concept in governmental accounting may lead to division of one legal entity (the government unit) into several economic or accounting entities called **funds.**

Clearly, the notion of an economic entity differs for business and local government. In the corporate context, the presence of common control over the affairs of several entities leads to the conclusion that one economic entity exists. In the context of local government, management control is influenced to a great extent by legal considerations. When several legal entities co-exist within a geographical area, there may be no common managerial control. The mayor of a city, for example, may have little or no control over a legally separate school district. Even within a single legal entity such as a city, not all control rests in the hands of management; laws of various types also exert considerable control. For example, a city's financial management may be influenced by:

1. The city charter.
2. Local ordinances.
3. State laws affecting city operations.
4. State or federal laws affecting the use of particular resources (for example, the federal revenue-sharing laws).
5. Bond covenants.

While legal considerations are not lacking in the corporate world, they are present and influential to a much greater degree in government.

Legislation and regulations define the ways in which resources may be spent, thus providing much of the legal control over government entities. It may be stipulated that resources derived from local property taxes be spent in certain ways, resources derived from a bond issue in other ways, and resources from federal revenue-sharing in yet other ways. One of the responsibilities of the management of local government is to ensure that resources are spent in the legally prescribed manners. This responsibility is often referred to as **stewardship,** meaning that management is entrusted with these resources by the community and must exercise certain specified responsibilities with respect to their use.

As a result of the stewardship concept, a single legal entity in local government is likely to be organized into several economic entities.

Each entity, called a **fund,** is defined as a set of resources that may be used for certain specified purposes or activities of the government unit.

The fact that there are different economic purposes and constraints related to resources results in the presence of several economic entities. Accounting focuses on these *economic entities*. The financial report of a government unit contains financial statements for each economic entity (fund) of the unit. In the local government context, therefore, the concept of economic entity leads to the presentation of multiple sets of financial statements for a single legal entity, whereas in the corporate context, the economic entity principle leads to a single set of statements for multiple legal entities.

The Eight Standard Funds

The affairs of a government unit may be organized into eight economic entities or funds. In a given local government unit, some or all of these **eight standard funds** will exist. We shall briefly describe each in terms of the source of its financial resources and the activities and purposes for which its resources are used. A city government is used as an example.

1. *General fund*—accounts for the basic services provided by city government, through the use of general revenue.
   a. Resources are derived from property taxes, sales taxes, general state aid, fees, fines, and so on.
   b. Resources are used for city administration, police, fire, courts, streets, parks, sanitation, and so on.

2. *Special revenue funds*—account for selected basic operations of the city, funded from special revenue sources.
   a. Resources are derived from state or federal aid for specific purposes (for example, federal revenue-sharing funds, which are limited to certain activities such as public safety); taxes levied for a certain purpose (for example, a school tax levied by a city), grants, and so on.
   b. Resources are used for the particular operations which are specified by the revenue source, as illustrated above.

3. *Capital projects funds*—account for the financing and construction or acquisition of major capital assets.
   a. Resources are derived primarily from proceeds of bond issues for specific projects; other sources may include state or federal aid, or allocation of general revenues (from general fund).
   b. Resources are used for construction or acquisition of buildings, major equipment, or public improvements such as roads, bridges, and sewer systems.

4. *Special assessment funds*—account for public improvements which are financed by specific assessments on property owners.
   a. Resources are derived from assessments on property owners who are served by the improvement, and allocation of general revenues (from general fund).
   b. Resources are used for construction or acquisition of improvements such as sewers, sidewalks, or street lighting.

5. ***Debt service funds***—account for the payment of principal and interest on the general long-term debt of the city.
   a. Resources are generally derived from transfers from other funds (the general fund or the capital projects fund) and from interest earned.
   b. Resources are used for payment of interest and principal; in some cases, resources are accumulated (and invested) in anticipation of future principal payments.

6. ***Enterprise funds***—account for certain business activities of a city in which goods or services are sold to the public, such as a city water department or a municipal golf course.
   a. Resources are derived from amounts charged to customers.
   b. Resources are used for operating expenses of the enterprise.

7. ***Internal service funds***—account for central services provided to other departments of the city; for example, a central supply unit which buys supplies in large quantities and issues them to various departments, a central vehicle maintenance shop, or a central computer center.
   a. Resources are derived from charges to other city departments; that is, transfers from other funds.
   b. Resources are used for operating expenses of the central service activities.

8. ***Trust and agency funds***—account for resources collected by the city on behalf of another entity and resources held by the city under a trust agreement.
   a. Resources are derived from collections on behalf of other entities, such as income taxes withheld from employees, and amounts received to be held in trust and used for a specific purpose, such as an endowment for the public library.
   b. Resources are used for transmittal of amounts collected to other entities, and for expenditures in accord with trust agreement.

These eight funds encompass all the activities of a city government. One (and only one) general fund will always exist. In the case of each of the other fund types, none, one, or several may exist. For example, if a city has no construction projects underway, a capital projects fund may not exist. On the other hand, if three projects are currently under construction, the city may use three capital projects funds or combine all three projects in one capital projects fund.

To further illustrate how the activities are structured into these eight funds, Exhibit 15.1 presents the fund structure of a typical school district. As noted earlier, some government units may not need all eight funds. There will, however, always be a general fund; this fund accounts for the basic operations of the government unit.

In summary, a local government consists of several economic entities. We next consider the general accounting principles applicable to these entities; later the typical financial statements for these entities are presented.

Exhibit 15.1   Fund Structure of a School District

Fund	Resources Derived From	Resources Used For
General	School tax; local, state, and federal aid; fees.	Administration, instruction, transportation, maintenance, debt service.
Special Revenue	Special state or federal aid (for example, Head Start Program).	Instruction and other costs related to specified program.
Capital Projects	Bond issues; state or federal aid, or transfers from general fund.	Construction, acquisition or renovation of school buildings; major equipment purchases (for example, fleet of buses).
Enterprise	Charges to customers of cafeteria, bookstore, and other enterprises; may be supplemented from other sources (for example, state aid for school lunch program).	Operating expenses of cafeteria, bookstore, or other enterprises.
Special Assessments	(Usually not applicable to a school district)	
Debt Service	Transfers from general or capital projects funds.	Payment of principal and interest.
Trust and Agency	Collections for others (for example, taxes withheld); gifts for specified purposes (for example, scholarship funds).	Transmittal of amounts collected; payment of scholarships.
Internal Service	Transfers from other funds for central services.	Costs of central services.

Accounting Principles for Local Government

As is the case with business accounting, accounting principles for local government have developed from several sources. While many principles and procedures have evolved from practice over the years, formal pronouncements have also played a role. Three major sources of pronouncements on accounting principles for local government exist: (1) the National Council on Governmental Accounting, (2) the American Institute of Certified Public Accountants, and (3) state governments.

National Council on Governmental Accounting   The National Council on Governmental Accounting (NCGA) has been the major standard-setting organization in the field of governmental accounting. The NCGA is sponsored and supported by the Municipal Finance Officers Association of the United States and Canada, a professional organization. For many years, the NCGA's book, *Governmental Accounting, Auditing, and Financial Reporting* (often referred to as *GAAFR* or the "blue book"), has served as the leading source of accounting principles for state and local government.[1] In 1979, *GAAFR* was restructured to become a series of official pronouncements. *Statement 1*, "Governmental Accounting and Financial Reporting Principles,"[2] covers the broad principles that underlie governmental accounting; subsequent statements deal with specific issues. For example, *Statement 2* is entitled "Grant, Entitlement, and Shared Revenue Accounting and Reporting by State and Local Governments."[3]

Other Sources   While the NCGA is the major source of principles for governmental accounting, it is not the only source. In 1974, the American Institute of Certified Public Accountants issued an audit guide entitled *Audits of State and Local Governmental Units.* In addition to establishing auditing standards, this document set forth accounting principles applicable to state and local governments. The principles set forth in this audit guide were influential in leading to some of the 1979 revisions in *GAAFR.* To date, the FASB has not taken any significant role in establishing governmental accounting standards, although it conceivably could become involved in the future.

Another source of accounting requirements is law or regulation. A state may specify certain accounting rules for all local government units within the state. In New York, for example, the State Department of Audit and Control has numerous accounting requirements to be followed by counties, cities, towns, school districts, and other units within the state. A possible future source of accounting principles for local government is the SEC. Local governments have been exempt from the reporting requirements of the securities laws. In recent years, however, concern over the solvency of municipalities has increased, accompanied by calls for registration and reporting requirements for municipal securities. Some municipalities have voluntarily issued formal prospectuses in response to these concerns. Increased regulation in this area appears likely.

Consideration is being given to the establishment of a Governmental Accounting Standards Board (GASB). Patterned after the FASB, this board would be responsible for issuing statements and interpretations on accounting and financial reporting by state and local government. At this writing, formation of a GASB is still in the discussion stage.

Types of Accounting for Funds   Differing characteristics of the economic entities in a local government require different types of accounting. In particular, business accounting, fiduciary accounting, and fund accounting are employed.

Business Accounting   Two of the eight funds—the enterprise fund and the internal service fund—conduct business activities and are sometimes referred to as **proprietary funds.** They sell goods and services either to the public or to

---

[1] Municipal Finance Officers Association of the United States and Canada, *Governmental Accounting, Auditing, and Financial Reporting* (Chicago: MFOA, 1980).

[2] National Council on Governmental Accounting, *Statement 1*, "Governmental Accounting and Financial Reporting Principles" (Chicago: MFOA, 1979).

[3] National Council on Governmental Accounting, *Statement 2* "Grant, Entitlement, and Shared Revenue Accounting and Reporting by State and Local Governments" (Chicago: MFOA, 1979).

units of the government. It is reasonable, therefore, that accrual accounting be applied to these funds as it is to commercial firms. Thus, for these two funds, the accounting procedures are already familiar. These funds will be discussed further in Chapter 17.

Fiduciary Accounting   The trust and agency funds hold and manage resources on behalf of others and are referred to as **fiduciary funds.** These resources may be amounts collected for transmittal to others or amounts held under some sort of formal trust agreement, to be used in a certain manner. Because fiduciary responsibilities exist, trust and agency funds generally use the same fiduciary accounting procedures presented in Chapter 4 for trusts and estates. We examine the application of fiduciary accounting to the trust and agency funds in Chapter 17.

Fund Accounting   The remaining five funds (general, special revenue, capital projects, special assessments, and debt service) are referred to as **governmental funds** and use a type of accounting known as **fund accounting.** The following sections discuss the various characteristics of this type of accounting.

Principles of Fund Accounting

Revenues and Expenditures   Fund accounting is concerned with changes in the resources available to each fund. Thus the focus is on accounting for the revenues and expenditures of each fund. In business accounting, revenues are amounts earned from the sale of goods and services. In fund accounting, **revenues** are inflows of resources, with no requirement that they be generated from the services provided by the government. Taxes, fees, and state aid all constitute revenues in fund accounting, but transfers from another fund and amounts borrowed are not considered revenues.

Since fund accounting is concerned with changes in resources, we are concerned with reporting **expenditures** (outflows of resources) rather than *expenses* (costs consumed in generating revenue or in delivering this period's goods and services). In fund accounting, payments for labor, materials, equipment, and repayment of debt all constitute expenditures.

Basis of Accounting   The emphasis on revenues and expenditures suggests that fund accounting would use cash-basis, rather than accrual-basis accounting. In fact, an in-between approach, known as a **modified accrual basis** (sometimes called a modified cash basis) **of accounting** is used.

Under the modified accrual approach, revenues are recognized when they become *measurable* and *available* (collectible within the current period or soon enough thereafter to be used to meet obligations of the current period). Some revenue items of a local government are assessed and collected in a manner that makes them subject to accrual, while others are not. Property taxes, for example, are accrued because (1) the total amount is known, since it is levied by the local government, (2) collection usually occurs within a short time, and (3) uncollectible amounts can be reasonably estimated. In many cases, grants from the state or federal government are also accrued. There are many revenue items of a local government that cannot be measured and recorded until they are actually collected; the cash basis is used for these items. Examples include traffic fines and sales and income taxes.

Generally, all expenditures are recorded on the accrual basis. The major exception is interest on general long-term debt and on special assessment fund debt. This interest is not accrued but is recorded when paid. Thus the modified accrual approach may be summarized as follows:

1. Some revenues are recorded on the accrual basis and other revenues are recorded on the cash basis.

2. All expenditures except certain interest payments are recorded on the accrual basis.

Budgetary Accounts   Accounting serves an important control function in local government—namely, to aid in ensuring that resources are spent in compliance with legal requirements. Legal restrictions on spending are usually expressed in the form of a **budget,** which prescribes both the total amount of spending allowed and the amounts in each expense category. A budget may be adopted by legislative/executive action (for example, passage by a city council and acceptance by a mayor) or by popular vote, as is the case with many school district budgets. Typically, any change in the total budget must be approved in the same way, while changes within the budget (transfers among budget components) usually require less formal approval (for example, a school board may approve budget transfers).

To aid in control of revenues and expenditures, *the budget is recorded in the accounts.* At the beginning of the year, the budgeted revenues and budgeted expenditures are entered in **budgetary accounts.** As actual revenues are received and resources are expended during the year, comparison with the budget is made regularly. This comparison helps to ensure that, in each category of the budget, actual spending does not exceed the authorized amount. Recording of budget data in the accounts is one of the key aspects of fund accounting.

Recording Purchase Orders   Budget data are recorded in the accounts to aid in maintaining control over expenditures. The budget establishes a legal spending limit, which must not be exceeded. Because of this constraint, it is important to know at any time not only the amount actually spent to date, but also the amount of unpaid bills and the amount of outstanding spending commitments. The amount of unpaid bills is handled conventionally by the use of accrual accounting (in governmental accounting, we use the term **vouchers payable** in place of accounts payable). We must, however, go beyond this to record outstanding spending commitments—contracts and purchase orders for goods and services yet to be delivered. When a purchase order is issued, the municipality commits some of its limited spending authority. If no record is kept, the danger exists that the government will overcommit itself and exceed the legal spending authority. Thus, purchase orders and other legally binding commitments for spending, known as **encumbrances** or **obligations,** are recorded in the accounts. The techniques for recording encumbrances are discussed in a subsequent section.

Fund Balance   Because a local government does not have owners, no stockholders' (or owners') equity is present. The equivalent of owners' equity in fund accounting is known simply as the **fund balance.** This account signifies the difference between the assets and liabilities of the entity. Portions of the fund balance are often "reserved" to signify a restriction on the spending of resources. Thus, total fund balance will consist of an *unreserved* portion, which signifies that assets are available for future spending, and one or more *reserves*, which signifies some limitation on the ability to spend.

Accounting for Fixed Assets and Long-Term Debt   For those entities in which fund accounting is used, fixed assets and long-term debt are generally absent from the balance sheet. These items are accounted for in special sets of accounts known as the **general fixed asset account group** and the **general long-term debt account group.** These two account groups are separate from the various funds and may contain items originating in several funds. They are not considered funds, since they have no resources to spend and no activities to carry out. These account groups will be fully discussed in Chapter 16.

Typical Entries in a Fund Accounting System

As mentioned earlier, the five governmental funds (general, special revenue, capital projects, special assessments, and debt service) use procedures known as **fund accounting.** As we discuss these five funds throughout the next two chapters, we will illustrate how fund accounting is applied to the particular activities and transactions of each fund. This task is made easier by first considering, in general terms, the typical entries of a fund accounting system. We will discuss the accounting for six major events or transactions. These six sets of entries will usually be present whenever fund accounting is used. The names of some accounts vary from one fund accounting system to another, but understanding the general entry type aids in coping with the varying terminology.

Entry 1: Recording the Budget   As mentioned earlier, the budget is recorded in the accounts to aid in controlling expenditures. A budget has two elements: planned revenues and planned expenditures. If the budget is *balanced*, these two amounts are equal, and the budget is recorded as:

Budgeted Revenues XX	
Budgeted Expenditures	XX

Budgeted Revenues is debited because it represents the expected inflow of resources to the fund (roughly analogous to receivables). Similarly, Budgeted Expenditures (often called Appropriations) is credited because it represents the expected outflow of resources from the fund (roughly analogous to payables). To illustrate, assume that expenditures of $800,000 are budgeted, and revenues are also expected to be $800,000. The budget entry would be:

Budgeted Revenues 800,000	
Budgeted Expenditures	800,000
To record budget for the year.	

It is not necessary that the budget be balanced in a particular fiscal period. A local government may plan to spend *less* than its anticipated revenue and thus to increase the net assets of the fund (which is called the Fund Balance). In this circumstance, the budget entry would show a credit to the fund balance. If revenues were expected to amount to $810,000, while expenditures were budgeted at $800,000, the unit is planning to increase its fund balance by $10,000 by spending less than it receives. The budget entry would be:

Budgeted Revenues	810,000	
Budgeted Expenditures		800,000
Fund Balance		10,000

To record budget for the year and planned increase in fund balance.

Alternatively, a local government may plan to spend *more* than its anticipated revenue, using resources accumulated in previous periods. The budget entry in this case would have a debit to the fund balance. If revenues were expected to amount to only $785,000, while expenditures were budgeted at $800,000, the unit is planning to decrease its fund balance by spending more than it receives this year. The budget entry would be:

Budgeted Revenues	785,000	
Fund Balance	15,000	
Budgeted Expenditures		800,000

To record budget for the year and planned decrease in fund balance.

The debit or credit to Fund Balance in the above entries signifies a planned decrease or increase in the unreserved portion of the fund balance. In subsequent entries, therefore, we designate this account as *Fund Balance—Unreserved*.

"Budgeted Revenues" and "Budgeted Expenditures" have been used here as generic titles, to illustrate the concept of the budget entry. As accounting for special funds is considered in subsequent chapters, more specific account titles will be employed in the budget entry. It is important to recognize, however, that while the account titles may vary from one fund to another, the concept of a budget entry remains the same.

Note that after the budget is recorded, the fund balance account shows the expected *year-end balance*. In the preceding example, where budgeted revenues were $785,000 and budgeted expenditures were $800,000, assume that the fund balance at the beginning of the year was $500,000. After the budget is recorded, the fund balance is $485,000. If the budgeted figures are achieved, $485,000 will be the amount of fund balance at the end of the year.

Entry 2: Recognizing Revenues   Under the modified accrual approach used in fund accounting, some revenues are recorded on the accrual basis, while others are recorded on the cash basis. The general forms of the entries are:

Receivables	XX	
Revenues		XX

for revenues recorded on the accrual basis and

Cash	XX	
Revenues		XX

for revenues recorded on the cash basis. Note that the account Revenues signifies the actual amount of revenues, as distinct from the estimated amount recorded in the Budgeted Revenues account. *Control accounts* are generally used in fund accounting. All revenues are credited to a single control account, and a subsidiary ledger is maintained on a detailed basis.

Entry 3: Issuing Purchase Orders   As discussed earlier, purchase orders are recorded in fund accounting, so that all commitments of resources are reflected in the accounts. Commitments in the form of outstanding purchase orders are known as **encumbrances.** At the time a purchase order is placed, the following entry is made:

Encumbrances .	. . . .	XX
Reserve for Encumbrances	. . . .	XX

The debit to Encumbrances represents a commitment of the fund's limited spending authority; it will become an expenditure when the goods or services are delivered. The credit to Reserve for Encumbrances represents a restriction of the fund balance. It signifies that, because of this commitment, the freedom to spend resources of the fund has been reduced. It is not yet a liability because the goods and services have not yet been delivered. The encumbrance entry is a temporary one. It is recorded when the purchase order is issued and is reversed when the goods or services are delivered.

For example, assume that a city places an order for office supplies on March 18, with the expected cost of the supplies being $18,500. To formally record this commitment, the following entry is made on March 18:

Encumbrances	. . . .	18,500
Reserve for Encumbrances	. . . .	18,500
To record purchase order for office supplies.		

This entry signifies that $18,500 of the office supplies budget has been committed. Suppose that the office supplies budget is $42,000 and that $8,000 has previously been spent. Recording the encumbrance of $18,500 on March 18 tells the management of the city that only $15,500 of the office supplies budget still remains:

Original Budget for Office Supplies	$42,000
Expended to Date	8,000
Unexpended Balance	$34,000
Outstanding Purchase Order	18,500
Uncommitted Balance	$15,500

Entry 4: Expenditures   When goods or services are received, an expenditure is recorded, following the modified accrual approach. If an encumbrance was previously recorded when these goods or services were ordered, we first reverse that entry:

Reserve for Encumbrances	. . . .	XX
Encumbrances .	. . . .	XX

The reversal signifies that the purchase order is no longer outstanding.

The expenditure is then recorded:

Expenditures .	. . . .	XX
Vouchers Payable	. . . .	XX

Expenditures is a control account; subsidiary ledgers are maintained for particular expenditure items. As noted earlier, *vouchers payable* is commonly used in place of *accounts payable* in fund accounting.

Continuing the example, assume that on June 3 the office supplies ordered on March 18 are delivered, accompanied by an invoice for $18,650. Two entries are required: (1) the previously recorded encumbrance must be reversed, and (2) the expenditure must be recorded.

Reserve for Encumbrances	18,500	
Encumbrances		18,500
To reverse encumbrance entry; goods delivered.		
Expenditures	18,650	
Vouchers Payable		18,650
To record cost of office supplies.		

It is not necessary that the amount of the encumbrance and the amount of the expenditure be equal. At the time the purchase order was placed, the exact cost of the goods or services may not have been determinable, and so an estimate may have been used. Note that the reversing entry is based on the amount previously encumbered ($18,500), while the expenditure entry is based on the actual cost ($18,650).

Entry 5: Cash Receipts and Payments These entries are straightforward. When the revenues previously accrued are collected, we make the following entry:

Cash	XX	
Receivables		XX

and when the expenditures previously accrued are paid, we record that payment as:

Vouchers Payable	XX	
Cash		XX

As noted earlier, when revenues accounted for on the cash basis are received, the entry is:

Cash	XX	
Revenues		XX

Similarly, if expenditures are paid without having been recorded as vouchers payable, the entry is:

Expenditures	XX	
Cash		XX

Entry 6: Closing Entries When closing entries are prepared at the end of the reporting period, both the *budgetary* accounts and the *actual* accounts must be closed. All closing entries are made to the Fund Balance. While a single combined closing entry is possible, use of two closing entries—one for revenues and the other for expenditures—aids in understanding the process.

As noted earlier, the fund balance of a government entity usually consists of an unreserved portion and one or more reserves. Closing entries are made to the unreserved portion. To close revenues, we must close both Budgeted Revenues (debit balance) and Revenues (credit balance) to the Unreserved Fund Balance. This may result in either a debit or a credit to Unreserved Fund Balance. A debit results if actual revenues are less than budgeted:

```
Revenues  .   .   .   .   .   .   .   .   .   .   .   .   .   . XX
Fund Balance—Unreserved   .   .   .   .   .   .   .   .   . XX
   Budgeted Revenues   .   .   .   .   .   .   .   .   .   .              XX
```

If actual revenues exceed the budget, Unreserved Fund Balance is credited.

If, at the end of the period, there are no outstanding purchase orders, we close Expenditures (debit balance) and Budgeted Expenditures (credit balance) to the Unreserved Fund Balance. In the case where actual expenditures are less than the amount budgeted, the entry is:

```
Budgeted Expenditures   .   .   .   .   .   .   .   .   .   . XX
   Expenditures  .   .   .   .   .   .   .   .   .   .   .   .             XX
   Fund Balance—Unreserved   .   .   .   .   .   .   .   .             XX
```

If actual expenditures exceed the budget, Unreserved Fund Balance is debited.

To illustrate, assume that budgeted revenues were $785,000 and budgeted expenditures were $800,000, and that actual revenues amounted to $787,000, while actual expenditures amounted to $791,000. The closing entries would be:

```
Revenues  .   .   .   .   .   .   .   .   .   .   . 787,000
   Budgeted Revenues  .   .   .   .   .   .   .                785,000
   Fund Balance—Unreserved  .   .   .   .   .                   2,000
To close revenues and budgeted revenues to fund
balance.

Budgeted Expenditures  .   .   .   .   .   .   . 800,000
   Expenditures  .   .   .   .   .   .   .   .                 791,000
   Fund Balance—Unreserved  .   .   .   .   .                   9,000
To close expenditures and budgeted expenditures to
fund balance.
```

As a result of these entries, the fund balance is increased by $11,000, because actual revenues exceeded the budget by $2,000, and actual expenditures were $9,000 less than planned. Recall that the budget entry at the beginning of the year was:

```
Budgeted Revenues  .   .   .   .   .   .   .   . 785,000
Fund Balance—Unreserved  .   .   .   .   .   .  15,000
   Budgeted Expenditures .   .   .   .   .   .   .              800,000
To record budget for the year and planned decrease in
fund balance.
```

While the fund balance was expected to decrease by $15,000, it actually decreased by only $4,000.

	Budgeted	Actual	Variance
Revenues	$785,000	$787,000	$ (2,000)
Expenditures	(800,000)	(791,000)	(9,000)
Change in Fund Balance . . .	$ (15,000)	$ (4,000)	$(11,000)

Note that the $15,000 debit to the fund balance in the budget entry and the $11,000 total credits to the fund balance in the closing entries together account for the $4,000 decrease during the year.

It is possible that outstanding purchase orders will exist at the end of the period. They are closed in the same manner as expenditures. In the case where actual expenditures plus encumbrances are less than budgeted expenditures, the closing entry is:

Budgeted Expenditures XX
    Expenditures   XX
    Encumbrances   XX
    Fund Balance—Unreserved   XX

Notice that the Reserve for Encumbrances is not closed. This account, which constitutes a reserved portion of the total fund balance, carries into the next time period. Accounting for the carryover of outstanding purchase orders will be discussed in Chapter 16.

Financial Statements for a Fund Accounting System

Since different types of accounting are used by the various fund entities, there are also variations in the financial statements presented. As each fund is discussed in Chapters 16 and 17, the specific financial statements for each will be given. For the present, we discuss the topic in general terms for entities which use fund accounting.

Balance Sheet   The **balance sheet** presents the assets, liabilities, and fund balance. As mentioned earlier, fixed assets and long-term debt are generally excluded from the fund's balance sheet and reported elsewhere. The fund's balance sheet therefore is limited to current assets (cash, temporary investments, receivables, and in some cases inventories), current liabilities, and fund balance. The general format of this statement appears as follows:

ASSETS:	LIABILITIES:
Cash	Vouchers Payable
Investments	Due to Other Funds
Receivables	
Due from Other Funds	**FUND BALANCE:**
	Reserved for _____
	Unreserved
Total Assets	Total Liabilities and Fund Balance

Statement of Revenues, Expenditures, and Changes in Fund Balance
The **statement of revenues, expenditures, and changes in fund balance** presents the revenues and expenditures of the period, along with other changes in the fund balance. The general format of this statement is as follows:

>   Revenues
> − Expenditures
> = Excess of Revenues over (under) Expenditures
> +/− Other Financing Sources or Uses (such as proceeds of bond issues and transfers to or from other funds)
> = Excess of Revenues and Other Sources over (under) Expenditures and Other Uses
> + Fund Balance—Beginning of Period
> = Fund Balance—End of Period

The fund balance referred to in this statement is the total fund balance, including any reserved portions.

In addition to the statement of revenues, expenditures, and changes in fund balance, a parallel statement showing the comparison between budget and actual data is presented. The format of the **budgetary comparison statement** is identical to the format of the statement of revenues, expenditures, and changes in fund balance, except that three columns of numbers are presented: budget, actual, and variance.

The Comprehensive Annual Financial Report The main financial report of a local governmental unit is known as a **comprehensive annual financial report (CAFR).** Two broad types of financial statements are included in the CAFR. One type is combined statements. **Combined statements,** as the name suggests, bring together information on several funds. The purpose is to provide an overview of the financial affairs of the government unit by combining some or all of the economic entities that comprise the unit. The following combined statements are presented:

1. Combined balance sheet covering all funds and account groups.
2. Combined statement of revenue, expenditures, and changes in fund balance for all *governmental* funds.
3. Budgetary comparison statements for the *general* and *special revenue* funds, and for any other *governmental* funds for which annual budgets have been legally adopted.
4. Combined statement of revenues, expenses, and changes in retained earnings for all *proprietary* funds.
5. Combined statement of changes in financial position for all *proprietary* funds.

Fiduciary funds are typically included either with the governmental funds (in item 2) or the proprietary funds (in items 4 and 5), although a separate combined statement may be prepared for the fiduciary funds.

A *combined* statement is different from a *consolidated* statement. A consolidated statement is based on the principle that one economic entity exists. To prepare a consolidated statement, transactions and relationships among the component entities are eliminated. For a combined statement, however, no eliminations are made. Several economic entities continue to exist but are reported together.

The second broad type of financial statement included in the CAFR is individual or combining statements. **Individual statements** are presented for the two *account groups*—general fixed assets and general long-term debt—and for any of the eight fund types containing only *one* fund account. **Combining statements** are presented where the government unit has *more than one* fund of a given type. For example, if three capital projects funds exist, a combining statement would show the accounts of each of the three along with totals.

In addition to these two sets of statements, the CAFR contains the independent auditor's report, notes to the financial statements, schedules providing further details on statement data, and statistical information, such as ten-year summaries of key accounting and tax data.

Thus the comprehensive annual financial report resolves the problem of presenting financial data on a government unit consisting of numerous economic entities by presenting two sets of statements. Combined statements focus on the overall status of the government unit, while individual and combining statements focus on the individual entities.

Disclosure   Disclosure by local government has lagged significantly behind disclosure by business firms. In a research study[4] published in 1976 by Coopers and Lybrand and the University of Michigan, covering forty-six cities, it was found that compliance with then-existing disclosure requirements was seriously deficient. Selected findings of this study are as follows:

Disclosure Requirement	Percent of Cities Not Complying
Disclosure of any excess of value of vested pension benefits over annual pension fund resources plus accruals	76%
Disclosure of accrued vacation and sick leave by employees	84
Disclosure of information on noncapitalized lease commitments	93
Disclosure of significant accounting policies	46

The revision of *GAAFR* in 1979 clarified the disclosure requirements for local government. Disclosure involves three components of the CAFR: notes to the financial statements, narrative information, and statistical tables. Notes to the financial statements must contain information necessary for fair presentation at the combined statements level, such as:

1.   Summary of significant accounting policies.
2.   Pension plan obligations.
3.   Accumulated unpaid employee benefits.
4.   Debt service requirements to maturity.
5.   Contingent liabilities and commitments such as noncapitalized leases and construction contracts.
6.   Interfund receivables and payables.
7.   Material violations of finance-related legal or contractual provisions.

Narrative information includes a description of the nature and purpose of the various funds, and such other information as may be required to understand the individual or combining statements. Statistical tables typically cover several years and include nonaccounting data. Examples of statistical tables include:

1.   General government expenditures by function and revenues by source —last ten years.
2.   Property tax levies and collections—last ten years.
3.   Assessed property values and tax rates—last ten years.
4.   Legal debt limit.
5.   Demographic statistics.

---

[4] Coopers & Lybrand and The University of Michigan, *Financial Disclosure Practices of the American Cities: A Public Report* (N.Y.: Coopers & Lybrand, 1976), pp. 30–33.

Accounting by State Government

Accounting and reporting principles for state government are less well developed than those for local government. There are many fewer units—fifty states compared to thousands of counties, cities, towns, villages, and school districts. While local government reports are routinely submitted to the states, states are not required to report to the federal government. Each state's financial report is directed to the citizens of the state. Moreover, a given state's system has evolved from its particular laws, regulations, and historical practices. As a result, there is considerable variety in state accounting and reporting.

State government accounting tends to be similar to local government accounting. The fund system and related accounting principles described in the preceding sections are generally applicable to state government. Therefore we will not discuss the mechanics of accounting and reporting at the state level. We will, however, briefly discuss the entity issue.

As is the case in local government, state government consists of a variety of subunits. In addition to the usual offices and agencies of the executive, legislative, and judicial branches of the state, there are also various boards, institutions (such as state hospitals and universities) and authorities (such as bridge or port authorities). Some of these may be semi-autonomous in that their management possesses such powers as the ability to issue bonds. For financial reporting purposes, it must be determined whether each of these subunits is a separate entity or a component of the state entity. The Council of State Governments has been working on the development of suggested accounting practices for state governments. In its issue paper, "Definition of Reporting Entity for State Government General Purpose Financial Reports," it offers this tentative entity definition:

> The reporting entity for general purpose financial reports of state government requires the inclusion of any governmental department, agency, institution, commission or other governmental organization for which the elected state officials have oversight responsibility. Oversight responsibility is derived from the state's power and includes, but is not limited to: selection of governing authority, designation of management, ability to significantly influence operations, accountability for fiscal matters, or scope of public service.[5]

If at least one of the five indicators of state oversight responsibility is clearly present, the unit in question should be considered as part of the state for reporting purposes.

As noted above, no clear source of accounting principles for state government exists. Usually, however, we look to the same sources as for local government, namely the NCGA, and to some extent the AICPA. The State Government Accounting Project of the Council of State Governments, cited above, is currently working to develop recommendations as to preferred accounting practices for state governments. This group does not view itself as a standard-setting body. Rather, it will submit its recommendations to the NCGA or another appropriate standard-setting body.

---

[5] Council of State Governments, State Government Accounting Project, "Definition of Reporting Entity for State Government General Purpose Financial Reports" (Lexington, Ky.: Council of State Governments, 1980), p. 8.

Accounting by the Federal Government

Accounting at the federal level differs in several ways from state and local government accounting. In this section, we discuss the financial organization and operations of the federal government and illustrate the recording of transactions and financial reporting.

Financial Organization

As is generally true of government at any level, the budgeting process is the first step in the sequence of financial operations for the federal government. The executive branch prepares a budget request and submits it to Congress. Following hearings and deliberation, Congress adopts a budget, which the president may sign or veto. Once a budget is approved, various agencies are involved in its administration and other aspects of the financial management of the government. We shall briefly discuss each agency.[6]

Office of Management and Budget The Office of Management and Budget (OMB) was established in 1970 as the successor to the Bureau of the Budget. Its major functions are:

1. To assist the president in the preparation of the budget and the formulation of the fiscal program of the government.

2. To supervise and control administration of the budget.

3. To assist the president in his effort to develop and maintain effective government by reviewing the organizational structures and management procedures of the executive branch to assure that they are capable of producing the intended results.

4. To evaluate the performance of federal programs and to serve as a catalyst in the effort to improve interagency and intergovernmental cooperation and coordination.

5. To assist the president by clearing and coordinating departmental advice on proposed legislation and recommendations for presidential action on bills passed by the Congress.

6. To assist in the consideration, clearance, and where necessary, the preparation of executive orders and proclamations.

7. To help develop regulatory reform proposals and programs for paperwork reduction.

8. To keep the president advised of the progress of activities by agencies with respect to those proposed, actually initiated, and completed. This, together with the relative timing of interagency activities, is necessary to assure that programs are coordinated and that money appropriated by the Congress is spent effectively, with the least possible overlapping and duplication.

9. To provide overall direction of procurement policies, regulations, and procedures for executive agencies.

OMB is headed by a director, a position which is viewed as cabinet-level.

---

[6] The agency descriptions are drawn from "Financial Management Functions in the Federal Government" published by the Joint Financial Management Improvement Program (sponsored by various federal agencies), August 1979.

Department of the Treasury   The Department of the Treasury has existed since 1789. Its head, the Secretary of the Treasury, has general responsibility for managing the government's finances. These responsibilities fall into two main areas: financial and accounting. In operating the federal financial system, the Department of the Treasury's major functions are:

1.   As the nation's treasurer, the department receives and disburses funds. Bank accounts are maintained at the Federal Reserve Bank and at thousands of private banks throughout the country.

2.   The department is the agency responsible for borrowing money necessary to meet operating obligations and for coordinating the debt activities of various federal agencies.

3.   The department is the federal government's banker. While operating through the private and Federal Reserve banks, checks are actually drawn on the U.S. Treasury. In addition, reconciliation functions are performed by the Treasury Department.

4.   The department is responsible for the physical production of money. It operates the Bureau of Engraving and Printing, which produces paper currency, and the Bureau of the Mint, which produces coin.

In addition to these financial functions, the Treasury maintains central accounting records on the government's financial transactions. These central accounts do not constitute a complete general ledger of all the government's assets and liabilities; rather they reflect those assets and liabilities directly related to cash operations (receipts, expenditures, borrowings, and so on). The accounts are maintained on the basis of reports from agencies as to deposits made and checks issued, and reports from the Federal Reserve system and other banks as to deposits received and checks paid. The Treasury also maintains subsidiary records for each federal agency.

The Treasury prepares certain financial reports which relate to the operations of the government as a whole. The major reports are:

1.   Daily Treasury Statement, showing cash and public debt transactions.

2.   Monthly Statement of the Public Debt of the United States.

3.   Monthly Treasury Statement of Receipts and Outlays of the United States Government, which includes the budget surplus or deficit.

4.   Annual Treasury Combined Statement of Receipts, Expenditures, and Balances of the United States Government.

Office of Personnel Management   The Office of Personnel Management (OPM) was established in 1978 to assume some of the functions formerly performed by the Civil Service Commission. The OPM has broad responsibility for managing the personnel function within the federal government, including responsibility for:

1.   Recruiting and examination of prospective employees.

2.   Managing the federal compensation and fringe benefit system.

3.   Employee relations, merit programs, discipline, affirmative action programs, and other areas of labor-management relations.

Other than its involvement in benefit programs such as retirement, life insurance, and health benefits, the OPM has limited involvement in financial management functions.

General Services Administration   The General Services Administration (GSA) was established in 1949 to provide property management services for the federal government. Its major functions include:

1.   Planning, acquisition, and management of public buildings.
2.   Inventory management.
3.   Management of the government's transportation equipment (for example, interagency motor pool).
4.   Management of the government's data processing and communications services.

Thus the GSA is responsible for management and reporting on the government's noncash assets.

General Accounting Office   The General Accounting Office (GAO) was established in 1921 as an agency of Congress. While the four agencies discussed previously are part of the executive branch of government, the GAO (and the two other agencies still to be discussed) are part of the legislative branch.

Under the direction of the comptroller general, the GAO has the following principal functions:

1.   Auditing the programs, activities, and financial transactions of the federal government and its agencies. Included in a GAO audit are examination of accounting records, examination of compliance with laws and regulations, reviews of the efficiency and economy of operations, and evaluation of the effectiveness of programs in light of desired results and legislative objectives.
2.   Establishing accounting principles, standards, and procedures for the federal government and reviewing agency accounting systems.
3.   Special studies for congressional committees or individual members of Congress.
4.   Settlement of claims by and against the federal government and collection of accounts owed to the government.

Congressional Budget Office   The Congressional Budget Office (CBO) was established in 1974 to provide Congress with budget-related information and analyses of alternative fiscal, budgetary, and programmatic policies. The CBO does not have direct management responsibilities; it is concerned with budgetary estimates and analysis.

Cost Accounting Standards Board   The Cost Accounting Standards Board (CASB) was established in 1970 to create uniform and consistent cost accounting policies in the federal government. Its major impact is on government contractors, who must follow the standards set by the CASB in any cost-plus or cost-reimbursement contracts with the federal government. Individual federal agencies must ensure that their contracts with external parties comply with the board's standards and procedures.

Fund Accounts

The accounts of the federal government are organized into several fund types. **General fund accounts** are used for receipts from general taxing and operating sources which are not dedicated to specific purposes and for expenditures arising from congressional authorization to spend general revenues. **Special fund accounts** are used for receipts earmarked by law for a specific purpose. **Revolving fund accounts** are used when there is a continuing cycle of operations, with continuing authority to spend receipts. **Management fund accounts** are used for intragovernmental activities. All of the above involve resources which are derived from the government's general taxing and revenue powers and from its business operations. In addition, **trust fund accounts** and **deposit fund accounts** are used where the federal government holds funds as a trustee or custodian.

Rather than illustrate the entire range of fund accounting for the federal government, we focus primarily on the accounting records maintained by a typical federal agency. Most often, an agency is included within the general fund, although it could be included elsewhere. For our discussions, we assume a general fund agency.

Financial Operations of a Federal Agency

Suppose that the Federal Seaweed Control Agency is appropriated $3,000,000 in the federal budget for the fiscal year 19X5–19X6 passed by Congress and signed by the President. This **appropriation** by Congress must undergo two more steps before the agency may spend resources. The executive branch, as represented by the Office of Management and Budget, must apportion the funds to the department in which the agency is located. This **apportionment** of funds is often done on a quarterly basis, to control the timing of spending by the agency. Moreover, some of the appropriated amount may not be apportioned; it may be held in reserve to cover unanticipated events. In our example, suppose the OMB apportions the $3,000,000 appropriation as follows:

First Quarter	$ 650,000
Second Quarter	700,000
Third Quarter	800,000
Fourth Quarter	700,000
Total Apportionment	$2,850,000
Reserve	150,000
Total Appropriation	$3,000,000

One further step remains; the agency head must allot the resources to operating officials. If, for example, there were several programs within the agency, the **allotment** would divide the resources among the various programs. At this point, the operating officials are able to obligate resources—to make spending commitments or **obligations** (these were called *encumbrances* in the local government context).

Budget Entries Because three steps are involved in providing spending authority to the agency—Congress, the OMB, and the agency head—three budget entries are needed. The first entry by the agency records the appropriation by Congress:

```
Fund Balance with U.S. Treasury  .    .    .    .    . 3,000,000
     Unapportioned Appropriations .    .    .    .    .                3,000,000
To record appropriation by Congress.
```

This entry signifies that the agency can potentially draw on $3,000,000 from the Treasury to pay its bills. Note, however, that this appropriation is as yet unapportioned by the OMB.

The second entry by the agency records the apportionment by the OMB for the first quarter of the year:

```
Unapportioned Appropriations .    .    .    .    .    . 650,000
     Unallotted Apportionments .    .    .    .    .    .                650,000
To record first quarter apportionment by OMB.
```

Subsequent apportionments are recorded later in the year, at the beginning of each quarter.

The third entry records the allotment by the agency head. Assuming that $200,000 is allotted to program A and $450,000 to program B, the entry is:

```
Unalloted Apportionments .    .    .    .    .    .    . 650,000
     Unobligated Allotments—Program A  .    .    .    .                200,000
     Unobligated Allotments—Program B  .    .    .    .                450,000
To record allotments to programs for first quarter.
```

As a result of these three budget entries, the manager of program A has $200,000 of first-quarter spending authority, and the manager of program B has $450,000.

Transaction Entries   As was discussed for local government accounting, an entry is made when a legal commitment to spend resources occurs. These commitments, known as **obligations** in federal accounting, arise from purchase orders, contracts, and the like. Suppose that, during July 19X5, program A incurs obligations of $76,150. These transactions are recorded in detail in an allotment ledger, as illustrated in Exhibit 15.2. At the end of July, the general ledger of the agency is updated by the following entry:

```
Unobligated Allotments—Program A.    .    .    .    . 76,150
     Unliquidated Obligations .    .    .    .    .    .    .                76,150
To record obligations incurred during July.
```

When recorded obligations are reversed, they are said to be **liquidated.** Suppose that, during July, obligations of $41,150 are liquidated, resulting in expenditures of $41,600. The details are recorded in the allotment ledger (see Exhibit 15.2), and the following entries are made in the general ledger:

```
Unliquidated Obligations .    .    .    .    .    .    . 41,150
     Unobligated Allotments—Program A .    .    .    .                41,150
To record obligations liquidated during July.

Unobligated Allotments—Program A.    .    .    .    . 41,600
     Expended Appropriations .    .    .    .    .    .    .                41,600
To record expenditure of appropriations during July.
```

In addition to the allotment ledger, which maintains a record of commitments of allotted funds, an accrued expenditures register is maintained to re-

Exhibit 15.2   Illustration of Allotment Ledger

COLUMN 8

Enter original allotments, allotment increases or withdrawals as evidenced by allotment advices.

COLUMN 9

Balances should be extended after each transaction or group of transactions is posted. The arithmetical effect on the balance in column 9 of the entries in columns 5 through 8 is as follows:
Column 5—Minus
Column 6—Plus
Column 7—Minus
Column 8—Plus

COLUMN 7

The amount of the obligations supported by purchase orders, contracts, and other obligation documents is entered in this column. Amounts entered in this column effect a decrease in the Unobligated Balance of Allotment.

COLUMN 6

The amount of the obligation previously entered as an "Obligation Incurred" is entered in this column. For partial liquidations of obligations, the amount of the accrued expenditure column by the same amount. Amounts in this column effect an increase in the Unobligated Balance of Allotment.

COLUMN 5

Enter amounts of accrued expenditures from expenditure vouchers or posting data sheets. Refunds are entered in this column as "red" or negative entries and they increase the Unobligated Balance of Allotment column by the same amount. Accrued expenditures for which no obligating documents have been issued are entered in this column and they decrease the Unobligated Balance of Allotments column by the same amount.

COLUMN 4

Enter for each accrued expenditure. If more than one object class involved, enter separately and bracket.

COLUMN 3

Titles of documents, names of vendors or creditors, or other description to explain the transaction.

COLUMN 2

Refer to the document file number. Where documents are summarized in block posting refer to the number assigned to the block posting document.

COLUMN 1

The dates in this column are the dates the transactions are entered in this ledger, regardless of the dates of the documents.

COLUMN 5

Totals for the fiscal year must equal the balance in General Ledger account "Expended Appropriations." Current month totals must agree with totals of Accounts to be Credited columns in Accrued Expenditures Register (Exhibit 15.3).

ALLOTMENT LEDGER

SHEET NO. 1

ALLOTMENT 100 SALARIES AND EXPENSES
DIVISION OR ACTIVITY OPERATIONS

DATE OF ENTRY	REFERENCE	DESCRIPTION	OBJECT CLASS	ACCRUED EXPENDITURES	OBLIGATIONS LIQUIDATED	OBLIGATIONS INCURRED	ALLOTMENTS	UNOBLIGATED BALANCE OF ALLOTMENTS
1	2	3	4	5	6	7	8	9
19X5 JULY 7	A.M. 1	ADVICE OF ALLOTMENT					250,000.00	250,000.00
8	M.D.R. 1	ESTIMATED PAYROLL FOR JULY				74,700.00		175,300.00
11	P.O. 1	EMPLOYER'S SHARE OF FICA AND INSURANCE				600.00		174,700.00
11	P.O. 3	FEDERAL SUPPLY SERVICE				350.00		174,350.00
11	T.R. 165	FELT AND TARRANT JOHN DOE TRANSPORTATION REQUEST				250.00		174,100.00
11	V.O. 1	PAYROLL NO. 1 7/1-7/2	01	9,700.00	9,700.00			173,850.00
		EMPLOYER'S SHARE OF FICA AND INSURANCE				250.00		173,850.00
20	V.O. 2	FELT AND TARRANT	15	300.00	300.00			173,850.00
			09	200.00	250.00			173,900.00
25	V.O. 2	PAYROLL NO. 2 7/3-7/16 EMPLOYER'S SHARE OF FICA AND INSURANCE	01	30,000.00	30,000.00			173,900.00
26	V.O. 4	FEDERAL SUPPLY SERVICE	15	300.00	300.00			173,900.00
27	V.O. 9	JOHN DOE-TRAVEL EXP	08	500.00	350.00			173,750.00
29	A.A. 2	ALLOTMENT OF JULY REIMBURSEMENTS	02	450.00	250.00		300.00	173,550.00 173,850.00
29	V.O. 6	REFUND OVERPAYMENT VO. 4	09	(50.00)				173,900.00
29	V.O. 7	A.T.&T CO. JULY TEL. BILL	04	200.00				173,700.00
		TOTALS CURRENT MONTH		41,600.00	41,150.00	76,150.00	250,300.00	173,700.00
		TOTALS SUBSEQUENT MONTHS		788,400.00	748,850.00	823,850.00	749,700.00	
		TOTALS FISCAL YEAR (ASSUME)		830,000.00	790,000.00	900,000.00	1,000,000.00	60,000.00
		FISCAL YEAR CLOSING		(830,000.00)	(790,000.00)	(790,000.00)	(830,000.00)	
		TRANSFER TO ALLOTMENT LEDGER FOR NEXT FISCAL YR.		110,000.00		110,000.00	170,000.00	60,000.00

JOURNAL ENTRY FOR MONTHLY CLOSING OF ALLOTMENT LEDGER:

Unobligated Allotments	76,150	
Unliquidated Obligations		76,150
Unliquidated Obligations	41,150	
Unobligated Allotments		41,150
Unobligated Allotments	41,600	
Expended Appropriations		41,600
To close Allotment Ledger for July		

Source: *Accounting Systems of U.S. Government Agencies*, compiled by Thomas R. Canada (Washington, D.C.: Graduate School Press, U.S. Department of Agriculture, 1968), p. 5–3.

Exhibit 15.3 Illustration of Accrued Expenditures Register

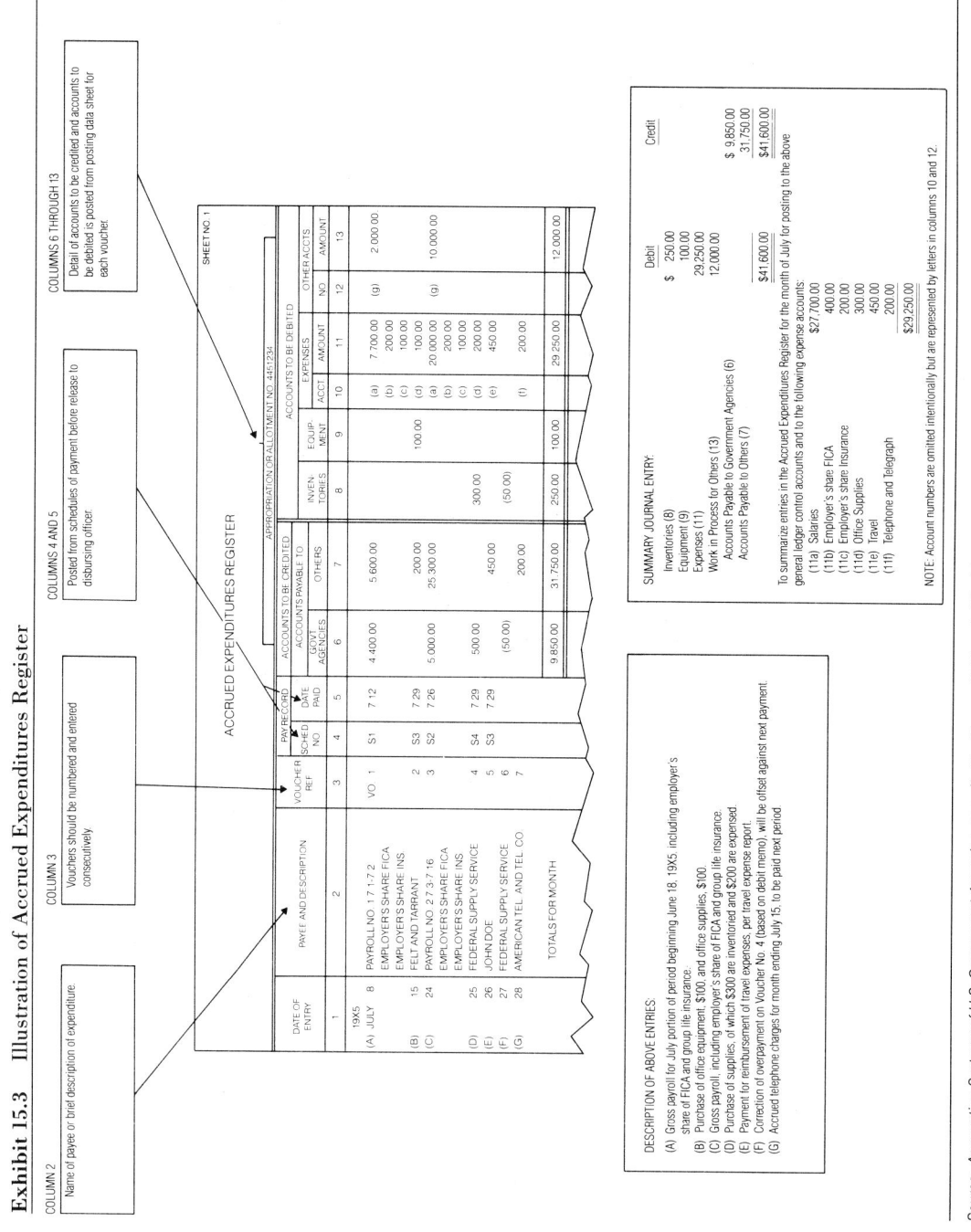

Source: *Accounting Systems of U.S. Government Agencies*, compiled by Thomas R. Canada (Washington, D.C.: Graduate School Press, U.S. Department of Agriculture, 1968), p. 5–11.

cord the details of expenditures (see Exhibit 15.3). From this register, information is taken to make the general ledger entries for actual expenditures of the agency. The $41,600 recorded in the above budgetary entry is now recorded as:

Inventories	250	
Equipment	100	
Expenses	29,250	
Work in Process	12,000	
Accounts Payable—Government Agencies		9,850
Accounts Payable—Others		31,750
To record accrued expenditures for July.		

When payment is made from the Treasury, it is recorded by the agency as:

Accounts Payable—Government Agencies	9,850	
Accounts Payable—Other	31,750	
Fund Balance with U.S. Treasury		41,600
To record payment of accounts payable.		

From this brief illustration, we see that the procedure for recording transactions at the federal level is similar to that at the local level. Budget entries are used to record spending authority, commitments are recorded, and expenditures are recorded on an accrual basis.

Financial Reporting   While agency reports may vary somewhat depending on the purposes and activities of the agency, they will generally include:

1. A balance sheet which sets forth the assets and liabilities of the agency, and the equity of the U.S. government. Unlike local government reporting, all assets—including fixed assets—are presented.

2. An operating statement showing the revenues and costs associated with the agency's programs and activities.

3. A statement of sources and applications of funds.

Other reports, such as comparisons of budgeted and actual expenditures and reports on the status of appropriations may also be included.

Overall Financial Reporting

Because of the scope and complexity of federal government operations, it has been difficult to achieve effective overall financial reporting. Emphasis in the past has been on budgetary reporting, and little attempt has been made to produce a single report covering the entire federal government.

In recent years, the Treasury has been working with an advisory committee of accountants and business people to develop a comprehensive report which emphasizes financial condition. One result of this project has been the development of prototype consolidated financial statements. Issued in 1977, these statements suggest what the federal government's statements would look like if consolidated, accrual-based statements were prepared. These are not official statements but the results of an experiment. They should be viewed as a step toward improving overall financial reporting at the federal level. The statements and notes (but not the various supplemental schedules) are reproduced in the chapter appendix.

Accounting for the Economy

The broadest type of government accounting is accounting for the economy as a whole. In a sense, this is not truly "government" accounting. Rather, it is known as **national income accounting.** While the data are collected and reported by the government, the reporting entity includes all segments of the economy—government, business, and individuals.

In accounting for the economy, the statistic most commonly presented is **gross national product (GNP),** which is a measure, in dollars, of the goods and services produced by the economy during a year. This figure is widely used as an indicator of the strength of the economy.

Gross national product may be measured in either of two ways; both are typically reported, as they emphasize different aspects of the economy. The **flow-of-products approach** focuses on *outputs*—the goods and services purchased by various segments of the economy. To eliminate double counting, intermediate products are eliminated. Thus, the automobile purchased by an individual is included, but the steel purchased by the automobile manufacturer is not. The goods and services generated by the economy are classified as follows:

> Goods and services purchased by individuals.
> Goods and services purchased by government.
> Goods and services purchased by business for investment (that is, fixed assets and inventories).
> Goods and services purchased by foreigners (exports), net of imports.

The alternative measure, the **flow-of-income approach,** focuses on *inputs*—payments to the various factors of production. Included are payments to labor (wages), to capital (depreciation, rents, interest, and profits), and to government (indirect taxes). The earnings of the economy, therefore, are classified as:

> Wages and benefits to employees.
> Net interest.
> Rental income of individuals.
> Depreciation.
> Income of unincorporated entities (proprietorships, partnerships, etc.).
> Income of corporate entities (before taxes).
> Indirect business taxes.

Several comments are applicable to this classification of earnings. Note that all earnings are shown before income taxes. The transfer to the government in the form of income taxes is not presented, as it does not represent a payment to a factor of production, but merely a transfer from one segment of the economy to another. The same treatment applies to transfer payments from the government to individuals, such as social security payments, unemployment compensation, and welfare. Since these are transfers rather than earnings, they are excluded.

Note, however, that *indirect* business taxes such as sales, excise, and import taxes paid by business are included. Unlike income taxes, these taxes are not transfers of earnings but are viewed as if they were payments for productive services. Rental income is identified for individuals only. Rental income earned by firms, if not eliminated as an intermediate service, is included in the firm's income. A major component of rental income of individuals is the imputed rental value of owner-occupied housing. Inclusion of this amount recognizes the "earnings" produced by all the nation's housing, whether or not rent is formally paid.

The two approaches to measuring gross national product are commonly presented side by side in a **national income and product statement.** The statement for the United States economy for a recent year is presented in Exhibit 15.4.

While the data for the national income and product statement are actually drawn from various statistics collected by the government, we can better understand the logic of the statement by viewing it as a consolidation of all the entities in the economy. To illustrate, suppose that the income statement of a typical firm is classified in the following manner:

Sales of goods and services:	Expenses:
To individual consumers	Goods and services purchased
To government	and consumed
To other firms for consumption	—from other firms
To other firms for investment	—from foreigners (imports)
To foreigners (exports)	Salaries, wages, and benefits
	Interest
	Rent
	Depreciation
	Indirect taxes
	Income before taxes

The sales revenue on the left side equals the expenses plus profit on the right side.

If we had an income statement of this type for each firm in the economy and consolidated by removing interfirm transactions and netting imports against exports, we would have:

Sales of goods and services:	Salaries, wages, and benefits
To individual consumers	Interest
To government	Rent
To other firms for investment	Depreciation
Net exports	Indirect business taxes
	Income before taxes of
	unincorporated firms
	Income before taxes of corporations

Exhibit 15.4   Illustration of National Income and Product Statement

United States
National Income and Product Statement
1979
(Amounts in Billions of Dollars)

Personal Consumption Expenditures . .	$1,528.6	Compensation of Employees $1,472.8
Gross Private Domestic Investment . . .	392.3	Proprietors' Income 130.3
Net Exports	(2.3)	Rental Income of Persons 26.6
Government Purchases of Goods and		Corporate Profits 180.8
Services	477.8	Net Interest 131.5
		National Income $1,942.0
		Indirect Business Taxes 191.1
		Other Adjustments 15.4
		Net National Product $2,148.5
		Capital Consumption Allowances . . . 247.9
Gross National Product	$2,396.4	Gross National Product $2,396.4

Source: President's Council of Economic Advisors, *Economic Report of the President* (Washington, D.C.: Government Printing Office, January 1980), various pages.

As can be seen by comparison with Exhibit 15.4, this assumed consolidation process yields the type of information presented in the national income and product statement. Transactions involving firms account for a good deal of national income and production. Transactions among individuals (including imputed rent) and transactions between individuals and government (excluding transfers) are the other major components. These transactions fit readily into the above format. For example, payment of salaries to government employees increases government purchases of goods and services on the left side and salaries on the right side.

This chapter has provided an overview of governmental accounting at the local, state, and federal levels, as well as an overview of national income accounting for the economy as a whole. Subsequent chapters will develop in detail various aspects of local government accounting.

Summary of Key Concepts

A local government unit is made up of several economic entities known as **funds.** Eight standard types of funds and two account groups exist, some or all of which may be used by a particular local government unit.

The general, special revenue, capital projects, special assessments, and debt service funds are known as **governmental funds** and use a method of accounting known as **fund accounting.** Fund accounting is characterized by use of the **modified accrual basis** for recording revenues and expenditures, and by inclusion of budgetary accounts.

The enterprise and internal service funds are known as **proprietary funds** because they are used to conduct business-type activities. **Accrual accounting** is used for proprietary funds.

The trust and agency funds are known as **fiduciary funds** and generally use fiduciary accounting principles.

Common financial statements for a fund include a **balance sheet** and a **statement of revenues, expenditures, and changes in fund balance.** For funds using budgetary accounting, a **budgetary comparison statement** is also presented.

The **comprehensive annual financial report** of a local government unit presents both **combined statements,** which give an overview of the financial affairs of the entire governmental unit, and **individual or combining statements** for each fund type and account group.

State government accounting generally follows the same principles as local government accounting.

Federal government accounting at the agency level is similar to state and local government accounting in a general way. Differences do exist in the level of complexity, terminology, and reporting.

The operations of the economy are reflected in a **national income and product statement.** This statement can be viewed as a consolidation of all the entities in the economy.

Consolidated Financial Statements of the United States Government

Statement of the Secretary of the Treasury	Beginning in 1949 with the recommendations of the Commission on Organization of the Executive Branch (Hoover Commission), the Federal Government has moved slowly but steadily towards the application of accrual accounting to the measurement of its financial operations. State and local governments have also trended in this direction.

This prototype report is the result of an experimental undertaking aimed at extending accrual accounting concepts to new areas of governmental accounting. The undertaking is intended to contribute to

> the improvement of accounting at all levels of government, Federal, state, and local;

> the development of accounting standards for public financial reporting by government entities; and

> the integration of governmental accounting standards with accounting standards applicable to the private sector.

This second prototype report should not be regarded as a financial statement in the conventional sense, but rather as a step in the evolution of comprehensive and understandable government financial reporting. It has not been prepared in accordance with any set of generally accepted accounting principles, as there are none for the U.S. Government. As the Comptroller General points out in his accompanying statement, there are a number of significant controversial issues that must be resolved before statements of this type can be certified. There is also disagreement among the members of the Advisory Committee on Federal Consolidated Financial Statements, Government officials responsible for accounting matters, and others as to how these issues should be resolved and also as to various portions of this prototype. Hence, the report should be recognized only for what it is—a preliminary approach to the complex and controversial task of presenting accurate and understandable information about the financial condition of the Government. *It is not the Government's report on its financial condition and it should not be so interpreted.*

This second prototype has been revised in major respects based upon recommendations of the advisory committee and reactions of the general public to the first prototype report published in late 1976. The basic statements of financial condition and operations have been delineated more fully. A number of supplemental schedules have been added to amplify various aspects of the Government's financial operations that are not captured in the basic statements. Both the basic statements and the supplemental schedules, however, are embryonic. Many conceptual and methodological issues must be resolved before reports such as this prototype can be represented as conforming to generally accepted accounting principles.

For example, among any national government's principal assets are its powers to tax and to create money. These are not represented among the assets in this prototype report. The outer continental shelf and some 704 million acres of public domain lands are likewise not included among the assets in this report; however, proposals have been made for valuing these lands for inclusion in future financial statements. How to carry these assets on a balance sheet will not be an easy issue to resolve.

On the liability side, much debate centers on the liability for accrued social security pensions. Some contend that social security benefits are current transfers of income and that no liability for future payments should be shown. Others contend that the full actuarial deficit—the difference between projected receipts and payments over the next 75 years—should be shown as a liability. This report continues, in modified form, the practice used in the first prototype of showing an amortized portion of the actuarial deficit. However, this is clearly not the appropriate final resolution of the issue; it needs further study and this will be done in the coming months.

Despite these and other conceptual issues and data deficiencies that are not yet resolved, it is important that governments press forward with the development of better financial measurement and reporting. Combined Federal, state, and local expenditures in 1976 amounted to 34 percent of the gross national product. Government borrowings in 1976 accounted for 40 percent of the new issues in the capital markets. Financial operations of this magnitude require more sophisticated accounting techniques than traditional governmental fund accounting provides.

The focus of governmental accounting traditionally has been on preventing overspending of appropriations. That is an essential purpose, but it is much too narrow for the large and complex institutions that governments have become. The focus of governmental accounting must be shifted to broader purposes— on facilitating better management of government programs and government finances and on enhancing public understanding of resources used in the conduct of government operations. Through the exploration of new accounting concepts, the adaptation of old concepts, and the exposure to the public of various accounting applications, this and subsequent reports can contribute to achieving those broader purposes.

During the past year, the advisory committee met to consider a number of issues and staff reports dealing with the shape and content of this report. The advisory committee members faced an unusually difficult task in that the problems with which they were confronted were many of the same fundamental issues the accounting profession has been actively debating, and because those problems had to be dealt with in a governmental context; something that had not been done before.

To date, the advisory committee, the General Accounting Office, and the Treasury have given primary attention to identifying the highest priority problems which need to be solved if governmental accounting is to be brought up to the level of the private sector. The complexity of the task is illustrated by a chart appearing at the end of this report on the valuation of assets. One of the advisory committee's recommendations was that assets be valued at their current values. The chart shows the wide gap that must be bridged before this can be accomplished.

As with the first prototype, we seek the reactions and comments of readers of this financial report.

W. MICHAEL BLUMENTHAL
Secretary of the Treasury
July 26, 1977

Statement of the Comptroller General of the United States

In commenting on an initial prototype report last year, we noted the need to make this report more comprehensive by providing information on the full range of Government activities. Significant progress has been made in the design and development of information that supplements the traditional statements. However, as with the first report, we must caution that this report must be considered preliminary and that before fully satisfactory financial statements can be prepared, many aspects of presenting information and determining appropriate amounts for assets and liabilities will require further study. For example, such controversial issues as the following must be resolved:

The basis for valuation of such diversified Federal assets as the public domain, defense weapon systems, and natural resources must be changed. In the attached statements, these assets are valued at cost. We agree with the preference expressed by the Advisory Committee on Federal Consolidated Financial Statements that Federal assets should be recorded and reported on a current value basis. Further study will be necessary to select the most appropriate current value method for each category of Federal asset and to determine the best source of the data needed to make the valuations.

The fair presentation of actual liabilities for Federal pension plans, social security payments and veterans benefits needs further consideration. Liabilities for some Federal pension plans that are not included in these financial statements need to be determined. Also, the method of determining the amounts of all these liabilities, as well as the method of presenting when payment will be required, needs further study.

The method of computing depreciation of Federal assets needs to be improved. The depreciation amounts used in these statements were based on broad calculations. Refinement of the methods used is desirable.

The effect of tax benefits on revenues needs further study. In many cases the data essential for analyzing the amounts of revenue which the Government has not received because of exemptions or deductions authorized by tax law is insufficient. Additional work is needed to improve the accuracy and scope of these computations.

The cost to the Government of interest subsidies on outstanding Government loans needs to be computed more precisely. The data currently available on interest subsidies represent only a very rough approximation of the costs of these subsidies to the Government. Efforts should be made to refine these data so that more accurate costs can be shown.

The time span of the Flow of Funds Statement should be increased. This Statement predicts cash basis revenues and expenditures in future years using certain basic assumptions reflected in the Federal budget. We believe this Statement should be expanded to cover at least a fifteen year period with information for each year provided in ranges which take into consideration varying economic conditions.

We have not examined or audited these statements. Such an audit would be impractical because these statements are of a preliminary nature and several difficult problems such as those described above remain to be resolved. Accordingly, we are not expressing an opinion on whether they fairly present the financial condition and results of Government operations for the periods of time they cover. We believe, however, that these preliminary statements will serve to highlight some of the critical financial problems that the Federal Government faces and will encourage more comprehensive financial reporting by government entities at all levels.

ELMER B. STAATS
Comptroller General of the United States
June 15, 1977

Introductory Statement to Notes

As is true of accounting in other types of economic entities, governmental accounting exists for the purpose of providing complete and accurate financial information, in proper form and on a timely basis, to those responsible for and concerned with the operations of governmental units and agencies. While the Federal Government presently prepares many types of statements for specialized users, these prototype Federal Consolidated Financial Statements have been prepared to serve the common needs of a variety of users, with emphasis on the general public, to help promote understanding of the overall financial condition of the Federal Government and to promote a more informed understanding of government's place in our economy. It is important to note that this report is a prototype: many aspects of the financial statements require further analysis. Only as the various problems are resolved can fully satisfactory statements be prepared. A change in the fiscal year required that amounts be reflected in the Consolidated Statement of Financial Position as of September 30, 1976, June 30, 1976, and June 30, 1975. The revenues and expenses for the three month Transition Quarter (July 1, 1976, to September 30, 1976) are shown separately in the Consolidated Statement of Operations.

The sources used in developing the statements were predominantly Treasury publications, supplemented by reports from both the civilian and military sectors of the Federal Government. For the most part, these publications and reports are a product of the agencies' accounting systems, which by law must conform in all material respects to the accounting principles, standards, and related requirements prescribed by the Comptroller General of the United States.

United States Government
Consolidated Statement of Financial Position
as of September 30, 1976, and June 30, 1976 and 1975
(amounts in billions)

ASSETS

(What the Government owns—resources that are available to pay obligations or to provide public services in the future)

	1976 Sept. 30	1976 June 30	1975 June 30
Cash and Monetary Reserves			
Operating Cash in the Treasury	$ 17.4	$ 14.8	$ 7.6
International Monetary Reserves (Note 1)	17.9	17.1	16.2
Other Cash	6.3	7.1	5.2
	$ 41.6	$ 39.0	$ 29.0
Receivables (Net of Allowances)			
Accounts Receivable	$ 5.4	$ 3.9	$ 5.5
Accrued Taxes Receivable (Note 2)	14.1	10.1	11.8
Loans Receivable (Note 3)	100.2	106.4	82.7
Advances and Prepayments	6.7	3.6	1.3
	$126.4	$124.0	$101.3
Inventories (at Cost) (Note 4)			
Goods for Sale	$ 13.5	$ 13.2	$ 11.2
Work in Process	.8	.8	.7
Raw Materials	1.4	1.6	2.8
Materials and Supplies for Government Use	35.4	35.5	31.2
Stockpiled Materials and Commodities	12.5	12.3	11.6
	$ 63.6	$ 63.4	$ 57.5
Property and Equipment (at Cost)			
Land (Note 5)	$ 7.6	$ 7.5	$ 7.0
Buildings, Structures, and Facilities (Note 6)	92.7	92.5	92.1
Military Hardware (Note 7)	133.5	133.5	126.6
Equipment (Note 7)	42.9	42.6	41.1
Construction in Progress	16.2	16.6	18.0
Other	1.7	1.8	2.1
	$294.6	$294.5	$286.9
Accumulated Depreciation (Note 8)	(147.2)	(145.1)	(136.5)
	$147.4	$149.4	$150.4
Deferred Charges and Other Assets	$ 20.2	$ 18.6	$ 16.7
Total Assets	$399.2	$394.4	$354.9

The accompanying notes are an integral part of this statement.

The maintenance of accounts on the accrual basis is a basic requirement for all Federal agencies. As of December 31, 1976, there were 338 accounting systems subject to approval by the Comptroller General. (The Comptroller General has approved the principles and standards of 98 percent of these accounting systems and the designs of 52 percent of the systems.) The great majority of information in this report is derived from these systems.

The accompanying financial statements include the accounts of all significant agencies and funds included in the Unified Budget of the United States

United States Government
Consolidated Statement of Financial Position
as of September 30, 1976, and June 30, 1976 and 1975
(amounts in billions)

LIABILITIES

(What the Government owes—obligations incurred in the past that will require cash or other resources in the future)

	1976		1975
	Sept. 30	June 30	June 30
Accounts Payable	$ 53.7	$ 45.7	$ 46.9
Unearned Revenue	9.8	9.5	8.3
Borrowings from the Public *(Note 9)*	494.6	476.6	394.4
Accrued Pensions under Retirement and Disability Plans *(Note 10)*			
Military Personnel	$ 119.3	$ 117.3	$ 96.6
Civilian Employees	133.9	130.9	118.0
Social Security	630.8	603.1	499.5
Veterans	113.4	113.6	117.3
	$ 997.4	$ 964.9	$ 831.4
Loss Reserves for Guarantee and Insurance Programs *(Note 11)*	$ 27.9	$ 25.3	$ 15.1
Other Liabilities	42.5	41.8	39.4
Total Liabilities	$1,625.9	$1,563.8	$1,335.5

FISCAL DEFICIT

(The accumulated amount by which the costs of Government activities have exceeded Government revenues)

Fiscal Deficit Beginning of Period	$ (1,169.4)	$ (980.6)	$ (833.2)
Current Period Fiscal Deficit	(29.6)	(85.2)	(63.9)
Current Noncash Provision for Social Security *(Note 12)*	(27.7)	(103.6)	(83.5)
Fiscal Deficit End of Period	$ (1,226.7)	$ (1,169.4)	$ (980.6)
Total Liabilities and Fiscal Deficit . . .	$ 399.2	$ 394.4	$ 354.9

The accompanying notes are an integral part of this statement.

Government. Agencies such as the U.S. Postal Service, the Export-Import Bank of the United States, and the Federal Financing Bank, which are classified as "off-budget" (not included in the budget), have also been included in the financial statements because they are wholly owned and are clearly within the scope of Government operations. Government-sponsored enterprises such as Federal Land Banks have been excluded because they are privately owned. The Federal Reserve System is excluded. Although the Government's power to tax and to create money may be considered its most important assets, these are not included in these statements because the concepts have not been developed to the point where valuation is possible.

Although the Advisory Committee on Federal Consolidated Financial Statements has generally agreed that assets should be shown on a current value ba-

United States Government Consolidated Statement of Operations
for the Transitional Quarter (TQ) ended September 30, 1976,
and the Years ended June 30, 1976 and 1975
(amounts in billions)

	1976		1975
REVENUES	TQ	June 30	June 30
Levied under the Government's Sovereign Power			
Individual Income Taxes	$ 38.8	$131.6	$122.4
Corporate Income Taxes	12.5	39.7	37.4
Social Insurance Taxes and Contributions . . .	25.8	92.7	86.4
Excise Taxes	4.5	16.9	16.6
Estate and Gift Taxes	1.5	5.2	4.6
Customs Duties	1.2	4.1	3.7
Miscellaneous	4.4	9.8	9.7
	$ 88.7	$300.0	$280.8
Earned through Government Business-Type Operations			
Sale of Goods and Services	$ 5.7	$ 14.8	$ 11.8
Interest	2.4	16.3	11.9
Other	4.0	17.6	16.8
	$ 12.1	$ 48.7	$ 40.5
Total Revenues	$100.8	$348.7	$321.3
EXPENSES BY FUNCTION (SEE ALSO SUMMARY OF EXPENSES BY OBJECT AND AGENCY)			
Agriculture	$ 1.9	$ 10.7	$ 14.5
Commerce and Transportation	6.3	17.6	15.4
Community and Regional Development	3.8	13.4	6.2
Education, Training, Employment, and Social Services .	6.6	17.9	14.4
General Government	3.2	12.2	7.9
General Science, Space, and Technology	1.4	4.3	3.7
Health	11.6	34.1	27.1
Income Security			
Military Personnel	4.8	28.1	23.1
Civilian Employees	5.5	21.2	17.0
Social Insurance	26.3	81.7	72.6
Veterans	1.6	4.7	14.2
Other	9.8	37.5	28.4
Interest	8.1	37.1	32.7
International Affairs	4.3	12.0	8.1
Law Enforcement and Justice	1.2	3.4	2.8
National Defense	22.6	65.6	73.3
Natural Resources, Environment, and Energy . . .	4.9	13.6	7.8
Revenue Sharing and General Purpose Fiscal Assistance	2.3	6.7	6.6
Veterans' Benefits and Services	4.2	12.1	9.4
Total Expenses	$130.4	$433.9	$385.2
Current Period Fiscal Deficit	$ (29.6)	$ (85.2)	$ (63.9)

SUMMARY OF EXPENSES BY OBJECT AND AGENCY	1976		1975
Expenses by object	TQ	June 30	June 30
Salaries and Employee Benefits	$ 8.3	$ 67.8	$ 63.9
Vendor Services and Supplies	24.1	68.5	67.3
Depreciation	2.1	8.6	7.7
Pensions, Health and Life Insurance	10.1	57.3	48.8
Casualty Insurance and Indemnities	35.5	103.0	87.1
Grants, Subsidies, and Contributions	42.2	91.6	77.7
Interest	8.1	37.1	32.7
Total Expenses	$130.4	$433.9	$385.2
Expenses by agency			
Legislative Branch	$ .2	$ .8	$ .7
The Judiciary	.1	.3	.3
Executive Branch			
Office of the President	4.3	11.5	22.1
Departments			
Agriculture	5.8	22.1	8.0
Commerce	.8	2.3	1.7
Defense	27.8	97.2	96.8
Health, Education and Welfare	43.2	132.1	107.9
Housing and Urban Development	4.4	15.6	9.7
Interior	1.5	4.2	3.3
Justice	.8	2.5	2.2
Labor	7.7	26.4	17.0
State	.4	1.2	.9
Transportation	3.8	12.7	9.0
Treasury: Interest	8.1	37.1	32.7
Other	3.2	9.8	9.8
Independent Agencies	18.3	58.1	63.1
Total Expenses	$130.4	$433.9	$385.2

The accompanying notes are an integral part of this statement.

sis, the current value method best suited for each type of asset has not yet been determined. The Valuation Methods Schedule [not reproduced] lists various current value methods applicable to each type of asset. This is one of the many conceptual as well as practical problems that the Treasury has begun to address and must resolve to improve the usefulness of these statements.

Notes to Financial Statements

1. International Monetary Reserves This category as of the latest period shown, September 30, 1976, comprises the following items: $11.6 billion in gold, which has been recorded at $42.22 per ounce, the statutory price at which gold is monetized by the issuance of Gold Certificates to the Federal Reserve System; $2.4 billion of Special Drawing Rights, which are an international reserve asset; and $3.9 billion representing the United States reserve position with the International Monetary Fund.

2. Accrued Taxes Receivable The September 30, 1976, total for taxes receivable represents $6.0 billion (net) for delinquent taxes and $8.1 billion of accrued corporate taxes. The amounts as of June 30, 1975, were $6.4 billion and $5.4 billion, respectively. No accrual has been made for individual income taxes. (A method for accruing these taxes is scheduled for study.) Likewise, assessed tax deficiencies pending settlement have not been included.

3. Loans Receivable   Outstanding loans and allowances for losses have been recorded as reported by the various lending agencies. No attempt has been made to evaluate the adequacy of the allowance for losses, but it is presumed to be understated and is under study. Interest rates and loan repayment terms vary considerably for outstanding loans, with rates ranging from 2 percent to 12 percent and terms from as short as 90 days to well over 40 years.

4. Inventories   Inventories include nondepreciable personal property and are generally stated at cost. The September 30, 1976, total for inventories comprises $47.8 billion for the Department of Defense and $15.8 billion for other agencies. The amounts as of June 30, 1975, were $42.8 billion and $14.7 billion, respectively. The inventory accounts do not include the weapons stockpile of the Energy Research and Development Administration, since the extent of this inventory is classified information.

5. Land   Land is valued at the cost paid by the Government. The cost of land acquired through donation, exchange, bequest, forfeiture, or judicial process is estimated by the General Services Administration at amounts the Government would have paid if purchased at the date of acquisition. Pending study of valuation methods, the outer continental shelf, other offshore lands, and the 704 million acres of public domain lands have not been included. In 1972 a committee of the House of Representatives estimated the value of public domain lands (93 percent of the total on-shore acreage owned by the Federal Government) to be $29.9 billion. Acreage owned by the Federal Government as of September 30, 1976, exclusive of off-shore lands, is summarized below by predominant usage.

Usage	Acres (millions)
Forest and Wildlife	504.6
Grazing	163.5
Parks and Historic Sites	26.0
Alaska Oil and Gas Reserves	23.0
Military (except Airfields)	18.4
Flood Control and Navigation	8.1
Reclamation and Irrigation	6.0
Industrial	2.9
Alaska Native Reserves	2.8
Airfields	1.9
Research and Development	1.6
Power Development and Distribution	1.5
Other Usages	1.8
Total	762.1

6. Buildings, Structures, and Facilities   This category consists of all real property owned by the Federal Government except land. The total reflects the acquisition cost of buildings and the costs of acquiring or erecting dams, utility systems, monuments, roads and bridges. The September 30, 1976, total for this category represents $61.7 billion for the Department of Defense and $31.0 billion for other agencies. The amounts as of June 30, 1975, were $57.2 billion and $34.9 billion, respectively.

7. Depreciable Personal Property   Equipment and military hardware are recorded at acquisition cost and include only depreciable personal property which is currently in use or in usable condition. The major components of each category are summarized below.

	Sept. 30, 1976	June 30, 1975
	(amounts in billions)	
Military Hardware		
Aircraft and Related Equipment	$ 57.3	$ 51.6
Ships and Service Craft	39.7	38.0
Combat and Tactical Vehicles	19.9	17.8
Missiles and Related Equipment	11.3	10.6
Other	5.3	8.6
Total	$133.5	$126.6
Equipment		
Department of Defense		
Industrial Plant Equipment	$ 14.3	$ 13.9
Communication and Electronics	4.2	4.9
Other	4.5	3.5
	$ 23.0	$ 22.3
Other Agencies	$ 19.9	$ 18.8
Total	$ 42.9	$ 41.1

8. Accumulated Depreciation   Most Government agencies do not calculate depreciation on property and equipment. For such agencies, accumulated depreciation was estimated on a straight line basis, based on available information. The useful lives applied to each classification of asset are as follows: buildings, structures, and facilities—50 years; ships and service craft—30 years; industrial plant equipment—20 years; all other depreciable assets—10 years.

Reported amounts were used for those agencies, for example, Tennessee Valley Authority and U.S. Postal Service, that do depreciate property and equipment. These agencies account for approximately 6 percent of the total accumulated depreciation reflected in the Consolidated Statement of Financial Position.

9. Borrowings From the Public   The gross amount of Federal debt outstanding has been reduced by intragovernmental holdings net of unamortized premiums and discounts. The largest such reduction reflects the holdings of Government trust funds. Significant intragovernmental holdings of Federal debt securities are summarized below. For additional information on borrowings from the public, see the Federal Debt Maturity Schedule in the supplementary section [not reproduced].

	Sept. 30, 1976	June 30, 1975
	(amounts in billions)	
Social Security Administration		
Federal Old Age and Survivors	$ 37.1	$ 39.9
Federal Disability Insurance	6.4	8.1
Federal Hospital Insurance	11.0	9.8
Federal Supplementary Medical Insurance	1.2	1.4
	$ 55.7	$ 59.2
Civil Service Commission		
Civil Service Retirement and Disability	$ 42.7	$ 38.6
Other	2.5	2.0
	$ 45.2	$ 40.6
Department of Labor—Unemployment	$ 4.9	$ 7.2
Department of Transportation		
Highway	$ 9.0	$ 9.6
Other	2.7	1.9
	$ 11.7	$ 11.5
Veterans Administration	$ 8.3	$ 8.1
Federal Deposit Insurance Corporation	6.6	6.2
Other	3.6	4.5
Total	$136.0	$137.3

As of September 30, 1976, foreign and international investors held approximately $75.0 billion of the debt outstanding with the public. The amount as of June 30, 1975, was $66.0 billion.

10. Accrued Pensions under Retirement and Disability Plans   The accounting for accrued pensions is subject to several different assumptions, definitions, and methods of calculation for the various retirement and disability plans. Specific methods applied to each of the major pension accruals are summarized below. Liabilities for approximately 30 other Government pension plans are not included because of insufficient data. Further study and analysis is required for adequate valuation and disclosure of pension liabilities.

Military personnel and civilian employees: Liabilities have been recorded based on the estimated present value of accrued benefits, as actuarially computed by the administering agencies.

Social security: Estimates for social security are based on the present value of the projected excess of benefits over contributions for present participants for the next 75 years.

Veterans: The liability for Veterans Administration benefits represents the computed present value of annual benefit payments estimated by the Veterans Administration to the year 2000.

11. Loss Reserves for Guarantee and Insurance Programs   For additional information on loss reserves for guarantee and insurance programs, see the Commitments and Contingencies Schedule in the supplementary section [not reproduced].

12. Current Noncash Provision for Social Security   The noncash provision for social security represents changes in the social security accrued liabilities between periods based on a 30-year amortization of the actuarial deficit. Accounting methods for this provision require additional study.

The noncash amounts are not included in the Statement of Operations because a substantial but indeterminate portion is not applicable to the current period. The Statement of Operations does include cash benefit payments.

13. Contingencies   Several Government agencies insure businesses and individuals against various types of risks. The amount of insurance coverage in force, representing the maximum risk exposure of the Government, is $1,566.9 billion as of September 30, 1976.

The Government also guarantees loans by nonGovernment enterprises to businesses and individuals. These guarantees become liabilities of the Government only when the Government is required to honor its guarantees. Loan guarantees in force at September 30, 1976, are $194.4 billion. For further information on contingencies, see the Commitments and Contingencies Schedule in the supplemental section [not reproduced].

14. Open-Ended Programs and Fixed Costs   The Government also commits itself to provide services by passing laws that make spending mandatory. Since a significant amount of future spending is fixed by law, it is very probable that the Government will pay for these programs in future years. Listed below are the programs for the Transition Quarter and Fiscal Year 1976 that can be terminated only if a law is changed.

	TQ	1976
	(amounts in billions)	
Payments for Individuals		
Social Security and Railroad Retirement	$20.7	$ 76.2
Federal Employees' Retirement and Insurance	4.3	15.6
Unemployment Assistance	4.2	19.8
Veterans Benefits	2.9	13.9
Medicare and Medicaid	7.0	26.3
Housing Payments	.6	2.5
Public Assistance Related Programs	4.9	20.2
	$44.6	$174.5
Net Interest	7.0	26.8
General Revenue Sharing	1.6	6.2
Other Open-Ended Programs and Fixed Costs	3.3	9.4
Total	$56.5	$216.9

Questions Q15.1   "Within each legal entity, the concept of economic entity dominates." Explain the meaning of this statement in terms of local government financial statement reporting.

Q15.2   In accounting for the activities of local governmental units, three types of accounting are followed: business accounting, fiduciary accounting, and fund accounting. How can you justify use of three types of accounting in one legal entity?

Q15.3   What are the sources for authoritative guidelines of governmental accounting principles and procedures?

Q15.4   What does the term *revenues* mean in business accounting? In fund accounting? Compare revenue recognition for business accounting to revenue recognition (modified accrual approach) for fund accounting.

Q15.5   Select the best answer for each of the following questions:
   1.   Under the modified accrual method of accounting used by a local government unit, which of the following would be a revenue most susceptible to accrual?
      a. Income taxes.
      b. Business licenses.
      c. Property taxes.
      d. Sales taxes.
   2.   Within a local government unit, two funds that are accounted for in a manner similar to a business entity are:
      a. General and debt service.
      b. Enterprise and general.
      c. Enterprise and trust and agency.
      d. Internal service and enterprise.
   3.   When used in fund accounting, the term *fund* usually refers to:
      a. A sum of money designated for a special purpose.
      b. A liability to other government units.
      c. The equity of a municipality in its own assets.
      d. A fiscal and accounting entity having a set of self-balancing accounts.

                                                                    (AICPA adapted)

Q15.6   Under fund accounting procedures, purchases of goods and services are recorded on the books at the time of order. How does this differ from the recording of purchases of goods and services following business accounting principles? Justify any differences in the treatment.

Q15.7   What is the effect on the fund balance of each of the following? (Answer "increase," "decrease," or "no effect.")
   1. Budgeted expenditures exceed budgeted revenues.
   2. Budgeted revenues exceed budgeted expenditures.
   3. Actual revenues equal budgeted revenues.
   4. Actual expenditures exceed budgeted expenditures.

Q15.8   Select the best answer for each of the following questions:

1.   Which of the following accounts is a budgetary account?
   a. Vouchers Payable.
   b. Expenditures.
   c. Encumbrances.
   d. Fund Balance.

2.   A town issues purchase orders to vendors and suppliers of $630,000. Which of the following entries should be made to record this transaction?

	Debit	Credit
a. Encumbrances	630,000	
Reserve for Encumbrances		630,000
b. Expenditures	630,000	
Vouchers Payable		630,000
c. Expenses	630,000	
Accounts Payable		630,000
d. Reserve for Encumbrances	630,000	
Encumbrances		630,000

3.   If a credit was made to the fund balance in the process of recording a budget for a local government unit, it can be assumed that:
   a. Budgeted expenditures exceed actual revenues.
   b. Actual expenditures exceed budgeted expenditures.
   c. Budgeted revenues exceed budgeted expenditures.
   d. Budgeted expenditures exceed budgeted revenues.

(AICPA adapted)

Q15.9   Compare the recording of the budget by local government with the recording of the budget by a federal agency.

Q15.10   Compare the recording of purchase orders by local government with the recording of purchase orders by a federal agency.

Exercises   E15.1   Following are several common activities or financial events in which a local government may participate:

1. Operations of a public library receiving the majority of its support from property taxes levied for that purpose.
2. Proceeds of a federal grant made to assist in financing the future construction of an adult training center.
3. Operations of a municipal swimming pool receiving the majority of its support from charges to users.
4. Monthly remittance to an insurance company of the lump sum of hospital/surgical insurance premiums collected as payroll deductions from employees.

5. Activities of a central motor pool which provides and services vehicles for the use of municipal employees on official business.

6. Activities of a municipal employee retirement plan which is financed by equal employer and employee contributions.

7. Collections of property taxes for the benefit of local sanitary, park, and school districts. The collections are periodically remitted to these units.

8. Activities of a street improvement project which is being financed by requiring each owner of property facing the street to pay a proportionate share of the total cost.

9. Activities of a central print shop offering printing services at cost to various city departments.

10. Transactions of a municipal police retirement system.

11. Activities of a municipal golf course which receives three-fourths of its total revenue from a special tax levy.

12. Self-supporting activities of government that are provided on a user charge basis.

13. Activities of a data processing center established to service all agencies within a government unit.

Required: For each of the above, indicate the type of fund in which the activity should be recorded by a local government and the type of accounting (business, fiduciary, or fund) that should be followed.

(AICPA adapted)

E15.2 Each of the following transactions relates to a city government:

1. A sinking fund is set up to accumulate and invest resources for the retirement of a general bond issue which matures in ten years.

2. The city receives a $50,000 grant from the federal government to institute a meal delivery program for senior citizens.

3. New curbing is being installed in a section of the city. The residents of that section will have an additional charge on their property tax bill during each of the next ten years to pay the cost of the curbing.

4. To remedy a flooding problem, the city plans a new drainage system in the southern part of the city. It is decided that this project will be financed by a general bond issue rather than by tax assessments to property owners.

5. The city establishes a retirement fund for its firefighters. Each year, 8 percent of the firefighters' wages is set aside by the city. The city administers the investment of funds and the payment of benefits.

6. Same as item 5, except that the city pays a premium to an insurance company, which is fully responsible for investment of funds and benefit payments.

7. The city has set up a computer services division, which handles payroll and other functions for all city agencies. Each agency is billed by the computer services division for the work done for that agency.

8. Fifteen new police cars are purchased, as provided in the general budget.

9. State aid funds are received. These funds may be used for any of the general operations of the city.

10. The city deducts federal income taxes from its employees' wages and periodically remits them to the federal government.

Required: Identify the fund in which each of the above would be recorded.

E15.3   The Anderson School District, an independent government unit, maintains several funds to account for its many activities. Following are several transactions:

1. Construction of a new library for the school district. Bonds were issued to finance the construction.
2. Receipt of a grant from the state to finance purchase of books for the new library.
3. Operating costs for the school cafeterias. Charges to students and faculty for food provide 85 percent of the operating costs.
4. Costs of operating and maintaining the school bus fleet, which are met by general school tax revenues.
5. Income from investments which were donated to the school district by a wealthy citizen. Investment income is used to provide scholarships to needy students.
6. Costs of operating school bookstores. Bookstores derive revenues from sale of books and stationery supplies and are self-sufficient.
7. Salaries for faculty and administration, which are paid out of general school tax revenues.

Required: Identify the type of fund in which each of the above should be recorded.

E15.4   Lance City owns a building which it rents to local organizations for meetings and social events. In December 19X0, the city received $400 from the Lance City Camera Club for use of the building on December 24, 19X0 and January 10, 19X1. The fiscal year for the city ends on December 31.

Required:

1. Assuming the building rental is handled through the general fund, record the cash receipt.
2. Assuming the building rental is handled through an enterprise fund, record the cash receipt.

E15.5   Following are several revenue items for a city government:

1. The police department collects $500 for traffic fines.
2. Interest ($650) on investments by a local government is earned but not yet received.
3. Property taxes of $4,500,000 are levied by a municipality.
4. Payment of $210,000 of the taxes levied in item 3 is received.
5. A county is notified that it has been awarded a $300,000 federal grant.
6. A city receives $5,000 rent in advance from an independent school district. The equipment rental relates to the city's upcoming fiscal year.

Required: For each item, make the proper journal entries under the accrual, modified accrual, and cash bases of accounting.

E15.6 The Newberry County budget for the 19X7 fiscal year included revenues of $3,502,000 and expenditures of $3,449,000.

Required: Prepare the closing entries for 19X7 under each of the following independent assumptions:
1. Actual revenues and expenditures equaled estimates.
2. Actual revenues were as expected, but actual expenditures exceeded estimates by $22,000.
3. Actual revenues of $3,500,000 equaled actual expenditures.
4. The net effect of the closing entries on the fund balance was zero. Actual revenues were $3,576,000.

E15.7 The Wildlife Preservation Commission, an agency of the federal government, was included in the annual budget passed by Congress for funding of $4,000,000 for the 19X1–X2 fiscal year. The Office of Management and Budget authorized the commission to spend $1,200,000 during the first quarter of the year. The chief commissioner of the agency divided this spending authority as follows:

Western Region Programs	$650,000
Central Region Programs	200,000
Eastern Region Programs	350,000

Required: Prepare the budget entries that should be recorded by the Wildlife Preservation Commission at July 1, 19X1, the beginning of the first quarter.

E15.8 Following are several transactions which may affect the national income and product statement:
1. A government employee earns a salary of $18,000.
   Answer: Compensation of employees increases by $18,000. Government purchases of goods and services increases by $18,000.
2. An individual pays a doctor's bill of $100 (assume no increase in the doctor's expenses).
3. An individual pays annual apartment rental of $4,000 to a corporation.
4. An individual pays annual apartment rental of $4,000 to an individual.
5. A couple owns the house in which they reside; estimated rental value is $5,000 per year.
6. A corporation pays $25,000 dividends to its shareholders.
7. An individual receives $6,000 in social security benefits.

Required: For each of the above, indicate the effect on the national income and product statement. The first one has been completed as an example.

E15.9 Identify the agency that performs each of the following financial management activities in the Federal government:
1. Auditing.
2. Budgetary administration.
3. Budgetary analysis for Congress.
4. Budgetary planning for the President.
5. Cash management.
6. Debt management.

7. Employee benefits.
8. Establishing accounting standards for government agencies.
9. Establishing accounting standards for government contractors.
10. Management of fixed assets.
11. Management of inventories.
12. Settlement of claims.

Problems **P15.1** **Fund Accounting for Alternative Forms of Purchase** The Blanche County treasurer's office currently buys computer time from a local private firm to process the payroll for county employees. The county water department, which is supported entirely by charges to customers, uses the same computer service to process its billings and collections. County managers are considering purchasing a computer to serve county needs. Several alternatives have been proposed:

Proposal 1 The county will purchase a small computer to handle payroll processing. The water department will continue to buy machine time from the private firm.

Proposal 2 The county will purchase a computer of adequate size to process both county payroll and water department billings and collections. A special fund will record the purchase and operating costs of the equipment. The treasurer's office and water department will be billed for the actual cost of computer services.

Proposal 3 The county will purchase a computer with excess capacity in anticipation of future computer needs. A special fund will record the purchase and operating costs of the equipment. Machine time not utilized by the county treasurer's office and water department will be sold to independent government units (such as school districts and townships). Such sales to outside parties are expected to account for 75 percent of computer usage.

Required:
1. Through what type of fund are the activities of the treasurer's office recorded? Through what type of fund are the activities of the water department recorded? How would a $15,000 purchase of computer time currently be recorded by the treasurer's office? By the water department?
2. For each of the three proposals, identify the fund which would record the purchase and operating costs of the computer.
3. If proposal 2 is accepted, how will receipt of $15,000 for computer time be recorded? Assume the $15,000 was not previously billed.
4. If proposal 3 is accepted, how will a billing to a school district for $20,000 of computer time be recorded?

P15.2 **Identification of Entry Types** Identified in Chapter 15 are six basic journal entry types encountered in fund accounting for local government:

Journal Entry Types

Budget	Expenditures
Revenues	Cash Receipts and Payments
Purchase Orders	Closing Entries

Required: Classify each of the following as to the entry type produced and make the entry (or entries). Unless specifically stated to be interrelated, assume each item is independent of the others.

1. A budget is approved anticipating $152,000 in revenue and authorizing $149,000 of expenditures.
2. Accounts payable of $890 are paid.
3. During the year, the government unit spent only $106,000 compared to $115,000 of expected outflows. The reporting period has ended. There are outstanding purchase orders of $250.
4. A purchase order for $400 of supplies is approved.
5. The supplies ordered in item 4 are received. The bill is for $400.
6. The supplies ordered in item 4 are received. The bill is for $410.
7. During the year, the municipality collected only $253,000 compared to the $262,000 expected. The reporting period has ended.
8. Taxes of $71,000 are accrued and then collected.
9. At the beginning of the fiscal year, the municipality expected to receive $474,000 and spend $479,000. The government unit actually received $476,000 and spent $476,000. Record the beginning and end-of-year entries.
10. Taxes of $82,000 are collected. No accruals were made.

P15.3 **Simple Fund Accounting for Local Government** The rural township of Barnesville provides a minimum of services to residents, all of which are accounted for in one fund. The budget approved by the town council at the beginning of the fiscal year 19X3 included expected revenues of $13,000 in taxes and $15,000 of anticipated expenditures. Cash on hand at the beginning of the year was $5,000. The fund balance was $5,000.

During the year, the following occurred:

1. Taxes of $12,050 were collected.
2. A community member died and left $2,000 to the township with no restrictions on the use of the money.
3. Cash expenditures for services provided (including labor, gasoline, and miscellaneous expenses) were $12,680.
4. Purchase orders were approved as follows: typewriter, $250; office supplies, $420; shop supplies, $340; tires, $325.
5. The office supplies bill was for $410. The shop supplies bill was for $360. The bill for tires totaled $325. All bills were paid.
6. At the end of the fiscal year, the typewriter had not been received or billed.

Required:

1. Make all the journal entries for the fund of the township of Barnesville, including closing entries.
2. Compute the fund balance as of the end of the fiscal year.

P15.4   **Recording Transactions and Closing Entries**   The January 1, 19X7, balance sheet for the single fund of the village of Owen is as follows:

Village of Owen
Fund Balance Sheet
January 1, 19X7

Cash	$30,000	Vouchers Payable	$43,000
Receivables	20,000	Fund Balance	7,000
		Total Liabilities and Fund	
Total Assets	$50,000	Balance	$50,000

Transactions for the village during 19X7 were:
  1. The village council approved a budget estimating revenues of $41,000 in property taxes and $10,000 in user charges. Property taxes are accrued on Owen's books. The budget authorized expenditures of $51,000.
  2. Receivables of $18,500 from last year were collected. Of the 19X7 tax levy, $26,500 was collected.
  3. Encumbrances of $50,300 were recorded. On December 31, 19X7, purchase orders of $13,000 were outstanding.
  4. Bills received exceeded the amounts encumbered by $200.
  5. Checks for $44,000 were mailed in payment of vouchers. No payments were made without vouchers.
  6. User charges of $11,000 were collected.

Required:
  1. Prepare journal entries to record the transactions for the village of Owen during 19X7.
  2. Prepare closing entries at December 31, 19X7, for the village of Owen.

P15.5   **Interpreting Financial Statements**   Financial statements of the City of Miami General Fund for the fiscal year ended September 30, 1976, appear in Exhibits 15.5, 15.6, and 15.7.

Required:
  1.   Answer the following questions regarding the general fund of the city of Miami.
     a. What is the fund balance at year-end?
     b. How much does the general fund owe to other city of Miami funds?
     c. What budget entry was made at the beginning of the year? (Include planned interfund transfers.)
     d. By what amount did the fund balance change from the beginning to end of year?
     e. By what amount was the fund balance expected to change?
     f. What amount of revenues, excluding interfund transfers, was received?
     g. Were actual expenditures for legal services more or less than planned expenditures? By what amount?

Exhibit 15.5   City of Miami Balance Sheet to Be Used in P15.5

City of Miami, Florida
General Fund
Balance Sheet
September 30, 1976

ASSETS

Cash		$ 119,894
Investments, at Cost		2,500,000
Taxes Receivable—Delinquent	$2,118,405	
Less Reserve for Estimated Losses	874,483	1,243,922
Interest and Penalties Receivable on Taxes	$ 9,130	
Less Allowance for Estimated Uncollectible Amounts .	8,341	789
Accounts Receivable		1,170,568
Total Assets		$5,035,173

LIABILITIES AND FUND BALANCE

Accrued Liabilities (Principally Salaries)	$ 884,158
Due to Other Funds	1,714,983
Accounts Payable and Other Liabilities	3,010,004
Fund Balance	(573,972)
Total Liabilities and Fund Balance	$5,035,173

Source: Adapted from City of Miami, Florida, Annual Financial Report, year ended September 30, 1976, pp. 38–39.

h. What amount was transferred from the general fund to other funds during the year?

i. What amount was transferred to the general fund from other funds during the year?

j. How much did the city receive in charges for recreation services during the year?

k. Compare your answer in item j to the planned recreation services receipts.

l. What revenue item was not anticipated by the city?

m. In how many cases did the city spend more than anticipated? Less than anticipated?

n. In how many cases did the city receive more money than anticipated? Less than anticipated?

o. What was the excess (deficiency) of actual tax revenues over budget?

p. Were revenues and transfers in greater or less than expenditures, encumbrances, and transfers out? By what amount?

q. What was the largest expenditure item?

r. Which revenue item, excluding transfers, provided the most resources to the city?

2.   The notes accompanying all the financial statements of the city of Miami, reproduced below, included a description of funds used by the city. Fill in the fund and account group titles for the following:

a. The _____ is the general operating fund of the city. General tax revenues and other receipts that are not allocated by law or contractual agreement to some other fund are accounted for in this fund. From the fund are paid the general operating expenses, the fixed charges, and the capital improvement costs that are not paid through other funds.

b. The _____ are used to account for revenues derived from specific taxes or other earmarked revenue sources which are required by law or regulation to finance particular functions or activities of government.

c. The _____ are used to account for the payment of interest and principal on the city's long-term debt.

d. The _____ are used to account for all resources used in the acquisition and construction of capital facilities and other fixed assets, with the exception of those that are financed by enterprise or internal service funds and special assessments.

e. The _____ are used to finance and account for the acquisition, operation, and maintenance of government facilities and services that are supported mainly by user charges to the general public.

f. The _____ are used to finance and account for certain services and commodities furnished to other funds within the city.

g. The _____ are used to account for monies and properties received and held by the city in a trustee, custodial, or agency capacity for other entities, such as employees, other governments, or nonpublic organizations. These funds are used to account for revenues and expenditures relating to most federal and state grants.

h. This group of accounts is established to account for all fixed assets of the city other than those accounted for in the enterprise and internal service funds. _____

i. This group of accounts is established to account for long-term debt not accounted for in enterprise funds. _____

P15.6 **Federal Agency Accounting** The International Cultural Commission is an agency of the State Department which sends U.S. cultural programs to perform in foreign countries and invites foreign cultural programs to perform in the United States. For the fiscal year beginning July 1, 19X3, the commission submitted the following budget to Congress: *(continued, bottom page 691)*

Cultural Export Program:		
Administrative Salaries	$700,000	
Other Administrative Costs	600,000	
Program Costs	350,000	$1,650,000
Cultural Import Program:		
Administrative Salaries	$550,000	
Other Administrative Costs	400,000	
Program Costs	200,000	1,150,000
General Administration:		
Salaries	$300,000	
Other Costs	520,000	820,000
Total Budgeted Costs		$3,620,000

Exhibit 15.6   City of Miami Budgetary Comparison Statement to Be Used in P15.5

City of Miami, Florida
General Fund
Statement of Revenues, Expenditures, Encumbrances,
and Transfers (Budget and Actual)
Year Ended September 30, 1976

	Budget	Actual
Revenues:		
Taxes:		
General Property Taxes	$19,031,184	$19,428,843
Penalties and Interest on Delinquent Taxes	60,000	183,941
Business and Excise Taxes	593,500	674,248
	$19,684,684	$20,287,032
Licenses and Permits:		
Business Licenses and Permits	$ 2,993,100	$ 3,000,369
Construction Permits	803,500	879,587
	$ 3,796,600	$ 3,879,956
Intergovernmental Revenue:		
Federal Grants	$ —	$ 871,304
State Grants	13,190,000	11,919,764
Other	1,717,455	2,023,740
	$14,907,455	$14,814,808
Intragovernmental Revenue:		
Engineering Services	$ 1,077,000	$ 1,256,720
Legal, Financial, and Other	375,503	325,940
	$ 1,452,503	$ 1,582,660
Charges for Services:		
Public Safety	$ 367,500	$ 410,834
Recreation	197,720	90,321
Other	137,500	56,436
	$ 702,720	$ 557,591
Miscellaneous Revenues:		
Interest	$ 1,200,000	$ 993,965
Rents	225,296	238,262
Other	464,000	726,525
	$ 1,889,296	$ 1,958,752
Total Revenues	$42,433,258	$43,080,799
Transfers from Other Funds	22,210,864	22,697,400
Total Revenues and Transfers	$64,644,122	$65,778,199
Expenditures and Encumbrances:		
General Government:		
Mayor and Commission	$ 204,316	$ 198,067
City Manager	546,413	566,102
City Clerk	112,093	127,985
Management Services	387,748	310,279
Finance	1,102,252	1,032,874
Legal	643,471	596,332
Employee Services	1,471,675	2,001,701
Civil Service	326,893	329,026
City Hall Operations	146,799	173,322
City Physician	146,994	132,731
Elections	85,895	67,938
	$ 5,174,549	$ 5,536,357

Exhibit 15.6   *continued*

	Budget	Actual
Public Improvements:		
Public Works	$ 3,955,834	$ 4,089,950
Building	1,260,462	1,152,292
Planning and Zoning	439,127	435,401
	$ 5,655,423	$ 5,677,643
Public Safety:		
Police	$20,001,410	$18,759,930
Fire	13,246,849	13,132,421
Communications	1,628,996	1,699,808
	$34,877,255	$33,592,159
Sanitation	$10,477,104	$10,400,131
Parks and Recreation	$ 4,001,752	$ 4,117,516
Other:		
Special Programs	$ 817,000	$ 631,674
Alterations and Improvements	267,599	90,755
Special Community Programs	160,011	151,912
Salary Adjustments	2,362,300	2,549,209
Miscellaneous	3,931,808	4,376,981
	$ 7,538,718	$ 7,800,531
Total Expenditures and Encumbrances	$67,724,801	$67,124,337
Transfers to Other Funds	184,162	184,162
Total Expenditures, Encumbrances, and Transfers	$67,908,963	$67,308,499
Deficiency of Revenues and Transfers over Expenditures, Encumbrances, and Transfers	$ 3,264,841	$ 1,530,300

Source: City of Miami, Florida, Annual Financial Report, year ended September 30, 1976, pp. 41–42.

Exhibit 15.7   City of Miami Change in Fund Balance to Be Used in P15.5

City of Miami, Florida
General Fund
Statement of Fund Balance
Year Ended September 30, 1976

Balance, September 30, 1975	$ 956,328
Excess (Deficiency) of Revenues and Transfers over Expenditures, Encumbrances, and Transfers	(1,530,300)
Fund Balance (Deficit), September 30, 1976	$ (573,972)

Source: City of Miami, Florida, Annual Financial Report, year ended September 30, 1976, p. 40.

Congress approved a budget of $3,820,000, adding $100,000 to the authorized program costs of each program. OMB apportioned one-half of the final budget to the commission on July 1, and one-half on January 1, 19X4. On each date, the chief commissioner allotted the budgeted amounts to the three unit managers.

Expenditures were obligated, liquidated, and accrued during the year as follows:

	July 1–December 31			January 1–June 30		
	Obligated	Accrued Expenditures	Obligations December 31	Obligated	Accrued Expenditures	Obligations June 30
General Administration:						
Salaries	$135,000	$120,000	$15,000	$150,000	$165,000	$ 0
Other	240,000	180,000	70,000	265,000	310,000	20,000
Export Program:						
Administrative						
Salaries . . .	320,000	300,000	20,000	360,000	370,000	0
Other						
Administrative .	280,000	260,000	35,000	280,000	300,000	15,000
Program Costs . .	220,000	140,000	90,000	175,000	250,000	45,000
Import Program:						
Administrative						
Salaries . . .	250,000	230,000	10,000	250,000	250,000	0
Other						
Administrative .	190,000	150,000	50,000	170,000	220,000	25,000
Program Costs . .	100,000	30,000	80,000	130,000	70,000	110,000

Actual payments recorded by the Treasury were $1,350,000 for July 1–December 31, 19X3, and $1,900,000 for January 1–June 30, 19X4.

Required:

1. Prepare journal entries to record the budget and the transactions of the International Cultural Commission for the year.
2. Prepare closing entries at June 30, 19X4. Assume that any amounts obligated as of year-end are carried forward and that unobligated spending authority lapses.
3. Prepare a balance sheet as of June 30, 19X4.
4. Prepare a statement comparing the commission's budgeted and actual expenditures for the year (include outstanding obligations in actual expenditures).

P15.7 **Analysis of Federal Consolidated Statements (Appendix)** Refer to the prototype consolidated statements of the U.S. Government reproduced in the chapter appendix. Answer each of the following questions for the September 30, 1976, statements (unless otherwise indicated).

1. What are the two largest asset items on the balance sheet?
2. What are the two largest liability items on the balance sheet?
3. Calculate the ratio of total assets to total liabilities.
4. The country's gold reserves are presented on the balance sheet at $11.6 billion, valued at the statutory price of gold at September 30, 1976. What amount would be shown at today's market price for gold?
5. Accrued taxes receivable are presented on the balance sheet at $14.1 billion. How much of this amount represents accrual of nondelinquent individual income taxes?
6. What percentage of the September 30, 1976, inventory is defense-related?
7. What is the average cost per acre of government land?
8. In the process of consolidation, what amount of intragovernmental debt was eliminated?

9. What are the two major sources of government revenue for the year ended June 30, 1976?
10. What two *functions* of the government resulted in the largest expenses during the year ended June 30, 1976?
11. What two *agencies* of the government accounted for the largest expenses during the year ended June 30, 1976?

P15.8 **National Income Accounting** The island nation of Hanover has a simple, self-sufficient economy, involving no imports or exports. The central accounting bureau has collected the following data on the three segments of the economy for 19X6:

Business Segment   The combined sales of all business firms in the economy (all of which are unincorporated) were $2,500,000, broken down as follows:

Sales to Individuals	$1,000,000
Sales to Government	500,000
Sales to Business—Consumption	800,000
Sales to Business—Investment	200,000
	$2,500,000

The combined expenses of all firms were:

Purchase and Use of Goods	$ 800,000
Salaries to Employees	700,000
Rent to Individuals	50,000
Depreciation	100,000
Indirect Business Taxes	400,000
	$2,050,000

Thus, pretax profits were $450,000; aftertax profits were $300,000.

Government Segment   The government's revenues came from income taxes and indirect business taxes. Government expenditures were $500,000 for purchases of goods and $500,000 for salaries to employees.

Household Segment   The income of individuals in the economy includes $200,000 as the imputed rental value of owner-occupied housing. Individuals paid income taxes of $600,000 (including the income taxes paid by business firms) and increased their net savings by $100,000 during the year.

Required: Prepare the national income and product statement for the nation of Hanover for 19X6.

Chapter 16

Accounting and Reporting for Routine Activities of Local Government

In this chapter, we consider the accounting aspects of the normal operating activities of local government. These activities are recorded and reported by the general and special revenue funds, which are studied in detail. All government units have a general fund, even if they have none of the other seven funds discussed in Chapter 15. Thus we examine the general fund first. The special revenue fund, also considered in this chapter, has activities and accounting very similar to those for the general fund. The chapter ends with a discussion of the special sets of accounts used for fixed assets and long-term debt. Funds which use fund accounting procedures, such as the general and special revenue funds, use these account groups.

Budget Formulation

The general and special revenue funds, two of the five funds which use fund accounting, require the recording of budget information in the accounts. The process of recording budget information is straightforward. However, the formulation of the budget may be a lengthy and difficult process.

Unlike business budgeting, which begins with a sales forecast, the budget formulation process in local government usually begins with *expenditure planning*. Activities and programs for the coming year are planned and their cost is estimated. When a tentative expenditure budget is complete, the revenue budget is prepared. First it must be decided whether the budget is to be balanced or is to provide for an increase or decrease in the fund balance. Then revenues from all sources other than the local property tax are estimated. Property taxes are the residual revenue and are planned in an amount necessary to achieve the required total revenue. If the resulting amount to be raised via property tax is unacceptable (for example, too large an increase is needed to achieve the total revenue), the process recycles until expenditures consistent with an acceptable level of property taxation are determined.

To illustrate, assume that the Wilford School District is formulating its general fund budget for 19X1–19X2. A detailed expenditure budget is prepared, which may be summarized as follows:

Central Administration	$ 480,000
Instruction	3,900,000
Operation and Maintenance	770,000
Transportation	600,000
Debt Service	850,000
Total Appropriations	$6,600,000

Next, a list of revenue sources other than the property tax is prepared:

State Aid	$2,000,000
Share of Local Sales Tax	400,000
Fees	200,000
Federal Aid	500,000
Total before Property Tax	$3,100,000

Assuming that the budget is to be balanced, $3,500,000 must be raised via property taxes. If this is deemed acceptable, a proposed tax rate is then calculated. Suppose that the assessed value of taxable property within the Wilford School District is $58,450,230. The tax rate is determined as follows:

$$\text{Tax rate} = \frac{\text{Amount to be raised by property tax}}{\text{Assessed value of taxable property}}$$

$$= \frac{\$3,500,000}{\$58,450,230}$$

$$= .05988.$$

Tax rates are commonly expressed as a rate per $1,000 of assessed valuation. Thus the rate for the Wilford School District would be $59.88 per $1,000 of assessed value, or 59.88 mills. Ideally, in setting the tax rate, the estimated percentage of uncollectible taxes should be taken into account. This would require that an amount greater than $3,500,000 be levied, so that expected collections are $3,500,000. For example, if 2 percent of the property tax levy is expected to be uncollectible, $3,571,428 (= $3,500,000/.98) must be levied in order to have expected revenue of $3,500,000. In many cases, however, property taxes are levied without regard for collectibility.

Budget approval must generally follow a specified legal process. A common process calls for a proposed budget to be presented by the executive (for example, mayor or school board president) of the local government to the legislative body for its approval. Ultimately, the budget approved by the legislature may differ from the proposed budget. The approved budget is then subject to acceptance or veto by the executive. Some jurisdictions provide that the executive must accept or veto the budget in its entirety; others permit veto of specific items in the budget. Another budget approval process used in some school districts requires that a budget be formulated by a school board and presented to the voters for acceptance or rejection. In either case, the process continues until a budget is accepted.

The General Fund

Once the budget is formulated and approved, the accounting process begins. We first consider the general fund, which accounts for the routine operations of a local government funded by general revenues.

Accounting for the General Fund

The general fund employs fund accounting, following the structure set forth in Chapter 15. We now discuss how this system applies to the general fund and consider several special situations.

Budget Entry   In the general fund, the title **Estimated Revenues** is used for the budgeted revenues account, and the title **Appropriations** is used for the budgeted expenditures account. Thus the entry for the balanced budget situation would be:

Estimated Revenues	XX	
Appropriations		XX

If the budget is not balanced, a debit or credit to Fund Balance—Unreserved is also required, as illustrated in Chapter 15.

Recording Property Tax Revenues   Under the modified accrual basis of accounting, some revenues are recorded on the accrual basis and some on the cash basis. Property tax revenue is a major example of a case where the accrual basis is used, because the amount of revenue can be estimated with reasonable accuracy and the probability of collection is very high. The amount of the tax levy, less an appropriate allowance for uncollectibles, should be recorded as revenue in the following manner:

Taxes Receivable—Current	XX	
Allowance for Uncollectible Taxes—Current		XX
Revenues		XX

The amount credited to Revenues is the *net amount* which the local government expects to collect. The net amount is recorded because it reflects the amount of spendable resources expected to be available. Property tax collections, which are a major source of revenue for most local governments, may not occur until after a few months of the fiscal year have elapsed. To provide operating cash for the period from the beginning of the fiscal year until collection, local governments often issue **tax anticipation notes.** These are short-term borrowings that are repaid from tax collections.

After a period of time has passed, the uncollected taxes will change from current to delinquent status. This balance should be reclassified to a Taxes Receivable—Delinquent account with a corresponding allowance for uncollectibles. The reclassification entries would be:

Taxes Receivable—Delinquent	XX	
Taxes Receivable—Current		XX
Allowance for Uncollectible Taxes—Current	XX	
Allowance for Uncollectible Taxes—Delinquent		XX

It is common to **fully reserve** delinquent taxes, which means that the amount of the allowance for uncollectibles should equal the amount of delinquent taxes receivable. To accomplish this, it may be necessary to adjust the amount of revenues originally recorded to bring the original estimate of uncollectible taxes into agreement with the delinquent amount.

To illustrate, assume that a city levies a property tax of $3,000,000, which is expected to be 95 percent collectible. The initial entry is:

Taxes Receivable—Current	3,000,000	
Allowance for Uncollectible Taxes—Current .		150,000
Revenues		2,850,000
To record tax levy.		

If $2,800,000 is collected, and the unpaid amounts are officially declared delinquent, the entries are:

Cash	2,800,000	
Taxes Receivable—Current		2,800,000
To record collections of property taxes.		
Taxes Receivable—Delinquent	200,000	
Taxes Receivable—Current		200,000
To reclassify unpaid taxes.		
Allowance for Uncollectible Taxes—Current . .	150,000	
Revenues	50,000	
Allowance for Uncollectible Taxes—		
Delinquent		200,000
To reclassify allowance for uncollectible taxes and increase it to $200,000.		

Note that the last entry makes the allowance equal to the amount of delinquent taxes. To increase the allowance to $200,000, Revenues (originally recorded as $2,850,000) must be reduced by $50,000. This adjustment has the effect of correcting the original entry to record the tax levy, so that Revenues shows the amounts actually collected and the Allowance for Uncollectible Taxes balance equals the amount of delinquent taxes receivable. Had the collections exceeded the amount originally entered as revenues, resulting in delinquent taxes being less than the allowance for uncollectible taxes, the adjusting entry would increase (credit) revenues and decrease (debit) the allowance.

If delinquent taxes are fully reserved, no revenue from these particular tax levies is anticipated. The criteria for accrual of revenue require that collection occur within a short time and the degree of collectibility be capable of reasonable estimation. These criteria are not met in the case of delinquent taxes. The collection process may take a long time, and its success is highly uncertain. As a result, revenue from delinquent taxes is not accrued. Any collections which do occur are recorded as revenues at time of collection. For example, a $10,000 collection of delinquent taxes would be recorded as:

Cash	10,000	
Allowance for Uncollectible Taxes—Delinquent . . .	10,000	
Taxes Receivable—Delinquent		10,000
Revenues		10,000
To record collection of delinquent taxes.		

In effect, revenues from delinquent taxes are recorded on the cash basis.

After additional time passes, delinquent taxes may become tax liens. **Tax liens** are legal claims against the taxed property, which may be satisfied by forcing sale of the property. Reclassification to a Tax Liens Receivable account, with a corresponding allowance for uncollectibles, should be made. Again, it is common to fully reserve tax liens. The entries are similar to those illustrated above for reclassifying taxes receivable from current to delinquent.

Purchase of Materials and Supplies   When an initial binding commitment of resources is made, in the form of a purchase order or contract for goods or services, an encumbrance is recorded. The encumbrance is reversed upon receipt of the goods or services, and the expenditure is recorded.

To illustrate, suppose that purchase orders for supplies are issued. The estimated cost of $46,000 is recorded as an encumbrance:

```
Encumbrances   .   .   .   .   .   .   .   .   .   .   46,000
    Reserve for Encumbrances   .   .   .   .   .   .              46,000
To record purchase orders for supplies.
```

Assume now that some of the supplies are received. The encumbered amount for the goods received was $38,000 but the invoice amount is $39,300. The following entries are made:

```
Reserve for Encumbrances   .   .   .   .   .   .   .   38,000
    Encumbrances   .   .   .   .   .   .   .   .   .   .              38,000
To reverse encumbrances for supplies received.

Expenditures .   .   .   .   .   .   .   .   .   .   .   39,300
    Vouchers Payable .   .   .   .   .   .   .   .   .              39,300
To record invoices for supplies received.
```

Two special problems with respect to accounting for materials and supplies merit further discussion. One is the presence of inventories, and the other is the existence of outstanding purchase orders at year-end.

Inventories   Two methods of inventory accounting exist for governmental funds: the purchases method, which treats inventory items as expenditures when *purchased*, and the consumption method, which treats inventory items as expenditures when *used*.

Under the **purchases method,** the cost of materials and supplies is charged to Expenditures as they are purchased, without regard to their consumption during the current period. Recall that a major objective of fund accounting is to account for the spending of resources as prescribed by a budget. Once materials and supplies have been purchased, spending authority has been used, and this important fact is recorded by debiting Expenditures. Whether the materials or supplies are currently consumed is of little importance insofar as spending authority is concerned.

Despite having recorded the purchase as an expenditure, it is still desirable to report on the financial statements the amount of materials and supplies in inventory at year-end. To accomplish this without changing the expenditure accounting for the purchase requires the following entry to establish the inventory:

```
Inventory   .   .   .   .   .   .   .   .   .   .   .   .   .   XX
    Reserve for Inventory   .   .   .   .   .   .   .   .   .              XX
```

The Reserve for Inventory account signifies that a portion of the fund's assets is no longer available for appropriation and expenditure. The inventory is an asset which can be used but cannot be expended to acquire goods and services. The Reserve for Inventory appears as part of the fund balance section on the balance sheet.

To illustrate, suppose that during the year supplies are purchased at a cost of $210,000. At time of purchase, the entry is:

Expenditures	210,000	
Vouchers Payable		210,000
To record purchase of supplies.		

Assume that, at year-end, supplies costing $33,000 remain in inventory. The year-end entry to establish the inventory is:

Inventory	33,000	
Reserve for Inventory		33,000
To record inventory at year-end.		

In subsequent years, inventory changes are easily recorded. Suppose that at the end of the following year, the inventory has decreased to $28,000. The year-end adjusting entry to reduce the inventory balance and the corresponding reserve by $5,000 is:

Reserve for Inventory	5,000	
Inventory		5,000
To adjust inventory to current year-end balance of $28,000.		

Under the **consumption method,** inventory is viewed as a spendable or consumable asset, similar to cash. Consequently, Inventory is debited at time of purchase, and Expenditures is debited only as the inventory is used. The entries under this approach are:

Inventory	XX	
Vouchers Payable		XX
To record purchase of supplies.		

Expenditures	XX	
Inventory		XX
To record use of supplies.		

No Reserve for Inventory account is needed. If such a reserve is established, however, it is created by debiting the Unreserved Fund Balance.

Outstanding Encumbrances at Year-End   At the end of the fiscal year, it is likely that there will be some purchase orders outstanding for goods or services which have been ordered but have not yet been received. Assume that purchase orders amounting to $27,000 were issued late in 19X1 and were still outstanding at year-end. At time of issue, the entry was:

Encumbrances	27,000	
Reserve for Encumbrances		27,000
To record purchase orders.		

The treatment of outstanding encumbrances at year-end and the treatment of the related expenditure in the subsequent year depend on whether the accounting system follows a legal or GAAP approach.

Under a **legal approach,** the budget is viewed in legal terms, namely as the authority to *commit the expenditure of resources* during a period of time. Thus, an encumbrance—a commitment to spend—constitutes a charge against the annual budget, irrespective of when the expenditure occurs. In terms of their effect on spending authority, outstanding encumbrances are equivalent to expenditures; that is, they are closed to the fund balance and are included in the budgetary comparison statements. In the succeeding year, the expenditures related to year-end encumbrances are recorded separately and are charged against the carryover reserve rather than against the subsequent year's budget.

Using the legal approach, the $27,000 of encumbrances outstanding at the end of 19X1 would be reflected in the closing entry as follows:

Appropriations	XX	
Fund Balance—Unreserved		XX
Expenditures		XX
Encumbrances		27,000

Closing the encumbrances at the end of 19X1 signifies that they are charged against the 19X1 budget. Note that the Reserve for Encumbrances account remains and will appear on the general fund balance sheet. This account carries over into 19X2 to signify that there are some transactions relating to the 19X1 budget yet to be completed. The goods and services will be received in 19X2 but will not be charged against the 19X2 budget. Various accounting procedures exist to properly record this situation; we shall illustrate one. At the beginning of 19X2, the Reserve for Encumbrances should be redesignated to signify that it involves purchase orders of the prior year:

Reserve for Encumbrances	27,000	
Reserve for Encumbrances—Prior Year		27,000
To reclassify purchase orders outstanding at beginning of 19X2.		

When the goods and services ordered in 19X1 are received in 19X2 at a cost of $26,600, a separate expenditures account is used:

Expenditures—Prior Year Encumbrances	26,600	
Vouchers Payable		26,600
To record invoices for goods and services ordered in 19X1.		

At the end of 19X2, an additional closing entry is required, to close the prior year encumbrances and related expenditures to the fund balance:

Reserve for Encumbrances—Prior Year	27,000	
Expenditures—Prior Year Encumbrances		26,600
Fund Balance—Unreserved		400
To close encumbrances carried over from 19X1 and related expenditures.		

The $400 credit to fund balance is in effect a correction of the 19X1 closing entry. That entry closed $27,000 of encumbrances against the fund balance. However, the actual charge for these goods and services was only $26,600. The entry to close 19X2 revenues, expenditures, and encumbrances would be unaffected by the above transactions.

Under a **GAAP approach,** the budget is viewed in terms of modified accrual accounting, namely the *expenditure of resources* during a period of time. Budgetary comparison statements compare expenditures recorded during the year (which do *not* include outstanding encumbrances) with a budget figure that indicates authority to spend during the year. Thus, a GAAP budget—one that measures authority to *spend* during the current year—consists of the current year's legal budget *plus* prior year appropriations carried over to the current year in the form of outstanding encumbrances.

Using the GAAP approach, the $27,000 of encumbrances outstanding at the end of 19X1 is reflected in the closing entry as follows:

Appropriations XX		
Fund Balance—Unreserved	XX	
Expenditures	XX	
Encumbrances	27,000	

Again the Reserve for Encumbrances remains, but it is considered part of the total fund balance. Moreover, the $27,000 of encumbrances does not appear on the 19X1 statement of revenues, expenditures, and changes in fund balance or on the 19X1 budgetary comparison statements.

In 19X2, the $27,000 encumbrance is restored to the accounts, in effect reversing part of the 19X1 closing entry:

Encumbrances 27,000		
Fund Balance—Unreserved	27,000	
To restore encumbrance carried over from 19X1.		

The subsequent expenditure is recorded in the same manner as all other 19X2 expenditures. At year-end, total expenditures for 19X2 include the $26,600 related to the carryover encumbrance. In the budgetary comparison statements for 19X2, total expenditures for 19X2 are then compared to a budget figure consisting of the 19X2 legal budget plus the carryover appropriation of $27,000.

The two methods may be summarized as follows. Assume for convenience that an encumbrance is outstanding at the end of 19X1.

1. Under the legal approach, the encumbered amount is treated as if it were an expenditure in 19X1:
   a. It is closed to the fund balance in 19X1.
   b. It is included in comparing budget to actual for 19X1.
   c. While the actual expenditure is recorded in 19X2, it is classified separately from 19X2 expenditures and is closed against the carried-over reserve for encumbrances. It does not affect the comparison of budget to actual for 19X2.

2. Under the GAAP approach, the encumbered amount is carried into 19X2:
   a. It is temporarily closed to the fund balance at the end of 19X1, but this entry is reversed in 19X2.
   b. It is *not* included in comparing budget to actual for 19X1.
   c. When the actual expenditure occurs in 19X2, it is included with all other 19X2 expenditures.
   d. In comparing budget to actual for 19X2, the encumbered amount from 19X1 is added to the 19X2 budget.

Interfund Transactions   Transactions among funds are common in local government. These transactions are of various types, each with its own accounting treatment. We shall discuss five types of **interfund transactions.**

Loans or **advances** are temporary transfers from one fund to another, with repayment expected. These are recorded as receivables or payables by the funds involved. Special account titles are used: Due from ＿＿＿ Fund and Due to ＿＿＿ Fund. Temporary interfund transfers may be used to provide initial financing for a particular activity. For example, suppose a particular project in the special revenue fund is to be supported by a federal grant. To provide for costs incurred prior to the actual receipt of the grant, the local government might advance $8,000 from the general fund to the special revenue fund. This transaction would be recorded in the general fund as:

    Due from Special Revenue Fund 8,000
        Cash   8,000
    To record advance to special revenue fund.

A parallel entry is required on the books of the special revenue fund:

    Cash 8,000
        Due to General Fund   8,000
    To record advance from general fund.

Reimbursements occur when fund A pays an expenditure properly applicable to fund B, and fund B subsequently repays fund A. Assuming fund A originally recorded the payment as an expenditure, the reimbursement is recorded as an expenditure by fund B and as a reduction of expenditures by fund A. For example, suppose that the general fund paid $4,000 for supplies which are properly chargeable to a special revenue fund project and recorded:

    Expenditures 4,000
        Cash   4,000
    To record purchase of supplies for special revenue fund
    project.

Subsequently, the special revenue fund reimburses the general fund for the supplies. The entry by the special revenue fund is:

    Expenditures 4,000
        Cash   4,000
    To record reimbursement to general fund for supplies.

and the entry by the general fund is:

    Cash 4,000
        Expenditures   4,000
    To record reimbursement from special revenue fund.

Note that, following the reimbursement, the expenditure is recorded in the proper fund, and there is no net effect on the general fund.

Quasi-external transactions are transactions which, if they involved an external party rather than another fund, would be treated as revenues or expenditures. The same accounting treatment applies when the transaction occurs between two funds. For example, if the general fund purchases supplies from an outside vendor, an expenditure is recorded by the general fund. If the supplies are purchased from an internal service fund, the accounting is identical: an expenditure is recorded by the general fund (and revenue is recorded by the internal service fund). Other examples of transactions of this type include:

1. Contributions to a pension trust fund.

2. Payments in lieu of property taxes by an enterprise fund.

3. Payments to an enterprise fund for utility services provided to city buildings.

Residual equity transfers occur when resources of a permanent equity nature are transferred from one fund to another. For example, if a city establishes an internal service fund, the initial equity of the fund might be provided by a transfer of general fund resources. Residual equity transfers are accounted for as direct changes in beginning fund balances.

Operating transfers involve legally authorized transfers of resources from the fund receiving the revenues to the fund which will make the expenditures. Unlike residual equity transfers, operating transfers are spent by the receiving fund in carrying on its activities. The general fund frequently supports the activities of other funds in this way. Some examples are:

1. Debt payments (principal and interest) on long-term debt originally incurred by the general or capital projects funds are commonly made from general fund resources. Money would be transferred from the general fund to the debt service fund.

2. A business activity of the local government such as the water department might be partially subsidized by general fund resources, which would be transferred to the enterprise fund.

3. A construction project might be financed in part by a bond issue and in part by general fund resources transferred to the capital projects fund.

Operating transfers are not considered revenues and expenditures. They are reported as Other Financing Sources (Uses) in the statement of revenues, expenditures, and changes in fund balance and in the budgetary comparison statements.

Financial Statements for the General Fund

Financial statements for the general fund typically include a balance sheet; a statement of revenues, expenditures, and changes in fund balance; and a budgetary comparison statement.

Balance Sheet The balance sheet of the general fund has the following format:

Assets:	Liabilities:
Cash	Vouchers payable
Short-term investments	Due to other funds
Taxes receivable, less allowance for uncollectible taxes	**Fund balance:**
Other receivables	Reserved for encumbrances
Due from other funds	Reserved for inventories
Inventories	Unreserved
Total Assets	Total Liabilities and Fund Balance

The balance sheet is unclassified. Fixed assets and long-term debt are excluded from the balance sheet and are recorded in separate account groups. Thus the assets of the general fund are limited to those which are able to be spent or otherwise consumed during the next fiscal period in carrying out the fund's activities. Similarly, the liabilities of the general fund are limited to claims that will be paid during the next fiscal year.

Exhibit 16.1   Illustration of General Fund Balance Sheet

City of Norwood
Balance Sheet—General Fund
June 30, 19X8

ASSETS

Cash	$ 51,000
Short-Term Investments, at Cost	1,850,000
Accounts Receivable (Net of $300 Allowance for Uncollectible Accounts)	1,200
Due from Other Governments	1,040,800
Total Assets	$2,943,000

LIABILITIES AND FUND BALANCE

Liabilities:	
Vouchers Payable	$ 239,000
Due to Other Funds	170,000
Total Liabilities	$ 409,000
Fund Balance:	
Reserved for Encumbrances	$2,265,000
Unreserved	269,000
Total Fund Balance	$2,534,000
Total Liabilities and Fund Balance	$2,943,000

Exhibit 16.1 presents a simple balance sheet for the general fund of a city. Note that only current assets are shown; these are the resources available for use in carrying on the particular activities of this fund. Note also that the total fund balance includes the reserve for encumbrances, which signifies that purchase orders were outstanding at year-end, along with the unreserved portion.

Statement of Revenues, Expenditures, and Changes in Fund Balance
The statement of revenues, expenditures, and changes in fund balance for the general fund summarizes all transactions affecting the *total fund balance* during the reporting period. The format of the statement is as follows:

> Revenues (Classified)
> − Expenditures (Classified)
> = Excess of Revenues over (under) Expenditures
> +/− Other Financing Sources (Uses) (such as proceeds of bond issues and transfers to or from other funds)
> = Excess of Revenues and Other Sources over (under) Expenditures and Other Uses
> + Fund Balance—Beginning of Period
> = Fund Balance—End of Period

Exhibit 16.2 Illustration of General Fund Statement of Revenues, Expenditures, and Changes in Fund Balance

City of Norwood
Statement of Revenues, Expenditures, and Changes
in Fund Balance—General Fund
For the Fiscal Year Ended June 30, 19X8

REVENUES:

Taxes	$6,453,000
Licenses and Permits	800,000
Charges for Services	1,500,000
Miscellaneous Revenues	879,000
Total Revenues	$9,632,000

EXPENDITURES:

General Government	$1,508,000
Public Safety	3,600,000
Health and Welfare	730,000
Education	3,080,000
Total Expenditures	$8,918,000
Excess of Revenues over (under) Expenditures	$ 714,000

OTHER FINANCING SOURCES (USES):

Operating Transfers In	$ 670,000
Operating Transfers Out	(850,000)
Total Other Financing Sources (Uses)	$ (180,000)
Excess of Revenues and Other Sources over Expenditures and Other Uses	$ 534,000
Fund Balance—July 1, 19X7	2,000,000
Fund Balance—June 30, 19X8	$2,534,000

The fund balance referred to in this statement is the *total* fund balance, including reserves. Exhibit 16.2 illustrates the statement of revenues, expenditures, and changes in fund balance.

Revenues are classified by *source*. For the general fund, major sources of revenue include taxes, intergovernmental revenues, licenses and permits, charges for services, and fines. Various types of expenditure classification also exist. For financial statement purposes, expenditures are often classified by character and function. Classification by *character* hinges on the time period(s) which the expenditures benefit. Common character classifications are *current expenditures*, *capital outlays*, and *debt service*. Classification by *function* identifies groups of related activities designed to accomplish a particular service or regulatory responsibility. Examples of functions are general government, public safety, education, highways, sanitation, health, and recreation. Other financing sources and uses include proceeds of long-term debt issues and operating transfers to or from the general fund. As noted earlier, residual equity transfers are reported as a change to the beginning fund balance.

Budgetary Comparison Statements   In addition to the statement of revenues, expenditures, and changes in fund balance discussed above, a parallel statement showing the comparison between budget and actual data is presented. The format of the budgetary comparison statement (formally called the **statement of revenues, expenditures, and changes in fund balance—budget and actual**) is identical to the format of the statement of revenues, expenditures, and changes in fund balance, except that three columns of numbers are presented:

Budget	Actual	Variance— Favorable (Unfavorable)

An illustration of a budgetary comparison statement appears in Exhibit 16.3. Note that the convention here differs from cost accounting. In cost accounting, favorable variances are commonly enclosed in parentheses, while in governmental accounting, parentheses are used for unfavorable variances.

Comprehensive Illustration of General Fund Accounting and Reporting

Ranford County maintains its general fund on a calendar year basis. On January 1, 19X2, the accounts of the general fund had the following balances:

Ranford County
Trial Balance
January 1, 19X2

Accounts	Debit	Credit
Cash	$ 80,000	
Taxes Receivable—Delinquent	15,000	
Due from Special Revenue Fund	10,000	
Supplies Inventory	5,000	
Vouchers Payable		$ 5,000
Fund Balance—Unreserved		83,000
Reserve for Supplies Inventory		5,000
Reserve for Encumbrances		2,000
Allowance for Uncollectible Taxes—Delinquent		15,000
	$110,000	$110,000

The 19X2 general fund budget included revenues from the following sources:

Property Taxes (Expected to Be 95% Collectible)	$200,000
State Aid	30,000
Fees and Licenses	8,000
Charges for Services	12,000
Miscellaneous	5,000

Expenditures for 19X2 were estimated to be:

General Services	$180,000
Supplies	18,000
Maintenance	14,000
Miscellaneous	6,000

Exhibit 16.3   Illustration of General Fund Budgetary Comparison Statement

City of Norwood
Statement of Revenues, Expenditures, and Changes
in Fund Balance—Budget and Actual—General Fund
For the Fiscal Year Ended June 30, 19X8

	Budget	Actual	Variance—Favorable (Unfavorable)
REVENUES:			
Taxes	$6,461,000	$6,453,000	$ (8,000)
Licenses and Permits	975,000	800,000	(175,000)
Charges for Services	1,604,000	1,500,000	(104,000)
Miscellaneous Revenues	866,000	879,000	13,000
Total Revenues	$9,906,000	$9,632,000	$(274,000)
EXPENDITURES:			
General Government	$1,764,000	$1,508,000	$ 256,000
Public Safety	3,334,000	3,600,000	(266,000)
Health and Welfare	839,000	730,000	109,000
Education	2,886,000	3,080,000	(194,000)
Total Expenditures	$8,823,000	$8,918,000	$ (95,000)
Excess of Revenues over (under) Expenditures	$1,083,000	$ 714,000	$(369,000)
OTHER FINANCING SOURCES (USES):			
Operating Transfers In	$ 665,000	$ 670,000	$ 5,000
Operating Transfers Out	(850,000)	(850,000)	—
Total Other Financing Sources (Uses)	$ (185,000)	$ (180,000)	$ 5,000
Excess of Revenues and Other Sources over Expenditures and Other Uses	$ 898,000	$ 534,000	$(364,000)
Fund Balance—July 1, 19X7	2,000,000	2,000,000	—
Fund Balance—June 30, 19X8	$2,898,000	$2,534,000	$(364,000)

In addition, the county decided to establish an internal service fund to purchase supplies used by the general fund and the special revenue fund. A permanent transfer of $20,000 from the general fund was authorized to enable the internal service fund to purchase an inventory base. For the first year of operation the general fund plans to subsidize $8,000 of the operating costs of the internal service fund.

Transactions during the Year   The events and transactions occurring during the year were recorded as follows.

1. The budget was recorded on January 2 as:

Estimated Revenues	255,000	
Appropriations		246,000
Fund Balance—Unreserved		9,000

To record 19X2 budget as follows:
Revenues from:
Property taxes $200,000

State aid .		30,000
Fees and licenses		8,000
Charges for services		12,000
Miscellaneous revenues .		5,000
Total revenues		$255,000
Appropriations for:		
General services		$180,000
Supplies .		18,000
Maintenance .		14,000
Capital transfer to internal service fund .		20,000
Operating transfer to internal service fund		8,000
Miscellaneous		6,000
Total appropriations .		$246,000

2. **Taxes were levied and recorded by the following entry.**

Taxes Receivable—Current .	200,000	
Allowance for Uncollectible Taxes—		
Current		10,000
Revenues		190,000

To record property tax levy, estimated to be 95% collectible.

3. **The county received $30,000 in state aid.**

Cash .	30,000	
Revenues		30,000

To record aid received from state government.

4. **Delinquent taxes of $4,000 were received; the remainder of 19X1 taxes were reclassified as tax liens.**

Cash .	4,000	
Allowance for Uncollectible Taxes—		
Delinquent	4,000	
Taxes Receivable—Delinquent .		4,000
Revenues		4,000

To record collection of delinquent taxes.

Tax Liens Receivable	11,000	
Allowance for Uncollectible Taxes—		
Delinquent	11,000	
Allowance for Uncollectible Tax Liens .		11,000
Taxes Receivable—Delinquent .		11,000

To reclassify uncollected delinquent taxes as tax liens and to fully reserve tax liens.

5. **The internal service fund was established, and the $28,000 authorized was transferred from the general fund.**

Fund Balance—Unreserved	20,000	
Cash .		20,000

To record permanent capital transfer to establish the internal service fund.

Operating Transfers Out .	8,000	
Cash .		8,000

To record authorized subsidy of internal service fund operating costs.

6. **Ranford County follows the GAAP approach for recording encumbrances outstanding at year-end. For the miscellaneous amounts en-**

cumbered for $2,000 but not received in 19X1, the bill received in 19X2 was $1,800. The bill was paid in cash.

Encumbrances	2,000	
Fund Balance—Unreserved		2,000
To restore encumbrances carried over from 19X1.		

Reserve for Encumbrances	2,000	
Encumbrances		2,000
To reverse encumbrances.		

Expenditures	1,800	
Cash		1,800
To record expenditures.		

7. Revenues were received as follows: $8,500 from fees and licenses, $11,800 from charges for services, and $5,300 from miscellaneous sources.

Cash	25,600	
Revenues		25,600
To record revenues.		

8. Supplies of $18,000 were ordered from the internal service fund.

Encumbrances	18,000	
Reserve for Encumbrances		18,000
To record ordering of supplies.		

9. Expenditures of cash were $6,200 for miscellaneous purchases and $40,000 for general services. For maintenance $14,000 was encumbered; for general services, $135,000.

Expenditures	46,200	
Cash		46,200
To record cash expenditures.		

Encumbrances	149,000	
Reserve for Encumbrances		149,000
To encumber resources for goods and services ordered.		

10. Supplies were received and the internal service fund was paid cash of $18,000. Ranford County follows the *purchases method* of accounting for inventory.

Reserve for Encumbrances	18,000	
Encumbrances		18,000
To reverse encumbrances.		

Expenditures	18,000	
Cash		18,000
To record payment for supplies.		

11. Current taxes of $183,000 were collected.

Cash	183,000	
Taxes Receivable—Current		183,000
To record collection of current taxes.		

12. Bills for goods and services ordered and received were as follows: maintenance, $14,000 and general services, $137,000. The total vouchers paid in 19X2 amounted to $152,000.

Reserve for Encumbrances	149,000	
Encumbrances		149,000
To reverse encumbrances.		
Expenditures	151,000	
Vouchers Payable		151,000
To record expenditures.		
Vouchers Payable	152,000	
Cash		152,000
To record payment of vouchers outstanding.		

13. Goods to be used in providing general services were ordered late in December but were not received in 19X2. The anticipated price of the goods was $1,300.

Encumbrances	1,300	
Reserve for Encumbrances		1,300
To encumber resources for goods ordered.		

14. Cash of $10,000 was received from the special revenue fund as repayment of a loan made in 19X1.

Cash	10,000	
Due from Special Revenue Fund . . .		10,000
To record repayment of loan.		

15. At year-end, a count of supplies showed inventory costing $7,000 was on hand.

Supplies Inventory	2,000	
Reserve for Supplies Inventory . . .		2,000
To adjust supplies inventory and reserve		
account from $5,000 beginning balance to		
$7,000 ending balance.		

16. Taxes uncollected at year-end were classified delinquent and fully reserved.

Revenues	7,000	
Taxes Receivable—Delinquent	17,000	
Allowance for Uncollectible Taxes—Current .	10,000	
Taxes Receivable—Current		17,000
Allowance for Uncollectible Taxes—		
Delinquent		17,000
To reclassify uncollected taxes as delinquent		
and fully reserved and to reduce revenues by		
the amount uncollected in excess of the		
estimated uncollectibles.		

The preclosing trial balance for Ranford County at December 31, 19X2, appears as follows:

Ranford County
Preclosing Trial Balance
December 31, 19X2

Account	Debit	Credit
Cash	$ 86,600	
Taxes Receivable—Delinquent	17,000	

Account	Debit	Credit
Tax Liens Receivable	11,000	
Supplies Inventory	7,000	
Encumbrances	1,300	
Expenditures	217,000	
Operating Transfers Out	8,000	
Estimated Revenues	255,000	
Vouchers Payable		$ 4,000
Revenues		242,600
Appropriations		246,000
Allowance for Uncollectible Taxes—Delinquent		17,000
Allowance for Uncollectible Tax Liens		11,000
Reserve for Supplies Inventory		7,000
Reserve for Encumbrances		1,300
Fund Balance—Unreserved		74,000
	$602,900	$602,900

The county's subsidiary records show the detail of the revenues and expenditure accounts as follows:

REVENUES

Property Taxes	$187,000
State Aid	30,000
Fees and Licenses	8,500
Charges for Services	11,800
Miscellaneous	5,300
Total Revenues	$242,600

EXPENDITURES

General Services	$177,000
Maintenance	14,000
Supplies	18,000
Miscellaneous	8,000
Total Expenditures	$217,000

Closing entries at December 31, 19X2, are as follows:

Revenues	242,600	
Fund Balance—Unreserved	12,400	
Estimated Revenues		255,000
To close revenues.		
Appropriations	246,000	
Operating Transfers Out		8,000
Expenditures		217,000
Encumbrances		1,300
Fund Balance—Unreserved		19,700
To close expenditures, encumbrances, and operating transfers.		

The financial statements for the general fund of Ranford County can now be prepared. The balance sheet appears as Exhibit 16.4.

Exhibit 16.4   Balance Sheet of Ranford County

Ranford County
Balance Sheet—General Fund
December 31, 19X2

ASSETS

Cash	$86,600
Taxes Receivable—Delinquent (net of $17,000 allowance for uncollectible taxes)	—
Tax Liens Receivable (net of $11,000 allowance for uncollectible tax liens) . .	—
Supplies Inventory	7,000
Total Assets	$93,600

LIABILITIES AND FUND BALANCE

Liabilities:	
Vouchers Payable	$ 4,000
Total Liabilities	$ 4,000
Fund Balance:	
Reserved for Supplies Inventory	$ 7,000
Reserved for Encumbrances	1,300
Unreserved	81,300
Total Fund Balance	$89,600
Total Liabilities and Fund Balance	$93,600

Note that the delinquent taxes receivable and tax liens receivable have both been fully reserved, signifying that no revenues are anticipated from these sources.

The statement of revenues, expenditures, and changes in the general fund balance is presented in Exhibit 16.5. The *total* fund balance (unreserved fund balance plus the reserves) appears on this statement. Since the purchases method was used for the supplies inventory, all purchases of supplies during the year are included in expenditures. The effect of the inventory increase, which increases the total fund balance, is shown under the caption "Other Financing Sources (Uses)."

The budgetary comparison statement for Ranford County appears in Exhibit 16.6.

The Special Revenue Fund

The special revenue fund is also used to account for operating activities of a local government. It is distinguished from the general fund in that the revenues (usually from state or federal grants) are directed to very specific activities or projects. For example, a local government might receive grants to provide a summer youth employment program, a drug abuse control program, and downtown redevelopment. In addition to special project grants, other restricted-use

Exhibit 16.5   Statement of Revenues, Expenditures, and Changes in Fund Balance of Ranford County

Ranford County
Statement of Revenues, Expenditures, and
Changes in Fund Balance—General Fund
For the Fiscal Year Ended December 31, 19X2

REVENUES:

Property Taxes	$187,000
State Aid	30,000
Fees and Licenses	8,500
Charges for Services	11,800
Miscellaneous	5,300
Total Revenues	$242,600

EXPENDITURES:

General Services	$177,000
Maintenance	14,000
Supplies	18,000
Miscellaneous	8,000
Total Expenditures	$217,000
Excess of Revenues over Expenditures	$ 25,600

OTHER FINANCING SOURCES (USES):

Increase in Supplies Inventory	$ 2,000
Operating Transfers Out	(8,000)
Total Other Financing Sources (Uses)	(6,000)
Excess of Revenues and Other Sources over Expenditures and Other Uses	$ 19,600
Fund Balance—January 1	$ 90,000 [a]
Less: Residual Equity Transfer	20,000
Adjusted Fund Balance—January 1	$ 70,000
Fund Balance—December 31	$ 89,600

[a] Unreserved Fund Balance	$83,000
Reserve for Supplies Inventory	5,000
Reserve for Encumbrances	2,000
	$90,000

money such as federal revenue-sharing, CETA, and urban renewal programs is handled in the special revenue fund. It is not unusual for hundreds of such programs to exist in a single local government. Thus the special revenue fund is likely to consist of several separate funds, many of which will further require detailed subsidiary records by project.

The special revenue fund involves many of the same types of activities as the general fund. The difference between the two lies in their sources of revenue. Revenue for the general fund comes from general sources such as property taxes, fees, and unrestricted state aid. The local government is free to allocate

Exhibit 16.6   Budgetary Comparison Statement for Ranford County

Ranford County
Statement of Revenues, Expenditures, and Changes
in Fund Balance—Budget and Actual—General Fund
For the Fiscal Year Ended December 31, 19X2

	Budget	Actual	Variance—Favorable (Unfavorable)
REVENUES:			
Property Taxes	$200,000	$187,000	$(13,000)
State Aid	30,000	30,000	—
Fees and Licenses	8,000	8,500	500
Charges for Services	12,000	11,800	(200)
Miscellaneous	5,000	5,300	300
Total Revenues	$255,000	$242,600	$(12,400)
EXPENDITURES:			
General Services	$180,000	$177,000	$ 3,000
Maintenance	14,000	14,000	—
Supplies	18,000	18,000	—
Miscellaneous	6,000	8,000	(2,000)
Total Expenditures	$218,000	$217,000	$ 1,000
Excess of Revenues over (under) Expenditures	$ 37,000	$ 25,600	$(11,400)
OTHER FINANCING SOURCES (USES):			
Increase in Supplies Inventory	$ —	$ 2,000	$ 2,000
Operating Transfers Out	(8,000)	(8,000)	—
Total Other Financing Sources (Uses)	$ (8,000)	$ (6,000)	$ 2,000
Excess of Revenues and Other Sources over Expenditures and Other Uses	$ 29,000	$ 19,600	$ (9,400)
Fund Balance—January 1	$ 90,000	$ 90,000	—
Less: Residual Equity Transfer	20,000	20,000	—
Adjusted Fund Balance—January 1	$ 70,000	$ 70,000	—
Fund Balance—December 31	$ 99,000	$ 89,600	$ (9,400)

this revenue among its various operating activities as it wishes. In the special revenue fund, on the other hand, each item of revenue is restricted to use for specified activities.

Because the special revenue fund involves the same type of activities as the general fund, the same accounting procedures are followed. Moreover, the financial statements of the special revenue fund parallel those of the general fund; that is, a balance sheet; statement of revenues, expenditures, and changes in fund balance; and budgetary comparison statement are presented. If several special revenue funds exist, *combining* balance sheets and statements of revenues, expenditures, and changes in fund balances are presented. These combining statements show the data for each fund as well as the total for

Exhibit 16.7   Illustration of Combining Balance Sheet

Name of Governmental Unit
Combining Balance Sheet—
All Special Revenue Funds
December 31, 19X2

ASSETS	Parks	State Gasoline Tax	Motor Vehicle License	Parking Meter	Juvenile Rehabil- itation	Totals December 31, 19X2	Totals December 31, 19X1
Cash	$39,525	$22,460	$ 5,420	$16,260	$17,720	$101,385	$ 91,459
Investments, at Cost . . .	16,200	—	—	15,000	6,000	37,200	25,000
Receivables:							
Taxes Receivable— Delinquent (Net of Allowance for Uncollectibles of $500) .	2,500	—	—	—	—	2,500	—
Accounts Receivable (Net of Allowance for Uncollectibles of $800) .	3,300	—	—	—	—	3,300	2,700
Accrued Interest . . .	25	—	—	—	—	25	—
Due from State Government .	—	47,250	28,010	—	—	75,260	62,400
Inventory of Supplies, at Cost .	1,100	990	702	1,066	1,332	5,190	5,190
Total Assets . . .	$62,650	$70,700	$34,132	$32,326	$25,052	$224,860	$186,749
LIABILITIES AND FUND BALANCES							
Liabilities:							
Vouchers Payable . . .	$10,000	$11,220	$ 4,260	$ 3,220	$ 5,150	$ 33,850	$ 23,414
Contracts Payable . . .	12,500	4,000	—	1,800	—	18,300	12,300
Judgments Payable . .	2,000	—	—	—	—	2,000	—
Due to General Fund . .	2,000	—	—	—	—	2,000	—
Total Liabilities . .	$26,500	$15,220	$ 4,260	$ 5,020	$ 5,150	$ 56,150	$ 35,714
Fund Balances:							
Reserved for Encumbrances . . .	$14,000	$16,500	$10,000	$ 500	$ 5,500	$ 46,500	$ 12,550
Reserved for Inventory of Supplies	1,100	990	702	1,066	1,332	5,190	5,190
Unreserved	21,050	37,990	19,170	25,740	13,070	117,020	133,295
Total Fund Balances .	$36,150	$55,480	$29,872	$27,306	$19,902	$168,710	$151,035
Total Liabilities and Fund Balances	$62,650	$70,700	$34,132	$32,326	$25,052	$224,860	$186,749

all special revenue funds. The format of combining statements is illustrated in Exhibits 16.7 and 16.8. Combining statements are not typically presented in the case of budgetary comparison statements because the format is unwieldy. If more detail beyond the combined statement is desired, budgetary comparison statements may be presented for each individual special revenue fund.

Exhibit 16.8   Illustration of Combining Statement of Revenues, Expenditures, and Changes in Fund Balance

Name of Governmental Unit
Combining Statement of Revenues, Expenditures, and Changes in
Fund Balances—All Special Revenue Funds
For the Fiscal Year Ended December 31, 19X2

	Parks	State Gasoline Tax	Motor Vehicle License	Parking Meter	Juvenile Rehabil- itation	Totals Year Ended December 31, 19X2	Totals Year Ended December 31, 19X1
REVENUES:							
Taxes	$189,300	$ —	$ —	$ —	$ —	$ 189,300	$ 168,400
Intergovernmental Revenues . .	—	422,500	201,000	—	207,600	831,100	749,990
Charges for Services .	—	—	—	79,100	—	79,100	71,420
Miscellaneous Revenues . .	70,700	—	—	600	325	71,625	63,614
Total Revenues . .	$260,000	$422,500	$201,000	$79,700	$207,925	$1,171,125	$1,053,424
EXPENDITURES:							
Public Safety . . .	$ —	$ —	$199,400	$80,900	$199,700	$ 480,000	$ 414,040
Highways and Streets .	—	417,000	—	—	—	417,000	346,414
Culture and Recreation .	256,450	—	—	—	—	256,450	238,419
Total Expenditures .	$256,450	$417,000	$199,400	$80,900	$199,700	$1,153,450	$ 998,873
Excess of Revenues over (under) Expenditures . .	$ 3,550	$ 5,500	$ 1,600	$ (1,200)	$ 8,225	$ 17,675	$ 54,551
Fund Balances— January 1 . .	32,600	49,980	28,272	28,506	11,677	151,035	96,484
Fund Balances— December 31 .	$ 36,150	$ 55,480	$ 29,872	$27,306	$ 19,902	$ 168,710	$ 151,035

Source: Reproduced with permission from National Council on Governmental Accounting, *Statement 1*, "Governmental Accounting and Financial Reporting Principles" (Chicago: Municipal Finance Officers Association of the United States and Canada, 1979), p. 42. © Copyright 1979 by Municipal Finance Officers Association of the United States and Canada.

Accounting for Fixed Assets

The various funds which comprise a local government account for fixed assets in different ways. Proprietary funds (enterprise and internal service funds) and fiduciary funds (trust and agency funds) include fixed assets on their balance sheets. The five governmental funds, on the other hand, exclude fixed assets from their balance sheets. The emphasis in fund accounting is on reporting of revenues and expenditures. The balance sheet of an entity using fund accounting focuses on financial assets—those which can be expended in a subsequent period—and does not list fixed assets, which cannot be expended. However, some accounting and reporting of fixed assets is desirable. To maintain accountability for these assets, records should be kept, showing the nature and cost[1] of each item of land, buildings, equipment, and improvements owned by

---

[1] If cost cannot be determined, it should be estimated, as in the case of assets which are constructed by the unit's own employees. Donated fixed assets are recorded at estimated fair market value at the time of donation.

the government unit. To provide information to financial statement users, a report on the investment in fixed assets is needed. What results is a separate set of records known as an **account group.** Thus, the **general fixed assets account group** is a set of records which account for the fixed assets acquired by a local government through its general, special revenue, capital projects, special assessments, and debt service funds.[2]

General Fixed Assets Account Group

The general fixed assets account group consists of two types of accounts. First, there are the asset accounts, showing the major classifications of fixed assets owned by a local government. Typical classifications are:

> Land
>
> Buildings
>
> Improvements (for example, streets, bridges, sewer systems)
>
> Construction in Progress (costs of uncompleted projects)
>
> Equipment

These accounts are used to record the cost of the assets. Second is a set of accounts showing the source of the fixed assets, that is, the specific funds through which the assets were acquired. These accounts are titled:

> Investment in General Fixed Assets—General Fund
>
> Investment in General Fixed Assets—Special Revenue Fund
>
> Investment in General Fixed Assets—Capital Projects Fund
>
> Investment in General Fixed Assets—Special Assessment Fund

If fixed assets are acquired by donation (for example, roads deeded to a town by a developer or a building turned over to a city by the federal government), an Investment in General Fixed Assets—Donations account is used. The sole function of the general fixed assets account group is to provide a record of fixed assets acquired by certain funds; it has no expendable resources, and thus cannot by itself acquire fixed assets. It is not a fund, only a set of accounts showing the amounts and sources of fixed assets.

Accounting for Fixed Asset Transactions

An acquisition of fixed assets by a fund using fund accounting requires two sets of entries: one is made by the fund itself to record the use of resources to acquire the assets, and one is made by the general fixed assets account group to record the acquisition of the assets and the source of the resources used to acquire them. For example, assume that highway equipment costing $400,000 is purchased by the general fund. The entry made in the *general fund* records the expenditure of resources:

Expenditures	400,000	
Vouchers Payable		400,000
To record purchase of highway equipment.		

Since fixed asset records are not maintained in the general fund, an entry must also be made in the *general fixed assets account group* as follows:

---

[2] These are the five governmental funds. The debt service fund would not be expected to acquire fixed assets so, as a practical matter, we are concerned with the fixed assets acquired by only four funds.

```
Equipment . . . . . . . . . . . .  400,000
    Investment in General Fixed Assets—General
    Fund . . . . . . . . . . . .              400,000
To record purchase of highway equipment by general
fund.
```

Depreciation of fixed assets is *not* recorded in governmental funds and thus is not shown in the general fixed assets accounts. The emphasis in fund accounting is on the expenditure of resources, not on the use of physical assets. This aspect of fund accounting has long been a center of controversy; many argue that depreciation should be recorded in governmental funds to better enable determination of the costs of government services. To date, however, this position has not been adopted.

A sale or other disposition of fixed assets also requires two sets of entries. Assume that old highway equipment, previously acquired with $150,000 of state grant funds (through the special revenue fund) is now sold for $30,000, with the proceeds going to the general fund. The entry in the *general fund* is:

```
Cash . . . . . . . . . . . . . .  30,000
    Revenues . . . . . . . . . . .            30,000
To record proceeds from sale of equipment.
```

The entry in the *general fixed assets account group* removes the previously recorded cost of the equipment.

```
Investment in General Fixed Assets—Special Revenue
    Fund . . . . . . . . . . . . .  150,000
    Equipment . . . . . . . . . .            150,000
To record disposition of equipment originally
purchased by special revenue fund.
```

Note that since the fixed assets have no book value in the general fund, no gain or loss is recognized. In the general fund, we simply record the proceeds as revenues.

Financial Statements for General Fixed Assets

The major financial statement for the general fixed assets account group is a balance-sheet-type statement called a **statement of general fixed assets**. The format of this statement is:

General Fixed Assets:	**Investment in General Fixed Assets:**
Land	General Fund
Buildings	Special Revenue Fund
Improvements	Capital Projects Fund
Equipment	Special Assessments Fund

An example is presented in Exhibit 16.9. In addition, a statement detailing the changes in general fixed assets during the year may be presented, as in Exhibit 16.10.

Accounting for Long-Term Debt

As was the case with fixed assets, long-term debt is accounted for in various ways by local governments. Proprietary and fiduciary funds present long-term debt on their own balance sheets. In addition, the balance sheet of the special assessments fund presents the long-term debt issued to finance its activities.

Exhibit 16.9   Illustration of Statement of General Fixed Assets

City of Anderson
Statement of General Fixed Assets
General Fixed Asset Group of Accounts
December 31, 19X8

GENERAL FIXED ASSETS:

Land	$ 40,000,000
Buildings	196,000,000
Improvements	19,000,000
Equipment	43,000,000
Total	$298,000,000

INVESTMENT IN GENERAL FIXED ASSETS FROM:

General Fund	$103,000,000
Special Revenue Funds	50,000,000
Capital Projects Funds	142,000,000
Special Assessment Funds	3,000,000
Total	$298,000,000

Exhibit 16.10   Illustration of Statement of Changes in General Fixed Assets

City of Anderson
Statement of Changes in General Fixed Assets
General Fixed Assets Group of Accounts
December 31, 19X8

	Land	Buildings	Improvements	Equipment	Total
General Fixed Assets, January 1, 19X8	$39,100,000	$187,150,000	$13,370,000	$37,500,000	$277,120,000
ADDITIONS:					
Expenditures from:					
General Fund	$ —	$ 50,000	$ —	$ 4,300,000	$ 4,350,000
Special Revenue Fund	600,000	600,000	30,000	700,000	1,930,000
Capital Project Fund	300,000	8,600,000	3,600,000	500,000	13,000,000
Special Assessments Fund	—	—	2,000,000	—	2,000,000
Total Additions	$ 900,000	$ 9,250,000	$ 5,630,000	$ 5,500,000	$ 21,280,000
	$40,000,000	$196,400,000	$19,000,000	$43,000,000	$298,400,000
DISPOSITIONS:					
Capital Projects Fund	—	400,000	—	—	400,000
General Fixed Assets, December 31, 19X8	$40,000,000	$196,000,000	$19,000,000	$43,000,000	$298,000,000

For the other four governmental funds,[3] long-term debt is excluded from the balance sheet and presented in a separate set of accounts known as the **general long-term debt account group.** As was the case with general fixed assets, this account group is used solely to provide a record of outstanding debt; *it does not engage in actual transactions.*

General Long-Term Debt Account Group

The primary account of the long-term debt group is the long-term liability account. This may be a single account (for example, Bonds Payable) or separate accounts for various classes of debt such as term bonds, serial bonds, and so forth.

To meet the requirements for a double entry system, accounts are provided to designate the amount of resources which will be required to pay the liabilities. There are two accounts of this type:

1.   *Amounts Available for Repayment of Long-Term Debt.* This account indicates the amount of resources which have already been set aside, usually in the debt service fund, for the eventual repayment of long-term debt.

2.   *Amounts to be Provided for Repayment of Long-Term Debt.* This account indicates the amount of resources which must be set aside in future years.

Accounting for Long-Term Debt Transactions

Issuance of long-term debt requires two sets of entries: one in the fund issuing the debt and spending the proceeds and one in the general long-term debt account group. For example, assume that $3,000,000 of long-term bonds are issued by the capital projects fund to finance the construction of a new school building. The receipt of proceeds of the bond issue is recorded by the *capital projects fund* as:

Cash 3,000,000
    Bond Proceeds   3,000,000
To record proceeds of bond issue for school
construction.

As was mentioned previously, bond proceeds are not considered revenue; rather, they are included in "other financing sources" on the statement of revenues, expenditures, and changes in fund balance. This point will be illustrated further in Chapter 17, when the capital projects fund is discussed. In addition to the entry in the capital projects fund, a record of the bond liability and the amount of resources needed in the future to repay the liability is entered in the *general long-term debt account group* as:

Amount to be Provided for Repayment of Bonds . 3,000,000
    Bonds Payable   3,000,000
To record bonds issued by capital projects fund.

The general long-term debt account group records only the *amount of principal* of the debt. Interest obligations are not shown, nor are any premium or discount on the original issue. Accounting for premium and discount is discussed in Chapter 17.

---

[3]   Again, the debt service fund is unlikely to issue long-term debt, and thus we are concerned only with debt issued by the general, special revenue, and capital projects funds.

Exhibit 16.11   Illustration of Statement of General Long-Term Debt

Blackstone County
Statement of General Long-Term Debt
June 30, 19X7

Amount Available for Repayment of Serial Bonds	$ 453,000
Amount to Be Provided for Repayment of Serial Bonds	9,184,000
Total	$9,637,000
Serial Bonds Payable	$9,637,000

Repayment of long-term debt also requires two sets of entries. Assume that $500,000 of long-term bonds mature this year, and that provision is made in the general fund budget for the retirement of these bonds. The entry in the *general fund* is:

Expenditures	500,000	
Cash		500,000
To record payment of principal of matured bonds.		

The entry in the *general long-term debt account group* is:

Bonds Payable	500,000	
Amount to be Provided for Repayment of Bonds .		500,000
To record retirement of matured bonds.		

If resources had been set aside in the debt service fund, our entries would be somewhat different. We shall consider this case when we discuss the debt service fund in Chapter 17.

Financial Statement for General Long-Term Debt

A **statement of general long-term debt** presents information on long-term debt at year-end. This statement presents *Bonds Payable* on the credit side, and the two accounts *Amount Available for Repayment of Long-Term Debt* and *Amount to be Provided for Repayment of Long-Term Debt* on the debit side. An example of such a statement is presented in Exhibit 16.11.

Summary of Key Concepts

The general fund usually requires a formal **budget determination process,** resulting in the calculation of a *property tax rate.*

Under the **modified accrual method of accounting,** certain revenues of the general fund are accrued, while others are recorded on the cash basis. In particular, property tax revenues are recorded on the accrual basis, with an allowance for uncollectible taxes.

Inventories may be accounted for either by the **purchases method,** which recognizes the expenditure at time of purchase, or by the **consumption method,** which recognizes the expenditure at time of use.

Alternative treatments also exist for **encumbrances outstanding at year-end.** Under the **legal approach,** encumbrances and expenditures both constitute charges against the current annual budget. Under the **GAAP approach,** expenditures are compared to a modified accrual budget, which is the annual budget plus carryover appropriations.

Various types of **interfund transactions** exist, each having distinct accounting treatment. **Operating transfers** must be distinguished from revenue and expenditure transactions.

Financial statements presented for the general fund include a **balance sheet,** a **statement of revenues, expenditures, and changes in fund balance,** and a **budgetary comparison statement.**

Fixed assets acquired by the general fund and by other governmental funds are recorded in the **general fixed assets account group.**

Long-term debt incurred by the general fund and by all other governmental funds except the special assessments fund is recorded in the **general long-term debt account group.**

Questions **Q16.1**   Briefly describe the budgeting process of a government unit.

Q16.2   Why are balance sheets of the governmental funds which use fund accounting unclassified as to current and noncurrent items?

Q16.3   Why are delinquent taxes often fully reserved? What effect does this procedure have on the balance sheet?

Q16.4   Explain the difference between temporary and permanent interfund transfers and give an example of each type.

Q16.5   The following was recorded in the general fund when equipment originally purchased by the special revenue fund was sold. What other journal entry was made in the government unit's accounts?

    Cash 6,000
        Revenues   6,000
    To record sale of equipment originally purchased for
    $7,500.

Q16.6   The following was recorded in the general long-term debt account group. What other journal entry was made in the government unit's accounts?

    Bonds Payable 850,000
        Amount to Be Provided for Repayment of Bonds   .   850,000
    To record payment of matured bonds by general fund.

Q16.7   What does the account entitled Amount Available for Repayment of Long-Term Debt represent, and where does it appear?

Q16.8   Select the best answer for each of the following multiple choice questions.
    1.   A city's general fund budget for the forthcoming fiscal year shows estimated revenues in excess of appropriations. The initial effect of recording this will result in an increase in:

a. Taxes receivable.
b. Fund balance.
c. Reserve for encumbrances.
d. Encumbrances.

2. What would be the effect on the general fund balance in the current year of recording a $15,000 purchase for a new fire truck out of general fund resources, for which a $14,600 encumbrance had been recorded in the general fund in the previous year, using the legal approach?
a. Reduce the general fund balance by $15,000.
b. Reduce the general fund balance by $14,600.
c. Reduce the general fund balance by $400.
d. Have no effect on the general fund balance.

3. In preparing the general fund budget of Brockton City for the forthcoming fiscal year, the city council appropriated a sum greater than expected revenues. This action of the council will result in:
a. A cash overdraft during that fiscal year.
b. An increase in encumbrances by the end of that fiscal year.
c. A decrease in the fund balance.
d. An increase in the fund balance. (AICPA adapted)

Q16.9 Select the best answer for each of the following multiple choice questions.

1. Which of the following should be accrued as revenues by the general fund of a local government?
a. Sales taxes held by the state which will be remitted to the local government.
b. Parking meter revenues.
c. Sales taxes collected by merchants.
d. Income taxes currently due.

2. Which of the following types of revenue would generally be recorded directly in the general fund of a government unit?
a. Receipts from a city-owned parking structure.
b. Property taxes.
c. Interest earned on investments held for retirement of employees.
d. Revenues of internal service funds. (AICPA adapted)

Q16.10 Select the best answer for each of the following multiple choice questions.

1. Authority granted by a legislative body to make expenditures and to incur obligations during a fiscal year is the definition of an:
a. Appropriation.
b. Estimated Revenue.
c. Encumbrance.
d. Expenditure.

2. What type of account is used to earmark the fund balance to liquidate the contingent obligations for goods ordered but not yet received?
a. Appropriations.
b. Encumbrances.
c. Expenditures.
d. Reserve for Encumbrances.

3. The Reserve for Encumbrances—Prior Year account represents amounts recorded by a government unit for:
    a. Anticipated expenditures in the next year.
    b. Anticipated expenditures for which purchase orders were made in the prior year but disbursement will be in the current year.
    c. Excess expenditures in the prior year that will be offset against the current year budgeted amounts.
    d. Unanticipated expenditures of the prior year that become evident in the current year.

(AICPA adapted)

Exercises E16.1 Legal requirements of Woten County set the maximum property tax rate at $60 per $1,000 of assessed value. Assessed value of taxable property within the county is $600,000,000. In preparing the county's general fund budget, appropriations of $40,000,000 were anticipated. State and federal aid to Woten County will be $13,000.000.

Required:

1. What is the maximum amount Woten County could receive from property tax revenues?
2. If the county plans a balanced budget, what will the tax rate be?

E16.2 The following information relates to actual revenues and expenditures for the town of Greenwood.

	Actual	Over (Under) Budget
REVENUES:		
Property Taxes	$3,000,000	$150,000
Fines	6,000	6,000
Intergovernmental	12,000	0
Sale of Services	500,000	(75,000)
Miscellaneous	4,000	(1,000)
EXPENDITURES:		
Services	2,050,000	55,000
Supplies	500,000	(76,000)
Other	950,000	32,000

Required:

1. What budget entry was made at the beginning of the year?
2. If the fund balance *before* the budget entry was $2,100,000, what is the fund balance after year-end closing entries?

E16.3 The following related entries were recorded in sequence in the general fund of a municipality.

Encumbrances	12,000	
Reserve for Encumbrances		12,000
Reserve for Encumbrances	12,000	
Encumbrances		12,000
Expenditures	12,350	
Vouchers Payable		12,350

Required: From the information given, answer the following multiple choice questions.

   1.   The sequence of entries indicates that

     a. An adverse event was foreseen and a reserve of $12,000 was created; later the reserve was cancelled, and a liability for the item was acknowledged.

     b. An order was placed for goods or services estimated to cost $12,000; the actual cost was $12,350, for which a liability was acknowledged upon receipt.

     c. Encumbrances were anticipated but later failed to materialize and were reversed. A liability of $12,350 was incurred.

     d. The first entry was erroneous and was reversed; an unrelated liability of $12,350 was recorded.

   2.   Assuming the legal approach to encumbrance accounting was followed, the entries

     a. Occurred in the same fiscal period.

     b. Did not occur in the same fiscal period.

     c. Could have occurred in the same fiscal period, but it is impossible to be sure of this.

     d. Would reflect the equivalent of a prior-period adjustment had the entity concerned been one operated for profit.

   3.   If the encumbrance equalled the appropriation for the items in the entries, what effect would the third entry have on the fund balance during closing?

     a. Increase the fund balance.

     b. Decrease the fund balance.

     c. Not affect the fund balance.

     d. Not affect the fund balance but affect the budget of the following fiscal period.

   4.   Entries similar to those for the general fund may also appear on the books of the municipality's

     a. General fixed assets account group.

     b. General long-term debt account group.

     c. Trust fund.

     d. Special revenue fund.

(AICPA adapted)

E16.4   On July 10, Marchville levied property taxes of $2,500,000. Based on past experience, city management estimated that the city would be unable to collect 4 percent of the taxes. Taxes were due September 30, but $800,000 was received before that date from taxpayers taking advantage of the 1 percent discount for early payment. Marchville treats discounts given as a reduction of revenues.

On January 1, outstanding taxes due of $150,000 were declared delinquent and were fully reserved. By the end of the fiscal year, 40 percent of the delinquent taxes had been collected. There were no taxes receivable, either current or delinquent, at the beginning of the fiscal year.

Actual expenditures were $2,000,000, the same amount as appropriations. All expenditures were cash transactions. The budget entry included $2,400,000 of estimated revenues. After the budget entry, the fund balance was $472,000.

Required:

1. Prepare the journal entries to record the property tax transactions.
2. State the balance sheet accounts and their respective balances relating to the property tax levy and collections as of the end of the fiscal year. Assume that the cash balance at the beginning of the fiscal year was $93,000.

E16.5   A year-end count of materials and supplies at Mooreland City showed inventories totaling $63,000 on hand. A similar count at the end of the previous year revealed inventories of $57,000. During the year, the city purchased materials and supplies of $160,500.

Required: Prepare the journal entries relating to inventory during the year, including any year-end adjustments, under the following assumptions:

1. The accounting focus is on expenditures for rather than consumption of inventories. The financial statements reflect year-end inventory balances.
2. The accounting focus is on consumption of inventories, viewing inventory as a spendable asset.

E16.6   The December 31, 19X0, balance sheet for the special revenues fund of Burnville showed $19,000 reserved for encumbrances. This figure represented $11,000 encumbered for office equipment and $8,000 for supplies. Early in 19X1, the equipment and supplies were delivered and bills received for $11,700 and $7,950, respectively.

Required: Prepare the journal entries for 19X1 relating to these events, using (1) the legal approach and (2) the GAAP approach.

E16.7   Interfund transfers of the general fund of North Weston City for 19X7 were:

	Transfers In	Transfers Out
1. To the special revenue fund to permit initial expenditures under a project to be fully supported by a federal grant		$18,000
2. To a special assessments fund as the city's contribution to a street lighting project		25,000
3. From the capital projects fund, unspent proceeds of a bond issue	$ 7,000	
4. To the enterprise fund as city's cost of services provided		12,000
5. To the internal service fund to temporarily finance a purchase of supplies		35,000
6. From the special revenue fund to repay advance . .	18,000	

Required: What accounts will appear on the 19X7 general fund balance sheet as a result of these transfers?

E16.8 The preclosing trial balance for the general fund of Graystone is given here:

Cash	$ 350,000
Taxes Receivable—Current	80,000
Allowance for Uncollectible Taxes—Current	(45,000)
Estimated Revenues	1,300,000
Expenditures	1,050,000
Expenditures—Prior Year Encumbrances	42,000
Encumbrances	30,000
Due from Other Funds	12,000
	$2,819,000
Vouchers Payable	$ 180,000
Due to Other Funds	21,000
Reserve for Encumbrances	30,000
Reserve for Encumbrances—Prior Year	45,000
Revenues	1,400,000
Appropriations	1,100,000
Fund Balance—Unreserved	43,000
	$2,819,000

Additional information:

1. At year-end, all uncollected taxes are deemed delinquent. Delinquent taxes are fully reserved.
2. A physical count of inventory revealed $25,000 of supplies on hand. Graystone discloses inventory available in the body of its financial statement.

Required:

1. Prepare all year-end adjusting and closing entries for the general fund of Graystone.
2. Prepare a year-end balance sheet for the general fund of Graystone.

E16.9 The following information relates to activities of the city of Wilsondale:

1. Wilsondale ordered fifteen police cars on February 15 at an expected total cost of $120,000. On April 28, the cars were delivered. The amount of the invoice was $123,500. Payment was made by the general fund on June 10.
2. On June 30, the city paid a semi-annual interest payment of $130,000 and a principal payment of $75,000 on general obligation bonds. Payment was made from the general fund.

Required: Prepare all necessary entries which the city of Wilsondale should make with respect to the above transactions. Identify for each entry the particular fund or account group in which the entry is being made.

E16.10 The Salinas City Statement of General Fixed Assets as of the beginning of the fiscal year follows:

Salinas City
Statement of General Fixed Assets
July 1, 19X0

GENERAL FIXED ASSETS		INVESTMENTS IN GENERAL FIXED ASSETS	
Land	$ 150,000	General Fund	$1,450,000
Buildings	1,000,000	Capital Projects Fund . .	500,000
Equipment	800,000		
Total	$1,950,000	Total	$1,950,000

During October 19X0, the city purchased a warehouse for $375,000, of which 40 percent was attributable to the land. The city began construction of a civic center in 19X0. The entire project was estimated to cost $800,000. By June 30, 19X1, $200,000 had been expended on the project, which was estimated to be one-fifth complete.

Old equipment originally costing $20,000 was scrapped, and new equipment was purchased for $35,000 early in 19X1.

Required: Prepare the *General Fixed Assets* portion of the June 30, 19X1, statement of general fixed assets for Salinas City.

E16.11 The village of Jamesville acquired the following fixed assets during 19X3:
1. Snow removal equipment was purchased by the general fund at a cost of $58,000.
2. A delivery van was purchased by the internal service fund at a cost of $8,300.
3. A building was purchased for $220,000 by the capital projects fund to serve as a youth center. The purchase was financed by a twenty-year bond issue.
4. Sewer lines were extended to an undeveloped section of the village at a cost of $700,000. This cost will eventually be paid by the property owners through special tax assessments. To cover the actual construction cost, bonds were issued by the special assessment fund.

Required: Prepare the entries needed in the village of Jamesville's general fixed assets accounts to reflect the above acquisitions.

E16.12 The county of Edgewater had the following transactions involving long-term debt during 19X6:
1. A $2,000,000 bond issue by the capital projects fund provided money for construction of new streets and bridges.
2. A $1,500,000 bond issue by the water authority (an enterprise fund) provided money for replacement of water mains.
3. A $3,300,000 bond issue by the special assessments fund provided money for improvements to the sewer treatment plant.
4. $100,000 of principal and $120,000 of interest was paid by the general fund on bonds issued in 19X4 for construction of a fire station.

5. Of the bond proceeds described in item 1, $80,000 was not spent on the project and was transferred to the debt service fund to be used for principal payments on the bonds in future years.

Required: Prepare the entries needed in the county of Edgewater's general long-term debt accounts.

Problems

P16.1   **Property Tax Levy**   In February 19X6, the city of Greenville began planning its budget for the fiscal year beginning July 1, 19X6. The following information was available:

General Fund Balance, January 1, 19X6	$ 352,000
Estimated Receipts from Property Taxes (January 1, 19X6–June 30, 19X6)	2,222,000
Estimated Revenue from Investments (January 1, 19X6–June 30, 19X7) .	442,000
Estimated Proceeds from Sale of General Obligation Bonds in August 19X6	3,000,000
	$6,016,000
Estimated Expenditures (January 1, 19X6–June 30, 19X6)	$1,900,000
Proposed Appropriations (July 1, 19X6–June 30, 19X7)	4,300,000
	$6,200,000

Additional information:

1. The general fund balance required by the city council for July 1, 19X7, is $175,000.
2. Property tax collections are due in March and September of each year. During the month of February 19X6, estimated expenditures are expected to exceed available funds by $200,000. Pending collection of property taxes in March 19X6, this deficiency will have to be met by the issuance of thirty-day tax anticipation notes of $200,000 at an estimated interest rate of 9 percent per annum.
3. The proposed general obligation bonds will be issued by the city water fund (an enterprise fund) and will be used for the construction of a new water pumping station.

Required: Prepare a statement as of January 1, 19X6, calculating the property tax levy required for the city of Greenville general fund for the fiscal year ending June 30, 19X7.

(AICPA adapted)

P16.2   **General Fund—Entries and Financial Statements**   The township of Wyatt finances its operations from revenues provided by property taxes, water distribution, fines levied by the municipal court, and interest on savings accounts.

Wyatt maintains only a general fund. The following information is available for the year ended December 31, 19X6:

1. General fund account balances on January 1, 19X6, were:

Cash in Savings Account	$ 620,000
Cash in Checking Accounts	384,800
Cash on Hand (Undeposited)	1,600
Water Department Supplies	36,400
Accounts Receivable—Water Customers	36,700
General Fund Balance	1,043,100
Reserve for Supplies	36,400

2. The budget for 19X6 adopted by the township commission and the transactions relating to the budget (with all current bills vouchered and paid on December 31, 19X6) for the year were:

	Budget	Actual
Property Taxes	$267,500	$267,500
Water Department Costs	665,000	643,600 [a]
Township Constable and Court Fees Paid by Township .	100,000	95,500 [a]
Water Revenues	300,000	320,600 [b]
Court Fines	125,000	110,250
Commissioners' Salaries and Expenses	60,000	54,700 [a]
Interest on Savings Accounts	20,000	22,400
Miscellaneous Expenses	12,000	26,100 [a]

[a] Cash expenditures.
[b] Billings.

3. All property taxes were collected.
4. A count of cash on December 31, 19X6, determined that there was $2,500 on hand that was not deposited until January 2, 19X7.
5. All outstanding water bills on January 1, 19X6, were collected during 19X6. All billings for water during 19X6 were paid with the exception of statements totaling $22,300, which were mailed to customers the last week of December.
6. All water department supplies were consumed during the year on the repair of water mains.

Required:

1. Prepare 19X6 journal entries for the township of Wyatt.
2. Prepare a balance sheet and a statement of revenues, expenditures, and changes in fund balance for Wyatt's general fund.

(AICPA adapted)

P16.3   **Special Revenue Fund**   In 19X4, Grand City established a special revenue fund to account for the addition of an aquarium to the city zoo. Work on the aquarium was scheduled to begin in January 19X5. Appropriations were not recorded until 19X5. Financing for the project was to be provided as follows:

From Federal Grant to Be Received in March 19X5	$ 90,000
From 19X4 General Fund Revenue	45,000
From 19X5 General Fund Revenue	45,000
	$180,000

The special revenue fund balance sheet for December 31, 19X4, was:

Grand City Special Revenue Fund
Balance Sheet
December 31, 19X4

ASSETS		LIABILITIES, RESERVES AND FUND BALANCE	
Cash	$ 13,000	Fund Balance	$135,000
Investments	32,000		
Accounts Receivable (Federal			
Grant)	90,000		
	$135,000		$135,000

During 19X5, the following occurred:

1. An appropriation of $180,000 was made for the project.
2. A contract for $175,000 for the addition to the aquarium was signed. Work was started, completed, and billed for $175,000.
3. Cash from the general fund and federal grant was received as scheduled.
4. Investments yielded $1,800 in revenues, $200 less than anticipated.
5. Vouchers remaining to be paid at year-end totaled $8,000.
6. Any remaining resources were reclassified for transfer to the general fund.

Required:

1. What was the 19X4 budget entry?
2. Prepare all 19X5 journal entries for the special revenue fund.
3. Prepare the balance sheet for the special revenue fund as of December 31, 19X5.

P16.4 General Fund—Adjustments and Statements The books for the town of Fountain Inn are maintained by an inexperienced bookkeeper. All transactions were recorded in the town's general fund for the fiscal year ended June 30, 19X6. The bookkeeper prepared the following trial balance:

Town of Fountain Inn
General Fund Trial Balance
June 30, 19X6

Cash	$ 12,900	
Accounts Receivable	1,200	
Taxes Receivable, Current	8,000	
Tax Anticipation Notes Payable		$ 15,000
Appropriations		350,000
Expenditures	344,000	
Estimated Revenues	290,000	
Revenues		320,000
Town Property	16,100	
Bonds Payable	36,000	
Fund Balance		23,200
Totals	$708,200	$708,200

Additional information:

1. The accounts receivable balance was due from the town's golf course, representing an advance made by the general fund. Accounts for the municipal golf course operated by the town are maintained in a separate enterprise fund.

2. The total tax levy for the year was $280,000, of which $10,000 was abated during the year. The town's tax collection experience in recent years indicates an average loss of 5 percent of the net tax levy for uncollectible taxes. At year-end, all taxes receivable are considered delinquent.

3. On June 30, 19X6, the town retired at face value 4 percent general obligation serial bonds totaling $30,000. The bonds were issued on July 1, 19X4, in the total amount of $150,000. Interest paid during the year was also recorded in the Bonds Payable account.

4. At the beginning of the year, the town council authorized a supply room with an inventory not to exceed $10,000. During the year, supplies totaling $12,300 were purchased and charged to Expenditures. The physical inventory taken at June 30 disclosed that supplies totaling $8,400 were used.

5. Expenditures for 19X6 included $2,600 applicable to purchase orders issued in the prior year. Outstanding purchase orders at June 30, 19X6, not recorded in the accounts, amounted to $4,100. The GAAP approach is used for outstanding encumbrances.

6. The amount of $8,200, due from the state for the town's share of state gasoline taxes, was not recorded in the accounts.

7. Equipment costing $7,500 was removed from service and sold for $900 during the year, and new equipment costing $17,000 purchased. These transactions were recorded in the Town Property account.

Required:

1. Prepare the adjusting and closing entries for the general fund of Fountain Inn and any corresponding entries to the general fixed assets and general long-term debt groups of accounts. Assume that general fixed assets and general long-term debt accounts were properly maintained in prior years.

2. Prepare a balance sheet and statement of changes in fund balance for Fountain Inn's general fund.

(AICPA adapted)

P16.5   Reconstructing Journal Entries   Balance sheets for the city of Golden's special revenue fund appear as shown below:

City of Golden
Special Revenue Fund
Balance Sheets
June 30, 19X1 and 19X0

ASSETS	19X1	19X0
Cash	$ 39,000	$ 10,000
Investments	140,000	200,000
Due from General Fund	50,000	—
Due from Federal Government	—	150,000
	$229,000	$360,000

LIABILITIES AND FUND BALANCE	19X1	19X0
Vouchers Payable	$ 87,000	$180,000
Reserve for Encumbrances	—	75,000
Fund Balance—Unreserved	142,000	105,000
	$229,000	$360,000

The budget entry made in July 19X0 was:

Estimated Revenues	50,000	
Fund Balance—Unreserved	13,000	
Appropriations		63,000
To record budget.		

Bills for the June 30, 19X0, encumbrances were $3,000 less than the amount committed. There were no unanticipated revenues. The legal approach is used for outstanding encumbrances.

Required: Reconstruct the journal entries for the year ended June 30, 19X1, for Golden's special revenue fund.

P16.6 **Statement of Revenues, Expenditures, and Changes in Fund Balance** Information concerning Dalton City's 19X1 general fund revenues and expenditures is given:

	Budgeted Amount	Actual Amount
Property Taxes	$432,000	$425,000
Licenses—Revenue	30,000	32,000
Permits—Revenue	37,500	35,000
Share of State Tax	60,000	58,000
Sale of Equipment	—	8,000
Interest Revenue	4,500	4,200
Gifts	—	7,000
General Government Expenditures	180,000	172,000
Public Safety Expenditures	105,000	106,000
Highway Expenditures	75,000	68,000
Health Services Expenditures	68,000	72,000
Education Expenditures	150,000	141,000

At year-end, the following amounts were encumbered:

For General Government	$6,000
For Public Safety	500
For Health Services	1,000
	$7,500

Required:
1. Property taxes are assessed at a rate of $48 per $1,000 assessed value. What is the assessed value of the taxable property in Dalton City?
2. What tax rate would give Dalton City a balanced budget?
3. Prepare a statement of revenues, expenditures, and changes in fund balance—budget and actual—for the Dalton City general fund.

P16.7 **General Fund and Account Groups—Corrections and Adjustments** During the fiscal year ending June 30, 19X7, all transactions of Salleytown were recorded in the general fund due to the inexperience of the town's bookkeeper. The trial balance of Salleytown's general fund is as follows:

Salleytown
General Fund Trial Balance
June 30, 19X7

Accounts	Debit	Credit
Cash	$ 16,800	
Short-Term Investments	40,000	
Accounts Receivable	11,500	
Taxes Receivable—Current	30,000	
Tax Anticipation Notes Payable		$ 50,000
Appropriations		400,000
Expenditures	382,000	
Estimated Revenue	320,000	
Revenues		360,000
General Property	85,400	
Bonds Payable	52,000	
Fund Balance		127,700
	$937,700	$937,700

The following information is also available:

1. The accounts receivable of $11,500 includes $1,500 due from the town's water utility. Accounts for the municipal water utility operated by the town are maintained in a separate fund.
2. The balance in Taxes Receivable—Current is now considered delinquent, and the town estimates that $24,000 will be uncollectible.
3. On June 30, 19X7, the town retired, at face value, 6 percent general obligation serial bonds totaling $40,000. The bonds were issued on July 1, 19X2, at face value of $200,000. Interest paid during the year ended June 30, 19X7, was charged to Bonds Payable.
4. During the year, supplies totaling $128,000 were purchased and charged to Expenditures. The town conducted a physical inventory of supplies on hand at June 30, 19X7, and this physical count disclosed that supplies totaling $84,000 were used. The purchases method is used.
5. Expenditures for the year ended June 30, 19X7, included $11,200 applicable to purchase orders issued in the prior year. Outstanding purchase orders at June 30, 19X7, not recorded in the accounts, amounted to $17,500. The legal approach is used.
6. On June 28, 19X7, the state revenue department informed the town that its share of a state-collected, locally-shared tax would be $34,000.
7. During the year, equipment with a book value of $7,900 was removed from service and sold for $4,600. In addition, new equipment costing $90,000 was purchased. The transactions were recorded in General Property.
8. During the year, 100 acres of land were donated to the town for use as an industrial park. The land had a value of $125,000. No recording of this donation has been made.

Required:

1. Prepare the formal reclassification, adjusting, and closing journal entries for the general fund as of June 30, 19X7.
2. Prepare the formal adjusting journal entries for the general long-term debt group of accounts and the general fixed assets group of accounts as of June 30, 19X7. Assume that proper entries were made in prior years.

(AICPA adapted)

P16.8 **General Fund—Comprehensive** The following summary of transactions was taken from the accounts of the West Columbia School District General Fund *before* the books had been closed for the fiscal year ended June 30, 19X5:

	Postclosing Balances June 30, 19X4	Preclosing Balances June 30, 19X5
Cash	$400,000	$ 700,000
Taxes Receivable	150,000	170,000
Allowance for Uncollectible Taxes	(40,000)	(70,000)
Estimated Revenues	—	3,000,000
Expenditures	—	2,842,000
Expenditures—Prior Year	—	58,000
Encumbrances	—	91,000
	$510,000	$6,791,000
Vouchers Payable	$ 80,000	$ 408,000
Due to Other Funds	210,000	142,000
Reserve for Encumbrances	60,000	151,000
Fund Balance—Unreserved	160,000	180,000
Revenues from Taxes	—	2,800,000
Miscellaneous Revenues	—	130,000
Appropriations	—	2,980,000
	$510,000	$6,791,000

Additional information:

1. A Taxes Receivable—Delinquent account is not used.
2. The estimated taxes receivable for the year ended June 30, 19X5, were $2,870,000, and taxes collected during the year totaled $2,810,000.
3. An analysis of the transactions in the Vouchers Payable account for the year ended June 30, 19X5, follows:

	Debit (Credit)
Current Expenditures	$(2,700,000)
Expenditures for Prior Year	(58,000)
Vouchers for Payment to Other Funds	(210,000)
Cash Payments during Year	2,640,000
Net Change	$ (328,000)

4. During the year, the general fund was billed $142,000 for services performed on its behalf by other city funds.
5. On May 2, 19X5, commitment documents were issued for the purchase of new textbooks at a cost of $91,000. The GAAP approach is used.

Required: Based upon the data presented above, reconstruct the original detailed journal entries that were required to record all transactions for the fiscal year ended June 30, 19X5, including the recording of the current year's budget. Prepare closing entries at June 30, 19X5.

(AICPA adapted)

P16.9   General Fund—Comprehensive   Data relating to the general fund of Pilotsville School District are as follows:

Pilotsville School District
General Fund
Balance Sheet
December 31, 19X6

ASSETS		LIABILITIES AND FUND BALANCE	
Cash	$36,600	Vouchers Payable	$22,000
Taxes Receivable—Current (Net		Due to Enterprise Fund . . .	7,000
of $8,000 Allowance for		Reserve for Encumbrances . .	4,600
Uncollectible Taxes) . . .	42,000	Reserve for Inventory . . .	17,000
Inventory	17,000	Fund Balance—Unreserved .	45,000
	$95,600		$95,600

Additional information:

1. The 19X7 budget included $287,000 in expected revenue, all from property taxes, and a $6,000 planned decrease in the fund balance. The tax levy was for $300,000.
2. Tax collections during 19X7 were:

19X6 Taxes	$ 45,000
19X7 Taxes	238,000
	$283,000

   Remaining 19X6 taxes were written off.
3. Taxes due at year-end are not considered delinquent but are 16 percent reserved.
4. Old school desks were sold for $800. The desks had originally cost $1,200.
5. New desks were purchased for $2,000. Neither transaction regarding the desks had been anticipated in the budget.
6. Vandalism to the schools resulted in $3,000 of unexpected repair and clean-up costs.
7. Actual total expenditures by the general fund were $291,000.
8. Supplies on hand at year-end totaled $13,000.
9. Although no vouchers payable were outstanding at the end of 19X7, $7,000 had been encumbered for goods ordered but not yet received. The GAAP approach is used.
10. The 19X6 encumbrance for $4,600 was canceled when the goods ordered were found to be defective.
11. Cash of $7,000 was transferred to the enterprise fund.

Required:

1. Prepare all the 19X7 journal entries for the school district's general fund.

2. Prepare a 19X7 balance sheet and a statement of revenues, expenditures and changes in fund balance for the general fund.

P16.10 **Acquisition and Disposition of Fixed Assets** At January 1, 19X3, the town of Bakersville compiled a current listing of its fixed assets and the means by which they were acquired.

	Cost
LAND:	
Site of Town Hall	$ 17,000
Site of Town Garage and Services Building	48,000
Town Park and Wildlife Preserve	160,000
BUILDINGS:	
Town Hall	775,000
Garage	380,000
Services Building	625,000
Park Buildings	63,000
EQUIPMENT:	
Office Equipment	116,000
Highway Equipment	843,000
Park Equipment	102,000
Other Equipment	477,000
IMPROVEMENTS:	
Streets	1,755,000
Sewers and Drainage	2,416,000
Park	288,000

The land and buildings, except for those related to the park, were financed by general obligation bonds through the capital projects fund. The park land was donated by a corporation which has a large plant in Bakersville. The town then applied for and received a state grant of $250,000 to develop the park. The cost of sewers and drainage were financed by assessments to property owners. All other fixed asset costs were paid from general fund appropriations.

During 19X3, the following transactions occurred:

1. Highway equipment purchased ten years ago at a cost of $62,000 was sold for $18,000.
2. New highway equipment costing $77,000 was purchased. An appropriation for this amount was included in the general fund budget.
3. A bond issue of $510,000 was approved to finance the construction of a youth center. Construction will begin in early 19X4.
4. Office equipment costing $2,000 was stolen and has not yet been replaced.
5. The town received a $40,000 federal grant to expand the wildlife preserve. It used the grant plus $5,000 of general fund resources to buy 200 acres of land adjoining the present site.

Required:

1. Record the transactions in the general fixed asset account group for 19X3.
2. Prepare a statement of general fixed assets as of December 31, 19X3, and a statement of changes in general fixed assets for the year.

Chapter 17

Accounting and Reporting for Nonroutine Activities of Local Government

Six funds—capital projects, special assessments, debt service, enterprise, internal service; and trust and agency—account for activities other than the routine operations of a government unit. Many of these activities are normal functions of government such as building schools, operating recreational facilities, and administering retirement benefits. However, they are outside the routine operating activities accounted for by the general and special revenue funds.

Recall that various types of accounting procedures are followed by these six funds. Capital projects, special assessments, and debt service funds follow fund accounting. Enterprise and internal service funds follow business accounting. Trust and agency funds follow fiduciary accounting. Each of the six and its respective accounting procedures are discussed in turn in this chapter.

Budget Formulation

Budget formulation for the six funds considered in this chapter is less involved than was the case for the general fund. Proprietary and fiduciary funds do not record budgets in the accounts and may not even require that formal budgets be adopted. Governmental funds other than the general and special revenue funds may or may not be required to prepare and record budgets, and the process of formulating and approving the budget may not be as complex as it was for the general fund. In the case of a debt service fund, for example, the budget is primarily dictated by required payments of principal and interest on debt. Thus the budget may be easily formulated by management and may not require legislative or voter approval. Budgets for the capital projects or special assessments funds, on the other hand, typically require more formal approval. The activities of these funds involve construction or acquisition of capital assets, which are usually financed by bond issues. These activities are discretionary, so the process of formulating and approving a budget is in effect a decision as to whether these activities should be undertaken.

The Capital Projects Fund

Government units may finance the acquisition or construction of fixed assets in various ways. The purpose of the assets and the means of financing their purchase or construction affect the accounting and reporting for these activities. Four principal alternatives exist:

1. Relatively small acquisitions, such as a purchase of a parcel of land or items of equipment, are often financed via the budget of the general (or special revenue) fund. The acquisition expenditure is recorded in the general fund, and the asset is recorded in the general fixed asset accounts.

2. Assets acquired by a proprietary fund (an enterprise or internal service fund) are fully accounted for by that fund. For example, if the city water division issues bonds and constructs a new pumping station, the transactions, the bond liability, and the assets are all recorded in the enterprise fund.

3. Assets financed by assessments to property owners, such as sidewalks or sewers, are accounted for in a special assessments fund. The receipt of proceeds from bond issues, the expenditures for construction, the collection of the assessments from the property owners, and the bond liability and subsequent payments thereon are all reported by the special assessments fund. The assets, however, are recorded in the general fixed asset accounts.

4. Asset acquisitions or construction projects which do not fall into any of the above categories are typically handled through a capital projects fund. Bonds are usually issued to provide the financing. The transactions relating to the acquisition or construction are recorded in the capital projects fund. The assets are recorded in the general fixed assets accounts, and the bond liability is recorded in the general long-term debt accounts.

Acquisition or construction accounted for in capital projects funds may initially be financed by a temporary advance from another fund and by short-term financing known as **bond anticipation notes,** which are short-term loans from a bank or other financial institution. When the long-term bonds are issued, these temporary loans are repaid. As will be discussed later, any bond proceeds not used for the project, along with any bond premium, are then used for debt service on the bond issue. Thus, the typical cash flow of a capital projects fund may be summarized as follows:

Sources of Cash	Uses of Cash
Advances from other funds Bond anticipation notes	Construction costs
Bond proceeds	Repay advances and bond anticipation notes Construction costs Interest and principal on bonds
Bond premium, if any	Interest and principal on bonds

Accounting for the Capital Projects Fund

To illustrate the accounting procedures for a capital projects fund, we will follow through a typical project. Assume that Lake City decides to construct a new fire station. A bond issue of $500,000 is authorized to meet the expected cost of construction. If a budget entry is recorded, it appears as follows:

```
Bonds Authorized—Unissued  .   .   .   .   .   .   500,000
    Appropriations  .   .   .   .   .   .   .   .   .           500,000
To record approval of project (construction of fire
station).
```

Note that **Bonds Authorized—Unissued** is a *budgeted revenues* account, signifying that the source of resources for the project will be the issuance of bonds.

Initial resources for the project might be temporarily advanced from another fund. This permits work to begin prior to the issuance of the bonds. Assume that, in our example, $12,000 is advanced from the general fund. The entry in the capital projects fund is:

```
Cash  .   .   .   .   .   .   .   .   .   .   .   .   .   12,000
    Due to General Fund  .   .   .   .   .   .   .   .           12,000
To record advance from general fund.
```

A parallel entry is made in the general fund.

Suppose that bids are taken for the construction of the fire station, and a contract for $495,000 is awarded to the qualified low bidder. This constitutes an encumbrance, which is recorded as:

```
Encumbrances  .   .   .   .   .   .   .   .   .   .   495,000
    Reserve for Encumbrances  .   .   .   .   .   .           495,000
To record award of contract for construction of fire
station.
```

Bonds are often not issued until the project is complete or nearly complete. In some cases, mortgage bonds are issued, with the property constructed serving as security for the debt. Such bonds are typically not issued until the construction is complete. In other cases, the city may delay issuing the bonds in anticipation of more favorable interest rates in the future. In either case, temporary financing is needed. This temporary financing often takes the form of *bond anticipation notes*. Assume that Lake City borrows $400,000 in this way to meet construction costs of the fire station. The entry is:

Cash	. . . .	400,000	
Bond Anticipation Notes Payable	. . . . .		400,000

To record temporary financing for fire station.

Cash not required immediately may be invested in certificates of deposit or other short-term investments:

Temporary Investments	. . . .	175,000	
Cash	. . . .		175,000

To record purchase of certificate of deposit.

Assume that $200,000 of vouchers are received, representing payments due for partial completion of the contract. Encumbrances are reversed and expenditures are recorded:

Reserve for Encumbrances	. . . .	200,000	
Encumbrances	. . . .		200,000

To reverse encumbrances for amount billed by contractor.

Expenditures	. . . .	200,000	
Vouchers Payable	. . . .		200,000

To record billing from contractor.

Contracts of this type often provide that a portion of each billing may be withheld by the city until the project is completed and passes inspection. This is known as a **retainage,** which helps protect the city against failure of the contractor to complete the project or against deficiencies which need to be remedied. If the Lake City contract provides for a 20 percent retainage, the contractor will be paid $160,000.

Vouchers Payable	. . . .	160,000	
Cash	. . . .		160,000

To record payment to contractor, less 20% retainage of $40,000 (= .2 × $200,000).

If desired, a separate account for Vouchers Payable—Retainage could be used. Later, when the project is completed and the contractor submits a second (final) bill for $298,000, the following entries are made:

Reserve for Encumbrances	. . . .	295,000	
Encumbrances	. . . .		295,000

To reverse balance of encumbrances on project.

Expenditures	. . . .	298,000	
Vouchers Payable	. . . .		298,000

To record billing from contractor.

To pay the contractor, Lake City liquidates the temporary investments and records $6,000 of earned interest:

Cash	. . . .	181,000	
Temporary Investments	. . . .		175,000
Revenues	. . . .		6,000

To record liquidation of temporary investments and interest earned.

Legal provisions specify how the interest earned on the temporary investments may be spent. In our example, Lake City may not use the $6,000 to meet construction costs but may apply it toward the interest on the bond anticipation notes. In other words, construction costs are limited to the $500,000 originally authorized.

The contractor is paid, with 20 percent retained by the city until the building passes final inspection:

```
Vouchers Payable  .   .   .   .   .   .   .   .   .   .   238,400
    Cash   .   .   .   .   .   .   .   .   .   .   .                238,400
To record payment to contractor, less 20% retainage of
$59,600 (= .2 × $298,000).
```

Assume now that the bonds are issued. The face amount of the bonds is $500,000, but they are issued at a premium such that Lake City receives $510,000. Bond proceeds and bond premium are not considered revenues or liabilities of the fund. Rather, they are classified as other financing sources and are reported on the statement of revenues, expenditures, and changes in fund balance. Thus, the entry is:

```
Cash   .   .   .   .   .   .   .   .   .   .   .   .   .   510,000
    Bond Proceeds .   .   .   .   .   .   .   .   .   .             500,000
    Bond Premium  .   .   .   .   .   .   .   .   .   .              10,000
To record issuance of $500,000 bonds for $510,000.
```

Again, legal provisions dictate how the $10,000 premium may be spent. Generally, the premium cannot be spent on construction costs of the project. The project was authorized for $500,000, and this authorization cannot be increased by the expedient of issuing bonds at a premium. Since a premium results from the fact that the bonds bear an interest rate higher than the market rate, any premium must normally be applied toward repayment of the principal and interest on the bonds. Thus a bond premium is usually transferred to the debt service fund. Bond discounts rarely occur in this context. If bonds were issued at a discount, the proceeds would be less than the amount authorized for the project, causing a potential cash shortage. To avoid this problem, the interest rate on the bonds is set high enough so that no discount results.

The proceeds of the face amount of the bond issue are used to pay off the bond anticipation notes, to repay the advance from the general fund, and to pay remaining amounts due the contractor. After the city officials have approved the completed project, they authorize payment of the retainages to the contractor. These events are recorded as follows:

```
Bond Anticipation Notes Payable  .   .   .   .   .   400,000
Expenditures   .   .   .   .   .   .   .   .   .   .     6,500
    Cash   .   .   .   .   .   .   .   .   .   .   .             406,500
To record repayment of bond anticipation notes, plus
interest of $6,500.

Due to General Fund   .   .   .   .   .   .   .   .    12,000
    Cash   .   .   .   .   .   .   .   .   .   .   .              12,000
To repay advance from general fund.

Vouchers Payable  .   .   .   .   .   .   .   .   .    99,600
    Cash   .   .   .   .   .   .   .   .   .   .   .              99,600
To record payment of retainages to contractor
($40,000 + $59,600).
```

The project is complete, but the capital projects fund shows a cash balance of $11,500, representing $10,000 of bond premium and $1,500 of unspent bond proceeds. Laws or regulations usually specify that unspent bond proceeds, like the bond premium, must be transferred to the debt service fund to be used for repayment of the bonds. Thus we close the accounts and transfer the cash balance.

Revenues	6,000	
Bond Proceeds	500,000	
Bond Premium	10,000	
Bonds Authorized—Unissued		500,000
Fund Balance—Unreserved		16,000

To close revenues, bond proceeds, and bond premium.

Appropriations	500,000	
Fund Balance—Unreserved	4,500	
Expenditures		504,500

To close expenditures ($504,500 = $200,000 + $298,000 + $6,500).

Operating Transfers Out	11,500	
Cash		11,500

To transfer balance to debt service fund.

Fund Balance—Unreserved	11,500	
Operating Transfers Out		11,500

To close transfers.

Capital projects often take more than one year to complete. Because the budget is usually established at the outset for the entire project, some modification must be made to the annual closing process. The following rules for closing entries exist when the project is not complete:

1. Close Estimated Revenues only to the extent of actual Revenues and close Bonds Authorized— Unissued only to the extent of Bond Proceeds. There will be no debit or credit to Fund Balance.

2. Close Appropriations only to the extent of Expenditures and Encumbrances. There will be no debit or credit to Fund Balance.

To illustrate, assume that in January 19X1, a capital project is authorized, and the following budget entry is recorded:

Bonds Authorized—Unissued	1,000,000	
Appropriations		1,000,000

To record approval of project.

Suppose that during 19X1 $400,000 of bonds were issued at par, that expenditures on the project were $280,000, and that $40,000 in encumbrances were outstanding. At the end of 19X1, the project is not yet complete. Closing entries at December 31, 19X1, are:

Bond Proceeds	400,000	
Bonds Authorized—Unissued		400,000

To close bond proceeds.

Appropriations	320,000	
Expenditures		280,000
Encumbrances		40,000

To close expenditures and encumbrances.

Note that no entries are made to fund balance and that $600,000 of bonds authorized but unissued and $680,000 of appropriations remain on the books for

19X2. At the beginning of 19X2, one additional entry is required to restore the open encumbrances to the accounts:

```
Encumbrances   .   .   .   .   .   .   .   .   .   .   40,000
    Fund Balance—Unreserved  .   .   .   .   .   .   .              40,000
    To restore encumbrances closed at December 31, 19X1.
```

Each capital project has a limited life. Once the project is completed and all bills are paid, any remaining resources are transferred (usually to the debt service fund). A government unit may, at any one time, have several projects underway. The capital projects fund, therefore, often consists of several individual project funds. Alternatively, if several projects are included in one fund, subsidiary records must be kept by project.

Interaction with Other Funds and Account Groups

Generally, activities carried on in the capital projects fund affect other funds and account groups. The interactions contained in the Lake City illustration are typical:

1. Cash was advanced from the general fund to the capital projects fund and subsequently repaid.

2. Excess cash left in the capital projects fund at the conclusion of construction was transferred to the debt service fund.

3. A building was constructed, requiring an entry in the general fixed assets account group.

4. Bonds were issued, requiring an entry in the general long-term debt account group.

The entries made in the other funds and account groups to reflect these interactions are presented in the following sections.

General Fund   The entries for the advance and subsequent repayment are straightforward:

```
Due from Capital Projects Fund  .   .   .   .   .   .   12,000
    Cash  .   .   .   .   .   .   .   .   .   .   .   .   .              12,000
    To record advance to capital projects fund.

Cash  .   .   .   .   .   .   .   .   .   .   .   .   .   12,000
    Due from Capital Projects Fund  .   .   .   .   .   .              12,000
    To record repayment of advance.
```

Debt Service Fund   The transfer of bond premium and unspent appropriations from the capital projects fund is considered an operating transfer to the debt service fund. It is a legally authorized transfer of resources generated in one fund to another fund, where they will be spent; namely, the payment of interest and principal on the bonds by the debt service fund. The entry is:

```
Cash  .   .   .   .   .   .   .   .   .   .   .   .   .   11,500
    Operating Transfers In  .   .   .   .   .   .   .   .              11,500
    To record transfer from capital projects fund.
```

General Fixed Assets Account Group   The cost of the new fire station must be recorded in the general fixed asset accounts. The cost would normally be recorded as $498,000, the amount paid to the contractor. Recall that an additional $6,500 was spent by the capital projects fund as interest on the bond anticipation notes. While an argument can be made for the inclusion of interest as a cost of the building, common practice is to exclude it. The entry is:

```
Buildings  .   .   .   .   .   .   .   .   .   .   .   498,000
    Investment in General Fixed Assets from Capital
        Projects Fund .   .   .   .   .   .   .   .   .                498,000
To record cost of new fire station.
```

If a capital project is only partially complete at year-end, an entry to a Construction in Progress account should be made. For example, assume that a highway project was partially complete at the end of 19X1, with a cost to date of $900,000. This would be recorded in the general fixed asset accounts as:

```
Construction in Progress   .   .   .   .   .   .   .   900,000
    Investment in General Fixed Assets from Capital
        Projects Fund .   .   .   .   .   .   .   .   .                900,000
To record 19X1 costs of highway project.
```

Suppose that the highway project is completed in 19X2 at an additional cost of $273,000. The entries in the general fixed asset accounts would be:

```
Construction in Progress   .   .   .   .   .   .   .   273,000
    Investment in General Fixed Assets from
        Capital Projects Fund   .   .   .   .   .   .                273,000
To record 19X2 costs of highway project.

Improvements  .   .   .   .   .   .   .   .   .   .   1,173,000
    Construction in Progress   .   .   .   .   .   .             1,173,000
To record completion of highway project.
```

General Long-Term Debt Account Group   While the proceeds from the issuance of bonds were recorded by the capital projects fund, the bond liability must be recorded in the general long-term debt accounts. At the time the bonds were issued, the following entry was made:

```
Amount to be Provided for Repayment of Bonds   .   .   500,000
    Bonds Payable .   .   .   .   .   .   .   .   .   .   .                500,000
To record issuance of bonds by capital projects fund
for construction of fire station.
```

Note that the premium was not recorded in the general long-term debt accounts.

Subsequently, $11,500 was transferred from the capital projects fund to the debt service fund, to be used for payment of principal and interest on the bonds. If this money will be used for interest, no entry should be made in the general long-term debt accounts. If, however, this money will be used for principal payments, this availability of resources must be reflected in the general long-term debt accounts as follows:

```
Amount Available for Repayment of Bonds   .   .   .   .   11,500
    Amount to be Provided for Repayment of Bonds   .   .                11,500
To record resources available in debt service fund.
```

Recall that the general long-term debt accounts show the amount of resources which must be provided in future budgets in order to repay the debts. As resources are actually set aside for this purpose, they are recorded as an "amount available" and the "amount to be provided" account is reduced.

Financial Statements for the Capital Projects Fund

A balance sheet and a statement of revenues, expenditures, and changes in fund balance are commonly presented for the capital projects fund. The balance sheet of a capital projects fund would include items such as the following:

Cash	Vouchers Payable
Temporary Investments	Contracts Payable
Due from Other Funds	Due to Other Funds
	Fund Balance:
	Reserved for Encumbrances
	Unreserved

If budgetary accounts are recorded and the project is incomplete, Bonds Authorized—Unissued also appears in the asset section and Appropriations appears in the fund balance section. In the Lake City illustration, the project was completed, the accounts were closed, and the fund balance was transferred to the debt service fund. Thus the balance sheet accounts all have zero balances.

The statement of revenues, expenditures, and changes in fund balance of a capital projects fund follows the format illustrated earlier for the general fund. The statement for the Lake City example appears in Exhibit 17.1.

In many cases, several capital projects funds exist at any one time. Thus, a combining balance sheet and a combining statement of revenues, expenditures, and changes in fund balance are presented. Combining statements show the accounts for each capital projects fund, along with totals for all such funds.

The Special Assessments Fund

Improvements constructed by government which benefit a limited, identifiable geographic area often are financed, at least in part, by the property owners benefited. For example, installation of sidewalks in a neighborhood is often financed by assessments to property owners in that neighborhood. Projects of this nature—streets, sidewalks, sewers, street lighting—are accounted for in a special assessments fund.

To ease the financial burden on the assessed parties, assessments are often spread over several years. Because funds to pay for the project will not be available immediately, financing is needed initially to pay the costs of the project. Bonds are often issued for this purpose. Thus the typical cash flow of a special assessments fund appears as follows:

Sources of Cash	Uses of Cash
Bond proceeds	Construction costs
Collection of assessments	Interest and principal on bonds

Recall that in the capital projects fund, bond proceeds are recorded as a source of financing. This is not the case in the special assessments fund. The

Exhibit 17.1 Illustration of Statement of Revenues, Expenditures, and Changes in Fund Balance for Capital Projects Fund

Lake City
Statement of Revenues, Expenditures,
and Changes in Fund Balance—Capital Projects Fund
For the Year Ended December 31, 19X0

REVENUES:

Interest Earned			$ 6,000

EXPENDITURES:

Capital Outlay	$498,000		
Interest—Temporary Financing	6,500	504,500	
Excess of Revenues over (under) Expenditures		$(498,500)	

OTHER FINANCING SOURCES (USES):

Bond Proceeds and Premium	$510,000		
Operating Transfers Out	(11,500)	498,500	
Excess of Revenues and Other Sources over (under)			
Expenditures and Other Uses		$ 0	
FUND BALANCE—JANUARY 1		0	
FUND BALANCE—DECEMBER 31		$ 0	

resources of a special assessments fund come from the assessments and any other permanent means of financing, such as a nonrepayable contribution from the general fund. The bond proceeds are recorded as a *liability* by the special assessments fund; repayment will also be recorded in this fund. The debt service fund and the general long-term debt account group are *not* used in accounting for the issuance and repayment of special assessment bonds.

Accounting for the Special Assessments Fund

To illustrate the accounting procedures for a special assessments fund, assume that Lake City is installing new street lights in a certain area. The lights are expected to cost $100,000. A ten-year serial bond issue will provide funds for construction, and residents of the affected area are to be assessed $140,000 over ten years. A serial bond issue is in effect a series of individual bond issues, each due in a different year. In our example, $10,000 of bonds mature in one year, $10,000 in two years, and so forth. The assessments collected each year are used to pay the principal of bonds maturing that year and the interest on all outstanding bonds.

Authorization of the project may or may not be recorded. If it is, the budget entry appears as:

Improvements Authorized	100,000	
Appropriations		100,000
To record approval of project (new street lighting).		

Suppose that 6 percent, ten-year serial bonds in the amount of $100,000 are issued at a $1,000 premium. As was the case in the capital projects fund, any bond premium is generally devoted to debt repayment rather than to providing additional resources for construction. Since both construction *and* debt service are handled by the special assessments fund, it may be convenient to establish two cash accounts to enhance control. Thus the issuance of the bonds is recorded as:

Cash—Construction	100,000	
Cash—Debt Service	1,000	
Bonds Payable		100,000
Bond Premium		1,000
To record issuance of 10-year, 6 percent serial bonds at 101.		

Bids are taken on the project and a contract is awarded for $97,000. This is recorded as an encumbrance:

Encumbrances	97,000	
Reserve for Encumbrances		97,000
To record award of contract for street lighting.		

The assessment of $140,000 is levied, payable over a ten-year period. As discussed earlier, this item constitutes a revenue to the special assessments fund and is recorded as:

Special Assessments Receivable—Current	14,000	
Special Assessments Receivable—Deferred	126,000	
Revenue		140,000
To record assessments levied.		

Some months later, the contract is completed, billed, and paid. The following entries are then recorded:

Reserve for Encumbrances	97,000	
Encumbrances		97,000
To reverse encumbrance.		
Expenditures	97,000	
Vouchers Payable		97,000
To record cost of completed street lighting.		
Vouchers Payable	97,000	
Cash—Construction		97,000
To record payment of contract.		

Since the project is complete, the remaining $3,000 from the bond proceeds is available for repayment of the bonds:

Cash—Debt Service	3,000	
Cash—Construction		3,000
To reallocate remaining construction cash to be used for debt service.		

Assume that at year-end the annual assessment is collected in full and the required payment on the serial bonds is made:

Cash—Debt Service	14,000	
Special Assessments Receivable—Current		14,000
To record collection of current year assessments.		
Bonds Payable	10,000	
Expenditures	6,000	
Cash—Debt Service		16,000
To record payment of annual interest and $10,000 of principal on bonds.		

Closing entries can now be made in the usual manner, closing actual revenues against budgeted revenues (Improvements Authorized) and actual expenditures against appropriations:

```
Revenues  . . . . . . . . . . . 140,000
Bond Premium . . . . . . . . . .   1,000
     Improvements Authorized . . . . . .           100,000
     Fund Balance—Unreserved  . . . . .             41,000
To close revenues and bond premium.

Appropriations . . . . . . . . . . 100,000
Fund Balance—Unreserved  . . . . . .   3,000
     Expenditures  . . . . . . . . . .           103,000
To close expenditures.
```

A fund balance of $38,000 remains. Although construction is complete, the fund will be active for nine more years, collecting the assessments and paying the principal and interest on the bonds. No further revenues are likely to be generated, but further expenditures (interest) will be incurred, gradually reducing the fund balance. Once the activities of the fund are completed (that is, once the bonds are paid), legal requirements govern the disposition of any remaining fund balance. The final year assessment could be reduced, effectively returning any fund balance to the property owners, or the balance could be transferred to the general fund. Similarly, legal guidelines would be followed if the fund had a deficiency, as might occur if some assessments prove uncollectible.

Interaction with Other Funds and Account Groups

Transactions by a special assessments fund have limited interaction with other funds and account groups. The general fund becomes involved if it provides temporary financing or if a portion of the cost of the improvements is funded through the general fund budget. In addition, the cost of the improvements must be recorded in the general fixed assets account group. For the Lake City illustration, the entry in the *general fixed assets account group* is:

```
Improvements . . . . . . . . . . . . 97,000
     Investment in General Fixed Assets—Special
     Assessments Fund . . . . . . . . . .           97,000
To record cost of street lighting.
```

Since the special assessments fund records its own bond liability and handles its own debt service, there is no interaction with either the debt service fund or the general long-term debt account group.

Financial Statements for the Special Assessments Fund

A balance sheet and a statement of revenues, expenditures, and changes in fund balance are presented for the special assessments fund. The balance sheet typically contains the following items:

Cash—Construction	Vouchers Payable
Cash—Debt Service	Contracts Payable
Special Assessments Receivable	Special Assessments Bonds
	Payable
	Fund Balance:
	Reserved for Encumbrances
	Unreserved

The unreserved fund balance is often designated for use for debt service, and may be so indicated on the balance sheet. For the Lake City illustration, the balance sheet is:

Lake City
Special Assessments Fund
Balance Sheet
December 31, 19X0

Cash—Debt Service	$ 2,000
Special Assessments Receivable	126,000
	$128,000
Bonds Payable	$ 90,000
Fund Balance:	
Unreserved—Designated for Debt Service	38,000
	$128,000

The statement of revenues, expenditures, and changes in fund balance follows the format previously discussed. For the Lake City illustration, the statement appears as follows:

Lake City
Special Assessments Fund
Statement of Revenues, Expenditures,
and Changes in Fund Balance
For the Year Ended December 31, 19X0

REVENUES:		
Special Assessments Levied		$140,000
EXPENDITURES:		
Capital Outlay	$97,000	
Debt Service—Interest	6,000	103,000
Excess of Revenues over Expenditures		$ 37,000
OTHER FINANCING SOURCES (USES):		
Bond Premium		1,000
Excess of Revenues and Other Sources over Expenditures and Other Uses		$ 38,000
FUND BALANCE—JANUARY 1		0
FUND BALANCE—DECEMBER 31		$ 38,000

As was the case with capital projects funds, several special assessments funds may exist, in which case combining statements are also presented.

The Debt Service Fund

Accounting treatment of long-term debt in governmental accounting depends in part on the source of cash used for repayment, the entity (fund) making the payment, and the fund incurring the debt. Debt may be recorded in the accounts of

Exhibit 17.2   Accounting for Long-Term Debt by Various Funds

Long-Term Debt Incurred By	Where Liability Is Recorded	Source of Resources to Repay Debt	Payment Made From
Special assessments fund	Special assessments fund	Assessments on property owners	Special assessments fund
Enterprise or internal service fund	Specific fund (enterprise or internal service)	Revenues from operations	Specific fund
Trust fund	Trust fund	Income of trust fund	Trust fund
General, special revenue, or capital projects fund	General long-term debt accounts	Provision in general fund budget Special tax levies Bond premium Proceeds of bond issue not spent on project	Debt service fund

the originating fund or in the general long-term debt account group. The primary role of the debt service fund is to receive cash from other funds and to use it either (1) to make current payments of principal and interest to debtholders or (2) to invest resources which are to be used for future principal payments.

A summary of the treatment of debt in governmental accounting is presented in Exhibit 17.2. Long-term debt incurred by an enterprise, internal service, trust and agency, or special assessments fund is recorded as a liability in those funds rather than in the general long-term debt accounts. Resources to repay the debt are generated by the operations of the related funds. Thus, payments of principal and interest are usually made directly by those funds to the bondholders. The debt service fund is not used for payments on such debt, unless the government unit deems it particularly convenient to make all debt payments from a single fund. In such a case, the enterprise, internal service, trust and agency, and special assessments funds would transfer money to the debt service fund, which in turn would pay the bondholders.

Long-term debt incurred by the general, special revenue, and capital projects funds is recorded as a liability in the general long-term debt accounts. Resources to repay the debt come primarily from the general fund budget, although special tax levies for debt retirement are also possible. As was illustrated earlier in the chapter, some resources for debt payment may be provided by bond premiums and unspent appropriations on capital projects. Payments on debt incurred by the general, special revenue, and capital projects funds are typically made through the debt service fund. In the following discussion, we assume the most common case—that the debt service fund handles payments on *general obligation debt* only and not on the debt of the special assessment, enterprise, internal service, and trust and agency funds. The typical cash flow of a debt service fund is shown next:

Sources of Cash	Uses of Cash
Transfers from general fund (budgetary appropriations for debt service)	Current payments of interest and principal on general obligation debt
Transfers from special revenue fund (proceeds of any special tax levies for debt service)	Investment for future principal payments
Transfers from capital projects fund (bond premium and unspent appropriations)	
Earnings on investments	
Liquidation of investments	

Accounting for the Debt Service Fund

Because the debt service fund employs fund accounting techniques, a budget for estimated revenues and appropriations *may* be recorded in the accounts but does not have to be, since the budget is usually the result of managerial design rather than a legal approval process. Resources of a debt service fund come from transfers from other funds and earnings on investments. Two estimated revenue accounts are used: **Required Additions** signifies the amount of transfers to be made from the general or special revenue funds (transfers from the capital projects fund are difficult to estimate and thus are often not budgeted), and **Required Earnings** signifies the estimated income from investments. Since the debt service fund is used to accumulate resources for future debt payment, annual appropriations usually differ from annual estimated revenues. In years in which resources are being accumulated toward future debt payments, appropriations will be less than estimated revenues; in years in which an accumulation is expended, appropriations will exceed estimated revenues.

To illustrate the sequence of entries, assume that Lake City establishes a debt service fund to make annual interest payments on a 5 percent, $500,000 general obligation bond issue and to accumulate resources for the future retirement of principal. A transfer of $50,000 to the debt service fund is appropriated in the general fund budget, and investment income for the year is estimated to be $2,700. The only planned expenditure is the $25,000 interest payment on the bonds. The budget entry for the debt service fund is:

Required Additions	50,000	
Required Earnings	2,700	
Appropriations		25,000
Fund Balance—Unreserved		27,700
To record budget.		

Assume that early in the year the $50,000 transfer is received from the general fund and is immediately invested in time deposits, government bonds, or other appropriate securities.

Cash	50,000	
Operating Transfers In		50,000
To record transfer from general fund.		
Investments	50,000	
Cash		50,000
To record purchase of investments.		

Later in the year, the interest payment on the bonds becomes due. Securities which had cost $24,000 are liquidated for $25,000, and the interest payment is made:

Cash	25,000	
Investments		24,000
Revenues		1,000
To record liquidation of securities costing $24,000.		

Expenditures	25,000	
Cash		25,000
To record payment of bond interest.		

If, at year-end, interest accrued on investments is $1,500, and $11,500 of bond premium and unspent appropriations are transferred from the capital projects fund, the following entries are made:

Investments	1,500	
Revenues		1,500
To record earnings on investments.		

Cash	11,500	
Operating Transfers In		11,500
To record transfer from capital projects fund.		

Despite the use of the modified accrual method for all governmental funds, interest on long-term debt is *not* accrued by the debt service fund. Rather it is recorded as an expenditure in the year in which the payment is made. Year-end closing entries are:

Operating Transfers In	61,500	
Revenues	2,500	
Required Additions		50,000
Required Earnings		2,700
Fund Balance—Unreserved		11,300
To close revenues and operating transfers in.		

Appropriations	25,000	
Expenditures		25,000
To close expenditures.		

After the closing entries, the accounts show cash of $11,500, investments of $27,500, and an unreserved fund balance of $39,000. The unreserved fund balance is designated for debt service.

Interaction with Other Funds and Account Groups

Several transactions of a debt service fund involve other funds and account groups. The two major interactions are: (1) transfers to the debt service fund must be recorded by the fund making the transfer and (2) the accumulation of resources available for repayment of debt must be noted in the general long-term debt accounts.

In our illustration, there were two transfers to Lake City's debt service fund. The transfer from the *general fund* is recorded on the general fund books as:

Operating Transfers Out	50,000	
Cash		50,000
To record transfer of appropriated contribution to debt service fund.		

Similarly, the entry for the transfer from the *capital projects fund* is recorded in that fund as:

```
Operating Transfers Out  .  .  .  .  .  .  .  .  .  11,500
    Cash  .  .  .  .  .  .  .  .  .  .  .  .  .  .  .              11,500
To record transfer of bond premium and unspent
appropriations to debt service fund.
```

At year-end, the debt service fund had accumulated $39,000. If this amount will be used for the future repayment of bond principal, it is recorded in the *general long-term debt account group* as:

```
Amount Available for Repayment of Bonds  .  .  .  .  39,000
    Amount to be Provided for Repayment of Bonds  .  .              39,000
To record amounts available in debt service fund.
```

Financial Statements for the Debt Service Fund

A balance sheet and a statement of revenues, expenditures, and changes in fund balance are typically presented for the debt service fund. The balance sheet for the Lake City illustration appears as follows:

Lake City
Debt Service Fund
Balance Sheet
December 31, 19X0

Cash	$11,500	Fund Balance:	
Investments	27,500	Unreserved—Designated for	
	$39,000	Debt Service	$39,000

The statement of revenues, expenditures, and changes in fund balance appears as:

Lake City
Debt Service Fund
Statement of Revenues, Expenditures,
and Changes in Fund Balance
For the Year Ended December 31, 19X0

REVENUES:

Earnings on Investments . . . . $ 2,500

EXPENDITURES:

Debt Service—Interest 25,000
Excess of Revenues over (under) Expenditures . . . . $(22,500)

OTHER FINANCING SOURCES (USES):

Operating Transfers In 61,500
Excess of Revenues and Other Sources over (under) Expenditures and
    Other Uses . . . . $ 39,000

FUND BALANCE—JANUARY 1 0

FUND BALANCE—DECEMBER 31 . . . . $ 39,000

The Enterprise and Internal Service Funds

Enterprise funds account for activities of government units which generate a substantial portion of their revenues by the sale of goods and services to outside parties. Typical activities of this nature are:

1. Utilities—municipal water, gas, and electricity.
2. Sanitation—sewer systems.
3. Recreational facilities—golf courses, marinas, swimming pools, tennis courts, and stadiums.
4. Commercial facilities—airports, ports, and farmers' markets.
5. Transportation facilities—bus, rapid transit, and toll bridges.
6. Public hospitals and health clinics.
7. Public housing projects.

In addition to user chargers, these activities are often subsidized by general government revenues. The principal source of revenue usually determines whether the activity is accounted for in an enterprise fund or in the general fund. If the majority of the activity's revenue is generated by charges to users, the activity should be accounted for in an enterprise fund; otherwise, it should be accounted for in the general fund.

Internal service funds account for centralized service activities of a government unit, where goods and services are sold to various departments and funds within the unit. Among the activities in this category are:

1. Central maintenance and repair services.
2. Central vehicle pool.
3. Central supply facilities.
4. Central print shop.
5. Central computer services.

Such activities are centralized so that cost savings may be realized through more efficient use of equipment, volume purchasing, and other economies of scale. The internal service fund pays the cost of operating the central service facility and sets user charges so as to produce sufficient revenues to recover costs.

Accounting and Reporting for Enterprise and Internal Service Funds

Enterprise funds and internal service funds employ the same accounting practices as do business entities. This means that they use full accrual accounting, distinguish between capital and expense items, and recognize depreciation on fixed assets.

The financial statements of enterprise and internal service funds are patterned after the financial statements of a business firm. The balance sheet has the same accounts and structure as a business balance sheet, with a minor exception in the equity section. While an enterprise or internal service fund has no capital stock and no stockholders, it is likely to have contributed capital, usually from the general fund. Thus there will be differences in terminology, but not in substance. Typical owners' equity items are at the top of page 756.

In addition, a statement of revenues, expenses, and changes in retained earnings and a statement of changes in financial position are presented. These

Business Firm	Enterprise or Internal Service Fund
Stockholders' Equity: Common Stock Paid-In Capital Retained Earnings	Fund Balance: Capital Contributed by General Fund Retained Earnings

also are very similar to the business counterparts. They are illustrated in Exhibits 17.4 and 17.5, following the discussion of trust funds. Because the same statement format is used by both enterprise or internal service funds and trust and agency funds, a single set of illustrations suffices.

The Trust and Agency Funds

Trust and agency funds, while commonly combined, consist of two distinct elements: trust funds and agency funds. While both involve resources collected, held, and paid out by the unit acting as a fiduciary, there are differences in terms of the purpose and duration of the fiduciary responsibility.

Agency Funds

Agency funds account for situations in which the government unit acts as collection agent for another entity. The two most common situations are employee deductions and tax collections. Deductions of various types (for example, federal and state taxes, health insurance, retirement contributions, union dues, payroll savings) are taken from the earnings of employees and periodically remitted on behalf of the employees to appropriate entities. In the case of tax collections, one government unit may collect taxes on behalf of another. For example, a state may collect income taxes or sales taxes on behalf of a city or county. A county may collect property taxes on behalf of other legal entities (cities, towns, or special districts) within its jurisdiction. In both situations, the resources are likely to be held for only a short time by the agency fund.

Accounting for Agency Funds   The majority of transactions of an agency fund fall into two categories: collection and payment. The entries for these two transaction types are straightforward. A collection requires a debit to cash and a credit to an appropriate liability account; a payment requires a debit to the liability and a credit to cash. Since most transactions involve the creation or settlement of a liability, we rarely find revenues or expenditures in an agency fund, and consequently an agency fund has little or no fund balance.

Trust Funds

Trust funds are used when the government unit holds, manages, and spends resources under terms of a trust agreement. Two general types exist. One type, often called a **nonexpendable trust fund,** requires that the principal be maintained intact and that the income be spent for a particular purpose. Examples include an endowment fund for the public library or a scholarship fund for students. The other type, called an **expendable trust fund,** does not maintain a distinction between principal and income; all resources of the fund may be spent for the specified purpose. A retirement (pension) fund is a common example. The fund receives resources from the local government, perhaps from the employees, and from earnings on investments. These resources are then used to pay retirement benefits. Note that, in contrast to agency funds, both types of trust funds normally hold resources for long periods of time.

Accounting for Trust Funds   Nonexpendable trust funds use the principles of fiduciary accounting outlined in Chapter 4. Distinction must be maintained between principal and income, resulting in reserved and unreserved fund balance accounts. To illustrate, assume that Lake City receives a $25,000 gift from a wealthy citizen, with the provision that the money be invested and income be used to purchase books for the library. The gift is credited to revenue and is closed to a reserved fund balance account to indicate the restriction on its spending. The entries are:

Cash	25,000	
Revenues		25,000
To record endowment for library.		

Investments	25,000	
Cash		25,000
To record investment of library endowment funds.		

Assume that during the remainder of the year $1,300 is earned on the investments, and $1,050 is spent to acquire library books.

Cash	1,300	
Revenues		1,300
To record earnings on investments.		

Expenditures	1,050	
Cash		1,050
To record purchase of library books.		

Closing entries would show an increase in the reserved fund balance of $25,000 and an increase in the unreserved fund balance of $250. Since the latter amount can be spent, it must be distinguished from the nonexpendable portion of the balance.

Revenues	26,300	
Expenditures		1,050
Fund Balance—Reserved for Endowment		25,000
Fund Balance—Unreserved		250
To close revenues and expenditures.		

Expendable trust funds may require only a single unreserved fund balance account or may also use reserves to signify the purpose for which the resources are held. In a pension fund, for example, an account entitled Fund Balance— Reserved for Retirement Pensions may be used. Transactions in an expendable trust fund typically involve revenues, expenditures, and investment activities. These present few accounting problems. Consider, for example, a firefighters' pension fund administered by a city. Employer contributions, employee contributions, and earnings on investments are all recorded as revenues. Payment of benefits to retirees or refunds of contributions to individuals leaving the system are recorded as expenditures.

Financial Statements for Trust and Agency Funds

Balance sheets are presented for both trust funds and agency funds. Beyond this, the statements differ. Since agency funds have few, if any, revenue and expenditure transactions, and hence little or no fund balance, a statement of revenues, expenditures, and changes in fund balance is not used. Rather, a **statement of changes in assets and liabilities** is used to show the agency fund's activity during the year. This statement is illustrated in Exhibit 17.3.

Trust funds, like proprietary funds, measure net income and changes in financial position. The statement of revenues, expenses, and changes in fund balance is illustrated in Exhibit 17.4, and the statement of changes in financial position is illustrated in Exhibit 17.5.

Summary of Key Concepts

The nonroutine activities of a local government are handled through six special entities: the capital projects, special assessments, debt service, enterprise, internal service, and trust and agency funds.

The **capital projects, special assessments,** and **debt service funds** are **governmental funds.** They use the modified accrual basis of accounting and the other fund accounting procedures. However, budgetary accounting is less important for these funds than for the general and special revenue funds.

The **enterprise** and **internal service funds** are **proprietary funds.** Their transactions, accounting, and financial statements closely parallel those for business firms.

The **trust and agency funds** are **fiduciary funds.** A combination of fiduciary accounting and fund accounting is employed.

Many transactions affect more than one fund or account group. Consideration of these **interactions** is very important in government accounting.

Questions   **Q17.1**   In governmental accounting, the budget for a fund may be entered in the accounting records. Briefly explain the purpose of this entry. For which of the eight fund types is a budget entry usually made?

Q17.2   A government unit may have several capital projects underway simultaneously. How must the accounting records and financial statements of the capital projects fund be structured so as to properly reflect this situation?

Q17.3   Improvement projects undertaken by a government unit may be financed by general revenues or by assessments to property owners. What criterion is often used in determining the source of financing for improvements?

Q17.4   The general fund of Taylor City transferred $15,000 to a special assessment fund. Under what assumptions would each of the following entries be made in the general fund?

1. Due from Special Assessments Fund 15,000
   Cash 15,000

2. Expenditures 15,000
   Cash 15,000

Exhibit 17.3   Agency Fund Statement of Changes in Assets and Liabilities

Name of Government Unit
Combining Statement of Changes in Assets and
Liabilities—All Agency Funds
For the Fiscal Year Ended December 31, 19X2

	Balance January 1, 19X2	Additions	Deductions	Balance December 31, 19X2
SPECIAL PAYROLL FUND				
ASSETS				
Cash	$ 6,000	$ 40,900	$ 43,550	$ 3,350
LIABILITIES				
Vouchers Payable	$ 6,000	$ 40,900	$ 43,550	$ 3,350
PROPERTY TAX FUND				
ASSETS				
Cash	$ 25,800	$ 800,000	$ 725,000	$100,800
Taxes Receivable (Net of Allowances for Uncollectibles)	174,200	1,205,800	800,000	580,000
Total Assets	$200,000	$2,005,800	$1,525,000	$680,800
LIABILITIES				
Due to Other Taxing Units:				
County	$180,000	$1,085,220	$ 652,500	$612,720
Special District	20,000	120,580	72,500	68,080
Total Liabilities	$200,000	$1,205,800	$ 725,000	$680,800
STUDENT ACTIVITY FUND				
ASSETS				
Cash	$ 1,600	$ 1,900	$ 1,650	$ 1,850
LIABILITIES				
Due to Student Groups	$ 1,600	$ 1,900	$ 1,650	$ 1,850
TOTALS—ALL AGENCY FUNDS				
ASSETS				
Cash	$ 33,400	$ 842,800	$ 770,200	$106,000
Taxes Receivable (Net of Allowance for Uncollectibles)	174,200	1,205,800	800,000	580,000
Total Assets	$207,600	$2,048,600	$1,570,200	$686,000
LIABILITIES				
Vouchers Payable	$ 6,000	$ 40,900	$ 43,550	$ 3,350
Due to Other Taxing Units	200,000	1,205,800	725,000	680,800
Due to Student Groups	1,600	1,900	1,650	1,850
Total Liabilities	$207,600	$1,248,600	$ 770,200	$686,000

Exhibit 17.4   Proprietary and Trust Funds Statements

Name of Government Unit
Combined Statement of Revenues, Expenses, and Changes in
Retained Earnings/Fund Balances
All Proprietary Fund Types and Similar Trust Funds
For the Fiscal Year Ended December 31, 19X2

	Proprietary Fund Types		Fiduciary Fund Types		Totals (Memorandum Only) Year Ended	
	Enterprise	Internal Service	Nonexpendable Trust	Pension Trust	December 31, 19X2	December 31, 19X1
Operating Revenues:						
Charges for Services .	$ 672,150	$88,000	$ —	$ —	$ 760,150	$ 686,563
Interest	—	—	2,480	28,460	30,940	26,118
Contributions . . .	—	—	—	160,686	160,686	144,670
Gifts	—	—	45,000	—	45,000	—
Total Operating Revenues . .	$ 672,150	$88,000	$ 47,480	$ 189,146	$ 996,776	$ 857,351
Operating Expenses:						
Personal Services . .	$ 247,450	$32,500	—	—	$ 279,950	$ 250,418
Contractual Services .	75,330	400	—	—	75,730	68,214
Supplies	20,310	1,900	—	—	22,210	17,329
Materials	50,940	44,000	—	—	94,940	87,644
Heat, Light, and Power	26,050	1,500	—	—	27,550	22,975
Depreciation . . .	144,100	4,450	—	—	148,550	133,210
Benefit Payments . .	—	—	—	21,000	21,000	12,000
Refunds	—	—	—	25,745	25,745	13,243
Total Operating Expenses . .	$ 564,180	$84,750	—	$ 46,745	$ 695,675	$ 605,033
Operating Income .	$ 107,970	$ 3,250	$ 47,480	$ 142,401	$ 301,101	$ 252,318
Nonoperating Revenues (Expenses):						
Operating Grants . .	$ 55,000	—	—	—	$ 55,000	$ 50,000
Interest Revenue . .	3,830	—	—	—	3,830	3,200
Rent	5,000	—	—	—	5,000	5,000
Interest Expense and Fiscal Charges . .	(92,988)	—	—	—	(92,988)	(102,408)
Total Nonoperating Revenues (Expenses) . .	$ (29,158)	—	—	—	$ (29,158)	$ (44,208)
Income before Operating Transfers . .	$ 78,812	$ 3,250	$ 47,480	$ 142,401	$ 271,943	$ 208,110
Operating Transfers In (Out)	—	—	(2,530)	—	(2,530)	(2,120)
Net Income . .	$ 78,812	$ 3,250	$ 44,950	$ 142,401	$ 269,413	$ 205,990
Retained Earnings/Fund Balances—January 1 .	2,088,544	6,550	139,100	1,040,800	3,274,994	3,069,004
Retained Earnings/Fund Balances— December 31 . . .	$2,167,356	$ 9,800	$184,050	$1,183,201	$3,544,407	$3,274,994

Source: Reproduced with permission from National Council for Governmental Accounting, *Statement 1*, "Governmental Accounting and Financial Reporting Principles" (Chicago: Municipal Finance Officers Association of the United States and Canada, 1979), p. 36. © Copyright 1979 by Municipal Finance Officers Association of the United States and Canada.

Exhibit 17.5 Statement of Changes in Financial Position—Proprietary and Trust Funds

Name of Government Unit
Combined Statement of Changes in
Financial Position—All Proprietary Fund Types and Similar Trust Funds
For the Fiscal Year Ended December 31, 19X2

	Proprietary Fund Types		Fiduciary Fund Types		Totals (Memorandum Only)	
	Enterprise	Internal Service	Non-expendable Trust	Pension Trust	December 31, 19X2	December 31, 19X1
SOURCES OF WORKING CAPITAL						
Operations:						
Net Income	$ 78,812	$ 3,250	$44,950	$142,401	$ 269,413	$ 205,990
Items Not Requiring (Providing) Working Capital:						
Depreciation	144,100	4,450			148,550	133,210
Working Capital Provided by Operations	$ 222,912	$ 7,700	$44,950	$142,401	$ 417,963	$ 339,200
Cash from Revenue Bond Construction Account	127,883				127,883	743,800
Contributions	672,666	—	—	—	672,666	—
Total Sources of Working Capital	$1,023,461	$ 7,700	$44,950	$142,401	$1,218,512	$1,083,000
USES OF WORKING CAPITAL						
Acquisition of Property, Plant, and Equipment	$ 324,453	$ 7,000	—	—	$ 331,453	$ 842,812
Retirement of General Obligation Bonds	50,000		—	—	50,000	50,000
Retirement of Revenue Bonds Payable	52,000		—	—	52,000	48,000
Repayment of Advance from General Fund	—	10,000	—	—	10,000	10,000
Net Decrease in Other Current Liabilities Payable from Restricted Assets	8,946	—	—	—	8,946	4,318
Net Increase in Other Restricted Assets	1,624	—	—	—	1,624	414
Total Uses of Working Capital	$ 437,023	$ 17,000	—	—	$ 454,023	$ 955,544
Net Increase (Decrease) in Working Capital	$ 586,438	$ (9,300)	$44,950	$142,401	$ 764,489	$ 127,456
ELEMENTS OF NET INCREASE (DECREASE) IN WORKING CAPITAL						
Cash	$ 119,276	$(20,300)	$ 4,310	$ 20,121	$ 123,407	$ 796,412
Investments			45,640	118,341	163,981	(84,286)
Receivables (Net of Allowances for Uncollectibles)	(5,570)		(5,000)		(10,570)	2,396
Due from Other Funds	(6,000)	(8,000)		2,189	(11,811)	(4,923)
Inventory of Supplies	11,250	14,000			25,250	(3,414)
Prepaid Expenses	460				460	520
Vouchers Payable	(72,471)	5,000			(67,471)	(42,427)
Contracts Payable	551,653			1,750	553,403	(525,400)
Accrued Liabilities	(12,160)				(12,160)	(11,422)
Net Increase (Decrease) in Working Capital	$ 586,438	$ (9,300)	$44,950	$142,401	$ 764,489	$ 127,456

Source: Reproduced with permission from National Council for Governmental Accounting, *Statement 1*, "Governmental Accounting and Financial Reporting Principles" (Chicago: Municipal Finance Officers Association of the United States and Canada, 1979), p. 38. © Copyright 1979 by Municipal Finance Officers Association of the United States and Canada.

Q17.5 Where should the liability for special assessment bonds which carry a secondary pledge of a municipality's general credit be recorded?

(AICPA adapted)

Q17.6 Describe the major differences that exist in the purpose of accounting and financial reporting and in the types of financial reports for a large city when compared to those for a large industrial corporation.

(AICPA adapted)

Q17.7 Why are inventories often ignored in accounting for local government units?

(AICPA adapted)

Q17.8 Select the best answers for the following multiple choice questions:
1. Premiums received on general obligation bonds are generally transferred to what fund or group of accounts?
    a. Debt service.
    b. General long-term debt.
    c. General.
    d. Special revenue.
2. A statement of changes in financial position is prepared for which fund?
    a. Enterprise.
    b. General.
    c. Special assessment.
    d. Agency.
3. Cash secured from property tax revenue was transferred for the eventual payment of principal and interest on general obligation bonds. The bonds had been issued when land was acquired several years ago for a city park. Upon the transfer, an entry would *not* be made in which of the following?
    a. Debt service fund.
    b. General fixed assets group of accounts.
    c. General long-term debt group of accounts.
    d. General fund.

(AICPA adapted)

Q17.9 Select the best answers for the following multiple choice questions:
1. An account for expenditures does *not* appear in which fund?
    a. Capital projects.
    b. Enterprise.
    c. Special assessment.
    d. Special revenue.
2. Which account represents the equity of a nonenterprise fund?
    a. Net assets.
    b. Fund balance.
    c. Reserves.
    d. Unencumbered balance.

3.   When should revenues from interest on assessments receivable be recorded in a special assessments fund?
   a. When legally due.
   b. When assessed.
   c. When collected in cash.
   d. When the amount is known.

(AICPA adapted)

Q17.10   Select the best answers for the following multiple choice questions:

1.   Which government fund would account for its fixed assets in a manner similar to a business organization?
   a. Enterprise.
   b. Capital projects.
   c. General fixed asset group of accounts.
   d. General.

2.   A city realized large capital gains and losses on securities in its library endowment fund. In the absence of specific instructions from the donor or state statutory requirements, the general rule of law holds that these amounts should be charged or credited to:
   a. General fund income.
   b. General fund principal.
   c. Trust fund income.
   d. Trust fund principal.

3.   Of the items listed below, those most likely to have parallel accounting procedures, account titles, and financial statements are:
   a. Special revenue funds and special assessment funds.
   b. Internal service funds and debt service funds.
   c. The general fixed assets group of accounts and the general long-term debt group of accounts.
   d. The general fund and special revenue funds.

4.   A city should use a capital projects fund to account for:
   a. Structures and improvements constructed with the proceeds of a special assessment.
   b. Proceeds of a bond issue to be used to acquire land for city parks.
   c. Construction in progress on the city-owned electric utility plant, financed by an issue of revenue bonds.
   d. Assets to be used to retire bonds issued to finance an addition to the city hall.

(AICPA adapted)

Exercises   E17.1   On January 14, 19X1, the city of Waterport authorized a $750,000 bond issue for the purchase of a building to be used as a community center. On May 3, the bonds were issued at par, and on June 1, the building was purchased and paid for. On November 1, the general fund paid the semi-annual interest of $30,000 on the bonds.

Required: Record all necessary entries for the above information. Identify the the fund or account group for each entry.

E17.2 The town of Kaley recently completed construction of a recreational facility which was accounted for in a capital projects fund. Bonds were issued at the onset of the project to finance construction. Legal constraints prevented use of the $800 premium on the bonds toward construction costs. The premium has not yet been transferred to the debt service fund. Temporary investments of bond proceeds yielded a 3 percent return, or $2,424.

Kaley awarded the construction contract for the facility to the lowest bidder. The contract called for a 15 percent retainage. Kaley's books show $11,550 due the contractor pending final inspection. All other amounts due the contractor have been remitted.

Required:
1. What was the face value of the bonds issued?
2. What was the amount of the contract awarded?
3. What was the original authorization for the project?
4. What is the fund balance after closing entries?

E17.3 At the beginning of fiscal year 19X2, Waller Town established a central supplies storehouse to service its several funds. The general fund contributed $25,000 (nonrefundable) to aid in the establishment. It was agreed that the storehouse would charge other funds for the purchase price of supplies plus 15 percent. During the year, the storehouse purchased $18,000 of supplies, paid operating expenses of $1,500, and billed other funds for $17,250. All accounts have been settled except $2,000 remaining to be collected from the general fund for supplies billed.

Required:
1. Prepare the balance sheet for the central supplies storehouse at the end of of fiscal 19X2.
2. State any effects of the transactions on the financial statements of the general fund of Waller Town. Assume the general fund bought supplies for $6,000 and used only $5,500 worth of supplies.

E17.4 In March 19X3, a resident of Randall City died, leaving her entire estate to the Randall City School District. The will specified that proceeds from the liquidation of the estate were to be invested, and investment income was to be used to provide scholarships for needy high school students. Three students were to be selected each year by the school superintendent. At the date of death, the fair market value of the estate was estimated to be $103,000. In December, the estate was liquidated, realizing $105,000. Administrative costs of the estate in 19X3 were $4,000. The net proceeds were then transferred to the school district and were invested in appropriate securities.

In 19X4, income from investments was $7,000. Administrative costs (all related to income) were $250. The first scholarships were awarded in 19X4 for a total of $5,000.

Required: Record the events described above in an appropriate fund. Include closing entries.

E17.5   The questions below apply to the funds and account groups for Ranchville. Assume each situation is independent of the others.
1.   Ranchville's water utility, which is an enterprise fund, submits a bill for $9,000 to the general fund for water service supplied to city departments and agencies. Submission of this bill results in:
  a.   Creation of balances which will be eliminated on the city's combined balance sheet.
  b.   Recognition of revenue by the water utility fund and of an expenditure by the general fund.
  c.   Recognition of an encumbrance by both the water utility fund and the general fund.
  d.   Creation of a balance which will be eliminated on the city's combined statement of revenues, expenditures, and changes in fund balances.
2.   The water utility transferred land and a building to the general city administration for public use at no charge to the city. On the water utility books, the land was carried at $4,000 and the building at a cost of $30,000, on which $23,000 depreciation had been recorded. In the year of the transfer, what would be the effect of the transaction?
  a.   Reduce retained earnings of the water utility by $11,000 and increase the fund balance of the general fund by $11,000.
  b.   Reduce retained earnings of the water utility by $11,000 and increase the total assets in the general fixed assets group by $11,000.
  c.   Reduce retained earnings of the water utility by $11,000 and increase the total assets in the general fixed assets group by $34,000.
  d.   Have no effect on a combined balance sheet for the city.
3.   The following information applies to the water utility fund:

Prepaid Insurance Paid in December 19X6	$ 43,000
Depreciation for 19X6	129,000
Provision for Doubtful Accounts for 19X6	14,000

What amount should be reflected in the statement of revenues and expenses (income statement) of the Ranchville water utility fund for the above items?
  a. $(43,000)
  b. $0
  c. $129,000
  d. $143,000.
4.   What will be the balance sheet effect of recording $50,000 of depreciation in the accounts of the water utility?
  a.   Reduce total assets of the utility fund and the general fixed assets group by $50,000.
  b.   Reduce total assets of the utility fund by $50,000 but have no effect on the general fixed assets group.

c. Reduce total assets of the general fixed assets group by $50,000 but have no effect on assets of the utility fund.

d. Have no effect on total assets of either the utility fund or the general fixed assets group.

5. Ranchville has approved a special assessments project in accordance with applicable laws. Total assessments of $500,000, including 10 percent for the city's share of the cost, have been levied. The levy will be collected from property owners in ten equal annual installments commencing with the current year. Recognition of the approval and levy will result in entries of:

a. $500,000 in the special assessments fund and $50,000 in the general fund.

b. $450,000 in the special assessments fund and $50,000 in the general fund.

c. $50,000 in the special assessments fund and $50,000 in the general fund.

d. $50,000 in the special assessments fund and no entry in the general fund.

6. Ranchville's debt service fund (for principal of term bonds) recorded required additions and required earnings of $15,000 and $7,000, respectively, for the fiscal year. The actual revenues and interest earnings were $16,000 and $6,500, respectively. What is the amount of actual additions and earnings to be recorded in the debt service fund and in the general long-term debt account group, respectively?

a. $22,500 and $22,000.

b. $22,000 and $22,000.

c. $22,500 and $22,500.

d. $22,500 and no entry.

7. Ranchville serves as collecting agency for the local independent school district and for a local fire district. For this purpose, Ranchville has created a single agency fund and charges the other entities a fee of 1 percent of the gross amounts collected. The service fee is treated as general fund revenue. During the latest fiscal year, a gross amount of $268,000 was collected for the independent school district and $80,000 for the fire district. As a consequence of the foregoing, Ranchville's general fund should:

a. Recognize receipts of $348,000.

b. Recognize receipts of $344,520.

c. Record revenue of $3,480.

d. Record encumbrances of $344,520.

8. When Ranchville realized $1,020,000 from the sale of a $1,000,000 bond issue, the entry in its capital projects fund was

```
Cash          . . .  .   .   . . .  .  . 1,020,000
    Bond Proceeds .    .   .  .  .   .   .           1,000,000
    Premium on Bonds .   .   .   . .  .  .              20,000
```

Recording the transaction in this manner indicates that:

a. The $20,000 cannot be used for the designated purpose of the fund but must be transferred to another fund.

    b. The full $1,020,000 can be used by the capital projects fund to accomplish its purpose.

    c. The nominal rate of interest on the bonds is below the market rate for bonds of such term and risk.

    d. A safety factor is being set aside to cover possible contract defaults on the construction.

(AICPA adapted)

E17.6 Often an entry on the books of one fund triggers corresponding entries in other funds of the government unit.

Required: Record any entries to other funds or account groups that correspond to the entries below. Identify the fund or account group for each entry made.

1. *General Fund*

Cash	12,000	
Due from Capital Projects Fund		12,000
To record repayment of advance.		

2. *Capital Projects Fund*

Bond Premium	8,000	
Cash		8,000
To transfer bond premium to debt service fund to be used for future repayment of principal.		

3. *Special Assessments Fund*

Cash	40,000	
Bonds Payable		40,000
To record issuance of bonds at par.		

4. *Special Assessments Fund*

Expenditures	40,000	
Vouchers Payable		40,000
To record final payment for improvements contract totaling $100,000.		

5. *Enterprise Fund*

Cash	18,000	
Capital Contributed from General Fund		18,000
To record transfer from general fund.		

E17.7 Name the fund(s) or group(s) of accounts which correctly answers the following questions:

1. An actuarial deficiency would appear in which fund?
2. "Excess of Net Billings to Departments over Costs" would appear as a caption in the financial statement of which fund?
3. Which type of fund can be either expendable or nonexpendable?
4. The account "Investment in Fixed Assets" appears where?
5. To provide for retirement of general obligation bonds, a city invests a portion of its receipts from general property taxes in marketable securities. Where should this investment activity be recorded?
6. Depreciation expense is recorded in which fund(s) or group(s) of accounts?

7. Where should the liability for general obligation bonds issued for the benefit of a municipal electric company and serviced by its earnings be recorded?

(AICPA adapted)

E17.8   List *all* the funds or groups of accounts in which the following situations require accounting recognition.

1. Part of the general obligation bond proceeds from a new issue was used to pay for the cost of a new city hall as soon as construction was completed. The remainder of the proceeds was transferred to repay the debt.
2. Equipment in general government service that had been constructed ten years before by a capital projects fund was sold. The receipts were accounted for as unrestricted revenue.
3. Cash was received from a special tax levy to retire and pay interest on general obligation bonds issued to finance the construction of a new city hall.
4. Fixed assets were acquired by a central purchasing and stores department organized to serve all municipal departments.
5. Several years ago a city provided for the establishment of a sinking fund to retire an issue of general obligation bonds. This year, the city made a $50,000 contribution to the sinking fund from general revenues and realized $15,000 in revenue from securities in the sinking fund. The bonds due this year were retired.
6. A municipal electric utility paid $150,000 out of its earnings for new equipment.
7. A municipality issued general obligation serial bonds to finance the construction of a fire station.
8. Expenditures of $200,000 were made during the year on the fire station in item 7 above.
9. A municipal electric utility issued bonds to be repaid from its own operations.

(AICPA adapted)

E17.9   During 19X1, the city of Reyland acquired a variety of assets.

Required: For each transaction listed below, identify any *asset accounts* debited at the time of the transaction. Specify the funds or account groups used.

1. Supplies of $800 were purchased by an internal service fund.
2. Early in the year, the general fund purchased supplies of $800. No inventory account is maintained by the general fund.
3. Sidewalks were installed at the expense of neighborhood property owners. Cost of installation was $4,000.
4. The city pool facility, which is financed by user charges, bought pool cleaning equipment for $450.
5. An ambulance garage was constructed by the capital projects fund for $80,000.
6. An ambulance was purchased by the general fund for $35,000.

E17.10   On January 1, a government unit issued 7 percent bonds at par for $70,000. On June 30, semi-annual interest became due and was paid.

Required: Make all the appropriate entries for January 1 and June 30 given the following independent assumptions. Explanations are not required. Identify each fund or account group affected.

1. The bonds were issued to finance special assessment construction.
2. The bonds were issued to finance city court expansion. General fund resources are transferred to debt service at the beginning of each year to finance annual interest charges.
3. The bonds were issued to finance city operations. General fund resources are transferred to debt service at the beginning of each year to finance annual interest charges.
4. The bonds were issued by a self-supporting city utility.
5. The bonds were issued by a police retirement fund.

Problems   P17.1   Transaction Recording—Various Funds   The following transactions represent practical situations frequently encountered in accounting for municipal governments. Each transaction is independent of the others.

1. The city council of Bernardville adopted a budget for the general operations of the city government during the new fiscal year. Revenues were estimated at $695,000. Legal authorizations for budgeted expenditures were $650,000.

2. Taxes of $160,000 were levied for the special revenue fund of Millstown. One percent was estimated to be uncollectible.

3. a. On July 25, 19X3, office supplies estimated to cost $2,390 were ordered for the city manager's office of Bullersville. Bullersville, which operates on the calendar year, does not maintain an inventory of such supplies.

   b. The supplies ordered July 25 were received on August 9, 19X3, accompanied by an invoice for $2,500.

4. On October 10, 19X3, the general fund of Washingtonville repaid to the utility fund a loan of $1,000 plus $40 interest. The loan had been made earlier in the fiscal year.

5. A prominent citizen died and left ten acres of undeveloped land to Harper City for a future school site. The donor's cost of the land was $55,000. The fair value of the land was $85,000.

6. a. On March 6, 19X3, Dahlstrom City issued 4 percent special assessment bonds payable March 6, 19X8, at face value of $90,000. Interest is payable annually. Dahlstrom City, which operates on the calendar year, will use the proceeds to finance a curbing project.

   b. On October 29, 19X3, the full $84,000 cost of the completed curbing project was accrued. Also, appropriate closing entries were made with regard to the project.

7. a. Conrad Thamm, a citizen of Basking Knoll, donated common stock valued at $22,000 to the city under a trust agreement. Under the terms

arships for needy students.

- b. On December 14, 19X3, dividends of $1,100 were received on the stock donated by Mr. Thamm.

8. a. On February 23, 19X3, the town of Lincoln, which operates on the calendar year, issued 4 percent general obligation bonds with a face value of $300,000 payable February 23, 19Z3, to finance the construction of an addition to the city hall. Total proceeds were $308,000. The bond premium is immediately transferred to the debt service fund.

- b. On December 31, 19X3, the addition to the city hall was officially approved, the full cost of $297,000 was paid to the contractor, and appropriate closing entries were made with regard to the project. (Assume that no entries have been made with regard to the project since February 23, 19X3.) Remaining cash is transferred to the debt service fund.

Required: For each transaction, prepare the necessary journal entries for all of the funds and groups of accounts involved. No explanation of the journal entries is required. Use the following headings for your solution:

Transaction Number	Journal Entries	Dr.	Cr.	Fund or Group of Accounts

In the far right column, indicate in which fund or group of accounts each entry is to be made, using the code shown here:

Funds:
General	G
Special revenue	SR
Capital projects	CP
Debt service	DS
Special assessments	SA
Enterprise	E
Internal service	IS
Trust and agency	TA

Groups of accounts:
General fixed assets	GFA
General long-term debt	LTD

(AICPA adapted)

P17.2   Transaction Recording—Various Funds   The fiscal year for the city of Cran ended on June 30, 19X7. An examination of the accounts on that date revealed the following:

1. On December 31, 19X6, the city paid $115,000 from the general fund to establish a central garage to service its vehicles, with $67,500 being applicable to the building, which has an estimated life of twenty-five years, $14,500 to land, and $33,000 to machinery and equipment which has an estimated life of fifteen years. A $12,200 cash contribution was received by the garage from the general fund on the same date.

2. The garage maintains no records, but a review of deposit slips and canceled checks revealed the following:

Collections for Services to City Departments Financed from the
General Fund $30,000
Office Salaries 6,000
Utilities 700
Mechanics' Wages 11,000
Materials and Supplies 9,000

3. The garage had uncollected billings of $2,000 from the general fund, accounts payable for materials and supplies of $500, and an inventory of materials and supplies of $1,500 at June 30, 19X7.

4. On June 30, 19X7, the city issued $200,000 in special assessment bonds at par to finance a street improvement project estimated to cost $225,000. The project is to be paid by a $15,000 levy against the city (payable in fiscal year 19X7–19X8) and $210,000 against property owners (payable in five equal annual installments beginning October 1, 19X7). The levy was made on June 30. A $215,000 contract was let for the project on July 2, 19X7, but work has not begun.

5. On July 1, 19X5, the city issued $400,000 in thirty-year, 6 percent general obligation term bonds of the same date at par and awarded a contract for $397,500 for the construction of a public health center. Construction was completed and the contractors fully paid a total of $397,500 in fiscal year 19X6–19X7. (Assume that no expenditures were recorded in 19X5–19X6.)

6. For the health center bonds, the city sets aside general fund revenues sufficient to cover interest (payable semi-annually on July 1 and January 1 of each year) and $5,060 to provide for the retirement of bond principal, the latter transfer being made at the end of each fiscal year and invested at the beginning of the next. These investments earned $304, the exact amount budgeted, during fiscal year 19X6–19X7. This $304 was received in cash and will be invested at the beginning of the next year.

Required: Assume that appropriate entries were made in the general fund. Prepare the necessary entries for the year ended June 30, 19X7, for all other funds and account groups. Do not prepare closing entries.

(AICPA adapted)

P17.3 **Capital Projects Fund** In a special election held on July 1, 19X7, the voters of the city of Nicknar approved a $10,000,000 issue of 6 percent general obligation bonds maturing in 19Z7. The proceeds of this sale will be used to help finance the construction of a new civic center. The total cost of the project was estimated at $15,000,000. The remaining $5,000,000 will be financed by an irrevocable state grant which has been awarded. A capital projects fund was established to account for this project and was designated the civic center construction fund.

The following transactions occurred during the fiscal year beginning July 1, 19X7, and ending June 30, 19X8:

1. On August 1, the general fund loaned $500,000 to the civic center construction fund for defraying engineering and other expenses.

2. Preliminary engineering and planning costs of $320,000 were paid to Akron Engineering Company. There had been no encumbrance for this cost.

3. On December 1, the bonds were sold at 101. The premium on bonds was transferred to the debt service fund to be used for future payment of bond principal.

4. On March 15, a contract for $12,000,000 was entered into with Candu Construction Company for the major part of the project.

5. Orders were placed on March 23 for materials estimated to cost $55,000.

6. On April 1, a partial payment of $2,500,000 was received from the state.

7. The materials that were previously ordered were received on June 7 at a cost of $51,000, and payment was made.

8. On June 15, a progress billing of $2,000,000 was received from Candu Construction for work done on the project. As per the terms of the contract, the city will withhold 6 percent of any billing until the project is completed.

9. The general fund was repaid the $500,000 previously loaned.

Required: Based upon the transactions presented above:

1. Prepare journal entries to record the transactions in the civic center construction fund for the period July 1, 19X7, through June 30, 19X8, and the appropriate closing entries at June 30, 19X8.

2. Prepare a balance sheet for the civic center construction fund as of June 30, 19X8.

(AICPA adapted)

P17.4 Capital Projects and Debt Service Funds The information below relates to the construction of a new recreation building in the city of Lander.

19X0 Transactions

1. A bond issue in the amount of $1,000,000 was authorized by vote on March 1, 19X0, to provide funds for the construction. The bonds are to be repaid in 20 annual installments, from a debt service fund, with the first installment due on March 1, 19X1.

2. An advance of $80,000 was received from the general fund to make a deposit on the land contract of $120,000. The deposit was made.

3. Bonds having a face value of $900,000 were sold for cash at 102. Since the cost of the land was much less than anticipated, the city decided to postpone sale of the remaining bonds.

4. Contracts amounting to $780,000 were awarded to the lowest bidder for the construction of the recreation center.

5. The temporary advance from the general fund was repaid, and the balance on the land contract was paid.

6. The architect certified that work in the amount of $640,000 had been completed, and bills for that amount were received.

7. Vouchers paid by the treasurer relative to the completed work amounted to $620,000.

8. The bond premium was transferred to the debt service fund.

19X1 Transactions

9. Due to engineering modifications in the construction plans, the contract was revised to $880,000. The remaining bonds were sold at 101.
10. The recreation center was completed and billed at a further cost of $230,000. The building passed final inspection.
11. The treasurer paid all bills.
12. The cash balance remaining was transferred to the debt service fund.

Interest on the bond issue is paid directly from the general fund. Transfers from the general fund to the debt service fund were $25,000 in 19X0 and $30,000 in 19X1. All cash was invested in certificates of deposit which yielded interest of $1,000 in 19X0 and $800 in 19X1. Expected investment income was $1,000 in each year. The first installment on the bonds ($45,000) was paid when due.

Required:

1. Prepare the journal entries for the recreation center fund for 19X0 and 19X1.
2. Prepare the balance sheet for the recreation center fund on December 31, 19X0.
3. Prepare the journal entries for the debt service fund and the general long-term debt account group for 19X0 and 19X1.

P17.5 **Special Assessments Fund** Early in 19X1, the town of Jacobs authorized widening of streets and installation of curbs in a residential area known as Woodside. The project was expected to cost $400,000 and to be financed by $50,000 from the 19X1 general fund budget and $350,000 from Woodside residents. Residents were assessed for equal principal payments over ten years plus interest on bonds as due. Ten-year, 6 percent bonds with a face value of $350,000 were issued at par on July 1, 19X1. Interest is due on December 31 and June 30. Proceeds from the bonds not currently needed to finance construction and proceeds of the assessments after payment of interest were invested in appropriate securities. Assessments to residents for interest are to be reduced by the prior year's earnings on investments.

Regarding the street improvement project, the following occurred:

1. Investments yielded $8,000 in 19X1 and $18,000 in 19X2. The balance in the cash account was $40,000 on December 31, 19X1, and $30,000 on December 31, 19X2.
2. Project costs of $400,000 were encumbered at the start of the project.
3. Construction costs billed in 19X1 were $150,000, of which $20,000 was not paid at year-end.
4. The improvement project was completed in 19X2 at a total cost of $400,000. All amounts due the contractor were paid.
5. Of the 19X1 assessment, $15,000 was not collected until 19X2. All 19X2 assessments were collected when due.

Required:

1. Prepare a schedule showing assessments due for 19X1 and 19X2.
2. Prepare 19X1 and 19X2 balance sheets for the special assessments street improvement fund.
3. What other funds or account groups are affected by the street improvement project?

P17.6   **Agency Fund**   In compliance with a newly enacted state law, Dial County assumed the responsibility of collecting all property taxes levied within its boundaries as of July 1, 19X5. A composite property tax rate per $1,000 of net assessed valuation was developed for the fiscal year ending June 30, 19X6, and is presented below:

Dial County General Fund	$ 60
Eton City General Fund	30
Bart Township General Fund	10
Composite Tax Rate	$100

All property taxes are due in quarterly installments and when collected are then distributed to the government units represented in the composite rate. In order to administer collection and distribution of such taxes, the county has established a tax agency fund.

Additional information:

1. In order to reimburse the county for estimated administrative expenses of operating the tax agency fund, the tax agency fund is to deduct 2 percent from the tax collections each quarter for Eton City and Bart Township. The total amount deducted is to be remitted to the Dial County general fund.

2. Current year tax levies to be collected by the tax agency fund are as follows:

	Gross Levy	Estimated Amount to Be Collected
Dial County	$3,600,000	$3,500,000
Eton City	1,800,000	1,740,000
Bart Township	600,000	560,000
	$6,000,000	$5,800,000

3. As of September 30, 19X5, the tax agency fund had received $1,440,000 in first quarter payments. On October 1, this fund made a distribution to the three government units.

Required: For the period July 1, 19X5, through October 1, 19X5, prepare journal entries to record the transactions described above for the following funds:

Dial County tax agency fund.
Dial County general fund.
Eton City general fund.
Bart Township general fund.

Your solution should be organized as follows:

Accounts	Dial County Tax Agency Fund		Dial County General Fund		Eton City General Fund		Bart Township General Fund	
	Debit	Credit	Debit	Credit	Debit	Credit	Debit	Credit

(AICPA adapted)

P17.7   **Budgeting for Various Funds**   The Laurens city council passed a resolution requiring a yearly cash budget by fund for the city beginning with its fiscal year

Exhibit 17.6   Cash Receipts and Disbursements, to Be Used in P17.7

CASH RECEIPTS

Taxes:

General Property . . .	$ 685,000
School	421,000
Franchise	223,000
	$1,329,000

Licenses and Permits:

Business Licenses . .	$ 41,000
Automobile Inspection Permits	24,000
Building Permits . .	18,000
	$ 83,000

Intergovernmental Revenue:

Sales Tax	$1,012,000
Federal Grants . . .	128,000
State Motor Vehicle Tax .	83,500
State Gasoline Tax . .	52,000
State Alcoholic Beverage Licenses	16,000
	$1,291,500

Charges for Services:

Sanitation Fees . .	$ 121,000
Sewer Connection Fees .	71,000
Library Revenues . . .	13,000
Park Revenues . . .	2,500
	$ 207,500

Bond Issues:

Civic Center	$ 347,000
General Obligation . .	200,000
Sewer	153,000
Library	120,000
	$ 820,000

Other:

Proceeds from the Sale of Investments . . .	$ 312,000
Sewer Assessments . .	50,000
Rental Revenue . . .	48,000
Interest Revenue . . .	15,000
	$ 425,000
Total Receipts . .	$4,156,000

CASH DISBURSEMENTS

General Government . . .	$ 671,000
Public Safety	516,000
Schools	458,000
Sanitation	131,000
Library	28,000
Rental Property . . .	17,500
Parks	17,000
	$1,838,500

Debt Service:

General Obligation Bonds	$ 618,000
Street Construction Bonds	327,000
School Bonds . . .	119,000
Sewage Disposal Plant Bonds	37,200
	$1,101,200
Investments	$ 358,000
State Portion of Sales Tax .	$ 860,200

Capital Expenditures:

Sewer Construction (Assessed Area) . .	$ 114,100
Civic Center Construction	73,000
Library Construction . .	36,000
	$ 223,100
Total Disbursements .	$4,381,000

---

ending September 30, 19X3. The city's financial director has prepared a list of expected cash receipts and disbursements, but he is having difficulty subdividing them by fund. The list is given in Exhibit 17.6.

The financial director provides you with the following additional information:

1. A bond issue was authorized in 19X2 for the construction of a civic center. Future civic center revenues are to account for 20 percent of the repayment of debt. The remainder is to come from general property taxes.

2. A bond issue was authorized in 19X2 for additions to the library. The debt is to be paid from general property taxes.

3. General obligation bonds are paid from general property taxes collected by the general fund.

4. Ten percent of the total annual school taxes represents an individually voted tax for payment of bonds, the proceeds of which were used for school construction.

5. In 19X0, a wealthy citizen donated rental property to the city. Net income from the property is to be used to assist in operating the library. The net cash increase attributable to the property is transferred to the library on September 30 of each year.

6. All sales taxes are collected by the city; the state receives 85 percent of these taxes. The state's portion is remitted at the end of each month.

7. Payment of the street construction bonds is to be made from assessments previously collected from the respective property owners. The proceeds from the assessments were invested and the principal of $312,000 will earn $15,000 interest during the coming year.

8. In 19X2, a special assessment in the amount of $203,000 was made on certain property owners for sewer construction. During fiscal 19X3, $50,000 of this assessment is expected to be collected. The remainder of the sewer cost is to be paid from a $153,000 bond issue to be sold in fiscal 19X3. Future special assessment collections will be used to pay principal and interest on the bonds.

9. All sewer and sanitation services are provided by a separate enterprise fund.

10. The federal grant is for fiscal 19X3 school operations.

11. The proceeds remaining at the end of the year from the sale of civic center and library bonds are to be invested.

Required: Prepare a budget of cash receipts and disbursements by fund for the year ending September 30, 19X3. All interfund transactions of cash are to be included.

(AICPA adapted)

P17.8   Comprehensive Fund Accounting   The balance sheet presented below was prepared by the city of Bayside's bookkeeper:

City of Bayside
Balance Sheet
June 30, 19X6

ASSETS

Cash	$ 160,000
Taxes Receivable—Current	32,000
Supplies on Hand	8,000
Marketable Securities	250,000
Land	1,000,000
Buildings	7,000,000
Total Assets	$8,450,000

LIABILITIES AND FUND BALANCE

Vouchers Payable	$ 42,000
Reserve for Supplies Inventory	8,000
Bonds Payable	3,000,000
Fund Balance	5,400,000
Total Liabilities and Fund Balance	$8,450,000

Additional information:

1. An analysis of the fund balance account disclosed the following:

Fund Balance, June 30, 19X5		$2,100,000
Add:		
Donated Land	$ 800,000	
Federal Grant-in-Aid	2,200,000	
Creation of Endowment Fund	250,000	
Excess of Actual Tax Revenue over Estimated Revenue	24,000	
Excess of Appropriations Closed Out over Expenditures and Encumbrances . . .	20,000	
Net Income from Endowment Funds . . .	10,000	3,304,000
		$5,404,000
Deduct:		
Excess of Cultural Center Operating Expenses over Income		4,000
Fund Balance, June 30, 19X6		$5,400,000

2. In July 19X5, land appraised at a fair market value of $800,000 was donated to the city for a cultural center which was opened on April 15, 19X6. Building construction expenditures for the project were financed from a federal grant-in-aid of $2,200,000 and from an authorized ten-year $3,000,000 issue of 7 percent general obligation bonds sold at par on July 1, 19X5. Interest is payable on December 31 and June 30. The fair market value of the land and the cost of the building are included in the Land and Fixed Assets accounts, respectively.

3. The cultural center receives no direct state or city subsidy for current operating expenses. A cultural center endowment fund was established by a gift of marketable securities having a fair market value of $250,000 at date of receipt. The endowment principal is to be kept intact. Income is to be applied to any operating deficit of the center.

4. It is anticipated that $7,000 of the 19X5–19X6 tax is uncollectible.

5. The physical inventory of supplies on hand at June 30, 19X6, amounted to $12,500.

6. Unfilled purchase orders for the general fund at June 30, 19X6, totaled $5,000.

7. On July 1, 19X5, an all-purpose building was purchased for $2,000,000. Of the purchase price, $200,000 was allotted to the land. The purchase had been authorized under the budget for the year ended June 30, 19X6.

Exhibit 17.7   Trial Balance for Anderson City, to Be Used in P17.9

Anderson City
General Fund Trial Balance
December 31, 19X9

	Debit	Credit
Cash	$ 207,500	
Taxes Receivable—Current	148,500	
Allowance for Uncollectible Taxes—Current		$ 6,000
Expenditures	760,000	
Revenues		992,500
Land	190,000	
River Bridge Bonds Authorized—Unissued	100,000	
Work in Process—River Bridge	130,000	
River Bridge Bonds Payable		200,000
Contracts Payable—River Bridge		25,000
Retained Percentage—River Bridge Contracts		5,000
Vouchers Payable		7,500
Fund Balance		300,000
Total	$1,536,000	$1,536,000

Required: Prepare a working paper showing adjustments and distributions to the proper funds or groups of accounts. The working paper should have the following column headings:
 1. Balance per Books
 2. Adjustments—Debit
 3. Adjustments—Credit
 4. General Fund
 5. City Cultural Center Endowment Fund:
     Principal
     Income
 6. General Fixed Assets Group of Accounts
 7. General Long-Term Debt Group of Accounts
Number all adjusting entries. Formal journal entries are not required. Supporting computations should be in good form.   (AICPA adapted)

P17.9   **Capital Projects and General Funds**   The books for Anderson City are maintained by an inexperienced bookkeeper. All transactions for the year were recorded in the city's general fund. The bookkeeper prepared the trial balance shown in Exhibit 17.7 for the year ended December 31, 1979.

Additional information:
 1. The budget for the year 19X9, not recorded on the books, estimated revenues and expenditures as $815,000 and $775,000, respectively.
 2. Outstanding purchase orders at December 31, 19X9, for operating expenses not recorded on the books totaled $2,500.
 3. Included in the Revenues account is a credit of $190,000 representing the value of land donated by the state as a grant-in-aid for construction of the River Bridge.

Exhibit 17.8   Trial Balance for City of Hayes, to Be Used in P17.10

City of Hayes
General Fund Trial Balance
June 30, 19X9

DEBITS

Cash	$ 127,180
Cash for Construction	174,000
Taxes Receivable—Current	8,000
Assessments Receivable—Deferred	300,000
Inventory of Materials and Supplies	36,000
Improvements Authorized	365,000
Estimated Revenues	3,785,000
Encumbrances	360,000
Expenditures	4,290,000
Total Debits	$9,445,180

CREDITS

Vouchers Payable	$ 69,090
Bonds Payable	300,000
Premium on Bonds	3,000
Reserve for Inventory	36,000
Reserve for Encumbrances	360,000
Appropriations	4,440,000
Interest Revenue	21,000
Fund Balance	106,090
Revenues	4,110,000
Total Credits	$9,445,180

4. The River Bridge bonds were sold at par.
5. The following items comprised the Expenditures account:

Current Operating Expenses	$472,000
Additions to Structures and Improvements	210,000
Equipment Purchases	10,000
General Obligation Bonds Paid	50,000
Interest Paid on General Obligation Bonds	18,000

6. A debt service fund is not to be used.
7. No taxes are considered delinquent as of December 31.

Required:

1. Make the journal entries necessary to set up the appropriate funds and account groups and correct the balances for each. Include closing entries.
2. Prepare the balance sheets for the general fund and any other fund(s) established in requirement 1. Do not prepare balance sheets for account groups.

(AICPA adapted)

P17.10   **General and Special Assessments Funds**   The trial balance of the general fund of the city of Hayes is given in Exhibit 17.8. Transactions were recorded in the general fund rather than establishing special purpose funds.

The following additional information is available:

1.   A physical inventory taken on June 30, 19X9, showed that materials and supplies with a cost of $37,750 were on hand at that date. Materials and supplies purchased during the year were correctly charged as expenditures.

2.   Current taxes are now considered delinquent, and it is estimated that $5,500 of such taxes will be uncollectible. Revenues were recorded at gross taxes receivable.

3.   On June 25, 19X9, the state revenue department informed the city that its share of a state-collected, locally-shared tax would be $75,000.

4.   New equipment for the police department was acquired at a cost of $90,000 and was properly recorded as an expenditure in the general fund.

5.   During the year, 100 acres of land were donated to the city for use as an industrial park. The land had a value of $250,000. No entry has been made.

6.   The city council authorized the paving and widening of certain streets at an estimated cost of $365,000, which included an estimated $5,000 cost for planning and engineering to be paid from the general fund. The remaining $360,000 was to be financed by a $10,000 contribution from the city in later years and $350,000 by assessments against property owners, payable in seven equal installments. A $5,000 appropriation was made for the city's share at the time the annual budget was recorded, and the total $365,000 was also recorded as an appropriation. The following information is also relevant to the street improvement project:

   a.   Property owners paid in full the $70,000 annual installment plus an additional $21,000 assessment for bond interest.

   b.   Special assessment bonds of $300,000 were authorized and sold at a premium of $3,000. The bond premium is to be used for interest payments.

   c.   The city's $15,000 share was recorded as an expenditure during the year. The $5,000 for planning and engineering fees was paid; the $10,000 contribution was not paid. Construction began July 5, 19X8, and the contractor has been paid $200,000 under the contract for construction which calls for performance of the work at a total cost of $360,000. This $360,000 makes up the balance in the Reserve for Encumbrances.

   d.   The Cash for Construction account was used for all receipts and disbursements relative to the project. It is made up of the proceeds of the bond issue and collection of assessment installments and interest minus payments to the contractor.

Required: Prepare a working paper to adjust the account balances at June 30, 19X9, and to distribute them to the appropriate funds or account groups. Do not make closing entries. Formal financial statements are not required.

(AICPA adapted)

Chapter 18

Accounting and Reporting by Nonprofit Organizations

Nonprofit organizations possess the following characteristics:

1. Significant amounts of the organization's resources are received from providers who neither expect to receive repayment nor expect to receive economic benefits proportionate to the resources provided.

2. The primary operating purposes of the organization are something other than providing goods or services at a profit.

3. There are no ownership interests that can be sold, transferred, or redeemed, or that convey entitlement to a share of resources in the event the organization is liquidated.[1]

These characteristics could apply to government units as well as nongovernment, nonprofit organizations. The two differ in their means of support: government units typically have taxing power as a means of compelling support, while nongovernment organizations depend upon voluntary contributions and user charges to provide resources. In this chapter, we use the term **nonprofit organizations** more narrowly, to mean private (nongovernment) organizations only.

Nonprofit organizations are numerous in today's society and include the following types:

1. Hospitals.

2. Colleges, universities, and other educational organizations.

3. Voluntary health and welfare organizations, such as the Red Cross and United Way.

---

[1] Statement of Financial Accounting Concepts No. 4, "Objectives of Financial Reporting by Nonbusiness Organizations" (Stamford, Conn.: FASB, 1980), par. 6.

4. Churches and other religious organizations.

5. Philanthropic foundations.

6. Professional organizations, such as the American Institute of Certified Public Accountants.

7. Trade organizations, such as the National Association of Retail Merchants.

8. Labor organizations, such as the United Auto Workers.

9. Civic and community groups, such as the League of Women Voters.

10. Social and fraternal organizations, such as a Veterans of Foreign Wars post.

11. Membership benefit organizations, such as the American Automobile Association.

Among these types of nonprofit organizations, we may identify three major approaches to the generation of financial resources and the provision of services:

1. Organizations which derive their support from voluntary contributions rather than user charges and offer their services to the public in general. Voluntary health and welfare organizations, churches, foundations, and civic groups tend to fall into this category.

2. Organizations which derive most of their support from user charges and offer services to the public in general. Hospitals and colleges tend to fall into this category.

3. Organizations which derive most of their support from member dues and provide services primarily to their members. Professional, trade, labor, social, and membership benefit organizations fall into this category.

Given these three different approaches, we may expect some differences in accounting and reporting practices. However, since such differences tend to be minor, there is sufficient similarity among the three that we may discuss accounting and reporting for nonprofit organizations in general.

Sources of Accounting Principles

Accounting principles for nonprofit organizations have developed over time, drawing from both business and governmental accounting practices. A **fund structure** is typically employed, dividing the organization into several accounting entities, as is the case in governmental accounting. However, many of the characteristics of fund accounting are not used by nonprofit organizations. Budgetary and encumbrance accounting and the modified accrual approach to revenue recognition are typically *not used* in nonprofit accounting. We will discuss these matters more fully in subsequent sections.

To date, no one authoritative body has emerged as the leader in standard setting for nonprofit organizations. For many years, the main standard-setting groups of the accounting profession (the APB, FASB, etc.) have concentrated on accounting standards for business firms and have largely ignored the nonprofit sector. Only recently has the FASB begun to deal with this area. As a result, many of the accounting principles for nonprofit organizations have developed informally through practice. However, three groups have played some formal role in the development of these accounting principles.

Industry Groups

Several groups have published materials which set forth accounting principles and procedures for a particular type of nonprofit organization. For example:

1. The United Way of America's *Accounting and Financial Reporting* presents information on general accounting principles, financial reporting, and financial control. It serves as a guide not only for member agencies of the United Way but also for other human service organizations.

2. The American Hospital Association has published a series of booklets dealing with accounting and financial management issues in hospitals. These are used extensively by hospitals throughout the country.

3. The National Association of College and University Business Officers has published a book entitled *College and University Business Administration*. Its recommendations on accounting for educational institutions have been widely adopted.

American Institute of Certified Public Accountants

The American Institute of Certified Public Accountants has issued a series of audit guides dealing with certain types of nonprofit organizations. While primarily designed to set standards for auditing these organizations, the guides also set forth the accounting and reporting principles which should be followed. Existing audit guides cover hospitals, colleges and universities, and voluntary health and welfare organizations.

Financial Accounting Standards Board

The Financial Accounting Standards Board has recently begun to consider the area of nonprofit organizations. Its initial effort is a statement of concepts entitled "Objectives of Financial Reporting by Nonbusiness Organizations." This statement identifies the factors that affect financial reporting by nonprofit organizations and establishes objectives that will serve as the foundation for subsequent adoption of specific accounting principles.

Fund Entities

The activities of nonprofit organizations, like those of local governments, are organized into funds for purposes of accounting and reporting. Depending on the nature and complexity of the organization, there may be a single fund or there may be several. Since many different types of organizations fall into the broad category of nonprofit organizations, considerable variation in the specific titles of funds exists. We can, however, identify the *general types of funds* that are often found in nonprofit accounting. In subsequent sections, we will discuss how these general types are employed in several specific types of nonprofit organizations.

Unrestricted Operating Fund

An **unrestricted operating fund,** also commonly called an **unrestricted current fund** or **general current fund,** is analogous to the general fund of a local government unit. This fund accounts for the day-to-day operating activities of the organization which are funded by resources having no restriction on their use. Such resources may come from voluntary contributions, user charges, unrestricted grants for operating purposes, and so on. Expenditures are made from the unrestricted operating fund to cover the costs of the primary services or activities of the organization.

Restricted Operating Fund

A **restricted operating fund,** also called a **restricted current fund,** is analogous to the special revenue fund of a local government. Expenditures from this fund also are made for the day-to-day operating activities or services of the organization. In this case, however, use of the fund's resources has been restricted by their provider to certain operating activities. Such resources typically come from grants or contributions. For example, a college may receive a grant for its history program, or a church may receive a contribution for its missionary work.

Plant Fund

The **plant fund** of a nonprofit organization, also called a **land, building, and equipment fund,** accounts for various aspects of the investment in land, buildings, and equipment. A plant fund is often a complex entity consisting of several subfunds; it may contain some or all of the following:

1. Unexpended resources which are to be used for the *acquisition* of land, buildings, or equipment (hereafter called plant assets). This component is analogous to the capital projects fund of a local government.

2. Resources set aside for the *renewal or replacement* of plant assets. When expended, the costs may be capitalized as additional plant assets or may be expensed. The resources of this component are usually transfers from operating funds set aside by management for future needs. There is no counterpart to this component in local governmental accounting.

3. Resources set aside for the *payment of interest and principal* on indebtedness related to past acquisitions of plant assets. This component is analogous to the debt service fund of a local government.

4. Information relating to *amounts already invested in plant assets* and the *unpaid balance of related indebtedness.* This component is analogous to both the general fixed assets and the general long-term debt account groups of a local government.

Endowment Fund

The **endowment fund** accounts for resources which the organization holds for the generation of income and is analogous to a trust fund of a local government. A *permanent endowment* consists of resources provided by outside donors or agencies who have stipulated that the principal is to be maintained indefinitely and is to be invested so as to produce income, which often must be spent in a specified way. A *term endowment* is similar, except that at some point the principal may be spent. A *quasi-endowment* (also called *funds functioning as endowment*) is resources which the management of the organization has set aside to be retained and invested for certain purposes. In this case, any restrictions are imposed by management rather than an outside donor and thus can be easily modified in the future.

Agency Fund

The **agency fund** of a nonprofit organization, also called a **custodian fund,** like the agency fund of a local government, accounts for resources held by the organization as a custodian or fiscal agent. For example, if a college holds the resources of student clubs and organizations, these resources would be recorded in an agency fund.

Loan Fund

A **loan fund,** found primarily in educational organizations, accounts for loans outstanding and resources available for lending to employees, students, and so on. A loan fund is usually said to be *revolving,* that is, the interest and principal payments on current loans provide the resources for future loans. The initial capital needed to establish the fund is typically provided either by outside gifts or allocation of internal resources. As a revolving, self-sustaining fund which primarily serves individuals within the organization, a loan fund is somewhat similar to an internal service fund of a local government.

Annuity Fund

An **annuity fund** accounts for resources acquired by a nonprofit organization in exchange for a promise to make specified payments to designated individuals for a given period of time. Many types of nonprofit organizations offer annuities as a means of deferred fund-raising. For example, assume an individual contributes $50,000 to a religious organization. In return, the organization agrees to pay the individual $4,000 annually for life. The organization invests the $50,000 and uses the income (and, if necessary, some of the principal) to make the annual payments. Upon the donor's death, the remaining funds become available to the organization for other uses. Annuity terms may vary from those in the above example; payments may be made to an individual other than the donor, or the payments may be for a specified number of years rather than for life.

Annuity agreements are attractive to both donors and organizations. Donors assure themselves (or others) of a specified income, while also assuring that the remaining funds will eventually go to the charity of their choice. In addition, there may be tax advantages to transferring assets to a charity while living rather than after death via bequest. From the organization's point of view, annuity agreements enable them to attract sizable contributions, even though it may be several years until the resources become available for the organization's programs.

A variation of an annuity agreement is a life income agreement. Such an agreement provides that *all* income earned on the contributed resources be paid annually to the donor for life. Under a life income agreement, therefore, the annual payment may vary, while under an annuity agreement the annual payment is fixed. Life income agreements may be recorded in the annuity fund or in a separate **life income fund.**

Annuity funds and life income funds have no direct counterparts in local governmental accounting. They are, however, similar to trust funds.

**Financial
Statements**

Financial statements of a nonprofit organization parallel those of a local government. A *balance sheet* presents the assets, liabilities, and fund balance of a particular fund. A *statement of revenues, expenditures (or expenses), and changes in fund balance* reports the activities of the period. The exact format and content of these statements varies somewhat among different funds and different organization types. They are illustrated for the various nonprofit organizations we consider in the following sections.

Voluntary Health and Welfare Organizations

Voluntary health and welfare organizations are very prevalent in our society. These organizations provide a wide variety of services, either to individuals or to broader segments of society, in the areas of health, social welfare, and community services. A brief list drawn from the multitude of services and organizations illustrates the pervasiveness and diversity of this category:

1. Health education and research (for example, American Heart Association).
2. Disaster relief (for example, American Red Cross).
3. Alcoholism and drug abuse counseling (for example, Alcoholics Anonymous).
4. Family counseling (for example, Planned Parenthood).
5. Social development (for example, Boys' Club).
6. Services to handicapped (for example, Goodwill Industries).

Voluntary health and welfare organizations are primarily supported by contributions, either to individual organizations or to "umbrella" organizations such as the United Way.

Accounting Principles

For many years, no formal pronouncements on accounting principles existed for voluntary health and welfare organizations. Practices were adapted from other areas of nonprofit accounting, such as hospitals and educational institutions. In 1964, the National Health Council and the National Social Welfare Assembly jointly published a guide entitled *Standards of Accounting and Financial Reporting for Voluntary Health and Welfare Organizations.* Known as the "black book," this guide came to be widely accepted as an authoritative source. Subsequently, the United Way of America published an accounting manual for use by its member agencies, incorporating the principles set forth in the black book. These principles were also the basis for an industry audit guide entitled *Audits of Voluntary Health and Welfare Organizations* published in 1966 by the AICPA and revised in 1973. Thus, three primary sources of accounting principles and practices by voluntary health and welfare organizations currently exist: the black book, the United Way manual, and the AICPA audit guide.

Types of Funds

The various types of funds employed by nonprofit organizations in general were discussed earlier in the chapter. The funds commonly found in voluntary health and welfare organizations are:

1. Unrestricted current fund.
2. Restricted current fund.
3. Plant fund (which includes unexpended resources for acquisition or replacement, net investment in fixed assets, and liabilities related to these assets).

4.   Endowment fund.

5.   Agency fund.

The following sections discuss and illustrate accounting and reporting for the above funds. Loan funds and annuity funds are usually not found in voluntary health and welfare organizations; they will be illustrated later.

Comprehensive Illustration

The Northeastern Heart Society supports research, education, and public awareness programs on the prevention of heart disease. Its resources are primarily generated from contributions, bequests, and grants. Its activities for the year ended December 31, 19X3, have been organized into four funds and are discussed in the following sections.

Unrestricted Current Fund   At January 1, 19X3, the balance sheet of the unrestricted current fund showed:

Cash	$117,000	Vouchers Payable	$ 33,000
Pledges Receivable (Net of $16,000 Allowance for Uncollectibles)		Fund Balance	148,000
	64,000		
	$181,000		$181,000

Contributions pledged during 19X3 amounted to $1,300,000, of which $1,150,000 was collected during the year. In addition, $67,000 of the pledges outstanding at January 1 was collected; the balance was written off. The society provides an allowance for uncollectibles equal to twenty percent of pledges outstanding at year-end. Revenue of $46,000 was earned from programs which the society conducted for employee groups of various corporations. The entries to record the above transactions are:

Pledges Receivable	1,300,000	
Revenue—Contributions		1,300,000
To record pledges during 19X3.		
Cash	1,150,000	
Pledges Receivable		1,150,000
To record collections of current pledges.		
Cash	67,000	
Pledges Receivable		67,000
To record collections of prior year pledges.		
Allowance for Uncollectible Pledges	13,000	
Pledges Receivable		13,000
To write off uncollected pledges from 19X2 ($13,000 = $80,000 − $67,000).		
Revenue—Contributions	27,000	
Allowance for Uncollectible Pledges . . .		27,000
To adjust allowance to 20% of year-end balance.		
Cash	46,000	
Revenue—Program Services		46,000
To record revenue from educational programs.		

Exhibit 18.1   Unrestricted Current Fund Financial Statements

Northeastern Heart Society
Unrestricted Current Fund
Balance Sheet
December 31, 19X3

Cash	$125,000	Vouchers Payable	$ 48,000
Pledges Receivable (Net of		Fund Balance	197,000
$30,000 Allowance for			
Uncollectibles)	120,000		
	$245,000		$245,000

Northeastern Heart Society
Unrestricted Current Fund
Statement of Revenues, Expenses,
and Changes in Fund Balance
For the Year Ended December 31, 19X3

REVENUES:

Contributions	$1,273,000	
Program Services	46,000	$1,319,000

EXPENSES:

Program Services:			
Research	$400,000		
Public Programs	350,000		
Corporate Programs	35,000	$ 785,000	
Supporting Services:			
General Administration	$210,000		
Fund Raising	175,000	385,000	1,170,000
Excess of Revenues over			
Expenses			$ 149,000

OTHER CHANGES IN FUND BALANCE:

Transfer to Plant Fund	100,000
Excess of Revenues over Expenses	
and Other Changes	$ 49,000
Fund Balance—Beginning of Year . . .	148,000
Fund Balance—End of Year	$ 197,000

Cash expenditures for 19X3 amounted to $1,255,000, as follows:

Research	$ 400,000
Public Awareness Programs	350,000
Corporate Programs	35,000
General Administration	195,000
Fund Raising	175,000
Transfer to Plant Fund	100,000
	$1,255,000

Exhibit 18.2   Restricted Current Fund Financial Statements

Northeastern Heart Society
Restricted Current Fund
Balance Sheet
December 31, 19X3

Cash	$57,000	Fund Balance	$57,000

Northeastern Heart Society
Restricted Current Fund
Statement of Revenues, Expenses,
and Changes in Fund Balance
For the Year Ended December 31, 19X3

REVENUES:

Grant	$200,000

EXPENSES:

Program Services	143,000
Excess of Revenues over Expenses	$ 57,000
Fund Balance—Beginning of Year	0
Fund Balance—End of Year	$ 57,000

Vouchers payable increased from $33,000 to $48,000; all unpaid vouchers at beginning and end of year relate to general administration costs. Entries to record the above are:

Expenses—Research	400,000	
Expenses—Public Programs	350,000	
Expenses—Corporate Programs	35,000	
Expenses—General Administration	210,000	
Expenses—Fund Raising	175,000	
Cash		1,155,000
Vouchers Payable		15,000
To record expenses for 19X3.		
Transfer to Plant Fund	100,000	
Cash		100,000
To record transfer to plant fund.		

Financial statements for the unrestricted current fund at December 31, 19X3, are presented in Exhibit 18.1.

Restricted Current Fund   During 19X3, the society received a federal grant of $200,000 to expand its public awareness programs into smaller communities where it had not previously been active. The grant period expires on March 31, 19X4; by the end of 19X3, $143,000 had been spent on the project. A restricted current fund was established to account for the grant. Financial statements at year-end appeared as shown in Exhibit 18.2.

Exhibit 18.3   Endowment Fund Financial Statements

Northeastern Heart Society
Endowment Fund
Balance Sheet
December 31, 19X3

Cash	$ 11,400	Fund Balance:	
Investments	728,500	Principal	$733,500
		Income	6,400
	$739,900		$739,900

Northeastern Heart Society
Endowment Fund
Statement of Revenues, Expenses,
and Changes in Fund Balance
For the Year Ended December 31, 19X3

REVENUES:

Bequests	$10,000	
Contributions	3,500	
Investment Income	80,000	$ 93,500

EXPENSES:

Scholarships	75,000
Excess of Revenues over Expenses	$ 18,500
Fund Balance—Beginning of Year	721,400
Fund Balance—End of Year	$739,900

Endowment Fund   Several years ago, the society received a $500,000 bequest to establish a scholarship fund. It was stipulated that the principal be maintained intact, with income used for scholarships. Subsequent bequests and contributions increased the principal of the fund to $720,000 by the beginning of 19X3. In addition, $1,400 of unexpended income was on hand at January 1, 19X3.

During 19X3, contributions of $3,500 and a bequest of $10,000 were received as additions to principal. Investment income was $80,000, and scholarships amounting to $75,000 were awarded and paid. At year-end, all but $5,000 of principal was invested.

Financial statements for the endowment fund appear as shown in Exhibit 18.3.

Plant Fund   Prior to 19X3, the society's only fixed assets were office equipment and a parcel of land bought in 19X2 as a building site. Thus the January 1, 19X3, balance sheet of the plant fund showed:

Land		$20,000	Fund Balance:		
Equipment	$30,000		Expended	$44,000
Accumulated				
Depreciation	6,000	24,000		
		$44,000		$44,000

Designation of a portion of the fund balance as *expended* signifies the amount of assets in the form of fixed, rather than expendable, assets. This is analogous to the Investment in General Fixed Assets found in local government accounting. Designation of a portion of the fund balance as *unexpended* signifies the amount of assets available for acquisition or replacement of plant assets or for debt service.

During 19X3, construction of an office building for the society was begun. $100,000 was transferred from the unrestricted current fund—half to be used for construction costs and half for debt service—and $300,000 was borrowed from the bank on a short-term building loan. When the building is completed, a mortgage will be obtained, and the building loan will be paid off. During 19X3, $240,000 was spent on construction costs, and $28,000 of interest was paid on the loan. Investment of excess cash balances in time deposits yielded $7,700 in interest revenue; the society's board of directors has authorized the use of this money for unanticipated construction costs. Depreciation on office equipment of $3,000 was charged to general administration.

The above information was recorded in the plant fund by the following entries:

Cash—Construction	50,000	
Cash—Debt Service	50,000	
Transfer from Unrestricted Current Fund		100,000
To record transfer from unrestricted current fund.		
Cash—Construction	300,000	
Loan Payable		300,000
To record building loan.		
Construction in Progress	240,000	
Cash—Construction		240,000
To record construction costs on building.		
Interest Expense	28,000	
Cash—Debt Service		28,000
To record interest paid on loan.		
Cash—Construction	7,700	
Interest Revenue		7,700
To record interest earned on time deposits.		
Expenses—General Administration	3,000	
Accumulated Depreciation—Equipment		3,000
To record depreciation on office equipment.		

The financial statements for 19X3 appear as shown in Exhibit 18.4.

Important Accounting Issues

The accounting procedures used to record transactions of voluntary health and welfare organizations (and other nonprofit organizations) are similar to those illustrated for local government. However, several special considerations exist, as will be discussed in the following sections.

Investments A voluntary health and welfare organization may invest endowment and other restricted resources on a long-term basis and may invest unrestricted resources on a temporary basis. Accounting questions arise in re-

Exhibit 18.4   Plant Fund Financial Statements

Northeastern Heart Society
Plant Fund
Balance Sheet
December 31, 19X3

Cash—Construction .		$117,700	Loan Payable . . .		$300,000
Cash—Debt Service .		22,000	Fund Balance:		
Land		20,000	Expended . . .		41,000
Equipment . . .	$30,000		Unexpended . .		79,700
Accumulated					
Depreciation . . .	9,000	21,000			
Construction in					
Progress		240,000			
		$420,700			$420,700

Northeastern Heart Society
Plant Fund
Statement of Revenues, Expenses,
and Changes in Fund Balance
For the Year Ended December 31, 19X3

REVENUES:

Interest		$ 7,700

EXPENSES:

General Administration	$ 3,000	
Interest	28,000	31,000
Excess (Deficiency) of Revenues over Expenses . . .		$ (23,300)

OTHER CHANGES IN FUND BALANCE:

Transfer from Unrestricted Current Fund	100,000
Fund Balance —Beginning of Year	44,000
Fund Balance—End of Year	$120,700

gard to the basis for carrying these investments on the balance sheet and the treatment of investment income, gains, and losses.

Three methods for presenting investments on the balance sheet are considered acceptable: *cost*, *market*, and *lower-of-cost-or-market*. The same method should be used for all funds. If the cost basis is used, market value should also be disclosed, and vice-versa.

The treatment of investment income, gains, and losses involves legal as well as accounting issues. The questions are: (1) whether gains and losses are expendable as income or are considered part of principal, and (2) whether *expendable* gains and losses and investment income earned by restricted or endowment funds may be spent for *unrestricted* uses. The usual answers to these questions are summarized as follows:

Fund Type	Investment Income	Gains	Losses
Unrestricted Fund	Unrestricted	Unrestricted	Unrestricted
Restricted Fund	Restricted unless legally available for unrestricted	Restricted unless legally available for unrestricted	Restricted
Endowment Fund	Unrestricted unless restricted by donor	Addition to principal unless donor or state law permits otherwise	Subtraction from principal unless donor or state law permits otherwise

If the cost method is used, only realized gains and losses are recorded. Under the market method, both realized and unrealized gains and losses are recorded. Under the lower-of-cost-or-market method, realized gains, realized and unrealized losses, and unrealized loss recoveries are recorded. The references to *gains* and *losses* in the above table thus must be interpreted in accordance with the method of accounting being used.

To facilitate the management of investments, a nonprofit organization may decide to combine the investments of several funds into a single portfolio or **investment pool.** Records must be maintained so that the equity of each fund in the pool can be determined. For example, assume that three funds originally contributed a total of $90,000 to an investment pool, as follows:

Fund	Contribution	Original Equity Percentage
A	$40,000	44.44%
B	35,000	38.89
C	15,000	16.67
	$90,000	100.00%

Whenever a change in the composition of the pool occurs—a fund invests or withdraws—new equity percentages should be calculated based on *current market values.* Assume that the investments in the pool have increased in value to $150,000 and that Fund C will invest an additional $100,000. The calculation of revised equity percentages proceeds as follows:

Fund	Original Equity Percentage	Allocation of Current Value	Value after Investment	Revised Equity Percentage
A	44.44%	$ 66,667	$ 66,667	26.67%
B	38.89	58,333	58,333	23.33
C	16.67	25,000	125,000	50.00
	100.00%	$150,000	$250,000	100.00%

If the market method were used to account for investments, each fund would report according to the above data. For example, the balance sheet of Fund A would show investments having a market value of $66,667 and a cost of $40,000.

Fixed Assets   Fixed assets of a voluntary health and welfare organization available for use in carrying out the organization's programs are recorded in the plant fund. *Purchased assets* are recorded at *cost*, and *donated assets* are recorded at *fair market value*. If a donated asset has a restricted use which prevents its disposition or use in certain programs, it is recorded in the restricted fund rather than the plant fund.

Depreciation practices vary widely. Some organizations record depreciation; others do not. Depreciation may be recorded on assets which are to be maintained and replaced out of operating revenues but not on assets which are to be maintained and replaced by contributions and grants. Ideally, depreciation on all assets should be recognized, so that the cost of the organization's programs and services is not understated.

Donations   Donations—of cash, goods, and services—often constitute the major source of support for voluntary health and welfare organizations. Donations may be received directly or indirectly through a parent or umbrella agency. Any restrictions placed on the use of the donated resources will determine the fund to be used.

Fund-raising activities by a nonprofit organization often result in promises of contributions known as **pledges.** Pledges of cash should be recorded as receivables on the accrual basis, with an allowance for uncollectible pledges based on past collection experience and the organization's collection practices (many organizations feel that public relations considerations prevent aggressive collection practices). For example, assume that a local Association for the Blind chapter holds an annual telethon on June 1, 19X1, to raise funds for the fiscal year beginning on that date. Callers to the telethon pledge $350,000 to the association, mostly in small amounts of $10 to $50. Past experience suggests that 30 percent of these pledges will not be collected. The organization should record:

Pledges Receivable	$350,000	
Allowance for Uncollectible Pledges		105,000
Revenue from Contributions		245,000
To record pledges net of estimated amount uncollectible.		

In this example, resources from the pledges are expected to be available within the current year and are considered to be current revenues. If the pledge is such that the normal collection period extends beyond the current year, a deferred revenue account should be used. For example, suppose a foundation awards a grant of $7,500 to the Association for the Blind, payable over three years, to support a special project. This would be recorded as:

Grants Receivable	7,500	
Revenue from Grants		2,500
Deferred Revenue		5,000
To record pledge of three-year grant from foundation.		

Donations of significant amounts of goods should be recorded at fair market value, if a clear basis for determining market value exists and if the goods are used in the organization's programs. For example, suppose medicine with a fair market value of $4,000 is donated to a health organization by a pharmaceutical company, and is used in a free clinic program. The entry would be:

```
Expenses—Free Clinic Program      . . . . . . .   4,000
     Revenue from Contributions .  . . . . . . .                4,000
To record donation of medicine.
```

On the other hand, goods whose value is difficult to determine, such as donations of used clothing to a social welfare agency, are usually not recorded.

Donations of services present a similar situation; some are recorded, others are not. Donated services are recorded if they meet the following conditions:

1. The services are a normal part of the organization's programs.

2. In the absence of volunteers, the services are performed by salaried personnel.

3. The organization controls the use and duties of volunteers.

4. There is a clearly measurable basis for the value of the services.

Many services do not meet these criteria and thus are generally not recorded. Examples include volunteers who provide auxiliary services which otherwise would not be provided and solicitors in fund-raising campaigns.

Colleges and Universities

Accounting and reporting for institutions of higher education is subject to some degree of variation because of the different "ownerships" which exist. Colleges and universities may be run by state government (as is, for example, Michigan State University), city government (as is City University of New York), or state and local government (the community colleges in New York State are jointly supported by the state and the county), or they may be private nonprofit institutions (as is Lehigh University). Profit-making organizations, such as proprietary business and secretarial schools, also exist. Our discussion here will focus primarily on *private nonprofit institutions*. Accounting for government-operated institutions involves a combination of accounting principles for colleges and universities with those for government units. Similarly, accounting for proprietary schools involves a combination of college and business accounting.

Accounting Principles

Accounting principles for colleges and universities are derived from two major sources. One is the work of professional education groups. The National Association of College and University Business Officers (NACUBO) through its Accounting Principles Committee and the American Council on Education have been especially influential. The other source is the accounting profession, which set forth accounting principles in an industry audit guide *Audits of Colleges and Universities*, published by the AICPA in 1973. The audit guide was heavily influenced by the previous work of the American Council on Education and NACUBO.

Types of Funds

All of the fund types discussed earlier in the chapter are commonly found in college and university accounting. These are: unrestricted current fund, restricted current fund, plant fund, endowment fund, agency fund, loan fund, and annuity and life income funds. Current funds (both unrestricted and restricted) account for the operating activities of the institution. Revenues of current funds are produced by:

1. Student tuition and fees. These should be reported at gross amount. Scholarships, tuition waivers, and similar reductions are considered expenses.
2. Government aid, grants, and contracts.
3. Gifts and private grants.
4. Endowment income.
5. Sales and services of educational departments, such as publications and testing services.
6. Revenues of auxiliary enterprises, such as food service, residence halls, campus store, and athletics.

Expenditures of current funds include such items as:

1. Instruction.
2. Research.
3. Extension and public service programs.
4. Libraries.
5. Student aid.
6. Student services (such as admissions, financial aid, and guidance).
7. Operation and maintenance of physical facilities.
8. General and administrative expenses.
9. Operating costs of auxiliary enterprises.
10. Transfers, whether voluntary or mandatory, to loan fund, plant fund (for example, for replacement of assets or for debt service), endowment funds, and others.

Important Accounting Issues

Colleges and universities follow accrual accounting. The accounting practices with respect to investments and donations are generally similar to those discussed for voluntary health and welfare organizations. Other issues are discussed below.

Depreciation   Depreciation of plant assets is not reported in the current funds, since these funds emphasize cash expenditures rather than operating expenses. Depreciation may be recorded in the plant fund, in which case it appears on the statement of changes in fund balance.

Loan Funds   Loan funds exist to provide loans to students or employees of the educational institution. Outstanding loans are carried as receivables, with an appropriate allowance for uncollectibles. Interest revenue on loans is usually recorded when collected rather than as it accrues.

   To illustrate, suppose that McKinley College transfers $100,000 from its unrestricted operating fund to establish a loan fund for its students. The transfer is recorded by the loan fund as:

Cash	100,000	
Fund Balance		100,000

To establish loan fund by transfer from unrestricted
operating fund.

During the first year, $28,000 is loaned to students, and $2,000 of interest and
$3,000 of principal are collected. At year-end, 3 percent of the outstanding bal-
ance is estimated to be uncollectible, and $1,200 of interest revenue has ac-
crued. Entries for the year are:

Loans Receivable	28,000	
Cash		28,000

To record loans made.

Cash	5,000	
Loans Receivable		3,000
Revenues		2,000

To record collections.

Bad Debt Expense	750	
Allowance for Doubtful Accounts		750

To record allowance for estimated uncollectibles.

Note that no entry is made for the accrued interest; interest revenue is recognized on a cash basis.

Following the closing entries, the balance sheet for the loan fund appears as:

McKinley College
Loan Fund
Balance Sheet
June 30, 19X0

Cash	$ 77,000	Fund Balance	$101,250
Loans Receivable (Net of $750			
Allowance for Doubtful			
Accounts)	24,250		
	$101,250		$101,250

Gains on Investments   The question of whether gains on endowment investments constitute principal or income is particularly relevant to colleges and
universities. Endowment income is a significant portion of the budget for many
private educational institutions. The treatment of gains influences the investment policies of the institution; if gains are not spendable, the institution is likely to invest in securities promising high current interest or dividend income
rather than securities with low current income but good future growth potential.
Such an investment policy may act against the institution's long-run interests;
investment in growth securities may be desirable to help offset the effects of inflation on the endowment. If a growth oriented investment policy is followed
and gains are not spendable, however, current budget problems may result.

    The question of the treatment of gains has been widely debated in recent
years. The traditional view that interest and dividends are spendable income
but that gains are not is based on a fiduciary viewpoint with respect to endowments. Under this point of view, the organization does not *own* its endowment,

but rather *administers it as a trustee* on behalf of the beneficiaries of the organization. Thus the endowment is viewed as a trust, and fiduciary accounting principles are applied, requiring a separation of principal and income and treatment of gains as a part of principal. The opposing view holds that considering an endowment as a trust is inappropriate. The organization is the absolute owner of the endowment, and corporate accounting principles, which do not involve a separation of principal and income, should apply.

A compromise position has emerged, known as a **total return approach,** which permits some spending of gains but also attempts to protect the principal. The nature of this approach and its legal status have been summarized as follows:

> This approach emphasizes total investment return—traditional yield plus or minus gains and losses. Some users of a total return approach account for the portion of gain utilized for general operating purposes as revenue instead of as a transfer. Practically all total return approaches emphasize the use of "prudence" and a "rational and systematic formula" in determining the portion of gains which may be appropriated for expenditures and call for the protection of endowment principal from the loss of purchasing power (inflation) as a primary consideration before appropriating gains. Some approaches embrace spreading (deferral and amortization) techniques to eliminate extreme short-term fluctuations in realized gains and losses which often occur as mere accidents of timing under the completed transaction method. Others would combine realized and unrealized gains in a spreading approach. Most total return approaches have been confined to appropriating only gains of quasi-endowment funds whereas some institutions have appropriated gains of virtually all such funds including true endowment. Some approaches restrict the gains available for appropriation to only realized gains whereas others have considered unrealized gains as available for appropriation also.
>
> In 1972 the National Conference of Commissioners on Uniform State Laws drafted the Uniform Management of Institutional Funds Act as a proposed clarification of the restrictions on trustees' and managers' powers to invest for growth. Among other things, it provides for a standard of prudent use of the excess of realized and unrealized appreciation of invested funds over the historic dollar value of the fund. The standard encompasses price level trends and economic conditions.
>
> Several states have enacted legislation since the late 1960s dealing with the gain utilization question. The new statutes are not consistent as to whether both realized and unrealized gains may be used, the degree to which principal should be protected, or retroactivity of application. One statute specifies that the historic dollar value of the fund should be adjusted from time to time to reflect the change in purchasing power of that historic dollar value before appropriating any gains. None of the statutes specifically discusses gain-spreading or related techniques. In some jurisdictions, appropriation of gains may be limited or prohibited by applicable statutory or common law.[2]

Thus, there is a trend toward eliminating or reducing the limitations on the spending of gains. This continues to be a subject of controversy.

---

[2]   American Institute of Certified Public Accountants, *Industry Audit Guide: Audits of Colleges and Universities* (N.Y.: AICPA, 1973), pp. 37–39; Copyright © 1973 by the American Institute of Certified Public Accountants, Inc.

Annuity and Life Income Funds   One means of fund-raising by colleges and universities (and by some other nonprofit organizations such as churches and religious groups) is the annuity or life-income agreement. A donor contributes a sum of money or other resources to the institution. In exchange, the institution agrees to make periodic payments, either to the donor or the other specified individuals, for a period of time. The time period may be a fixed number of years or may be the lifetime of the beneficiary. At the termination of the agreement period, any remaining resources are typically available to the institution for restricted or unrestricted use. If the periodic payment is a fixed amount, the agreement is called an **annuity;** if the payment is defined as the amount of income earned on the contributed assets, it is a **life income agreement.**

In the case of annuity funds, the contributed assets are recorded at either donor's cost or, preferably, fair market value. The present value of the annuity payments should be calculated and recorded as a liability. The difference is recorded as fund balance. It is not appropriate to merely debit assets and credit fund balance, as would be done for endowment funds.

Life income funds, on the other hand, are treated in a manner similar to endowment funds. The future payments to beneficiaries are equal to future income, and thus no present value exists for the liability.

To illustrate, suppose that an elderly alumnus, who has a life expectancy of nine years, donates $50,000 to McKinley College under an annuity agreement whereby he is to receive $7,000 annually for life. It is determined that a 10 percent discount rate is appropriate. The present value of the liability is calculated as:

$7,000 \times$ Present value of an ordinary annuity of (9 years, 10%) = $7,000 \times 5.759 = $40,313.

The contribution is recorded as:

Cash	50,000	
Annuity Payable		40,313
Annuity Fund Balance		9,687
To record contribution and corresponding annuity agreement.		

Suppose further that $40,000 was invested at 12 percent, and $10,000 remained in a savings account at 6 percent. Entries for the first year are as follows:

Investments	40,000	
Cash		40,000
To record investment of $40,000 at 12%.		
Cash	5,400	
Annuity Fund Balance		5,400
To record income for year from investments ($4,800) and from savings account ($600).		
Annuity Payable	2,968	
Annuity Fund Balance	4,032	
Cash		7,000
To record annuity payment and corresponding reduction in liability.		

In the third entry above, the reduction in the liability was calculated as follows:

Original Liability (Present Value of $7,000 for 9 Years at 10%: $7,000
  × 5.759) $40,313
Liability after One Year (Present Value of $7,000 for 8 Years at 10%:
  $7,000 × 5.335) 37,345
  Reduction in Liability . . . . $ 2,968

This calculation is analogous to the use of the effective interest method for long-term debt. The balance sheet of the annuity fund appears as follows:

McKinley College
Annuity Fund
Balance Sheet
June 30, 19X0

Cash	$ 8,400	Annuity Payable	$37,345
Investments	40,000	Fund Balance	11,055
	$48,400		$48,400

If the same contribution were made under a life income agreement, no initial liability would be calculated. The donor is entitled to receive whatever income is generated each year. Assuming the same facts as above, the entries for a life income fund would be:

Cash 50,000
  Life Income Fund Balance 50,000
To record contribution under life income agreement.

Investments 40,000
  Cash 40,000
To record investment of $40,000 at 12%.

Cash 5,400
  Life Income Payable 5,400
To record income for year from investments and from
savings account and corresponding obligation to donor.

Life Income Payable 5,400
  Cash 5,400
To record payment of current income to donor per
agreement.

The balance sheet would appear as:

McKinley College
Life Income Fund
Balance Sheet
June 30, 19X0

Cash	$10,000	Fund Balance	$50,000
Investments	40,000		
	$50,000		$50,000

If an organization has both annuity and life income agreements, a combined balance sheet is often presented.

Hospitals

As was the case with colleges and universities, hospitals may be government, private nonprofit, or proprietary organizations. Thus, aspects of governmental or business accounting may be present. Our focus in this discussion is on the voluntary (that is, private nonprofit) hospitals, although many of the accounting principles apply also to government or proprietary hospitals. Similarly, many of the accounting principles apply to health care institutions other than hospitals, such as rehabilitation centers and nursing homes.

Accounting Principles

Accounting principles for hospitals derive from two major sources. The American Hospital Association has issued several publications relating to accounting, cost determination, and internal control by hospitals. The AICPA has published a *Hospital Audit Guide* which discusses accounting principles for hospitals.

Types of Funds

A voluntary hospital is likely to employ at least the following funds: unrestricted current fund, restricted current fund, plant fund (usually limited to resources for plant expansion and replacement), endowment fund, and agency fund. Other funds might be present in certain circumstances. For example, a teaching hospital (one which educates doctors or nurses in addition to providing patient services) may have funds common to educational institutions, such as a loan fund.

Current fund revenues of a hospital (both restricted and unrestricted) come from patient services and other operating and nonoperating sources. Patient service revenue is recorded on an accrual basis, using the hospital's established rates, and consists of:

1. Revenue from daily patient services such as room, board, general nursing, medical, and surgical services.

2. Revenue from other medical services such as operating room and emergency room.

3. Revenue from ancillary services such as blood bank, laboratory, pharmacy and anesthesiology.

These revenues are initially recorded at gross amounts. However, full rates may not be collected from all patients. Thus, gross revenues should be reduced by the following allowances:

1. Charity allowances—full or partial reductions in charges for indigent patients.

2. Courtesy allowances—reductions in charges for employees, clergy, and so on.

3. Contractual adjustments—differences between a hospital's rate and the rate established by contractual agreements with third-party payers such as Blue Cross.

4. Allowance for uncollectible accounts.

Other operating revenue includes sales to patients and others of nonmedical goods and services (such as telephone calls, gift shop, cafeteria, and parking lot), revenue from educational programs, and gifts or grants for specified purposes. Nonoperating revenue includes such items as unrestricted gifts, unrestricted income from endowments, and donated services.

Important Accounting Issues	Again, many of the accounting issues discussed earlier, especially those with respect to investments and donations, apply to hospitals. Additional issues are discussed below. One aspect that affects much of hospital accounting is the need for *extensive cost accounting*. Most nonprofit organizations pay little attention to cost accounting, but for hospitals it is essential. A large percentage of a hospital's patient service revenues are paid not by the patients themselves, but by **third-party payers**—Blue Cross, Medicare, Medicaid, and private insurance plans. Because many of these pay on a cost-reimbursement basis, hospitals generally attempt to determine the *full cost* (not variable cost) of their services. The need for costing affects many other accounting procedures.
	Depreciation Property, plant, and equipment and related liabilities are included in the unrestricted fund. Thus the plant fund for a hospital differs from plant funds for other nonprofit organizations. A hospital plant fund typically contains *only* resources set aside for expansion or replacement of plant.
	Depreciation is recorded and is included in operating expenses of the unrestricted fund. Recording of depreciation is essential if all costs of providing services are to be recognized.
	Cost Finding As mentioned earlier, much of a hospital's revenue is based on cost reimbursement for services rendered. **Cost finding** is the process of first segregating all direct costs by cost centers, and then allocating overhead costs to the revenue-producing operations of the hospital. Various methods of cost allocation may be employed, ranging from direct allocation to step methods to simultaneous equation methods. These methods are typically covered in cost accounting courses and are not discussed here.
Overview of Nonprofit Accounting	Accounting for nonprofit organizations involves a combination of the principles and procedures used by local government with those used by business. This chapter has discussed one type which is supported primarily by voluntary contributions and two which are supported in large part by user charges. While many other types of nonprofit organizations exist, their accounting and reporting tend to parallel that discussed for voluntary health and welfare organizations, colleges, or hospitals. Because of the comparative lack of standard setting by a single body, procedures developed by various industry groups are widely used.
Summary of Key Concepts	**Nonprofit organizations** have an objective other than providing goods and services at a profit. Resource providers do not expect direct benefits, and there are no equity interests.
	A **fund structure** is commonly used for nonprofit organizations. The fund structure has some similarities to and some differences from the fund structure for local government. Of particular note is the **plant fund,** which possesses char-

acteristics of a local government's capital projects fund, debt service fund, general fixed assets account group, and general long-term debt account group all in one fund. Also, the **loan fund** and the **annuity fund** of a nonprofit organization have no counterparts in governmental accounting.

Financial statements for a nonprofit organization typically consist of a **balance sheet** and a **statement of revenues, expenses, and changes in fund balance.**

Investments of nonprofit organizations may be valued using the **cost, market,** or **lower-of-cost-or-market method.** Treatment of investment income, gains, and losses depends upon the nature of the fund holding the investments. The question of whether **gains** constitute **principal or income** is an important and unresolved issue.

Accounting for **donations** is typically on the accrual basis for **cash donations,** with revenue deferred if the cash will not be available until a subsequent year. **Donations of goods and services** may not be recorded at all under certain circumstances; when such donations are recorded, fair market value is used.

Cost determination, while important to virtually all nonprofit organizations, is particularly vital to hospitals because of third-party reimbursements. **Cost allocation,** including recognition of depreciation, is important in hospital accounting.

Questions

Q18.1 Compare the objectives and sources of revenues of (1) local government and (2) nonprofit organizations.

Q18.2 What are the major sources of accounting and reporting standards for voluntary health and welfare organizations?

Q18.3 Explain the difference between restricted and unrestricted funds in nonprofit accounting. What counterparts do these funds have in governmental accounting?

Q18.4 What is the purpose of a loan fund? How are resources for the fund provided?

Q18.5 What is the accounting treatment for debt incurred for construction by a nonprofit organization? Contrast this treatment to that by a local government.

Q18.6 How should gains and losses on sales of investments held by a voluntary health and welfare organization be recorded?

Q18.7 Select the best answer for each of the following multiple choice questions:
1. Which of the following receipts is properly recorded in the restricted current fund by a university?
   a. Tuition.
   b. Student laboratory fees.
   c. Housing fees.
   d. Research grants.

2.   What is the recommended method of accounting to be used by colleges and universities?
    a.   Cash.
    b.   Modified cash.
    c.   Restricted accrual.
    d.   Accrual.

3.   In the loan fund of a college or university, each of the following types of loans would be found *except:*
    a.   Student.
    b.   Staff.
    c.   Building.
    d.   Faculty.

(AICPA adapted)

Q18.8   The following multiple choice questions refer to the accounts of a large nonprofit hospital which properly maintains four funds: current unrestricted, current restricted, endowment, and plant. For each question, select the best answer.

1.   The endowment fund consists of several small endowments, each for a special purpose. The hospital treasurer has determined that it would be legally possible and more efficient to pool the assets and allocate the resultant revenue. The soundest basis on which to allocate revenue after assets are pooled and comply with the special purposes of each endowment would be to:
    a.   Determine market values of securities or other assets comprising each endowment at the time of transfer to the pool and credit revenue to each endowment on that pro rata basis.
    b.   Determine book value of each endowment at the time of transfer to the pool and credit revenue to each endowment on that pro rata basis.
    c.   Apportion future revenue in the moving-average ratio that the various endowments have earned revenue in the past.
    d.   Ask the trustee who administers the pooled assets to make the determination, since the trustee is in a position to know which assets are making the greatest contribution.

2.   How should charity service, contractual adjustments, and bad debts be classified in the statement of revenues and expenses for the hospital?
    a.   All three should be treated as expenses.
    b.   All three should be treated as deductions from patient-service revenues.
    c.   Charity service and contractual adjustments should be treated as revenue deductions, while bad debts should be treated as an expense.
    d.   Charity service and bad debts should be treated as expenses while contractual adjustments should be treated as a revenue deduction.

3.   To assure the availability of money for improvement, replacement, and expansion of plant, it would be most desirable for the hospital to:
    a.   Use accelerated depreciation to provide adequate funds for eventual replacement.

b. Use the retirement or replacement system of depreciation to provide adequate funds.

c. Sell assets at the earliest opportunity.

d. Transfer cash from the current unrestricted fund to the plant fund in amounts at least equal to the periodic depreciation charges.

(AICPA adapted)

Exercises   **E18.1**   Funds X and Y of the VHW Organization, a voluntary health and welfare organization, pool their idle resources for investment purposes. At the beginning of the year, each fund contributed $30,000 to the pool. During the year, the value of the investments increased 10 percent. At the end of the year, Fund X withdrew $5,000 from the investment pool and Fund Y contributed $7,000. The net addition was immediately invested.

Required:

1. Compute the percentage of equity in the investment pool held by each fund at year-end after the transactions described above.

2. What amount would be presented under the "Investments" caption on the end-of-year balance sheet for each fund if VHW uses the cost method for reporting investments? If VHW uses the market method?

E18.2   The following items relate to a nonprofit college:

1. An alumna donates cash for purchase of library books.

2. An alumna donates cash, stipulating that income generated by investment of the cash be paid to the donor during the donor's lifetime. At the donor's death, the gift and all future income belongs to the college.

3. An alumna donates cash, stipulating that income generated by investment of the cash be used for student scholarships. The principal is to remain intact.

4. A gymnasium is constructed.

5. Salaries to faculty are paid.

6. Loans are made to faculty members.

7. Student activity fees for student organizations are collected with tuition payments.

8. Depreciation on the gymnasium is computed.

Required: For each item, identify the type of fund in which the event or activity should be recorded.

E18.3   Hopeville Retreat is a nonprofit organization that counsels former drug addicts in readjusting to productive community life. Donations provide the major support for Hopeville Retreat. During 19X2, the following gifts were received by the organization:

1. Cash from fund-raising campaign, $25,000.

2. Cash from rehabilitated clients of the organization, $10,000.

3. Clothing donated by a local department store. Cost to the store was $2,800. Market value was $3,600.

4. A television set valued at $300 donated by a private citizen.
5. Medicine used for drug withdrawal symptoms, donated by a pharmaceutical company. Cost of drugs was $3,000; market value was $5,000.
6. Secretarial and bookkeeping services for necessary paperwork and record-keeping performed by volunteers, valued at $7,000.
7. Door-to-door fund solicitation time donated by local high school students. The organization estimates this service to be worth $2,800 when valued using minimum wage rates.
8. Free radio announcements of the fund-raising campaign given by a local radio station. The normal charge for advertisements of comparable length is $400.

Required: For each gift, indicate at what amount the donation would be recorded on the books of Hopeville Retreat.

E18.4   The following items relate to a voluntary health and welfare organization:
1. A gift of cash is received with no stipulations as to use.
2. The organization borrows money to finance construction of a new office building.
3. Money is collected and held for distribution to an unaffiliated organization.
4. Money is collected and held for distribution to the beneficiaries of one of the organization's programs.
5. An automobile is donated for use in transporting officials on organization business.
6. Depreciation is computed on the automobile in item 5.
7. General revenues are set aside to repay the loan in item 2.
8. Used toys are collected for holiday distribution to needy children.

Required: For each item, identify the type of fund in which the event or activity should be recorded.

E18.5   First Baptist Church of Lawton has followed a policy of recording gross pledges to its missionary fund as revenues and writing off uncollected pledges in the year following the pledge. In 19X9, the church decided to establish an allowance for uncollectible pledges based on pledges and collections for the first five years of the fund. Data pertaining to the missionary fund appear below.

Year	Pledged	Collected	
19X3	$1,000	$ 600	
19X4	1,500	110	(19X3 pledges)
		1,200	(19X4 pledges)
19X5	1,200	150	(19X4 pledges)
		960	(19X5 pledges)
19X6	3,000	2,550	(19X6 pledges)
19X7	2,500	2,000	(19X7 pledges)
19X8	2,800	250	(19X7 pledges)
		2,000	(19X8 pledges)

Required:

1. Establish an allowance for uncollectible pledges and correct the church's books as of the beginning of 19X9. Uncollected 19X8 pledges have not yet been written off. All uncollected pledges for years prior to 19X8 have been written off.

2. During 19X9, $3,000 was pledged. Of the $2,500 which was collected that year, $400 applied to 19X8 pledges. The remaining 19X8 pledges were written off. Record the 19X9 transactions related to pledges.

E18.6 Canton College, a nonprofit organization, maintains the following funds:

Unrestricted current fund.

Restricted current fund—scholarships.

Plant fund.

Agency fund.

Loan fund.

Required: For each of the transactions below, specify the fund(s) affected and record the journal entry. Explanations may be omitted.

1. The school's general fund-raising campaign generates pledges of $80,000. Past history shows pledges to be 90 percent collectible.
2. A previously recorded pledge for scholarship money is received ($7,000).
3. An employee borrows $1,000 from the school and signs a note for repayment within one year.
4. Student activity fees of $6,000 are transferred to student organizations.
5. Salaries of $20,000 are paid to employees. An accrual had not been recorded.
6. A loan of $11,000 is taken to buy audiovisual equipment.
7. An $800 scholarship is awarded.

E18.7 On January 1, 19X0, Patricia Dahlene gave Stokely College $100,000 in cash with the provision that the cash be invested in income-producing securities. Actuarial estimates set Dahlene's life expectancy at fifteen years from the date of the gift. The annual discount rate associated with the arrangements outlined below is 8 percent.

Required: Specify the fund affected and record Patricia Dahlene's gift on the college's books under each of the following *independent* arrangements.

1. The college is to pay Patricia Dahlene $7,500 every December 31 of her remaining life. If earnings of the principal are insufficient to meet the payments, then the principal is to be depleted. Any earnings exceeding the required payment can be spent by the college without restriction. Gains and losses on principal assets must be added to (deducted from) principal. Upon Dahlene's death, remaining resources become available to the college with no restriction as to use.

2. The college is to pay Patricia Dahlene all earnings of the principal for life. Any gains and losses pertaining to principal assets are treated as income and therefore affect payments to the donor. Upon Dahlene's death, remaining resources become available to the college with no restrictions as to use.

E18.8 Davis College's plant fund had the following balance sheet at June 30, 19X7:

Davis College
Plant Fund
Balance Sheet
June 30, 19X7

Cash	$ 70,000	Mortgage Payable . . .	$4,600,000
Land	400,000	Fund Balance	2,020,000
Buildings	3,700,000		
Equipment	2,450,000		
	$6,620,000		$6,620,000

During the year ended June 30, 19X8, the following transactions occurred:
1. Resources in the amount of $500,000 were transferred from the unrestricted current fund.
2. Resources in the amount of $80,000 were transferred from the restricted current fund and spent on the purchase of audiovisual equipment.
3. Interest of $330,000 and principal of $200,000 were paid on the mortgage.
4. The college does not record depreciation on its assets.

Required: Prepare the balance sheet and the statement of revenues, expenses, and changes in fund balance for the plant fund for the year ended June 30, 19X8.

Problems P18.1 **Budgeting for a College** Crosby College, a nonprofit school, is developing its budget for the upcoming 19X1–19X2 academic year. The following data relate to the current academic year (19X0–19X1):

	Lower Division (Freshman/Sophomore)	Upper Division (Junior/Senior)
Average Number of Students per Class . . .	25	20
Average Salary of Faculty Members	$24,000	$24,000
Average Number of Credit Hours Carried each Year per Student	33	30
Enrollment Including Scholarship Students . .	2,000	1,360
Average Faculty Teaching Load in Credit Hours per Year (8 Classes of 3 Credit Hours) . . .	24	24

Additional information:
1. For 19X1–19X2, lower division enrollment is expected to increase by 10 percent, while the upper division's enrollment is expected to remain stable. Faculty salaries will be increased by a standard 8 percent, and additional merit increases to be awarded to individual faculty members will be $150,000 for the lower division and $135,000 for the upper division.
2. The current budget is $384,000 for operation and maintenance of plant and equipment; this includes $180,000 for salaries and wages. Experience of the past three months suggests that the current budget is realistic but that expected increases for 19X1–19X2 are 8 percent in salaries

wages and $18,000 in other expenditures for operation and maintenance of plant and equipment.

3. The budget for the remaining expenditures for 19X1–19X2 is as follows:

Administrative and General $280,000
Library 220,000
Health and Recreation 150,000
Athletics 240,000
Insurance and Retirement 330,000
Interest 96,000

4. The college expects to award fifteen tuition-free scholarships to the lower division students and ten to upper division students. Tuition is $44 per credit hour, and no other fees are charged.

5. Budgeted revenues for 19X1–19X2 are as follows:

Endowments $342,000
Net Income from Auxiliary Services 500,000
Athletics 460,000

The college's remaining source of revenue is an annual support campaign held during the spring.

Required:

1. Compute by division (a) the expected enrollment, (b) the total credit hours to be carried, and (c) the number of faculty members needed for 19X1–19X2.
2. Compute the budget for 19X1–19X2 faculty salaries by division.
3. Compute the 19X1–19X2 tuition revenue budget by division.
4. Compute the amount which must be raised during the annual support campaign in order to cover the 19X1–19X2 expenditures budget.

(AICPA adapted)

P18.2 **Investment Pools** Modern Families is a voluntary health and welfare organization that specializes in family counseling. Three of the organization's funds (family planning, FP; marriage counseling, MC; and single parenting, SP) were financed by grants from donors who restricted the use of the gifts. The resources of the funds not required for current operations are combined in an investment pool. On January 1, 19X7, the date of the investment pool's establishment, the following contributions were made:

FP $40,000
MC 20,000
SP 40,000

These monies were invested in securities as follows:

Security A: 100 shares at $80 each.

Security B: 270 shares at $100 each.

Security C: 1,000 shares at $30 each.

Security D: 500 shares at $70 each.

Dividends received on the securities were distributed pro rata rather than being reinvested.

During 19X7, the following occurred:

1. On June 30, SP contributed $20,600 to the investment pool, FP withdrew

$20,600, and MC withdrew $5,760. Shares of security D were sold to finance the net withdrawal.

2. On September 30, FP contributed $17,000, and SP withdrew $9,400. The net cash inflow was invested in security D.

3. Market values of the securities fluctuated as follows:

	March 31	June 30	September 30	December 31
Security A	$ 90	$94	$94	$90
Security B	100	98	97	98
Security C	30	30	30	33
Security D	70	72	76	76

Required:

1. Determine the equity percentage in the investment pool of each fund as of January 1, March 31, June 30, September 30 and December 31.

2. Determine the amount each fund would present as investments on its respective December 31, 19X7, balance sheet if Modern Families follows the cost method of accounting for investments.

3. Determine the amount each fund would present as investments on its respective December 31, 19X7, balance sheet if Modern Families follows the market method of accounting for investments.

4. Determine the amount each fund would present as investments on its respective December 31, 19X7, balance sheet if Modern Families follows the lower-of-cost-or-market method of accounting for investments.

P18.3   Hospital Accounting—Insurance Reimbursements   Grady Hospital completed its first year of operation as a qualified institutional provider under the health insurance (HI) program for the aged and wishes to receive maximum reimbursement for its allowable costs from the government. The following financial, statistical, and other information is available:

1.   The hospital's charges and allowable costs for departmental inpatient services were:

Departments	Charges for HI Program Beneficiaries	Total Charges	Total Allowable Costs
Inpatient Routine Services (Room, Board, Nursing)	$425,000	$1,275,000	$1,350,000
Inpatient Ancillary Service Departments:			
X-ray	$ 56,000	$ 200,000	$ 150,000
Operating Room	57,000	190,000	220,000
Laboratory	59,000	236,000	96,000
Pharmacy	98,000	294,000	207,000
Other	10,000	80,000	88,000
Total Ancillary	$280,000	$1,000,000	$ 761,000
Totals	$705,000	$2,275,000	$2,111,000

2. For the first year, the reimbursement settlement for inpatient services may be calculated at the option of the provider under either of the following apportionment methods:

   a. *The departmental RCC (ratio of cost centers) method* provides for listing on a departmental basis the ratios of beneficiary inpatient charges to total inpatient charges with each department beneficiary inpatient charge ratio applied to the allowable total cost of the respective department.

   b. *The combination method (with cost finding)* provides that the cost of routine services be apportioned on the basis of the average allowable cost per day for all inpatients applied to total inpatient days of beneficiaries. The residual part of the provider's total allowable cost attributable to ancillary (nonroutine) services is to be apportioned in the ratio of the beneficiaries' share of charges for ancillary services to the total charges for all patients for such services.

3. Statistical and other information:

   a. Total inpatient days for all patients, 20,000.

   b. Total inpatient days applicable to HI beneficiaries (600 aged patients whose average length of stay was 12.5 days), 7,500.

   c. A fiscal intermediary acting on behalf of the government's medicare program negotiated a fixed allowance rate of $90 per inpatient day subject to retroactive adjustment as a reasonable cost basis for reimbursement of covered services to the hospital under the HI program. Interim payments based on an estimated 500 inpatient days per month were received during the twelve-month period subject to an adjustment for the provider's actual cost experience.

Required:

1. Prepare schedules computing the total allowable cost of inpatient services for which the provider should receive payment under the HI program and the remaining balance due for reimbursement under each of the following methods:

   a. Departmental RCC method.

   b. Combination method (with cost finding).

2. Under which method should Grady Hospital elect to be reimbursed for its first year under the HI program, assuming the election can be changed for the following year with the approval of the fiscal intermediary? Why?

3. Grady Hospital wishes to compare its charges to HI program beneficiaries with published information on national averages for charges for hospital services.

   Compute the following (show your computations):

   a. The average total hospital charge for an HI inpatient.

   b. The average charge per inpatient day for HI inpatients.   (AICPA adapted)

P18.4 Nonprofit Organization Accounting   The following data are available concerning Somerset Blood Bank, a nonprofit organization:

1. Blood is furnished to the blood bank by volunteers and when necessary by professional donors. During the year, 2,568 pints of blood were taken from volunteers and professional blood donors.

Exhibit 18.5   Balance Sheet for Somerset Blood Bank, to Be Used in P18.4

Somerset Blood Bank
Balance Sheet

ASSETS	June 30, 19X1	June 30, 19X2
Cash	$ 2,712	$ 2,093
U.S. Treasury Bonds	15,000	16,000
Accounts Receivable—Sales of Blood:		
Hospitals	1,302	1,448
Individuals	425	550
Inventories:		
Blood	480	640
Supplies and Serum	250	315
Furniture and Equipment, Less Depreciation	4,400	4,050
Total Assets	$24,569	$25,096
LIABILITIES AND FUND BALANCE		
Accounts Payable—Supplies	$ 325	$ 275
Fund Balance	24,244	24,821
Total Liabilities and Fund Balance	$24,569	$25,096

2. Volunteer donors who give blood to the bank can draw against their accounts when necessary. An individual who requires a blood transfusion has the option of paying for the blood used at $25 per pint or replacing it at the blood bank. Hospitals purchase blood at $8 per pint.

3. Somerset Blood Bank has a reciprocal arrangement with a number of other banks that permits a member who requires a transfusion in a different locality to draw blood from the local bank against his account in Somerset. The issuing blood bank charges a set fee of $14 per pint to the home blood bank.

4. If blood is issued to hospitals but is not used and is returned to the blood bank, there is a handling charge of $1 per pint. Only hospitals are permitted to return blood. During the year, 402 pints were returned. The blood being returned must be in usable condition.

5. Blood can be stored for only twenty-one days and then must be discarded. During the year 343 pints were outdated. This is a normal rate of loss.

6. The blood bank sells serum and supplies at cost to doctors and laboratories. These items are used in processing blood and are sold at the same price that they are billed to the blood bank. No blood bank operating expenses are allocated to the cost of sales of these items.

7. Inventories of blood are valued at the sales price to hospitals. The sales price to hospitals was increased on July 1, 19X1. The inventories are as shown at the bottom of page 813.

8. The financial statements are shown as Exhibits 18.5 and 18.6.

Exhibit 18.6   Statement of Cash Receipts and Disbursements for Somerset Blood Bank, to Be Used in P18.4

Somerset Blood Bank
Statement of Cash Receipts and Disbursements
For the Year Ended June 30, 19X2

Balance, July 1, 19X1:			
Cash in Bank			$ 2,712
U.S. Treasury Bonds			15,000
Total			$17,712
Receipts:			
From Hospitals:			
Hillcrest Hospital	$7,702		
Good Samaritan Hospital	3,818	$11,520	
Individuals		6,675	
From Other Blood Banks		602	
From Sales of Serum and Supplies		2,260	
Interest on Bonds		525	
Gifts and Bequests		4,928	
Total Receipts			26,510
Total to Be Accounted For			$44,222
Disbursements:			
Laboratory Expense:			
Serum	$3,098		
Salaries	3,392		
Supplies	3,533		
Laundry and Miscellaneous	277	$10,300	
Other Expenses and Disbursements:			
Salaries	$5,774		
Dues and Subscriptions	204		
Rent and Utilities	1,404		
Blood Testing	2,378		
Payments to Other Blood Banks for Blood			
Given to Members Away from Home	854		
Payments to Professional Blood Donors	2,410		
Other Expenses	1,805		
Purchase of U.S. Treasury Bond	1,000	15,829	
Total Disbursements			26,129
Balance, June 30, 19X2:			$18,093
Cash in Bank			$ 2,093
U.S. Treasury Bonds			16,000
Total			$18,093

Inventories of Blood

	Pints	Sales Price	Total
June 30, 19X1	80	$6	$480
June 30, 19X2	80	8	640

Required:

1. Prepare a statement on the accrual basis of the total expense of taking and processing blood.
2. Prepare a schedule computing (a) the number of pints of blood sold and (b) the number of pints withdrawn by members.
3. Prepare a schedule computing the expense per pint of taking and processing the blood that was used.

(AICPA adapted)

P18.5 **Sources and Uses of Cash** The General Medical Institute is a nonprofit corporation without capital stock, which accounts for its activities in a single fund. Its comparative financial statements appear as Exhibits 18.7 and 18.8.

Additional information:

1. Accounts receivable—patients are stated net of the allowance for doubtful accounts, which amounted to $10,000 at October 31, 19X2, and $14,600 at October 31, 19X3. During the year, bad debts totaling $800 were written off.
2. The research activities are net of research grants aggregating $10,000. Included as a research expense is depreciation of $6,600 on special research equipment.
3. During 19X3, the construction of a new building was begun. The estimated cost of the building and equipment is $1,000,000. The expansion is being financed as follows:

Grant from Government	$ 335,000
Mortgage (Repayment to Begin upon Completion of Building) .	500,000
Special Features Installed at the Request of Government Agencies and to Be Paid for by the Agencies	80,000
Institute Funds	85,000
Total	$1,000,000

4. New therapy equipment costing $15,000 was purchased in 19X3 and replaced therapy equipment with a book value of $5,000 which was sold for $3,000.
5. To obtain additional cash for working capital, investments with a cost of $50,000 were sold during July.

Required: Prepare a statement accounting for the increase in cash for the year ended October 31, 19X3, to be included in the annual report of the General Medical Institute. The statement should set forth information concerning cash applied to or provided by:

1. Operations.
2. Research activities.
3. Acquisitions of assets.
4. Other sources of funds.

(AICPA adapted)

P18.6 **Multifund Balance Sheets** The bookkeeper for the Jacob Vocational School resigned on March 1, 19X8, after preparing the general ledger trial balance and analysis of cash as of February 28, 19X8. These statements appear in Exhibits 18.9 and 18.10.

At the end of the fiscal year, August 31, 19X8, an examination of the records showed the following:

1. D. E. Marcy donated 100 shares of Trans, Inc., stock in September 19X7 with a market value of $110 per share at the date of donation. The terms of

Exhibit 18.7   Statements of Revenues and Expenses for General Medical Institute, to Be Used in P18.5

The General Medical Institute
Comparative Statements of Revenues and Expenses
For the Years Ended October 31, 19X3 and 19X2

	19X3	19X2	Increase (Decrease)
REVENUE FROM SERVICES RENDERED			
Services to Patients	$360,000	$304,000	$ 56,000
Less Free Services	36,000	38,000	(2,000)
Net Revenue from Services Rendered	$324,000	$266,000	$ 58,000
OPERATING EXPENSES			
Departmental Expenses:			
Medical Services	$ 32,700	$ 29,300	$ 3,400
Medicine and Supplies	14,600	10,500	4,100
Nursing Services	89,900	76,200	13,700
Therapy Services	34,300	31,300	3,000
Dietary	40,700	37,100	3,600
Housekeeping and Maintenance	37,300	29,500	7,800
Administration and Other	33,700	23,400	10,300
General Expenses:			
Rental of Leased Premises (Net)	—	3,100	(3,100)
Depreciation—Building and Equipment	9,900	8,300	1,600
Provision for Uncollectible Accounts	5,400	3,500	1,900
Interest Expense	6,500	—	6,500
Loss on Sale of Equipment	2,000	—	2,000
Other	16,200	6,500	9,700
Total Expenses	$323,200	$258,700	$ 64,500
Excess of Revenues from Services Rendered over Expenses of Patient Care	$ 800	$ 7,300	$ (6,500)
OTHER INCOME (EXPENSES)			
Research	$ (13,300)	$ (13,200)	$ (100)
Gain on Sale of Investments	18,600	3,500	15,100
Investment Income	16,500	13,300	3,200
Contributions	10,300	14,800	(4,500)
Grant from Government Designated for Expansion	335,000	—	335,000
Miscellaneous	2,700	1,500	1,200
Total Other Income	$369,800	$ 19,900	$349,900
Excess of Revenues over Expenses	$370,600	$ 27,200	$343,400

the gift provide that the stock and any income thereon are to be retained intact. At any date designated by the board of directors, the assets are to be liquidated and the proceeds used to assist the school's director in acquiring a personal residence. The school will not retain any financial interest in the residence.

2. E. T. Pearce donated 6 percent bonds in September 19X7 with par and market values of $150,000 at the date of donation. Annual payments of $3,500 are to be made to the donor during his lifetime. Earnings in excess of these payments are to be used for current operations in the following

Exhibit 18.8   Balance Sheets for General Medical Institute, to Be Used in P18.5

The General Medical Institute
Comparative Balance Sheets
October 31, 19X3 and 19X2

ASSETS	19X3	19X2	Increase (Decrease)
Cash	$ 28,600	$ 18,500	$ 10,100
Accounts Receivable—Patients (Net) . .	75,500	55,500	20,000
Investments (Cost)	413,100	463,100	(50,000)
Prepaid Expenses	2,200	1,600	600
Land, Building, Equipment (Net)	327,200	333,700	(6,500)
Construction in Progress	793,800	—	793,800
Total Assets	$1,640,400	$872,400	$768,000

LIABILITIES AND FUND BALANCE	19X3	19X2	Increase (Decrease)
Accounts Payable—Construction . . .	$ 110,800	—	$110,800
Less Receivables from Government Agencies	80,000	—	80,000
Accounts Payable—Construction (Net) . .	$ 30,800	—	$ 30,800
Accounts Payable—Current Operations . .	11,800	$ 10,200	1,600
Mortgage Payable	365,000	—	365,000
Total Liabilities	$ 407,600	$ 10,200	$397,400
Fund Balance:			
Balance, November 1	$ 862,200	$835,000	$ 27,200
Excess of Revenues over Expenses for Year	370,600	27,200	343,400
Balance, October 31	$1,232,800	$862,200	$370,600
Total Liabilities and Fund Balance . . .	$1,640,400	$872,400	$768,000

fiscal year. Upon the donor's death the fund is to be used to construct a school cafeteria.

3. No transactions have been recorded on the school's books since February 28, 19X8. An employee of the school prepared the following analysis of the checking account for the period from March 1 through August 31, 19X8:

Balance, March 1, 19X8			$288,900
Deduct: General Current Operating			
Expenses	$14,000		
Purchase of Equipment	47,000	$61,000	
Less Student Fees		8,000	
Net Expenses		$53,000	
Payment for Director's Residence .	$11,200		
Less Sale of 100 Shares of Trans, Inc., Stock	10,600	600	53,600
Total			$235,300
Add: Interest on 6% Bonds		$ 9,000	
Less Payments to E. T. Pearce . . .		3,500	5,500
Balance, August 31, 19X8			$240,800

Exhibit 18.9 Trial Balance for Jacob Vocational School, to Be Used in P18.6

Jacob Vocational School
General Ledger Trial Balance
February 28, 19X8

DEBITS

Cash for Current Operations	$258,000
Cash for Restricted Current Uses	30,900
Stock Donated by D. E. Marcy	11,000
Bonds Donated by E. T. Pearce	150,000
Building	33,000
Land	22,000
General Current Operating Expenses	38,000
Faculty Recruitment Expenses	4,100
Total	$547,000

CREDITS

Mortgage Payable on Fixed Assets	$ 30,000
Income from Gifts for General Operations	210,000
Income from Gifts for Restricted Uses	196,000
Student Fees	31,000
Fund Balances	80,000
Total	$547,000

Required: Prepare August 31, 19X8, balance sheets for the four funds of Jacob Vocational School: unrestricted current fund, restricted current fund, plant fund, and annuity fund.

(AICPA adapted)

P18.7 **Hospital Cost Accounting** Bowman Hospital, a nonprofit organization, is preparing a preliminary budget for the year ending June 30, 19X2. Projections for room requirements for inpatients by type of service are:

Type of Patient	Total Patients Expected	Average Number of Days in Hospital Regular	Average Number of Days in Hospital Medicare	Private	Semiprivate	Ward
Medical	2,100	7	17	10%	60%	30%
Surgical	2,400	10	15	15	75	10

Of the patients served by the hospital, 10 percent are expected to be Medicare patients, all of whom are expected to select semiprivate rooms. Both the number and proportion of Medicare patients have increased over the past five years. Daily rentals per patient are: $80 for a private room, $70 for a semiprivate room and $50 for a ward.

Operating room charges are based on man-minutes (number of minutes the operating room is in use multiplied by number of personnel assisting in the operation). The per man-minute charges are $.26 for inpatients and $.44 for outpatients. Studies for the current year show that operations on inpatients are divided as follows:

Type of Operation	Number of Operations	Average Number of Minutes Per Operation	Average Number of Personnel Required
A	800	30	4
B	700	45	5
C	300	90	6
D	200	120	8
	2,000		

The same proportion of inpatient operations is expected for the next fiscal year, and 180 outpatients are expected to use the operating room. Outpatient operations average twenty minutes and require the assistance of three persons.

Budgeted expenses for the year ending June 30, 19X2, by departments, are:

General Services:	
Maintenance of Plant	$ 100,000
Operation of Plant	55,000
Administration	195,000
All Others	384,000
Revenue Producing Services:	
Operating Room	136,880
All Others	2,200,000
	$3,070,880

The following information is provided for cost allocation purposes:

	Square Feet	Salaries
General Services:		
Maintenance of Plant	12,000	$ 80,000
Operation of Plant	28,000	50,000
Administration	10,000	110,000
All Others	36,250	205,000
Revenue Producing Services:		
Operating Room	17,500	30,000
All Others	86,250	605,000
	190,000	$1,080,000

Basis of Allocations:
   Maintenance of plant—salaries
   Operation of plant—square feet
   Administration—salaries
   All other general service costs—8% to operating room, 92% to other revenue-producing departments

Required: Prepare schedules showing the computation of:
   1. The number of patient days (number of patients multiplied by average stay in hospital) expected by type of patients and service.
   2. The total number of man-minutes expected for operating room services for inpatients and outpatients. For inpatients, show the breakdown of total operating room man-minutes by type of operation.
   3. Expected gross revenue from room charges.
   4. Expected gross revenue from operating room services.
   5. Cost per man-minute for operating room services. Use the step-down

Exhibit 18.10   Analysis of Cash for Jacob Vocational School, to Be Used in P18.6

Jacob Vocational School
Analysis of Cash
For the Six Months Ended February 28, 19X8

Unrestricted Cash for Current Operations:			
Balance, September 1, 19X7		$ 80,000	
Add: Student Fees	$ 31,000		
Gift of W. L. Jacob	210,000	241,000	
		$321,000	
Deduct: General Current Operating			
Expenses	$ 38,000		
Payment on Land and Building . .	25,000	63,000	$258,000
Cash for Restricted Uses:			
Gift of W. L. Jacob for Faculty Recruitment .		$ 35,000	
Less Faculty Recruitment Expenses . . .		4,100	30,900
Checking Account Balance, February 29, 19X8 .			$288,900

method of cost allocation (costs of the general service departments are allocated in the following order: maintenance of plant, operation of plant, administration, all others).

(AICPA adapted)

P18.8   **University Accounting**   Presented in Exhibit 18.11 is the current funds balance sheet of Mayville University as of the end of its fiscal year ended June 30, 19X7.

The following transactions occurred during the fiscal year ended June 30, 19X8:

1. On July 7, 19X7, a gift of $100,000 was received from an alumnus. The alumnus requested that one-half of the gift be used for the purchase of books for the university library and the remainder be used for the establishment of a scholarship fund. The alumnus further requested that the income generated by the scholarship fund be used annually to award a scholarship to a qualified disadvantaged student. On July 20, 19X7, the board of trustees resolved that the resources of the newly established scholarship fund would be invested in savings certificates. On July 21, 19X7, the savings certificates were purchased.

2. Revenue from student tuition and fees applicable to the year ended June 30, 19X8, amounted to $1,900,000. Of this amount, $66,000 was collected in the prior year, and $1,686,000 was collected during the year ended June 30, 19X8. In addition, at June 30, 19X8, the university had received cash of $158,000, representing fees for the session beginning July 1, 19X8.

3. During the year ended June 30, 19X8, the university had collected $349,000 of the outstanding accounts receivable at the beginning of the year. The balance was determined to be uncollectible and was written off against the allowance account. At June 30, 19X8, the allowance account was increased to $11,000.

Exhibit 18.11   Current Funds Balance Sheet, to Be Used in P18.8

Mayville University
Current Funds Balance Sheet
June 30, 19X7

ASSETS

Current Funds:
Unrestricted:
Cash $210,000
Accounts Receivable—
Student Tuition and
Fees, Less Allowance
for Doubtful Accounts
of $9,000   341,000
State Appropriations
Receivable   .   .   .   75,000 $626,000
Restricted:
Cash   .   .   .   .   . $ 7,000
Investments   60,000   67,000

Total Current Funds   .   . $693,000

LIABILITIES AND FUND BALANCES

Current Funds:
Unrestricted:
Accounts Payable   .   . $ 45,000
Deferred Revenues .   .   66,000
Fund Balances .   .   .   515,000 $626,000

Restricted:
Fund Balances .   .   .   67,000

Total Current Funds   .   . $693,000

4. Interest charges of $6,000 were earned and collected on late student fee payments.
5. The state appropriation was received. An additional unrestricted appropriation of $50,000 was made by the state but had not been paid to the university as of June 30, 19X8.
6. An unrestricted gift of $25,000 cash was received from alumni of the university.
7. During the year, pre-19X7 investments of $21,000 were sold for $26,000. Investment income amounting to $1,900 was also received. Gains and losses on the sale of investments by the restricted current fund are considered to be restricted. Gains and losses on the sale of investments by the endowment fund are treated as adjustments of principal.
8. During the year, unrestricted operating expenses of $1,777,000 were recorded. At June 30, 19X8, $59,000 of these expenses remained unpaid.
9. Restricted cash of $13,000 was spent for authorized purposes during the year.
10. The accounts payable at June 30, 19X7, were paid during the year.
11. During the year, $7,000 interest was earned and received on the savings certificates purchased in accordance with the board of trustees resolution, as discussed in transaction 1.

Required:
1. Prepare journal entries to record in summary the above transactions for the year ended June 30, 19X8. Each journal entry should be numbered to

correspond with the transaction described above. Your answer sheet should be organized as follows:

	Current Funds				Endowment Fund	
	Unrestricted		Restricted			
Accounts	Dr.	Cr.	Dr.	Cr.	Dr.	Cr.

2. Prepare a statement of revenues, expenditures, and changes in fund balances for the year ended June 30, 19X8.

(AICPA adapted)

Index